PACIFIC NORTHWEST CAMPING DESTINATIONS

RV And Car Camping Destinations In
Oregon, Washington, And British Columbia

3rd Edition

MIKE *and* TERRI CHURCH

ROLLING HOMES PRESS

Published by
Rolling Homes Press
161 Rainbow Dr., #6157
Livingston, TX 77399-1061
www.rollinghomes.com

Printed in the United States of America
First Printing 2012

Publisher's Cataloging in Publication

Church, Mike.
Pacific Northwest camping destinations : RV and car camping destinations in
    Oregon, Washington, and British Columbia / Mike and Terri Church-Third
    Edition
    p.cm.
    Includes index.
    Library of Congress Control Number: 2012901038
    ISBN 978-0982310120

1. Camping–Northwest, Pacific–Guidebooks 2. Recreational vehicle living–
Northwest, Pacific–Guidebooks. 3.Camp sites, facilities, etc–Northwest, Pacific–
Guidebooks. 4. Northwest, Pacific–Guidebooks. I. Church, Terri. II. Title.

GV191.42.N75C48 2012   2012 901038
796.54'09795-dc21

This book is dedicated to the next generation of Northwest campers -

Giovanni, Chiyo, Sophie, Emily, Miye, Ellen, Perry, Matt, Ben, Jace, Allison, Natalya, Kelsey, Julie, Brett, Jackson, Aiden, Jeremy, Tiffany, Ashlyn, Lauryn, Jon, and Kate.

Warning, Disclosure, and Communication With The Authors and Publishers

Half the fun of travel is the unexpected, and self-guided camping travel can produce much in the way of unexpected pleasures, and also complications and problems. This book is designed to increase the pleasures of Pacific Northwest camping and reduce the number of unexpected problems you may encounter. You can help ensure a smooth trip by doing additional advance research, planning ahead, and exercising caution when appropriate. There can be no guarantee that your trip will be trouble free.

Although the authors and publisher have done their best to ensure that the information presented in this book was correct at the time of publication they do not assume and hereby disclaim any liability to any party for any loss or damage caused by errors, omissions, or any other cause.

In a book like this it is inevitable that there will be omissions or mistakes, especially as things do change over time. If you find inaccuracies we would like to hear about them so that they can be corrected in future editions. We would also like to hear about your enjoyable experiences. If you come upon an outstanding campground or destination please let us know, those kinds of things may also find their way to future versions of the guide or to our internet site. You can reach us by mail at:

Rolling Homes Press
161 Rainbow Dr., #6157
Livingston, TX 77399-1061

You can also communicate with us by sending an email through our web site at:

www.rollinghomes.com

Other Books by Mike and Terri Church
and
Rolling Homes Press

Traveler's Guide To
Alaskan Camping

Traveler's Guide To
Mexican Camping

Traveler's Guide To
Camping Mexico's Baja

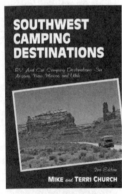

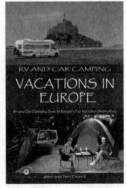

Southwest
Camping Destinations

Traveler's Guide To
European Camping

RV and Car Camping
Vacations in Europe

A brief summary of the above books is provided on pages 718 to 719

Rollinghomes.com has updated information for each of our books which comes from information submitted by others and also from our travels between editions. This information is updated until we begin the process of researching and writing a new edition. Once we start the research process there is just no time to update the website and the new information goes in the next edition. Just go to our Website at www.rollinghomes.com and click on the *Online Updates* button to review updates.

Updates Online

www.rollinghomes.com

TABLE OF CONTENTS

CHAPTER 5

9

Preface

Pacific Northwest Camping Destinations is one of two books in our Camping Destinations Series. The other is *Southwest Camping Destinations* which describes both traveling and snowbird destinations and campgrounds in Arizona, New Mexico, southern Utah, and southeast California. We also write and publish the Traveler's Guide Series including the books *Traveler's Guide to Alaskan Camping*, *Traveler's Guide to Mexican Camping*, *Traveler's Guide to Camping Mexico's Baja*, *Traveler's Guide To European Camping*, and *RV and Car Camping Vacations in Europe*.

Once again this new version, the third, of Pacific Northwest Camping Destinations contains much more information than the editions that preceded it. This time it has gone from 608 pages to 720 pages. We describe 141 destinations rather than 129. And now there are 1,310 campgrounds, an increase of 13%.

Our guidebooks are designed for both RV and car camping travelers in the Continental U.S. and Alaska, adjoining Canada and Mexico, and Europe. These books are travel guides aimed at a large part of the traveling public that has been virtually ignored by traditional travel book publishers – camping travelers. There are lots of travel guides available, but very few include the information that the camping traveler needs for a fun-filled and comfortable trip.

We have not attempted to include all of the campgrounds in the Pacific Northwest in this book, the large catalog-style guides take care of that. Instead, we've selected destinations and campgrounds that stand out. You'll find a brief description of what each destination has to offer in the way of attractions, then a listing of some of the better campgrounds in the area.

We are always looking for a way to make our guides more useful and easier to use and there is an important change in this edition of the book. Near the beginning of each destination chapter we've added a series of maps that we call our Campground Location Index Maps. It's worth your time to take a good look at these..They make the layout of the chapter and the campground locations crystal clear. Shaded areas on the map show the area covered by each destination section. There's a block that shows where to find the details about that destination and its campgrounds. The scale of the maps is large enough to show an icon for every one of the campgrounds in the book so that you can have a good idea of what you will find before even turning to the destination description.

Our campground descriptions deserve a little explanation. You'll note that we've made heavy use of icons or pictograms to convey information in a compact format. We think you'll find them very useful. By using the pictograms we've allowed ourselves room to use text to try to give you a better feel for what the campground offers and to give useful driving instructions for finding it. You'll also find latitude and longitude so that you can easily use a GPS-based mapping program for navigation and we've included maps showing approximate locations for each campground.

There's another improvement to the books that should be useful. We now include each of the Interstates in Washington and Oregon as well as the Trans-Canada Highway as destinations. The Interstate destinations are located near the front of the destination chapters and inlcude descriptions of the campgrounds or references to where you can find them for every campground convenient to a traveler on the Interstates. That means that when you're on the big highways and covering a lot of distance each day it's easy to look in the book and find a good place to stop for the night.

This book covers the states of Washington and Oregon, and also the province of British Columba as far north as Dawson Creek and the foot of the Cassiar Highway. Just coincidentally, that's exactly where the coverage of our Alaska book, Traveler's Guide to Alaskan Camping, starts. Folks traveling to Alaska or northwest travelers planning to visit northern British Columbia will probably want to have both books on hand.

Once again we've had a lot of fun researching and writing this book. It's been a chance to visit family members and friends in the region and to revisit some great camping destinations. We'll continue to visit the Pacific Northwest most years as we travel between Alaska and Mexico and we hope to meet you somewhere along the way.

PACIFIC NORTHWEST

THE OREGON COAST

BC'S YOHO NATIONAL PARK

WASHINGTON'S MT RAINIER

Chapter 1
Introduction

The Pacific Northwest is a wonderful camping destination. It is hard to think of another place in the world with such a diverse range of natural attractions and with such good highway access to them. While it is a temptation to think of the Northwest as just two regions, the rainy west of the mountains and the dry east of the mountains, the Northwest is really much more complex. Here's a quick rundown on the geographical layout.

Much of the Pacific Ocean coastline is easily accessible because there are highways running along almost the entire length. In the south, in Oregon, there are charming small towns and larger regional centers. Farther north, in Washington, there are fewer people and wilder beaches. In the far north Vancouver Island is really wild, the only way to visit the coast is along remote highways that stretch westward to isolated small towns. If you want to explore the coastline north and south from the towns you'll have to walk or use a boat.

Inland from the coast are a range of coastal mountains. In Washington some of this range is the Olympic National Park. In Oregon the coastal range isn't quite as spectacular, but much of it is partially protected as national forest. Geologically speaking, Vancouver Island in British Columbia is really part of this coastal range too.

Between the coastal range and the Cascade Mountains is a flat region with most of the Northwest's people. Here you'll find the big cities: Vancouver, Seattle, and Portland. But this region isn't all cities, there's also the Willamette Valley, Puget Sound, Vancouver Island's east coast, and B.C.'s Sunshine Coast.

Moving eastward, the next range of mountains are the Cascades. Geologically the Cascade Mountains are a young range. They're much higher than the coastal range, and have steep slopes and deep valleys. They form a barrier to moisture that creates one of the most memorable features of the Northwest – while the western part of the region is wet and lush the eastern part is dry, much is actual desert. The Cascades are full of interesting destinations. There are national parks and monuments: the North Cascades, Rainier, St Helens, and Crater Lake. The mountains are cut by transportation routes that are destinations themselves including but not limited to the Fraser Canyon, the Columbia Gorge, and the North Cascades Highway.

In British Columbia the Cascades get confused. Almost the entire southern part of the province is mountainous, to the traveler there's really no well-defined separation between the Cascade Range and the Rocky Mountains. But the Columbia River starts in B.C., and farther south its valley widens to form the Columbia Basin that occupies much of the dry eastern part of the state of Washington. Eastern Oregon is dry too, but here the topography is a high, dry, rugged plateau. Ranges like the Blue Mountains provide pine-covered relief from parched lower elevations.

Camping Travel

We realize that not everyone who uses this book will be an experienced camper. Certainly not everyone has or even wants to travel in their own personal RV. Camping is becoming more and more popular each year as more people recognize the unique benefits of this type of travel. Traveling in your own car or RV, sleeping in your own mobile bed, visiting the great outdoors but having the comforts of home, and saving lots of money doing it – that's camping travel.

You don't need an RV to travel this way. During the summer months you can comfortably camp out of the back of your car. For just a small investment you can equip yourself with everything you need to stay in a campground. Today's camping equipment is inexpensive and usually pretty well designed. You don't need expedition-quality gear for car camping, and there is no reason to spend extra money to get something that is ultra-light weight. You're not going to be carrying this equipment on your back. It is much more important to get equipment that will be comfortable. Get a big tent, they're not really expensive. You don't have to sleep on the ground, there are foam and air mattresses, not to mention cots, that are almost as comfortable as your bed at home

If sleeping in a tent seems a little more like roughing it than you are willing to accept you still can camp. Rental RVs are readily available. Later in this chapter you'll find information about renting RVs in Portland, Seattle, and Vancouver. When you check prices remember that the RV provides both transportation and lodging, you'll also spend less on food because you can easily cook in the RV and won't have to eat every meal in a restaurant. It won't take long to feel at home at the wheel of your rental RV, most roads aren't crowded, and you'll be surprised at the great views that you'll have from that high RV seat. When renting we recommend that you don't get a RV that is larger than you need. Big is not necessarily better with RVs, especially when you are traveling most of the time. If you have kids along consider having them sleep in a tent, they'll probably like it better anyway.

This is a good place to mention RV maneuverability. When you are parked comfortably in a campsite you want the biggest RV possible, but when you are on the road you want the smallest one possible. We've all seen the huge RVs traveling the interstate, usually pulling a tow car (often called a "toad" by RVers). Those RVs are fine when you are in an RV park but they're not really very convenient when on the road. For the type of travel outlined in this book you'll be much happier in a smaller RV. It will be easier to park when shopping, easier to fill with gas at a station, and be more economical. Most importantly, drivers of smaller RVs have many more choices when it comes to picking a campsite.

Once you reach the destinations you're going to want to be able to drive around to see the sights, go shopping, and conveniently get around. Fortunately, most of the destinations in this book aren't crowded urban areas so you can use an RV for local access. Those with really big RVs will want to have a "toad" or (in the case of those pulling trailers) use their towing vehicle. Rental motorhomes in the 18 to 22 foot range are not too difficult to maneuver and park so you won't need a "toad" if you have one of those. In urban areas it is probably best to just rely on public transportation. Portland, Seattle, Vancouver and many smaller cities have good systems and decent service from most RV parks.

Tour Routes

In Chapter 2 of this book we outline several tours that you can follow to enjoy much of what the Northwest has to offer. They all start at one of what we call the gateway cities: Portland, Seattle, and Vancouver, B.C. Each includes six or seven destinations that offer good RV facilities and things to see and do. The idea is that you can spend a week traveling and know that you will enjoy each of the stops you make. Actually, it would be easy to spend two or three weeks on each route, but that is up to you. These routes are just ideas. You can take it from there.

Campgrounds

Campgrounds in the Northwest can be classified in many ways, but we think of them as described below. When they are available we've tried to provide a range of campground types to choose from at each destination. The type you like will depend upon how much you value hookups, amenities, natural settings, convenience and cost.

Commercial campgrounds provide the widest range of amenities. They are owned by companies or individuals and must make at least a small profit to stay open. This does not necessarily mean that they are always the most expensive campground choice since the government-owned campgrounds have been raising their rates in recent years. Commercial campgrounds almost always offer hookups, dump stations, and hot showers, they also often have swimming pools and other amenities. A big advantage of commercial campgrounds is that they usually will accept reservations over the phone with no additional charge. They are often the only type of campground that is located near or inside a town. Parking sites in commercial campgrounds are usually closer to each other than those in government campgrounds, land is a big cost to a commercial campground but is pretty much free to the government. Commercial campgrounds have been forced to enlarge sites to remain viable so most can deal fairly well with large RVs.

Washington and Oregon state campgrounds are similar to each other. Most are located in scenic or historical locations. Government campgrounds tend to have lots of land so parking sites are spread farther apart than in a commercial campground and landscaping is usually very nice. Sites themselves can be large enough for the largest RVs although this varies, older campgrounds were built when RVs were smaller and many have not been updated. State campgrounds in Washington and Oregon often have hookups, but not always. They also often provide showers, although there is sometimes a small charge in the form of a coin-operated timer. State campgrounds are much more likely to allow campfires than commercial campgrounds, usually wood can be purchased at the campground. During the summer most state campgrounds now have an on-site "host". Usually the host is an RVer who parks in one of the sites and helps run the campground by collecting fees, marking reserved sites, providing information, and helping state employees keep the facility clean, safe, and organized. Many state campgrounds in Washington and

Oregon are now on a reservation system although the system is not nearly as convenient or inexpensive as the system provided by commercial campgrounds. State campgrounds at popular destinations are often crowded, particularly on weekends, to use them you must either reserve a space or arrive early in the day. The reservation system is described under the *Campground Reservations* heading below.

British Columbia provincial campgrounds are similar to Washington and Oregon state campgrounds. They are located in scenic areas, they tend to have lots of acreage, and sites are often plenty large enough for big RVs. Provincial campgrounds, on the other hand, do not usually have utility hookups, and they often do not have showers. There is a reservation system, it is described under the *Campground Reservations* heading below. Provincial campgrounds often lower fees in early October because fewer amenities are available in the winter.

U.S. Forest Service campgrounds and RSTBC campgrounds in BC are the least developed type of campground listed in this book. These are located in the national or provincial forests, they are usually fairly small and usually do not have hookups or showers. Many have vault toilets instead of flush ones. Sites are usually separated by vegetation but can be small, particularly in old campgrounds built before the advent of big RVs. On the other hand, these are the least expensive campgrounds and often the least crowded with the best natural setting. They're particularly good for tent campers and those with small maneuverable RVs.

Other federal campgrounds are a mixed bag. The ones in this book are mostly national park campgrounds. They range from the beautiful and highly-developed sites in Canada's Banff National Park to the basic sites at most U.S. national parks. See the individual entries in this book for more details.

For many travelers camping is just not camping without a campfire. European visitors seem to particularly enjoy them, maybe because they don't find campfires in European campgrounds. Many commercial campgrounds do not allow campfires, probably due to burning restrictions in urban areas and the supervision and clean-up that fires require. Most state, provincial, and federal campgrounds do allow campfires although burning restrictions are often in effect in dryer areas.

You will not be able to find sufficient firewood on the ground in any of the campgrounds listed in this book. That means that you must either bring your own or purchase it at the campgrounds. Most campgrounds that allow fires do sell firewood firewood and prefer that you do not bring your own to avoid spreading insects from one area to another.

Campground Reservations

The destinations in this book are popular. If you are traveling during the period from Memorial Day (end of May) to Labor Day (beginning of September), as most travelers do, you will find that campgrounds are sometimes full when you arrive. To avoid a late-in-the-day search for a place to stay all you have to do is take the time to reserve a space. We have indicated whether campgrounds accept reservations in the individual campground listings in this book.

It is easy to make reservations at virtually all commercial campgrounds. Almost all accept MasterCard or Visa charges and some even have toll-free numbers. Best of all, there is almost always no additional charge for making a reservation.

Federal, state, and provincial campgrounds are another story. The good news is that many do now accept reservations. The bad news is that most charge a substantial fee to make reservations and most use a sub-contractor for the reservation-taking process. Government campgrounds usually require that you make reservations several days in advance. Information about how to make state and provincial campground reservations is listed at the beginning of the *Oregon, Washington,* and *British Columbia* chapters. You'll find much more about reservation systems in the introductory material to these campground chapters.

Renting an RV

It is not necessary to own your own RV to enjoy the destinations and campgrounds described in this book. You can easily rent an RV in Portland, Seattle, or Vancouver. Here are a few of the firms in that business. Give them a call or drop them a line for information about RVs and rates. Don't forget to ask if they will pick you up at the airport if that is important to you.

Portland Area

Cruise America, Mt Scott Motors, 8400 SE 82nd Ave, Portland, OR 97266; (503) 777-9833

RV Gold, 1570 SE Paloma Ct, Gresham, OR 97080; (503) 491-1592 or (888) 491-0592; roger@rvgold.com

RV Northwest, 4350 SW 142 Avenue, Beaverton, OR 97005; (503) 641- 9140, (877) 641-9140

RVs To Go Portland, 27975 SW Parkway Ave, Wilsonville, OR 97070; (503) 570-6131 or (800) 787-8646

Seattle Area

Cruise America – Seattle, 12201 Hwy 99 South, Everett, WA 98204; (425) 355-8935

Cruise America, Destination Rentals, 7014 6th Ave, Tacoma, WA 98409; (253) 566-4373

Five Corners RV, 16068 Ambaum Blvd S, Seattle, WA 98148; (206) 241-6111 or (800) 249-6860

Western Motorhome Rentals, 19303 Highway 99, Lynwood, WA 98036; (800) 800-1181

Vancouver Area

Candan RV Center, 20257 Langley Bypass, Langley, BC V3A 6K9; (604) 534-8128 or (800) 922-6326

Cruise Canada – Vancouver, 7731 Vantage Way, Vancouver, BC V4G 1A6; (604) 946-5775 or (800) 983-3189

Cruise America – Gammon Motor Cars, 2397 W Railway, Abbotsford, BC V2S 2E3; (604) 850-0321

Go West Campers International Ltd, 32 Fawcett Road, Coquitlam, BC V3K 6X9; (604) 528-3900 or (800) 661-8813

El Monte RV – Vancouver, 5242 Pacific Hwy, Ferndale, WA 98248; (360) 380-3300 or (888) 337-2214

Fraserway RV Centre Ltd, 747 Cliveden Place, Delta BC V3M 6C7; (604) 527-1102 or (800) 661-2441; fraserway@fraserway-rv.com

Border Crossing

It is very likely that you will be crossing the US-Canadian border while traveling in the Pacific Northwest. This is easy to do if you are properly prepared.

A passport or equivalent travel document is required for U.S. or Canadian citizens crossing into the US. Canada does not require a passport to enter Canada but does require some documentation. As a practical matter, however, U.S. citizens have to get back into the U.S. so they will have to have the U.S. documentation anyway, and that's accepted for travel into Canada too. Passport equivalent documents include NEXUS cards, U.S. Passport Cards, and Enhanced Drivers Licenses. Most people, however, will be using passports. If you have children along it is very important to have certified copies of their birth certificates and permission letters from parents if they are not yours. Passports may not be required for children under 16 years of age if they are under adult supervision, but you should check with Canadian and U.S. government agencies to make sure that you have exactly what is required if you are traveling with children.

For your vehicle you'll want the following: registration, up-to-date license tags and proof of insurance. Make sure you have your vehicle registration with you and if you are not the registered owner a signed statement that it is OK to take it out of the country. Check to make sure your automobile insurance is good in the country you are traveling to. For U.S. RVers: you can get a Canadian Non-Resident Interprovincial Motor Vehicle Liability Insurance Card from your insurance company. It is likely that you will not have to show any of these documents but having them on hand is definitely nice if you are asked for them.

Guns are a problem in Canada, don't try to take one in from the U.S. unless yours is a hunting trip. If it is a hunting trip check with Canadian officials before you leave home about regulations. Never fib about weapons at the border, vehicles are often searched and penalties are steep.

Many people like to carry pepper spray for defense against bears. This can be a problem at the border going into Canada. Sprays designed for defense against people definitely aren't allowed. With bear spray the border agent has quite a bit of discretion so be polite. A good way to avoid problems is to just wait until you are in Canada before buying bear spray, it's readily available there.

RVers carry more food and liquor than most travelers and there are restrictions that they must consider. Always answer truthfully when asked about food by a border official. Here again, fibbing can get you in big trouble. Most of the time they're going to take a look anyway so you're likely to get caught. It's best to keep inventories of liquor, tobacco, meat, eggs, fruits, and vegetables very low since there are restrictions, many of them constantly changing, on all of these items.

Pets in the form of dogs and cats are not a real problem. You should have records from a licensed veterinarian identifying each animal and showing-up-to-date rabies vaccinations. Your vet should know what paperwork is required.

For more information about border crossing details and requirements please check the *Pacific Northwest Links* page of our website, www.rollinghomes.com. The internet is a good source of information but links frequently change, our *Pacific Northwest Links* page has several border information links and we keep them up to date.

Ferries

Washington State Ferries operate in Puget Sound. For schedules and information call (206) 464-6400. Reservations are not taken for most runs. One special route is of interest. There is a Washington State ferry route from Anacortes (north of Seattle) to Victoria. This can be used to travel between the U.S. and Vancouver Island without visiting the Vancouver area. Reservations are essential for this route. For schedules and information call (206) 464-6400. The Washington State Ferries website is excellent, there's a link from www.rollinghomes.com.

The British Columbia Ferry Corporation operates ferries between Vancouver Island and the Mainland. Ferries also connect the Sunshine Coast with the road system. For schedules and information call (888) 223-3779. The B.C. Ferry Corporation has a web site with lots of information, check our web site at www.rollinghomes.com for a link to the site.

A ferry also operates across the Straight of Juan de Fuca between Victoria and Port Angeles Washington. This ferry is run by a private company, Black Ball Transport. For schedules, information, and reservations call 360 457-4491 in Port Angeles, 250 386-2202 in Victoria.

Visitor Information

We're strong believers in the usefulness of local traveler's information offices. British Columbia, Washington, and Oregon all have fine offices in virtually every town. We've given their telephone numbers and mailing addresses if available at the end of each chapter so that you can send for information before you leave home. When you are on the road you will find that the offices are well signed from most town approaches, just follow the signs to the office. They can provide you with maps, a listing of sights to see, opening times, and locations for any service you may require. Most towns also maintain a web site with useful information, you can find links to them at www.rollinghomes.com.

Internet Resources

Every day there are more and more websites devoted to information about destinations, campgrounds, interesting sites, parks, and transportation. New sites appear and old ones disappear or change addresses. We've found that the only way to maintain a current listing is to set up our own Internet site. The address is **www.rollinghomes.com** and has current links to a large variety of sites that will be of interest to readers of this guide. Don't ignore this resource, it can make your trip much more rewarding.

When to Go

Camping in the Northwest is pretty much a spring, summer, and fall activity. We give dates for the period that each listed campground is open in the individual chapters. While it may be possible to visit most areas during the winter and stay at campgrounds most people would probably not find the experience enjoyable. Winter in the Northwest, at least on the west side of the Cascade Mountains, is wet and cool. Temperatures seldom fall below freezing but there are few sunny days and daytime temperatures are often in the low forty's (Fahrenheit). On the east side of the Cascades winter weather is generally much cooler, often below freezing, but the skies tend to be clearer.

The camping season generally runs from the last half of April to the end of September with the most popular period between Memorial Day (end of May) and Labor Day (beginning of September).

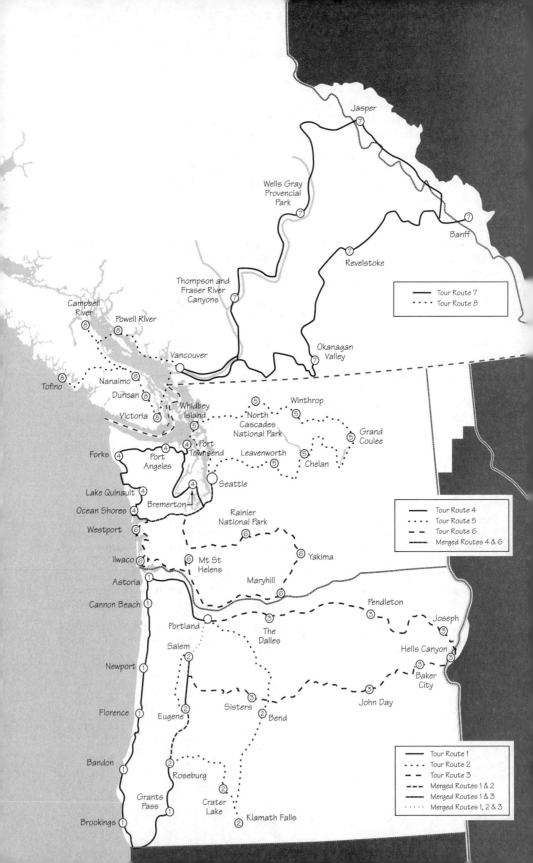

Jasper ⑦

Wells Gray
Provencial
Park
⑦

Banff ⑦

Revelstoke ⑦

Thompson and
Fraser River
Canyons ⑦

Okanagan
Valley ⑦

Campbell
River ⑧

Powell River ⑧

Vancouver ○

	Tour Route 7
⋯	Tour Route 8

Tofino ⑧

Nanaimo ⑧

Duncan ⑧

Victoria ⑧

Whidbey
Island ⑤

Winthrop ⑤

North
Cascades
National Park ⑤

Grand
Coulee ⑤

Forks ④

Port
Angeles ④

Port
Townsend ④

Leavenworth ⑤

Chelan ⑤

Lake Quinault ④

Seattle ○

④

Bremerton ④

Rainier
National Park ⑥

	Tour Route 4
⋯	Tour Route 5
– –	Tour Route 6
–	Merged Routes 4 & 6

Ocean Shores ④

Westport ⑥

Yakima ⑥

Ilwaco ⑥

Mt St
Helens ⑥

Maryhill ⑥

Astoria ①

Cannon Beach ①

Pendleton ③

Joseph ③

Portland ○

The Dalles

Hells Canyon ✕ ③

Salem

③

Baker
City ③

Newport ①

Sisters ③

John Day ③

Florence ①

Eugene ②

Bend ②

Bandon ①

Roseburg ②

Grants
Pass ①

Crater
Lake ②

Klamath Falls ②

Brookings ①

	Tour Route 1
⋯	Tour Route 2
– –	Tour Route 3
–	Merged Routes 1 & 2
–	Merged Routes 1 & 3
⋯	Merged Routes 1, 2 & 3

Chapter 2
Suggested Touring Routes

This chapter contains eight tours of the Pacific Northwest. There are three tours from Portland, three from Seattle, and two from Vancouver. We've included these tours because the Northwest has so much to offer that it can be tough to decide where to go and what to see. You can use the suggested tours as a starting point and cut them or expand them as you like.

Each suggested tour has either seven or eight driving days. That means you can do them in a long week, but that would be a hard week of driving. If you only have a week consider cutting out some of the destinations.

TOUR 1 – THE OREGON COAST

Summary: This tour starts in Portland, Oregon. You'll travel quickly south to reach the extreme south end of Oregon's Pacific coast, then leisurely wander north on US-101 to return to Portland. Please note that coaches over 40 feet long are restricted from traveling a section of this route, see the *Big Coaches* section below.

High Points

- » The Oregon Caves
- » Oregon Coast lighthouses and jetties
- » Rogue River from a jet-powered mail boat
- » Oregon Dunes National Recreation Area
- » Sea Lion Caves
- » Yaquina Head near Newport
- » Cannon Beach

»   Seaside
»   Historic Astoria and Lewis and Clark's Fort Clatsop

General Description

This tour makes a quick dash south from Portland but then makes a leisurely return north along the full length of Oregon's Pacific coast. As you drive south on Interstate Highway 5 through the Willamette Valley you may feel that you are missing lots of interesting stops, and you are. But save that until later. After one day on the interstate things start to get interesting. You'll cross the coastal mountains and by the afternoon of the second day you are on the coast. There is so much to see and do that you may want to spend a month returning north to Portland. The total distance of this tour is 779 miles (1,255 km), driving time about 21 hours over 8 days.

The Roads

During the first day you'll be traveling down Interstate 5 (I-5), the major north-south highway on the west coast of the United States. On day two you'll leave the interstate at Grants Pass and head southwest through the Siskiyou Mountains along winding US-199. Note that coaches over 40 feet long are not allowed on the California section of this road, see the *Big Coaches* section below. At the coast you'll join the coastal US-101. This road has been designated as the **Pacific Coast National Scenic Byway**, and it lives up to its name, it is really scenic. The standard of the road varies, but it is mostly good two-lane highway allowing vehicles of any size to easily and safely maintain the speed limit.

US-101 is well marked with mileage posts. These start in Astoria in the north and reach mile 363 at the Oregon-California border. They make a great way to locate campgrounds and interesting sights, we'll use them extensively in describing this tour.

Practical Tips

You will quickly notice that our favored campgrounds on this loop are in Oregon state parks. This is generally true throughout Oregon but particularly along the coast. Any private campground owner will tell you that government campgrounds have an unfair advantage – lots of prime real estate. Many other states do not take advantage of this, but Oregon and Washington do. The state campgrounds offer full hookups (in at least two cases even cable TV), beautiful settings and landscaping, lots of room, and a reservation system.

The reservation system is key. From Memorial Day to Labor Day the coast is very popular and reservations are usually necessary, especially on weekends. Make them as soon as you can, particularly if you are traveling on weekends or holidays. We describe the reservation system under *Oregon State Campgrounds* in the *Oregon* chapter of this book.

The Oregon Coast changes with the seasons. It's a great destination all year long and many campgrounds remain open during the entire year, but it's a completely different place in the winter than in the middle of the summer. This is one of the few tours in this book that is fine for winter travel although you may have to deal with snow during the drive from Grants Pass to Brookings. When snow is a problem you can use a different route to reach the coast, perhaps US-20 from south of Salem to Newport would be the best choice but there are several alternatives. During wet winter weather the coastal US-101 is sometimes closed by landslides, regional news programs will have reports if this happens. The road usually reopens within a day or two. In the winter you don't really need to worry about making reservations at the campgrounds.

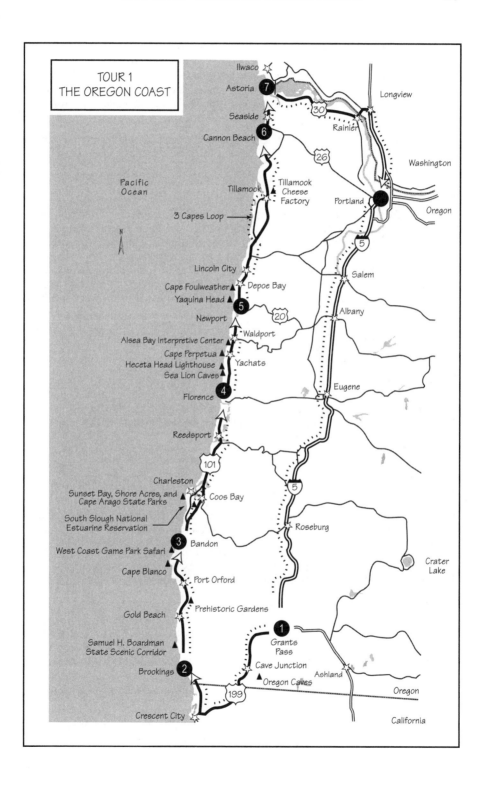

TOUR 1
THE OREGON COAST

Ilwaco
Astoria 7
Longview
Seaside 30
Cannon Beach 6
Rainier
Washington
Pacific
Ocean
Tillamook
Tillamook Cheese
Factory
Portland
Oregon
3 Capes Loop
N
Lincoln City
Cape Foulweather Depoe Bay
Yaquina Head 5
Newport 20
Albany
Waldport
Alsea Bay Interpretive Center
Cape Perpetua
Heceta Head Lighthouse Yachats
Sea Lion Caves
4
Florence Eugene
Reedsport
101
Charleston
Sunset Bay, Shore Acres, and
Cape Arago State Parks
Coos Bay 5
South Slough National
Estuarine Reservation
Roseburg
West Coast Game Park Safari 3 Bandon
Crater
Lake
Cape Blanco
Port Orford
Gold Beach
Prehistoric Gardens
1
Samuel H. Boardman
State Scenic Corridor
Grants
Pass
Brookings 2
Cave Junction
Ashland
Oregon Caves
Oregon
199
Crescent City
California

Whale watching is a very popular pastime on the coast. Gray whales winter in Baja California and summer in the far north, therefore they pass the Oregon coast twice. During December, January, and early February they are going south; in March, April and May they are headed north. A small population also summers in Oregon waters. You can see the whales from high points on shore and also take whale-watching boat trips from several ports.

Fishing is another popular activity along the coast. You can fish from charter boats from many ports, fish in salt water along the beaches, or fish the estuaries and rivers along the coast.

Big Coaches

The State of California restricts coaches over 40 feet long from traveling many roads. One of these is US-199 between the California border and its intersection with US-101 near Crescent City. Coaches over 40' long will need to modify this touring route. One idea would be to travel south on I-5 to Redding and then west on US-299 to the coast at Arcata. From there you would follow US-101 north to Brookings. From Ashland this is a total driving distance of 375 miles (605 km), so you'd probably want to overnight somewhere in California, perhaps Arcata. Alternately you could travel west on SR-20 from Albany to Newport, overnight there or in Florence, and then continue on to Brookings the next day. Since both Florence and Newport are already overnight stops on this tour route when heading north you could bypass one of them northbound and shorten the tour by one day.

DAY 1 – DESTINATION GRANTS PASS – 245 MILES (395 KM), 4 HOURS

From Portland we'll head south on Interstate 5 (I-5). This is a major four-lane highway that actually runs the length of the westernmost states from Blaine on the Canadian border to Tijuana on the Mexican border. It's almost never within sight of the ocean, only between Los Angeles and San Diego.

From Portland the highway runs straight down the length of the Willamette Valley. There are coastal mountains on the right and the Cascades on the left. After leaving the Portland metropolitan area you'll drive through farming country and pass the towns of Salem, Albany, and Eugene. After Eugene the highway begins to climb to pass across the Middle Range before dipping into the Umpqua River Valley where Roseburg is located and then climbing again over a pass to reach the Rogue River Valley and Grants Pass.

You'll stop for the night near the town of *Grants Pass*, see page 149 for a description of the area and the available campgrounds. If you want to make a shorter day of it we also describe the campgrounds along the entire length of I-5 in our *Interstate 5 Corridor* section (page 77).

DAY 2 – DESTINATION BROOKINGS – 198 MILES (158 KM), 3 HOURS

From Grants Pass follow US-199 southwestward. US-199 is a mostly two-lane road but it's OK for RVs to 40 feet. Coaches over 40 feet are not legal on this road on the California side of the border, see the *Big Coaches* section above. Portions of US-199 are winding and somewhat narrow, so take it easy on those sections. Drivers with large coaches or trailers or who have less experience might want to consider taking one of the alternate routes described in the *Big Coaches* section above.

About twenty-eight miles (45 km) from Grants Pass you'll reach **Cave Junction**, from here a small paved road leads east 20 miles (32 km) to the **Oregon Caves**. This side trip is

THE SCENIC SOUTHERN OREGON COASTLINE

well worth your while, the caves are unique in the Northwest. They have formations from mineral-laden water flows. Unfortunately the road is not recommended for large RVs. If you have a smaller vehicle available (tow vehicle or towed car) you can leave your larger RV or trailer in the parking lot at the visitor center in Cave Junction and make the side trip in it. See *Oregon Caves National Monument* on page 197 for information about campgrounds in this area if you decide to spend more time..

Some 15 miles (24 km) beyond Cave Junction you reach the California border. During some seasons you'll be stopped and asked if you have any fruits on board, then you're on your way. You're in California, but not for long. After 35 miles (56 km), much of it along highway bordered by tall redwoods (this portion of the road is named the Redwood Highway), you'll see the sign for US-101 north to the Oregon border and, six miles (10 km) beyond, Brookings. See page 114 for information about *Brookings* and the campgrounds there. If you are interested in a jet boat ride up the Rogue River you might consider traveling on another 28 miles (45 km) to *Gold Beach* (page 146) to overnight there.

🚐 DAY 3 – DESTINATION BANDON – 84 MILES (135 KM), 3 HOURS

The 29-mile (47 km) section of coastline from Brookings north to Gold Beach is very scenic. The road closely follows the coastline which is alternately rocky cliffs and sandy beaches. From Mile 353 to Mile 343 you are in the **Samuel H. Boardman State Scenic Corridor**. There are many pull-offs giving you the opportunity to make short walks and take some photos from scenic viewpoints.

The town of **Gold Beach** is located at Mile 328. It sits at the mouth of the Rogue River. Jet boat trips from here are very popular. See the *Gold Beach* destination description at page 146.

You might find a visit to the **Prehistoric Gardens** at Mile 313.1 interesting, particularly if you have some youngsters along. There are full-sized dinosaur replicas in a rain forest setting.

Farther north **Port Orford** is the western-most incorporated city in the contiguous U.S. See *Port Orford* (page 202) for more information. Don't miss **Cape Blanco**, just to the north and accessed via the road from Mile 296.6.

Just south of Bandon you'll pass by an interesting stop, the **West Coast Game Park Safari**. It's at Mile 281.5 and features 75 different species.

Finally, at Mile 270 you'll reach your destination for the day, the town of *Bandon*. See page 107 for information and campgrounds. If you choose to stop before reaching Bandon you might take a look at the description of things to do and campgrounds in the sections of this book covering *Gold Beach* (page 146), or *Port Orford* (page 202).

▇ DAY 4 – DESTINATION OREGON DUNES NEAR FLORENCE – 72 MILES (116 KM), 2 HOURS (TO FLORENCE)

Coos Bay lies north of Bandon. The route below bypasses much of the town by passing through Charleston and then rejoining US-101 north of the city.

Drive north from Bandon and take the left turn at Mile 256.9 marked Charleston. The Seven Devils Road soon passes **South Slough National Estuarine Reservation**. You'll find a visitor's center and paths down to and around the estuary. Continuing on you'll enter Charleston and see signs pointing left for **Sunset Bay State Park**, **Shore Acres State Park**, and **Cape Arago State Park**. See *Charleston* (page 129) for more about this area. If you wanted to add a day to this tour this might be a nice place to do it.

Follow the highway across the bridge from Charleston and northeast through suburbs of Coos Bay. You'll eventually hit Hwy 101 again. Turn north and you'll soon be entering Oregon's dune country. For about 40 miles (65 km) between Coos Bay and Florence the highway passes inland of a large dune field. See *Reedsport and the Oregon Dunes* (page 220) for more about this area. You can overnight in one of the many campgrounds serving the dunes area or continue north to Florence. See our *Waldport and Florence* section (page 247) for more about that area.

▇ DAY 5 – DESTINATION NEWPORT – 50 MILES (81 KM), 2 HOURS

From Florence continue north on US-101.

The twenty miles (32 km) or so between Mile 186 and Yachats at Mile 165 are within the Siuslaw National Forest and are very scenic. The *Waldport and Florence* destination description (page 247) describes the section north to Waldport at Mile 156. Along the way you'll pass **Sea Lion Caves** (Mile 179.3), **Heceta Head Lighthouse** (Mile 178.3), and the **Cape Perpetua Interpretive Center** (Mile 167.3).

At Mile 165 you'll pass through little **Yachats**, and then at Mile 156 reach **Waldport**. Just south of the big bridge is the **Alsea Bay Interpretive Center**. To the north the flat coastline is less scenic, at Mile 143 you'll find that you are approaching Newport. See *Lincoln City to Newport* (page 177) for information about the area and its campgrounds.

▇ DAY 6 – DESTINATION CANNON BEACH – 110 MILES (177 KM), 4 HOURS

Driving north from Newport you'll pass the **Yaquina Head** entrance at Mile 137.6 and pass around **Cape Foulweather** at about Mile 131. Little **Depoe Bay** (Mile 128.0) is so scenic that almost everyone stops for a look. You'll reach Lincoln City at about Mile 120.

This entire section of road is described under *Lincoln City to Newport* (page 177).

At Mile 90.4 turn off US-101 and follow the **Three Capes Loop** toward Pacific City. This scenic loop and Tillamook at the other end are described under *Tillamook and the Three Capes Loop* (page 240).

After a stop in Tillamook at the **Tillamook Cheese Visitor's Center** you can continue north. From Tillamook US-101 winds its way north through a series of towns along the Tillamook Bay, Nehalem Bay, and the coast. These are **Bay City** (Mile 60.8), **Garibaldi** (Mile 55.6), **Barview** (Mile 53.7), **Rockaway Beach** (Mile 50.8), **Wheeler** (Mile 47.0), **Nehalem** (Mile 44.7), **Manzanita** (Mile 43.0), and finally, Cannon Beach. You can spend the night in Cannon Beach which is described in our section titled *Astoria, Seaside and Cannon Beach* (page 99) or stop sooner at a campground farther south. These are described in our section titled *Nehalem Bay and Manzanita* (page 193).

▦ DAY 7 – DESTINATION ASTORIA – 25 MILES (40 KM), 1 HOUR

Today's drive is a short one, but en route you'll pass through **Seaside**, one of the most-visited cities on the coast, and end the day near **Astoria** which is one of the coast's most historical sites. There's lots to see so don't spend too much time eating a leisurely breakfast in Cannon Beach.

Just 3 miles (5 km) north of Cannon Beach at Mile 25 you'll begin to pass through the road-side outskirts of Seaside. Seaside is described in our section titled *Astoria, Seaside and Cannon Beach* (page 99).

Continuing north you will spot the southern access road to Fort Stevens and Warrenton at Mile 7.5. There's another access road at Mile 6.5. Three of the Astoria area campgrounds are along this road. Astoria is northeast across the long bridge across the mouth of the Youngs River. Again, see the *Astoria, Seaside and Cannon Beach* section (page 99) for information about things to do and campgrounds in Astoria.

▦ DAY 8 – DESTINATION PORTLAND – 95 MILES (153 KM), 2 HOURS

From Astoria it is an easy drive back to Portland along US-30. This highway generally follows the south bank of the Columbia but is seldom within view of the river. For most of the distance it is a decent two-lane road. It is possible to cross the river at a bridge from Rainier in Oregon to Longview in Washington. There you can pick up the I-5 interstate, the same highway we followed south from Portland on this trip. I-5 follows the north bank of the Columbia to Portland and is quicker than US-30. It also offers easier access to Portland campgrounds.

TOUR 2 – CENTRAL OREGON LOOP

Summary: This tour starts in Portland, Oregon. It crosses the Cascade Mountains near Portland and then travels down the east side of the range as far as the California border. Then you return north through Crater Lake National Park and the length of the Willamette Valley.

High Points

> » Mt Hood
> » Mt Bachelor
> » Cascade Lakes Highway
> » Newberry National Volcanic Monument

- » High Desert Museum
- » Klamath Basin National Wildlife Refuges
- » Lava Beds National Monument
- » Crater Lake National Park
- » Umpqua River Valley
- » McKenzie River Valley
- » Robert Aufderheide Memorial Drive
- » Willamette Valley

General Description

On this tour you will have a chance to explore Oregon's section of the Cascade Mountains. First you'll cross the mountains from Portland and drive south along the eastern slopes. You'll visit Bend and Klamath Falls. Then you'll drive northwest to spend some time at Crater Lake National Park before descending to the western slopes. There, in Oregon's historical heartland, you'll visit the towns of Roseburg, Eugene, and Salem. Each has its own access to the wild Cascades to the east, as well as covered bridges, wineries, and historical sites in the fertile farming country nearby. Total driving distance is 659 miles (1,063 km), time on the road about 17 hours.

Oregon's Cascades are much more accessible than Washington's. While Washington has only six east-west highways, Oregon has 10 of them. Rather than zigzag our way back and forth across the mountain range we'll only cross twice, once in the north and again toward the south. Both of the routes you will follow are very suitable for big RVs of all kinds with easily handled two-lane highways and medium grades.

On the east side of the mountains and headed south the tour follows US-97 which is mostly two lanes and fairly flat. There is quite a lot of traffic on US-97 but it moves right along.

On the west side of the mountains headed north you'll travel on either the I-5 interstate or good rural roads.

Even though the tour only crosses the Cascades twice it still gives you the opportunity to drive in the mountains. It's also easy to drive into the mountains on day trips from Bend, Eugene and Springfield. If you are driving an unwieldy larger RV you can leave it parked in the campground and do the exploring in your tow car.

Practical Tips

This would generally be considered a summer tour. Some of the destinations, however, do offer possibilities in the winter. On the east side of the Cascades the weather is usually decent, and you'll see that the campgrounds at lower elevations around Bend are open all year. This is a very popular winter sports area with Mt Bachelor's skiing nearby. The Klamath Falls area also has its winter attractions, during the months of December through February the area attracts the Lower 48's largest concentration of bald eagles.

A problem with a winter visit is the higher elevations, of course. Crater Lake National Park is snowed in until June most years so in winter you'll probably be better off to cross westward to I-5 using US-97 to Weed. Once you make it north to Roseburg you'll again find the valley campgrounds to be open, although winter days are short and the weather generally wet.

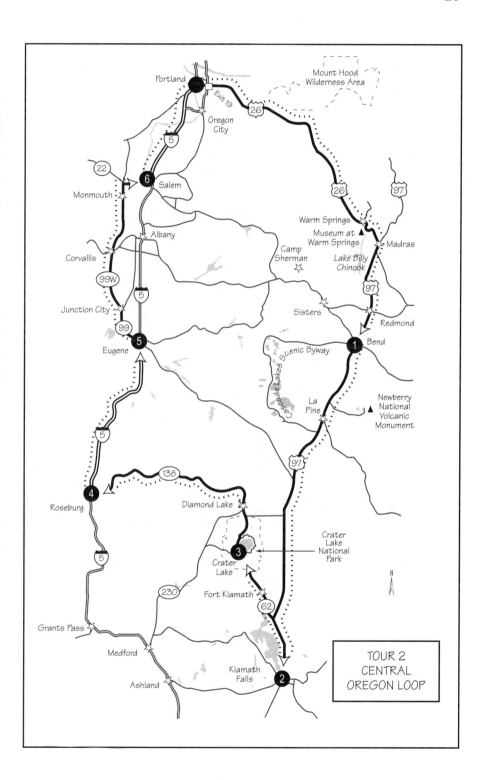

TOUR 2
CENTRAL
OREGON LOOP

▆ DAY 1 – DESTINATION BEND – 165 MILES (266 KM), 4 HOURS

From the ring road around the east side of Portland (I-205) take Exit 19 and follow the signs for Hwy 26. Once you leave the populated areas around Gresham the highway will take you up across the south slopes of Mt Hood and down the far side into the dry country on the eastern slopes of the Cascade Mountains. As you start to descend you'll be amazed at how fast the evergreens disappear and the temperatures rise.

The town of Warm Springs is in the 600,000-acre Warm Springs Indian Reservation. Attractions in this area include the **Museum at Warm Springs** as well as **Lake Billy Chinook** to the south. See our section titled *Warm Springs and Madras* (page 257) for more about the region as well as a wealth of interesting places to stay.

South from Madras on US-97 you'll pass through Redmond and in just a few more miles reach the northern outskirts of Bend. The Bend area is full of attractions. See the following sections of this book for information: *Bend and La Pine* (page 110), *Camp Sherman and the Metolius River* (page 118), *Cascade Lakes Scenic Byway Loop* (page 122), *Newberry National Volcanic Monument* (page 194), and *Redmond and Sisters* (page 217).

▆ DAY 2 – DESTINATION KLAMATH FALLS – 138 MILES (223 KM), 3 HOURS

The drive from Bend to Klamath Falls couldn't be simpler. You just follow US-97 south. The road is mostly two-lane although there are many places where it has been widened to three or four lanes for passing, there is quite a bit of traffic along this highway since it is the main north-south corridor on the east side of Oregon's Cascades. See our *Klamath Falls* section (page 166) for things to do and places to stay in Klamath Falls.

▆ DAY 3 – DESTINATION CRATER LAKE NATIONAL PARK – 54 MILES (87 KM), 2 HOURS (TO CRATER LAKE LODGE)

From Klamath Falls drive north on Hwy 97 toward Bend. The intersection with Hwy 62 is 20 miles (32 km) north, turn on to Hwy 62 and follow it 30 miles (48 km) through Fort Klamath to the south entrance of the park.

If you plan to camp in the park you have arrived. However, camping opportunities in the park are limited. If you plan to go on to a campground outside the park you should have plenty of time to drive the road around the crater, stop and take in some of the sights, and then drive on out to those campgrounds. See our sections titled *Crater Lake National Park* (page 141) and *Rogue Umpqua Scenic Byway* (page 229) for information about things to do and places to stay in the area.

▆ DAY 4 – DESTINATION ROSEBURG – 107 MILES (173 KM), 3.5 HOURS

When you are ready to depart Crater Lake make your way out the north entrance. Soon after you pass the entrance station the road intersects SR-138. Head westward toward Roseburg. Four miles (6 km) after that intersection you'll come to another, this one with SR-230 toward Medford and Grants Pass. At this point you are very near Diamond Lake.

From Crater Lake SR-138 leads down the canyons of the Clearwater and North Fork of the Umpqua River to Roseburg. This is a very scenic route with many places to pull off and enjoy views of the river and surrounding mountains. See our sections titled *Rogue Umpqua Scenic Byway* (page 229) and *Roseburg and the Umpqua Valley* (page 235) for information about this area and places to stay.

▆ DAY 5 – DESTINATION EUGENE – 70 MILES (113 KM), 1.25 HOURS

The route from Roseburg to Eugene is an easy one, just follow the I-5 freeway north. See our section titled *Eugene* (page 143) for information about things to do and places to stay.

◼ DAY 6 – DESTINATION SALEM – 80 MILES (129 KM), 2.5 HOURS

While it is possible to drive right up I-5 from Eugene to Salem, a distance of 59 miles (95 km), there is a better alternate route. This is the old US-99.

Follow US-99 out of Eugene toward Junction City. At first the highway is lined with commercial activities of various kinds with quite a few stoplights, but soon you'll be driving through flat quiet farming country.

At Junction City the highway splits into US-99 West and US-99 East. Much of the old US-99 East is parallel to or covered by the I-5 Interstate but US-99 West remains a good countryside route.

Forty-three miles (69 km) north of Junction City is **Corvallis**. Corvallis is a pleasant city with a population of about 50,000. It is home to Oregon State University.

From Corvallis continue north on US-99. You'll pass through little Monmouth and then catch SR-22, the Willamina-Salem Highway, east to Salem. See our section titled *Salem* (page 237) for things to do and places to see in the Salem area.

◼ DAY 7 – DESTINATION PORTLAND – 45 MILES (73 KM), 1 HOUR

The drive north to Portland goes by pretty quickly. You're barely on the road before you start to arrive in the suburbs. Portland is described in our section titled *Portland* (page 204).

TOUR 3 – EASTERN OREGON LOOP

Summary: This tour starts in Portland, Oregon. It heads eastward through the Columbia Gorge and then across the Blue Mountains as far as Hells Canyon, then returns westward through the John Day country and crosses the Cascades near Sisters, Oregon.

High Points

- » Columbia River Scenic Highway
- » Bonneville and The Dalles Dams
- » Wallowa Lake
- » Hells Canyon
- » Oregon Trail
- » John Day Fossil Beds
- » Metolius Meadows
- » McKenzie Pass

General Description

This tour crosses northern Oregon to the Idaho border, then returns along a more southerly route. Along the way it stops for the night at a variety of interesting places. Most nights are spent in or near popular outdoor destinations although, surprisingly, the route does not pass through or near any national parks. It, however, does visit a national scenic area, a national recreation area and a national monument. The total driving distance of this tour is 853 miles (1,376 km), driving time will be about 24.5 hours.

The first day is spent near Portland as you tour the southern shore of the Columbia Gorge. The following day the route travels east to Pendleton where you can spend the night at

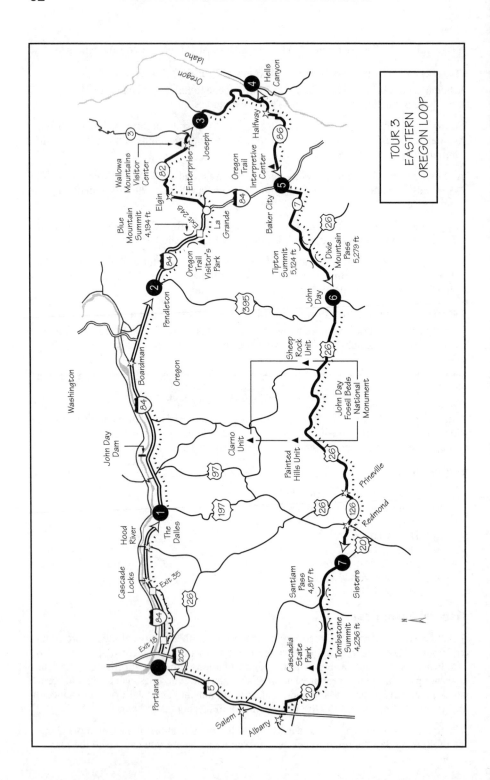

an Indian-owned resort offering a golf course and a casino. Day 3 heads into the wild northeast corner of the state for a night at beautiful Wallowa Lake. The next day's route follows small (but paved) roads through the Wallowa National Forest to the spectacular Hells Canyon. Heading westward finally you can visit the Oregon Trail in Baker City. Day 6 offers a visit to the John Day Fossil Beds National Monument and then you'll spend the final evening in scenic Sisters near the famous Metolius River.

The Roads

You'll find lots of variety in this chapter. The first day you'll visit one of the most famous roads in the country – the **Columbia River Scenic Highway**. This is a very scenic but narrow road so larger RVs may want to drive directly to Cascade Locks via I-84, park the RV in a campground, and then explore the highway in a smaller tow car or truck.

The following two days will find you on I-84, a major east-west freeway route, for most of the time. When you do leave I-84, however, you'll be on paved two-lane highways for most of the remainder of the trip. Only on the last day will you again drive on a freeway when you join I-5 south of Albany to drive north to Portland.

Practical Tips

For RVers this is a summer or fall trip. The road between Joseph and Hells Canyon is not open in the winter and many campgrounds throughout the route are also not open in the winter.

For the most part this route is not as heavily traveled as the *Oregon Coast Tour* but reservations are still a good idea, particularly in the state park campgrounds.

You can easily combine this tour with the *Central Oregon Loop Tour* to make a two or three week trip. The last night on this tour is spent at Sisters which is just a few miles from Bend, the first night's stop on that tour.

The theme of this tour could easily be the **Oregon Trail**. Locations with Oregon trail exhibits along the way are the **Columbia Gorge Discovery Center and Waasco County Historical Museum** in The Dalles, the **Tamástslikt Cultural Institute** just outside Pendleton, **Oregon Trail Visitor's Park** near the Blue Mountains summit east of Pendleton, and the **Oregon Trail Interpretive Center** near Baker, Oregon.

▄ DAY 1 – DESTINATION THE COLUMBIA GORGE – 93 MILES (150 KM), 3 HOURS (TO THE DALLES)

From Portland follow I-84 eastward. The Dalles is 85 miles (137 km) from Portland. See our section titled *Columbia Gorge* (page 132) for information about the area and its campgrounds.

Smaller RVs (to about 25 feet) will want to leave I-5 at Exit 18 and follow the **Columbia River Scenic Highway** (US-30) eastward to Exit 35. It's very scenic and passes a number of spectacular waterfalls. If you're in a big RV and want to drive the highway in a tow car consider overnighting in Cascade Locks and driving back to see the highway. Cascade Locks campgrounds are covered in the *Columbia Gorge* section (page 132).

▄ DAY 2 – DESTINATION PENDLETON – 119 MILES (192 KM), 2 HOURS

The route from the Columbia Gorge to Pendleton follows I-84. The distance from Cascade Locks to Pendleton is 162 miles (261 km), from The Dalles to Pendleton the distance is 119 miles (192 km).

From The Dalles eastward the highway continues to follow the Columbia River. At first you will be following the shore of **Celilo Lake** behind The Dalles Dam but soon you will spot **John Day Dam**. Above it the Columbia is called Lake Umatilla. About 50 miles (81 km) east of John Day Dam you will reach Boardman and the highway leaves the river and cuts inland for 54 miles (87 km) to Pendleton through a rolling landscape filled with irrigation circles. See the *Pendleton* section (page 201) for information about Pendleton attractions and campgrounds.

🚐 DAY 3 – DESTINATION JOSEPH AND LAKE WALLOWA – 121 MILES (195 KM), 3 HOURS (TO JOSEPH)

Wallowa Lake and the adjoining town of Joseph lie about 50 miles (81 km) northeast, as the crow flies, of Baker City Oregon. The drive from Pendleton is very scenic, first on I-84 through the Blue Mountains and then from La Grande on back roads through farming country and then through wooded canyons.

From Pendleton take I-84 eastward. Almost immediately you'll reach the long grade up into the Blue Mountains. The scenery changes quickly from dry grasslands to pine forests. Emigrant Springs State Park, an alternate campground for Pendleton, is just off the freeway at Exit 234.

You'll pass the Blue Mountains Summit (elevation 4,194 feet) and reach an interesting stop, the **Oregon Trail Visitor's Park**. To reach it take Exit 248 and follow a winding road for 3 miles (5 km) to the park. You'll find a short trail that leads up the hill to a section of the **Oregon Trail**, ruts are visible and an interpretive trail and volunteers help you make sense of what you see.

Back on the freeway you'll soon descend into the Grand Ronde Valley. There are several exits for the town of La Grande, take Exit 261 which is marked for Elgin. You will want to go left toward the northeast, but you might want to make a brief detour to the right to take a look at La Grande. The area is described in the *La Grande and the Grande Ronde Valley* (page 170) section of this book.

Head out of La Grande on SR-82, this highway takes a few unexpected turns but you will have no problem following it if you just watch for signs for Elgin and then Enterprise. If you zero your odometer when you leave the freeway you'll reach Elgin at 19 miles (31 km), Enterprise at 63 miles (102 km) , and Joseph at 70 miles (113 km).

You may want to make two stops in Enterprise before going on to Joseph. Just before you arrive in town you'll pass the **Wallowa Mountains Visitor Center**. A stop here will bring you up to speed on the area's attractions. Then, in Enterprise you'll find the last large supermarket in this neck of the woods, you might stop and pick up groceries for the next few nights.

See the *Wallowa Lake Region* (page 252) for information about things to do and places to see in this area.

🚐 DAY 4 – DESTINATION HELLS CANYON – 68 MILES (110 KM), 3 HOURS (TO COPPERFIELD)

The drive from Wallowa Lake to Hells Canyon is described in our section titled *Hells Canyon Scenic Byway* (page 158). There are a number of national forest campgrounds along the route. When you reach Hells Canyon take a look at the section titled *Hells Canyon* (page 153) for information about things to do and campgrounds in the area.

▥ DAY 5 – DESTINATION BAKER CITY – 70 MILES (113 KM), 2 HOURS

From Hells Canyon SR-86 leads west to Baker City. For the most part this road runs through open range and irrigated farmland with one decent summit with a good climb just past the town of Halfway, the top is at 3,653 feet.

As you approach Baker City you will spot the **Oregon Trail Interpretive Center** on top of Flagstaff Hill to your right. This is a must-see attraction. See the *Baker City and Sumpter* section (page *104*) for more about the Baker City area and places to stay.

▥ DAY 6 – DESTINATION JOHN DAY – 79 MILES (127 KM), 2.5 HOURS (TO JOHN DAY)

From Baker City and Sumpter travel eastward on SR-7. East of Sumpter you'll climb over 5,124 foot Tipton Summit and then link up with US-26 and travel westward. The highway soon crosses another summit, this one the 5,279 foot Dixie Mountain Pass, and finally reaches the town of John Day.

See the *John Day Country* section (page 160) for things to do and campgrounds in the area.

▥ DAY 7 – DESTINATION SISTERS – 155 MILES (250 KM), 5 HOURS

The drive from John Day to Sisters follows US-26 eastward to Prineville, then branches south on SR-126 to pass through Redmond and on to Sisters. Until the highway reaches the Prineville area this is a very sparsely populated area of Oregon, and also extremely scenic with miles and miles of open pine forest.

Along the way you'll have the opportunity to visit two of the sections of the **John Day Fossil Beds National Monument**. They are described in the *John Day Country* section (page 160) and include the Sheep Rock section near Mile 38 of this day's drive and the Painted Hills section near Mile 66 of the drive.

Prineville, a possible place to overnight if you're running late, is covered in our *Prineville* section (page 212). See the *Redmond and Sisters* section (page 217) for places to stay and things to do in the Sisters area. *Camp Sherman and the Metolius River* (page 118) are nearby and make a good alternate with their many national forest campgrounds.

▥ DAY 8 – DESTINATION PORTLAND – 148 MILES (239 KM), 4 HOURS

From Sisters the easiest route back to Portland for big RVs is US-20 across Santiam Pass (4,817 feet) and Tombstone Summit (4,236 feet) to Interstate I-5 just south of Albany.

Cascadia State Park, 59 miles (95 km) from Sisters, makes a good place to take a break. The park is located along the South Santiam River at the site of a spring long famous for its healthful soda water. There's an historic covered bridge nearby. Once you reach I-5 it's about 55 freeway miles (89 km) north to Portland. See our *Portland* section (page 204) for things to do and places to stay in the Portland area.

TOUR 4 – WASHINGTON'S OLYMPIC PENINSULA LOOP

Summary: This tour starts in Seattle, Washington. After crossing Puget Sound near Tacoma you circle the Olympic Peninsula with visits to mountains, a hot spring, ocean beaches, and resorts.

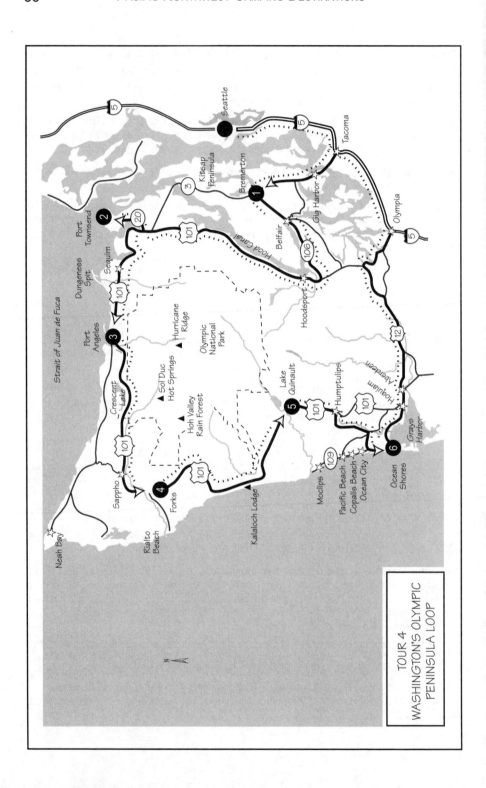

TOUR 4
WASHINGTON'S OLYMPIC
PENINSULA LOOP

High Points

- » Hood Canal
- » Kitsap Peninsula
- » Port Townsend
- » Olympic National Park
- » Hurricane Ridge
- » Olympic Mountains
- » Dungeness Spit
- » Sol Duc Hot Springs
- » Rialto Beach
- » Hoh Valley Rain Forest
- » The North Beaches
- » Grays Harbor

General Description

This is the shortest of the Washington tours. Northwest residents often drive the Olympic loop over a weekend. That's pretty fast, it wouldn't give you time to enjoy an area that is filled with natural wonders. Total distance driven on this tour is 511 miles (824 km), driving time should be about 13 hours.

The tour follows Interstate 5 south from Seattle to Tacoma. In Tacoma you leave I-5 and cross the Tacoma Narrows to the Kitsap Peninsula. The campgrounds along Hood Canal make a good place to stop for the night.

During the following days the tour leads you north to Port Townsend and then Port Angeles along the Strait of Juan de Fuca and then circles on around the Olympic Peninsula. This is a sparsely populated region famed for natural attractions and dominated by Olympic National Park.

Finally, on the last day of the tour you reach the ocean-side resort of Ocean Shores. You'll find a lot to do here and in the small towns stretched along the beaches to the north as well as in Hoquiam and Aberdeen to the east.

The Roads

The greater part of this tour follows US-101 in a loop around the Olympic Peninsula. You will be driving this two-lane paved highway from a point near Hoodsport on the Hood Canal until you reach Aberdeen, a distance of 252 miles (406 km). This is a uniformly good road, no problem at all for RVs.

Practical Tips

Like the *Oregon Coast Tour* from Portland this tour can be fun at any time of the year. During the winter you must expect a lot of rain, but temperatures rarely descend below about 40 degrees Fahrenheit. Coastal storms actually attract visitors during the winter.

You could easily combine this tour with our Southern Washington tour in either of two ways. From Aberdeen you could head south to Westport and then do the entire Southern Washington tour in a counter-clockwise direction. Alternately, instead of returning to Seattle you could drive to Packwood and start the tour in a clockwise direction.

It is also easy to connect with the Vancouver Island tour by taking a ferry north from Port Angeles to Victoria.

■ DAY 1 – DESTINATION THE KITSAP PENINSULA – 69 MILES (111 KM), 2 HOURS (TO BREMERTON)

Rather than deal with the crowded and somewhat expensive (especially for RVs) ferries that ply the waters of Puget Sound we'll do an end run and drive around the south end of the sound.

From Seattle head south on I-5. You'll pass through Tacoma and take Exit 132 (marked for Gig Harbor) and US-16 to drive across the **Tacoma Narrows Suspension Bridge**. Don't give it a thought, but this is the bridge that replaced the infamous "Galloping Gertie", that bridge collapsed in 1940. If you want to investigate Tacoma you could spend the evening here, see our *Tacoma* section (page 447) for things to do and places to stay including campgrounds near Gig Harbor.

Stay on US-16 as it leads north to Bremerton. See the *Kitsap Peninsula and Bainbridge Island* section (page 349) for things to do and places to stay on the Kitsap Peninsula.

■ DAY 2 – DESTINATION PORT TOWNSEND – 102 MILES (165 KM), 3 HOURS

From the Kitsap Peninsula you have a choice. You can travel directly to Port Townsend using SR-3 and the Hood Canal Floating Bridge. From Bremerton to Port Townsend using this route the distance is 48 miles (77 km).

Alternately, you can follow the south and west shores of Hood Canal using SR-106 and US-101. From Bremerton to Port Townsend using this route is a distance of 102 miles (165 km). This is by far the most scenic route, much of it is described in our *Hood Canal* section (page 341). There are many campgrounds along the canal so this is a good place to add an extra day to the tour.

Eventually the highway leaves the shore of the canal and approaches the north shore of the Olympic Peninsula. Just before you get there you will see a sign for Port Townsend (SR-20). Take the right turn and in 13 miles (21 km) you will find yourself entering one of the most interesting towns on the peninsula. See the *Port Townsend* section (page 413) for information about Port Townsend.

■ DAY 3 – DESTINATION THE PORT ANGELES AREA – 46 MILES (74 KM), 1.5 HOURS (TO PORT ANGELES)

The direct route to Port Angeles doesn't take long, the distance is very short. You'll re-trace your steps back to US-101, then follow that highway for 35 miles (56 km) west to Port Angeles. Between Port Townsend and Port Angeles you'll pass through Sequim. See our *Sequim* section (page 434) for more about this town. Port Angeles is just beyond, see our *Port Angeles and the North Olympic Park* section (page 406) for details about what to do and where to stay. Sequim and Port Angeles are so close to each other that you can spend the night in either one.

■ DAY 4 – DESTINATION FORKS, HOH VALLEY AND RIALTO BEACH – 56 MILES (90 KM), 1.5 HOURS (TO FORKS)

As you head west from Port Angeles you'll pass north of the **Olympic National Park** past extremely scenic **Crescent Lake**. This region is described in our *Port Angeles and the North Olympic Park* section (page 406).

After 44 miles (71 km) you'll reach a town, really a populated intersection, called Sappho. SR-113, which joins the highway here, will take you north to join SR-112 as it connects Port Angeles with **Neah Bay**. This can be an interesting side trip if you have the time. It is described in our *Neah Bay, Sekiu and Lake Ozette* section (page 385). Forks, just 11 miles (18 km) beyond the intersection, is described in our *Forks and the Western Sections of Olympic National Park* section (page 327).

⊞ DAY 5 – DESTINATION LAKE QUINAULT AND THE KALALOCH COAST – 67 MILES (108 KM), 1.5 HOURS (TO LAKE QUINAULT)

From Forks US-101 travels south. After 13 miles (21 km) you'll see the Upper Hoh Road going east to the **Hoh Rain Forest Visitor Center** in Olympic National Park. It's well worth the 32 mile (52 km) roundtrip drive to visit the place. Then the highway curves back out to the coast and passes **Ruby Beach** and **Kalaloch Lodge** before again passing inland toward **Lake Quinault**. This entire section is covered in our *Forks and the Western Sections of Olympic National Park* section (page 327). You could overnight in the Hoh Valley, at Kalaloch Lodge, or at Lake Quinault. Take your pick.

⊞ DAY 6 – DESTINATION OCEAN SHORES AND THE NORTH BEACHES – 41 MILES (66 KM), 1 HOUR (TO OCEAN SHORES)

Back on US-101 and headed south you have a choice of routes. The main highway will take you directly to Hoquiam with little delay. From there you can cut west to the North Beaches area. This is the route to take if you are in need of supplies, there is a better choice of stores in Hoquiam than you will find in the little towns along the coast.

A more direct route, all on paved roads, takes you west on back roads to Moclips at the north end of the North Beaches coastal strip. From there you can follow the coast road south. This back road leaves US-101 at Humptulips near Mile 109 of US-101. Drive west 12 miles (19 km) to Copalis Crossing, then at the T intersection turn right and follow signs for Moclips north 10 miles (16 km) to a point on the coastal SR-109 just south of Pacific Beach. From there you can drive south on SR-109 to Copalis (8 miles (13 km)), Ocean City (11 miles (18 km)) or Ocean Shores (16 miles (26 km)).

See our *Ocean Shores and the North Beaches Area* section (page 393) for information about the area and places to camp.

⊞ DAY 7 – DESTINATION SEATTLE – 130 MILES (210 KM), 2.5 HOURS

The drive back to Seattle is quick and easy. Follow SR-109, US-101 and US-12 eastward through Hoquiam and Aberdeen. You'll hit 4-lane highway on the far side of Aberdeen and never really have to slow down much, except during rush hours, as you travel east to an intersection with I-5 just south of Olympia, then north through Tacoma to Seattle.

TOUR 5 – WASHINGTON'S NORTH CASCADE LOOP

Summary: This tour starts in Seattle, Washington. You'll drive north and cross the North Cascades Highway to the Methow Valley. In eastern Washington you'll visit the sunny Grand Coulee area, then return through apple country and Stevens Pass.

High Points

- » Ferry to Whidbey Island
- » Deception Pass
- » North Cascades National Park
- » Winthrop and the Methow Valley
- » Grand Coulee Dam

»   Lake Chelan
»   Leavenworth Alpine Village

General Description

The well-known Cascade Loop is one of the most heavily promoted tourist routes in the state of Washington. Deservedly so, this tour is definitely a great way to spend a week or two. You'll have a chance to enjoy a variety of landscapes: islands and seashores, rugged evergreen-clad mountains, piney ranchland, and the dry coulee country of eastern Washington. The total distance is 587 miles (947 km), total driving time about 17 hours.

You'll start your journey with a short ferry ride to Whidbey Island. The ferry runs from Mukilteo, which is just north of Seattle, to Clinton. The drive up the island offers several interesting side trips and stops. You don't have to use a ferry to get off Whidbey Island, the bridge at **Deception Pass** at the north end of the island not only brings you back to the mainland, it offers you one of the most scenic views in the state. Actually, this bridge doesn't really take you to the mainland, it takes you to Fidalgo Island. From there it is easy to travel onward since this so-called island is really only separated from the mainland by what is little more than a wide canal.

From Fidalgo Island you'll travel on SR-20 up the Skagit Valley to the North Cascades National Park. After spending a night in or near the park you drive on eastward descending into the Methow Valley. Winthrop is the center of activity in the Methow, it's a friendly little town with a western theme.

Your route continues eastward the next day, you cross Loup Loup Pass, drive through the Colville Indian Reservation, and stop for the night at one of the world's manmade wonders, Grand Coulee Dam. The Grand Coulee area has more than just the dam, the surrounding area is a water-sports paradise.

If you liked Grand Coulee you'll probably also like Lake Chelan. It too offers a lot for water-oriented RVers, but there's more. The apple orchards on the surrounding hills give its own unique flavor.

From Chelan you'll start back through the mountains toward Seattle. Your route takes you down the Columbia River and then up the Wenatchee River Valley through fruit orchards and past fruit stands. You'll spend the night in Leavenworth, an unabashedly tourist-oriented town with a Bavarian motif.

Finally, to return to Seattle you'll follow US-2 across Stevens Pass. At 4,061 feet this pass is about 1,400 feet lower than Washington Pass on the North Cascades Highway, it stays open all winter long.

The Roads

This tour almost exclusively follows two-lane highways. All are suitable for any RV.

SR-20, the North Cascades Highway, is only open in the summer. Crews do not clear it of snow so when the snow starts falling in November the road is closed from Mile 134 near Diablo to Mile 171. It doesn't open again until about mid-April, the date depends upon how much snow fell the preceding winter.

Highway 2, which you will follow to return back across the Cascades from the east side is also a two-lane road. This is a well-traveled highway, you'll share the road with lots of

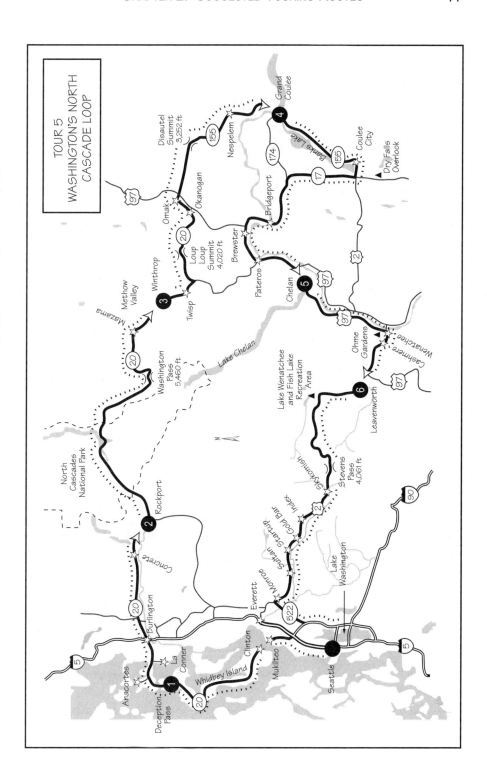

TOUR 5
WASHINGTON'S NORTH
CASCADE LOOP

others because many people like to drive this scenic route as an alternative to the massive freeway that crosses Snoqualmie Pass to the south.

Practical Tips

Like almost all the tours in this book this one is long if you really only have a week to do it. Fortunately you can easily bypass some of the stops and spend time in the ones that have the most appeal to you. A quick look at our route map will show you that it is particularly easy to bypass the stops at Whidbey Island and Grand Coulee, and thereby save yourself some driving miles too.

If you decide that the ferry ride to Whidbey Island isn't particularly appealing because of the expense or time involved you can easily bypass it by driving north on Interstate 5 to Mount Vernon and then driving westward a relatively short distance on SR-20 to the tour's first-night campgrounds. You'll retrace only a short part of this route the following day on your way to the North Cascades National Park.

As we mentioned above this is definitely a summer- and fall-only route since the North Cascades Highway (SR-20) is not open during the winter. Let the opening dates for the highway define proper season for this tour, all of the other destinations on this tour have excellent weather for the entire time that the North Cascades Highway is open.

▨ DAY 1 – DESTINATION WHIDBEY ISLAND OR THE SKAGIT VALLEY – 60 MILES (97 KM), 3 HOURS (TO DECEPTION PASS VIA FERRY)

For the first day's drive of this tour you have a choice of routes. If you have the time and feel like taking a ferry ride you can take the ferry from Mukilteo to Whidbey Island and then drive up the island to the evening's destination. If you want to save the ferry toll you can drive farther north and then cut west to the same destination. We'll describe both routes.

For the leisurely ferry route drive north on I-5 for about 12 miles (19 km) to Exit 182 and follow the signs northwest to Mukilteo. A ferry from there provides frequent service to the town of Clinton on the south end of Whidbey Island. Our *Whidbey Island* section (page 459) describes the island and the campgrounds there.

If you don't want to take the ferry just drive north on I-5 for about 60 miles (97 km) to Exit 230. Drive west on US-20 to reach **Deception Pass** at the north end of Whidbey Island. Our section titled *Skagit Valley* (page 436) describes the area and campgrounds.

▨ DAY 2 – DESTINATION NORTH CASCADES NATIONAL PARK – 57 MILES (92 KM), 2 HOURS (TO ROCKPORT)

From Deception Pass continue following SR-20 northeast. After a few winding miles there's a stop sign where our SR-20 meets what appears to be a major highway. Here a spur of SR-20 (known as 20W) goes left to Anacortes, we go right following what is still the same SR-20 we have been following up Whidbey Island. The road passes over the Swinomish Channel as a four-lane road, crosses farming country for a few miles, narrows to two lanes, and passes under I-5 and into the strip mall area on the outskirts of Burlington. You'll soon see a sign for SR-20 that jogs you north for about a mile before you are directed east on Avon Ave.

You are now established on the **North Cascades Highway**, still called SR-20. For the next 143 miles (231 km), until you reach a junction just south of Twisp, you won't have to make many route choices. The highway is well supplied with mile markers, you'll soon see Milepost 61 and then a sign telling you that Winthrop, on the far side of the Cascade Mountains, is 131 miles (211 km) ahead. The section titled *North Cascades National Park* (page 389) describes the road across the mountains, the park area, and the available campgrounds.

Day 3 – Destination Winthrop – 94 miles (152 km), 3 hours

Continue east on SR-20. From Washington Pass the road descends steeply for a few miles, then follows the Methow Valley on in to Winthrop. See our section titled *Winthrop and the Methow Valley* (page 462) for information about this area.

Day 4 – Destination Grand Coulee – 99 miles (160 km), 2.5 hours

From Winthrop head south on SR-20. You'll pass through Twisp and about 2 miles (3 km) south find the intersection where US-20 heads east over Loup Loup Summit. Watch carefully so that you do not miss the turn, although you would expect that US-20 would be the main road it really appears to be a minor side road.

It is 29 miles (47 km) from the intersection near Twisp to the twin towns of Okanogan and Omak. Loup Loup Summit at 4,020 feet presents no real problems even for large RVs, there are two forest service campgrounds near the summit. While it is possible to bypass Okanogan and Omak by jogging south to US- 97 near the western edge of Okanogan it is really not worth the bother, just head straight ahead through the towns, it is more interesting.

In Omak you will see the direction signs pointing right for SR-155. You'll pass across a fairly narrow bridge and then enter the Colville Indian Reservation. As you follow the highway the 50 miles (81 km) across the reservation to Grand Coulee Dam you'll pass across one more pine-clad summit, Disautel Summit at 3,252 feet, and also pass through Nespelem. This is the burial place of Chief Joseph, famous chief of the Nez Percé. Visits to his grave are discouraged. Just south of Nespelem you can stop at the Coleville Indian Agency for information about the reservation. You may also want to visit the **Coleville Tribal Museum** in the town of Grand Coulee if you have an interest in the native American connection here.

The section titled *Grand Coul*ee (page 336) outlines things to do and places to stay in the area.

Day 5 – Destination Chelan – 110 miles (177 km), 2.5 hours

Today's route is rather convoluted, but it passes by and through some interesting sites and country.

From the Grand Coulee Dam area head south on SR-155 along the eastern shore of Banks Lake. Basalt-topped cliffs dominate the landscape along most of the length of the lake. **Steamboat Rock**, almost an island, is impressive and hard to miss. At the south end of the lake you will join US-2 and pass through Coulee City and across the top the low Dry Falls Dam which forms the south end of Banks Lake. A few miles beyond the dam take the side trip south for 2 miles (3 km) to the **Dry Falls Overlook**. There is a small but interesting visitor center there describing the unusual geological history of the area.

Back on US-2 watch for the intersection with SR-17 in about 2 miles (3 km). You want to turn north here. SR-17 goes north through farm land studded with scattered rocks. Eventually, after 21 miles (34 km) you will join SR-174 and drive west to the Columbia at Bridgeport. **Chief Joseph Dam**, second largest electricity-producing dam in the U.S., is located here. The section titled *Lake Pateros Region* (page 355) describes the region and lists the available campgrounds.

Continuing west along the north shore of Lake Pateros you'll pass through Brewster and Pateros, and pass little Wells Dam. Finally you'll spot US-97 Alt branching right to climb the hill to Chelan.

The section titled *Chelan* (page 314) describes the area and the campgrounds there.

⛟ DAY 6 – DESTINATION LEAVENWORTH – 53 MILES (85 KM), 1.25 HOURS

From Chelan follow US-97 Alt west along the south shore of the lake and then south through scenic Knapp Coulee and down to the Columbia. The highway follows the river south past Rocky Reach Dam toward Wenatchee.

As you approach the northern outskirts of Wenatchee watch for signs for US-2. Just before you reach the intersection you will see a sign pointing right for **Ohme Gardens**. These hillside gardens are well worth a stop. The Wenatchee area is described in the section titled *Wenatchee* (page 454).

Once established on US-2 you will follow the Wenatchee River Valley westward through fruit tree orchards. After passing Cashmere the valley narrows and the evergreens take over, before long you'll find yourself approaching Leavenworth.

The Leavenworth area is described in our section titled *Leavenworth* (page 360). Just beyond is another interesting area, see *Lake Wenatchee and Fish Lake Recreation Area* (page 358).

LEAVENWORTH MIGHT MAKE YOU THINK YOU'RE IN BAVARIA

⊞ DAY 7 – RETURN TO SEATTLE – 114 MILES (184 KM), 3 HOURS

From Leavenworth US-2 leads westward and over Stevens Pass. The pass is 4,061 feet and located 33 miles (53 km) from Leavenworth. Stevens Pass Ski Area at the top of the pass is a popular destination during the winter for Seattle-area skiers.

Once past the summit the road descends steeply to the Skykomish River Valley and passes through a string of little towns: Skykomish, Index, Gold Bar, Startup, Sultan, and finally, Monroe. In Monroe watch for signs for SR-522 on the west side of town. SR-522 will take you southwest to I-405, the Seattle ring road on the east side of Lake Washington.

TOUR 6 – WASHINGTON'S SOUTHERN LOOP

Summary: Starts in Seattle, Washington. On this tour you'll visit Rainier National Park, tour the Yakima Valley wine district, see the north side of the Columbia Gorge, travel up the Spirit Lake Memorial Highway to view Mt St Helens, then circle west to visit Washington State's southern Pacific Coast.

High Points

» Mt Rainier National Park
» Yakima Wine Country
» Columbia Gorge
» Mt St Helens National Monument
» Long Beach Peninsula and Willapa Bay
» Grays Harbor

General Description

This one-week tour will take you to a large variety of landscapes and climates. In seven days you'll visit mountains, productive farmlands, dry grasslands, an active river corridor, and even the Pacific Coast. Of the three Washington State tours in this book this one visits areas that are probably a little less well-known than the others, yet in many ways it is the best of the three. You'll visit a national park, a national scenic area, and a national volcanic monument. The total distance covered is 766 miles (1,236 km) or an average of about 110 miles (177 km) each day, not at all an uncomfortable distance. Total driving time should be about 20 hours.

From Seattle you'll drive south on I-5 and then east to spend the night near (or in) Mt Rainier National Park. The next day you cross the Cascades through White Pass to the Yakima Valley. From there you head southward to spend the night on the shores of the Columbia River. Traveling westward you will visit Mt St Helens National Monument and then continue westward along the lower Columbia River to the river mouth at Ilwaco and the Long Beach Peninsula. Finally, you'll circle north around Willapa Bay to Westport and then return to Seattle.

The Roads

All of the roads that you will travel on this tour are paved and fairly heavily traveled, big RVs will find no particular obstacles. Almost all of the roads are two-lane although about 200 miles (323 km) of the trip are on the I-5 Interstate or four-lane roads between Aberdeen and Olympia.

About the only places you might have some concern if you are driving a big RV would be

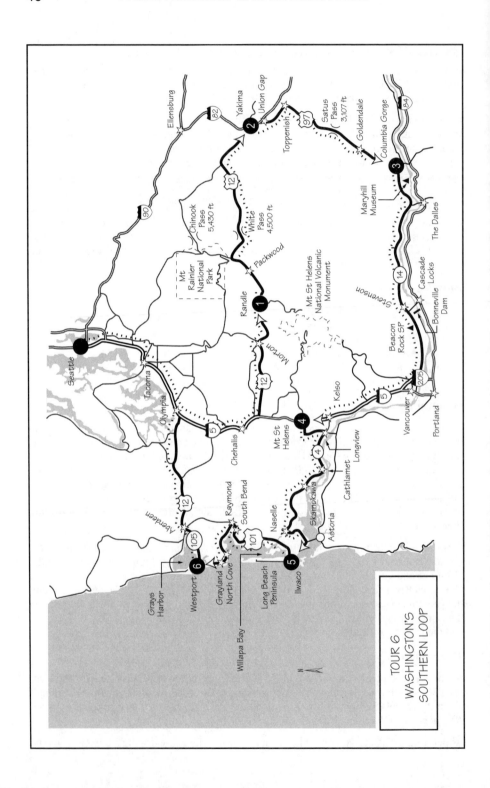

the side-trips up the mountain in Mt Rainier National Park and again up the mountain at Mt St Helens National Park. Tow cars are handy at these destinations.

Practical Tips

There is a lot to see and do on this trip. Although the tour is laid out as a 7-day trip you will probably find that you could use more time in the schedule to enjoy the various destinations. It is very easy to cut two or three days from the itinerary by traveling I-5 back to Seattle from Mt St Helens rather than making a visit to the coast. It would also be possible to spend an enjoyable week just visiting the beaches and not even crossing the Cascades.

If you have a lot of time it is also easy to combine this tour with several of the others. When you examine the maps you will see that a combination with Tour 4 of the Olympic Peninsula makes a lot of sense. You could also combine it with Tour 1 of the Oregon Coast or Tour 3 of Eastern Oregon.

⏩ DAY 1 – DESTINATION RANDLE AND MT RAINIER NATIONAL PARK – 140 MILES (226 KM), 3.5 HOURS (TO RANDLE)

From Seattle head south on I-5. Avoid the rush hour, traffic between Seattle and Tacoma can be bad. Take Exit 68 south of Chehalis and follow US-12 eastward through Morton and Randle. This area and its campgrounds are described in our *Mt Rainier National Park* (page 374) and *Cowlitz River Lakes Region* (page 323) sections.

⏩ DAY 2 – DESTINATION YAKIMA – 89 MILES (144 KM), 2.5 HOURS

SR-123 into the park branches off US-12 about 7 miles (11 km) northeast of Packwood. US-12 continues east over 4,500 foot White Pass. This road is open year round and presents no problems for larger RVs. The crest of the pass is occupied by the White Pass ski area which is probably best known for the Mahre brothers. These two Olympic skiers grew up skiing here. The climb from the intersection to the pass is 13 miles (21 km), have someone keep an eye on the back window for views of Mt Rainier. Watch for The Palisades turnout, a good place to stop for the view and to see the interesting basalt cliff-side columns.

After the pass the road descends through dryer country, pines begin to appear. You pass Rimrock Lake behind Tieton Dam and follow the Tieton River through canyons rimmed by basalt cliffs. There are several small Forest Service campgrounds along the way. Thirty-four miles (55 km) from the pass US-12 meets SR-410, a summer-only route over 5,430-foot Chinook Pass, and together they soon become a 4-lane highway and continue the 17 miles (27 km) east to Yakima. US-12 meets the I-82 freeway just north of Yakima.

The Yakima area is described in our section titled *Yakima and the Yakima Valley* (page 465).

⏩ DAY 3 – DESTINATION MARYHILL – 79 MILES (127 KM), 2 HOURS

US-97 branches off I-82 just south of Union Gap on the south side of Yakima. For the first 15 miles (24 km) it is a four-lane highway with some side road access.

Just outside **Toppenish** after passing the **Yakama Nation Heritage Center,** the road branches to the right and becomes a two lane highway. This part of the drive, from Union Gap until crossing Satus Pass about 34 miles (55 km) south of Toppenish, is on the Yakama Indian Reservation. It is mostly grasslands with the occasional wooded drainage. As the road climbs you will encounter more trees.

After crossing Satus Pass (3,107 feet) and entering Klickitat County don't be surprised if you encounter a good cross-wind. The Columbia Gorge is famous for its winds, and they often extend far inland from the river.

Sixteen miles (26 km) south of the pass you'll pass the town of Goldendale, a good place to gas up. Goldendale is home of the **Goldendale Observatory**. In the evening visitors are allowed to use the telescope here to view the planets and stars. The observatory is located in Goldendale Observatory State Park just north of town, a good spot for views of mounts Hood, St Helens, Adams, and Rainier.

After passing Goldendale you'll soon start descending into the Columbia Gorge. US-97 meets SR-14 which follows the river's north shore. Follow the signs for US-97 as it jogs down the steep hillside to the river. This area is described in the section titled *Goldendale and Maryhill Region* (page 334).

⬛ DAY 4 – DESTINATION MT ST HELENS NATIONAL VOLCANIC MONUMENT – 160 MILES (258 KM), 4 HOURS (TO SILVER LAKE)

From the eastern end of the Columbia Gorge drive along the Washington shore on SR-14. This is a two-lane highway and not nearly as busy as I-84 on the Oregon shore of the river.

The distance from Maryhill to the I-205 freeway at Vancouver, Washington is 95 miles (153 km). Along the way you'll have excellent views of the far side, the river traffic and the windsurfers.

This is a long day's drive and there are several good place to stop and stretch your legs.

About 55 miles (89 km) west of the Maryhill Museum, about a mile west of the town of Stevenson, you might enjoy a visit to the new **Columbia Gorge Interpretive Center**. It is architecturally impressive and houses a variety of objects from the area including a fish wheel, a steam engine, and the largest collection of rosaries in the world.

A few miles farther west you reach **Bonneville Dam.** You can either cross the river on the Bridge of the Gods to the Cascade Locks area and visit the main visitor center (described in the *Oregon* chapter under *Columbia Gorge*, page 132) or visit the newer Second Powerhouse on the Washington side.

Back on the road you won't get far before you reach **Beacon Rock State Park**. The huge Beacon Rock is 848 feet high. It's the core of an ancient volcano and has a path (with railings) all the way to the top.

When you reach I-205 head north toward Seattle, you'll soon merge onto I-5 and after driving a little less than an hour reach Exit 49, your turnoff for Mt St Helens.

This area and its campgrounds are described in our *Mt St Helens National Volcanic Monument* section (page 381).

⬛ DAY 5 – DESTINATION ILWACO AND LONG BEACH – 90 MILES (145 KM), 2.5 HOURS

To reach the Long Beach Peninsula from Mt St Helens National Monument you will follow SR-4, the Ocean Beach Hwy, which runs westward on the north shore of the Columbia River. This is not as fast a route as US-30 on the south side of the river. If you are in a hurry you can cross the river into Oregon at Longview and then return when you reach Astoria.

From the Mt St Helens campgrounds near Castle Rock drive south on I-5 a few miles to Exit 39. This is marked as the exit for SR-4. Follow the signs through Longview and soon you'll be leaving town and spot the river off to the left. The highway follows the river until it reaches Cathlamet, then it jogs inland for a short distance, returns to the river at Skamokawa, and then goes inland to climb over a range of hills. Near Naselle take the left onto SR-401 which will take you back to the river. You'll pass the Astoria-Megler Bridge and spot Astoria on the far shore of the river. Ilwaco is just 11 miles (18 km) ahead.

This area is described in the section titled *Ilwaco and Long Beach* (page 347).

Day 6 – Destination Westport – 80 miles (129 km), 2.5 hours

To reach Westport you follow US-101 east and then north around the eastern shore of Willapa Bay. At Raymond, just past South Bend and 45 miles (73 km) from the Long Beach area, turn westward toward the coast again and follow the highway through North Cove and Grayland. You'll reach an intersection where the stub road to Westport meets SR-105 and, continuing north three miles (5 km), soon find yourself in Westport.

This area is described in the section titled *Westport* (page 457)

Day 7 – Destination Seattle – 128 miles (206 km), 3 hours

The drive back to Seattle is an easy one, most roads are limited access highways. Follow SR-105 east to Aberdeen. Turn eastward on US-12. You'll soon hit 4-lane highway and never really have to slow down much, except during rush hours, as you travel east to an intersection with Interstate 5 just south of Olympia, then north on I-5 through Tacoma to Seattle.

TOUR 7 – BRITISH COLUMBIA MAINLAND LOOP

Summary: This tour starts in Vancouver, British Columbia. It travels eastward to the Okanagan Valley, then even farther east to the Rocky Mountain national parks: Yoho, Banff, and Jasper. As you turn back toward Vancouver you'll visit two more parks, Mt Robson and Wells Gray, before descending through the Fraser Canyon to the coast.

High Points

- » Okanagan Valley
- » Canadian Rockies including Yoho, Banff, and Jasper National Parks
- » Lake Louise
- » Icefields Parkway and the Columbia Icefield
- » Mt Robson
- » Wells Gray Provincial Park and Helmcken Falls
- » Fraser River Canyon

General Description

Inland British Columbia represent one of the premier RVing destinations in North America. This is a spectacularly beautiful region, you'll see more impressive mountain scenery here than anywhere else you are likely to ever take an RV.

This is a huge area. While it would theoretically be possible to make this entire tour in one week we definitely would not recommend that you try to do so. At the end of your trip you would be exhausted. You would also feel like you had missed more than you had seen. The distances are long and the miles are packed with things to see while several

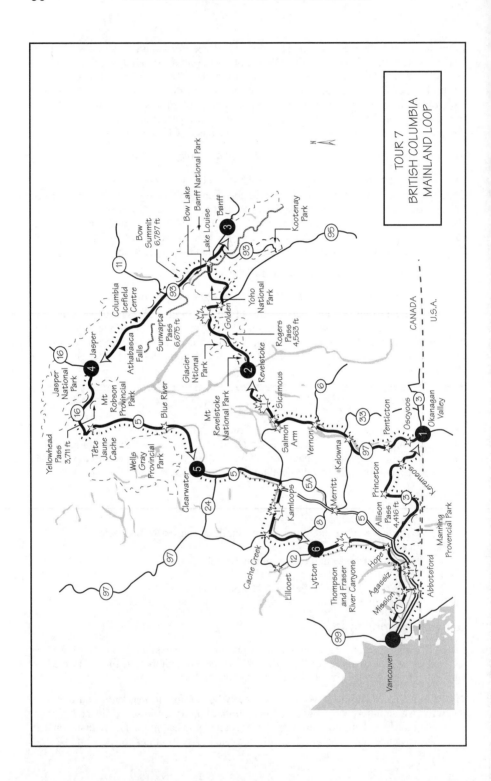

individual destinations offer plenty to keep you busy for several days. Our advice: plan on at least two weeks if you want to do this entire trip. Driving distance for the tour is 2,018 km (1,251 miles), approximate driving time is 32 hours.

The route starts at the coast in the province's largest city, Vancouver. As you drive up the Fraser River Valley you will be crossing a very civilized area of farms and small towns. However, when you reach Hope you leave all this and immediately begin climbing into a much more sparsely populated region. Highway 3 crosses both the Hozameen and Okanagan Ranges and passes through Manning Provincial Park before descending into irrigated fruit-growing country in the Okanagan Valley.

After spending some time in the valley this tour heads north to Salmon Arm where it joins the transcontinental Highway 1 and turns eastward. After stopping for a night near Revelstoke in the Columbia River Valley you'll climb to cross through Glacier National Park and the Dogtooth Range, descend to cross over the Columbia River once again, and then ascend into the Canadian Rockies through Yoho National Park to Banff National Park.

When you've had a chance to see all there is to see in Banff you can head north along the Icefields Parkway past the Columbia Icefield to Jasper National Park. Jasper too has a lot to offer, but after a couple of days it is time to begin the drive back toward Vancouver. During the day you'll pass through Mt Robson Provincial Park and then spend the night either in or near Wells Gray Provincial Park.

Continuing southward you'll follow a slightly out-of-the-way route to thread your way down the impressively scenic Thompson and Fraser River Canyons. You'll spend the night in the canyons and then continue south to meet the expressway near Hope and retrace your way down the Fraser Valley to Vancouver.

The Roads

Virtually all of the roads on this tour are of the two-lane variety. On the other hand, although they are two-lane roads they are in excellent condition with good shoulders and frequent passing lanes and rest areas. This is a mountainous route, it starts at sea level and travels over may passes reaching its highest altitude on the Icefields Parkway in Banff National Park, 2,067 meters (6,787 feet). If you have toured Colorado this may not seem high but rest assured that you will be more than satisfied by the mountains you find along this route.

Practical Tips

Since this tour traverses fairly high mountain country, particularly in Banff and Jasper National Parks, it is a summer trip. Plan to start no earlier than May and to be out of the mountains before the end of September. Even within these boundaries it is very possible that you might receive a dusting of snow during the night.

In this section you'll find lots of ways to make a one-week tour into a two or three-week one. Here's one way to shorten things a bit. One way to make more time is to use the new Highway 5, also known as the Coquihalla Highway. Using the Coquihalla from Hope to Merritt and then the Okanagan Connector from Merritt to Kelowna you can cut the first day's 7 hour drive down to only 4 to 5 hours. On your way home, if you've overstayed along the way, you can drive directly from Clearwater to Vancouver and cut an entire day from your itinerary by following the Coquihalla Highway from Kamloops to Hope.

◤ DAY 1 – DESTINATION THE OKANAGAN VALLEY – 371 KILOMETERS (230 MILES), 6.5 HOURS (TO OSOYOOS)

From Vancouver point your RV's nose east and follow the Trans-Canada Highway to the town of Hope. The entire 188 kilometer (117 mile) distance is along a multi-lane limited access freeway.

Hope forms a kind of transportation crossroads. In or near the town three major routes intersect. Highway 1 heads north from town up the Fraser Canyon. Highway 5, also called the Coquihalla Highway, provides a quick and direct toll route north to Kamloops. And finally, Highway 3 , the Crowsnest Highway, winds its scenic way east. You'll be following Highway 3 but first you might want to stop and take a look at Hope. The section titled *Hope* (page 539) describes the area and campgrounds.

Highway 3 is a fine two-lane highway, but it does cross some healthy mountains. From Hope to Osoyoos at the south end of Canada's section of the Okanagan Valley is a distance of 246 kilometers (153 miles). The highest point along the route is Allison Pass in Manning Provincial Park with an altitude of 1,352 meters (4,416 feet).

Deep in the Cascades the highway enters **Manning Provincial Park**. There are four campgrounds in the park, all are suitable for RVs. The campgrounds, a visitor center, and the Manning Park Resort with a restaurant and other services are all located near each other about 42 kilometers (26 miles) east of Hope. For more about this area see the *Manning Provincial Park* section (page 563).

Continuing east you'll begin to notice that the countryside is becoming much dryer. You'll pass through the ranch and lumber town of Princeton and then, 198 kilometers (123 miles) from Hope enter Keremeos. You can't miss the huge number of fruit stands along the highway in this town, you're entering British Columbia's fruit country. A combination of warm sunny weather and abundant water from irrigation make this the country's fruit basket. Expect to find cherries by the end of June, apricots in July, peaches just a little later, pears toward the end of August, and apples in September. Fruit ripens first in the southern Okanagan and later in the north because the south is warmer. In this book the *Similkameen Valley* section (page 618) has more about his area.

Just 48 more kilometers (30 miles) along Hwy 3 and you will arrive in Osoyoos, the south end of Canada's Okanagan Valley, almost on the U.S. border.

The *Okanagan Valley* section (page 579) describes the area and some of its campgrounds.

◤ DAY 2 – DESTINATION REVELSTOKE – 321 KILOMETERS (199 MILES), 4.5 HOURS

From the Okanagan Valley follow Hwy 97 north to intersect the Trans-Canada highway (Hwy 1) near Salmon Arm and Sicamous. Both of these towns are on the shore of **Shuswap Lake**. See the *Shuswap* section (page 613) for more about this region.

The distance from Salmon Arm to Revelstoke through the Monashee Mountains is only 104 kilometers (64 miles) so you'll soon find yourself approaching Revelstoke. The *Revelstoke* section (page 610) describes the attractions and campgrounds of this area.

◤ DAY 3 – DESTINATION BANFF NATIONAL PARK – 233 KILOMETERS (145 MILES), 3 HOURS (TO LAKE LOUISE)

From Revelstoke to Banff National Park Highway 1 follows the original route of the Canadian Pacific Railway. This portion of the railroad was one of the most problematic when it was being built in the 1880s because of the terrain it crosses. Today, for highway

WILDLIFE IS COMMON IN THE CANADIAN NATIONAL PARKS

travelers, that translates into a scenic and interesting day of driving.

East of Revelstoke just 72 kilometers (45 miles) the highway crosses **Rogers Pass** (1,387 meters, 4,563 feet) in the middle of Glacier National Park. See the *Glacier National Park* section (page 535) for more about this area.

Continuing westward the highway descends to the Columbia River at the town of Golden. Here the river is flowing north, not south. From Golden the road ascends the valley of the Kicking Horse River and soon enters Yoho National Park. See the section titled *Yoho National Park and Golden* (page 673) for more about this area.

You'll enter Banff National Park at the eastern border of Yoho National Park. See the section titled *Banff National Park* (page 494) for information about this area and its campgrounds.

🚐 DAY 4 – DESTINATION JASPER NATIONAL PARK – 232 KILOMETERS (144 MILES), 5 HOURS (TO JASPER TOWNSITE)

The route to be followed today is entirely along the 230 kilometer (143 mile) Icefields Parkway stretching from an intersection on the Trans-Canada Highway near Lake Louise north through the mountains to Jasper. Don't hurry along this highway, there is plenty of magnificent scenery and many places to stop, enjoy the view, and even take some hikes.

Like most Canadian national parks there is a day fee for the use of Banff and Jasper National Parks. It is possible to drive through Banff Park on Highway 1 without paying the fee, but not the Icefield Parkway. There are kiosks on both ends of the Icefields Parkway to collect the fee.

Some 35 kilometers (21 miles) from the start of the Parkway you'll come to **Bow Lake**. From here you'll see no more of the Bow River. There's a viewpoint where you can look across the turquoise-colored lake and see Num-Ti-Jah Lodge and the Bow Glacier beyond.

Six kilometers (4 miles) beyond Bow lake the highway crests Bow Summit at 2,067 meters (6,787 feet). This is the highest point on the Parkway.

Seventy-five kilometers (47 miles) north of the intersection with Highway 1 the Parkway crosses the North Saskatchewan River. To the west is the Howse Valley. The North Saskatchewan River and the Howse Valley were one of the early passes used by explorers and fur traders to cross the Rocky Mountains. Highway 11 heads east from here to Rocky Mountain House and Red Deer.

Sunwapta Pass (2,035 meters, 6,675 feet) marks the boundary between Banff National Park and Jasper National park. A few kilometers north of the pass is the huge **Columbia Icefield Centre**. This is an observatory with great views across the valley to the Athabasca Glacier and the Columbia Icefield. It also serves as the embarkation point for bus tours onto the glacier. Busses leave the Centre and drive to edge of the glacier, there passengers change to special vehicles with huge tires called snocoaches to actually drive out onto the glacier. As an alternative you can drive to the foot of the glacier yourself and take a short hike for a close look. The Icefield Centre also houses a Parks Canada Visitor Centre.

It is well worth a short side trip off the highway to take a look at **Athabasca Falls**. The access road is actually a short section of Highway 93A which was an older version of today's highway that runs north along the western side of the valley parallel to today's road for about 25 kilometers. The turn for Athabasca Falls is well marked, it is 73 kilometers (45 miles) north of the Columbia Icefield Centre. The Athabasca River drops over a ledge and tumbles through a narrow canyon. Overlooks and a pedestrian bridge offer excellent views, a great place for pictures.

Thirty kilometers (19 miles) beyond the falls the Icefield Parkway intersects Highway 16 which crosses the Rockies through Yellowhead Pass. If you continue straight on across the highway you will find yourself in Jasper townsite. See the section titled *Jasper National Park* (page 542) for more about this area.

⬛ DAY 5 – DESTINATION WELLS GRAY PROVINCIAL PARK – 318 KILOMETERS 197 MILES), 5.5 HOURS (TO CLEARWATER)

From the Jasper townsite area we'll follow Hwy 16 westward across Yellowhead Pass (1,131 meters, 3,711 feet), and into **Mt Robson Provincial Park**. You'll be driving along the upper Fraser River Valley and pass Yellowhead and Moose Lakes. **Mt Robson** is the highest mountain in the Canadian Rockies (3,954 meters, 12,972 feet). You can stop at the visitor center near the western border of the park some 62 kilometers (38 miles) west of Yellowhead Pass. From the visitor center you have a spectacular view of the mountain. The reason it is so impressive is that the visitor center sits at an altitude of only about 850 meters (2,800 feet) and is only 11 kilometers from the mountain, you definitely get the full effect. See the *Mt Robson and Valemount* section (page 566) for more about this area.

From Mt Robson Provincial Park the highway continues westward until it meets Highway 5 near Tête Jaune Cache. Turn south here toward Kamloops. The highway climbs over a low pass and then follows the North Thompson River Valley through the small town of Blue River and eventually reaches Clearwater. See the section titled *Wells Gray*

Provincial Park (Clearwater River Corridor Section) and Clearwater (page 662) for information about this area and its camping possibilities.

◾ Day 6 – Destination Thompson and Fraser River Canyons – 286 kilometers (177 miles), 4 hours (to Lytton)

From Clearwater we follow Highway 5 and the North Thompson River for 115 kilometers (71 miles) south to Kamloops. See the section titled *Kamloops* (page 547) for more about the region and its campgrounds. Here you have a choice. If you want to get back to Vancouver a day early you can continue on Highway 5, known as the Coquihalla Highway, from here to Hope. This is a high speed toll highway that will cut several driving hours from the trip back to Vancouver.

On the other hand, if you have another day and wish to see one of the most impressive river canyons and railroad/road engineering projects in the world, head westward from Kamloops on Highway 1. This is our old friend, the Trans-Canada Highway, last seen in Banff National Park. From Kamloops the road travels along Kamloops Lake and then parallel to the Thompson River. When it reaches Cache Creek the highway turns south and soon you are in the Thompson River Canyon. See the section titled *Thompson and Fraser River Canyons* (page 637) for information about the area and its camping possibilities.

◾ Day 7 – Destination Vancouver – 256 kilometers (159 miles), 3.5 hours

Once Highway 1 crosses to the west bank of the Fraser River you have reached the lower reaches of the canyon. The road remains on the west side for 42 kilometers (26 miles) until it crosses again at Hope.

Just before reaching Hope you have a route choice. If you are in a hurry you can continue on to Hope and then follow Highway 1 back to Vancouver, this is the same highway that you drove when you were heading east on the first day of this tour.

If you have more time you can follow Highway 7 along the north side of the Fraser River. This is a much smaller two-lane highway. You can follow it all the way to Vancouver or cross over the Fraser River to intersect Highway 1 near Agassiz (near Bridal Falls on Hwy 1) or Mission (near Abbotsford on Hwy 1).

Tour 8 – British Columbia's Sunshine Coast and Vancouver Island Loop

Summary: This tour starts in Vancouver, British Columbia. Hop up the Sunshine Coast to Powell River using a combination of ferries and roads, then cross to Vancouver Island. Visit the west coast of the Island at Tofino, then head southward to Victoria before returning to Vancouver, again by ferry.

High Points

- » The Sunshine Coast
- » Ferry rides up the Sunshine Coast and through the Gulf Islands
- » Campbell River and great salmon fishing
- » Pacific Rim National Park
- » First Nations Culture
- » Victoria

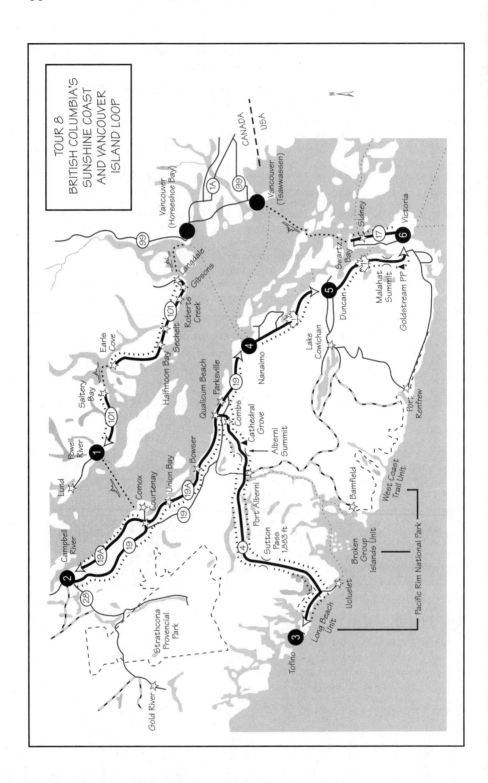

TOUR 8
BRITISH COLUMBIA'S
SUNSHINE COAST
AND VANCOUVER
ISLAND LOOP

General Description

One of the most popular destinations in the Pacific Northwest is Vancouver Island. This large island is easily accessible using frequent ferries from near Vancouver on the mainland. On the island you'll find British Columbia's capital, Victoria, as well as remote beaches, northwest Indian culture (called First Nations in Canada), some of the best salmon fishing in the world, and pristine evergreen forests. An added bonus of this tour is the Sunshine Coast which stretches over 100 kilometers (62 miles) north from the city of Vancouver along the mainland and offers surprisingly good weather and warm water because it is in the rain shadow of Vancouver Island's mountains.

The tour starts at the Horseshoe Bay ferry terminal just north of Vancouver. On the first day you take two ferry rides and do some driving on scenic two-lane roads as you travel up the Sunshine Coast to Powell River. Later, when you are ready, you take another ferry across to Vancouver Island. On the Island you visit Campbell River, and then work your way down the island with visits to Tofino, Nanaimo, Duncan, and finally the Victoria area in the south. This circular route ends with another ferry trip through the Gulf Islands to Tsawwassen which is located on the mainland just south of the city of Vancouver.

This is a relaxed tour with relatively short distances between most of your stops. Many days you will have time for a significant amount of sightseeing or just plain enjoying the outdoors. There are also plenty of reasons to expand this tour into a two or three week trip.

The Roads and Ferries

The ferries used in this circular tour are all operated by the British Columbia Ferry Corporation, also known as BC Ferries. It is not possible to make reservations for these crossings. Reservations are not usually necessary anyway. However, it is best to avoid travel on weekends during the high season: late May, June, July, August and early September, to avoid long lines. There is a special fare plan for this circle route which is known as the Circlepac and which will net you a discount of about 15%. If your RV is over 7 feet high or 20 feet long you will be paying more than the normal passenger vehicle rate for ferry travel. See the individual route sections for other information about the ferries. You will find additional information about the ferries in Chapter 1.

For the most part the roads traveled on this tour are very good. Few are more than two-lane highways, but they are adequate for all types of RVs and there are no high passes. You will find much more information about the roads in the individual sections of this chapter. Total driving distance on this tour is 815 kilometers (505 miles) with 23 hours on the road (including ferries).

Practical Tips

It is best to make this tour during the summer, say from May to September. The months of April and October are acceptable if you don't mind some rain and have a good warm RV in which to spend the night. You will find that some campgrounds are open year-round, some folks love to visit the wild western coast around Tofino just for the winter storms.

It is pretty easy to shorten this loop if you don't have time for the whole thing. One way would be to cut out the Sunshine Coast and Campbell River by taking a ferry directly from Horseshoe Bay to Nanaimo. You could still make the drive out to Tofino (day three's destination) or skip that too.

🚐 DAY 1 – DESTINATION POWELL RIVER – 127 KILOMETERS (79 MILES) (DOES NOT INCLUDE FERRY), 5 HOURS (DOES INCLUDE FERRY)

The first segment of today's drive is a 45-minute ferry ride from Horseshoe Bay across Howe Sound to Langdale. There are frequent ferries from Horseshoe Bay (approximately every two hours) so you don't have to worry much about your schedule there, but you should check when you buy your ticket to see when the Earls Cove to Saltery Bay ferry runs. Otherwise you might find yourself waiting for quite a long period at the dock in Earls Cove, particularly if you arrive there in the early afternoon. The travel time given above for this day's drive includes a half-hour for loading and unloading at each of the ferry landings.

When you leave the boat in Langdale you are on the Sunshine Coast proper. Some folks call this area the Lower Coast. Highway 101 runs north near the coast for 79 kilometers (49 miles) through the communities of Gibsons, Roberts Creek, Sechelt, Halfmoon Bay, Madeira Park, and Pender Harbor to Earls Cove. See the section titled *Sunshine Coast (Lower)* (page 629) for information about the attractions and campgrounds in this area.

The ferry from Earls Cover to Saltery Bay also runs approximately every two hours, but there is a 4-hour gap in the schedule in the afternoon. This run takes about 50 minutes and crosses Jervis Inlet. The coast north from Saltery Bay to Powell River could properly be called the Upper Sunshine Coast but it is so dominated by the town of Powell River that most folks just call it Powell River. The distance from Saltery Bay to Powell River is 27 kilometers (17 miles). See the section titled *Sunshine Coast (Upper)* (page 631) for more about this area and its campgrounds.

🚐 DAY 2 – DESTINATION CAMPBELL RIVER – 48 KILOMETERS (30 MILES) (DOES NOT INCLUDE FERRY), 3.5 HOURS (INCLUDING FERRY)

The ferry from Powell River to Little River near Comox on Vancouver Island makes the trip only a few times each day. Make sure to check the schedule so that you don't over-sleep. The crossing takes about an hour and a half.

From Comox follow Highway 19A north to Campbell River. By selecting Hwy 19A as you near Campbell River you'll come into town along the coast.

See the section titled *Campbell River* (page 513) for information about the area and its campgrounds.

🚐 DAY 3 – DESTINATION TOFINO – 268 KILOMETERS (166 MILES), 5 HOURS

The drive from Campbell River to Tofino takes you south through the Comox Valley region to Qualicum Beach and then all the way across the island to the west coast. While the drive sounds ambitious it really is no problem.

From Campbell River follow Highway 19 south. After 45 kilometers (28 miles) you'll reach Courtenay and drive through an area of strip malls and giant supermarkets. Watch for signs for Highway 19A, it is the road that follows the coast south. A new section of Hwy 19 passes farther inland and is not as scenic. You'll pass several small seaside towns including Union Bay, Fanny Bay, Bowser, and finally reach Qualicum Beach. This is an attractive stretch of ocean-side country, it is one of the places you could spend the night on Day 4 after returning from the west coast.

At Qualicum Beach you will spot Highway 4 heading up the hill to the west toward Port Alberni and eventually Tofino. Turn here and you'll pass through the business district,

THERE IS LOTS TO DO TO KEEP YOU BUSY DURING YOUR STAY AT TOFINO

cross under the inland Highway 19, and then pass the little town of Coombs. Pull over and take a look around. You'll probably enjoy visiting the old Coombs General Store, Frontier Town, antique shops, and the Old Country Market. Don't miss the goats on the roof! Heading west from Coombs toward Port Alberni watch for the sign for **Butterfly World**, it's a tropical garden filled with butterflies and birds. Farther west you'll see the signs for Qualicum Falls Provincial Park. There's a good campground here as well as hiking paths to see the falls. A little farther west you'll find yourself passing through an area of huge trees, mostly Douglas Firs. There's a pull-off parking area here and you can follow trails through **Cathedral Grove** in MacMillan Provincial Park.

The road soon rises and passes over low Alberni Summit (375 meters, 1230 feet) and then descends to pass through the northern edge of the town of Port Alberni. See the section titled *Port Alberni* (page 592) for more about this area.

About 48 kilometers (30 miles) beyond Port Alberni you'll reach 250-meter (820 foot) Sutton Pass and then the road descends and in another 10 kilometers (6 miles) you will reach a T intersection. Ucluelet is to the left (6 kilometers, 4 miles) and Tofino to the right (33 kilometers, 20 miles). Most of the Long Beach section of Pacific Rim National Park is also to the right. For now turn to the right, you can come back and explore Ucluelet later if you desire.

See the section titled *Tofino, Ucluelet, and the Pacific Rim National Park* (page 642) for more about this area and its campgrounds.

⛟ DAY 4 – DESTINATION NANAIMO – 215 KILOMETERS (133 MILES), 4 HOURS (TO NANAIMO)

To drive to Nanaimo you must retrace your trip westward on Highway 4 as far as Qualicum Beach. You might stop and take a look at Ucluelet which we bypassed on the outbound trip.

When you have backtracked across the island and again reached the east coast in Qualicum Beach, turn south. Just south of Qualicum Beach is Parksville, which, like Qualicum Beach, has many campgrounds. You can overnight here or farther south near Nanaimo. See the section titled *Oceanside* (page 575) for more about this area and its campgrounds.

Highways 19 and 19A merge just south of Parksville, then 16 kilometers (10 miles) south, they split again with the new Highway 19 Nanaimo Parkway (bypass route) being the preferred route to the Nanaimo campgrounds. See the section titled *Nanaimo* (page 571) for more about the area and its campgrounds.

⛟ DAY 5 – DESTINATION DUNCAN AND COWICHAN LAKE – 52 KILOMETERS (32 MILES), 1 HOUR (TO DUNCAN)

Duncan lies only an hour's drive south of Nanaimo along what is designated as Highway 1. It's really the same highway that you have been following south along the east side of Vancouver Island, but here it is considered to be the final kilometers of the Trans-Canada Highway that begins in Newfoundland and ends in Victoria.

For information about the area and campgrounds surrounding Duncan see *Cowichan Valley: Chemainus, Duncan, and Cowichan Lake* (page 526).

⛟ DAY 6 – DESTINATION VICTORIA – 56 KILOMETERS (35 MILES), 1 HOUR

From Duncan it is only a short drive south to Victoria. Twenty-nine kilometers (18 miles) south of Duncan the highway climbs to the **Malahat Summit**, there is a great viewpoint but access from the southbound lanes is limited, you may have to drive another kilometer or so to a good turnaround if you want to stop and enjoy the view.

A few kilometers after the summit viewpoint you pass through Goldstream Provincial Park. This park has an excellent campground and is convenient to Victoria. It also has a number of hiking trails through first-growth forest of Douglas Fir and cedar as well as waterfalls and look-out points.

Once you pass Goldstream Park you're only a short distance from Victoria and it is time to start watching for the city campgrounds. See the section titled *Victoria* (page 656) for information about the area and its campgrounds.

⛟ DAY 7 – DESTINATION VANCOUVER – 48 KILOMETERS (30 MILES) (DOES NOT INCLUDE FERRY), 3.5 HOURS (INCLUDING FERRY)

The ferry back to Vancouver departs from Swartz Bay at the north end of the Saanich Peninsula. To get there just drive north on Hwy 17 from Victoria for 32 kilometers (20 miles). Ferries run frequently. They dock at Tsawwassen which is only a half hour drive south of Vancouver.

Chapter 3
How to use the
Destination Chapters

The chapters titled Oregon, Washington, and British Columbia are the meat of this book. Each starts with an index map, it's an easy way to see how the destination sections later in the chapter will fit together. The chapters begin with general descriptions of the landforms and regions of each state or province. Then there's information about the government campgrounds and their reservations systems (if any).

Within the first few pages of each chapter you'll find a series of **Campground Location Maps**. They are an overview of the campgrounds located in the chapter, and an easy way to locate exactly the information you need.

These maps contain a lot of information. First, the general location of every campground in the book is shown on these maps. Each campground is represented by a symbol which tells you what kind it is: commercial, state or provincial, federal, or local. Lightly shaded boxes enclose the campground clusters, these boxes indicate which destination section of the book describes the campgrounds. There is a small information box alongside each one with the name of the section and page number where it starts.

Finally you'll come to the *Destinations and Their Campgrounds* section. Each destination section includes a map to give you the lay of the land and to pinpoint campground locations. The maps are for the most part pretty easy to interpret, there is a symbol key on the following page.

We have selected destinations that are great places to visit in an RV. These are places with convenient campgrounds as well as lots to see and do. Some of these are cities and towns, others are general recreational areas that may cover quite a bit of territory. We give you some background information about the place and also describe some of the attractions that you might want to visit.

MAP LEGEND

══84══	Major Freeway	(97)	Secondary Road No.	·············	State Border
────	Other Paved Roads	(20)	Other Road No.	─ ─ ─	Country Border
─·■·─	Unpaved Roads	🍁	Canadian National Hwy	┼─┼─┼	Railroad
═□═	Freeway Off-ramp	🚌	Campground (40 ft) (See Page 65)	·▲·	Ferry Route
═□═ Exit 2	Off-ramp – Name Indicated	🚐	Campground (RVs Under 40 ft)	✿	City or Town
(5)	Freeway Number	⊡	Campground - Location Only, No Description	◉	Roundabout
▒▒	City Center	⚠	Tent Only Campground	) (	Mountain Pass
■	Federal Campground	☐	State Campground	▲	Area of Interest
○	Local Campground	Ashland Pg 79	Destination Section and Pg No	✈	Major Airport
				✈	Other Airport
				●	Commercial Campground

Campground Information

Immediately after the name of the campground we give the opening and closing dates. Then there is contact information for making reservations or making inquiries by phone or email.

A location line gives the campground location with respect to some nearby landmark. Then there's a line with latitude and longitude that can be used with a GPS to assist in finding the campground. At the end of the line is the approximate elevation of the campground.

Next is a group of pictograms or symbols. These are designed to convey important information about the campground at a glance. For your convenience abbreviated keys to these symbols are located on the back inside cover to this book.

FREE	Free	$$$ / $$$	Over $25 and up to $30
$	Up To $5	$$$ / $$$$	Over $30 and up to $35
$$	Over $5 and up to $10	$$$$ / $$$$	Over $35 and up to $40
$$$	Over $10 and up to $15	$$$$ / $$$$$	Over $40 and up to $45
$ / $$$	Over $15 and up to $20	$$$$$ / $$$$$	Over $45 and up to $50
$$ / $$$	over $20 and up to $25	Over $50	Over $50

The first symbols are for price. Since campground prices do change frequently this is really an approximation, but it is the price that was in effect when the book was issued. It is the price in U.S. dollars for a standard full-hookup site with 30-amp power (if available) for a 30-foot RV. RVers willing to park without hookups or with partial hookup sites are often quoted a lower price. If you are tent camping you may find that no-hookup tent sites are often available for considerably less. If you are in a larger RV requiring a pull-thru site, 50-amp power, or yours is a premium or view site you will probably find that the price is higher.

The remaining symbols are as follows:

 Tents – The campground does allow tent campers.

 Rentals – The campground has rental cottages of some kind for those who do not want to sleep in a tent or RV. They may be yurts, motel rooms, cabins, or even tepees.

 20 Amp Electric – Low amp electrical hookups are available. High-amp hookups are not as important in the Northwest as they are in some other places since air conditioning is usually not necessary. In the hot desert country on the eastern side of the mountains it may be. Most low amp electrical hookups have 20 amp breakers but occasionally you'll find a 15 or even 10 amp circuit.

 30 Amp Electric – 30 amp electrical outlets are available.

 50 Amp Electric – 50 amp electrical outlets are available. Usually 30-amp sites are also available at campgrounds with 50-amp sties.

 Water – There is water at some or all of the sites. If there is no symbol then water is at faucets or a pump not at the sites. If there is no water we indicate so in the text section.

 Sewer – The sewer symbol means that there are sewer drains available at some or all sites.

 Dump – Indicates that there is a dump station (sani-station in Canada) available.

 Flush Toilets – Almost all of the campgrounds listed in this book have toilets, the toilet symbol in our descriptions shows which ones are flush toilets. You may also run into pit or vault (outhouse-style) toilets, particularly in provincial or federal campgrounds. If there are no toilets at all it will be obvious from the text.

 Showers – Hot showers are available. There may be an additional fee for showers, usually in the form of a coin box that takes quarters or loonies (Canadian one-dollar coins).

 Fires – Campfires are allowed, usually at individual sites but sometimes at a central or community fire pit. Plan on either bringing firewood along with you or buying it at the campground, you won't be able to pick wood off the forest floor either because it is prohibited or because there have been too many folks there ahead of you. Cutting standing trees is never permitted. Temporary fire bans are sometimes in effect.

 Swimming – Swimming is available either on-site or very nearby. It may be a swimming pool, lake, river, or even the ocean if folks customarily swim there. There are almost never lifeguards, you swim at your own risk. If the swimming is outdoors (not an inside pool) it will be seasonal.

 Playground – There is a playground for children with swings, slides and the equivalent or there are horseshoes, a play field, or provisions for some other type of sports.

Telephone – There is a pay phone or courtesy phone available

Cell Phone – The campground has at least weak cell phone coverage.

TV – TV hookups are available at some or all sites.

WI-Fi – Indicates that Wi-Fi (wireless internet) is available in the campground. Wi-Fi access is the fastest changing amenity offered by campgrounds today. Campgrounds are adding Wi-Fi access at a pretty good clip. If this is important to you don't hesitate to ask before making a reservation or perhaps call ahead as you approach your destination to determine the current offerings of the campgrounds you are considering.

Free Wi-Fi – Wi-Fi is not only available – it's free. Since Wi-Fi is such a new thing many campground owners are feeling their way on this. We're finding that many that charged at first are now offering it for free, but also that some that originally didn't charge now are. If you like free Wi-Fi you should let campgrounds owners know it.

Groceries – Many campgrounds have small stores. We've included this symbol if the store appears to have enough stock to be useful, or if there is an off-site store within easy walking distance.

Restaurants – Few campgrounds in the U.S. or Canada have restaurants, but if they do, or if there is one within easy walking distance, we include the restaurant symbol.

Laundry – The campground has self-operated washers.

Propane – The campground offers either bottled propane or a propane fill station.

Ice – Either block or cubed ice is available for ice chests or drinks.

Handicap – The wheelchair symbol indicates that at least partial handicapped access is provided. These provisions vary considerably, you should call the information number listed for the campground to get more details if this is a consideration for you.

No Pets – No dogs or cats are allowed. Virtually all campgrounds require leashes and the majority restrict number, size, and breed. Call the information number to inquire if this might apply to you.

Reservations – Reservations are taken. Please refer to the *Government Lands and Their Campgrounds* sections at the beginning of the Destinations chapters for information about making reservations at government campgrounds. Commercial campgrounds are easier, just call the listed telephone number.

Credit Cards – Either Master Card or Visa is accepted.

Good Sam – Many campgrounds give a discount to members of the Good Sam Club. We include the symbol if they are official Good Sam campgrounds. We find that the standards required for listing by Good Sam mean that in general these campgrounds stand out as having decent facilities, good management, and relatively fair prices. For club information call (800) 234-3450 or see their website at www.goodsamclub.com.

 Escapees – The Escapee symbol means that discounts are offered to members of the Escapees RV Club. Call (888) 757-2582 or (936) 327-8873 for more information or see their website – www.escapees.com.

 FMCA – Discounts are available to FMCA members. Call (800) 543-3622 or (513) 474-3622 for more information if you own a qualifying motorhome, or check the website at www.fmca.com.

 Passport America – Passport America discount cards are accepted. Most campgrounds offering this discount also will sell you the card.

 Coast to Coast – This is a Coast to Coast park.

 40 Foot RVs – Coaches to 40 feet will fit in the park. See RV Size below for more about this.

In the text portion of the campground listing we try to give you some feeling for the campground as well as detailed instructions for how to find it. We've included a count of the number of sites in a campground so that you'll have an idea of the size of the campground. These are our count and may vary from the owner's count, particularly if there are tent sites at the campground since the exact number of these is often difficult to distinguish.

RV Size

Our Big Rig symbol means that there is room for coaches to 40 feet to enter the campground, maneuver, and park. Usually this means we've seen them do it. The driver we saw may have been a better driver than most so exercise caution. If you pull a fifth-wheel you'll have to use your own judgment of how your RV handles compared with a coach. If you drive an even larger 45-foot coach you can at least use our symbol as a starting point in making your campground decisions. There's usually more in the write-up itself about this, including site lengths, and we also usually mention pull-thrus if available. Always evaluate the campground and assigned space yourself before attempting to maneuver and park, the final decision is yours. A properly trained outside spotter is essential, most RV accidents occur during the parking phase.

Units of Measurement

The region covered by this guide uses two different sets of measurements. Canada is on the metric system while the U.S. uses miles and gallons.

We've given mileages in both kilometers and miles. In the U.S. the miles come first, in British Columbia the kilometers do.

Here are some handy conversion factors:

1 km = .62 mile	1 liter = .26 U.S. gallon
1 mile = 1.61 km	1 U.S. gallon = 3.79 liters
1 meter = 3.28 feet	1 kilogram = 2.21 pounds
1 foot = .3 meters	1 pound = .45 kilogram

Convert from °F to °C by subtracting 32 and multiplying by 5/9
Convert from °C to °F by multiplying by 1.8 and adding 32

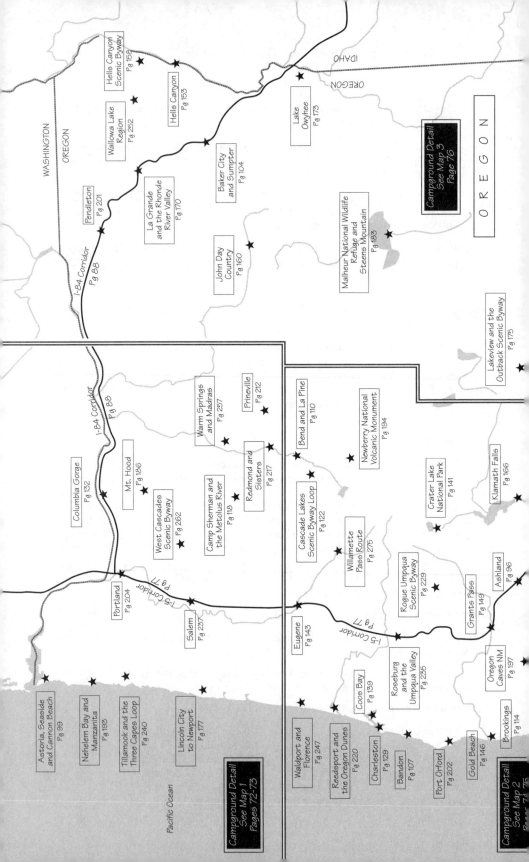

WASHINGTON

OREGON

OREGON

IDAHO

O R E G O N

Campground Detail
See Map 3
Page 76

Hells Canyon
Scenic Byway
Pg 158

Wallowa Lake
Region
Pg 252

Hells Canyon
Pg 153

Baker City
and Sumpter
Pg 104

Lake
Owyhee
Pg 175

Pendleton
Pg 201

La Grande
and the Rhonde
River Valley
Pg 170

John Day
Country
Pg 160

Malheur National Wildlife
Refuge and Steens Mountain
Pg 183

I-84 Corridor
Pg 88

Lakeview and the
Outback Scenic Byway
Pg 175

I-84 Corridor
Pg 88

Columbia Gorge
Pg 132

Mt. Hood
Pg 186

Warm Springs
and Madras
Pg 257

Prineville
Pg 212

Bend and La Pine
Pg 110

West Cascades
Scenic Byway
Pg 262

Camp Sherman and
the Metolius River
Pg 118

Redmond
and Sisters
Pg 217

Newberry National
Volcanic Monument
Pg 194

Portland
Pg 204

I-5 Corridor
Pg 77

Cascade Lakes
Scenic Byway Loop
Pg 122

Crater Lake
National Park
Pg 141

Klamath Falls
Pg 166

Salem
Pg 257

Willamette
Pass Route
Pg 275

Rogue Umpqua
Scenic Byway
Pg 229

Eugene
Pg 143

I-5 Corridor
Pg 77

Roseburg
and the
Umpqua Valley
Pg 235

Grants Pass
Pg 149

Ashland
Pg 96

Astoria, Seaside
and Cannon Beach
Pg 99

Nehelem Bay and
Manzanita
Pg 193

Tillamook and the
Three Capes Loop
Pg 240

Lincoln City
to Newport
Pg 177

Campground Detail
See Map 1
Pages 72-73

Pacific Ocean

Waldport and
Florence
Pg 247

Reedsport and
the Oregon Dunes
Pg 220

Coos Bay
Pg 139

Charleston
Pg 129

Bandon
Pg 107

Port Orford
Pg 202

Gold Beach
Pg 146

Oregon
Caves NM
Pg 197

Brookings
Pg 114

Campground Detail
See Map 2

Oregon is a varied and beautiful state. The people who live here, as in Washington and British Columbia, are very outdoors oriented, and that means that there are lots of camping opportunities.

Like Washington the state of Oregon is cut from north to south by a mountain range, the Cascades. This causes a dramatic division of the state. These mountains isolate the eastern part of the state from the marine climate of the west. That means that eastern Oregon is hot and dry in the summer and cold and dry in the winter. The western part of the state has a much wetter and more moderate climate. The summers are pleasantly warm but don't offer as many clear days as in the east, the winters almost never see snow, but they do see a lot of rain.

It's an amazing fact that although Oregon is full of natural wonders it is only home to one national park. Crater Lake is one of the more remote national parks in the country, but also one of the easiest to explore in your own vehicle. The drive around the crater rim makes it a snap.

REGIONS AND THEIR CAMPGROUND RESOURCES

Oregon Coast

One of the top camping destinations in the entire country is the Oregon Coast. The region changes with the seasons. It's a great destination all year long and many campgrounds remain open during the entire year, but it's a completely different place in the winter than in the middle of the summer. This is one of the few destination areas in Oregon that is fine for winter camping travel. During wet winter weather the coastal highway, US-101, is sometimes closed by landslides. Regional news programs will have reports if this hap-

COQUILLE RIVER LIGHTHOUSE NEAR BANDON ON THE OREGON COAST

pens. The road generally opens within a day or two. In the winter you don't really need to worry about making reservations at the campgrounds.

Whale watching is a very popular pastime on the coast. Gray whales winter in Baja California and summer in the far north, therefore they pass the Oregon coast twice. During December, January, and early February they are going south, in March, April and May they are headed north. A small population also summers in Oregon waters. You can see the whales from high points on coast and also take whale-watching voyages from several ports.

Fishing is another popular activity along the coast. You can fish from the charter boats that are based at many ports, fish in salt water along the beaches, or fish the estuaries and rivers along the coast. Every destination described in this region offers fishing possibilities.

In this book you will find a full selection of Oregon Coast campgrounds. There are 125 of them here including 71 commercial campgrounds, 18 state campgrounds, 19 federal Forest Service or BLM campgrounds and 17 municipal or county campgrounds. The following sections list almost all campgrounds along the Oregon coast from north to south: • *Astoria, Seaside and Cannon Beach,* • *Nehalem Bay and Manzanita,* • *Tillamook and the Three Capes Loop,* • *Lincoln City to Newport,* • *Waldport and Florence,* • *Reedsport and the Oregon Dunes,* • *Coos Bay,* • *Charleston,* • *Bandon,* • *Port Orford,* • *Gold Beach,* and • *Brookings.*

Willamette Valley and Portland

A low range of mountains, the Coastal Range, separates the Oregon coast from the Willamette Valley which stretches south from Portland. The valley is both the largest population center of Oregon and an important farming and recreational area. I-5 crosses the Willamette Valley from north to south, and then continues on to the California border. The following is a listing of the destinations in this book along the I-5 corridor from north to south: *Interstate 5 Corridor • Portland, • Salem, • Eugene, • Roseburg and the Umpqua Valley, • Grants Pass, and • Ashland and Medford.*

Cascade Mountains

The Cascade Mountains extend an average of about 80 miles (130 km) from west to east. This is a young range geologically and it shows. Hillsides are steep and valleys are narrow. There are some major volcanic peaks in Oregon's Cascades including Mt Hood (11,235 ft.), the Three Sisters (all a little over 10,000 ft.), Mt Bachelor (9,065 ft.), Broken Top (9,173 ft.) and Mount Mazama, home to Crater Lake (with the south rim to near 8,000 ft.), Mt Scott (8,926 ft.), and Mt McLoughlin (9,295 ft.). Crater Lake National Park is the only national park in Oregon. Our Cascade Mountains destinations are *Camp Sherman and the Metolius River,* • the *Willamette Pass Route,* • *Rogue-Umpquah Scenic Byway*, and • *Crater Lake National Park.* Other destinations which include some Cascade Mountain campgrounds border the range to the north, west and east, they are: • *Columbia Gorge,* • *West Cascades Scenic Byway,* • *Redmond and Sisters,* • *Bend and La Pine*, and • *Cascade Lakes Scenic Byway Loop..*

Columbia River

The northern border of Oregon is the Columbia River. The Columbia has always been an important transportation corridor so it offers quite a bit of history. It also is very scenic with waterfalls as well as huge lakes behind massive dams. Three destination sections in this book cover the area: • *Highway 84 Corridor,* • *Columbia Gorge* and • *Goldendale and Maryhill Region* (this section is in Chapter 5).

Bend Area

East of the Cascades Oregon is composed of high plateau country with smaller dry mountain ranges. Just east of the Cascades the area around Bend stands out as a really great camping destination. It's so good that in this book a total of eight different destination sections describe the area: *Warm Springs and Madras • Camp Sherman and the Metolius River,* • *Prineville* • *Redmond and Sisters,* • *Bend and La Pine,* • *Cascade Lakes Scenic Byway Loop,* • *Willamette Pass Route, and* • *Newberry National Volcanic Monument.*

The East

There are other destinations east of the Cascades. They tend to be widely scattered in this almost-empty landscape. In this book you'll find: • *Interstate 84 Corridor,* • *Pendleton,* • *Wallowa Lake Region,* • *Hells Canyon Scenic Byway,* • *Hells Canyon,* • *Baker City and Sumpter,* • *La Grande and the Grande Ronde Valley,* • *Upper John Day Country* • *Klamath Falls,* • *Lakeview and the Outback Scenic Byway,* • *Malheur National Wildlife Refuge and Steens Mountain* and • *Lake Owyhee.*

OREGON

GOVERNMENT LANDS AND THEIR CAMPGROUNDS

Oregon State Campgrounds

Oregon has one of the best state campgrounds systems in the country. There are 52 State of Oregon parks that have campgrounds. Forty-eight of the most interesting and accessible are listed in this book.

We think that these campgrounds are the cream of the crop in Oregon. Given a choice most campers choose to stay in a state campground if one is convenient. Any private campground owner will tell you that government campgrounds have an unfair advantage – lots of prime real estate. Many other states do not take advantage of this, but Oregon does. The state campgrounds offer hookups, beautiful settings and landscaping, lots of room, and even an excellent reservation system.

These campgrounds cater to all types of campers. Tenters will find hiker/biker walk-in sites as well as vehicle accessible sites. RVers will find long, wide sites suitable for big RVs, often with full hookups, sometimes even with cable TV. Restrooms often offer good showers as part of the package, not an extra cost add-on. If you are looking for even more in the way of sleeping quarters, there are often cabins, yurts, or teepees that will get you out of the weather. Finally, Oregon state park campgrounds all accept credit cards at the park, even when there is only a self-registration kiosk.

The reservation system is key. From Memorial Day to Labor Day state campgrounds are very popular and reservations are often necessary, especially on weekends. Make them as soon as you can, particularly if you happen to have a large RV since sites for big RVs with slide-outs are at a premium in the state park campgrounds. About half of the Oregon state parks accept reservations, the others are first-come, first served.

Reservations for State of Oregon campgrounds are easy to make. For a telephone reservation call (800) 452-5687. The internet address for reservations is www.reserveamerica. com. Both of these systems have information about site size, so if you have a big RV they can assign you an appropriate location. You can also check site availability on the website and then call the telephone number to make your reservation. Reservations can be made from 9 months to two days in advance, they cost $8 per reservation. The fee applies to each site reserved, no matter for how long, it's not a per-day fee. Note however, that there is a 14 day limit on stays in most Oregon state campgrounds.

Oregon state parks cost less in the winter. From October 1 to April 30 it's Discovery Season and rates are about 20% lower. Summer rates for no-hookup vehicle campsites are from $17 to $21, winter rates from $13 to $17. Summer rates for hookup campsites are from $20 to $28, winter rates from $16 to $23. There are also inexpensive hiker/biker (no parking pad) tent sites, the charge is generally $6 per person for these sites.

Federal Campgrounds

In this chapter you'll find a variety of federal campground types. These include National Forest campgrounds in 10 different national forests: Siuslaw, Rogue River, Siskiyou, Umpqua, Willamette, Mt Hood, Deschutes, Ochoco, Freemont-Winema, and Wallowa-Whitman. They also include other campgrounds also administered by the National Forest Service including those in the Crooked River National Grasslands, Newberry National Monument, Columbia Gorge National Scenic Area, and Oregon Dunes National Recreation Area. There are also national park campgrounds in Crater Lake National Park, and

BLM and Corps of Engineers campgrounds in a variety of other federal lands areas. In all there are 180 federal campgrounds in the Oregon chapter.

Most RVers think of federal lands campgrounds as best for tent campers and small RVs. Many are, but you'll also find some big-rig campgrounds including a few with utility hookups. Look in our *Baker City and Sumpter, Crater Lake National Park, Maryhill Region*, and *Waldport and Florence* sections for federal campgrounds offering hookups. It is possible to use a big RV in some Federal campgrounds and we've included a lot of information in this chapter that will help you decide which ones are right for you and your camping vehicle.

Seniors can get a discount on most federal government campgrounds. If you're a U.S. citizen or permanent resident and 62 years old you can buy a Senior Pass. The cost is $10 for life, it gets you half off on most federal campground fees as well as free access to national parks and other federal lands.

Many campgrounds on federal lands can be reserved. Most use the National Recreation Reservation Service. Access is via the www.recreation.gov website or telephone – (877) 444-6777. From outside the U.S. the number is (518) 885-3639. Individual campground write-ups in this book tell which federal campgrounds can be reserved. Most campsites have a $9 fee per reservation when made on the internet, $10 per reservation when made over the phone. Campground reservations can be made up to 6 months in advance.

CAMPGROUND LOCATION INDEX MAPS

On the following pages you'll find three Campground Location Index Maps for Oregon. These maps show the approximate location of every campground as described in this chapter. The shaded areas show which section covers each campground shown. It's an easy matter to turn to the proper section where you'll find a detailed map, a description of the area, and detailed descriptions of all of the campgrounds. Note that there are four types of symbols used for the campgrounds:

- ■ Federal
- ☐ State
- ● Commercial
- ○ Local Government

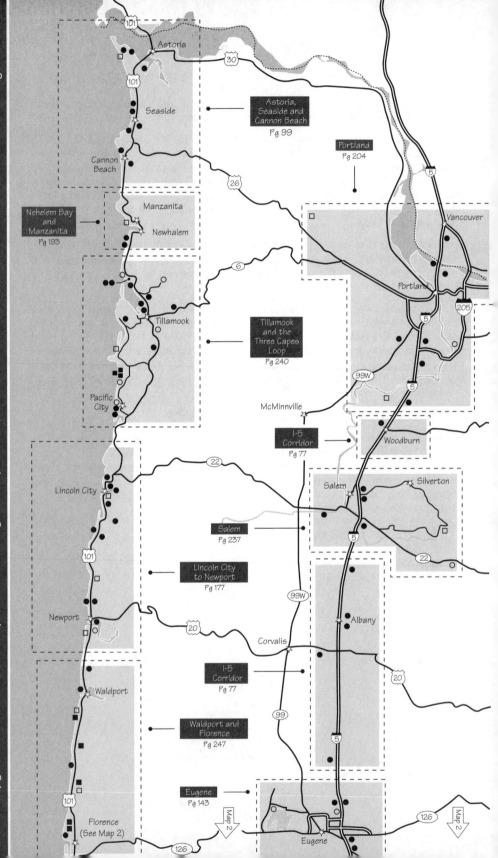

Campground Location Index Map * Northern Oregon * Map 1

Astoria

101

30

101

Astoria,
Seaside and
Cannon Beach
Pg 99

Portland
Pg 204

Seaside

5

Vancouver

Cannon
Beach

26

Manzanita

Nehelem Bay
and
Manzanita
Pg 193

Newhalem

6

Portland

205

Tillamook
and the
Three Capes
Loop
Pg 240

99W

Pacific
City

McMinnville

Woodburn

I-5
Corridor
Pg 77

5

22

Salem

Silverton

Lincoln City

Salem
Pg 237

5

22

Lincoln City
to Newport
Pg 177

99W

Newport

20

Albany

Corvalis

20

I-5
Corridor
Pg 77

99

Waldport

Waldport and
Florence
Pg 247

5

101

Eugene
Pg 143

Map 2

Map 2

Florence
(See Map 2)

126

Eugene

126

Map 2

Map 2

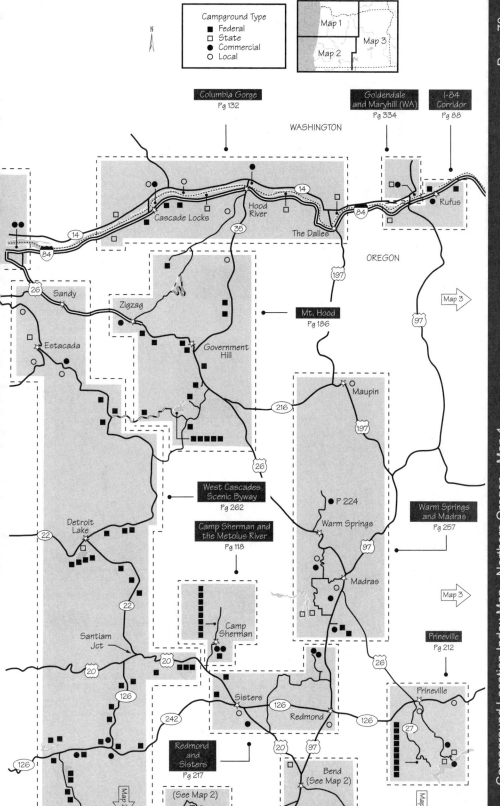

Campground Location Index Map * Northern Oregon * Map 1

Campground Type
■ Federal
□ State
● Commercial
○ Local

Map 1
Map 2
Map 3

Columbia Gorge
Pg 132

Goldendale
and Maryhill (WA)
Pg 334

I-84
Corridor
Pg 88

WASHINGTON

14

Cascade Locks

Hood
River

The Dalles

84

Rufus

OREGON

197

26

Sandy

Zigzag

Estacada

Government
Hill

Mt. Hood
Pg 186

216

Maupin

197

97

Map 3

26

West Cascades
Scenic Byway
Pg 262

P 224

Warm Springs

Warm Springs
and Madras
Pg 257

22

Detroit
Lake

Camp Sherman and
the Metolus River
Pg 118

97

Madras

Map 3

22

Camp
Sherman

Prineville
Pg 212

Santiam
Jct

20

20

26

Prineville

126

Sisters

27

242

126

Redmond

126

Redmond
and
Sisters
Pg 217

20

97

Map 2

126

Bend
(See Map 2)

Map 2

(See Map 2)

35

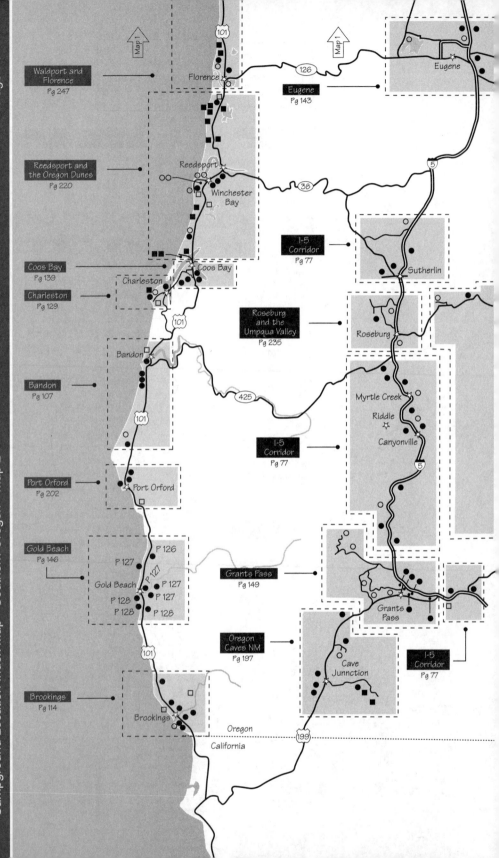

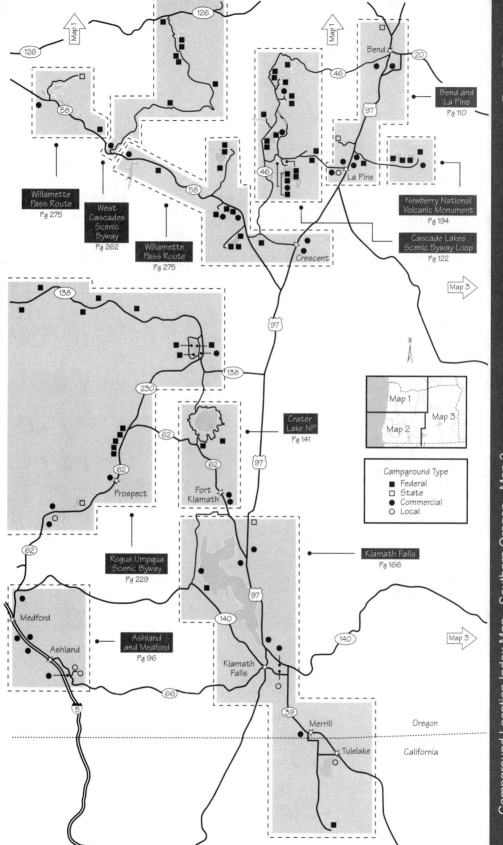

126

Map 1

126

58

Willamette
Pass Route
Pg 275

West
Cascades
Scenic
Byway
Pg 262

Willamette
Pass Route
Pg 275

Map 1

46

Bend

20

97

Bend and
La Pine
Pg 110

La Pine

Newberry National
Volcanic Monument
Pg 194

46

Crescent

Cascade Lakes
Scenic Byway Loop
Pg 122

Map 3

97

138

138

230

62

62

62

62

Prospect

Fort
Klamath

Crater
Lake NP
Pg 141

97

N

Map 1

Map 3

Map 2

Campground Type

■ Federal
□ State
● Commercial
○ Local

Rogue Umpqua
Scenic Byway
Pg 229

Klamath Falls
Pg 166

62

Medford

Ashland

Ashland
and Medford
Pg 96

97

140

Klamath
Falls

140

Map 3

5

66

39

Merrill

Oregon

Tulelake

California

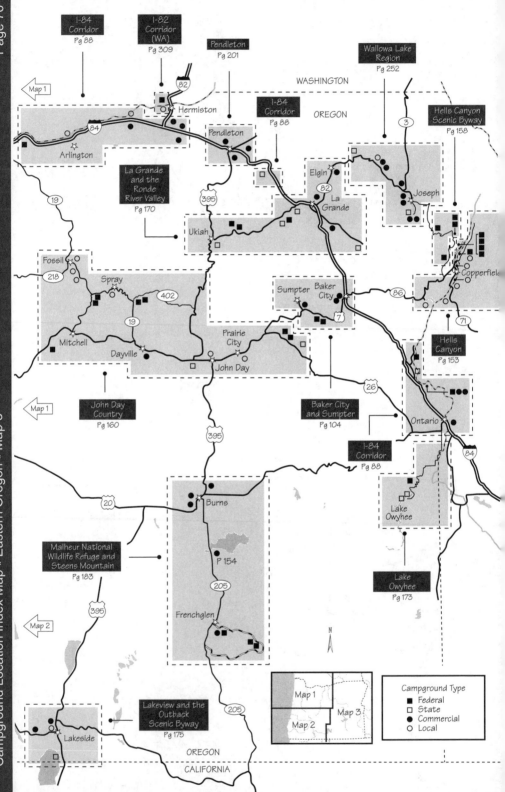

I-84 Corridor
Pg 88

I-82 Corridor (WA)
Pg 309

Pendleton
Pg 201

Wallowa Lake Region
Pg 252

Hells Canyon Scenic Byway
Pg 158

Map 1

WASHINGTON

OREGON

Hermiston

Pendleton

I-84 Corridor
Pg 88

Arlington

La Grande and the Ronde River Valley
Pg 170

Elgin

La Grande

Joseph

Ukiah

Fossil

Spray

Sumpter

Baker City

Copperfield

Mitchell

Dayville

Prairie City

John Day

Hells Canyon
Pg 153

Map 1

John Day Country
Pg 160

Baker City and Sumpter
Pg 104

Ontario

I-84 Corridor
Pg 88

Burns

P 154

Lake Owyhee

Malheur National Wildlife Refuge and Steens Mountain
Pg 183

Lake Owyhee
Pg 173

Map 2

Frenchglen

N

Lakeview and the Outback Scenic Byway
Pg 175

Lakeside

OREGON

CALIFORNIA

Map 1

Map 2

Map 3

Campground Type
■ Federal
□ State
● Commercial
○ Local

OREGON

DESTINATIONS AND THEIR CAMPGROUNDS

INTERSTATE 5 CORRIDOR

Interstate 5 (I-5) is the main north-south corridor in western Oregon and Washington. It runs 585 miles (944 km) from the Canadian border just south of Vancouver south through the largest population centers of the Pacific Northwest including Bellingham, Seattle, Tacoma, Portland, Salem, and Eugene.

The campgrounds listed below are located in Oregon, see the Interstate 5 Corridor section in the Washington chapter for campgrounds in that state. Note that many of the campgrounds along the I-5 Corridor are described under other destination sections in this chapter. If so, we've given a page reference to make finding them easy.

Interstate 5 Corridor Campgrounds

⮕ **Exit 308**

● **JANTZEN BEACH RV PARK** *(Listed under Portland, page 210)*

⮕ **Exit 307**

● **COLUMBIA RIVER RV PARK** *(Listed under Portland, page 209)*

⮕ **Exit 291**

● **ROAMER'S REST RV PARK** *(Listed under Portland, page 211)*

⮕ **Exit 289**

● **RV PARK OF PORTLAND** *(Listed under Portland, page 210)*

⮕ **Exit 286**

● **PHEASANT RIDGE RV RESORT** *(Listed under Portland, page 211)*

⮕ **Exit 278**

● **AURORA ACRES RV PARK** *(Listed under Portland, page 211)*

⮕ **Exit 271**

● **PORTLAND-WOODBURN RV PARK**
   (Open All Year)

   Res & Info: (888) 988-0002, www.woodburnrv.com, info@woodburnrv.com
   Location: Woodburn, I-5 Exit 271

   GPS Location: 45.15306 N, 122.88222 W, 100 Ft

150 Sites – This is a modern big-rig park near the freeway with some convenient restaurants out front including a Starbucks and an Elmer's. There's an outlet mall next door. There are lots of 60-foot pull-thrus as well as 40 foot back-ins. The park also has a swimming pool. Take Exit 271 from I-5 and turn west. In .3 mile (.5 km) turn right and in another .1 mile (.2 km) you'll see the RV park entrance to the right.

⮕ **Exit 256**

● **PHOENIX RV PARK** *(Listed under Salem, page 239)*

⮕ **Exit 255**

● **HEE HEE ILLAHEE RV RESORT** *(Listed under Salem, page 239)*

OREGON

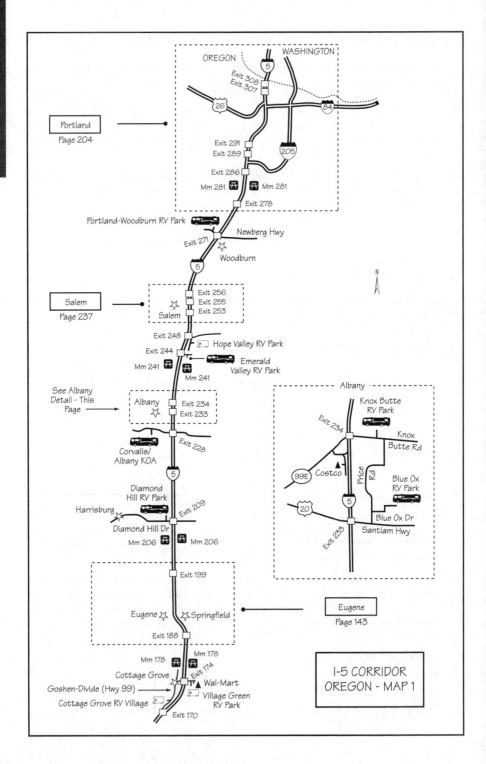

OREGON   WASHINGTON

Exit 308
Exit 307

26

84

Portland
Page 204

Exit 291
Exit 289

205

Exit 286

Mm 281   Mm 281

Exit 278

Portland-Woodburn RV Park

Exit 271   Newberg Hwy

Woodburn

5

Salem
Page 237

Exit 256
Exit 255
Exit 253

Salem

Exit 248

Exit 244   Hope Valley RV Park

Mm 241   Emerald
              Valley RV Park
      Mm 241

See Albany
Detail - This
Page

Albany

Exit 234
Exit 233

Exit 228

Corvalis/
Albany KOA

5

Diamond
Hill RV Park

Harrisburg   Exit 209

Diamond Hill Dr

Mm 206   Mm 206

Exit 199

Eugene   Springfield   Eugene
                                Page 143

Exit 188

Mm 178   Mm 178

Cottage Grove   Exit 174

Goshen-Divide (Hwy 99)   Wal-Mart

Cottage Grove RV Village   Village Green
                              RV Park

Exit 170

Albany

Knox Butte
RV Park

Exit 234   Knox
                     Butte Rd

99E   Costco

Price Rd

20   Blue Ox
                RV Park

Blue Ox Dr

Exit 233   Santiam Hwy

5

I-5 CORRIDOR
OREGON - MAP 1

➲ *Exit 253*

● **SALEM CAMPGROUND AND RVS** *(Listed under Salem, page 239)*

➲ *Exit 244*

● **EMERALD VALLEY RV PARK** *(Open All Year)*
Res and Info: (503) 363-0701,
manager@emeraldvalley-rvp.com,
www.emeraldvalley-rvp.com
Location: I-5 Exit 244

GPS Location: 44.79215 N, 123.03311 W, 200 Ft

52 Sites – This is a new park located right next to I-5 at Exit 244. Sites are pull-thrus to 60 feet and back-ins to 45. They are gravel surfaced. There is no shade or picnic tables. Take Exit 244 and drive east, you'll see the entrance right away.

➲ *Exit 234*

● **KNOX BUTTE RV PARK** *(Open All Year)*
Res and Info: (800) 510-6620, 541 928-9033,
knxpark@hotmail.com,
www.knoxbuttervpark.com
Location: Albany, I-5 Exit 234

GPS Location: 44.64500 N, 123.05528 W, 2,300 Ft

76 Sites – This is a small older residential park with friendly management and some sites for travelers, including a few tent sites. It's across from the Albany Fairgrounds and Expo Center. There are pull-thrus and back-ins to 55 feet. North bound traffic take Exit 234, southbound Exit 234A. Go east for .3 mile (.5 km) on Knox Butte Road, the campground is on the left.

➲ *Exit 233*

● **BLUE OX RV PARK** *(Open All Year)*
Reservations: (800) 336-2881
Information: (541) 926-2886,
www.proaxis.com/~blueoxrvpark
Location: Albany, I-5 Exit 233

GPS Location: 44.63250 N, 123.05111 W, 200 Ft

150 Sites – This is a modern big-rig park with indoor pool and spa. Although it's convenient to the freeway it is far enough away from the traffic to avoid much of the noise. There are residents here but also a lot of traveler sites, they are pull-thrus to 65 feet. Take Exit 233 from I-5 and drive east on US-20. In .2 miles (.3 km) turn left on Price Rd. and in another .1 mile (.2 km) you'll see the long entrance road on your right.

➲ *Exit 228*

● **CORVALIS/ALBANY KOA** *(Open All Year)*
Reservations: (800) 562-8526,
www.koa.com/campgrounds/
albany/
Information: (541) 967-8521,
www.koa.com/campgrounds/
albany/
Location: Albany, OR

GPS Location: 44.56368 N, 123.15319 W, 200 Ft

100 Sites – This sometimes very busy KOA is located in wide-open farming country some distance west of I-5, about half way to Corvalis. Sites are back-ins and pull-thrus to about 65 feet. Amenities include a seasonal outdoor swimming pool. From Exit 228 of I-5 drive west for 4.8 miles (7.7 km). Turn left on Oakville Rd S and you'll see the campground entrance on the left in .2 mile (.3 km).

⮕ **Exit 209**

● **DIAMOND HILL RV PARK** *(Open All Year)*
Res and Info: (541) 995-9279,
    manager@diamondhillrvpark.com,
    www.diamondhillrvpark.com
Location: I-5 Exit 209

GPS Location: 44.28306 N, 123.06333 W, 300 Ft

90 Sites – The Diamond Hill is an older park, apparently an ex-KOA. There are many residential rigs including mobile homes. Some traveler sites are available, they include pull-thrus to 60 feet and back-ins to about 40 feet. Take Exit 209 from I-5. Drive west on Diamond Hill Dr. for .3 miles (.5 km), the campground is on the right.

⮕ **Exit 199**

● **EUGENE KAMPING WORLD** *(Listed under Eugene, page 146)*

● **EUGENE PREMIER RESORTS RV** *(Listed under Eugene, page 146)*

⮕ **Exit 188**

● **DEERWOOD RV PARK** *(Listed under Eugene, page 145)*

⮕ **Exit 163**

○ **PASS CREEK DOUGLAS COUNTY PARK** *(Open All Year)*
Information: (541) 942-3281, www.co.douglas.or.us/parks.asp
Location: 25 Miles (40 Km) S of Eugene

GPS Location: 43.72250 N, 123.20861 W, 300 Ft

30 Sites – This is one of those simple but good campgrounds near the freeway that make great overnight stops. This one has long paved back-in sites to 60 feet with full hookups for RVs. Sites are separated by expanses of lawn and there are shade trees. Tents are pitched in an area of lawn. Leave I-5 at Exit 163 and then follow signs north along the west side of the freeway to the park. Exit 163 is 25 miles (40 km) south of Eugene and 35 miles (56 km) north of Roseburg.

⮕ **Exit 148**

● **RICE HILL RV PARK** *(Open All Year)*
Res and Info: (866) 236-0121,
    ricehilervpark@msn.com,
    www.ricehill-rvpark.com
Location: I-5 Exit 148

GPS Location: 43.54194 N, 123.28639 W, 400 Ft

44 Sites – This is a small but new big-rig park not far away from the freeway on an exit with several service stations including a truck stop. Sites include 75-foot pull-thrus as well as back-ins, they're paved and have patios and picnic tables. Northbound access is easy, just take Exit 148 and proceed to the intersection with Long John Road. Follow Long John left for .4 mile (.6 km) to the campground entrance on your left. Southbound take Exit 148. Then follow the road next to the freeway southbound for .2 mile (.3 km),

OREGON

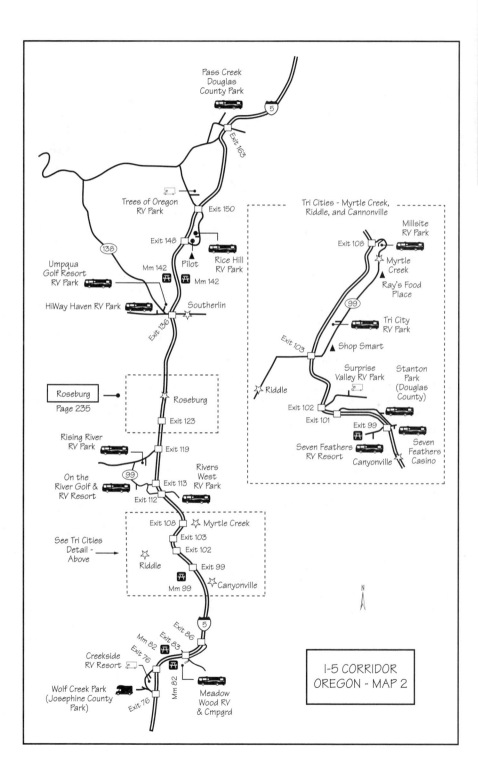

Pass Creek
Douglas
County Park

5

Exit 163

Trees of Oregon
RV Park

Exit 150

Tri Cities - Myrtle Creek,
Riddle, and Cannonville

Millsite
RV Park

Exit 108

Myrtle
Creek

Ray's Food
Place

Exit 148

138

Mm 142   Pilot

Rice Hill
RV Park

Mm 142

99

Umpqua
Golf Resort
RV Park

Tri City
RV Park

HiWay Haven RV Park

Southerlin

Exit 103   Shop Smart

Exit 136

Surprise
Valley RV Park

Stanton
Park
(Douglas
County)

Roseburg
Page 235

Roseburg

Exit 102

Riddle

Exit 101

Exit 123

Exit 99

Rising River
RV Park

Exit 119

Seven Feathers
RV Resort

Seven
Feathers
Casino

Canyonville

99

Rivers
West
RV Park

On the
River Golf &
RV Resort

Exit 113

Exit 112

Exit 108   Myrtle Creek

Exit 103

See Tri Cities
Detail -
Above

Exit 102

Riddle

Exit 99

Mm 99   Canyonville

N

5

Exit 86

Mm 82   Exit 83

Exit 76

Creekside
RV Resort

Mm 82

Wolf Creek Park
(Josephine County
Park)

Exit 76

Meadow
Wood RV
& Cmpgrd

I-5 CORRIDOR
OREGON - MAP 2

it will go under the freeway. Then proceed .7 mile (1.1 km) past the gas stations to the campground entrance which is on your left.

➲ **Exit 136**

● **HI-WAY HAVEN RV PARK** *(Open All Year)*
   Res and Info: (800) 552-5699, (541) 459-4557,
                      manager@hiwayhaven.com,
                      www.hiwayhaven.com
   Location: Sutherlin, I-5 Exit 136

   GPS Location: 43.38708 N, 123.35249 W, 400 Ft

100 Sites – This unusual park specializes in drive-in movies, it was once a drive-in theater and even sometimes shows movies. The big yellow barn makes it an easy RV park to spot from the distance. All sites are full-hookup pull-thrus to 60 feet. Interior roads are paved, sites are gravel. The park is far enough from the freeway to avoid traffic noise. Take Exit 136 from I-5 and go west for .2 miles (.3 km) on SR-138. At a Y take the left for Fort McKay road and drive .5 mile (.8 km), the campground is on the right.

● **UMPQUA GOLF RESORT RV PARK** *(Open All Year)*
   Res and Info: (541) 459-4423,
                      parkmanager@umpquarvresort.com
   Location: Sutherlin, I-5 Exit 136

   GPS Location: 43.38778 N, 123.34722 W, 400 Ft

41 Sites – This is a modern new RV park associated with an 18-hole professional golf course. Breakfast and lunch snacks are available at the golf clubhouse. Sites are pull-thrus to 65 feet and back-ins to 45. Interior roads are paved and so are the parking slots. Sites have picnic tables, this is a very well kept park. Take Exit 136 from I-5 and go west for .4 miles (.6 km) on SR-138. The campground entrance is on the right.

➲ **Exit 123**

○ **DOUGLAS COUNTY FAIRGROUNDS** *(Listed under Roseburg, page 236)*

➲ **Exit 119**

● **RISING RIVER RV PARK** *(Open All Year)*
   Res and Info: (800) 854-4279, (541) 679-7256,
                      risingrv@charter.net. www.risingriverrv.com
   Location: I-5 Exit 119

   GPS Location: 43.13389 N, 123.39611 W, 400 Ft

70 Sites - This park has an active entrance area, the access road threads between an older mobile home park and sales lot. Most lots here are permanently occupied but there are a few available for travelers. These are full-hookup pull-thrus to 60 feet and back-ins to 50 feet. You can walk down to the adjacent South Umpqua River. Take Exit 119 from I-5 and follow SR-99 for 2 miles (3.2 km) to the southwest. Turn left on Grange Road and bear to the right to the park.

➲ *Exit 113*

● ON THE RIVER GOLF AND RV RESORT
   (Open All Year)
   Reservations: (800) 521-5556
   Information: (541) 679-3505,
                www.ontherivergolf-rv.com
   Location: I-5 Exit 113

   GPS Location: 43.08028 N, 123.38472 W, 500 Ft

53 Sites – This little RV park is on the bank of the South Umpqua River and has a small 6 hole pitch-and-put par 3 golf course and fish ponds. The RV sites here are pull-thrus to 60 feet and back-ins to 40, most with full hookups. There are also tent sites. Swimming and fishing are possible in the river and there are community fire-pits on the river bank. From Exit 113 of I-5 on the west side of the freeway follow the road that goes north and west until it meets SR-99, a distance of .7 miles (1.1 km). Turn right and follow SR-99 for 1.2 miles (1.9 km) until you approach the bridge over the South Umpqua, the campground is on the left just short of the bridge.

➲ *Exit 112*

● RIVERS WEST RV PARK *(Open All Year)*
   Res and Info: (888) 863-7602
   Location: I-5 Exit 112

   GPS Location: 43.05944 N, 123.33972 W, 500 Ft

117 Sites – This is a very tidy well-run campground located right next to the freeway but also on the bank of the South Umpqua River. A long row of evergreens between the park and the freeway somewhat lessens the road noise, this is a very convenient park for travelers. Sites are pull-thrus to 70 feet and back-ins to 50 feet but many are shorter. Some sites are full hookups but many are partial or no-hookup and there are tent sites too. Fishing and swimming in the river are possible. Take Exit 112 and go to the former rest area (now blocked off) on the east side of the freeway. The access road to the RV park is Ruckles Road which is on the opposite side of the road from the rest area entrance and goes south along the freeway on the east side for .3 mile (.5 km) to the campground.

➲ *Exit 108*

● MILLSITE RV PARK *(Open May 15 to Sept 15)*
   Information: (541) 863-3171
   Location: I-5 Exit 108

   GPS Location: 43.02417 N, 123.29361 W, 500 Ft

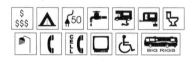

11 Sites – This is a nice little municipal campground, usually with a host, not far off the freeway right in the little town of Myrtle Creek. It's a small campground with 11 paved back-in sites to 80 feet and full hookups. They have picnic tables and some shade. Tenters pitch on the lawn behind the sites and park in an RV site, the tenting charge is the same as a full-hookup RV site. A good clean restroom has push-button hot showers and there's also a dump station here and water fill for folks from outside the park (extra fee of $5 for drop-in dumpers). Take Exit 108 and drive east .6 mile (1 km). Turn right at 4th Ave and you're there.

⮥ Exit 103

● **TRI CITY RV PARK** *(Open All Year)*
Res and Info: (541) 860-5000,
                    info@tricityrvpark.com,
                    www.tricityrvpark.com
Location: I-5 Exit 103

GPS Location: 42.98778 N, 123.32000 W, 600 Ft

70 Sites – This is a newer campground designed for big rigs. They have full hookups including 50 amp power, cable TV, telephone, and Wi-Fi at the sites. Many are wide pull-thrus to 80 feet. It's a handy location near the freeway, near Seven Feathers Casino, and near Myrtle Creek. Take Exit 103 and follow SR-99 north on the east side of the freeway for one mile, the RV park is on your left.

⮥ Exit 101

○ **STANTON PARK** *(Douglas Country) (Open All Year)*
Information: (541) 440-4500
Location: I-5 Exit 101

GPS Location: 42.94639 N, 123.29306 W, 600 Ft

42 Sites – Stanton Park is a mature county park with a nice campground. The sites are paved and located off two paved loops, they include pull-thrus to about 45 feet and back-ins to 40 feet. Half the sites have hookups, they have picnic tables and fire pits. The park adjoins the South Fork of Umpqua River, there's a popular local swimming beach at a pool in the river below the park. Take Exit 101 and follow the road along the northeast side of the freeway to the east for 1.5 miles (2.4 km). The park entrance is on the left.

⮥ Exit 99

● **SEVEN FEATHERS RV RESORT** *(Open All Year)*
Res and Info: (888) 677-7771,
                    www.sevenfeathersrvresort.com
Location: I-5 Exit 99

GPS Location: 42.93746 N, 123.29535 W, 700 Ft

191 Sites – This casino has a brand-new big-rig park
on the west side of the interstate, the casino itself is on the east side. The park is very upscale, most people feel that the price is really reasonable in view of the amenities. These are pull-thru sites to 65 feet and back-ins to 60 feet. The facilities are very nice with indoor pool and spa, fitness center, library, and gift shop. The nearby truck center has a restaurant, deli, and store. There's a shuttle to the casino which has restaurants and gambling, of course.

In addition to the RV park the casino has a parking lot where overnighting is allowed. It's on the east side of the freeway near the casino. GPS location is 42.94157 N, 123.28565 W. You must check in at the player's club to stay there.

The facilities here straddle the freeway and there's an underpass so access is easy both north and southbound at Exit 99.

➲ *Exit 86 Southbound, Exit 83 Northbound*

● **MEADOW WOOD RV AND CAMPGROUND**
  (Open All Year)
  Res and Info: (541) 832-3112
  Location: I-5 Exit 83 and 86

  GPS Location: 42.76028 N, 123.34333 W, 1,400 Ft

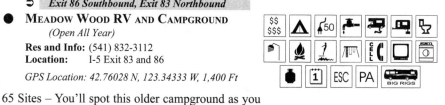

65 Sites – You'll spot this older campground as you pass it northbound since it's next to the freeway. Access is from the next exit north using a long driveway. Sites include pull-thrus to 50 feet and back-ins to 40 feet. Only a few sites have sewer but most have electricity and water. Northbound access isn't bad. Take Exit 83 and drive east for .2 miles (.3 km). Turn south on Autumn Road and follow it south for 1 mile (1.6 km) to the campground entrance. There's a steep hill and part of the distance is gravel. Southbound take Exit 86 and travel south for 3 miles on the road on the east side of the interstate. When you arrive at Exit 83 follow the Exit 83 instructions from above.

➲ *Exit 76*

○ **WOLF CREEK PARK** *(Josephine County Park)*
  (Open All Year)
  Information: (541) 474-5285, www.co.josephine.or.us
  Location: Wolf Creek, I-5 Exit 76

  GPS Location: 42.69472 N, 123.40194 W, 1,200 Ft

35 Sites – This county campground has sites set in a heavily treed area with sites to 30 feet on gravel, packed earth, and forest duff. It's a fine campground for smaller RVs and tent campers. Some sites have water and electric hookups and a dump at the campground dump station is included. There's a high dump fee for those from outside the campground. Sites have fire pits and picnic tables. Restrooms are vault toilets and there's a host. Take Exit 76 and drive west into Wolf Creek. In .6 mile (1 km) turn north on Front St., and in another .1 mile (.2 km) turn left on Main Street. After another .3 mile (.5 km) you'll enter the campground. The famous Wolf Creek Inn is nearby, you'll pass it on the way in to the campground.

➲ *Exit 71*

● **SUNNY VALLEY RV PARK** *(Open All Year)*
  Res and Info: (541) 479-0209
  Location: I-5 Exit 71

  GPS Location: 42.63037 N, 123.38363 W, 1,200 Ft

40 Sites – The Sunny Valley RV Park is an older former KOA with easy access from the interstate. There's a scenic covered bridge a short distance away on the far side of the interstate. Sites here are pull-thrus and back-ins to 45 feet as well as tent sites. The Wi-Fi does not reach the sites but can be used in the office and on the patio. Take Exit 71 and drive .1 mile (.2 km) south on the west side of the freeway, the campground is on the right.

OREGON

OREGON

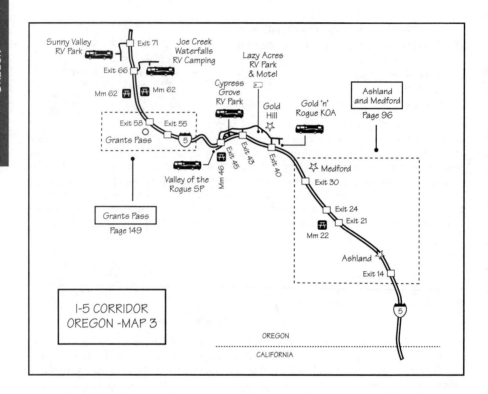

I-5 CORRIDOR
OREGON -MAP 3

⇨ **Exit 66**

● **JOE CREEK WATERFALLS RV CAMPING**
   (Open All Year)
   Res and Info: (541) 479-7974,
                    www.joecreekrv.com
   Location: I-5 Exit 66
   GPS Location: 42.57139 N, 123.36444 W, 1,200 Ft

54 Sites – Most sites in this scenic campground are rented on a monthly basis but they have a few RV and tent sites for travelers. Sites are pull-thrus to 60 feet. The campground has access to the nearby Jumping Joe Creek with waterfalls and swimming holes. There's a well-stocked convenience store out front. Take Exit 66 and go north on the access road on the east side of the interstate for .3 miles (.5 km). Turn right on Jumpoff Joe Creek Road and follow it for .4 mile (.6 km), the campground is on the right.

⇨ **Exit 58**

● **ROGUE VALLEY OVERNIGHTERS** *(See Grants Pass, Page 150)*

● **JACKS LANDING RV RESORT** *(See Grants Pass, Page 151)*

⇨ **Exit 55**

● **MOON MOUNTAIN RV RESORT** *(See Grants Pass, Page 151)*

● **RIVERPARK RV RESORT** *(See Grants Pass, Page 151)*

● **BRIDGEVIEW RV RESORT** *(See Grants Pass, Page 151)*

➲ *Exit 45B*

☐ **VALLEY OF THE ROGUE STATE PARK**
    (Open All Year)

Reservations: www.reserveamerica.com,
        (800) 452-5687
Information: (541) 582-1118, (800) 551-6949,
        www.oregonstateparks.org
Location: 32 Miles (52 Km) N of Ashland
        Along I-5

GPS Location: 42.41056 N, 123.13056 W, 1,000 Ft

167 Sites – This is a popular state park with a very convenient location. It's located right next to I-5 between Grants Pass and Medford. The sites here are paved sites off loops with both pull-thru and back-in sites, many over 50 feet long, some as long as 83 feet. The grounds are grass-covered and have many attractive shade trees. This park is unusual for a state campground because it has both Wi-Fi (from a commercial vendor, there is a fee) and a laundry room and machines. There's also a boat launch on the Rogue River and a hiking trail along the river. Other activities are fishing and fish-watching (salmon) in the river and river swimming in the summer. To reach the park take Exit 45B from I-5. This is 10 miles (16 km) south of Grants Pass and 13 miles (21 km) north of Medford.

➲ *Exit 45A*

● **CYPRESS GROVE RV PARK** *(Open All Year)*
  Res and Info: (800) 758-0719,
        www.cypressgrovervpark.com
  Location: I-5 Exit 45A

GPS Location: 42.41972 N, 123.12389 W, 1,000 Ft

45 Sites – Cypress Grove is handy to the interstate. It's a park with mostly long-term residents but also has spaces for travelers. Sites are pull-thrus to 65 feet and back-ins to 55 feet but maneuvering room can be tight. Take Exit 45A and turn north on the Rogue River Highway (SR-99). The campground is on the right almost immediately.

➲ *Exit 40*

● **GOLD 'N' ROGUE KOA** *(Open All Year)*
  Reservations: (800) 562-8506, www.koa.com
  Information: (541) 855-7710,
        medfordkoa@msn.com
  Location: I-5 Exit 40

GPS Location: 42.42722 N, 123.03778 W, 1,000 Ft

96 Sites – Like most KOAs this one is set up for family camping with a pool, tent sites, and rental cabins. Sites include pull-thrus to 65 feet and back-ins to 55 feet. Take Exit 40 and drive northeast for .2 mile (.3 km) Turn right on Blackwell Road and you'll see the entrance on the right in another .5 mile (.8 km).

➲ *Exit 30*

● **LAKEWOOD RV PARK** *(See Ashland and Medford, page 96)*

➲ *Exit 24*

● **HOLIDAY RV PARK** *(See Ashland and Medford, page 96)*

● **PEAR TREE RESORT** *(See Ashland and Medford, page 97)*

⊃ **Exit 21**

● **AMERICAN RV RESORT** *(See Ashland and Medford, page 97)*

⊃ **Exit 14**

● **GLENYAN CAMPGROUND** *(See Ashland and Medford, page 98)*

INTERSTATE 84 CORRIDOR

Interstate 84 (I-84) is the main east-west corridor in Oregon. It runs 377 miles (608 km) from the Idaho border just west of Boise west through remote western Oregon, threads the Columbia Gorge, and ends in Portland.

The campgrounds listed below are located in Oregon (actually, one is in Idaho and one in Washington). They're listed from west to east. Note that many of the campgrounds along the I-84 Corridor are described under other destinations sections in this chapter. If so, we've given a page reference to make finding them easy.

Interstate 84 Corridor Campgrounds

⊃ **Exit 14**

● **ROLLING HILLS MOBILE TERRACE AND RV PARK** *(See Portland, page 209)*

● **PORTLAND FAIRVIEW RV PARK** *(See Portland, page 209)*

⊃ **Exit 35**

☐ **AINSWORTH STATE PARK** *(See Columbia Gorge, page 133)*

⊃ **Exit 41 Eastbound Only**

■ **EAGLE CREEK CAMPGROUND** *(See Columbia Gorge, page 137)*

⊃ **Exit 44**

○ **PORT OF CASCADE LOCKS MARINE PARK** *(See Columbia Gorge, page 135)*

● **CASCADE LOCKS KOA** *(See Columbia Gorge, page 135)*

■ **HERMAN CREEK CAMPGROUND** *(See Columbia Gorge, page 136)*

⊃ **Exit 51**

■ **WYETH CAMPGROUND** *(See Columbia Gorge, page 136)*

⊃ **Exit 56**

☐ **VIENTO STATE PARK** *(See Columbia Gorge, page 137)*

⊃ **Exit 64**

● **BRIDGE RV PARK AND CAMPGROUND** *(See Columbia Gorge, page 137)*

⊃ **Rest Area at Mile 73 Westbound Only**

☐ **MEMALOOSE STATE PARK** *(See Columbia Gorge, page 138)*

⊃ **Exit 97**

☐ **DESCHUTES RIVER STATE RECREATION AREA** *(Open All Year)*

Reservations:	www.reserveamerica.com, (800) 452-5687
Information:	(541) 739-2322, (800) 551-6949, www.oregonstateparks.org
Location:	13 Miles (21 Km) E of The Dalles

GPS Location: 45.63389 N, 120.90806 W, 100 Ft

59 Sites – The Deschutes River empties into the Columbia about 4 miles (6 km) west of

OREGON

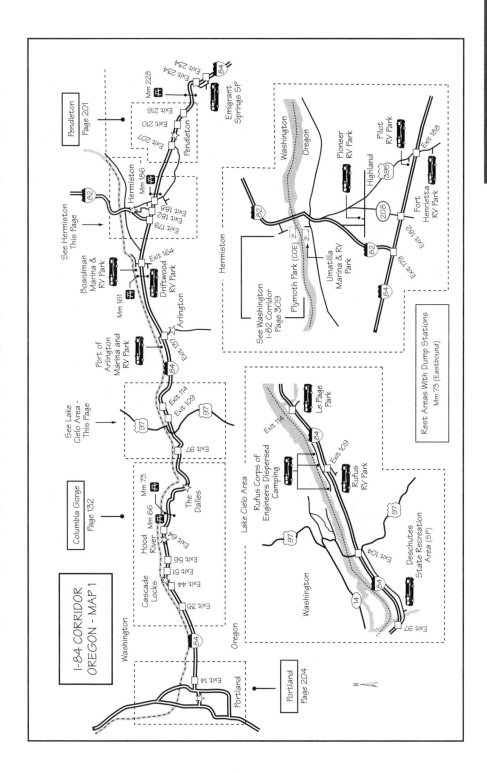

the US-97 bridge. This state campground is very popular with river-lovers, both those floating the river and those who launch their power boats at the ramp on the far side of the river at Heritage Landing. Fishing for salmon is good in the Columbia and trout fishing is good in the Deschutes. The first two miles of the Deschutes are reserved for bank fishermen. Several hiking trails are on the east bank of the Deschutes. There's also a mountain bike trail that stretches 17 miles up the river on an old railroad bed. There are separate non-hookup and hookup camping areas. Tent and non-hookup campers are on grass in open fields, all hookup sites are back-ins. About half of the hookup sites are over 40 feet, the longest is almost 60 feet. Campfires are not allowed from July 1 to Sept 30. The water system is drained in winter. To reach the campground take Exit 97 from I-84 and follow the frontage road on the south side of the highway east for 3 miles (5 km) to the campground entrance.

➲ **Exit 109**

● **RUFUS RV PARK** *(Open All Year)*
   Res and Info: (541) 739-2272, www.rufusrvpark.com
   Location: Rufus, OR

   GPS Location: 45.69266 N, 120.73701 W, 200 Ft

60 Sites – The Rufus RV Park is an older park. It's on the south side of the highway above the town of Rufus. The sites all have full hookups and they are OK for carefully driven big rigs. Some are pull-thrus. Take Exit 109 and on the south side of the highway turn right on W 1st Street and drive .4mile (.6 km) west to Wallace. Turn up the hill here and in .1 mile (.2 km) you'll reach the campground on the right. The sites are on the bench above the office and restrooms.

■ **RUFUS CORPS OF ENGINEERS DISPERSED CAMPING** *(Open All Year)*
   Information: (541) 506-7819
   Location: Exit 109 I-64

   GPS Location: 45.69346 N, 120.75526 W, 200 Ft

100 Sites – If you take Exit 109 and drive toward the water you can go either downstream or upstream on a paved access road that borders the river. In both directions there are spots where you can camp for 14 days out of every 30. Although signs say to camp in designated areas the fact is that other signs only designate the spots where you can't camp, most lots are OK. There are several paved parking areas to the right toward the dam and a large gravel area with a vault toilet at the end of the road to the south. Both are commonly used for camping both by Indian fishermen (who fish here with nets under treaty rights) and travelers. No fires are allowed and pets must be on leashes. There is no potable water.

➲ **Exit 114**

■ **LE PAGE PARK** *(Open April 1 to Oct 30 – Varies)*
   Reservations: www.recreation.gov, (877) 444-6777
   Information: (541) 506-7819
   Location: 27 Miles (44 Km) E of The Dalles

   GPS Location: 45.72778 N, 120.65306 W, 200 Ft

22 Sites – This is a small Corps of Engineers park located where the John Day River flows into Lake Umatilla behind John Day dam on the Columbia River. It's a very nice little campground with large back in and pull-thru sites including waterfront hookup sites to 50 feet. The campground has a manned entrance booth, a boat ramp and a swimming

Oregon

beach. To reach the campground take Exit 114 from I-84, the campground is located right at the exit.

⊃ Exit 137

○ **Port of Arlington Marina and RV Park** *(Open All Year)*
Information: (541) 454-2868
Location: Arlington, OR

GPS Location: 45.72281 N, 120.20724 W, 200 Ft

10 Sites – The Port of Arlington has two types of camping. There's a small full hookup RV park (often full of monthly units) and two areas for camping without utilities. One is a paved lot near the restrooms and the other a large gravel next to the river. The charge for parking in the lots with no utilities was $9 last time we visited. The small hookup park has three pull-thrus to 50 feet and back-ins that are smaller. The restroom building has no showers. Take Exit 137 from I-84 which will take you to the small town on the south side of the highway. On the eastern side of the small harbor take Arlington Port Road which will take you back under the highway a short distance to the port and its camping areas.

⊃ Exit 164

● **Driftwood RV Park** *(Open All Year)*
Res and Info: (800) 684-5543,
customerservice@driftwood-rv.com,
www.driftwood-rv.com
Location: 3 Miles S of I-84 Exit 164

GPS Location: 45.82148 N, 119.71972 W, 300 Ft

103 Sites – The Driftwood is a large modern big-rig park quite a distance from the interstate. It has a large community of semi-permanent rigs but also has room for travelers. Sites are paved or gravel, all pull-thrus to 50 feet. All are full-hookups. Amenities include a tennis court, basketball court, and indoor swimming pool. From I-84 Exit 164 drive south on S Main St for 1.3 miles (2.1 km). Turn right on Kunze Lane and proceed .9 mile (1.5 km), the campground entrance is on the right.

○ **Boardman Marina and RV Park** *(Open All Year)*
Reservations: (888) 481-7217, park@visitboardman.com
Information: (541) 481-7217, www.visitboardman.com
Location: 1 Mile N of I-84 Exit 164

GPS Location: 45.84341 N, 119.70786 W, 200 Ft

67 Sites – This municipal campground is a beautiful facility on the shore of the Columbia River. RV sites are both back-ins and pull-thrus to 80 feet and there are four tent sites with pitching on grass. The RV sites are paved, well separated, and surrounded by lawn with trees for shade. They have picnic tables and patios. There is a bike trail along the water and a nearby park with playground, swimming beach, and boat ramp. This campground has a 14 day stay limit. From I-84 take Exit 164 and drive north for .7 miles (1.1 km) to a T. Turn left and the campground entrance is on the right in .2 mile (.3 km).

⊃ Exit 179

Just a few miles north on I-82 are two riverfront RV parks that make good stops. They have easy on and off access and are described in the Highway I-82 section of the Washington chapter.

OREGON

● PLYMOUTH RV PARK *(See Interstate 82 Corridor, page 310)*

● UMATILLA MARINA AND RV PARK *(See Interstate 82 Corridor, page 311)*

➲ **Exit 182**

● PIONEER RV PARK *(Open All Year)*
Reservations: (888) 408-6100,
                 pioneeerv@charterinternet.com
Information: (541) 564-9286, www.pioneer-rv.com
Location: 4 Miles North of I-84 Exit 182

GPS Location: 45.83553 N, 119.31862 W, 400 Ft

102 Sites – This is a modern no-nonsense big rig campground. There's a large population of semi-permanent residents in this park, as in most commercial parks in the Hermiston area. Roads and sites are paved with strips of nice grass between them. There are back-in and pull-thru sites to 60 feet. Take Exit 182 and drive north on Hwy 207 for 3.8 miles (6.1 km). Turn left on W Highland Ave, the park is on the right in .3 mile (.5 km).

➲ **Exit 188**

● PILOT RV PARK *(Open All Year)*
Res and Info: (541) 449-1189,
                  manager@pilotrvpark.com,
                  www.pilotrvpark.com
Location: I-84 Exit 188

GPS Location: 45.76513 N, 119.20711 W, 600 Ft

40 Sites – This RV park is located behind a Pilot truck stop so it has easy access to a Subway restaurant, a McDonalds, and a small store. Many of the sites have semi-permanent residents. All sites are paved full-hookups with picnic tables on patios. Some sites are pull-thrus to 75 feet. From the exit drive north just a short distance to the station. The park is at the rear.

○ FORT HENRIETTA RV PARK *(Open All Year)*
Res and Info: (541) 571-3597, ecpl@centurytel.net
Location: Echo, WA some 1.7 miles S of I-84
                  Exit 188

GPS Location: 45.74208 N, 119.19814 W, 600 Ft

14 Sites - This is a small municipal campground located where the Oregon Trail crossed the Umatilla River just east of Echo, Oregon. There are 7 back-in sites with full hookups and two pull-thrus to 40 feet with water and electric. There are also 5 tent sites with pitching on gravel. A building on-site has restrooms and showers. Next door is the local skate-board park. From Exit 188 of I-84 drive south on the Old Pendleton River Road. Soon you'll descend a hill and see the town of Echo ahead. At 1.2 miles (1.9 km) turn right on N Dupont St, immediately crossing some railroad tracks. In 3 blocks or .2 mile (.3 km) turn right on Main St. The campground is on the left in another .1 mile (.2 km).

➲ **Exit 207**

● THE LOOKOUT RV PARK *(See Pendleton, page 201)*

➲ **Exit 210**

● PENDLETON KOA *(See Pendleton, page 201)*

➲ **Exit 216**

● WILDHORSE CASINO RV PARK *(See Pendleton, page 202)*

➲ *Exit 234*

☐ **EMIGRANT SPRINGS STATE HERITAGE AREA**
　　(Open All Year)

Reservations: www.reserveamerica.com, (800) 452-5687
Information: (541) 983-2277, (800) 551-6949,
　　　　　　　www.oregonstateparks.org
Location: 20 Miles (32 Km) E of Pendleton

　GPS Location: 45.54000 N, 118.46194 W, 3,800 Ft

51 Sites – Emigrant Springs is handy to the interstate and makes a great overnight stop if you're traveling through the region. The campground is along the route of the Oregon Trail and has an information kiosk. It's set in old–growth pines, really a beautiful place.

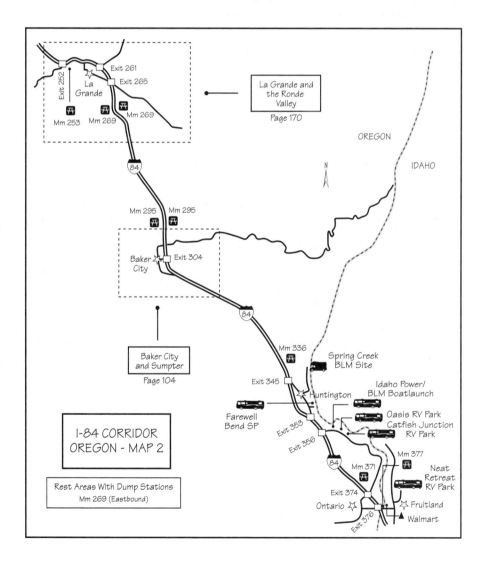

Sites are all back-ins. A few reach 55 feet in length and many are over 40 feet. In winter a few sites, with power, remain open but there is no water. There is also a horse campground here. To reach the campground take Exit 234 from I-84, the campground is on the south side of the highway. That's 20 miles (32 km) east of Pendleton.

➲ **Exit 252**

☐ **HILGARD JUNCTION STATE PARK**
   (See La Grande and the Grande Ronde Valley, page 172)

■ **BIRD TRACK SPRING CAMPGROUND**
   (See La Grande and the Grande Ronde Valley, page 172)

➲ **Exit 261**

● **LA GRANDE RENDEZVOUS RV RESORT**
   (See La Grande and the Grande Ronde Valley, page 171)

➲ **Exit 265**

● **EAGLES HOT LAKE RESORT** *(See La Grande and the Grande Ronde Valley, page 170)*

➲ **Exit 304**

● **OREGON TRAILS WEST RV PARK** *(See Baker City and Sumpter, page 105)*

● **MOUNTAIN VIEW HOLIDAY TRAV-L-PARK** *(See Baker City and Sumpter, page 105)*

➲ **Exit 345**

■ **SPRING CREEK BLM SITE** *(Open All Year)*
   Information: (541) 473-3144
   Location: On Snake River 6 Miles East of I-84 Exit 345

   GPS Location: 44.37542 N, 117.23805 W, 2,100 Ft.

30 Sites – This BLM site is on the shore of the upper end of the Brownlee Reservoir of the Snake River. It has tent sites with fire pits in three grassy areas and three gravel lots for RV parking with no defined sites. Any size rig would fit in the park but access is best for coaches to about 35 feet. There is also a boat launch. Take Exit 345 from I-84. On the east side of the interstate follow Hwy 30 south for 2.7 miles (4.3 km) to Huntington. In Huntington continue straight on E. Washington Street and the Snake River Road to follow the rail lines to the east. In another 2.6 miles (4.3 km) you'll reach the Snake River and turn north. The campground is on the right .9 mile (1.5 km) after you reach the river.

➲ **Exit 353**

☐ **FAREWELL BEND STATE PARK** *(Open All Year)*
   Reservations: www.reserveamerica.com, (800) 452-5687
   Information: (541) 869-2365, (800) 551-6949,
                   www.oregonstateparks.org
   Location: Exit 353 of I-84

   GPS Location: 44.30356 N, 117.22756 W, 2,100 Ft

120 Sites – This beautiful Oregon state park is very convenient to the interstate and great place to stop. The location has historical significance. Here the Oregon Trail left the Snake River to travel inland, it was a place for travelers to rest before the arduous trek across the mountains to Oregon City near today's Portland. The park occupies the bank of the Brownlee Reservoir, a popular fishing and water sports lake. It has a boat ramp and docks. There are 30 tent sites and about 90 RV sites. They have electricity and are both back-ins and pull-thrus to about 60 feet. These are paved sites with lots of grass separating them and trees for shade. In winter most sites are closed and there are no reservations

OREGON

taken but ten hookup sites and many no hookup/tent sites remain open for travelers. Take Exit 353 and drive north for just .9 mile (1.5 km) to the park entrance on the right.

➲ **Exit 356**

■ **IDAHO POWER/BLM BOAT LAUNCH** *(Open All Year)*
Location: Along Snake River about 3 miles east of I-84 Exit 356

GPS Location: 44.26271 N, 117.12772 W, 2,100 Ft

5 Sites – A mostly undeveloped boat launch site where camping is allowed with a 14 day limit. There is a vault toilet and one picnic table with fire grate. About five RVs can park here although sites are not laid out, don't block the boat ramp. Two campgrounds (described below) adjoin to the east upriver. From Exit 356 drive east for 2.9 miles (4.7 km), the facility is on the left.

● **OASIS RV PARK** *(Open All Year)*
Res and Info: (541) 262-3504
Location: Along Snake River about 3 miles east of Exit 356

GPS Location: 44.26365 N, 117.12541 W, 2,100 Ft

28 Sites – A neatly laid out campground on the banks of the Snake River. It's popular with fishermen and also makes a convenient place to spend the night. Sites include pull-thrus to 65 feet and have picnic tables. From Exit 356 drive east for 3.0 miles (4.8 km), the campground is on the left.

● **CATFISH JUNCTION RV PARK**
    (Open All Year)
Res and Info: (541) 262-3833,
    dandjsilva@ruralnetwork.net,
    www.catfishjunctionrvpark.com
Location: Along Snake River about 3 miles east of I-84 Exit 356

GPS Location: 44.26382 N, 117.12414 W, 2,100 Ft

40 Sites – A campground along the Snake River just past the two listed above. Amenities include a boat ramp and fish cleaning station. There are many tents sites as well as 20 RV sites including partial hookup pull-thrus to 60 feet as well as back-in full hookup and dry sites. From Exit 356 drive east for 3.1 miles (5.0 km), the campground is on the left.

➲ **Exit 376**

● **NEAT RETREAT RV PARK** *(Open All Year)*
Res and Info: (208) 452-4324,
    info@neatretreatrvpark.com,
    www.neatretreatrvpark.com
Location: Fruitland, ID

GPS Location: 44.03514 N, 116.92430 W, 2,100 Ft

40 Sites – This park, just across the border in Idaho, is easy to reach from the highway. It has some long-term residents and a mobile home section but also sites for traveling RVers and tenters. From Exit 376 drive east on East Idaho Avenue for 1.2 miles (2 km) past a big Walmart and across the Snake River to N. Whitley Dr. Turn left and in just .5 mile (.8 km) take the right at NW 24th Street. Bear left almost immediately to drive north on N. Alder Dr. for a short distance to the campground which is at the end.

ASHLAND AND MEDFORD

Ashland (population 20,000) is probably best known for the **Oregon Shakespeare Festival**. It runs from late February to October in three different venues, including an outdoor theater. Performances each year include many different productions, both Shakespeare and modern. It is best to get your tickets before you arrive in town. The nearby town of Jacksonville offers the **Britt Pavilion** with many music performances of all genres during the year. Ashland is also known for its **Lithia water**, you can try it at water fountains downtown and in Lithia Park.

Several towns and interesting destinations line I-5 to the north of Ashland, several of the campgrounds listed for Ashland are actually along I-5 to the north.

Medford (area population 207,000) is the big town of the area. It is located about 12 miles (19 km) north of Ashland. As the big city Medford acts as the business and medical center for a region known for its fruit. A popular stop in Medford is **Harry and David's Country Village**. You probably know them for their mail-order gift baskets. There are signs on I-5 directing you to the store. Medford has a **Pear Blossom Festival** in mid-April and hosts the **Jackson County Fair** on the third weekend of July.

Tent campers visiting Ashland will enjoy the Emigrant Lake Campground when it is open. Otherwise the Glenyan Campground is an excellent choice. If you don't mind the long drive the Valley of the Rogue State Park (see page 87) is also good. For really big RVs the easiest choices are along the freeway and include Valley of the Rogue State Park, Holiday RV Park, and Pear Tree Resort. The Glenyan is our favorite and any RV can fit with careful driving.

Ashland And Medford Campgrounds

● **LAKEWOOD RV PARK** *(Open All Year)*
Res and Info: (541) 830-1957,
Lakewood@country.net,
www.lakewoodrvpark.com
Location: Medford, OR

GPS Location: 42.42095 N, 122.84512 W, 1,300 Ft

45 Sites – This is a simple big rig park with many long-term rigs but room for some travelers. It has pull-thru sites to 50 feet. The park is quite a distance from I-5 but convenient for shopping including at a nearby Costco. From Exit 30 off I-5 in Medford head northeast on Hwy 62, the Crater Lakes Highway. After 5.5 miles (8.9 km) watch closely for the sign and turn right into Merry Lane. The next road is Hwy 140, the Lake of the Wood Highway. If you reach it you've gone too far. Once on Merry the campground is one block in on the right.

● **HOLIDAY RV PARK** *(Open All Year)*
Reservations: (800) 452-7970
Information: (541) 535-2183, kprv@aol.com
Location: 10 Miles (16 Km) N of Ashland

GPS Location: 42.28306 N, 122.81861 W, 1,500 Ft

110 Sites – This is a modern big-rig park with narrow pull-thrus to 70 feet and also shorter back-ins. Some sites are very narrow. Amenities include an outdoor heated pool. There's a McDonalds nearby. It's conveniently

OREGON

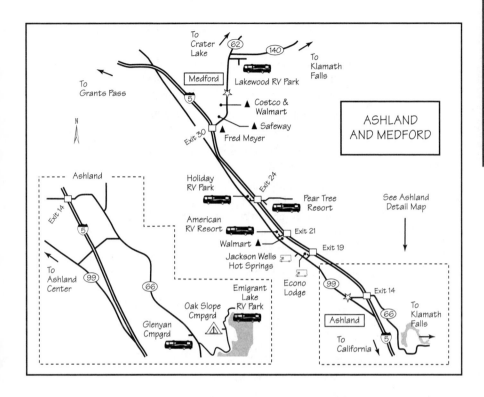

located just west of I-5 at Exit 24. This is 10 miles (16 km) north of Ashland's Exit 14.

● **PEAR TREE RESORT** *(Open All Year)*
Res and Info: (800) 645-7332, (541) 535-4445
Location: 10 Miles (16 Km) N of Ashland

GPS Location: 42.27874 N, 122.81047 W, 1,500 Ft

31 Sites – The Pear Tree is a much smaller resort than the Holiday and is located off the same freeway exit. This is a campground behind a motel. There are sizeable back-in sites and pull-thrus to 75 feet. Amenities include a seasonal outdoor swimming pool and hot tub. You can also walk next door to a restaurant. Take Exit 24 from I-5 and travel south on the access road on the east side of the freeway for .1 mile (.2 km) to the campground.

● **AMERICAN RV RESORT** *(Open All Year)*
Res and Info: (541) 535-6632
Location: 7 Miles (11 Km) N of Ashland Along I-5

GPS Location: 42.24667 N, 122.77667 W, 1,600 Ft

63 Sites – The American is an older resort and has a lot of long-term residents. Sites are back-ins. Although some are as long as 50 feet the park prefers RVs no longer than 40 feet. A paved bike trail runs next to the park along Bear Creek and there is a seasonal swimming pool.

The campground is located just west of I-5 at Exit 21. This is 7 miles (11 km) north of Ashland at Exit 14.

● **GLENYAN RV PARK AND CAMPGROUND**
    (Open All Year)

Reservations: (877) 453-6926,
    info@glenyanrvpark.com
    www.glenyanrvpark.com
Information: (541) 488-1785,
    info@glenyancampground.com
Location: 5 Miles (8 Km) E of Ashland on SR-66

    GPS Location: 42.15528 N, 122.62944 W, 2,100 Ft

68 Sites – The Glenyan is the closest and most convenient campground for a visit to Ashland and has long been a popular choice for visitors. It's a very friendly campground. Sites here are set in trees and no two are alike. There are back-ins and pull-thrus to 70 feet with full or partial hookups. There are also nice tents sites around a meadow and along Neil Creek There's a seasonal outdoor swimming pool as well as Wi-Fi in the office, it does reach a few of the sites. To reach the campground drive east from Ashland at Exit 14 of I-5 on SR-66. The campground entrance is on the right 3.0 miles (4.8 km) from I-5.

○ **OAK SLOPE CAMPGROUND**
    (Open April 15 to Oct 15 – Varies)

Reservation: www.jacksoncountyparks.com
Information: (541) 774-8183, parksinfo@jackoncounty.org,
    www.jacksoncountyparks.com
Location: 6 Miles (10 Km) E of Ashland on SR-66

    GPS Location: 42.15667 N, 122.61833 W, 2,200 Ft

42 Sites – This is one of two campgrounds overlooking Emigrant Lake Reservoir in the Emigrant Lake Jackson County Park. The other is The Emigrant Lake RV Park which has hookups, see below. Oak Slope Campground does not have hookups and is a tent campground. Access roads are paved but narrow and sites are on a hillside giving good views of the lake below. They have fire pits and picnic tables. The campground is located across the park road from the lake and day-use area. Farther along the road are a dump station and the RV park. There is also a large water slide and boat launch in the park. To reach the campground drive east from Ashland at Exit 14 of I-5 on SR-66. The entrance road to the park is on the left 3.2 miles (5.2 km) from I-5. When you follow the access road the campground is on the left in .9 mile (1.5 km).

○ **EMIGRANT LAKE RV PARK** *(The Point)*
    (Open March 16 to Oct 31 – Varies)

Reservations: (541) 774-8183, benchml@jacksoncounty.org
Information: (541) 774-8183, parksinfo@jacksoncounty.org,
    www.jacksoncountyparks.com
Location: 6 Miles (10 Km) E of Ashland on SR-66

    GPS Location: 42.16111 N, 122.61639 W, 2,300 Ft

32 Sites – This county RV park has nice paved sites overlooking the Emigrant Lake Reservoir. Some stretch to 50 feet, most are long back-ins with only three pull-thrus. Reservations are very important here, this is a popular place. To reach the campground drive east from Ashland at Exit 14 of I-5 on SR-66. The entrance road to the park is on the left 3.2 miles (5.2 km) from I-5. When you follow the access road the campground is at the end in 1.3 mile (2.1 km).

ASTORIA, SEASIDE, AND CANNON BEACH

Some folks claim **Astoria** (population 10,000) is the oldest town in this part of the country, but that can be disputed since it has not been continually occupied since the early days of Fort Astoria. Astoria was founded in 1811 as a fur-trading post, but later abandoned. Only since the 1840s was the town site permanently occupied, and by that time Oregon City on the outskirts of today's Portland had begun to grow.

The Columbia River is the town's reason for existence. Even today the river pilots that guide the huge ships across the bar are based here. There's an excellent museum, the **Columbia River Maritime Museum**, that gives the whole fascinating story on Columbia River shipping.

Another river-oriented site here is the huge Astoria Bridge. You can't miss it because it towers over the little town and stretches 4.1 miles (6.6 km) north across the Columbia to Washington State. On a nice day the drive across is well worth the time it takes for the great views. Once across you might look around. The **Lewis and Clark Campsite Heritage Area** just 2.4 miles (3.9 km) to the west occupies the spot where Lewis and Clark first saw the Pacific Ocean. At 3.0 miles (4.8 km) is **Fort Columbia State Park**. This was a second fort (of three) guarding the entrance to the Columbia, Fort Stevens was on the south bank and Fort Canby was farther west on the north shore.

Back in Astoria there are at least two more must-see attractions. The **Astoria Column**, erected by the Northern Pacific Railroad in 1926, offers great views after a 164-step

THE EXCELLENT COLUMBIA RIVER MARITIME MUSEUM IN ASTORIA

climb up the interior spiral stairway. The **Flavel House Museum** is a Victorian-style mansion built by Oregon's first steamship captain, it has the original furnishings and was built in 1883.

Finally, one of the campgrounds just to the south, Fort Stevens State Park, has a great deal of historical interest. Fort Stevens was built during the Civil War. It was also shelled by a Japanese submarine during World War II. You can find out more at the **Museum** in the park. At the far north end of the park is a huge **jetty** jutting out into the Pacific. It was designed to help protect the entrance to the Columbia and to help control the sand bars that want to close the shipping channels. It is not entirely successful, extensive dredging is still required and the entrance to the Columbia is one of the world's more dangerous shipping routes, particularly during winter storms.

The area near the mouth of the Columbia River is well-known for its fishing, and also as a fairly treacherous piece of water. Fishing charters from both Astoria and Warrenton/ Hammond are available.

Astoria celebrates the **Astoria Warrenton Crab and Seafood Festival** on the last week-end in April and the **Scandinavian Midsummer Festival** sometime in the second half of June.

South of Astoria, at Mile 7, old Highway 101 leads 3 miles (5 km) east to **Fort Clatsop National Memorial**. This is where the Louis and Clark Expedition spent the winter of 1805-1806.

Fourteen miles (23 km) south of Astoria is **Seaside**. The center of town is between the highway and the ocean. The town is about 100 years old, and the main business here has always been tourism. Seaside has a variety of attractions. There's the two-mile paved **Promenade** along the beach, shopping and restaurants along **Broadway**, and the **Seaside Aquarium**. If you are interested in the town's history visit the **Seaside Museum**. There almost always seems to be something going on in Seaside, particularly in the summer, check at the Seaside Chamber of Commerce for information.

Cannon Beach (population 1,600), 6 miles (10 km) south of Seaside, is cute and upscale. There's an excellent beach, big rocks called sea stacks just offshore, and lots of little res-taurants, shops and galleries. Cannon Beach hosts a **Sandcastle Day** about the middle of June as well as the **Stormy Weather Arts Festival** near the beginning of November. One of Cannon Beach's big advantages in the way of ambiance is that the highway bypasses the town.

Adjoining Cannon Beach to the north is **Ecola State Park**. It encompasses **Tillamook Head**, there is a hiking trail through the park from Cannon Beach to Seaside. Captain William Clark of the Lewis and Clark expedition is thought to have viewed the Cannon Beach area from a vantage point in the park, it was probably the farthest point south along the coast reached by the expedition.

The campgrounds below are listed from north to south. We've done this all along the Oregon coast. If you're traveling from north to south this book covers virtually all camp-grounds along the coast. The destinations after this one fall in this order: • *Nehalem Bay and Manzanita,* • *Tillamook and the Three Capes Loop,* • *Lincoln City to Newport,* • *Waldport and Florence,* • *Reedsport and the Oregon Dunes,* • *Coos Bay,* • *Charleston,* • *Bandon,* • *Port Orford,* • *Gold Beach,* • *Brookings.* See the index map at the beginning of this chapter for easy orientation.

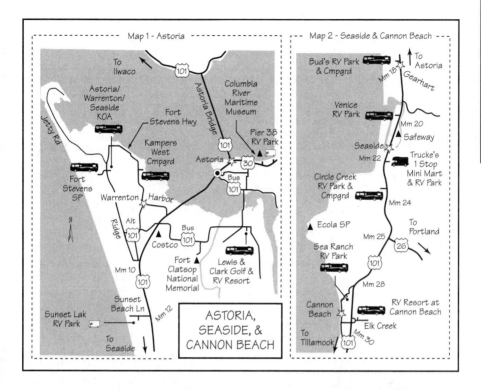

Map 1 - Astoria

Map 2 - Seaside & Cannon Beach

ASTORIA, SEASIDE, & CANNON BEACH

Astoria, Seaside, and Cannon Beach Campgrounds

● **LEWIS AND CLARK GOLF AND RV PARK** *(Open All Year)*
   Res and Info: (503) 338-3386, www.astoriaoregonrvpark.com
   Location: 3 Miles (5 Km) S of Astoria

   GPS Location: 46.15124 N, 123.83640 W, Near Sea Level

35 Sites – This pleasant modern RV park is right next to a 9-hole
golf course just outside Astoria. Sites are back-ins to 70 feet and
pull-thrus to 60 feet. It's for self-contained rigs. Easiest access is from the intersection
of Hwy 101 and Hwy 101 Business some 3 miles (5 km) south of Astoria. The turn is
marked with a sign for the airport and Lewis and Clark National Historical Park. Turn
east on Business Hwy 101 and follow it as it curves around the airport, crosses the Lewis
and Clark Bridge, and becomes Youngs River Road. Some 5.1 miles (8.2 km) from
where you left the main Hwy 101 you'll see the RV park entrance on the right.

☐ **FORT STEVENS STATE PARK** *(Open All Year)*
   Reservations: www.reserveamerica.com,
                  (800) 452-5687
   Information: (503) 861-1671, (800) 551-6949,
                  www.oregonstateparks.org
   Location: 6 Miles (10 Km) SW of Astoria

   GPS Location: 46.18222 N, 123.96250 W, Near Sea Level

496 Sites – This is the largest state campground in Oregon. The parking area for check-

ing in is larger than some of the other campgrounds. Sites have large paved parking pads, many suitable for the largest RVs and some are pull-thrus. There are also yurt rentals, a hiker/biker area, 14 miles (23 km) of bicycle and hiking trails, a lake with swimming beach and boat launch, and a very long Pacific beach. This large state park is a former military fort which protected the mouth of the Columbia River from the time of the Civil War until after World War II. You can tour the old batteries and a museum You can drive to the campground by heading northwest from either Mile 6.5 or Mile 7.5 of US-101. Signs will guide you along back roads to the campground.

● **ASTORIA / WARRENTON/ SEASIDE KOA**
(Open All Year)
Reservations: (800) 562-8506, www.koa.com
Information: (503) 861-2606, astoriakoa@aol.com,
www.astoriakoa.com
Location: 6 Miles (10 Km) W of Astoria

GPS Location: 46.18444 N, 123.95611 W, Near Sea Level

255 Sites – This large KOA is located right across from the entrance to Fort Stevens State Park and offers a commercial alternative with virtually the same location. This too is a huge campground with facilities to match and excellent management. Sites include pull-thrus and back-ins to 55 feet. Amenities include a very large indoor year-round swimming pool, hot tub, mini golf, and a snack bar. There are also bicycle rentals, very handy for those bike trails at Fort Stevens State Park across the street. Follow the directions given for the state park above to reach the campground.

● **KAMPERS WEST KAMPGROUND** *(Open All Year)*
Reservations: (800) 880-5267
Information: (503) 861-1814,
kamping@kamperswest.net,
www.kamperswest.com
Location: 5 Miles (8 Km) SW of Astoria

GPS Location: 46.18472 N, 123.92833 W, Near Sea Level

175 Sites – This is a large, older, big-rig campground near the Columbia River. It caters to fishermen with boat trailer parking, fish-cleaning tables and seafood cooking areas. Sites are back-ins to 55 feet on gravel and grass. The grass sites are also used by tent campers. The campground is located near Warrenton. From US-101 about 2 miles (3 km) south of Astoria follow E. Harbor Drive west to Warenton where it curves north and becomes Fort Stevens Highway. Some 2.8 miles (4.5 km) from US-101 you will see the campground on the right.

● **BUD'S RV PARK AND CAMPGROUND**
(Open All Year)
Res and Info: (800) 730-6855, (503) 738-6855,
www.budsrv.com
Location: 2 Miles (3 Km) N of Seaside

GPS Location: 46.03806 N, 123.91333 W , Near Sea Level

36 Sites – This campground is located behind a convenience store. There is a large area with grass for tent camping and also back-in RV sites. Each of these has a patio and picnic table. Most sites are back-ins to about 25 feet long but a few can take large RVs to 40 feet. The campground is located on the west side of US-101 at the north end of Gearhart, which is just outside Seaside to the north.

● **VENICE RV PARK** *(Open All Year)*
   Res and Info: (503) 738-8851, www.shopseaside.com/vrv/
   Location: Northern Edge of Seaside

   GPS Location: 46.01083 N, 123.91194 W, Near Sea Level

20 Sites – This local RV park has many full-time resident trailers, but about 20 spaces are set aside for travelers too. It's an old RV park with simple facilities and RVs are really packed in. Traveler sites are back-ins and pull-thrus to 70 feet. Maneuvering room is tight and spaces are narrow. Slide-outs are not recommended. The Neawanna River runs along the side of the park. The RV park is located just off US-101 on the west side near the northern edge of Seaside.

● **TRUCKE'S 1 STOP MINI MART AND RV PARK** *(Open All Year)*
   Information: (503) 738-8863
   Location: Seaside

      GPS Location: 45.98056 N, 123.92611 W, Near Sea Level

13 Sites – Trucke's is a very simple RV park. It's a lot next to a gas station and convenience store. There are 13 back-in sites on grass to 35 feet in length. Only electric hookups are available. Watch for Trucke's on the east side of US-101 toward the southern end of the strip of business that line the highway as it passes through Seaside.

● **CIRCLE CREEK RV PARK AND CAMPGROUND**
      (Open April 1 to Nov 1)
   Res and Info: (503) 738-6070, info@circlecreekrv.com,
                www.circlecreekrv.com
   Location: 1 Mile (1.6 Km) S of Seaside

   GPS Location: 45.96528 N, 123.92472 W, Near Sea Level

64 Sites – Circle Creek is Seaside's premier campground. In fact it's the only large full-service traveler's campground servicing Seaside. The sites here are widely spaced back-in and pull-thru sites to 60 feet. Extensive areas of clipped grass separate the sites. Reservations are recommended all summer long, even during the week. The campground is located about 1 mile (1.6 km) south of Seaside on the west side of US-101.

● **SEA RANCH RV PARK** *(Open All Year)*
   Res and Info: (503) 436-2815,
                www.cannon-beach.net/searanch/
   Location: Cannon Beach

   GPS Location: 45.90194 N, 123.95639 W, Near Sea Level

80 Sites – Many people think this is the most ideally located campground on the Oregon coast, it's within walking distance of central Cannon Beach. It's also a stable and horse rides are available. Sites here are irregularly laid out in an area of trees. There are tent sites, small vehicle camping sites, and back-in sites to 55 feet. Maneuvering room for big RVs is limited but parking is definitely possible. Swimming is in the river. If you take the northern exit (near Mile 28) to Cannon Beach you'll see the campground on the left in just .3 mile (.5 km).

○ **RV RESORT AT CANNON BEACH** *(Open All Year)*

   Res and Info: (503) 436-2231, (800) 847-2231,
                  info@cbrvresort.com, www.cbrvresort.com
   Location: 1 Mile (2 Km) E of Cannon Beach

   GPS Location: 45.88889 N, 123.95556 W, Near Sea Level

100 Sites – This resort is Cannon Beach's big-rig RV resort. It's city owned and run by a private company. There are back-in and pull-thru sites to 60 feet. Amenities include an indoor swimming pool and an hourly shuttle to Cannon Beach and Seaside. If you want to walk you can be at the beach in a half mile, central Cannon Beach is just under a mile on foot. The campground is located just east of US-101 at the middle Cannon Beach exit at Mile 29.5.

BAKER CITY AND SUMPTER

Although the **Oregon Trail** passes near Baker City (population 10,000) the town really dates from the gold mining period of the 1860s. Located on I-84 Baker City is more than a spot to stop for gas and a quick bite, the town has a surprising number of interesting nearby tourist attractions.

First on the list must be the **National Historic Oregon Trail Interpretive Center**. Completed in 1992 this modern museum presents a fascinating look at the Oregon Trail. The trail itself passes below, you can see the ruts from the center but there are walking trails leading down for a closer look. In the center itself you pass along a winding path past

BE SURE TO VISIT THE NATIONAL HISTORIC OREGON TRAIL INTERPRETIVE CENTER

OREGON

dioramas, slide shows, and exhibits – plan on at least an hour to take it all in. We RVers should especially appreciate this monument to some of the first of our tribe. If you look close you'll see that many of the large mural-type pictures are attributed to well known RVing author Bill Moeller. There is quite a bit of RV parking at the center.

In Baker City itself you might want to visit the **Geiser Grand Hotel**, dating from 1889, has been restored and is designated as a National Historic Landmark.

Baker's annual celebration is the **Miner's Jubilee**, held during the third week of July.

From Baker follow SR-7 westward out of town. The road follows the Powder River toward the old dredge tailing piles near Sumpter. Twenty miles (32 km) after leaving town you'll pass the entrance road for Union Creek Campground. Four and eight-tenths miles (7.7 km) farther along take a left to visit **Railroad Park**. From here, on weekends and holidays from Memorial Day to the end of September, you can ride to the dredge at Sumpter behind a historic steam locomotive, the **Stump Dodger**. Driving on, in just 2.3 miles (3.7 km), you'll reach a junction, take a right and visit the historic gold mining town of Sumpter.

Sumpter offers a number of attractions. The main street is lined with several restaurants, small stores, and other tourist-oriented establishments. The most interesting attraction, however, is the dredge at the **Sumpter Valley Dredge State Heritage Area**. Neglected for many years the dredge had sunk in its pond, but has been raised and is being restored. You can wander through it now, it is already a well-done exhibit that will only get better.

Baker City and Sumpter Campgrounds

● MOUNTAIN VIEW HOLIDAY TRAV-L-PARK
     (Open All Year)
Reservations: (800) 806-4824
Information: (541) 523-4824,
                 mtviewrv@oregontrail.net,
                 www.mtviewrv.com
Location: Baker City

GPS Location: 44.79444 N, 117.84139 W, 3,400 Ft

100 Sites – The campground for travelers is located behind a mobile home park and is very clean and well-managed. This is a big-rig park with pull-thru sites to 70 feet. The buildings have a western theme and amenities include a summer swimming pool and year-round hot tub. Easiest access to the campground is from I-84 at Exit 302. Go west from the intersection and follow the highway as it immediately turns to the south. In .5 miles (.8 km) take the right onto Hughes Lane. One mile (1.6 km) after the turn you'll see the campground entrance on your left.

● OREGON TRAILS WEST RV PARK
     (Open All Year)
Reservations: (888) 523-3236
Information: (541) 523-3236
Location: Baker City

GPS Location: 44.80278 N, 117.81806 W, 3,400 Ft

60 Sites – This is an older commercial park but it is very convenient to the freeway and has long pull-thrus to about 55 feet. Back-ins around the perimeter of the park are full of resident rigs, pull-thrus in the middle are used for travelers. These sites are separated by grass and have picnic tables. The tent sites here are very large grassy areas, some with

OREGON

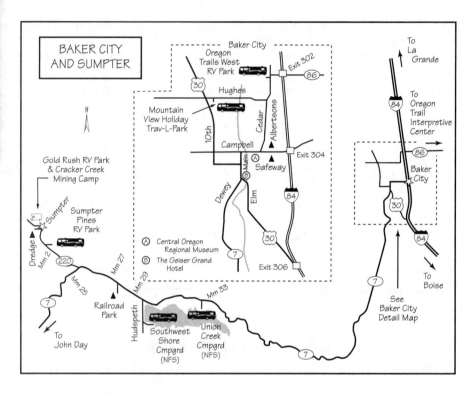

BAKER CITY AND SUMPTER

fences for separation and most are located toward the front of the park away from the RVs. The campground has a gas station and small convenience store out front. Take Exit 302 from I-84, you'll see the campground on the west side of the highway. This exit is also the one where SR-86 from Hells Canyon reaches the interstate.

■ UNION CREEK CAMPGROUND

(Open May 1 to Sept 30 – Varies)

Reservations: www.recreation.gov, (877) 444-6777
Information: (541) 523-6391
Location: 17 Miles (27 Km) SW of Baker City

GPS Location: 44.69139 N, 118.02972 W, 4,100 Ft

74 Sites – This large Wallowa-Whitman National Forest campground is unusual, it has electrical, water, and sewer hookups. The park covers a very large area on the shore of Phillips Reservoir. Access roads are wide, paved loops and sites are large enough to handle RVs to 45 feet. It's actually a good big-rig park. The campground is located 17 miles (7 km) from Baker City and 10 miles (6 km) from Sumpter on SR-7.

■ SOUTHWEST SHORE FOREST CAMPGROUND

(Open All Year, Maintained Only Memorial Day to Sept 30 – Varies)

Information: (541) 523-6391
Location: 23 Miles (37 Km) SW of Baker City

GPS Location: 44.67583 N, 118.08389 W, 4,100 Ft

16 Sites – This smaller Wallowa-Whitman National Forest campground

OREGON

occupies the southwest shore of Phillips Reservoir. There is no drinking water at this campground but the sites are large, many to 60 feet, and the internal roads are wide enough to allow big RVs to maneuver. The campground access road is a loop so you can check it without unhooking if you have a big rig, but the route through the campground is deceiving so be careful. To reach the campground drive south on Hudspeth Road from an intersection on SR-7 that is 22 miles (35 km) west of Baker City and 7 miles (11 km) east of Sumpter. Some 1.1 miles (1.8 km) south of the intersection turn left on gravel Lake Road, you'll soon see the campground entrance on your left.

● **SUMPTER PINES RV PARK**
(Open All Year)

Res and Info: (541) 894-2328,
reservations@
sumpterpinesrvpark.com,
www.sumpterpinesrvpark.com

Location: .6 Miles (1 Km) S of Sumpter

GPS Location: 44.73361 N, 118.19583 W, 3,700 Ft

21 Sites – This is a small and very pleasant commercial RV park located just outside Sumpter. It makes an excellent base for exploring the area and has full-hookup back-in and pull-thru sites to 60 feet set in trees. There is a separate tent camping area with vehicle parking next to the tent sites. The campground is located just .6 miles (1 km) south of Sumpter on the road into town, SR-220.

BANDON

For such a small town Bandon (population 3,000) has lots to offer. Today's visitors know the town as an artist's colony and laid-back tourist town with interesting attractions including cranberry farms. The cute little Old Town sits just south of the harbor. Bandon is located near the mouth of the Coquille River and has its own jetties and lighthouse. It has been a port attracting visitors since the 1800s.

Once you have set yourself up in a campground take a stroll around the **Old Town,** also called Bandon By The Sea. The **Chamber of Commerce** is located along the highway at the entrance to the area. You'll find shops and good restaurants. Don't miss the stores selling cranberry sweets and products. There's even a museum - **The Bandon Historical Society Museum**, located in the old Coast Guard Station.

If you approached Bandon from the south you may have noticed fields that are surrounded by dikes and flooded with water. Those aren't rice paddies, they're **cranberries**. Bandon actually produces about 5% of the country's crop. The big event of the year is the **Cranberry Festival** in the first half of September.

Bandon has good beaches and also a good selection of sea stacks - big rocks offshore. You can best see them from **Beach Loop Drive** which follows the coast on the south side of the Coquille River. The **Bandon State Natural Area** and **Face Rock Scenic Viewpoint** provide several beach access points, necessary since this stretch of coast is fairly built up with private residences and motels.

Bandon is also a fishing town. Charter boats are available at the boat basin next to the old town. The Coquille River offers salmon, and in the lower section it is possible to catch crabs. Surf fishing is popular from the beach north and south of the river mouth.

Bandon's lighthouse, the **Coquille River Lighthouse**, is located on the north bank of the river near the mouth. It makes a good photograph from town but to reach it you must follow US-101 north to Bullards Beach State Park. The same road provides access to the campground, the lighthouse, and long sandy Bullards Beach. This lighthouse is not operational. The state park also offers hiking trails and the river mouth area of the park is popular with windsurfers.

About six miles (10 km) south of Bandon you'll find the **West Coast Game Park Safari** at Mile 281.5. This is a large private zoo with a reported 75 different species. Some of the animals are free-roaming while others are in exhibit areas.

Bandon Campgrounds

☐ **BULLARDS BEACH STATE PARK** *(Open All Year)*

Reservations: www.reserveamerica.com, (800) 452-5687
Information: (541) 347-3501, (800) 551- 6949,
www.oregonstateparks.org
Location: 1.5 Miles (2.4 Km) N of Bandon

GPS Location: 43.15222 N, 124.39833 W, Near Sea Level

185 Sites – This large state park campground is on the north side of the Coquille River. The campground is away from the beach and set in a large grove of shore pines. A mile-long paved trail leads to the beach and the Coquille River Lighthouse. The campground offers a hiker-biker camp as well as dry, full-hookup, and partial-hookup back-in vehicle camping sites. Some of the hookup sites are as long as 64 feet, many are over 50 feet long. The campground entrance road goes west to the campground and day-use area about a mile north of Bandon, just north of the bridge over the Coquille.

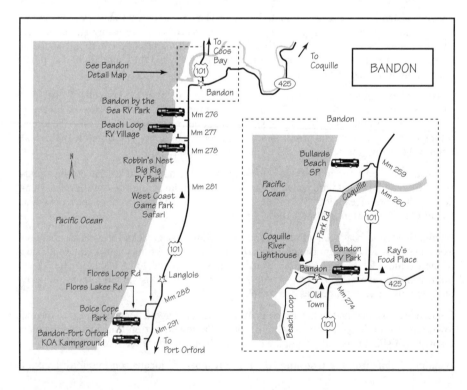

● **BANDON RV PARK** *(Open All Year)*
　Res and Info: (541) 347-4122,
　　　　　　　　bandonrvpark@bandonrvpark.org,
　　　　　　　　www.bandonrvpark.org
　Location:　Bandon

　GPS Location: 43.11917 N, 124.40250 W, Near Sea Level

44 Sites – This small RV park doesn't have a lot of extra amenities but has full hookups and an excellent location, you can easily stroll in to Bandon's Old Town. There are gravel sites, with back-ins to 55 feet and pull-thrus to 70 feet. The campground is located right in Bandon about a half-mile east of the downtown harbor and right on Highway 101. Reservations are recommended year-round.

● **BANDON BY THE SEA RV PARK** *(Open All Year)*
　Res and Info: (541) 347-5155,
　　　　　　　　www.bandonbythesearvpark.com
　Location:　2 Miles (3 Km) S of Bandon

　GPS Location: 43.08417 N, 124.41583 W, 100 Ft

90 Sites – Despite the name this campground is not by the sea. Instead, it is located along US-101 south of Bandon. There are back-in and pull-thru sites to 60 feet. The campground is on the west side of US-101, 2.3 miles (3.7 km) south of where the highway makes its 90° turn in Bandon to head south.

● **ROBBIN'S NEST BIG RIG RV PARK** *(Open All Year)*
　Res and Info: (541) 347-2175, bandonbluesky@aol.com
　Location:　3 Miles (5 Km) S of Bandon

　GPS Location: 43.06778 N, 124.41528 W, 100 Ft

23 Sites – Robbin's Nest is a modern big-rig RV park located on US-101 south of Bandon. There are back-in and pull-thru sites to 80 feet. There's a small grocery store across the street. The campground is on the west side of US-101, 3.4 miles (5.5 km) south of where the highway makes its 90° turn in Bandon to head south.

● **BEACH LOOP RV VILLAGE** *(Open All Year)*
　Res and Info: (541) 347-2100,
　　　　　　　　beachloop@hughes.net,
　　　　　　　　www.beachloopvillage.com
　Location:　4 Miles SW of Bandon

　GPS Location: 43.06917 N, 124.42833 W, 100 Ft

24 Sites – RV sites here include one 60 foot pull-thru and back-ins to 45 feet. There are also rental units. Many additional sites in this park are occupied by permanent units. From the point where US-101 make its 90° turn in Bandon drive south for 3.4 miles (5.5 km). Turn right on Beach Loop Dr and the campground will be on the right in .6 miles (1 km).

○ **BOICE COPE PARK** *(Open All Year)*
　Location:　17 Miles (27 Km) S of Bandon

　GPS Location: 42.90167 N, 124.50194 W, Near Sea Level

34 Sites – This Curry County park is a little off the beaten path

and is not well known but it's definitely worth a visit. The campground overlooks Floras Lake and the beach with trails leading out to the beach. The lake is popular with wind surfers and the campground fills up on good windy weekends. A reader board explains that at one time in the early 1900s there were plans to dredge an outlet to the lake and turn this into a lucrative port along this otherwise shelterless coast. Unfortunately, it turned out that the lake was higher that the ocean so if an outlet was dug it would drain itself empty into the ocean. All of the disappointed settlers of the new town that had formed in anticipation of the port then moved away. Sites here are back-ins to 45 feet arranged around a large lawn area. There are also tent sites. From US-101 near Mile 288.5, 14 miles (23 km) south of Bandon, turn seaward on Flores Loop Road. In 1.1 miles (1.7 km) turn right onto Flores Lake Road. In another 1.4 miles (2.3 km), make a 90° left, then turn right onto Boice Cope Road and you'll reach the park in another .3 mile (.5 km).

● **BANDON / PORT ORFORD KOA KAMPGROUND**
    (Open March 1 to Nov 15)

Reservations: (800) 562-3298, www.koa.com
Information: (541) 348-2358,
             koacamp@harborside.com
Location: 17 Miles (27 Km) S of Bandon

   GPS Location: 42.87750 N, 124.46861 W, 100 Ft

70 Sites – This KOA serves both Bandon and Port Orford. It is also handy for visiting the popular Game Park Safari, 9.4 miles (15 km) to the north. Sites here are set in a native forest for a woodsy setting. There are long pull-thrus to 80 feet as well as a variety of other sites. There's also a seasonal swimming pool. The campground is near Mile 291.5. That's 17 miles (27 km) south of Bandon and 9 miles (15 km) north of Port Orford.

BEND AND LA PINE

The Bend area (population about 77,000) offers a wealth of outdoor recreational opportunities. The town is large enough to offer pretty much anything you would need, it makes a great base.

The **Deschutes National Forest** is to the west and south. It has miles of trails and back roads. There are dozens of Forest Service campgrounds in the forest, at least 25 are convenient to the Bend area. The Deschutes River is very popular for white-water rafting.

Just south of Bend (about 3 miles) you'll find the **High Desert Museum.** With live animals, western art, and historical dioramas this is a nationally-acclaimed do-not-miss attraction.

Bend area has at least 24 **golf courses** nearby, it would be hard to find a better place to get out on the fairways.

Bend celebrates the **Bend Summer Festival** on the second weekend in July.

Six other listings in this chapter are near Bend and can easily be reached on day trips. These are • *Camp Sherman and the Metolius River,* • *Cascade Lakes Scenic Byway Loop,* • *Warm Springs and Madras,* • *Newberry National Volcanic Monument,* • *Redmond and Sisters,* and • *Prineville.*

Bend and La Pine Campgrounds

☐ **TUMALO STATE PARK** *(Open All Year)*
Reservations: www.reserveamerica.com, (800) 452-5687
Information: (541) 382-3586, (800) 551-6949,
www.oregonstateparks.org
Location: 4 Miles W of Bend

GPS Locations: 44.12861 N, 121.33056 W, 3,200 Ft

77 Sites – Tumalo State Park is located not far west of Bend along the Deschutes River. Sites here are all back-ins and a few reach 50 feet, several exceed 40 feet. There are also hiker/biker tent sites. Swimming and fishing are both possible in the river and there are nice hiking trails. The park is located south of US-20 some 4 miles (6 km) west of Bend.

● **SCANDIA RV PARK** *(Open All Year)*
Res and Info: (541) 382-6206, scandiarv@hwy97.net
Location: Bend

GPS Location: 44.03028 N, 121.31194 W, 3,800 Ft

85 Sites – Although this is an older campground with quite a few permanent residents it has a separate new section for big RVs. Pull-thru sites vary in size but reach 60 feet and are well-spaced in this section. There are also tent-camping sites in this park. The Scandia is in southern Bend off the business US-97 loop. If you are driving south on the main US-97 highway exit to the east on SE Powers Rd. which

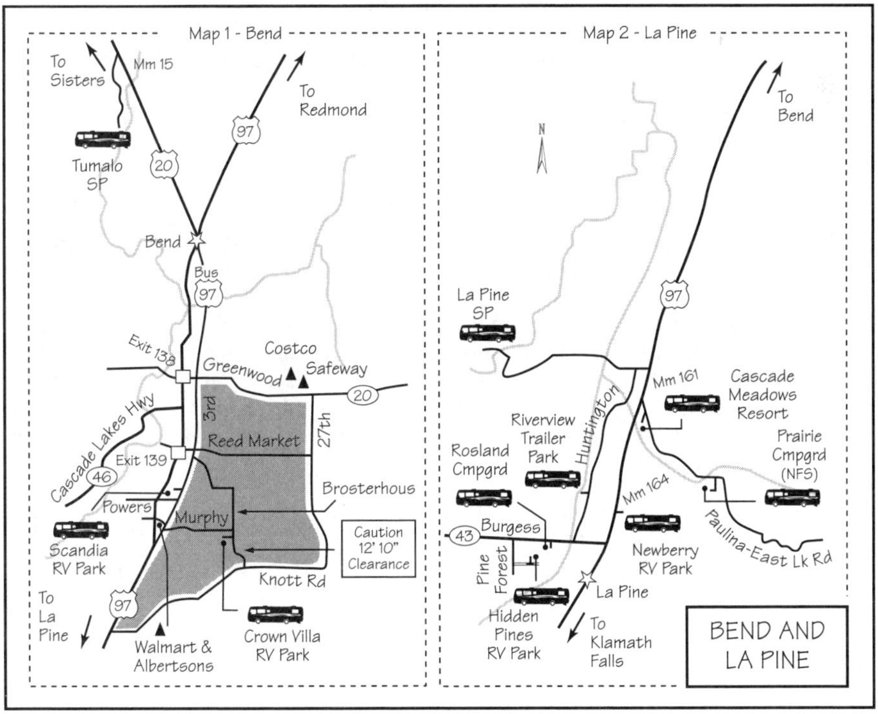

Map 1 - Bend

To Sisters
Mm 15
To Redmond
97
Tumalo SP
20
Bend
Bus 97
Exit 138
Costco
Greenwood
Safeway
20
Cascade Lakes Hwy
3rd
Reed Market
27th
Exit 139
46
Brosterhous
Powers
Murphy
Caution 12' 10" Clearance
Scandia RV Park
Knott Rd
To La Pine
97
Walmart & Albertsons
Crown Villa RV Park

Map 2 - La Pine

To Bend
N
La Pine SP
97
Mm 161
Cascade Meadows Resort
Riverview Trailer Park
Huntington
Prairie Cmpgrd (NFS)
Rosland Cmpgrd
Mm 164
Paulina-East Lk Rd
43
Burgess
Newberry RV Park
Pine Forest
La Pine
Hidden Pines RV Park
To Klamath Falls

BEND AND LA PINE

OREGON

is about 2 miles (3 km) south of the center of town. Drive east one block to business US-97, also called SE 3rd Street. Turn left and the campground will be on the left almost immediately.

● **CROWN VILLA RV PARK** *(Open All Year)*
Res and Info: (541) 388-1131, (866) 500-5300,
info@crownvillarvresort.com,
www.crownvillarvresort.com
Location: Bend

GPS Location: 44.01667 N, 121.29528 W, 3,700 Ft

115 Sites – This is a really first-class RV resort catering to big RVs. Most sites are back-ins but they're 90 feet long and separated by well-groomed lawns and shaded by large trees. There is no swimming pool but there is a hot tub, tennis courts, and a putting green. The campground is located in southeast Bend. From central Bend drive south on US-97 about 2.5 miles (4 km) to SW Pinbrook. Turn east and drive a block to SE 3rd Street (also called Bus US-97), then jog south a short distance and turn east again on SE Murphy Road. In 1.2 mile (1.9 km) turn right on SE Brosterhous Rd and the campground entrance in on the right in just a short distance.

● **HIDDEN PINES RV PARK** *(Open All Year)*
Res and Info: (541) 536-2265, hprvpk@inbox.com
Location: 26 Miles (42 Km) S of Bend

GPS Location: 43.69472 N, 121.52139 W, 4,200 Ft

24 Sites – Hidden Pines is a small family-run park located away from the main highways in a residential neighborhood near La Pine. It's a clean and well-managed park. Some pull-thru sites extend to 65 feet and there are grassy tent sites. From US-97 24 miles (39 km) south of Bend or 2 miles (3 km) north of La Pine turn west on Burgess Rd. In 2.4 miles (3.9 km) turn south on Pine Forest Road and drive 3 blocks. Turn left on Wright Ave, drive a block, and the campground is on the left.

● **RIVERVIEW TRAILER PARK** *(Open All Year)*
Res and Info: (541) 536-2382
Location: 24 Miles (39 Km) S of Bend

GPS Location: 43.71583 N, 121.48889 W, 4,200 Ft

28 Sites – This is another campground located away from the highway near La Pine. It has long back-in sites to 70 feet with lots of maneuvering room as well as a grassy tenting area. There are many long-term rigs here, about half of the sites are open for travelers. From the intersection of Hwy 97 and Hwy 43 in La Pine drive west on Hwy 43 for .9 miles (1.5 km). Turn north on S Huntington Rd and the campground is on the left after another .8 miles (1.3 km).

■ **PRAIRIE CAMPGROUND** *(Open May 15 to Oct 15 – Varies)*
Information: (541) 383-5300
Location: 23 Miles (37 Km) S of Bend

GPS Location: 43.72500 N, 121.42333 W, 4,300 Ft

17 Sites – This small Deschutes National Forest campground is located near the inter-section of US-97 and the road up to Newberry National Monument. It's an inexpensive campground close to Hwy 97 with big sites and is seldom full. Sites here are large pull-

thrus to 45 feet. The campground is off the access road to the Newberry Volcanic National Monument (Paulina-East Lake Rd.). From US-97, 20 miles (32 km) south of Bend and 6 miles (10 km) north of La Pine, drive east on Paulina-East Lake Rd for 2.8 miles (4.5 km), the campground entrance is on your right.

● **CASCADE MEADOWS RESORT**
  (Open All Year)
  Res and Info: (541) 536-2244,
          thepinedrop@hotmail.com
  Location: 20 Miles (32 Km) S of Bend

  GPS Location: 43.75028 N, 121.45889 W, 4,200 Ft

117 Sites – Cascade Meadows is a large big-rig park conveniently located at the junction of US-97 and the highway up to Newberry Volcanic National Monument. This is a membership park but it accepts non-members as well. Amenities include a restaurant, swimming pool, and hot tub. The campground has full-hookup pull-thru sites with picnic tables to 70 feet separated by grass and also tent camping. The junction is located 20 miles (32 km) south of Bend and 6 miles (10 km) north of La Pine. The access to the park is off the Paulina-East Lake Rd which is the access road to the monument.

☐ **LA PINE STATE PARK** *(Open All Year)*
  Reservations: www.reserveamerica.com, (800) 452-5687
  Information: (541) 536-2071, (800) 551- 6949,
          www.oregonstateparks.org
  Location: 19 Miles (31 Km) S of Bend

  GPS Location: 43.77444 N, 121.53750 W, 4,200 Ft

128 Sites – This large state park straddles the Deschutes River. There is room for big RVs with many pull-thru and back-in full-hookup sites over 50 feet long. The park is also home to "Big Red". It's the largest ponderosa pine in Oregon, or at least the biggest that people know about. Nice hiking trails follow both sides of the river and the fishing is good. The campground entrance is off US-97 some 19 miles (31 km) south of Bend and 7 miles (11 km) north of La Pine.

● **NEWBERRY RV PARK** *(Open All Year)*
  Res and Info: (541) 536-7596, www.NewberryRV.com,
          NewberryRVF@gmail.com
  Location: 23 Miles (37 Km) S of Bend

  GPS Location: 43.71250 N, 121.47361 W, 4,200 Ft

38 Sites – The Newberry is a modern big-rig RV park. It's a large flat park next to the highway with gravel-surfaced back-in and pull-thru sites to 55 feet at the northern edge of the town of La Pine.

○ **ROSLAND CAMPGROUND** *(Open May 15 to Oct 15 – Varies)*
  Information: (541) 536-2223, www.lapineparks.org
  Location: 1 Mile (1.6 Km) E of La Pine

  GPS Location: 43.70279 N, 121.50557 W, 4,200 Ft

11 Sites – This campground is operated by the La Pine Park and Recreation District. It's a small little-known campground in a convenient location, a real find. It has large pull-thru sites suitable for any size RV, one site has power hookup, the rest are economical dry sites

and tent sites with pitching on grass. From the intersection of Hwy 97 and Hwy 43 in La Pine drive west on Hwy 43 for 1.5 miles (2.4 km), the campground entrance is on the left.

BROOKINGS

Brookings (population 6,400) is the most southerly town on the Oregon coast. The town is increasingly popular and growing, largely because it has better weather than most towns along the coast. Warm air descending from the Rogue Valley mixes with marine air to produce comfortable temperatures year round. Unfortunately, as is common along the entire coast, there is still lots of rain, particularly in the winter.

About 75% of the **Easter lilies** produced in the U.S. come from near Brookings. Early July is the time to see large fields of blooming flowers.

There are three business centers in Brookings with a downtown area on high ground north of the Chetco River and smaller unincorporated Harbor along the south shore of the Chetco River outlet. There are also many stores and other businesses strung out along the highway south of town.

A **State Welcome Center** (open May through October, 8 a.m. to 6 p.m. on Monday-Saturday and 9 a.m. to 5 p.m. on Sunday) is located at a rest area near Mile 355.6. This is just across the highway from the Harris Beach State Park and about a half-mile north of Brookings. The welcome center has pamphlets covering the whole state and is designed to provide information for folks driving north from California. There is parking for RVs.

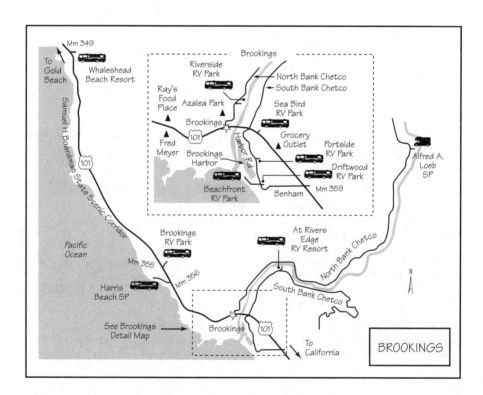

While you are in Brookings you may want to visit **Brookings Harbor** for a meal at one of the seafood restaurants and perhaps even book a fishing charter. Brookings Harbor is said to be the safest port on the Oregon coast. Many coastal ports have dangerous entrances due to waves coming across the sandbars at river and estuary entrances. Fishing excursions are available for salmon and rockfish in the summer.

There's river fishing at Brookings too, the Chetco for steelhead (winter) and salmon (fall) and the Winchuck River a little to the south for rainbows and cutthroat.

The town is proud of **Azalea Park**, a small park just north of the river with many Azaleas, they bloom from April to June. It's a pleasant place for a picnic. **Harris Beach State Park** is located just north of town. It's a great place to camp but also has a day-use area with picnic tables overlooking huge rocks and a beach that is large enough to allow you to indulge in some beachcombing. Inland from Brookings along the Chetco River near Loeb State Park is the **Redwood Nature Trail** which runs through some of the world's northernmost redwoods. Drive eight miles (13 km) east on North Bank Road to reach the trail.

The 29-mile (47 km) section of coastline from Brookings north to Gold Beach is very scenic. The road closely follows the coastline which is alternately rocky cliffs and sandy beaches. From Mile 343 to Mile 353 you are in the **Samuel H. Boardman State Scenic Corridor**. There are many pull-offs giving you the opportunity to make short walks and take some photos from scenic viewpoints.

Brookings Campgrounds

● **WHALESHEAD BEACH RESORT** *(Open All Year)*
Reservations: (800) 943-4325
Information: (541) 469-7446, whaleshead@charter.net,
www.whalesheadresort.com
Location: 6 Miles (10 Km) N of Brookings

GPS Locations: 42.14722 N, 124.35333 W, 200 Ft

51 Sites – This park perches above the highway and the ocean north of Brookings. Since it's on the inland side of the highway there's a tunnel to the beach. At one time there were over 140 RV sites here but only 51 remain, the remainder are occupied by park units. Sites are back-ins occupying terraces, the terrain here is steep. Some are as long as 55 feet, many have cedar decks with picnic tables. When you drive in to register a circular drive leads you around the main registration and restaurant building. It looks like it will be tight but it's not bad. The entrance of the park is on the east side of US-101 at Mile 349.2.

● **BROOKINGS RV PARK** *(Open All Year)*
Res and Info: (541) 469-6849,
www.brookingsrv.com
Location: 1 Mile (2 Km) N of
Brookings

GPS Location: 42.07333 N, 124.30583 W, 200 Ft

43 Sites – This is the only campground located at the northern approaches to Brookings other than Harris Beach State Park. It occupies a site on the hillside above US-101 and is popular with long-term residents. Because it sits on a hillside it often has sunshine when the other campgrounds in the area still have fog. The campground has back-in and pull-thru sites to about 50 feet, most are shorter. The entrance road is near Mile 355.3. Stay left at the Y and climb the hill for .3 miles (.5 km) to the campground entrance.

☐ **HARRIS BEACH STATE PARK** *(Open All Year)*
Reservations: www.reserveamerica.com,
            (800) 452-5687
Information: (541) 469-2021, (800) 551-6949,
            www.oregonstateparks.org
Location: ½ Mile (1 Km) N of Brookings

GPS Location: 42.06806 N, 124.31139 W, 100 Ft

149 Sites – Yes, this state campground does have TV hookups at many of the sites, it also offers a laundry room. It is conveniently located at the northern edge of Brookings and has a beautiful beach area bordered by very photogenic rocks as well as the largest offshore island along the coast. The campground is above the beach in trees with most sites having no views, but the day area below on the beach is just a nice stroll down the hill. Sites are back-ins with many to 50 feet and even a bit larger. The entrance road is near Mile 355.9.

☐ **ALFRED A. LOEB STATE PARK** *(Open All Year)*
Information: (541) 469-2021, (800) 551-6949,
            www.oregonstateparks.org
Location: 7 Miles E of Brookings

GPS Location: 42.11278 N, 124.18806 W, 100 Ft

48 Sites – Alfred A. Loeb is located quite a distance inland from Brookings along the Chetco River. It's in a Myrtlewood forest with some trees over 200 years old. Sites here are all back-ins, many exceed 40 feet but access is poor so 35 feet is about the maximum appropriate rig size. There is a riverside trail to a nearby redwood forest (the trees are at the northernmost point in their range here) and also fishing in the Chetco. From Brookings follow North Bank Chetco River Road eastward for 7.3 miles (11.8 km) to the campground.

● **RIVERSIDE RV RESORT** *(Open All Year)*
Res and Info: (541) 469-4799,
              chetcocharlie@riverside-rv.com
              www.riverside-rv.com
Location: .5 Miles (1 Km) E of Brookings

GPS Location: 42.05972 N, 124.26833 W, Near Sea Level

30 Sites – A very pleasant small RV park along the bank of the Chetco River near Brookings. It's popular with long-term residents, reservations are a must. It has tent sites that are good for bicycle and motorcycle campers. For RVers there are a few pull-thrus to 65 feet but most sites are back-ins, several reach 55 feet and a few are longer. From Brookings follow North Bank Chetco River Road .4 mile (.6 km) east to the campground entrance.

● **AT RIVERS EDGE RV RESORT** *(Open All Year)*
Res and Info: (541) 469-3356, (888) 295-1441,
              stay@riversedge.com,
              www.atriversedge.com
Location: 2 Miles (3 Km) E of Brookings

GPS Location: 42.07083 N, 124.25250 W, Near Sea Level

126 Sites – The park occupies a large cleared area on the south bank of the Chetco. There's a steep narrow entrance road that can be intimidating, if you don't trust your driving or brakes don't come here. Facilities are modern and well maintained. There are

many back-in spaces with cement patios and 10 new long pull-thrus to 60 feet. Amenities include a small boat ramp and a clubhouse with an exercise and game room. Follow the South Bank Chetco Road eastward for 1.3 miles (2.1 km) to the park.

○ **BEACHFRONT RV PARK** *(Open All Year)*
 Res and Info: (541) 469-5867, (800) 441-0856,
  www.port-brookings.harbor.org
 Location: Brookings Harbor

GPS Location: 42.04306 N, 124.26583 W, Near Sea Level

133 Sites – The Beachfront is operated by the Port of Brookings. It has sites not 50 feet from the water between the marina and the ocean. Access is not controlled, there is a stream of automobile traffic in front of the RVs, and also public parking. The restrooms are grim cement block units and access is not limited to campground residents. Sites are both back-ins and pull-thrus to 60 feet. There are tent sites here behind the row of RVs, the surface for these is grass. There's a restaurant and the harbor and boat ramp are nearby. To reach the park follow the Harbor Road toward the water from the south end of the bridge over the Chetco. The park will be on your right in 1 mile (2 km).

● **PORTSIDE RV PARK** *(Open All Year)*
 Res and Info: (541) 469-6616, (877) 787-2752,
  www.portside-rvpark.com
 Location: Brookings Harbor

GPS Location: 42.04833 N, 124.26389 W, Near Sea Level

85 Sites – The Portside actually has about 90 sites, but close to half of them are taken up by nice park model homes. This definitely changes the character of an RV park. Some people will like it and some won't. Across the road is the Portside Suites hotel with a restaurant. Most sites are back-ins to 50 feet long but there are some longer pull-thrus to 65 feet. To reach the park follow the Harbor Road toward the water from the south end of the bridge over the Chetco. The park will be on your left in .5 mile (.8 km).

● **DRIFTWOOD RV PARK** *(Open All Year)*
 Res and Info: (541) 469-9089,
  info@driftwoodrvpark.com,
  www.driftwoodrvpark.com
 Location: Brookings Harbor

GPS Location: 42.04278 N, 124.26278 W, Near Sea Level

106 Sites – The Driftwood is a friendly and pleasant park located near the boat harbor, a lot of people really like this place. It's not right on the edge of the bay and doesn't have the ocean right outside the window but it's nearby. Most sites in this park are 40 feet long although there are some pull-thrus to 60 feet. Some sites have instant-on telephone and the park has free Wi-Fi. To reach the park follow the Harbor Road toward the water from the south end of the bridge over the Chetco. The park will be on your left in .9 mile (1.4 km).

● **SEA BIRD RV PARK** *(Open All Year)*
 Res and Info: (541) 469-3512,
  www.seabirdrv.com
 Location: Brookings

GPS Location: 42.05417 N, 124.26333 W, 100 Ft

60 Sites – The Sea Bird is probably the most popular campground in Brookings. The low price has a lot to do with that. It's a simple well-run park with both back-in and pull-thru sites to 50 feet. The park is located on the east side of US-101 just south of the Chetco bridge.

CAMP SHERMAN AND THE METOLIUS RIVER

The **Metolius River** springs from the ground as a good-sized clear mountain river. It is thought to pass underground from the nearby mountains. After emerging the river flows through a beautiful area of ponderosa pine and grasslands. The Metolius is a famous fishing spot (fly fishing only), the area is extremely scenic with many hiking trails. The commercial center of the region is called Camp Sherman, it amounts to little more than a store and post office. There are quite a few homes and resorts set in seclusion among the pines in the surrounding area. To get there just follow US-20 some 9 miles (15 km) toward Salem and then take the Camp Sherman road (Rd. 14) to the right. After 2.7 miles (4.4 km) there is a fork, take the right (Rd. 14) to visit the source of the Metolius River and the National Forest Service campgrounds downstream. A left at the fork puts you on Rd. 1419 and a drive through an area of lodges and other facilities. You can take a right after another 2.2 miles (3.5 km) to reach the Camp Sherman Store which has groceries, gas, a deli, and a post office.

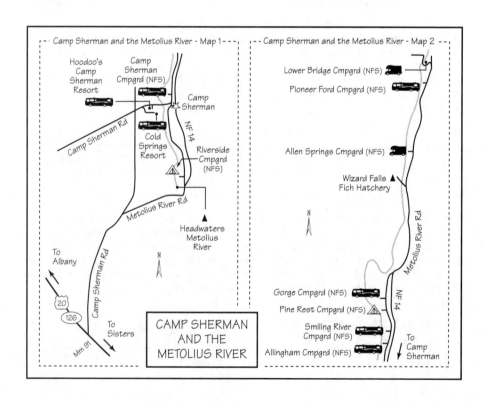

OREGON

Camp Sherman and the Metolius River Campgrounds

● **HOODOO'S CAMP SHERMAN RESORT**
(Open All Year)

Reservations: reservations@campshermanrv.com
Information: (541) 595-6514, (541) 822-3799,
               www.campshermanrv.com
Location: Camp Sherman

GPS Location: 44.46000 N, 121.64722 W, 2,900 Ft

30 Sites – The Camp Sherman Resort is probably the best stop for travelers who want full hookups in the Camp Sherman area. There are full and partial hookup sites to 45 feet. Parking is on grass or gravel in a mowed lawn area. Restrooms and showers here are available for a fee to folks staying at the other campgrounds nearby. To reach this campground take the SW Camp Sherman Road from US-20 some 10 miles (16 km) northwest of Sisters. Follow the road north taking the left fork at 2.6 miles (4.2 km). Four and eight tenths miles (7.7 km) from where you left US-20 follow SW Camp Sherman Road to the right, the campground is on the right .4 mile (.6 km) from the corner.

● **COLD SPRINGS RESORT** *(Open All Year)*

Res and Info: (541) 595-6271,
               lodging@coldspringsresort.com,
               www.coldspringsresort.com
Location: Camp Sherman

GPS Location: 44.45778 N, 121.64611 W, 2,900 Ft

25 Sites – This campground is primarily for long-term campers but maintains about 10 sites for travelers. These back-in sites are used by coaches to 40 feet but careful maneuvering is required. To reach the campground take the SW Camp Sherman Road from US-20 some 10 miles (16 km) northwest of Sisters. Follow the road north taking the left fork at 2.6 miles (4.2 km). Four and eight tenths miles (7.7 km) from where you left US-20 follow SW Camp Sherman Road to the right, the campground entrance road is on the right .2 mile (.3 km) from the corner.

■ **RIVERSIDE CAMPGROUND** *(Open May 15 to Oct 15 – Varies)*

Information: (541) 383-5300, www.hoodoo.com
Location: Stretches South of Camp Sherman

GPS Location: 44.43917 N, 121.63361 W, 2,900 Ft

16 Sites – The Riverside is a Deschutes National Forest walk-in tent campground that stretches along the Metolius River Road between Camp Sherman and the Head of the Metolius. There are parking pull-offs along the dirt road, the campsites are scattered near the Metolius River about 75 yards from the parking sites. There are picnic tables and fire pits as well as vault toilets and hand-operated water pumps. To reach the campground take the SW Camp Sherman Road from US-20 some 10 miles (16 km) northwest of Sisters. Follow the road north taking the right fork at 2.6 miles (4.2 km). Four and three tenths miles (6.9 km) from where you left US-20 you'll see the campground sign on the left.

■ **CAMP SHERMAN CAMPGROUND** *(Open All Year)*
Reservations: www.recreation.gov, (877) 444-6777
Information: (541) 383-5300, www.hoodoo.com
Location: .4 Mile (.6 km) N of Camp Sherman

GPS Location: 44.46333 N, 121.63889 W, 2,900 Ft

15 Sites – This is the first of the riverside Deschutes National Forest vehicle campgrounds you reach as you travel north (downstream) along the Metolius. It has sites to 50 feet and is on the east side of the river like the other sites listed below. Exercise care entering this campground in larger RVs. To reach the campground take the SW Camp Sherman Road from US-20 some 10 miles (16 km) northwest of Sisters. Follow the road north taking the left fork at 2.6 miles (4.2 km). Four and eight tenths miles (7.7 km) from where you left US-20 follow SW Camp Sherman Road to the right. You'll pass the entrance to the Camp Sherman Resort, cross a bridge over the Metolius, and pass the Camp Sherman store. Just after passing the store follow SW Metolius River Rd. to the left and you'll see the campground entrance on the left in .4 miles (.6 km).

■ **ALLINGHAM CAMPGROUND** *(Open May 15 to Sept 15 – Varies)*
Information: (541) 383-5300, www.hoodoo.com
Location: 1 Mile (1.6 Km) N of Camp Sherman

GPS Locations: 44.47194 N, 121.63778 W, 2,900 Ft

10 Sites – Allingham is the next Deschutes National Forest campground to the north of the Camp Sherman Campground along the Metolius. It's small with narrow access roads but some sites are 50 feet long and fairly large RVs use it with careful maneuvering. To reach the campground follow the instructions in the previous write-up, the entrance to Allingham is .6 miles (1 km) beyond that for the Camp Sherman National Forest Campground.

■ **SMILING RIVER CAMPGROUND** *(Open May 13 to Sept 25 – Varies)*
Reservations: www.recreation.gov, (877) 444-6777
Information: (541) 383-5300, www.hoodoo.com
Location: 1.3 Mile (2.1 Km) N of Camp Sherman

GPS Location: 44.47500 N, 121.63639 W, 2,900 Ft

36 Sites – This is the next Deschutes National Forest campground north along the Metolius. Although this is considered an RV campground it has huge ponderosa pines closely bordering the road and making access with anything larger than a 30 foot coach pretty difficult. Yet we see 40 foot RVs in the campground and sites do exceed that length. To reach the campground follow the directions given for the Camp Sherman National Forest Campground. Then drive another .9 miles (1.5 km) north to reach the entrance for Smiling River.

■ **PINE REST CAMPGROUND** *(Open All Year)*
Information: (541) 383-5300, www.hoodoo.com
Location: 1.7 Mile (2.7 Km) N of Camp Sherman

GPS Location: 44.48155 N, 121.63789 W, 3,000 Ft

7 Sites – Pine Rest is a small Deschutes National Forest campground on the east shore of the Metolius. This is a tent campground with parking for small vehicles at most sites. Interior roads are paved but parking is on dirt. There is a picnic shelter overlooking the river but no potable water. This campground remains open all year long, there are reduced

services and smaller fee from about Oct 15 to May 1. To reach the campground follow the directions given for the Camp Sherman National Forest Campground. Then drive another 1.3 miles (2.1 km) north to reach the entrance for Pine Rest.

■ **Gorge Campground** *(Open May 12 to Sept 19 – Varies)*
　Information:　(541) 383-5300, www.hoodoo.com
　Location:　　2 Mile (3.2 Km) N of Camp Sherman

GPS Location: 44.48506 N, 121.63881 W, 2,900 Ft

18 Sites – Gorge Campground is a Deschutes National Forest Campground set on the east bank of the Metolius River. Some sites here are long and with careful maneuvering it is possible to get large RVs into then although slide-outs can be a problem. There is not potable water at the campground. To reach the campground follow the directions given for the Camp Sherman National Forest Campground. Then drive another 1.6 miles (2.6 km) north to reach the entrance for Gorge Campground.

■ **Allen Springs Campground** *(Open All Year)*
　Information:　(541) 383-5300, www.hoodoo.com
　Location:　　5.3 Mile (8.5 Km) N of Camp Sherman

GPS Location: 44.52984 N, 121.62959 W, 2,800 Ft

16 Sites – Allen Springs is a Deschutes National Forest Campground on east bank of the Metolius River. Sites here are as long as 36 feet but are suitable for coaches to about 30 feet due to lack of maneuvering room. Many of the site are walk-in tent sites. The campground is open all year but there are reduced services and rates from Oct 11 to May 14 (Varies). There is no potable water at this campground. To reach the campground follow the directions given for the Camp Sherman National Forest Campground. Then drive another 4.9 miles (7.9 km) north to reach the entrance for Allen Springs.

■ **Pioneer Ford Campground** *(Open May 12 to Sept 19 – Varies)*
　Information:　(541) 383-5300, www.hoodoo.com
　Location:　　6.8 Miles (11 Km) N of Camp Sherman

GPS Location: 44.55084 N, 121.62188 W, 2,800 Ft

20 Sites – Pioneer Ford is a Deschutes National Forest Campground on the east bank of the Metolius River in large Ponderosa Pines. Sites here are larger than in most of the campgrounds along the river. Some exceed 70 feet but careful maneuvering is required. Roads are paved with parking on gravel. To reach the campground follow the directions given for the Camp Sherman National Forest Campground. Then drive another 6.4 miles (10.3 km) north to reach the entrance for Allen Springs.

■ **Lower Bridge Campground** *(Open May 1 to Oct 10 – Varies)*
　Information:　(541) 383-5300, www.hoodoo.com
　Location:　　7.4 Miles (11.9 Km) N of Camp Sherman

GPS Location: 44.55722 N, 121.62041 W, 2,900 Ft

10 Sites – The small Lower Bridge Campground slopes toward the river just north of the highway where it crosses the Metolius on Bridge 99. The sites here are as large as 30 feet but most are not level and it can be hard to park. Water is from a faucet. To reach the campground follow the directions given for the Camp Sherman National Forest Campground. Then drive another 7 miles (11.3 km) north to reach the entrance for Lower Bridge.

CASCADE LAKES SCENIC BYWAY LOOP

An interesting drive southwest from Bend is known as the **Cascade Lakes Byway**. This spectacularly scenic two-lane paved road heads west from Bend to **Mt Bachelor**, a very popular winter ski area. In the summer you can ride the lift up the mountain for the view. The highway passes around the north side of the mountain and then south along a chain of lakes. The highway in this section is called the Cascade Lakes Highway (NF-46).

After passing the mountain you will find that a maze of Forest Service roads – some paved, some not – offer the opportunity to do lots of exploring, fishing, and camping. The road beyond Mt Bachelor is closed by snow in winter.

For the campgrounds shown below we've shortened the loop. Forty-nine miles (79 km) from Bend turn east on South Century Drive (NF-42). Then, 9 miles (15 km) from that intersection, the route turns right on Burgess Road and continues 11 miles (18 km) to US-97 at a point 22 miles (35 km) south of Bend and 2 miles (3 km) north of La Pine. The entire loop as outlined here is paved although side roads to campgrounds are often gravel.

The many lakes in the area vary in size and usage. Some are reservoirs and others are not. Most lakes are carefully managed and stocked to maximize the fishing possibilities. Here's a brief roundup of the lakes bordered by campgrounds we've listed below.

Sparks Lake is a very shallow natural lake with a surface area of about 800 acres. Much of the lake is surrounded by lava flows making access difficult for fishermen without boats. This is fly-fishing-only water and the lake has a 10 mph speed limit. Brook and cutthroat trout are present.

Elk Lake is a deep natural lake with a surface area of about 300 acres. It's a fairly deep lake and very clear. There are small kokanee and the lake is heavily stocked with brook trout. Boat speed is limited to 10 mph.

Hosmer Lake is a shallow clear 160-acre lake offering great views of the mountains to the northeast. It's a fly-fishing-only lake with populations of Atlantic salmon, brook trout, and rainbows. This is also a great canoeing lake. There are actually two lakes here connected by a long channel. No engines are allowed, but electric motors are OK.

Big and Little Lava Lakes are actually only connected during unusually high water levels during the spring. Little Lava Lake is the source of the Deschutes River which flows south through Craine Prairie Reservoir and Wickiup Reservoir before turning north to flow into the Columbia. These are old spring-fed natural lakes with a combined surface area of about 500 acres. Fishermen will find rainbows and brook trout.

Craine Prairie Reservoir is a large shallow lake with a surface area of about five square miles. It was first created in 1922 by damming the Deschutes River. This is an extremely productive fishing lake. It's most famous for its "crainebows". These, of course, are large rainbow trout, said to grow in this friendly environment at a rate of two inches per month during the summer. Whitefish, brook trout, kokanee, and largemouth bass are also present.

North Twin Lake is a small, fairly deep circular lake with a surface are of about 130 acres. The lake is heavily stocked with rainbows. Motors are not allowed.

South Twin Lake is another small, fairly deep circular lake. It has a surface area of about

100 acres and, like North Twin, is heavily stocked with rainbows. No motors are allowed on the lake.

Wickiup Reservoir is another reservoir formed by damming the Deschutes River. Wickiup is deeper than Crane Reservoir but water levels vary greatly. Surface area of the lake when full is 10,300 acres. Wickiup is known for its very large brown trout. Fishing is usually excellent in the lake with rainbows, brook trout, kokanee, coho salmon and whitefish also present.

The campgrounds below are arranged along a route that follows the Cascade Lake Highway (FR-46) west and then south for 49 miles (79 km). Then it turns east on FR-42 and Burgess Road to return to US-97 just north of La Pine. The distance from Bend that is listed assumes you travel this route. From Rock Creek Campground eastward it's actually

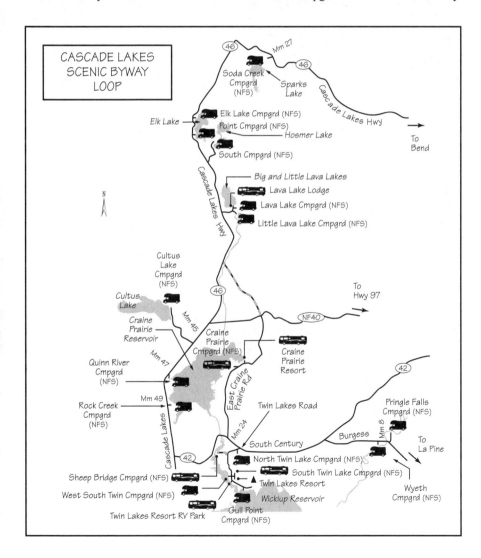

CASCADE LAKES
SCENIC BYWAY
LOOP

SPECTACULAR VIEW OF MT BACHELOR FROM THE CRANE PRAIRIE RESORT

shorter to travel south from Bend on US-97 and then eastward on FR-42 or Burgess Road to the campgrounds.

Cascade Lakes Scenic Byway Loop Campgrounds

■ **SODA CREEK CAMPGROUND** *(Open June 1 to Sept 30 – Varies)*
Information: (541) 383-5300, www.hoodoo.com
Location: 26 Miles (42 Km) W of Bend

GPS Location: 44.02500 N, 121.72806 W, 5,400 Ft

10 Sites – Soda Creek is a Deschutes National Forest campground. It is one of the closest of the national forest campgrounds to Bend but it is only suitable for tent camping or RVs to about 30 feet. The campground has no potable water but there is a vault toilet, tables, and fire pits. A trail leads to Sparks Lake. Watch for the sign for Sparks Lake on the Cascade Lakes Highway 23 miles (37 km) west of Bend. Turn south onto the lake road and then almost immediately turn right into the campground.

■ **ELK LAKE CAMPGROUND** *(Open May 15 to Sept 30 – Varies)*
Information: (541) 383-5300, www.hoodoo.com
Location: 33 Miles (53 Km) SW of Bend

GPS Location: 43.98000 N, 121.80917 W, 4,900 Ft

23 Sites – Elk Lake is a Deschutes National Forest Campground. The entrance for this campground is right off the paved Cascade Lakes Highway. It is a lakeside campground with a resort next door where you can find rental boats and a restaurant. The campground has a beach area and a boat ramp and some of the sites reach 26 feet in length. There is a good sign at the entrance, it's 30 miles (48 km) west of Bend.

POINT CAMPGROUND *(Open May 25 to Sept 30 – Varies)*
Information: (541) 383-5300, www.hoodoo.com
Location: 31 Miles (50 Km) SW of Bend

GPS Location: 43.96667 N, 121.80861 W, 4,900 Ft

OREGON

10 Sites – Just south of the Elk Lake Campground is the smaller but very similar Point Campground (Deschutes National Forest). It too has sites to 26 feet and has a boat ramp and beach. Some sites are along the lake. Watch for the entrance road 31 miles (50 km) west of Bend on the Cascade Lakes Highway.

SOUTH CAMPGROUND *(Open May 15 to Sept 30 – Varies)*
Information: (541) 383-5300, www.hoodoo.com
Location: 34 Miles (55 km) SW of Bend

GPS Location: 43.96139 N, 121.79000 W, 5,000 Ft

23 Sites – This Deschutes National Forest campground along Hosmer Lake has pull-thru sites suitable for RVs to 26 feet with the limiting factor being maneuvering room and a bad access road. There is no potable water at this campground but there are picnic tables, fire pits, outhouses and a boat ramp. To reach the campground drive 32.5 miles (52 km) west from Bend on the Cascade Lakes Highway. Turn east on the access road at the sign and drive 1.2 miles (1.9 km) to the campground.

LAVA LAKE CAMPGROUND *(Open May 15 to Oct 15 – Varies)*
Information: (541) 383-5300, www.hoodoo.com
Location: 36 Miles (58 Km) SW of Bend

GPS Location: 43.91333 N, 121.76694 W, 4,800 Ft

44 Sites – This is a large national forest campground suitable for larger RVs than most in this area. The forest service says the campground is good for RVs to 30 feet but you'll see RVs to 35 feet in here. The Lava Lake Lodge, right next door, has a dump station and showers. There is also a boat ramp at the campground. To reach the campground drive west on the Cascade Lakes Highway for 35 miles (56 km). Turn east on Lava Lake Road and follow it .8 miles (1.3 km) to the campground.

LAVA LAKE RESORT *(Open April 20 to Oct 31 – Varies)*
Res and Info: (541) 382-9443
Location: 36 Miles (58 Km) SW of Bend

GPS Location: 43.91444 N, 121.76806 W, 4,800 Ft

24 Sites – This lodge, sitting next to Lava Lake, has full hookup back-in sites for RVs to 45 feet. The lodge rents boats and has a store and dump and water fill station open to folks not staying at the campground for a fee. To reach the campground drive west on the Cascade Lakes Highway for 35 miles (56 km). Turn east on Lava Lake Road and follow it .8 miles (1.3 km) to the campground.

LITTLE LAVA LAKE CAMPGROUND *(Open May 15 to Oct 15 – Varies)*
Reservations: www.recreation.gov, (877) 444-6777
Information: (541) 383-5300, www.hoodoo.com
Location: 36 Miles (58 Km) SW of Bend

GPS Location: 43.91067 N, 121.76410 W, 4,700 Ft

13 Sites – This campground is on Little Lava Lake, the source of the Deschutes River.

A lava flow separates Little Lava from Lava Lake. There are some nice tent sites on the river. Some vehicle sites are as long as 40 feet but access is poor so the campground is best for RVs to 30 feet. One site is a pull-thru, the rest are back-ins. The campground is just .6 (1 km) from Lava Lake Lodge, see above. Access is from the same road that leads to Lava Lake Lodge and Lava Lake Campground. To reach the campground drive west on the Cascade Lakes Highway for 35 miles (56 km). Turn east on Lava Lake Road and follow it .7 miles (1.1 km) to the campground.

■ **CULTUS LAKE CAMPGROUND** *(Open May 25 to Sept 25 – Varies)*
Information: (541) 383-5300, www.hoodoo.com
Location: 48 Miles (77 Km) SW of Bend

GPS Location: 43.83374 N, 121.83416 W, 4,700 Ft

55 Sites – Cultus Lake is one of the few in the area that allows the use of high-powered watercraft. It's popular with water-skiers and other water sports lovers. Sites here are back-ins with a few pull-thrus. Access is poor and it is difficult to level rigs in many sites so this campground is best for RVs to 35 feet although a few sites would take larger rigs. Both interior roads and parking pads are gravel. There is a dock and a boat ramp at the day use area near the campground. From Bend drive west and then south on the Cascade Lakes Highway for 43 miles (69 km). Turn west on the Cultis Lake road and follow it for 2 miles (3.2 km) to the campground.

■ **QUINN RIVER CAMPGROUND** *(Open April 1 to Sept 15 – Varies)*
Information: (541) 383-5300, www.hoodoo.com
Location: 45 Miles (73 Km) SW of Bend

GPS Location: 43.78722 N, 121.83556 W, 4,400 Ft

41 Sites – Quinn River Campground is a Deschutes National Forest campground that is located on the shore of Crane Prairie Reservoir. Sites here are paved off paved roads and will take RVs to 35 feet, there is also a boat ramp. The access road to the campground is on the Cascade Lakes Highway 45 miles (73 km) from Bend.

■ **ROCK CREEK CAMPGROUND** *(Open April 1 to Sept 30 – Varies)*
Information: (541) 383-4700,
Location: 47 Miles (76 Km) SW of Bend

GPS Location: 43.76583 N, 121.83639 W, 4,400 Ft

32 Sites – This is another Deschutes National Forest campground along the western shore of Crane Prairie Reservoir. The back-in sites are located off two loop drives and measure to 50 feet but limited maneuvering room makes 35 feet the practical maximum for RV size here. There is a boat ramp at the campground. The access road to the campground is on the Cascade Lakes Highway 47 miles (76 km) from Bend.

■ **CRANE PRAIRIE CAMPGROUND** *(Open April 20 to Oct 15 – Varies)*
Reservations: www.recreation.gov, (877) 444-6777
Information: (541) 383-5300, www.hoodoo.com
Location: 57 Miles (92 Km) SW of Bend

GPS Location: 43.79722 N, 121.75833 W, 4,400 Ft

140 Sites – This is the largest of the Deschutes National Forest camp-
grounds on the Crane Prairie Reservoir. The sites here are off five different loops, most are back-ins. There are some sites to at least 45 feet in length, roads are paved while parking pads are gravel. Many sites are right on the lake although the larger sites are

away from the water. There is a boat ramp, of course. The campground is adjacent to the Crane Prairie Resort which provides limited groceries, coin-operated showers, and a laundry which are available to people staying at the national forest campground. To reach the campground from Bend drive west on the Cascade Lakes Highway for 49 miles (79 km), then turn left on Forest Road 42, also called South Century Drive. Drive for 3.8 miles (6.2 km) and then turn left onto East Crane Prairie Road (also called NF-4270). The campground will be on your left in another 4.4 miles (7.1 km).

● **CRANE PRAIRIE RESORT**
   (Open May 1 to Oct 15 – Varies)
   Res and Info: (503) 383-3939, (541) 383-3939,
                    www.crane-prairie-resort-guides.com
   Location: 57 Miles (92 Km) SW of Bend

   GPS Location: 43.79806 N, 121.75806 W, 4,400 Ft

36 Sites – This is a commercial campground with full-hookup sites. Some sites are 75 feet long, the campground is suitable for any size RV. The resort has canoe and boat rentals and a small store with fishing tackle and some groceries. Note that there is not a dump site or any dumping available for folks from outside the campground but that campsites do have sewer hookups. Showers are available for folks not staying at the resort, it's only a short walk from the huge Crane Prairie Campground. The view of the mountains to the north over the docks and lake is fantastic. To reach the campground from Bend drive southwest on the Cascade Lakes Highway for 49 miles (79 km), then turn left on Forest Road 42, also called South Century Drive. Drive for 3.8 miles (6.1 km) and then turn left onto East Crane Prairie Road (also called NF-4270). The campground will be at the end of the road in 4.5 miles (7.3 km).

■ **NORTH TWIN LAKE CAMPGROUND** *(Open April 1 to Oct 15 – Varies)*
   Information: (541) 383-5300, www.hoodoo.com
   Location: 54 Miles (87 Km) SW of Bend

   GPS Location: 43.73389 N, 121.76417 W, 4,300 Ft

20 Sites – This Deschutes National Forest campground on North Twin Lake has sites to about 40 feet but limited maneuvering room means that 35 feet is the practical maximum RV size. There is no drinking water but there is a boat ramp. The Twin Lakes service area (see *Twin Lakes Resort* listing below) is about 2.5 miles (4 km) distant. To reach the campground from Bend drive west on the Cascade Lakes Highway for 49 miles (79 km), then turn left on Forest Road 42, also called South Century Drive. Drive for 4.5 miles (7.3 km) and turn right onto Twin Lake Road. The campground is on the left in another .2 miles (.3 km).

■ **SHEEP BRIDGE CAMPGROUND** *(Open April 20 to Oct 15 – Varies)*
   Information: (541) 383-5300, www.hoodoo.com
   Location: 54 Miles (87 Km) SW of Bend

   GPS Location: 43.73222 N, 121.78389 W, 4,400 Ft

23 Sites – The sites in this Deschutes National Forest campground are not clearly marked off but there is lots of room to park. This is a campground where parking big RVs of any size is possible if they are carefully driven. The access road is .5 mile (.8 km) of gravel. The Twin Lakes service area (see *Twin Lakes Resort* listing below) is about 2 miles (3 km) distant. The campground is located on the Deschutes channel of Wickiup Reservoir which is known for its brown trout. To reach the campground from Bend drive west on

the Cascade Lakes Highway for 49 miles (79 km), then turn left on Forest Road 42, also called South Century Drive. Drive for 4.5 miles (7.3 km) and turn right onto Twin Lake Road. The campground entrance road is on the right in another .7 miles (1.3 km).

■ **TWIN LAKES RESORT**
(Open April 20 to Oct 15 – Varies)
Res and Info: (541) 593-6526,
www.twinlakesresortoregon.com
Location: 55 Miles (89 Km) SW of Bend

GPS Location: 43.71477 N, 121.77157 W, 4,400 Ft

22 Sites – This resort serves as a service center of sorts for the campgrounds in the Twin Lakes and Wikiup Reservoir area. The store and restaurant overlook South Twin Lake and there is a shower building and laundry nearby. The resort has a campground too, although it is .2 miles (3 km) farther south on the west side of Twin Lake Road and overlooks the reservoir rather than South Twin Lake. Just a little further south along Twin Lakes Road is a Forest Service dump station that serves the area. The Twin Lakes Resort camping area has many back-in sites to 50 feet with full hookups. There are showers and flush toilets at the campground in addition to those at the resort. To reach the campground from Bend drive west on the Cascade Lakes Highway for 49 miles (79 km), then turn left on Forest Road 42, also called South Century Drive. Drive for 4.5 miles (7.3 km) and turn right onto Twin Lakes Road. The resort entrance road is on the left in 1.9 miles (3.1 km), the campground is on the right in another .2 miles (.3 km).

■ **SOUTH TWIN LAKE CAMPGROUND**
(Open April 20 to Oct 15 – Varies)
Information: (541) 383-4700,
Location: 55 Miles (89 Km) SW of Bend

GPS Location: 43.71639 N, 121.77111 W, 4,300 Ft

21 Sites – This Deschutes National Forest campground sits just to the north of the Twin Lakes Resort on the shore of South Twin Lake. There is a boat ramp. A few of the sites reach 40 feet and carefully driven 40-foot coaches do camp here. The South Twin Lake store, restaurant, showers and laundry are conveniently located just across a parking lot. To reach the campground from Bend drive west on the Cascade Lakes Highway for 49 miles (79 km), then turn left on Forest Road 42, also called South Century Drive. Drive for 4.5 miles (7.3 km) and turn right onto Twin Lakes Road. The campground entrance road is on the left in 1.9 miles (3.1 km).

■ **WEST SOUTH TWIN CAMPGROUND**
(Open April 1 to Sept 25 – Varies)
Information: (541) 383-4700,
Location: 55 Miles (89 Km) SW of Bend

GPS Location: 43.71472 N, 121.77278 W, 4,300 Ft

24 Sites – This is another Deschutes National Forest campground in the cluster around Twin Lakes Resort. This one is just across the road and overlooks the inlet arm of Wickiup Reservoir. There is a boat ramp for Wickiup Reservoir here too. It's an easy stroll to the resort and the facilities there. The sites in this campground are off a paved loop road. Some reach 40 feet but because of limited maneuvering room we recommend that coaches no longer than 35 feet use this campground. To reach the campground from Bend drive west on the Cascade Lakes Highway for 49 miles (79 km), then turn left on Forest Road

42, also called South Century Drive. Drive for 4.5 miles (7.3 km) and turn right onto Twin Lakes Road. The campground entrance road is on the right in 1.9 miles (3.1 km).

■ **GULL POINT CAMPGROUND** *(Open April 20 to Oct 15 – Varies)*
Reservations: www.recreation.gov, (877) 444-6777
Information: (541) 383-4700, 541 338-7869
Location: 55 Miles (89 Km) SW of Bend

GPS Location: 43.70528 N, 121.75778 W, 4,300 Ft

74 Sites – This is a large Deschutes National Forest campground located on the north shore of Wickiup Reservoir. While some sites reach 45 feet, maneuvering room limits recommended RV size to 35 feet. There is a dump station just to the north of the campground and the Twin Lake Resort is about 1.1 miles (1.8 km) distant. To reach the campground from Bend drive west on the Cascade Lakes Highway for 49 miles (79 km), then turn left on Forest Road 42, also called South Century Drive. Drive for 4.5 miles (7.3 km) and turn right onto Twin Lakes Road. The campground entrance road is on the right in 3 miles (4.8 km).

■ **WYETH CAMPGROUND** *(Open April 20 to Oct 15 - Varies)*
Information: (541) 383-4700,
Location: 61 Miles (98 Km) SW of Bend

GPS Location: 43.73778 N, 121.61611 W, 4,200 Ft

5 Sites – Wyeth is a tiny Deschutes National Forest campground located on the shore of the Deschutes River. It is a take-out point for floaters since it is just above Pringle Falls. The few sites are small and uneven, they limit use to tent campers and RVs to about 25 feet. There is no potable water at this campground, just the river. To reach the campground from Bend drive west on the Cascade Lakes Highway for 49 miles (79 km), then turn left on Forest Road 42, also called South Century Drive. Drive for 9 miles (15 km) and turn right on Burgess Road. After another 3 miles (5 km) follow the access road right for a short distance to the campground.

■ **PRINGLE FALLS CAMPGROUND** *(Open May 1 to Oct 31 – Varies)*
Information: (541) 383-4700,
Location: 61 Miles (98 Km) SW of Bend

GPS Location: 43.74833 N, 121.60361 W, 4,200 Ft

7 Sites – Pringle falls is a very small Deschutes National Forest campground with a narrow and rough access road, it is only suitable for RVs to about 25 feet. Sites are back-ins arranged off a sandy central clearing. There are vault toilets but no water other than what is in the Deschutes River which runs past the campground. To reach the campground from Bend drive west on the Cascade Lakes Highway for 49 miles (79 km), then turn left on Forest Road 42, also called South Century Drive. Drive for 9 miles (15 km) and turn right on Burgess Road. After another 3.5 miles (5.6 km) follow the access road left to the campground.

CHARLESTON

Between Reedsport and Gold Beach is Coos Bay, center of commercial life on the southern Oregon coast. **Charleston**, just to the west, is also an interesting destination. It is a fishing village, with more convenient access to the ocean for fishing boats than Coos Bay and North Bend which are located farther from the estuary mouth. In Charleston you'll

OREGON

find, a fishing pier, fishing charter companies, restaurants, and shops. This is also a popular crabbing location.

From Charleston you'll see signs pointing toward the coast for **Sunset Bay State Park**, **Shore Acres State Park**, and **Cape Arago State Park**. These three small state parks along the shore offer a variety of options. **Shore Acres State Park** is the former estate of a timber magnate: Louis J. Simpson. There are formal gardens with roses, azaleas, and rhododendrons, and also a Japanese garden. There's a bluff-top lookout with views along the rocky coast. **Cape Arago State Park**, at the end of the road, also offers a coastal lookout, often with views of sea lions and seals, not to mention the occasional whale. The park also has excellent tide pools. **Sunset Bay State Park,** the first park you come to, has a small bay where the water gets warm enough for the hardy to swim. It also has a campground.

Charleston Campgrounds

● **Charleston Marina RV Park**
   (Open All Year)
   Res and Info: (541) 888-9512,
                rvpark@charlestonmarina.com,
                www.charlestonmarina.com
   Location: Charleston

   GPS Location: 43.34333 N, 124.32556 W, Near Sea Level

115 Sites – Charleston Marina RV Park is very popular with fishermen, it bills itself as a working fishing village. It's also a good place to base yourself even if you have no interest in the area's fishing at all. Unlike some marina campgrounds this one doesn't overlook the marina, it's a block or so from the boats. The campground has a few tent sites, also two rental yurts. The RV sites here occupy a large lot and are basic parking spaces. They are back-ins and pull-thrus to 50 feet. Most are wide sites designed to let you park your boat trailer next to the RV. In Charleston go north on Boat Basin Road from the corner in Charleston on the Cape Arago Highway that is just west of the bridge. Drive north about .2 mile (.3 km) to Kingfisher Dr., turn right, and you'll soon see the campground entrance on your left.

○ **Bastendorff Beach County Campground**
   (Open All Year)
   Information: (541) 396-3121, coospark@co.coos.or.us
                www.co.coos.or.us/ccpark/bastendorff/
                Bastendorff.html
   Location: 2 Miles W of Charleston

        GPS Location: 43.34083 N, 124.34917 W, 100 Ft

100 Sites – Bastendorff Beach County Campground sits on a hillside overlooking the Pacific just west of Charleston. The sites are off four loops. There are tents sites (including hiker/bicyclist sites) as well as RV sites. Almost all of the RV sites are back-ins, but some extend to 45 feet. To reach the campground travel west from Charleston on the Cape Arago Highway. In 1.7 miles (2.7 km) you'll see the Bastendorff Beach Road going right. The campground is a short distance up this road on the right.

■ **Bastendorff Beach Boondocking** *(Open All Year)*
   Information: (541) 756-0100
   Location: 2 Miles W of Charleston

        GPS Location: 43.34978 N, 124.34129 W, Near Sea Level

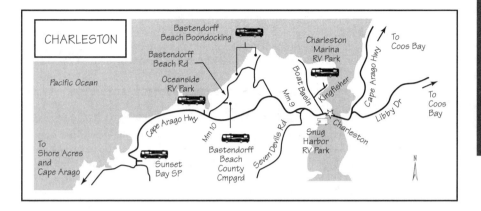

25 Sites – The land near the water below the Bastendorff Beach County Campground is managed by the Bureau of Land Management and some of it is open to tent and RV camping. Much of it is sand and beach scrub and it is a popular spot for locals to break in their sand rigs. There are signs posted at parking areas along the beach with maps showing which areas are OK for overnighting. There is no fee. Vault toilets are available and there is a 24 hours every 14 days limit to stays here. There is no potable water. To reach the area follow the instructions given above to reach the Bastendorff Beach County Campground but continue past the campground entrance and down the hill. The BLM area begins near the first pull-offs for the beach, signs are posted.

● **OCEANSIDE RV PARK** *(Open All Year)*
    Res and Info: (541) 888-2598, (800) 570-2598,
                mail@oceansidervpark.net,
                www.oceansidervpark.net
    Location: 2 Miles (3.2 Km) W of Charleston

    GPS Location: 43.33944 N, 124.35444 W, Near Sea Level

83 Sites – The Oceanside is a real find. It's a full-hookup park suitable for larger RVs, and it's just a short stroll from a good beach. There are few commercial campgrounds offering this amenity within a hundred miles north or south. Sites here are in two parts. An older section is near the entrance, but a nicer new section is nearer the beach with full-hookup back-ins and pull-thrus to 60 feet. Don't let the older rigs discourage you from entering the campground. Maneuvering room is decent and there are no obstructions to your slides. The campground is located 1.8 miles (2.9 km) west of Charleston on the Cape Arago Highway, the entrance is on the right just after you pass Bastendorff Beach Road.

☐ **SUNSET BAY STATE PARK** *(Open All Year)*
    Reservations: www.reserveamerica.com, (800) 452-5687
    Information: (541) 888-4902, (800) 551-6949,
                www.oregonstateparks.org
    Location: 5 Miles (8 Km) W of Charleston

    GPS Location: 43.33056 N, 124.37083 W, Near Sea Level

130 Sites – Sunset Bay is a pleasant state park campground. The campsites are in a small valley, across from the entrance road is the day use area on a beautiful little half-moon of beach. Trails from the park lead along the cliffs to Shore Acres State Park and Cape Arago to the south. There are vehicle tenting sites as well as a hiker/biker camping area.

RV sites here include both partial and full hook-up parking as well as yurts and dry sites. The RV sites here aren't as long as at some Oregon State Park campgrounds, but there are 41 sites from 40 to 51 feet. Some have electricity and water, other are full hookups. The entrance to the campground is 5.1 miles (8.2 km) from Charleston on the Cape Arago Highway.

COLUMBIA GORGE

The section of the Columbia Gorge covered in this section stretches from the eastern suburbs of Portland to The Dalles. The first miles, as far as Cascade Locks, are the most impressive with most of the interesting stops. The Columbia River Scenic Highway is one of the prime attractions of the Gorge, but it is narrow with limited parking and not suitable for RVs over about 25 feet. A tow car or smaller RV are essential for visiting this attraction. If you have a larger RV you might drive directly from Portland to Cascade Locks on Interstate 84, a distance of 35 miles (56 km), and park your RV. Use your smaller vehicle to tour the western section of the Scenic Highway.

The **Historic Columbia River Scenic Highway** was completed in 1915. It was considered an engineering triumph and was built as much as a scenic attraction as a transportation route. I-84 obliterated much of the highway but two good sections remain. The first is about 23 miles (37 km) long and runs between Exit 18 of I-84 to Exit 35. This section of road has famous scenic viewpoints and many waterfalls. The second section leaves I-84 at Exit 69 and climbs the bluffs to Rowena Crest Viewpoint before descending to meet I-84 at Exit 76, just west of The Dalles.

To follow the scenic highway from west to east (again, in a vehicle no longer than 25 feet) leave I-84 at Exit 18. You will follow the quiet Sandy River for several miles before starting to climb. Make a stop at the **Portland Women's Forum State Scenic Viewpoint** for an excellent view of the Crown Point Vista House ahead and slightly lower against the backdrop of the Gorge. This is a very popular photographic viewpoint. In just over a mile you will arrive at the **Vista House**, the views here are outstanding and there's also a gift shop and some exhibits about the highway and local wildflowers.

After the Vista House the highway descends and the waterfalls start. They're all different and all worth a stop. In order they are **Latourell Falls, Shepperds Dell, Bridal Veil, Wahkeena Falls, Multnomah Falls, Oneonta Gorge**, and **Horsetail Falls**. Multnomah Falls is the best known and has the best facilities. There is a lodge with restaurant and information office as well as good paved trails up to a scenic walking bridge just below the falls. The falls themselves have a drop of 620 feet and are clearly viewable from the lodge below.

You'll reach I-84 at Exit 35 after passing Ainsworth State Park Campground. In just 5 miles (8 km) you'll reach the **Bonneville Dam** exit. This dam offers one of the best of the many dam touring opportunities on the Columbia, if you want to see a dam close up this is a good one. There is plenty of room for parking big RVs here. Take a look at the visitor's center which has exhibits and a fish-viewing room. Just a short walk from the center you can view the generator room. This dam also has huge locks, you may be lucky enough to watch a tug with barges passing through. Finally, the dam has a fish hatchery with a unique sturgeon-viewing pond.

Exit 44 for Cascade Locks (for traffic from the west) is four miles (6 km) beyond Bonneville Dam. **Cascade Locks** (population 1,100) is a small town and a good base for a visit to the western end of the gorge. Before the Bonneville Dam was built there was a set of locks here to let boats on the river bypass the **Cascades of the Columbia**, a treacherous series of rapids. Bonneville Dam flooded the locks, but there is a pleasant waterfront park, and the top of the drowned locks are still above lake level. You can take a cruise on the **Columbia Gorge sternwheeler** which is based here during the summer. There is a bridge across the river at Cascade Locks, it is called the **Bridge of the Gods**. The name comes from an Indian legend, probably based upon the fact that a huge landslide once stopped up the Columbia at this point. The **Cascades Crest Trail**, a long-distance hiking trail following the entire crest of the Cascades, crosses the Columbia on the bridge.

Eastward from Cascade Locks you continue to follow I-84. You'll want to make a stop at **Hood River** (population 5,800). This little town has become the windsurfing capital of the U.S. Drive down the hill and across the railroad and park next to the river, if there's wind there will be lots of **windsurfers**. Watching them can be very entertaining.

Also in Hood River is the terminal for the **Mount Hood Railroad**. They offer scenic and dinner train trips up the Hood River Valley to the south.

East of Hood River is another chance to leave I-84 and follow the original US-30 (Historic Columbia River Scenic Highway). Take Exit 69. The road climbs onto the cliffs above the river. There is an excellent overlook with lots of parking room some 12 miles (19 km) along, it's called **Rowena Crest Viewpoint** and offers great views up and down the river. From there the road once again descends and rejoins I-84 at Exit 76.

Next stop is The Dalles (population 12,300). There's a new attraction here, the **Columbia Gorge Discovery Center and Waasco County Historical Museum**. It is a very well-done facility, particularly the Waasco County section. Take Exit 82 and follow the signs. They have lots of parking for big RVs.

Just past The Dalles is the second dam on the river. Take Exit 88 for **The Dalles Dam**. Due to security concerns identification and preregistration are required, see *Information Resources* at the end of the chapter for contact information.

Camping in the Gorge will make you very aware that this is a transportation corridor. Road noise from the highway is a factor, but the railroads are the real attention-getters. Most campgrounds are near the railroads, and some are in places where the trains make a lot of noise with their warning horns because there are level crossings. In the campground descriptions below we note the campgrounds that are particularly affected.

Columbia Gorge Campgrounds

☐ **AINSWORTH STATE PARK** *(Open March 15 to Oct 31 – Varies)*
Information: (503) 695-2301, (800) 551-6949,
www.oregonstateparks.org
Location: 9 Miles (15 Km) W of Cascade Locks

GPS Location: 45.59611 N, 122.05028 W, 900 Ft

51 Sites – Ainsworth is located toward the eastern end of the most scenic section of the Historic Columbia River Highway. Large RVs shouldn't drive the highway because it is narrow and crowded but it is OK to access this campground as described below. The campground is a jewel. The park area is small but it has large pull-thru sites to 60 feet and good restrooms. It's also the most convenient place for RVers to leave their RVs while they take a smaller vehicle to visit the highway and falls to the west. The Gorge 400 trail leads west from the campground to Multnomah Falls and be-

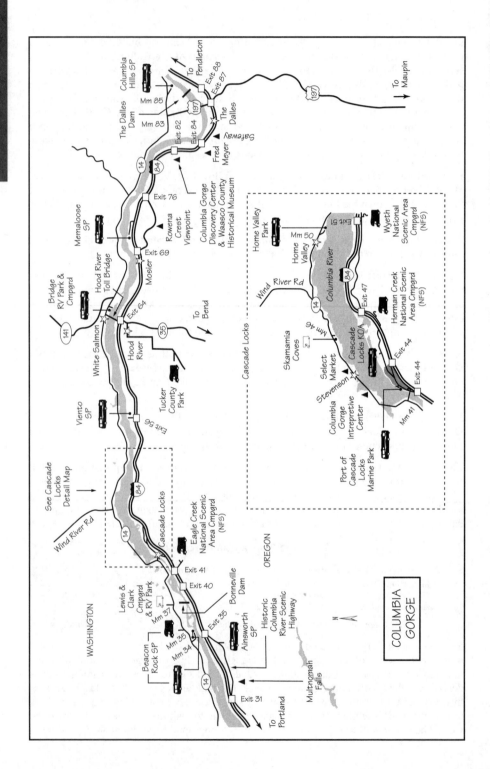

COLUMBIA GORGE

OREGON

yond. From I-84 take Exit 35. Then drive west on the Historic Columbia River Highway for .3 mile (.5 km) to the campground.

● **PORT OF CASCADE LOCKS MARINE PARK** *(Open All Year)*
   Information: (541) 374-8619, www.sternwheeler.com
   Location: Cascade Locks

   GPS Location: 45.66750 N, 121.89556 W, 100 Ft

16 Sites – This is a small beautifully-located campground in a municipal riverside park in Cascade Locks. The Columbia Gorge sternwheeler docks nearby. Sites are back-ins to 40 feet. They're gravel sites with picnic tables surrounded by nice grass and not far from the river. A new restroom building at the park has flush toilets and hot showers. The fly in the ointment at this park is that you must use a railroad underpass to enter the park and it only allows RVs to 12 feet high. To reach the campground follow entrance signs from the center of Cascade Locks which is most easily reached by taking Exit 44 from I-84.

● **CASCADE LOCKS KOA** *(Open Feb 20 to Oct 15)*
   Reservations: (800) 562-8698, www.koa.com
   Information: (541) 374-8668,
                    cascadelockskoa@clbb.net
   Location: Cascade Locks

   GPS Location: 45.67861 N, 121.86833 W, 100 Ft

80 Sites – This KOA is decently located for basing yourself to visit the Historic Columbia River Scenic Highway and its waterfalls, particularly for those with children along. However, train noise is a major problem since the busy track is very near and level crossings require constant horn blowing. Some sites are very long pull-thrus and there is a swimming pool (summer only). To reach the campground from the west take Exit 44 from I-84. Follow the main road through town, Wa-na-pa Street, and then turn north on Forest Lane Road. You'll see the campground on the left 1 mile (1.6 km) from the turn.

☐ **BEACON ROCK STATE PARK** *(Open All Year)*
   Information: (509) 427-8265, (360) 902-8844,
                    www.parks.wa.gov
   Location: North Side of Columbia, 30 Miles (49 Km)
                    W of White Salmon, WA

   GPS Location: 45.63421 N, 122.02384 W, 400 Ft.

33 Sites – Beacon Rock is the huge rock on the north side of the Columbia River about 35 miles (56 km) east of Vancouver, WA. It's a lot of fun to climb the path to the top of the rock, but there are also three different places to camp in this state park.

The GPS listed in the heading is for the main campground. It has 27 small sites off a paved loop on the hillside above Beacon Rock. This is a CCC-era campground. These sites are great for tent campers with cars and a few are able to accommodate vans or pickup campers. Flush toilets and showers are provided in a modern building and several hikes have trailheads near the camping area. This campground is not open in winter.

The second camping area is two sites near the park's boat launch. To reach it drive west from Beacon Rock on Hwy 14 for just .8 mile (1.3 km) there's a road that leads south .6 mile (1 km) to the ramp. There are two tent sites here. The parking for one is about 30 feet, the other is only large enough for a van or car. Nearby is a modern building with handicap-accessible flush toilets and showers. The GPS for this location is 45.62171 N, 122.02108 W.

Finally, if you drive directly inland from the boat launch for .4 mile (.6 km) you will find the Woodard Creek Campground. It has five full-hookup back-in sites to 40 feet. An older restroom building with flush toilets and showers is nearby. The GPS location of this camping area is 45.61999 N, 122.02955 W. It is open all year.

This is a Washington State Park and is on the north side of the river. Easiest access is from Cascade Locks in Oregon. Cross the Bridge of the Gods at the south end of town and at the T with Hwy 14 turn left. You'll reach the state park in 6.8 miles (11 km).

○   **HOME VALLEY PARK** *(Open All Year)*
Information: (509) 427-2980
Location: N Side of Columbia, 10 Miles (16 Km) E of
          Cascade Locks via Bridge of the Gods

         GPS Location: 45.70864 N, 121.77446 W, Near 100 Ft

24 Sites – Home Valley is a simple and inexpensive municipal campground. The campground shares the park with the local baseball diamond. Sites here are gravel back-ins in trees. Some have views of the river. They vary in length and a few reach 40 feet in length but poor maneuvering room means the campground is best for RVs of 35 feet or less. There are picnic tables, fire pits, and chemical toilets. The campground is on the Washington side of the river. If you are on the Oregon side you can cross at the Bridge of the Gods in Cascade Locks. On the far side of the bridge turn right on Hwy 14. In 9.1 miles (14.7 km) you'll see the campground entrance on the right.

■   **WYETH NATIONAL SCENIC AREA CAMPGROUND**
      (Open May 1 to Sept 30)
Information: (541) 308-1700, www.fs.fed.us/r6/columbia/forest/
Location: 6 Miles E of Cascade Locks

         GPS Location: 45.68944 N, 121.77194 W, 400 Ft

19 Sites – This is one of three Columbia River Gorge National Scenic Area campgrounds run by the Forest Service. These are great little parks, reasonably priced. Wyeth is the prettiest of them all. Access is limited by site size to 30 feet. Sites themselves are paved back-ins off paved roads with picnic tables and fire pits. There is a 14-day time limit here. The Wyeth and Gorge hiking trails lead south from the park and there is a host. The campground is most easily reached by taking Exit 51 from I-84. Then follow the access road westward on the south side of the highway for a very short distance. The campground entrance is on the left. Access from the highway is extremely easy.

■   **HERMAN CREEK NATIONAL SCENIC AREA CAMPGROUND**
      (Open May 1 to Sept 30)
Information: (541) 308-1700, www.fs.fed.us/r6/columbia/forest/
Location: 2 Miles (2 Km) E of Cascade Locks

         GPS Location: 45.68250 N, 121.84417 W, 100 Ft

7 Sites – Herman Creek sits on a ridge above the highway. It's one of the few campgrounds in the region that is set up for horses, several of the sites have tie rails for them. It will take tents and RVs to 30 feet although the steep narrow entrance drive may give RVers a few bad moments. Once up the ridge the road makes a small loop through the campground. Herman Creek and the Cascade Crest Trails lead into the mountains south

of the campground. The stay limit here is 14 days. Access is a little convoluted. From the east on I-84 take Exit 47, then follow Forest Lane southwest on the south side of the highway for .5 mile (.8 km) to the entrance on your left. From the west take Exit 44 from I-84. Drive through Cascade Locks and in 1 mile (1.6 km) turn left on Forest Lane. Follow Forest Lane for 1.9 miles (3.1 km) until it passes under I-84. Then follow the frontage road to the left for .4 mile (.6 km) to the campground.

■ **EAGLE CREEK NATIONAL SCENIC AREA CAMPGROUND**
(Open May 1 to Sept 30)
Information: (541) 308-1700, www.fs.fed.us/r6/columbia/forest/
Location: 6 Miles (10 Km) W of Cascade Locks

GPS Location: 45.64083 N, 121.92639 W, 400 Ft

18 Sites – Dating from 1915, this is the first National Forest Service campground constructed in the US. It is also the first one with flush toilets. This campground sits on a ridge above the Eagle Creek fish hatchery. Sites in the park would take some RVs to 35 feet but there is a sharp hairpin on the access road and tight interior roads that put a practical limitation of about 30 feet on the campground. Even in an RV that short it is important to be careful. Westbound on I-84 take Exit 41 and follow the access road to the hatchery and around back to the campground. There is no access eastbound so continue to Exit 40, reverse course, and use Exit 41.

☐ **VIENTO STATE PARK** *(Open March 15 to Oct 31 – Varies)*
Information: (541) 374-8811, (800) 551-6949,
www.oregonstateparks.org
Location: 6 Miles (10 Km) W of Hood River

GPS Location: 45.69778 N, 121.66750 W, 100 Ft

74 Sites – This is a beautiful state park with one big problem. The railroad runs right next to the park and there is a level crossing to provide access to the lower part of the park along the river. That means that every train going by blows its horn, and that goes on all day and night, approximately every 15 minutes. Otherwise it's a very enjoyable place with good facilities, back-in sites to 50 feet, and access to the river for windsurfing. It's seldom full, for good reason. There are some very small vehicle access sites on the south side of the freeway farther from the highway that provide a quieter location for tent campers. Access is from Exit 56 of I-84. The main campground is on the north side of the highway beyond the day use area.

● **BRIDGE RV PARK AND CAMPGROUND**
(Open All Year)
Res and Info: (509) 493-1111, (888) 550-7275,
bridgerv@bridgerv.com,
www.bridgerv.com
Location: White Salmon, WA

GPS Location: 45.72250 N, 121.48778 W, 100 Ft

50 Sites – An almost-new park with both a grassy tent area and paved back-in and pull-thru sites to 65 feet. The campground is actually on the Washington side even though we talk about this area in the Oregon chapter in this book. It's easy to reach the campground from Oregon. Just cross the Hood River Bridge from Hood River, Oregon to White Salmon, Washington. On the north side turn right on SR-14 and you'll see the entrance to the RV park in .1 mile (1.6 km), just beyond the Union 76 station.

○ **TUCKER COUNTY PARK** *(Hood River County)*
    (April 1 to Oct 31 – Varies)
Information: (541) 386-4477
Location: 7 Miles (11 Km) S of Hood River

GPS Location: 45.65083 N, 121.56000 W, 400 Ft

94 Sites – This county park next to the Hood River has a day use area as well as a campground. There are three loops, they're back-in spaces to 30 feet with picnic tables and fire pits with grills. To reach the park head south from downtown Hood River on 13th Street. This quickly becomes SR-281. In about 5 miles (8 km) you'll cross a bridge over the Hood River and then almost immediately see the Mile 5 marker. Just beyond turn right following the signs for Dee and Parksdale. In another .3 mile (.5 km) turn right into the park entrance.

☐ **MEMALOOSE STATE PARK CAMPGROUND**
    (Open March 11 to Oct 31 – Varies)
Reservations: www.reserveamerica.com, (800) 452-5687
Information: (541) 478-3008, (800) 551-6949,
    www.oregonstateparks.org
Location: 6 Miles (10 Km) W of Hood River

GPS Location: 45.69583 N, 121.34417 W, 200 Ft

110 Sites – This is the largest of the state campgrounds in the Gorge area. It's also reportedly located in the hottest part of the Gorge. Fortunately it has nice shade trees. This campground has large paved back-in sites (to 55 feet) off two paved loops in an open park-like setting overlooking the river, it's popular with big-rig owners. While the railroad runs below the park there is not a crossing so noise isn't too bad. Access is from the rest area near Mile 73 of I-84 westbound. There is no direct access eastbound. Instead, drive past and take Exit 76 to make a U-turn and return to enter the park.

☐ **COLUMBIA HILLS STATE PARK** *(April 1 to Oct 31)*
Information: (509) 767-2277
Location: 6 Miles (10 Km) NW of The Dalles

GPS Location: 45.64387 N, 121.10611 W, 100 Ft

18 Sites – Columbia Hills State Park is known for the pictographs and petroglyphs that were moved here when the reservoir formed by building The Dalles Dam flooded the valley. Some of the rock art can be viewed near the campground, more if it can be seen as part of a guided tour. The park is situated on the north shore of the Columbia River in Washington state, and also boasts Horsethief Lake, an arm of the reservoir cut off by a railroad bed. Most of the campsites are located on a gravel pad overlooking a grassy day-use park which is situated on Horsethief Lake. These are side-by-side back-ins and are not separated from each other. There are 12 sites, eight have electrical and water hookups and four have no hookups. The hookup sites and some of the no-hookup sites are long and fine for RVs to 45 feet as they extend into a gravel maneuver area. There are also six tent sites with pitching pads and fences for protection against the wind from the west that often sweeps this park. There are boat launches on both the lake and the reservoir. From Exit 87 of I-84 drive north on Hwy 197 across the Columbia and continue for 3.3 miles (5.3 km) At the intersection with Hwy 14 turn right and drive 1.6 miles (2.6 km). The state park entrance is on the right.

COOS BAY

The city of Coos Bay, with a population of about 16,000, is the largest city on the Oregon coast. The town of North Bend is next door and together they are often called the Bay Area. The city is situated near the outlet of the Coos River but is a bit inland, the town of Charleston, described separately in this book, is nearer to the mouth of the river.

The city serves as the supply center for this section of the coast and for that reason is of interest to RVers. Most attractions and campgrounds in the area are either to the north and described in this book in the *Reedsport and the Oregon Dunes* section, or to the west and described in the *Charleston* section. Coos Bay does have some large RV parks, including the very nice one at The Mill Casino on the waterfront, described below.

Coos Bay Campgrounds

● **THE MILL CASINO RV PARK** *(Open All Year)*
Res and Info: (800) 953-4800, (541) 756-8800,
Location: Coos Bay

GPS Location: 43.39803 N, 124.21930 W, Near Sea Level

150 Sites – The Mill Casino, which overlooks the waterfront in Coos Bay, has a new, upscale, and very reasonably priced RV Park. Sites are landscaped, paved pull-thrus to 60 feet and back-ins

COOS BAY

to 45 feet. Some are next to the bay, there's a slightly higher price for these. A shuttle will run you across the parking lot to the Casino where you can get an additional 15% off the campground price by joining the Millionaires Club. At the casino you'll also find three restaurants, entertainment, and, of course, gambling. The casino and RV park are hard to miss as you travel US 101 along Coos Bay just north of the central part of town. Use the main casino entrance. Signs will direct you through the huge parking lot to the RV park. You will see many RVs parking in the lot, see the entry below.

● **THE MILL CASINO PARKING LOT** *(Open All Year)*
Information: (541) 756-8800
Location: Coos Bay

GPS Location: 43.39803 N, 124.21960 W, Near Sea Level

200 Sites – The Mill Casino has a very large parking lot to the north of the casino buildings. Self contained RVs are allowed to overnight for free at the north end of the lot. You must check in with the RV park for security reasons. To reach the lot just follow the instructions given above for the Mill Casino RV Park.

● **LUCKY LOGGERS RV PARK** *(Open All Year)*
Res and Info: (888) 267-6003, (541) 267-6003,
www.luckyloggersrv.net
Location: Coos Bay

GPS Location: 43.35977 N, 124.20918 W, Near Sea Level

78 Sites – The Lucky Logger is the closest RV to central Coos Bay and has a very handy location, but it's an older park that needs attention. It is with easy strolling distance of both a Safeway and a Fred Meyer and actually within walking distance of downtown. The park has a lot of long-term residents but caters to travelers too. Sites are almost all back-ins, they extend to 40 feet. There are also just a few pull thrus to 50 feet. From Hwy 101 as it passes through central Coos Bay turn east on Johnson Avenue. Follow it a few blocks and just past the Safeway turn left and enter the park at the end of the block.

● **ALDER ACRES RV PARK** *(Open All Year)*
Res and Info: 888 400-7275, 541 269-0999,
alderacresrv@charter.net,
www.alderacres.com
Location: Coos Bay

GPS Location: 43.38053 N, 124.24620 W, 100 Ft

90 Sites – Alder Acres is another Coos Bay RV park with a lot of long term residents but which also caters to travelers. The traveler sites are pull-thrus to 60 feet. This is an open park with no shade, both access roads and site are paved. It's clean and has good management. The park is located along the road that connects downtown Coos Bay with Charleston. From Central Coos Bay follow the signs for Charleston. They'll take you west on Central Avenue, and then onto the Empire – Coos Bay Highway. About 2 miles (3 km) from Coos Bay you'll see the campground on the left.

● **MIDWAY RV PARK** *(Open All Year)*
Res and Info: 541 888-9300,
www.midwayrvparkcoosbay.com
Location: Coos Bay

GPS Location: 43.37261 N, 124.28904 W, 100 Ft

59 Sites – This RV Park bills itself as being midway

between Coos Bay and Charleston. It's the largest and nicest of several parks located along the Cape Arago Highway in western Coos Bay. Sites here are mostly back-ins to about 60 feet although there are just a few slightly longer pull-thrus. The sites are separated by tall hedges giving some privacy, this is a well-maintained park. From Hwy 101 just south of the Mill Casino Entrance along Coos Bay turn west on Newmark Street. As you drive west this becomes the Cape Arago Hwy. In 2.8 miles (4.5 km) the highway make a 90 degree left turn and heads south. In another 1.5 mile (2.4 km) you'll see the campground entrance on the left. It's best to drive past this entrance and turn left on Kellogg Blvd to enter through the side entrance on that street.

CRATER LAKE NATIONAL PARK

Crater Lake was designated a national park in 1902. The primary attraction here is the deep blue lake in the volcanic caldera of Mount Mazama. The caldera and lake are a fairly recent geologic occurrence, the mountain blew off its top about 7,500 years ago, well within the time that this region was populated by Native Americans. The explosion is calculated by geologists to have been 42 times as powerful as the recent eruption of Mt St. Helens. The lake in the caldera is definitely one of the scenic wonders of the world. It is the deepest lake in the U.S. at 1,932 feet.

A 37-mile (60 km) road circles the rim of the caldera offering many viewpoints. While some folks follow the rim drive in their RVs it is best to use a smaller vehicle if you have one available. The road is narrow in many places and parking at viewpoints is sometimes tight, particularly on weekends and during August.

Facilities in the park are limited. There are two visitor centers. **Steele Visitor Center**

WIZZARD ISLAND AT BEAUTIFUL CRATER LAKE

OREGON

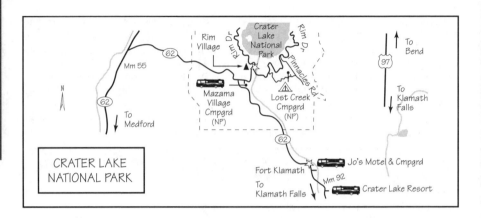

is open all year, the **Rim Visitor Center** is only open during the summer when melting snow allows the opening of the rim drive. This varies from year to year, usually the road is open from early July to about the end of October.

One popular activity in the park is the narrated **boat tour** of the lake. It takes about an hour and forty-five minutes and circles the lake with a stop at Wizard Island. To take the tour you must walk the 1-mile **Cleetwood Cove Trail** down to the lake, not too difficult on the way down but another story climbing the 700 vertical feet back out. Remember, you are at an altitude of 6,176 feet at the lake's surface. Don't try this unless you are in reasonably good shape. At the peak of the season there are 9 trips each day, tickets are sold at the parking lot.

Camping sites inside the park are limited, that's OK because there are lots of possibilities within easy driving distance but outside the park boundaries. Mazama Village Campground is the only possibility inside the park for RVs. There's also a tent-only campground called Lost Creek Campground. To the west of the national park there are several campgrounds we've covered in the *Rogue-Umpqua Scenic Byway* section of this chapter that make great bases for a visit. Another area with campgrounds offering good access to the park is east of the southern park entrance.

Crater Lake National Park Campgrounds

■ **Mazama Village Campground**
  (Open June 15 to Oct 3 – Varies)
  Reservations: (888) 77-4crater, reserve-cl@xanterra.com,
  http://www.craterlakelodges.com/What-to-
  Know-808.html
  Information: (541) 594-3100,
  www.nps.gov/crla/planyourvisit/
  campgrounds.htm
  Location: Crater Lake National Park

  GPS Location: 42.86722 N, 122.16583 W, 6,000 Ft

212 Sites – Mazama is the largest campground in the park and the only one that will take RVs. No hook-up sites predominate and there are quite a few pull-thrus, some wide and some not. This campground is carefully managed and each site is color coded by size, the managers know which sites will fit which RVs. There are only 10 or so electrical hookup

sites. Unfortunately, the RV sites with electricity are some of the smaller ones in the campground, even the pull-thrus are narrow. Near the entrance gate is a services building with store, showers, and a laundry. In the campground itself there are restrooms with flush toilets and one restroom building in the campground has additional showers. The campground is located at the newly renovated Mazama Village which is just inside the south (Annie Springs) entrance to the park. It's about 7 miles (11 km) from Rim Village overlooking the caldera and lake.

LOST CREEK CAMPGROUND *(Open July 15 to Oct 5 – Varies)*
Information: (541) 594-3100, www.nps.gov/crla/planyourvisit/campgrounds.htm
Location: Crater Lake National Park

GPS Location: 42.87944 N, 122.03889 W, 6,300 Ft

16 Sites – Lost Creek Campground is a vehicle-accessible tent camping area. RVs are not allowed. There is water at the campground. To reach Lost Creek follow Rim Drive 11 miles (18 km) counter-clockwise from Rim Village. Turn right away from the lake on Pinnacles Road and you'll see the campground entrance road in 3.1 miles (5 km).

CRATER LAKE RESORT
   (Open May 1 to Oct 31 – Varies)
Res and Info: (541) 381-2349, crtrlkrst@aol.com,
           www.craterlakeresort.com
Location: 18 Miles (29 Km) SE of Crater Lake
           National Park

GPS Location: 42.68444 N, 121.97250 W, 4,200 Ft

24 Sites – This little motel and campground along Fort Creek is a very pleasant place to stay. It's 18 miles (29 km) from the southern entrance to the park so it's convenient to the park but away from the congestion. The full-hookup RV sites back up to the little river and some reach 40 feet. Partial hookup sites that back up to the front fence will take even larger RVs on a grass surface and there is tenting on several pleasant lawn areas. You can fish or canoe on the crystal-clear creek. The campground is located on the east side of SR-62 two miles (3 km) south of Fort Klamath.

JO'S MOTEL & CAMPGROUND *(formerly Fort Klamath RV Park)*
   (Open May 1 to Oct 31 – Varies)
Res and Info: (541) 381-2234 , www.josmotel.com
Location: 16 Miles (26 Km) SE of Crater Lake National Park

GPS Location: 42.70361 N, 121.99500 W, 4,100 Ft

11 Sites – This small campground behind a motel is located in the little town of Fort Klamath next to the Wood River. It's 16 miles (26 km) from the south entrance of the park. All site are back-ins, some are electric and water sites to 40 feet. There is also a separate walk-in tent-camping area nearer the river. There are community fire pits and a dump station is available for an extra charge. Watch for the sign on the east side of the road as you pass through Fort Klamath.

EUGENE

Eugene (population 156,000), home to the University of Oregon, has a lot to offer. Actually, this is a twin city, Springfield (population 52,000) is just to the east. Often considered one of the most livable middle-sized towns in the U.S., Eugene has the cultural

OREGON

attractions of a university town and the outdoor attractions of the nearby McKenzie River Valley climbing east into the Cascades.

Eugene is laced with **bike paths**, particularly along the Willamette River. If you are a biker rider, jogger, or walker you should take advantage of them.

The **University of Oregon** campus covers 250 acres near downtown Eugene. It is very attractive and a good place for a stroll. It has two good museums: the **Museum of Art** and the **Museum of Natural History**.

Eugene occupies the south end of the fertile Willamette Valley. There are several small **wineries** in the area that deserve a visit.

State Route 126 leads east toward Bend up the **McKenzie River Valley**. While Sisters is 90 miles (145 km) away, you can find a lot to enjoy by just making a side trip as far as McKenzie Bridge, 50 miles (81 km) up the valley. Watch for the **Goodpasture** covered bridge at about Mile 22 just west of Vida. You can make an excellent loop trip out of the drive by following the paved **Robert Aufderheide Memorial Drive** (a National Forest Service Byway), from a point five miles (8 km) short of McKenzie bridge, south 57 miles (92 km) to meet SR-58 and then return 41 miles (66 km) to Eugene on that highway. As you near Eugene on SR- 58 you'll have a chance to visit 5 more covered bridges. See the sections titled *West Cascades Scenic Byway* and *Willamett Pass Route* for more about this drive and campgrounds along the way.

The Eugene area campgrounds below are described from south to north.

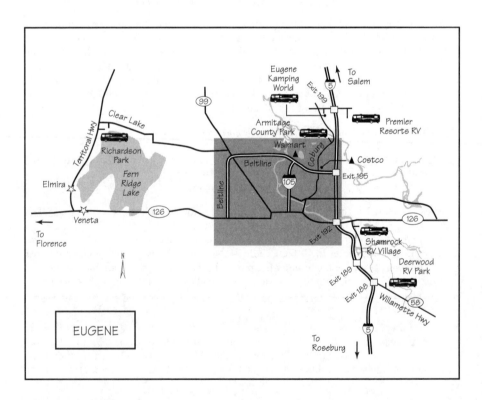

OREGON

Eugene Campgrounds

● **DEERWOOD RV PARK** *(Open All Year)*
Reservations: (877) 988-1139, info@deerwoodrvpark.com
Information: (541) 988-1139, www.deerwoodrvpark.com
Location: 3 Miles (5 Km) S of Eugene

GPS Location: 43.99583 N, 123.00111 W, 400 Ft

75 Sites – This new big-rig park is certainly a convenient and popular stop in a town that has plenty of big-rig spaces. It's south of the town, however, while most of the other big-rig sites are north of town. Sites are back-ins and pull-thrus to 90 feet. To reach the park take Exit 188 from I-5 south of Eugene. Follow the access road north on the east side of the highway to the park entrance.

● **SHAMROCK VILLAGE RV PARK** *(Open All Year)*
Reservations: (877) 877-1004, www.shamrockvillagepark.com
Information: (541) 747-7473, manager@shamrockvillagepark.com
Location: Eugene

GPS Location: 44.04083 N, 123.02806 W, 400 Ft

157 Sites – This is the only RV park we list that is actually in town. It's a popular spot when the Ducks have an at-home game. This older campground has a lot of long-term resident RVs but there are traveler sites in two areas. One has full-hookup pull-thrus to 50 feet that require careful driving if your RV is at all large. The others are partial hookup 30-amp parallel parking sites along the river with no sewer hookup. To most easily reach the campground from I-5 take Exit 189 at the southern edge of town. Then travel north on Franklin Blvd. on the east side of the freeway for 1.9 miles (3.1 km) to the campground entrance. It's on the right.

○ **RICHARDSON PARK** *(Open April 15 to Oct 15)*
Res and Info: (541) 682-2000, www.lanecounty.org/parks
Location: 13 Miles (21 Km) W of Eugene

GPS Location: 44.11944 N, 123.32083 W, 300 Ft

97 Sites – This large county park is on the shore of Fern Ridge Lake to the west of Eugene. The campground is a little out of the way but sites are large and surrounded by grassy lawns, it's a very pleasant campground. Sites here are back-ins and pull-thrus and reach 70 feet or more, good for big RVs. The park has many water-related amenities including docks, boat launch, and a swimming area. The lake is popular with sailboarders. To reach the campground follow SR-126 west from Eugene. You'll pass south of Fern Ridge Lake and after about 13 miles (21 km) near Veneta turn north on Territorial Highway. In another 4.6 miles (7.4 km) the road to the park goes east and the campground entrance is .2 mile (.3 km) from that turn.

○ **ARMITAGE COUNTY PARK**
Res and Info: (541) 682-2000, www.lanecounty.org/parks
Location: 4 Miles (6 Km) NW of Eugene

GPS Location: 44.11034 N, 123.05310 W, 300 Ft.

37 Sites – This Lane County Park is located nor far off I-5 to the north of Eugene on the banks of the McKenzie River. It has large paved sites off paved roads with little shade in the camping area but lots of grass. Tent campers pitch on the grass next to the individual RV sites. There are back-ins and

pull-thrus to 60 feet. The park has a boat launch. Take Exit 199 from I-5 north of Eugene and drive west for .7 mile (1.1 km). Turn left on Coburg Road and drive 2.4 mile (3.9 km), the entrance is on the right.

● **EUGENE PREMIER RESORTS RV** *(Open All Year)*
Reservations: (888) 710-8451,
www.premierrvresorts.com
Information: (541) 686-3152,
premiereugene@msn.com
Location: 4 Miles (6 Km) N of Eugene

GPS Location: 44.13389 N, 123.04833 W, 400 Ft

150 Sites – This is the most upscale of the RV parks just north of Eugene. The same company also has nice resorts in Lincoln City and Salem in Oregon as well as Clarkston, Washington and Redding, California. Sites are paved pull-thrus to 65 feet and back-ins to 50 feet with patios. Amenities include a swimming pool. Take Exit 199 from I-5 and head east, the campground will be on your right next to the freeway.

● **EUGENE KAMPING WORLD** *(Open All Year)*
Reservations: (800) 343-3008
Information: (541) 343-4832,
www.eugenekampingworld.com
Location: 4 Miles (6 Km) N of Eugene

GPS Location: 44.13417 N, 123.05639 W, 400 Ft

132 Sites – This older campground offers tent camping sites as well as a variety of RV sites including many pull-thrus to 70 feet. Amenities include mini golf and a game room, there's a Country Pride Restaurant nearby. This campground is on the opposite side of the freeway from the Premier Resorts park. Take Exit 199 from I-5 and head west. Just past the big Travel America truck stop turn into the entrance road. Be careful here, it's easy to make a mistake and turn into the truck stop.

GOLD BEACH

Gold Beach is 27 miles (44 km) north of Brookings and 26 miles (42 km) south of Port Orford at the mouth of the Rogue River. A jet-boat trip up the river is one of the most popular day trips along the entire Oregon Coast, most people thoroughly enjoy it. Until a road was built to reach the small town of Agnes, some 32 miles (52 km) up the Rogue, mail was delivered by mail boat. Today you can drive to Agnes, but the boats are more fun! Contact Jerry's Rogue Jets. A variety of trips are offered.

Fishing is also good in the area. The Rogue is a famous fishing river, and offshore fishing is also popular.

The campgrounds below are listed from north to south.

OREGON

Gold Beach Campgrounds

● **HONEY BEAR CAMPGROUND AND RV RESORT**
  (Open All Year)
  Reservations: (800) 822-4444
  Information: (541) 247-2765, www.honeybearrv.com
  Location: 17 Miles (27 Km) N of Gold Beach

  GPS Location: 42.53667 N, 124.39722 W, 100 Ft

85 Sites – This is an unusual campground, great for an overnight stop or an extended stay. The owners run a German restaurant and specialty food shop (Black Forest Sausage Kitchen) on the property. People stop here for the German food specialties like sausages, honey-cured hams, and rye breads that are sold out of the little store. The camping area is nicely landscaped and occupies a hillside away from the beach. There's easy walking access to the ocean and also stocked fish ponds on the property. The scattered sites mean Wi-Fi is not good. Sites line several loops, many are pull-thrus to 60 feet. There is also excellent tent camping. The park is located just a short distance off US-101, the route is well signed. The turn off US-101 is at Mile 318.3. This is 17 miles (27 km) south of Port Orford and 9 miles (15 km) north of Gold Beach.

● **NESIKA BEACH RV PARK** *(Open All Year)*
  Res and Info: (541) 247-6077, www.nesikarv.com
  Location: 6 Miles (10 Km) N of Gold Beach

  GPS Location: 42.50139 N, 124.41361 W, Near Sea Level

38 Sites – This small RV park along a quiet road back from the beach is popular with longer-term tenants but also has a few spaces for travelers including tent campers. Most sites are back-ins to 40 feet although there are just a couple of longer pull-thrus. Maneuvering space is tight for larger RVs. The campground is located on Nesika Beach Road which leaves US-101 near Mile 321. The campground is signed from the intersection.

● **LEX'S LANDING** *(Open All Year)*
  Res and Info: (541) 247-0909, (800) 290-6208,
                  info@lexslanding.com,
                  www.lexslanding.com
  Location: 1 Mile (2 Km) NE of Gold Beach

  GPS Location: 42.43056 N, 124.41028 W, Near Sea Level

30 Sites – Lex's has installed a long line of big-rig, back-in and pull-thru RV sites to 50 feet overlooking the river from the north bank. There's a new restroom and laundry building too, it overlooks the RV sites. Other amenities include a grocery store, boat ramp, and dock. This campground is on North Bank Rogue River Road which goes eastward on the north bank of the Rogue, it's about .2 mile (.3 km) from the intersection with US-101.

● **INDIAN CREEK RECREATION PARK** *(Open All Year)*
  Reservations: (877) 537-7704
  Information: (541) 247-7704, indiancreek@harborside.com,
                  www.indiancreekrv.com
  Location: 1 Mile (2 Km) E of Gold Beach

  GPS Location: 42.42750 N, 124.40361 W, 100 Ft

116 Sites – This campground is on the south side of the

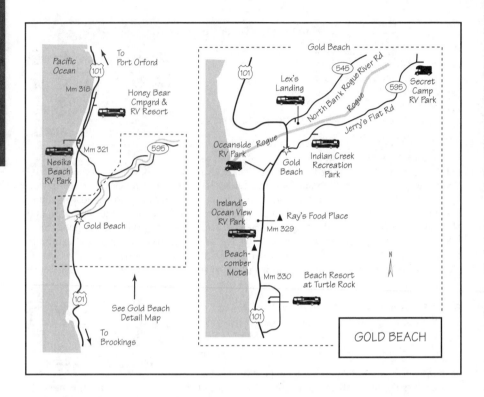

GOLD BEACH

Rogue River east of Gold Beach. Sites are on the opposite side of the road from the river and behind a small store and restaurant. The park is popular with fishermen and can be crowded during the fishing season. Most sites are back-ins to 45 feet, there are also some pull-thrus to 60 feet. The campground also has nice tent-camping sites on grass. From Gold Beach follow Jerry's Flat Road east along the south shore of the Rogue for .7 mile (1.2 km) to the campground.

● **SECRET CAMP RV PARK** *(Open All Year)*
Reservations: (888) 308-8338
Information: (541) 247-2665, www.secretcamprvpark.com
Location: 3 Miles E of Gold Beach

GPS Location: 42.44444 N, 124.36861 W, 100 Ft

25 Sites – This tiny campground is excellent for tent campers
and smaller RVs. It has a couple of long pull-thrus but most sites are back-ins to about 35 feet. The campground is located off Jerry's Flat Road on the south side of the Rogue about 3 miles (5 km) from the intersection with US-101.

● **OCEANSIDE RV PARK** *(Open All Year)*
Res and Info: (541) 247-2301, www.oceansiderv1.com
Location: Gold Beach

GPS Location: 42.42028 N, 124.42639 W, Near Sea Level

90 Sites – If you like the ocean this will be your pick in Oceanside. It's located on the south bank of the mouth of the Rogue River. A bonus is that the gold beach airstrip is right next door. The campground has pull-thrus to 55 feet and back-ins to 40 feet. From US-101 in Gold Beach about .6 mile (1 km) south of the bridge over the Rogue follow signs west for the RV park.

● **IRELAND'S OCEAN VIEW RV PARK** *(Open All Year)*
  Res and Info: (541) 247-0148, www.irelandsrusticlodges.com
  Location: Gold Beach

  GPS Location: 42.40222 N, 124.42250 W, Near Sea Level

32 Sites – Ireland's is the most attractive of the Gold Beach RV parks. It's located right next to the beach. Sites are paved and separated by lawn. The pull-thrus are 50 feet long, the back-ins about 35 feet. The campground isn't visible from the road, the entrance is just north of the Beachcomber Motel on the west side of US-101. That's toward the south end of Gold Beach, about 1.8 miles (2.9 km) south of the Rogue River bridge. You park and then walk 100 yards up the highway to the Gold Beach Inn to check in.

● **BEACH RESORT AT TURTLE ROCK** *(Open All Year)*
  Reservations: (800) 353-9754,
                    turtlereserverations@earthlink.net
  Information: (541) 247-9203, www.turtlerockresorts.com
  Location: 2 Miles (3 Km) S of Gold Beach

  GPS Location: 42.38889 N, 124.41694 W, Near Sea Level

100 Sites – Turtle Rock is located along an unpopulated section of the coast just south of Gold Beach. The campground itself is located in a very large parcel of land on the east side of the highway, there is a trail that leads under the highway to the beach. Sites here are back-ins to about 40 feet and pull-thrus to 55+ feet. There are also luxury rental cottages. To reach the campground leave US-101 at Mile 330.2. Head east on County 637 for .4 mile (6 km) and you'll see the campground entrance on the right.

GRANTS PASS

The town of **Grants Pass** (population 35,000) is a pleasant and quiet town located about 40 miles (65 km) north of Ashland. It occupies the banks of the Rogue River, you may decide to take a ride on the river from this inland base. You can also take a jet boat ride from the mouth of the river in Gold Beach, take a look at that section for more information. From Grants Pass the river flows into the coastal mountains and becomes a designated Wild and Scenic River. You can ride a jet boat from downtown Grants Pass and through **Hellgate Canyon**, the jet boats are not permitted to run all the way down the river to the coast. The Rogue is popular for fishing and river raft trips, Grants Pass is a center for companies that specialize in guiding these activities.

It is also possible to take a scenic drive to Hellgate Canyon. To do so take Exit 61 from I-5 about 3 miles (5 km) north of Grants Pass. Drive west through Merlin and you'll soon be in the canyon. You probably won't want to drive much past the town of Galice which serves as civilization in this part of the valley. It is actually possible to drive all the way across the Coast Range on a paved road but it is not suitable for larger RVs. To do it you'll want to take the left a mile or so before you reach Galice. Grants Pass annual events include the **Boatnik Festival** on Memorial Day, and the **Josephine County Fair** in mid-August.

Twenty miles (32 km) north of Grants Pass at Exit 76 you might enjoy a stop at **Wolf Creek Inn State Heritage Site.** Now a state park, this may be the oldest hotel in the state, it dates to the early 1880s when it was a stage-coach stop. It has eight rooms, but RV travelers will be more interested in the meals served in the dining room which is decorated as it was in the early days. Just south, at Exit 71, is the **Applegate Trail Interpretive Center**. The Applegate Trail was a southern route of the Oregon Trail, there's also a covered bridge nearby.

Grants Pass Campgrounds

● **ROGUE VALLEY OVERNIGHTERS** *(Open All Year)*
Res and Info: (541) 479-2208,
roguevalleyovernighters@hotmail.com,
www.roguevalleyovernighters.com
Location: Grants Pass, I-5 Exit 58

GPS Location: 42.45944 N, 123.32306 W, 1,000 Ft

110 Sites – This is an older urban RV park behind a Subway and across from a Wendy's. It's a pleasant campground with trees between the sites. It has many long-term residents but also some sites for travelers. These are pull-thrus to 70 feet and some back-ins to about 30 feet. Take Exit 58 and turn downhill to the south on 6th Street. In just .2 miles (.3 km) you'll see the Subway and campground on your right.

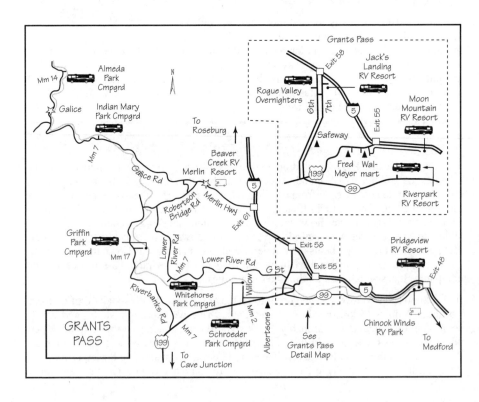

● **JACKS LANDING RV RESORT** *(Open All Year)*
  Reservations: (866)-RV-Jacks, www.jackslandingrv.com
  Information: (541) 472-1144, rvjacks@echoweb.net,
                  www.jackslandingrv.com
  Location: Grants Pass, I-5 Exit 58

  GPS Location: 42.46139 N, 123.31861 W, 1,100 Ft

54 Sites – Jack's Landing is a big-rig park located right next to the interstate in Grants Pass. It's a modern park with paved roads and parking and manicured landscaping. It has pull-thrus to 80 feet and back-ins to 60 feet. Take Exit 58 and turn downtown to the south on 6th street. Get in the left lane and turn left on N. Hillcrest Drive which is the second cross street, then left again on 7th so you're headed back the way you came. Get in the right lane and turn right on Morgan in a little less than a block to reach the park.

● **MOON MOUNTAIN RV RESORT** *(Open All Year)*
  Res and Info: (877) 479-1145, info@moonmountainrv.com,
                   www.moonmountainrv.com
  Location: Grants Pass, I-5 Exit 55

  GPS Location: 42.43639 N, 123.27278 W, 1,000 Ft

40 Sites – Moon Mountain is a well-kept park with paved roads and gravel sites, it's located next to the interstate although access is somewhat roundabout. It has pull-thrus to 60 feet and back-ins to 45 feet. Take Exit 55 from I-5 and travel west on SR-199 for .2 mile (.3 km). Turn left on Agnes Road and drive .2 miles (.3 km). Turn left on Foothill Blvd. (which becomes Pearce Park Rd.) and drive another 1.4 miles (2.3 km) to the campground.

● **RIVERPARK RV RESORT** *(Open All Year)*
  Reservations: (800) 677-8857
  Information: (541) 479-0046, www.riverparkrvresort.com
  Location: Grants Pass, I-5 Exit 55

  GPS Location: 42.42528 N, 123.28278 W, 800 Ft

50 Sites – This is a beautiful quiet park on the shore of the Rogue River east of Grants Pass and well away from the freeway. Sites are all back-ins, they stretch to 50 feet. They have picnic tables and shade. To reach the park take Exit 55 from I-5. Travel west on US-199 past big box stores for 1.8 miles (2.9 km). Just after crossing the Rogue River you'll turn left on Parkdale Dr (signed for SR-99) and then in .3 miles (.5 km) left on SR-99. Follow SR-99 for 2.5 miles (4 km) to the campground entrance, it's on your left.

● **BRIDGEVIEW RV RESORT** *(Open All Year)*
  Res and Info: (541) 582-5980
  Location: Grants Pass, I-5 Exit 48

  GPS Location: 42.43139 N, 123.17417 W, 1,000 Ft

40 Sites – This is another RV park along the Rogue River. It's a decent park with dock, paved sites off a paved loop and some nice landscaping. The sites are pull-thrus to about 40 feet and back-ins to 35 feet. Take Exit 48 from I-5 and drive south across the river to a T, about .2 miles (.3 km). Turn right on SR-99 and you'll see the campground on the right in another .1 mile (.2 km).

OREGON

○ **ALMEDA PARK CAMPGROUND** *(Open All Year)*
Reservations: www.reserveamerica.com, (800) 452-5687
Information: (541) 474-5285
Location: 22 Miles (35 Km) NW of Grants Pass

GPS Location: 42.60657 N, 123.58095 W, 700 Ft

34 Sites – This Josephine County park has tent and irregularly shaped no-hookup RV sites, both back-ins and pull-thrus, to 50 feet and longer. A rental yurt is available. Sites and roads are packed dirt, there are picnic tables, fire pits, and water faucets. It's pretty far out along the Rogue River which explains the lack of electricity. There's a ramp for rafts. Almeda is about three miles beyond Galice along the river road. From Exit 61 of I-5 travel west on the Merlin Galice Road for 19 miles (31 km) to the park entrance, it's on the right.

○ **INDIAN MARY PARK CAMPGROUND** *(Open All Year)*
Reservations: www.reserveamerica.com, (800) 452-5687
Information: (541) 474-5285
Location: 15 Miles (24 Km) W of Grants Pass

GPS Location: 42.55249 N, 123.54046 W, 800 Ft

92 Sites – Indian Mary is the largest of the RV parks in the Josephine County system and is the flagship park so it's pretty nice. It's located along the Rogue River and has a boat ramp. Interior roads are paved and so are the RV sites, there's lots of grass and shade trees. This is a very popular place for recreational rafters from town, there's a raft company based down by the ramp. There are back-in sites to 45 feet with full and partial hookups. There is also a rental yurt. From Exit 61 of I-5 travel west on the Merlin Galice Road for 10.4 miles (16.8 km) to the park entrance, it's on the right.

○ **WHITEHORSE PARK CAMPGROUND** *(Open All Year)*
Reservations: www.reserveamerica.com, (800) 452-5687
Information: (541) 474-5285
Location: 7 Miles (11 Km) W of Grants Pass

GPS Location: 42.43710 N, 123.45790 W, 800 Ft

42 Sites – Whitehorse is a small park near the north bank of the Rogue to the west of Grants Pass. Most sites here are for tents but there are also eight RV sites with full hookups, some to 45 feet, as well as a rental yurt. Other amenities include a boat ramp, flush toilets and showers. From Hwy 199 in central Grants Pass drive west on SW G Street for 1.3 miles (2.1 km). Turn left on Lincoln Road for .5 mile (.8 km), then right on Lower River Road. Now follow Lower River Road for 6 miles (10 km) to the park entrance.

○ **SCHROEDER PARK CAMPGROUND** *(Open All Year)*
Reservations: www.reserveamerica.com, (800) 452-5687
Information: (541) 474-5285
Location: 3 Miles (5 Km) W of Grants Pass

GPS Location: 42.43465 N, 123.37611 W, 800 Ft

51 Sites – Schroeder is the closest of the Josephine County Parks to Grants Pass. Like most of the others it too is along the Rogue River, this time on the south shore. Over half of the sites here have full hookups, the rest are set aside for tenters. Many of the RV sites are pull-thrus to 60 feet. There are two rental yurts. Amenities include heated toilet and shower building as well as a boat ramp and nearby tennis/

basketball court. From Exit 55 of I-5 drive west on Hwy 199 for 4.7 miles (7.6 km). Turn right at the sign for the campground and follow Willow north for 1.3 mile (2.1 km) to the park.

○ **GRIFFIN PARK CAMPGROUND** *(Open All Year)*
   Reservations: www.reserveamerica.com, (800) 452-5687
   Information: (541) 474-5285
   Location: 14 Miles (23 Km) W of Grants Pass

   GPS Location: 42.46261 N, 123.48733 W, 300 Ft

19 Sites – Griffin is a Josephine County park on the bank of the Rogue River. It has full-hookup sites, both back-ins and pull-thrus to 50 feet. There are 4 tents sites and a rental yurt. From Exit 55 of I-5 in Grants Pass drive west toward Cave Junction on Hwy 199 for 9.2 miles (14.8 km). Turn north on Riverbanks Rd and follow it for 6.1 miles (9.8 km). Turn right on Griffin Road and follow it for .7 mile (1.1 km) to the park.

HELLS CANYON

Hells Canyon stretches along the Oregon-Idaho border for 110 miles (177 km) from Ox-bow Dam to the Oregon-Washington border in the north. The canyon is sometimes called the deepest in the U.S. with a depth of about 8,900 feet. This is measured from the top of nearby He Devil Mountain so purists might be right is saying that the Grand Canyon is actually a deeper canyon. Regardless, Hells Canyon is impressive, particularly from the bottom. The bordering ridges average 5,500 feet above the river.

The portion of the canyon that we are concerned with here is the top part, a 30-mile (48 km) stretch actually beginning above the canyon with road access along the entire length. There are three dams in this area operated by the Idaho Power Company: Brownlee, Oxbow, and Hells Canyon. These dams are very controversial in ecological circles since they do not have fish ladders and act as a barrier to the migration of salmon up the Snake River. Some people would like to see the dams removed entirely.

As with most of this type of controversy there are arguments for keeping the dams. In addition to economic and flood control arguments there is the one about the recreational potential of the lakes behind the dams. In this case the recreational opportunities are out-standing. The three lakes offer flat-water water sports opportunities, vehicle-accessible camping along the shores, sightseeing, and excellent fishing.

State Route 86 reaches the river from the direction of Baker, Oregon at Copperfield, a few miles below Oxbow Dam. The river here is actually a narrow lake, Hells Canyon Res-ervoir. You can cross the lake on a bridge into Idaho and follow an excellent paved road to the left or down river for 23 miles (37 km) to a point just beyond Hells Canyon Dam. The scenery along this section of road is spectacular with barren cliffs rising thousands of feet from the river. The drive has been designated a Scenic Drive by the state of Idaho. When you reach **Hells Canyon Dam** you can drive across it and then descend a steep road to a National Forest information center. This center is at a put-in point for popular float trips of the lower canyon which is designated as a wild river for 31.5 miles (50.8 km) and then as a scenic river for another 36 miles (58 km). Large RVs (over about 26 feet or towing a trailer) will not want to make this final crossing of the dam and descent to the information center because there is a sharp switchback and limited maneuvering room at the information center. Drivers of large RVs should watch carefully for the appearance

OREGON

VIEWPOINT AT NATIONAL FOREST INFORMATION CENTER AT HELLS CANYON DAM

of the dam ahead, about the time they see it they will reach a large flat turn-around area, the last place to do so before the dam. Unfortunately there are no warning signs so you are on your own.

From Copperfield the road also extends upriver on the Oregon side of the river. It soon passes **Oxbow Dam**, which is barely visible off to the left and not accessible by road, and runs along the shore of Oxbow Reservoir. This section of road is not as impressive as the section downstream but it's still outstanding. After 11 miles (18 km) the road crosses the river just below hulking **Brownlee Dam** and then climbs the cliff face to reach huge Brownlee Reservoir. After following the shore of the reservoir for a few miles the road heads east into Idaho and away from the river toward Cambridge, Idaho.

Hells Canyon Campgrounds

○ **COPPERFIELD PARK** *(Open All Year)*
Information: (800) 422-3143, (541) 785-3323,
www.idahopower.com
Location: Hells Canyon

GPS Location: 44.97389 N, 116.85778 W, 1,700 Ft

72 Sites – This campground, run by Idaho Power, is extremely nice. Sites are separated and surrounded by clipped grass and shade trees. Facilities are excellent with paved sites. Most sites are back-ins but there are also a few pull-thrus, some will take RVs to 45 feet. There are also ten dedicated tent sites. The park sits on the bank of Hells Canyon Reservoir. It's the first campground you'll see as you arrive on SR-86 from the west. There's a boat launch about a mile downstream along a gravel road from the intersection near the campground. The stay limit here is 14 days.

■ **BIG BAR CAMPGROUND** *(Open All Year)*
Information: (208) 628-3916
Location: Hells Canyon

GPS Location: 45.12377 N, 116.74261 W, 1700 Ft

Approx. 50 Sites – Big Bar Payette National Forest Recreation Site is a former orchard site located on the east shore of Hells Canyon Reservoir. There is a boat ramp here and a large gravel parking lot with a helicopter pad. RVs of any size can camp in the lot, stay well clear of the pad. There are also some beautiful lakeside locations to the north but they can only be accessed on very uneven rough roads so access to them is limited to small RVs to about 25 feet. The only facilities here are a vault toilet and some rock fire rings. To reach the campground cross the bridge near Copperfield Park and follow the road north along the lakeshore for another 13 miles (21 km).

○ **HELLS CANYON PARK** *(Open All Year)*
Information: (800) 422-3143, (541) 785-3323,
www.idahopower.com
Location: Hells Canyon

GPS Location: 45.04639 N, 116.81417 W, 1,700 Ft

38 Sites – This is an Idaho Power campground located on the east shore of Hells Canyon Reservoir. There is a tent camping area where you pitch on grass away from your vehicle. There are also 22 power and water RV sites that are parallel parking along a wide driveway, some are right next to the lake. There are also four back-in overflow sites with

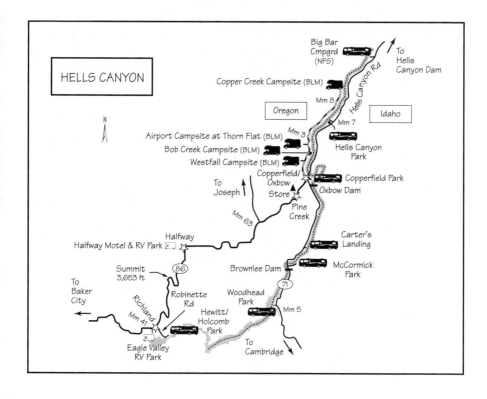

only power hookups in a gravel lot next to the boat ramp. RV sites will take RVs to 40 feet, some longer depending upon the other RVs parked in front and behind. To reach the campground cross the bridge near Copperfield Park and follow the road north along the lakeshore for 6 miles (10 km).

○ **CARTER'S LANDING** *(Open All Year)*
  Information: (800) 422-3143, (541) 785-3323, www.idahopower.com
  Location: Hells Canyon

GPS Location: 44.87833 N, 116.86167 W, 1,800 Ft

10 Sites – This is another Idaho Power camping area. Carter's Landing is a small basic camping area along the shore of Oxbow Reservoir with no hookups. There are some picnic tables, barbecues and fire rings. There's also a vault toilet and a boat launch. RVs of any size can park here and there's lots of maneuvering room. From Copperfield Park go south. You'll see the campground on the left in 7 miles (11 km).

○ **McCORMICK PARK** *(Open All Year)*
  Information: (800) 422-3143, (541) 785-3323,
                www.idahopower.com
  Location: Hells Canyon

GPS Location: 44.85083 N, 116.89528 W, 1,800 Ft

37 Sites – McCormick Park is an Idaho Power campground. It is on the shore of Oxbow Reservoir with Brownlee Dam looming over it in the south. This campground isn't as polished as Copperfield, Hells Canyon or Woodhead Park. There are 8 tent sites with nice sand tent pads and vehicle parking at each site. RV sites are back-ins around a very large open circle, they will take RVs of any size. These sites have power hookups but no water. There are, however, water faucets for filling with water and also a dump station. The park also has a large overflow area for RVs, the charge here is $6.00 per night. There is also a boat ramp. From Copperfield drive south along the shore of Oxbow Lake. In 11 miles (18 km) you'll cross the bridge below Brownlee Dam, the campground entrance is immediately beyond on the left.

○ **WOODHEAD PARK** *(Open All Year)*
  Information: (800) 422-3143, (541) 785-3323,
                www.idahopower.com
  Location: Hells Canyon

GPS Location: 44.80472 N, 116.91944 W, 2,100 Ft

139 Sites – This is the largest and the nicest of the Idaho Power campgrounds in the canyon. It sits on rocky outcrops above Brownlee Reservoir. Most sites have great views. The sites have water and electric hookups and are of various sizes with some to 55 feet. Most sites are back-ins but there are a few pull-thrus. Both roads and sites are paved. There's a large boat ramp area dividing the campground into two sections but both are accessed from the same entry road. The campground is the farthest to the south in the Canyon. From the direction of Baker zero your odometer when you reach Copperfield. Turn right and follow Oxbow Reservoir and then Brownlee Reservoir for 15 miles (24 km) to the campground.

■ **WESTFALL BLM CAMPSITE** *(Open All Year)*
  Information: (541) 523-1256
  Location: West shore Hells Canyon Reservoir

GPS Location: 44.99046 N, 116.85511 W, 1,700 Ft

7 Sites – Westfall Campsite is the first campsite on the gravel and dirt road running north from Oxbow on the west side of the Hells Canyon Reservoir which is variously called Lakeshore Road, Idaho Power Road, Ballard Creek Rd. and Homestead Rd. It's 1.2 miles (1.9 km) from Oxbow. RV sites here are on three terraces in trees across the road from the lake. It's good for small RVs (to about 30 feet) and tent campers with vehicles. There are also some walk-in tent sites. Picnic tables, fire pits, and a vault toilet are provided but no water. Stays are limited to 14 days.

■ **BOB CREEK BLM CAMPSITE** *(Open All Year)*
　Information: (541) 523-1256
　Location:　West shore Hells Canyon Reservoir

　　　　　GPS Location: 44.99766 N, 116.85000 W, 1,700 Ft

13 Sites – This is another small BLM campground, this time on the water side of the road. There are a variety of site types irregularly situated, all with tables and fire pits. It's best for rigs to about 30 feet. There are vault toilets and a boat ramp suitable only for small boats and canoes. No water is provided and the stay limit is 14 days. The site is at 1.8 miles (2.9 km) on Lakeshore Road.

■ **AIRPORT BLM CAMPSITE AT THORN FLAT** *(Open All Year)*
　Information: (541) 523-1256
　Location:　West shore Hells Canyon Reservoir

　　　　　GPS Location: 45.01071 N, 116.84915 W, 1,700 Ft

13 Sites – Airport Campsite has larger sites arranged irregularly on the inland side of the road. Most are back-ins but a few are pull-thrus to 35 feet. Picnic tables, fire rings, and vault toilets are provided but no water. The campground is on Lakeshore Road at 2.8 miles (4.5 km).

■ **COPPER CREEK BLM CAMPSITE** *(Open All Year)*
　Information: (541) 523-1256
　Location:　West shore Hells Canyon Reservoir

　　　　　GPS Location: 45.07914 N, 116.78621 W, 1,700 Ft

10 Sites – Copper Creek Campsite is the last campsite on the gravel and dirt road running north from Oxbow on the west side of the Hells Canyon Reservoir which is variously called Lakeshore Road, Idaho Power Road, Ballard Creek Rd. and Homestead Rd. It's 8.9 miles (14.4 km) from Oxbow, the last 2.6 miles (4.2 km) are marked as being suitable for only rigs or rig combinations to 20 feet because the road is narrow and has few places to turn around or pass oncoming traffic. The campsite is a large sloping field between the road and the lake. Unfortunately, the slope makes camping impossible for either RVs or tents except on the flat ground near the lake. There are not defined sites or picnic tables. Vault toilets are provided but no water. The time limit at this campground is 14 days.

○ **HEWITT/HOLCOMB PARK** *(Open All Year)*
　Res and Info: (541) 893-6147,
　　　　　hewittpark@eagletelephone.com,
　　　　　www.bakercounty.net/parks&recreation
　Location:　Near Richland, 28 Miles (45 Km) W of Hells
　　　　　Canyon

　　　　　GPS Location: N 44.75806 N, 117.12417 W, 2,100 Ft

40 Sites – This campground is located on the far western arm of Brownlee Reservoir

where it backs up into the Powder River Valley. This is much closer to Baker City than the rest of the Hells Canyon campgrounds listed above. It's not actually in the canyon at all, but if you have a boat it gives access to the same lake. This is a municipal park with a boat ramp. The spaces are back-ins around the edge of the asphalt parking lot. The spaces will take RVs to 40 feet without getting in the way of traffic circulation in the lot. There are also separate tent sites with camping on grass. The park is southeast of Richland. This town is 39 miles (63 km) east of Baker City on SR-86 and about 28 miles (45 km) west of Hells Canyon. To reach the campground travel east from town on SR-86. In .7 mile (1.1 km) turn south on Robinette Road, you'll reach the campground in 1.4 miles (2.3 km).

HELLS CANYON SCENIC BYWAY

The drive from Wallowa Lake to Hells Canyon runs through the Wallowa-Whitman National Forest. It is the most scenic section of the Hells Canyon Scenic Byway which actually runs from La Grande to Baker. This is an extremely pleasant drive on paved forest service roads. It has been designated an Oregon State Scenic Byway and an All American Road and a National Forest Byway by the federal government.

In spring and fall it is a good idea to contact the Forest Service at (541) 426-5546 for information about the condition of the road, it is not cleared in winter.

From near the center of Joseph follow Highway 350 east toward Imnaha and Furguson Ridge. After 8.1 miles (13.1 km) take the right turn marked Highway 39 and Wallowa

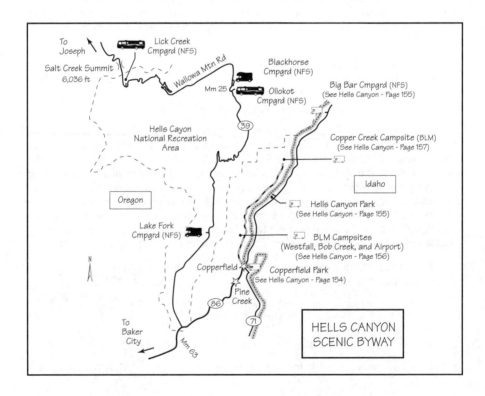

Mountain Road. Signs will tell you it is now 64 miles (103 km) to Halfway and 37 miles (60 km) to the Hells Canyon Scenic Overlook.

You soon enter the Wallowa-Whitman National Forest. The road climbs to Salt Creek Summit which is 8 miles (13 km) from the junction. Five miles (8 km) after the summit the road enters **Hells Canyon Recreation Area**.

Twenty-four miles (39 km) from the summit you'll see a sign directing you left to **Hells Canyon Overlook**. This three-mile (5 km) spur road is paved, follow it to a nice overlook area with great views of Hells Canyon. You can't actually see the river from here, but it will give you a much different view of the canyon that the one you see from the bottom.

Back at the main road continue south. The road descends in 19 miles (31 km) to meet US-86. Turn left and follow US-86 down to the river, a distance of 8 miles (13 km). Two miles (3 km) before reaching the river you'll pass through Pine Creek which has gasoline and a small grocery store.

Hells Canyon Scenic Byway Campgrounds

LICK CREEK CAMPGROUND *(Open June 15 to Oct 15 – Varies)*
Information: (541) 523-6391
Location: 24 Miles (39 Km) SE of Joseph

GPS Location: 45.15722 N, 117.03389 W, 5,400 Ft

12 Sites – This Wallowa-Whitman National Forest camping area next to Lick Creek has some big sites to 60 feet, both back-in and pull-thru. There's lots of room to maneuver. There are also tent-only sites. No water is provided. The campground is 24 miles (39 km) from Joseph and 36 miles (58 km) from the junction with SR-86.

BLACKHORSE CAMPGROUND *(Open June 15 to Oct 15 – Varies)*
Information: (541) 523-6391
Location: 36 Miles (58 km) SE of Joseph

GPS Location: 45.15639 N, 116.87500 W, 4,000 Ft

16 Sites – Sites in this Wallowa-Whitman National Forest campground are off a loop road that has two entrances on the highway. A few sites will take RVs to 35 feet, most sites are smaller. The access road is narrow and makes entering the sites difficult for larger RVs so this campground is best for RVs to 30 feet and for tents. No water is provided. The campground is 36 miles (58 km) from Joseph and 24 miles (39 km) from the junction with SR-86.

OLLOKOT CAMPGROUND *(Open April 15 to Oct 15 – Varies)*
Information: (541) 523-6391
Location: 37 Miles (60 Km) SE of Joseph

GPS Location: 45.15167 N, 116.87694 W, 4,000 Ft

12 Sites – This Wallowa-Whitman National Forest campground is located in a light, open forest and is near the highway with a good paved access road. It's on the Imnaha River. There's a turn-around circle at the end of the access road but it's small and doesn't allow enough room for turning if you're towing. There are sites to 50 feet here but due to access difficulties the campground is best for RVs to 40 feet and for tents. There is a hand water pump. The campground is 37 miles (60 km) from Joseph and 23 miles (37 km) from the junction with SR-86.

■ **LAKE FORK CAMPGROUND** *(Open April 15 to Oct 15 – Varies)*
Information: (541) 523-6391
Location: 51 Miles (82 Km) SE of Joseph

$$ ▲ 🔥 ♿

GPS Location: 45.00944 N, 116.91250 W, 3,300 Ft

10 Sites – Sites in this Wallowa-Whitman National Forest campground are off two narrow loop roads, sites will take RVs to about 30 feet. No water is provided. The campground is 51 miles (82 km) from Joseph and 9 miles (15 km) from the junction with SR-86.

JOHN DAY COUNTRY

John Day is a town of 1,750 souls. Today it is the largest town in Grant County, although Canyon City (population 725), two miles (3 km) south, is the county seat. In the 1860s these towns served the nearby **Strawberry Mountain gold fields**. You can visit the fields near Canyon City, the **Grant County Historical Museum** has exhibits describing this period.

During the 1800s large numbers of Chinese came to the west from southern China. They worked the railroads and fish canneries, and they also worked the mines. John Day had one of the largest Chinese populations in the western mining areas, and the tiny **Kim Wah Chung and Co. Museum** in John Day offers a fascinating look back at this period. It occupies the rickety building that served as home, store, opium den, card room, and Chinese herbal pharmacy for a pair of Chinese entrepreneurs. The building was locked up and remained undisturbed for years following the owner's deaths. When reopened it was a treasure house of interesting things including Chinese herbs and groceries from the early part of the century.

LOTS OF OPPORTUNITIES FOR PHOTOGRAPHY ON THE BLUE BASIN HIKING TRAILS

The **Grant County Fair** is held in John Day during the second week of August.

To the west of John Day are the three units of the **John Day Fossil Beds National Monument**. There is a brand-new visitor center located on SR-19 some 2 miles (3 km) north of its intersection with US-26 and 40 miles (65 km) from John Day.

The visitor center is located in the **Sheep Rock section** of the monument. Other interesting attractions in this section are **Picture Gorge** (which you pass through just before reaching the visitor center), **Sheep Rock** to the east of the visitor center, **Blue Basin** with hiking trails 3 miles (5 km) north of the visitor center, and the **Forsee Area**, also with hiking trails, about 7 miles (11 km) north of the visitor center.

There are two other sections of this monument. Far to the north, off SR-218 near the town of Fossil, is the **Clarno Unit**. The prime attraction here is the **Palisades**, a rugged cliff rising from the flatlands. There are several trails here offering you a look at plant fossils.

The other section of the monument is known as the **Painted Hills**. Just west of Mitchell, 66 miles (106 km) west of John Day along US-26, a small paved road leads north into the section. You'll find an overlook offering you the opportunity to take photos of smoothly rounded hills with bands of colored minerals. The area also offers hiking trails and a small rest area with picnic tables and restrooms.

John Day Country Campgrounds

■ **OREGON CAMPGROUND** *(Open May 15 to Sept 15 – Varies)*
Information: (541) 523-3691
Location: 37 Miles (60 Km) E of John Day

GPS Location: 44.54639 N, 118.34250 W, 4,900 Ft

6 Sites – This tiny Wallowa-Whitman National Forest campground is right off US-26 in the Blue Mountains. It's just east of 5,109 ft. Blue Mountain Pass and serves as the entrance to an Oregon Off Highway Vehicle Area. There's parking for the off-highway area in the campground. Although one site is over 60 feet long maneuvering room is limited and the campground is best for RVs to 30 feet. The campground is located 9 miles (15 km) southeast of Austin Junction and 12 miles (19 km) northwest of Unity.

■ **YELLOW PINE CAMPGROUND** *(Open May 15 to Sept 15 – Varies)*
Information: (541) 523-6391
Location: 40 Miles E of John Day

GPS Location: 44.52917 N, 118.31250 W, 4,500 Ft

21 Sites – This is a larger Wallowa-Whitman National Forest campground. It's a very pretty place set in an open grove of towering pines. There are sites here to 40 feet but limited maneuvering room means that 35 foot RVs are the practical maximum. The campground is located 11 miles (18 km) southeast of Austin Junction and 10 miles (16 km) northwest of Unity.

☐ **UNITY LAKE STATE RECREATION SITE**
      (Open April 1 to Oct 31)
Information: (541) 932-4453, (800) 551-6949,
                www.oregonstateparks.org
Location: 48 Miles (77 Km) E of John Day

GPS Location: 44.50167 N, 118.18444 W, 4,100 Ft

35 Sites – Unity Lake State Campground is located on the shore of Unity Lake, a reser-

OREGON

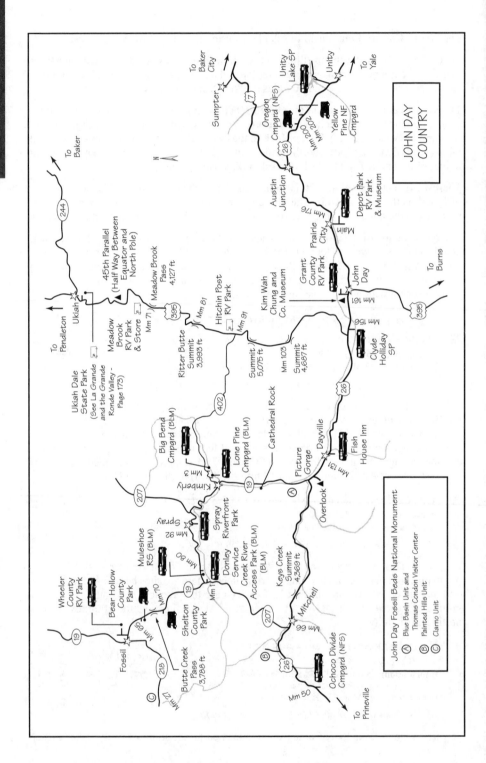

JOHN DAY COUNTRY

voir, in open grasslands east of the Blue Mountains along US-26. There is a hiker-biker tent camping area in this park as well as very large RV sites including some pull-thrus to 100 feet long. There are also rental cabins and a boat ramp. There is a swimming area and a boat dock, as well as a launching area. To reach the campground follow US-26 19 miles (31 km) southeast from Austin Junction or 2 miles (3 km) northwest from Unity. Turn north on Dooley Mountain Highway, the campground entrance is on the left in 2.4 miles (3.9 km).

○ **DEPOT PARK RV PARK AND MUSEUM**
  (Open May 1 to Oct 31 – Varies)
  Res and Info: (541) 820-3605
  Location: 13 Miles (21 Km) E of John Day

  GPS Location: 44.45778 N, 118.70694 W, 3,500 Ft

20 Sites – Depot Park is a Prairie City municipal campground located on the grounds of the city museum. There are tent camping sites on grass as well as 20 full-hookup RV sites including several pull-thrus to 60 feet long. Parking is paved and there are picnic tables and fire pits. The campground is just a few blocks from the center of this little town. To find the campground turn south on Main Street from Front Street (SR-26) in the center of town. The campground will be on your left in about 3 blocks, a distance of .3 miles (.5 km).

○ **GRANT COUNTY RV PARK** *(Open All Year)*
  Res and Info: (541) 575-0110, (541) 575-0946 after hours
  Location: John Day

  GPS Location: 44.42111 N, 118.95389 W, 3,000 Ft

25 Sites – The Grant County RV Park is located on the Grant County Fairgrounds in John Day. The famous Kim Wah Chung Museum is nearby. This campground has long pull-thru sites to 70 feet with full hookups as well as back-in sites and tent camping. To reach the campground drive north on NW Bridge Street from an intersection in the middle of town a block west of the intersection of US-26 and US-395. In four blocks you'll see the fairground entrance used by campers signed on the right. There is a self-registration sign and lockbox near the entrance gate.

☐ **CLYDE HOLLIDAY STATE RECREATION SITE**
  (Open March 1 to Nov 31)
  Information: (541) 932-4453, (800) 551-6949,
                   www.oregonstateparks.org
  Location: 7 Miles (11 Km) W of John Day

  GPS Location: 44.41611 N, 119.08944 W, 3,200 Ft

31 Sites – State parks are scarce in this part of the state. This is one of the nicest. It's a small shady oasis in a fairly parched area. The park borders the John Day River which is pretty small at this point. Sites are paved back-ins with electricity and water, most longer than 50 feet. There is also a separate hiker-biker tent-camping area tucked away in a corner of the park and also some teepees for rent. There are shade trees here, welcome in this hot dry climate and a walking trail runs along the river. The campground is on the south side of US-26 some 7 miles (11 km) west of John Day.

● **FISH HOUSE INN** *(Open All Year)*
Information: fishinn@highdesertnet.com, www.fishhouseinn.com
Location: In Dayville, 31 Miles (50 Km) W of John Day

GPS Location: 44.46722 N, 119.53500 W, 2,400 Ft

7 Sites – This is a great little commercial campground in a small town. It's exceptionally neat and tidy. The seven sites are all back-ins with full hookup and are about 70 feet long. Watch for the Fish House Inn sign on the south side of US-26 as it passes through Dayville. This is about 31 miles (50 km) west of John Day and about 8 miles (13 km) east of the new John Day Fossil Beds National Monument visitor center at Sheep Rock.

■ **LONE PINE CAMPGROUND** *(Open As Weather Allows)*
Information: (503) 808-6002
Location: 58 Miles (94 Km) NW of John Day

GPS Location: 44.77778 N, 119.62472 W, 1,800 Ft

4 Sites – This small BLM campground is just a small cleared lot next to the north fork of the John Day River. There are picnic tables and fire pits next to the river as well as a vault toilet. Some sites will take any size RV although you'll have to exercise care entering and leaving. No water is provided. The campground is located 1.8 miles (2.9 km) east on Hwy 402 of the intersection of SR 19 and Hwy 402. This is 19 miles (31 km) north of the Sheep Rock Visitor Center of John Day Fossil Beds National Monument.

■ **BIG BEND CAMPGROUND** *(Open As Weather Allows)*
Information: (503) 808-6002
Location: 59 Miles (95 Km) NW of John Day

GPS Location: 44.78083 N, 119.61028 W, 1,900 Ft

4 Sites – Another small BLM campground set along the north fork of the John Day River. Sites here are down a short grade and next to the river. It's good for tents or RVs. Big RVs can get in here but might have to drop their tows in order to maneuver. The only water is in the river. The campground is located 3.0 miles (4.8 km) east on Hwy 402 from the intersection of SR-19 and Hwy 402. This is 20 miles (32 km) north of the Sheep Rock Visitor Center of John Day Fossil Beds National Monument.

○ **SPRAY RIVERFRONT PARK** *(Open As Weather Allows)*
Information: (541) 468-2069
Location: In Spray, 69 Miles (111 Km) NW of John Day

GPS Location: 44.82694 N, 119.79389 W, 1,700 Ft

7 Sites – The town of Spray has a riverfront park campground located just south of the village. The park has seven no-hookup designated sites, five are long pull-thru parking sites. The river runs next to the park, there are some shade trees, and vault toilets are provided. This campground has water and there is a boat ramp. To reach the campground turn south on Parish Creek Road (1st Ave.) in the town of Spray. Spray is on SR-19 some 21 miles (34 km) north and west of the Sheep Rock Visitor Center of John Day Fossil Beds National Monument and 32 miles (52 km) south and east of the town of Fossil.

■ **MULESHOE RECREATION SITE** *(Open As Weather Allows)*
Information: (541) 468-2069
Location: 80 Miles (129 Km) NW of John Day

GPS Location: 44.80750 N, 119.96639 W, 1,600 Ft

10 Sites – This is a good BLM campground for both tents and big RVs. There are six 70-foot back-in sites overlooking the river as well as smaller vehicle accessible tent or small RV sites and a walk-in tent area with two tables and fire pits. This campground also has a boat launch, but no water other than the river. The campground is located 11 miles (18 km) west of Spray on the south side of SR-19.

■ **DONLEY SERVICE CREEK RIVER ACCESS PARK** *(Open All Year)*
Information: (503) 808-6002
Location: 82 Miles (132 Km) NW of John Day

GPS Location: 44.79306 N, 120.00083 W, 1,600 Ft

10 Sites – This BLM recreation area has 4 walk-in campsites for tent campers. There is also a large gravel lot suitable for any size RV but this RV area has no fire pits or picnic tables. This campground has no water except from the river, there is a boat launch. The recreation area is on the east side of SR-207 some .3 miles (.5 km) south of the intersection with SR-19 which is 13 miles (21 km) west of Spray.

○ **SHELTON COUNTY PARK** *(Open April 15 to Nov 15 – Varies)*
Information: (541) 763-2400
Location: 10 Miles (16 Km) S of Fossil on Hwy 19

GPS Location: 44.89528 N, 120.09099 W, 3,300 Ft.

45 Sites – This county park has many irregular sites set in pines, mostly back-ins. Some are big sites, any size RV should be able to find a spot but interior roads and soft surfaces mean the practical limit is about 35 feet. The sites are off two long interior roads with loops at the ends that allow those who are towing to easily turn. There are picnic tables and fire pits at each site, vault toilets, and water outlets scattered around the campground. The campground is on the west side of Hwy 19 some 21 miles (34 km) northwest of Spray and 10 miles (16 km) south of Fossil.

○ **BEAR HOLLOW COUNTY PARK** *(Open April 15 to Nov 15 – Varies)*
Information: (541) 763-2400
Location: 6 Miles (10 Km) S of Fossil on Hwy 19

$$ ▲ 🔥
♿

GPS Location: 44.93923 N, 120.12488 W, 3,300 Ft.

15 Sites – This county park is also set in Pines with irregular sites. They have picnic tables and fire-pits and there are vault toilets. Sites and roads make 35 feet the practical maximum RV size here. The campground is on the west side of Hwy 19 some 25 miles (40 km) northwest of Spray and 6 miles (10 km) south of Fossil

○ **WHEELER COUNTY RV PARK** *(Open All Year)*
Information: (541) 763-4560
Location: Fossil, OR

GPS Location: 44.99782 N, 120.21097 W, Alt 2,600 Ft

12 Sites – The little town of Fossil hosts the Wheeler County Fairgrounds. There is an RV parking area at the fairgrounds that is open to travelers when it's not reserved for an event. The major events are the fair in August and the 4th of July. There are some long-term rigs here and facilities are older but it's a decent place to spend the night. There are full-hookups and long gravel back-in sites (they are pull-thrus if the park isn't full). A dedicated restroom building offers toilets and showers. From Hwy 19 one block east of the intersection with Hwy 218 turn north in to town on Main Street. In 3 blocks turn right on 4th Street, the park is two blocks ahead.

■ OCHOCO DIVIDE CAMPGROUND
(Open May 25 to Nov 15 – Varies)
Information: (541) 416-6500
Location: 85 Miles (137 Km) W of John Day

$$ \quad \triangle \quad \textcolor{gray}{\spadesuit} \quad \&\text{ BIG RIGS}$$

GPS Location: 44.50000 N, 120.38667 W, 4,600 Ft

30 Sites – Ochoco Divide is a large Ochoco National Forest campground located in ponderosa pines high in the mountains at the top of Ochoco Pass. The campground has walk-in tent sites as well as vehicle accessible tent and RV sites to 60 feet, some are pull-thrus. This campground is a popular overnight stop with many one-nighters but there is also a good hiking trail system with trailheads just west of the campground. This easily accessible campground is just off US-26 some 31 miles (50 km) east of Prineville.

KLAMATH FALLS

Founded in 1876 and originally called Linkville, the town of Klamath Falls (population 21,000) occupies the Klamath Basin. It is surrounded by national wildlife refuges set aside for migrating birds. The refuges extend south across the California border. At one time there were even more wetlands in the area, many were drained to create farmland early in the century.

Many visitors to the town come for the bird-watching. There's something to see all year long. A good place to start is with a visit to the **Refuge Headquarters and Visitors**

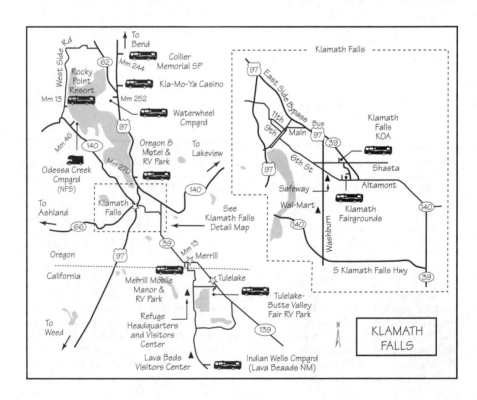

Center about 5 miles (8 km) west of Tulelake which is across the border in California, about 14 miles (23 km) south of Klamath Falls. There are actually six different refuges in the area. They offer auto tour routes, canoe trails, walking trails, and photography blinds.

In Klamath Falls you will probably enjoy a visit to the **Favell Museum of Western Art and Indian Artifacts.** This is an outstanding museum with exhibits including a huge arrowhead collection, Indian artifacts from all the western states, a miniature firearm collection, and western art created by over 300 artists including Charles Russell.

The **Kla-Mo-Ya Casino** is located in the small town of Chiloquin about 22 miles (35 km) north of Klamath Falls on US- 97.

Lava Beds National Monument is in California, but not far from Klamath Falls. The monument actually adjoins the wildlife refuges to the south. The monument is a large area covered by shield volcano lava beds. Hundreds of lava tube caves make this a popular and easy place to explore underground. It's as dry as the wildlife refuges are wet. There is a visitors center and also a campground in the monument. The visitor center sells inexpensive protective helmets, highly recommended if you plan to do any spelunking. The area was the scene of the Modoc Indian War, several sites in the monument are related to that 1872 conflict. To get there drive south on SR-39 (which becomes SR-139 in California) to Tulelake, about 4 miles (6 km) beyond Tulelake you'll see the entrance to the monument. From there a paved road circles around the south end of Tule Lake Wildlife Refuge and then south through the monument to the visitor center and campground.

Klamath Falls Campgrounds

● **KLAMATH FALLS KOA** *(Open All Year)*
   Reservations: (800) 562-9036, www.koa.com
   Information: (541) 884-4644,
          kfallskoa@charterinternet.com
   Location: Klamath Falls

   GPS Location: 42.21389 N, 121.74639 W, 4,100 Ft

80 Sites – This is a full-service KOA with all that that means. There are a variety of sites, many under shady cottonwoods, including a grassy tent camping area and back-in and pull-thru sites to 55 feet. Amenities include a seasonal swimming pool and also gasoline sales out front. The campground is located on the east side of Klamath Falls about 2 miles (3 km) from the central area. Easiest access is from the East Side Bypass (SR-39) which becomes SR-140 to Lakeview. Turn west on Shasta and the campground is on the right just .1 mile (.2 km) from the corner.

○ **KLAMATH FAIRGROUNDS** *(Open All Year)*
   Information: (541) 883-3796, www.kcfairgrounds.org
   Location: Klamath Falls

   GPS Location: 42.20848 N, 121.74332 W, 4,100 Ft

38 Spaces – The fairgrounds are located right in town and are a very convenient place to stay if you happen to be here when there are no events using the facilities. The best camping area is inside the fenced grounds. There are 24 pull-thru spaces to 60 feet with full hookups (50 amps) and a nearby restroom with showers. However, the gate to this area is locked at nine and opened again at seven in the morning so it's not good if you want to be out late. Outside the fence on the west side of the grounds is a large open grassy area

with 14 back-in sites with 30-amp outlets and water faucets. There is lots more room here for dry camping and tents are OK. Reservations are not accepted and the fairgrounds and event center are busy most of the year. The schedule of events is posted on the website. Registration is at the fairgrounds office and when the office is closed a maintenance person is suppose to collect the camping fee. The fairgrounds are very near the KOA. Easiest access is from the East Side Bypass (SR-39) which becomes SR-140 to Lakeview. Turn west on Shasta and in .1 miles (.2 km) turn left on Crest. The Fairgrounds entrance is about .4 miles (.3 km) to the south, it's on the right.

● **OREGON 8 MOTEL AND RV PARK**
   (Open All Year)
   Res and Info: (541) 883-3431,
                    www.oregonmotel8rvpark.com
   Location: 2 Miles (3 Km) N of Klamath Falls

   GPS Location: 42.27500 N, 121.81111 W, 4,100 Ft

32 Sites – The RV park here is a large gravel lot behind an older hotel. The RV park is neat and clean and has large pull-thrus to 60 feet with parking on gravel. Some sites have grass separating them. The campground has a seasonal pool and a lounge area with TV. The Oregon 8 is located 2 miles (3 km) north of Klamath Falls on the east side of US-97.

● **WATERWHEEL CAMPGROUND** *(Open All Year)*
   Res and Info: (541) 783-2738
   Location: 21 Miles (34 Km) N of Klamath Falls

   GPS Location: 42.52472 N 121.88694 W, 4,200 Ft

34 Sites – The Waterwheel has a pleasant streamside location along the Williamson River north of Klamath Falls near the Kla-Mo-Ya Casino. Tent camping is possible on a small island in the river reached by a footbridge. Some of the RV parking is on grass next to the river and there are also pull-thrus to 70 feet just back from the river. This is a popular fishing location and the campground has a small boat launch area and also a dock. The campground is located about 21 miles (34 km) north of Klamath Falls on the west side of US-97.

● **KLA-MO-YA CASINO** *(Open All Year)*
   Information: (888) 552-6692
   Location: 22 Miles (35 Km) N of Klamath Lake

   GPS Location: 42.53589 N, 121.88452 W, 4,200 Ft.

This casino allows overnight parking for RVs. Parking is on gravel or specially designated paved RV parking spaces, these are about 40 feet long. There is also a dump and water fill station in the parking lot. You must register with security in the casino if you wish to overnight. There is a large travel center with gas and a small store nearby. From Klamath Falls drive 22 miles (35 km) north on US 395. The casino is on the east side of the road just north of where Hwy 62 goes west to Crater Lake.

☐ **COLLIER MEMORIAL STATE PARK**
   (Open April 15 to Oct 31 – Varies)
   Information: (541) 783-2471, (800) 551-6949,
                    www.oregonstateparks.org
   Location: 30 Miles (48 Km) N of Klamath Falls

   GPS Location: 42.64306 N, 121.87500 W, 4,200 Ft

OREGON

68 Sites – A large campground with paved full hookups and big sites (both back-ins and pull-thrus over 45 feet long) along the Williamson River. This river is a well-known trout fishery. Nearby is a state-run outdoor logging museum and pioneer village. The campground is located about 30 miles (48 km) north of Klamath Falls on the east side of US-97.

● **ROCKY POINT RESORT** *(Open April 1 to Nov 1)*
Res and Info: (541) 356-2287, rvoregon@aol.com,
www.rockypointoregon.com
Location: 32 Miles (52 Km) NW of Klamath Falls

GPS Location: 42.47944 N, 122.08667 W, 4,300 Ft

34 Sites – The resort sits along the shore of Upper Klamath Lake on the Upper Klamath Wildlife Refuge & Canoe Trail. This is on the opposite side of the lake from Klamath Falls, a distance of about 32 miles (51 km) by road. The resort has 18 full-hookup sites with some pull-thrus to 50 feet as well as partial hookup and tent sites. The resort rents canoes, kayaks, pedal boats, and motorboats and sells fishing supplies. From SR-140 25 miles (40 km) north of its intersection with SR-66 near Klamath Falls drive north on West Side Road for 3 miles (5 km). You'll see signs leading you to the lakeshore and resort.

■ **ODESSA CREEK CAMPGROUND** *(Open May 1 to Sept 30 – Varies)*
Information: (541) 883-6714
Location: 25 Miles NW of Klamath Falls

GPS Location: 42.43000 N, 122.06111 W, 4,200 Ft

6 Sites – This is a very small Freemont-Winema National Forest campground that is best for very small RVs and tent campers. It is located at the point where Odessa Creek enters Upper Klamath Lake and is considered something of a birding hotspot, particularly for woodpeckers. A canoe is useful for accessing the nearby marsh. One site near the entrance will take RVs to 30 feet, the rest are very small sites. There is no potable water at the campground. Follow SR-140 north along the west side of Klamath Lake for 23 miles (37 km) from the intersection of SR-140 and SR-66 near Klamath Falls. Near Mile 46 turn on the marked gravel road and drive .9 miles (1.5 km) east to the campground.

● **MERRILL MOBILE MANOR AND RV PARK** *(Open All Year)*
Res and Info: (541) 798-1654, merrillmobilemanor@hotmail.com
Location: Merrill, 14 Miles (23 Km) SE of Klamath Falls

GPS Location: 42.02345 N, 121.60478 W, 4,000 Ft

32 Sites – A small RV park with many long-term guests but also with spaces for travelers. These are gravel full-hookup pull-thrus and back-ins to 50 feet. The campground is located on the south side of Hwy 39 toward the western end of the town of Merrill.

○ **TULELAKE-BUTTE VALLEY FAIR RV PARK** *(Open All Year)*
Information: (530) 667-5312, tulefair@cot.net
Location: Tulelake, CA, 25 Miles (40 KM) SE of Klamath Falls

GPS Location: 41.95080 N, 121.48112 W, 4,000 Ft

35 Sites – This small fairgrounds offers tent sites with pitching on grass and back-in grass RV sites to 45 feet with full hookups. Restrooms with showers are available. Payment is at a kiosk near the entrance From Hwy

OREGON

139 passing through the town of Tulelake drive west on E St for seven blocks or .6 mile (1 km) and turn left on Park Street, the campground is at the end of the street two blocks ahead.

■ **INDIAN WELL CAMPGROUND** *(Open All Year)*
Information: (530) 667-2282
Location: Lava Beds National Monument, 42 Miles (68 Km S of Klamath Falls)

GPS Location: 41.71770 N, 121.50413 W, 4,500 Ft

43 Sites - This is the only campground in California's Lava Beds National Monument. The monument is famous for its lava tube caves. The campground is located within walking distance of the visitor center. Sites are off two paved loops. There are short back-in sites and also long parallel parking areas next to camping sites, some will take RV combinations to about 45 feet. Sites have picnic tables, fire pits, and some shade. There's plenty of maneuvering room. Restrooms have flush toilets but no showers. The campground is just down the hill from the visitor center.

LA GRANDE AND THE GRANDE RONDE VALLEY

At the eastern edge of the Blue Mountain Range you'll find the huge Grande Ronde Valley and La Grande (population 13,000). On the east side of the valley is the Wallowa Range. Both of these ranges are crossed by I-84 and the valley is a popular overnight stop for travelers.

Historically, this fertile valley was shared by many Indian tribes including the Nez Perce, Cayuse, Umatilla, Walla Walla and Shoshone during the summer. It was called The Valley of Peace.

Today La Grande is the home of Eastern Oregon University. Attractions in the valley include the **Union County Museum** in Union, The **Eastern Oregon Fire Museum** in La Grande, and the **Manuel Museum** at Hot Lake Springs. The **Eagle Cap Excursion Train** between Elgin and Minam is popular in the summer.

La Grande and the Grande Ronde Campgrounds

● **EAGLES HOT LAKE RV PARK**
(Open All Year)
Res and Info: (800) 994-LAKE,
(541) 963-5253,
www.eagleshotlakerv.com
Location: 8 Miles (13 Km) SE of La Grande

GPS Location: 45.24488 N, 117.96988 W, 2,700 Ft

110 Sites – This campground is not far southeast of La Grande but seems a world away. It's quiet here, and adjacent to the Ladd Marsh Wildlife Area and Nature Trails, a large wetlands area. The RV sites here are gravel off gravel access roads. They're all long pull-thrus to 90 feet with full hookups. There are also tent sites with pitching on grass. Amenities include a pool in summer and a community fire pit. Easiest access is from Exit 265 of I-84. From there drive southeast on the La Grande Baker Highway, Hwy 203, for 4.9 miles (7.9 km). Turn right on Hot Lake Lane and follow this gravel road for .5 mile (.8 km) to the campground.

● **LA GRANDE RENDEZVOUS RV PARK** *(Open All Year)*
Res and Info: 541 962-0909, rvresort@eoni.com,
www.lagrandeonline.com/
LaGrandeRendezvousRVResort/
Location: La Grande

GPS Location: 45.33337 N, 118.07108 W, 2,700 Ft

102 Sites – For folks traveling through the area on I-84 this is the most convenient RV park in town. In fact, it's the only RV park we list that is actually in La Grande. It's a basic big rig park with full-hookup pull-thrus to 70 feet. There are also tent sites. Take Exit 261 from I-84 and turn northwest on Island Avenue. In just .2 mile (.3 km) turn left on Riddle Road, then immediately left again. The RV park is just ahead.

☐ **CATHERINE CREEK STATE PARK**
(Open April 15 to Oct 15 – Varies)
Information: (800) 452-5687
Location: 21 Miles (34 Km) SE of La Grande

GPS Location: 45.15227 N, 117.74424 W, 3,200 Ft

20 Sites – This campground is well off the interstate. It is situated next to a small creek in a canyon not far southeast of the little town of Union. Sites here are back-ins and pull-thrus to 40 feet off a gravel loop road along little Highway 203. There are no hookups but water is available in faucets. From Exit 265 of I-84 travel southeast on the La Grande

LA GRANDE
AND THE GRANDE
RONDE RIVER VALLEY

– Baker Highway for 10.9 miles (17.6 km). In the town of Union turn east on the Medical Springs Highway (Hwy 203) and you'll reach the campground in another 8.1 miles (13.1 km).

☐ **HILGARD JUNCTION STATE PARK** *(April 15 to Oct 15 – Varies)*
Information: (800) 551-6949
Location: 9 Miles (15 Km) W of La Grande

GPS Location: 45.34166 N, 118.23449 W, 3,000 Ft

17 Sites – Hilgard is conveniently located right next to the freeway but also next to the Grande Ronde River. Sites are all back-ins with no hookups, and only reach 30 feet. To reach the campground you drive through a nice grassy day use area. Take Exit 252 from I-84 and you'll find the campground just south of the interstate.

■ **BIRD TRACK SPRING CAMPGROUND** *(Open June 1 to Oct 30 – Varies)*
Information: (541) 963-7186
Location: 15 Miles (24 Km) SW of La Grande

GPS Location: 45.29986 N, 118.30709 W, 3,100 Ft

21 Sites – This Wallowa-Whitman National Forest campground is situated in an open forest of pines and is located across the highway from the Bird Track Springs Interpretive Area and nature trail. Sites are back-ins to 80 feet. Water is from a hand pump. From Exit 252 of I-84 drive southwest on Hwy 244 for 5.6 miles (9 km) to the campground.

☐ **RED BRIDGE STATE PARK** *(April 15 to Oct 15 – Varies)*
Information: (800) 551-6949
Location: 17 Miles (27 Km) SW of La Grande

GPS Location: 45.28977 N, 118.33185 W, 3,200 Ft

20 Sites – Red Bridge is located along Hwy 244 in the Blue Mountains next to the Grande Ronde River. There are 10 back-in vehicle sites to about 40 feet and another 10 or so tent sites with pitching on grass. The camping area is adjacent to a rest area and has large expanses of grass. From Exit 252 of I-84 drive southwest on Hwy 244 for 7.4 miles (11.9 km) to the campground.

■ **BEAR WALLOW CAMPGROUND** *(Open June 1 to Oct 30 – Varies)*
Information: (541) 427-3231
Location: 42 Miles (68 Km) SW of La Grande

GPS Location: 45.18457 N, 118.75338 W, 3,900 Ft

7 Sites – Bear Wallow is a small Umatilla National Forest Campground. It is next to Bear Wallow Creek and has an interpretive trail. Sites are off a loop and are back-ins, some to 45 feet although maneuvering room is limited. There is no potable water available at the campground. From Exit 252 of I-84 drive southwest on Hwy 244 for 35 miles (56 km) to the campground.

■ **LANE CREEK CAMPGROUND** *(Open June 1 to Oct 30 – Varies)*
Information: (541) 427-3231
Location: 4   3 Miles (70 Km) SW of La Grande

GPS Location: 45.18928 N, 118.76595 W, 3,800 Ft

6 Sites – Lane Creek is another small Umatilla National Forest Campground just off Hwy 244. It has narrow back-in sites to 40 feet. Maneuvering and parking is difficult because

of the narrow sites so this campground is best for RVs to about 35 feet. There is no potable water available in the campground. From Exit 252 of I-84 drive southwest on Hwy 244 for 36 miles (58 km) to the campground.

☐ **UKIAH DALE FOREST STATE CAMPGROUND** *(Open All Year)*
   Information: (800) 551-6949
   Location: 55 Miles (89 Km) SW of La Grande

   GPS Location: 45.12381 N, 118.97585 W, 3,300 Ft

27 Sites – This Oregon state campground is located next to Camas Creek, a tributary of the North Fork of the John Day River. The sites are all back-ins off a loop road, they extend to about 45 feet. From Exit 252 of I-84 drive southwest on Hwy 244 for 47 miles (76 km) to the intersection with Hwy 395. Turn left and you'll see the campground entrance in another 1.4 miles (2.3 km).

● **HU NA HA RV PARK** *(Open May 1 to Oct 15 - Varies)*
   Res and Info: (541) 437-2253, trichards@cityofelginor.org
   Location: Elgin, OR

   GPS Location: 45.56258 N, 117.91031 W, 2,600 Ft

56 Sites – This newer city campground, located in Elgin some 28 miles (45 km) from La Grande on the road in to the Wallowa Lake region, is conveniently situated for a stop if you're headed in to the lake. It's a modern park with back-ins and pull-thrus to 65 feet. These are gravel sites separated by grass. In Elgin turn south on S 8th Ave as you pass through town on Hwy 204. In four blocks turn east on Cedar Street, you'll see the campground on the left in another .3 mile (.5 km).

LAKE OWYHEE

Lake Owyhee fills the valley behind Owyhee Dam, running for over 50 miles to the south. It's a popular but somewhat remote destination for fishermen and water sports lovers in Eastern Oregon.

The river and lake are named for two fur trappers from Hawaii who were killed by Indians in 1819. At that time the Sandwich Islands were seldom called Hawaii, and the spelling hadn't settled on what we use today.

The state park campgrounds are located on the east shore of the reservoir toward the south end. Access is via a very scenic paved road that runs about ten miles up the Owyhee Canyon. Then things get interesting as the road climbs the cliff face to the top of the 417-foot high dam and then winds along next to the lake on a narrow and sometimes steep ledge. Pickups pulling boat trailers are common here and pretty large RVs use the campgrounds. The state does not post a restriction on RV size and we've seen 35-foot fifth wheels and 40 foot coaches in here. It takes a confident driver to try this. It's best to drive it in something smaller before committing your large RV.

Actually, the drive in is one of the best parts of a trip to the park. Much of the Owyhee River, including the section through the canyon below the dam has been designated a Wild and Scenic River by Congress. The canyon is very scenic and has quite a few places where the BLM allows boondock camping. This section of river is a popular fishery for stocked brown and rainbow trout.

OREGON

Lake Owyhee Campgrounds

☐ **LAKE OWYHEE STATE PARK –**
  MCCORMACK CAMPGROUND *(Open April 15 to Oct. 31)*

Reservations: www.reserveamerica.com, (800) 452-5687
Information: (541) 339-2331, (800) 551-6949,
            www.oregonstateparks.org
Location: 45 Miles (74 km) SW of Ontario, OR

GPS Location: 43.61463 N, 117.25024 W, 2,600 Ft

39 Sites – McCormack is the first of the two state park campgrounds located near each other on the east shore of Owyhee Reservoir. The campground is located on a rocky point extending into the lake. The 31 RV sites here are paved back-ins to 55 feet, they have 30-amp electrical outlets and water. Tent sites are available as well as two rental tepees. There is a building with flush toilets and showers, a dump station, and a boat ramp. Marine fuel, ice, and firewood are available for purchase since this is a fairly remote park.

From I-84 take Exit 374 and follow the signs for Owyhee State Park. They'll take you south on Hwy 201 for 12.8 miles (20.6 km) to Nyassa. Here take a right on Succor Creek Hwy and follow it as it heads generally southward for another 7.9 miles (12.7 km). Turn right on Owyhee Ave and drive west for 4.2 miles (6.8 km). Turn left on Owyhee Lake Road which soon reaches the river and follows it through a canyon for 18.6 miles (30 km) to the foot of Owyhee Dam. Here the road climbs to the lake level (over 400 feet) and then follows the lakeshore for 3.5 exciting miles (5.6 km) to the campground entrance.

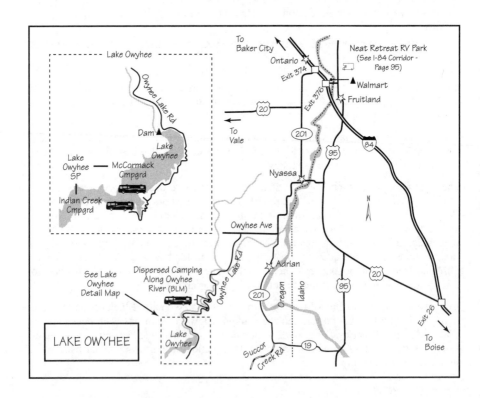

☐ **LAKE OWYHEE STATE PARK –**
    INDIAN CREEK CAMPGROUND *(Open April 15 to Oct 31)*

Reservations: www.reserveamerica.com, (800) 452-5687
Information: (541) 339-2331, (800) 551-6949,
              www.oregonstateparks.org
Location: 46 Miles (74 km) SW of Ontario, OR

GPS Location: 43.60951 N, 117.25698 W, 2,600 Ft

35 Sites – The Indian Creek Campground has 35 sites. Twenty six have electrical and water hookups and nine have no hookups. Sites are back-ins to 45 feet, parking is on gravel, and the electrical sites have 50-amp power. Restrooms here are vault toilets, for showers and the dump station you have to go back up the road to McCormack campground.

To reach the campground follow the instructions above for McCormack Campground. Continue for another 1 mile (1.6 km) to Indian Creek Campground.

■ **BLM DISPERSED CAMPING ALONG OWYHEE RIVER**
Information: (541) 473-3144
Location: 37 Miles (60 Km) SW of Ontario, OR

GPS Location: 43.68643 N, 117.21053 W, 2,100 Ft

Approx. 15 Sites – The Owyhee River below the dam is well known as a Spring and Fall brown and rainbow trout fishery. There are several areas between the highway and the river where it is possible to pull an RV well off the highway or pitch a tent and spend the night. There are portable toilets at most of them. If you zero your odometer at the well-signed Snively Hot Springs (18.8 miles from Nyassa and 12 miles below the dam) there are areas at 5.5 miles (8.9 km), 6.8 miles (11.0 km) and 9.6 miles (15.5 km). See the instructions for McCormack Campground above for the route to drive from I-84 in Ontario.

LAKEVIEW AND THE OUTBACK SCENIC BYWAY

While most folks driving south from Bend to Klamath Falls just follow Hwy 97 there is another less direct route. This is **The Outback Scenic Byway** which follows SR-31 south from La Pine (29 miles (47 km) south of Bend on US-97) to Valley Falls, then US-395 south to Lakeview, and then SR-140 west to Klamath Falls. The drive is probably named as it is because the country it traverses resembles the remote Australian outback. Along the way you can visit **Fort Rock**, a formation that stands in for Australia's Ayers rock to make the comparison even more realistic. If you take this route plan on a long day, the distance from Bend to Klamath Falls is 270 miles (435 km). You could make it a two-day trip by spending the night near Lakeview in one of the following campgrounds.

Lakeview and the Outback Scenic Byway Campgrounds

☐ **GOOSE LAKE STATE RECREATION AREA**
    (Open April 10 to Oct 10 – Varies)
Information: (541) 947-3111, (800) 551-6949,
              www.oregonstateparks.org
Location: 13 Miles (21 Km) S of Lakeview

GPS Location: 41.99333 N, 120.31833 W, 4,700 Ft

48 Sites – Goose Lake State Park is right on the border between California and Oregon. The park offers lake swimming, boating, and fishing – it's also a great place for waterfowl viewing. Sites are paved back-ins to 50 feet with electric and water hookups. There's also

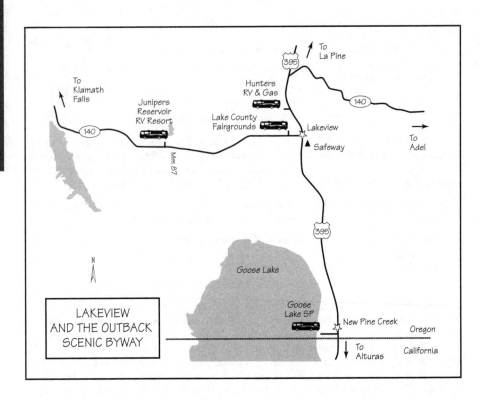

LAKEVIEW AND THE OUTBACK SCENIC BYWAY

a dump station. From Lakeview drive 12 miles (19 km) south on US-395. Then, at the state line, drive 1 mile (2 km) west on State Line Road to the campground.

● **HUNTERS RV AND GAS**
   (April 15 to Oct 31– Varies)
   Res and Info: (541) 947-4968, dkbayes@tnet.biz
                huntersrvpark@gooselake.com
   Location: 1 Mile (2 Km) N of Lakeview
   GPS Location: 42.21722 N, 120.36472 W", 4,800 Ft

40 Sites – Hunter's RV is the only choice here for year-round campsites in a commercial campground. It's nothing fancy, just RV sites behind a gas station, small convenience store, and café. Parking is on gravel with sites to at least 60 feet. There are quite a few long-term residents here but also space for travelers. The campground is on the west side of US-395 about a mile (.2 km) north of Lakeview.

○ **LAKE COUNTY FAIRGROUNDS** *(Open April 15 to Oct 30 – Varies)*
   Information: (541) 947-2925
   Location: Lakeview
   GPS Location: 42.19472 N, 120.36278 W, 4,700 Ft

25 Sites – The fairgrounds in Lakeview have a camping area. It's a gravel lot near the entrance with 14 pull-thru sites to 55 feet. There's much more area without hookups for dry camping. The sites have electric and water hookups and there's also a dump station. Showers and restrooms are available on the east lawn and showers

OREGON

cost $2. The fairgrounds does not allow fires and no picnic tables are provided. The fairground entrance and camping are right off SR-140 (North Fourth Street) .8 mile (1.3 km) west of the intersection with US-395.

● **JUNIPERS RESERVOIR RV RESORT**
(Open May 1 to Oct 15)
Res and Info: (541) 947-2050,
junipers@junipersrv.com,
www.junipersrv.com
Location: 9 Miles W of Lakeview

GPS Location: 42.18306 N, 120.53278 W, 4,700 Ft

45 Sites – This campground is located near Junipers Reservoir on a working cattle ranch to the west of Lakeview. There are grassy tent sites and full-hookup pull-thrus to 80 feet. The reservoir has good fishing and birding. The resort is located north of SR-140 some 9 miles (15 km) west of Lakeview.

LINCOLN CITY TO NEWPORT

As you drive down the Oregon coast **Lincoln City** appears at about Mile 113. It continues for about 7 miles (11 km). With a population of over 7,000 people this is one of the largest cities on the coast and it draws many tourists. The attraction is the beach. You will find access at **Roads End State Recreation Site** at Mile 112.8, the **D River Wayside** at Mile 115, and at **Siletz Bay** at Mile 118. Inland at Lincoln City is **Devil's Lake**, several of the campgrounds listed below are near the lake. It's a shallow lake with a large winter population of ducks. Fishing for rainbow trout, perch, and bass is possible in the lake too. Finally, the **Chinook Winds Casino** is located in Lincoln City, and so is **the Tanger Outlet Centers** shopping mall.

After crossing the **Siletz River** the road widens and is separated by a divider. You're now in the community of **Lincoln Beach**. The ocean is a short distance to the west of the road, and while there isn't much in the way of an actual business district here, there are two RV parks, both described below. At the south end of Lincoln Beach **Fogarty Creek State Recreation Area** gives access to beach and tide pools, and just a bit farther south **Boiler Bay State Wayside** is a place to watch the ocean boil against the rocky shoreline.

At Mile 128.0 you'll find yourself in tiny **Depoe Bay**. As you cross the bridge look inland to see one of the smallest and snuggest harbors along the entire coast. Then stop and take a look at the very narrow entrance to the harbor. Depoe Bay was the site of the charter-fishing sequence in the movie *One Flew Over the Cuckoo's Nest*. You can catch a whale-watching cruise from the harbor or check out the many shops and restaurants.

When Captain Cook arrived in 1778 he must not have been enjoying the weather when he first spotted the continent at the cape he named **Cape Foulweather**. There is an excellent viewpoint and a small shop just down from the highway on a short access road from Mile 131.2.

A little over a mile south a road leads west to the small town of Otter Crest and a parking area and viewpoint for the **Devil's Punchbowl**. The Punchbowl is a bowl that has been worn in the rocks by the wave action. If waves and tide are right the vertical spray can be impressive. Watch for the turn at Mile 132.5. Turn-around room for big RVs is limited. It's also a good place for an impressive coastal picture to the south.

Just north of Newport, at Mile 137.6, a road leads to **Yaquina Head**. Formally designated the Yaquina Head Outstanding Natural Area it is run by the Bureau of Land Management and has seen improvements over the last few years that now make it one of the most interesting stops along the coast. The head is occupied by Yaquina Head lighthouse, tallest along the Oregon coast. Offshore is Colony Rock, a sea-bird rookery where you can sometimes see puffins. Yaquina Head has a new and very nice visitors center with excellent exhibits about the tide pools and nearby lighthouse.

Newport (population 10,000) is one of the two most popular tourist destination towns along the coast, the other is Seaside to the north. One reason is that Newport is only two highway hours from Portland.

In town the main attraction is probably the **Old Town** situated along the north shore of Yaquina Bay. Here you'll find a variety of tourist-trap-type attractions including restaurants, shops, Oregon Undersea Gardens and, believe it or not, a Ripley's Believe It or Not! The Old Town can be a lot of fun, and the presence of an actual working fish-processing plant or two is a nice touch. Large murals grace the walls of some buildings.

Seaward from the Old Town, west of the bridge, is **Yaquina Bay State Park**. There you'll find **Yaquina Bay Lighthouse**, views of the harbor entrance, and trails to the beach. A little farther north is **Nye Beach**, an old and established beachside neighborhood where most resort hotels are located.

South of the big bridge over the outlet of Yaquina Bay are two ocean-oriented attractions. These are the **Oregon Coast Aquarium** and the **Hatfield Marine Science Center**. The very impressive aquarium is probably best known as the former home of Keiko the killer whale, but don't let Keiko's absence stop you from visiting. The aquarium is modern and

PASSAGES OF THE DEEP AT THE OREGON COAST AQUARIUM

well thought out with great displays of the region's marine life including tide pools, a seabird aviary, jellyfish, seals, sea lions, and sea otters. The science center next door is a branch of Oregon State University and has a public wing with marine displays.

Newport has a big charter fishing fleet. Also offered are whale-watching tours and boat tours of local oyster beds and the harbor.

Newport's big event is in February, the **Newport Seafood and Wine Festival**, there's also **Loyalty Days and Sea Faire** in May.

Lincoln City to Newport Campgrounds

● LINCOLN CITY KOA *(Open All Year)*
    Reservations: (800) 562-3316, www.koa.com
    Information: (541) 994-2961,
                  lincolnkoa@harborside.com
    Location: 2.5 Miles (4 Km) E of Lincoln City

   GPS Location: 44.99194 N, 123.97833 W, Near Sea Level

70 Sites – This small KOA has a pleasant location in a country setting to the east of Devil's Lake. It's not on the water, you must walk about a quarter-mile to the community park if you want to enjoy the lake. There are sites here of all types including some for tents as well as full-hookup pull-thrus to 50 feet. To reach the campground follow East Devil's Lake Road southward from US-101 about .5 mile (.8 km) north of Lincoln City. In 1 mile (1.6 km) turn left into NE Park Lane and almost immediately you'll see the campground entrance on your right.

● DEVIL'S LAKE RV PARK *(Open All Year)*
    Res and Info: (800) 460-0616, (541) 994-3400,
                info@devilslakerv.com,
                www.devilslakerv.com
    Location: Lincoln City

   GPS Location: 44.99583 N, 123.99806 W, 100 Ft

85 Sites – This is a big-rig park occupying a sloping site that overlooks the north end of Devil's Lake. It's not on the lake, however. Many sites are terraced pull-thrus to 65 feet long. Both sites and roads are paved. It is located just southeast of US-101 at the north entrance to Lincoln City.

● LOGAN ROAD RV PARK *(Open All Year)*
    Res and Info: (877) 564-2678, (541) 994-4261,
                www.loganroadrvpark.com
    Location: Lincoln City

   GPS Location: 44.99944 N, 124.00389 W, 100 Ft

51 Sites – This RV park is a modern big-rig park. It occupies the upper end of a large parking lot near the Chinook Winds Casino, the main reason many people stay here. Sites and driveways are paved and separated by small grassy plots, there are back-in sites and also pull-thrus to 50 feet with plenty of room for slide-outs. There is a shuttle to the casino but it's really not much of a walk, only about 300 yards. In Lincoln City turn northwest on Logan Road which is .2 miles (.3 km) north of the Mile 113 marker. You'll pass a Safeway store (on your left) and come to the campground entrance in .2 miles (.3 km).

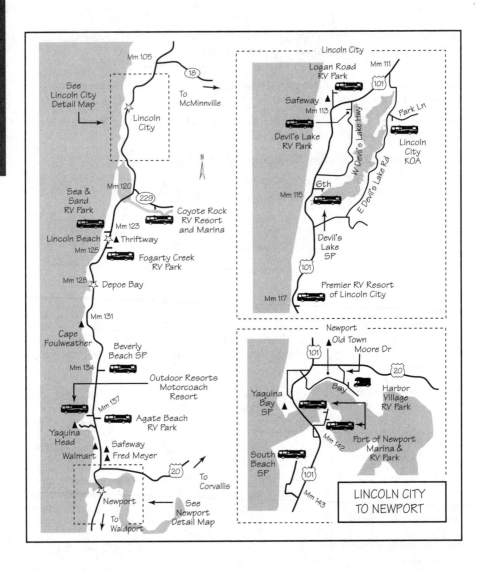

DEVIL'S LAKE STATE RECREATION AREA
(Open All Year)

Reservations: www.reserveamerica.com, (800) 452-5687
Information: (541) 994-2002, (800) 551-6949,
www.oregonstateparks.org
Location: Lincoln City

GPS Location: 44.97028 N, 124.01278 W, Near Sea Level

87 Sites – This state park campground is located away from the ocean near Devil's Lake. All sites here are back-ins but some reach 55 feet in length. To enter the park turn east on NE 6th Dr from US-101, that's between Mile 114 and 115. The entrance is just a short distance down this road on the right. A day use area has a separate entrance off US-101

about a half-mile (1 km) south. The day use area has a boat ramp and also some moorage slips and connects with the campground via a nature trail.

● **Premier RV Resort of Lincoln City**
    (formerly Oceanview RV Village) (Open All Year)
  Reservations: (877) 871-0663
  Information: (541) 996-2778, village@harborside.com
  Location: Lincoln City

GPS Location: 44.93472 N, 124.02139 W, Near Sea Level

92 Sites – This modern big-rig campground is located on the east side of US-101, some sites have views of the ocean. Sites are mostly back-ins although there are a few pull-thrus too. Most sites are between 40 and 50 feet although a few are longer. Watch for the RV park on the east side of US-101 near Mile 117.4.

● **Coyote Rock RV Resort and Marina**
    (Open All Year)
  Info and Res: (541) 996-6824,
        coyrock@harborside.com,
        www.coyote-rock.com
  Location: 3 Mile (5 Km) S of Lincoln City

GPS Location: 44.88180 N, 123.97757 W, Near Sea Level

94 Sites – This RV resort and marina is on the north bank of the Siletz River about 2 miles inland from the Hwy 101 bridge. This river is known for its spring and fall Chinook salmon runs and that makes this a popular RV park. Fishermen appreciate the ramp, docks, and boat rentals. There are tent camping sites as well as both back-in and pull-thru RV sites to 58 feet, many along the water. From the intersection just north of the Siletz River bridge, about 1 mile (1.6 km) south of Lincoln City, drive inland on the Siletz Highway for 2.1 miles (3.4 km) to the resort.

● **Sea and Sand RV Park** *(Open All Year)*
  Res and Info: (877) 821-2231, (541) 764-2313,
        www.seaandsandrvpark.com
  Location: Lincoln Beach

GPS Location: 44.86056 N, 124.03917 W, Near Sea Level

110 Sites – The Sea and Sand is a recently refurbished park stretching a long distance from the highway down to the ocean. The sites in back are called forest sites and are much less expensive than those near the ocean. The best sites are back-ins that overlook the beach just below. Sites are back-ins and pull-thrus to 40 feet. The campground is located near Mile 123.4 in Lincoln Beach, 4.5 miles (7.3 km) north of the Depoe Bay bridge.

● **Fogarty Creek RV Park**
  Res and Info: (541) 764-2228
  Location: Lincoln Beach

GPS Location: 44.84359 N, 124.04721 W, Near Sea Level

53 Sites – This older RV park sits along the highway on the inland side of the boulevard through Lincoln Beach. It has quite a few long-term residents, but also space for travelers. Sites are pull-thrus and back-ins to 42 feet. There's a restaurant next door. The campground is located near Mile 124.8 in Lincoln Beach, 3.1 miles (5.0 km) north of the Depoe Bay Bridge.

□ **BEVERLY BEACH STATE PARK** *(Open All Year)*
   Reservations: www.reserveamerica.com,
                    (800) 452-5687
   Information: (541) 265-9278, (800) 551-6949,
                    www.oregonstateparks.org
   Location: 6 Miles (10 Km) N of Newport

GPS Location: 44.72889 N, 124.05500 W, Near Sea Level

256 Sites – Beverly Beach is a large state park occupying a wide ravine that opens out onto a beautiful beach. Access to the beach is under US-101 but the bridges are high above. The sites here are both back-ins and pull-thrus, many will take RVs over 45 feet and the roads and parking pads are paved. The campground is located at Mile 134 on the east side of US-101 about 6 miles (10 km) north of Newport and 5.9 miles (9.5 km) south of the Depoe Bay bridge.

● **AGATE BEACH RV PARK** *(Open All Year)*
   Res and Info: (541) 265-7670
   Location: 2 Miles (3 Km) N of Newport

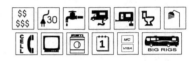

GPS Location: 44.68167 N, 124.06222 W, 100 Ft

32 Sites – This is a small older RV park located on the east side of US-101 in the community of Agate Beach. It's a comfortable park in a convenient location, and reasonably priced. Sites are back-ins, many of the full-hookup sites will take RVs to 40 feet. Sites with just electricity and water hookups are better for shorter RVs. The campground is located near Mile 137.3 on the east side of US-101. It's 2 miles (3 km) north of Newport and 9.1 miles (14.7 km) south of the Depoe Bay bridge.

● **OUTDOOR RESORTS MOTORCOACH RESORT**
   (Open All Year)
   Res and Info: (541) 265-3750 , (800) 333-1583,
                    stay@orapacificshores.com,
                    www.pacificshoresrv.com
   Location: 2 Miles (3 Km) N of Newport

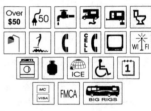

GPS Location: 44.68333 N. 124.06389 W, 100 Ft

210 Sites – This is a first class big-rig park. Only motor-coaches and Class-C units at least 30 ft. long are allowed to stay here. Sites are all full-hookup back-ins to 70 feet. It's a location overlooking the beach with two swimming pools, saunas, Jacuzzis, fitness center, and a convenience center. The campground is on the ocean side of US-101 2 miles (3 km) north of Newport and 9.1 miles (14.7 km) south of the Depot Bay bridge.

● **HARBOR VILLAGE RV PARK** *(Open All Year)*
   Res and Info: (541) 265-5088,
                    gocamping@harborvillagervpark.com,
                    www.harborvillagervpark.com
   Location: Newport

GPS Location: 44.63083 N, 124.03861 W, Near Sea Level

140 Sites – Despite limited facilities, not too many traveler sites, smallish parking spaces, and many permanent residents, this older RV park has one big advantage - location. You can easily walk a few blocks west along the edge of the harbor to Newport's old town. About 50 of the sites are available for travelers. Most of these are smaller sites but a few will take RVs to 35 feet. The Wi-Fi here is only available in the office and at a few

nearby sites. Reservations are definitely recommended in all seasons. From the junction of US-101 and SR-20 in town go .5 miles (.8 km) east on SR-20, turn south on SE Moore Dr and drive down to the waterfront, turn left and you'll see the campground entrance in about a block on the left.

● **PORT OF NEWPORT MARINA AND RV PARK**
    (Open All Year)
    Res and Info: (541) 867-3321, www.portof.com
    Location: 1 Mile (2 Km) S of Newport

GPS Location: 44.62083 N, 124.04944 W, Near Sea Level

150 Sites – The marina campground in Newport is located on the south side of the bay. It's away from the Old Town but convenient to one of Newport's top attractions, the Oregon Coast Aquarium. There are two sections to this RV park. Near the marina office is a modern big-rig park with back-ins and pull-thrus to 60 feet. A smaller Annex area adjoins a motel to the south of the large marina parking lot. It has 46 back-in sites to 40 feet long and its own set of restrooms. The two RV camping areas are about 200 yards apart and both are managed out of the office in the marina building at the larger modern campground. The Annex sites are less expensive and fall in our over $30 and up to $35 range. The entry road for the marina leaves US-101 just south of the big bridge over the Yaquina Bay outlet.

☐ **SOUTH BEACH STATE PARK** *(Open All Year)*
    Reservations: www.reserveamerica.com, (800) 452-5687
    Information: (541) 867-4715, (800) 551-6949,
                  www.oregonstateparks.org
    Location: 2 Miles (3 Km) S of Newport

GPS Location: 44.60417 N, 124.06139 W, Near Sea Level

227 Sites – This large state park campground is conveniently located not far south of Newport. Campsites are quite a distance back from the beach here, there are hiking trails to reach it. The sites are all back-ins with electricity and water hookups. They stretch to 60 feet but the largest number fall into the 40 to 50 foot range. There is also a hiker-biker camp area and a number of rental yurts. The campground entrance road goes west from US-101 about 1.5 miles (2.4 km) south of Newport's Yaquina River bridge.

MALHEUR NATIONAL WILDLIFE REFUGE AND STEENS MOUNTAIN

In the far southeast corner of Oregon there are several closely located attractions that make a great RVing destination. A variety of campgrounds provide good overnight possibilities and daytime destinations will keep you busy for several days.

Malheur National Wildlife Refuge covers 187,000 acres and incorporates large wetland areas including Malheur and Harney Lakes. The refuge headquarters can be reached by paved road although it's a little out of the way, a few miles east of SR-205 and south of Malheur Lake. There you'll find a small museum, well known in the birding community for its 200 mounted birds. The headquarters is a source for bird lists and information about tour routes through the refuge and the grounds are known for good birding. For birders, early spring is the best time to visit the refuge. During the first week of April nearby Burns celebrates the **John Scharff Migratory Bird Festival**.

South of the refuge is the tiny town of **Frenchglen**, population about 15. It's home of the Frenchglen Hotel, a state historical wayside, and serves home style meals for its guests which are also available to non-hotel guests if they make reservations. Nearby sights, related to the historic French Ranch, are the P Ranch with its long barn, the Round Barn, and the Sod House Ranch. Near Frenchglen are two decent campgrounds, the Page Springs BLM Campground and the Steens Mountain Resort, they're described below.

Steens Mountain is a huge fault-block mountain which slopes gradually upward from Frenchglen to a height of 9,733 feet and then falls off abruptly on the east side for great views of the Alvord playa below, not to mention southeast Oregon and parts of Idaho and Nevada. Access is via the 66-mile Steens Mountain Loop, a gravel and dirt road most suitable to high clearance vehicles but with large portions passable in a passenger car. Check in Frenchglen for road conditions before traveling the route, it's generally only open from mid-July through October because of snow.

Since the Malheur-Steens area is so remote it's nice to know that there's a service center of sorts nearby. **Burns** (population 3,000) is about 25 miles (40 km) north of the Malheur area and has stores and service stations, as well as several of the better places to camp while visiting the area. You might want to visit the **Harney County Historical Museum** for a look at the history of this cattle-oriented town.

Malheur National Wildlife Refuge and Steens Mountain Campgrounds

● **BURNS RV PARK** *(Open March 1 to Nov 15 - Varies)*
Reservations: (800) 573-7640
Information: (541) 573-7640, www.burnsrvpark.com
Location: Burns

GPS Location: 43.59806 N, 119.04917 W, 4,100 Ft

50 Sites – This well-kept park is on the north side of
Burns. Sites are shaded by cottonwoods, great for tents. There are pull-thrus to 75 feet and back-ins to 60 feet. US-20/395 makes a 90° turn in central Burns and heads north. The north-south street is also called Broadway. Some .9 miles (1.5 km) north of this turn you'll see the RV park on the right.

● **OLD CAMP CASINO** *(Open All Year)*
Reservations: (888) 343-7568
Informatio: (541) 573-1500, www.oldcampcasino.com
Location: Burns

GPS Location: 43.58333 N, 119.07917 W, 4,200 Ft

17 Sites – This small casino (slots and bingo) in Burns has its own RV park. There are 17 full-hookup pull-thru sites to 55 feet with parking on gravel and little in the way of landscaping. A new building next to the sites offers restrooms with showers. It's a short walk to the casino which has a restaurant. From central Burns drive west on US-395 (E Monroe Street). The highway curves to the south but don't follow, instead continue straight on W Monroe and you'll soon see the casino on the left. The campground is down the hill behind it.

● **THE SANDS RV PARK** *(Open All Year)*
Information: (541) 573-9071
Location: Hines

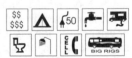

GPS Location: 43.56833 N, 119.07889 W, 4,100 Ft

15 Sites – The Sands is a very simple little commercial RV park located in Hines, a small

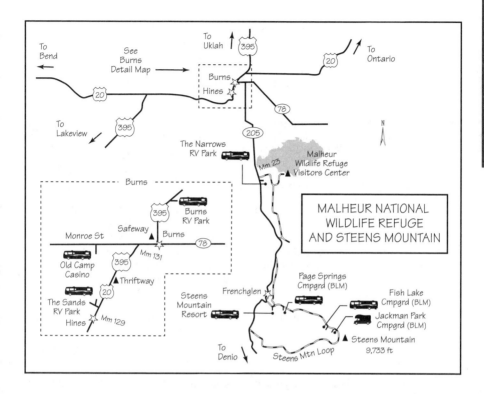

town just a mile or so southwest of Burns along US-395/20. The sites are in a grassy lot behind a small A-frame building which contains restrooms and a pay station. Sites are back-ins and pull-thrus to about 45 feet with full hookups. There are also sites for dry camping and also for tents. This campground is unattended. Watch for it on the north side of the highway as you drive through Hines, it's on the corner of US-20 and W. Conley Ave.

● **THE NARROWS RV PARK** *(Open All Year)*
   Res and Info: (800) 403-3292, (541) 495-2006,
                www.thenarrowsrvpark.com
   Location: 24 Miles (39 Km) S of Burns

   GPS Location: 43.25722 N, 118.95778 W, 4,100 Ft

50 Sites – The Narrows is a newer RV park conveniently located near the Malheur Refuge. There's a restaurant, small store, gas pumps, and the RV park in a large gravel lot to the east. It offers pull-thru and back-in sites to 50 feet as well as tent sites and a rental yurt. The Narrows is located at the junction of SR-205 and County Road 405 which is the road that runs out to the refuge headquarters and museum. This is 24 miles (39 km) south of Burns and 34 miles (55 km) north of Frenchglen.

■ **PAGE SPRINGS CAMPGROUND** *(Open All Year)*
   Information: (541) 573-4400
   Location: 3 Miles (5 Km) E of Frenchglen

   GPS Location: 42.80556 N, 118.86750 W, 4,200 Ft

36 Sites – Page Springs is a BLM campground. It occupies an area next to the Donner and Blitzen River, just east of Frenchglen. Sites are off two gravel roads in an open grassy area with scattered cottonwoods and junipers. These are big sites, some exceeding 60 feet. Almost all are back-ins but a few serve as pull-thrus. From Frenchglen drive east on Steens Loop Road for 2.9 miles (4.7 km). Just after the bridge over the Donner und Blitzen River you'll find the campground entrance on the right.

● **STEENS MOUNTAIN RESORT** *(Open All Year)*
Res and Info: (800) 542-3765 or (541) 493-2415,
SteensMtnResort@centurytel.net,
www.steensmountainresort.com
Location: 3 Miles (5 Km) E of Frenchglen

GPS Location: 42.80806 N, 118.87250 W, 4,200 Ft

76 Sites – Steens Mountain Resort is a rustic commercial campground located between Frenchglen and Page Springs Campground. The sites here are off gravel loop roads. They're on a gradual sloping hillside and are somewhat irregular. Some are pull-thrus as long as 100 feet. There are full hookup and partial hookup sites as well as tent sites, rental cabins and modular units. From Frenchglen drive east of Steens Loop Road for 2.8 miles (4.5 km) Turn right onto Resort Lane and follow this access road for .2 miles (.3 km) to the campground.

■ **FISH LAKE BLM CAMPGROUND** *(Open July 15 to Nov 1 – Varies)*
Information: (541) 573-4400
Location: 16 Miles (26 Km) E of Frenchglen

GPS Location: 42.74036 N, 118.64370 W, 7,400 Ft

23 Sites – Fish Lake BLM Campground is located next to little Fish Lake. This is a stocked lake and is very popular with fishermen in small boats. Some of the sites here are OK for RVs to 40 feet although few large rigs come up here because access is on a gravel road from Frenchglen. From Frenchglen drive east on Steens Loop Road for 18 miles (29 km) to the campground entrance. This is a gravel road but does not usually require a high clearance vehicle on the section up to the campground.

■ **JACKMAN PARK BLM CAMPGROUND** *(Open July 15 to Nov 1 – Varies)*
Information: (541) 573-4400
Location: 18 Miles (29 Km) E of Frenchglen

GPS Location: 42.71982 N, 118.62660 W, 7,800 Ft

6 Sites – Jackman Park Campground is a small BLM campground. The entrance road leads about .2 miles back to small sites set in small trees. The only amenities are vault toilets. From Frenchglen drive east on Steens Loop Road for 18 miles (29 km) to the campground entrance. This is a gravel road but does not usually require a high clearance vehicle on the section up to the campground.

MT HOOD

Mt Hood, at 11,240 feet, towers above Portland to the east. It's a relatively young (geologically speaking) volcanic peak, one of many between Mt Rainier in Washington and Mt Shasta in northern California.

With five ski areas Mt Hood is a very popular winter destination. Since the Mt Hood National Forest surrounds the mountain it's a very popular summer destination too, with lots of campgrounds and trails. You'll notice that many of the national forest campgrounds we list take reservations, that's because on weekends this area is a magnet for Portland-based campers.

There's relatively good access to the mountain by road. US-26 runs from Portland across the southern face of the mountain. It crosses Blue Box Pass at 4,024 feet before descending into Madras and the Bend area. SR-35 cuts north along the east side of the mountain to connect up with I-84 at Hood River. Both of these highways provide access to a number of campgrounds not far from the highway.

The main center of civilization on the mountain is Government Camp, 28 miles (45 km) east of Sandy. Here you'll find stores and restaurants. This is also where the 6 mile (10 km) road up to **Timberline Lodge** begins. It's worth the drive up to see the CCC-era lodge, it's open to the public as a restaurant, hotel, and ski resort.

You'll see that a number of the campgrounds listed below are off the main roads in the Timothy Lake Area in lower country to the south of the mountain. Access to these is easy via the paved Skyline Rd. from Mile 66 of SR-26.

Mt Hood Campgrounds

● **MT HOOD VILLAGE RESORT**
(Open All Year)

Res and Info: (503) 622-4011,
(800) 255-3069,
mthoodrvinfo@mhchomes.com,
www.RVontheGO.com
Location: 14 Miles (23 Km) E of Sandy

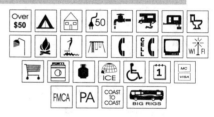

GPS Location: 45.35917 N, 121.99611 W, 1,200 Ft

345 Sites – Mt Hood Village is a huge RV park with full facilities. It's in the community of Welches and is the closest campground to Portland of those listed under this heading. This is an Encore resort, part of a large camping resort chain. They have a few tent sites but the facility is more oriented to rental cabins and RVs with pull-thrus and back-ins to 60 feet. The extensive amenities include a large indoor pool. Rates from the middle of September to the middle of May are considerably lower than those in the summer, the icon above is the summer rate. The campground is on the south side of US-26 at Mile 38.5.

■ **TOLL GATE CAMPGROUND** *(Open May 15 to Sept 15 – Varies)*
Reservations: www.recreation.gov, (877) 444-6777
Information: (503) 622-3191
Location: 19 Miles (31 Km) E of Sandy

GPS Location: 45.32167 N, 121.90556 W, 1,600 Ft

14 Sites – This is an older Mt Hood National Forest campground, in fact it has quite a bit of depression-era CCC stonework. It sits next to the Zigzag River and very near the highway. It's in an area of heavy evergreen tree growth, also lots of moss. Water is from faucets and sites have picnic tables and fire pits. Sites are off a narrow paved loop, most are back-ins to 30 feet although there is a short pull-thru and a parallel parking site in a wide spot. The campground is at Mile 44.7 of US-26.

OREGON

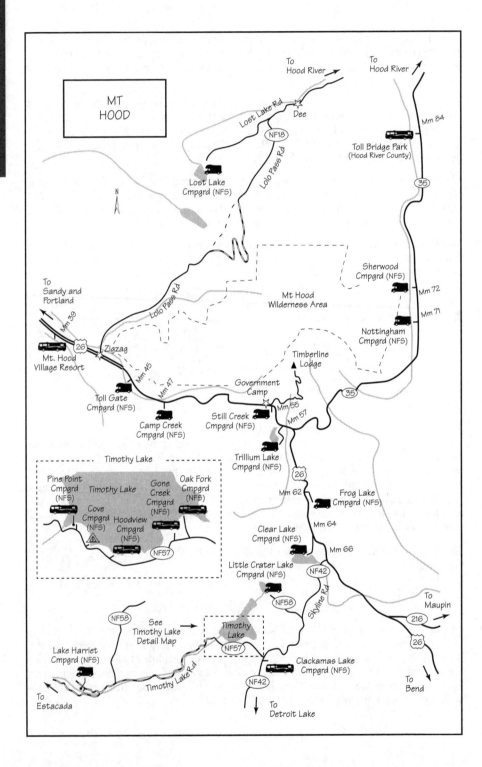

OREGON

■ **CAMP CREEK CAMPGROUND** *(Open May 15 to Sept 15 – Varies)*
Reservations: (877) 444-6777, www.recreation.gov
Information: (503) 622-3191
Location: 21 Miles (34 Km) E of Sandy

GPS Location: 45.30389 N, 121.86694 W, 2,100 Ft

24 Sites – The Mt Hood National Forest's Camp Creek Campground is very similar to Toll Gate Campground, it's larger and will take slightly larger RVs. Again it's a depression-era CCC campground with evergreens and moss. Sites are off two paved loops, mostly back-ins and some suitable for RVs to 30 feet. Water is from a hand pump and sites have picnic tables and fire pits. The campground is off US-26 at Mile 47.2.

■ **STILL CREEK CAMPGROUND** *(Open June 1 to Sept 5 – Varies)*
Reservations: www.recreation.gov, (877) 444-6777
Information: (503) 622-3191
Location: 29 Miles (47 Km) E of Sandy

GPS Location: 45.29472 N, 121.73833 W, 3,800 Ft

27 Sites – This Mt Hood National Forest campground has an unusual layout. Sites are off a paved loop road with the ones on the first portion of the loop angled backwards making it difficult to use them with an RV. The second half of the loop has sites angled properly with back-ins to 30 feet. Part way through the loop there's a Y, a road leaves the campground here that is a back road to Trillium Lake Campground, see below. Still Creek sites have picnic tables and fire pits, water is from faucets, and some of the sites are paved. The access road for Still Creek leaves US-26 at Mile 54.4, it's .4 mile (.6 km) down the hill to the sites.

■ **TRILLIUM LAKE CAMPGROUND** *(Open May 15 to Oct 10 – Varies)*
Reservations: www.recreation.gov, (877) 444-6777
Information: (503) 622-3191
Location: 31 Miles 50 Km) E of Sandy

GPS Location: 45.27028 N, 121.73278 W, 3,600 Ft

57 Sites – This is a Mt Hood National Forest Campground on the shore of 60-acre Trillium Lake. It's a modernized campground with paved back-in and pull-thru sites to 40 feet off paved loop roads. The campground has picnic tables and fire pits, water is from faucets. There's a nice two-mile trail around the lake as well as a boat ramp at a day use area, no engines are allowed on the lake. To most easily reach the campground leave US-26 at Mile 56.7 and follow the signs on paved forest service roads for 1.3 miles (2.1 km) to the campground.

■ **FROG LAKE CAMPGROUND** *(Open June 15 to Oct 15 – Varies)*
Reservations: www.recreation.gov, (877) 444-6777
Information: (503) 622-3191
Location: 35 Miles E of Sandy

GPS Location: 45.22417 N, 121.69444 W, 3,900 Ft

32 Sites – This handy Mt Hood National Forest campground is located near, but not on, 10-acre Frog Lake. Sites are all back-ins suitable for RVs to about 30 feet. This is an area of mixed evergreens without a lot of underbrush. There's a day-use area nearby with access to the lake and a small boat ramp, engines are not allowed. To reach the campground take the exit at Mile 62 of US-26. You'll enter a large parking lot, used as a Snowpark in the winter, the campground and day-use area entrances are to your right.

■ **CLEAR LAKE CAMPGROUND** *(Open June 1 to Oct 10 – Varies)*
Reservations: www.recreation.gov, (877) 444-6777
Information: (541) 352-6002
Location: 38 Miles (62 Km) E of Sandy

GPS Location: 45.17944 N, 121.69722 W, 3,500 Ft

27 Sites – This Mt Hood National Forest campground is on the east shore of 500-acre Clear Lake, really a reservoir with a water level that fluctuates. Sites are off a paved loop road, many are narrow pull-thrus or pull-offs although there are also back-ins. Some sites are as long as 45 feet but they're narrow and access is poor so the campground is best for RVs no larger than 30 feet. Water is from a hand pump, there is a swimming area and a boat ramp. Power boats are allowed but have a 10 mph speed limit. To reach the campground take paved FR 2630 from Mile 64.5 of US-26. It's a mile to the campground.

■ **NOTTINGHAM CAMPGROUND** *(Open May 1 to Sept 30 – Varies)*
Information: (541) 352-6002
Location: 26 Miles (42 Km) S of Hood River

GPS Location: 45.36778 N, 121.57028 W, 3,400 Ft

20 Sites – This Mt Hood National Forest campground is on the bank of the East Fork of Hood River. It's in an open area of dry-country pines. Sites here are unpaved back-ins to 30 feet off a dirt and gravel road next to the river. Sites have picnic tables and fire pits, water is not provided. Access to the campground is off SR-35 near Mile 70.

■ **SHERWOOD CAMPGROUND** *(Open May 1 to Oct 15 – Varies)*
Information: (541) 352-6002
Location: 25 Miles (42 Km) S of Hood River

GPS Location: 45.39444 N, 121.57056 W, 3,100 Ft

11 Sites – This small Mt Hood National Forest campground is immediately adjacent to SR-35 on the bank of the East Fork of Hood River. You can actually access some of the sites directly from the highway. This is an old campground and sites will only take cars and RVs to about 25 feet. There are fire pits and picnic tables as well as a vault toilet but no provision for water. The campground is near Mile 72 of SR-35.

■ **TOLL BRIDGE PARK** *(Hood River County)*
     (Open April 1 to Oct 31 – Varies)
Res and Info: (541) 352-5522,
          reservations@co.hood-river.or.us
Location: 15 Miles S of Hood River

GPS Location: 45.51833 N, 121.56833 W, 1,600 Ft

89 Sites – This campground is in a county park along the East Fork Hood River. In addition to the campground there's a popular day-use area with a cooking and eating shelter. The campground has a variety of sites off four loops: an RV loop, a tent loop, the East Loop and the West Loop. RV sites 1-20 are full hookup back-ins sites to 40 feet. The tent loop has parking pads and room for tents. The other two loops have paved parking pads, some are long pull-thrus to 60 feet, and they have water and electric hookups. The restrooms are in a cement block building and there's a dump station nearby. This park has a host. From SR-35 turn east on Toll Bridge Road at Mile 84, you'll see the park entrance on the right in .3 mile (.5 km).

■ **LOST LAKE CAMPGROUND** *(Open May 1 to Oct 31 – Varies)*
Information: (541) 352-6002, (541) 386-6366, www.lostlakeresort.org
Location: Lost Lake

GPS Location: 45.49972 N, 121.81667 W, 3,100 Ft

120 Sites – Mt Hood National Forest's Lost Lake Campground occupies
the eastern shore of Lost Lake. The lake is about 240 acres in size and popular for fishing and boating (no engines allowed). The campground is adjacent to Lost Lake Resort
which is on the lake and has cabins, some groceries, rental boats, and hot showers (for
an extra charge). The campground itself is off several loops. Loops A,B, C and D are the
loops for RVs with D having some long pull-thrus. Loop E is walk-in tent sites and loop
F is a premium tent-only loop near the lake. Finally, there is a horse camp loop. Many
sites have paved parking pads, all have picnic tables and fire pits. There's a boat ramp and
excellent hiking trails from the campground including a three-mile trail around the lake.
Due to the long back-road access route and limited maneuvering room we recommend
the campground only for RVs to 30 feet. Easiest access is from the north in the Hood
River Valley. From the small town of Dee the Lost Lake Road goes southwest for 13.5
miles (21.8 km) to the campground.

■ **LITTLE CRATER LAKE CAMPGROUND**
   (Open June 1 to Sept 25 – Varies)
Reservations: www.recreation.gov, (877) 444-6777
Information: (503) 622-3191
Location: Near Timothy Lake

GPS Location: 45.14833 N, 121.74528 W, 3,300 Ft

16 Sites – This Mt Hood National Forest campground is situated next to Little Crater
Lake which is very small and in an artesian wetland area just above Timothy Lake. All
of the sites are back-ins, a few to 30 feet. A short stub trail, the Little Crater Lake Trail,
connects with the Pacific Crest Trail less than a quarter-mile away. To reach it from the
Mt Hood area take the cut-off at Mile 66 of SR-26. Follow Skyline Rd. (also called NF-
42) for 4.1 miles (6.6 km). Turn right on to NF-58 and drive 2.2 miles (3.5 km) to the
campground entrance.

■ **OAK FORK CAMPGROUND** *(Open May 20 to Sept 10 – Varies)*
   Reservations: www.recreation.gov, (877) 444-6777
   Information: (503) 622-3191
   Location: Timothy Lake

GPS Location: 45.11151 N, 121.76975 W, 3,300 Ft

47 Sites – This Mt Hood National Forest campground is one of five located on the south
shore of Timothy Lake. The lake is a reservoir with a surface area of about 1,400 acres.
It's a popular swimming and water sports lake, engines are allowed but there's a 10 mph
speed limit. There's a trail along the south shore as well as the 14-mile Timothy Lake
Trail around the lake. A network of trails in this area offer miles of hiking including connections to the Cascade Crest Trail. This campground is the farthest east of the five. It has
a boat ramp, a dock, and small beaches. Sites are off two loops. Like all the campgrounds
along the lake, it can be hard to level a rig here. There are just a few sites for large RVs
and slides can be a problem because larger sites tend to be narrow pull-thrus. Sites to 30
feet are common. Water is from a hand pump. To reach the campground take the cut-off at
Mile 66 of SR-26. Follow Skyline Rd. (also called NF-42) for 8.2 miles (13.2 km). Take a
right at the Y and in 1.3 miles (2.1 km) you'll see the campground entrance on the right.

■ **GONE CREEK CAMPGROUND** *(Open May 15 to Oct – Varies)*
Reservations: www.recreation.gov, (877) 444-6777
Information: (503) 622-3191
Location: Timothy Lake

GPS Location: 45.11056 N, 121.77444 W, 3,300 Ft

44 Sites – This is another of the Mt Hood National Forest campgrounds located along the south shore of Timothy Lake. There is a boat ramp here and small beaches. Sites are off two loops. This is the most congested of the five campground along the lake and while there are some sites exceeding 40 feet they are too narrow for slide-outs. Sites to 30 feet are common. Water is from faucets. To reach the campground take the cut-off at Mile 66 of SR-26. Follow Skyline Rd. (also called NF-42) for 8.2 miles (13.2 km). Take a right at the Y and in 1.5 miles (2.4 km) you'll see the campground entrance on the right.

■ **HOODVIEW CAMPGROUND** *(Open May 15 to Sept 5 – Varies)*
Reservations: www.recreation.gov, (877) 444-6777
Information: (503) 622-3191
Location: Timothy Lake

GPS Location: 45.10750 N, 121.79222 W, 3,100 Ft

43 Sites – Another Mt Hood National Forest campground on the south shore of Timothy Lake. It has great views of Mt Hood across the lake. The campground has a boat ramp, a dock, and small beaches. Sites are off two loops and this park has slightly more room to maneuver and park than the first two. Still, big rig sites are scarce. To reach the campground take the cut-off at Mile 66 of SR-26. Follow Skyline Rd. (also called NF-42) for 8.2 miles (13.2 km). Take a right at the Y and in 2.5 miles (4.0 km) you'll see the campground entrance on the right.

■ **COVE CAMPGROUND**
Information: (503) 622-3191
Location: Timothy Lake

GPS Location: 45.10985 N, 121.79894, 3,200 Ft

10 Sites – This is a walk-in tent campground along the lakeshore. Sites have picnic tables and fire pits and there is a vault toilet. Parking for cars is very limited, only enough for four vehicles and it's right out on the road. The campground is probably best for bicycle travelers. To reach the campground take the cut-off at Mile 66 of SR-26. Follow Skyline Rd. (also called NF-42) for 8.2 miles (13.2 km). Take a right at the Y and in 2.9 miles (4.7 km) you'll see the campground sign on the right.

■ **PINE POINT CAMPGROUND** *(Open May 15 to Sept 20 – Varies)*
Reservations: www.recreation.gov, (877) 444-6777
Information: (503) 622-3191
Location: Timothy Lake

GPS Location: 45.11278 N, 121.80167 W, 3,200 Ft

25 Sites – This is the smallest of the Mt Hood National Forest campgrounds on the south shore of Timothy lake. It's more open than the other three vehicle campground here and the large rigs sites allow use of slides. Sites are off a single paved loop, all but one are back-ins, some as long as 40 feet. To reach the campground take the cut-off at Mile 66 of SR-26. Follow Skyline Rd. (also called NF-42) for 8.2 miles (13.2 km). Take a right at the Y and in 3.2 miles (5.1 km) you'll see the campground entrance on the right.

■ **CLACKAMAS LAKE CAMPGROUND**
(Open May 25 to Sept 15 – Varies)
Reservations: www.recreation.gov, (877) 444-6777
Information: (503) 622-3191
Location: Near Timothy Lake

GPS Location: 45.09500 N, 121.74889 W, 3,400 Ft

46 Sites – Clackamas Lake is a small marshy lake but fishing is possible. There's a board walk offering access. The Mt Hood National Forest campground here has one loop with back-ins and a few pull-thrus to 40 feet. Miller Trail connects with the Pacific Crest Trail about two miles away. To reach the campground take the cut-off at Mile 66 of SR-26. Follow Skyline Rd. (also called NF-42) for 8.2 miles (13.2 km). Take a left at the Y and in .2 miles (.3 km) you'll see the campground entrance on the left.

■ **LAKE HARRIET CAMPGROUND** *(Open May 1 to Sept 15 - Varies)*
Reservations: www.recreation.gov, (877) 444-6777
Information: (503) 622-3191
Location: Near Timothy Lake

GPS Location: 45.07354 N, 121.95899 W, 2,000 Ft.

11 Sites – This Mt Hood National Forest campground at the east end of little Lake Harriet is a good base for those planning to fish this popular little lake. The sites are off a gravel in and out road with a loop at the end, some reach 35 feet in length. Water is from a hand pump. The campground is near the Timothy Lake Road. Easiest access is from SR-224. Timothy Lake Road Leaves SR-224 at Mile 50, 25 miles (40 km) south of Estacada. Follow Timothy Lake Road east for 6.3 miles (10.1 km), then turn left at the sign for Lake Harriett Campground. Follow the gravel road for another 1 mile (1.6 km) to the campground on the left.

NEHALEM BAY AND MANZANITA

Nehalem Bay offers easy to access crabbing and fishing opportunities. The spit of land that forms the bay is occupied by a large and very popular state park. There is a great beach. Cannon beach is near to the north and Tillamook to the south. What more could you want.

Nehalem Bay and Manzanita Campgrounds

☐ **NEHALEM BAY STATE PARK** *(Open All Year)*
Reservations: www.reserveamerica.com, (800) 452-5687
Information: (503) 368-5154, (800) 551-6949,
                   www.oregonstateparks.org
Location: 1 Mile (2 Km) S of Manzanita

GPS Location: 45.70306 N, 123.93472 W, Near Sea Level

290 Sites – Nehalem Bay campground occupies a spit between Nehalem Bay and the ocean. It's just south of the village of Nehalem and shares a long, wide beach with the town. Campsites are sheltered behind dunes but the beach is extremely accessible. There's a boat launch at the park, not to mention an airstrip. RV sites are all back-ins. Many are over 50 feet long, over half are 40 feet or longer. In addition to the 265 RV sites with electricity there is a hiker/biker area, a horse camp with 17 sites, an airport camp with six sites for fly-in campers, and 18 yurts. To reach the campground watch for the sign just south of Manzanita, other signs will take you 2 miles (3 km) on back roads to the campground.

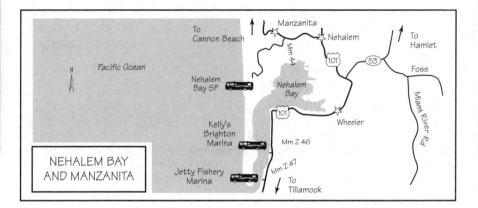

● **KELLY'S BRIGHTON MARINA** *(Open All Year)*
Res and Info: (503) 368-5745,
kellysbrightonmarina@gmail.com,
www.kellyscrabs.com
Location: Brighton

GPS Location: 45.66917 N, 123.92472 W, Near Sea Level

26 Sites – This marina on Nehalem Bay has back-in sites overlooking the marina. Camping is on gravel in a lot shared by parked cars, in wet weather there are puddles and mud. RVs to 45 feet can park toward the north end without getting in the way. A small restroom building services the RV sites. There is also a very small grassy area with no nearby vehicle parking north of the buildings and boat launch for tenters. Fishermen love this place because it has the facilities they need – boat launch, moorage, rental boats, and guided fishing trips. The campground is located right off US-101 as it runs along the bay 6 miles (10 km) south of Nehalem and 3.6 miles (5.8 km) north of Rockaway Beach.

● **JETTY FISHERY MARINA** *(Open All Year)*
Res and Info: (503) 368-5746, (800) 821-7697,
info@jettyfishery.com,
www.jettyfishery.com
Location: 1 Mile (2 Km) S of Brighton

GPS Location: 45.65972 N, 123.92917 W, Near Sea Level

30 Sites – Like the Brighton Marina mentioned above this place is also a fisherman's destination. They too have docks, marina, and boat launch. RV sites are back-ins near the entrance and there is a separate large tent area on grass to the north. Most RV sites will take RVs to 45 feet with no problem. The campground is located right off US-101 as it runs along the bay 6.7 miles (10.8 km) south of Nehalem and 2.9 miles (4.7 km) north of Rockaway Beach.

NEWBERRY NATIONAL VOLCANIC MONUMENT

South of Bend is the **Newberry National Volcanic Monument**. This national monument is a little unusual in that it is managed by the Forest Service rather than the National Park Service. That's largely because it's more efficient that way since the monument is surrounded by the Deschutes National Forest. The monument preserves a large section of interesting volcanic terrain.

There are two important destinations in the monument: **Lava Lands Visitor Center** and the **Newberry Volcano**. The visitor center is located 12 miles (19 km) south of Bend, just to the west of US-97. It has newly updated exhibits, and a bookstore. There's also a road up to the Lava Butte Lookout at the top of a small volcano.

The larger **Newberry Volcano** also has a road into the caldera. There are two lakes in the caldera: Paulina Lake and East Lake. All of the campgrounds listed below are located in the Newberry Volcano caldera and near the lakes.

There is a dump station as you enter the Newberry Caldera between Mile 12 and 13. The campgrounds below are beyond that point, none have their own dump station. The campgrounds are listed from end of the road back toward the west.

Newberry National Volcanic Monument Campgrounds

■ CINDER HILL CAMPGROUND *(Open June 1 to Sept 30 – Varies)*
   Reservations: www.recreation.gov, (877) 444-6777
   Information: (541) 383-4000
   Location: Newberry Caldera

GPS Location: 43.72917 N, 121.19472 W, 6,400 Ft

110 Sites – This is the campground at the end of the paved road. It sits on the east side of East Lake and stretches for a long distance along the shoreline. There is a boat launch here and room to pull boats up on the beach. Most sites reach 30 feet and maneuvering room is good for rigs of that size. There are also some long pull-thrus to about 55 feet but most of these are narrow and for large rigs careful maneuvering and parking is required. From US-97 some 20 miles (32 km) south of Bend and 6 miles (10 km) north of La Pine follow the Paulina-East Lake Rd east as it climbs to the monument. The campground is 18.3 miles (30 km) from the junction with US-97.

● EAST LAKE RESORT AND RV PARK
   (Open May 15 to Oct 20 – Varies)
   Res and Info: (541) 536-2230, www.EastLakeResort.com
   Location: Newberry Caldera

GPS Location: 43.72278 N, 121.19306 W, 6,400 Ft

40 Sites – This resort serves as a place to get supplies, showers, and do laundry for the campers in the monument. The main resort buildings are

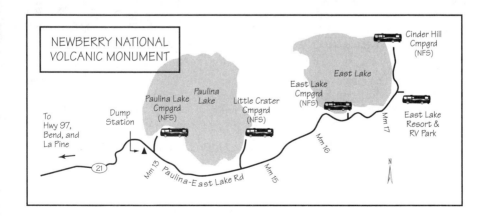

VIEW ACROSS EAST LAKE FROM THE EAST LAKE CAMPGROUND

on the lakeshore and amenities here include a boat ramp, restaurant, rooms, and small grocery store. On the upper side of the highway there is a campground with both back-in and long (75 foot) pull-thru sites with water and electricity. The dump station is included; it costs $10 if you're not staying in the RV park. There is a shower building and laundry at the campground, they are also available (for a fee) to campers in the other campgrounds along the lakes. Wi-Fi is available for a fee at the lakeshore buildings but not the campground. From US-97 some 20 miles (32 km) south of Bend and 6 miles (10 km) north of La Pine follow the Paulina-East Lake Rd east as it climbs to the monument. The campground is 18 miles (29 km) from the junction with US-97.

■ **EAST LAKE CAMPGROUND** *(Open June 1 to Oct 15 – Varies)*
Information: (541) 383-4000
Location: Newberry Caldera

GPS Location: 43.71778 N, 121.21000 W, 6,400 Ft

29 Sites – This campground occupies the south shore of East Lake. Sites vary in size but some reach 40 feet including some pull-thrus right on the lakeshore. There is a boat ramp at the campground. From US-97 some 20 miles (32 km) south of Bend and 6 miles (10 km) north of La Pine follow the Paulina-East Lake Rd east as it climbs to the monument. The campground is 16.9 miles (27 km) from the junction with US-97.

■ **LITTLE CRATER CAMPGROUND** *(Open June 1 to Oct 15 – Varies)*
Information: (541) 383-4000
Location: Newberry Caldera

GPS Location: 43.71056 N, 121.24361 W, 6,400 Ft

OREGON

50 Sites – This waterfront campground is on the east shore of Paulina Lake. Many sites are pull-thrus and there are also long back-ins, some to 70 feet. There is a boat ramp at the campground. From US-97 some 20 miles (32 km) south of Bend and 6 miles (10 km) north of La Pine follow the Paulina-East Lake Rd east as it climbs to the monument. The campground is 14.9 miles (24 km) from the junction with US-97.

■ **Paulina Lake Campground** *(Open May 20 to Oct 20 – Varies)*
  Reservations: www.recreation.gov, (877) 444-6777
  Information: (541) 383-4000
  Location: Newberry Caldera

GPS Location: 43.70972 N, 121.27250 W, 6,400 Ft

69 Sites – Pauline Lake Campground is the first you reach as you enter the monument. It occupies the south shore of Paulina Lake and has two entrances and two boat ramps. Many of the sites here are 60-foot pull-thrus but they tend to be difficult for really big RVs because they are sharply curved. From US-97 some 20 miles south (32 km) of Bend and 6 miles (10 km) north of La Pine follow the Paulina-East Lake Rd east as it climbs to the monument. The campground is 13.3 miles (21 km) from the junction with US-97.

Oregon Caves National Monument

The Oregon Caves National Monument is an interesting stop in Southcentral Oregon. Located just southwest of Grants Pass there are both commercial and Forest Service campgrounds conveniently located for use as a base while visiting the monument.

Discovered in 1874 and declared a national monument in 1909, this cave is made of metamorphosed limestone, in other words, it's marble. There are lots of formations from mineralized water so it's an interesting cave. There are also several good hiking trails in the monument as well as a great old lodge, the Oregon Caves Chateau.

Access to the monument is from **Cave Junction**, located 28 miles (45 km) west of Grants Pass on US-199. The Illinois Valley Visitor Center is at the junction. Since large RVs are not recommended past Grayback Campground at Mile 11.5 of the road up to the monument it is possible to leave your coach or trailer in the parking lot of the visitor center while you drive your smaller vehicle (assuming you have one) up to the cave.

Cave tours are offered from late March though the end of November. You can only enter the cave as part of a tour. The tours are moderately strenuous with lots of steps, some are really closer to ladders than steps. Children are required to be at least 42 inches in height to enter the caves. The tours take 90 minutes. In addition to the normal tour the staff also offers a candlelight tour (the last tour each day) as well as an introduction to caving tour on Saturdays that goes off the normal tour route. No reservations are taken for tours, it's first-come, first served.

Oregon Caves National Monument Campgrounds

● **Mountain Man RV Park** *(Open All Year)*
  Res and Info: (541) 592-2656
  Location: 2 Miles (3.2 Km) S of Cave Junction

  GPS Location: 42.13500 N, 123.66444 W, 1,400 Ft

54 Sites – This is an older park but it has a nice traveler section at the west side of the campground with spacious

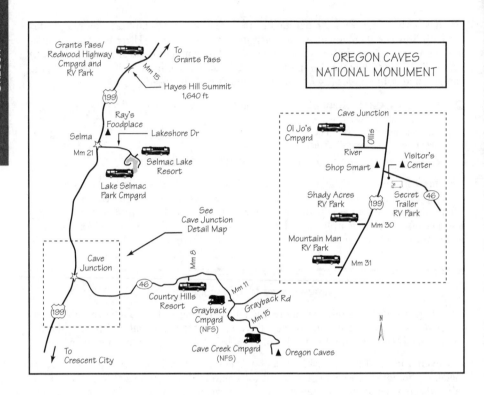

sites, grass, and lots of room. There are also rest room facilities dedicated to this section. Sites are pull-thrus and back-ins to 60 feet. The park is off US-199 some 2 miles (3.2 km) south of the junction with SR-46, the highway leading up to Oregon Caves National Monument.

● **SHADY ACRES RV PARK** *(Open All Year)*
    Res and Info: (541) 592-3702
    Location: 1 Mile (1.6 Km) S of Cave Junction

    GPS Location: 42.14774 N, 123.65540 W, 1,400 Ft

47 Sites – This older park sits behind an RV supply store. There are both traveler and full-time sites in the park, they are back-ins and pull-thrus to 60 feet. The campground is off US-199 1 mile (1.6 km) south of the junction with SR-46, the highway leading up to Oregon Caves National Monument.

● **COUNTRY HILLS RESORT** *(Open All Year)*
    Res and Info: (541) 592-3406 or (800) 99 RV'ING
    Location: 8 Miles (12.9 Km) E of Cave Junction

    GPS Location: 42.16389 N, 123.51083 W, 1,400 Ft

32 Sites – Country Hills sits near to the national forest, the closest commercial park to the caves. This is a small motel with a pleasant camping area some distance behind that has big trees for shade and a small creek alongside. Tent and RV sites are irregularly shaped, surfaces are

gravel and packed soil. Two of the RV sites are long pull-thrus, the rest are back-ins but many are pretty large. Just a few sites have full hookups, most of the RV sites have just water and electricity. There is a dump station. Swimming is in the creek. Wi-Fi is available only up near the office. The campground is on SR-46, the road leading up to the caves, it's about 8 miles (12.9 km) from the junction.

■ **GRAYBACK CAMPGROUND** *(Open May 26 to Sept 30 – Varies)*
Information: (541) 592-4000
Location: 11.5 Miles (18.5 Km) W of Cave Junction

GPS Location: 42.14222 N, 123.46056 W, 1,900 Ft

40 Sites – Sites in this Siskiyou National Forest campground are off two paved loop roads. They're back-in sites, some to 40 feet, but limited maneuvering room means that this campground is best for RVs to 30 feet. Picnic tables, fire pits, a large picnic shelter, and flush toilets are provided. The Forest Service recommends that you not take trailers past this campground, from here on up to the caves the road is narrow and has lots of curves. Visitors are permitted to leave their RVs in the day use area of this campground while visiting the caves although you must access the parking area through the somewhat narrow access road in the campground. Those with big rigs would be better off leaving their RV at the visitor center parking lot in Cave Junction. The campground is on SR-46, the road leading up to the caves, it's 11.5 miles (18.5 km) from the junction.

■ **CAVE CREEK CAMPGROUND** *(Open May 26 to Sept 15 – Varies)*
Information: (541) 592-4000
Location: 15.8 Miles (25.5 Km) E of Cave Junction

GPS Location: 42.11808 N, 123.43583 W, 2,500 Ft

18 Sites – This Siskiyou National Forest campground has paved sites off a paved loop road. Although a few are parallel parking style to 40 feet, access roads are narrow, as is the main road. In fact, trailers are not recommended past Grayback Campground, see above. The campground is best for RVs without trailers to 25 feet. There's a 1.8 mile (2.9 km) trail leading from the campground up to the monument. The campground is on SR-46, the road leading up to the caves, it's 15.8 miles (25.5 km) from the junction.

● **OL JO'S CAMPGROUND**
Res and Info: (541) 592-4207,
www.oljorvcampground.com
Location: Cave Junction, OR

GPS Location: 42.17349 N, 123.66136 W, 1,300 Ft

30 Sites – This is a simple but well-kept modern big-rig park located at the northern edge of Cave Junction, well off the main road. Sites here are paved pull-thrus and back-ins to 50 feet. They are surrounded by lawn. There are also tent sites with water, fire rings, picnic tables and BBQs. A common area has a large-screen TV and pool table. From central Cave Junction drive west on W River Street for .4 mile (.6 km). Turn right on N Ollis Rd and drive until it T's in .2 miles (.3 km). Turn left and you'll reach the campground in .3 mile (.5 km).

OREGON

● **GRANTS PASS/REDWOOD HIGHWAY**
    CAMPGROUND AND RV PARK *(Open All Year)*

Reservations: (800) 562-9036,
              redwoodhwycampground@msn.com
Information: (541) 476-6508,
              www.redwoodhwycampground.com
Location: 14 Miles (23 Km) W of Grants Pass

    GPS Location: 42.34675 N, 123.56226 W, 1,200 Ft

35 Sites – This former KOA is located half way between Grants Pass and Cave Junction so it is a possible spot to stay for visits to both the city and the Marble Caves. There are pull-thrus and back-ins to 50 feet. From Grant's Pass drive west on US-199 for about 14 miles (23 km), the campground is on the right near Mile 14.5.

○ **LAKE SELMAC PARK CAMPGROUND** *(Open All Year)*
    Reservations: www.reserveamerica.com, (800) 452-5687
    Information: (541) 474-5285,
    Location: 8 Miles (13 Km) N of Cave Junction

      GPS Location: 42.43465 N, 123.37611 W, 800 Ft

83 Sites – Lake Selmac is the largest of the Josephine County RV Parks near Grants Pass. It's the only one with campsites that is not located on the Rogue River. Instead it's out near Cave Junction and makes a great place to stay when visiting the attractions in that area. Lake Selmac is a pretty little reservoir lake. The camping sites here are in five different areas around the lake called Osprey, Heron, Teal, Eagle and Mallard. As you approach the lake from the west you'll come to a Y. To the left are a private resort (see below) and Eagle and Mallard Loops. To the right at the Y are Osprey, Heron, and Teal Loops. Eagle, Heron, and Teal loops are for tents with small parking slots, all have sites along the water and there is quite a bit of shade, tents are pitched on packed earth sites. Mallard Loop has back-in full hookup sites in an open area (and also some tent sites) while Osprey has a combination of 36 tent and hookup sites in trees including many full-hookup sites to 50 feet. Both Eagle and Osprey have restrooms with flush toilets and showers, the other loops have vault toilets. There is a dump station on the Osprey Loop. Several yurts are available as well as boat launches, picnic areas, and swimming areas. From Hwy 199 about 22 miles (35 km) southwest of Grants Pass or 8 miles (13 km) north of Cave Junction drive south on Lakeshore Drive for 2 miles (3.2 km) to the Y. Campgrounds are in both directions as described above.

● **LAKE SELMAC RESORT** *(Open All Year)*
    Res and Info: (541) 597-2277, info@lakeselmac.com,
                www.lakeselmac.com
    Location: 8 Miles (13 Km) N of Cave Junction

    GPS Location: 42.26319 N, 123.57454 W, 1,300

35 Sites – This resort is located right across the road from Selmac Lake. It's not part of the county park like the other campgrounds around the lake. Sites here are pull-thrus to 60 feet and back-ins to 40. Some are full-hookup and others partial. There are also tent sites. Amenities include a store, boat rentals, and mini-golf. From Hwy 199 about 22 miles (35 km) southwest of Grants Pass or 8 miles (13 km) north of Cave Junction drive south on Lakeshore Drive for 2 miles (3.2 km) to the Y. The resort is to the left.

PENDLETON

Pendleton (population 17,000) bills itself as "The real west". The little town does indeed have a western flavor. It is very well known for its **Pendleton Round-Up**, a 4-day rodeo held during mid-September. Make sure you have reservations if you visit during the round-up, you'll have lots of company. You should also buy your tickets to the rodeo early to avoid being disappointed.

The name Pendleton may make you think of wool blankets. This is the home of the **Pendleton Blanket Mill**. The company began operations in 1909 when it started making woolen Indian blankets, today they have mills scattered around the country. The one in Pendleton has a store and gives tours of the factory.

Four miles (6 km) east of Pendleton is the **Wildhorse Resort**. This entertainment complex, run by the Confederated Tribes of the Umatilla Indian Reservation, has a casino, an 18-hole golf course, an RV park, and a museum. The museum is known as the **Tamástslikt Cultural Institute** and describes the Cayuse, Umatilla and Walla Walla tribes and cultures and their interaction with the travelers on the Oregon Trail. The easiest way to enjoy the resort is to stay at the convenient RV park.

If you take I-84 eastward almost immediately you'll reach the long grade up into the Blue Mountains. The scenery changes quickly from dry grasslands to pine forests. Emigrant Springs State Park is just off the freeway at Exit 234 and is described at page 93.

Heading even farther eastward you'll pass the Blue Mountains Summit (elevation 4,194 feet) and reach an interesting stop, the **Oregon Trail Visitor's Park**. To reach it take Exit 248 and follow a winding road for 3 miles (5 km) to the park. You'll find a short trail that leads up the hill to a section of the Oregon Trail, ruts are visible and an interpretive trail and volunteers help you make sense of what you see.

Pendleton Campgrounds

● **PENDLETON/MOUNTAIN VIEW KOA** *(Open All Year)*
  Reservations: (866) 562-7560, www.koa.com
  Information: (541) 276-1041, pendletonkoa@gmail.comt,
  www.nwfamilyrvresorts.com
  Location: Pendleton

  GPS Location: 45.66000 N, 118.78028 W, 1,300 Ft

107 Sites – This is a modern big-rig park. It has pull-thru sites to 65 feet and also tent sites. Access from the freeway is easy, the campground is located just south of the Red Lion that is easy to spot from the highway. Take Exit 210 from I-84. Turn south and take the first right onto Southwest Nye Ave. Follow Nye for one block and then turn left onto SE 3rd St., the campground is a block ahead and to the right.

● **THE LOOKOUT RV PARK** *(Open All Year)*
  Reservations: (877) 604-6014
  Information: (541) 276-6014
  Location: Pendleton

  GPS Location: 45.67667 N, 118.84056 W, 1,100 Ft

30 Sites – This simple park on the west side of Pendleton

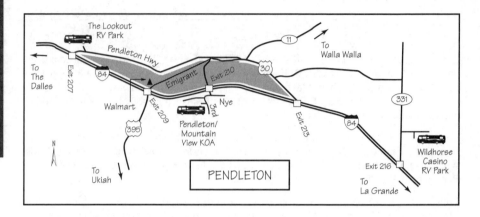

is located on a hillside. Sites are all long pull-thrus to 60 feet. This is a decent big-rig overnight stop but it has little ambiance, everything here is paved. The Wi-Fi signal is best if you're near the restrooms, otherwise it may not be useable. To find the park take Exit 207 from I-84, you'll see it on the hillside on the north side of the exit.

● **WILDHORSE CASINO RV PARK** *(Open All Year)*
Reservations: (800) 654-9453
Information: (541) 278-2274,
        www.wildhorseresort.com
Location: 4 Miles (6 Km) E of Pendleton

GPS Location: 45.64833 N, 118.67556 W, 1,400 Ft

100 Sites – Just a short drive east of Pendleton is the entertainment complex of the Confederated Tribes of Umatilla. You'll find a good big-rig RV park and also, within walking distance, a casino, a golf course, and a museum. Some pull-thru sites are 60 feet in length, others are long back-ins. They are surrounded by clipped grass and are well separated but offer no shade. There is a swimming pool with spa and restrooms with hot showers. There's also a separate tent-camping area with a community fire ring. You can walk about a quarter-mile to the casino which has a restaurant, there is also a free shuttle bus for transportation to the casino, museum, or golf course. To reach the campground take Exit 216 from I-84 about 4 miles (6 km) east of Pendleton. Follow signs .3 mile (.5 km) north to the access road for the complex. The RV park entrance is .3 mile (.5 km) up the entrance boulevard, on the right.

PORT ORFORD

Port Orford is the western-most incorporated city in the contiguous U.S. You'll pass through this small town at Mile 301 of US-101 along the Oregon coast. Take the time to stop at **Battle Rock Wayside** at the south end of town for views and steep access to the beach. Those with small and easy to maneuver RVs can turn toward the ocean at the sign in town and drive out to the **Port Orford Heads Wayside**. There's a trail to a headland which can be an excellent whale-watching spot but turn-around room is limited.

Cape Blanco is the westernmost point in the contiguous U.S. You reach it by taking a five-mile (8 km) paved road from Mile 296.6 of US 101. That's just north of Port Orford. The lighthouse on the cape is the oldest on the Oregon coast, there's also a small state park campground with electrical hookups. There are hiking trails all across Cape Blanco with magnificent views.

Port Orford Campgrounds

☐ **CAPE BLANCO STATE PARK** *(Open All Year)*
Information: (541) 332-6774, (800) 551-6949,
www.oregonstateparks.org
Location: 8 Miles (13 Km) N of Port Orford

GPS Location: 42.83139 N, 124.54972 W, 200 Ft

53 Sites – The Cape Blanco State Park occupies Cape Blanco. On the end is the oldest remaining lighthouse on the Oregon Coast, the Cape Blanco Lighthouse, which dates from 1870. The campground sites are off a loop. They are all back-in sites, some to 65 feet with many longer than 40 feet. There is also a hiker/biker tent camping area and a horse camp. There are many trails on the cape, the lighthouse is .7 mile (1.1 km) west of the campground. The entrance road to Cape Blanco leaves US-101 near Mile 296.6. This is 3 miles (5 km) north of Port Orford. From the highway drive 4.7 miles (7.6 km) toward the cape and turn left to enter the campground.

● **ELK RIVER RV PARK** *(Open All Year)*
Res and Info: (541) 332-2255
Location: 4 Miles (6 Km) NE of Port Orford

GPS Location: 42.77389 N, 124.47028 W, Near Sea Level

55 Sites – This commercial campground is a bit out of

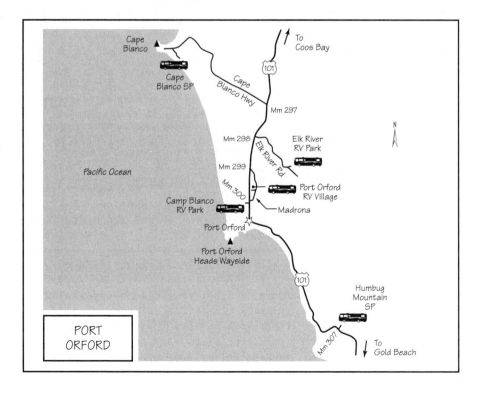

town. It's very relaxed and popular with salmon fishermen, has a boat ramp, and has quite a few long-term residents. Sites here will take big RVs, many are pull-thrus to 60 feet. To reach the campground turn east on Elk River Road from US-101 near Mile 297.6. The campground entrance is 1.7 miles (2.7 km) from the highway.

● **PORT ORFORD RV VILLAGE** *(Open All Year)*
  Res and Info: (541) 332-1041,
                portorfordrv@gmail.com,
                www.portorfordrv.com
  Location: 1 Mile N of Port Orford
  GPS Location: 42.76111 N, 124.49417 W, 100 Ft

47 Sites – This is an older park with enthusiastic and friendly owners, a popular place. Most sites here are back-ins to 40 feet but there are a few even longer pull-thrus. Tent camping is on grass. To reach the campground turn east on Madrona Ave at Mile 300 at the north end of Port Orford, the campground will be on your left in .5 miles (.8 km).

● **CAMP BLANCO RV PARK** *(Open All Year)*
  Res and Info: (541) 332-6175, www.campblanco.com
  Location: Port Orford
  GPS Location: 42.75472 N, 124.49750 W, 200 Ft

25 Sites – This small RV park is neat as a pin and very well run. Sites are back-ins and pull-thrus to 60 feet. Although there's no laundry at the campground there's a laundromat across the street, even better. An unusual feature here is the "boatel", an old fishing boat that has been converted into a rental room – very cute. The RV park is located near the northern entrance to Port Orford, it's on the west side of US-101.

☐ **HUMBUG MOUNTAIN STATE PARK** *(Open All Year)*
  Reservations: www.reserveamerica.com, (800) 452-5687
  Information: (541) 332-6774, (800) 551-6949,
                www.oregonstateparks.org
  Location: 6 Miles (10 Km) S of Port Orford
  GPS Location: 42.68833 N, 124.43361 W, Near Sea Level

95 Sites – This state park campground is located away from the coast and the sites are right next to the highway. There's a trail to the summit of Humbug Mountain from the campground and another to the beach. The campground has a hiker-biker camp as do most Oregon state campgrounds on the Oregon coast, they're well-used by hikers traveling the coastal trail. Most of the vehicle sites here are back-ins. Only 39 have hookups, none have sewer drains. They reach 90 feet, 20 are over 40 feet. The campground is on the east side of the highway near Mile 307.9. This is 6 miles (10 km) south of Port Orford and 21 miles (34 km) north of Gold Beach.

PORTLAND

The Portland region, with a population of about 2,300,000, is by far the largest concentration of people in Oregon. The area population depends, of course, upon how you define the region. The population is fairly dense as far south as Salem and also crosses the Columbia to Vancouver, Washington.

Portland is a young city by any standards, it was founded around 1844 when the first land claim was staked in what is now downtown Portland. Although the city is older than Seattle it is only older by a few years. The location is said to have been used for years as a seasonal campsite by Indians, there was a village nearby on Sauvie Island near the mouth of the Willamette.

Actually, by the time Portland was founded, Europeans had been in the neighborhood for quite a few years too. Fort Vancouver, across the Columbia River, was an important Hudson's Bay Company post beginning in 1825.

Like Seattle, much of Portland's early growth came as a timber port to fuel the demand for lumber in booming San Francisco down the west coast. Gold had been discovered in the Sacramento River Valley and San Francisco was growing rapidly. Portland served as a gateway to the Willamette River Valley which was attracting large numbers of settlers who traveled the Oregon Trail. It became much easier to reach Portland when the railroad arrived in 1883.

Lewis and Clark passed near Portland in 1805 so Portland celebrated the fact 100 years later with the Lewis and Clark Centennial Exposition, actually a world's fair. Huge numbers of tourists attended the exposition and many decided to move to Portland. The population of the city leaped ahead during the next decade.

With the development of the Columbia River Valley's farming and industry during the 1900s Portland has become even more important as a transportation hub. Today, based on total tonnage, the city is the west coast's largest port.

Portland and its suburbs sprawl 25 miles (40 km) from east to west and 25 miles (40 km) from north to south. The northern border of the city is the Columbia River although Vancouver, Washington, on the north side of the river definitely qualifies as a suburb. The Willamette River runs right through the center of town with the downtown area on the west bank some 10 miles (16 km) from where the Willamette meets the Columbia.

Just west of the city center is a range of hills, much of them is covered by Washington Park and Forest Park. On the far side of the hills are the suburbs of Beaverton and Hillsboro. To the east rises Mt Hood, on the lower slopes is the suburb of Gresham. South of Portland along the Willamette are many more suburbs, among them Milwaukee, Lake Oswego, West Linn, Oregon City, Tualatin, and Tigard.

Highway I-5 runs north and south through the center of Portland. Near downtown I-5 follows the east bank of the Willamette opposite the downtown business district. There is a short ring-road freeway, I-405, that leaves I-5 north of downtown, circles around the west side of the district, and then rejoins I-5 after less than four miles (6 km). There's a much longer ring-road freeway, I-205, around the east side of Portland. It leaves I-5 north of the Columbia River and makes a 36-mile (58-km) loop around the east side of the city before rejoining I-5 at the far southern border of the Portland suburbs. I-84 from the east also ends near the city center, it joins I-5 on the east bank of the Willamette River opposite downtown after having come in through eastern Portland.

Portland has an award-winning public transportation system. The crown jewel is the Max light rail system with extensions running far east to Gresham and west to Hillsboro. Extensions go north to the airport and Expo Center. Portland also has an excellent bus system.

Central Portland has a real parking problem, that means that you will probably want to visit using the public transportation system. Unfortunately the Max light rail system does not serve any of Portland's campgrounds, you'll have to use the bus at least part of the way. Once you reach downtown, however, there is free bus service in the central core and busses and the Max system provide easy access to the places you will probably want to visit.

Portland provides one bus route that is of particular interest to visitors. This is Bus 63, nicknamed **Art, The Cultural Bus**. It provides access to many of Portland's cultural attractions including the **Memorial Coliseum, Oregon Convention Center, Oregon History Center, Oregon Museum of Science and Industry (OMSI), Pacific Northwest College of Art, Portland Art Museum, Portland Center for the Performing Arts, Tom McCall Waterfront Park, River Place shops and marina, Oregon Zoo, Japanese Garden, International Rose Test Garden, World Forestry Center and the Vietnam Memorial**.

Public transportation in central Portland is conveniently centered around the downtown Transit Mall. This is eleven-block-long area between 5th and 6th Avenues is closed to all traffic except public transportation. The Tri-Met (transit) main office is located at Pioneer Courthouse Square.

Once you have arrived in downtown Portland you might want start your tour by making your way to **Pioneer Courthouse Square**. It adjoins the transit mall and is bounded by Broadway, 6th Ave., Morrison, and Yamhill. Here you'll find the Tri-Met transit office and you'll also be in the center of downtown Portland's attractions. You are also in the center of Portland's upscale shopping district. Portland is a popular shopping destination with visitors because Oregon does not have a sales tax.

To find the **Greater Portland Convention and Visitor's Center** you can stroll east toward the river on Salmon St. to the three World Trade Center buildings. Across the street is **Governor Tom McCall Waterfront Park**. It stretches about a mile along the Willamette River and offers an excellent place for a promenade on a nice day. At the south end of the park is the **RiverPlace Marina** development with upscale shops and restaurants.

To really appreciate Portland you should know the names and locations of the various districts. Many are within easy walking distance of downtown, particularly since Portland's blocks are small, some downtown are only 200 feet square.

Four of the districts have their southern borders along W. Burnside Street, an east-west thoroughfare five blocks north of Pioneer Courthouse Square. The farthest west is called the **Northwest District**. Bounded on the west by NW 27th Ave. and on the east by NW 18th Ave. The district is just west of the I-405 ring road but still less than a mile from Pioneer Courthouse Square if you head northwest on Morrison. The whole district is filled with refurbished Victorian homes, many now serving as boutiques, coffee houses, book shops, theaters, pubs, and restaurants. The center of the action is known as **Nob Hill**, NW 21st through 23rd Ave.

The next district to the east and just east of the I-405 ring road is **The Pearl**, bounded on west by NW 15th Ave. and east by NW 8th Ave. It's an up-and-coming district of restored warehouses with art galleries and condominium conversions. Here you'll find one of Portland's best-known stores–**Powell's Books**. Covering a full block at 10th and Burnside this bookstore is the largest independent bookstore in the world.

The next district to the east is **Chinatown**. The Chinatown gates are at 4th and Burnside. Merging in from the east is **Old Town**. Many of the buildings here are from the 1880s, Portland had a fire in 1872 that razed much of this area and resulted in the building of these cast iron-fronted buildings typical of the period.

Now we've followed the districts eastward all the way to the river, there are two more just to the south. **Skidmore Historic District** and **Yamhill Historic District** adjoin the Riverfront Park from Burnside south to about Salmon St. Both are much like the **Old Town** district to the north. A popular attraction in the Skidmore District is the **Saturday Market**, a street crafts market held on Saturday and Sunday all year except in the dead of winter and located just south of Burnside near the Skidmore Fountain.

There are also a couple of interesting shopping districts on the east side of the Willamette. The **Hawthorne District** is along east-west Hawthorne Boulevard from about SE 17th to SE 55th Ave. It has kind of a counter-culture (or maybe 1960s) atmosphere and offers second-hand shops, book stores, cafes and galleries.

More mainstream is the huge **Lloyd Center** shopping mall. It is located about 10 blocks east of the river near the Memorial Coliseum and the Oregon Convention Center. The easiest way to get there is via the Gresham-bound Max.

Antique hunters will want to visit the **Sellwood District**. To reach it start at the Sellwood Bridge, Portland's southernmost. Drive east on Tacoma for 7 blocks to SE 13th and you are there. From Tacoma St. north to about Bybe St. you'll find many antique shops and also some good restaurants.

Portland is known for its city parks, but the best must be huge **Washington Park**. It is located in the hills west of downtown Portland and is easily accessible either by taking the Hillsboro-bound Max and getting off at the zoo stop or from US-26 west of downtown at the Zoo Exit. In the park are a number of Portland's most popular attractions including

VIEW OF PORTLAND WITH MT HOOD AS A BACKDROP FROM WASHINGTON PARK

OREGON

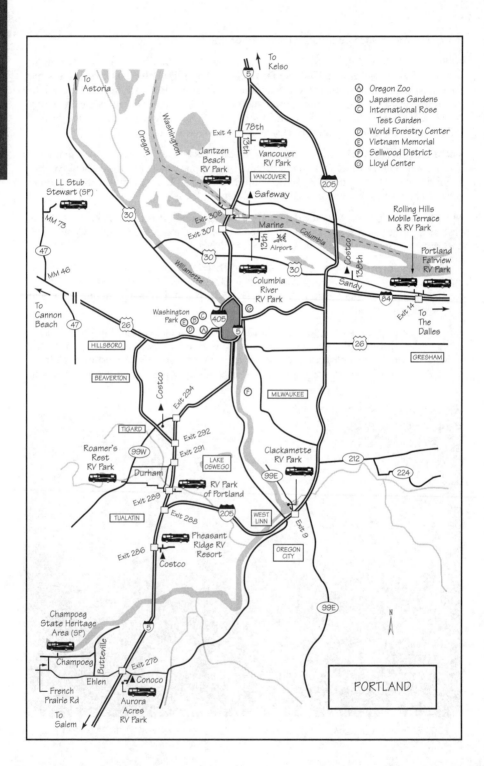

To Kelso

To Astoria

Oregon

Washington

Exit 4   78th
13th
Jantzen Beach RV Park
Vancouver RV Park
VANCOUVER

205

LL Stub Stewart (SP)
MM 73

47

MM 46

30

Safeway

Exit 308
Exit 307
Marine
13th   Airport
Columbia
30

Rolling Hills Mobile Terrace & RV Park

Costco
13.8th
Sandy

Portland Fairview RV Park

84
Exit 14
To The Dalles

Willamette

Columbia River RV Park

To Cannon Beach   47   26

HILLSBORO

Washington Park Ⓔ Ⓑ Ⓒ
Ⓓ Ⓐ   405   G
5

26   GRESHAM

BEAVERTON   Costco   Exit 294

Ⓕ   MILWAUKEE

TIGARD

Roamer's Rest RV Park   99W   Exit 292
Exit 291
LAKE OSWEGO

Durham

Clackamette RV Park   212

99E   224

RV Park of Portland

Exit 289

TUALATIN   Exit 288   205   WEST LINN   Exit 9

Pheasant Ridge RV Resort
Exit 286   Costco   OREGON CITY

Champoeg State Heritage Area (SP)   99E

5

Butteville
Champoeg
Ehlen   Exit 278
Conoco
French Prairie Rd   Aurora Acres RV Park
To Salem

N

Ⓐ Oregon Zoo
Ⓑ Japanese Gardens
Ⓒ International Rose Test Garden
Ⓓ World Forestry Center
Ⓔ Vietnam Memorial
Ⓕ Sellwood District
Ⓖ Lloyd Center

PORTLAND

the **Washington Park Zoo, International Rose Test Garden, Japanese Gardens**, Hoyt **Arboretum**, and the **World Forestry Center**.

Science, and technology buffs will probably enjoy the **Oregon Museum of Science and Industry** (OMSI). Located on the east bank of the Willamette, OMSI covers 18 acres and offers a variety of hands-on technology-inspired exhibits including a decommissioned submarine, an Omnimax theater, a giant walk-through heart, a shaking earthquake room, and even the bridge of the Starship Enterprise.

Portland Campgrounds

● **PORTLAND FAIRVIEW RV PARK** *(Open All Year)*
Reservations: (877) 777-1047
Information: (503) 661-1047,
   info@portlandfairviewrv.com,
   www.portlandfairviewrv.com
Location: Portland

GPS Location: 45.54333 N, 122.44389 W, 100 Ft

407 Sites – This is a huge and modern big-rig RV park on the east side of Portland. If you are arriving on I-84 from the east access to the campground is very convenient. The park has over 400 sites, all have full hookups, many are large pull-thrus to 60 feet. Parking is on paved pads with patios separated by well-tended grass. Sites are arranged on several terraces sloping shallowly to the north toward the Columbia River. Amenities include nice restrooms, swimming pool, recreation room, exercise room playground, and laundry. A small market is nearby. To use public transportation to get to downtown Portland you take a bus from just outside the campground. To reach the campground take Exit 14 from I-84 east of Portland. Drive north one-quarter mile (.4 km) to Sandy Boulevard, turn right, and you'll see the campground on your left almost immediately.

● **ROLLING HILLS MOBILE TERRACE AND RV PARK**
   (Open All Year)
Res and Info: (503) 666-7282
Location: Portland

GPS Location: 45.54556 N, 122.45472 W, 100 Ft

137 Sites – This is another choice for camping on the east side of Portland. This campground is just down the street from the Portland Fairview. It's an older campground with quite a few long-term residents but the services are adequate and the traveler sites are mostly pull-thrus to about 50 feet. There is a swimming pool here too. Take Exit 14 from I-84 east of Portland and travel north a quarter-mile to Sandy Boulevard. Turn left and you'll see the campground entrance on the right in .3 mile (.5 km).

● **COLUMBIA RIVER RV PARK** *(Open All Year)*
Res and Info: (503) 285-1515; (888) 366-7725:
   manager@columbiariverrv.com,
   www.columbiariverrv.com
Location: Portland

GPS Location: 45.59974 N, 122.65248 W, Near Sea Level

150 Sites – This modern big rig campground is very convenient if you're arriving in Portland from the north. It has paved pull-thrus and back-ins to 60 feet, all with full hookups.

Take Exit 307 and drive east for 1.5 mile (2.4 km) on Marine Dr. Turn right on 13th and the campground entrance is on your right.

● **VANCOUVER RV PARK** *(Open All Year)*
   Reservations: (877) 756-2972
   Information: (360) 695-1158, vancouverrv@juno.com,
                   www.vancouverrvparks.com
   Location: Vancouver, WA

   GPS Location: 45.67722 N, 122.65861 W, 100 Ft

152 Sites – This campground is north of the Columbia in Vancouver, Washington. It's just off the I-5 freeway and make a handy campground for visits to Portland. It's a modern big-rig park with back-in and pull-thru sites to 55 feet. Take Exit 4 from I-5. Drive east on NE 78th Street for two blocks and turn south on NE 13th Ave. The campground is on the left about halfway down the block.

● **JANTZEN BEACH RV PARK** *(Open All Year)*
   Reservations: (800) 443-7248
   Information: (503) 289-7626, www.jantzenbeachrv.com
   Location: Portland

   GPS Location: 45.61611 N, 122.68583 W, Near Sea Level

169 Sites – This campground is one of the closest to central Portland and it is an easy campground to reach if you are approaching from the north. It is located on Hayden Island which is an island in the Columbia River crossed by I-5 as it enters Portland. Sites here are back-ins and pull-thrus to 60 feet. Amenities include a swimming pool in the summer. Near the campground is a large shopping center but actually the area is a comparatively quiet retreat considering how close it is to central Portland. Quiet, except that like all RV parks along the Columbia through Portland there's lots of aircraft noise from jets approaching and departing Portland International. Bus transportation is available to downtown from near the campground. Take Exit 308 which is marked Jantzen Beach, then follow the campground signs 1/2 mile (.8 km) on Hayden Island Drive to the west of the freeway on the north bank of the island.

○ **CLACKAMETTE RV PARK** *(Open All Year)*
   Information: (503) 496-1201,
                   http://www.orcity.org/parksandrecreation/
   clackamette-park-rv-park
   Location: Portland

   GPS Location: 45.37000 N, 122.60306 W, Near Sea Level

35 Sites – This city park has RV camping sites along the Willamette River just north of where I-205 crosses near Oregon City. It's a gravel lot with back-ins and pull-thrus to 40 feet. There is a dump station, the fee is $5. Take Exit 9 from I-205. Drive north on SR-99E for only .3 mile (.5 km), the campground entrance is on the left.

● **RV PARK OF PORTLAND** *(Open All Year)*
   Reservations: (800) 856-2066
   Information: (503) 692-0225,
                   office@rvparkofportland.com
                   www.rvparkofportland.com
   Location: Portland

   GPS Location: 45.38306 N, 122.74500 W, 100 Ft

112 Sites – This is an older park but in good condition. The park has quite a few long-term residents but it's well managed and maintained and OK for travelers. Sites are pull-thrus, most are 60 feet long but access is tight. Take Exit 289 from I-5 in Tualatin, at the southern edge of Portland. Drive east on SW Nyberg Rd for .3 mile (.5 km), the campground is on the left.

● **PHEASANT RIDGE RV RESORT** *(Open All Year)*
　　Res and Info: (800) 532-7829, (503) 682-7829
　　　　　　　　www.pheasantridge.com,
　　　　　　　　service@pheasantridge.com
　　Location: Portland

　　GPS Location: 45.33583 N, 122.76194 W, 200 Ft

130 sites – This is a big rig park with large pull-thrus and back-ins to 60 feet and lots of modern amenities including an indoor pool. It's also close to shopping including Costco and Camping World. Take Exit 286 and drive east for .3 mile (.5 km) on SW Elligsen Rd, the campground entrance is on the left.

● **ROAMER'S REST RV PARK** *(Open All Year)*
　　Reservations: (877) 478-7275
　　Information: (503) 692-6350, info@roamersrestrvpark.com,
　　　　　　　　www.roamersrestrvpark.com
　　Location: Portland

　　GPS Location: 45.39250 N, 122.80056 W, 100 Ft

93 Sites – This excellent modern campground is a popular place to stay for folks spending some time in Portland. The compact site slopes steeply to the Tualatin River. Restrooms are nice, there are individual rooms with toilet, shower and sink. Sites here vary but they are paved off paved roads, separated by nice grass, and there are quite a few pull-thrus to 60 feet and longer. Reach the campground most easily by taking Exit 291 from I-5. Drive southwest on Carman Dr. to join SW Upper Boones Ferry Rd heading south. At .5 mile (.8 km) from the freeway turn right on SW Durham Road and follow Durham west for 2.2 miles (3.5 km) to SR-99W (SW Pacific Hwy). Turn left and in .8 mile (1.3 km) you'll see the campground entrance on the right.

● **AURORA ACRES RV PARK** *(Open All Year)*
　　Res and Info: (503) 678-2646,
　　　　　　　　reservations@AuroraAcresRV.com
　　　　　　　　www.auroraacresrv.com,
　　Location: Portland, I-5 Exit 278
　　GPS Location: 45.23194 N, 122.80722 W, 100 Ft

130 Sites – The Aurora Acres is a tidy campground that is very conveniently located just off I-5 in an uncongested area. It's a good stop if you're approaching Portland during the rush hour or if you just don't want to deal with the city until tomorrow. Wi-Fi doesn't reach the sites, just the clubhouse and office. They have pull-thrus to 60 feet and 40-foot back-ins. There's a seasonal swimming pool and a recreation hall. Take Exit 278 and drive east, the campground is on the right in about 100 yards.

☐ **L.L. STUB STEWART STATE PARK** *(Open All Year)*
Reservations: www.reserveamerica.com, (800) 452-5687
Information: (503) 324-0606, (800) 551-6949,
              www.oregonstateparks.org
Location: 30 Miles (48 Km) E of Portland

GPS Location: 45.73639 N, 123.19222 W, 900 Ft

131 Sites – This is Oregon's first new full service state campground in 30 years. It's bound to be popular since it's so close to Portland. RV sites are back-ins to 60 feet and with full hookups off two paved loop roads. There are also tent sites as well as hike-in primitive campsites, a cabin area, and a horse camp. Unlike most Oregon parks this one has very few trees in the camping area, that's good if you brought along your TV satellite antenna. Wi-Fi is available at the welcome center. The park has about 15 miles of trails for non-motorized use. Easiest access from Portland is to drive west on US-26. If you start at I-405 take Exit 1 and drive 28 mile (45 km) west. Turn right on SR-47 near Mile 45.5 following signs for Vernonia and the park entrance is on the right in another 4 miles (6 km). Reservations are highly recommended during weekends throughout the year.

☐ **CHAMPOEG STATE HERITAGE AREA** *(Open All Year)*
Reservations: www.reserveamerica.com, (800) 452-5687
Information: (503) 678-1251, Ext. 225, (800) 551-6949,
              www.oregonstateparks.org
Location: 20 Miles (32 Km) S of Portland

GPS Location: 45.24972 N, 122.88000 W, Near Sea Level

82 Sites – Champoeg is a historical park, it is set in one of the first locations settled in the Willamette Valley. It's about 6 miles (10 km) from I-5 but it's still a handy place to stop, particularly if you're approaching Portland from the south and just don't want to drive in to the city in the evening traffic. Sites here vary but many are back-ins exceeding 55 feet. There are also 10 long pull-thrus, and a hiker-biker tent camp., From I-5 south of Portland take Exit 278. Drive west on Ehlen Rd. NE for 1.6 mile (2.6 km), then turn right on Butteville Rd NE. After another 1.7 mile (2.7 km) turn left on Champoeg Road NE and you'll see the campground entrance on the right in another 2.8 mile (4.5 km).

PRINEVILLE

Prineville (population 9,000) is located about 17 miles (27 km) east of Bend, an easy drive on SR-126. One attraction for campers in the Prineville area is the Prineville Reservoir, about 16 miles (26 km) south of town. Here the Crooked River and Bowman Dam form a 3,030 acre lake that is popular for fishing, swimming, and boating of all kinds. Anglers will find rainbows as well as bass and crappie in the lake. Three of the RV parks listed below are on the shores of the reservoir, one is in town.

Another nearby attraction is the Lower Crooked River Recreation Area running northward from the Bowman Dam on the Prineville Reservoir through a deep basalt canyon. The Crooked River is a National Wild and Scenic River. This section is known for its rainbow trout fly fishing and wonderful scenery. There are 9 Bureau of Land Management Campgrounds along the river, all are described below.

OREGON

Prineville Campgrounds

○ **CROOK COUNTY RV PARK** *(Open All Year)*
Reservations: (800) 609-2599
Information: (541) 447-2599,
ccrvpark@crestviewcable.com,
www.prineville-crookcounty.org
Location: Prineville

GPS Location: 44.29306 N, 120.84556 W, 2,800 Ft

81 Sites – The town of Prineville hosts a very nice big-rig campground that is actually a county park. It is right next to the county fairgrounds. The managers live on site. Many sites are 65-foot pull-thrus with full hookups including cable. There is also a grassy tent-camping area. In central Prineville drive south on South Main. The campground is on your left in .7 mile (1.1 km).

● **SUN ROCKS RV RESORT** *(Open All Year)*
Res and Info: (541) 447-6540,
sunrocksrv@coinet.com,
www.sunrocksrvresort.com
Location: 12 Miles (19 Km) South of Prineville

GPS Location: 44.16833 N, 120.72236 W, 3,500 Ft

95 Sites – This RV park is located just two miles from the Prineville Reservoir. Although it's not on the lake it does have a solar-heated pool and a spa. Campfires are in community

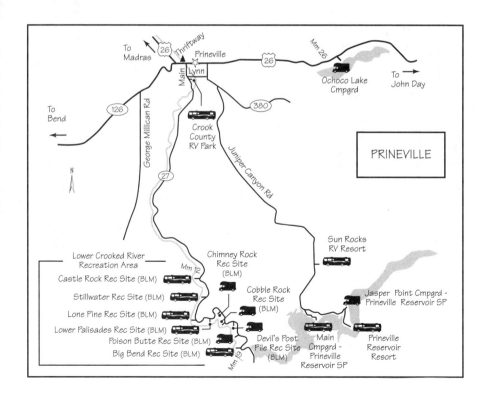

fire pits. About 40 of the sites here are back-ins or pull-thrus to 75 feet. The rest are large tent sites between the hookup sites and the road. From Prineville drive south on SR-380 (Combs Flat Rd.) for 1.3 miles (2.1 km). Then turn right on SE Juniper Canyon Road and follow the road 10.7 miles (17.3 km) to the campground, the entrance is on the left.

☐ **PRINEVILLE RESERVOIR – MAIN CAMPGROUND STATE PARK** *(Open All Year)*

Reservations: www.reserveamerica.com, (800) 452-5687
Information: (541) 447-4363, (800) 551-6949, www.oregonstateparks.org
Location: 14 Miles (23 Km) S of Prineville

GPS Location: 44.13056 N, 120.72194 W, 3,200 Ft

67 Sites – This is one of two campgrounds at Prineville Reservoir State Park. This is the larger of the two and has sites with sewer, the other does not. Sites here aren't as long as at many Oregon state campgrounds but many are over 40 feet and a couple reach 50 feet. They're all back-in sites. The lakeside campground is popular for water sports and has boat ramp, boat moorages in summer, fishing pier, and swimming area. There's a dump station at Jasper Point Campground, see below. From Prineville drive south on SR-380 (Combs Flat Rd.) for 1.3 miles (2.1 km). Then turn right on SE Juniper Canyon Road and follow the road to the campground entrance in another 13 miles (21 km).

☐ **PRINEVILLE RESERVOIR – JASPER POINT CAMPGROUND STATE PARK** *(Open May 1 to Sept 30)*

Information: (541) 447-4363, (800) 551-6949, www.oregonstateparks.org
Location: 16 Miles (26 Km) S of Prineville

GPS Location: 44.13500 N, 120.69472 W, 3,200 Ft

30 Sites – This is the second Prineville Reservoir State Park campground. It's the smaller of the two and has fewer facilities, but it has the only dump station in the park. It also has a boat launch. Some people swim along the small rocky beach next to the boat launch, but most people use it as a place to beach their boats and other watercraft. Sites here are smaller than at the main campground, but they're better separated and some overlook the water. They're suitable for RVs to about 35 feet, some present leveling problems since they're not quite flat. To reach the campground continue past the entrance to the main campground for another 2.1 miles (3.4 km).

● **PRINEVILLE RESERVOIR RESORT**
    (Open May 15 to Labor Day – Varies)
Res and Info: (541) 447-7468, www.prinevillereservoirresort.com
Location: 17 Miles (27 Km) S of Prineville

GPS Location: 44.12333 N, 120.68750 W, 3,200 Ft

70 Sites – This is a private resort located on the shore of Prineville Reservoir. Sites vary in size but 40-foot RVs can be accommodated, they have electricity and water hookups Most sites are 15 amp although there are a few located back from the water with 30 amps. Camping is on an open dirt lot that gradually slopes down to the shore of the lake. Many sites are along the beach. There's a marina here with a boat ramp, boat rentals, and marine gas sales as well as a store and cafe. To reach the resort continue on past the Jasper Point Campground for another 1.1 miles (1.8 km) to the end of the road.

○ **OCHOCO LAKE CAMPGROUND** *(Open April 1 to Oct 31 – Varies)*
Information: (541) 447-1209
Location: 6 Miles (10 km) E of Prineville

GPS Location: 44.30524 N, 120.70084 W, 3,100 Ft

22 Sites – This Crook County campground is located east of town
on Ochoco Lake. Sites are back-ins to 45 feet, some are paved and
some gravel. Maneuvering room is limited, the campground is difficult for RVs over 40
feet. Restrooms have flush toilets and showers and there is a boat ramp and a dock. From
Prineville drive east on Hwy 26 for 6 miles (10 km) to the lake.

■ **CASTLE ROCK RECREATION SITE** *(Open All Year)*
Information: (541) 416-6700
Location: 11 Miles (18 Km) South of Prineville

GPS Location: 44.15817 N, 120.83412 W, 2,900 Ft

6 Sites – This is a BLM campground in the Lower Crooked River Recreation Area. The
sites are arranged near the river off an access road with a turnaround loop at the end. Two
large sites will take RVs to 40 feet, the rest are small. Picnic tables, fire pits, vault toilets
and trash service are provided. There is no potable water. No fee is charged from November 1 to March 31 but the campground remains open. From the center of Prineville at
3rd and Main Street drive south on Main Street which is also Hwy 27. Follow the paved
highway for 12.2 miles (19.7 km) to the campground, it's on the right.

■ **STILLWATER RECREATION SITE** *(Open All Year)*
Information: (541) 416-6700
Location: 13 Miles (21 Km) South of Prineville

GPS Location: 44.14505 N, 120.82926 W, 3,000 Ft

11 Sites – This is a BLM campground in the Lower Crooked River Recreation Area. The
sites are arranged near the river with a loop to the right with sites 1 to 6 and a stub road to
the left with the rest. There are a few long back-ins for RVs to 40 feet but most sites are
small. There's quite a bit of maneuvering room for this area. Picnic tables, fire pits, vault
toilets and trash service are provided. There is no potable water. No fee is charged from
November 1 to March 31 but the campground remains open. From the center of Prineville at 3rd and Main Street drive south on Main Street which is also Hwy 27. Follow the
paved highway for 13.4 miles (21.6 km) to the campground, it's on the right.

■ **LONE PINE RECREATION SITE** *(Open All Year)*
Information: (541) 416-6700
Location: 14 Miles (23 Km) S of Prineville

GPS Location: 44.12945 N, 120.83714 W, 3,000 Ft

6 Sites – This is a BLM campground in the Lower Crooked River Recreation Area. The
sites are arranged near the river off a stub road with a tight turnaround circle at the end. A
couple of the sites will take any size RV but maneuvering room is limited and parking difficult for larger units. Picnic tables, fire pits, vault toilets and trash service are provided.
There is no potable water. No fee is charged from November 1 to March 31 but the campground remains open. From the center of Prineville at 3rd and Main Street drive south on
Main Street which is also Hwy 27. Follow the paved highway for 14.6 miles (23.5 km) to
the campground, it's on the right.

LOWER PALISADES RECREATION SITE *(Open All Year)*
Information: (541) 416-6700
Location: 15 Miles (24 Km) S of Prineville

GPS Location: 44.13096 N, 120.82406 W, 3,000 Ft

14 Sites – This is a BLM campground in the Lower Crooked River Recreation Area. The sites are arranged near the river off two stub roads. There's also one site near the highway which is some distance above and behind the campground. Several sites here are large pull-thrus, this may be the best of the Recreation Area campgrounds for large RVs. Despite this, careful maneuvering is required by large rigs because access is somewhat cramped. Picnic tables, fire pits, vault toilets and trash service are provided. There is no potable water. No fee is charged from November 1 to March 31 but the campground remains open. From the center of Prineville at 3rd and Main Street drive south on Main Street which is also Hwy 27. Follow the paved highway for 15.4 miles (24.8 km) to the campground, it's on the right.

CHIMNEY ROCK RECREATION SITE *(Open All Year)*
Information: (541) 416-6700
Location: 16 Miles (26 Km) S of Prineville

GPS Location: 44.13539 N, 120.81436 W, 3,000 Ft

16 Sites – This is a BLM campground in the Lower Crooked River Recreation Area. The sites are arranged near the river off two stub roads, one to the right and one to the left. This campground really seems to be intended as a tent campground. Despite this RVs can parallel park next to many of the sites so it works for large rigs. There's pretty good maneuvering room too with wide access roads. There's a hand water pump making this the only one of the campgrounds in the Recreation Area with potable water. Picnic tables, fire pits, vault toilets and trash service are provided. The popular Chimney Rock Trail leaves the road just across the highway. No fee is charged from November 1 to March 31 but the campground remains open. From the center of Prineville at 3rd and Main Street drive south on Main Street which is also Hwy 27. Follow the paved highway for 16.4 miles (26.4 km) to the campground, it's on the right.

COBBLE ROCK RECREATION SITE *(Open All Year)*
Information: (541) 416-6700
Location: 16 Miles (26 Km) S of Prineville

GPS Location: 44.12787 N, 120.81037 W, 3,000 Ft

14 Sites – This is a BLM campground in the Lower Crooked River Recreation Area. The sites are arranged near the river off a narrow loop road that is difficult to negotiate with large rigs. Although some sites reach 40 feet this campground is best for smaller RVs. Picnic tables, fire pits, vault toilets and trash service are provided. No fee is charged from November 1 to March 31 but the campground remains open. From the center of Prineville at 3rd and Main Street drive south on Main Street which is also Hwy 27. Follow the paved highway for 17.0 miles (27.4 km) to the campground, it's on the right.

DEVIL'S POST PILE RECREATION SITE *(Open All Year)*
Information: (541) 416-6700
Location: 17 Miles (27 Km) S of Prineville

GPS Location: 44.12887 N, 120.80065 W, 3,000 Ft

7 Sites – This is a BLM campground in the Lower Crooked River Recreation Area. The

irregular sites are arranged near the river off a stub road. Some sites to 40 feet but little maneuvering room, this campground is best for smaller rigs. Picnic tables, fire pits, vault toilets and trash service are provided. No fee is charged from November 1 to March 31 but the campground remains open. From the center of Prineville at 3rd and Main Street drive south on Main Street which is also Hwy 27. Follow the paved highway for 17.6 miles (28.4 km) to the campground, it's on the right.

■ **POISON BUTTE RECREATION SITE** *(Open All Year)*
   Information: (541) 416-6700
   Location: 17 Miles (27 Km) S of Prineville

   GPS Location: 44.11947 N, 120.79742 W, 3,000 Ft

5 Sites – This is a BLM campground in the Lower Crooked River Recreation Area. The sites are small and access difficult, the campground is best for RVs not exceeding 30 feet. Picnic tables, fire pits, vault toilets and trash service are provided. No fee is charged from November 1 to March 31 but the campground remains open. From the center of Prineville at 3rd and Main Street drive south on Main Street which is also Hwy 27. Follow the paved highway for 18.2 miles (29.3 km) to the campground, it's on the right.

■ **BIG BEND RECREATION SITE** *(Open All Year)*
   Information: (541) 416-6700
   Location: 18 Miles (29 Km) S of Prineville

   GPS Location: 44.11218 N, 120.79395 W, 3,100 Ft

15 Sites – This is a BLM campground in the Lower Crooked River Recreation Area. Many sites overlook the river. This campground has been upgraded so that there is a paved handicap site. There are also three walk-in tent sites. Several sites will take large RVs and maneuvering room is pretty good. Picnic tables, fire pits, vault toilets and trash service are provided. No fee is charged from November 1 to March 31 but the campground remains open. From the center of Prineville at 3rd and Main Street drive south on Main Street which is also Hwy 27. Follow the paved highway for 18.9 miles (30.4 km) to the campground, it's on the right.

REDMOND AND SISTERS

Redmond (population 26,000), is the northernmost of the big towns along US-97 as it passes along the east side of the Cascades through Oregon. Along with Bend the city forms the commercial nucleus of the region.

Sisters (population 1,000) is one of those theme towns, it may remind you of Leavenworth or Winthrop in Washington. It's located just 19 miles (31 km) west of Redmond. Sisters is a cute little place with a number of restaurants, shops, and art galleries. Plan to spend an hour or two wandering around.

Popular events in Sisters include the **Sisters Rodeo** in early June and the **Sisters Quilt Show** over the Fourth of July weekend.

These towns serve as a good base for exploring some beautiful countryside. The town of Bend is only 21 highway miles (34 km) south of Redmond so you might consider some of the same sights covered in the *Bend and La Pine* section. The attractions listed in this book under *Camp Sherman and the Metolius River*, the *Cascade Lakes Highway*, and *Newberry National Volcanic Monument* are also near.

A popular drive from Sisters is the **McKenzie-Santiam Pass Loop**. This 82 mile (132 km) loop is a designated a National Forest Scenic Byway. The loop follows SR-242 westward from Sisters and across **McKenzie Pass**. There you'll find the **Dee Wright Observatory**, built of lava and offering an easy wheelchair-accessible trail through a lava flow. After the pass the road descends to the intersection with SR-126. Turn north and follow this highway up the McKenzie River Valley. See our *West Cascades Scenic Byway* section for information about the campgrounds and sights in the McKenzie River Valley. Watch for signs for **Koosah and Sahalie Falls**, both are easily accessible. You'll come to another intersection, this time US-20. Turn east here and it will take you over **Santiam Pass** and past the Metolius River Recreation Area back to Sisters. The first portion of the route, SR-242, is narrow and steep and not suitable for large RVs, that's why it is listed here only as a day trip. Also, snow closes this portion of the loop from November until late June.

Redmond and Sisters Campgrounds

● **CROOKED RIVER RANCH RV PARK**
(Open All Year)
Reservations: (800) 841-0563
Information: (541) 923-1441,
rvpark@crookedriverranch.com,
www.crookedriverranch.com
Location: 13 Miles (21 Km) N of Bend

GPS Location: 44.42361 N, 121.23833 W, 2,600 Ft

101 Sites – The Crooked River Ranch RV Park is operated as part of this large housing development. The campground sits in a wide canyon, next door is a nice golf course and there's a large swimming pool. Sites here include pull-thrus and back-ins to 60 feet as well as good tent sites. To reach the campground turn west on NW Lower Bridge Road from US–97 some 4 miles (6.5 km) north of Redmond and on the northern edge of the small town of Terrebonne. Drive west for 2.2 miles (3.5 km) and turn right on NW 43rd St. Follow this road north as it curves through the development and down into the canyon, you'll see the campground sign at 5.3 miles (8.5 km) from the turn onto NW 43rd.

● **RIVER RIM RV PARK** *(Open All Year)*
Res and Info: (541) 923-7239, riverrimrv@prodigy.net
Location: 13 Miles (21 Km) N of Bend

GPS Location: 44.43389 N, 121.24472 W, 2,500 Ft

24 Sites – This is a smaller RV park located in the canyon not far from the Crooked River Ranch RV Park. This one is not owned by the homeowner's association and has few amenities, but it's still popular. Sites here will take larger RVs, many are back-ins to about 60 feet but there are also some pull-thrus. To reach this campground follow the directions for Crooked River Ranch RV Park above, the entrance for the River Rim is .4 miles (.6 km) beyond that for the Crooked River.

○ **REDMOND EXPO CENTER RV PARK** *(Open All Year)*
Res and Info: (541) 548-2711, www.expo.deschutes.org
Location: 2 Miles (3 Km) S of Redmond

GPS Location: 44.23333 N, 121.18667 W, 3,000 Ft

116 Sites – The Redmond Expo Center, used by Affin-

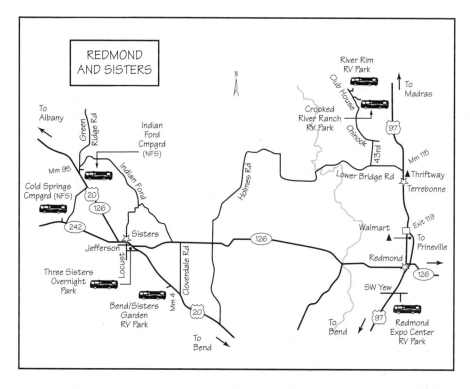

REDMOND AND SISTERS

ity and FMCA for some of their big national rallies, has a campground. It is available to individual campers when there are no events in progress requiring its use. It's a first class-big rig park with paved drives and parking as well as a central building with restrooms, showers, and a laundry. Sites are pull-thrus to 55 feet and back-ins to 40 feet with full hookups as well as ten walk-in sites for tents with pitching on grass. Raised grills are provided as are picnic tables. The fairgrounds are located just south of Redmond on the east side of US-97. From US-97 take the SW Yew Ave. and head east. In .3 mile (.5 km) turn right on SW 19th Street (it's the first right after the tracks) and watch for the campground on the left.

■ **INDIAN FORD CAMPGROUND** *(Open May 12 to Oct 10 – Varies)*
Information: (541) 549-7700, www.hoodoo.com
Location: 5 Miles (8 Km) NW of Sisters

GPS Location: 44.35833 N, 121.61111 W, 3,200 Ft

25 Sites – Indian Ford Deschutes National Forest Campground has a handy location just off SR-20 just 5 miles (8 km) northwest of Sisters. Although it's right next to the highway it's popular because it's so convenient to Sisters. It's set in tall ponderosa pines, some sites reach 50 feet and there is plenty of room to maneuver. There is no potable water at this campground.

■ **COLD SPRINGS CAMPGROUND** *(Open May 12 to Oct 10 – Varies)*
Information: (541) 549-7700, www.hoodoo.com
Location: 4 Miles (6.5 Km) W of Sisters

GPS Location: 44.31000 N, 121.63000 W, 3,400 Ft

23 Sites – This Deschutes National Forest campground sits 4 miles (6 km) west of Sisters just off SR-242. It is very popular with birders. Sites are located off a long loop road that winds through big trees. Some are pull-thrus, many of these and also many of the back-ins reach 45 feet. There is a hand pump for water.

○ **THREE SISTERS OVERNIGHT PARK**
   (Open April 8 to Nov 1 – Varies)
   Information: (541) 323-5220, www.ci.sisters.or.us/parks.html
   Location: Sisters

   GPS Location: 44.28750 N, 121.54194 W, 3,100 Ft

60 Sites – This municipal campground is located on the eastern approaches to Sisters just south of US-20. It has gravel back-in RV sites, some exceeding 60 feet, with either full-hookups or no hookups. Seven pull-thrus are available. There are also sites for tents with pitching on grass. This is a fairly open campground with scattered tall pines. There is a dump station which requires a separate payment. The campground is close enough for walking in to town, less than a half mile (.8 km) distant. Easiest access is off South Locust Street.

● **BEND/SISTERS GARDEN RV RESORT**
   (Open All Year)

   Reservations: (888) 503-3588,
   www.bendsistersgardenrv.com
   Information: (541) 516-3036,
   bendsistersgardenrv@gmail.com
   Location: 4 Miles (6.5 Km) SE of Sisters

   GPS Location: 44.25028 N, 121.48861 W, 3,200 Ft

96 Sites – This resort stands out as one of nicest big-rig parks in the Northwest. All roads and sites are paved and have patios, picnic tables, and fire pits. Sites are back-ins and pull-thrus to 70 feet, all have full hookups. They are well spaced with grass separating them with scattered trees providing quite a bit of shade. The whole RV park is a garden with lots of flowers in season and large green areas. Amenities include pool, spa, store, playground, meeting building, and a long dog walk. The resort is on the south side of US-20 about 4 miles (6.5 km) southeast of Sisters.

REEDSPORT AND THE OREGON DUNES

For about 47 miles (76 km) between Florence and Coos Bay the highway passes inland of a large area of shifting sand dunes. Much of the area is incorporated into the **Oregon Dunes National Recreation Area**. Many visitors come here to roar across the dunes on sand buggies, it can be a lot of fun. Others enjoy hiking through sections closed to motorized vehicles or visit the beaches. If you didn't bring your own sand buggy they can easily be rented in the area.

The official center of the dunes area is **Reedsport** at Mile 211.5 of U.S. 101, a town of about 5,000 near the mouth of the Umpqua River, the largest river between the Columbia and the Sacramento. Reedsport is the location of the **Oregon Dunes National Recreation Area Visitor Center**. SR-38 joins US-101 here, if you drive 3 miles (5 km) east you'll reach the **Dean Creek Elk Viewing Area**, a refuge where you can usually see and photograph elk.

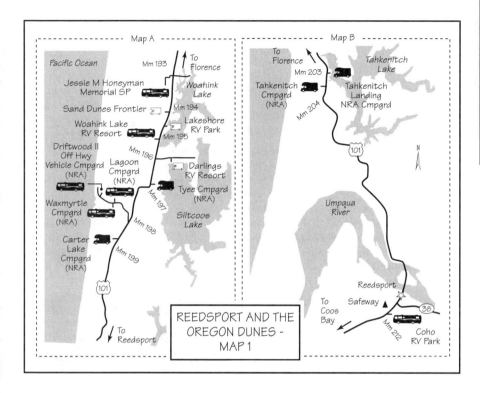

REEDSPORT AND THE
OREGON DUNES -
MAP 1

About 10 miles (16 km) north of Reedsport is the **Oregon Dunes Overlook** at Mile 200.8. Boardwalks and ramps make it easy to see and understand the dunes. As you continue north on U.S. 101 you'll pass Jessie M Honeyman State Park (see camping below), and arrive at Florence at Mile 191.

One of the centers for RVing in this area is Winchester Bay about three miles (5 km) south of Reedsport. Both Reedsport and Winchester Bay are actually located on the Umpqua River but Winchester Bay is closer to the mouth. You'll find 7 campgrounds below that are located in this area. There is a very nice harbor here as well as access to ATV areas in the dunes to the south. Watch for the road west to **Umpqua Lighthouse State Park** south of Reedsport near Mile 217 and just south of Winchester Bay. There is also access directly from Winchester Bay. The lighthouse overlooks the south shore of the mouth of the Umpqua River. This is also the location of the **Umpqua River Whale Watching Station**, whales are often sighted in the estuary.

Sand dunes dominate this coast. Access and use is restricted and regulated by the Oregon Dunes Recreation Area, administered as part of the Siuslaw National Forest. Some areas allow all terrain vehicle (ATV) use, others are just for hikers.

The campgrounds below are listed from north to south.

Reedsport and the Oregon Dunes Campgrounds

☐ **JESSIE M HONEYMAN MEMORIAL STATE PARK**
(Open All Year)
Reservations: www.reserveamerica.com, (800) 452-5687
Information: (541) 997-3641, (800) 551-6949,
www.oregonstateparks.org
Location: 3 Miles (5 Km) S of Florence

GPS Location: 43.92556 N, 124.11167 W, 200 Ft

355 Sites – Honeyman is a beach campground but the
beach here is on Cleawox Lake, not the ocean. Sand dunes separate the campground from the ocean and you can hike through them to reach the coast some two miles (3 km) distant. There's another day-use area on much larger Woahink Lake which is across the highway. It has a boat ramp. In summer Honeyman has no access for ATV riders to the dunes, but in winter from October 1 to April 30 access is allowed from one loop. This is Oregon's second largest state campground. Sites are back-ins to 55 feet, a large number of them are longer than 40 feet. The H loop is best for RVs with slide-outs. The entrance to Honeyman is directly off US-101 at Mile 193.5, about 2.6 miles (4.2 km) south of the Florence bridge.

● **WOAHINK LAKE RV RESORT** *(Open All Year)*
Res and Info: (800) 659-6454, (541) 997-6454,
www.woahinklakerv.com
Location: 4 Miles (7 Km) S of Florence

GPS Location: 43.90333 N, 124.11611 W, Near Sea Level

75 Sites – This is a modern family-run commercial
campground. The campground has access at the back to the dunes so it is a good place to stay if you have your own buggy. It also has its own dock on Woahink Lake across the highway from the campground. Sites are back-ins and pull-thrus to 65 feet. There is a community fire pit. The campground entrance is on the west side of US-101 near Mile 195.5, about 4.3 miles (6.9 km) south of the Florence bridge.

■ **TYEE CAMPGROUND** *(Open May 1 to Sept 30 – Varies)*
Reservations: www.recreation.gov, (877) 444-6777
Information: (541) 750-7000
Location: 6 Miles (10 Km) S of Florence

GPS Location: 43.88417 N, 124.12056 W, 100 Ft

14 Sites – Tyee is an old Oregon Dunes National Recreation Area campground with vehicle accessible sites suitable only for small rigs like cars and vans with lengths to 20 feet. The attraction at the campground is its boat launch onto little Siltcoos River, a popular canoe trail and fishing location. The entrance to the campground is at Mile 196.8, about 5.6 miles (9.0 km) south of the Florence bridge.

■ **DRIFTWOOD II OFF HIGHWAY VEHICLE**
CAMPGROUND *(Open All Year)*

Reservations: www.recreation.gov, (877) 444-6777
Information: (541) 750-7000
Location: 8 Miles (13 Km) S of Florence

GPS Location: 43.88083 N, 124.14806 W, Near Sea Level

OREGON

67 Sites – Driftwood II Oregon Dunes NRA Campground is primarily an ATV camp-ground. Sites are back-ins to 40 feet in five large paved lots. ATVers have direct access to the dunes. Picnic tables and fire pits adjoin the lots. The modern restrooms here even have showers. To reach the campground turn west on the paved road marked Siltcoos Recreation Area. It leaves US-101 near Mile 198, about 6.8 miles (11.0 km) south of the Florence bridge. Driftwood II is the last of three campgrounds along the road, it is 1.2 mile (1.9 km) from US-101.

■ **WAXMYRTLE CAMPGROUND** *(Open June 6 to Oct 3 – Varies)*
   Reservations: www.recreation.gov, (877) 444-6777
   Information: (541) 750-7000
   Location: 8 Miles (13 Km) S of Florence

          GPS Location: 43.87694 N, 124.14333 W, Near Sea Level

55 Sites – This Oregon Dunes NRA campground is extremely attractive, almost like a garden. Waxmyrtle Beach Trail leaves from the entrance of the campground and there is also access to Stagecoach Trailhead. Sites are back-ins and pull-thrus to 70 feet. To reach the campground turn west on the paved road marked Siltcoos Recreation Area. It leaves US-101 near Mile 198, about 6.8 miles (11.0 km) south of the Florence bridge. Waxmyrtle is one of two campgrounds with entrances on opposite sides of the road about .8 mile (1.3 km) from the highway. It's the one on the left.

■ **LAGOON CAMPGROUND** *(Open May 1 to Sept 30 - Varies)*
   Reservations: www.recreation.gov, (877) 444-6777
   Information: (541) 750-7000
   Location: 8 Miles (13 Km) S of Florence

          GPS Location: 43.87861 N, 124.14222 W, Near Sea Level

39 Sites – Located just across the road from Waxmyrtle Campground, this Oregon Dunes NRA campground is also very nice. Sites are back-ins and pull-thrus to 70 feet. To reach the campground turn west on the paved road marked Siltcoos Recreation Area. It leaves US-101 near Mile 198, about 6.8 miles (11.0 km) south of the Florence bridge. The campground entrance is on the right about .8 miles (1.3 km) from the highway.

■ **CARTER LAKE CAMPGROUND** *(Open May 1 to Sept 30 – Varies)*
   Reservations: www.recreation.gov, (877) 444-6777
   Information: (541) 750-7000
   Location: 8 Miles (13 Km) S of Florence

          GPS Location: 43.86083 N, 124.14167 W, Near Sea Level

23 Sites – This NRA campground has sites that are large enough for 30 foot RVs. The campground is located on the west side of the highway near Mile 199 at the north end of Carter Lake. This is 7.6 miles (12.3 km) south of the Florence Bridge.

■ **TAHKENITCH LANDING CAMPGROUND** *(Open All Year)*
   Reservations: www.recreation.gov, (877) 444-6777
   Information: (541) 750-7000
   Location: 8 Miles (13 Km) N of Reedsport

          GPS Location: 43.79972 N, 124.14667 W, Near Sea Level

27 Sites – This NRA campground has sites set off a loop overlooking the boat landing at Tahkenitch Lake. They are small sites with parking on grass, only suitable for tent campers and smaller rigs like vans and pickup campers. There is no potable water at this

campground. A boat ramp is located .3 miles (.5 km) to the north. The campground is on the east side of the highway near Mile 203. This is 12.2 miles (19.7 km) south of the Florence bridge and 8.2 miles (13.2 km) north of Reedsport.

■ **TAHKENITCH CAMPGROUND** *(Open May 1 to Sept 30)*
Reservations: www.recreation.gov, (877) 444-6777
Information: (541) 750-7000
Location: 8 Miles (13 Km) N of Reedsport

GPS Location: 43.79528 N, 124.14889 W, Near Sea Level

30 Sites – This is a Oregon Dunes NRA campground with back-in sites to about 25 feet. Nearby Three Mile Lake Trail leads from a parking area to the lake and out to the ocean beach. Tahkenitch Lake is across the highway. The campground is on the west side of US-101 near Mile 204. This is 7.5 miles (12.1 km) north of Reedsport.

● **COHO RV PARK** *(Open All Year)*
Res and Info: (541) 271-5411
Location: Reedsport

GPS Location: N 43.69722 N, 124.11194 W, Near Sea Level

49 Sites – The Coho is an older commercial campground situated right in Reedsport. It's nothing fancy but the price is right and it's a popular place for fishing enthusiasts. There are back-in sites and pull-thrus to 60 feet with parking on gravel. Watch for the campground sign on the east side of the highway in Reedsport about .8 mile (1.3 km) south of the bridge.

<!-- Map image: REEDSPORT AND THE OREGON DUNES - MAP 2 -->

Map A

Salmon Harbor Marina

Salmon Harbor RV

To Florence
Reedsport

Winchester Bay

Discovery Point Resort & RV Park

Winchester Bay RV Resort

Mm 215

Surfwood Cmpgrd

Half Moon Bay Cmpgrd

Mm 217

Windy Cove - Section A & B

Umpqua Lighthouse SP

William M Tugman SP

Mm 221

Mm 222

Eel Creek Cmpgrd (NRA)

REEDSPORT AND THE OREGON DUNES - MAP 2

Map B

Pacific Ocean

Spinreel OHV Cmpgrd (NRA)

Mm 225

Riley Ranch County Park

Mm 227

Oregon Dunes KOA Kampground and RV Resort

Mm 229

Trans-Pacific Parkway

Horsfall OHV Cmpgrd (NRA)

Mm 232

Wild Mare Horse Camp (NRA)

Bluebill Cmpgrd (NRA)

To Coos Bay

OREGON

● **SURFWOOD CAMPGROUND** *(Open All Year)*
  Res and Info: (541) 271-4020
  Location: 2 Miles (3 Km) S of Reedsport

  *GPS Location: 43.67444 N, 124.15917 W, Near Sea
  Level*

150 Sites – The Surfwood is a large older RV
park located a few miles north of Winchester Bay. Sites are back-ins and pull-thrus to 50
feet, they are separated by lines of high shrubs so they're somewhat private. The park is
popular with folks who like this coast but want to park away from the water and ATV activity. There is a seasonal swimming pool and ATVs can be rented, they must be trailered
to the sand. The campground entrance road is at Mile 215. This is about .8 mile (1.3 km)
northeast of the Winchester Bay cutoff.

○ **HALF MOON BAY ATV CAMPGROUND – DOUGLAS COUNTY
    PARK** *(Open All Year)*

  Reservations: (541) 957-7001
  Information: (541) 271-5634, www.co.douglas.or.us/parks/
  Location: Winchester Harbor

            GPS Location: 43.66375 N, 124.20174 W, Near Sea Level

45 Sites – This new county campground is designed for ATV campers. It has big back-
in and pull-thrus sites to 125 feet (only one, most are shorter but still long). These are
separated sites, not a parking lot. Interior roads and sites are gravel. The campground is
situated between the ocean and the dunes, not immediately next to either but very close to
both. From Mile 215.9 of US-101 drive west on Salmon Harbor drive for 1.7 miles (2.7
km). The campground entrance is on the right.

● **DISCOVERY POINT RESORT AND RV PARK**
    (Open All Year)
  Res and Info: (541) 271-3443,
                www.discoverypointresort.com
  Location: Winchester Bay

  GPS Location: 43.66778 N, 124.19667 W, Near Sea Level

75 Sites – Discovery Point is the nearest commercial
campground to the dunes in the Winchester Bay area. It
caters to ATVers, often large parties of them. ATVs are available for rent. Tent campers
are welcome. ATV users dominate this campground, if you don't like them you won't like
this park. Some pull-thru RV sites reach 45 feet long and they are very wide. Wi-Fi is at
the office hotspot. From Mile 215.9 of US-101 drive west on Salmon Harbor drive for 1.3
miles (2.1 km). The campground entrance is on the left.

○ **WINCHESTER BAY RV RESORT** *(Open All Year)*
  Res and Info: (541) 271-0287,
                salmonh@codouglas.or.us,
                www.marinarvresort.com
  Location: Winchester Bay

  GPS Location: 43.67639 N, 124.18444 W, Near Sea Level

138 Sites – The Winchester Bay RV Resort is a Douglas County campground. It's very
upscale, one of the nicest places to stay, particularly in a big RV, along this section of
the coast. Sites are all paved and landscaped. They are back-ins and pull-thrus to 60 feet.

You have a choice of waterfront sites overlooking the marina or outer bay or interior sites where the views aren't quite so good. There's a nice paved walking trail around the exterior. Also, no ATV operation is allowed. From Mile 215.9 of US-101 drive west on Salmon Harbor drive for .5 miles (.8 km). The campground entrance is on the right.

☐ **UMPQUA LIGHTHOUSE STATE PARK**
(Open All Year)

Reservations: www.reserveamerica.com, (800) 452-5687
Information: (541) 271-4118, (800) 551-6949,
                www.oregonstateparks.org
Location: 1 Mile (2 Km) South of Winchester Bay

GPS Location: 43.66194 N, 124.19361 W, 100 Ft

44 Sites – This campground is along Maria Lake, just south of the Umpqua Lighthouse. Sites are arranged both off the entrance road and one loop. They are all back-ins, some around 50 feet or longer and several more over 40 feet. Although this campground is accessible from Salmon Harbor Drive it is easier to go west on an access road from Mile 216.7 of US-101, about .8 mile (1.3 km) south of the Salmon Harbor Drive junction with US-101 in Winchester Bay.

○ **WINDY COVE SECTION A** *(Open All Year)*
Information: (541) 271-4138,
                www.co.douglas.or.us/parks/campgrounds.asp
Location: Winchester Bay

GPS Location: 43.67528 N, 124.18028 W, Near Sea Level

28 Sites – This is the first of two sections of the Windy Cove Douglas County campground. These are older campgrounds that preceded the Winchester Bay RV Resort across the street. The sites are back-ins from 32 to 60 feet long. From Mile 215.9 of US-101 drive west on Salmon Harbor drive for .2 miles (.3 km). The campground entrance is on the left.

○ **WINDY COVE SECTION B** *(Open All Year)*
Reservations: (541) 957-7001
Information: (541) 271-5634,
                www.co.douglas.or.us/parks.htm
Location: Winchester Bay

GPS Location: 43.67500 N, 124.18556 W, Near Sea Level

69 Sites – This campground is the second of the Douglas County Windy Cove campgrounds. It is nearer to the dunes and popular with ATVers. The sites are located off two loops. One loop has back-in full-hookup sites to 60 feet. The second loop is much smaller back-in no-hookup sites. From Mile 215.9 of US-101 drive west on Salmon Harbor drive for .6 miles (1 Km). The campground entrance is on the left.

○ **SALMON HARBOR MARINA** *(Open All Year)*
Information: (541) 271-0287
Location: Winchester Bay

GPS Location: 43.67806 N, 124.18056 W, Near Sea Level

140 Sites – In addition to all of the hook-up camping at Winchester Bay the marina provides five large parking areas for dry camping. Two of these are gravel lots that extend into the bay with back-in parking next to the water and picnic tables and grills. Three

others are paved parking lots a little back from the water but near the waterfront lots. These have no tables or barbecues. Parking slots are from 50 to 60 feet long. There are restrooms nearby with flush toilets and showers. There is also a dump station. From Mile 215.9 of US-101 drive west on Salmon Harbor Drive for .1 mile (.2 km). Turn right into the large lot and look for the signs designating which areas are the camping sections of the lot.

☐ **WILLIAM M TUGMAN STATE PARK CAMPGROUND**
   (Open All Year)

Reservations: www.reserveamerica.com, (800) 452-5687
Information: (541) 271-4118, (800) 551-6949,
              www.oregonstateparks.org
Location: 5 Miles (8 Km) S of Winchester Bay

   GPS Location: 43.60028 N, 124.17806 W, 100 Ft

94 Sites – This state park is located on the east side of the highway near Eel Lake. There is a day use area on the lake with a fishing dock. The campground sites are off three loops. All sites are paved back-ins from 28 to 60 feet, many exceed 40 feet in length so this is a decent big-rig park although there are no sewer connections, just a dump station. The campground entrance road is near Mile 221.3 of US-101. This is 8.1 miles (13.1 km) south of Reedsport and 12.3 miles (19.8 km) north of the Coos Bay suspension bridge.

■ **EEL CREEK CAMPGROUND** *(Open All Year)*
Reservations: www.recreation.gov, (877) 444-6777
Information: (541) 271-6000
Location: 6 Miles (10 Km) S of Winchester Bay

   GPS Location: 43.58833 N, 124.18639 W, Near Sea Level

52 Sites – Access to this Oregon Dunes NRA campground is directly off US-101. There is dune access for hikers but not ATVs from this park. The John Dellenbach trail leads through the dunes to the beach, a distance of about three miles (4.8 km) one way. A parking area for hikers not staying in the campground is located south of the park with a separate entrance. The sites here are back-ins and pull-thrus, they are suitable for RVs to about 35 feet. The campground entrance is on the west side of US-101 at Mile 222.3. This is 9.1 miles (14.7 km) south of Reedsport and 11.3 miles (18.2 km) north of the Coos Bay suspension bridge.

■ **SPINREEL OHV CAMPGROUND** *(Open All Year)*
Reservations: www.recreation.gov, (877) 444-6777
Information: (541) 271-6000
Location: 9 Miles (15 Km) N of the Coos Bay Bridge

   GPS Location: 43.56917 N, 124.20361 W, Near Sea Level

36 Sites – Spinreel is an Oregon Dunes NRA campground that is primarily for ATV users. There is access to the dunes and ATVs can sometimes be rented near the entrance to the campground. There is also a large parking lot for day-use ATVers. Campsites are all back-ins here, they reach 60 feet although maneuvering room is a little tight. These sites are separated sites, not parking-lot style. The campground entrance road is off US-101 at Mile 224.2. This is 11.1 miles (17.9 km) south of Reedsport and 9.3 miles (15 km) north of the Coos Bay suspension bridge.

○ **RILEY RANCH COUNTY CAMPGROUND** *(Open All Year)*
Res and Info: (541) 396-3121,
                    www.co.coos.or.us/ccpark/Riley_Ranch/
                    RileyRanch.html
Location: 7 Miles (11 Km) north of the Coos Bay Bridge

GPS Location 43.51679 N, 124.21962 W, Near Sea Level

92 Sites – This is a new Coos Bay County park. In addition to the campground (which has no ATV dune access) there is a day-use area which is extremely popular with ATVers. Butterfield Lake, stocked with trout, is adjacent to the campground and so is Oregon Dunes NRA. Sites here are all back-ins and are long, some to 90 feet. When we visited there was no dump site and only one (very nice) restroom building but both are planned in the near future. The campground entrance road is off US-101 at Mile 227. This is 13.7 miles (22.1 km) south of Reedsport and 6.7 miles (10.8 km) north of the Coos Bay bridge.

● **OREGON DUNES KOA KAMPGROUND**
    AND RV RESORT *(Open All Year)*

Reservations: (800) KOA-4236, www.koa.com,
                        (800) 562-4236
Information: (541) 756-4851,
                        www.oregonduneskoa.com
Location: 4 Miles (6.5 Km) N of the Coos
                        Bay Bridge

GPS Location: 43.50139 N, 124.21944 W, Near Sea Level

69 Sites – This KOA caters to the ATV crowd. Sites are set in a large open lot and many are long pull-thrus, some to 85 feet. The campground entrance road is off US-101 at Mile 228.8. This is 15.5 miles (25 km) south of Reedsport and 4.9 miles (7.9 km) north of the Coos Bay bridge.

■ **HORSFALL OHV CAMPGROUND** *(Open All Year)*
Reservations: www.recreation.gov, (877) 444-6777
Information: (541) 271-6000
Location: 2 Miles (3 Km) NW of the Coos Bay Bridge

GPS Location: 43.44250 N, 124.24639 W, Near Sea Level

70 Sites – This is another Oregon Dunes NRA campground with ATV access to the dunes. The sites are parking-lot style in paved lots with sites to 50 feet. There are picnic tables and fire pits along the edges, tenters can set up there off the asphalt. There is also a loading ramp. To reach the campground follow Trans-Pacific Parkway west from Mile 232.7. This is .7 mile (1.1 km) north of the Coos Bay bridge. In 1 mile (1.6 km) take the right fork, the campground is on the right about 1.5 miles (2.4 km) from US-101.

■ **BLUEBILL CAMPGROUND** *(Open May 1 to Sept 30 – Varies)*
Reservations: www.recreation.gov, (877) 444-6777
Information: (541) 271-3611
Location: 4 Miles (6 Km) NW of the Coos Bay Bridge

GPS Location: 43.45111 N, 124.26278 W, Near Sea Level

18 Sites – Bluebill is a small campground. It is one of the three NRA campgrounds in the immediate area. Bluebill has back-in sites (and one pull-thru) for RVs, they are from 30 to 80 feet long, off a loop drive. The campground is located near the shore of Bluebill Lake, there is a one-mile trail around the lake. To reach the campground follow Trans-Pacific

OREGON

Parkway west from Mile 232.7. This is .7 mile (1.1 km) north of the Coos Bay bridge. In 1 mile (1.6 km) take the right fork, the campground is on the left about 2.8 miles (4.5 km) from US-101.

■ **WILD MARE HORSE CAMP** *(Open All Year)*
   Reservations: www.recreation.gov, (877) 444-6777
   Information: (541) 271-6000
   Location: 2 Miles (3.2 Km) NW of the Coos Bay Bridge

   GPS Location: 43.44972 N, 124.26722 W, Near Sea Level

12 Sites – This NRA campground is designed for folks with horses. Twelve of the sites have room for parking a trailer and also small corrals and hitching posts. These are back-in sites to about 55 feet. The campground is about a half-mile from the beach. To reach the campground follow Trans-Pacific Parkway west from Mile 232.7. This is .7 mile (1.1 km) north of the Coos Bay bridge. In 1 mile (1.6 km) take the right fork, the campground is on the left about 3.0 miles (4.8 km) from US-101.

ROGUE-UMPQUA SCENIC BYWAY

The Rogue-Umpqua Scenic Byway offers the chance to make a quick loop into Oregon's Cascade Mountains from I-5. The total distance, without side-trips, is just a little over 160 miles (258 km). Along the way you'll have lots of chances to stop for the night at a variety of campgrounds including national forest, state, county, and private campgrounds.

Basically, the byway follows the river valleys of the upper Umpqua and Rogue River. We've arranged the campgrounds below so you're traveling up the Rogue from Medford and then down the Umpqua to Roseburg.

Both of these rivers are well-known fishing rivers. The Umpqua is said to be the best summer steelhead river in the US.

Near the farthest east point of the loop is the Umpqua National Forest's Diamond Lake Recreation Area. Four of the campgrounds listed below are near this lake. It has swimming beaches, 11 miles (18 km) of paved hiker/biker trails circling the lake, boat ramps, and is a popular rainbow trout fishery. One of the campgrounds at the lake is a commercial big-rig RV park with full hookups. There is also a commercial lodge offering a restaurant, pizza joint, service station, grocery stores, laundry, fishing charters and bike rentals.

This route offers excellent access to Crater Lake NP. Since the campgrounds in the park aren't great you might want to consider staying in one of the campgrounds along this route and making a day trip into the park. Excellent places to stay for this include: Joseph Stewart State Park, Prospect RV Park, Union Creek Campground, Farewell Bend Campground, Broken Arrow Campground, Diamond Lake RV Park, and Diamond Lake Campground.

Rogue-Umpqua Scenic Byway Campgrounds

● **ROGUE RIVER RV PARK** *(Open All Year)*
   Reservations: (800) 775-0367
   Information: (541) 878-2404, www.rogueriverrv.com
   Location: 20 Miles (32 Km) N of Medford

   GPS Location: 42.61503 N, 122.81139 W, 1,400 Ft

OREGON

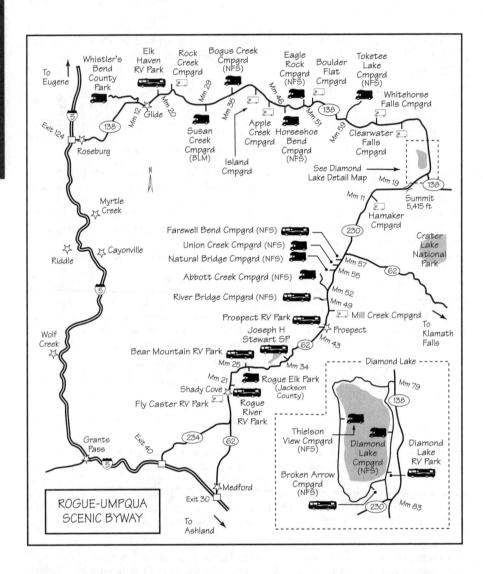

80 Sites – This is a large park on the bank of the Rogue River just north of the bridge in Shady Cove. Many long-term units are in this park, but they also have sites for travelers. These are 60-foot pull-thrus with full hookups. Campsites are both paved and gravel-surfaced off paved access roads. There are rental cabins and also a boat ramp. You're in a small town here so it's easy to walk to a restaurant. The entrance is at Mile 20.2 of SR-62.

● **BEAR MOUNTAIN RV PARK** *(Open All Year)*
   Res and Info: (541) 878-2400
   Location: 25 Miles (40 Km) N of Medford

   GPS Location: 42.66182 N, 122.76022 W , 1,500 Ft

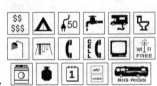

35 Sites – Bear Mountain RV Park is sited across the

highway from the Rogue. Sites are back-ins to 40 feet around a central lawn area. Although there are long-term units in this park there are usually just a few sites available for travelers. The campground entrance is at Mile 25.3 of SR-62.

○ **ROGUE ELK PARK** *(Jackson County) (April 15 to Oct 15)*
  Reservations: www.jacksoncountyparks.com
  Information: (541) 774-8183,
               www.jacksoncountyparks.com
  Location: 25 Miles (40 Km) N of Medford

GPS Location: 42.66250 N, 122.75250 W, 1,500 Ft

37 Sites – This county campground is sited between the Rogue River and the highway. Camping is in two areas. To the right as you enter is a paved loop with 29 sites for RVs to 35 feet. These are back-ins and 14 have electric and water hookups, the others have no hookups. To the left as you enter is a parking lot and on the far side a line of short gravel-surfaced sites along the river with no hookups, they'll take tent campers with automobiles as well as vans or pickup campers. There's a restroom building, showers and a dump station ($5 fee). The campground entrance is near Mile 25.8 of SR-62.

☐ **JOSEPH H STEWART STATE RECREATION AREA**
    (Open March 1 to Oct 31)
  Reservations: www.reserveamerica.com, (800) 452-5687
  Information: (541) 560-3334, (800) 551-6949,
               www.oregonstateparks.org
  Location: 33 Miles (53 Km) N of Medford

GPS Location: 42.68278 N, 122.61500 W, 2,000 Ft

201 Sites – This large state campground is adjacent to
the Lost Creek Reservoir on the Rogue River. It's a popular lake for boating, swimming, and fishing. Campsites are off 4 loops a little back from the lake. They're all paved back-ins, some to 80 feet. Many have electrical and water hookups. Some distance from the campsites there's a marina with store and café. The entrance to the campground is near Mile 34.2 of SR-62.

● **PROSPECT RV PARK**
    (also known as Crater Lake RV Park) (Open All Year)
  Res and Info: (541) 560-3399,
               www.prospectrvpark.com
  Location: 42 Miles (68 Km) NE of Medford

GPS Location: 42.75472 N, 122.49444 W, 2,500 Ft

57 Sites – This big rig park caters to visitors who find this area a convenient place to stay when visiting Crater Lake and the attractions of the Rogue Valley. It's just outside the border of the Rogue River National Forest, about 35 miles from Crater Lake. Sites are wide back-ins and pull-thrus to 65 feet. Sites are paved and so are the access roads. The campground entrance is at Mile 43.7 of SR-62.

■ **RIVER BRIDGE CAMPGROUND** *(Open July 1 to Sept 6)*
  Information: (541) 560-3400
  Location: 50 Miles (81 Km) NE of Medford

GPS Location: 42.82158 N, 122.49322 W, 2,700 Ft

11 Sites – River Bridge is a small unimproved Rogue River National Forest campground

a bit off the highway. It is situated near a bridge over a quiet section of the Rogue River. Sites vary in size with several to 35 feet and the ones at the entry reach 45 feet, if only because they extend into a gravel entry area. From SR-62 take the road at Mile 49, it's marked for the campground. Follow the small gravel road for .9 mile (1.5 km) to the entrance on the right just before the campground.

■ **ABBOTT CREEK CAMPGROUND** *(Open May 15 to Oct 31 – Varies)*
Information: (541) 560-3900, www.roguerec.com
Location: 52 Miles (84 Km) NE of Medford

GPS Location: 42.88389 N, 122.50639 W, 3,000 Ft

25 Sites – This Rogue River National Forest campground along little Abbott Creek is a little out of the way, it also has sites set aside for off-road vehicle users. It will take larger RVs than many small Forest Service campgrounds, several sites reach 40 feet but lack of maneuvering room limits coaches to about 35 feet. There is a hand pump for water. From SR-62 take the road at Mile 51.7, it's marked for the campground. Follow this paved road for 3.5 miles (5.6 km) to entrance.

■ **NATURAL BRIDGE CAMPGROUND** *(Open May 15 to Oct 30 – Varies)*
Information: (541) 560-3900
Location: 19 Miles (31 Km) W of Crater Lake National Park

GPS Location: 42.89250 N, 122.46278 W, 3,300 Ft

17 Sites – Natural Bridge is the smallest of the three Rogue River National Forest campgrounds in a stretch along the Rogue River here. Trails lead along the river letting you view the lava tubes where the river passes underground. There is no drinking water in this campground. Some site are 50 feet long but limited narrow roads and lack of maneuvering room means that coach size should be limited to about 35 feet. From the intersection of SR-62 and SR-230 travel southwest for 2.6 miles (4.2 km) to the campground entrance. This is 19 miles (31 km) from the south entrance to Crater Lake National Park.

■ **UNION CREEK CAMPGROUND** *(Open May 15 to Oct 30 – Varies)*
Information: (541) 560-3900, www.roguerec.com
Location: 17 Miles (27 Km) W of Crater Lake National Park

GPS Location: 42.90639 N, 122.44833 W, 3,200 Ft

78 Sites – This large Rogue River National Forest campground is situated on both sides of Union Creek where it empties into the Rogue and is best for RVs to about 30 feet. There are a few sites to 40 feet but narrow roads and big trees limit maneuvering room. Check with the host or walk the road before attempting to take a big RV in here. From the intersection of SR-62 and SR-230 travel southwest for 1.4 miles (2.3 km) to the campground entrance. This is 17 miles (27 km) from the south entrance to Crater Lake National Park.

■ **FAREWELL BEND CAMPGROUND** *(Open May 15 to Oct 20 – Varies)*
Information: (541) 560-3900, www.roguerec.com
Location: 16 Miles (26 Km) W of Crater Lake National Park

GPS Location: 42.91583 N, 122.43444 W, 3,100 Ft

61 Sites – Farewell Bend Rogue River National Forest campground is the best of the three campgrounds along here for RVs. There are sites from 46 to 65 feet long and they are angled making entry possible for larger RVs. Still, remember that this is a national

forest campground and exercise caution. A trail leads from the campground to the Rogue Gorge Viewpoint. From the intersection of SR-62 and SR-230 travel southwest for .5 mile (.8 km) to the campground entrance. This is 16 miles (26 km) from the south entrance to Crater Lake National Park.

■ **BROKEN ARROW CAMPGROUND** *(Open May 15 to Sept 5 – Varies)*
   Information: (541) 498-2531
   Location: 4 Miles (6 Km) N of Crater Lake National Park

   GPS Location: 43.13250 N, 122.14667 W, 5,200 Ft

147 Sites – Broken Arrow is one of two large Umpqua National Forest campgrounds near Diamond Lake. This one is on flat ground away from the lake, and as a result the sites tend to be easier to access and more suitable for larger RVs. There are back-ins and pull-thru sites to 50 feet. It is south of the lake. From the Diamond Lake entrance off SR-230 near the junction of SR-230 and SR-138 drive north for .7 mile (1.1 km). Turn left and the entrance to the campground is on the left in .6 mile (1 km).

● **DIAMOND LAKE RV PARK**
   (Open May 15 to Oct 1)
   Res and Info: (541) 793-3318, dlrvp@chatlink.com,
                www.diamondlakervpark.com
   Location: 4 Miles (6 Km) N of Crater Lake National
                Park

   GPS Location: 43.13889 N, 122.13389 W, 5,300 Ft

110 Sites – This is the closest full-hookup big-rig campground to Crater Lake. It sits away from Diamond Lake but does offer back-in and pull-thru sites to 60 feet. Sites are gravel. From the Diamond Lake entrance off SR-230 near the junction of SR-230 and SR-138 drive north for 1 mile (1.6 km). The campground is on the right.

■ **DIAMOND LAKE CAMPGROUND** *(Open May 15 to Oct 31 – Varies)*
   Reservations: www.recreation.gov, (877) 444-6777
   Information: (541) 498-2531,
   Location: 5 Miles (8 Km) N of Crater Lake National Park

   GPS Location: 43.15917 N, 122.13333 W, 5,200 Ft

238 Sites – This huge Umpqua National Forest campground occupies a sloping site on the east shore of Diamond Lake. Some sites reach 35 feet but maneuvering room is tight. There are two boat ramps. From the Diamond Lake entrance off SR-230 near the junction of SR-230 and SR-138 drive north for 2.7 miles (4.4 km). The entrance is on the left.

■ **THIELSON VIEW CAMPGROUND** *(Open May 15 to Oct 15 – Varies)*
   Information: (541) 498-2531
   Location: 10 Miles (16 Km) N of Crater Lake National Park North Entrance

   GPS Location: 43.16942 N, 122.16801 W, 5,200 Ft

60 Sites – This smaller Umpqua National Forest Campground is located on the west side of Diamond Lake. Sites here are back-ins and pull-thrus to about 40 feet but roads are narrow and access difficult so we don't recommend it for large RVs. There is a boat ramp and a dock. Easiest access is from SR-138 some 4.3 miles (6.9 km) north of the intersection with SR-230. Turn west and follow signs for 3.5 miles (5.6 km) to the campground entrance.

■ **TOKETEE LAKE CAMPGROUND** *(Open All Year)* | $$ | ▲ | ♨ | ♿ |
Information: (541) 498-2531
Location: 57 Miles (92 Km) E of Roseburg

GPS Location: 43.27250 N, 122.40528 W, 2,400 Ft

33 Sites – Note that this campground closed for at least a year on September 27, 2010 due to a hydroelectric project. The campground is located off the main highway in the North Umpqua Valley above Toketee Dam and Lake. It's an Umpqua National Forest campground. No potable water is provided. Site size and maneuvering room limit access to coaches to 30 feet. There is a boat ramp at the campground. From SR-138 near mile marker 59, about 57 miles (92 km) from Roseburg, turn north on NF Road 34. At .3 mile (.5 km) take the left fork and climb for another 1.1 miles (1.8 km) passing the Toketee Dam and Lake to the campground entrance near the upper end of the lake.

■ **EAGLE ROCK CAMPGROUND** *(Open May 20 to Sept 30 – Varies)* | $$ | ▲ | ♨ | ♿ |
Information: (541) 496-3532
Location: 49 Miles (79 Km) E of Roseburg

GPS Location: 43.29583 N, 122.55472 W, 1,600 Ft

25 Sites – Eagle Rock Umpqua National Forest campground has sites to 45 feet but limited maneuvering room limits coach size to about 30 feet. There is no drinking water available at this campground. From SR-138 near Mile 51, about 49 miles (79 km) from Roseburg watch for the campground entrance on the north side of the road.

■ **HORSESHOE BEND CAMPGROUND** *(Open May 20 to Sept 30)* | $$$ | ▲ | 🚻 | ♨ | ♿ |
Information: (541) 496-3532
Location: 44 Miles (71 Km) E of Roseburg

GPS Location: 43.28806 N, 122.62722 W, 1,300 Ft

26 Sites – This is one of the more upscale Umpqua National Forest campgrounds along the river. The restrooms have flush toilets and many of the campsites are right on the riverbank. There are sites exceeding 40 feet but limited maneuvering room means the campground is best for coaches to 35 feet. From SR-138 near Mile 46, about 44 miles (71 km) from Roseburg watch for the campground entrance on the south side of the road.

■ **BOGUS CREEK CAMPGROUND** *(Open May 20 to Oct 15)* | $$$ | ▲ | 🚻 | ♨ | ♿ |
Information: (541) 496-3532
Location: 33 Miles (53 Km) E of Roseburg

GPS Location: 43.32417 N, 122.80056 W, 1,100 Ft

15 Sites – The Umpqua National Forest Bogus Creek Campground has sites off two loops on the far side of the highway from the river. This campground has very narrow access roads limiting coach size to about 30 feet. From SR-138 near Mile 35, about 33 miles (53 km) from Roseburg, watch for the campground entrance on the north side of the road.

■ **SUSAN CREEK CAMPGROUND** *(Open April 25 to Nov 15)* | $$$ | ▲ | 🚻 | 📶 |
Information: (541) 440-4930, www.or.blm.gov/roseburg | ♨ | ☕ | ♿ |
Location: 27 Miles (44 Km) E of Roseburg

GPS Location: 43.29778 N, 122.89500 W, 1,000 Ft

29 Sites – Sites in this BLM campground reach 40 feet but limited maneuvering room limits practical coach size to 35 feet. From the day-use area downstream there is a one-

mile trail to Susan Falls. The campground is located near Mile 29 off SR-138, about 27 miles (44 km) from Roseburg.

● **ELK HAVEN RV PARK** *(Open All Year)*
   Res and Info: (541) 496-3090, (888) 552-0166,
                     vacation@elkhavenrv.com,
                     www.elhavenrv.com
   Location: 18 Miles (29 Km) E of Roseburg

   GPS Location: 43.32417 N, 123.05194 W, 700 Ft

43 Sites – Elk Haven is a commercial big-rig park with pull-thrus and back-ins to 55 feet in a large open field near the highway. There are several fishing ponds on the property and an above-ground seasonal swimming pool. The campground is off SR-138 near Mile 20 about 18 miles (29 km) east of Roseburg.

○ **WHISTLER'S BEND COUNTY PARK** *(Open All Year)*
   Information: (541) 673-4863, www.douglas.or.us/parks.asp
   Location: 13 Miles (21 Km) E of Roseburg

   GPS Location: 43.30944 N, 123.21167 W, 600 Ft

28 Sites – Whistler's Bend is a Douglas County park located just outside Roseburg to the east. This is a large park, with a small campground located on the shore of the Umpqua River. There are shade trees and views across the river, a very pleasant place. Good restrooms are situated above the camping area near some rental yurts. There are tent sites as well as back-ins to 35 feet. To reach the campground turn north off SR-138 near Mile 12, about 10 miles (16 km) east of Roseburg. Follow the signs for 2.7 miles (4.4 km) to the park entrance and then up and over a low pass to the campground.

ROSEBURG AND THE UMPQUA VALLEY

Little Roseburg (population 21,000) is the main town of the Umpqua Valley. The Umpqua River, like the Rogue farther south, actually flows from the Cascades and then through the Coastal Mountains to the Pacific. At Roseburg the valley widens and becomes good farmland. Roseburg is an old town for Oregon, it was established by the Hudson Bay Company in 1836 as a fur-trading post.

Probably the best known of Roseburg's sights is the **Wildlife Safari**. It is located just northwest of Winston which is about 7 miles (11 km) south of Roseburg. At Wildlife Safari you drive your vehicle through fenced areas filled with wildlife from Africa, Asia, and North America on a 3-mile loop.

The Umpqua Valley is also a **wine-growing region**. Pick up a tour map at the visitor center that will lead you on a circuit of the valley's wineries and tasting rooms. You'll need the map to find these small wineries hidden on back roads.

Roseburg also has an excellent museum - The **Douglas County Museum of Cultural and Natural History**. It is located right next to the RV park at the Douglas County Fairgrounds. Take Exit 123 from I-5 and follow the signs.

Roseburg hosts the **Douglas County Fair** the second week of August.

OREGON

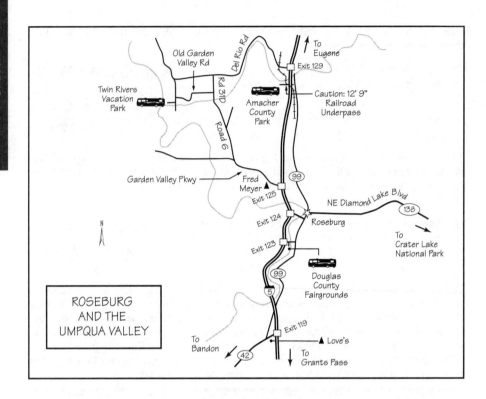

ROSEBURG
AND THE
UMPQUA VALLEY

Roseburg and the Umpqua Valley Campgrounds

○ **DOUGLAS COUNTY FAIRGROUNDS** *(Open All Year)*
Information: (541) 957-7010
Location: Roseburg

GPS Location: 43.19306 N, 123.35944 W, 400 Ft

50 Sites – This is a self registration campground right next to the freeway as you enter Roseburg from the south. It's stark but functional and a great place to stop if you're traveling I-5 and just want to stop and spend the night somewhere simple. The fair here is just before the middle of August and it will be full then, but otherwise there's usually plenty of room. There are a few pull-thrus to 55 feet as well as many back-in sites to about 35 feet. Sites have electricity and water and there is a dump station. The dump station is included if you are staying in the park, $5 if you are not. Restrooms are across the road. Take Exit 123 from I-5 and follow signs to the campground on the east side of the highway.

● **TWIN RIVERS VACATION PARK**
   (Open All Year)
Res and Info: (541) 673-3811,
              twinr.v.@earthlink.net,
              www.twinriversrvpark.com
Location: 7 Miles (11 Km) W of Roseburg

GPS Location: 43.26889 N, 123.43639 W, 300 Ft

75 Sites – This is a big-rig park that offers a lot more than just big spaces and good hook-ups. It's a little out of the way, about 6 miles (10 km) from the freeway west of town next to the Umpqua River, but if you plan to stay for more than a night in the area it's worth the drive. The sites are separated by lawns and trees and you are well away from any road noise. There are tent sites with camping on grass and also long pull-thrus 75 feet and back-ins to 45 feet. Management here is excellent. Next door is River Forks County Park which has a boat ramp and swimming in the river. To most easily reach the campground take Exit 125 from I-5. Drive west on NW Garden Valley Parkway for 2 miles (3 km), then turn north on County Road Six. In 3 miles (5 km) you'll come to a Y, turn left on County Road 31D. In another 1.4 miles (2.3 km) turn left on Old Garden Valley Road and you'll see the campground on the left in .9 mile (1.5 km).

○ **AMACHER COUNTY PARK** *(Open All Year)*
Information: (541) 957-7001, www.douglas.or.us/parks.asp
Location: 5 Miles (8 Km) N of Roseburg

GPS Location: 43.28083 N, 123.35639 W, 400 Ft

30 Sites – Amacher is a small county park located almost under a freeway bridge and railway trestle north of Roseburg. Other than the freeway noise this is a nice place with paved back-in sites to 30 feet separated by lawn. Tent sites are on the perimeter and they have fire pits while the RV sites do not. The entryway has a height limitation marked as twelve foot, nine inches as it passes under a trestle. The park is on the bank of the North Umpqua River. On the other side of the river, a nice walk, is a fish ladder where you can watch salmon traveling up the river. Take Exit 129 from I-5. Drive south on SR-99 on the east side of the highway and cross the Umpqua River on a long and fairly narrow bridge. The campground entrance is on the west side of the highway on the south end of the bridge.

SALEM

Salem (population 155,000), Oregon's state capital, is an excellent base for exploring the upper Willamette Valley. This region was the goal of most of the trekkers of the Oregon Trail. Oregon City, 35 miles (56 km) north of Salem is considered the end of the Oregon Trail.

Since Salem is one of the older towns in the Willamette Valley you would expect the central area to have some sights of interest and you wouldn't be mistaken. Start at **Mission Mill Village** which is easy to find since it houses an information center for the city. There is also a wool museum set in the buildings of the old Thomas Kay Woolen Mill. Just follow the information signs posted near the entrances to town.

From the Mission Mill Village you can visit the other sites of downtown Salem including **Willamette University**, the **State Capitol and grounds** and surrounding **historic area, Deepwood Estate and Gardens, Bush House Museum and Conservatory,** and the **Bush Barn Art Center**.

The Salem area is home to a large collection of **covered bridges** dating from the early 20th century. You can follow a loop visiting six of these bridges from Exit 253 off I-5 in Salem. The loop goes east on SR-22, then loops south to Albany on SR-226 from Mehama and Lyons. You'll need a guide pamphlet available from most area visitor's centers to find all of the bridges since they are tucked away on side roads.

Near Salem is the premier Oregon **wine growing area**. It is centered around McMin-

OREGON

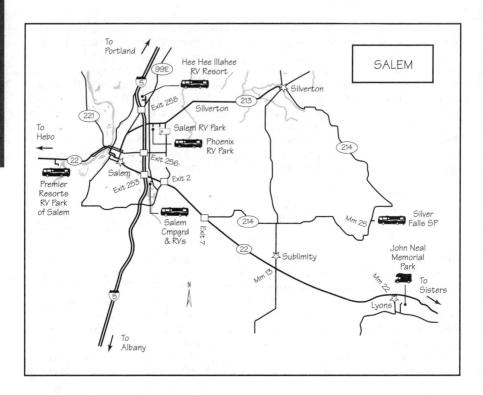

nville in Yamhill County to the west of Salem. The county has some 30 wineries, many offer tours. Pick up a guide to the wineries at the McMinnville tourist information center or other area information centers.

The area between Salem and Portland is full of interesting historical sites, particularly **Oregon City**, **Aurora**, and **Champoeg**. A driving tour from Salem north on I-5 to Oregon City, then south on 99E, west on country roads to Champoeg State Park, and then returning to Salem can make an interesting day trip. Once again, check with local information centers for more details.

The **Evergreen Aviation and Space Museum** is located near McMinnville about 30 miles (48 km) northwest of Salem. It's the home of Howard Hugh's huge **Spruce Goose** seaplane as well as many other aircraft. There's also a water park.

If you have kids along they will probably be ready for something less historical after visiting all of the above. The answer is **Enchanted Forest**, a theme park located right along the I-5 freeway at Exit 248.

Salem Campgrounds

● **PREMIER RESORTS RV PARK OF SALEM**
   (Open All Year)
   Res and Info: (503) 364-7714, (877) 364-9990,
          www.premierrvresorts.com
   Location: 4 Miles (6 Km) W of Salem

   GPS Location: 44.93056 N, 123.12333 W, 100 Ft

180 Sites – This campground is on the western approaches to Salem. That's a little inconvenient if you're traveling I-5 and looking for a place to spend the night but even so many folks think it's worth the trouble to come out here. This is an upscale big-rig campground with pull-thru sites to 55 feet. Amenities include a swimming pool, a library/card room, a business center, meeting rooms, *a* game and exercise room, and free Wi-Fi. Watch for the resort on the south side of SR-22 some 4.2 miles (6.8 km) west of the bridges over the Willamette as you leave Salem.

● **SALEM CAMPGROUND AND RVs**
    (Open All Year)
Reservations: (800) 826-9605
Information: (503) 581-6736,
           www.salemrv.com
Location: Salem

GPS Location: 44.91222 N, 122.98528 W, 200 Ft

220 Sites – This is one of the older Salem campgrounds and has quite a few long-term residents but it continues to have decent facilities and is a reliable and decently priced park. There are tent sites here with tents pitched on grass in a treed area and also RV sites of various types including pull-thrus to 65 feet. Take Exit 253 from I-5 and head east on the North Santiam Hwy (SR-22). Take the Lancaster Dr. SE off-ramp in just .2 mile (.3 km) and go south on Lancaster for 100 yards. Turn right into Hagers Grove Rd. SE, the campground is at the end of the road in .3 mile (.5 km), just past a Home Depot.

● **HEE HEE ILLAHEE RV RESORT** *(Open All Year)*
    Res and Info: (877) 564-7295, www.heeheerv.com
    Location: Salem

    GPS Location: 44.98787 N, 122.99247 W, 200 Ft

140 Sites – This new big-rig campground is located just off the freeway at the northern edge of Salem. It has pull-thrus to 75 feet and back-ins to 45 feet. Amenities include an outdoor swimming pool and indoor spa. From I-5 take Exit 258 and head north on Portland Road NE. In .2 mile (.3 km) turn left on Astoria Drive NE and you'll soon see the RV park on the left.

● **PHOENIX RV PARK** *(Open All Year)*
    Reservations: (800) 237-2497
    Information: (503) 581-249,
           www.phoenixrvpark.com
    Location: Salem

    GPS Location: 44.96917 N, 122.98056 W, 100 Ft

107 Sites – This is a modern big-rig campground with back-ins and pull-thrus to 70 feet. Wi-Fi is included in the rate for one day only. Take Exit 256 from I-5 and drive east on Market St. NE to Lancaster Dr. NE, about 5 blocks or .3 mile (.5 km). Turn north on Lancaster and drive 1.2 miles (1.9 km) to Silverton Road NE. Turn right and you'll see the campground entrance on the right in .1 mile (.2 km).

☐ **SILVER FALLS STATE PARK** *(Open All Year)*
    Reservations: www.reserveamerica.com, (800) 452-5687
    Information: (503) 873-8681, (800) 551-6949,
           www.oregonstateparks.org
    Location: 22 Miles (35 Km) E of Salem

    GPS Location: 44.87194 N, 122.64944 W, 1,300 Ft

OREGON

100 Sites – This is Oregon's largest state park – by area. It has ten waterfalls, lots of trails, and a large campground. Many sites here are back-ins over 50 feet long, some stretch to 80 feet. To reach the campground drive east on SR-22 about 6 miles (10 km) to the junction with SR-214, then follow SR- 214 some 16 miles (26 km) to the park.

○ **JOHN NEAL MEMORIAL PARK** *(Open April 15 to Oct 15 – Varies)*
Res and Info: (541) 967-3917, www.co.linn.or.us/parks
Location: 22 Miles (35 Km) E of Salem

GPS Location: 44.78278 N, 122.60833 W, 700 Ft

40 Sites – John Neal is a small Linn County park in the town of Lyons. The park is on the bank of the North Santiam River and has a boat ramp. Some sites overlook the river, the longer ones are about 30 feet. From Salem drive east on SR-22 about 21 miles (34 km). Turn right and follow SR-226 into Lyons. In 1.1 mile (1.8 km) follow the main street left until you reach North 13th Street. Turn left and the park is about three blocks ahead.

TILLAMOOK AND THE THREE CAPES LOOP

Most people probably know **Tillamook** for its cheese, and cheese factories are a big part of the draw here. The **Tillamook Cheese Visitors Center** is north of town along US-101 at Mile 63.9. There is another factory nearby, the **Blue Heron French Cheese Company**, at Mile 65. Our favorite attraction in Tillamook is the **Tillamook Naval Air Station Museum**. It is located south of town near Mile 68.1. The museum is housed in a huge blimp hanger, you really can't miss it. Inside is a collection of World War II fighters and bombers along with other interesting aircraft.

THE TILLAMOOK CHEESE FACTORY IS A HIGHLIGHT OF A VISIT TO TILLAMOOK

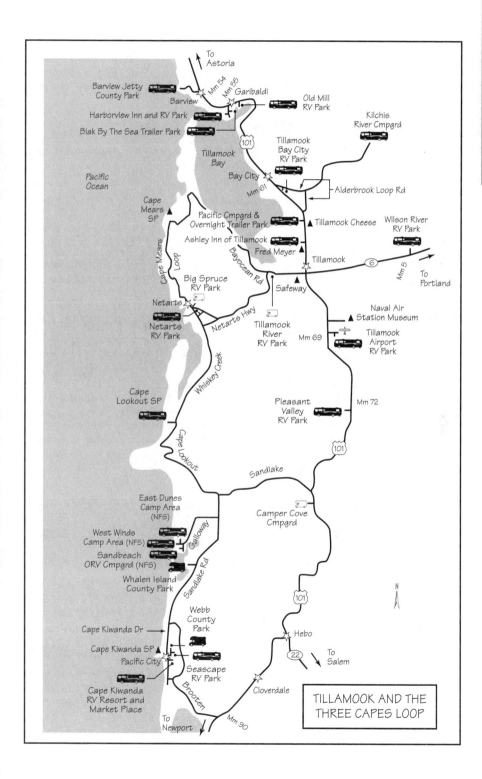

TILLAMOOK AND THE
THREE CAPES LOOP

As you drive between Tillamook and Lincoln City you may want to leave US-101 and follow the **Three Capes Loop**. The north junction is in Tillamook at the west end of Third Street, the south junction is at Mile 90.4. The 28-mile (45 km) loop will lead you past **Netarts, Cape Lookout, Cape Kiwanda, and Pacific City.** A side trip from near Netarts will take you to **Oceanside** and **Cape Mears**.

Tillamook and the Three Capes Loop Campgrounds

○ **BARVIEW JETTY COUNTY PARK** *(Open All Year)*
   Res and Info: (503) 322-3522, parks@co.tillamook.or.us,
                    www.co.tillamook.or.us/gov/parks
   Location: 12 Miles (19 Km) N of Tillamook

   GPS Location: 45.56889 N, 123.94528 W, Near Sea Level

315 Sites – This county campground rivals the state campgrounds along the coast in size and facilities. It occupies the peninsula at the base of the north jetty protecting the entrance to Tillamook Bay. There are back-in and pull-thru full-hookup spaces to 50 feet and lots more RV and tent camping spaces with no hookups. The campground entrance is located 2.3 miles (3.7 km) south of Rockaway Beach and 1.8 miles (2.9 km) west of Garibaldi off US-101.

● **HARBORVIEW INN AND RV PARK** *(Open All Year)*
   Res and Info: (503) 322-3251, www.harborviewfun.com
   Location: 9 Miles (15 Km) N of Tillamook

   GPS Location: 45.55608 N, 123.91528 W, Near Sea Level

30 Sites – The Harborview Inn is located near the marina at Garibaldi. There are 30 RV sites behind the motel. Their location is actually better than that of the motel since they overlook the water and most have great views. This is a nicely laid out little park with back-in spaces to 50 feet. They have full hookups and are separated by grass. The waterfront sites are a little more expensive than the others. A hotel room has been redone to provide restrooms for the park. There is no restaurant at the motel but there is one right across the street. In Garibaldi follow S 7th Street out to the marina. The motel is on your right about .2 mile (.3 km) from where you left US 101.

● **BIAK BY THE SEA TRAILER PARK**
      (Open All Year)
   Res and Info: (503) 322-2111
   Location: 9 Miles (15 Km) N of Tillamook

   GPS Location: 45.55722 N, 123.91417 W, Near Sea Level

64 Sites – This is one of several RV parks dedicated to fisherman near the marina at Garibaldi. Sites are back-ins and pull-thrus on gravel to 40 feet. In Garibaldi follow S 7th Street out to the marina, the campground is the one on the left about .1 mile (.2 km) from where you left US-101.

● **OLD MILL RV PARK** *(Open All Year)*
   Res and Info: (503) 322-0322, www.oldmill.us
   Location: 9 Miles (15 Km) N of Tillamook

   GPS Location: 45.55847 N, 123.91066 W, Near Sea Level

200 Sites – This is the third of the RV parks near the Garibaldi marina. Unlike the first two it's located on the

east side of the marina. Sites here are back-ins to about 40 feet and very long pull-thrus. There's a huge building out front that's used for special events, but it also houses the office and laundry. In Garibaldi follow 3rd Street south across the railroad tracks to the RV park. It's just a block, you can see it from the highway.

○ **KILCHIS RIVER CAMPGROUND**
 (Open May 1 to Sept 30 – Varies)
 Res and Info: (503) 842-6694,
  www.co.tillamook.or.us/gov/parks/
  Campgrounds.htm
 Location: 10 Miles (16 Km) NE of Tillamook

GPS Location: 45.53753 N, 123.78490 W, 100 Ft

67 Sites – Feel like getting away from the ocean for a while? In the unlikely event that you do, this Tillamook County campground might be a good choice. It's located a few miles back in the mountains, in the deep wooded valley of the Kilchis River. The park has many tent sites as well as a lot of back-in vehicle sites as long as 35 feet. There are also three longer pull-thru sites, they're 40 to 45 feet long. The campground has no hookups but does have a dump station. There's also a boat launch on the river. From US 101 some .5 mile (1 km) south of Bay City and 4.3 miles (6.9 km) north of Tillamook drive east on Alderbrook Loop Road. After 1.7 miles (2.7 km) continue straight onto Kilchis River Road and follow it for another 4.1 miles (6.6 km) to the park which is at the end of the road.

● **TILLAMOOK BAY CITY RV PARK**
 (Open All Year)
 Reservations: (800) 200-2075
 Information: (503) 377-2124,
  www.tillamookbaycityrvpark.com
 Location: 4 Miles (6 Km) N of Tillamook

GPS Location: 45.51111 N, 123.87528 W, Near Sea Level

46 Sites – The Tillamook Bay City RV Park is one of the nicer and better maintained campgrounds along the highway north of Tillamook. The RV and tent sites are in a grassy well-clipped field. The RV sites are back-ins and pull-thrus to 60 feet. There are several community fire pits and also individual fire pits in the tent camping area. Although the campground is located along US-101 the entrance is off Alderbrook Loop Road which leaves US-101 just .5 mile (1 km) south of Bay City and 4.3 miles (6.9 km) north of Tillamook.

● **ASHLEY INN OF TILLAMOOK** *(Open All Year)*
 Res and Info: (503) 842-7599
 Location: Tillamook

GPS Location: 45.47670 N, 123.84542 W, Near Sea Level

20 Sites – This is a modern multi-story motel with RV sites to the side and behind. These are back-in and parallel parking sites to 50 feet. Access roads are paved, so are the parking pads, and there are lawns between the sites. It's well cared for. Sites have electric and water hookups but no sewers, there is a dump station. There are also no dedicated restroom or showers so only self-contained rigs are accepted. The hotel has a continental breakfast which is included in the price, and also an indoor salt water swimming pool. The motel is on the west side of Hwy 101 at the northern edge of Tillamook, it's .5 mile (.8 km) south of the Tillamook Cheese factory.

OREGON

● PACIFIC CAMPGROUND AND
    OVERNIGHT TRAILER PARK *(Open All Year)*
    Res and Info: (503) 842-5201
    Location: Tillamook

GPS Location: 45.48670 N, 123.84653 W, Near Sea Level

42 Sites – This campground and RV park has a lot of long-term residents but also has sites for travelers. The gravel RV sites are pull-thrus to 40 feet. The park is on the west side of Hwy 101 at the northern edge of Tillamook, it's just north of the Tillamook Cheese Factory.

● WILSON RIVER RV PARK *(Open All Year)*
    Res and Info: (503) 842-2750, www.wilsonriverrv.com
    Location: 4 Miles (7 Km) East of Tillamook

GPS Location: 45.46801 N, 123.74853 W, 100 Ft

69 Sites – This campground has about a half-mile of frontage along the Wilson River, and fishing is important to the people who stay here. Sites are pull-thrus and back-ins to 60 feet, some along the river. From Tillamook drive east on Hwy 6 for about 4.5 miles (7.3 km), the campground entrance is on the left.

● NETARTS RV PARK *(Open All Year)*
    Res and Info: (503) 842-7774, www.netartsbay.com
    Location: 6 Miles (10 Km) W of Tillamook

GPS Location: 45.42639 N, 123.93833 W, Near Sea Level

83 Sites – This is a nice upscale resort overlooking the ocean at Netarts Bay which is on the ocean west of Tillamook. Sites are in two areas. An older section of the park has sites overlooking the water and also behind the main resort buildings along a canal. Some of these sites will take RVs to 45 feet but many restrict slide-outs. There is also a newer area of the park inland which has long back-in sites that can easily handle large modern RVs with slides. Amenities include boat rentals. To reach the RV park follow SR-6 west from Tillamook. Follow signs for Netarts and as you approach the town you'll see the campground signs pointing to your left. If you miss the sign just continue to Netarts, turn south along the coast, you'll see the RV park on your left in just .5 mile (1 km) from the turn.

☐ CAPE LOOKOUT STATE PARK *(Open All Year)*
    Reservations: www.reserveamerica.com, (800) 452-5687
    Information: (503) 842-4981, (800) 551-6949,
                www.oregonstateparks.org
    Location: 10 Miles (16 Km) SW of Tillamook

GPS Location: 45.36278 N, 123.96917 W, Near Sea Level

212 Sites – This is one of the nicer Oregon State coastal campgrounds because the camping area is right next to the wide sandy beach. The park has a hiker/biker tent camp as well as many vehicle accessible sites. There are a limited number of hookup sites, only 39 of them. Many sites here exceed 40 feet, some reach 60. There are no pull-thrus and many sites are difficult to access with longer RVs because they leave the driveway at a 90-degree angle. To reach the campground follow signs west from Tillamook on 3rd Street which becomes SR-6 or Netarts Highway West. In 4.4 miles (7.1 km) take the left fork at the Y, the road becomes Whiskey Creek Road. Ten miles (16 Km) from Tillamook you'll see the entrance on the right.

OREGON

■ SAND BEACH ORV CAMPGROUND *(Open All Year)*
Reservations: www.recreation.gov, (877) 444-6777
Information: (541) 750-7127
Location: 18 Miles (29 km) W of Tillamook

GPS Location: 45.28417 N, 123.95500 W, Near Sea Level

101 Sites – Sand Beach is a Siuslaw National Forest campground. It's primarily an ORV (off road vehicle) campground with access to large areas of sandy dunes. This is the northernmost of these ORV campgrounds along the Oregon coast. You'll find several more listed under *Reedsport and the Oregon Dunes* below. There are actually three camping areas in the immediate vicinity. The main campground, Sand Beach, is a normal Forest Service type campground with separated back-in sites to about 45 feet. Many are extra large to allow parking for ATV trailers. There are also two large paved lots called the East Dunes Camp Area and the West Winds Camp Area where overnight camping is allowed in RVs. These two parking-lot style campgrounds cost less ($10 per night) and reservations are not available in them. All three areas have handicapped-accessible restrooms with flush toilets but no hookups. Some of the sites in the main camping area overlook the beach along Sandlake estuary. Access is easiest from US-101 south of Tillamook. Follow Sandlake Road west from its junction with US-101 some 10.5 miles (17 km) south of Tillamook. After 4.4 miles (7.1 km) Sandlake makes a 90-degree turn, the Cape Lookout Road continues straight. Turn left and in 1 mile (2 km) turn right on Galloway Rd. Follow Galloway 2.3 miles (3.7 km) to the campground.

○ WHALEN ISLAND COUNTY PARK *(Open May 1 to Sept 30 – Varies)*
Res and Info: (503) 965-6085, parks@co.tillamook.or.us,
                  www.tillamook.or.us/gov/parks
Location: 18 Miles (29 Km) SW of Tillamook

GPS Location: 45.27278 N, 123.94944 W, Near Sea Level

34 Sites – This is a small Tillamook County campground located along the east side of the Sandlake estuary. Sites are near the water in an open area bordered by trees. Sites are not clearly laid out, people park where you can level the RV or where there is a level spot for the tent. Picnic tables and fire pits are provided. Access is easiest from US-101 south of Tillamook. Follow Sandlake Road west from its junction with US-101 some 10.5 miles (17 km) south of Tillamook. After 4.4 miles (7.1 km) Sandlake makes a 90-degree turn, the Cape Lookout Road continues straight. Turn left and in 3.5 miles (5.6 km) you'll see the campground on the right.

○ WEBB COUNTY PARK *(Open All Year)*
Res and Info: (503) 965-5001, parks@co.tillamook.or.us,
                  www.co.tillamook.or.us/gov/parks
Location: 27 Miles (44 Km) SW of Tillamook

GPS Location: 45.21639 N, 123.96861 W, Near Sea Level

38 Sites – There is a small cluster of campgrounds located just south of Cape Kiwanda in the town of Pacific City. They are inland from the beach but really just across the highway. This county park is the smallest of them. The sites are back-ins on grass. Some will take RVs to 35 feet although most are shorter and better for smaller RVs and tents. It's a nice little campground. Easiest access is from US-101. From the junction with Brooten Road about 24 miles (39 km) south of Tillamook drive northwest about 2.7 miles (4.4 km) to the center of Pacific City. Jog toward the beach on Pacific Ave and then turn north

on Cape Kiwanda Dr. for 1.1 mile (1.8 km) to the cluster of campgrounds on your right. This campground is the farthest north of the group.

● **SEASCAPE RV PARK** *(Open All Year)*
   Res and Info: (503) 965-7006, tomichivillagervpark@
   earthlink.net, www.seascaperv.com
   Location: 24 Miles (39 Km) SW of Tillamook

   GPS Location: 45.21583 N, 123.96889 W, Near Sea Level

40 Sites – This campground is the second from the north in the cluster of campgrounds north of Pacific City. It's an older park. There are large back-in and pull-thru sites to 56 feet. From the junction of US-101 with Brooten Road about 24 miles (39 km) south of Tillamook drive northwest about 2.7 miles (4.4 km) to the center of Pacific City. Jog toward the beach on Pacific Ave and then turn north on Cape Kiwanda Dr. for 1.1 mile (1.8 km) to the cluster of campgrounds on your right.

● **CAPE KIWANDA RV RESORT AND MARKET PLACE** *(Open All Year)*

   Res and Info: (503) 965-6230,
   capekiwanda@oregoncoast.com,
   www.capekiwandarvresort.com
   Location: 24 Miles (39 Km) SW of Tillamook

   GPS Location: 45.21472 N, 123.96861 W, Near Sea Level

180 Sites – The final campground in the cluster at Cape Kiwanda is the largest. It has nice amenities including an indoor swimming pool, a grocery store, and a pizza restaurant. There are tent sites here, as well as back-ins and pull-thrus, a few of the latter reach 60 feet. From the junction of US-101 with Brooten Road about 24 miles (39 km) south of Tillamook drive northwest about 2.7 miles (4.4 km) to the center of Pacific City. Jog toward the beach on Pacific Ave and then turn north on Cape Kiwanda Dr for 1.1 mile (1.8 km) to the cluster of campgrounds on your right.

○ **TILLAMOOK AIRPORT RV PARK** *(Port of Tillamook Campground)*
   (Open May 25 to Sept 30 – Varies)
   Information: (503) 842-7152, (503) 842-2413, www.potb.org
   Location: 2 Miles (3 Km) S of Tillamook

   GPS Location: 45.41889 N, 123.82028 W, Near Sea Level

52 Sites – This is a campground located on the west side of the Tillamook airport. The best-known feature of this airport is the air museum which is located in a huge World War II blimp hanger on the far side of the field. The campground is gravel roads and sites in an open field. There are picnic tables and fire pits. Not a lot of work was done in constructing the sites or making them useable. Most parking areas are higher than the surrounding ground and pretty narrow but they are as long as 50 feet. Amenities are limited to a restroom building over by the airport gate, several hundred yards away. Still, the price is good, and sites are usually available. There is no access across the airport to the museum, you must drive around to reach it. The campground is located on the east side of US-101 about 2.3 miles (3.7 km) south of Tillamook.

● **PLEASANT VALLEY RV PARK** *(Open All Year)*
Res and Info: (503) 842-4779,
                www.pleasantvalleyrvpark.com
Location: 6 Miles (10 Km) S of Tillamook

GPS Location: 45.37056 N, 123.80528 W, 100 Ft

76 Sites – This commercial RV park is one of the
nicest in the area. Sites are pull-thrus to 65 feet under
shade trees. Facilities are in good condition and the
park is well run. It's located on the west side of US-101 about 6.3 miles (10.2 km) south
of Tillamook.

WALDPORT AND FLORENCE

Waldport (population 2,100) is about 14 miles (23 km) south of Newport. The highway
crosses the new Alsea Bay Bridge here, and at the south end of the bridge is the **Alsea
Bay Interpretive Center** with displays covering transportation along the coast.

South of Waldport the twenty miles (32 km) between Yachats at Mile 165 and Mile
186 are very scenic. They're in the Siuslaw National Forest. You may want to stop at
the **Cape Perpetua Interpretive Center** at Mile 167.3. The center, run by the Forest
Service, has exhibits covering the forest and coastline in this area. Nature trails and tide
pools are accessible from the center. This is also another popular whale-watching site.
There is adequate parking for larger RVs.

Heceta Head Lighthouse is one of the most scenic of the eight along the Oregon coast.

SEA LIONS ON THE ROCKS NEAR SEA LION CAVE

You can walk to the lighthouse using a trail that leads from **Heceta Head Lighthouse State Scenic Viewpoint** at Mile 178.3. There is also a bed and breakfast here in the former assistant lighthouse keeper's house, **Heceta House**.

Sea Lion Caves, at Mile 179.3, have long been a do-not-miss stop for travelers along the coast. This is a commercial operation. An elevator drops through the cliff to a lookout window which lets visitors watch a colony of undisturbed Stellar sea lions in a large natural sea cave. In the distance you can also see the Heceta Head Lighthouse to the north. Parking is limited for RVs, it's best to visit the caves in a tow car or smaller RV. Just north of the caves is a pull-off where you can sometimes see sea lions on the rocks and in the water below. This is also an excellent spot to get a photo of the Heceta Head Lighthouse to the north and to watch for whales.

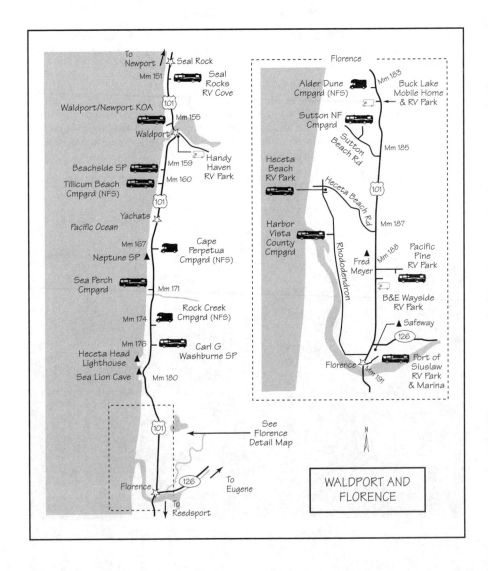

Florence (population 8,500), originally a lumber mill town, is located near the mouth of the Siuslaw River. It has become an attractive tourist destination, particularly in the **Old Town** area along the waterfront. Like the old towns in several other cities along the coast this one has interesting shops and restaurants, Florence is not as flashy as some. There's also a marina and a very convenient RV park run by the port.

The Siuslaw River is navigable for 20 miles (32 km) upstream and fishing for a variety of species is popular.

Golfers will probably appreciate the Sandpines Golf Course and the Ocean Dunes Golf Links, both take advantage of the rolling dunes in the area.

Florence has a **Rhododendron Festival** during the third week of May.

Waldport and Florence Campgrounds

● **SEAL ROCKS RV COVE** *(Open All Year)*
   Res and Info: (541) 563-3955, info@sealrocksrv.com,
   www.sealrocksrv.com
   Location: 5 Miles (8 Km) N of Waldport

   GPS Location: 44.49250 N, 124.08250 W, Near Sea Level

58 Sites – This small RV park sits above the highway with ocean views. No two sites are alike. They include tents sites, partial hookup sites, a few pull-thrus, and some long back-ins with full-hookups to 60 feet. The RV Park is located on the east side of US-101 near Mile 151 about 9 miles (15 km) south of Newport and 5 miles (8 km) north of Waldport.

● **WALDPORT/NEWPORT KOA** *(Open All Year)*
   Reservations: (800) KOA-3443
   Information: (541) 563-2250, orcstkoa@casco.net
   Location: 1 Mile (2 Km) N of Waldport

   GPS Location: 44.43556 N, 124.07528 W, 100 Ft

91 Sites – The Waldport KOA has a location with fantastic views of Waldport's Alsea Bay bridge just to the south. It's a popular place, reservations are essential all summer long. There is a trail to the beach. Sites here run the usual KOA gamut with cabins, tent sites, back-ins and pull-thrus. Some sites reach 60 feet in length. The campground is on the west side of US-101 just north of Waldport's bridge.

☐ **BEACHSIDE STATE PARK CAMPGROUND**
   (Open March 1 to Oct 31 - Varies)
   Reservations: www.reserveamerica.com, (800) 452-5687
   Information: (541)563-3220, (800) 551-6949,
   www.oregonstateparks.org
   Location: 3 Miles (5 Km) S of Waldport

   GPS Location: 44.38222 N, 124.08861 W, Near Sea Level

76 Sites – As the name suggests this small state campground is located right next to a long beach. Most sites are 40 feet long back-ins but maneuvering room is limited so care is required when parking and many sites limit use of slide-outs. There are no sewer connections and no dump station at this campground. The entrance is on the west side of US-101 near Mile 159. That's 3 miles (4.8 km) south of Waldport.

■ **TILLICUM BEACH NATIONAL FOREST CAMPGROUND** *(Open All Year)*

Reservations: www.recreation.gov, (877) 444-6777
Information: (541) 563-4800
Location: 4 Miles (6 Km) S of Waldport

GPS Location: 44.36639 N, 124.09139 W, Near Sea Level

60 Sites – Tillicum Beach Siuslaw National Forest Campground is one of the few national forest campgrounds in this part of the US with electrical hookups, seven of these sites have them. It's just south of the mouth of the Alsea River. The campground is set just above the long beach, access is easy. Sites are back-ins and pull-thrus, many reach 40 feet. The campground is on the west side of US-101 at Mile 160.5. It is 4 miles (6.5 km) south of Waldport.

■ **CAPE PERPETUA CAMPGROUND** *(Open May 15 to Sept 15 – Varies)*

Reservations: www.recreation.gov, (877) 444-6777
Information: (541) 547-3289
Location: 11 Miles (18 Km) S of Waldport

GPS Location: 44.28222 N, 124.10722 W, 100 Ft

38 Sites – This national forest campground occupies an inland valley south of the Cape Perpetua and north of Captain Cook Point and the coastal Neptune State Park. Hiking trails run throughout the cape area giving access from the campground to the interpretive center, overlooks, inland trails, and also trails to the ocean. Sites are shorter back-ins for small RVs to about 25 feet. They're all off one long access road that follows Cape Creek up the valley. The campground entrance is near Mile 167, about 11 miles (17.7 km) south of Waldport.

● **SEA PERCH RV RESORT** *(Open All Year)*

Res and Info: (541) 547-3505, seaperch@peak.org, www.seaperchrvpark.com
Location: 14 Miles (23 Km) S of Waldport

GPS Location: 44.23028 N, 124.10944 W, Near Sea Level

27 Sites – The Sea Perch, as you would expect, perches above the ocean. It's a very nice little commercial park with good views from almost all the sites and easy access to the beach. Sites are back-ins and pull-thrus to 60 feet. There is a community fire ring. The campground is on the west side of US-101 near Mile 171.

■ **ROCK CREEK CAMPGROUND** *(Open May 20 to Sept 5 – Varies)*

Reservations: www.recreation.gov, (877) 444-6777
Information: (541) 563-4800
Location: 18 Miles S of Waldport

GPS Location: 44.18472 N, 124.11500 W, Near Sea Level

15 Sites – This little Siuslaw National Forest campground is on the east side of US-101. The sites are all back-ins to 25 feet arranged off a road which runs inland along Rock Creek. Watch for the entrance near Mile 174.

☐ **CARL G. WASHBURNE MEMORIAL STATE PARK**
   (Open All Year)
   Information: (541) 547-3416, (800) 551-6949,
                   www.oregonstateparks.org
   Location: 14 Miles (23 Km) N of Florence

   GPS Location: 44.16000 N, 124.11306 W, Near Sea Level

65 Sites – The campground in this smaller state park is on the east side of the highway, there is a day use area and dump station on the beach side. The campground has access to a good trail system including trails north to Cape Perpetua. Sites here are all back-ins and stretch to 55 feet, most are over 40 feet long. The campground is near Mile 176 of US-101 just north of Heceta Head. It's about 20 miles (32 km) south of Waldport and 14 miles (23 km) north of Florence.

■ **ALDER DUNE CAMPGROUND** *(Open All Year)*
   Information: (541) 563-4800
   Location: 7 Miles (11 Km) N of Florence

   GPS Location: 44.06902 N, 124.10191 W, Near Sea Level

39 Sites – This Siuslaw National Forest campground is located just west of US-101 between Alder and Dune Lakes. There is a trail around Alder Lake. The dunes nearby can be walked, off-road vehicles are not allowed. Sites are back-ins to 35 feet, many will not accept RVs with slide-outs. The campground is located at Mile 183.5.

■ **SUTTON CAMPGROUND** *(Open All Year)*
   Reservations: www.recreation.gov, (877) 444-6777
   Information: (541) 563-4800
   Location: 3 Miles (5 Km) N of Florence

   GPS Location: 44.05417 N, 124.10750 W, Near Sea Level

80 Sites – Sutton is another modern Siuslaw National Forest campground with electrical hookups. There are big sites here, some to 60 feet and many in the 34 to 40 foot range. Trails leave from the campground to follow Cottonwood Creek, cross Alder Dune to Alder Dune Campground, and also to go to Cottonwood Lake. The campground is located off Sutton Beach Road which goes west from US-101 at Mile 185.5, about 3 miles (5 km) north of Florence. The campground is on the right .7 mile (1.1 km) from the highway.

○ **HARBOR VISTA COUNTY CAMPGROUND** *(Open All Year)*
   Reservations: (541) 997-5987, www.lanecounty.org/parks
   Information: (541) 682-2000, www.lanecounty.org/parks
   Location: 4 Miles (6 Km) NW of Florence

   GPS Location: 44.01528 N, 124.12500 W, 100 Ft

44 Sites – This is a well-kept county campground with paved sites and electrical hookups. There are vistas from the campground of the coast, but not from the sites. Sites are all back-ins, some as long as 55 feet. To drive to the campground turn west from US-101 on Heceta Beach Road from Heceta Junction, about a mile north of Florence. Follow the road northwest for 1.9 mile (3.1 km) and turn left on North Rhododendron Drive just after passing Heceta Beach RV Park. Now drive 1.2 miles (1.9 km) south on N. Rhododendron and turn right on Jetty Road North, you'll see the campground entrance on the left almost immediately.

OREGON

● **HECETA BEACH RV PARK** *(Open All Year)*
  Res and Info: (541) 997-7664,
  hecetabeachrvpark@yahoo.com,
  www.hecetabeachrv.com
  Location: 3 Miles NW of Florence

GPS Location: 44.03278 N, 124.12861 W, Near Sea Level

56 Sites – This campground is not on the beach, but you can walk there in about five minutes through a residential neighborhood. The RV park has grassy tent sites. The RV sites here are back-ins and pull-thrus from 50 to 60 feet. They are separated by hedges. A good-size mini-mart is out front, as well as a laundry and a recreation room. To drive to the campground turn west from US-101 on Heceta Beach Road from Heceta Junction, about a mile (2 km) north of Florence. Follow the road northwest for 1.9 miles (3.1 km) and you'll see the campground on the left.

● **PACIFIC PINE RV PARK** *(Open All Year)*
  Res and Info: (541) 997-1434,
  http://www.touroregon.com/happyplacervpark/
  index.html
  Location: Florence

GPS Location: 44.00222 N, 124.09972 W, Near Sea Level

64 Sites – Pacific Pine is a newer RV park designed for big RVs. It's located next to a storage locker facility. Sites are back-ins and pull-thrus, mostly about 55 feet long and separated by strips of grass and shrubs. Watch for the sign on the east side of US-101 on the northern approaches to town.

○ **PORT OF SIUSLAW RV PARK AND MARINA**
  (Open All Year)
  Res and Info: (541) 997-3040
  Location: Florence

GPS Location: 43.96889 N, 124.10111 W, Near Sea Level

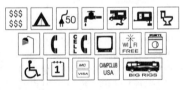

105 Sites – The Port of Siuslaw (Florence) operates this RV park next to their marina. It has a nice location inland from the Old Town, within easy walking distance of the shops and restaurants there. Tenters have grass and trees away from the water or grass along the bank of the estuary. RV sites are all back-ins and reach 55 feet. Some back up to the water and do not have sewer, some are back-ins on an open area, and others are back-ins in trees. For easiest access follow Nopal Street southeast from US-101 from a point about .3 mile (.5 km) north of the bridge, the turn is marked with a campground sign. In two blocks turn left on 1st and the campground is at the end of the street.

WALLOWA LAKE REGION

The Wallowa Lake Region is located in the far northeast corner of Oregon. Easiest access is from I-84 at La Grande. Take Exit 261 which is marked for Elgin.

Head out of La Grande on Highway 82, this highway takes a few unexpected turns but you will have no problem following it if you just watch for signs for Elgin and then Enterprise. If you zero your odometer when you leave the freeway you'll reach Elgin at 19

JOSEPH IS KNOWN FOR ITS FOUNDRIES PRODUCING BRONZE STATUES

miles (31 km), Enterprise at 63 miles (102 km), and Joseph at 70 miles (113 km).

You may want to make two stops in Enterprise before going on to Joseph. Just before you arrive in town you'll pass the **Wallowa Mountains Visitor Center**. A stop here will bring you up to speed on the area's attractions. Then, in Enterprise you'll find the last large supermarket in this neck of the woods, you might stop and pick up groceries for the next few nights.

The small town of Joseph and nearby Wallowa Lake make a very attractive destination. Almost anyone can find something of interest in this area.

Joseph itself is a small town with a population of some 1,300 people. The town is known for its foundries that produce bronze statues of all sizes, most with western themes. There are showrooms and you can tour a couple of the foundries, just ask at the showrooms.

The Wallowa Lake area was the traditional summer home of the Nez Percé Indians. You can visit the **Wallowa County Museum** in Joseph to learn more about them. South of town and overlooking the lake you'll find **Chief Joseph's grave**. This is the grave of old Chief Joseph, father of the Chief Joseph who led his people toward Canada in 1877.

Wallowa Lake is a 4-mile-long jewel extending from near Joseph back into high mountains. At the south end of the lake is a tourist area with the state park, a couple of private RV campgrounds, miscellaneous attractions for the tourist hordes, and some trailheads for hikes into the Wallowa Mountains. The lake is very popular for water sports of all kinds including water skiing and fishing. The top tourist attraction here must be the **Mount Howard Tram** which lifts visitors to 8,200 feet for several miles of hiking trails and great views in all directions.

Joseph celebrates **Chief Joseph Days** in late July and **Alpenfest** on the third weekend after Labor Day.

Wallowa Lake Region Campgrounds

☐ **MINAM STATE RECREATION AREA** $$ 🏕 ♨ 🚐 BIG RIGS
   (Open April 1 to Oct 10 – Varies)
   Information: (800) 551-6949,
                      www.oregonstateparks.org
   Location: 36 Miles (58 KM) NW of Joseph

   GPS Location: 45.63694 N, 117.72861 W, 2,400 Ft

24 Sites – This is a small campground with a minimum of facilities, more like a traditional national forest campground than most Oregon state parks. It is located next to the Wallowa River, a really beautiful location. You can fish the river for rainbows on a riverside trail or use this as an access point for floating the Wallowa and Grande Ronde. Twelve sites are very large paved back-ins, some to 70 feet, the other 12 are large unpaved areas. This is an open campground with few trees. The 1.5-mile (2.4 km) gravel entrance road leaves SR-82 some 13 miles (21 km) east of Elgin and 20 miles (32 km) west of Lostine.

○ **WALLOWA LION'S RV PARK** *(Open April 15 to Sept 30 – Varies)*   FREE 🏕 🚐 ♨ | CELL 🚐 BIG RIGS
   Location: In Wallowa, 25 Miles (40 Km) NW of Joseph

   GPS Location: 45.57694 N, 117.53583 W, 2,800 Ft

20 Sites – This camping area is little more than a grassy park but the price is right, it's

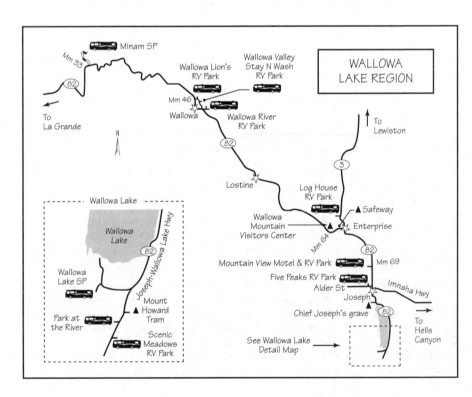

free. There are no hookups but any size RV can park on the grass here and there are port-a-potties. There is also a nearby dump station with potable water, also free and also run by the Lions. Donations are accepted. The campground is located toward the northern edge of the small town of Wallowa. You'll see the sign pointing east as you enter town from the north, it's just beyond the railroad tracks.

● **WALLOWA VALLEY STAY N WASH RV PARK**
    (Open All Year)
Telephone: (541) 886-6944
Location: In Wallowa, 25 Miles (40 Km) NW of Joseph

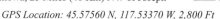

    GPS Location: 45.57560 N, 117.53370 W, 2,800 Ft

15 Sites – This is a small campground on a back street in Wallowa. The sites are located behind a laundromat which has showers and restrooms. Sites are back-ins and pull-thrus to 45 feet with full hookups. The RV park is located a short distance east of the Wallowa Lion's RV Park described above. To find the park follow those for the Lion's and then continue another block or so down the street.

● **WALLOWA RIVER RV PARK** *(Open April 15 to Oct 15 – Varies)*
Information: (541) 886-7002, (866) 886-7002, wrrv@uci.net
Location: In Wallowa, 24 Miles (39 Km) NW of Joseph

    GPS Location: 45.57028 N, 117.52250 W, 2,100 Ft

31 Sites – This is a handy small campground at the southern edge of Wallowa. It has 50-foot pull-thru sites and full hookups. At the southern edge of Wallowa where the highway curves to meet 1st Street follow 1st to the east, the campground is on the left in .1 mile.

● **LOG HOUSE RV PARK**
    (Open All Year)
Res and Info: (541) 426-4027
Location: Enterprise, 7 Miles (11 Km)
    N of Joseph

    GPS Location: 45.43778 N, 117.28611 W, 3,700 Ft

30 Sites – This park is located on the northern approaches to Enterprise. It has a western theme and big sites with pull-thrus to 60 feet. From central Enterprise follow SR-3 north toward Lewiston for .9 mile (1.5 km) to the campground, it's on the left overlooking town.

● **MOUNTAIN VIEW MOTEL AND RV PARK**
    (Open All Year)
Reservations: (866) 262-9891,
    mike@rvmotel.com
Information: (541) 432-2982,
    www.rvmotel.com
Location: 1 Mile N of Joseph

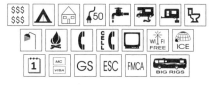

    GPS Location: 45.38083 N, 117.23028 W, 3,900 Ft

40 Sites – The Mountain View is a motel with a good campground in the rear. It's away from the crowds down at the southern end of Wallowa Lake and is a handy campground for visits to Joseph. Sites are long back-ins that will take RVs to 45 feet with lots of room to park a tow car. There are also three pull-thrus to 65 feet. Watch for the motel and camp-

ground on the west side of the highway about a mile north of central Joseph.

● **FIVE PEAKS RV PARK** *(Open April 1 to Nov 30)*
Res and Info: (541) 432-4605, 888 432-4605,
www.5peaksrvpark.com
Location: Joseph

GPS Location: 45.35702 N, 117.23123 W, 4,100 Ft

5 Sites – This small RV park is the only one actually in central Joseph. There are 5 back-in sites, they'll take 40 foot rigs. RVs must be self-contained, there are no restrooms. This is a nice place next to the owner's residence, it's only 2 blocks to Main Street in the middle of town. In central Joseph turn west on W Alder Street. Drive one block and then turn right. The park is at the end of the block, straight ahead.

☐ **WALLOWA LAKE STATE PARK** *(Open All Year)*
Reservations: www.reserveamerica.com,
(800) 452-5687
Information: (541) 432-4185, (800) 551-6949,
www.oregonstateparks.org
Location: 6 Miles (10 Km) S of Joseph

GPS Location: 45.28083 N, 117.21278 W, 4,400 Ft

210 Sites – This state park is actually world famous, National Geographic once chose it as one of the six best state parks in the west. There is lots to do here and the setting is magnificent. There is a boat launch and swimming area along the lake shore. Within walking distance you'll find restaurants, mini-golf, the tram to the top of Mount Howard, horse rides, and go-karts. Sites are very large with many longer than 60 feet. In winter 10 sites remain open, but there is no water available. To reach the campground just follow Highway 82 south 6 miles (10 km) from Joseph. The road reaches the lake at 2 miles (3 km), then follows the eastern lake shore for 4 miles (6 km) to the south end. At a Y there go right to the park entrance. This is a very popular park, even during the week you should have reservations or arrive very early in the day.

● **PARK AT THE RIVER** *(Open All Year)*
Res and Info: (541) 432-4704, (541) 432-8800,
info@eaglecapchalets.com,
www.eaglecapchalets.com
Location: 6 Miles (10 Km) S of Joseph

GPS Location: 45.27639 N, 117.20917 W, 4,400 Ft

48 Sites – This medium-sized RV park is quiet and will take RVs to 50 feet and longer in its well-separated back-in sites. It is affiliated with Eagle Cap Chalets across the street, they have a swimming pool, hot tub, and café. Wi-Fi here is a hot spot at the café. Most sites are back-ins to 50 feet but there are a couple of pull-thrus to 70 feet. All sites have full hookups. At the Y at the south end of Wallowa Lake go left, the campground is on the right in .3 mile (.5 km).

● **SCENIC MEADOWS RV PARK**
(Open May 15 to Oct 1 – Varies)
Res and Info: (541) 432-9285
Location: 6 Miles (10 Km) S of
Joseph

GPS Location: 45.27444 N, 117.20972 W, 4,400 Ft

20 Sites – A nice little well-run RV park with amenities some will like and others hate including a go-kart track (right next to the camping sites), mini-golf, and horses. Kids love it. There are four tent sites, the 160 remaining RV sites are mostly back-ins but there are 4 pull-thrus to 45 feet. Most sites have only electricity and water but there is a dump station. Located in the south Wallowa Lake tourist area. From the Y at the south end of Wallowa Lake go left, the campground is on the left in .4 mile (.6 km).

WARM SPRINGS AND MADRAS

Ninety-five miles (153 km) after leaving US-205 in Portland and heading southeast across the shoulder of Mt Hood you will reach the town of Warm Springs in the 600,000-acre **Warm Springs Indian Reservation**. You may want to take a break and tour **The Museum at Warm Springs**. It documents the heritage of the tribes that make up the Confederated Tribes of Warm Springs: the Wasco, Paiute and Warm Springs (Walla Walla) Tribes. If you decide to stay a while you can drive north on Hwy 3 to **Kah Nee Ta Vacation Resort** which boasts an RV park and a golf course as well as the **Indian Head Gaming Center**, a casino.

In another 14 miles (23 km) along US-26 you will reach Madras and US-97, the east-of-the-Cascades north-south highway. Nearby are several reservoirs that make great camping destinations.

The largest of these is **Lake Billy Chinook**. This reservoir fills a stunning canyon behind Round Butte Dam. The canyon is formed by three rivers: the Deschutes, the Metolius, and the Crooked Rivers. The reservoir has 72 miles (116 km) of shoreline and 4,000 surface acres. Water sports of all kinds are popular in the reservoir and there is fishing for Kokanee, trout, and bass.

Warm Springs and Madras Campgrounds

● **KAH NEE TA HIGH DESERT RESORT**
    AND CASINO *(Open All Year)*

Res and Info: (541) 553-1112,
                www.Kahneeta.com
Location: Warm Springs

GPS Location: 44.86167 N, 121.20028 W, 1,400 Ft

51 Sites – Kah Nee Ta is a very upscale resort with a large RV park adjoining a very nice swimming pool that is fed by hot springs. It's located on the Warm Springs Reservation. There are a number of very colorful teepees that can be rented for camping but other tents are not allowed. The casino is within walking distance and the area has hiking trails too. The campground is very popular with vacationing families since there's so much to do. This is a destination in itself which is good since it's remote from other attractions. Sites in the RV park are full-hookup back-ins and pull-thrus to 60 feet. To reach the campground drive north from Warm Springs on BIA-3 for 11.5 miles (18.5 km). The route is well signed.

○ **MAUPIN CITY PARK** *(Open 15 to Oct 31 – Varies)*

Information: (541) 395-2252, citypark@cityofmaupin.com,
                www.cityofmaupin.com
Location: Maupin

GPS Location: 45.17300 N, 121.07426 W, 900 Ft

OREGON

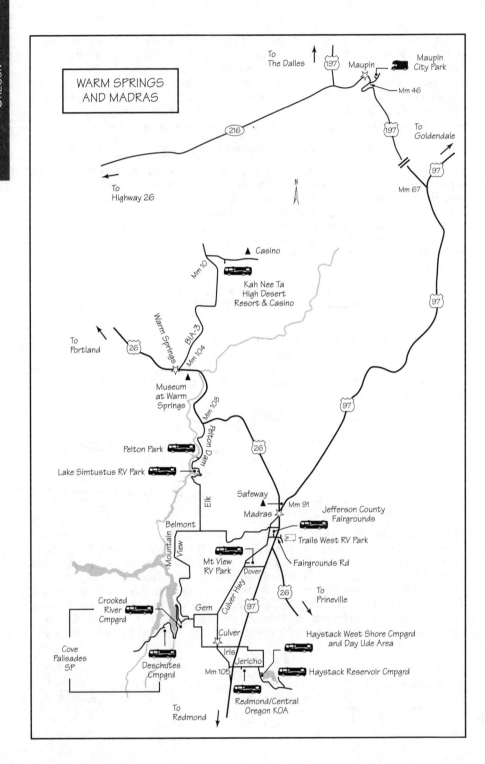

WARM SPRINGS
AND MADRAS

To The Dalles

197 Maupin

Maupin City Park

Mm 46

216

197

To Goldendale

97

Mm 67

To Highway 26

N

97

Casino

Kah Nee Ta High Desert Resort & Casino

Mm 10

Warm Springs

BIA-3

Mm 104

26

To Portland

Museum at Warm Springs

Mm 108

97

Pelton Dam

26

Pelton Park

Lake Simtustus RV Park

Elk

Safeway

Mm 91

Madras

Jefferson County Fairgrounds

Belmont

Trails West RV Park

Mountain View

Mt View RV Park

Dover

Fairgrounds Rd

Crooked River Cmpgrd

Gem

Culver Hwy

97

26

To Prineville

Cove Palisades SP

Culver

Iris

Jericho

Mm 105

Haystack West Shore Cmpgrd and Day Ude Area

Deschutes Cmpgrd

Haystack Reservoir Cmpgrd

Redmond/Central Oregon KOA

To Redmond

47 Sites – This is a city campground located just outside town along the Deschutes River. It has tent sites with pitching on grass as well as 28 paved full-hookup back-ins to 35 feet with parking on pavement strips. Although the strips are a little short 40 foot rigs just fit in many sites, they just have to use some of the grass. There's a raft ramp at the campground, this is a popular access point on the Deschutes for floaters. From Maupin cross the river to the southeast on Hwy 197, you'll see the left turn for the park and campground almost immediately.

○ **PELTON PARK** *(Open April 20 to Sept 25 – Varies)*
    Res and Info: (541) 325-5292, peltonpark@pgn.com,
                 www.portlandgeneral.com/parks,
                 (541) 475-0516 (store and marina)
    Location: 13 Miles (21 Km) NW of Madras

    GPS Location: 44.68722 N, 121.23389 W, 1,500 Ft

70 Sites – This campground is operated by Portland General Electric and the Confederated Tribes of Warm Springs. It is situated on the shore of Lake Simtustus, the reservoir behind Pelton Dam. Sites are back-ins to 50 feet but the maneuvering room is limited and the campground is recommended only for RVs to 40 feet. Amenities include a marina with groceries and a small restaurant as well as a covered cooking area with electric burners that is very handy for tent campers. The campground can be reached from US-26 (the Warm Springs Highway) at a point 4 miles (6 km) southeast of Warm Springs. Turn south on NW Pelton Dam Road and follow it 3.4 miles (5.5 km) to the campground.

● **LAKE SIMTUSTUS PARK** *(Open All Year)*
    Res and Info: (541) 475-1085, www.lakesimtustusrvresort.com
    Location: 15 Miles (24 Km) NW of Madras

    GPS Location: 44.67417 N, 121.23222 W, 1,600 Ft

90 Sites – This campground spills down the steep cliff on the east side of Lake Simtustus. The good access road makes it possible for large RVs to easily reach the terraces and lakeside. All sites are full-hookup back-ins to 45 feet. This campground also has a dock, boat ramp, and kayak rentals. Best access for large RVs is from the north. From US-26 (the Warm Springs Highway) at a point 4 miles (6 km) southeast of Warm Springs turn south on NW Pelton Dam Road and follow it 5.0 miles (8.1 km) to the campground.

○ **JEFFERSON COUNTY FAIRGROUNDS** *(Open All Year)*
    Information: (541) 325-5050
    Location: Madras

    GPS Location: 44.61990 N, 121.13531 W, 2,300 Ft

66 Sites – The fairgrounds in Madras has a large RV park. It's a basic park but the price is very reasonable and facilities are pretty good. Parking is in a large gravel lot with full-hookup back-in and pull-thru sites to about 75 feet. A dedicated restroom building has flush toilets and showers. Near the entrance is a dump station, there is a fee for its use. From central Madras turn west on Southwest Fairgrounds Road. In just .1 mile (.2 km) turn right into the signed entrance for the RV park and follow the road back to the RV park.

● **MOUNTAIN VIEW RV PARK** *(Open All Year)*
   Res and Info: (541) 546 3049
   Location: 3 Miles (5 KM) Southwest of Madras in
                     Metolius

   GPS Location: 44.59539 N, 121.16977 W, 2,500 Ft

60 Sites – This is a well-kept campground with quite a
few long-term residents, but also quite a few spaces for travelers. Sites are back-ins and
pull-thrus to 65 feet. Parking is on gravel and spaces are separated by rows of shrubs.
From Hwy 97 about 2 miles (3 km) south of Madras near Mile 98.4 turn west on SW
Dover Lane. There is a sign at the turn. Proceed for 1.2 miles (2 km) to a stop sign in
the town of Metolius. Turn right and the park is on the right in another .3 miles (.5 km).

☐ **CROOKED RIVER CAMPGROUND – COVE PALISADES**
   STATE PARK) *(Open All Year)*

   Reservations: www.reserveamerica.com, (800) 452-5687
   Information: (541) 546-3412, (800) 551-6949,
                     www.oregonstateparks.org
   Location: 14 Miles (23 Km) SW of Madras

   GPS Location: 44.54222 N, 121.25556 W, 2,300 Ft

91 Sites – Cove Palisades has two campgrounds and they are so different that we have
listed them separately here. This one is located on the east side of the reservoir and is not
near the water. It is on a bench well above the lake. Sites are all back-ins in a large grassy
field, all with electricity and some with water. Many sites are over 40 feet long, some are
over 50 feet. The campground is most easily accessed from US-97 some 7 miles (11 km)
south of Madras and 15 miles (24 km) north of Redmond. Turn west on SW Iris Lane and
drive 2.3 miles (3.7 km). Turn right on SW Feather Drive and drive north for 1.2 miles
(1.9 km). Now turn left on SW Fisch Lane for .5 miles (.8 km) and follow it as it turns 90°
to the north and becomes SW Frazier Dr. In .5 mile (.8 km) take the left on SW Jordan Rd.
and follow it another .9 miles (1.5 km) to the park entrance, which is on the left.

☐ **DESCHUTES CAMPGROUND – COVE PALISADES**
   STATE PARK) *(Open May 1 to Sept 15 – Varies)*

   Reservations: www.reserveamerica.com, (800) 452-5687
   Information: (541) 546-3412, (800) 551-6949,
                     www.oregonstateparks.org
   Location: 19 Miles (31 Km) SW of Madras

   GPS Location: 44.53889 N, 121.27806 W, 2,100 Ft

174 Sites – Deschutes Campground is a little harder to reach than Crooked River but is
still accessible to big RVs. It is located down in the canyon on a peninsula between the
Deschutes and Crooked River Arms. Ninety-two sites are tent sites, The rest are full-
hookup pull-thrus and back-ins to 60 feet with paved parking pads. There is a good trail
system from the campground. To reach the campground follow the instructions given
above for the Crooked River Campground. Drive right by that campground entrance
and follow the road for another 4.7 miles (7.6 km) as it winds down into the canyon,
follows Crooked Arm south and crosses a bridge to the peninsula and then climbs to the
Deschutes Campground entrance.

● **REDMOND/CENTRAL OREGON KOA**
(Open March 1 to Nov 15)
Reservations: (800) 562-1992, www.koa.com
Information: (541) 546-3046,
        madraskoa@msn.com,
        http://madras-koa.com
Location: 11 Miles (18 Km) S of Madras

GPS Location: 44.50111 N, 121.17833 W, 2,700 Ft

80 Sites – This is a typical KOA with full facilities including a swimming pool. The location is somewhat out of the way for a campground that isn't a destination in itself (for most people anyway) but it's close to the Haystack Reservoir for those folks wanting more than the federal campgrounds there have to offer. There are gravel back-ins and pull-thrus to 60 feet, including full and partial hookup sites. To reach the campground turn east from US-97 some 9 miles (15 km) south of Madras and 15 miles (24 km) north of Redmond on SW Jericho Lane. You'll see the campground on the right in .6 mile (1 km).

■ **HAYSTACK RESERVOIR CAMPGROUND**
(Open April 15 to Oct 15 – Varies)
Information: (541) 475-9272
Location: 14 Miles (23 Km) S of Madras

GPS Location: 44.49056 N, 121.13972 W, 2,800 Ft

24 Sites – This is a Crooked River National Grasslands campground. National grasslands are run by the same folks who run national forests, the USDA Forest Service. The campgrounds here are much like you would expect a national forest campground to be. This campground is set on the shore of a small reservoir known as Haystack Reservoir. There are no hookups but the sites are nice back-ins. The reservoir is popular for both fishing and water sports. This is an open sunny campground with fairly long sites, many are pull-thrus exceeding 45 feet. Both roads and sites are paved. Water is from a hand pump but there is also an RV fill station. To reach the campground turn east from US-97 some 9 miles (15 km) south of Madras and 15 miles (24 km) north of Redmond on Jericho Lane. Follow the road east for 1.3 miles (2.1 km). Turn right on SW Haystack Drive and follow it for 2.3 miles (3.7 km) as it curves around the south side of the reservoir to the campground entrance which is on the east side of the lake.

■ **HAYSTACK WEST SHORE CAMPGROUND AND DAY USE AREA**
(Open All Year)
Information: (541) 475-9272
Location: 12 Miles (19 Km) S of Madras

GPS Location: 44.49361 N, 121.16000 W, 2,800 Ft

14 Sites – This is a day use area and campground, the dedicated camping sites have been added in the last few years. They are back-in along the shore and up to 32 feet long but because many open into a large gravel area they will take rigs of any size. There's a boat ramp and dock here too. No potable water is provided. To reach the campground turn east from US-97 some 9 miles (15 km) south of Madras and 15 miles (24 km) north of Redmond on Jericho Lane. Follow the road east for 1.3 miles (2.1 km). Turn right on SW Haystack Drive and follow it for .4 mile (.6 km) as it curves around the west side of the reservoir to the campground entrance.

OREGON

OREGON

WEST CASCADES SCENIC BYWAY

The West Cascades Scenic Byway is a route running north-south along the west side of the Cascade Mountains. It begins in Estacada, just southeast of Portland, and ends in Westfir – Oakridge on SR-58, some 183 miles (295 km) to the south. Along the way you'll travel on a variety of road including:

•   From Estacada to Detroit Lake the route is a paved highway variously labeled as SR-206, Clackamas River Road, National Forest 46, and Breitenbush Rd. Total distance on this section is 71 miles (15 km). Although some of this portion of the route is national forest road it's all paved and fine for carefully driven RVs.

•   From Detroit Lake to the Santiam Junction the route follows SR-22. Total distance 32 miles (52 km).

•   From the Santiam Junction to the junction with SR-126 the route is on Hwy 20/126. This section is only 3 miles (5 km).

•   From the Hwy 20/126 junction south on SR-126 to a junction just west of McKenzie Bridge. Total distance of this section is 29 miles (45 km).

•   Finally there's the Willamette National Forest's Aufderheide Memorial Drive between the junction just west of McKenzie Bridge on SR-126 to the Westfir-Oakridge community along SR-58, a distance of 48 miles (77 km). This section too is a national forest road. It's paved and again, fine for carefully driven RVs.

Along this entire drive you'll find few pockets of civilization. Other than Estacada and Westfir-Oakridge there are no towns of much size. Fuel is available at both ends of the route and also in both Detroit Lake and McKenzie Bridge.

The route is almost entirely inside two national forests: Mt Hood and Willamette. You'll find that the majority of campgrounds listed are national forest campgrounds. If you're searching for hookups you can find them, see the Detroit Lake and McKenzie Bridge areas for those.

Since Estacada, the starting point of the byway, is a bit out of the way, it helps to know how to get there. The easiest access is from I-205, Portland's ring route. Take Exit 12 from the freeway and follow SR-224 up the Clackamas River for 17 miles (27 km) to the town.

In addition to the campgrounds along the scenic byway, you'll find that we've listed a few to the east of the byway along US-20 as it climbs across Santiam Pass. These are national forest campgrounds and a visit won't take you far off the route.

West Cascades Scenic Byway Campgrounds

○ **METZLER PARK** *(Clackamas County) (May 1 – Sept 30)*
     Res and Info: (503) 353-4415, www.co.clackamas.or.us
     Location: 5 Miles (8 Km) S of Estacada

     GPS Location: 45.22861 N, 122.36472 W, 600 Ft

75 Sites – Metzler is a beautiful county campground set in a bend of Clear Creek. It's possible to swim in the creek and there are local hiking trails. Sites are in two areas. Sites 1 through 27 are in the South

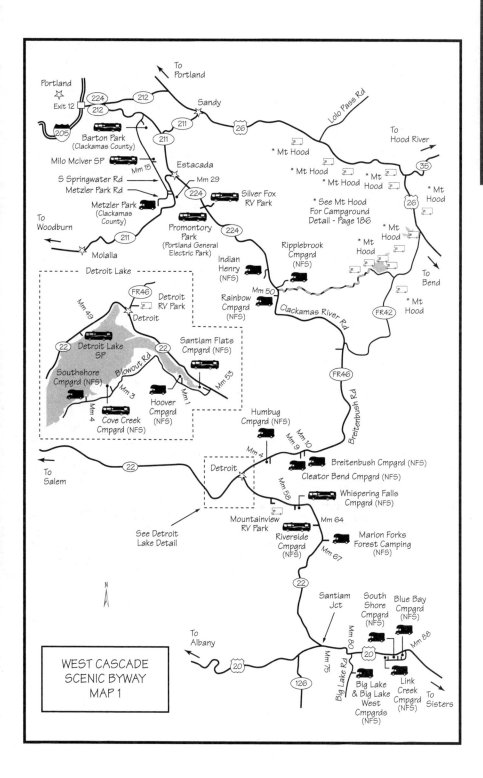

WEST CASCADE
SCENIC BYWAY
MAP 1

Campground. They have electrical and water hookups and a few of these back-in sites reach 40 feet. The North Campground has a combination of hookup and no-hookup sites and again, just a few of these back-ins reach 40 feet. Due to restricted maneuvering room we recommend the park to RVs no larger than 35 feet. From Estacada head south on SR-211. In 4 miles (6.5 km) turn right on South Springwater Road. In .5 mile (.8 km) you'll come to a T. Turn left here onto Metzler Park Road and in 1.9 miles (3.1 km) you'll reach the entrance kiosk.

☐ **MILO MCIVER STATE PARK** *(March 15 to Oct 30 – Varies)*

Reservations: www.reserveamerica.com, (800) 452-5687
Information: (503) 630-7150, (800) 551-6949,
www.oregonstateparks.org
Location: 4 Miles (6 Km) W of Estacada

GPS Location: 45.30000 N, 122.38194 W, 700 Ft

53 Sites – This is a large state park set along the Clackamas River. Rafting, canoeing and kayaking are popular but there are also hiking and biking trails, a model airplane field, and a disk golf course. The campground is on two loops. There's a nine site tent loop and another with 44 back-in RV sites with water and electric hookups. Some sites are as long as 80 feet. To reach the park drive south from Estacada on SR- 211 for 1 mile (1.6 km). Turn right on S. Haydon Rd. then in 1.1 mile (1.8 km) go right on South Springwater Road. The park entrance is on the right in another 1.2 miles (1.9 km).

○ **BARTON PARK** *(Clackamas County)(Open May 1 to Oct 31)*

Res and Info: (503) 353-4415, www.co.clackamas.or.us
Location: 8 Miles (13 Km) NW of Estacada

GPS Location: 45.38528 N, 122.40778 W, 200 Ft

98 Sites – This park is also located along Clackamas River. The raft float from Milo McIver State Park to here is about six miles and is very popular. So is the fishing. Campsites are in three different areas. There are a variety of sites from tent sites up to pull-thrus to 60 feet with electric and water hookups. From Estacada follow SR-211 north for 7.7 miles (12.4 km) to Barton Corner. Turn left here, the park entrance is .3 miles (.5 km) ahead.

● **SILVER FOX RV PARK** *(Open All Year)*

Res and Info: (503) 630-7000,
silverfoxpark@cascadeaccess.com,
www.silverfoxrvpark.com
Location: 6.5 Miles (10.5 Km) W of Estacada

GPS Location: 45.22417 N, 122.24111 W, 800 Ft

70 Sites – This commercial RV park sits on the hillside above the upper end of North Fork Reservoir and the Promontory Park campground described below. Most RV sites for travelers are in a large gravel lot at the back of the campground. Sites are almost all back-ins to 60 feet. From Estacada drive east on SR-224 for 6.5 miles (10.5 km), the park is on the left.

○ **PROMONTORY PARK** *(Portland General Electric Park)*
(Open May 25 to Sept 30 – Varies)

Res and Info: (503) 630-7229, (503) 464-8515,
www.portlandgeneral.com
Location: 6.5 Miles (10.5 Km) E of Estacada

GPS Location: 45.22250 N, 122.24333 W, 700 Ft

OREGON

50 Sites – Promontory Park is a recreation area run by Portland General Electric at the upper end of 350-acre North Fork Reservoir. There are boat launch and swimming facilities, a dock, a fishing lake for youngsters, and a campground. Sites here are back-ins ranging from 35-feet down. From Estacada drive east on SR-224 for 6.5 miles (10.5 km), the park is on the right.

■ **INDIAN HENRY** *(Open May 20 to Sept 30 – Varies)*
   Reservations: www.recreation.gov, (877) 444-6777
   Information: (503) 630-6861
   Location: 21 Miles (34 Km) SE of Estacada

GPS Location: 45.10860 N, 122.07586 W, 1,200 Ft.

83 Sites – As you drive down SR-224 through the Mt Hood National Forest you'll find many small national forest campgrounds including Lazy Bend, Carter Bridge, Armstrong, Ripplebrook, Rainbow, Riverside, and River Ford. For the most part these are small campgrounds, but the exception is Indian Henry. Here you'll find a large old campground with three loops next to the Clackamas River and Whale Creek. The loop roads and sites are paved but roads are narrow and sites are small, this campground was built long before large rigs. While a few sites are as long as 30 feet you must use extreme care parking. There is a dump station here but it is closed and cannot be used. This campground has problems with falling limbs and tree blowdowns and may be closed either temporarily or permanently. From Estacada drive southeast on SR-224 for 20.1 miles (32.4 km). Turn right just before the bridge on NF-4620, the campground entrance is .5 mile (.8 km) ahead.

■ **RIPPLEBROOK CAMPGROUND** *(Open May 15 to Sept 15)*
   Reservations: www.recreation.gov, (877) 444-6777
   Information: (503) 630-6861
   Location: 25 Miles (40 Km) SE of Estacada

GPS Location: 45.07944 N, 122.0415 W, 1,400 Ft

14 Sites – Ripplebrook is one of the smaller Mt Hood National Forest campgrounds along SR-224. Campsites overlook a small creek, a nice location. Sites are off an out and back access road with a loop at the end. Site sizes and shapes are very irregular. Most are short but one near the entrance is 40 feet and a couple others are 35. Maneuvering room is tight. There is no potable water. The campground is located just north of the intersection of Timothy Lake Road and SR-224 at the Mile 50 marker.

■ **RAINBOW CAMPGROUND** *(Open May 15 to Sept 15 - Varies)*
   Information: (503) 630-6861
   Location: 25 Miles (40 Km) SE of Estacada

GPS Location: 45.07743 N, 122.04465 W, 1,400 Ft

17 Sites – This is another Mt Hood National Forest campground, it's just across the road from the Ripplebrook. Sites here are off a loop road and are small. They too are extremely irregular and only reach about 25 feet in length with many smaller than that. There is no potable water at the campground.

■ **BREITENBUSH CAMPGROUND** *(Open May 15 to Sept 15 – Varies)*
   Reservations: www.recreation.gov, (877) 444-6777
   Information: (801) 226-3564
   Location: 9.2 Miles (14.8 km) N of Detroit Lake

GPS Location: 44.78111 N, 121.99139 W, 2,000 Ft

30 Sites – This Willamette National Forest campground is adjacent to the Breitenbush River. The sites are off two paved loops, parking is on paved pads. Sites have picnic tables and fire pits. Some sites reach 45 feet and longer but due to limited maneuvering room the forest service recommends a maximum trailer length of 24 feet. This is a popular campground and on weekends you must stay for two days, on holidays for three days. The campground is on the east side of FR 46 some 9.2 miles (14.8 km) north of the intersection with SR-22 at Detroit Lake.

■ **CLEATOR BEND CAMPGROUND** *(Open May 15 to Sept 30 – Varies)*
Information: (801) 226-3564
Location: 8.7 Miles (14 Km) N of Detroit Lake

GPS Location: 44.77833 N, 121.99861 W, 2,100 Ft

9 Sites – This small Willamette National Forest campground along the Breitenbush River has back-ins and one pull-thru off a paved loop road with sites to 30 feet. It is on the east side of FR 46 some 8.7 miles (14 km) north of the intersection with SR-22 at Detroit Lake.

■ **HUMBUG CAMPGROUND** *(Open May 5 to Sept 30 – Varies)*
Information: (503) 854-3366
Location: 4.4 Miles (7.1 Km) N of Detroit Lake

GPS Location: 44.77222 N, 122.07861 W, 1,800 Ft

21 Sites – This is a nice modern Willamette National Forest Service campground with large paved sites off a paved loop road. There are pull-thrus to 70 feet and back-ins to at least 50 feet. Unfortunately, maneuvering room is tight so we recommend the park to carefully driven RVs no longer than 35 feet and the forest service says trailers to 30 feet. The campground is on the east side of FR 46 some 4.4 miles (7.1 km) north of the intersection with SR-22 at Detroit Lake.

☐ **DETROIT LAKE STATE PARK** *(Open All Year)*
Reservations: www.reserveamerica.com, (800) 452-5687
Information: (503) 854-3346, (800) 551-6949,
          www.oregonstateparks.org
Location: N Shore of Detroit Lake

GPS Location: 44.72889 N, 122.17556 W, 1,600 Ft

311 Sites – This is a very large state campground on the shore of Detroit Lake, a reservoir on the North Santiam River. The lake is very popular for watersports (including powered) and the park has a swimming area and dock. Sites are off many paved loops and have paved parking pads. Some sites are full hookups, there are also electric and water sites as well as many no-hookup tent and RV sites. All sites are back-ins, many exceed 50 feet. The campground is located on the north shore of the reservoir off SR-22 about 1.5 miles (2.4 km) west of its intersection with FR 46.

■ **SOUTHSHORE CAMPGROUND** *(Open May 15 to Sept 15 – Varies)*
Information: (503) 854-3366
Location: S Shore of Detroit Lake

GPS Location: 44.70500 N, 122.17389 W, 1,600 Ft

30 Sites – This Willamette National Forest campground is on the south shore of Detroit Lake and has a boat ramp. Sites are off three paved loops and parking pads are paved. There are pull-thru and back-ins sites to 35 feet. Actually, there are some pull-thrus to 70

OREGON

feet but they are considered double sites and you pay two fees to use them, pretty pricey. Sites have picnic tables and fire pits and there are vault toilets. From the intersection of FR 46 and SR-22 drive south 2.8 miles (4.5 km) to Blowout Road (near Mile 53). Turn west here and follow the paved road for 4.2 miles (6.8 km) to the campground.

■ **COVE CREEK CAMPGROUND** *(Open May 15 to Sept 30 – Varies)*
  Reservations: www.recreation.gov, (877) 444-6777
  Information: (503) 854-3366
  Location: S Shore of Detroit Lake

       GPS Location: 44.70861 N, 122.15944 W, 1,600 Ft

63 Sites – This Willamette National Forest campground is on the south
shore of Detroit Lake. It's the most big-rig friendly of the Forest Service campgrounds on the lake but not all sites will take big rigs. There are back-ins to 50 feet and pull-thrus to 60 feet. Maneuvering room isn't bad. Access roads are paved and so are parking pads, the campground has flush toilets and coin-op showers. It also has a boat ramp and dock. From the intersection of FR 46 and SR-22 drive south 2.8 miles (4.5 km) to Blowout Road (near Mile 53). Turn west here and follow the paved road for 3.5 miles (5.6 km) to the campground.

■ **HOOVER CAMPGROUND** *(Open April 15 to Sept 30 – Varies)*
  Reservations: www.recreation.gov, (877) 444-6777
  Information: (503) 854-3366
  Location: S Shore of Detroit Lake

       GPS Location: 44.71194 N, 122.12278 W, 1,600 Ft

36 Sites – This Willamette National Forest campground is on the North Santiam River arm of Detroit Lake, near the far east end of the lake. Again, this campground charges double for long pull-thrus and maneuvering room is limited so we recommend it only for RVs to 35 feet. The forest service says maximum trailer length is 30 feet. There's a boat launch and fishing platforms, also a short nature trail. From the intersection of FR 46 and SR-22 drive south 2.8 miles (4.5 km) to Blowout Road (near Mile 53). Turn west here and follow the paved road for 1 mile (1.6 km) to the campground.

■ **SANTIAM FLATS CAMPGROUND** *(Open All Year)*
  Information: (503) 854-3366
  Location: E Shore of Detroit Lake

       GPS Location: 44.71111 N, 122.11389 W, 1,600 Ft

30 Sites – This Willamette National Forest campground is a flat parking area on the east shore of Detroit Lake near the inlet. It's unusual, but still considered a Forest Service campground. There is a fee and it has a vault toilet. There is no potable water. Sites are ill defined and any size RV can fit, so can tents of course although this campground is best for RVs. At busy times the campground is really packed. There are some picnic tables and fire pits.

■ **WHISPERING FALLS CAMPGROUND** *(Open May 15 to Sept 30 – Varies)*
  Information: (541) 854-3366
  Location: 5 Miles (8 Km) S of Detroit Lake

       GPS Location: 44.68833 N, 122.01000 W, 1,900 Ft

16 Sites – This Willamette National Forest campground is a small older campground sitting above the West Fork of the Santiam River, the campground is named after a small

falls on the far side of the river. It's set in a dense evergreen forest. Access to the river is not possible from the individual sites but there is a trail down to the bank. Sites here are surprisingly large, some pull-thrus and back-ins reach 60 feet. The forest service says maximum trailer size is 30 feet. The access road is paved but a little ragged, there's a vault toilet and sites have fire pits and picnic tables. The campground is located at about Mile 58.5 of SR-22.

■ **RIVERSIDE CAMPGROUND** *(Open May 15 to Sept 30 – Varies)*
Reservations: www.recreation.gov, (877) 444-6777
Information: (503) 854-3366
Location: 11 Miles (18 Km) S of Detroit Lake

GPS Location: 44.64222 N, 121.94500 W, 2,300 Ft

38 Sites – This Willamette National Forest campground occupies a site on the east shore of the West Fork of the Santiam River. Sites are off two out-and-back access roads along the river, they have turning loops at the end. Sites here are back-ins to about 45 feet. Maneuvering room is tight, exercise caution. The forest service recommends a maximum trailer length of 24 feet. Since this is a popular campground you must stay at least two days on weekends, three days on holidays. The campground is located at about Mile 64.2 of SR-22.

■ **MARION FORKS FOREST CAMPING** *(Open All Year)*
Information: (503) 854-3366
Location: Marion Forks, 13 Miles (21 Km) S of Detroit Lake

GPS Location: 44.61139 N, 121.94750 W, 2,500 Ft

15 Sites – To get to this Willamette National Forest campground you turn into the parking lot for the Marion Forks Fish Hatchery which is just to the south of the Marion Creek Bridge. Immediately after turning into the hatchery a smaller gravel road goes to the left to run along Marion Creek and sites 1-7 are located along this road. This area is suitable for RVs to 25 feet. On entering the hatchery if you continue through to the back of the parking lot, a rough paved loop road leads to sites 8-15. These sites are back ins and some are as long as 50 feet but because very limited maneuvering room this area is best for RVs no larger than 35 feet. The Forest Service says maximum trailer length is 24 feet. Sites are under a dense forest of evergreens. There are vault toilets, fire pits, and picnic tables. The campground is located on the east side of the road at about Mile 66.5 of SR-22.

■ **BIG LAKE AND BIG LAKE WEST CAMPGROUNDS**
    (Open July 5 to Oct 15 – Varies)
Reservations: www.recreation.gov, (877) 444-6777
Information: (503) 854-3366
Location: Big Lake

GPS Location: 44.37972 N, 121.86944 W, 4,600 Ft

49 Sites – These Willamette National Forest campground occupy the northwest shore of 250 acre Big Lake. It's a popular natural lake for boating and some fishing. The sites here are back-ins and pull-thrus to 35 feet in an area of lodge pole pines. Some sites are on the lakeshore and boats can be pulled up in front. To reach the campgrounds go south from Mile 80 of US-20 on Big Lake Road, this is also the access road to Hoodoo Ski Area. In .8 miles (1.3 km) you come to a Y, the resort is to the right, the campgrounds to the left. In another 2.4 miles (3.9 km) you'll reach the campgrounds.

■ **BLUE BAY CAMPGROUND** *(Open May 15 to Sept 15 – Varies)*
Reservations: (877) 444-6777, www.recreation.gov
Information: 541-549-7700
Location: Suttle Lake

GPS Location: 44.41944 N, 121.73222 W, 3,500 Ft

25 Sites – This is the first of three Deschutes National Forest campgrounds on 240-acre Suttle Lake. The lake is popular for power boats as well as fishing. The 3.2-mile Suttle Lake Shoreline Trail circles the lake. Sites in this campground are off two paved loops, most sites are either waterfront or have a water view. Sites are both pull-thrus and back-ins to 45 feet but due to limited maneuvering room the campground is best for RVs to 35 feet. To reach the campground take NF-2070 south from Mile 87.4 of US-20. The campground entrance is on the right in .9 mile (1.5 km).

■ **SOUTH SHORE CAMPGROUND** *(Open May 25 to Sept 20 – Varies)*
Reservations: www.recreation.gov, (877) 444-6777
Information: (541) 225-6300
Location: Suttle Lake

GPS Location: 44.42028 N, 121.73556 W, 3,500 Ft

24 Sites – South shore is the middle of three Deschutes National Forest campgrounds on Suttle Lake. This one has both back-in and pull-thru sites to about 45 feet off paved loop roads. Limited maneuvering room make parking an RV over about 35 feet pretty tough. The campground has a boat ramp and fish cleaning station. To reach the campground take NF-2070 south from Mile 87.4 of US-20. The campground entrance is on the right in 1 mile (1.6 km).

■ **LINK CREEK CAMPGROUND** *(April 25 to Nov 25 - Varies)*
Reservations: www.recreation.gov, (877) 444-6777
Information: (541) 225-6300
Location: Suttle Lake

GPS Location: 44.41583 N, 121.75556 W, 3,500 Ft

31 Sites – This is the last of the three Deschutes National Forest campgrounds on Suttle Lake, and the most used. Sites here are set in scattered pines and are both back-ins and pull-thrus to 60 feet. Maneuvering room is restricted so careful driving is important but large rigs do use this campground. Access roads are paved and some, but not all, pads are paved. Ice and some simple food items are available across the street. There's a boat ramp at the campground. To reach the campground take NF-2070 south from Mile 87.4 of US-20. The campground entrance is on the right in 2.1 miles (3.4 km).

■ **COLDWATER COVE CAMPGROUND** *(Open June 15 to Oct 15 – Varies)*
Reservations: www.recreation.gov, (877) 444-6777
Information: (541) 822-3381
Location: 18 Miles (29 Km) NE of McKenzie Bridge

GPS Location: 44.35583 N, 121.9947 W, 3,100 Ft

33 Sites – Coldwater Cove Willamette National Forest Service Campground is located on the shore of Clear Lake, headwaters of the McKenzie River. The campground is set in an old lava flow on the east side of the lake off two paved loops. Sites are paved and some reach 35 feet. The Forest Service says maximum trailer length is 30 feet. Nearby Clear Lake Resort has a restaurant. There are trails to Koosah Falls and Sahalie Falls. The

OREGON

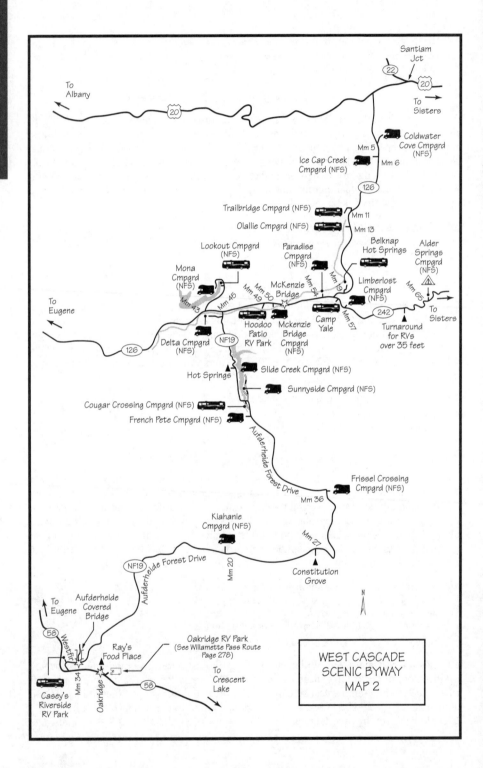

WEST CASCADE
SCENIC BYWAY
MAP 2

access road to the campground goes east from SR-126 near Mile 5.3

■ **ICE CAP CREEK CAMPGROUND** *(Open May 25 to Sept 15 – Varies)*
Information: (541) 822-3381
Location: 17 Miles NE of McKenzie Bridge

GPS Location: 44.34306 N, 121.99972 W, 2,800 Ft

21 Sites – Ice Cap is a small, older Willamette National Forest Service campground on Carman Reservoir on the McKenzie River. Parking is on dirt and duff off a paved loop road. Many sites are for tents, some will take RVs to 30 feet although leveling may be difficult. The Forest Service recommends trailers to 30 feet. There is no potable water at this campground. Koosah and Sahalie Falls are nearby. The entrance to the campground is near Mile 5.5 of SR-126.

■ **TRAILBRIDGE CAMPGROUND**
        (Open April 25 to Oct 25 - Varies)
Information: (541) 822-3381
Location: 13 Miles NE of McKenzie Bridge

GPS Location: 44.28306 N, 122.04417 W, 2,100 Ft

40 Sites – Trail Bridge Willamette National Forest Campground is located on the Trail Bridge Reservoir on the McKenzie River. It's a popular fishing destination. To access the campground you must exit Hwy 126 and pass through a single-lane access route past a small power plant. You'll drive under a gantry (lots of room) right next to the turbines and emerge on the other side on a one lane paved road with pull-offs which leads to the camping area. At the campground a gravel loop road leads past a variety of camping sites many of which are in open gravel or grass areas with sites defined by the placement of a picnic table and a rock or metal fire ring. Near the entrance to the camping area there are vault toilets and water faucets. There's a pay phone at the power plant. The campground also has a boat ramp. The access road leads west from Mile 10.8 of SR-126.

■ **OLALLIE CAMPGROUND** *(Open April 15 to Oct 25 – Varies)*
Reservations: www.recreation.gov, (877) 444-6777
Information: (541) 822-3381
Location: 11 Miles NE of McKenzie Bridge

GPS Location: 44.25556 N, 122.03944 W, 2,000 Ft

16 Sites – This Willamette National Forest campground is located on the McKenzie River. Paved sites are set off two paved loops. The first or upper loop is best for larger RVs, several sites on this loop are pull-thrus to 70 feet although they are narrow. The lower loop is unsuitable for large RVs and has spaces for RVs to about 25 feet. It's next to the river and much quieter than the upper loop since it's farther from the highway. There's a boat ramp for rafts and drift boats at this campground and fishing is popular. The entrance is near Mile 12.9 of SR-126.

● **BELKNAP HOT SPRINGS** *(Open All Year)*
Res and Info: (541) 822-3512,
        www.BelknapHotSprings.com
Location: 5 Miles E of McKenzie Bridge

GPS Location: 44.19222 N, 122.05056 W, 1,600 Ft

57 Sites – This little-known destination has one of the nicest RV parks in the northwest. It's a hot spring resort with a lodge, rental cabins, and

two nice hot pools. Sites are in three locations. The lower sites are back-ins (or pull-ins) down by the main lodge building with water and electric sites to about 38 feet. There's a pool at the main building and the sites front on the McKenzie River. An upper RV campground has back-in sites to 60 feet and full and partial hookups, the second pool is nearby. There are tent sites both across the river and near the upper pool. Wi-Fi is available at the lodge but not at the sites. Reservations are recommended. Nearby Camp Yale (see below) has the same ownership and serves as a sort of overflow camping area, it also has a dump station that can be used by Belknap guests. The resort entrance is near Mile 18.7 of SR-126, very near the intersection with SR-242, the McKenzie Highway.

● **CAMP YALE** *(Open All Year)*
   Res and Info: (541) 822-3512,
                    www.BelknapHotSprings.com
   Location: 5 Miles (8 Km) E of McKenzie Bridge

GPS Location: 44.18167 N, 122.06889 W, 1,600 Ft

16 Sites – With the same ownership as Belknap Hot Springs this campground serves as a kind of alternate camping area for the resort. There are 16 back-in 45-foot sites with full hookups. There's also a dump station that can be used by Belknap guests. Camp Yale is located off SR-242, the McKenzie Highway, .3 mile (.5 km) from it's intersection with SR-126.

■ **LIMBERLOST CAMPGROUND** *(Open May 20 to Sept 30 – Varies)*
   Information: (541) 822-3381
   Location: 6 Miles (10 Km) E of McKenzie Bridge

GPS Location: 44.17361 N, 122.05361 W, 1,700 Ft

13 Sites – This tiny Willamette National Forest campground has 13 sites off a narrow loop road. It's suitable only for tent campers or very small RVs like pickup campers and vans. The campground is located on SR-242, the McKenzie Highway, about 1.4 miles (2.3 km) east of the intersection with SR-126.

■ **ALDER SPRINGS CAMPGROUND** *(Open When Snow Allows)*
   Information: (541) 822-3381
   Location: 15 Miles (24 Km) E of McKenzie Bridge

GPS Location: 44.17889 N, 121.91528 W, 2,700 Ft

6 Sites – Alder Springs is a small tent-only Willamette National Forest campground. There are six sets of tables and fire pits just off the road, also a vault toilet. In the late fall, winter, and spring when SR-242 is closed over McKenzie Pass the barrier is just east of this campground. The campground is located near Mile 66 of SR-242, about 10 miles (16 km) from its intersection with SR-126.

■ **PARADISE CAMPGROUND** *(Open May 15 to Oct 25 – Varies)*
   Reservations: www.recreation.gov, (877) 444-6777
   Information: (541) 822-3381
   Location: 4 Miles (6 Km) E of McKenzie Bridge

GPS Location: 44.18444 N, 122.09000 W, 1,600 Ft

64 Sites – This Willamette National Forest campground is set along the McKenzie River in an old growth forest. It was built by the CCC so it has some history. The campground is dark and access roads are narrow. Sites, however, are large with some pull-thrus as long as 70 feet. Unfortunately, maneuvering room is scarce and we recommend the camp-

ground for RVs no longer than 35 feet. The McKenzie National Recreation Trail runs past the campground and continues upstream beyond Clear Lake. There's a launch ramp here for rafters and drift-boat fishermen. The campground access road leaves SR-126 near Mile 54.

■ **McKenzie Bridge Campground** *(Open April 20 to Sept 30 – Varies)*
   Reservations: www.recreation.gov, (877) 444-6777
   Information: (541) 822-3381
   Location: McKenzie Bridge

GPS Location: 44.17611 N, 122.17417 W, 1,300 Ft

20 Sites – This Willamette National Forest campground borders the McKenzie River in a heavy evergreen forest. Many sites are near the river and these are long back-in and pull-thru sites. Unfortunately, maneuvering room is tight so we recommend the campground only for RVs to 35 feet. There's a launching area for rafts and drift boats. The campground access road leaves SR-126 near Mile 49.7, just west of McKenzie Bridge.

● **Hoodoo Patio RV Park** *(Open All Year)*
   Res and Info: (541) 822-3596, reservations@patiorv.com,
                www.patiorv.com
   Location: 1 Mile (2 Km) W of McKenzie Bridge

   GPS Location: 44.17576 N, 122.19128 W, 1,300 Ft

70 Sites – This older commercial campground is operated by the same folks who manage many of the forest service campgrounds in the Northwest. Some sites are along the river and others are near the road with carports, they're especially handy if you're here in the winter. All sites except one are back-ins to 45 feet. The campground is on the south side of SR-126 next to the McKenzie River, it's near Mile 49 and not far west of McKenzie Bridge.

■ **Mona Campground** *(Open May 15 to Sept 15 – Varies)*
   Information: (541) 822-3381
   Location: 10 Miles (16 Km) W of McKenzie Bridge

GPS Location: 44.20056 N, 122.26306 W, 1,300 Ft

23 Sites – This Willamette National Forest campground occupies a high bank on the north side of Blue River Reservoir. The roads and parking pads are paved, sites are pull-thrus and back-ins to 35 feet. To reach the campground turn north from SR-126 onto Blue River Reservoir Road near Mile 44. This is 6 miles west of McKenzie Bridge. Follow Blue Water Reservoir Road north for 4.2 miles (6.8 km) as it curves around the northeast end of the reservoir to the campground.

■ **Lookout Campground** *(Open April 20 to Oct 2 – Varies)*
   Information: (541) 822-3381
   Location: 10 Miles (16 Km) W of McKenzie Bridge

GPS Location: 44.20361 N, 122.26056 W, 1,300 Ft

20 Sites – This is a dispersed parking area on the east end of the Blue River Reservoir. It's an open parking area near the boat launch area so any size RV can park on the gravel here. There are no amenities other than the nearby vault toilets but there is usually a host. To reach the campground turn north from SR-126 onto Blue River Reservoir Road near Mile 44. This is 6 miles west of McKenzie Bridge. Follow Blue Water Reservoir Road north for 3.5 miles (5.6 km) as it curves around the northeast end of the reservoir to the campground.

■ **DELTA CAMPGROUND** *(Open April 20 to Oct 20 – Varies)*
   Information: (541) 822-3381
   Location: 5 Miles (8 Km) W of McKenzie Bridge

   GPS Location: 44.16278 N, 122.27722 W, 1,100 Ft

38 Sites – This Willamette National Forest campground occupies a delta at the confluence of the McKenzie River and the South Fork of the McKenzie River. The campground sits in a beautiful old growth evergreen forest. Sites aren't large and the access road is cramped, our recommended RV size here is 30 feet. Water is available via a hand pump and there is a barrier-free nature trail. From the intersection of SR-126 and the Aufderheide Forest Drive head south for just .2 mile (.3 km), the campground entrance road goes to the west.

■ **SLIDE CREEK CAMPGROUND** *(Open April 30 to Sept 30 – Varies)*
   Information: (541) 822-3381
   Location: 16 Miles (26 Km) S of McKenzie Bridge

   GPS Location: 44.07583 N, 122.22500 W, 1,700 Ft

16 Sites – Slide Creek Campground is one of the Willamette National Forest campgrounds near Cougar Reservoir, it's on the east side of the reservoir on a side road. There is a boat ramp here as well as the campgrounds. The sites in the campgrounds are small and off a narrow loop road with no views of the lake. The sites are suitable only for tent camping and small RVs. From an intersection just south of the reservoir drive 1.3 mile (2.1 km) on the gravel access road up the east side of the reservoir to the campground.

■ **SUNNYSIDE CAMPGROUND** *(Open May 15 to Sept 15 – Varies)*
   Information: (541) 822-3381
   Location: 15 Miles (24 Km) S of McKenzie Bridge

   GPS Location: 44.06028 N, 122.22056 W, 1,700 Ft

13 Sites – This is a small Willamette National Forest campground near the shore of the Cougar Reservoir. The campsites are arranged off one access road with a small turnaround at the end. Sites are small, suitable only for automobiles, vans, and pickup-campers. From an intersection just south of the reservoir drive .1 mile (.2 km) on the gravel access road up the east side of the reservoir to the campground.

■ **COUGAR CROSSING CAMPGROUND** *(Open All Year)*
   Information: (541) 822-3381
   Location: 15 Miles (24 Km) S of McKenzie Bridge

   GPS Location: 44.05750 N, 122.22000 W, 1,700 Ft

12 Sites – Although this large open lot in the Willamette National Forest looks more like a rest area than a campground it's a good overnight place for large RVs. There are tent sites in the trees as well as several vehicle camping sites where any size rig can park. Amenities include picnic tables, fire pits, and a vault toilet. There is no potable water. The campground is adjacent to the intersection at the south end of the Cougar Reservoir.

■ **FRENCH PETE CAMPGROUND** *(Open May 15 to Sept 15 – Varies)*
   Information: (541) 822-3381
   Location: 16 Miles (26 Km) S of McKenzie Bridge

   GPS Location: 44.04278 N, 122.20861 W, 1,900 Ft

17 Sites – This Willamette National Forest campground has back-in sites to 30 feet off a

paved loop. There's a hand pump for water. The campground is in a grove of Douglas fir and alder next to the South Fork of the McKenzie River. Just to the north is the trailhead for French Pete Trail which leads three miles up French Creek to the east into the Three Sisters Wilderness and connecting trails

■ **FRISSEL CROSSING CAMPGROUND** *(Open May 15 to Sept 15 – Varies)*
Information: (541) 822-3381
Location: 27 Miles (44 Km) S of McKenzie Bridge

GPS Location: 43.95750 N, 122.08500, 2,600 Ft

12 Sites – This Willamette National Forest campground is set in a grove of huge Douglas firs. It sits along the South Fork of the McKenzie River just upstream from the confluence with the Roaring River. Sites here are pull-thrus and back-ins to 35 feet off a loop drive but access is tight. Water is available at a hand pump. The campground is on the east side of the Aufderheide Forest Drive near Mile 36. From here southbound the road crosses up and over a divide from the McKenzie watershed to the Willamette watershed.

■ **KIAHANIE CAMPGROUND** *(Open May 25 to Oct 30 – Varies)*
Information: (541) 782-2283
Location: 20 Miles (32 Km) NW of Westfir

GPS Location: 43.88472 N, 122.25667 W, 2, 200 Ft

18 Sites – This Willamette National Forest campground occupies a site on the bank of the North Fork of the Willamette River in an old growth forest. This is a designated Wild and Scenic River. This is not a stocked river and fly fishing is allowed for the native fish. Sites are back-ins and pull-thrus, some suitable for RVs to 30 feet. The Forest Service says trailers up to 24 feet. Water is from a hand pump. The campground is near Mile 20 of the Aufderheide Forest Drive, about 20 miles (32 km) from Westfir and 43 miles (69 km) from McKenzie Bridge.

● **CASEY'S RIVERSIDE RV PARK** *(Open All Year)*
Res and Info: (541) 782-1906,
        www.caseysrvpark.com
Location: Westfir

GPS Location: 43.75611 N, 122.52861 W, 1,000 Ft

56 Sites – Casey's is a nice modern park with paved roads and parking pads situated along the Middle Fork of the Willamette River. They have pull-thrus to 75 feet and back-ins to 50. Amenities include a seasonal pool, boat ramp, and there's fishing in the river. To reach the campground turn north off SR-58 at Mile 31.3 for Westfir. In .3 miles (.5 km) you'll see the campground on the left.

WILLAMETTE PASS ROUTE

One of the most direct crossings of the Cascade Mountains in is Oregon SR-58 through Willamette Pass. It runs from the Eugene region to connect with US-97 about 55 miles (89 km) south of Bend. The pass altitude is 5,126 feet.

In the Cascades the highway passes through both the Willamette and the Deschutes National Forests.

Near Mile 55 there's a viewpoint for **Salt Creek Falls**, Oregon's second highest waterfall at 286 feet. There's also a 2.5 mile (4.0 km) trail to **Diamond Creek Falls**.

OREGON

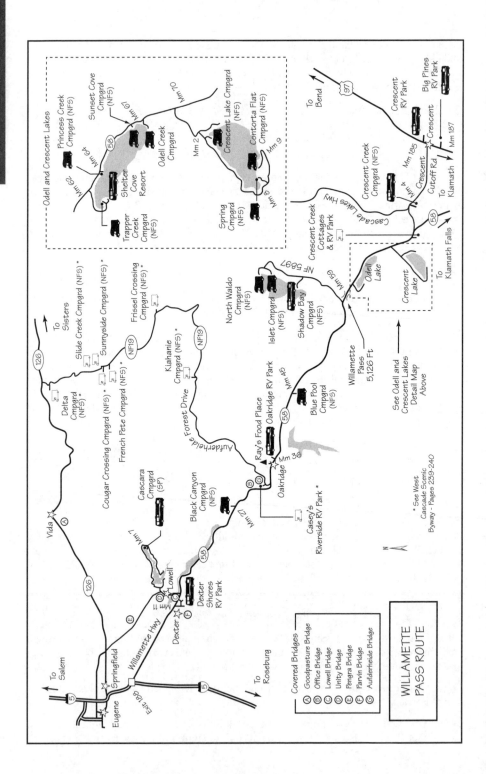

Covered Bridges
- Ⓐ Goodpasture Bridge
- Ⓑ Office Bridge
- Ⓒ Lowell Bridge
- Ⓓ Unity Bridge
- Ⓔ Pengra Bridge
- Ⓕ Parvin Bridge
- Ⓖ Aufderheide Bridge

WILLAMETTE PASS ROUTE

* See West Cascade Scenic Byway - Pages 239–240

OREGON

THE WESTFIR COVERED BRIDGE (ALSO CALLED OFFICE BRIDGE) NEAR OAKRIDGE

A little farther on , but still on the west side of the pass, **Waldo Lake** is about 5 miles (8 km) north of the highway. This large lake at 5,400 feet, is thought to be one of the three purest lakes in the world. The other two are Crater Lake, not far away, and a lake in Siberia. There's a 21-mile hiking trail around the lake. There are also several campgrounds, see below.

Once across the pass there are two more large lakes south of the highway. These are Odell and Crescent Lakes, both with campgrounds described below.

Willamette Pass Route Campgrounds

● **DEXTER SHORES RV PARK** *(Open All Year)*
Reservations: (866) 558-9777
Information: (541) 937-3711,
          www.dextersshoresrv.com
Location: 14 Miles (23 Km) E of Eugene

GPS Location: 43.91333 N, 122.80972 W, 600 Ft

61 Sites – This is a popular local RV park with good access to a day-use park on nearby Dexter Reservoir. There are some resident units here, but also a separate large area for travelers. These traveler RV sites are back-ins and pull-thrus to 65 feet. There are also tent sites in a separate area with picnic tables and fire pits. Travel east from Exit 188 of I-5 on SR-58, the Willamette Highway, for 11.1 miles (17.9 km). The campground entrance is signed on the right

OREGON

☐ **FALL CREEK STATE RECREATION AREA -**
CASCARA CAMPGROUND *(Open May 1 to Sept 30)*

Information: (541) 937-1080, (800) 551-6949,
           www.oregonstateparks.org
Location: 26 Miles (42 Km) E of Eugene

GPS Location: 43.97222 N, 122.66694 W, 900 Ft

47 Sites – This campground is in Fall Creek State Recreation Area on Fall Creek Reservoir. Cascara is a popular swimming and water sports park (including personal watercraft and water skiing) in the summer. Water levels in the reservoir are low in the fall and the park tends to be pretty much empty then. There are good tent sites and back-ins to 40 feet although there are no hookups here. There are also walk-in tent sites along the shoreline of the reservoir. The campground has a swimming area and a boat ramp. If you follow the route below to reach the park you'll see two of the region's covered bridges. Travel east from Exit 188 of I-5 on SR-58, the Willamette Highway, for 12.7 miles (20.5 km). Turn left toward Lowell just past the Lowell covered bridge and pass through Lowell (the road make a two-block jog to the left in Lowell) and drive 2.8 miles (4.5 km) until you see the Unity covered bridge ahead. Don't cross it, instead turn right and follow Big Fall Creek Road 8 miles (13 km) to the park.

■ **BLACK CANYON CAMPGROUND** *(Open May 27 to Oct 11 – Varies)* $ $$$ ▲ 🔥 [1]

Reservations: www.recreation.gov, (877) 444-6777
Information: (541) 782-2283
Location: 28 Miles (45 Km) E of Eugene

GPS Location: 43.80556 N, 122.56472 W, 1,000 Ft

74 Sites – This large Willamette National Forest campground is set in a dense forest of cedars and hemlocks. The access roads inside the park are paved but very narrow and winding making it suitable only for tent campers and coaches to about 30 feet. Black Canyon is located at the upper end of Lookout Point Reservoir. It's really on the Middle Fork of the Willamette River before it flows into the lake but at high water levels the lake does reach the campground. There is a boat ramp. Travel east from Exit 188 of I-5 on SR-58, the Willamette Highway, for 27 miles (44 km). The campground entrance is signed on the left.

● **OAKRIDGE RV PARK** *(Open All Year)*

Res and Info: (541) 782-2611, mgr@arborinnmotel.
           net,
           www.oakridgervpark.com,
Location: Oakridge

GPS Location: 43.74111 N, 122.45972 W, 1,200 Ft

25 Sites – This commercial campground in Oakridge is on the same grounds as the Arbor Inn Motel. It has pull-thru and back-in sites to 55 feet. Access roads are paved and parking is on gravel. The campground is on the north side of SR-58 at Mile 36.

■ **BLUE POOL CAMPGROUND** *(Open April 23 to Sept 18 – Varies)* $$$ ▲ 🚻 🔥 ♿

Information: (541) 782-2283
Location: 9 Mile (15 Km) E of Oakridge

GPS Location: 43.70972 N, 122.29833 W, 1,900 Ft

24 Sites – Blue Hole Willamette National Forest Campground is located right next to SR-58 along Salt Creek. There are two narrow paved loop roads set in huge cedars and

Douglas firs. Small sites and narrow roads limit practical RV size to 25 feet. Water is from faucets and there is a restroom with flush toilets. The campground is on the south side of the highway near Mile 44.5.

■ SHADOW BAY CAMPGROUND *(Open July 20 to Sept 30 – Varies)*
   Reservations: www.recreation.gov, (877) 444-6777
   Information: (541) 782-2283
   Location: Waldo Lake

   GPS Location: 43.69778 N, 122.04250 W, 5,400 Ft

90 Sites – This large Willamette National Forest campground has back-ins sites to 35 feet off six loops near the south shore of Waldo Lake. None of the sites are along the lake but those on Loop F are nearest. There's a swimming beach and a boat ramp. Note that the Forest Service warns about mosquitoes at this campground. At Mile 59 on SR-58 turn north on NF-5897 for Waldo Lake. After driving 6.5 miles (10.5 km) turn left on NF-5896, signed for Shadow Bay. In another 1.6 miles (2.6 km) you'll see the campground entrance on the right.

■ NORTH WALDO CAMPGROUND *(Open July 17 to Oct 4 – Varies)*
   Reservations: www.recreation.gov, (877) 833-6777
   Information: (541) 782-2283
   Location: Waldo Lake

   GPS Location: 43.75972 N, 122.00389 W, 5,400 Ft

58 Sites – North Waldo is a Willamette National Forest campground on the northeast shore of Waldo Lake. It is the most-used campground on the lake, perhaps because it has fewer mosquitoes. Sites are off a paved loop road and are limited to 35 foot in length. There's a swimming beach and a boat ramp at the campground. At Mile 59 on SR-58 turn north on NF-5897 for Waldo Lake. In 12.2 miles (19.7 km) you'll come to a T. Turn right here and in .3 miles (.5 km) you'll come to the campground.

■ ISLET CAMPGROUND *(Open July 18 to Oct 17 – Varies)*
   Information: (541) 782-2283
   Location: Waldo Lake

   GPS Location: 43.74750 N, 122.00806 W, 5,400 Ft

55 Sites – This Willamette National Forest Service campground is on the eastern shore of Waldo Lake. Sites are back-ins to 30 feet off one loop road. The campground has a swimming beach at the nearby day use area as well as a boat launch. At Mile 59 on SR-58 turn north on NF-5897 for Waldo Lake. In 12.2 miles (19.7 km) you'll come to a T. Turn left here and in 1.2 miles (1.9 km) you'll enter the campground.

■ TRAPPER CREEK CAMPGROUND *(Open May 20 to Oct 10 – Varies)*
   Reservations: www.recreation.gov, (877) 833-6777
   Information: (541) 433-3200
   Location: Odell Lake

   GPS Location: 43.58250 N, 122.04444 W, 4,800 Ft

32 Sites – This Deschutes National Forest campground is located on the southwest shore of Odell Lake. It's the most spacious of the campgrounds on Odell Lake. Paved sites are off a long paved loop and some sites reach 35 feet. Next door is the Shelter Cove Resort which has a general store, see below. Although people swim in the lake there is no designated swimming beach. To reach the campground leave SR-58 at Mile 62.7 and

turn south onto the Odell Lake West Access Road. Follow it for 1.9 miles (3.1 km) to the campground.

● **SHELTER COVE RESORT**
    (Open All Year – Reduced Service in Winter)
  Reservations: (800) 647-2729
  Information: 433-2548, www.sheltercoveresort.com
  Location: Odell Lake

  GPS Location: 43.58028 N, 122.04028 W, 4,800 Ft

72 Sites – This private resort has cabins and an RV park. Sites have electrical hookups, water is available, and there's a sewer pump-out service if you don't want to move your rig over to the dump station. Some sites will take RVs to 45 feet. There are docks and swimming is in the lake. The resort also has a general store. Reach the resort by leaving SR-58 at Mile 62.7 and turn south onto Odell Lake West Access Road. Follow it for 2.1 miles (3.4 km) to the resort.

■ **PRINCESS CREEK CAMPGROUND** *(Open April 25 to Sept 15 – Varies)*
  Information: (541) 433-3200
  Location: Odell Lake

  GPS Location: 43.58611 N, 122.00917 W, 4,800 Ft

32 Sites – Princess Creek Deschutes National Forest Campground occupies a fairly narrow area between SR-58 and Odell Lake. Sites are arranged off two long loops, some sites are waterfront and are considered premium sites with a higher price. Some sites here are as long as 45 feet however maneuvering room is poor and the campground is best for RVs only to 30 feet. There is no potable water at this campground. There's a boat ramp at the campground and boats can be pulled up in front of some sites. The lake is used for swimming but there is no designated swimming beach. The entrance to the campground is directly off SR-58 at approximately Mile 63.9.

■ **SUNSET COVE CAMPGROUND** *(Open April 25 to Oct 10 – Varies)*
  Information: (541) 433-3200
  Location: Odell Lake

  GPS Location: 43.56417 N, 121.96472 W, 4,800 Ft

21 Sites – Much like Princess Creek described above this Deschutes National Forest campground is situated between the highway and Odell Lake. Here too there are a few sites which could take larger RVs but lack of maneuvering room makes the campground suitable only for RVs to 30 feet. There's a boat ramp and no designated swimming beach. The entrance to the campground is directly off SR-58 at about Mile 66.4.

● **ODELL CREEK CAMPGROUND**
    (Open May 10 to Oct 10 – Varies)
  Reservations: (800) 434-2540
  Information: (541) 433-2540, www.odelllakeresort.com
  Location: Odell Lake

  GPS Location: 43.54972 N, 121.96222 W, 4,600 Ft

31 Sites – The sites in this former USFS campground are arranged off an out and back road along the lakeshore. These back-ins sites are long enough for 30 foot RVs and have picnic tables and fire pits. The campground is managed from the Odell Lake Resort across the creek which has a boat ramp and restaurant. At Mile 67.5 of SR-58 turn south

on East Odell Lake Road, you'll see the campground in .4 mile (.6 km).

■ **CRESCENT LAKE CAMPGROUND** *(Open All Year – Snow Dependant)*
  Reservations: www.recreation.gov, (877) 833-6777 (Yurts Only)
  Information: (541) 433-3200
  Location: Crescent Lake

GPS Location: 43.50194 N, 121.97722 W, 4,800 Ft

47 Sites – This Deschutes National Forest campground is on the north side of Crescent Lake. There are back-in and pull-thru sites suitable for RVs to about 35 feet. Rental yurts are available all year long, only the yurts are reservable. Some sites are on the lakeshore (premium add-on to fee) and there is a boat ramp. To reach the campground turn south on the Crescent Lake Highway from Mile 69.5 of SR-58. In 2.3 miles (3.7 km) turn right and in another .3 mile (.5 km) turn left into the campground access road.

■ **SPRING CAMPGROUND** *(Open May 15 to Sept 30 – Varies)*
  Information: (541) 433-3200
  Location: Crescent Lake

GPS Location: 43.46167 N, 122.01611 W, 4,800 Ft

77 Sites – This is the largest of the Deschutes National Forest campgrounds on Crescent Lake. The campground covers quite a large area, vegetation is a thin pine forest so there's lots of light. Many of the sites are along the lake shore, sites are pull-thrus and back-ins suitable for RVs to 35 feet. To reach the campground turn south on the Crescent Lake Highway from Mile 69.5 of SR-58. In 2.3 miles (3.7 km) turn right and then proceed around the lake counter-clockwise for 6.2 miles (10 km) to the campground entrance on the left.

■ **CONTORTA FLAT CAMPGROUND**
     (Open May 15 to Sept 30 – Varies)
  Information: (541) 433-3200
  Location: Crescent Lake

GPS Location: 43.46111 N, 122.00667 W, 4,800 Ft

18 Sites – This Deschutes National Forest campground on the south shore of Crescent Lake is in an open area with few trees. The roads and ground surface are dirt so when it's windy or when there's traffic through the campground dust can be a problem. These are back-ins sites with no separating vegetation, pretty much like a commercial RV park but without the hookups, they reach 35 feet in length. Some of the sites are directly adjacent to the wide beach. You can pull your boat up there or swim although there's no formal swimming beach. To reach the campground turn south on the Crescent Lake Highway from Mile 69.5 of SR-58. In 2.3 miles (3.7 km) turn right and then proceed around the lake counter-clockwise for 7 miles (11.3 km) to the campground entrance on the left.

■ **CRESCENT CREEK CAMPGROUND** *(Open May 15 to Sept 30 – Varies)*
  Information: (541) 433-3200
  Location: 8 Miles (13 Km) W of Crescent

GPS Location: 43.49750 N, 121.84333 W, 4,400 Ft

9 Sites – This little Deschutes National Forest campground is a popular spot for birders with some nice trails from the campground. Sites are off a gravel loop road, there are both pull-thrus and back-ins to 50 feet. From Crescent drive west on the Crescent Cutoff for 8.4 miles, the campground is on the left.

● **CRESCENT RV PARK** *(Open all Year)*
Res and Info: (541) 433-2950,
www.crescentrvpark.com
Location: Crescent

GPS Location: 43.46500 N, 121.69222 W, 4,400 Ft

30 Sites – This is a simple older RV park located next to the highway just north of Crescent. It has gravel roads and parking with some trees. Tent sites are arranged under trees next to the highway. RV sites are mostly back-ins with a few pull-thrus, sites extend to 45 feet. The park is at Mile 185 of US-97, on the north edge of Crescent.

● **BIG PINES RV PARK** *(Open All Year)*
Res and Info: (800) 351-2785 or (541) 433-2785,
www.bigpinesrvpark.com
Location: Crescent

GPS Location: 43.44908 N, 121.70530 W, 4,400 Ft

31 Sites – This is a nice modern big rig park with
widely spaced sites and lots of grass and trees. The sites are back-ins and pull-thrus to 60 feet. They have picnic tables and fire pits. The campground is on the east side of Hwy 97 at the south end of Crescent.

Information Resources

See our Internet site at www.rollinghomes.com for Internet information links.

Ashland and Medford

Ashland Chamber of Commerce, 110 East Main Street (PO Box 1360), Ashland, OR 97520; (541) 482-3486; sandra@ashlandchamber.com

Oregon Shakespeare Festival, 15 S Pioneer Street, Ashland, OR 97520; (541) 482-2111 for brochure, (541) 482-4331; for tickets, boxoffice@osfashland.org

Astoria, Seaside and Cannon Beach

Astoria Visitors Center, 111 W Marine Dr (PO Box 176), Astoria, OR 97103; (503) 325-6311; visitors@oldoregon.com

Astoria-Warrenton Highway 101 Visitor Center, 143 S Highway 101, Warrenton, OR 97146; (503) 861-1031

Cannon Beach Information Center, 207 N Spruce St (PO Box 64), Cannon Beach, OR 97110; (503) 436-2623; chamber@cannonbeach.org

Columbia River Maritime Museum, 1972 Marine Drive, Astoria, OR 97103; (503) 325-2323

Flavel House, 441 8th St, Astoria, OR 97103; (503) 325-2203

Fort Clatsop National Memorial, 92343 Fort Clatsop Rd, Astoria, OR 97103-9197; (503) 861-2471

Seaside Aquarium, 200 N Promenade, Seaside, OR 97138; (503) 373-6211; aquarium@ seasideaquarium.com

Seaside Museum and Historical Society, 570 Necanicum Dr, Seaside, OR 97138; (503) 738-7065

Seaside Visitors Bureau, 7 N Roosevelt Drive, Seaside, OR 97138; (503) 738-3097 or (800) 306-2326; info@seasideor.com

Baker City and Sumpter

Baker County Chamber of Commerce and Visitors Bureau, 490 Campbell St Baker, OR 97814; (541) 523-5855 or (888) 523-5855; info@visitbaker.com

National Historic Oregon Trail Interpretive Center, 22267 Oregon Highway 86 (PO Box 987), Baker City, Oregon 97814-0987; (541) 523-1843; BLM_OR_NH_Mail@blm.gov

Sumpter Valley Railroad, PO Box 389, Baker City, OR 97814-0389; (541) 894-2268; info@svry.com

Bandon

Bandon Chamber of Commerce, 300 Second Street (PO Box 1515), Bandon, OR 97411; (541) 347-9616

West Coast Game Park Safari, 46914 Hwy 101, Bandon, OR 97411; (541) 347-3106; info@gameparkssafari.com

Bend and La Pine

Deschutes National Forest, 63095 Deschutes Market Road, Bend, OR 97702; (541) 383-5300

Central Oregon Visitors Association, 661 SW Powerhouse Dr. Ste 1301, OR 97702; (541) 389-8799 or (800) 800-8334; info@visistcentraloregon.com

High Desert Museum, 59800 South Hwy 97, Bend, OR 97702; (541) 382-4754

La Pine Chamber of Commerce, 51425 Hwy 97, Suite A (PO Box 616) La Pine, OR 97739; (541) 536-9771; info@lapine.org

Sunriver Area Chamber of Commerce, Building #13, Village at Sunriver, 57100 Beaver Drive (PO Box 3246), Sunriver, OR 97707; (541) 593-8149; info@sunriverchamber.com

Brookings

Brookings-Harbor Chamber of Commerce, 16330 Lower Harbor Rd (PO Box 940), Brookings, OR 97415; (541) 469-3181; chamber@wave.net

Oregon State Welcome Center, 14433 US-101, Brookings, OR 97415; (541) 469-4117; crisseywc@netzero.net

Camp Sherman and the Metolius River

Deschutes National Forest, 63095 Deschutes Market Road, Bend, OR 97702; (541) 383-5300

Metolius Recreation Association, PO Box 64, Camp Sherman, OR 97730; (541) 595-6117

Cascade Lakes Scenic Byway Loop

Deschutes National Forest, 63095 Deschutes Market Road, Bend, OR 97702; (541) 383-5300

Charleston

Charleston Visitor Information Center, 91141 Cape Arago Hwy (PO Box 5735), Charleston, OR 97420; (541) 888-2311

South Slough National Estuarine Research Reserve, 61907 Seven Devils Road (PO Box 5417), Charleston, OR 97420; (541) 888-5558

Columbia Gorge

Bonneville Dam Visitor Center, US Corps of Engineers, Cascade Locks, OR 97014-0150; (541) 374-8820

Columbia River Gorge National Scenic Area, USDA Forest Service, 902 Wasco, Suite 200, Hood River, OR 97031; (541) 308-1700

Columbia Gorge Discovery Center, 5000 Discovery Drive, The Dalles, OR 97058; (541) 296-8600

Hood River Chamber of Commerce, 720 E Port Marina Drive, Hood River, OR 97031; (541) 386-2000 or (800) 366-3530; info@hoodriver.org

Mount Hood Railroad, 110 Railroad Ave, Hood River Oregon 97031; (541) 386-3556 or (800) 872-4661

Port of Cascade Locks Visitors Center, 355 WaNaPa St (PO Box 307), Cascade Locks, OR 97014; (541) 374-8619

The Dalles Chamber of Commerce, 404 W 2nd St, The Dalles, OR 97058; (541) 296-2231 info@thedalleschamber.com

Coos Bay

Bay Area C of C, 145 Central Ave., Coos Bay, OR 97420; (541) 266-0868; timmslater@ oregonsbayarea.org

Coos Bay Visitors Center, 50 Central Ave (P.O. Box 210), Coos Bay, OR 97420; (541) 269-0215 or (800) 824-8486; cheryl@oregonsbayarea.org

Crater Lake National Park

Crater Lake National Park, PO Box 7, Crater Lake, OR 97604; (541) 594-3000

Umpqua National Forest, 2900 NW Stewart Parkway, Roseburg, OR 97471; (541) 957-3200

Eugene

Eugene and Lane County Convention and Visitors Association, 754 Olive Street (PO Box 10286), Eugene, OR 97401; (541) 484-5307 or (800) 547-5445; info@TravelLane-County.org

Gold Beach

Gold Beach Visitors Center, 94080 Shirley Lane (PO Box 375), Gold Beach, OR 97444; (541) 247-7526 or (800) 525-2334; visit@goldbeach.org

Jerry's Rogue Jets, 29985 Harbor Way (PO Box 1011), Gold Beach, OR 97444; (800) 451-3645 or (541) 247-4571; jerrys@roguejets.com

Grants Pass

Applegate Trail Interpretive Center, 500 Sunny Valley Loop, Sunny Valley, OR 97497; (541) 472-8545

Grants Pass-Josephine County Chamber of Commerce, 1995 W Vine St, Grants Pass, OR 97526; (541) 476-7717; gpcoc@grantspasschamber.org

Wolf Creek Inn, 100 Front St, Wolf Creek, OR 97497; 541 866-2474; WolfCreekInnkeepers@fontier.com

John Day Country

Grant County Chamber of Commerce, 301 W Main, John Day, OR 97845; (541) 575-0547 (800) 769-5664; gcadmin@gcoregonlive.com

John Day Fossil Beds National Monument, 32651 Hwy 19, Kimberly, OR 97848; (541) 987-2333

Klamath Falls

Discover Klamath, 205 Riverside Dr. Suite B, Klamath Falls, OR 97601; (800) 445-6728 or (541) 882-1501; info@discoverklamath.com

Favell Museum of Western Art and Indian Artifacts, 125 W Main, Klamath Falls, OR 97601; (541) 882-9996

Klamath Basin National Wildlife Refuge, 4009 Hill Rd, Tulelake, CA 96134; (530) 667-2231; r8kbwebmaster@fws.gov

Kla-Mo-Ya Casino, 34333 Hwy 97 N, Chiloquin, OR 97624; (541) 783-7529

Lava Beds National Monument, PO Box 1240, Tulelake, CA 96134; (530) 667-8113

La Grande and the Grande Ronde Valley

Eastern Oregon Fire Museum, 102 Elm St., La Grande, OR; (541) 963-8588

Manuel Museum, Hot Lake Springs, 66172 Hwy 203 (PO Box 1043), La Grande, OR 97850; (541) 963-4685; info@hotlakesprings.comn

Union County Museum, Main Street, Union, OR; (541) 562-6003

Lakeview and the Outback Scenic Byway

Lake County Chamber of Commerce, 126 North E Street, Lakeview, OR 97630; (541) 947-6040; ahenry@lakecountychamber.org

Lincoln City to Newport

Depoe Bay Chamber of Commerce, 223 SW Hwy 101, Ste B (PO Box 21), Depoe Bay, OR 97341; (541) 765-2889 or (877) 485-8348

Greater Newport Chamber of Commerce, 555 SW Coast Hwy, Newport, OR 97365; (541) 265-8801 or (800) 262-7844; info@newportchamber.org

Lincoln City Visitor & Convention Bureau, 801 SW Hwy 101, Suite 1, Lincoln City, OR 97367; (541) 994-8378 or (800) 452-2151; events@lincolncity.org

Malheur National Wildlife Refuge and Steens Mountain

Frenchglen Hotel State Heritage Site, Frenchglen, OR 97736; (541) 493-2825 or (800) 551-6949

Harney County Chamber of Commerce, 484 North Broadway, Burns, OR 97720; (541) 573-2636; info@harneycounty.com

Malheur National Wildlife Refuge, 36391 Sod House Lane, Princeton, OR 97721; (541) 493-2612

Mt Hood

Mt Hood Information Center, 24403 E Welches Rd, Welches, Suite 103, OR 97067; (503) 622-4822, (888) 622-4822; infoctr@mthood.info

Mt Hood National Forest, Forest Headquarters, 16400 Champion Way, Sandy, OR 97055; (503) 668-1700

Mt Hood National Forest, Zigzag Ranger District, 70220 E Highway 26, Zigzag, OR 97049; (503) 622-3191

Timberline Lodge, 27500 E Timberline Road, OR 97028; (503) 272-3311

Nehalem Bay and Manzanita

Nehalem Bay Area Chamber of Commerce, 36005 7th St (PO Box 601), Nehalem, OR 97131; (503) 368-5100

Newberry National Volcanic Monument

Lava Lands Visitor Center, 58201 South Hwy 97, Bend, OR 97707; (541) 593-2421

Oregon Caves National Monument

Illinois Valley Chamber of Commerce Visitor Information Center, 201 Caves Hwy (PO Box 312), Cave Junction, OR 97523; (541) 592-3326; ivchamberofcommerce@cavenet.com

Oregon Caves Information Station, Oregon Caves National Monument, 19000 Caves Hwy, Cave Junction, OR 97523; (541) 592-2100

Pendleton

Pendleton Chamber of Commerce, 501 S Main, Pendleton, OR 97801; (541) 276-7411 or (800) 547-8911; info@pendletonchamber.com

Pendleton Round-Up, 1205 SW Court (PO Box 609), Pendleton, OR 97801; (800) 457-6336 or (541) 276-2553

Wildhorse Casino and Resort, 72777 Hwy 331, Pendleton, OR 97801; (800) 654-9453; info@wildhorseresort.com

Port Orford

Port Orford Chamber of Commerce, PO Box 637, Port Orford, OR 97465; (541) 332-8055; chamber@portorfordchamber.com

Portland

International Rose Test Garden, 400 SW Kingston, Ave, Portland, OR 97201; (503) 823-3636

Oregon City Chamber of Commerce, 2895 S Beavercreek Road, Ste 103 (PO Box 226), Oregon City, OR 97045; (503) 656-1619; chamberinfo@oregoncity.org

Oregon's Mt Hood Territory, 150 Beavercreek Road, Ste 245, Oregon City, OR 97045; (503) 655-8490

Oregon Museum of Science and Industry, 1945 SE Water Ave, Portland, OR 97214-3354; (503) 797- 4000 or (800) 955-6674; info@omsi.edu

Portland Oregon Visitors Association Visitor Center, 701 SW 6th Ave #1, Portland, OR 97204; (503) 275-8355

Washington Park Zoo, 4001 SW Canyon Rd, Portland, OR 97221; (503) 226-1561

Prineville

Ochoco National Forest, 3160 NE 3rd St, Prineville, OR 97754; (541) 416-6500

Prineville-Crook County Chamber of Commerce, 102 NW Second Street, OR 97754; (541) 447-6304; info@visitprineville.org

Redmond and Sisters

Redmond Chamber of Commerce, 446 SW 7th, Redmond, OR 97756; (541) 923-5191; info@visitredmondoregon.com

Sisters Area Visitor Information Center, 291 E Main Avenue (PO Box 430), Sisters, OR 97759; (541) 549-0251; info@sisterscountry.com

Reedsport and the Oregon Dunes

Oregon Dunes National Recreation Area Visitor Center, 855 Highway 101 S, Reedsport, OR 97467; (541) 271-6000

Reedsport/Winchester Bay Chamber of Commerce, 855 Hwy Ave, Reedsport, OR 97467; (541) 271-3495 or (800) 247-2155; rdollar@reedsportcc.org

Siuslaw National Forest, 4077 SW Research Way, Corvallis, Oregon 97339; (541) 750-7000

Rogue Umpqua Scenic Byway

Rogue River-Siskiyou National Forest, High Cascades Ranger District, 47201 Highway 62, Prospect, OR 97536; (541) 560-3400

Shady Cove-Upper Rogue Chamber Visitor and Convention Bureau, 21800 Crate Lake Hwy 62 (PO Box 1573), Shady Cove, OR 97539; (541) 878-2404; chamber@shadycoveup-perrogue.org

Umpqua National Forest, Diamond Lake Ranger District, 2020 Toketee Ranger Station Road, Idleyld Park, OR 97447; (541) 498-2531

Umpqua National Forest, North Umpqua Ranger District, 18782 North Umpqua Highway, Glide, OR 97443; (541) 496-3532

Roseburg and the Umpqua Valley

Colliding Rivers Information Center, 18782 N Umpqua Hwy, Glide, OR 97443; (541) 496-0157

Douglas County Museum of History and Natural History, 123 Museum Drive, Roseburg, OR 97471; (541) 957-7007; museum@co.douglas.or.us

Roseburg Visitors and Convention Bureau, 410 SE Spruce (PO Box 1262), Roseburg, OR 97470; (541) 672-9731 and (800) 444-9584; info@visitroseburg.com

Wildlife Safari, 1790 Safari Road (PO Box 1600), Winston, OR 97496: (541) 679-6761

Salem

Enchanted Forest, 8462 Enchanted Way SE, Turner, OR 97392; (503) 363-3060 or (503) 371-4242

Evergreen Aviation & Space Museum, 500 NE Captain Michael King Smith Way, McMinnville, OR 97128; (503) 434-4185

Salem Convention & Visitors Association, 1313 Mill St SE, Salem, OR 97301; (800) 874-7012 or (503) 581-4325; information@travelsalem.com

Visitor Services, Oregon State Capitol, 900 Court Street NE, Salem, OR 97310; (503) 986-1388

Tillamook and the Three Capes Loop

Pacific City-Nestucca Valley Chamber of Commerce, PO Box 75, Cloverdale, OR 97112; (503) 392-4340;manager@pcnvchamber.org

Tillamook Chamber of Commerce, 3705 Hwy 101 N, Tillamook, OR 97141; (503) 842-7525

Waldport and Florence

Florence Area Chamber of Commerce, 290 Hwy 101, Florence, OR 97439; (541) 997-3128

Waldport Chamber of Commerce, 620 NW Spring St (PO Box 669), Waldport, OR 97394; (541) 563-2133; chamber@peak.org

Yachats Area Chamber of Commerce and Visitor Center, 241 Hwy 101 (PO Box 728); Yachats, OR 97498; (541) 547-3530 or (800) 929-0477; info@yachats.org

Wallowa Lake Region

Wallowa County Chamber of Commerce, 309 South River Street, Suite B (PO Box 427), Enterprise, OR 97828; (541) 426-4622 or (800) 585-4121; info@wallowacountychamber.com

Wallowa Mountains Visitor Center (National Forest Service), Enterprise, OR 97828; (541) 523-5546

Warm Springs and Madras

Crooked River National Grassland, 813 SW Hwy 97, Madras, OR 97741; (541) 475-9272

Madras-Jefferson County Chamber of Commerce, 274 SW 4th St (PO Box 770), Madras, OR 97741; (541) 475-2350 or (800) 967-3564; office@madraschamber.com

Museum at Warm Springs, 2189 Hwy 26 (PO Box 909), Warm Springs, OR 97761; (541) 553-3331

West Cascades Scenic Byway

Estacada Chamber of Commerce, 475 SE Main (PO Box 298), Estacada, OR 97023; (503) 630-3483

Mt Hood National Forest, Clackamas River Ranger District – Estacada Ranger Station, 595 NW Industrial Way, Estacada, OR 97023; (503) 630-6861

Willamette National Forest, McKenzie Ranger District, 57600 McKenzie Highway, McKenzie Bridge, OR 97413; (541) 822-3381; r6_willamette_wwweb_frontdesk@fs.fed.us

Willamette Pass Route

Deschutes National Forest, Crescent Ranger District, 136471 Hwy 97 N (PO Box 208), Crescent, OR 97733; (541) 433-3200

Willamette National Forest, Middle Fork Ranger District, 46375 Highway 58, Westfir, OR 97492; (541) 782-2283; r6_willamette_wwweb_frontdesk@fs.fed.us

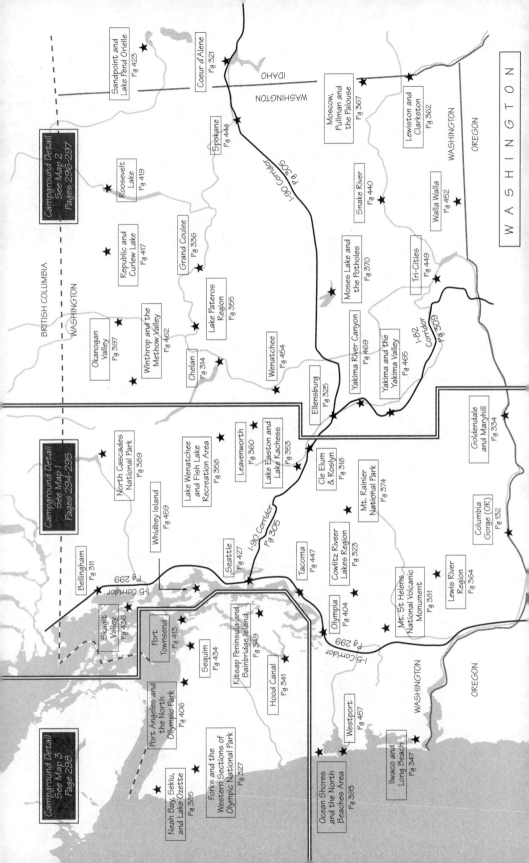

WASHINGTON

BRITISH COLUMBIA

WASHINGTON

IDAHO

WASHINGTON

OREGON

WASHINGTON

OREGON

Campground Detail
See Map 2
Pages 296-297

Campground Detail
See Map 1
Pages 294-295

Campground Detail
See Map 3
Page 298

Sandpoint and
Lake Pend Oreille
Pg 423

Coeur d'Alene
Pg 321

Spokane
Pg 444

Moscow,
Pullman and
the Palouse
Pg 367

Lewiston and
Clarkston
Pg 362

Roosevelt
Lake
Pg 419

Snake River
Pg 440

Walla Walla
Pg 452

Republic and
Curlew Lake
Pg 417

Grand Coulee
Pg 356

Moses Lake and
the Potholes
Pg 370

Tri-Cities
Pg 449

Lake Pateros
Region
Pg 355

I-82
Corridor
Pg 309

Okanogan
Valley
Pg 397

Winthrop and the
Methow Valley
Pg 462

Wenatchee
Pg 454

Yakima River
Canyon
Pg 469

Chelan
Pg 314

Yakima and the
Yakima Valley
Pg 465

I-90 Corridor
Pg 305

Ellensburg
Pg 325

North Cascades
National Park
Pg 389

Lake Wenatchee
and Fish Lake
Recreation Area
Pg 358

Leavenworth
Pg 360

Goldendale
and Maryhill
Pg 334

Whidbey Island
Pg 459

Lake Easton and
Lake Kachees
Pg 353

Cle Elum
& Roslyn
Pg 318

Mt. Rainier
National Park
Pg 374

Bellingham
Pg 311

I-5 Corridor
Pg 299

Seattle
Pg 427

Columbia
Gorge (OR)
Pg 132

I-90 Corridor
Pg 305

Tacoma
Pg 447

Cowlitz River
Lakes Region
Pg 323

Lewis River
Region
Pg 364

Skagit
Valley
Pg 436

Mt. St. Helens
National Volcanic
Monument
Pg 381

Port
Townsend
Pg 413

Olympia
Pg 404

Sequim
Pg 434

Kitsap Peninsula and
Bainbridge Island
Pg 349

I-5 Corridor
Pg 299

Port Angeles and
the North
Olympic Park
Pg 406

Hood Canal
Pg 341

Neah Bay, Sekiu,
and Lake Ozette
Pg 385

Forks and the
Western Sections of
Olympic National Park
Pg 327

Westport
Pg 457

Ocean Shores
and the North
Beaches Area
Pg 383

Ilwaco and
Long Beach
Pg 347

Chapter 5
Washington

Like the rest of the Pacific Northwest, Washington State has a mild but wet west half and a dry eastern half. The Cascade Mountains make the difference as they isolate the eastern half of the state from the influence of the Pacific Ocean.

Washington state has three National Parks. These are the Olympic National Park, the North Cascades National Park, and Mt Rainier National Park. At first glance these all seem to be parks celebrating mountains, but that's not entirely true. The Olympic National Park has a section that encompasses a great deal of the Pacific coast of the state.

While this chapter is titled *Washington* we have also included a few northern Idaho destinations. We just couldn't bring ourselves to leave them out.

REGIONS AND THEIR CAMPGROUND RESOURCES

Olympic Peninsula

The dominating feature of the Olympic Peninsula is the Olympic Mountains that occupy the center. These mountains make up the largest portion of Olympic National Park. The mountainous interior is circled by a mostly two-lane highway. It's a good road so there's decent access to the entire peninsula.

The Olympic Peninsula is remote, it's also pretty wet. Those two characteristics make the area a great camping destination. It's important to know that the amount of rainfall varies a lot depending upon where you are in relation to the mountains. Along the western front of the range it's so wet that the area is considered a rain forest. On the east and northeast side of the mountains there's a lot less rain. The town of Sequim is known for the fact that it sits in the "rain shadow" of the Olympic Mountains.

The Olympic Peninsula destinations in this book ring the mountains. Traveling counter-clockwise they are as follows: • *Port Townsend,* • *Sequim,* • *Port Angeles and the North Olympic National Park, and* • *Forks and the Western Sections of Olympic National Park.*

Pacific Coast

Washington's Pacific coast isn't nearly as well known as Oregon's. That means it's usually not nearly so crowded. There are good campgrounds along the coast, including some great state parks. The water's a little cooler than farther south but the coast is wilder and just as much fun to visit. Here are the coastal destinations from north to south: • *Neah Bay, Sekiu, and Lake Ozette,* • *Forks and the Western Sections of Olympic National Park,* • *Ocean Shores and the North Beaches Area,* • *Westport, and* • *Ilwaco and Long Beach.*

Puget Sound

The most populous area of Washington State is the Puget Sound region. That doesn't mean that you can't camp here. You'll find lots of spots in the many less dense areas, many near a saltwater beach. And don't forget that you can camp when you visit the cities too. From north to south here are the destinations in this chapter in the Puget Sound area and along the I-5 corridor: • *Bellingham,* • *Skagit Valley,* • *Whidbey Island,* • *Kitsap Peninsula and Bainbridge Island,* • *Hood Canal,* • *Seattle,* • *Tacoma, and* • *Olympia.*

Cascade Mountains

Just as they do in Oregon to the south, Washington's Cascade mountains measure about 80 miles (130 km) from west to east. Those in Washington are even more rugged and impenetrable that those farther south. There are only four east-west highway crossings (five counting along the Columbia River). One of these, the North Cascades Highway, is closed by snow in winter. Major mountains in the Washington Cascades include Mt Baker (10,778 ft.), Mt Rainier (14,408 ft.), Mt Adams (12,307 ft.) and Mt St Helens (8,364 ft.). Two of the state's three national parks are also located in the Cascades. These are the Cascade Mountains destinations in this book listed from north to south: • *North Cascades National Park,* • *Winthrop and the Methow Valley,* • *Chelan,* • *Lake Wenatchee and Fish Lake Recreation Area,* • *Leavenworth,* • *Lake Easton and Lake Kachess,* • *Cle Elum and Roslyn,* • *Mt Rainier National Park,* • *Cowlitz River Lakes Region,* • *Mt St Helens National Volcanic Monument, and* • *Lewis River Region.*

East of the Cascades

Eastern Washington is a popular summer destination because the weather is reliably good and the Columbia and Snake Rivers and their reservoirs provide a way to keep cool. Most of eastern Washington is in the Columbia Basin, the huge area drained by the Columbia River. Many of the destinations listed in this book are actually located along the river, or at least close by. The Columbia is dammed along almost its entire length, it's really a series of big lakes. Destinations in Washington state east of the Cascades are the following: • *Winthrop and the Methow Valley,* • *Okanogan Valley,* • *Republic and Curlew Lake,* • *Lake Pateros Region,* • *Chelan,* • *Wenatchee,* • *Grand Coulee,* • *Roosevelt Lake,* • *Ellensburg,* • *Moses Lake and the Potholes,* • *Spokane,* • *Yakima and the Yakima Valley,* • *Yakima River Canyon,* • *Tri-Cities,* • *Snake River,* • *Walla Walla,* • *Lewiston, ID and Clarkston, WA, and* • *Moscow, ID, Pullman, WA, and the Palouse.*

Northern Idaho

We've included a few destinations in this book that are really in Idaho, not Washington.

THE IMPRESSIVE CASCADE MOUNTAINS ON THE NORTH CASCADES HIGHWAY

They're great places to visit, they're not far away, and it would be a shame to leave them out just because they're in Idaho. These destinations are: • *Coeur d'Alene,* • *Sandpoint and Lake Pend Oreille,* • *Lewiston, ID and Clarkston, WA, and* • *Moscow, ID, Pullman, WA, and the Palouse.*

GOVERNMENT LANDS AND THEIR CAMPGROUNDS

Washington State Campgrounds

Washington state has one of the best campground systems in the country. Like those in Oregon, most Washington campgrounds offer hookups as well as restrooms with flush toilets and hot showers. Many campgrounds can handle big rigs. These state campgrounds are the best choice for a place to spend the night in many destination areas. In addition to individual campsites many parks offer group areas, cabins, platform tents, or yurts.

Washington state campgrounds always charge for showers, they usually use coin boxes that take quarters. The campgrounds only accept credit cards if there is a manned entry booth. If a self-pay system is in effect credit cards are not accepted.

The website for Washington state parks is at www.parks.wa.gov. It's a nice website with descriptions of the campgrounds. You can also get information about the state campgrounds by calling the overall information number of (360) 902-8844. Each park can also be called although these numbers are not always monitored, the telephone numbers are listed in our individual campground descriptions.

Reservations for state parks can be made by using the state's reservation website www.

parks.wa.gov/reservations/ or by calling (888) CAMPOUT ((888) 226-7688). A fee (on-line $6.50, phone $8.50) is charged for each reservation no matter how many days it covers. An additional $5 fee is charged non-residents for each reservation. Not all state parks accept reservations, we tell you which ones do in the individual entries in this chapter. At most campgrounds reservations are only accepted for individual campsite camping during the period from May 15 to September 15, reservations are not considered necessary during the remainder of the year. Only Cape Disappointment, Deception Pass, Dosewallips, Grayland Beach, Kitsap Memorial, Ocean City, Pacific Beach, Steamboat Rock and Fort Worden accept year-round reservations. A few others, including Pearrygin Lake, Riverside, Wenatchee Confluence, Sun Lakes, and Lake Chelan have different reservation window dates, see the individual write-ups for these dates. Reservations can be made as much as 9 months in advance or as little as 1 day before arrival date.

There are a few state campsites that do accept reservations but that are not included in the overall reservation system. The only ones listed in this book is Fort Worden and Fort Townsend, see the individual write-up below for information about this.

Camping fees in Washington state campgrounds are pretty uniform from campground to campground. During the peak season (May 15 to Sept 15) they charge $21 for tent and no-hookup sites, $29 for partial hookup sites, and $31 for full hookup sites. There's also an additional $3 to $5 added for certain "high use" parks. Many of the parks listed in this book fall into that category. Finally, there's an additional $3 to $5 additional charged for select premium campsites in some parks. In our experience that means waterfront sites when available. In the off season (Sept 16 to May 14) it's $21 for a standard site, $27 for a partial hookup site, and $29 for a full hookup site.

Washington State offers state campground discounts for state residents who have reached the age of 62 years. This Off-Season Senior Citizen Pass costs $50 and gives free camping from October 1 to March 31 and from Sunday through Thursday in April. You'll still have to pay $6 for electricity.

Washington now offers an annual **Discover Pass** for $30. This pass allows day use of state parks as well as being required for Department of Natural Resources campgrounds that were formerly free. The pass is not required in state parks if you pay a camping fee. Daily passes (rather than the annual pass) are available and cost $10. The pass is available at parks if they have manned kiosks, online at https://fishhunt.dfw.wa.gov/, or at recreational license vendors.

Federal Campgrounds

Washington state has a lot of federal land and many federal campgrounds. They fall into the categories of national park campgrounds, national forest campgrounds, and BLM campgrounds.

The three national parks in Washington are the Olympic National Park, the North Cascades National Park, and Rainier National Park. Campgrounds in these parks are listed under • *Port Angeles and North Olympic National Park,* • *Neah Bay, Sekiu, and Lake Ozette,* • *Forks and the Western Sections of Olympic National Park,* • *Hood Canal,* • *North Cascades National Park,* • *and Mt Rainier National Park.* The park service also administers the Roosevelt National Recreation Area above Grand Coulee Dam, you'll find campgrounds in this area listed in • *Grand Coulee* and in • *Roosevelt Lake.*

Washington has many national forests including Wenatchee, Olympic, Gifford Pinchot, Mt Baker-Snoqualmie, and Okanogan. You'll find national forest campgrounds listed in the following destination sections: • *Cle Elum and Roslyn*, • *Forks and the Western Sections of Olympic National Park*, • *Hood Canal*, • *Lake Easton and Lake Kachess*, • *Lake Wenatchee and Fish Lake Recreation Area*, • *Leavenworth*, • *Okanogan Valley*, • *Port Angeles and Northern Olympic National Park*, • *Rainier National Park*, • *Winthrop and the Methow Valley*.

Northern Idaho national forests include the Kaniksu National Forest, see • the *Sandpoint and Lake Pend Oreille* section for a campground in this forest.

BLM campgrounds described in this chapter are all located in • the *Yakima River Canyon* section.

Many campgrounds on Federal lands can be reserved. Most use the National Recreation Reservation Service. Access is via the www.recreation.gov website or telephone number – (877) 444-6777. From outside the U.S. the number is (518) 885-3639. Individual campground write-ups in this book tell which federal campgrounds can be reserved. Most campsites have a $9 fee per reservation when made on the internet, $10 per reservation when made over the phone. Campground reservations can be made up to 6 months in advance.

CAMPGROUND LOCATION INDEX MAPS

On the following pages you'll find three Campground Location Index Maps for Washington. These maps show the approximate location of every campground as described in this chapter. The shaded areas show which section covers each campground shown. It's an easy matter to turn to the proper section where you'll find a detailed map, a description of the area, and detailed descriptions of all of the campgrounds. Note that there are four types of symbols used for the campgrounds:

■ Federal
□ State
● Commercial
○ Local Government

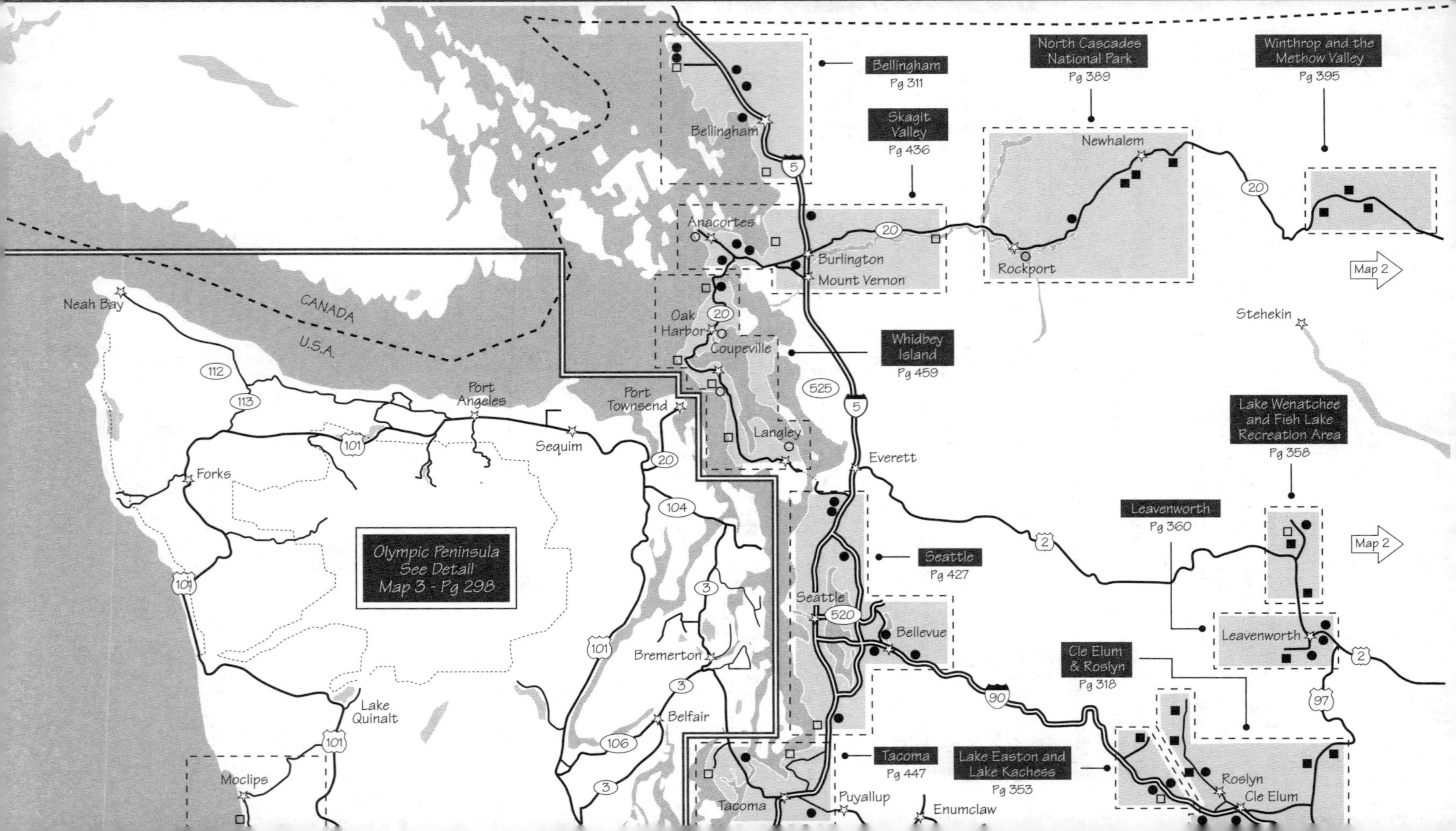

Campground Location Index Map * Western Washington * Map 1

Winthrop and the Methow Valley Pg 395

Map 2

Stehekin

Lake Wenatchee and Fish Lake Recreation Area Pg 358

Map 2

Leavenworth

20

North Cascades National Park Pg 389

Newhalem

Rockport

97

Roslyn
Cle Elum

Leavenworth Pg 360

Cle Elum & Roslyn Pg 318

Leavenworth Pg 360

2

90

Bellingham Pg 311

Skagit Valley Pg 436

20

Burlington
Mount Vernon

Whidbey Island Pg 459

Seattle Pg 427

Bellevue

520

Lake Easton and Lake Kachess Pg 353

Tacoma Pg 447

Enumclaw

Puyallup

Bellingham

5

Anacortes

Oak Harbor

20

Coupeville

Landley

525

Everett

Seattle

Tacoma

5

Port Townsend

20

104

3

Bremerton

Belfair

3

106

Sequim

101

Olympic Peninsula See Detail Map 3 - Pg 298

Port Angeles

Lake Quinalt

CANADA
U.S.A.

112

113

Forks

101

101

Neah Bay

Moclips

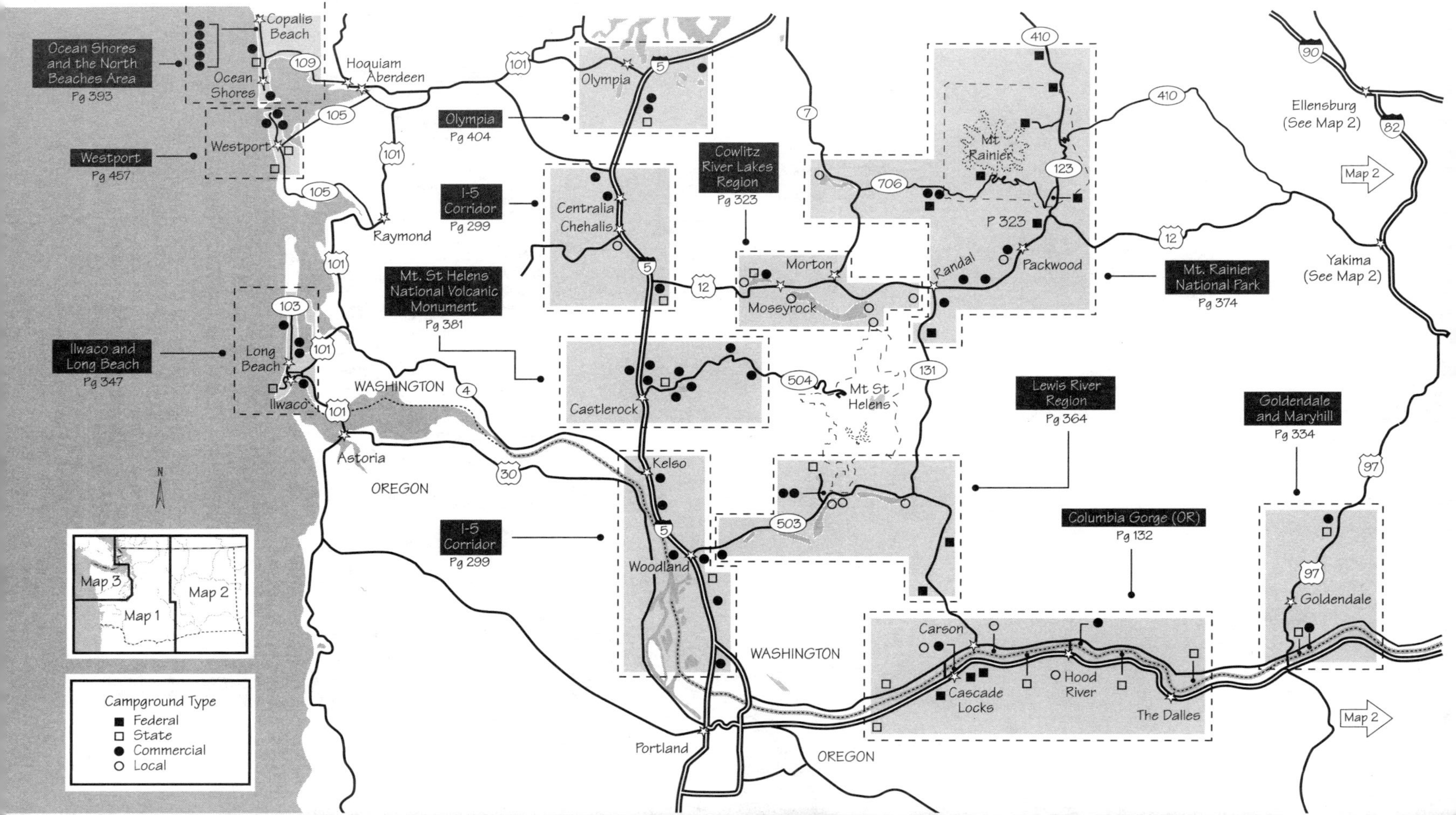

Campground Location Index Map * Western Washington * Map 1

Map 2

Ellensburg (See Map 2)

Yakima (See Map 2)

Map 2

Goldendale
97
Goldendale and Maryhill
Pg 334

Mt. Rainier National Park
Pg 374

The Dalles

Columbia Gorge (OR)
Pg 132

Hood River

Lewis River Region
Pg 364

Cascade Locks

Packwood

Mt. Rainier

Randal

Carson

Morton

Mt St Helens

WASHINGTON

OREGON

Cowlitz River Lakes Region
Pg 323

Mossyrock

Kelso

Woodland

Portland

Olympia

Centralia Chehalis

Castlerock

Olympia
Pg 404

I-5 Corridor
Pg 299

Mt. St Helens National Volcanic Monument
Pg 381

Raymond

WASHINGTON

OREGON

I-5 Corridor
Pg 299

Hoquiam Aberdeen

Astoria

Copalis Beach

Ocean Shores

Westport

Long Beach

Ilwaco

Ocean Shores and the North Beaches Area
Pg 393

Westport
Pg 457

Ilwaco and Long Beach
Pg 347

N

Map 2

Map 1

Map 3

Campground Type
■ Federal
□ State
● Commercial
○ Local

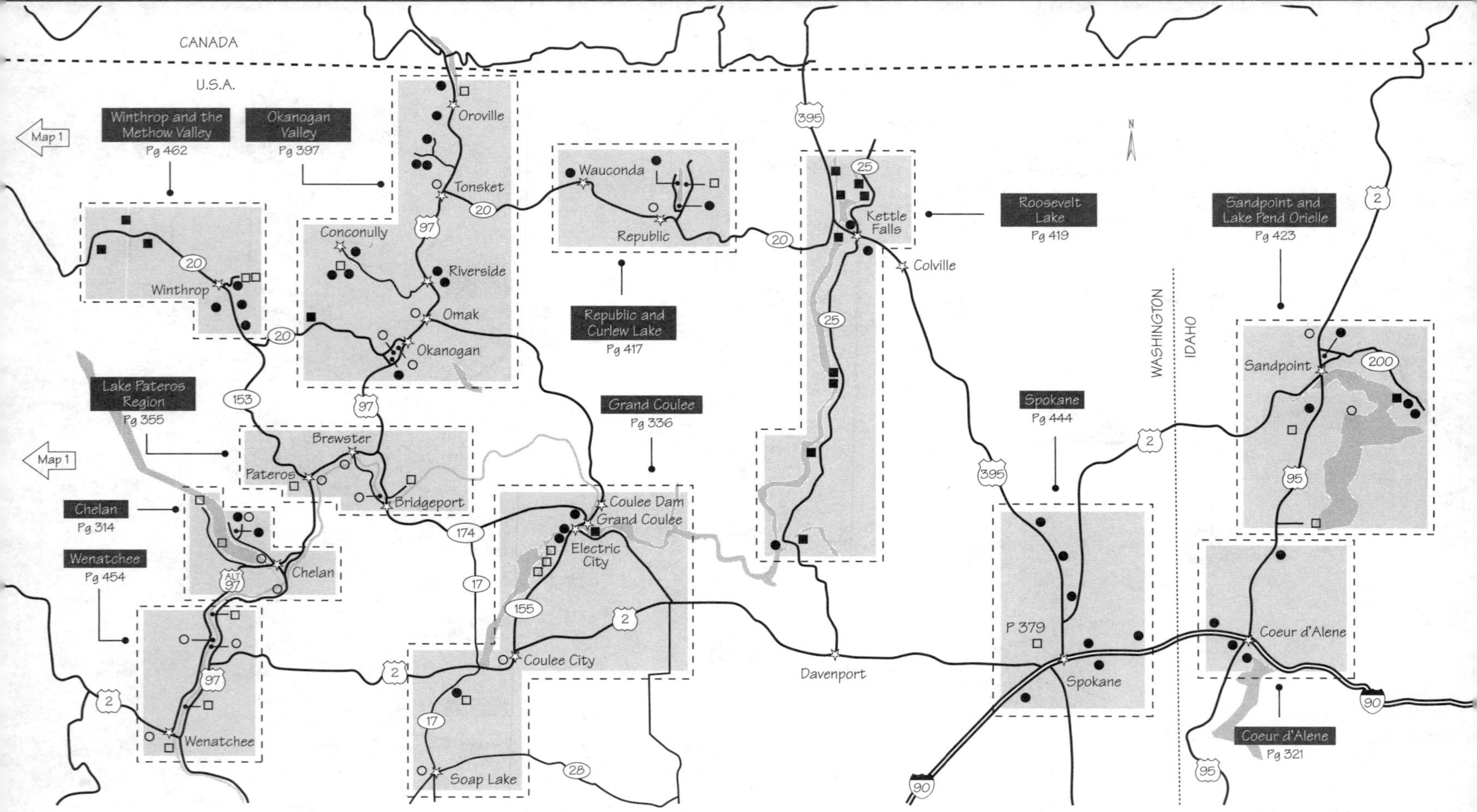

Campground Location Index Map * Eastern Washington * Map 2

CANADA
U.S.A.

Map 1

Winthrop and the Methow Valley
Pg 462

Okanogan Valley
Pg 397

Lake Pateros Region
Pg 355

Map 1

Chelan
Pg 314

Wenatchee
Pg 454

Grand Coulee
Pg 336

Republic and Curlew Lake
Pg 417

Roosevelt Lake
Pg 419

Spokane
Pg 444

Sandpoint and Lake Pend Oreille
Pg 423

Coeur d'Alene
Pg 321

IDAHO
WASHINGTON

N

Winthrop
Oroville
Tonasket
Conconully
Riverside
Omak
Okanogan
Brewster
Bridgeport
Pateros
Chelan
Wenatchee
Soap Lake
Coulee City
Electric City
Grand Coulee
Coulee Dam
Wauconda
Republic
Kettle Falls
Colville
Davenport
Spokane
Sandpoint
Coeur d'Alene

P 379
P 397

2
95
90
2
395
25
20
97
153
155
174
17
28
2
90
95

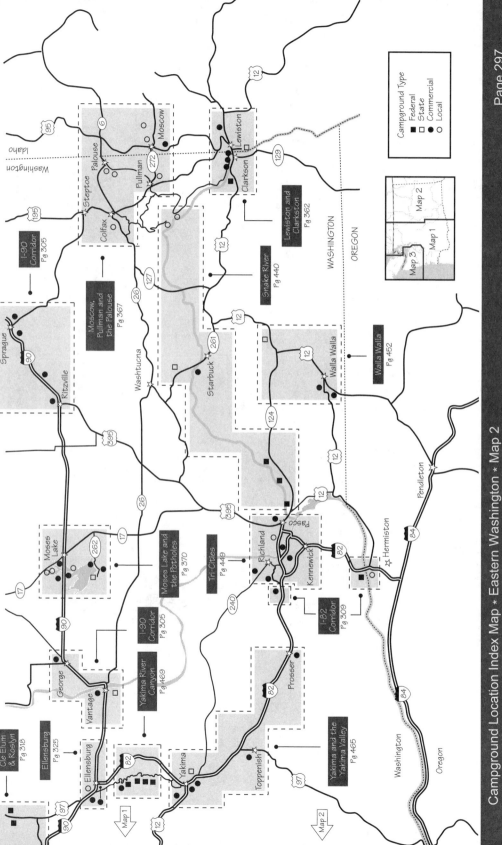

Campground Location Index Map * Eastern Washington * Map 2

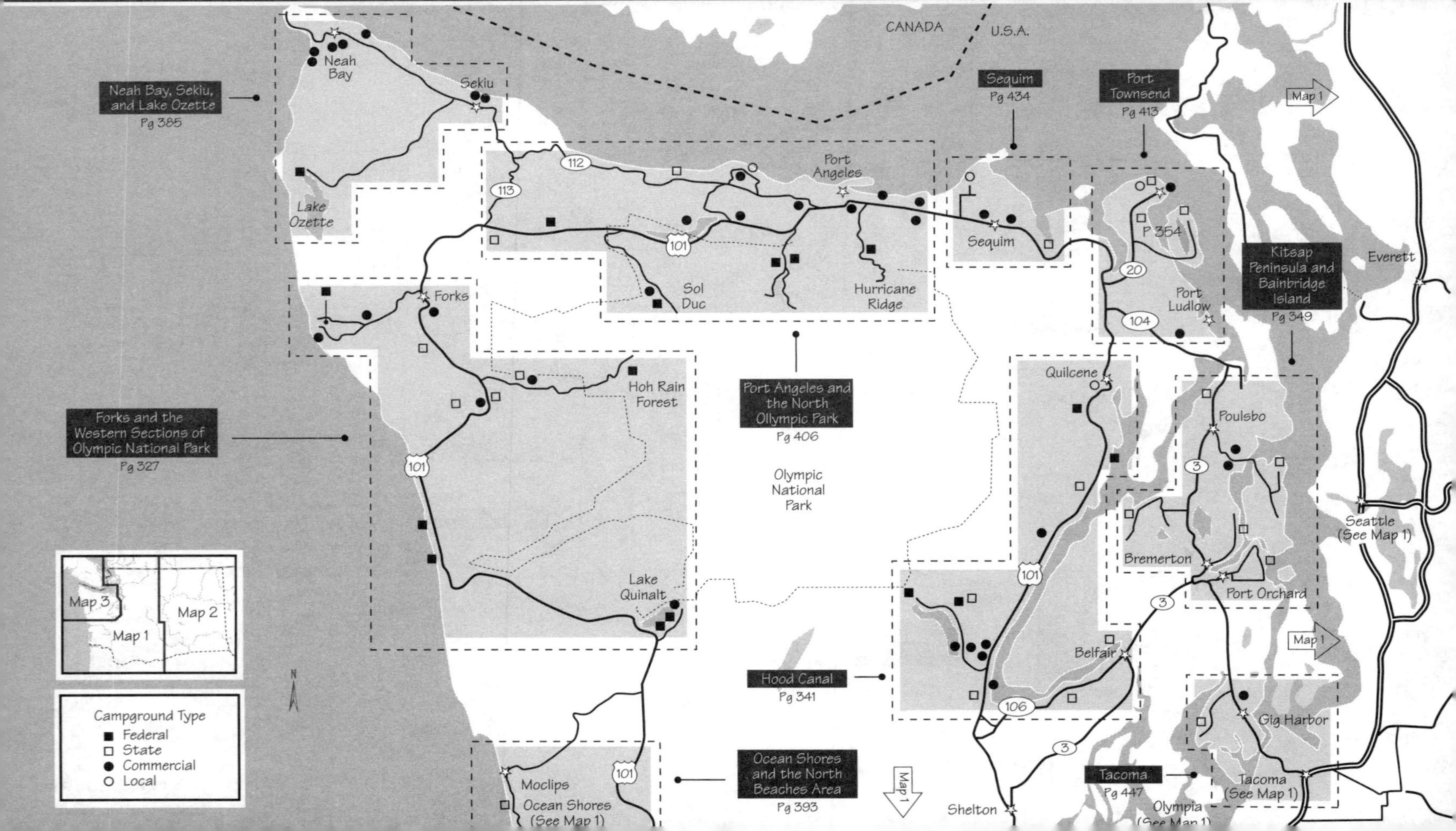

Campground Location Index Map * Olympic Peninsula * Map 3

Kitsap Peninsula and Bainbridge Island
Pg 349

Port Townsend
Pg 413

Port Ludlow
Pg 354

Sequim
Pg 434

Port Angeles and the North Olympic Park
Pg 406

Hurricane Ridge

Port Angeles

Sol Duc

Hoh Rain Forest

Lake Quinalt

Olympic National Park

Hood Canal
Pg 341

Ocean Shores and the North Beaches Area
Pg 393

Ocean Shores (See Map 1)

Moclips

Forks and the Western Sections of Olympic National Park
Pg 327

Forks

Neah Bay, Sekiu, and Lake Ozette
Pg 385

Neah Bay

Sekiu

Lake Ozette

CANADA

U.S.A.

Everett

Seattle (See Map 1)

Poulsbo

Port Orchard

Gig Harbor

Tacoma (See Map 1)

Olympia (See Map 1)

Bremerton

Belfair

Shelton

Quilcene

Tacoma
Pg 447

Map 1

Map 1

Map 1

Map 1

Campground Type
Federal
State
Commercial
Local

Map 2

Map 1

Map 3

N

DESTINATIONS AND THEIR CAMPGROUNDS

INTERSTATE 5 CORRIDOR

Interstate 5 (I-5 is the main north-south corridor in western Washington and Oregon. It runs 585 miles (944 km) from the Canadian border just south of Vancouver, BC south through the largest population centers of the Pacific Northwest including Bellingham, Seattle, Tacoma, Portland, Salem and Eugene.

The campgrounds listed below are located in Washington, see the *Interstate 5 Corridor* section in the Oregon chapter for campgrounds in that state. Note that many of the campgrounds along the I-5 Corridor are listed under other destinations sections in this chapter. If so, we've given a page reference in this section to make finding them easy.

Interstate 5 Corridor Campgrounds

> ➲ *Exit 266*

☐ **BIRCH BAY STATE PARK** *(Listed under Bellingham, page 313)*

> ➲ *Exit 263*

⬤ **THE CEDARS RV RESORT** *(Listed under Bellingham, page 313)*

WASHINGTON

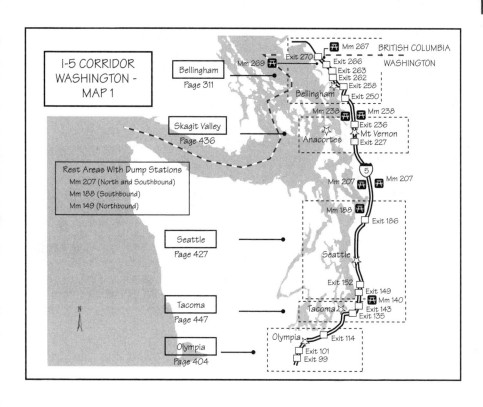

➲ **Exit 262**

● **NOR'WEST RV PARK** *(Listed under Bellingham, page 313)*

➲ **Exit 258**

● **BELLINGHAM RV PARK** *(Listed under Bellingham, page 313)*

➲ **Exit 250**

☐ **LARRABEE STATE PARK** *(Listed under Bellingham, page 314)*

➲ **Exit 236**

● **BURLINGTON/ANACORTES KOA** *(Listed under Skagit Valley, page 439)*

➲ **Exit 227**

● **MT. VERNON RV PARK** *(Listed under Skagit Valley, page 437)*

➲ **Exit 186**

● **LAKESIDE RV PARK** *(Listed under Seattle, page 431)*

● **MAPLE GROVE RV PARK** *(Listed under Seattle, page 431)*

➲ **Exit 152**

● **SEA-TAC KOA** *(Listed under Seattle, page 433)*

➲ **Exit 149**

☐ **SALTWATER STATE PARK** *(Listed under Seattle, page 433)*

➲ **Exit 143**

☐ **DASH POINT STATE PARK** *(Listed under Tacoma, page 448)*

➲ **Exit 135**

● **MAJESTIC MOBILE MANOR RV PARK** *(Listed under Tacoma, page 448)*

➲ **Exit 114**

● **NISQUALLY PLAZA RV PARK** *(Listed under Olympia, page 406)*

➲ **Exit 101**

● **OLYMPIA CAMPGROUND** *(Listed under Olympia, page 405)*

➲ **Exit 99**

☐ **MILLERSYLVANIA STATE PARK** *(Listed under Olympia, page 404)*

● **AMERICAN HERITAGE CAMPGROUND** *(Listed under Olympia, page 405)*

➲ **Exit 88**

● **OUTBACK RV PARK** *(Open All Year)*
Res and Info: (360) 273-0585,
         outbackrvpark@hotmail.com,
         www.outbackrvpark.com
Location: Rochester, I-5 Exit 88

GPS Location: 46.81028 N, 123.05750 W, 100 Ft

58 Sites – This is a modern park on a flat parcel, there are no trees but it is landscaped. The park has pull-thrus to 55 feet and longer back-ins. Southbound take Exit 88, northbound take Exit 88B. Drive west on US-12 for 2.5 miles (4 km), the park is on the left.

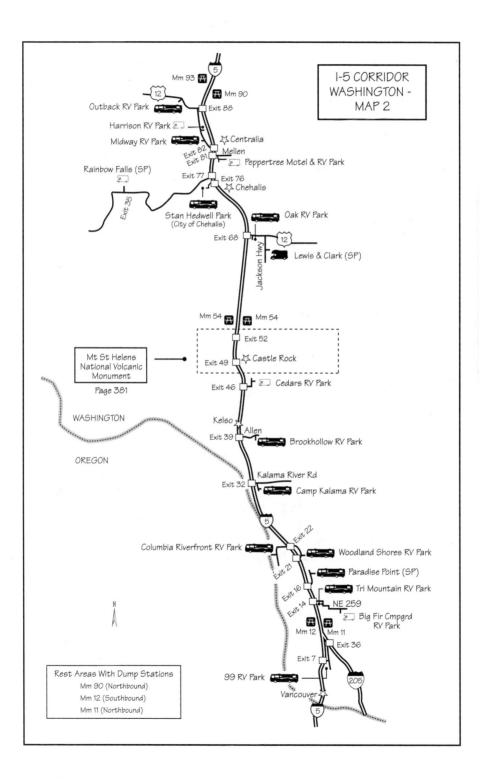

I-5 CORRIDOR
WASHINGTON -
MAP 2

Mm 93
Mm 90
Outback RV Park
Exit 88
Harrison RV Park
Midway RV Park
Centralia
Exit 82
Mellen
Exit 81
Peppertree Motel & RV Park
Rainbow Falls (SP)
Exit 77
Exit 76
Chehalis
Exit 35
Stan Hedwell Park
(City of Chehalis)
Oak RV Park
Exit 68
Jackson Hwy
12
Lewis & Clark (SP)
Mm 54
Mm 54
Exit 52
Mt St Helens
National Volcanic
Monument
Page 381
Exit 49
Castle Rock
Exit 46
Cedars RV Park
WASHINGTON
Kelso
OREGON
Exit 39
Allen
Brookhollow RV Park
Kalama River Rd
Exit 32
Camp Kalama RV Park
Columbia Riverfront RV Park
Exit 22
Woodland Shores RV Park
Exit 21
Paradise Point (SP)
Exit 16
Tri Mountain RV Park
Exit 14
NE 259
Big Fir Cmpgrd
RV Park
Mm 12
Mm 11
Exit 36
Exit 7
205
99 RV Park
Vancouver
5

WASHINGTON

Rest Areas With Dump Stations
Mm 90 (Northbound)
Mm 12 (Southbound)
Mm 11 (Northbound)

N

● **Exit 82**

● **MID-WAY RV PARK** *(Open All Year)*
Reservations: (800) 600-3204
Information: (360) 736-3200
           midwayrv@cen.quick.com
Location: Centralia, I-5 Exit 82

    GPS Location: 46.73528 N, 122.99472 W, 100 Ft

60 Sites – This is a mature but nice park with paved roads, ornamental trees and shrubs, and a mini-mart out front. Sites are pull-thrus and back-ins to 65 feet. Take Exit 82 from I-5 and drive northwest on Harrison Ave for .8 mile (1.3 km). Turn left on Galvin Rd and drive .3 mile (.5 km), the campground is on the left.

● **Exit 76**

○ **STAN HEDWELL PARK** *(City of Chehalis)*
        (Open April 1 to Nov 24)
Information: (360) 748-6664
Location: Chehalis

          GPS Location: 46.64000 N, 122.96306 W, 100 Ft

29 Sites – This city park is close to the freeway and reasonably priced. Tent camping is inexpensive and pitching is on grass. RV Sites are all back-ins, some to 45 feet with parking on gravel or grass. There are electricity and water hookups and a dump station. Sites have picnic tables and fire pits and are well separated. There's normally a host at this campground. It's set in trees near the city's playing fields. Take Exit 76 from I-5 and drive southwest .3 mile (.5 km) on Rice Road. The park entrance is on the right, follow signs to the camping area.

● **Exit 68**

● **OAK RV PARK** *(Open All Year)*
Res and Info: (360) 262-9221, info@oakrvpark.com,
           www.oakrvpark.com
Location: 8 Miles (13 km) S of Chehalis,
           I-5 Exit 68

    GPS Location: 46.54667 N, 122.87056 W, 400 Ft

32 Sites – This is an older RV park located behind a Texaco station just east of I-5, very handy. There are pull-thrus to 60 feet and much smaller back-ins. Take Exit 68 and drive east, the campground is on your right just .2 miles (.3 km) east of the interstate.

☐ **LEWIS AND CLARK STATE PARK** *(Open All Year)*
Information: (360) 864-2643, (360) 902-8844
Location: I-5 Exit 68

      GPS Location: 46.52167 N, 122.81472 W, 400 Ft

40 Sites – Lewis and Clark State Park is known as one of the last major stands of old growth forest in the state with Douglas Fir and red cedar. The sites in this campground are in two areas, most are no-hookup sites in a forested area, others are full-hookup sites across the road from the forested campground and day use area. The 25 no-hookup sites will take RVs to about 35 feet, they have picnic tables and fire pits. Most of the 8 hookup sites have full hookups in back-in sites suitable for RVs to about 35 feet, maneuvering room is tight for these sites. There are also horse sites and a hiker/biker camping area. Amenities include hiking and equestrian trails. Take Exit 68 and drive east on US-12 for

2.7 miles (4.4 km). Turn right on the Jackson Hwy and in 1.6 miles (2.6 km) you'll reach the park. Turn right into the park for the dry sites. Don't turn but continue straight a short distance for the hookup sites, they're on the left.

➲ **Exit 52**

● **TOUTLE RIVER RV RESORT**

(Listed under Mt St Helens National Volcanic Monument, page 382)

● **PARADISE COVE RV PARK**

(Listed under Mt St Helens National Volcanic Monument, page 383)

➲ **Exit 49**

● **MT ST. HELENS RV PARK**

(Listed under Mt St. Helens National Volcanic Monument, page 383)

➲ **Exit 39**

● **BROOKHOLLOW RV PARK** *(Open All Year)*

Reservations: (800) 867-0453
Information: (360) 577-6474, camping@Kalama.com,
                 www.brookhollowrvpark.com
Location: I-5 Exit 39

GPS Location: 46.14444 N, 122.87917 W, 100 Ft

132 Sites – Brookhollow is a very nice big rig park with widely-spaced paved parking with patios and picnic tables off paved drives. There are pull-thrus to 60 feet and back-ins to 45 feet. From Exit 39 of I-5 drive east for 1 mile (1.6 km) to the campground, the entrance is on the right.

➲ **Exit 32**

● **CAMP KALAMA RV PARK** *(Open All Year)*

Res and Info: (800) 750-2456,
                  campkalama@kalama.com,
                  www.kalama.com/~campkalama
Location: I-5 Exit 32

GPS Location: 46.03677 N, 122.85561 W, 100 Ft

115 Sites – An older but well-kept park just east of the interstate. Sites are gravel and grass with quite a bit of shade. They have pull-thrus to 90 feet and long back-ins too, also tent sites. There's a restaurant. Take Exit 32 and drive east for just .1 mile (.2 km). Turn right on Meeker Drive which parallels the interstate heading south, The campground is on the left in .4 mile (.6 km).

➲ **Exit 22**

● **COLUMBIA RIVERFRONT RV PARK**
   (Open All Year)

Res and Info: (800) 845-9842,
                  info@colriverfrontrv.com,
                  www.colombiariverfrontrv
                  park.com
Location: I-5 Exit 22

GPS Location: 45.91222 N, 122.80194 W, Near Sea Level

75 Sites – This is a very nice campground but its best feature is the waterfront location with great views of the passing ships on the river out front. There's also a seasonal swim-

ming pool. They have pull-thrus to 80 feet and back-ins to 40 feet. Take Exit 22 from I-5 and head west toward the river on Dike Road. At 1.8 miles (2.9 km) at a T go left. You'll reach the campground in another 1.2 miles (1.9 km).

➲ *Exit 21*

● **WOODLAND SHORES RV PARK** *(Open All Year)*

Res and Info: (360) 225-2222, woodlandshores@aol.com,
www.woodlandshoresrv.com
Location: Woodland, I-5 Exit 21

GPS Location: 45.90667 N, 122.73917 W, Near Sea Level

57 Sites – This little campground is tucked in next to the Lewis River in the little town of Woodland. It's beautifully maintained. Parking is on paved pads, some sites are right along the river. They have pull-thrus to 60 feet and back-ins to 45. Take Exit 21 from I-5 and drive .2 miles (.3 km) northeast and turn right on Millard Ave to the park.

➲ *Exit 16*

☐ **PARADISE POINT STATE PARK**
(Open May 13 to Sept 14)

Reservations: www.parks.wa.gov/reservations/,
(888) 226-7688
Information: (360) 263-2350
Location: I-5 Exit 16

GPS Location: 45.86611 N, 122.70444 W, 100 Ft

76 Sites – Paradise Point is just off the interstate but buffered with trees. It has 18 sites with electric and water hookups as well as lots of dry sites. Parking is on paved back-in sites to 40 feet. The day use area has a small beach on the East Fork of the Lewis River where both swimming and fishing are possible. Take Exit 16 and follow the access road north on the east side of the interstate for .8 mile (1.3 km) to the entrance.

➲ *Exit 14*

● **TRI MOUNTAIN RV PARK** *(Open All Year)*

Res and Info: (360) 887-8983
Location: I-5 Exit 14

GPS Location: 45.81500 N, 122.68222 W, 200 Ft

81 Sites – A good modern park with not a lot of frills. There are restaurants in a nearby strip mall. The campground has pull-thrus to 55 feet and back-ins to 45. Take Exit 14 from I-5 and drive east and then south on Pioneer. You'll see the campground on the right in .4 mile (6 km).

➲ *Exit 7*

● **99 RV PARK** *(Open All Year)*

Res and Info: (360) 573-0351, rvpark99@hotmail.com
Location: I-5 Exit 7

GPS Location: 45.71389 N, 122.65139 W, 100 Ft

90 Sites – Most of the sites in this park are occupied by long term residents but some sites are available for travelers. There are pull-thrus to 70 feet and back-ins to 40 feet. Access to this park can be confusing because it is very near the point where I-5 is joined by I-205 (Portland's ring route). In fact, it's between the

two. Southbound on I-5 you take the I-205 exit and then immediately (the exit is actually part of the turn ramp) take Exit 36 to the right. Drive straight and in about .5 mile (.6 km) you'll see the RV park on the right. Northbound on I-5 take Exit 7. Drive east a block on NE 134th Street and then turn south on SR-99. The campground will be on your right in about .3 mile (.5 km). Northbound in I-205 take Exit 35. Drive west to SR-99, turn south, and the campground is on your right in about .3 mile (.5 km).

INTERSTATE 90 CORRIDOR

Interstate 90 (I-90) is the main east west road corridor in Washington. It runs 300 miles (484 km) from Seattle to the border with Idaho. In the listing below we've extended the route a few miles into Idaho to include the Coeur d'Alene area.

Note that many of the campgrounds along the I-90 corridor are listed under other destinations sections of this chapter. If so, we've given a page reference in this section to make finding them easy.

Interstate 90 Corridor Campgrounds

➲ **Exit 11**

● **TRAILER INNS RV PARK** *(Listed under Seattle, page 432)*

➲ **Exit 13**

○ **VASA PARK RESORT AND BALLROOM** *(Listed under Seattle, page 432)*

WASHINGTON

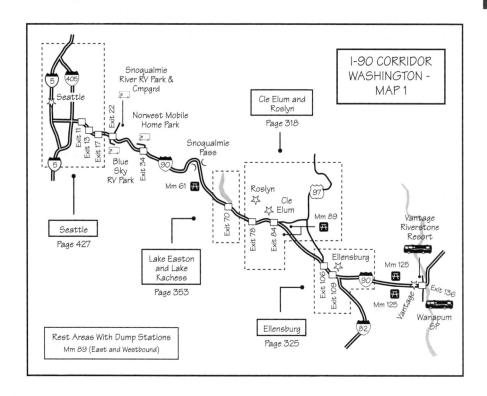

WASHINGTON

⮑ *Exit 17*

● **ISSAQUAH VILLAGE RV PARK** *(Listed under Seattle, page 432)*

⮑ *Exit 70*

● **LAKE EASTON RESORT** *(Listed under Lake Easton and Lake Kachess, page 354)*

● **SILVER RIDGE RANCH** *(Listed under Lake Easton and Lake Kachess, page 355)*

☐ **LAKE EASTON STATE PARK** *(Listed under Lake Easton and Lake Kachess, page 354)*

⮑ *Exit 78*

● **SUN COUNTRY GOLF AND RV RESORT** *(Listed under Cle Elum and Roslyn, page 319)*

⮑ *Exit 84*

● **WHISPERING PINES RV PARK** *(Listed under Cle Elum and Roslyn, page 318)*

⮑ *Exit 106*

● **ELLENSBURG KOA KAMPGROUND** *(Listed under Ellensburg, page 327)*

⮑ *Exit 109*

● **DAYS INN** *(Listed under Ellensburg, page 326)*

⮑ *Exit 136*

● **VANTAGE RIVERSTONE RESORT** *(Open All Year)*
   Res and Info: 509 856-2800, www.vantagewa.com
   Location: .   3 Mile (5 Km) North of I-90 Exit 136

   GPS Location: 46.94497 N, 119.99042 W, 600 Ft

120 Sites – This is an older but very large RV park that is conveniently near the highway. Sites here are full-hook-up, partial hookups, and no hookup back-ins and pull-thrus to 40 feet. They are surrounded by grass and many are shaded by trees. There is also tent camping on grass nearer the river. Wi-Fi is available at the office which is also a small store with a restaurant next door. It's a great place to stay if there's a concert at the Gorge.

☐ **WANAPUM STATE PARK**
     (Open March 18 to Nov 1 – Varies)
   Reservations: www.parks.wa.gov/reservations/,
                (888) 226-7688
   Information: (509) 856-2700
   Location: 2.7 Mile (4.4 Km) South of I-90 Exit 136

   GPS Location: 46.90418 N, 119.99174 W, 500 Ft

50 Sites – This beautiful state park campground is located on the west side of Wanapum Lake, the reservoir of Wanapum Dam which is 2.1 miles (3.4 km) downstream from the campground. There is a boat launch at the park as well as a sandy swimming beach in the day use area. Sites are situated on green lawns overlooking the water. Roads are paved and sites are gravel. There are full-hookup back-ins and spacious full-hookup pull-thrus to 70 feet.

⮑ *Exit 151*

● **SHADY TREE RV PARK AND CAMPGROUND** *(Open All Year)*
   Information: (509) 785-3101
   Location: .1 Mile (.2 Km) N of I-90 Exit 151

   GPS Location: 47.10405 N, 119.82894 W, 1,100 Ft

50 Sites – This is an older park behind a decades-old farmhouse.

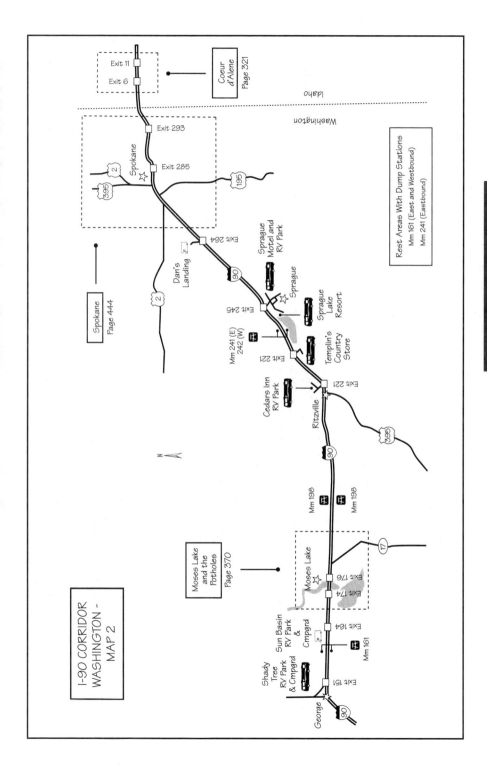

I-90 CORRIDOR WASHINGTON - MAP 2

Coeur d'Alene Page 321

Idaho

Washington

Exit 11

Exit 6

Exit 293

Exit 285

Spokane

2

395

195

Rest Areas With Dump Stations
Mm 161 (East and Westbound)
Mm 241 (Eastbound)

WASHINGTON

Exit 264

Dan's Landing

90

2

Spokane Page 444

Sprague Motel and RV Park

Sprague

Exit 245

Sprague Lake Resort

Mm 241 (E) 242 (W)

Exit 221

Templin's Country Store

Cedars Inn RV Park

Exit 221

Ritzville

395

N

90

Mm 198

Mm 198

Moses Lake and the Potholes Page 370

Moses Lake

17

Exit 176

Exit 174

Sun Basin RV Park & Cmpgrd

Exit 164

Mm 161

Shady Tree RV Park & Cmpgrd

Exit 151

George

90

There are many long-term residents but also a few sites for travelers. Sites are all back-ins with parking on gravel off a gravel loop. A few have picnic tables. Some are as long as 50 feet. Take Exit 151 and drive north on SR 281 for only a short distance, turn right on SR 283, the campground is on the right just after the turn. This is another popular Gorge concert campground.

➲ **Exit 174**

● **SUNCREST RESORT** *(Listed under Moses Lake and the Potholes, page 372)*

● **SUNRISE RESORTS PIER FOUR** *(Listed under Moses Lake and the Potholes, page 372)*

➲ **Exit 176**

● **LAKE FRONT RV PARK** *(Listed under Moses Lake and the Potholes, page 372)*

➲ **Exit 221**

● **CEDARS INN RV PARK** *(Open All Year)*
Res and Info: (509) 659-1007,
                    reservations@cedarsinnritzville.com,
                    www.cedarsinnritzville.com
Location: Ritzville, WA

GPS Location: 47.11935 N, 118.36382 W, 1,800 Ft

39 Sites – This is a campground behind a large modern motel. It's located just off the interstate at an exit with several gas stations, small stores, and a park. Sites are gravel pull-thrus to 40 feet off gravel interior roads. Wi-Fi is available in the motel lobby but not at most of the sites. There is a swimming pool and a small restaurant next door. Take Exit 221 from I-90 and drive north .1 mile (.2 km). Turn right on Smitty Road and after about a block you'll see the entrance to the motel parking lot on the left. Turn in and park to register, the RV park is ahead and beyond the swimming pool.

➲ **Exit 231**

● **TEMPLIN'S COUNTRY CORNER** *(Open All Year)*
Information: (509) 659-0198
Location: I-90 Exit 231 on the south side of the highway

GPS Location: 47.20923 N, 118.22709 W, 1,800 Ft

8 Sites – Templin's is a truck stop with restaurant and small store located just off the interstate. To the west they have eight pull-thru RV sites with power and water. It's not fancy, but the price is good. Restrooms are only available when the restaurant is open so this is a campground for self-contained rigs.

➲ **Exit 245**

● **SPRAGUE MOTEL AND RV PARK** *(Open All Year)*
Res and Info: (509) 257-2615, www.spraguemotel.com
Location: Sprague, WA

GPS Location: 47.30008 N, 117.97238 W, 1,800 Ft

13 Sites – This is a small recently-upgraded RV park be-
hind a friendly family-run motel. Sites are gravel back-ins and pull-thrus to 40 feet sepa-
rated by small plots of lawn. Downtown Sprague is just a short distance away. Take Exit 245 and drive south for .7 miles (1.1 km) to 4th Street. Turn right, then right again at the next intersection onto South B Street. Proceed north 3 blocks and turn right on 1st Street. Follow 1st east for .1 mile (.2 km) to the motel which is on the right.

● SPRAGUE LAKE RESORT *(Open April 1 to Oct 15)*
  Res and Info: (509) 257-2864, www.spraguelakeresort.com
  Location: Sprague, WA

  GPS Location: 47.28855 N, 118.02249 W, 1,800 Ft

26 Sites – This is a lakeside fishing resort that's a bit like an oasis in the dry countryside around Sprague. The interior loop road is gravel, parking is on grass. Most sites are back-ins or tent sites but there are also a few pull-thrus to 35 feet. There's a boat ramp and dock and some sites are along the lake, all sites are near the lake. Take Exit 245 and drive south for .7 miles (1.1 km) to 4th Street. Turn right, then right again at the next intersection onto South B Street. Proceed north 3 blocks and turn left on 1st Street. Drive west through town and in .5 mile (.8 km) take the left fork onto Max Harder Road East. Continue east for 1.6 mile (2.6 km) to Sprague Lake Resort Road and turn right. Follow the entrance road .3 mile (.5 km) to the resort. There are several direction signs along the route so it's easy to follow.

⊃ **Exit 285**

● PARK LANE MOTEL SUITES AND RV PARK *(Listed under Spokane, page 444)*

● TRAILER INNS RV PARK *(Listed under Spokane, page 445)*

⊃ **Exit 293**

● SPOKANE KOA *(Listed under Spokane, page 447)*

⊃ **Exit 6 (Idaho)**

● COEUR D'ALENE RV RESORT *(Listed under Coeur d'Alene, page 322)*

⊃ **Exit 11 (Idaho)**

● RIVER WALK RV PARK *(Listed under Coeur d'Alene, page 322)*

● BLACKWELL ISLAND RV PARK *(Listed under Coeur d'Alene, page 322)*

INTERSTATE 82 CORRIDOR

Interstate 82 (I-82) is a north-south road corridor connecting I-90 in eastern Washington with I-84 in eastern Oregon. It runs only 153 miles (247 km) from Ellensburg in Washington to Hermiston in Oregon. We've listed the campgrounds from north to south.

Note that many of the campgrounds along the I-82 corridor are listed under other destinations sections of this chapter. If so, we've given a page reference in this section to make finding them easy.

Interstate 82 Corridor Campgrounds

⊃ **Exit 31**

● YAKIMA TRAILER INNS RV PARK *(Listed under Yakima and the Yakima Valley, page 468)*

⊃ **Exit 33**

☐ YAKIMA SPORTSMAN STATE PARK *(Listed under Yakima and the Yakima Valley, page 467)*

⊃ **Exit 34**

● CIRCLE H RV PARK *(Listed under Yakima and the Yakima Valley, page 467)*

⊃ **Exit 80**

● WINE COUNTRY RV PARK *(Listed under Yakima and the Yakima Valley, page 468)*

WASHINGTON

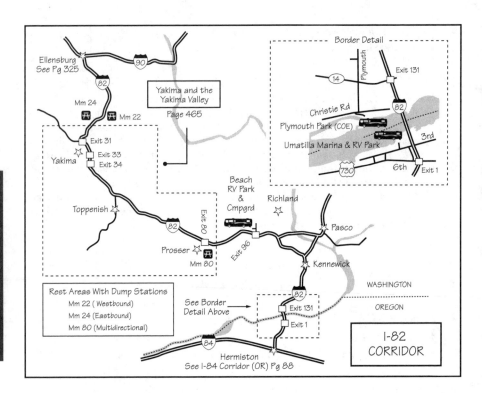

➲ **Exit 96**

● **BEACH RV PARK AND CAMPGROUND** *(Open All Year)*
Res and Info: (509) 588-5959, reservations@beachrv.net,
www.beachrv.net
Location: Exit 96 of I-82

GPS Location: 46.25433 N, 119.47666 W, 400 Ft

110 Sites – This campground with access to the Yakima River is conveniently located. It tends to be a long-term residential park and it is recommended that you call ahead if you are thinking of visiting. Sites vary but include some long paved pull-thrus to about 70 feet. From Exit 96 of I-82 drive north for .2 miles (.3 km) and turn left at the sign for the entrance.

➲ **Exit 131**

■ **PLYMOUTH PARK** *(Open April 1 to Oct 31)*
Reservations: www.recreation.gov, (877) 444-6777
Information: (541) 506-7819, (509) 783-1270
Location: 1.6 Mile (2.6 Km) West of Exit 131 of I-82

GPS Location: 45.93368 N, 119.35067 W, 200 Ft

32 Sites – This Corps of Engineers campground on the north
side of Lake Umatilla, is across from the town of Umatilla in Oregon. The waterfront at the campground is on a waterway with an island between the campground and the lake itself. Sites are paved pull-thrus off paved roads and extend to 40 feet. Half of the sites

have full hookups and half have electricity and water. There is also a day use area located about a mile west of the campground which has a swimming beach, boat ramp, and dock. Take Exit 131 from I-82 and drive west on SR-14 for .7 mile (1.1 km). Turn left on South Plymouth Road and follow it south for .7 mile (1.1 km). Turn left on Christie Road and the campground entrance is on the left in about .2 mile (.32 km).

➲ *Exit 1 (Oregon)*

○ **UMATILLA MARINA AND RV PARK** *(Open All Year)*
    Res and Info: (541) 922-3939
    Location: Exit 1 of I-82

    GPS Location: 45.92359 N, 119.33095 W, 300 Ft

35 Sites – The RV park here is a large grass field overlooking the marina just west of the I-82 bridge. The sites here are gravel back-ins and pull-thrus to 60 feet with full hookups. There are also tent sites. Take Exit 1 from I-82. Just west of the freeway follow Brownell Blvd. north for .3 miles (.5 km) to 3rd Street. Turn left on 3rd and drive west for about .3 miles (.5 km) to Quincy Ave. Turn right and find the campground entrance just ahead on the right.

BELLINGHAM

Whatcom County's largest town and the farthest north major city along the I-5 corridor is Bellingham (population 81,000). Founded in 1852 as a sawmill town Bellingham has gone through phases as a coal town, a gold stampede supply town, a railroad town, and a fishing and salmon-packing town. Today it's the home of Western Washington University and also the southern terminus of the Alaska Marine Highway System.

The center for tourist activities in Bellingham is **Fairhaven** on the south side of the city. It's also the port for the Alaska ferries. Fairhaven is most easily reached from I-5 by taking Exit 250 and heading west on the Old Fairhaven Parkway. From June to September there is a farmer's market in Fairhaven on Wednesdays.

North from Fairhaven along the waterfront there is quite a bit of recent tourist development to replace the older industries that are disappearing from the city. There are waterfront trails, a new luxury hotel, a marina, restaurants, and waterfront parks.

South from the Fairhaven district is **Chuckanut Drive**. This narrow highway along a steep hillside overlooking Samish Bay was opened in 1896. It was the main route for travelers from the south and was famous as a very scenic road. Today it's too narrow for big RVs, anything over 18,000 pounds GVW is not allowed and drivers of wide-bodied RVs will be uncomfortable when they meet traffic. The scenic, narrow section only extends 10 miles (16 km) south of Bellingham, then you're in the flats of the Skagit Valley.

Bellingham has an interesting museum, the regional **Whatcom Museum of History and Art** which in addition to historical displays also has some natural history exhibits. Bellingham is a good place to take **water tours**. Perhaps you could catch the Alaska State Ferry up the Inside Passage as a deck passenger. If you don't have time for that you might instead try a day-long boat tour through the San Juan Islands to Victoria, B.C. and back.

Tent campers will find Bellingham a bit of a challenge with the two nearest state parks pretty far from the center of things. Larrabee State Park is probably the best bet but The Cedars is a possibility with easy access even if it's pretty far north of town. Big rig camp-

WASHINGTON

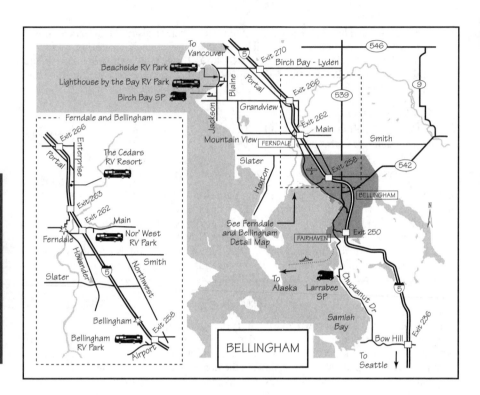

ers are well taken care of by the commercial campgrounds, all are good for them. The state parks, however, don't service big rigs very well in this area.

Bellingham Campgrounds

● **LIGHTHOUSE BY THE BAY RV PARK** *(Open All Year)*
Res and Info: (360) 371-5603, (604) 800-1505,
info@lighthousebythebay.com,
www.lighthousebythebay.com
Location: Birch Bay

GPS Location: 48.91783 N, 122.73812 W, Near Sea Level

100 Sites – This nicely maintained RV park has full-hookup back-in sites to 58 feet. Roads are paved. It's about .3 miles (.5 km) from the beach. From I-5 take Exit 270. Drive west on Birch Bay-Lynden Road for 2.8 miles (4.5 km). Turn left on Blaine Road (Hwy 548) and drive south 1.3 mile (2.1 km). Turn right on Alderson Road and drive west, the campground is on the right in .5 miles (.8 km).

● **BEACHSIDE RV PARK** *(Open All Year)*
Res and Info: (800) 596-5962, (360) 371-5962,
www.beachsidervpark.com
Location: Birch Bay

GPS Location: 48.91872 N, 122.74483 W, Near Sea Level

72 Sites – Despite the name, this campground is really located across the street and a bit

back from the beach. Sites here are full hookup back-ins and pull-thrus to 60 feet. From I-5 take Exit 270. Drive west on Birch Bay-Lynden Road for 2.8 miles (4.5 km). Turn left on Blaine Road (Hwy 548) and drive south 1.3 mile (2.1 km). Turn right on Alderson Road and drive west to Beach Bay Drive, a distance of .8 mile (1.3 km). Turn right here and you'll see the entrance to the campground on the right.

☐ **BIRCH BAY STATE PARK** *(Open All Year)*
  Reservations: www.parks.wa.gov/reservations/,
             (888) 226-7688
  Information: (360) 371-2800, (360) 902-8844,
             birchbay@parks.wa.gov,
             www.parks.wa.gov
  Location: 20 Miles (32 Km) N of Bellingham

  GPS Location: 48.90306 N, 122.76056 W, Near Sea Level

167 Sites – This state park campground occupies a ridge overlooking the beach at the south side of Birch Bay. Along the beach is a day-use area where it is possible to swim and a boat launch. Most sites here are non-hookup but there is an area with 20 hookup sites (three with sewer) in the North Campground for RVs to about 30 feet. There are larger sites, including some pull-thrus but no hookups, for RVs to 35 feet in the South Campground. Some sites reach 60 feet but maneuvering room limits accessibility. From I-5 take Exit 266 and follow Grandview Road (SR-548) westward for 5.8 miles (9.4 km). Turn right onto Jackson Road and then in .8 mile (1.3 km) turn left into Helweg Road. The campground entrance is just ahead.

● **THE CEDARS RV RESORT** *(Open All Year)*
  Res and Info: (360) 384-2622
  Location: 9 Miles (15 Km) N of Bellingham

  GPS Location: 48.87056 N, 122.58528 W, Near Sea Level

260 Sites – The Cedars is a very nice resort for tents and RVs conveniently located just north of Ferndale with easy freeway access. RV sites are back-ins and pull-thrus to 65 feet. Amenities include a seasonal swimming pool, instant-on telephone at the sites, and Wi-Fi. From I-5 take Exit 263 and drive north on Portal Way. The campground will be on your left in .9 mile (1.5 km).

● **NOR'WEST RV PARK** *(Open All Year)*
  Res and Info: (360) 384-5038,
             nwrvparkferndale@yahoo.com
  Location: 7 Miles (11 Km) N of Bellingham

  GPS Location: 48.84583 N, 122.56972 W, Near Sea Level

27 Sites – This modern, small and tidy RV park is very popular. Reservations are necessary all through the summer months. Sites are paved back-ins and pull-thrus to 60 feet. From I-5 take Exit 262 and follow Main Street east for .3 mile (.5 km). The campground entrance is on the right.

● **BELLINGHAM RV PARK** *(Open All Year)*
  Reservations: (888) 372-1224
  Information: (360) 752-1224, bellrvpark@msn.com,
             www.bellinghamrvpark.info
  Location: Bellingham

  GPS Location: 48.78750 N, 122.52000 W , 100 Ft

WASHINGTON

56 Sites – The most convenient park to Bellingham is this modern big-rig park just off the freeway. All of the sites here are 65-foot pull-thrus. Restrooms are exceptionally nice. Take Exit 258 from I-5 as it passes through Bellingham. You'll spot the park on the west side of the freeway.

☐ **LARRABEE STATE PARK** *(Open All Year)*
   Reservations: www.parks.wa.gov/reservations/,
               (888) 226-7688
   Information: (360) 676-2093, (360) 902-8844,
               larrabee@parks.wa.gov, www.parks.wa.gov
   Location: 5 Miles (8 Km) S of Bellingham

GPS Location: 48.65361 N, 122.49028 W, 100 Ft

85 Sites – This state campground is located south of Bellingham at the north end of Chuckanut Drive. It's a venerable campground, in fact it was the first Washington state park. Sites here are arranged off a narrow loop. Many sites are gravel but 11 of the full hookup sites are paved. Although there are some long sites, limited maneuvering room makes this campground only suitable for RVs to 30 feet. There are also eight primitive walk-in tent sites. There is also a boat launch. Note that a busy rail line runs right through this park. The campground must be approached from the north if you are in an RV because Chuckanut Drive to the south is very narrow and long rigs are restricted. From I-5 take Exit 250. Drive west on Old Fairhaven Parkway for 1.2 miles (1.9 km) until you reach Chuckanut Drive North. Turn south and you'll reach the campground in 5.1 miles (8.2 km).

CHELAN

The town of Chelan (population 3,500) occupies a moraine at the south end of 55-mile-long (89 km) **Lake Chelan**. Chelan is mostly known for two things in Washington state, its apples and the lake which is a popular recreation destination for folks from far around. In fact, most weekends during the summer find Chelan packed with visitors, many from west of the mountains.

During spring, summer, and fall the area's **apple orchards** are hard to miss. There are about 10,000 acres planted in Red Delicious, Golden Delicious, and other varieties. One of the best things about Chelan is that popular as it is with tourists, the orchards remain an important part of the economy and the atmosphere here. Chelan apples are thought to be better than those grown in many other locations because the lake tends to moderate the temperatures in the valley.

One of the best places to see apples is on the slopes above **Manson**, located about 8 miles (13 km) up the east shore of the lake from Chelan. The town promotes a 16-mile (26 km) **scenic driving loop** that offers views of the lake, orchards, and surrounding area. It's also an excellent bicycle route – as long as you don't mind some hills. Manson hosts two apple-related festivals during the year: the **Manson Apple Blossom Festival** is in early May and the **Manson Harvest Festival** is in the middle of October.

There are also more and more vineyards in the Chelan area. In October the **Chelan Crush** offers the opportunity to visit area vineyards, particularly on the first and second weekends of the month.

There's also a **casino** in Manson, the Mill Bay Casino, and it allows overnight RV parking in it's lot, see below.

The deep and narrow Lake Chelan winds its way back into the Cascades, the far north end is actually inside the North Cascades National Park Service Complex. One of the popular things to do in Chelan is to take a ferry ride to **Stehekin** which is at the north end of the lake. These ferries do not carry vehicles. At least one boat each day leaves in the morning and returns in the afternoon, in summer more boats operate and there is even a high-speed catamaran making two trips each day. A one-way trip on the cat takes only an hour and 15 minutes. In Stehekin you can wander around the isolated little town or take one of several tours offered to visitors. Stehekin is an important access point to the North Cascades National Park, there is a park information center and a shuttle bus to help you access nearby tent campgrounds and trails.

Chelan itself has a full plate of both sports and cultural related attractions. During the year the town hosts events related to arts and crafts, hang gliding, music, mountain biking, fine arts, hydro racing, running and fishing. There should be something for everyone.

At the south end of the lake near Chelan the main focus on the lake is water sports. You have a choice of personal water craft, water skiing, even sailing. The water is a little chilly, even in the middle of the summer, but the air is warm so no one seems to mind.

Chelan in the summer is a very busy place. Reservations are highly recommended. The Lakeshore and Lake Chelan State Park are the big campgrounds in the area. Both are good for tent camping although the state park is best. For big rigs the Lakeshore is the most popular choice. Sometimes during the week there is room up above Manson at the Kamei and Wapato Lake campgrounds when everything else is full. They're also much quieter and more pleasant when things are busy, but they're not near Lake Chelan either.

WASHINGTON

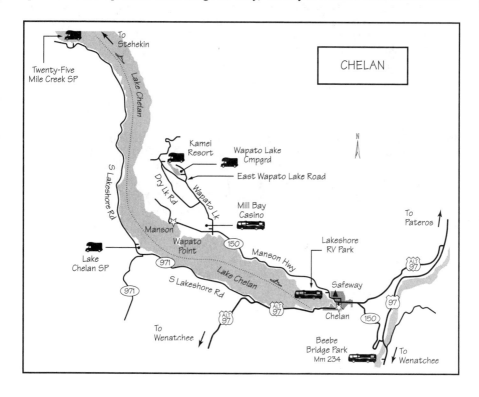

WASHINGTON

Chelan Campgrounds

○ **LAKESHORE RV PARK** *(Open All Year)*
Res and Info: (509) 682-8023,
www.chelancityparks.com
Location: Chelan

GPS Location: 47.84472 N, 120.02444 W, 1,200 Ft

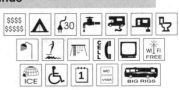

165 Sites – The largest and most convenient of the Chelan campgrounds is located right in town on the shore of the lake. This is a city campground, it's very nice. The park has restrooms with hot showers, a swimming beach, tennis courts and a playground. Best of all, it's just a short stroll to the center of town as well as a nearby Safeway. Sites are back-ins and pull-thrus, some as long as 60 feet. Some sites have large tent pads. Wi-Fi is useable only near the office. Rates are considerably less expensive during shoulder and off seasons. The campground is on the lakeshore near where the road heads out to Manson. If you follow signs for Manson from any of the entrances to Chelan you'll see it on your left as you start out of town.

● **MILL BAY CASINO** *(Open All Year)*
Information: (509) 687-6911
Location: Manson

GPS Location: 47.88513 N, 120.13266 W, 1,100 Ft

50 Sites – The casino has a large dirt parking lot to the west of the paved parking lot. Overnight parking by RVs is allowed. RVers should register with security people in the casino upon arrival. To reach Mill Bay Casino head out of Chelan along the lakeshore toward Manson. Turn right in 5.8 miles (9.4 km) on Wapato Lake Road. In just .2 mile (.3 km) you'll see the casino entrance on your left. After you enter the RV area is straight ahead beyond the paved parking area.

● **KAMEI RESORT** *(Open Late April to Labor Day – Varies)*
Res and Info: (509) 687-3690
Location: 10 Miles (16 Km) N of Chelan

GPS Location: 47.92139 N, 120.17528 W, 1,300 Ft

50 Sites – Kamei is a small private campground located on the shore of Wapato Lake in the hills above Lake Chelan. It's good for RVs to about 35 feet. The campground is located in a beautiful area full of apple orchards and fishing in the small lake can be pretty good. There's a boat ramp and boat rentals. To reach Kamei Resort head out of Chelan along the lakeshore toward Manson. Turn right in 5.8 miles (9.4 km) on Wapato Lake Road. You'll pass the Mill Bay Casino and in 3.6 miles (5.8 km) see the campground on your right.

○ **WAPATO LAKE CAMPGROUND** *(Open April 15 to Sept 15)*
Res and Info: (509) 687-6037, info@mansonparks.com,
http://mansonparks.com/WapatoLakeCampground.
html
Location: 9 Miles (15 Km) N of Chelan

GPS Location: 47.91333 N, 120.15361 W, 1,300 Ft

50 Sites – This is a small lakeside City of Manson park located at the southeast end of little Wapato Lake, the same lake that Kamei Resort borders. Some spaces here will take RVs to 35 feet. Pets are limited, none are allowed on major holidays and only one pet per

site is allowed at other times. Some of these sites are waterfront, it's a nice little park with decent facilities. A boat ramp is next door and there is a swimming beach at the park. To reach Wapato Lake Campground head out of Chelan along the lakeshore toward Manson. Turn right in 5.8 miles (9.4 km) on Wapato Lake Road. You'll pass the Mill Bay Casino and in 2.3 miles (3.7 km) see East Wapato Lake Road going right. Turn right and in another .2 miles (.3 km) you'll see the campground on your left.

☐ **LAKE CHELAN STATE PARK** *(Open All Year)*
Reservations: (888) 226-7688, www.parks.wa.gov
Information: (509) 687-3710, (360) 902-8844,
    www.parks.wa.gov
Location: 9 Miles (15 Km) W of Chelan,

GPS Location: 47.87389 N, 120.19972 W, 1,200 Ft

144 Sites – This campground is very popular with tent campers as there are over 100 tent sites and only 35 utility sites. Many sites are shaded. The maximum RV size that will comfortably fit in this very popular state park is about 30 feet, all sites are back-ins. There's a sandy swimming beach and a boat launch. The campground is located 9 miles (15 km) from Chelan up the western shore of the lake. It is an extremely popular campground, reservations are a must all summer long. This park accepts reservations from May 15 to September 30.

☐ **TWENTY-FIVE MILE CREEK STATE PARK**
    (Open March 31 to Oct 9 – Varies)
Reservations: www.parks.wa.gov/reservations/, (888) 226-7688
Information: (509) 687-3610, (360) 902-8844, www.parks.wa.gov
Location: 20 Miles (32 Km) NW of Chelan

GPS Location: 47.99250 N, 120.25944 W, 1,200 Ft

67 Sites – This state campground is at the end of the road that goes up the west side of Lake Chelan. There is a small boat harbor here with a boat ramp as well as a small store alongside the ramp. The entrance road is steep but paved and some sites will take RVs to 30 feet. Most people using this campground are in smaller rigs or tents. To reach the campground just drive SR-971 up the west side of the lake, the campground is at about Mile 10, some 9.7 miles (15.6 km) beyond Lake Chelan State Park.

○ **BEEBE BRIDGE PARK** *(Open April 1 to Nov 1)*
Information: (509) 661-4551
Location: 4 Miles (6.5 Km) SE of Chelan

GPS Location: 47.80715 N, 119.97278 W, 700 Ft

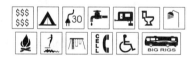

46 Sites – Beebe Bridge is Chelan County PUD park located on the Entiat Reservoir of the Columbia River. It's the closest Columbia River park to Chelan, about 3.6 miles (5.8 km) away. Like many of the campgrounds along the river this one is a beautiful place with large expanses of grass, paved roads and paved sites. There are pull-thru sites to 60 feet and back-ins to 45 feet. Sites have electricity and water hookups, there is a dump station. Other amenities includes a swimming beach, boat launch, and tennis courts. From Chelan take the Chelan Falls Road (SR-150) at the east end of town down to the river, a distance of about 3.1 miles (5 km). When you reach Hwy 97 turn right and cross the river, the park is on the right as soon as you reach the other side.

CLE ELUM AND ROSLYN

Little **Cle Elum** (population 1,900), is located where I-90 departs the Cascade Mountains as it heads east. This is Ponderosa pine country, with a much sunnier and dryer climate than just a few miles to the west. Just 2 miles (3 km) northwest of Cle Elum is little Roslyn (population 900), close enough that they are really almost one community. The main service center is Cle Elum which is near the freeway and has shopping and restaurants including a supermarket.

These towns began at the end of the 19th century as coal-mining communities. Even today you can see evidence of this, particularly in Roslyn where the immigrant cemetery dating from its mining days is one of the attractions.

Today this area is actually beginning to be a bit of a bedroom community for Seattle, 80 miles (130 km) away across Snoqualmie Pass. It's a 1.5 hour drive, assuming that snow doesn't slow you to a stop in the pass during the winter. Some folks can live with that, the trade-off is more winter sunshine. For other Seattle-area residents this is a great place for a weekend get-a-way.

Roslyn is probably best known today as the setting for the television series **Northern Exposure**. Although the town of Cicily was supposed to be in Alaska the show was actually filmed here. You'll probably recognize several of the shooting locations.

From Cle Elum the Wenatchee National Forest is very accessible. SR-903 goes north through Roslyn and then Ronald for many miles. It's known as the Salmon La Sac Road and three of the forest service campgrounds listed below are located along the road. From Cle Elum it's 25 miles (40 km) northeast to Blewett Pass on US-97. This busy highway connects with the Wenatchee Valley and passes through the national forest. Two forest service campgrounds along this highway as it climbs to the pass are listed below. There are many dirt roads allowing access to back country from US-97.

Tent campers here will be attracted by the Wenatchee National Forest campgrounds, all a bit out of town but in attractive settings in the woods. None of the forest service campgrounds are good for really big rigs. If you have one of them the place to go is the Whispering Pines, it's conveniently located just off the freeway. If you're a golfer, however, you'll probably want to stay at the Sun Country Golf and RV Resort. The best big rigs forest service sites are at Salmon La Sac, but exercise caution.

Cle Elum and Roslyn Campgrounds

● **WHISPERING PINES RV PARK** *(Open All Year)*
Res and Info: (509) 674-7278, whisperingpines@inlandnet. com,
         www.whisperingpines.cjb.net
Location: Cle Elum

GPS Location: 47.18917 N, 120.93667 W, 2,000 Ft

35 Sites – The Whispering Pines is a modern campground set up for big rigs with both full hookup and partial hookup sites. Nearby is a RV parts store and service facility run by the same owners, very convenient. Sites include pull-thrus and back-ins to 60 feet. The campground is located on the south side of Interstate 90. Westbound on I-90 take Exit 84 and then turn left and go south .2 miles (.3 km) to the campground. Eastbound on I-90 there is no Exit 84 so you should continue on to Exit 85. A U-turn is difficult so just drive

into Cle Elum and in 2.3 miles (3.7 km) from the exit turn left at the stoplight onto Oaks Avenue and follow it across the railroad tracks and freeway to the campground, a distance of .6 miles (1 km) from the stoplight.

● **SUN COUNTRY GOLF AND RV RESORT**
  (Open April 15 to Oct 15 – Varies)
  Res and Info: (509) 674-2226, www.golfsuncountry.com
  Location: 5 Miles (8 Km) W of Cle Elum

  GPS Location: 47.18750 N, 121.05056 W, 1,900 Ft

25 Sites – This small 9-hole golf resort also has RV sites. While there are 25 back-in sites with parking on grass only about four are suitable for longer coaches because the front of the sites drop off making leveling very difficult. Note that rates are lower from Monday through Thursday. To reach the campground take Exit 78 from I-90, about 5 miles (8 km) west of Cle Elum. Drive south .1 mile (.2 km) to Sun Country Road (also called Nelson Siding Road). Turn left and follow the road .4 miles (.6 km) up and over a hill to the golf resort.

● **THE LAST RESORT** *(Open All Year)*
  Res and Info: (509) 649-2222, creek@inlandnet.com,
                     www.thelastresortwa.com
  Location: 9 Miles (15 Km) NW of Cle Elum

  GPS Location: 47.27417 N, 121.07417 W, 2,300 Ft

15 Sites – The Last Resort is a restaurant and convenience store with a few RV sites

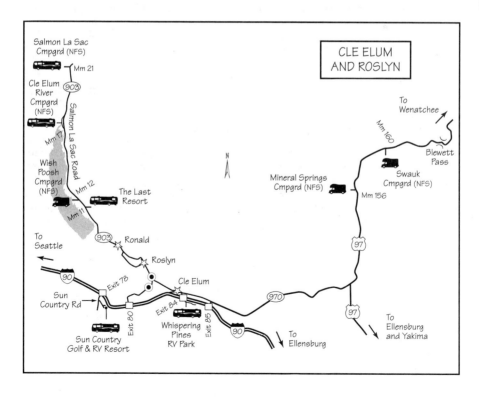

on the hillside at the rear. Although some sites have full hookups the ones available for traveler use are usually electricity-only back-in sites. The only restrooms are in the convenience store and are not available when it is closed, there are no showers. The campground is on the east side of the Salmon La Sac Road near Mile 11 about 5 miles (8 km) north of Roslyn.

■ **WISH POOSH CAMPGROUND** *(Open May 27 to Sept 5 – Varies)*
Reservations: www.recreation.gov, (877) 444-6777
Information: (509) 852-1100
Location: 10 Miles (16 Km) NW of Cle Elum

GPS Location: 47.27972 N, 121.08611 W, 2,300 Ft

33 Sites – This Wenatchee National Forest campground is located on the shore of Cle Elum Lake. The campground has a large boat ramp area and a swimming beach. Some sites have room for RVs to 40 feet but maneuvering room is limited and access for really big rigs is difficult so the campground is best for RVs to 30 feet. The campground is located on the west side of the Salmon La Sac Road near Mile 12 about 5 miles (8 km) north of Roslyn.

■ **CLE ELUM RIVER CAMPGROUND** *(Open May 27 to Sept 5 – Varies)*
Information: (509) 852-1100
Location: 15 Miles (24 Km) NW of Cle Elum

GPS Location: 47.35056 N, 121.10528 W, 2,200 Ft

23 Sites – This is a smaller Wenatchee National Forest campground with the sites all back-ins off one road that runs parallel to the Salmon La Sac Road about 100 yards away. Sites overlook the flood plain of the Cle Elum River but it is too far in the distance to enjoy and not visible from the sites. The campground is located on the west side of the Salmon La Sac Road near Mile 17 about 10 miles (16 km) north of Roslyn.

■ **SALMON LA SAC CAMPGROUND** *(Open May 27 to Sept 5 – Varies)*
Reservations: (877) 444-6777, www.recreation.gov
Information: (509) 656-0366
Location: 18 Miles (29 Km) N of Cle Elum

GPS Location: 47.40389 N, 121.09778 W, 2,300 Ft

66 Sites – Salmon La Sac is a very large Wenatchee National Forest campground with sites that can be reserved so it is a popular place. It is situated between the Cooper and Cle Elum rivers. On weekends there is a two night minimum stay required, on holidays 3 days are required. One of the loops has some large pull-thru sites suitable for RVs to 40 feet. Water is from a hand pump. The campground is located on the west side of the Salmon La Sac Road near Mile 21 about 14 miles (23 km) north of Roslyn.

■ **SWAUK CAMPGROUND** *(Open May 27 to Sept 5 – Varies)*
Information: (509) 852-1100
Location: 21 Miles (34 Km) NE of Cle Elum

GPS Location: 47.32889 N, 120.65750 W, 3,000 Ft

24 Sites – This small Wenatchee National Forest campground is located along US-97, the Blewett Pass highway between Cle Elum and the Wenatchee Valley. Road noise is a definite problem here. The sites are located off a small loop beyond a rest area, they are suitable for RVs to 25 feet. The campground is located near Mile 160, about 21 miles (34 km) northeast of Cle Elum.

■ **MINERAL SPRINGS CAMPGROUND** *(Open May 27 to Sept 5 – Varies)*
Information: (509) 852-1100
Location: 17 Miles (27 Km) NE of Cle Elum

GPS Location: 47.29000 N, 120.69944 W, 2,700 Ft

8 Sites – Another very small Wenatchee National Forest campground right next to US-97, the Blewett Pass highway between Cle Elum and the Wenatchee Valley. It's very near the highway so road noise is a problem. Sites are small and suitable for RVs to 25 feet. The campground is located near Mile 156, about 17 miles (27 km) northeast of Cle Elum.

COEUR D'ALENE, IDAHO

Coeur d'Alene (population 44,000), located on the north shore of Lake Coeur d'Alene, is a friendly-sized city in a beautiful lakeside setting. It has long been a tourist destination and offers a good selection of restaurants and shopping. Coeur d'Alene is only 30 miles (48 km) east of Spokane, Washington on Interstate 90.

Beginning with the construction of the 18-story **Coeur d'Alene Resort** on the lakeshore in town in 1986 local businessman Duane Hagadone has almost single-handedly developed the town into an international destination. Related developments are the **Coeur d'Alene Resort Golf Course** just east of town and **Silverwood Theme Park** to the north. Don't miss a walk through the resort and along the waterfront.

Another golf attraction in the area is the **Circling Raven Golf Club** in Worley, about 26 miles (42 km) south of Coeur d'Alene on US-95.

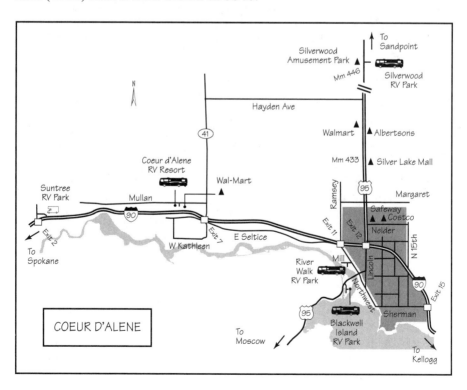

The big attraction, though, must be the lake. **Lake Coeur d'Alene** is a huge alpine lake extending 25 miles (40 km) from north to south. It's popular for all sorts of waters sports, from houseboats to kayaking. You'll see an amazing collection of watercraft on the lake on any warm summer day.

The drive around the lake is popular too. Take I-90 east 7 miles (11 km) to Exit 22. Turn south on little two-lane SR-97. This road follows the eastern shoreline south for 36 miles (58 km) to join SR-3 before reaching St Maries. **St Maries** is known for the wild-rice grown in the neighborhood. You better stop and pick some up before heading east on SR-5 along the short south shore and then north on US-95 back to Coeur d'Alene. US-95 doesn't follow the lake shore so it's not very scenic. A much longer but more scenic alternate to get back to town would be to follow SR-3 southeast from St Maries to meet SR-6. Drive southwest through Harvard, Princeton, and Potlatch to catch US-95 north again to Coeur d'Alene. All together this route is 175 miles (282 km), it makes a long day. An alternate would be to spend the night at one of the RV parks listed in this book under *Moscow, Pullman and the Palouse*.

Coeur d'Alene Campgrounds

● **RIVER WALK RV PARK** *(Open All Year)*
Reservations: (888) 567-8700
Information: (208) 765-5943, riverwalkrvpark@yahoo.com
Location: Coeur d'Alene

   GPS Location: 47.69056 N, 116.80139 W, 2,100 Ft

43 Sites – This is the smallest of the Coeur d'Alene parks listed in this book and also the closest to the lakefront in town. It's small but well run and maintained. Sites here can handle RVs to 36 feet. Reservations are recommended. From I-90 take Exit 11 and head south toward the center of town. In .7 mile (1.1 km) turn right onto W. Mill Ave., the campground entrance will be on your left almost immediately.

● **BLACKWELL ISLAND RV PARK**
   (Open April 1 to Oct 15)
Reservations: (888) 571-2900
Information: (208) 665-1300, www.idahorvpark.com
Location: 1 Mile (1.6 Km) W of Coeur d'Alene

GPS Location: 47.68056 N, 116.80250 W, 2,100 Ft

172 Sites – This is a modern big-rig campground with sites to 70 feet and lots of maneuvering room located just across the Spokane River from central Coeur d'Alene. This is a riverfront campground and amenities include a beach, a boat dock, a boat ramp, and a meeting room. Easiest access from I-90 is to take Exit 12 and head south on Lincoln Way which is also US-95. In .7 mile (1.1 km) turn right on West Walnut Avenue (also US-95) and follow it for .7 mile (1.1 km) across the river. Just beyond the river you'll see the big RV park on your left and the entrance road.

● **COEUR D'ALENE RV RESORT** *(Open All Year)*
   Res and Info: (208) 773-3527
   Location: 7 Miles (11 Km) W of Coeur d'Alene

      GPS Location: 47.71389 N, 116.91250 W, 2,100 Ft

189 Sites – Despite the name this huge RV park is in Post Falls, about 6 miles (10 km) west of Coeur d'Alene. This

is a big-rig park with back-ins and pull-thrus to 72 feet. The stand-out amenity is the building which houses the offices, restrooms, lounge area and indoor swimming pool. Also nice is the nearby Walmart. Wi-Fi only works in the office area. To reach the park take Exit 7 from I-90 and drive north on SR-41 for .2 miles (.3 km). Turn left on East Mullan Avenue and drive .8 miles (1.3 km), past the Walmart, to the campground entrance which is on the left.

● **SILVERWOOD RV PARK** *(Open May 1 to Oct 5)*
   Res and Info: (208) 683-3400,
                 www.silverwoodthemepark.com/rv-park.php
   Location: 18 Miles N of Coeur d'Alene

   GPS Location: 47.90743 N, 116.70405 W, 2,300 Ft

160 Sites – This is a big rig RV park associated with the impressive Silverwood Theme Park across the highway. There are tent-only sites as well as full-hookup back-in and pull-thru sites (mostly back-in) to 65 feet with parking on gravel or dirt. There's also a overflow area (but with a hefty fee) for overnighting if the campground is full. From the junction of US-95 and I-90 (Exit 12) near Coeur d'Alene drive north 16 miles (25.8 km) to the park, the campground is on the right.

COWLITZ RIVER LAKES REGION

US Highway 12, also called the White Pass Scenic Byway, leaves I-5 at Mile 68, about 35 miles (56 km) south of Olympia and 60 miles (97 km) north of Vancouver, WA. It heads eastward following the valley of the Cowlitz River toward the southern entrances of Mt Rainier National Park and the White Pass which give access to the Yakima Valley.

Along the way are two large lakes formed by hydroelectric dams. As is the normal practice when dams form such lakes, several excellent campgrounds have been built on the lake shores to provide recreational opportunities.

The first of the lakes is Mayfield Lake, which is the reservoir behind the Mayfield Dam. Campgrounds on the lake include a state park, a Tacoma Power campground, and a commercial campground. Mayfield's water level is relatively stable making it ideal for waterfront campgrounds.

The second lake, Riffe Lake, is much larger than Mayfield. It's the reservoir behind

WASHINGTON

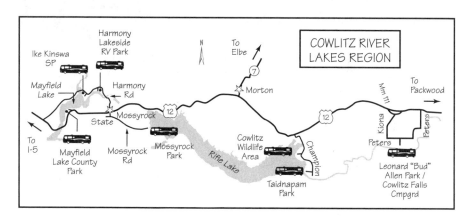

Mossy Rock Dam. At 600 feet this is the tallest dam in the Pacific Northwest. This lake is 13 miles long and hosts three Tacoma Power campgrounds.

Finally, a bit farther east, there's another hydroelectric project, the Cowlitz Falls Project. It too has an associated Lewis County Public Utility District campground.

Cowlitz River Lakes Region Campgrounds

○ **MAYFIELD LAKE COUNTY PARK** *(Open April 15 to Oct 15)*
   Reservations: (888) 226-7688, www.tacomapower.com/parks
   Information: (360) 985-2364
   Location: 3.4 Miles (5.5 Km) West of Mossyrock

   GPS Location: 46.53287 N, 122.55676 W, 300 Ft

54 Sites – This is a Tacoma Power campground on Mayfield Lake. Sites here are pull-thrus and back-ins to 45 feet with just a few that are larger than that, up to about 60 feet. Roads are paved and so are parking pads. Some of the sites are along the lake shore. There is a boat launch and swimming beach. From Mossyrock drive west for 3.4 mile (5.5 km) on Hwy 12. Turn north into Beach Road and in .3 miles (.5 km) you'll see the park entrance on the right.

☐ **IKE KINSWA STATE PARK** *(Open All Year)*
   Reservations: www.parks.wa.gov/reservations/,
                     (888) 226-7688
   Information: (360) 983-3402, (360) 902-8844,
                     www.parks.wa.gov
   Location: 3.7 Mile (6 Km) N of Mossyrock, WA

   GPS Location: 46.55407 N, 122.53015 W, 400 Ft

101 Sites – This state park is located on the north shore of Mayfield Lake. Campsites are off three loops in heavy timber, none are on the lakeshore. There are back-in and pull-thru sites to 60 feet as well as a hiker/biker tent camp area. Roads are paved and parking is on asphalt or gravel. There is a day use area with swimming beach and boat launch. From Mossyrock drive north on Harmony Road to the park entrance, a distance of 3.7 miles (6 km).

● **HARMONY LAKESIDE RV PARK** *(Open All Year)*
   Res and Info: (877) 780-7275, (360) 983-3804,
                     harmonyrvpark@aol.com,
                     www.harmonylakesidervpark.com
   Location: 2.3 Mile (3.7 Km) N of Mossyrock, WA

   GPS Location: 46.55786 N, 122.50379 W, 400 Ft

80 Sites – This is a commercial RV park on the north side of Mayfield Lake. Sites here are gravel pull-thrus and back-ins to 60 feet separated by grass. There is a marina area with docks, boat slips, and rental watercraft. From Mossyrock drive north 2.3 miles (3.7 Km) on Harmony Road to the RV Park entrance. It's on the left.

○ **MOSSYROCK PARK** *(Open All Year Except Dec 20 – Jan 1)*
   Reservations: (888) 226-7688, www.tacomapower.com/parks
   Information: (360) 983-3900
   Location: 3 Miles (4.8 Km) SE of Mossyrock, WA

   GPS Location: 46.51627 N, 122.42348 W, 800 Ft

WASHINGTON

152 Sites – Mossyrock is a Tacoma Power campground located at the west end of Riffe Lake. It's a large campground with back-in and pull-thru sites to 60 feet off four loops. Amenities include a swimming beach, boat launch, laundry, store, and fast-food stand. From Hwy 12 in Mossyrock drive south on Williams Street for .3 mile (.5 km). At the T turn left on East State Street and follow it for 3 miles (4.8 km) to the park entrance.

○ **TAIDNAPAM PARK** *(Open All Year Except Dec 20 – Jan 1)*
   Reservations: (888) 226-7688, www.tacomapower.com/parks
   Information: (360) 497-7707
   Location: 20 Miles (32 Km) East of Mossyrock, WA

    GPS Location: 46.46866 N, 122.16471 W, 800 Ft

163 Sites – Taidnapam is a Tacoma Power park at the east end of Riffe Lake. It has back-in and pull-thru sites to 65 feet. This is a beautiful modern park. Amenities include a fishing bridge, boat ramp, and swimming area. From Mossyrock follow Hwy 12 east for 16 miles (25.8 km) to Cosmos Road. Follow Cosmos south for .1 mile (.2 km) to Champion Haul Road and turn left. Now follow Champion 3.9 miles (6.3 km) to the park. All of this route is paved.

○ **COWLITZ WILDLIFE AREA**
   Location: 18 Miles (29 Km) East of Mossyrock, WA

    GPS Location: 46.46866 N, 122.16471 W, 800 Ft

Approx. 20 Sites – This is an mostly undeveloped camping area on the east end of Riffe Lake that is run by Tacoma Power. The only amenity is a vault toilet. Camping is in a gravel lot and a few spaces along the lake. From Mossyrock follow Hwy 12 east for 16 miles (25.8 km) to Cosmos Road. Follow Cosmos south for .1 mile (.2 km) to Champion Haul Road and turn left. Now follow Champion 1.7 miles (2.7 km) to the park. All of this route is paved.

○ **LEONARD "BUD" ALLEN PARK / COWLITZ FALLS CAMPGROUND** *(Open May 13 to Sept 11 - Varies)*
   Res and Info: (360) 497-7175, www.lcpud.org
   Location: 28 Miles (45 Km) East of Mossyrock, WA
    GPS Location: 46.50490 N, 122.01500 W, 900 Ft

62 Sites – Cowlitz Falls is a Lewis County PUD campground located on the Cowlitz River. It has gravel and paved back-in and pull-thru sites to 45 feet off paved access roads. Amenities include a boat launch ramp, nature trails, softball and soccer fields, volleyball court and horseshoe pit. From Mossyrock drive east on Hwy 12 for 24 miles (38.6 km) to near Milepost 111. Turn right on Savio Road and follow it for 1.2 mile (1.9 km) to Kiona Road. Turn right and follow it for 2.2 miles (3.5 km) as it becomes Peters Road and then makes a 90 degree left turn. Now follow Peters for another .9 mile (1.4 km) to the park entrance on the right.

ELLENSBURG

Ellensburg (population 18,000) is probably best known for its Labor Day celebration, the Ellensburg Rodeo. It's in the center of the ranching area in western Washington. It's also a college town, home of the Central Washington University.

Ellensburg, once you get downtown away from the freeway, is a nice little town. You'll

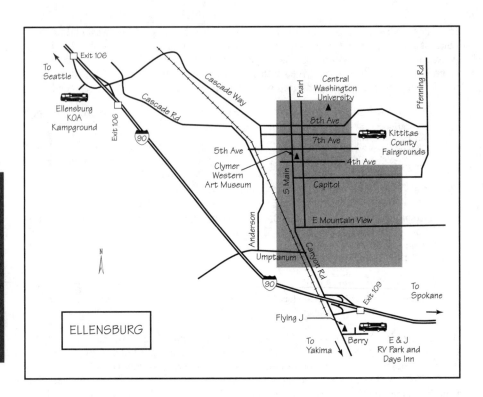

want to visit the **Clymer Western Art Museum** and take a look at the **Ellensburg Bull** statue on 4th and Perl. There's also a cowboy statue one block up on fifth. The **university campus** is just at the northeast edge of the central district and offers a **Japanese garden** and an **art gallery**.

On Labor day there's the **Ellensburg Rodeo**, but at the same time there's the **Kittitas County Fair**. Both are held in the fairgrounds just east of downtown and stretching northward. Another popular event is the **Ellensburg National Art Show and Auction** in late May.

All of the campgrounds listed below are fairly near town but the only one that lets you easily wander around the center in the evening is the fairgrounds.

Ellensburg Campgrounds

● **E & J RV PARK AND DAYS INN** *(Open All Year)*
Reservations: (888) 889-9870
Information: (509) 933-1500
Location: Ellensburg

GPS Location: 46.97056 N, 120.53556 W, 1,500 Ft

79 Sites – This campground behind a Day's Inn is a
very large paved lot with long sites, many are pull-thrus. It has lots of amenities including an indoor swimming pool and spa. There are back-ins and pull-thrus to 70 feet. Take Exit 109 from I-10. Drive south for .2 mile (.3 km) and turn left onto Berry Road just beyond

the Flying J truck stop. In another .1 mile (.2 km) you'll see the hotel and campground on the left.

● **ELLENSBURG KOA KAMPGROUND**
  (Open Jan 1 to Nov 16)
  Reservations: (800) 562-7616, www.koa.com
  Information: (509) 925-9319,
                ellensburgkoa1@hotmail.com
  Location: Ellensburg

  GPS Location: 47.00556 N, 120.59444 W, 1,500 Ft

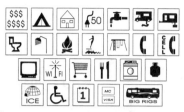

140 Sites – This is an older KOA but it has a very nice location next to the Yakima River. It has back-in and pull-thru sites to 55 feet. Amenities include a boat ramp. Take Exit 106 from I-90. Turn south and immediately you'll see the KOA entrance on your left.

○ **KITTITAS COUNTY FAIRGROUNDS**
  (Open All Year)
  Res and Info: (800) 426-5340, (509) 962-7639,
                www.co.kittitas.wa.us/fairgrounds
  Location: Ellensburg

  GPS Location: 46.99778 N, 120.53361 W, 1,600 Ft

200 Sites – This is a great place to stay if there are no events in progress. Call to find out. The fairgrounds has lots of hookup sites with electricity and water in many locations, but the ones used by travelers are back-in sites with parking on grass. Restroom facilities including showers are nearby. The fairgrounds are within easy walking distance of the center of town. Easiest access is from Main Street in the center of downtown. Drive east on 7th Ave. At the east end you'll find a big paved parking lot, park here and go find the office to check in. The office is at the west edge of the fairgrounds between 5th and 6th and is open until 5 p.m. If the office is closed folks generally just park and pay in the morning.

FORKS AND THE WESTERN SECTIONS OF OLYMPIC NATIONAL PARK

When logging was going full blast **Forks** (population 3,500) was known as the logging capital of the Olympic Peninsula. It probably still is the capital but the tourist industry is getting more and more important to the local economy. This might seem surprising since Forks is the rainiest town in the state with an annual rainfall of over 100 inches. One factor is the popular Twilight novels. They are set in Forks and attract large numbers of fans.

Forks is the center of an interesting region on the western border of the Olympic National Park. From Forks there is good access to an otherwise isolated coastal section of the park as well as the rain forests on the western slope of the Olympic Mountains.

The town of **Forks** lines both sides of US-101. You'll find several restaurants as well as a good-sized supermarket, the best places to get supplies on the northwest side of the peninsula. There is also a **National Park Information Center**. South of town is the **Forks Visitor's Center** and next door the **Forks Timber Museum**. Forks holds an annual celebration during the week ending with the **Fourth of July**, it has traditional logging contests as well as a fun run and other activities.

From US-101 just north of Forks a 14-mile (23 km) paved road runs west to the coast. At the end of the road is the Quileute Indian town of **La Push**. Just before reaching La

WASHINGTON

RIALTO BEACH IS ONE OF WASHINGTON STATE'S MOST SCENIC BEACHES

Push you'll see parking areas for the National Park's **Third Beach** and **Second Beach**. You must hike to these beaches, 1.3 miles (2 km) to Third and .5 miles (.8 km) to Second. **First Beach** is accessible from La Push itself.

About 11 miles (18 km) along the road from Forks to La Push you'll reach **Mora Junction**. If you turn north here you'll be able to follow a road leading past the big national park campground called Mora to **Rialto Beach**. Rialto Beach is located just across the Quillayute River outlet from La Push, it is one of the most scenic of all Washington State beaches and is known for its accumulation of driftwood.

Also easily accessible from Forks is the Olympic National Park's **Hoh Rain Forest**. Drive south from Forks for 12 miles (19 km), then turn east on the Upper Hoh Road. This 18-mile (29 km) paved road leads to the Olympic National Park's Hoh Rain Forest Visitor Center. There is a large national park campground near the visitor center and there are several very good hiking trails allowing you to wander through one of the very few temperate rain forests in the world.

South from the Hoh River Valley Cut-off US-101 soon curves west to the coast. For about 12 miles (19 km) it runs along the ocean with frequent parking areas and trails leading short distances down the hill to the beach. **Ruby Beach**, the farthest north, is a good place to stop and walk down to the beach. Those red pebbles on the beach are not rubies, they're garnets. The island offshore is Destruction Island, it has its own lighthouse.

Watch for the **Kalaloch Lodge** above the beach just off the road, the Kalaloch Campground is nearby, so is **Kalaloch Visitor Information Center**. Consider taking a break here and looking around, you might decide to stay. The highway soon turns inland and passes through Queets. The gravel **Queets River Road** leads inland for 14 miles (23 km) from an intersection about 8 miles (13 km) east of Queets on US-101 giving access to trails and also a primitive campground inside the park.

The **Lake Quinault area** provides visitors with very accessible rain forest access. The lake itself is actually part of the Quinault Indian Reservation but south of the lake is Olympic National Forest land and the north is Rainier National Park land. There are several campgrounds along the south shore of the lake. A **trail system** on the hillside above provides an excellent way to get out in the rain forest among the tall trees on trails that are fun but not too challenging. The **world's largest Sitka spruce** is just east of the Lake Quinault Rain Forest Village. The south shore is also home to the venerable **Lake Quinault Lodge**, built in 1926 and certainly worth a look-through.

There's quite a selection of campgrounds in this region. Where you stay will probably de-

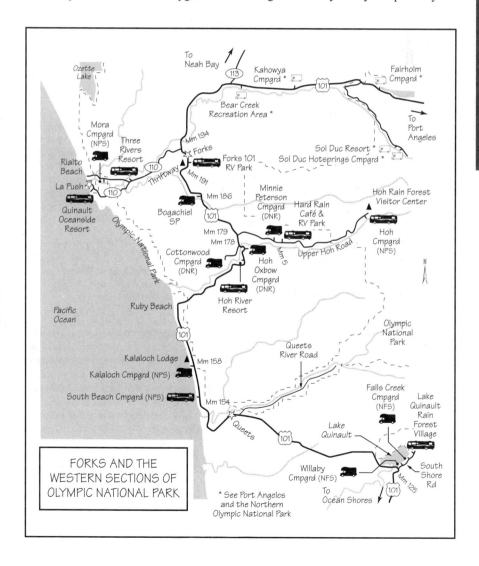

FORKS AND THE
WESTERN SECTIONS OF
OLYMPIC NATIONAL PARK

* See Port Angeles
and the Northern
Olympic National Park

WASHINGTON

pend upon your interests. Tent campers will enjoy all of the national park campgrounds. Many of these will also take RVs but have no hookups. For those who don't need hookups and whose rigs aren't too large the Washington Department of Natural Resources campgrounds are priced right. Commercial parks in the area are a good alternative for RVers who must have hookups, several will take the largest rigs.

Forks and the Western Sections of Olympic National Park Campgrounds

● **FORKS 101 RV PARK** *(Open May 1 to Oct 1 – Varies)*
Reservations: (800) 962-9964,
Information: (360) 374-5073, www.forks-101-rv-park.com
Location: Forks

GPS Location: 47.94194 N, 124.38500 W, 300 Ft

36 Sites – This is a commercial campground right in Forks.
If you want to be in town, this is the place. There are back-ins and pull-thrus to over 70 feet. All are full-hookup sites. A large grocery store is right across the road. Watch for the campground on the east side of the highway near the south end of town.

■ **MORA CAMPGROUND** *(Open All Year)*
Information: (360) 565-3130
Location: 13 Miles (21 Km) W of Forks

GPS Location: 47.91667 N, 124.60667 W, Near Sea Level

94 Sites – This large Olympic National Park campground sits in a grove of huge hemlocks and Sitka spruces along the Quillayute River some two miles (3 km) from the coast at Rialto Beach. A few sites in the campground will take RVs to 35 feet with careful maneuvering. Most sites, however, are best for RVs to 25 feet. Give up the hook-ups for a night to appreciate the big trees and lush vegetation of this part of the state. It is located right off the road to Rialto Beach, you can't miss it.

● **THREE RIVERS RESORT** *(Open All Year)*
Res and Info: (360) 374-5300,
      threerivers@centurytel.net,
      www.forks-web.com/threerivers
Location: 9 Miles (15 Km) W of Forks

GPS Location: 47.91306 N, 124.53417 W, 100 Ft

19 Sites – This little resort has rental cabins, gas sales, a convenience store and a restaurant. It is located at the confluence of the Quillayute, Sol Duc, and Bogachiel Rivers and is popular with fishermen, guided fishing trips are offered. There are RV and tent camping sites in a grove of trees to the rear. Some sites have electricity and water hookups, a few have sewer, others have no hookups. They vary in size but some will take RVs to 35 feet. To reach the campground head west on the La Push Road (SR-110). It leaves US-101 about 1 mile (2 km) north of Forks. The campground is located right where Mora Road to Rialto Beach goes right 7.8 miles (12.6 km) from US-101.

● **QUILEUTE OCEANSIDE RESORT** *(Open All Year)*
Res and Info: (360) 374-5267, (800) 487-1267,
      www.quileuteoceanside.com
Location: La Push

GPS Location: 47.90361 N, 124.63000 W, Near Sea Level

42 Sites – This is a full-hookup big-rig campground

that is right on the beach in La Push. This is an open beach, popular with surfers. Two nearby beaches are accessible via good hiking trails. Sites are back-ins to 60 feet. Restrooms are located at the back of the store, a long walk from the sites. Their use is not limited to campground residents and they were not clean when we visited. To reach the campground head west on the La Push Road (SR-110). It leaves US-101 about 1 mile (1.6 km) north of Forks. The campground is located near the entrance to La Push, 13.6 miles (21.9 km) from US-101. While you may spot some sites behind the store don't stop there, go on to the offices of Quileute Oceanside Resort on the left about a quarter-mile beyond. You can pull in there and check in at the office.

☐ **BOGACHIEL STATE PARK** *(Open All Year)*
Information: (360) 374-6356, (360) 902-8844, www.parks.wa.gov
Location: 5 Miles (8 Km) S of Forks

GPS Location: 47.89417 N, 124.36417 W, 200 Ft

42 Sites – Many of the campgrounds nearby do not have dump stations or showers. Bogachiel is where those campers come for both of those services. The campground has tent and RV sites although only six have hookups (power and water only). Although some of the sites exceed 40 feet in length, the lack of maneuvering room limits users of this campground to rigs of about 35 feet. The dump station is accessible to larger rigs. The campground is located off US-101 about 5 miles (8 km) south of Forks and 7.5 miles (12 km) north of the cutoff to the Upper Hoh Road.

☐ **MINNIE PETERSON WASHINGTON STATE DEPARTMENT OF NATURAL RESOURCES CAMPGROUND** *(Open All Year)*
Information: (800) 264-0890
Location: 17 Miles (27 Km) SE of Forks

GPS Location: 47.81889 N, 124.17444 W, 200 Ft

9 Sites – Eight sites in this campground are off a loop road, another is a walk-in. It's a nice tent-camping campground and will also take RVs to about 35 feet. There is no drinking water at the campground. Use of the campground requires that you have either an annual Washington State Discover Pass or a Washington State One-day Pass. Passes cannot be purchased at the campground, see the discussion under *Washington State Parks* above. The campground is on the north side of the Upper Hoh Road 4.7 miles (7.6 km) from US-101.

● **HARD RAIN CAFÉ AND RV PARK** *(Open All Year)*
Res and Info: (360) 374-9288, info@hardraincafe.com ,
www.hardraincafe.com
Location: 18 Miles (29 Km) SE of Forks

GPS Location: 47.81694 N, 124.15389 W, 200 Ft

20 Sites – The Hard Rain is a small rural store and restaurant with a few tent and 13 RV sites in the rear. These are back-ins that will take any size rig, half have electric and water and the remainder are full hookups. There is also a restroom with shower. The campground is located on the north side of the Upper Hoh Road 5.8 miles (9.4 km) from US-101 and 12.1 miles (19.5 km) from the end of the road at the Hoh Rain Forest Visitor Center.

■ **HOH OLYMPIC NATIONAL PARK CAMPGROUND** *(Open All Year)*
Information: (360) 565-3130, www.nps.gov/olym/
Location: 31 Miles (50 Km) SE of Forks

GPS Location: 47.85944 N, 123.93611 W, 500 Ft

88 Sites – This Olympic National Park campground is adjacent to the Hoh Rain Forest Visitor Center and trails. It's a great place to stay and enjoy the area. Expect rain! Sites are off three loops and there are back-ins and some pull-thrus that will accept RVs to 40 feet. The campground is 18 miles (29 km) from US-101.

☐ **COTTONWOOD WASHINGTON STATE DEPARTMENT OF NATURAL RESOURCES CAMPGROUND** *(Open All Year)*
Information: (800) 264-0890
Location: 17 Miles (27 Km) S of Forks

GPS Location: 47.78000 N, 124.29111 W, 100 Ft

9 sites – This campground is located some distance from US-101 and requires driving on a little gravel but it's really pretty convenient. The nine sites are off two loops. No potable water is provided. Although some sites are as long as 55 feet a lack of maneuvering room makes 35 feet the practical maximum. The campground is located off the Lower Hoh Road. Use of the campground requires that you have either an annual Washington State Discover Pass or a Washington State One-day Pass. Passes cannot be purchased at the campground, see the discussion under *Washington State Parks* above. This road leaves US-101 13.7 miles (22.1 km) south of Forks, about 1.2 miles (1.9 km) south of the junction for the Upper Hoh Road. Follow the paved road southwest for 2.1 miles (3.4 km). Then turn left on a gravel road and follow it .8 mile (1.3 km) to the campground.

☐ **HOH OXBOW WASHINGTON STATE DEPARTMENT OF NATURAL RESOURCES CAMPGROUND** *(Open All Year)*
Information: (800) 264-0890
Location: 14 Miles (23 Km) S of Forks

GPS Location: 47.80944 N 124.24944 W, 200 Ft

7 Sites – This campground is located inside an oxbow turn of the Hoh River and right next to US-101. There is no drinking water at the campground. Sites are located off a loop, a few of the back-ins will take RVs to 35 feet and there is one pull-thru of about the same length. Some sites are along the river. Use of the campground requires that you have either an annual Washington State Discover Pass or a Washington State One-day Pass. Passes cannot be purchased at the campground, see the discussion under *Washington State Parks* above. The campground entrance is on the east side of the highway about 14.4 miles (23.2 km) south of Forks.

● **HOH RIVER RESORT** *(Open All Year)*
Res and Info: (360) 374-5566, www.hohriverresort.com
Location: 16 Miles (26 Km) S of Forks

GPS Location: 47.78972 N, 124.25056 W, 100 Ft

25 Sites – This is an older campground behind a country convenience store with gas pumps. It's very popular with fishermen. Sites are in an open area. They are back-ins that will take RVs to 40 feet. The resort is on the west side of US-101 some 15.6 miles (25.2 km) south of Forks.

■ **KALALOCH OLYMPIC NATIONAL PARK CAMPGROUND**
(Open All Year)

Reservations: (800) 365-2267, http://reservations.nps.gov
Information: (360) 565-3130, www.nps.gov/olym
Location: 33 Miles (53 Km) S of Forks

GPS Location: 47.61278 N, 124.37500 W, 100 Ft

170 Sites – This Olympic National Park campground has a desirable location above a wild beach. It has tent and RV sites suitable for RVs to 35 feet and is very convenient to the highway. The campground is located within walking distance of the Kalaloch Inn and Park Service Information Center. Note that although you can drive through this part of the park without paying the national park entrance fee, if you stay at the campground you'll have to pay it. The campground is near Mile 158 of US-101, about 33 miles (53 km) south of Forks and 61 miles (98 km) north of Hoquiam.

■ **SOUTH BEACH OLYMPIC NATIONAL PARK CAMPGROUND** *(Open May 25 to Sept 30 – Varies)*

Information: (360) 565-3130, www.nps.gov/olym
Location: 36 Miles (58 Km) S of Forks

GPS Location: 47.56556 N, 124.35972 W, Near Sea Level

Approx. 50 Sites – South Beach serves as a sort of overflow to nearby Kalaloch campground. We actually like it better. It's a large open bench above the beach. Parking is on grass and gravel. Since sites are not delineated any size rig will fit. There are picnic tables and fire pits as well as a restroom building with flush toilets. Off season there are only vault toilets. The campground is located 3.4 miles (5.5 km) south of Kalaloch Campground and is just a short distance off US-101 overlooking a great beach.

● **LAKE QUINAULT RAIN FOREST VILLAGE** *(Open All Year)*

Information: (800) 255-6936, (360) 288-2535,
mail@rfv.com, www.rainforestresort.com
Location: 69 Miles (111 Km) S of Forks

GPS Location: 47.47528 N, 123.83111 W, 200 Ft

31 Sites – This resort has been here on the south shore of beautiful Lake Quinault for many years. It is located just down the road from famous Lake Quinault Lodge. All spaces are back-ins with room for big rigs. A word of warning about winter camping at this campground. The sites sit very near the lake and in winter the lake level sometimes rises to cover them. It is hard for them to forecast when this might happen, if the lake is up the campground is closed. It is best to call ahead to check. Restrooms are closed in winter. Wi-Fi is available only in the café which is some distance from the RV sites. To reach the campground just follow the South Shore Road from Mile 125.5 of US-101. The resort is about 3.2 miles (5.2 km) from the highway.

■ **FALLS CREEK CAMPGROUND**
(Open Memorial Day to Labor Day – Varies)

Information: (360) 288-2525
Location: 68 Miles (110 Km) S of Forks

GPS Location: 47.46944 N, 123.84500 W, 200 Ft

31 Sites – This is a small Olympic National Forest campground just .2 miles (.3 km) east of Lake Quinault Lodge. Vehicle access is very cramped, sites here are best for tent camp-

ers and rigs to 16 feet. There are walk-in tent sites in addition to the vehicle sites. The campground has a boat ramp. Note that to use a boat on the lake a Quinault Indian Nation Tribal Fishing Permit and boat decal are required. To reach the campground follow South Shore Road from Mile 125.5 of US-101 for 2.4 miles (3.9 km) to the entrance.

■   **WILLABY CAMPGROUND** *(Open Memorial Day to Sept 30 – Varies)*
　　Information: (360) 288-2525
　　Location:　　67 Miles (108 Km) S of Forks

　　　　GPS Location: 47.46222 N, 123.85750 W, 200 Ft

34 Sites – Like Falls Creek this is an Olympic National Forest campground for tents and smaller rigs to 21 feet. Access is better than at Falls Creek because sites are located along a paved loop road. There's a boat ramp here. Note that to use a boat on the lake a Quinault Indian Nation Tribal Fishing Permit and boat decal are required. To find the campground follow South Shore Road from Mile 125.5 of US-101 for 1.6 (2.6 km) miles to the entrance.

GOLDENDALE AND MARYHILL REGION

This region forms the eastern gateway to the Columbia Gorge which extends from the Maryhill area west for about 90 miles (145 km). US-97, the major north-south route on the east side of the Cascades, crosses the Columbia here. There are several unusual sights nearby, it is a small fruit-growing region, and the river offers dams, fishing, and windsurfing.

There are two sights here connected with the eccentric railroad heir Sam Hill. Hill was the son-in-law of railroad baron James J. Hill, builder of the Great Northern Railway. Hill's story is too involved to relate here, but you'll become familiar with it as you take a look at the two structures he built nearby.

The first is a concrete replica of Stonehenge in England. This **northwest Stonehenge** sits on a site which might have been more appropriate to a replica of the Parthenon in Athens. It overlooks the gorge from a hilltop just above the first two campgrounds mentioned below. To reach it you just follow the small paved road through fruit-tree orchards and the historic village of Maryhill, then up the hillside, a distance of about two miles (3 km) from the campgrounds. During the season you will find fruit stands between the campgrounds and the village.

Another nearby Sam Hill edifice is the **Maryhill Museum of Art**. Hill built the place as a mansion but didn't live there, reportedly because his wife refused to live in such a remote and windy place. At first glance you may think that the curators are hard-pressed to find exhibits for the museum, the collection is very eclectic. However, you'll find the varied exhibits well worth the stop. This museum draws a lot of people, especially considering its very remote and out-of-the-way location. The exhibits include an excellent collection of American Indian artifacts, memorabilia related to Queen Marie of Romania (a family friend), French fashion from the 1940's, and photos of Sam's work with road building in the northwest during the early part of the last century. The museum is located a few miles west of the campgrounds along SR-14.

Up the hill to the north is the town of **Goldendale** (population 3,500). Goldendale is a small agricultural town. The main attraction is the **Goldendale Observatory State Park**, Goldendale is relatively cloud-free and therefore good for an observatory. There is a large 24.5 inch Cassegrain telescope which is open to the public.

Goldendale and Maryhill Region Campgrounds

☐ **MARYHILL STATE PARK** *(Open All Year)*
Reservations: www.parks.wa.gov/reservations/,
        (888) 226-7688
Information: (509) 773-5007, (360) 902-8844,
Location: 17 Miles E of The Dalles

    GPS Location: 45.68194 N, 120.83361 W, 100 Ft

72 Sites – This State of Washington campground is located right on the banks of the Columbia. It is very popular with windsurfers, expect it to fill up early on summer weekends. The terrain is very flat, large grassy areas separate the RVs and there is lots of shade. Many sites are long pull-thrus that can easily take RVs to 65 feet. One section has 20 vehicle accessible tent sites, gravel pitching pads are provided, only cars and vans can park at these sites. Amenities include a swimming beach and a boat launch. You'll spot the campground next to the river as you descend the hill on US-97. It is just upriver from the Sam Hill Memorial Bridge where US-97 crosses the Columbia.

● **PEACH BEACH CAMPGROUND**
    (Open All Year)
Res and Info: (509) 773-4927
Location: 17 Miles (27 Km) E of The Dalles

        GPS Location: 45.68444 N, 120.81778 W, 100 Ft

82 Sites – Located just east of the state campground, this RV Park is so similar to the state

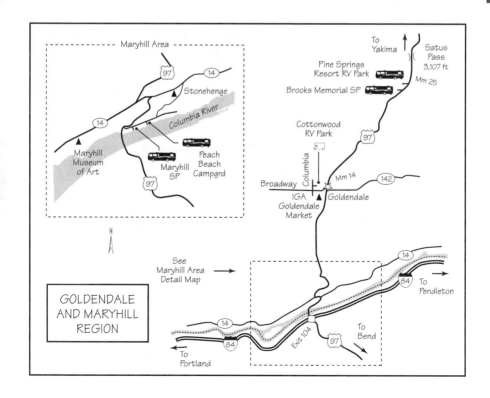

park that it might be an extension. The major difference is that the campground isn't quite so structured and it's also less expensive. Sites are long back-ins or pull-thrus to 70 feet, parking is on gravel with grass between sites. Take the exit for the state campground off US-97. Drive past the state campground entrance and another .6 mile (1 km), then turn right into Peach Beach at the far end of the state campground.

☐ **BROOKS MEMORIAL STATE PARK** *(Open All Year)*
Information: (509) 773-4611
Location: 12 Miles (19 Km) N of Goldendale

GPS Location: 45.95157 N, 120.66714 W, 2,600 Ft

45 Sites – Brooks Memorial is set in the high pine country of Satus Pass. It's popular with folks from the hot country in the Yakima Valley to the north and the Columbia Valley to the south because summer temperatures are cooler here. There are miles of hiking and biking trails in the park. The hookup sites in this park are back-ins to 60 feet. From Goldendale drive north toward Yakima on Hwy 97. The campground is on the left.

● **PINE SPRINGS RESORT RV PARK** *(Open All Year)*
Information: (509) 773-4434, pinespringsresort@wildblue.net,
              www.pinespringsresort.net
Location: 12 Miles (19 Km) N of Goldendale

GPS Location: 45.95116 N, 120.66428 W, 2,600 Ft

21 Sites – This is a small campground behind a bar, grill, and store next to the Brooks Memorial State Park in Satus Pass. The sites are under pines and there are back-ins and pull-thrus to about 38 feet. From Goldendale drive north toward Yakima on Hwy 97. The campground is on the left after 12 miles (19 km).

GRAND COULEE

As you drive into the town of Coulee Dam from the north you couldn't possibly miss the massive dam spanning the river valley ahead. **Grand Coulee Dam** was one of the big government programs of the 1930s. It was a huge project with several aims. It was to provide work for thousands of men. It was to provide irrigation water for an extensive area. And it was to provide lots of electricity. Today there are 11 dams on the Columbia south of the Canadian border. This is the largest of them and by far the most impressive. It also provides a benefit that may not have been deemed to be very important by its planners and builders, the dam has created two huge lakes that are recreation areas in a region that almost always has beautiful weather during the summer.

The large lake behind the dam is known as **Roosevelt Lake**. Access to this lake from the Grand Coulee Dam area is limited. There is one federal campground on the lake near the dam with road access. Road access to the remainder of Roosevelt Lake requires that you travel eastward and detour away from the lake. For more about the campgrounds on upper Roosevelt Lake see the *Roosevelt Lake* section of this chapter.

There is a second more convenient lake, however. **Banks Lake**, created as part of the Grand Coulee irrigation scheme, dominates recreation in the area. It stretches some 30 miles (48 km) south from Grand Coulee's towns, and is shallow enough to become quite warm in summer. Banks Lake attracts water sports lovers from all over the state.

There are actually four towns surrounding the dam. **Coulee Dam** (population 1,000) is situated below the dam, **Elmer City** (population 300) is downstream along the Columbia (north). **Grand Coulee** (population 900) and **Electric City** (population 1,000) are just above the dam along the shore of Banks Lake (south).

The dam provides the focus for many tourist activities in the area. The first stop is the U.S. Bureau of Reclamation's **Visitor Arrival Center**. It is located just below the dam on the left bank (as you face downstream). Stop here to find out about the tours and evening laser light show. Tours are generally available but not always, it depends upon the security level in effect when you visit.

During the summer there is a nightly **laser light show** projected on the face of the dam. It's a fun evening activity and takes about 35 minutes. The time of the show varies during the year from 10 p.m. to 8:30 p.m. depending upon when it gets dark. A good place to park and watch is **Crown Point**, located far above the dam about 2 miles (3.2 km) outside Grand Coulee off SR-174 in the direction of Bridgeport.

There's more to this area than the dam and lakes however. The **Grand Coulee** is actually a valley that stretches south from the dam as far as Soap Lake, about 45 miles (73 km). It is said to have been formed during the Ice Age Floods. These huge floods inundated western Washington periodically during the last ice age. A huge lake, Lake Missoula, was repeatedly formed when the ice blocked the Clark Fork River in Montana. The lake would periodically break through the ice dam causing tremendous floods which would rush through western Washington and out through the Columbia Gorge. The whole thing is explained with exhibits at the **Sun Lakes-Dry Falls Visitor Center** which overlooks the Dry Falls Cliffs on SR-17 south of Coulee City. Exhibits there say that the floods would crash over the 350-foot cliffs with a water depth of 400 feet, and a width that was 5 times what Niagara Falls is today.

WASHINGTON

PLENTY OF ROOM FOR RV PARKING AT THE GRAND COULEE DAM

Grand Coulee Campgrounds

○ **SMOKIAM CITY CAMPGROUND**
   (Open April 15 to Oct 15 – Varies)
Information: (509) 246-1211,
                  www.soaplakecity.org/5848/16901.
                  html
Location: Soap Lake

GPS Location: 47.39222 N, 119.48389 W, 1,000 Ft

43 Sites – This is a Soap Lake municipal campground. It's located on the south shore of
Soap Lake, convenient for taking a dip in the lake. Some sites are large back-ins suitable

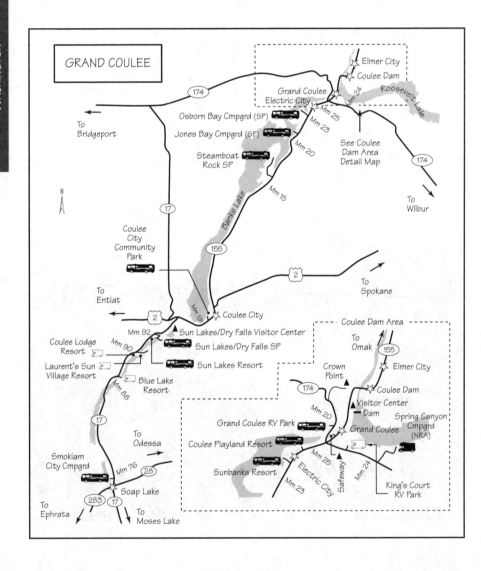

for RVs to 45 feet with full hookups. You'll see the campground on the lakeshore as you leave Soap Lake driving north on SR-17.

☐ **SUN LAKES DRY FALLS STATE CAMPGROUND**
(Open All Year)
Reservations: www.parks.wa.gov/reservations/, (888) 226-7688
Information: (509) 632-5583, (360) 902-8844
Location: 5 Miles (8 Km) S of Coulee City

GPS Location: 47.58944 N, 119.39056 W, 1,100 Ft

191 Sites – This state campground shares an idyllic location at the foot of Dry Falls with a commercial camping resort and a golf course. Park Lake is excellent for swimming and water sports and there is a small marina and a good boat launch available. The campground sits away from the lake and is actually two different campgrounds now that a new full-hookup big-rig campground has been completed at a location about a quarter-mile (.4 km) east and above the older camping area. Sites in the new campground are 60 feet long, the older sites are crowded together and best for smaller rigs although some have hookups. Other amenities include a park store, laundromat, boat rentals, and nearby golf. Unlike most Washington State Parks the reservation window for this park is April 15 to Sept 15. The entrance road to the campground is toward the bottom of the Dry Falls grade on SR-17. It's 5 miles (8 km) southwest of Coulee City.

● **SUN LAKES RESORT**
(Open April 1 to Oct 17 – Varies)
Res and Info: (509) 632-5291, www.sunlakesparkresort.com
Location: 5 Miles (8 Km) S of Coulee City

GPS Location: 47.59083 N, 119.39528 W, 1,100 Ft

121 Sites – This resort is located in the same area as Sun Lakes Dry Falls State Campground. It's run by a concessionaire on state park land. Sites here are in an area back from the lake and the back-in and pull-thru sites reach 65 feet in length. Amenities include a swimming pool, grocery store, kiosk food takeout, swimming beach, nearby golf course, and a boat launch and marina shared with the state park. The entrance road to the campground is toward the bottom of the Dry Falls Grade on SR-17. It's 5 miles (8 km) southwest of Coulee City. After turning on the state park entrance road you'll see this resort on the right just after the dump station and before you reach the state park camping area.

○ **COULEE CITY COMMUNITY PARK** *(Open April 1 to Oct 31)*
Information: (509) 632-5043, (509) 632-5331, www.couleecity.com
Location: Coulee City

GPS Location: 47.61667 N, 119.29278 W, 1,500 Ft

100 Sites – This city park has lots of room for campers, both in tents and RVs. It's on the south shore of Banks Lake. Tents are pitched on grass, RV sites are both back-ins and pull-thrus to 60 feet. The park is in the middle of town on the shore of the lake, the main highway runs right along here so it's hard to miss.

WASHINGTON

☐ **STEAMBOAT ROCK STATE PARK** *(Open All Year)*
Reservations: www.parks.wa.gov/reservations/,
                (888) 226-7688
Information: (509) 633-1304, (360) 902-8844,
                www.parks.wa.gov
Location: 8 Miles (13 Km) S of Electric City

GPS Location: 47.85306 N, 119.13194 W, 1,500 Ft

126 Sites – This is a very popular state campground located along Banks Lake on a peninsula formed by Steamboat Rock, the formation looms over the campground. It's great for water sports. The long back-in sites here reach 50 feet. The campground entrance is on SR-155 some 8 miles (13 km) south of Electric City and 17 miles (27 km) north of Coulee City. This park accepts reservations year-round.

☐ **JONES BAY AND OSBORNE BAY CAMPGROUNDS** *(Open All Year)*
Location: (Jones) 3 Miles (5 Km) S of Electric City
Location: (Osborne) 2 Miles (3 Km) S of Electric City

GPS Location (Jones): 47.89056 N, 119.07722 W, 1,500 Ft
GPS Location (Osborne): 47.92333 N, 119.05972 W, 1,500 Ft

44 Sites (Jones) and 36 Sites (Osborne) – These two smaller campsites are really part of Steamboat Rock State Park. They're remote from the rest of the park and the campsites have no hookups and no potable water. Both are waterside campgrounds. The sites at Jones Bay are spread over a large area with each site having access to the water, those in Osborne Bay are along the edge of a large parking lot. Both locations have boat ramps. From the entrance to Steamboat Rock State Park drive north 7.5 miles (12.1 km) to Jones Bay, 10.2 miles (16.5 km) to Osborne Bay.

● **SUNBANKS RESORT** *(Open All Year)*
Reservations: (888) 822-7195,
                info@sunbanksresort.com
Information: (509) 633-3786,
                www.sunbanksresort.com
Location: Electric City

GPS Location: 47.92778 N, 119.05583 W, 1,500 Ft

210 Sites – This large resort-style RV park occupies a peninsula projecting into Banks Lake just south of Electric City. There are a variety of site types at this campground, most are irregularly laid out and few will take larger rigs. There are a line of large sites designed for big rigs located just in front of the huge log main building. These have full hookups with 50-amp power and are the only real choice if you have a big rig (sites to 60 feet). They're good sites with views across a lawn to the lake. The rest of the RV sites in the resort have only electricity and water hookups or no hookups. There is a dump station. Many sites are on grass along the lake, you can tie your boat up in front of your camp. There are also quieter sites on the hill overlooking everything, choose one of these for a little more seclusion. The resort has a large main lodge built of logs. It houses the reception office, a small store, a bar, and a restaurant. Wi-Fi is only available in or near the building. There's also mini golf, a sandy beach, a boat launch, rental dock space, and rental boats of various kinds. This place is very busy in summer with a lot going on. To reach the resort head south just a short distance along the east shore of Banks Lake from Electric City. The campground is on the right just before the highway starts across a levee.

● **COULEE PLAYLAND RESORT** *(Open All Year)*
Res and Info: (509) 633-2671,
www.couleeplayland.com
Location: Electric City

GPS Location: 47.93444 N, 119.02972 W, 1,500 Ft

100 Sites – This waterside campground at the north
end of Electric City offers long sites suitable for any length rig. It's an older campground,
the location is the draw. There's a grocery store and a boat launch. This is the only place
on the lake to get fuel for your boat.

■ **SPRING CANYON CAMPGROUND** *(Open April 15 to Oct 15 - Varies)*
Information: (509) 633-9188
Location: 3 Miles (5 Km) E of Electric City

GPS Location: 47.93306 N, 118.93944 W, 1,400 Ft

87 Sites – A handy Lake Roosevelt National Recreation Area campground with room for RVs to about 30 feet overlooking Roosevelt
Lake. The campground is located about 3 miles (5 km) east of Grand Coulee on the south
shore of the lake. There are no hookups but there is a boat launch and a very popular
beach at the day use area below the campground. Many sites have great views. Some
sites are under sun shelters which limit height to between 9 and 11 feet, each one has the
clearance marked on the front. For many more Lake Roosevelt National Recreation Area
campgrounds on the upper end of the lake see the *Lake Roosevelt* section of this chapter.

● **GRAND COULEE RV PARK** *(Open All Year)*
Res and Info: (509) 633-0750, (800) 633-0750,
grandcouleervpark@gmail.com,
www.grandcouleedam.com/gcrv/
Location: Grand Coulee

GPS Location: 47.95028 N, 119.00139 W, 1,600 Ft

51 Sites – Grand Coulee RV Park is a small commercial campground offering full hookups. It's a good base for exploring the area if you aren't interested in a waterside location.
The park is very convenient to the lookout point at Crown Point, a good place to watch
the laser light show on the face of the dam in the evening. There are back-in and pull-
thru sites to 60 feet. The campground is located off SR-174 which leaves Grand Coulee
toward Bridgeport. It's .9 miles (1.5 km) from the junction of SR-174 with SR-155 in
Grand Coulee.

HOOD CANAL

The word canal is really not an accurate description of the **Hood Canal**. Actually, this canal is really a 70-mile-long (115 km) inlet. On a map the canal appears to be a giant hook
which forms the western boundary of the Kitsap Peninsula. Because the canal is so long
and shallow its waters are fairly warm. It is quite popular with water sports enthusiasts.
Oysters grow here, you will probably see them if you walk the beaches. Many folks from
the more populous regions of Puget Sound have summer cabins along the shore of the
canal. In winter the water is clear and scuba divers love it.

Belfair is located at the very end of the long warm-water Hood Canal, and also at the base
of the Kitsap Peninsula. From there SR-106 leads westward along the south edge of the

canal for 20 miles (32 km). Where the canal turns north SR-106 intersects with US-101. US-101 follows the west side of the canal northward for 40 miles (65 km) through the small communities of Hoodsport, Lilliwaup, and Brinnon to Quilcene. Just west of the canal are the Olympic Mountains and Olympic National Park. A few small roads climb to give access to this forest area.

Many of the campgrounds listed below are located at or near sea level along or near these two highways. However, five of them are located along a two-lane paved road that rises from Hoodsport on the west shore of the canal. These five include an Olympic National Park campground as well as an Olympic National Forest campground, a state Department of Natural Resources campground, and two commercial campgrounds.

Hood Canal Campgrounds

☐ **BELFAIR STATE PARK** *(Open All Year)*
 Reservations: www.parks.wa.gov/reservations/,
       (888) 226-7688
 Information: (360) 275-0668, (360) 902-8844
 Location: 3 Miles (5 Km) SW of Belfair

 GPS Location: 47.43056 N, 122.87722 W, Near Sea Level

167 Sites – This large state park campground at the end of Hood Canal offers many sites including large RV sites near the water. These RV sites are back-ins and pull-thrus to 60 feet and since they're set in an open grass field there is no problem with slide-outs. Many more sites are forest-type back-ins for tent-campers and smaller rigs. Swimming is in a small salt water lake at the beach. The campground is near Belfair. From the center of town west of the Safeway follow Clifton Lane north. Clifton becomes SR-300 and 3.5 miles (5.6 km) from the Safeway you'll reach the park entrance.

☐ **TWANOH STATE PARK** *(Open All Year)*
 Information: (360) 275-2222, (360) 902-8844
 Location: 8 Miles (13 Km) W of Belfair

 GPS Location: 47.37750 N, 122.97278 W, Near Sea Level

47 Sites – This state campground is situated on the south shore of Hood Canal. There is a day use area with swimming in Hood Canal and boat ramp on the canal side of the highway. The small camping area is on the opposite side. This is an older forest-type campground with cramped entry roads. There are back-in and pull-thru sites, a few to 45 feet long, but lack of maneuvering room limits use to RVs of about 35 feet. About half the sites have hookups. The campground is located on SR-106 some 8.5 miles (13.7 km) west of Belfair.

☐ **POTLATCH STATE PARK** *(Open All Year)*
 Reservations: www.parks.wa.gov/reservations/, (888) 226-7688
 Information: (360) 877-5361, (360) 902-8844
 Location: 2 Miles (3 Km) N of the Intersection of US-101 and
       SR-106

 GPS Location: 47.36194 N, 123.15806 W, Near Sea Level

93 Sites – This campground too is located on Hood Canal, but it is on the west side where the canal cuts north along the eastern edge of Olympic National Park. There is a day use area along the water but the main campground is on the mountain side of the highway. There are back-in and pull-through sites to 60 feet in length. The campground is located

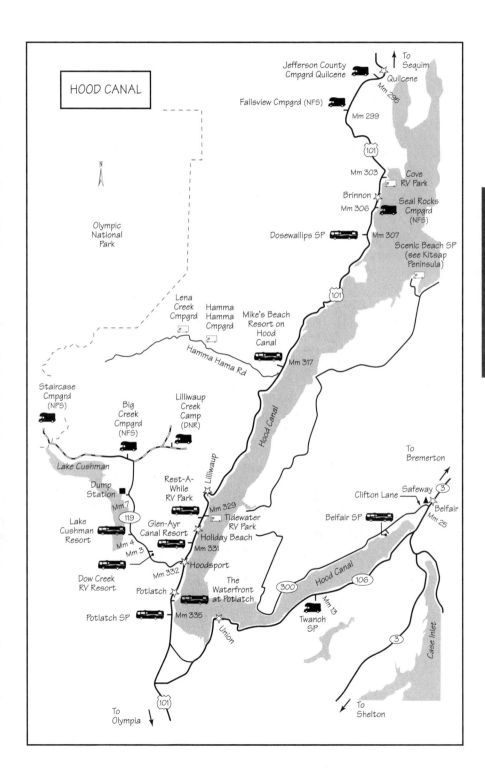

HOOD CANAL

Jefferson County
Cmpgrd Quilcene

To
Sequim

Quilcene
Mm 295

Fallsview Cmpgrd (NFS)
Mm 299

101

Mm 303

Cove
RV Park

Brinnon
Mm 306

Seal Rocks
Cmpgrd
(NFS)

Dosewallips SP
Mm 307

Scenic Beach SP
(see Kitsap
Peninsula)

Olympic
National
Park

101

Lena
Creek
Cmpgrd

Hamma
Hamma
Cmpgrd

Mike's Beach
Resort on
Hood
Canal

Hamma Hama Rd

Mm 317

Hood Canal

Staircase
Cmpgrd
(NPS)

Big
Creek
Cmpgrd
(NFS)

Lilliwaup
Creek
Camp
(DNR)

Lake Cushman

To
Bremerton

Dump
Station

Rest-A-
While
RV Park

Lilliwaup

Clifton Lane

Safeway

3

Mm 7

119

Glen-Ayr
Canal Resort

Mm 329

Tidewater
RV Park

Belfair SP

Belfair
Mm 25

Lake
Cushman
Resort

Mm 4
Mm 3

Holiday Beach
Mm 331

Hood Canal

Dow Creek
RV Resort

Mm 332

Hoodsport

Potlatch

The
Waterfront
at Potlatch

300

106

Potlatch SP
Mm 335

Union

Twanoh
SP

Mm 13

3

Case Inlet

101

To
Olympia

To
Shelton

WASHINGTON

on the west side of Hood Canal off US-101 some 2 miles (3.2 km) north of its intersection with SR-106.

● **THE WATERFRONT AT POTLATCH** *(Open All Year)*
Res and Info: (360) 877-9422, canal@hctc.com,
www.thewaterfrontatpotlatch.com
Location: 3 Miles (5 Km) N of the Intersection of US-101 and SR-106

GPS Location: 47.37028 N, 123.15889 W, Near Sea Level

14 Sites – These are premium RV sites set alongside and in front of a hotel on the shore of Hood Canal. There are pull-thrus to 60 feet and back-ins to 45. All sites overlook the canal, this is a prime location. The hotel is along US-101 some 2.6 miles (4.2 km) north of its intersection with SR-106.

■ **BIG CREEK CAMPGROUND** *(Open May 15 to Sept 25 – Varies)*
Information: (360) 877-5254
Location: 9 Miles (15 Km) W of Hoodsport

GPS Location: 47.49250 N, 123.21000 W, 900 Ft

25 Sites – Big Creek is an Olympic National Forest Campground. Sites here are forest-type with back-ins to about 30 feet. Access is via the SR-119 that climbs from Hoodsport about 5.3 miles (8.5 km) north of the intersection of US-101 and SR-106. In 9.3 miles (15 km), after passing Lake Cushman, you will come to a T. Turn left here and in just .1 mile (.2 km) you'll see the campground on your right.

■ **STAIRCASE NATIONAL PARK CAMPGROUND**
(Open May 20 to Sept 26 – Varies)
Information: (360) 565-3130
Location: 16 Miles (26 Km) W of Hoodsport

GPS Location: 47.51528 N, 123.32944 W, 800 Ft

56 Sites – Staircase is an Olympic National Park campground. It's a forest-type campground located just beyond the far west end of Lake Cushman along the North Fork of the Skokomish River. Sites here are almost all back-ins, limited maneuvering room limits use to RVs to 30 feet. Note that it's inside the Olympic National Park and therefore requires payment of a park entrance fee in addition to the camping fee. Access is via the SR-119 that climbs from Hoodsport about 5.3 miles (8.5 km) north of the intersection of US-101 and SR-106. In 9.3 miles (15 km), after passing Lake Cushman, you will come to a T. Turn left here and follow the road to the end, about 6.4 more miles (10.3 km). Just before coming into the park you'll have about 3.8 mile (6.1 km) of gravel, the rest is paved.

☐ **LILLIWAUP CREEK CAMP** *(Open May 15 to Sept 15 – Varies)*
Information: (800) 264-0890
Location: 11 Miles (18 Km) W of Hoodsport

GPS Location: 47.50361 N, 123.17639 W, 1,100 Ft

11 Sites – Lilliwaup is a small forest-style Washington Department of Natural Resources campground with a loop access road and sites to about 30 feet. It's a good tent-camping and small RV campground with no amenities other than vault toilets and nearby trails. There is no potable water. Use of the campground requires that you have either an annual Washington State Discover Pass or a Washington State One-day Pass. Passes cannot be purchased at the campground, see the discussion under *Washington State Parks* above.

Access is via the SR-119 that climbs from Hoodsport about 5.3 miles (8.5 km) north of the intersection of US-101 and SR-106. In 9.3 miles (15 km), after passing Lake Cushman, you will come to a T. Turn right here, the road becomes gravel. In 1.5 mile (2.4 km) at the junction take the right fork, the campground is on the left in another .3 mile (.5 km).

● **LAKE CUSHMAN RESORT** *(Open All Year)*
   Res and Info: (360) 877-9630, (800) 588-9630,
      resort@lakecushman.com,
      www.lakecushman.com
   Location: 5 Miles (8 Km) W of Hoodsport

   GPS Location: 47.42917 N, 123.21889 W, 700 Ft

74 Sites – This resort on the shore of Lake Cushman has a small store and restaurant overlooking the lake. It also has 22 water and electric hookup sites, all back-ins, and many more no-hookup smaller sites. Most of the large sites will accept slide-outs. While there is no dump station there is one a few miles down the road at Camp Cushman. Other amenities include a boat ramp and docks. Access is via SR-119 that climbs from Hoodsport about 5.3 miles (8.5 km) north of the intersection of US-101 and SR-106. You'll reach the campground in 4.8 miles (7.7 km).

● **DOW CREEK RV RESORT** *(Open all Year)*
   Res and Info: (360) 877-5022
   Location: 3 Miles (5 Km) W of Hoodsport

   GPS Location: 47.41052 N, 123.18768 W, 600 Ft

77 Sites – Dow Creek is a Sunrise Resort. While this is a membership resort it does accept reservations from non-members. There are back-in and pull-thrus sites to about 45 feet. Parking is on gravel off paved access roads. Access is via SR-119 that climbs from Hoodsport about 5.3 miles (8.5 km) north of the intersection of US-101 and SR-106. You'll reach the campground in 3 miles (5 km).

● **GLEN-AYR CANAL RESORT** *(Open All Year)*
   Res and Info: (360) 877-9522, (866) 877-9522,
      glenayr@hctc.com, www.glenayr.com
   Location: 1 Mile (1.6 Km) N of Hoodsport

   GPS Location: 47.42028 N, 123.13083 W, Near Sea Level

36 Sites – The Glen-Ayr is located across the road from the shore of Hood Canal. They have a beach and dock on the water. There are 8 pull-thrus to 65 feet and many back-ins, some to 40 feet. There is a large indoor hot tub situated to overlook the canal from the resort side. The Glen-Ayr is located north of Hoodsport, 5.3 miles (8.5 km) north of the intersection of US-101 and SR-106.

● **REST-A-WHILE RV PARK** *(Open All Year)*
   Res and Info: (360) 877-9474, (866) 637-9474,
      info@restawhile.com
      www.restawhile.com
   Location: 2 Miles (3 Km) N of Hoodsport

   GPS Location: 47.44083 N, 123.11889 W,
      Near Sea Level

73 Sites – The campground office here is a small country convenience store. Sites are located near the canal and also across the road. There are both pull-thrus to 60 feet and

back-ins to 45 feet with full hookups. There is also a small restaurant on site and others nearby. The campground is located north of Hoodsport, 8.1 miles (13.1 km) north of the intersection of US-101 and SR-106.

● **MIKE'S BEACH RESORT ON HOOD CANAL** *(Open All Year)*
    Information: (360) 877-5324, reservations@mikesbeachresort.com,
                      www.mikesbeachresort.com
    Location: 14 Miles (23 Km) N of Hoodsport

   GPS Location: 47.56826 N, 123.01547 W, Near Sea Level

28 Sites – This camping area is on the west side of the highway a few hundred feet south of Mike's Beach Resort. The resort itself is on the water side of the highway and has a dock, kayak and boat rentals, a play area, and offers shellfish gathering on the rocky beach. This is a popular scuba destination and air is available. There are 13 back-in RV sites to 45 feet with electricity and water hookups, a few have sewer too. There are also 15 tent sites. Restrooms are a portable toilet. The camping area is at Mile 317.7 of US-101.

☐ **DOSEWALLIPS STATE PARK** *(Open All Year)*
    Reservations: www.parks.wa.gov/reservations/,
                       (888) 226-7688
    Information: (360) 796-4415, (360) 902-8844
    Location: 25 Miles (40 Km) N of Hoodsport

   GPS Location: 47.68528 N, 122.90083 W, Near Sea Level

125 Sites – The largest part of the campsites in this park are pinwheel-style back-ins off 8 circles. Some reach 40 feet, full hookup sites are available. There are also a few back-in sites on the east side of the highway. These are accessed by driving under a bridge from the park on the west side of the highway and have no hookups. The park has shoreline along Hood Canal and also along the Dosewallips River. There is swimming in the river. The campground is located 30 miles (48 Km) north of the intersection of US-101 and SR-106, about two miles (3 km) south of Brinnon. This park accepts reservations year-round.

■ **SEAL ROCKS CAMPGROUND** *(Open May 10 to Sept 25 – Varies)*
    Information: (360) 765-2200
    Location: 26 Miles (40 Km) N of Hoodsport

   GPS Location: 47.70778 N, 122.89333 W, Near Sea Level

42 Sites – This older Olympic National Forest campground is one of the few National Forest campgrounds in the state located along the ocean. The roads are cramped here and although there are some longer sites we recommend it for RVs no longer than 30 feet. The campground is located near the northern end of the stretch of US-101 along Hood Canal. It is 32 miles (52 km) north of the intersection of US-101 and SR-106.

■ **FALLSVIEW CAMPGROUND** *(Open May 10 to Sept 25 – Varies)*
    Information: (360) 765-2200
    Location: 33 Miles (53 Km) N of Hoodsport

   GPS Location: 47.79056 N, 122.92500 W, 500 Ft

30 Sites – This Olympic National Forest campground is located in Walker Pass and offers a trail to a waterfall near the campground. Sites are off two loops. Many are long narrow pull-thrus and back-ins but sites and roads are narrow so we recommend the campground

for RVs to 35 feet, many sites will not take slide-outs. There is no potable water at this campground. The campground is located 39 miles (63 km) north of the intersection of US-101 and SR-106 and just 3 miles (5 km) south of Quilcene.

○ **Jefferson County Campground Quilcene** *(Open All Year)*
   Location: Quilcene

   GPS Location: 47.82173 N, 122.87959 W, Near Sea Level

11 Sites – This Jefferson County campground in the small town of Quilcene has no-hookup sites for tent campers or those with small RVs to 30 feet. There's a vault toilet, playground, covered picnic shelter, and water faucet. Across the road is the Loggers Landing Restaurant. The campground is located at about Mile 295 of Hwy US-101.

ILWACO AND LONG BEACH

During the late 1800s the **Long Beach Peninsula**, like Seaside in Oregon to the south, was a beach resort frequented by folks from Portland. During the middle 1900s the peninsula was almost forgotten, but lately it has begun to be noticed again.

There are actually two centers of interest here. First there's the area near the mouth of the Columbia near Ilwaco. Second is the Long Beach Peninsula itself which starts just a few miles north of Ilwaco and runs northward for 28 miles (45 km). The peninsula forms the western border of Willapa Bay, famous for its oysters.

Ilwaco (population 1,000) is a fishing town. It is located a few miles east of the mouth of the Columbia on the north shore. In addition to serving fishermen, the town also hosts the Cape Disappointment Coast Guard Station. This is the Coast Guard's lifeboat school, it is located here because there are lots of opportunities to practice in the wild surf of the Columbia bar. The Coast Guard station is actually right next to one of the nicest Washington state parks, **Cape Disappointment**. This park, in addition to a fine campground, has **two lighthouses**, a nice beach, miles of trails, and the excellent **Lewis and Clark Interpretive Center**. There's also a great view of the mouth of the Columbia, complete with ships crossing the bar, from the interpretive center or the nearby lighthouse.

Historically the **Long Beach Peninsula** (also sometimes called the North Beach Peninsula) was connected to the river port at Ilwaco by a narrow-gauge railroad. Today the rail lines have been replaced by a road, SR-103. As you drive up the peninsula you'll find a number of small towns: Seaview, Long Beach, Klipsan Beach, Ocean Park, Surfside, Nahcotta, and Oysterville. Most of the tourist activities center around the town of Long Beach, that's where you'll find the majority of the restaurants and shops. The real attraction is out of sight to the west, it's the longest beach in the continental U.S. The peninsula finally ends at Leadbetter Point State Park, an excellent birding location. As you return (and if you are an oyster fan) stop in Nahcotta to visit the **Willapa Bay Oysterhouse Interpretive Center** and perhaps to buy oysters and other seafood at the wharf (in season).

Long Beach (population 1,400) is definitely a tourist town, it hosts several annual events. Early in the season, in May, there's the **Ragtime Rhodie Dixieland Jazz Festival**. There's also a Fourth of July event called **Fireworks Off The Boardwalk**. Biggest of all is the **Washington State International Kite Festival** the third week of August.

WASHINGTON

Ilwaco and Long Beach Campgrounds

☐ **CAPE DISAPPOINTMENT STATE PARK** *(Open All Year)*

Reservations: www.parks.wa.gov/reservations/,
　　　　　　　(888) 226-7688
Information: (360) 642-3078, (360) 902-8844,
　　　　　　　www.parks.wa.gov/parks/
Location: 3 Miles (5 Km) SW of Ilwaco

GPS Location: 46.28333 N, 124.05583 W, Near Sea Level

240 Sites – Formerly called Fort Canby, this is one of the most popular parks in the state. The attraction is the great beaches, two scenic lighthouses, and a Lewis and Clark interpretive center. The park occupies the point on the north side of the mouth of the Columbia River. RV sites are back-ins off circles, they reach 45 feet in length. From central Ilwaco

WASHINGTON

ILWACO AND LONG BEACH

To Westport

Ocean Park
Ocean Park Resort
Mm 10
To Nahcotta, Oysterville, and Surfside

Klipsan Beach
Evergreen Court
Westgate Cabins & RV Park
Mm 8

103

Pegg's Over 55 RV Park
Anderson's RV Park On the Ocean
Mm 5
Willapa Bay

Pacific Holiday RV Resort
Mm 4
Land's End RV Park
Mm 3
Mermaid Inn & RV Park
The Crows Nest RV Park

Peninsula Hwy

Driftwood RV Park
Mm 2
Long Beach
Sand Castle RV Park
Pacific Ocean
Oceanic RV Park

Seaview
Sid's Market

101

Sou'Wester Lodge, Cabins, & RV Park
Mm 14
Eagle's Nest Resort
Ilwaco
Mm 9

Ilwaco/ Long Beach KOA

Robert Gray

101

Mm 6

Cape Disappointment SP
Beacon Charters & RV Park

N

River's End Cmpgrd & RV Park
To Astoria

Columbia River

follow the signs west for the park. The entrance is 3.3 miles (5 Km) from the intersection in town. This park accepts reservations year-round.

● **ILWACO / LONG BEACH KOA KAMPGROUND**
(Open May 30 to Sept 30 – Varies)
Reservations: (800) 562-3258, www.koa.com
Information: (360) 642-3292, ilwacokoa@hotmail.com
Location: 2 Miles (3 Km) E of Ilwaco

GPS Location: 46.32139 N, 124.00528 W, Near Sea Level

90 Sites – Probably because it's located a bit east of Il-waco the KOA usually has room when other nearby campgrounds are full, a good thing to know in this popular area. Sites include long pull-thrus with parking on grass. It's at the intersection of US-101 and SR-401.

● **SAND CASTLE RV PARK** *(Open All Year)*
Res and Info: (360) 642-2174, www.sandcastlerv.com
Location: Long Beach

GPS Location: 46.35889 N, 124.05361°W, Near Sea Level

45 Sites – This is a small RV park convenient to the attractions of central Long Beach. There are tent sites as well as back-ins to 50 feet with full hookups and parking on grass. It's located on the east side of SR-103 near Mile 2.

● **DRIFTWOOD RV PARK** *(Open All Year)*
Res and Info: (360) 642-2711, (888) 567-1902, www.driftwood-rvpark.net
Location: Long Beach

GPS Location: 46.36167 N, 124.05389 W, Near Sea Level

56 Sites – This is one of the larger Long Beach camp-grounds with some of the best facilities. There are back-in and pull-thru sites to 50 feet. The park is at the northern edge of town near Mile 2 of State Route 103.

● **ANDERSEN'S RV PARK ON THE OCEAN**
(Open All Year)
Reservations: (360) 642-2231, (800) 645-6795
Information: (360) 642-2231, info@andersensrv.com, www.andersensrv.com
Location: 2 Mile (3 Km) N of Long Beach

GPS Location: 46.40222 N, 124.05389 W, Near Sea Level

60 Sites – This campground is located next to the beach about 3.5 miles (5.6 km) north of central Long Beach. Two long lines of long back-in sites to 50 feet stretch from the office and other buildings out toward the shore. It's a well-run friendly park and very popular. The campground is on the west side of SR-103 at Mile 5 north of Long Beach.

KITSAP PENINSULA AND BAINBRIDGE ISLAND

West of the Seattle/Tacoma metro area, across Puget Sound, is a rural region known as the **Kitsap Peninsula**. Access for many to this area is by Washington State Ferry. In fact, the ferries make access so easy that this area, the Kitsap Peninsula and the connected Bainbridge Island, are a bedroom community for Seattle.

Another access route, and this one is better for RVs of any size larger than a van, is the suspension bridge linking Tacoma with the west side of the sound. Almost immediately you will find yourself in another world. You pass from the crowded Seattle-Tacoma metropolis to the green countryside of rural western Puget Sound and the Kitsap Peninsula. You might want to stop and take a look at **Gig Harbor**, sometimes called the Northwest's Sausalito. The little waterfront town is filled with small shops and has a nice nautical flavor. It's so close to Tacoma that we've included its campground under the *Tacoma* heading elsewhere in the chapter, but it's a good base for exploring the Kitsap Peninsula.

Stay on SR-16 as it leads north to Bremerton. Just short of that city the highway will meet SR-3. You can turn left here and in 8 miles (13 km) be in Belfair. Belfair has a nice state park campground along Hood Canal, we've listed it in the *Hood Canal* section. It too can make a nice base for exploring the Kitsap Peninsula.

If you decide to head north and explore the peninsula you might want to make your first stop **Port Orchard**. This little harbor town is a good place to shop for antiques, art, or just plain knickknacks.

Port Orchard is directly across Sinclair Inlet from much larger **Bremerton**, known as the home of the Puget Sound Naval Shipyard. You'll have to drive around the west end of Sinclair Inlet to get there if you want to take your car. The alternative is a passenger-only ferry running across the inlet. The waterfront in Bremerton is the center of interest. There you'll find a boardwalk and shipyard-related sights including the destroyer **Turner Joy** which is open to self-guided tours, and the **Bremerton Naval Museum**. There are a number of moth-balled ships in Bremerton, you can take a commercial harbor tour to see them but you are not allowed on board the ships.

If you find that you enjoy the Bremerton Naval Museum you may want to drive a few miles north on SR-3 through Silverdale and then turn east on SR-308 to Keyport. There you'll find the **Naval Underwater Museum**. The Kitsap Peninsula plays an important part in supporting the U.S. submarine fleet. Along the west coast of the peninsula on Hood Canal is the **Bangor Trident Nuclear Submarine Base** and Keyport is home to the **Naval Undersea Warfare Center**, neither is open for tours, however.

Since you've come so far north already you might as well visit **Poulsbo**, it's only about three miles (5 km) farther north. Poulsbo is another cute harbor town offering antiques and shops. The difference here is that Poulsbo is proud of its Norwegian heritage and shows it off with Scandinavian-theme architecture and products.

Beyond Poulsbo SR-305 connects with Bainbridge Island. Bainbridge has one of the ferry ports for Seattle arrivals and departures as well as many homes. It also has a nice state park campground.

You will see that when visiting the Kitsap Peninsula you have a wide choice of state campgrounds. For tent campers in smaller vehicles or on bicycles these are easily accessible from Seattle by ferry and make good weekend destinations, particularly when reservations are available.

In addition to the campgrounds listed below several others are located nearby and allow easy access to the area. Gig Harbor (listed under *Tacoma* in this book) has a good commercial campground. There's also a nice state park campground near Belfair (that will take big rigs and offers hookups and reservations). It's listed in the *Hood Canal* section of this book.

If you are visiting the Northwest and would like to visit Seattle in a unique way you might

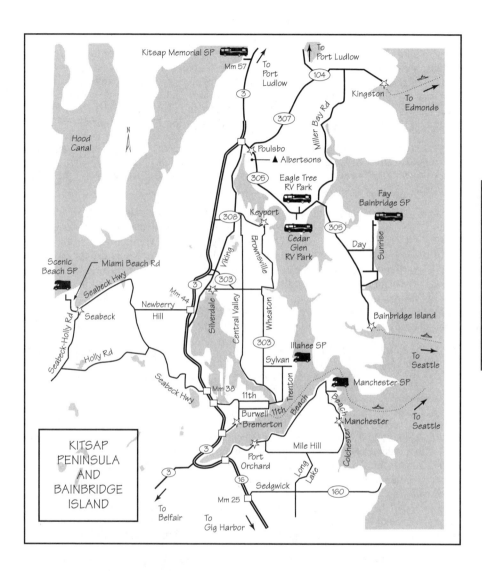

consider camping on the Kitsap Peninsula or Bainbridge Island and using the ferry to visit the city. Leave your vehicle and walk on. The ferries dock right downtown and you can walk or use public transportation to get around Seattle.

Kitsap Peninsula and Bainbridge Island Campgrounds

MANCHESTER STATE PARK *(Open All Year)*

Reservations: www.parks.wa.gov/reservations/, (888) 226-7688

Information: (360) 871-4065, (360) 902-8844, www.parks.wa.gov

Location: 6 Miles (10 Km) E of Port Orchard

GPS Location: 47.57667 N, 122.55472 W, Near Sea Level

50 Sites – This state campground is located on the Puget Sound shoreline to the east of Port Orchard. The camping area is away from the water. Campsites are forest-type and include some pull-thrus. While some sites reach 60 feet narrow roads and poor access limit RV size to about 35 feet. Access to this park involves driving on narrow back roads. One route would be to head east along the waterfront from Port Orchard on Beach Drive East. The road follows the waterfront to the northeast and then turns south to head inland. Five miles (8 km) from Port Orchard you'll see the sign for the park on the left.

☐ **ILLAHEE STATE PARK** *(Open All Year)*
    Information: (360) 478-6460, (360) 902-8844, www.parks.wa.gov
    Location: Bremerton

GPS Location: 47.59556 N, 122.59861 W, Near Sea Level

25 Sites – This state park is located just northeast of Bremerton along the shore of Puget Sound. The small forest-type campground is away from the water and is located on a hillside with narrow access roads. There are only two sites with hookups at this park, most sites are without utility hookups. Carefully driven 40-foot rigs do use the park, but access is difficult. The park also has a small boat ramp and a wide, gently-sloping beach. To reach the campground most easily follow SR-303 some 6.7 miles (10.8 km) southeast from its intersection with SR-3 near Silverdale. SR-303 starts as NW Waaga Way, then becomes Wheaton Way after it turns south toward Bremerton. Turn east on Sylvan Way (SR-306) and follow it 1.5 miles (2.4 km) to the campground entrance.

● **CEDAR GLEN RV PARK** *(Open All Year)*
    Res and Info: (360) 779-4305,
        cedarglenmhpllc@embarqmail.com,
        www.cedarglenmhp.com
    Location: 2 Miles (3 Km) E of Poulsbo

GPS Location: 47.70556 N 122.59694 W, 100 Ft

36 Sites – This small, very neat commercial campground south of the highway is associated with a much larger mobile home park on the north side. Most sites are occupied by long-term RVs but there are often sites for travelers. Sites are long gravel back-ins to 100 feet off a straight gravel access road. Slide-outs are not a problem. The check-in office and laundry are at the mobile home park. Restrooms reserved to the RV park are at the RV park location. Follow SR-305 southeast from its intersection with SR-3 near Poulsbo. The campground is on the right in 4.9 miles (7.9 km). If you are coming the other way from Bainbridge Island the campground is 1.5 miles (2.4 km) from the bridge.

● **EAGLE TREE RV PARK** *(Open All Year)*
    Res and Info: (360) 598-5988, info@eagletreerv.com,
        www.eagletreerv.com
    Location: 3 Miles (5 Km) E of Poulsbo

GPS Location: 47.70611 N, 122.59028 W, 200 Ft

88 Sites – The Eagle Tree is a newer big-rig park.
Gravel sites are situated among tall cedars. There are full-hookup back-in and pull-thru sites from 40 to 80 feet in length which will accommodate slide-outs. Follow SR-305 southeast from its intersection with SR-3 near Poulsbo. The campground is on the left in 5.3 miles (8.5 km). If you are coming the other way from Bainbridge Island the campground is 1.1 miles (1.8 km) from the bridge.

☐ **FAY BAINBRIDGE STATE PARK** *(Open All Year)*
  Information: (206) 842-3931, (360) 902-8844, www.parks.wa.gov
  Location: 8 Miles (13 Km) N of Bainbridge Island Ferry Terminal

  GPS Location: 47.70278 N, 122.50778 W, Near Sea Level

36 Sites – This campground has both tent sites in a forest setting and RV and tent sites near the beach with views across the Sound. The RV sites are all back-ins and a few will accept RVs to 40 feet. These sites are not separated by trees so slide-outs present no problems. This campground is on Bainbridge Island and is the closest state campground to the ferry. From the bridge onto the island follow SR-305 south and turn left on NE Day Road W. Coming the other way this intersection is 4.3 miles (6.9 km) from the ferry terminal. Follow Day Road east for 1.3 miles (2.1 km) until you reach Sunrise Dr. NE. Follow Sunrise north for 1.6 miles (2.6 km) to the campground entrance which is on the right.

☐ **KITSAP MEMORIAL STATE PARK** *(Open All Year)*
  Reservations: www.parks.wa.gov/reservations/, (888) 226-7688
  Information: (360) 779-3205, (360) 902-8844, www.parks.wa.gov
  Location: 4 Miles (6.4 Km) S of the Hood Canal Bridge

  GPS Location: 47.81778 N, 122.65000 W, Near Sea Level

39 Sites – Kitsap Memorial is on the west side of the peninsula on the shore of Hood Canal. The camping sites here are back-ins to 40 feet in an open area. The restroom building is fairly new and one of the nicest in the state with individual shower rooms, you'll think you're in an Oregon state park except that you have to feed them with quarters here. There are also spiffy rental cabins. Campsites do not have a water view but are just across a grassy field from the small and narrow beach. The entrance road to the park is off SR-3 just 2.9 miles (4.7 km) south of the Hood Canal Floating Bridge. This park accepts reservations year-round.

☐ **SCENIC BEACH STATE PARK** *(Open All Year)*
  Reservations: www.parks.wa.gov/reservations/, (888) 226-7688
  Information: (360) 830-5079, (360) 902-8844, www.parks.wa.gov
  Location: 9 Miles (15 Km) SW of Silverdale

  GPS Location: 47.64722 N, 122.84667 W, Near Sea Level

52 Sites – Scenic Beach is another state campground on Hood Canal. The beach here is small and narrow. Campsites are all forest-type off paved roads on two loops. There are back-ins to 50 feet and pull-thrus that are even longer but access roads are narrow making the campground only suitable for RVs to 35 feet. The campground is somewhat isolated since it is located away from the main thoroughfares on the island. From SR-3 near Silverdale drive west on NW Newberry Hill Road. In 2.8 miles (4.5 km), at the T turn right on Seabeck Hwy. NW and follow this road as it goes north and then turns west to follow the shoreline. In 5.1 miles (8.2 km) turn right on Miami Beach Road and follow it to the campground, another 1.4 miles (2.3 km).

LAKE EASTON AND LAKE KACHESS

For Seattle area residents the Lake Easton and Lake Kachess region is a convenient wilderness destination. Exit 70, the epicenter of the campgrounds in the area, is (of course), 70 miles (113 km) from the beginning of I-90 in Seattle. It's an easy drive in the summer with at least four lanes all the way.

WASHINGTON

This area is the headwaters of the Yakima River. Both Lakes Easton and Kachess are dammed reservoirs offering water sport activities. Kachess is much larger and more remote. It's 5 miles (8 km) north of the highway and covers 6,535 acres. Fishing is possible for kokanee, rainbows and cutthroats. Lake Easton is much smaller and good for small unpowered boats. It's really more of a wide spot in the river than a lake. While 10 horsepower engines are allowed the many stumps in the lake make it easy to have an accident with a powered boat.

This area is in the Wenatchee National Forest and back country can be accessed using trails and logging roads. It is also crossed by the **John Wayne Trail and Iron Horse Trail State Park**. This trail extends from Cedar Falls on the west side of the Cascades across the state to the Idaho border. It follows an abandoned railroad right-a-way and can be used by hikers, bikers, and horseback riders.

The Lake Easton area is also a popular winter sports destination with miles of cross country ski trails, nearby snow machine country, and even overnight parking at the state park.

This area has camping opportunities for everyone. Tenters will enjoy any of the government campgrounds although only the state park offers showers. Most RVers seem to favor the state campground. When it's full the commercial campgrounds provide overflow room for those desiring hookups.

Lake Easton and Lake Kachess Campgrounds

■ **LAKE KACHESS CAMPGROUND** *(Open May 1 to Sept 30 – Varies)*
Reservations: www.recreation.gov, (877) 444-6777
Information: (509) 656-0366
Location: 5 Miles (8 Km) NE of I-90 Exit 62

GPS Location: 47.35528 N, 121.24972 W, 2,200 Ft

182 Sites – This is a very large Wenatchee National Forest campground on the shores of Kachess Lake. Sites are off six loops and there are two boat ramps. Most sites here are only suitable for RVs to 30 feet but there are some pull-thru sites along one loop that will take RVs to 40 feet. To reach the campground take Exit 62 from I-90 and drive 5 miles (8 km) northeast on the paved Kachess Lake Road.

● **LAKE EASTON RESORT** *(Open All Year)*
Information: (509) 656-2255
Location: I-90 Exit 70

GPS Location: 47.24694 N, 121.18722 W, 2,300 Ft

123 Sites – This is an older membership campground but travelers are accommodated if the campground has room. It does often fill up during summer weekends and no reservations are accepted. Take Exit 70 from I-90. Go east along the road that parallels the south side of the freeway for a short distance, the entrance is on the right.

□ **LAKE EASTON STATE PARK**
    (Open May 6 to Oct 10 – Varies, Snow Park all Winter)
Reservations: www.parks.wa.gov/reservations/, (888) 226-7688
Information: (509) 656-2230, (360) 902-8844, www.parks.wa.gov
Location: I-90 Exit 70

GPS Location: 47.24444 N, 121.18583 W, 2,200 Ft

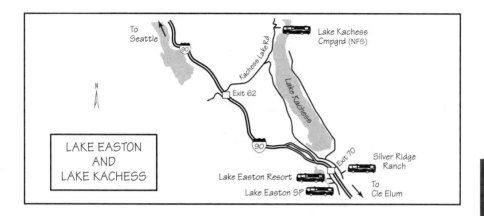

135 Sites – This is a popular lakeside campground. It has swimming and a boat ramp as well as offering easy access to the John Wayne Pioneer Trail. In winter it is used as a Sno-Park offering overnight parking in a large cleared lot for the large number of people who come to this area for winter activities. Sites and access allow large RVs to use the park, some sites will take combinations to 60 feet. Take Exit 70 from I-90 and travel east on the road that parallels the freeway on the south side, you'll see the campground entrance on the right in just .4 mile (.6 km).

● **SILVER RIDGE RANCH** *(Open All Year)*

Res and Info: (877) 656-0275,
(509) 656-0275,
miki@silverridgeranch.com,
www.silverridgeranch.com

Location: I-90 Exit 70

GPS Location: 47.24927 N, 121.18511 W, 2,100 Ft

75 Sites – This campground and bed and breakfast is just off the freeway. It's popular with horse owners in summer because of the miles of trails nearby, also with snow machine owners in winter for the same reason. There are 45 back-in and pull-thru RV sites to 40 feet, and also 30 tent sites. Shade is provided by evergreens, sites are dirt and gravel off gravel roads. From Exit 70 off I-90 drive north to the T on the north side of the freeway, turn right and you'll see the campground entrance on the left in .2 miles (.3 km).

LAKE PATEROS REGION

Lake Pateros fills the Columbia River valley behind Wells Dam at Mile 515.8 of the Columbia River. The upper end of the 30-mile (48 km) lake is near Chief Joseph Dam at Mile 545.1 of the Columbia. The valley at this point turns to the east toward the Grand Coulee and the massive dam there.

This section of the river doesn't get a lot of tourist attention, but maybe it should. Lake Pateros, and also Lake Rufus Wood behind Chief Joseph Dam, offer hot weather, water-sports, and fishing.

Pateros (population 700) is the town farthest downriver on the lake. This is a fruit growing region and fruit processing is clearly the town's main business. There's a municipal park along the waterfront for walking and camping. There are also two large tanks on the hillside above town that you'll probably notice, they've been beautified with a reflector art installation by eastern Washington artist Richard Elliot. The three annual celebrations in Pateros are the **Apple Pie Jamboree** about the middle of July, the **Pateros Fun Run** (a motorcycle rally) at the end of July, and **Pateros Hydro Classic** on Lake Pateros in mid August.

Other towns in the area are **Brewster** (population 2,200) and **Bridgeport** (population 2,000). Both have city campgrounds.

East of Brewster an interesting stop is **Fort Okanogan**. The access road goes south from SR-17 just east of its intersection with US-97. Here you'll find a state information center which overlooks the confluence of the Columbia and Okanogan Rivers. Fort Okanogan was a fur-trading station located near the confluence during the 1800s. The actual sites (there were two of them) of the forts are far below near the rivers, you can look through a couple of sighting contraptions at the center to see where they once stood.

Fishing is popular in both lakes. Lake Pateros has salmon, steelhead, walleye and bass while Lake Rufus Woods in known for its big rainbows as well as walleye and kokanee. On Lake Rufus Woods if you are shore fishing outside the state park you need a Coleville Tribe fishing license in addition to your Washington state license.

For both tent campers and RVers the best campgrounds in this region are the state campgrounds. The Marina Park in Bridgeport is also a nice possibility.

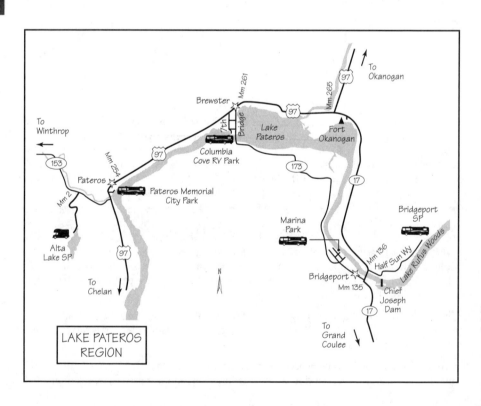

Lake Pateros Region Campgrounds

☐ **BRIDGEPORT STATE PARK** *(Open April 1 to Oct 31 – Varies)*
Reservations: www.parks.wa.gov/reservations/, (888) 226-7688
Information: (509) 686-7231, (360) 902-8844, www.parks.wa.gov
Location: 3 Miles (5 Km) NE of Bridgeport

GPS Location: 48.01444 N, 119.60083 W, 900 Ft

34 Sites – Bridgeport State Park is on the north side of Rufus Woods
Lake behind Chief Joseph Dam on the Columbia River. This is a
beautiful campground, nice and green because there's lots of water available. Amenities
include a swimming beach, boat launch, and a very green 18-hole golf course. Fishing,
wind-surfing, and warm-water boating are popular activities here. There are back-ins and
pull-thrus to 45 feet. To reach the campground follow the access road north for 2 miles (3
Km) from a junction with SR-17 just across the bridge from Bridgeport.

○ **MARINA PARK** *(Open April 15 to Oct 30 – Varies)*
Res and Info: (509) 686-4747 (April - Oct) or
(509) 686-4041 (Nov - March),
clerk@nwi.net
Location: Bridgeport

GPS Location: 48.01417 N, 119.67750 W", 700 Ft

22 Sites – This riverside campground in Bridgeport is a little gem and also a real value.
It's a municipal campground. There are back-in and pull-through sites to 60 feet and also
a boat ramp. The small campground even has a host. The park is located toward the western end of the town of Bridgeport, follow Columbia Ave. west and then turn north toward
the river on 7th Street to the campground.

○ **COLUMBIA COVE RV PARK** *(Open May 1 to Oct 31 – Varies)*
Res and Info: (509) 689-3464
Location: Brewster

GPS Location: 48.09111 N, 119.78389 W, 700 Ft

24 Sites – This is another city campground near the river. Not
quite as nice as the one in Bridgeport this campground offers similar amenities. There's a
nearby boat launch and even a swimming pool next door. Overflow sites with power only
are nearby. Sites are back-ins and pull-thrus to 40 feet. To reach the campground follow
7th Street to the water from US-97 in central Brewster.

○ **PATEROS MEMORIAL CITY PARK** *(Open All Year)*
Information: (509) 923-2571
Location: Pateros

GPS Location: 48.05269 N, 119.89978 W, 700 Ft

13 Sites – It is possible to park along the street at the waterfront city park in Pateros for
a small fee. The park has restrooms with flush toilets and showers as well as an outdoor
kitchen area, horseshoe pits and docks. There is a stand with payment envelopes near the
kitchen area.

☐ **ALTA LAKE STATE PARK** *(Open March 21 to Oct 31 – Varies)*
  Reservations: www.parks.wa.gov/reservations/, (888) 226-7688
  Information: (509) 923-2473, (360) 902-8844, www.parks.wa.gov
  Location: 4 Miles (6 Km) SW of Pateros

      GPS Location: 48.02944 N, 119.93611 W, 1,200 Ft

123 Sites – Alta Lake is an alpine lake accessible by road. It's a
unique place for a large state campground and very popular. There are a variety of site
types. A large open grassy field is used by both tenters and RVers not needing hookups.
Additional back-in sites off loops are small but some have water and electric hookups to
about 25 feet. Finally, one loop has a paved parking lot-style area with hookups sites to
38 feet. There are swimming and watersports possibilities in the lake (including personal
watercraft) with docks and launch ramps although launching is difficult when water levels are down. There are also hiking trails from the campground and a nearby 18-hole golf
course. A small grocery operates in the park. Reservations for campsites can be made for
the period April 1 to Oct 31. The road to the campground leaves SR-153 about 1.7 miles
(2.7 km) west of Pateros. It climbs to the south, it's 1.8 miles (2.9 km) to the campground
from the intersection.

LAKE WENATCHEE AND FISH LAKE RECREATION AREA

About 20 miles (32 km) north of Leavenworth in the Wenatchee National Forest the
Wenatchee River valley holds two interesting lakes and miles of hiking trails.

The largest of the lakes is **Lake Wenatchee**. This is a large glacial lake. Near the south
shore are two campgrounds. One is a large state park with two separate campgrounds
(the park is bisected by the Wenatchee River, the outlet of the lake), the other is a modern
national forest campground. Lake Wenatchee offers swimming and boating as well as
fishing. The lake has salmon, trout, perch and whitefish.

Nearby is the much smaller **Fish Lake**. This is a popular fishing lake with at least two
commercial fishing lodges offering campsites along the shore. It's a 500 acre lake offering stocked rainbows, German browns, perch, and bass.

This area is a popular winter destination too. There are miles of cross country ski trails
and you can ice fish in Fish Lake. The day-use area of the state park remains open in
winter as a camping area.

Lake Wenatchee and Fish Lake Recreation Area Campgrounds

☐ **LAKE WENATCHEE STATE PARK** *(Open April 15 to Oct 11 –*
  Varies, In Winter A Plowed Lot Is Open For Camping)
  Reservations: www.parks.wa.gov/reservations/, (888) 226-7688
  Information: (509) 763-3101, (360) 902-8844, www.parks.wa.gov
  Location: 19 Miles (31 Km) N of Leavenworth

      GPS Locations: 47.81250 N, 120.72111 W
      and 47.80306 N, 120.71806 W, 1,800 Ft

197 Sites – This is a very large state campground in two dif-
ferent sections separated by a mile or so. The two areas are called the North and South
campground and they are split by the Wenatchee River. The nearby lake is the attraction
here, there's a popular swimming beach near the south campground. The South Campground is older, has no hookups, and is suitable for RVs to about 30 feet. The North

Campground has the hookups and some sites are suitable for RVs to 45 feet. It's about a quarter-mile (.4 km) from the lake. There are miles of equestrian trails near the campgrounds and horses are available for rental. To reach the campgrounds drive north from Leavenworth on US-2 for 16 miles (26 km), then turn north on SR-207. The entrance to the South Campground is in 3.5 miles (5.6 km), the North is another mile (1.6 km).

■ **NASON CREEK CAMPGROUND** *(Open May 1 to Sept 30 – Varies)*
Information: (509) 664-9200
Location: 19 Miles (31 Km) N of Leavenworth

GPS Location: 47.80083 N, 120.71500 W, 1,800 Ft

73 Sites – This large Wenatchee National Forest campground is located just outside the gates of the south section of Lake Wenatchee State Park. Most of the campground is a modern forest service campground with paved interior roads and large sites (some pull-thrus) suitable for large rigs of any size. To reach the campgrounds drive north from Leavenworth on US-2 for 16 miles (26 km), then turn north on SR-207. The entrance to the campground is in 3.5 miles (5.6 km) on the left.

● **COVE RESORT** *(Open May 1 to Sept 30 – Varies)*
Information: (509) 763-3130,
www.coveresortatfishlake.com
Location: 20 Miles (32 Km) N of Leavenworth

GPS Location: 47.82889 N, 120.71361 W, 1,900 Ft

110 Sites – This north woods style fishing resort has a dock for fishing as well as rental

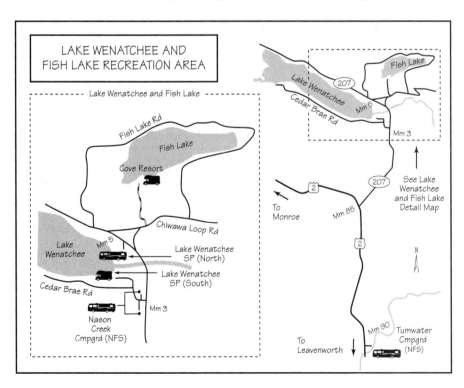

rowboats and a boat ramp. Fishing tackle and advice are offered in the office. In the woods behind are lots of campsites, some with hookups and others without. Most sites will only take rigs to 30 feet but a few near the main buildings will take RVs to about 35 feet. To reach the resort drive north from Leavenworth on US-2 for 16 miles (26 km), then turn north on SR-207. In 4.2 miles (6.8 km) turn right on Chiwawa Loop Road and you'll see the resort entrance road on the left in .5 mile (.8 km). There is a .8 mile (1.3 km) gravel driveway.

■ **TUMWATER CAMPGROUND** *(Open May 1 to Oct 31 – Varies)*
Information: (509) 664-9200
Location: 10 Miles (16 Km) N of Leavenworth

GPS Location: 47.67833 N, 120.73444 W, 1,700 Ft

84 Sites – Conveniently located right off US-2, Tumwater Wenatchee Forest Campground has paved back-in sites (and 3 pull-thrus) to about 40 feet and is set in pine trees and situated next to Chiwaukum Creek. To reach the campground drive north on US-2 for 10 miles (16 km) from Leavenworth. The entrance is between Mileposts 90 and 91.

LEAVENWORTH

Leavenworth (population 2,000) is a small out of the way town that has recreated itself as a tourist destination. Beginning in the early 60s Leavenworth's business community began to build and rebuild using a Bavarian theme. Today the buildings, together with a stunning location surrounded by mountains, actually does look somewhat Bavarian.

Best of all, at least in the view of the businesses in town, some 1.5 million people each year visit Leavenworth to shop, dine, and enjoy the events scheduled throughout the year. It would be hard to drive through town on US-2 and not stop for at least a quick look around. A better plan is to stay at one of the nearby campgrounds and spend at least an evening.

Leavenworth is full of shops, restaurants, and art galleries. They provide a lot to keep you busy any day of the year. But the town also hosts special events. These include **Maifest** in early May, **Kinderfest** on the fourth of July, a **Summer Theater** in July and August, a **Chamber Music Festival** in July, an **Autumn Leaf Festival** in late September, **Wenatchee River Salmon Festival** in early October, **Oktoberfest** in the first half of

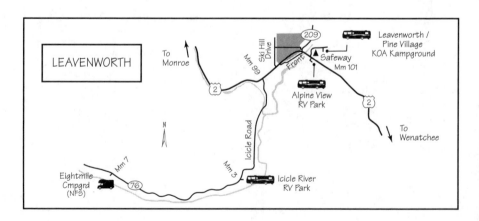

October, **Christkindlmarkt** in late November, and lots more. Check with the Chamber of Commerce for exact dates and information about additional events.

Leavenworth Campgrounds

● **LEAVENWORTH / PINE VILLAGE KOA**
    KAMPGROUND *(Open All Year)*

Reservations: (800) 562-5709, www.koa.com
Information: (509) 548-7709, pkoa@hotmail.com
Location: 1 Mile (2 Km) NE of Leavenworth

GPS Location: 47.59861 N, 120.63944 W, 1,100 Ft

135 Sites – This is a handy place to stay if you are interested in visiting the village for shopping or to visit a restaurant. The large campground sits in tall evergreens above the Wenatchee River. There's a shuttle bus to take you in to town, the distance is less than a mile. This is a large KOA with a full list of amenities. Sites are back-ins and pull-thrus to 65 feet. Careful maneuvering is required for some sites. The campground is located on the east side of town. From US-2 you'll see signs pointing north just east of the bridge next to the Safeway, the campground is .6 mile (1 km) up the road, the entrance is on the right.

● **ALPINE VIEW RV PARK**
    Res and Info: (888) 548-8439, (509) 548-8439,
                 www.alpineviewrvpark.com
    Location: Leavenworth, WA

GPS Location: 47.59581 N, 120.64619 W, 1,100 Ft

40 Sites – The Alpine View is a rustic older park that is the closest campground to the center of Leavenworth. It's the only campground that will let you comfortably walk in to the center of the village, the distance is about a half-mile. Sites are set in trees, some have picnic tables and fire pits. They are back-ins mostly to 40 feet although there are four pull-thrus. Access is tight. The campground is next to Hwy 2 so it's convenient but noise may be a problem. The campground is located at the eastern edge of town across the highway from the Safeway.

● **ICICLE RIVER RV PARK** *(Open April 1 to Oct 18 – Varies)*
    Res and Info: (509) 548-5420, icicleriverrv@yahoo.com,
                 www.icicleriverrv.com
    Location: 3 Miles (5 Km) SW of Leavenworth

GPS Location: 47.54944 N, 120.68694 W, 1,200 Ft

114 Sites – Farther from town than the KOA, this campground has beautiful sites, some along the river. Sites are back-ins to 40 feet. To reach the campground drive 1 mile (1.6 km) west on US-2 to Icicle Road from central Leavenworth. Turn left here and drive 3 miles (5 km) to the campground which is on the left.

■ **EIGHTMILE CAMPGROUND** *(Open May 1 to Oct 15 – Varies)*
    Information: (509) 548-6977
    Location: 7 Miles (11 Km) SW of Leavenworth

GPS Location: 47.55083 N, 120.76472 W, 1,900 Ft

45 Sites – Eightmile Wenatchee National Forest campground is in a very scenic location

in the canyon of Icicle Creek. There are many hiking trails in the area. Sites here are suitable for RVs to 30 feet, space for parking a second vehicle is scarce. There are paved roads and sites, tent pads are gravel. To reach the campground drive 1 mile (1.6 km) west on US-2 to Icicle Road from central Leavenworth. Turn left here and drive 6.7 miles to the campground which is on the left.

LEWISTON AND CLARKSTON

The sister cities of **Lewiston, Idaho** (population 31,000) and **Clarkston, Washington** (population 7,200) are located at the confluence of the Clearwater River where it joins the Snake River. It's interesting to note that Lewiston has the lowest altitude of any city in Idaho. Because temperatures are higher here than elsewhere in the state it's considered Idaho's banana belt.

Thanks to a series of 8 dams along the Columbia and Snake Rivers (Bonneville, The Dalles, John Day, McNary, Ice Harbor, Lower Monumental, Little Goose, Lower Granite) this is the farthest inland flat-water port in the United States. Tugs and barges export the products of the region's farms: largely wheat, lentils, and peas.

Lewis and Clark passed through here and were befriended by the local Nez Percé tribe. The **Lewis and Clark Discovery Center** is located at Hells Gate State Park, about 3.5 miles (5.6 km) south of town up the east bank of the Snake River.

East of town is the Nez Percé reservation which has a casino (and campground) as well as the **Nez Percé National Historical Sites Park** with its **Museum of Nez Percé Culture**.

Jet boat tours up the Snake River are very popular. It's a long run, the canyon begins a full 50 miles (80 km) south of Lewiston. Most tours leave from the marina at Hells Gate State Park. Several of the companies offering these tours are listed at the end of this chapter.

The twin town has a great bike/walking path called the **Clearwater and Snake River National Trail**. It runs for almost 20 miles along both shores of the Snake River and also east along the Lewiston levee following the Clearwater river.

Lewiston and Clarkston Campgrounds

● **GRANITE LAKE PREMIER RV RESORT** *(Open All Year)*
  Info and Res: (509) 751-1635 or (800) 989-4578,
  www.premierrvresorts.com
  Location: Clarkston

  GPS Location: 46.42417 N, 117.04306 W, 700 Ft

75 Sites – This is a very nice big-rig campground located in Clarkston on the shore of the Snake River, just below its confluence with the Clearwater. They have paved sites with patios, both back-ins and pull-thrus to 55 feet. In the summer there's a pool and spa. Start in Clarkston on US-12. Drive north on 5th St. toward the river, pass the Costco, and the campground is at the end of the street.

● **AHT' WY PLAZA RV** *(Open All Year)*
  Information: (208) 746-0723
  Location: 5 Miles (8 Km) E of Lewiston

  GPS Location: N 46.43694 N, W 116.90500 W, 700 Ft

32 Sites – This older RV park is associated with the Clearwater River Casino which is located nearby. Sites are irregular full-hookup pull-thrus and back-ins to 60 feet. These are dirt sites with shade. Restrooms have hot showers and there is a pool. The casino has a restaurant. Campers park and then check in at the casino. From Lewiston drive east on US-12 for about 5 miles (8 km). You'll pass the casino and find the campground just beyond.

☐ **HELLS GATE IDAHO STATE PARK**
   (Open All Year)
   Reservations: (866) 634-3246,
                     www.parksandrecreation.idaho.gov
   Information: (208) 799-5015,
                     www.parksandrecreation.idaho.gov
   Location: Lewiston

   GPS Location: 46.37028 N, 117.05361 W, 700 Ft

93 Sites – This Idaho State Park is located along the Snake River not far above its confluence with the Clearwater River in Lewiston and Clarkston. Jet boat tours of the Snake River Canyon leave from docks at the park and the Lewis and Clark Discovery Center is located at the park. The camping area here is a shaded area near the river with sites off three paved loops. They have full-hookup, partial-hookup, and dry sites including back-ins and pull-thrus to 70 feet. The day-use area next door has a large sandy beach for swimming. From Lewiston follow Snake River Avenue up the east side of the Snake River for 3.5 miles (5.6 km) to the park.

WASHINGTON

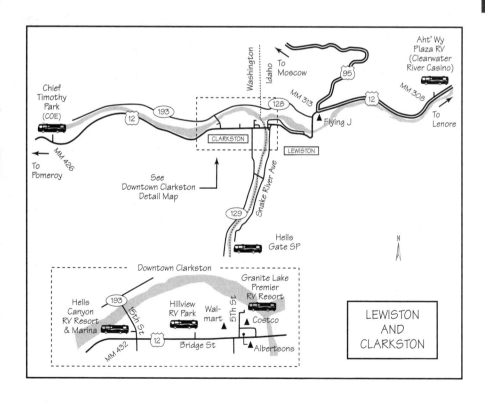

● **HILLVIEW RV PARK** *(Open All Year)*
Reservations: (866) 758-6299
Information: (509) 758-6299, hillviewrvpark@yahoo.com
Location: Clarkston

GPS Location: 46.41972 N, 117.05472 W, 700 Ft

100 Sites – This urban RV park in Clarkston is handy and
not as expensive as the other parks in town. Sites are both back-ins and pull-thrus to 65
feet, most are full-hookup sites. The campground is on the north side of Bridge Street
(US-12) at 12ᵗʰ Street in central Clarkston.

● **HELLS CANYON RV RESORT AND MARINA**
(Open All Year)
Res and Info: (509) 758-6963,
hellscanyonresort@clearwire.net,
www.hellscanyon.net
Location: Clarkston

GPS Location: 46.42083 N, 117.06917 W, 700 Ft

50 Sites – This is a marina, restaurant, and RV resort
complex on the Snake River at the western edge of Clarkston. It's a modern big-rig park
with paved back-in and pull-thru sites to 60 feet with patios. All sites are full hookups.
Amenities include the marina, an indoor swimming pool, indoor hot tub, and a restaurant.
The park is north of US-12 at the western edge of Clarkston where 15ᵗʰ Street goes north
to cross the Snake River.

■ **CHIEF TIMOTHY PARK**
(Open May 1 to Oct 31 – Varies)
Reservations: www.recreation.gov, (877) 444-6777
Information: (509) 758-8613,
www.nww.usace.army.mil.
Location: 6 Miles (10 Km) W of Clarkston

GPS Location: 46.41528 N, 117.19417 W, 700 Ft

49 Sites – Chief Timothy is an island in the Snake River accessible by a small bridge from
the south shore not far west of Clarkston. This is a privately managed Corps of Engineers
campground. There are tent sites as well as lots of pull-thrus to 60 feet. These are full,
partial, and no-hookup sites. Some sites are waterfront and there are also a few rental
yurts. Amenities include a swimming beach, boat launch, and bike trails. The entrance is
off US-12 near Mile 426, about 6 miles (10 km) west of Clarkston.

LEWIS RIVER REGION

The Lewis River, like the Cowlitz to the north of Mt St Helens, runs westward to meet
the Columbia. The Lewis is south of Mt St Helens, and it too has dams and reservoirs
that host popular campgrounds. The lakes with campgrounds are Yale Lake and the Swift
Reservoir.

Unlike the Cowlitz River area the Lewis River area is relatively unpopulated and includes
the south approaches to Mt St Helens Volcanic Monument and a section of Gifford Pinchot National Forest.

There are several tourist attractions in the area. Most popular is probably the **Ape Cave**.
It's a 13,000 foot lava tube, the longest in the U.S. You can walk the entire length of the

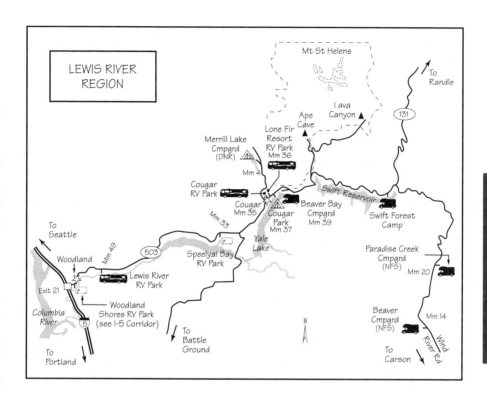

cave. Most children love it.

A popular but difficult hike is this area is the one to the **southern rim of Mt St Helens**. The trail starts not far beyond Ape Cave and climbs 4.5 miles and 4,500 feet to the rim. It's very difficult, sometimes dangerous, and weather is a big factor.

Lewis River Region Campgrounds

● **LEWIS RIVER RV PARK** *(Open All Year)*
Res and Info: (360) 225-9556
Location: 5 Miles (8 Km) E of Exit 21 of I-5

GPS Location: 45.93859 N, 122.67130 W, Near Sea Level

70 Sites – This is a rural residential RV park with quite a few sites for travelers. The campground is behind and next to a country store, and on the banks of the Lewis River. Sites are back-ins, some to 45 feet. Amenities include a seasonal swimming pool. From Exit 21 on I-5 follow the Lewis River Road (Hwy 503) west about 5 miles (8 km) to the store and campground.

● **COUGAR RV PARK** *(Open All Year)*
Res and Info: (360) 238-5224,
www.cougarrv.net
Location: Cougar

GPS Location: 46.04857 N, 122.30737 W, 500 Ft

40 Sites – This RV park in the small town of Cougar has tent camping as well as full-hookup back-in and pull-thru sites to 55 feet. You can easily walk to the nearby restaurant and store. From Exit 21 on I-5 follow the Lewis River Road (Hwy 503) west about 28 miles (45 km) to Cougar and the campground.

● **LONE FIR RESORT RV PARK** *(Open All Year)*
   Res and Info: (360) 238-5210, www.lonefirresort.com
   Location: Cougar

   GPS Location: 46.05096 N, 122.30319 W, 500 Ft

36 Sites – The Lone Fir has tent camping and back-in sites to 60 feet as well as a couple of slightly longer pull-thrus. There is a restaurant and a seasonal swimming pool too. From Exit 21 on I-5 follow the Lewis River Road (Hwy 503) west about 28 miles (45 km) to Cougar and the campground which is just beyond the Cougar RV Park described above.

○ **COUGAR PARK** *(Pacific Power and Light)*
   (Open May 25 to Sept 10 – Varies)
   Res and Info: (503) 813-6666
   Location: 1 Mile (2 Km) E of Cougar

   GPS Location: 46.05491 N, 122.29145 W, 400 Ft

45 Sites – Cougar Park is a Pacific Power and Light campground on Yale Reservoir. It's a tent-only vehicle accessible campground, RVs go to the nearby Beaver Bay campground described below. There's a swimming beach here as well as restroom buildings with toilets and showers. From Exit 21 on I-5 follow the Lewis River Road (Hwy 503) west about 29 miles (47 km) to the entrance road. Turn here and in a short distance you'll reach the park.

○ **BEAVER BAY RECREATION AREA**
   (Open April 25 to Sept 28 – Varies)
   Information: (503) 813-6666
   Location: 2 Miles (3 Km) E of Cougar

   GPS Location: 46.06038 N, 122.26698 W, 500 Ft

63 Sites – Beaver Bay is a Pacific Power and Light Company RV campground on Yale Reservoir. Access is constricted but with careful driving and scouting ahead you can access RV sites, including some pull-thrus, to about 45 feet. Many are much smaller. Amenities include restrooms with flush toilets and showers, a dump station, host, swimming beach, and boat launch. From Exit 21 on I-5 follow the Lewis River Road (Hwy 503) west about 31 miles (50 km) to the entrance road.

□ **MERRILL LAKE CAMPGROUND** *(DNR)*
   (Open May 15 to Sept 15 – Varies)
   Location: 4 Miles (6 Km) N of Cougar

   GPS Location: 46.09470 N, 122.31981 W, 1,500 Ft

7 Sites – Merrill Lake Campground is a Washington Department of Natural Resources campground. Camping is free but to stay here you must have a current State Parks/Recreation Pass and there is a three day limit. The sites are walk-in tent sites but there are parking spaces for vehicles the size of cars or vans. There are picnic tables, fire pits, vault toilets, and a hand water pump. The water must be treated to be potable. Merrill Lake is fly fishing only with a five mile an hour speed limit. Fishing from boats with engines

is prohibited. To reach the campground drive north on FS Road 8100 from the junction on Hwy 503 about a half-mile west of Cougar. The road is signed as Kalama Recreation Area. There are signs to the campground, the distance is 4.7 miles (7.6 km).

○ **SWIFT FOREST CAMP** *(Open April 28 to Nov 30 – Varies)*
Information: (503) 813-6666
Location: 18 Miles (29 Km) E of Cougar

GPS Location: 46.05414 N, 122.03927 W, 900 Ft

93 Sites – Swift Forest Camp is a Pacific Power and Light Company campground on the Swift Reservoir. It's fairly upscale with paved roads and paved parking sites off two loop roads. Sites are back-ins to 30 feet. Amenities include flush toilets, a dump station, a boat ramp, and swimming beach. From Exit 21 on I-5 follow the Lewis River Road (Hwy 503) west about 46 miles (74 km) to the entrance road.

■ **PARADISE CREEK CAMPGROUND** *(Open May 15 to Sept 15 – Varies)*
Reservations: www.recreation.gov, (877) 444-6777
Information: (360) 891-5000
Location: 20 Miles (33 Km) N of Carson, WA

GPS Location: 45.95001 N, 121.93644 W, 1,500 Ft

42 Sites – This Gifford Pinchot National Forest campground has paved roads and sites as well as some tent pads. Sites are back-ins to about 35 feet. Easiest access to this campground is from Hwy 14 on the north side of the Columbia River at Carson. Drive 14 miles (23 km) north on the Wind River Road, then north another 6 miles (10 km) on Forest Road 30 to the campground.

■ **BEAVER CAMPGROUND** *(NFS)*
(Open May 15 to Sept 15 – Varies)
Reservations: www.recreation.gov, (877) 444-6777
Information: (509) 395-3400
Location: 20 Miles (33 Km) N of Carson

GPS Location: 45.85507 N, 121.95650 W, 1,000 Ft

24 Sites – This is another nice Gifford Pinchot National Forest campground with paved roads and parking. Sites are mostly back-ins to about 30 feet. Access is from Hwy 14 on the north side of the Columbia River at Carson. Drive 13 miles (21 km) north on Wind River Road to the campground.

MOSCOW, PULLMAN, AND THE PALOUSE

These two college towns are located just a few miles from each other on opposite sides of the Washington-Idaho state line. The climate here is ideal for summer visits with clear bright sunny days and comfortable evenings.

Moscow (population 24,000) is the home of the **University of Idaho**. The campus (with an enrolment of about 14,000) overlooks the town from the southwest. In addition to the campus, attractions in Moscow include the old-fashioned and active **central business district**, the **Appaloosa Museum and Heritage Center**, the **Idaho Forest Fire Museum**, and the **Latah County Historical Museum**. Bikers and walkers appreciate the 9-mile (14.5 km) bike trail connecting Moscow with Pullman.

Pullman (population 30,000) is home to **Washington State University**. The university

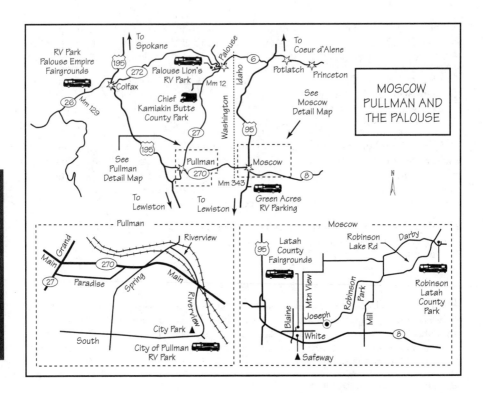

has 22,000 students so it considerably augments the town's population and social life. Pullman is similar to Moscow with a pleasant downtown area and an attractive campus. The school here runs its own creamery. You wouldn't want to visit this area and not purchase some of their famous **Cougar Cheese**, particularly the Cougar Gold!

Moscow and Pullman are surrounded by an area of rolling cropland known as the **Palouse**. This scenic area produces dry peas, lentils, and wheat. In fact, the Palouse is the dry pea and lentil capital of the nation. Pullman hosts the **National Lentil Festival** during the second half of August. For a view of the Palouse your best bet is **Steptoe Butte**. The 3,612-foot-tall quartzite outcrop is a Washington state park. It is located about 30 miles (48 km) north of Pullman beyond Colfax. Unfortunately there is no campground.

Moscow, ID, Pullman, WA and the Palouse Campgrounds

○ **CITY OF PULLMAN RV PARK** *(Open April 1 to Nov 30)*
   Res and Info: (509) 334-4555, (509) 338-3228
   Location: Pullman

   GPS Location: 46.72556 N, 117.17083 W, 2,400 Ft

29 Sites – This is a small city campground. Sites are back-ins to 40 feet. Tents are pitched on grass next to the Palouse River. Restroom facilities are limited to port-a-potties. From SR-270 between Pullman and Moscow you want to drive north on NE Spring Street. This is the first street west of the

railroad overpass which is about a half-mile east of Main in downtown Pullman. Follow NE Spring and then NE Riverview around to the right and under the highway for .4 mile (.6 km) to the campground entrance.

○ **LATAH COUNTY FAIRGROUNDS** *(Open All Year)*
Information: (208) 883-5722
Location: Moscow

GPS Location: 46.72361 N, 116.98417 W, 2,600 Ft

5 Sites – This fairgrounds in Moscow has 5 full-hookup back-ins to 45 feet. Restrooms are portable toilets. There is also a dump station. The fairgrounds are conveniently located near the Safeway on the east side of town. There are frequent weekend events at this small fairgrounds, often the camping sites are occupied. It is always a good idea to call ahead to check availability. From central Moscow head east on SR-8. Turn north on White Street, the street just west of the Tesoro. It will take you behind the Safeway. Go one block, turn right, and you'll soon see the fairgrounds entrance on your left.

● **GREEN ACRES RV PARKING** *(Open All Year)*
Information: (208) 882-7487
Location: 1 Mile (2 Km) S of Moscow

GPS Location: 46.69639 N, 117.00750 W, 2,700 Ft

6 Sites – Although facilities are minimal this is a convenient place for self-contained rigs. Sites are back-ins and pull-thrus and some will take RVs to 45 feet. There is no potable water available. The RV park is located just off the east side of US-95 some 1.5 miles (2.4 km) south of Moscow.

○ **ROBINSON LATAH COUNTY PARK** *(Open All Year)*
Res and Info: (208) 883-5709
Location: 5 Miles (8 Km) E of Moscow

GPS Location: 46.75444 N, 116.90833 W, 2,700 Ft

8 Sites – This little county park is located in the countryside just east of Moscow. There are five back-in RV sites that will take RVs to 45 feet. There is also a separate tent-camping area with three grass sites. From Moscow drive east on SR-8. About .2 miles (.3 km) past the Safeway turn left on Mountain View Road. There is a sign at this turn and at the other turns on the route to the park. In .5 miles (.8 km) turn right on Joseph Street and follow the signs for 4.4 miles (7.1 km) to the park.

○ **CHIEF KAMIAKIN BUTTE COUNTY PARK** *(Open All Year)*
Location: 12 Miles (19 Km) N of Pullman

GPS Location: 46.87000 N, 117.15306 W, 2,900 Ft

7 Sites – This small campground occupies a wooded butte in the middle of Washington's famous wheat-growing country. The butte is covered with Ponderosa Pine and the 3.5-mile Pine Ridge Trail begins at a day use area near the campground. Sites here are small, in fact vehicles over 18 feet are prohibited. The campground is best for tents or perhaps small vans. Sites have picnic tables and fire rings and there is a vault toilet. Access to the park is signed off SR-27 about 11 miles (18 km) north of Pullman. Turn west onto Fugate Road, drive 1.1 miles (1.8 km) and turn left onto Kamiak Butte Park Road. You'll reach the day-use are in .8 mile (1.3 km), drive through to the campground entrance.

○ **PALOUSE LIONS RV PARK** *(Open All Year)*
Res and Info: (509) 878-1811,
          www.visitpalouse.com/rvpark.html
Location: Palouse, WA

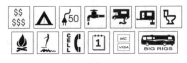

GPS Location: 46.90957 N, 117.08035 W, 2,400 Ft

10 Sites – This is a small campground for self-contained RVs in the town of Palouse. There are back-in and pull-thru sites to 75 feet with full hookups. Use of the municipal swimming pool is included. You can easily walk to the center of town, about two blocks. From central Palouse drive west on W Main Street, in just two blocks you'll see the RV park on the right.

○ **RV PARK PALOUSE EMPIRE FAIRGROUNDS** *(Open All Year)*
Res and Info: (509) 397-6238 or 3753,
          www.palouseempirefair.org
Location: 4 Miles (6 Km) W of Colfax

GPS Location: 46.86694 N, 117.43583 W, 2,100 Ft

30 Sites – The Palouse Empire Fairgrounds are in a rural location away from any towns. The fair is held in early September and there are activities at the fairgrounds on Labor Day, but at other times the campground is likely to be almost empty. They have a grassy field with RV hookups for electricity and water, there is also a dump station. Restrooms have flush toilets but no showers. The fairgrounds are located about 4 miles (6 km) west of Colfax on SR-26. The access gate for the camping area is on the west side of the complex.

MOSES LAKE AND THE POTHOLES

Moses Lake (population 20,000) is located at the center of Washington state in a region with hot dry summers and cold, but clear, winters. If fact, the weather here is clear so predictably that the local airport is a beehive of flying activity. Much of the country's large aircraft flight training takes place out of the Moses Lake airport because it's so big, so remote, and has such decent weather. Of course it's also conveniently close to the Boeing factories in Seattle. Moses Lake has even been designated an alternate landing site for the space shuttle.

Recreational activities are centered around two large lakes. **Moses Lake** itself practically surrounds the town and to the south is the large **Potholes Reservoir**. Water sports of all types are popular. Even the fishing is good with warm water species like walleye, trout, bass, perch, crappie, and catfish.

There are other attractions. In town there's the **Moses Lake Museum and Art Center** with an extensive collection of native American artifacts as well as changing art exhibits. For physical fun try the **Surf'n Slide Water Park** a large water park with 200-foot slides, a beach area, and other attractions.

Just south of Moses Lake is the **Grand County Off Road Vehicle Area**. It's located in an area of sand dunes and has no facilities, but camping is allowed. Follow Division Street south or take Exit 174 and drive south. Both enter the off-road area.

Moses Lake is also a well known birding area. Hotspots are south of town and include the northern border of Potholes Reservoir as well as the **Seep Lakes Wildlife Area** and **Columbia National Wildlife Refuge** south of the reservoir.

Moses Lake and the Potholes Campgrounds

○ **MOSES LAKE CASCADE CAMPGROUND**
   (Open April 15 to Sept 15 – Varies)
   Res and Info: (509) 764-3805, (509) 766-9240,
                 www.mlrec.com/cascade-camping_23.html
   Location: 2 Miles (3 Km) W of Moses Lake

   GPS Location: 47.13944 N, 119.31111 W, 1,000 Ft

85 Sites – This is a municipal campground set on the shore of Moses Lake to the west of the central part of the town of Moses Lake. Parking here is on grass and most of the back-in sites are suitable for RVs to about 30 feet. A few sites are designated for RVs to 38 feet. To reach the campground leave I-90 at Exit 176. Drive north on SR-171 for 2.8 miles (4.5 km) and turn left on S. Alder Street. Drive .4 mile (.6 km) across the bridge and turn left on West Valley Road. Follow West Valley for 1.6 miles (2.6 km) until it curves to the right and descends the hillside, you'll see the campground along the shore of the lake below. Turn left into the entrance and then immediately left again to access the campground.

○ **GRANT COUNTY FAIRGROUNDS** *(Open All Year)*
   Information: (509) 765-3581,
                 www.gcfairgrounds.com/campgrounds.html
   Location: Moses Lake

   GPS Location: 47.14502 N, 119.30882 W, 1,100 Ft

550 Sites – The fairgrounds in Moses Lake has extensive camping facilities including

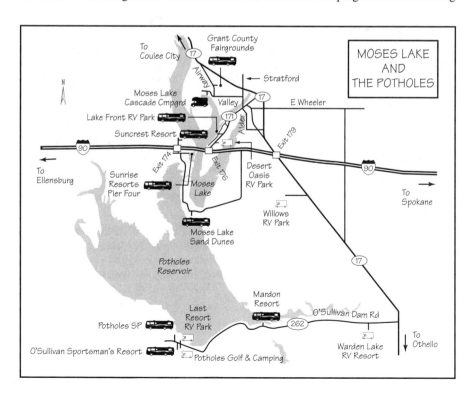

tent, full hookup, and partial hookup sites. There are dump stations, restrooms with showers, and even Wi-Fi. As always with a fairground campsite it's best to call ahead to see if there is an event in progress or if there are special access or check-in procedures. To reach the campground leave I-90 at Exit 176. Drive north on SR-171 for 2.8 miles (4.5 km) and turn left on S. Alder Street. Drive .4 mile (.6 km) across the bridge and turn left on West Valley Road. Follow West Valley for 1.4 miles (2.3 km) and then turn right on Airway Dr NE. You'll soon see the campground entrance on the right.

● **LAKE FRONT RV PARK** *(Open All Year)*
   Res and Info: (509) 765-8294
   Location: Moses Lake

   GPS Location: 47.11013 N, 119.30764 W, 1,000 Ft

42 Sites – This is a small campground that is located on the lakeshore near downtown Moses Lake. It was formerly called the Big Sun Resort. It's an older place but is being renovated, sites have been enlarged and some are now over 55 feet long. These have pull-in access directly off the city street. Exit I-90 at Exit 176 and drive north on SR-171. At .6 mile (.9 km) you'll see the sign for the campground, turn left and drive a block to the campground. Park on the street, there's always lots of room, and walk into the park to check in.

● **SUNCREST RESORT** *(Open All Year)*
   Res and Info: (509) 765-0355,
                infor@suncrestresort.com,
                www.suncrestresort.com
   Location: 5 Miles (8 Km) SW of Moses Lake

   GPS Location: 47.10806 N, 119.34278 W, 1,000 Ft

83 Sites – Suncrest is a nice park located just off I-90 just outside and to the west of Moses Lake. Although it's not on the lakeshore there's a beautiful pool and huge hot tub (60-person capacity!) Sites are paved back-ins and pull-thrus to 65 feet. They are narrow but slides will fit. Access is via Exit 174 of I-90. Drive north a short distance and you'll see the entrance.

● **SUNRISE RESORTS PIER FOUR**
      (Open All Year)
   Res and Info: (509) 765-6319,
                www.sunriseresorts.com/
                pier4.jsp
   Location: Moses Lake

   GPS Location: 47.10204 N, 119.32775 W, 1,000 Ft

180 Sites – The Pier Four sits on the shore of Moses Lake just south of the freeway crossing and next to Moses Lake State Park. It has paved pull-thru and back-in sites separated by grass. Amenities include a pool, Jacuzzi, beach area on the lake, and a boat ramp. This is a member resort but non members are welcomed and can make reservations. From I-5 take Exit 174 and drive south to Sage Road, it's a block or so. Turn left and follow Sage Rd for .8 mile (1.3 km) to the park.

☐ **POTHOLES STATE PARK** *(Open All Year)*
Reservations: www.parks.wa.gov/reservations/,
                        (888) 226-7688
Information: (509) 346-2759, (360) 902-8844,
                        www.parks.wa.gov
Location: 22 Miles (35 Km) S of Moses Lake

  GPS Location: 46.97361 N, 119.34750 W, 1,000 Ft

121 Sites – This campground is located on the shores of the Potholes Reservoir to the south of Moses Lake. This reservoir and the area to the south, known as the Seep Lakes, are very popular with birders. It's also an important part of the Columbia River irrigation scheme. The state park is a large one and sites extend to 50 feet since they are back-ins off large circles that are paved in the middle. The park is water oriented with boat ramps, a dock, and a swimming area. Water levels in the reservoir fluctuate quite a bit from spring to fall. There are also large grassy areas that are great for kids. Take Exit 179 from I-90 and drive south on SR-17 for 9.9 miles (16 km). Turn right on the O'Sullivan Dam Road which is also known as SR- 262. It will lead you 12.3 miles (19.8 km) to the campground entrance; you'll cross the large earth dam en route.

● **O'SULLIVAN SPORTSMAN'S RESORT**
      (Open All Year)
Reservations: (888) 346-2447
Information: (509) 346-2447, osullivan@nwi.net,
      www.osullivansportsmanresort.com
Location: 21 Miles (34 Km) S of Moses Lake

   GPS Location: 46.97000 N, 119.34528 W, 1,000 Ft

160 Sites – This is a membership campground located near the state park. It usually has room for non-members. The campground is not located next to the water but has large back-in and pull-thru sites for RVs to 45 feet and good amenities including a seasonal swimming pool and cable TV. Take Exit 179 from I-90 and drive south on SR-17 for 9.9 miles (16 km). Turn right on the O'Sullivan Dam Road which is also known as SR-262. It will lead you 11.2 miles (18.1 km) to the campground entrance; you'll cross the large earth dam en route.

● **MARDON RESORT** *(Open All Year)*
Reservations: (800) 416-2736
Information: (509) 346-2651, info@mardonresort.com,
                        www.mardonresort.com
Location: 20 Miles (32 Km) S of Moses Lake

  GPS Location: 46.96583 N, 119.32000 W, 1,000 Ft

184 Sites – This is a large and venerable resort located on the shore of Potholes Reservoir. There are many long-term residents and also many tent and RV sites for travelers. Sites are back-ins and pull-thrus to 50 feet. Amenities include a grocery store, restaurant, and swimming beach. Take Exit 179 from I-90 and drive south on SR-17 for 9.9 miles (16 km). Turn right on the O'Sullivan Dam Road which is also known as SR- 262. It will lead you 10 miles (16.1 km) to the campground entrance; you'll cross the large earth dam en route.

WASHINGTON

○ **MOSES LAKE SAND DUNES** *(Open All Year)*
  Information: (509) 762-1160 (Grant County Sheriff's Office)
  Location: 5 Miles (8 Km) S of Moses Lake

GPS Location: 47.06143 N, 119.32655 W, 1000 Ft

This is a 3,000 acre area of sand dunes located between the Potholes Reservoir and Moses Lake. It's also called the Grant County ORV Area. It's an official ORV area and a Washington State ORV sticker is required. The only facilities are vault toilets. There is lake access. Overnight camping is allowed with the sticker. From I-5 take Exit 174 and drive south to Sage Road, it's a block or so. Turn left and follow Sage Rd for .3 mile (.5 km) to the east. Turn right on S Sand Dunes Road and follow it about 4 miles (6.5 km) to the off road vehicle area.

MT RAINIER NATIONAL PARK

The centerpiece of this national park is 14,411 ft. Mt Rainier. It's the tallest mountain in the Cascades, the tallest along the west coast until you reach Mt Whitney in California. This was an early national park, it was created in 1899 and many of the structures in the park were built by the CCC during the 1930s.

Think of the park as having two centers of interest for vehicle-based visitors. One centers around the visitor center at **Paradise** on the south side of the mountain, the other centers around the visitor center at **Sunrise** on the northeast side of the mountain. Of course, if you are a hiker the entire park is open to you.

Paradise sits at the 5,400-foot level of the mountain. Most people who climb the mountain start from the huge Paradise parking lot. There is a year-round visitor center here. You'll also want to visit the old Paradise Inn. If the weather allows you can follow trails through the surrounding meadows and enjoy the wildflowers and the views.

There may be two centers of interest but there are three entrance to the park. Campgrounds tend to be near these entrances, both inside and outside the park. It's best not to take large RVs (say over 25 feet) up onto the mountain since roads are steep and narrow. Instead park them at one of the campgrounds near the entrances and use a tow car to access Paradise or Sunshine. Note that no fuel is available inside the park. Also note that both the Stevens Canyon Road (from the Ohanepecosh Entrance) and the Sunrise Road are closed by snow in winter.

The **Nisqually Entrance** is located at the far southwest corner of the park. This is often thought of as the main entrance. It provides the shortest access route to the Paradise area on the south side of the mountain. Campgrounds near this entrance are the first ones listed below: Cougar Rock Campground, Mounthaven Resort, Gateway Inn, Big Creek Campground and Alder Lake Park. Not far inside the entrance is Longmire, which has the only hotel in the park that is open year-round. At Longmire you can take a look at the **National Park Inn** and the **Longmire Museum**. The short and easy **Trail of the Shadows** lets you explore the immediate area. The highway distance to Paradise from the Nisqually Entrance is 17 miles (27 km).

Also giving access to Paradise, but with a much longer access route, is **Ohanapecosh Entrance**. It's near the southeast corner of the park. Near this entrance are Ohanapecosh Campground, La Wis Wis Campground, and the Packwood RV Park. The Stevens Canyon Road leads from this entrance to Paradise, a distance of 21 miles (34 km). From

Ohanapecosh the highway climbs over Backbone Ridge, descends to cross the Muddy Fork of the Cowlitz River at Box Canyon, and then climbs through Stevens Canyon to reach the high country at Paradise. The lower elevations crossed by the highway are largely covered with old-growth evergreen forest. An excellent way to enjoy the trees is to hike the 1.5 mile (2.4 km) **Grove of the Patriarchs interpretive trail**. It's located near the entrance. Another good stop is the one at **Reflection Lakes** for a photo of the mountain.

On the eastern border of the park but outside the park entrances SR-410 and then SR-123 cross Cayuse Pass at 4,694 feet. This highway connects Enumclaw to the north with US-12 which crosses south of the park. SR-410 is also the location of the third entrance to the park, the White River Entrance. Campgrounds handy to this entrance are White River Campground, The Dalles Campground, and Silver Springs Campground. It's 15 miles (24 km) from SR-410 up to Sunrise. The road passes White River Campground, the Frying Pan Creek Trailhead, and then loops its way up the side of the mountain to the meadows around Sunrise. You'll find a visitor's center here, also the **Sunrise Lodge**, and lots of trails. Sunrise is as high as you can get on the mountain in your car, 6,400 feet, and is only accessible and open from July to early September.

Near the White River Entrance but toward the east away from the park SR-410 climbs to cross Chinook Pass. You might want to take a short side trip up to Lake Tipsoo just below the pass for great views back westward to the mountain (assuming good weather).

The campgrounds along US-12 south of the mountain aren't quite as convenient to Mt Rainier as the ones near the entrances but they have an additional benefit. From the area of Randle you can easily access the eastern viewpoints of **Mt St Helens National Monu-**

GOOD WALKING TRAILS AT THE PARADISE VISITOR CENTER AT MT RAINIER

WASHINGTON

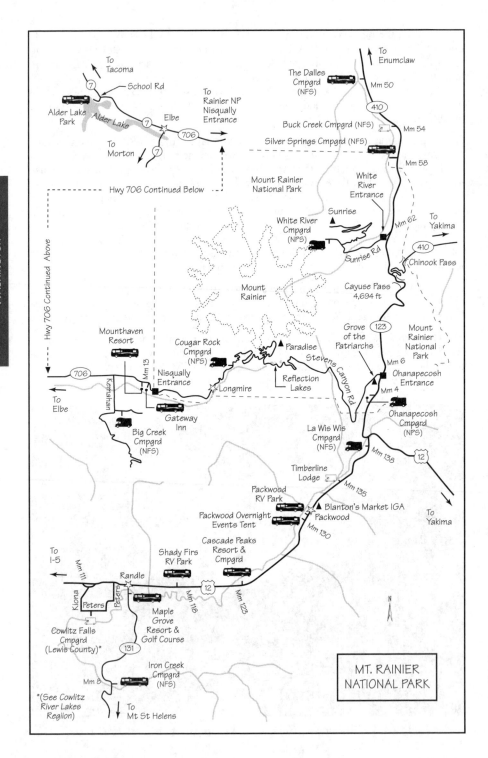

MT. RAINIER
NATIONAL PARK

ment. Campgrounds listed below that are in this area are Cascade Peaks Resort and Campground, Shady Firs RV Park, Maple Grove Resort and Golf Course, and Iron Creek Campground. The campgrounds in this chapter listed under *Cowlitz River Lakes Region* are pretty good places to stay while visiting the park too.

To access the Windy Ridge Viewpoint, which has great views of the caldera blowout on Mt St Helens, you drive south from Randle on forest service roads a distance of 36 miles (58 km). The route is well signed, the road is paved, and the view is spectacular. It's also a lot less crowded than the main viewpoints accessible from farther west. See the *Mt St Helens* section for information about access and campgrounds on that side.

Mt Rainier National Park Campgrounds

■ **COUGAR ROCK CAMPGROUND** *(Open May 25 to Oct 15 – Varies)*
Reservations: www.recreation.gov, (800) 365-2267
Information: (360) 569-2211
Location: 9 Miles (15 Km) Inside Nisqually Entrance,

GPS Location: 46.76750 N, 121.79222 W, 3,200 Ft

200 Sites – Cougar Rock is the main Mt Rainier National Park Campground for the southwest part of the park. It is convenient for visits to the Paradise Visitor Center. There is a recommended size limit here of coaches to 35 feet and trailers to 27 feet (although the campground is set on uneven ground so sites are irregular and many are much shorter). Most sites are back-ins but there are a few narrow pull-thrus. Some sites have timber-framed tent pads. Reservations are available and are definitely necessary from late July 1 to Labor day. The campground is 8.6 miles (14 km) inside the Nisqually Entrance, 8.9 miles (14.4 km) from Paradise Visitor Center.

● **MOUNTHAVEN RESORT** *(Open All Year)*
Reservations: (800) 456-9380
Information: (360) 569-2594, info@mounthaven.com,
                www.mounthaven.com
Location: .8 Mile (1.3 Km) Outside Nisqually Entrance
GPS Location: 46.74861 N, 121.92750 W, 2,000 Ft

16 Sites – This resort is located very near the southwest entrance to the park and is a good base if you like more amenities than the park campgrounds offer. It has cabins and good long RV sites to 60 feet with full hookups under big trees. The campground is known for its quiet and is well-managed, amenities include a hot tub. The resort is located on the south side of the highway .8 mile (1.3 km) outside the Nisqually entrance to the park.

● **GATEWAY INN** *(Open All Year)*
Res and Info: (360) 569-2506,
                info@gatewayinnonline.com,
                www.gatewayinnonline.com
Location: .   .2 Mile (.3 Km) Outside Nisqually Entrance
GPS Location: 46.74184 N, 121.92032 W, 1,900 Ft

12 Sites – The Gateway Inn is a restaurant, small store, motel, and RV park just outside the park entrance. RV sites are full and partial hookup back-ins to 40 feet. There are no permanent restroom facilities but a portable toilet is available in summer to accommodate tent campers. The inn is located on the south side of the highway about .2 mile (.3 km) outside the Nisqually entrance to the park.

WASHINGTON

■ **BIG CREEK CAMPGROUND** *(Open May 25 to Sept 25 – Varies)*
  Reservations: www.recreation.gov, (877) 444-6777
  Information: (360) 497-1100
  Location: 5 Miles (8 Km) From Nisqually Entrance

GPS Location: 46.73583 N, 121.97083 W, 1,800 Ft

29 Sites – This is a Gifford Pinchot National Forest campground convenient to the southeast entrance to Rainier Park. Both roads and sites are paved. Some sites here will take coaches to 35 feet but access roads are narrow so exercise caution. Water is from faucets and there is usually a host. From a point on SR-706 some 3.5 miles (5.6 km) west of the Nisqually entrance to the park drive south on Kemahan Rd. In 1.4 miles (2.3 km) the road makes a 90° left and in another .5 mile (.8 km) you'll see the entrance on your right.

○ **ALDER LAKE PARK** *(Open Jan 2 – Dec 19)*
  Reservations: (888) 226-7688
  Information: (360) 569-2778
  Location: 16 Miles (26 Km) West of Nisqually
                   Entrance to Mt Rainier Nat Park

GPS Location: (46.799314 N, 122.29421 W, 1,200 Ft

173 Sites – This large Tacoma Power campground on Alder Lake makes a decent base for exploring Mt Rainier National Park since it's only 16 miles (26 km) west of the Nisqually Entrance to the park. Sites are located in four campgrounds including one removed 4 miles from the others at Rocky Point and have full, partial, or no hookups. Sites are back-ins and sometimes narrow pull-thrus to 50 feet. Access roads require careful driving and it can be difficult to level rigs on many sites. Amenities include a boat ramp, playgrounds and swimming beach. The campground is located off School Road which leaves SR-7 about 5.6 miles (9.0 km) northwest of Elbe which is 10.3 miles (16.6 km) west of the Nisqually entrance to Mt Rainier National Park.

■ **OHANAPECOSH CAMPGROUND**
    (Open May 25 to Oct 10 – Varies)
  Reservations: www.recreation.gov, (800) 365-2267
  Information: (360) 569-2211
  Location: 2 Miles (3 Km) S of Ohanapecosh Entrance

GPS Location: 46.73278 N, 121.56917 W, 1,900 Ft

188 Sites – Ohanapecosh is an older national park campground that serves the southeastern portion of the park. It is set in huge evergreens and tends to be a little dark. Roads are paved and parking pads are gravel. Sites were laid out in the days of much smaller rigs, the park recommends a size limit of 27 feet for trailers (and 5th wheels) and 32 feet for motorhomes. The limits are due to both site size and access road complications. Reservations are available and can be important from late June to Labor Day because this is a busy campground. The campground entrance is actually outside the park entrance station but the campground is in the park. It's 1.8 miles (2.9 km) south on SR-123 from the entrance road.

■ **LA WIS WIS CAMPGROUND** *(Open May 15 to Sept 30 – Varies)*
  Reservations: www.recreation.gov, (877) 444-6777
  Information: (360) 494-0600
  Location: 6 Miles (10 Km) E of Packwood

GPS Location: 46.67778 N, 121.57750 W, 1,400 Ft

115 Sites – This Gifford Pinchot National Forest campground is convenient to the south-east entrance to the park. It's an older campground with small sites suitable for RVs to about 30 feet. It borders the Clear Fork of the Cowlitz River, trout fishing is possible. There are short trails to the Blue Hole on the Ohanapecosh River and to Purcell Falls. The entrance to the campground is on the north side of the highway .6 miles (1 km) south of the intersection of US-12 and SR-123. It's 6 miles (10 km) east of Packwood and 6.1 (9.8 km) miles from the Ohanapecosh Entrance to the Park.

● **PACKWOOD RV PARK** *(Open All Year)*
  Res and Info: (360) 494-5145
  Location: Packwood

  GPS Location: 46.60611 N, 121.67250 W, 1,000 Ft

89 Sites – Located in the middle of Packwood, this old RV park is a relaxed place in a relaxed town. You can stroll across the street to a restaurant or the grocery store, things couldn't be more convenient. The campground is set under large trees providing lots of shade. Parking is on grass with room for any size rig. Full hookups are available, as are sites with electricity and water only. Some sites are pull-thrus suitable for RVs to 45 feet. Sites are located in two places, some next to the office and others across the street in a large grassy lot. The campground sits near the center of town, it is well-signed and hard to miss.

○ **PACKWOOD OVERNIGHT EVENTS TENT** *(Open All Year)*
  Information: (360) 494-0808, www.packwoodonline.com
  Location: Packwood

  GPS Location: 46.60160 N, 121.67596 W, 1,000 Ft

10 Sites – The city of Packwood has a small no-hookup camper area next to their Senior Citizen center. It offers no hookups, just a grassy lot. A water faucet is available but there are no restrooms.

■ **WHITE RIVER CAMPGROUND** *(Open June 25 to Sept 15 – Varies)*
  Information: (360) 569-2211
  Location: 43 Miles (69 Km) SE of Enumclaw

  GPS Location: 46.90222 N, 121.63889 W, 4,400 Ft

112 Sites – White River is the Mt Rainier National Park campground that services the northeast portion of the park. The entrance to this area is called the White River entrance and one road leads up to the Sunrise Visitor Center. This campground is off that road. It sits in a valley with the mountain looming at the top. Climbers often start here to head up this side of the mountain. There are several trails including one that climbs steeply to Sunrise and another that leads to an overlook of Emmons Glacier. Sites here are remark-ably short, most would not accommodate a 25-foot RV comfortably, but there are a few that will take very carefully driven 30-footers. The campground entrance is on the left 5.3 miles (8.6 km) from the White River Entrance and 10 miles (16 km) from Sunrise.

■ **THE DALLES CAMPGROUND**
  (Open Memorial Day to Labor Day – Varies)
  Reservations: www.recreation.gov, (877) 444-6777
  Information: (360) 825-6585
  Location: 26 Miles (42 Km) SE of Enumclaw

  GPS Location: 47.06833 N, 121.57694 W, 2,100 Ft

45 Sites – The Dalles Mt Baker-Snoqualmie National Forest campground is situated next to the White River along the SR-410, the Mather Parkway, as it climbs toward Chinook and Cayuse Passes. It's situated in dense old growth evergreens. Sites here vary a great deal in size from back-ins suitable only for RVs to 22 feet to a few large back-in sites that will just barely take a 45-footer. There's a half-mile barrier-free nature trail and a very large old-growth Douglas-fir nearby. The campground is located 26 miles (42 km) southeast of Enumclaw and 12 miles (19 km) north of the cutoff to Sunrise.

■ SILVER SPRINGS CAMPGROUND
   (Open Memorial Day to Labor Day – Varies)
Reservations: www.recreation.gov, (877) 444-6777
Information: (360) 825-6585
Location: 32 Miles (52 Km) SE of Enumclaw

   GPS Location: 46.99333 N, 121.53222 W, 2,700 Ft

56 Sites – This is a second national forest campground located along SR-410, the Mather Parkway, as it climbs toward the passes. This one too is along the White River. There are a few more large sites in this campground but it is very similar to The Dalles, described above. The campground is located 32 miles (52 km) southeast of Enumclaw and 6 miles (10 km) north of the cutoff to Sunrise.

● CASCADE PEAKS RESORT AND CAMPGROUND
   (Open All Year)
Reservations: (866) 255-2931
Information: (360) 494-9202, (360) 494-7931,
           www.cascadervresort.com
Location: 7 Miles (11 Km) W of Packwood

   GPS Location: 46.53417 N, 121.77750 W, 900 Ft

700 Sites – This is a very large campground. It has a lot of amenities and sells memberships and individual sites. Travelers are welcome, however. Amenities include two swimming pools, a hot tub and sauna. Sites are varied with tent areas, full-hookups for RVs to 45 feet, and many electric and water sites set in trees. The campground is located north of US-12 some 8 miles (13 km) east of Randle and 7 miles (11 km) west of Packwood.

● SHADY FIRS RV PARK *(Open All Year)*
Res and Info: (360) 497-6108
Location: 2 Miles (3.2 Km) East of
           Randle, WA

   GPS Location: 46.53458 N, 121.90920 W, 900 Ft

35 Sites – This small older park has grass RV sites under evergreens off paved gravel roads as well as a tent camping area and a small store. It's located just east of Randle on the north side of the highway.

● MAPLE GROVE RESORT AND GOLF COURSE
   (Open All Year)
Information: (360) 497-2742,
           www.kmresorts.com/resorts/maple-
           grove
Location: Randle

   GPS Location: 46.52972 N, 121.95417 W, 800 Ft

175 Sites – This is another membership resort but

does accept Good Sam members and other affiliations. Call to check. It often has room for travelers during the week in the summer and all week the rest of the year. Amenities include a nine-hole golf course and an indoor swimming pool and hot tub. The campground is in two areas. There's a big-rig park with pull-thrus suitable for 45 footers in a big open field. There's also a shaded area with smaller sites much like a forest service campground but with electrical hookups in about half of the 78 sites. The campground is located just south of the intersection of US-12 and SR-131 in Randle.

■ IRON CREEK CAMPGROUND *(Open May 20 to Sept 26 – Varies)*
   Reservations: www.recreation.gov, (877) 444-6777
   Information: (360) 497-1100
   Location: 9 Miles (15 Km) S of Randle

   GPS Location: 46.42833 N, 121.98528 W, 1,100 Ft

98 Sites – This campground in the Gifford Pinchot National Forest makes a great base for exploring both Rainier and the east side of Mt St Helens. For a national forest campground it's a big place with almost 100 sites. It can accommodate big rigs with sites to 45 feet and adequate maneuvering room. It sits on the Cispus River, fishing is possible. From Randle drive south on SR-131. At the fork at .9 miles (1.5 km) stay right, you'll reach the campground 9.2 miles (14.8 km) south of Randle.

MT ST HELENS NATIONAL VOLCANIC MONUMENT

When Mt St Helens blew on May 18, 1980 it created a unique tourist attraction. The thousands of square miles of devastated landscape make an impressive destination, and a lot of effort and money have been spent to make the mountain accessible. The area is now known as **Mount St Helens National Volcanic Monument**. Easiest access for motorized travelers is from the west and that's what we'll talk about in this sections. See the *Mt Rainier National Park* section for information about approaching the mountain from the east.

A parkway, the **Spirit Lake Memorial Highway**, leads from Exit 49 of I-5 some 51 miles (82 km) eastward toward the mountain. Most of the parkway was built after the eruption. It is wide and beautiful, suitable for any rig. The only problem is that after the Hoffstadt Bluffs Visitor Center at Mile 27 the road climbs rather steeply, sometimes with seven percent grades. You can leave trailers or big rigs at the visitor center and use the tow car to drive on up.

Along the road there are now no less than 4 information centers. This must be the highest concentration of such places in the world and a trip to the mountain for most people is largely a drive from one center to the next. If you do want to get off the road and explore however, you can do so. There are a number of hiking trails accessible from the parkway.

The first stop is **Mount St Helens Visitor Center**. It is about 5 miles (8 km) from I-5 and run by the Forest Service. It has exhibits that make a great introduction to your drive up to the mountain with background information about the eruption. The mountain is not visible from this center.

Stop number two is **Hoffstadt Bluffs Visitor Center** at Mile 27. This center is the most commercial of the four, it seems to be dedicated mostly to selling souvenirs and services. From here you can take a helicopter tour, have a meal in a large restaurant, or buy a souvenir.

VIEW OF MT ST HELENS FROM THE JOHNSTON RIDGE OBSERVATORY

The third center is called **The Charles W. Bingham Forest Learning Center** and is at Mile 33. This one is a Weyerhaeuser operation and explores the timber and logging aspects of the eruption. A huge amount of timber was blown down, much was destroyed but a lot was salvaged. Weyerhaeuser is now doing a lot of replanting. Don't miss this stop, we find it the most interesting of all the centers, it is very well done.

Finally, at Mile 51, is **Johnston Ridge Observatory**. This new center is very close to the mountain, just 5 miles (8 km) from the crater. You can actually see the new swelling lava dome inside the crater because the crater walls on this side were blown out during the eruption. The observatory is so close to the mountain that it is sometimes closed when geologists report that the mountain is active. Johnston Ridge overlooks the devastated Spirit Lake and gives you the best idea of the massive devastation caused by the eruption.

Mt St Helens National Volcanic Monument Campgrounds

● **TOUTLE RIVER RV RESORT** *(Open All Year)*
Res and Info: (360) 274-8373, greatrvresort@aol.com,
          www.greatrvresort.com
Location: I-5 Exit 52, West Side

GPS Location: 46.32385 N, 122.91460 W, 100 Ft

305 Sites – Toutle River is a new, very large, upscale RV park. It's located next to the freeway, with a busy train track on the far side. RV sites are pull-thrus and back-ins to 75 feet. Tent camping is on grass. Since it's a new park there is little shade, newly planted trees will take a while to grow. Amenities include a pool, store, movie pavilion, disc golf, pickleball, sauna, hot tub, poolside and grill. Campfires are in a group

fire pit. Take Exit 52 from I-5 and you'll find the campground entrance on the west side of the highway.

● **Paradise Cove RV Park** *(Open All Year)*
   Res and Info: (360) 274-6785
   Location: I-5 Exit 52, East Side

   GPS Location: 46.32317 N, 122.91078 W, 100 Ft

50 Sites – This older park is primarily a residential park but it does have a few sites available for travelers although few stop here. Sites are haphazardly arranged with parking on grass or gravel. Sites are back-ins and stretch to 45 feet. Take Exit 52 from I-5, the campground is on the east side.

● **Mt St Helens RV Park** *(Open All Year)*
   Res and Info: (360) 274-8522, MSHRVP@aol.com ,
                     www.mtsthelensrvpark.com
   Location: 2 Miles (3 Km) E of I-5 Exit 49

   GPS Location: 46.30611 N, 122.87667 W, 400 Ft

88 Sites – This modern RV park, not far from I-5
Exit 49, makes an excellent base for your visit to Mt St Helens. The sites are arranged on a terraced hillside. Sites are back-ins to 46 feet, both partial and full hookup. Full hookups including cable are available. The campground can provide information and advice about a trip up the mountain. Amenities include a laundry, recreation hall, and playground. To find the campground take Exit 49 from I-5. Drive east on SR-504 for 2

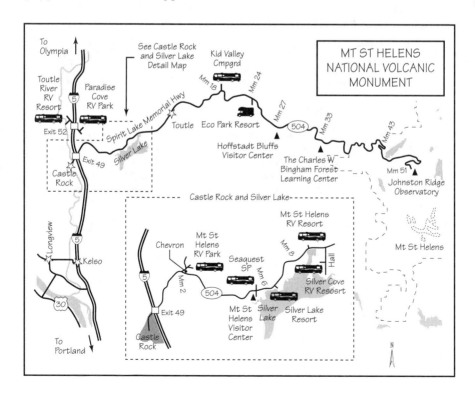

WASHINGTON

miles (3 km). Turn left on Tower Road, you'll see the campground entrance on the right soon after the turn.

☐ SEAQUEST STATE PARK *(Open All Year)*
  Reservations: www.parks.wa.gov/reservations/, (888) 226-7688
  Information: (360) 274-8633, (360) 371-2800,
                www.parks.wa.gov
  Location: 6 Miles (10 Km) E of I-5 Exit 49

  GPS Location: 46.29583 N, 122.81778 W, 400 Ft

88 Sites – This state park offers sites set in huge evergreens. Most sites are suitable for RVs to about 35 feet but the full-hookup area has open side-by-side sites suitable for RVs to 40 feet. The campground is just off SR-504 and a convenient location for a visit to the monument. From Exit 49 on I-5 follow SR-504 east toward the mountain for 6 miles (10 km), the entrance is on the left.

● SILVER LAKE RESORT *(Open All Year)*
  Res and Info: (360) 274-6141,
                contact@silverlake-resort.com,
                www.silverlake-resort.com
  Location: 6 Miles (10 Km) E of I-5 Exit 49

  GPS Location: 46.29724 N, 122.80553 W, 400 Ft

30 Sites – This is a small family run lakeside resort with RV and tent sites arranged between the resort buildings at the lake and the highway. RV sites are back-ins to 40 feet, access can be tight for larger rigs and trailers. There are also several tent sites. Amenities include a boat dock and ramp. From Exit 49 on I-5 follow SR-504 east toward the mountain for 6.1 miles (9.8 km), the resort entrance is on the right.

● MT ST HELENS RV RESORT *(Open All Year)*
  Res and Info: (360) 274-2701,
                office@mtsthelensrvresort.com,
                www.mtsthelensrvresort.com
  Location: 8 Miles (13 Km) E of I-5 Exit 49

  GPS Location: 46.31972 N, 122.77472 W, 400 Ft

46 Sites – This is a roadside fishing resort across the highway from Silver Lake with a dock and rental boats. The restaurant and bar here seem to be very popular with the motorcycle crowd. On the hillside behind the restaurant are RV sites with back-ins and pull-thrus to 50 feet. Nice tents sites are located below and to the right at the edge of the trees. From Exit 49 on I-5 follow SR-504 east toward the mountain for 8.2 miles (13.2 km), the entrance is on the left.

● SILVER COVE RV RESORT *(Open All Year)*
  Res and Info: (360) 967-2057,
                silvercovervresort@comcast.net,
                www.silvercovervresort.com
  Location:

  GPS Location: 46.31247 N, 122.76228 W, 400 Ft

160 Sites – Silver Cove is a large and fairly new big-rig RV park along the shore of Silver Lake. Sites are back-ins with a few pull-thrus to 65 feet. Some sites are along canals connecting to the lake for boat access to sites. From Exit 49 on I-5 follow SR-504 east toward the mountain for 9.1 miles (14.6 km) to Hall Road. Turn right and in another .5 mile (14.6 km) you'll see the entrance on the right.

● **KID VALLEY CAMPGROUND** *(Open All Year)*
   Res and Info: (360) 274-9060, kidvalley@kalama.com,
                www.kidvalley.com
   Location: Mile 18.3 of Spirit Lake Hwy

   GPS Location: 46.37389 N, 122.60944 W, 700 Ft

28 Sites – This small campground is the closest to the mountain with hookups. There are 20 back-in RV sites to 45 feet, some full and some partial hookup. The campground also has tent camping. The 19 Mile House Restaurant and a store are nearby. The campground is located at Mile 18.3 of the Spirit Lake Highway.

● **ECO PARK RESORT** *(Open All Year)*
   Res and Info: (877) 255-1980 or (360) 274-7007,
                www.ecoparkresort.com
   Location: Mile 24.1 of Spirit Lake Hwy

   GPS Location: 46.35500 N, 122.52611 W, 1,100 Ft

8 Sites – The Eco Park Resort offers the closest campground to the Mt St. Helens observatories. There's a café and gift shop up by the highway and RV sites, yurts, and rental cabins in the valley below. Sites here are back-ins on gravel, some long enough for RVs to 35 feet. Sites have no hookups but water faucets are nearby, there are picnic tables at the sites but no fire pits. The campground is located off the Spirit Lake Highway at Mile 24.1.

NEAH BAY, SEKIU, AND LAKE OZETTE

If you travel north from Forks and then west along the Strait of Juan de Fuca you'll reach the Makah Indian fishing town of **Neah Bay**. This is the home of the **Makah Cultural and Research Center**, one of the best such museums in the U.S. You can drive on past Neah Bay to the **Cape Flattery Lookout** which offers impressive views of the rocky coast at the most northwesterly point in the Lower 48.

Heading out to Neah Bay you'll pass Sekiu at the west end of Clallam Bay. This is a top salmon fishing destination and has a number of fishing-oriented RV parks with docks for fishing fanatics.

From the road out to Neah Bay another road goes south to **Ozette Lake**. There's a small National Park Service campground at the end of the road and a parking lot. The two three-mile plank trails and a three mile walk along the beach to connect them make up the **Ozette Triangle**, one of the most popular hikes on the Olympic Peninsula, if not in all of Washington state.

Neah Bay, Sekiu, and Lake Ozette Campgrounds

● **HOBUCK CAMPGROUND** *(Open All Year)*
   Information: (360) 645-2663, www.hobuckbeachresort.com
   Location: 3 Miles (5 Km) SW of Neah Bay

   GPS Location: 48.34002 N, 124.66352 W, Near Sea Level

300 Sites – This Makah owned dispersed camping area next to Hobuck Beach is a huge grassy field. On sunny weekends; and often on rainy, windy ones too; it's full of surfer rigs. There are no dedicated sites so RVs and tents are scattered around the field, wherever the owners like the ambiance. There are no tables or fire pits but you can build a fire

IMPRESSIVE VIEWS AND GREAT BIRD WATCHING AT CAPE FLATTERY LOOKOUT

where you need it. There are chemical toilets and also a restroom building with flush toilets and showers. The building has outside faucets for rinsing sandy wetsuits. The office has Wi-Fi which is only usable when you are nearby, not in the campground. The route to the resort is well signed from the west end of the waterfront highway in Neah Bay. The signs will lead you south 3 miles (5 km) to the campground entrance. There is a small office next to the highway for checking in.

● **HOBUCK RV PARK** *(Open All Year)*
   Information: (360) 645-2663, www.hobuckbeachresort.com
   Location: 3.5 Miles (7 Km) SW of Neah Bay

   GPS Location: 48.33208 N, 124.65876 W, Near Sea Level

20 Sites – This is a full hookup RV park located just south down the beach from the no-hookup campground described above. Management is the same. Sites are back-ins to 40 feet, closely spaced, on gravel. Recently about half of the campground has been filled with rental park models, it was much larger in prior years. There is a restroom building with flush toilets and showers. The office up the road is the Wi-Fi hotspot. The route to the resort is well signed from the west end of the waterfront highway in Neah Bay. The signs will lead you south 3 miles (5 km) to the tent campground entrance. There is a small office next to the highway for checking in. Once you've done the RV park is another .6 mile (1 km) farther south along the road.

● **VILLAGE RV PARK** *(Open All Year)*
   Information: (360) 640-4113
   Location: Neah Bay

   GPS Location: 48.36567 N, 124.61308 W, Near Sea Level

24 Sites – Located on Bayview, the waterfront avenue in Neah Bay, this campground is certainly simple. It's across the street from the water. Sites are back-ins to 45 feet in a lot next to a house. It's for self-contained RVs since there are no restroom facilities. As you enter Neah Bay from the east just continue along the main road until you see the campground on the left, it's about half way around the bay.

● **THE CAPE MOTEL AND RV PARK** *(Open All Year)*
   Res and Info: (360) 645-2250
   Location: Neah Bay

   GPS Location: 48.36639 N, 124.60668 W, Near Sea Level

50 Sites – This is the largest and most popular RV park that is actually in town. You can easily walk to the store or restaurant from the campground. The place isn't overly structured, people are here to enjoy the area and what it offers. Sites are back-ups to 45 feet with parking on grass or gravel. As you enter Neah Bay from the east watch for the park on the left not long after entering town.

● **SNOW CREEK RESORT** *(Open All Year)*
   Res and Info: (800) 883-1464, (360) 645-2284,
                       www.snowcreekwa.com
   Location: 3 Miles (5 Km) E of Neah Bay

   GPS Location: 48.35276 N, 124.54748 W, Near Sea Level

40 Sites – This is a fishing oriented dock and launch facility

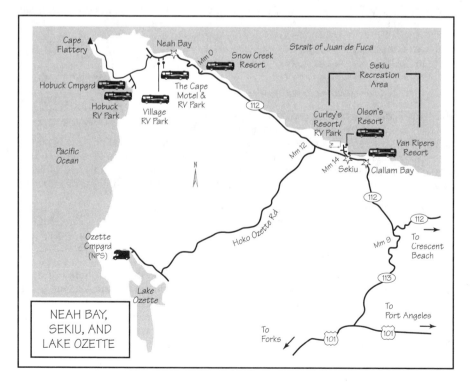

NEAH BAY,
SEKIU, AND
LAKE OZETTE

with camping and RV sites located not far east of Neah Bay. Their rail launching set-up can handle fairly large boats and there are buoys off the rocky beach for mooring. Fishing tackle and scuba air are available. The RV and tent sites are located between the road and the waterfront office, also on the bluff above and on the far side of the road. These campground facilities are basic and cramped but the folks who fill this place don't really care, they appreciate the boat facilities and the fishing. Sites are back-ins to about 40 feet. The sites near the office are crowded, the few on the bluff behind have more room but are a little remote for most people. The cement-block restrooms are utilitarian. The campground is located between Sekiu and Neah Bay. From the cutoff to the Sekiu Recreation Area the distance is 14.3 miles (23.1 km). From Neah Bay it's about 3 miles (5 km).

● **OLSON'S RESORT** *(Open All Year)*
  Information: (360) 963-2311, www.olsonsresort.com
  Location: Sekiu Recreation Area

  GPS Location: 48.26548 N, 124.29970 W, Near Sea Level

200 Sites – Olson's is the largest campground in the Sekiu Recreation Area. They have multiple lots with both full-hookup and no hookup sites. Sites will take large RVs, the no-hookup site are not assigned, you find your own spot to set up. Five restroom buildings provide toilets and showers. Parking is on gravel, dirt, or mud; fires are allowed. If there's no fire ring you can make your own. No reservations are taken. The office building doubles as a small store. Olson's has a big marina with docks and launch facilities. The Sekiu Recreation Area is on the west side of Clallam Bay near the Mile 15 marker of Hwy 112. That's 19 miles (31 km) west of the road's intersection with Hwy 101 and about 16 miles (26 km) east of Neah Bay. From the highway follow Front Street .4 mile (.6 km) north, the office is on the right.

● **VAN RIPERS RESORT** *(Open All Year)*
  Information: (360) 963-2334, www.vanripersresort.com
  Location: Sekiu Recreation Area

  GPS Location: 48.26548 N, 124.29970 W, Near Sea Level

100 Sites – Van Ripers is smaller than Olson's but similar. RV and tent sites are in two areas and include full and partial hookup pull-thru and back-in sites as well as tent sites. The Sekiu Recreation Area is on the west side of Clallam Bay near the Mile 15 marker of Hwy 112. That's 19 miles (31 km) west of the road's intersection with Hwy 101 and about 16 miles (26 km) east of Neah Bay. From the highway follow Front Street .3 mile (.5 km) north, the office is on the right.

■ **OZETTE OLYMPIC NATIONAL PARK CAMPGROUND** *(Open All Year)*
  Information: (206) 963-2725
  Location: 23 Miles (37 Km) SW of Sekiu

  GPS Location: 48.15350 N, 124.66751 W, Near Sea Level

15 Sites – This small national park campground is located on the north shore of Ozette Lake. It's adjacent to a ranger station and the parking lot where two trails lead out to the coast. The campground itself has 15 back-in sites, most will take RVs to 30 feet, some a bit larger. Parking is on grass and there are picnic tables and fire pits. Restrooms are at the ranger station near the trailhead and parking lot, they have flush toilets but no showers. Swimming is in the lake or the nearby shallow river. There is also a boat ramp and dock.

This is a popular campground and reservations are not taken, it's best to arrive early in the day. The access road to the campground is called the Hoko Ozette Road. It heads south from an intersection on Hwy 112 about 2 miles (3 km) west of Sekiu and 14 miles (23 km) east of Neah Bay. Hoko Ozette Road is paved and the campground and parking lot are at the end, a distance of 21 miles (34 km) from the intersection with Hwy 112.

NORTH CASCADES NATIONAL PARK

You may be surprised at the nature of this national park. Although we sometimes call it a national park in this book it is technically a national park complex. The **North Cascades National Park Service Complex** is actually composed of three parts: **North Cascades National Park**, **Ross Lake National Recreation Area**, and **Lake Chelan National Recreation Area**. SR-20 actually never enters the national park itself, instead the park is split by the Ross Lake NRA, and the road passes through this NRA.

The reason for this is that long before the park was established three dams were built here by Seattle City Light to provide Seattle with power. They form three lakes: little Gorge Lake, larger Diablo Lake, and huge Ross Lake. There are also two Seattle City Light company towns inside the NRA.: Newhalem and Diablo. The park itself lies to the north and south and has little in the way of man-made intrusions. Only trails and boats provide access.

Newhalem itself presents a very neat and well-tended appearance. Seattle City Light employees who work at the dams live here. Seattle City Light maintains a **visitor center** in Newhalem, it's a good place to check for information about local sights and hikes since most short ones are related to City Light facilities. Just a few miles further along, on a side road from near Mile 126, is another Seattle City Light town, **Diablo**.

There are a wealth of **hiking opportunities** in this park. Passenger boats ply both Diablo and Ross Lake, you can catch a ride to the beginning points for many wilderness hikes. Register with the back-country ranger station in Marblemount or at the ranger stations in Sedro-Woolley or Winthrop (if you are coming the other way) before your hike if you plan to camp overnight. Also, you should be aware that if you park at a trailhead in the national forests to the west and east (not the park complex though) you need a Northwest Forest Pass available at forest service offices.

Shorter hikes from the road that do not require registration include the River Loop Trail, Newhalem Rockshelter Trail, To Know a Tree Trail, Trail of the Cedars, and Ladder Creek Falls Trail, all in the Newhalem area. There's also the Thunder Woods trail at Mile 131, the Ross Dam Trail (Mile 134), Happy Creek Forest Walk (Mile 135), and Ruby Creek Trail (Mile 138).

For us, however, the main attraction is the road. It has long reached as far as the town of Diablo. In 1972 a new portion opened that continued on over the Cascades. The road is spectacular because it travels through true wilderness. There are no towns, just mountains everywhere. This new road is only open in the summer, during the winter it is closed from Mile 134 to Mile 171. Open dates depend upon the snow, usually the road is open from mid April to some time in November. Highlights of this new portion of road are the **overlooks** at **Diablo Lake** (Mile 131) and **Ross Lake** (Mile 135), and **Rainy Pass** (4,855 feet at Mile 157) and **Washington Pass** (5,277 feet at Mile 162).

If you are approaching the park from the west you'll want to make a stop at the **North Cascades National Park Service Complex Headquarters** in Sedro-Woolley. It's at about Mile 64 and located right next to the road. They can give you information about activities in the park ahead. They can also give you the status of campgrounds in the park and tell you whether any sites remain available. This information is invaluable in making your plans for the evening stop.

Driving east from Sedro-Woolley you will be following the Skagit River Valley and pass through the towns of Concrete, Rockport, and Marblemount. Near Rockport SR-530, which forms a loop from the south that starts near Arlington, joins the highway. If you want hookups when you stop for the night the commercial campground in Marblemount or one of the two campgrounds near Rockport make a good place to stop. They are listed under campgrounds below. These campgrounds are outside the national recreation area.

The stretch of road eastward to Marblemount closely follows the **Skagit River**. The Skagit has been designated a **Wild and Scenic River** and during the winter hosts one of the largest gatherings of **bald eagles** in the lower 48 states. The section of river between Rockport and Newhalem is a prime viewing area from mid-December through February. About 500 bald eagles gather in the area during this time. There is a two-day **Upper Skagit Bald Eagle Festival** held in the area at the beginning of February each year. People come to see eagles perch in trees overlooking the river or munch on decaying salmon along the gravel bars.

The town of Marblemount, at Mile 106, is your last chance for gas on this side of the mountains. Don't forget to check your gauge. Marblemount is also home to the park's **Wilderness Information Center** where you get back-country permits for the park.

At about Mile 111 you actually enter the park. Before you know it you will be entering the Seattle City Light company town of Newhalem. Before you really reach the town, at about Mile 120, you'll see the sign for the right turn into the **North Cascades Visitor Center** and Newhalem Campground. The visitor center is well worth a stop, It is the most important Park Service facility in the park, there are exhibits and a very well done slide show.

Gorge Lake, behind **Gorge Dam**, is the smallest of the three dam-created lakes. It covers 210 acres. The dam here was built in the 1920s. You can see most of Gorge Lake from the highway which passes along its northern shore.

At the east end of Gorge Lake the road crosses to the south side of the Skagit River. The original road goes on in to **Diablo**, the new road passes south of **Diablo Lake** which is the second largest of the lakes and covers an area of 910 acres. The road dips down to the shore of the lake at Colonial Creek at Mile 130. There is a large campground here as well as a boat launch. There is an excellent view of this lake from the **overlook** at Mile 131, just up the hill past the campground.

Ross Lake behind **Ross Dam** is the largest of the lakes. There is no road access to Ross Lake, the best view is from the **Ross Lake Overlook** at Mile 135.

Before you know it you will be past the lake area and climbing toward Rainy Pass. Once you leave the lakes you also leave the NRA, you're now in the Okanogan National Forest. **Rainy Pass** is 4,860 feet high (Mile 157). There's a picnic area and trails there. In fact, the Pacific Crest National Scenic Trail crosses the road at the pass.

Five miles farther along is **Washington Pass**, 5,477 feet (Mile 162). A stop here is essential, the view from the overlook is spectacular. You look across the valley at Liberty

OVERLOOK ABOVE DIABLO LAKE

Bell and the Early Winter Spires, also straight down at the highway climbing from the east side of the pass.

From Washington Pass the road descends steeply for a few miles, then follows the Methow Valley on in to Winthrop.

The campgrounds listed below are arranged from west to east. There are other campgrounds listed in this book convenient to the area. To the west see the *Skagit Valley* section for more campgrounds, to the east see *Winthrop*.

North Cascades National Park Campgrounds

○ **HOWARD MILLER STEELHEAD COUNTY PARK**
   (Open All Year)
   Res and Info: (360) 853-8808, hmsp@fidalgo.net
   Location: Rockport

   GPS Location: 48.48444 N, 121.59639 W, 200 Ft

59 Sites – This campground is in the town of Rockport. Our guess is that when the campground is full Rockport's population doubles. There's a small store and a tavern above the campground for limited supplies. This is a large open grassy campground right next to the Skagit River. Sites are large, some to 60 feet long, and there are no trees to block your slide-out. Some sites are along the river. Roads are paved and so are parking pads. You might not even notice Rockport from the main road. It is near Mile 98 and inside the angle formed by the intersection of SR-20 and SR-530. There are two entrances to the campground, one signed off SR-20 which brings you down through the village, the other off 530 just north of the bridge.

● **ALPINE RV PARK AND CAMPGROUND** *(Open All Year)*
   Res and Info: (360) 873-9002, alpinervpark@hotmail.com,
                www.aikenworld.com/alpine/
   Location: Marblemount

   GPS Location: 48.55083 N, 121.42417 W, 300 Ft

32 Sites – This reasonably-priced commercial campground is a
good alternative to the state and federal campgrounds in the area. It's a basic campground
but has the facilities you need. Big rigs will find that the back-in sites will take RVs to
45 feet and longer and there's plenty of room to maneuver. The campground is located
on the north side of the highway just east of Marblemount and 12 miles (19 km) west of
Newhalem.

■ **GOODELL CAMPGROUND** *(Open May 15 to Oct 15 – Varies)*
   Information: (360) 856-5700
   Location: Newhelem

   GPS Location: 48.67194 N, 121.27083 W, 400 Ft

21 Sites – This is a small national park campground located just down the highway from
the Newhalem Creek Campground. It's on the north side of the river and a popular put-in
point for the rafting companies. It's an older campground with back-in sites to about 30
feet. Roads are paved while parking pads are gravel. Some sites are next to the river. The
campground entrance road is .5 miles (.8 km) west of Newhalem.

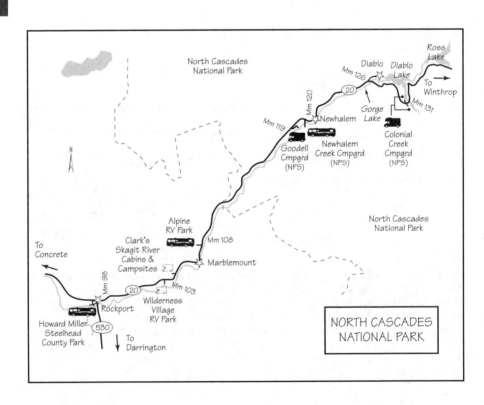

NORTH CASCADES
NATIONAL PARK

■ **NEWHALEM CREEK CAMPGROUND** *(Open All Year)*
Reservations: www.recreation.gov, (877) 444-6777
Information: (360) 856-5700
Location: Newhalem

GPS Location: 48.67083 N, 121.26083 W, 400 Ft

116 Sites – Newhalem is the most civilized and probably the busiest of the park's campgrounds. Although it is left open in the winter the water is turned off about the middle of October and on again about May 1. Sites here are paved and located off paved loop roads with pull-thru and back-in sites to 45 feet. A few sites have pads for tents. The campground is at the western approaches to Newhalem. The main visitor center for the park is located in the same area.

■ **COLONIAL CREEK CAMPGROUND** *(Open All Year)*
Information: (360) 856-5700
Location: 9 Miles (15 Km) E of Newhalem

GPS Location: 48.68833 N, 121.09500 W, 1,200 Ft

145 Sites – This large North Cascades National Park campground is located just west of the point where the highway is barricaded during the winter. It's right where the highway crosses an arm of Diablo Lake. Sites are located on both sides of the highway. The campground is an older one, it's not designed for big rigs. The largest practical size for RVs here is 30 feet and most sites just don't have room for slide-outs. Leveling can be difficult. Some tent sites are near the water and there are some pads for pitching tents. While the campground is theoretically open all year the snow isn't usually cleared and there is no water in winter. The campground is located 9.5 miles (15.3 km) east of Newhalem and 63 miles (102 km) west of Winthrop.

OCEAN SHORES AND THE NORTH BEACHES AREA

The **North Beaches Area** stretches from Ocean Shores on the north point of the entrance to Grays Harbor for about 30 miles (48 km) north to the Quinault Indian Reservation. The name North Beaches refers to the fact that these beaches are north of the mouth of Grays Harbor. There are also fine beaches south of Grays Harbor, see the *Westport* section for more about this area. The North Beaches are the closest Pacific beaches to Seattle, they can be reached in about 3 hours by freeway, so you will find much more activity here than on the more remote beaches to the north in the Olympic National Park.

There are a number of small towns along the coast. From south to north they are **Ocean Shores**, **Ocean City**, **Copalis Beach**, **Pacific Beach**, **Moclips**, and, finally, inside the Quinault Indian Reservation, **Taholah**. The towns north of Ocean Shores are small, most have little more than a few motels, campgrounds, and restaurants. The beaches out front are wide and solid, driving is allowed on many of them. One of the big attractions is the razor clams. There are beds of clams in front of the towns, when the tide is particularly low and the season open you'll usually find hundreds of folks digging clams on the beach. The beaches are great when there are no clams too, you can ride a bicycle, fly a kite, surf fish, or just comb the tide line.

Ocean Shores (population 5,600) is a different story. This town was developed during the 1960s as a resort and retirement haven. It has big beachside motels, a golf course, restaurants and shops, a casino, and even a lake and canals that offer decent fishing. Ocean Shores has a marina just inside the mouth of Grays Harbor, the somewhat down-at-the-heels commercial campground is located at the marina. You can arrange a fishing charter here or, during the summer, catch a small walk-on only passenger ferry across the mouth of Grays Harbor to Westport.

Ocean Shores hosts a large number of events. These include the **Beachcombers Fun Fair** in early March, the **Ocean Shores International Kite Challenge** in June, and the **Jazz at the Beach** in November. Check with the chamber of commerce for dates and other events.

Just outside Ocean Shores is the modern Quinault Beach Resort Casino. It's a good place to have some fun but even better, it also allows RVers to park in its lot which overlooks the beach. See the description below.

Two larger towns, **Hoquiam** (population 9,000) and **Aberdeen** (population 16,900), are about 20 miles (32 km) east of Ocean Shores. These larger towns make a good place to pick up supplies. They also have their own attractions. The **Grays Harbor Historical Seaport** in Aberdeen is the home port for the **Lady Washington**. This is a full-sized sailing replica of one of the ships in which an expedition led by Captain Gray discovered both the Columbia River and Grays Harbor in 1788. Although the Lady Washington is usually at sea visiting other areas, there is an interpretive center and museum.

A little west of Hoquiam you'll find the entrance road for **Bowerman Basin**. This is a wildlife refuge, during late April and early May it is a wonderful place to view thousands of shorebirds.

The campgrounds below are listed from north to south. Along this coast the state parks are without a doubt the nicest sites for both tents and RVs. The commercial campgrounds provide a decent back-up, many of them also accept tents. The last place to fill is usually Quinault Maritime Resort RV Park and Campground.

Ocean Shores and the North Beaches Area Campgrounds

☐ **PACIFIC BEACH STATE PARK** *(Open All Year)*
Reservations: www.parks.wa.gov/reservations/, (888) 226-7688
Information: (360) 276-4297, (360) 902-8844, www.parks.wa.gov
Location: 15 Miles (24 Km) N of Ocean Shores

GPS Location: 47.20583 N, 124.20278 W, Near Sea Level

64 Sites – RV sites here are in an open area next to the beach with no trees. Views are great and the beach very accessible. This is a very popular campground, particularly during open clam tides. Sites are back-ins, some extend to 60 feet and nearly all will accept 45-footers. About two-thirds have electrical hookups and there is a dump station with water. The campground is located right in the town of Pacific Beach and is well signed from the entrance road to town. This park accepts reservations year-round.

● **COPALIS BEACH SUNRISE RESORT** *(Open All Year)*
Res and Info: (360) 289-4278, www.sunriseresorts.com
Location: 7 Miles (11 Km) N of Ocean Shores

GPS Location: 47.11139 N, 124.17611 W, Near Sea Level

78 Sites – The Sunrise is a membership club resort but will allow non-members. It has large sites with about half of them being pull-thrus to 60 feet. Restroom are older but serviceable. It's a big place, the main attraction is the beachside location. The resort is

located right in Copalis, follow the signs on Heath Road from SR-109 which passes just inland of the town.

● **DUNES RESORT** *(Open All Year)*

Res and Info: (360) 289-3873, (877) 386-3778, OlympicBeaches@aol.com, www.olympicbeaches.com

Location: 6 Miles (10 Km) N of Ocean Shores

GPS Location: 47.10694 N, 124.17611 W, Near Sea Level

34 Sites – This is the first of a string of campgrounds stretching south from Copalis Beach. All of these campgrounds face the ocean but are separated from the beach by

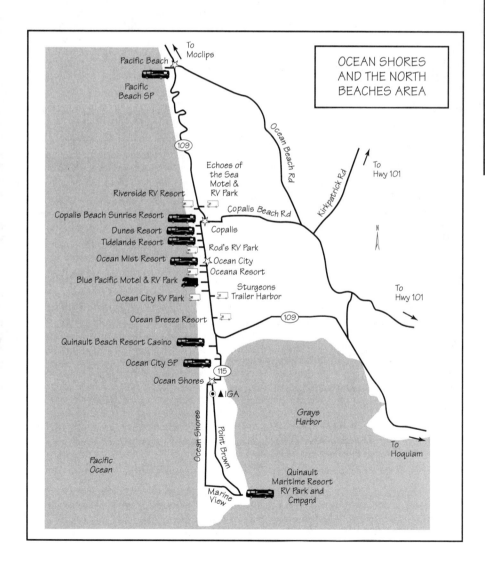

OCEAN SHORES AND THE NORTH BEACHES AREA

small but difficult-to-cross Connor Creek. This campground has a rowboat (the Titanic) that can sometimes be pulled across the water using a hand line. There are six tent sites and 28 back-in RV sites to 40 feet which occasionally take 45 footers. The facilities are old but were well-maintained and in good shape when we visited. The entrance road is off SR-109 a few hundred yards south of Copalis.

● **TIDELANDS RESORT** *(Open All Year)*
   Res and Info: (360) 289-8963, mail@tidelandresort.com,
                 www.TidelandsResort.com
   Location: 6 Miles (10 Km) N of Ocean Shores

   GPS Location: 47.10278 N, 124.17556 W, Near Sea Level

80 Sites – Sites in this park are in large grassy fields next to the beach dunes. The campground is separated from the ocean by Connor Creek. There is lots of room for tent campers and 42 RV sites in two areas. Nine are pull-thrus with full hookups and cable for rigs to about 35 feet. The remainder of the RV sites are back-ins with water and electric hookups for rigs of any size. Facilities here are old but service-able. The resort is located about .4 miles (.6 km) south of Copalis with the access road off SR-109.

● **OCEAN MIST RESORT** *(Open All Year)*
   Information: (360) 289-3659,
                 www.kmresorts.com/1-oceanmist.shtml
   Location: 5 Miles (8 Km) N of Ocean Shores

   GPS Location: 47.08389 N, 124.16861 W, Near Sea Level

140 Sites – The Ocean Mist is a K&M membership campground. Non-members are allowed to stay here if there is room. This campground too is near the ocean with some sites on the ocean side of the creek (members only) and some on the highway side. There's a hot tub during the summer season. All sites are full-hookup with cable TV. The back-in sites will take RVs to 40 feet. The resort is located about 1.8 miles (2.9 km) south of Copalis with the access road off SR-109.

● **BLUE PACIFIC MOTEL AND RV PARK** *(Open All Year)*
   Res and Info: (360) 289-2262, www.bluepacificmotel.com
   Location: 5 Miles (8 Km) N of Ocean Shores

   GPS Location: 47.07694 N, 124.16806 W, Near Sea Level

19 Sites – This is a small but well-run and well-maintained campground and motel. It too is separated from the ocean by Connor Creek. The grassy camping area has back-in sites, some with full hookups and some with electricity and water only. They will accept RVs to 38 feet. The RV park is located about 2 miles (3 km) south of Copalis with the access road off SR-109.

● **QUINAULT BEACH RESORT CASINO**
   Information: (360) 289-9466
   Location: 1.5 Miles (2.4 Km) N of Ocean Shores

   GPS Location: 47.04110 N, 124.17061 W, Near Sea Level

Approx. 50 Sites – This beachside casino has a large gravel lot for parking RVs. There are no dedicated RV services but it's free and it has a great location overlooking the beach grass and beach beyond. The casino itself has a restaurant and restrooms, of course. The entrance to the casino is .5 miles (.8 km) south of the intersection of SR-109 and SR-115 (on the Ocean Shores access highway). To reach the RV parking area you drive through the parking lot and to the left. You'll see the RVs parked ahead. Check in with the concierge at the casino.

☐ **OCEAN CITY STATE PARK** *(Open All Year)*
Reservations: www.parks.wa.gov/reservations/,
(888) 226-7688
Information: (360) 289-3553, (360) 902-8844,
ocean.city@parks.wa.gov
www.parks.wa.gov
Location: 1 Mile (2 Km) N of Ocean Shores

GPS Location: 47.03167 N, 124.15861 W, Near Sea Level

178 Sites – This is a very large state campground located next to the beach. Only a small number (29) have hookups, but many of the sites are large (to 50 feet) with room for big rigs and good maneuvering room. The entrance to the campground is a half mile (.8 km) south of the intersection of SR-109 and SR-115 (on the Ocean Shores access highway). This park accepts reservations year-round.

● **QUINAULT MARITIME RESORT AND RV PARK**
(Open March 1 to Oct 31 – Varies)
Information: (360) 276-8215, ext 239
Location: Ocean Shores

GPS Location: 46.94806 N, 124.13111 W, Near Sea Level

100 Sites – This campground is located next to the marina where the ferry to Westport docks. That means that it is quite a distance south of the central business district but convenient to both Damon Point State Park and the Oyhut State Game Refuge at the far south end of the peninsula. The facilities here are old and poorly maintained. We assume that sometime soon this site will be used for another development of some kind. Still, the large pull-thru sites with full hookups attract a good number of campers, particularly when everything else in the area is full. To reach the campground follow signs to the marina. As you arrive in Ocean Shores on US-115 take Point Brown Avenue (to the left after the sharp right turn as you arrive in town) and follow it south for 5.5 miles (8.9 km).

OKANOGAN VALLEY

The Okanagan River Valley, an important agricultural and recreational destination in British Columbia, continues south of the border with a different spelling. In the U.S. it's the Okanogan, even the river name changes.

Washington State's Okanogan isn't nearly as heavily populated or economically important as that of B.C. US-97 runs the length of the valley beside the river and there are a string of small towns along it – Oroville, Tonasket, Riverside, North Omak, Omak, and Okanogan. The largest population center is the sister towns of Okanogan and Omak with a combined population of about 7,500.

To the west of the valley are the foothills of the Cascades with many small reservoirs offering campgrounds, cooler temperatures, and fishing. Probably the most popular of these are the two reservoirs at the small town of **Conconully**, four of the campgrounds listed below are in Conconully. Much of this area is part of the **Okanogan National Forest**.

The best known event in the valley is the **Omak Stampede**. It's held during the second

WASHINGTON

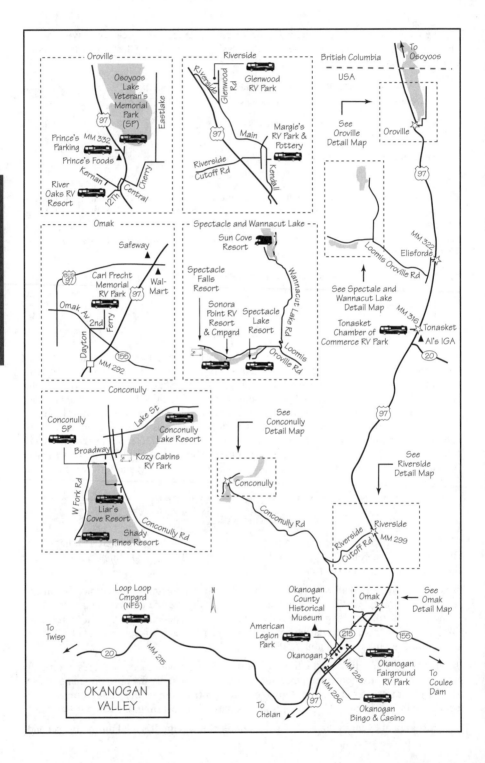

week of August. This big rodeo is best known for its Suicide Race in which riders plunge down a steep hill into the river, horses are sometimes killed doing this and it's very controversial. Other attractions of the Stampede include an Indian Encampment with Native American drumming and dancing.

Okanogan Valley Campgrounds

☐ **OSOYOOS LAKE VETERAN'S MEMORIAL PARK**
    (Open All Year)
    Reservations: www.parks.wa.gov/reservations/,
                (888) 226-7688
    Information: (509) 476-3321, www.oroville-wa.com
    Location: Oroville

GPS Location: 48.94972 N, 119.43417 W, 900 Ft

86 Sites – This park sits on the shore of Osoyoos Lake which stretches to the north into Canada. Sites here are set on a large lawn, some are waterfront. These are big gravel back-in sites to 45 feet. The campground has flush toilets and coin-op showers, also a dump station. A day-use area has a swimming beach and boat ramp, the lake is popular for swimming and fishing for small-mouth bass, kokanee, and rainbow trout. In winter RV campers may park in the picnic area parking lot although the campsites are not open. The entrance road to the park leaves US-97 at the northern edge of Oroville, near Mile 332.7. That's 3.8 miles (6.1 km) south of the Canadian border.

● **RIVER OAKS RV RESORT** *(Open All Year)*
    Res and Info: (509) 476-2087, www.riveroaksrv.com
    Location: Oroville

GPS Location: 48.93778 N, 119.44306 W, 900 Ft

50 Sites – This modern campground has both permanent and traveler sites. The traveler sites are back-ins around the perimeter of the campground. They're all long back-ins suitable for any size RV, parking is on gravel. The campground is in Oroville. Near the center of town go west on Twelfth Ave, after one block turn north on Ironwood Street, and in another block turn left on Kernan Street. The campground entrance is on the left in .1 mile (.2 km).

● **PRINCE'S PARKING** *(Open All Year)*
    Location: Oroville

GPS Location: 48.94917 N, 119.43722 W, 1,000 Ft

58 Sites – Prince's Parking is the bargain park in Oroville. It's not pretty, but it's cheap. All sites are long back-ins with power. There's an inexpensive dump station and water fill site as well as restrooms and laundry. The sites are on a gravel bench on the west side of US-97 at the north edge of Oroville, they look across the highway over the lake.

○ **TONASKET CHAMBER OF COMMERCE RV PARK**
    (Open April 15 to Oct 15 – Varies)
    Information: (509) 486-4429
    Location: Tonasket

GPS Location: 48.71028 N, 119.43667 W, 900 Ft

8 Sites – Tonasket is located along US 97 about 16 miles (26 km) south of Oroville. The chamber of commerce office for the town has eight RV slots. These are back-in spaces with full hookups. They're long spaces since they open onto a large parking lot, any size

RV will fit. Restroom facilities are limited to a wheelchair-accessible port-a-pottie but there is a dump station. It's free to folks staying in the campground, there's a $4 fee if you just stop to use it. The chamber of commerce is on the west side of the highway at the northern entrance to town.

● **GLENWOOD RV PARK** *(Open April 1 to Nov 15)*
  Res and Info: (509) 322-2280
  Location: Riverside

  GPS Location: 48.50944 N, 119.51333 W, 800 Ft

30 Sites – This tidy shaded campground is located in the small town of Riverside. There are pull-thru and back-in sites to 50 feet as well as tent sites. From US-97 at Mile 299.7 (the northernmost of three exits for Riverside) drive southeast on Riverside Rd. In .3 mile (.5 km) turn left on Glenwood Rd and you'll see the campground on the left in .1 mile (.2 km).

● **MARGIE'S RV PARK AND POTTERY**
    (Open All Year)
  Res and Info: (509) 826-5810, margierv@bossig.com,
                www.margies-rvpark.com
  Location: Riverside

       GPS Location: 48.50083 N, 119.50528 W, 800 Ft

55 Sites – This is a well-kept park in a residential setting. There are tent sites as well as pull-thrus and back-ins to 55 feet. Some sites are full-hookup, others have power and water. From US-97 at Mile 298.6 (the southernmost of three exits for Riverside) drive northeast for .3 mile (.5 km), the campground entrance is on the right.

○ **CARL PRECHT MEMORIAL RV PARK**
    (Open March 1 to Oct 31 – Varies)
  Information: (509) 826-1170, kristim@omakcity.com,
                www.omakcity.com/rv_park.html
  Location: Omak

    GPS Location: 48.41111 N, 119.51778 W, 800 Ft

68 Sites – This campground is one of the best places to stay in the region. It's a full-hook-up campground on the Omak Stampede Grounds. These are paved pull-thru and back-in sites to 70 feet, surrounded by grass under shade trees. Reservations are not accepted and there is a five day stay limit. Easiest access to the park is from US-97. Take the exit marked for the Stampede Grounds at Mile 291.4. This puts you on Dayton Street which leads directly north to the entrance of the park, a distance of .3 miles (.5 km).

○ **AMERICAN LEGION PARK** *(Open All Year)*
  Location: Okanogan

       GPS Location: 48.37111 N, 119.57139 W, 700 Ft

20 Sites – In Okanogan next to the Okanogan County Historical Museum is a park where overnight RV parking is allowed. This is parallel parking on gravel next to a grassy area with picnic tables. A poorly maintained restroom building offers flush toilets and showers, this is also where the pay station is located. The stay limit here is 72 hours. On Saturdays a farmers market is held here so you have to park at the far north or south ends of the lot on Friday night. The campground is located off SR-215 (Bus US-97) just north of central Okanogan. Take the SR-20 Exit from US-97 at Mile 286.4. Drive west for .5 mile

(.8 km) to a T. Turn right here onto SR-215 and follow it north for 1.5 miles (2.4 km), the park is on the right.

● **OKANOGAN BINGO AND CASINO** *(Open All Year)*
Information: (800) 559-4643
Location: Okanogan

GPS Location: 48.35389 N, 119.58583 W, 900 Ft

20 Sites – This small casino allows RV parking for free in their gravel parking lot. There is room for about 20 RVs of any size to park, a limited number of them can run a long cord for low-amp electricity. There are restrooms in the casino and a port-a-potty in the parking lot. You must go into the casino and get a club card but there is no charge. The casino is on the west side of US-97 near Mile 286.6.

○ **OKANOGAN FAIRGROUND RV PARK**
(Open April 1 to October 30 – Varies)
Information: (509) 422-1621
Location: Okanogan

GPS Location: 48.37775 N, 119.55177 W, 700 Ft

100 Sites – The Okanogan Fairgrounds offers RV and tent camping when the facility is not being used for the fair, which is first weekend after Labor Day. Tent camping is on grass. RV sites are in three different locations with full-hookup sites to 60 feet. From US-97 near mile 288 turn west on Cameron Lake Road. In a short distance turn right on Rodeo Trail Road in 1 mile (1.6 km) you'll see the fairgrounds entrance on the left.

● **LIAR'S COVE RESORT**
(Open Jan 7 to Oct 30)
Res and Info: (509) 826-1288 or (800) 830-1288,
liarscoveresor@yahoo.com
www.liarscoveresort.com
Location: Conconully

GPS Location: 48.55056 N, 119.74750 W, 2,300 Ft

40 Sites – Liar's Cove is a relaxed resort on the shore of Conconully Reservoir next to Conconully State Park. Some sites will take RVs to 45 feet, they have full hookups and patios. Amenities include a small store, boat dock, and boat rentals. To reach the park leave US-97 near Mile 298.9 at Riverside and head west on Riverside Cutoff. After 4.9 miles (7.9 km) you'll come to a T. Turn right here onto Conconully Road and in another 9.7 miles (15.6 km) you'll see the resort entrance on your left.

□ **CONCONULLY STATE PARK**
(Open March 15 to Nov 30 – Varies)
Information: (509) 826-7408, (360) 902-8844,
ww.parks.wa.gov
Location: Conconully

GPS Location: 48.55667 N, 119.75111 W, 2,300 Ft

84 Sites – This park occupies the northern shore of Conconully Reservoir and has boat launches and docks. Sites are in three areas. An older RV area has 9 gravel pull-thru sites to 60 feet but no electrical hookups. The second area is parking on grass near picnic tables and fire pits with grills under huge willow trees. There are 15 RV sites with electric and water hookups in this area in addition to many grass tent sites. A third area is to the south-

east along the lakeshore. To reach the park leave US-97 near Mile 298.9 at Riverside and head west on Riverside Cutoff. After 4.9 miles (7.9 km) you'll come to a T. Turn right here onto Conconully Road and in another 10.1 miles (16.3 km) you'll arrive in the village of Conconully, the state park is on your left.

● **SHADY PINES RESORT**
(Open April 15 to Oct 30 – Varies)
Reservations: (800) 552-2287
Information: (509) 826-2287,
www.shadypinesresort.com
Location: Conconully

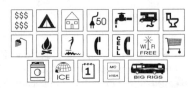

GPS Location: 48.54278 N, 119.75889 W, 2,300 Ft

23 Sites – Shady Pines is a family-owned resort on the west side of Conconully Reservoir. The 20 sites are on two levels with both full and partial hookups. There are pull-thru and back-ins to 40 feet. Each has a picnic table. There is a community fire pit. The resort has a gift shop and boat rentals as well as a launching ramp. To reach the park leave US-97 near Mile 298.9 at Riverside and head west on Riverside Cutoff. After 4.9 miles (7.9 km) you'll come to a T. Turn right here onto Conconully Road and in another 10.1 miles (16.3 km) you'll arrive in the village of Conconully. Take the first left after the state park onto Broadway and drive on around the lake for 1.2 miles (2 km) to the resort.

● **CONCONULLY LAKE RESORT**
(Open April 25 to Oct 30 – Varies)
Res and Info: (509) 826-0813, (800) 850-0813
Location: Conconully

GPS Location: 48.56472 N, 119.73250 W, 2,300 Ft

11 Sites – This is the only campground in this section that is located on the upper lake. The resort buildings and the campsites here are separated by a parking and government boat-launch area with vault toilets. The sites are pull-in sites along the lake shore with full hookups. They're long sites and will accept 45 foot RVs. Other facilities are in the resort at the far side of the gravel parking lot. To reach the park leave US-97 near Mile 298.9 at Riverside and head west on Riverside Cutoff. After 4.9 miles (7.9 km) you'll come to a T. Turn right here onto Conconully Road and in another 10.1 miles (16.3 km) you'll arrive in the village of Conconully. Continue through town for three blocks and then turn right on Lake Street. Follow Lake for .9 miles (1.5 km) to the campground.

● **SPECTACLE LAKE RESORT**
(Open April 1 to Oct 30 – Varies)
Res and Info: (509) 223-3433,
www.spectaclelakeresort.com,
spectaclelake@okcom.org
Location: Lakes West of Okanogan Valley

GPS Location: 48.80917 N, 119.53222 W, 1,300 Ft

50 Sites – This lakeside resort has motel rooms and camping sites. The sites here are in 2 areas. Some are pull-in sites on the lake shore and are full hookup with 20 amp power. The others are set in a grassy lawn under trees behind the motel building without a lake view but do have 30 amp power. These sites are back-in parking on grass and are full hookup. Although the resort has sites to take larger RVs parking is somewhat cramped so it would be best for larger RVs to call ahead and make sure there is room. RV park guests

can use all resort facilities including the heated swimming pool, docks, boat launch, exercise room, horseshoe pits, play areas, recreation hall, and basketball and volleyball courts. Row boats and motor boats are available for rent. From Ellisforde, at about Mile 321.4 on US 97 between Oroville and Tonasket turn west following signs for Spectacle Lake and Loomis. In .6 mile (1 km) at the T turn left, and then in another 1.3 miles (2.1 km) turn right following signs for Many Lake Recreation Area and Loomis. This puts you on the Loomis-Oroville Road. Follow it for 5.8 miles (9.4 km). Turn left on Holmes Road and you'll reach the resort in .6 mile (1 km).

● **SONORA POINT RV RESORT AND CAMPGROUND**
    (Open April 1 to Oct 31 – Varies)
    Res and Info: (509) 223-3700, info@sonorapointresort.com,
              www.sonorapointresort.com
    Location: Lakes West of Valley

     GPS Location: 48.80944 N, 119.55500 W, 1,300 Ft

50 Sites – This is a second resort on Spectacle Lake. It was formerly called the Rainbow Resort but has been renamed and is going to be developed into a much larger place. When we visited, however, things were pretty much unchanged. The sites here are full and partial hookups, both back-in and pull-thru, to 80 feet. There's a beach, a boat ramp and dock. Swimming is in the lake. Fire pits are available on the lake shore. There are two fifth wheels available as overnight rentals. From Ellisforde, at about Mile 321.4 on US 97 between Oroville and Tonasket turn west following signs for Spectacle Lake and Loomis. In .6 mile (1 km) at the T turn left, and then in another 1.3 miles (2.1 km) turn right following signs for Many Lake Recreation Area and Loomis. This puts you on the Loomis-Oroville Road. Follow it for 7.6 miles (12.3 km), the resort is on the left.

● **SUN COVE RESORT** *(Open April 20 to Oct 15 – Varies)*
    Res and Info: (509) 476-2233, suncove@nvinet.com,
              www.thesuncoveresort.com
    Location: Lakes West of Valley

     GPS Location: 48.87833 N, 119.51167 W, 1,800 Ft

40 Sites – Sun Cove is a lakeside resort set on the east side of Wannacut Lake to the west of the Okanogan Valley. This is a three-mile-long lake popular for fishing and relaxed water sports, there's an eight mile speed limit so fast boats and watercraft aren't an option. The resort has sites in two different areas. There are 27 sites with full-hookups as you enter the resort, they are behind the motel units and have no lake view. There are also additional sites in another area with lake view but no hookups and gravel surfaces. Due to a long narrow entry road and lack of maneuvering room the campground is suitable for RVs to about 35 feet. The resort offers a restaurant, small store, rental motel units, a dock area, boat ramp, and a heated swimming pool. From Ellisforde, at about Mile 321.4 on US 97 between Oroville and Tonasket turn west following signs for Spectacle Lake and Loomis. In .6 mile (1 km) at the T turn left, and then in another 1.3 miles (2.1 km) turn right following signs for Many Lake Recreation Area and Loomis. This puts you on the Loomis-Oroville Road. Follow it for 5.1 miles (8.2 km) and then turn right on the Wannacut Lake Road. In another 3.9 miles (6.3 km) turn right under an arch for Sun Cove Resort. A narrow dirt road leads another 1 mile (1.6 km) to the resort.

WASHINGTON

■ **LOUP LOUP CAMPGROUND** *(Open May 1 to Oct 15 – Varies)*
Information: (509) 996-4000
Location: Mountains West of Valley

GPS Location: 48.39667 N, 119.90222 W, 4,100 Ft

25 Sites – This Okanogan National Forest campground is at a much higher altitude than the other campgrounds in this section. It's set in a forest of larch and pines off SR-20 between Okanogan and Twisp. There is a ski area nearby and many trails through the forest. This campground is suitable for carefully driven RVs to 40 feet since it has back-in and pull-thru sites to 60 feet off a good gravel access road. Water is available but not at the sites. To reach the campground travel west from Okanogan on SR-20 for about 17 miles (27 km) to Mile 214.8. Turn north on NF-42, a paved road, and drive .5 mile (.8 km). Turn right at the sign for the campground and then in .6 mile (1 km) turn left into the campground.

OLYMPIA

Olympia (population 46,000) is located along I-5 at the southern end of Puget Sound. The city is the capital of Washington State and the attractions for a tourist mostly relate to that fact. Together with nearby Tumwater and Lacey the area has a population of about 95,000 people. In addition to the government activities Olympia is home to Evergreen State College. This is a strategic location for travelers because it's where US-101 and SR-8, the roads to the Olympic Peninsula and coast, intersect I-5.

Most of the interesting government buildings can be visited including the domed **Legislative Building**, the **Temple of Justice**, the **Capitol Conservatory**, and the **Governor's Mansion**. There is also a **State Capitol Museum** and a **Vietnam Memorial**.

If you're more interested in outdoor activities you should try visits to **Percival Landing Park** (Olympia's waterfront) on Budd Inlet or the **Olympia Farmer's Market**. The market is in operation from Thursday to Sunday in summer and is located on Capitol Way to the north of the central area.

Olympia Campgrounds

☐ **MILLERSYLVANIA STATE PARK** *(Open All Year)*
Reservations: www.parks.wa.gov/reservations/,
                (888) 226-7688
Information: (360) 753-1519, (360) 902-8844,
                www.parks.wa.gov
Location: 15 Miles (24 Km) SE of Olympia

GPS Location: 46.90972 N, 122.90694 W, 200 Ft

180 Sites – Millersylvania sits on the shore of Deep Lake, about 7 miles (11 Km) as the crow flies southeast of Olympia. Campsites here are of two types. There are water and electric hookup sites in a large open field with pull-thrus and back-ins to 70 feet and lots of slide-out room. There are also back-in forest-type sites (with a few pull-thrus) with no hookups that are great for tents and smaller rigs. Campsites are away from the lake but it's an easy stroll and there are two buoyed swimming beaches. Take Exit 99 from I-5 about 11 miles (18 km) south of Olympia. Drive east on SR-121 (93rd Ave. SE) for 1.5 miles (2.4 km) and turn right on Tilley Rd. S. Drive 3 miles (5 km) south, the campground entrance is on the right.

● **AMERICAN HERITAGE CAMPGROUND**
  (Open All Year)
  Res and Info: (360) 943-8778,
                   olycamp@comcast.net,
                   www.americanheritage
                   campground.com
  Location: 7 Miles (12 Km) S of Olympia

GPS Location: 46.94861 N, 122.92806 W, 200 Ft

100 Sites – This commercial campground has the feel of a state park with forest-type back-in sites to 60 feet under tall Douglas-firs. Full-hookup, partial-hookup, and no-hookup sites are available. Amenities include a swimming pool in the summer months. The campground is owned and managed by the same people who own the Olympia Campground, listed below. During the winter (from Labor Day to Memorial Day) you must go to that campground first to check in. To go directly to the campground take Exit 99 from I-5 about 11 miles (18 km) south of Olympia. Drive east on SR-121 (93rd Ave. SE) for .4 mile (.6 km) and turn south on Kimmie St. SW. The campground is just ahead on the left.

● **OLYMPIA CAMPGROUND** *(Open All Year)*
  Res and Info: (360) 352-2551,
                   olycamp@comcast.net,
                   www.olympiacampground.com
  Location: 10 Miles (16 Km) SE of Olympia

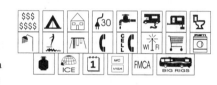

GPS Location: 46.96694 N, 122.92167 W, 100 Ft

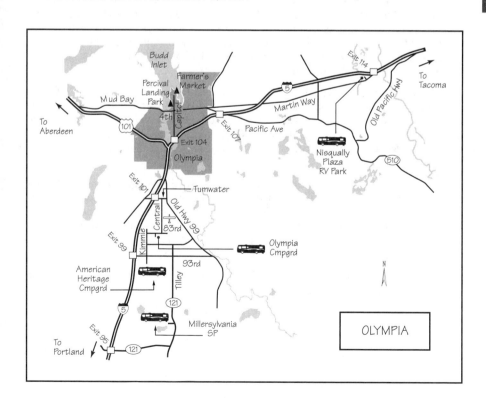

90 Sites – This family-run campground sits behind a Texaco service station and quick-stop convenience store. The sites at the front of the park are long pull-thrus to 65 feet with hookups and room for slides, those at the rear are forest-type back-ins. Amenities include a seasonal swimming pool. Take Exit 101 from I-5 about 9 miles (15 km) south of Olympia. Drive east on Tumwater Blvd. SW for .5 miles (.8 km) and turn south on Central St. SW. Drive .5 miles (.8 km) south on Central and at the T turn right on 83rd Ave. You'll see the Texaco just ahead on the left, the campground entrance is on the east side.

● **NISQUALLY PLAZA RV PARK** *(Open All Year)*
   Res and Info: (360) 491-3831
   Location: 7 Miles (11 Km) N of Olympia

   GPS Location: 47.06667 N, 122.72278 W, Near Sea Level

50 Sites – Nisqually Plaza is conveniently located next to I-5. It's primarily a long-term campground, not a traveler place, but we list it because there are generally a few sites available for travelers and it is convenient for an overnight stop. There is a swimming pool but it is unheated, even in summer. Sites are all back-ins, most reach 60 feet and have room for slide-outs. Take Exit 114 from I-5. This is about 7 miles (11 km) north of central Olympia. You'll see the campground on the east side of the highway.

PORT ANGELES AND THE NORTH OLYMPIC PARK

With a natural harbor in a very convenient location at the mouth of Puget Sound it is no wonder that **Port Angeles** (population 19,000) is a fishing and ferry port. You can join a fishing charter for salmon or bottom fish or take a ferry across the Strait of Juan de Fuca to Victoria for a day trip. For a view of the city and the mountains in the park to the south drive out **Ediz Hook**, the sand spit which forms the harbor. Port Angeles hosts the **Clallam County Fair** the third weekend of August.

The big attraction of Port Angeles is, of course, access to the northern reaches of **Olympic National Park**. The 17-mile (27 km) road up to **Hurricane Ridge** actually begins in Port Angeles. This is an excellent drive for those desiring views of the park's high country without much hiking. Thirty miles (48 km) east from Port Angeles on US-101 the **Sol Duc Road** also gives access to the park and hot springs there. You'll find hiking trails from both roads.

The presence of the park might make you forget the southern coastline of the Strait of Juan de Fuca. Don't let it, there are many coastal destinations in the region. Some are listed in the sections of this book covering *Sequim* (to the east) and *Forks* and *Neah Bay, Sekiu, ad Lake Ozette* (to the west). Closer to Port Angeles are the sites along the Straight of Juan de Fuca accessible from SR-112 to the west of Port Angeles. These include Salt Creek County Park and Crescent Beach. Both offer camping sites.

It is possible to travel to Canada from Port Angeles by ferry. You can go over to Victoria as a day trip on foot or in a vehicle, or you can cross on the ferry in your RV to explore the region. See the *Victoria* section in the British Columbia chapter for more information about that area.

Campgrounds below are listed from east to west. For hookups near Port Angeles we prefer the Elwha Dam RV Park. Tent campers have lots of choices, particularly in the park. Families with children will like the KOA. Farther west the Sol Duc Hot Springs area is a

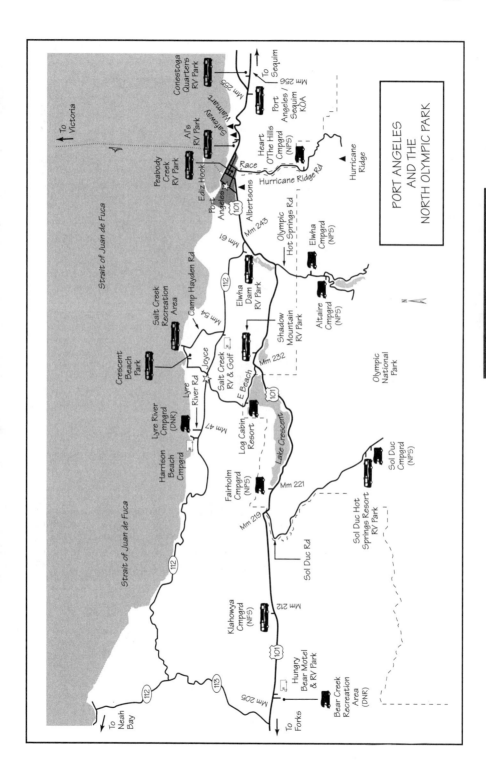

PORT ANGELES
AND THE
NORTH OLYMPIC PARK

favorite for both tent and RV camping, there are even hookups. Along the coast the Salt Creek County Park is an excellent choice, and it now offers hookups.

Port Angeles and the North Olympic Park Campgrounds

● **CONESTOGA QUARTERS RV PARK** *(Open All Year)*
Res and Info: (360) 452-4637, (800) 808-4637
Location: 6 Miles (10 Km) E of Port Angeles

    GPS Location: 48.09611 N, 123.29083 W, 300 Ft

34 Sites – This is an older RV park with simple facilities. Parking is on grass or gravel, there are back-in and pull-thru sites to 50 feet. The RV park is on the north side of US-101 about 7 miles (11 km) west of Sequim and 6 miles (10 km) east of Port Angeles.

● **PORT ANGELES / SEQUIM KOA**
    (Open March 18 to Oct 31)
Reservations: (800) 562-7558, www.koa.com
Information: (360) 457-5916,
           portangeleskoa@wavecable.com,
           www.portangeleskoa.com
Location: 5 Miles (8 Km) E of Port Angeles

    GPS Location: 48.09472 N, 123.30528 W, 300 Ft

120 Sites – Located mid-way between Sequim and Port Angeles this KOA has all of the normal KOA amenities including both big sites and tent sites, swimming pool, mini golf, bike rentals, and movies. Sites include pull-thrus to 60 feet. The campground is located on the south side of US-101 about 8 miles (13 km) west of Sequim and 5 miles (8 km) east of Port Angeles.

● **AL'S RV PARK** *(Open All Year)*
Res and Info: (360) 457-9844
Location: Port Angeles

    GPS Location: 48.10889 N, 123.38444 W, 100 Ft

41 Sites – Al's is a basic but well-managed and maintained small park. There are lots of long-term residents but also several spaces for travelers. The park has back-in spaces to 35 feet although room can sometimes be found for longer rigs. A small lawn area provides tent campers with a place to pitch their tent. The campground is located at the eastern edge of Port Angeles. A sign on US-101 points you north on North Brook Ave. Almost immediately jog left onto N. Lees Creek and the campground is on the right in .3 miles (.5 km).

● **PEABODY CREEK RV PARK** *(Open All Year)*
Res and Info: (360) 457-7092, (800) 392-2361,
           peabodyrv@peabodyrv.com,
           www.peabodyrv.com
Location: Port Angeles

    GPS Location: 48.11583 N, 123.43139 W, Near Sea Level

36 Sites – The Peabody Creek is an older RV park located in a ravine in central Port Angeles. It's a unique place due to its central location which lets you walk anywhere in town. There are quite a few long-term residents but also traveler sites. Most sites here are small (to about 30 feet), maneuvering room is limited. The managers say they can

WASHINGTON

SWEEPING VIEW FROM THE HURRICANE RIDGE HIKING TRAILS

accommodate RVs to 45 feet however. Tenters often use the small grassy area set aside for them. The campground is located off Lincoln Street which is the route US-101 takes going through town. It is on the east side of the street, opposite 2nd Ave.

■ **HEART O'THE HILLS CAMPGROUND** *(Open All Year)*
Information: (360) 565-3130
Location: 5 miles (8 Km) S of Port Angeles

GPS Location: 48.03583 N, 123.42778 W, 1,800 Ft

105 Sites – This federal campground, like most of those in Olympic National Park, is best for tent campers and those with smaller RVs. The managers recommend rigs to 21 feet although they note that there are some sites to 35 feet. With caution rigs to 35 feet can use this campground although most sites would not allow the use of slide-outs. The campground is located off the Hurricane Ridge Road. From central Port Angeles drive south on S. Race Street. This becomes Hurricane Ridge Road. You'll soon pass the park visitor center and in another 5.1 miles (8.2 km) will reach the campground entrance.

● **ELWHA DAM RV PARK** *(Open All Year)*
Res and Info: (360) 452-7054, (877) 435-9421,
paradise@elwhadamrvpark.com,
www.elwhadamrvpark.com
Location: 5 Miles (8 Km) W of Port Angeles

GPS Location: 48.09750 N, 123.55306 W, 300 Ft

60 Sites – Although it is some distance outside town this is our favorite park when we

visit Port Angeles. There is a large grassy area with shade if you want it for tent camp-ers. The park has some long term residents but they are along the border of the park and separate from the traveler sites. Some traveler sites are pull-thrus to 60 feet. A separate tent area covers a large area. There is a hiking trail to the Lower Elwha Dam. To reach the campground turn north on SR-112 which leaves US-101 about 4 miles (6.5 km) west of Port Angeles. Follow SR-112 for .7 mile (1.1 km), turn left into Lower Dam Road, then turn left again immediately into the campground entrance.

■ **ALTAIRE CAMPGROUND** *(Open May 15 to Oct 15 – Varies)*
Information: (360) 565-3130
Location: 12 Miles (19 Km) W of Port Angeles

GPS Location: 48.00972 N, 123.59111 W, 400 Ft

30 Sites – This Olympic National Park campground is at a pretty little place along the El-wha River. Sites are back-ins and pull-thrus off one loop. It's a narrow road but RVs to 35 feet can manage to use the campground if they are extremely cautious. It's better for tent campers and smaller rigs. To reach the campground turn south on Olympic Hot Springs Road from US-101 about 7 miles (11 km) west of Port Angeles. You'll pass through a park entrance booth and then see the campground on your right just after crossing the Elwha at 4.7 miles (7.6 km).

■ **ELWHA CAMPGROUND** *(Open All Year)*
Information: (360) 565-3130
Location: 10 Miles (16 Km) W of Port Angeles

GPS Location: 48.02806 N, 123.58889 W, 300 Ft

41 Sites – This Olympic National Park campground is located in a dense stand of Doug-las-Fir and Hemlocks. It's a little dark but a nice campground anyway. There are back-in and pull-thru sites to 40 feet but an extremely narrow access loop road closely bordered by big trees makes 25 feet the maximum practical RV size for this park. To reach the campground turn south on Olympic Hot Springs Road from US-101 about 7 miles (11 km) west of Port Angeles. You'll pass through a park entrance booth and then see the campground on your left at 2.9 miles (4.7 km).

○ **SALT CREEK RECREATION AREA** *(Open All Year)*
Res and Info: (360) 928-3441,
ccpsc@olypen.com,
www.clallam.net/Parks/SaltCreek.html
Location: 15 Miles (24 Km) W of Port Angeles

GPS Location: 48.16167 N, 123.69889 W, 100 Ft

92 Sites – This is a Clallam County Campground. Camping is in two areas. There is a forest-type campground with back-in sites to 40 feet. There is also a large grassy area overlooking the water with back-ins and pull-thrus to 50 feet, many with electricity and water hookups. This site was a military base until after WWII. Now it offers beach access (from a point to the west), and a marine life sanctuary with tide pools. About 4 miles (6.4 km) west of Port Angeles turn north on SR-112. Follow SR-112 for 7.2 miles (11.6 km) and turn north on Camp Hayden Road. You'll reach the campground in another 3.5 miles (5.6 km).

CRESCENT BEACH PARK *(Open All Year)*
Reservations: (866) 690-3344, www.olypen.com/crescent
Information: (360) 928-3344, crescent@olypen.com,
Location: 15 Miles (24 Km) W of Port Angeles

GPS: 48.15917 N, 123.71139 W, Near Sea Level

36 Sites – Crescent Beach Park is very unique, it has its
own beach. The beach is about a half-mile long, in summer the water gets warm enough
for swimming and when the weather is right this can be a surfing destination too. The
highway runs about 100 yards back from the beach and the campground is on the south
side of it. Parking is on grass, any size rig will fit just fine and it's also good tent camping.
About 4 miles (6 km) west of Port Angeles turn north on SR-112. Follow SR-112 for 7.2
miles (11.6 km) and turn north on Camp Hayden Road. You'll reach the campground in
another 4.2 miles (6.8 km).

☐ **LYRE RIVER WASHINGTON DEPARTMENT OF NATURAL**
   RESOURCES CAMPGROUND *(Open All Year)*

Information: (360) 374-6131
Location: 19 Miles (31 Km) W of Port Angeles

GPS Location: 48.15000 N, 123.83306 W, 100 Ft

9 Sites – Lyre River is a very small and dark forest-type campground in dense trees. Sites
are small and there is little or no maneuvering room, it's OK for RVs to about 25 feet
but even rigs this small will have to struggle to turn around. Fishing for steelhead and
salmon is possible in the Lyre River. Use of the campground requires that you have either
an annual Washington State Discover Pass or a Washington State One-day Pass. Passes
cannot be purchased at the campground, see the discussion under *Washington State Parks*
above. About 4 miles (6.4 km) west of Port Angeles turn north on SR-112. Follow SR-
112 15 miles (24 km) and turn north on E. Lyre River Rd. at the campground sign. The
campground entrance is about .5 miles (.8 km) from the highway.

● **SHADOW MOUNTAIN RV PARK** *(Open All Year)*
Reservations: (877) 928-3043
Information: (360) 928-3043, info@shadomt.com,
                www.shadowmt.com
Location: 13 Miles (21 Km) W of Port Angeles

GPS Location: 48.08528 N, 123.71000 W, 600 Ft

54 Sites – This campground occupies terraces on the
hillside behind a Texaco station and convenience
store along the highway west of Port Angeles. Sites are full-hookup back-ins to 45 feet
with good maneuvering room. There are also tent sites in a separate meadow. Amenities
include miniature golf. The Wi-Fi hotspot is at the store and does not reach most sites.
From Port Angeles travel west 13 miles (21 km) along US-101 to the campground.

● **LOG CABIN RESORT**
   (Open May 20 to Sept 18 – Varies)
Res and Info: (360) 928-3325,
                 www.logcabinresort.net
Location: 14 Miles (23 Km) W of Port
              Angeles

GPS Location: 48.09556 N, 123.79028 W, 500 Ft

38 Sites – About 15 miles (24 km) west of Port Angeles is beautiful Lake Crescent. On the north shore is an old resort, originally established in 1895. There is a small lodge with a restaurant and cabins, swimming and fishing out front, boat ramp and dock, and a fine but rustic little RV park. Sites are back-ins with full hookups. A few extend to 35 feet but most are shorter. Parking is on grass. To reach the resort start at the junction of US-101 and SR-112 which is about 3 miles (5 km) west of Port Angeles. Drive west 10.8 miles (17.4 km) on US-101 Just before you reach the east end of the lake East Beach Rd., a well-marked but narrow paved road, goes right. Follow the road behind cabins along the lake shore for about three miles (5 km) to the resort.

■ **FAIRHOLM CAMPGROUND** *(Open April 1 to Oct 15 – Varies)*
Information: (360) 565-3130
Location: 25 Miles (40 Km) W of Port Angeles

GPS Location: 48.07000 N, 123.91833 W, 600 Ft

88 Sites – Fairholm is an older Olympic National Park campground located right off the highway at the west end of Crescent Lake. It's best for tent campers, the Park Service recommends that RVs no longer than 21 feet use this campground. From Port Angeles drive west on US-101 for 25 miles (40 km) to the campground.

● **SOL DUC HOT SPRINGS RESORT RV PARK**
    (Open March 15 to Oct 15 – Varies)
Reservations: (866) 4-SOL-DUC
Information: (360) 327-3583, pamsdr@aol.com,
                 www.visitsolduc.com
Location: 38 Miles (61 Km) W of Port Angeles

GPS Location: 47.96889 N, 123.86139 W, 1,700 Ft

17 Sites – This hot springs resort has occupied the same location since the early part of the last century. There are rental cottages, a restaurant, a snack bar, and several hot pools. There is also an RV campground. It has 17 back-in sites around a large gravel lot, there is room for any rig. Only electricity and water are available, there is a dump station (extra charge) a little farther up the road. Behind the sites are picnic tables and fire pits. The resort is a short walk away, the restrooms are located there. To reach the resort head west from Port Angeles for 26 miles (42 km). Turn south on the Sol Duc Road, the campground is on the right in 12.5 miles (20.2 km). The RV park entrance is separate from the one for the resort, it is just beyond the main entrance.

■ **SOL DUC OLYMPIC NATIONAL PARK CAMPGROUND** *(Open All Year)*
Information: (360) 565-3130
Location: 39 Miles (63 Km) W of Port Angeles

GPS Location: 47.96611 N, 123.85694 W, 1,700 Ft

82 Sites – About .2 mile (.3 km) beyond the Sol Duc resort is a park campground. The sites are located off two loops. A few of the sites will take RVs to 35 feet, narrow roads and sites require cautious driving. Many sites do not have room for slide-outs. Loop A is better for RVs than loop B. To reach the resort head west from Port Angeles for 26 miles (42 km). Turn south on the Sol Duc Road, the campground is on the right in 12.7 miles (20.5 km). The entrances for loops A and B are separate, they are located just beyond the dump station.

■ **KLAHOWYA NATIONAL FOREST CAMPGROUND**
   (Open May 15 to Sept 15 – Varies)
Information: (360) 374-6522
Location: 34 Miles (55 Km) W of Port Angeles

GPS Location: 48.06333 N, 124.11056 W, 700 Ft

57 Sites – This Olympic National Forest campground is good for tents and RVs to 40 feet. The campground sits alongside the Sol Duc River. There are hiking trails from the campground and fishing for salmon and steelhead is possible. There's also a boat ramp for drift boats. From Port Angeles drive west for 34 miles (55 km) on US-101, the campground entrance is on the right.

☐ **BEAR CREEK DEPARTMENT OF NATURAL**
      RESOURCES RECREATION AREA *(Open All Year)*

Information: (360) 374-6131
Location: 40 Miles (65 Km) W of Port Angeles

GPS Location: 48.06611 N, 124.23972 W, 500 Ft

15 Sites – This small campground is located right next to the highway and is a good place to overnight. Sites are back-ins and pull-thrus off a loop road. Limited maneuvering room limits use to RVs to 35 feet. Use of the campground requires that you have either an annual Washington State Discover Pass or a Washington State One-day Pass. Passes cannot be purchased at the campground, see the discussion under *Washington State Parks* above. From Port Angeles drive west for 40 miles (65 km) on US-101, the campground is on the south side of the highway.

PORT TOWNSEND

Port Townsend (population 8,800) is not particularly large or economically important today, but at one time this was the major metropolis on Puget Sound. The city was established in 1851. It had an extremely handy location at the entrance to Puget Sound so in the days of sailing ships it was the logical place for a port to serve the area. The town is filled with historic Victorian buildings dating from this era when Port Townsend ruled the sound. Unfortunately for Port Townsend, railroads eventually reached the northwest, and they led to Tacoma and Seattle, not Port Townsend.

The resulting economic bust in Port Townsend was very beneficial to today's tourist trade. The movers and shakers eventually moved out but left the town pretty much as it was at the end of the nineteenth century. Over 70 commercial buildings and homes in the town date from the era and have been preserved.

Port Townsend actually has two old business areas and one new one. As you come into town from the south you will be in the newest one. Behind the Safeway on the left is a parking lot where you can leave your rig and ride a shuttle in to town, parking for big rigs is very limited downtown. Just past the Safeway you will see the Visitor Information Center. They can give you a map of the town with directions for finding some of the more interesting older buildings.

Continuing straight ahead you will soon find yourself in the **historic waterfront district** of town along Water Street. The handsome old buildings in this part of town are filled with shops and restaurants, this is the place to do some poking around.

WASHINGTON

The third business area in Port Townsend is up on the bluff overlooking the waterfront. This was once the "sophisticated" shopping area, a place to shop for ladies who didn't want to have to visit the rowdy waterfront area below. To get there you'll probably drive. While you are doing that take the time to wend your way to the north and take a look at **Fort Worden**. The fort occupies a commanding position near Point Wilson. Now a state-owned conference center (with two campgrounds), the fort was once one of three that guarded the entrance to the sound. The **Coast Artillery Museum** at the fort will show you how it all worked.

Port Townsend celebrates a **Rhododendron Festival** in May and a **Wooden Boat Festival** in September.

You will notice that there is a ferry dock in Port Townsend. Using it you can make the short crossing to Whidbey Island. Whidbey has many campgrounds, see the *Whidbey Island* section of this guide. It is also possible to take a passenger ferry (no vehicles) from Port Townsend to either Victoria, B.C. or to Seattle.

Port Townsend Campgrounds

FORT TOWNSEND STATE PARK *(Open April 1 to Nov 15 – Varies)*
Reservations: (360) 344-4431, fwcamping@parks.wa.gov
Information: (360) 385-3595, (360) 902-8844, www.parks.wa.gov
Location: 3 Miles (5 Km) S of Port Townsend

GPS Location: 48.07444 N, 122.78889 W, 100 Ft

44 Sites – This state park encompasses the former Fort Townsend which dated from 1856. An interpretive trail with 13 stations helps you explore the site. While this is a waterfront state park the campsite are in two locations away from the water. Sites 1 to 27 are forest-type sites in a loop with narrow roads, a sign at the entryway limits use to vehicles under 21 feet. Sites 28 to 40 are narrow pull-thru sites to 38 feet. They will not accommodate slide-outs and the turn to exit the area is very tight, big rigs would need to back out. We recommend that RVs no longer than 30 feet use this area. The campground is located south of Port Townsend along Port Townsend Bay. The Old Fort Townsend Road leaves SR-20 about 2 miles (3 km) south of Port Townsend, it leads east for 1.3 miles (2.1 km) to the park.

JEFFERSON COUNTY FAIRGROUNDS *(Open All Year)*
Information: (360) 385-1013, jeffcofairgrounds@olypen.com, www.jeffcofairgrounds.com
Location: Port Townsend

GPS Location: 48.13222 N, 122.78389 W, Near Sea Level

81 Sites – The fairgrounds are located just west of Port Townsend and make a good inexpensive place to stay while visiting the town. Parking is in a very large grassy field with full, partial, and no hookup sites suitable for any size rig. There's a self check-in system so the site is unattended. There are dedicated restrooms for the campground and they are generally kept in decent shape. From SR-20 as you enter Fort Townsend from the west you will see both the fairgrounds and Fort Worden (see below) signed to the left on Kearney Street. Turn left here and drive .3 mile (.5 km) on Kearney. At the T turn left on Blaine and then take the first right onto San Juan Ave. Now follow San Juan north for 1.5 miles (2.4 km) to where it makes a 90-degree left and becomes 49th. Drive east about four blocks and turn left on Jackman Street. The entry gate is a block and a half ahead on the left.

☐ **FORT WORDEN STATE PARK** *(Open All Year)*
Reservations: (360) 344-4431, www.fortworden.org
Information: (360) 344-4431, (360) 344-4400,
(360) 902-8844, www.fortworden.org
Location: Port Townsend

GPS Location: 48.13389 N, 122.76472 W, Near Sea Level

80 Sites – Camping at Fort Worden is in two areas known as the Beach and Upper campgrounds. The beach sites are near Point Wilson and really are not on the beach, but they're near it. These are long paved back-in and pull-thru sites to 70 feet in an open area of grass. The upper campground sites are about a mile (1.6 km) away. These are all back-ins to about 55 feet on gravel. This state park has its own reservation system and does not

WASHINGTON

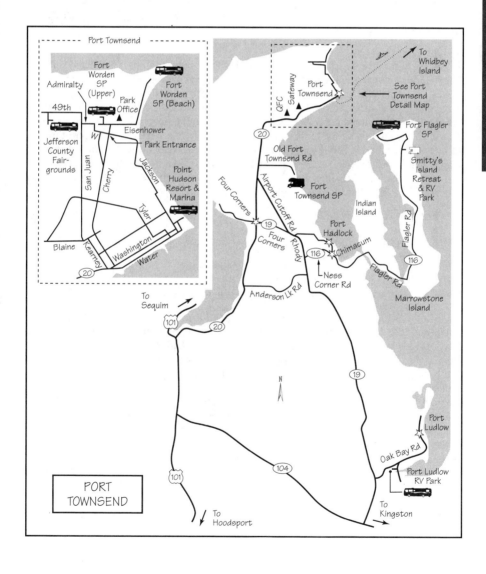

use the system used by the other Washington state parks. From SR-20 as you enter Fort Townsend from the west you will see both the fairgrounds and Fort Worden signed to the left on Kearney Street. Turn left here and drive .3 mile (.5 km) on Kearney. At the T turn left on Blain and then take the first right onto San Juan Ave. Now follow San Juan north for 1.4 miles (2.3 km). Turn right on Admiralty Street and follow it as it turns right and then left, you'll reach the state park entrance in .5 mile (.8 km). Turn left into the park, proceed ahead for two blocks to Eisenhower Ave, turn right and you'll soon see the reception office on the left. Park and go inside to check in.

● **POINT HUDSON RESORT AND MARINA**
(Open All Year)
Reservations: (800) 228-2803
Information: (360) 385-2828, info@portofpt.com , www.portofpt.com/point_hudson.htm
Location: Port Townsend

GPS Location: 48.11833 N, 122.75056 W, Near Sea Level

44 Sites – For convenience it is hard to beat this little campground. It is located right on Point Hudson which is at the north end of Port Townsend's waterside business area. From this campground you can easily stroll to the center of town to shop or visit a restaurant in the evening. The resort was once a Coast Guard station and the tidy white-painted buildings maintain the atmosphere. So does the location on the point where you can keep an eye on all the passing ships, ferries, and yachts. Sites here are back-ins and pull-thrus to 45 feet. The location is very exposed in windy weather. It is not difficult to find. The main drag along the waterfront is known as Water Street. As you approach the end of the street you will see the RVs directly ahead. You must jog left on Monroe Street for two blocks to Jefferson St. to enter the campground.

☐ **FORT FLAGLER STATE PARK**
(Open March 1 to Nov 1 – Varies)
Reservations: www.parks.wa.gov/reservations/, (888) 226-7688
Information: (360) 385-1259, (360) 902-8844, www.parks.wa.gov, fort.flagler@parks.wa.gov
Location: 17 miles (27 Km) SE of Port Townsend

GPS Location: 48.09417 N, 122.69750 W, Near Sea Level

120 Sites – Fort Flagler is located just 2.5 miles (4 km) from Port Townsend across Port Townsend Bay. You can easily see the town from the campground area, but getting there in your rig is a little more involved. Campsites at Fort Flagler are in two areas, an upper campground and the beachside campground. Sites are paved and are both long pull-thrus and back-ins to 45 feet. Fifty-eight of them offer full hookups. On a clear day Mt Baker is clearly visible. The roundabout (and only) route to the campground is as follows. From the Four Corners intersection on SR-20 drive east on SR-19. Four Corners is 4 miles (6.5 km) south of Fort Townsend and 6 miles (9.7 km) north of the intersection of US-101 and SR-20 at the foot of Discovery Bay. Follow Four Corners Road 1.3 miles (2.1 km) east to the intersection with Rhody Drive and then follow Rhody south 1.2 miles (1.9 km) to Ness Corner Road. Follow Ness Corner Road (SR-116) east for 10.5 miles (16.9 km) as it crosses onto Indian Island and then Marrowstone Island and leads you directly to the park entrance. The road changes names along the way but the route is well signed.

● **PORT LUDLOW RV PARK** *(Open All Year)*
Res and Info: (360) 437-9377
Location: 14 Miles (23 Km) S of Port Townsend

GPS Location: 47.91988 N, 122.70496 W, 100 Ft

37 Sites – Port Ludlow is an upscale marina and housing development on the coast about 14 miles south of Port Townsend. The campground here is older but in relatively good shape, sites are full-hookup back-ins and pull-thrus, most 35 to 40 feet long. They are set in trees, much like a state park. The paved access roads are narrow making parking difficult for larger RVs. Nearby are a golf course and the marina. From Port Townsend drive south on SR-19 for 12.5 miles (20.2 km) to the road leading east to Port Ludlow. Drive east 1.4 miles (2.3 km) and make a right turn and then an immediate right to enter the campground.

REPUBLIC AND CURLEW LAKE

Little Republic (population 1,100) is a former gold mining town located in a fairly remote area of northeast Washington. It's in a valley between the Okanogan Highlands and the Kettle Range, about 90 miles (145 km) northwest of Spokane and just 25 miles (40 km) south of the Canadian border.

The privately operated **Stonerose Interpretive Center and Fossil Site** features Eocene epoch fossils. Digging is permitted with a permit. The **Fairy County Fairgrounds** are

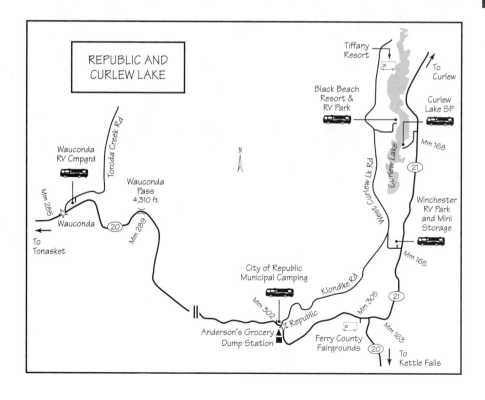

WASHINGTON

in Republic, the fair is held on Labor day. Other celebrations include **Prospectors Days** and the **Republic Motorcycle Rally** in June and the **Washington Open Fiddle Contest** in mid-August.

Most area campgrounds are located on or near Curlew Lake, which is about 8 miles (13 km) by road to the northeast. The lake is some 7 miles (11 km) long and fairly narrow. It's a popular fishery for trout and bass and is also great for swimming and other water sports including skiing, kayaking, and sailing.

Republic and Curlew Lake Campgrounds

○ CITY OF REPUBLIC MUNICIPAL CAMPING
   (Open April 1 to Oct 31 – Varies)
   Information: (509) 775-3216
   Location: Republic, WA

   GPS Location: 48.64786 N, 118.73917 W, 2,500 Ft

6 Sites – The City of Republic allows RVs to park along North Kean Street near the center of town. There is room for about six rigs to parallel park next to a small park. There are six electrical boxes next to the road, and the park has a shelter, tables, and restrooms. RVs are allowed to park here from 6 pm until 8 am. Kean is one block west of Clark, Republic's main street, and the RV parking area is along the block on the north side of where State Route 20 comes in to town from the west. There is a dump station located at the south entrance to town, a $3 donation is suggested for its use.

● WAUCONDA RV CAMPGROUND *(Open April 1 to Oct 31 - Varies)*
   Information: (509) 486-2511,
                   Joe&Cheryl@waucondarvcampground.com,
                   www.waucondarvcampground.com
   Location: 17 Miles (27 Km) W of Republic

   GPS Location: 48.73264 N, 119.00613 W, 3,500 Ft

25 Sites – Wauconda is a former mining town now owned by one couple. The camping area occupies the grounds of an old school with no other buildings nearby. There are nine full hookup back-in RV sites to about 60 feet. There is also a large grassy field for tent camping and a teepee available for rental. Restroom facilities are limited to a portable toilet. The campground is signed from US 20 about 17 miles (27 km) west of Republic and 24 miles (39 km) east of Tonasket.

□ CURLEW LAKE STATE PARK
   (Open April 1 to Oct 31 - Varies)
   Information: (509) 775 3592, (360) 902-8844,
                   www.parks.wa.gov
   Location: 8 Miles (13 Km) NE of Republic

   GPS Location: 48.71914 N, 118.66235 W, 2,300 Ft

84 Sites – Curlew Lake, located about 8 miles (13 km) from Republic, is popular for fishing and boating. This state park is located on the lakeshore. There are back-in and pull-thru RV sites to 40 feet, some with full hookups and some with electricity only. There are also vehicle accessible no-hookup sites as well as walk-in tent sites on grass and along the lakeshore. The park offers a boat ramp and dock as well as a swimming area. From the south end of Republic follow Hwy 21 to the northeast for 8.5 miles (13.7 km) to the park entrance on the left. The paved park access road will take you .5 miles (.8 km) down to the campground.

● **WINCHESTER RV PARK AND MINI STORAGE**
    (Open All Year)
Res and Info: (509) 775-1039,
                 relaxing@winchesterrvpark.com,
                 www.winchesterrvpark.com
Location: 5 Miles (8 Km) NE of Republic

GPS Location: 48.67926 N, 118.66636 W, 2,400 Ft

40 Sites – Winchester is a well-maintained modern RV park with large paved sites separated by well-clipped grass. Sites are pull-thrus to 100 feet and back-ins to 55 feet. Tent camping is on grass. From the south end of Republic follow Hwy 21 east for 5.1 miles (8.2 km). Turn west on West Curlew Lake Road and almost immediately you'll see the campground entrance on the left.

● **BLACK BEACH RESORT AND RV PARK**
    (Open April 1 to Oct 31 - Varies)
Res and Info: (509) 775-3989, bbresort@bossig.com,
                 www.blackbeachresort.com
Location: 13 Miles (21 Km) NE of Republic

GPS Location: 48.72845 N, 118.66722 W, 2,300 Ft

112 Sites – Black Beach is an older resort on the west shore of Curlew Lake. Parking is on grass with large sites for parking an RV, a tow car, and perhaps a boat trailer. Some sites are on the lake. There is a boat launch, some older docks, a small motel, and a small store. This is a popular old-fashioned fishing resort and many of the guests have been coming here for a lot of years. From the south end of Republic follow Hwy 21 east for 5.1 miles (8.2 km). Turn west on West Curlew Lake Road and follow it west and then north for 3.8 mile (6.1 km). Turn right on Black's Beach Road and follow it east to the resort.

ROOSEVELT LAKE

Roosevelt Lake is the reservoir behind Grand Coulee Dam. It's 130 miles (210 km) long. Much of the lake itself and a lot of the south shore make up the **Coulee Dam National Recreation Area**. A large portion of the north shore is the Colville Indian Reservation and part of the south shore is the Spokane Indian Reservation.

The NRA is administered by the National Park Service. The lake is a popular destination for water sports including house boat rentals. Many federal campgrounds line the south shore and a good number have boat launch facilities.

The town of **Kettle Falls** (population 1,600) is located near the upper end of the lake and is connected by good roads to the Spokane area. Historically, the falls were an important Indian fishing location but they were submerged when the lake formed behind Grand Coulee Dam. The lake also flooded the original town and it was moved to the present location in 1940. Kettle Falls is the main source of supplies when visiting the area.

Near Kettle Falls and overlooking the lake is **St Paul's Mission**. The restored Catholic mission was originally built in 1847 to serve the large number of Indians who lived at Kettle Falls during the fishing season.

Farther west where the Spokane River once met the Columbia River is **Fort Spokane**. It was built in 1880 above a series of rapids that were also a popular Indian fishing location. Today there are a museum and visitor center at the site.

The campgrounds listed below are located on the upper end of Roosevelt Lake. There are additional campgrounds, including one national park campground on the lakeshore, near Grand Coulee Dam on the lower lake. See the *Grand Coulee* section of this chapter for them.

Roosevelt Lake Campgrounds

■ **KAMLOOPS ISLAND CAMPGROUND –**
   LAKE ROOSEVELT NRA *(Open All Year)*

Information: (509) 633-9441
Location: 6 Miles (10 Km) NW of Kettle River

GPS Location: 48.67777 N, 118.11647 W, 1,300 Ft

17 Sites – This is a small Lake Roosevelt National Recreation Area campground located in the far north end of Roosevelt Lake at the mouth of the Kettle River inlet. The island has road access. Campsites are back-ins in pines. Some are as long as 30 feet. Parking pads are paved and so are the roads. Water is from a hand pump. From Kettle Falls drive west on Hwy 395 for 2.7 miles (4.4 km) to Hwy 20. Turn north and drive 3.3 miles (5.3 km). Turn right onto Northport Flat Creek Road and then in just .1 mile (1.6 km) turn left into the paved campground entrance road.

■ **KETTLE RIVER CAMPGROUND –**
   LAKE ROOSEVELT NRA *(Open All Year)*

Information: (509) 633-9441
Location: 9 Miles (15 Km) NW of Kettle Falls

GPS Location: 48.71636 N, 118.12336 W, 1,300 Ft

13 Sites – Kettle River Campground is another small Lake Roosevelt National Recreation Area campground at the northern end of Lake Roosevelt along the Kettle River inlet. The campground occupies a small peninsula with pine trees. Sites are back-ins and pull-thrus to about 35 feet off a loop road. Campground roads are paved and so are the parking pads. From Kettle Falls drive west on Hwy 395 for 2.7 miles (4.4 km) to Hwy 20. Turn north and drive 6.1 miles (9.8 km). Turn right, cross the railroad tracks, and follow the paved access road for .7 miles (1.1 km) to the campground.

■ **KETTLE FALLS CAMPGROUND –**
   LAKE ROOSEVELT NRA *(Open All Year)*

Reservations: www.recreation.gov, (877) 444-6777
Information: (509) 633-9441
Location: 4 Miles (6 Km) SW of Kettle Falls

GPS Location: 48.60075 N, 118.12223 W, 1.300 Ft

76 Sites – This is a fairly large Lake Roosevelt National Recreation Area campground. It's the closest to Kettle Falls and quite popular. Sites here are back-ins and pull-thrus to about 45 feet. Access roads are paved and so are parking pads, the campground sits in a dense grove of pines. Roads are narrow and the campground can be crowded so careful maneuvering is required of big rigs. In addition to scattered vault toilets there are comfort stations with flush toilets, water comes from faucets. There is a very popular boat launch as well as a store and houseboat rental facility. Drive west from Kettle Falls and turn left on South Boise Road just before Lake Roosevelt Bridge over the lake, about 2 miles (3 km). Follow the road south for 1.9 miles (3.1 km) to the campground entrance.

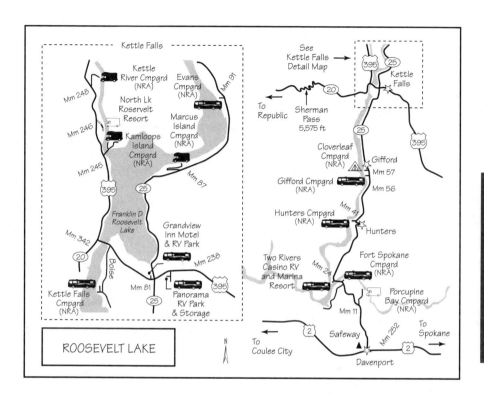

ROOSEVELT LAKE

● **GRANDVIEW INN MOTEL AND RV PARK**
   (Open All Year)
   Res and Info: (888) 488-6733, (509) 738-6733,
                  www.grandviewinnandrvpark.com
   Location: Kettle Falls

   GPS Location: 48.60633 N, 118.07634 W, 1,500 Ft

23 Sites – The Grandview is a motel with a small RV park located at the western entrance to Kettle Falls. Sites are full-hookup gravel back-ins to 60 feet and they are separated by grass. As you approach Kettle Falls from the west you'll see the motel on the left at the intersection of Hwy 395 and Hwy 25.

● **PANORAMA RV PARK AND STORAGE**
   (Open All Year)
   Res and Info: (509) 738-6831, (800) 227-6352
   Location: Kettle Falls

   GPS Location: 48.60863 N, 118.06220 W, 1,600 Ft

62 Sites – The Panorama is an older RV park and storage facility located right in Kettle Falls. There are pull-thrus to 60 feet and back-ins to 40 feet. This campground has a lot of long-term residents but is also used by travelers. In Kettles Falls from the intersection of Hwy 395 and Hwy 25 drive east .7 mile (1.1 km) and turn south on Juniper Street. Cross the railroad tracks and take the first right on 6th Avenue. The campground is directly ahead.

■ **Evans Campground – Lake Roosevelt NRA**
   (Open All Year)
   Information: (509) 633-9441
   Location: 9 Miles (15 Km) N of Kettle Falls

   GPS Location: 48.69996 N, 118.01768 W, 1,300 Ft

43 Sites – Evans is one of the few Lake Roosevelt NRA camp-grounds with a dump station. It also has a boat ramp so it's well used even though reservations are not available. Sites are large here and paved with wide paved access roads so it's fine for larger rigs. The campground is in a thin forest of pines and some sites are right along the lakeshore. From the intersection of Hwy 395 and Hwy 25 in Kettle Falls drive north for 9.3 miles (15 km) to the entrance on the left.

■ **Marcus Island Campground –**
   Lake Roosevelt NRA *(Open All Year)*
   Information: (509) 633-9441
   Location: 6 Miles (10 Km) N of Kettle Falls

   GPS Location: 48.66909 N, 118.05315 W, 1,300 Ft

20 Sites – Marcus Island is a smaller Lake Roosevelt campground with minimal facilities although there is a boat ramp. Sites are off a long stub road with a small turning circle at the end, the campground is best for RVs only to 30 feet. Water is from a hand pump. From the intersection of Hwy 395 and Hwy 25 in Kettle Falls drive north for 5.6 miles (9 km) to the entrance on the left.

■ **Cloverleaf Campground – Lake Roosevelt NRA**
   (OpenAll Year)
   Information: (509) 633-9441
   Location: 24 Miles (39 Km) S of Kettle Falls

   GPS Location: 48.29726 N, 118.14587 W, 1,400 Ft

9 Sites – Cloverleaf is a small tent-only campground near the town of Gifford, WA. Gifford Campground, suitable for RVs and described below, is just to the south. This is a walk-in campground and is also used by boat campers so there is a boat dock but no launch ramp. Restrooms are vault toilets and there is a water pump. From Kettle Falls drive south on Hwy 25 for 24.1 miles (38.7 km), the campground is on the left.

■ **Gifford Campground – Lake Roosevelt NRA**
   (Open All Year)
   Information: (509) 633-9441
   Location: 25 Miles (40 Km) S of Kettle Falls

   GPS Location: 48.28708 N, 118.14340 W, 1,300 Ft

42 Sites – Gifford is a beautiful waterfront Lake Roosevelt NRA campground. Sites here are back-ins with a few pull-thrus and reach 45 feet. Roads and sites are paved, some sites are along the lake. There's a boat ramp and a dock, as well as a dump station. From Kettle Falls drive south on Hwy 25 for 25 miles (40 km) to the campground entrance.

■ **Hunters Campground – Lake Roosevelt NRA**
   (Open All Year)
   Information: (509) 633-9441
   Location: 39 Miles (63 Km) S of Kettle Falls

   GPS Location: 48.12473 N, 118.23129 W, 1,300 Ft

39 Sites – This Lake Roosevelt National Recreation Area campground is relatively remote but has good facilities. Sites have paved pads off paved roads, some are just back from the lake and have good views. Comfort stations have flush toilets and there is a dump station and a boat ramp and dock. From Kettle Falls drive south on Hwy 25 for 39 miles (40 km) to the entrance road in Hunters, WA. From there it's about a mile (1.6 km) out to the campground.

● **TWO RIVERS CASINO RV AND MARINA RESORT** *(Open All Year)*

Res and Info: (509) 722-4029,
www.two-rivers-resort.com
Location: 24 Miles (39 Km) N of Davenport, WA

GPS Location: 47.90601 N, 118.32526 W, 1,300 Ft

130 Sites – This casino, campground, and marina is the nicest facility on Lake Roosevelt. The RV park has paved roads and sites, they are separated by grass and have patios. Most sites are back-ins to about 45 feet although there are just a few large pull-thrus as well as tent sites. There's also an overflow area for RVers with no hookups but with a substantial fee. The casino is nearby and also a marina with houseboat rentals. From Davenport, WA, drive north on Hwy 25 to the facility which is just across the bridge from the Fort Spokane visitor center and campground. Coming from the north it's 60 miles (97 km) from Kettle Falls.

■ **FORT SPOKANE CAMPGROUND– LAKE ROOSEVELT NRA** *(Open All Year)*

Reservations: www.recreation.gov, 877 444-6777
Information: (509) 633-9441
Location: 23 Miles (37 Km) N of Davenport, WA

GPS Location: 47.90875 N, 118.30916 W, 1,300 Ft

67 Sites – The Fort Spokane Campground is conveniently located near Fort Spokane visitor center and across the bridge from the Two Rivers Casino. Sites here are paved off paved roads, there are large back-ins and pull-thrus. Note that reservations are available here, and a good idea on weekends since the campground is more easily accessible than many on the north section of the lake. Amenities include a boat ramp and dock. From Davenport drive north on Hwy 25 for 23 miles (37 km), the campground is on the right.

SANDPOINT AND LAKE PEND OREILLE, IDAHO

Sandpoint (population 7,400) is located on the northwest shore of beautiful Lake Pend Oreille. This is an attractive little lakeshore town with plenty of shopping and restaurants. The town also has a number of art galleries. The **Bonner County Historical Museum** offers local history and Native American artifacts. Sandpoint has walking and bicycle trails and a number of nearby golf courses. The city hosts quite a few events during the year. Among them are the **Northern Idaho Timberfest** in early June, **Sandpoint Wooden Boat Festival** in July, the **Festival at Sandpoint** music festival in early August, and the **Bonner County Fair and Rodeo** in late August.

A major attraction near Sandpoint is **Schweitzer Mountain Resort**. This regional ski area offers both winter and summer attractions. There's skiing from late November to early April. In summer the chairlifts are used for sightseeing and there are hiking trails,

WASHINGTON

mountain biking, and horseback riding. It's only 11 miles (18 km) up to the slopes from Sandpoint.

Lake Pend Oreille is the largest lake in Idaho. It has a surface area of 180 square miles and over 100 miles of shoreline. It's also a deep lake with depths in some places of over 1,100 feet. That means it has excellent fishing for cold water fish like rainbows and lake trout.

Only one campground below is near Sandpoint. The others are scattered around the lake or along the highway south of Sandpoint. There's a good selection with forest service, state, and commercial campgrounds all represented.

Sandpoint and Lake Pend Oreille, Idaho Campgrounds

○ **BONNER COUNTY FAIRGROUNDS** (Open All Year)
Res and Info: (208) 263-8414
Location: Sandpoint

GPS Location: 48.31025 N, 116.55733 W, 2,100 Ft

33 Sites – At the north end of the Bonner County Fairgrounds there's a newly renovated camping area. RV sites are paved back-ins off a paved driveway with lots of grass. Sites are about 45 feet long, some a little longer. There are electrical and water hookups at all sites as well as a dump station. Tents can be pitched on the grass. The center of the campground has a picnic shelter and there are barbeque grills. There's also a new restroom building with showers. Reservations are a good idea because the campground is used by people attending various events on the grounds including the fair during the second half of August. From the intersection of SR-200 and US-2 in Ponderay just north of Sandpoint drive west on the Schweitzer Cutoff Road for .5 miles (.8 km) to Boyer Road. Turn right and drive north a short distance, the entrance is on the left. Drive on back to the campground, if the fairground office is closed there is a host to check you in.

● **HI DEE HO RV PARK** (Open All Year)
Res and Info: (800) 763-3922, (208) 263-3922,
              sbayless@lakerv.com,
              www.lakerv.com
Location: 2 Miles (3 Km) N of Sandpoint

GPS Location: 48.29750 N, 116.54528 W, 2,100 Ft

46 Sites – This is a modern big-rig campground with large pull-thru sites suitable for rigs longer than 45 feet and 50-amp power. It is operated in conjunction with a RV service center and parts store and has an excellent restroom and laundry building. It's located in an industrial park but is the closest park in this guide to the town of Sandpoint. From the intersection of SR-200 and US-2 in Ponderay just north of Sandpoint drive .5 miles (8 km) north on US-2, the entrance is on the right.

● **ISLAND VIEW TRAILER PARK** (Open May 1 to Nov 1)
Res and Info: (208) 264-5509,
              stevemisha@coldwellbanker.com,
              http://www.sandpoint.com/go/islandview/
Location: 21 Miles (34 Km) E of Sandpoint

GPS Location: 48.20889 N, 116.28778 W, 2,000 Ft

55 Sites – This is a smaller RV resort located on the Hope Peninsula on the east shore of Lake Pend Oreille. This peninsula is a game reserve, deer are very plentiful. Because the

location is a little off the beaten path most residents here stay for several months but there are usually some spaces for travelers and it's a very pleasant RV park. Sites vary in size, they are back-ins and pull-thrus to 60 feet. Amenities include a boat launch and marina. The Hope Peninsula road leaves SR-200 some 18 miles (29 km) east of Sandpoint and 7 miles (11 km) north of Clark Fork. It's 1.9 miles (3.1 km) from the cutoff to the resort.

● **BEYOND HOPE RESORT** *(Open May 1 to Oct 1)*

Reservations: (877) 270-HOPE,
    www.beyondhoperesort.com
Information: (208) 264-5251, www.beyondhoperesort.com
Location: 21 Miles (34 Km) E of Sandpoint

  GPS Location: 48.21528 N, 116.28528 W, 2,000 Ft

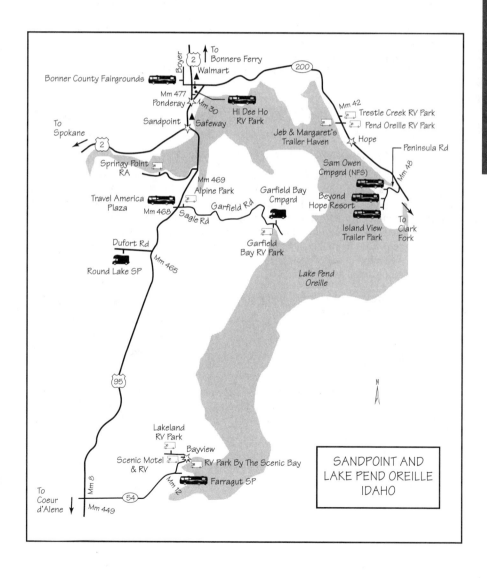

SANDPOINT AND
LAKE PEND OREILLE
IDAHO

60 Sites – This campground is located near the Island View but much larger. Amenities include a boat launch, marina, and restaurant. Parking is on grass, sites will take large rigs. A weekly pump-out service is available for sites not having sewer. The Hope Peninsula road leaves SR-200 some 18 miles (29 km) east of Sandpoint and 7 miles (11 km) north of Clark Fork. It's 1.4 miles (2.3 km) from the cutoff to the resort.

■ **SAM OWEN CAMPGROUND** *(Open May 12 to Sept 25 – Varies)*
Reservations: www.recreation.gov, (877) 444-6777
Information: (208) 264-0209
Location: 20 Miles (32 Km) E of Sandpoint

GPS Location: 48.21944 N, 116.28500 W, 2,000 Ft

81 Sites – This is a large Kaniksu National Forest campground located on the Hope Peninsula on the east side of Lake Pend Oreille. There is a beach area for swimming, campsites are located in the trees behind. Some of these sites will take RVs to 45 feet but maneuvering room is tight. There is a dump and water fill station, a fee is charged for those not camping here. The Hope Peninsula road leaves SR-200 some 18 miles (29 km) east of Sandpoint and 7 miles (11 km) north of Clark Fork. It's 1.1 miles (1.7 km) from the cutoff to the campground entrance.

○ **GARFIELD BAY CAMPGROUND** *(Open May 1 to Sept 30)*
Information: (208) 265-1438
Location: 14 Miles (23 Km) S of Sandpoint

GPS Location: 48.19000 N, 116.43444 W, 2,200 Ft

24 Sites – This is a small forest service-type campground run by Bonner County that climbs a hillside behind Garfield Bay on the west shore of Lake Pend Oreille. It's quite a climb to the campground from the lakeshore, about a quarter mile. Sites here are small, a couple are suitable for RVs to about 30 feet. On the shore of the lake down the hill is a park with wheelchair-accessible flush toilets, swimming beach, boat launch, and dump station but the restrooms in the campground are outhouses. From US-95 some 5 miles (8 km) south of Sandpoint follow Sagle Road and then Garfield Road east 8.7 miles (14.0 km) to the campground entrance.

● **TRAVEL AMERICA PLAZA** *(Open All Year)*
Res and Info: (208) 263-6522, (208) 263-7511
Location: 5 Miles (8 Km) S of Sandpoint

GPS Location: 48.20306 N, 116.56694 W, 2,200 Ft

76 Sites – This campground occupies a large field behind a gas station, restaurant, and quick-stop grocery along the highway south of Sandpoint. Sites are pull-thrus to 60 feet with parking on grass between gravel drives. Restrooms and the laundry are in a new building. Sign in at the grocery store out front. The campground is on the west side of the highway 5 miles (8 km) south of Sandpoint.

□ **ROUND LAKE STATE PARK** *(Open All Year)*
Reservations: (888) 922-6743, www.idahoparks.org
Information: (208) 263-3489, rou@idpr.state.id.us,
www.idahoparks.org
Location: 10 Miles (16 Km) S of Sandpoint

GPS Location: 48.16667 N, 116.63694 W, 2,200 Ft

52 Sites – This campground is on a lake to the west of Lake Pend Oreille and south of Sandpoint. Some sites will take RVs to 30 feet. There is a swimming beach, a boat launch, and a two-mile (.3 km) nature trail around the lake. Only electric motors are allowed on Round Lake. To reach the campground follow US-95 south from Sandpoint for 8 miles (12.9 km). Turn west on Dufort Road, the campground entrance is on the left in 1.9 miles (3.1 km).

☐ **FARRAGUT STATE PARK** *(Open All Year)*
   Reservations: (888) 922-6743, www.idahoparks.org
   Information: (208) 683-2425, far@idpr.state.id.us,
                   www.idahoparks.org
   Location: 30 Miles (48 Km) S of Sandpoint

   GPS Location: 47.94972 N, 116.60611 W, 2,100 Ft

183 Sites – This, the most popular state park in Idaho, occupies a huge area that was formerly the Farragut Naval Station. There are three campgrounds here with a total of 183 sites. Amenities include a swimming beach, bicycle trails, a museum and two disk golf courses. Some sites will take RVs to 45 feet. The access road is the four-lane SR-54 which heads east from US-95 some 25 miles (40 km) south of Sandpoint. In 4.3 miles (6.9 km) you'll see the exit on the right for the campground headquarters and sign-in station.

SEATTLE

The Seattle Metropolitan Area is the Northwest's giant with an area population (including Everett, Tacoma, and the Eastside) of almost 3,300,000 people. Access to Seattle is easy. Seattle-Tacoma International Airport (locally called Sea-Tac) provides connections to national and international flights. If you happen to be arriving in your own vehicle the city is conveniently located at the intersection of the west coast's I-5 and east-west I-90 which connects this part of the Northwest with points east. Seattle makes an extremely interesting tourist destination. It is a very popular with visitors from both the U.S. and other countries.

Driving in Seattle can be confusing and the roads congested. Roads must detour around lakes and hills. A major highway, I-5, runs north and south right through the middle of the city, sometimes it is as much of a barrier as the hills, lakes, and canals. A ring-road freeway, I-405 circles east of Lake Washington, others were planned but never built. Two major freeways connect I-5 and I-405 across Lake Washington on floating bridges. One of those sank several years ago, but it has been replaced. Even with all this concrete there is not nearly enough highway for the number of cars, so be sure to avoid the extended rush hours.

The city has only a very limited light rail system, but it does have a pretty good bus system. Most of the campgrounds listed below have decent bus transportation available that can get you to downtown Seattle. Unfortunately it is more difficult to use the busses from the campgrounds to reach the outlying neighborhoods and suburbs since the lines tend to radiate from the center rather than circle it. That means that you will probably want to use the bus to go downtown because both traffic and parking are difficult there. When bound for destinations away from the city center you will probably want to use your tow car or smaller RV.

Seattle has two other transportation options, both are tourist destinations in their own right. The state's ferry fleet serves the far shore of Puget Sound from a terminal in downtown Seattle. No visit to Seattle would be complete without a ferry outing. Also, Seattle still has its monorail, originally built for the 1964 World's Fair. The monorail's usefulness is limited but it does provide a good way to visit the Space Needle and Seattle Center from downtown.

Seattle's **central downtown area** is fairly compact, about 9 blocks deep from the water up to the I-5 freeway and 13 wide from Jefferson to Olive. The streets in this section don't run north and south like they do in most of the rest of Seattle, they are cocked at a 45-degree angle to parallel the waterfront. The area is compact, but walking it can be tiring because the streets climb steeply uphill from the water. It is good to know that bus service in the central area is free, just climb on and ride.

When you arrive in town you will probably alight near the uptown shopping district centered around **Westlake Center** at 4th and Pine at the north end of the downtown area. There are a cluster of large stores here including the flagship Nordstrom department store. Westlake is also the terminal for the monorail, more on that later.

Directly toward the water from Westlake is one of Seattle's most famous attractions. **Pike Place Market**, at 1st and Pike, is an actual operating farmer's market, but much more. In addition to produce you'll find fish, exotic foods of all kinds, arts and crafts, and even restaurants. It's set in several funky buildings dating from 1907, although there are lots of upscale additions in the vicinity.

Just down 1st Avenue from the market is the **Seattle Art Museum**. It offers permanent displays of Asian and Northwest Indian art as well as temporary traveling exhibits. You can find the museum by watching for the **Hammer Man** sculpture out front, you really can't miss it.

From the market or museum you can descend to the waterfront using either stairs or a handy elevator. The **downtown Seattle waterfront** stretches for over a mile from Pier 70 next to Myrtle Edwards Park in the northwest to the Colman Dock ferry terminal (Pier 52) in the southeast. The piers between the two offer restaurants, stores, a marina, and even public parks. The area draws crowds on any sunny day. Don't miss the **Seattle Aquarium** on Pier 59. You can easily travel the length of the waterfront on a streetcar running on the far side of the road, the streetcar line turns inland at the south end of the waterfront and runs east through Pioneer Square to the International District.

At the south end of the waterfront is Colman Dock, the terminal for the **Washington State Ferry System**. Walk onto a ferry for an inexpensive two-hour round trip ride to the far side of the sound. You'll find commercial tour-boat operators along the waterfront, they'll take you on a **sightseeing tour** of Elliott Bay or through the ship canal. You can also travel to **Tillicum Island** for a traditional-style salmon bake.

To the south of the central downtown area is the **Pioneer Square Historical District**. This is the original Seattle. The whole swampy mess burned down in 1893 and handsome brick buildings were built as replacements. Later, fill from projects to flatten Seattle's hills (called the Regrade) was used to raise the street levels and fill the tidelands to the south. Today you'll see two huge sports arenas built on the fill, one for baseball and one for football. The center of the action in this part of town is tiny **Pioneer Square.** It is located at the foot of Yesler, the original "**Skid Road**" and near the location of Seattle's first large employer, the steam-powered Yesler's Mill. The mill is long gone but the square and surrounding streets do offer lots of shops and restaurants. Here you can take a tour of Seattle's "**underground**". The underground is actually the first floors of the nearby build-

PIONEER SQUARE AT THE FOOT OF THE ORIIGINAL "SKID ROAD"

ings. When the streets were raised during the Regrade the first floors of these buildings were abandoned, entrances were moved up to the second floors.

East of the Pioneer Square area is Seattle's **International District**. One easy way to reach it is to ride the trolley from the waterfront or Pioneer Square area. Covering about 30 blocks the district is filled with Chinese, Japanese, Korean, Filipino, and Southeast Asian shops and restaurants. Worth a walk-through is the large Uwajimaya Asian supermarket.

Back at the central shopping district you have one more thing to do. Hop on the monorail and ride to the **Seattle Center**. This was the site of the 1964 World's Fair and continues to offer a number of attractions including the **Space Needle**, the **Pacific Science Center**, and even an amusement park. You can ride the elevator to the top of the Space Needle for the view or tour the child-friendly exhibits of the Science Center.

North of the downtown Seattle area and probably most easily reached using your own set of wheels is another of Seattle's popular attractions. The **Hiram M. Chittenden Locks** mark the beginning of the canal that connects the salt water Puget Sound with Lake Washington. You can watch work boats and yachts as they float up and down and also take a peek through **viewing windows** at the fish ladder that lets salmon and steelhead bypass the locks.

If you drive eastward near the north shore of the canal you'll pass through Ballard, Fremont, and Wallingford and find yourself in the **University District**. Most of the stores and restaurants here are along the north-south 45th Avenue, usually just called the "Ave". The campus lies just a block east of the Ave and is huge, 35,000 students attend class here. The University grounds are very attractive, you'll enjoy a walk on the campus.

Because Seattle used to be home to Boeing it is known for aviation, and there are two

WASHINGTON

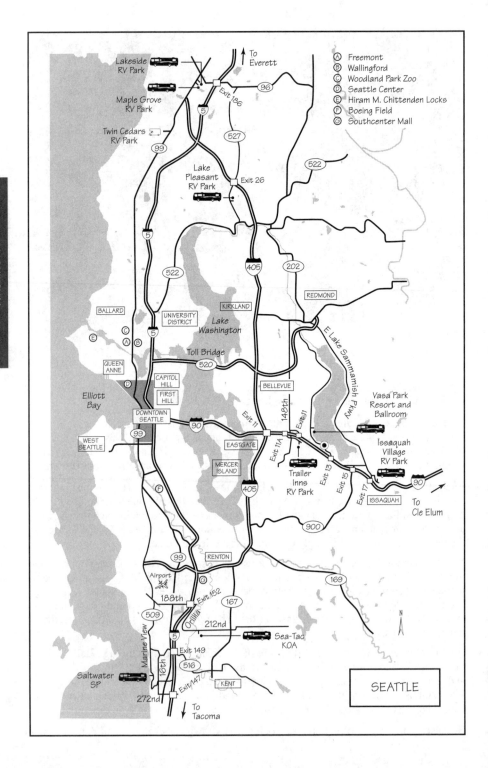

To Everett

Lakeside RV Park

Maple Grove RV Park

Twin Cedars RV Park

Exit 186

96

5

527

99

Lake Pleasant RV Park   Exit 26

522

522

405

202

REDMOND

BALLARD

UNIVERSITY DISTRICT

KIRKLAND

Lake Washington

5

Ⓒ

Ⓔ

Ⓐ Ⓑ

QUEEN ANNE

Toll Bridge

520

CAPITOL HILL

FIRST HILL

BELLEVUE

Ⓓ

Elliott Bay

DOWNTOWN SEATTLE

99

90

Exit 11

148th

Exit 11

E Lake Sammamish Pkwy

Vasa Park Resort and Ballroom

WEST SEATTLE

EASTGATE

Exit 11A

MERCER ISLAND

Trailer Inns RV Park

Exit 13

Exit 15

Exit 17

Issaquah Village RV Park

90

Ⓕ

405

ISSAQUAH

To Cle Elum

900

99

RENTON

169

Airport

Ⓖ

188th   Exit 152

Orilla

167

509

212nd

Sea-Tac KOA

Marine View

5

Exit 149

516

16th

KENT

Saltwater SP

Exit 147

272nd

To Tacoma

N

SEATTLE

A   Freemont
B   Wallingford
C   Woodland Park Zoo
D   Seattle Center
E   Hiram M. Chittenden Locks
F   Boeing Field
G   Southcenter Mall

interesting aviation-oriented destinations. The first is the **Museum of Flight**, which is located south of downtown along the west side of Boeing Field. The museum has a collection of more than 40 aircraft including the first Air Force 1 (a Boeing 707), a B-17, a B-29, a Concorde, and a Blackbird supersonic spy plane. North of Seattle at Paine Field near Everett is the **Boeing 747, 767, 777, 787 Production Facility**. Tours of this huge hanger are very popular, call first to inquire about the best time to arrive. You reach it by driving west from Exit 189 off I-5 near Everett and then following the signs.

None of Seattle's campgrounds are near the center of town. For RVers the best choice probably depends upon the direction from which you arrive. Tenters are not well served. Most campgrounds, even if they would accept tenters, do not have proper sites for tents. The best tent campgrounds are Vasa Park, the KOA, and the Lakeside. Also, campers, even tent campers if they have the necessary transportation to get to the ferry terminal, might consider camping on the Kitsap Peninsula or Bainbridge Island and using the ferries to access Seattle.

Seattle Campgrounds

● **LAKESIDE RV PARK** *(Open All Year)*
  Reservations: (800) 468-7275
  Information: (425) 347-2970, (425) 742-7333
  Location: 20 Miles (32 Km) N of Downtown
                   Seattle

  GPS Location: 47.88583 N, 122.26083 W, 500 Ft

160 Sites – The Lakeside is a large big-rig park with pull-thrus to 55 feet and shorter back-ins, there are also some grassy tent sites. Most of the campground is paved but the asphalt is somewhat offset by the small adjoining lake and walking trail. Facilities are modern and there is bus service available nearby to both Seattle and Everett. This campground is north of Seattle off Interstate 5, actually in southern Everett. Take Exit 186, drive west on 128 St. SW for 1.5 miles (2.4 kilometers), turn left on US-99 and you'll see the campground on the left in .2 miles (.3 km)

● **MAPLE GROVE RV PARK** *(Open All Year)*
  Reservations: (866) 793-2200
  Information: (425) 423-9608,
                   info@maplegroverv.com,
                   www.maplegroverv.com
  Location: 20 Miles (32 Km) N of Downtown
                   Seattle

  GPS Location: 47.88472 N, 122.26028 W, 500 Ft

87 Sites – The Maple Grove is located just south of the Lakeside RV Park in southern Everett. It is also a big-rig park with sites including pull-thrus to 55 feet. They have excellent restrooms and like the Lakeside above also have good bus service. Take Exit 186 from I-5, drive west on 128 St. SW for 1.5 miles (2.4 kilometers), turn left on US-99 and you'll see the campground on the left in .2 miles (.3 km)

● **LAKE PLEASANT RV PARK** *(Open All Year)*
  Reservations: (800) 742-0386
  Information: (425) 487-1785
  Location: 20 Miles (32 Km) NE of
                   Downtown Seattle

  GPS Location: 47.78000 N, 122.21667 W, 100 Ft

WASHINGTON

190 Sites – This is a very unusual park for Seattle. Sites are set around a small lake, a great location. Most sites are back-ins around the lake, some are parallel-type parking. There are also some pull-thrus away from the lakeshore. Some sites are as long as 65 feet in length. Take Exit 26 from I-405 and head south on SR-527 (Bothell Everett Hwy). In 1.2 miles (1.9 km), as you descend a hill, slow and watch for the entrance on your left. Exercise extreme caution as the traffic moves right along through here and it's easy to miss the entrance.

● **TRAILER INNS RV PARK** *(Open All Year)*
  Res and Info: (800) 659-4684, (425) 747-9181,
  www.trailerinnsrv.com
  Location: 10 Miles (16 Km) E of Downtown Seattle

  GPS Location: 47.57639 N, 122.13306 W, 300 Ft

100 Sites – The closest campground to downtown Seattle, this one is located up the hill from the Eastgate interchange right next to I-90 on the east side of Lake Washington. The campground is an older one, really a large paved lot with the RVs parked very close to-gether. Many rigs are long-term. There are pull-thru spaces to 62 feet for carefully driven big rigs as well as back-ins to 34 feet. Amenities include a good indoor swimming pool, hot tub, and sauna. There is a lot of traffic noise due to the location. The entrance roads are somewhat confusing because Eastgate has lots of freeway on- and off-ramps. From the east take Exit 11 marked Eastgate. Drive south across the freeway, then turn left at the frontage road (signed) and drive about a half mile (.8 km) east to the entrance. From the west on I-90 take Exit 11A (which is east of the intersection of I-405 and I-90). You'll come to a stop sign at the top of the ramp, proceed directly ahead onto the frontage road and you'll see the campground on the right in about a half-mile (.8 km).

● **ISSAQUAH VILLAGE RV PARK** *(Open All Year)*
  Reservations: (800) 258-9233
  Information: (425) 392-9233,
  issaquahrv@earthlink.net,
  http://home.earthlink.net/~issaquahrv
  Location: 16 Miles (26 Km) E of Downtown Seattle

  GPS Location: 47.53667 N, 122.03111 W, 100 Ft

55 Sites – Issaquah, which is 20 miles (32 km) east of Seattle, may seem a long way from the city. Just remember that thousands of commuters make the trip every day. The camp-ground is modern and has mostly back-in sites, most to about 60 feet. To reach the park take Exit 17 from I-90 and drive north on East Lake Sammamish Parkway SE. In just 250 yards turn right into 229th Ave. SE. Go just one block and turn right on SE 66th, the park will be on your left in another .5 mile (.8 km).

○ **VASA PARK RESORT AND BALLROOM**
  (Open May 15 to Oct 15)
  Res and Info: (425) 746-3260, sawink@comcast.net,
  www.vasaparkresort.com
  Location: 13 Miles (21 Km) E of Downtown Seattle

  GPS Location: 47.57639 N, 122.11333 W, Near Sea Level

22 Sites – Vasa Park is a small swimming resort on the shore of Lake Sammamish to the

east of Seattle. It's a popular place for the local kids during the summer and also an un-usual camping destination. At the north end of the resort is an area set aside for camping. There are back-in RV sites with full hookups as well as back-in grass-covered sites for tent campers and RVs with partial hookups. Full-hookup sites are about 50 feet in length while the partials are longer, about 80 feet. Amenities include a bath house with laundry, food service kiosk in summer, swimming beach, and boat ramp. The main downside to this park is that there is no convenient bus service, you'll have to walk about a mile to catch one. Take Exit 13 from I-90 between Eastgate and Issaquah. Drive north on West Lake Sammamish Parkway past a roundabout for 1 mile (1.6 km), the campground en-trance is on the right just at the end of the curve. Watch you speed, the police monitor this section of road constantly.

● SEA-TAC KOA *(Open All Year)*

Reservations: (800) 562-1892, www.koa.com
Information: (253) 872-8652,
seattlekoa@aol.com,
www.seattlekoa.com
Location: 15 Miles (24 Km) S of
Downtown Seattle

GPS Location: 47.41194 N, 122.26250 W, Near Sea Level

150 Sites – This KOA is a nice one and if you are approaching Seattle from the south it's about your only choice for a campground unless you want to travel to those on the northern or eastern approaches to the city. Even though it's called the Seattle Tacoma KOA it's quite a distance from Tacoma. Sites are back-ins and pull-thrus to 70 feet. There are also grassy tent sites. Amenities include a seasonal outdoor swimming pool, pancake breakfasts in summer, nearby bike trails, and a bus to Seattle within 6 blocks. Take Exit 152 from I-5, this is 12 miles (19 km) from central Seattle and 19 miles (31 km) north of central Tacoma. Follow Orilla Road south on the east side of the freeway as it descends into the valley. In 2.4 miles (3.9 km) you'll see the campground on your right.

☐ SALTWATER STATE PARK *(Open All Year)*

Reservations: www.parks.wa.gov/reservations/,
(888) 226-7688
Information: (253) 661-4956, (360) 902-8844,
www.parks.wa.gov
Location: 20 Miles (32 Km) S of Downtown Seattle

GPS Location: 47.37278 N, 122.32250 W, Near Sea Level

48 Sites – Saltwater is a little far off the beaten path to be convenient for visitors to Se-attle. On the other hand, if you are looking for a non-commercial campground near the city this is one of the few possibilities. The beach area has a food kiosk and is a popular scuba-diving destination. The campground is in a valley inland. Near the entry are large back-ins to 55 feet as well as a few pull-thrus. Farther back is an area with smaller sites only suitable for tent campers, both car campers and hiker/bikers. Campfires are not al-lowed in this park, but you can use charcoal or propane barbecues. The campground is located quite a distance from I-5 and it is necessary to pick your way through the com-mercial and residential areas of Des Moines to reach it. Take Exit 149 from I-5 and head west on the Kent Des Moines Road (SR-516). In 2 miles (3 km) you'll reach Marine View Drive (SR-509). Follow Marine View 1.5 miles (2.4 km) south to the park.

SEQUIM

Between Port Townsend and Port Angeles you'll find yourself driving though the town of **Sequim**, a popular retirement town due to a well-publicized annual rainfall that is far less than that of most of western Washington due to the "rain-shadow effect" of the Olympic Mountains to the southwest.

The **Dungeness Spit** is directly north of town, this is a national wildlife refuge. The 5.5-mile (8.9 km) spit is the longest natural one in the world and an excellent place to see seabirds. There is also a campground at the base of the spit in Clallam County's Dungeness Recreation Area. In town you might want to visit the **Museum and Arts Center** which houses exhibits related to mastodons dug up nearby. The find was unusual because there was a spear point found between the ribs of one of the beasts, evidence that they were hunted by early Americans. For more active animals there is the **Olympic Game Farm** located north of town, it is home to many animals that starred in TV and movies and has a large collection of endangered and unusual animals as well as a petting farm and aquarium. There are also some wineries in the area, the **7 Cedars Casino**, and a golf course.

Outdoor-oriented tent and RV campers will find the Dungeness Recreation Area campground to be their best bet in this area. Big rig RVers will probably enjoy the small but modern and well-done Gilgal Oasis.

Sequim Campgrounds

☐ **SEQUIM BAY STATE PARK** *(Open All Year)*
Reservations: www.parks.wa.gov/reservations/, (888) 226-7688
Information: (360) 902-8844, (360) 371-2800,
www.parks.wa.gov
Location: 4 Miles (6 Km) E of Sequim

GPS Location: 48.04056 N, 123.02972 W, 100 Ft

89 Sites – Sequim Bay State Park is a shoreline park with a boat ramp. Campsites are away from the water and there is no real beach. The sites are small here and off three loops. One loop is to the right as you enter and has back-in full hookup sites in an open area that are long enough for RVs to about 30 feet. The Upper Loop is to the left as you enter and has forest-type sites, a sign restricts rig length here to 25 feet due to the narrow roads. Straight ahead when you enter is the lower loop. These sites are forest-type sites on a hillside, RVs to about 30 feet should be able to use this area. A trail leads under the highway to tennis courts a baseball field, horseshoes, and the paved Discovery Trail. The campground is on the north side of US-101 about 4 miles (6.4 km) east of Sequim.

● **GILGAL OASIS RV PARK** *(Open All Year)*
Reservations: (888) 445-4251
Information: (360) 452-1324, info@gilgaloasisrvpark.com,
www.gilgaloasisrvpark.com
Location: Sequim

GPS Location: 48.07722 N, 123.09056 W, 100 Ft

29 Sites – Gilgal Oasis is a modern but small big-rig RV park located near the center of Sequim. There are back-in sites to 50 feet and pull-thru sites to 60 feet. All sites are paved and have full hookups. From Washington Street in central Sequim turn south on South Brown Road (opposite the QFC store) for just a block to the park.

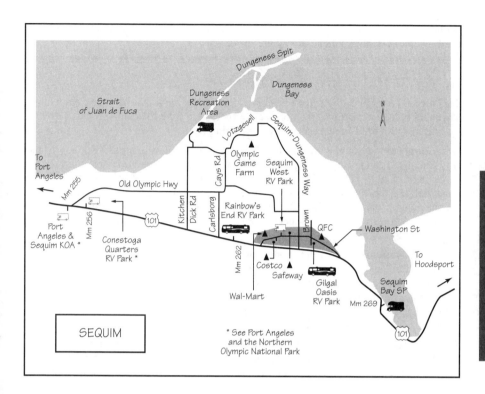

SEQUIM

* See Port Angeles and the Northern Olympic National Park

● **RAINBOW'S END RV PARK** *(Open All Year)*
Reservations: (877) 638-3863
Information: (360) 683-3863,
office@rainbowsendrvpark.com,
www.rainbowsendrvpark.com
Location: 1 Mile (2 Km) W of Sequim

GPS Location: 48.07778 N, 123.16028 W, 200 Ft

44 Sites – The Rainbow End is a popular commercial park located just west of Sequim. It's a well-kept older park and sites here vary a lot in size, there are back-ins and pull-thrus to 55 feet. The park is on the north side of US-101 about 1 mile (2 km) west of Sequim.

○ **DUNGENESS RECREATION AREA** *(Open Feb 1 to Sept 30)*
Res and Info: (360) 683-5847, ccpdu@olypen.com,
www.clallam.net/countyparks
Location: 6 Miles (10 Km) N of Sequim

GPS Location: 48.13833 N, 123.19583 W, 100 Ft

66 Sites – This is a Clallam County Recreation Area located at the foot of the Dungeness Spit which is a National Wildlife Refuge. Hiking in the area, particularly on the spit, is excellent. Sites here are back-ins to 40 feet but lack of maneuvering room makes 35 foot RVs the practical maximum. The campground is located north of Sequim near the coast. Easiest access is by using Kitchen Dick Road. Kitchen Dick goes north from US-101

about 3 miles (5 km) west of Sequim. Follow Kitchen Dick for 3.2 miles (5.2 km) to the north, then jog right and then left to enter the park.

SKAGIT VALLEY

This area is a popular day trip or weekend destination for folks from the Seattle area. There are quite a cluster of attractions easily accessible from the campgrounds below. A tow car or small RV is a real advantage for visiting them.

Deception Pass is the narrow channel that separates the north end of Whidbey Island from Fidalgo Island. Two soaring bridges span the gap, they provide opportunities for some great pictures. The water in the passage below runs pretty fast, it is fun to watch boats fighting the current. The pass is within Deception Pass State Park, you can walk beaches within the park on both Whidbey Island and Fidalgo Island. See the *Whidbey Island* section for more about Deception Pass State Park and the other Whidbey Island campgrounds.

Ferries run from the town of **Anacortes** on Fidalgo Island into the **San Juan Islands**. It can be hard to get a vehicle onto these ferries (auto service is chronically inadequate to the San Juans) but there is usually plenty of room for walk-on passengers. The islands are very scenic, we suggest the ride out to Friday Harbor on San Juan Island. You can easily explore Friday Harbor on foot, have a nice meal, and then catch another ferry back to Anacortes. This is definitely a day-long trip.

The little town of **La Conner** attracts hordes of visitors from Seattle on any sunny week-end. It sits next to the Swinomish Channel separating Fidalgo Island from the mainland and has lots of little shops and restaurants. This is a particularly popular destination dur-

A FERRY RIDE THROUGH THE SCENIC SAN JUAN ISLANDS

ing the **Skagit Valley Tulip Festival** during the first half of April each year. Acres and acres of tulips and daffodils fill the fields of the Skagit delta between La Conner and Mount Vernon.

Skagit Valley Campgrounds

☐ **RASAR STATE PARK** *(Open All Year)*
Reservations: www.parks.wa.gov/reservations/, (888) 226-7688
Information: (360) 826-3942, (360) 902-8844,
www.parks.wa.gov
Location: 25 Miles (40 Km) NE of Mt Vernon

GPS Location: 48.51861 N, 121.90167 W, 100 Ft

49 Sites – Rasar is one of the newer parks in the Washington state park system. It is near the Skagit River, a trail leads from the campground to the river. Over 500 bald eagles winter on the river and this is a popular bird-watching campground. Facilities are excellent. Sites will take RVs to 40 feet. To reach the campground drive east from Sedro Woolley for 16 miles (26 km). Turn south on Russell Road and drive .7 miles (1.1 km). At the intersection turn right and you'll reach the campground in another 1.2 miles (1.9 km).

● **MOUNT VERNON RV PARK** *(Open All Year)*
Reservations: (800) 385-9895
Information: (360) 428-8787
Location: Mt Vernon

GPS Location: 48.42306 N, 122.35139 W, Near Sea Level

81 Sites – This is an meticulously groomed, excellent urban campground in a pleasant little town. It's very popular and reservations are recommended. Sites include large pull-thrus to 80 feet, it's a good big-rig campground. From central Mt Vernon SR-536 goes west toward Anacortes. If you zero your odometer as you leave the bridge over the Skagit River you'll see the campground on your right in .5 miles (.8 km).

☐ **BAY VIEW STATE PARK** *(Open All Year)*
Reservations: www.parks.wa.gov/reservations/, (888) 226-7688
Information: (360) 757-0227, www.parks.wa.gov
Location: 11 Miles (18 Km) W of Mt Vernon

GPS Location: 48.48861 N, 122.47917 W, Near Sea Level

76 Sites – Bay View has sites in three locations. There are a few back-in sites with electricity and water outside the entry kiosk. These sites are the most suitable for RVs and some will take RVs to 55 feet. Another group of back-in electrical and water hookup sites surround a grassy field inside the park, they handle RVs to about 35 feet. Finally, many sites with no hookups are in an area of trees, some of these are as long as 40 feet but maneuvering room is limited so they're best for tent camping or RVs to 30 feet. There is a newer restroom building now, a big improvement. Although the campground has a dump station it has been closed for some time. This is a good campground for birders. Just down the road is the 2.2-mile (3.5 km) Padilla Bay Shore Trail which runs along a dike overlooking a tidal estuary. Also nearby is the Breazeale Padilla Bay Interpretive Center. To reach the campground turn north from SR-20 on the Bayview-Edison Road, the intersection is 6.3 miles (10.2 km) west of I-5 Exit 230 or 2.1 miles (3.4 km) east of the Swinomish Channel bridge. Drive north 3.7 miles (6 km) to the campground.

WASHINGTON

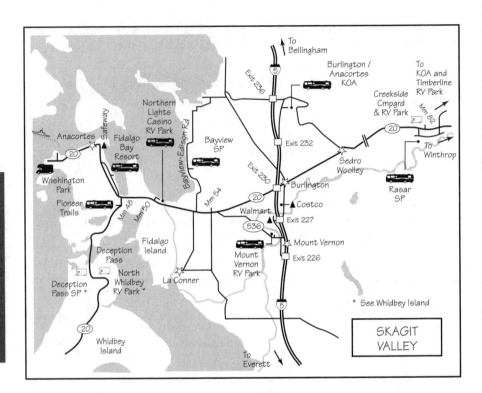

● **FIDALGO BAY RESORT** *(Open All Year)*
   Res and Info: (800) 727-5478, (360) 293-5353,
                    reserve@fidalgobay.com,
                    www.fidalgobay.com
   Location: 13 Miles (21 Km) W of Mt Vernon

   *GPS Location: 48.48194 N, 122.59306 W,
      Near Sea Level*

150 Sites – A nice big-rig RV park next to Fidalgo Bay just outside Anacortes. It has a great view of the March Point refinery across the bay. There are back-in and pull-thru sites to 70 feet, all are full-hookup sites. Some sites are beachfront and there is a boat ramp. To find it drive .3 mile (.5 km) northwest on the SR-20W spur toward Anacortes from its intersection with SR-20 as it comes north from Oak Harbor and Deception Pass. Turn north onto Fidalgo Bay Road and follow it 1.2 miles (1.9 km) to the resort.

● **NORTHERN LIGHTS CASINO RV PARK** *(Open All Year)*
   Res and Info: (888) 288-8883, (360) 293-2691,
                    www.swinomishcasino.com
   Location: 9 Miles (15 Km) W of Mt Vernon

   GPS Location: 48.45917 N, 122.51944 W, Near Sea Level

35 Sites – This casino has a new RV park located behind it just across the railroad tracks from Padilla Bay. This is a big-rig park with back-ins and pull-thrus to 55 feet. It's good only for self-contained campers since there are no restroom

facilities other than those in the casino itself. If the campground is full the casino allows overflow no-hookup camping in it's parking lot. The casino is located Off SR-20 just west of the bridge over the Swinomish Channel. This is 8.6 miles (13.9 km) west of Exit 230 on I-5 and 5 miles (8 km) east of Anacortes.

● **PIONEER TRAILS** *(Open All Year)*
    Res and Info: (360) 293-5355,
          www.pioneertrails.com
    Location: 13 Miles (21 Km) W of Mt Vernon

GPS Location: 48.45528 N, 122.58694 W, 200 Ft

150 Sites – This is a big-rig campground in a grove of large evergreens. Even with the trees, though, it's not dark. There are pull-thru sites to 70 feet and back-ins to 60 feet. Eleven and six-tenths miles (18.7 km) west of Exit 230 off I-5 and 2 miles east of Anacortes highway SR-20 cuts south toward Whidbey Island. The campground is .5 mile (.8 km) south of this intersection on the west side of the highway.

○ **WASHINGTON PARK** *(Open All Year)*
    Reservations: (360) 293-1918
    Information: (360) 293-1927.
          http://www.cityofanacortes.org/Parks/
          WaPark/wa_park.htm
    Location: 3 Miles (5 Km) W of Anacortes

GPS Location: 48.49889 N, 122.69278 W, Near Sea Level

70 Sites – Washington Park is a city campground with back-in and pull-thru sites in a forested area. It's a dark campground but there is a great beach area nearby as well as good hiking trails. For tent campers it is excellent, it's also OK for RVs to about 30 feet. Rig size is limited by narrow roads and lack of maneuvering room more than site size, a few of the sites actually reach over 40 feet. The campground occupies a point of land just west of the San Juan Islands ferry terminal in Anacortes. From central Anacortes follow the ferry terminal signs west on 12th Street and then Oakes Ave. After 3.1 miles (5 km) the road forks with the ferry to the right. Go straight ahead on Sunset Ave. instead and you'll reach the campground in another .8 mile (1.3 km).

● **BURLINGTON/ANACORTES KOA**
    (Open All Year)
    Reservations: (800) 562-9154,
          www.koa.com
    Information: (360) 724-5511
    Location: 11 Miles (18 Km) N of Mt Vernon

GPS Location: 48.55222 N, 122.33389 W, Near Sea Level

130 Sites – Facilities are normal KOA standard, like all of them it's a good place if you have kids along. Amenities include an indoor pool and hot tub. Sites vary but there are both tent sites and big-rig sites to 65 feet. These are back-ins to 45 feet and pull-thrus to 65 feet. The campground is located not far off I-5 north of Burlington and Mt Vernon. Take Exit 236 and head east and down the hill. At the intersection with old US-99 in .8 mile (1.3 km) turn right. In just .2 mile (.3 km) turn left into N. Green Road and the campground will be on your left almost immediately.

WASHINGTON

WASHINGTON

SNAKE RIVER

The campgrounds covered in this section are set along the lower Snake River between Lewiston/Clarkston and the Tri-Cities.

This section of river is a series of reservoirs behind four dams, listed here in a downstream direction from east to west. The dams were all built by the Corps of Engineers and serve two purposes: production of electrical power and enhancement of commercial navigation up the river to Lewiston/Clarkston. It's interesting to note that the deep-water channel from Portland to Lewiston/Clarkston is deep enough to float barges twice as heavy as those that travel the Mississippi.

The lower Snake River dams are very controversial, many environmentalists would like to see them removed. All of these dams have fish ladders and locks to allow barges to pass.

Lower Granite Lock and Dam – This dam was completed in 1972 and contains Lower Granite Lake. The lake extends upstream to Lewiston, a distance of 39 miles. Lower Granite Dam has a fish-viewing room as well as a visitor center offering movies, displays, and tours. Driving across the dam is restricted, call (888) 326-4636 for hours when driving across is allowed. Picture identification is required.

Little Goose Lock and Dam – Little Goose was completed in 1970. Behind it is Lake Bryan which extends to the foot of Lower Granite dam, a distance of 37 miles. Little Goose Dam has a fish-viewing room where you can watch salmon ascending the fish ladder. Driving across the dam is restricted, call (888) 326-4636 for hours when driving across is allowed. Picture identification is required.

Lower Monumental Lock and Dam – Lower monumental was finished in 1969. Behind the dam is Lake Herbert G. West which extends 28 miles east to the foot of Little Goose Dam. Driving across the dam is restricted, call (888) 326-4636 for hours when driving across is allowed. Picture identification is required.

Ice Harbor Lock and Dam – Located 9.2 river miles from the mouth of the Snake at Pasco. It was completed in 1961. Behind the dam is Lake Sacajawea which stretches 32 miles upstream to the base of Lower Monument Dam. There is a fish-viewing room and visitor center at this dam on the south shore. There is no public road across the dam.

There are marinas on all of these lakes, see the campground descriptions below for the location of many of them. Watersports of all types are very popular and fishing for sturgeon, salmon, and steelhead is often excellent.

Snake River Campgrounds

○ **WAWAWAI COUNTY PARK** *(Open All Year – Limited Facilities in Winter)*
Information: (509) 397-6238
Location: Near North Shore of Lower Granite Lake

$$$ ▲

GPS Location: 46.63583 N, 117.37278 W, 700 Ft

9 Sites – This is a small Corps of Engineers campground operated by Whitman County. The nine sites are all paved and located in an area with lots of vegetation and trees. Sites are small but paved and located off an in-and-out access road with a turn-around at the end. Some are pull-thrus, they will take carefully driven RVs to about 35 feet. There are picnic tables and fire pits but campfires are not allowed in summer. The park has a short trail leading to a birding platform. Easiest access is from Lewiston. On the north side of

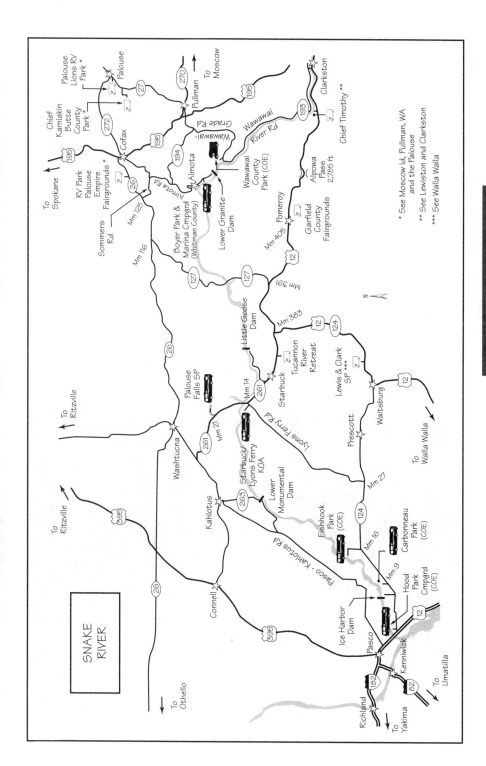

SNAKE RIVER

* See Moscow Id, Pullman, WA and the Palouse

** See Lewiston and Clarkston

*** See Walla Walla

WASHINGTON

the river opposite the city follow Wawawai River Road (SR-193) to the west along the lake a distance of 25 miles (40 km). The road will then turn up a valley and the campground entrance will soon appear on the left.

○ **BOYER PARK AND MARINA CAMPGROUND**
(Open All Year – Limited Facilities in Winter)

Info and Res: (509) 397-3208, www.bpark.biz, www.portwhitman.com

Location: North Shore Lake Bryan

GPS Location: N 46 41'03" W 117 26'53", 600 Ft

54 Sites – This Whitman County marina and park is located on the shore of Lake Bryan, a reservoir on the Snake River which is popular for fishing and water sports. The park has lots of facilities including a swimming beach, a marina, docks, boat launch, and snack bar. There's also a 3.5 mile bike trail along the lake shore. Sites are full and partial hookup back-ins to 60 feet. There's also a tent-camping area. Best access is from the north since the nearby Granite Dam where US-94 crosses the river has restricted crossing hours. From the south end of Main Street in Colfax drive southwest on Almota Road for 19 miles (31 km) to the campground.

● **STARBUCK / LYONS FERRY MARINA KOA**
Open March 1 to Nov 30 – Varies)

Reservations: (800) 562-5418, www.koa.com

Information: (509) 399-8020, lyonsferrymarina@columbiainet.com.com

Location: South Shore Lake West

GPS Location: N 46.58528, W 118.21944, 500 Ft

UNOBSTRUCTED VIEW OF PALOUSE FALLS FROM THE STATE PARK OVERLOOK

58 Sites – This park has recently become a KOA. It is located on the south side of the river opposite Lyons Ferry Park. There are 18 paved back-in sites to 45 feet, most with full hookups behind the marina. There are also some tent sites. Amenities include a restaurant, grocery, and bait and tackle shop. The park is on the south shore of the Snake River where SR-261 crosses. The entrance is on the west side of the highway.

☐ **PALOUSE FALLS STATE PARK** *(Open April 20 to Sept 20 – Varies)*
Information: (509) 646-9218, (260) 902-8844
Location: 7 Miles (11 Km) N of Lake West

GPS Location: N 46.66361, W 118.22806, 900 Ft

10 Sites – Palouse Falls drops 200 unobstructed feet as the Palouse River descends to empty into the Snake. This park has a great overlook offering an unobstructed view of the sight. It also has ten nearby camping sites. These are best for tents but RVs are allowed and the parking lot for the overlook means that there is room to park an RV to about 40 feet. There are no hookups, but there are picnic tables, fire pits, and a vault toilet. The entrance road to the park leaves SR-261 some 5.5 miles (8.9 km) north of the bridge over the Snake River. It's another 2 miles (3.2 km) on a gravel road to the overlook and campground.

■ **FISHHOOK PARK** *(Open May 20 to Sept 11 – Varies)*
Reservations: www.recreation.gov, (877) 444-6777
Information: (509) 547-7781, (509) 547-2048,
www.nww.usace.army.mil
Location: S Shore of Lake Sacajawea

GPS Location: N 46.31611, W 118.76556, 500 Ft

61 Sites – This is a beautiful Corps of Engineers park on the shore of Lake Sacajawea, a reservoir on the Snake River. It is grass covered and shaded with back-in and pull-thru sites to 55 feet off paved loops. Some sites have beautiful setting along the lake shore. There are also tents sites in a large grassy area near the lake. Near the entrance is a day use area with a swimming beach, docks, and boat launch facilities. Start at the intersection where SR-124 leaves US-12 just east of the mouth of the Snake River where it empties into the Columbia at Pasco. Drive east on SR-124 for 16 miles (25.8 km) to Fishhook Park Road. Turn left and follow this road 4.5 miles (7.3 km) to the park.

■ **CHARBONNEAU PARK** *(Open All Year)*
Reservations: www.recreation.gov, (877) 444-6777
Information: (509) 547-2048,
www.nww.usace.army.mil/corpsoutdoors/
Location: S Shore of Lake Sacajawea

GPS Location: N 46.25806, W 118.84306, 400 Ft

67 Sites – This is another gorgeous Corps of Engineers campground along the Snake River, this one on Lake Sacajawea just above Ice Harbor Dam. The sites here are off two paved loops, surrounded by grass and shaded. They are back-ins and pull-thrus to 60 feet with full or partial hookups. Fifteen sites are overflow sites with no hookups. Amenities include a marina, docks, launch ramp, swimming beach, and snack bar. From October 1 to April 30 there are no utilities, and no fee. Start at the intersection where SR-124 leaves US-12 just east of the mouth of the Snake River where it empties into the Columbia at Pasco. Drive east on SR-124 for 8.5 miles (13.5 km) to Sun Harbor Dr. Turn left and follow this road 1.8 miles (2.9 km) to the park.

■ **HOOD PARK CAMPGROUND**
    (Open May 1 to Sept 30 – Varies)
    Reservations: www.recreation.gov, (877) 444-6777
    Information: (509) 547-2048,
        www.nww.usace.army.mil/corpsoutdoors/
    Location: S Shore Snake River Near Pasco

    GPS Location: N 46.21500, W 119.01389, 300 Ft

83 Sites – This is the farthest downstream of the beautiful Corps of Engineers camp-grounds on the Snake River. This one's on Lake Wallula, not far from where the Snake and the Columbia come together. The park is situated on the lake with the McNary Wildlife Refuge behind. The sites here are paved pull-thrus and back-ins to 60 feet with electricity and water hookups, there's also a dump station and 15 overflow sites. Other amenities include a swimming beach, boat ramp, and docks. The campground is located just east of the intersection where SR-124 leaves US-12 just east of the mouth of the Snake River.

SPOKANE

Spokane (population 210,000) is Washington's largest city east of the Cascades. The city sits astride I-90 just 18 miles (29 km) from the Idaho border. It serves as a business center for eastern Washington and also northern Idaho and western Montana.

The centerpiece of the town has to be **Riverfront Park** (not to be confused with River-side State Park). This 100 acre area around **Spokane Falls** was turned into an interesting park in preparation for the 1974 World's Fair and Exposition. You'll find a gondola offer-ing views of the falls as well as an amusement park and IMAX theater.

Spokane has an impressive museum, the **Northwest Museum of Arts and Cultures**. It overlooks the Spokane River on the west side of town. It has a very large collection of indigenous artifacts as well as exhibits on Northwest history and art.

Spokane is also home to **Gonzaga University**. The campus is located north of the river east of the city center. Attractions here include the Bing Crosby Memorabilia Room (he was an alumnus) and the **Jundt Art Museum**.

One of our favorite Spokane attractions is the 37-mile (60 km) **Spokane Centennial Trail**. This paved bike trail follow the Spokane River all the way from the Idaho Border, through the city, and then through Riverside State Park on the west side as far as Nine Mile Falls.

Spokane Campgrounds

● **PARK LANE MOTEL SUITES AND RV PARK**
    (Open All Year)
    Res and Info: (509) 535-1626,
        reservations@parklanemotel.com,
        www.parklanemotel.com
    Location: 2 Miles (3 Km) E of Downtown Spokane

    GPS Location: 47.65694 N, 117.34500 W, 1,900 Ft

19 Sites – This is a popular RV park located behind a small motel in the big-box store area along Sprague Ave. east of central Spokane. There are back-in sites to 40 feet. Only self-contained rigs are accepted because there are no restrooms for the RV park. Sites have instant-on telephone (you get a phone and phone book when you check in) as well as free

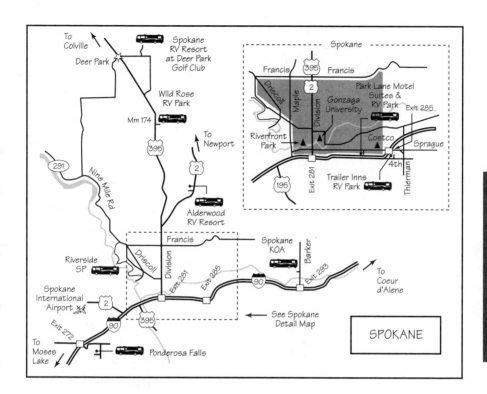

Wi-Fi which is useable from your rig in the park. Take Exit 285 from I-90 and drive west for 1.1 miles (1.8 km), the motel is on the left.

● **TRAILER INNS RV PARK** *(Open All Year)*
Reservations: (800) 659-4864
Information: (509) 535-1811, www.trailerinnsrv.com
Location: 3 Miles (5 Km) E of Downtown Spokane
   GPS Location: 47.65444 N, 117.32278 W, 1,900 Ft

97 Sites – Trailer Inns has large parks like this one in Spokane, Yakima, and Seattle. All are older paved parks with closely spaced rigs and many long-term tenants, but all can accept large rigs (with careful maneuvering). Sites here are back-ins and pull-thrus to 55 feet. This one is conveniently located near I-90 east of central Spokane. To reach the park take Exit 285 and drive east for about .3 miles (.5 km). Turn right on S. Thieman St. and drive 3 blocks, then turn right on E. 4th Ave. and you'll see the campground entrance on the right in another .3 mile (.5 km).

☐ **RIVERSIDE STATE PARK** *(Open All Year)*
Reservations: www.parks.wa.gov/reservations/,
   (888) 226-7688
Information: (509) 465-5064, (360) 902-8844,
   www.parks.wa.gov
Location: 4 Miles (6 Km) W of Downtown Spokane

   GPS Location: 47.69583 N, 117.49444 W, 1,800 Ft

33 Sites – West of central Spokane along the Spokane River is a large state park. It has a small campground. Sites are in two closely located areas. An older area near the entrance booth is best for tents and smaller RVs. Two of these sites have full hookups. Below is a new area near the river with 14 large sites with electricity and water that are suitable for RVs to 45 feet and longer. Swimming here is in the river. Access to this campground is a little roundabout. From I-90 take Exit 281 and drive north on Division Street (US-2). In 4.2 miles (6.8 km) turn left on E. Francis Ave. Follow Frances and then W. Nine Mile Rd. west for 3.8 miles (6.1 km). Turn left following signs to the park and wind through the trees along the river for another 2.1 miles (3.4 km) to the campground entrance. Reservations are available April 15 to October 31.

● **WILD ROSE RV PARK** *(Open All Year)*
   Res and Info: (509) 276-8853, wildroserv@aol.com
   Location: 15 Miles (24 Km) N of Central Spokane

   GPS Location: 47.86999 N, 117.42029 W, 2,000 Ft

67 Sites – The Wild Rose is a well-kept residential RV Park. A number of sites are available for travelers. Sites are gravel pull-thrus and back-ins with patios to 55 feet. To reach the park take Exit 281 from I-90 in central Spokane. Drive north through the center of town on N Division Street, also called Hwy 395. Continue for 15 miles (24 km), the RV park entrance is on the right.

● **SPOKANE RV RESORT AT DEER PARK GOLF CLUB**
   (Open April 1 to November 1)
   Res and Info: (877) 276-1555, www.spokanervresort.com
   Location: 20 Miles (32 Km) N of Spokane

   GPS Location: 47.96893 N, 117.44745 W, 2,100 Ft

61 Sites – This is a new big-rig resort and golf course in the town of Deer Park, located a few miles north of Spokane. The sites here are privately owned condominium sites, but many are available for travelers. Sites are full-hookup back-ins to 60 feet. There's a swimming pool and spa, and an excellent 18-hole golf course. From I-90 take Exit 281 and drive north on city streets through Spokane on Hwy 395. Twenty-two miles (35.5 km) from the freeway turn right on E. Crawford Ave. Proceed 1.8 mile (2.9 km) to North Country Club Drive, turn left, and follow signs 1 mile (1.6 km) to the campground office.

● **ALDERWOOD RV RESORT** *(Open All Year)*
   Reservations: (888) 847-0500
   Information: (509) 467-5320,
                  alderwood@air-pipe.com,
                  www.alderwoodrv.com
   Location: 9 Miles (15 Km) N of
                  Downtown Spokane

   GPS Location: 47.78528 N, 117.35472 W, 1,900 Ft

108 Sites – This is a modern campground on the north side of Spokane. Facilities are good including heavily landscaped sites, an indoor swimming pool, and free Wi-Fi at the sites. RV sites are back-ins and pull-thrus to 70 feet. The campground is located off US-2 on the north side of Spokane. From I-90 take Exit 281 and drive north on city streets through Spokane on Hwy 395. In 6.0 miles (9.7 km) take the right fork onto Hwy 2. In another 4.2 miles (6.8 km) you'll see the RV park entrance on the left.

● SPOKANE KOA *(Open All Year)*
Reservations: (800) 562-3309,
www.koa.com
Information: (509) 924-4722
Location: 14 Miles (23 Km) E of
Downtown Spokane

GPS Location: 47.68472 N, 117.15472 W, 2,000 Ft

160 Sites – This is a fairly standard KOA with an seasonal outdoor pool. It's easy to access from the interstate and it's a large flat open lot so it's a good big-rig park with sites to 70 feet. The nearby trains are hard to ignore. To reach the campground from I-90 take Exit 293 east of Spokane and drive north on North Barker Road for 1.2 miles (1.9 km), the campground is on your left.

● PONDEROSA FALLS
(Open All Year)
Res and Info: (509) 747-9415, (800) 494-7275
Location: 11 Miles (18 Km) W of
Downtown Spokane

GPS Location: 47.58250 N, 117.54306 W, 2,500 Ft

188 Sites – This is a membership campground located quite a distance west of Spokane. Sites here can take RVs to 45 feet and larger, they're set in trees. Amenities include instant-on telephones, an indoor pool and lots of playgrounds and sports equipment including mini-golf. Non-members are welcome with reservations. From Exit 272 of I-90 about 6 miles (10 km) west of Spokane drive east on West Hallett Road for about 2 miles (3.2 km) following signs for the park. Turn right on Thomas Mallen Road and the park entrance will be on your right in .7 mile (1.1 km).

TACOMA

Tacoma (population 198,000) is located about 35 miles (56 km) south of Seattle along I-5. This second-largest city on Puget Sound has long been known for its smell. Even today under certain weather conditions you'll be aware of the one remaining pulp mill as you drive by. Fortunately the campgrounds are some distance from the city.

Tacoma is one of the least expensive places to live in the area. As the region grows Tacoma has become a desirable place to live and to visit.

The centerpiece of rebuilding Tacoma's downtown is the restored **Union Station**. This railroad station was built in 1911, it had actually been boarded up when it was chosen to be redone as the federal courthouse. Near the station you'll find two good museums. One is the excellent **Washington State History Museum**. The second is a new museum, the **Tacoma Art Museum**. Not far away, and linked to these museums by the **Chihuly Bridge of Glass**, is the new **Museum of Glass**. Together these museums will keep you busy all day long.

Tacoma also has a great park. **Point Defiance Park** to the west of the city covers 700 waterfront acres. It has gardens and a zoo and aquarium.

In addition to the four campgrounds listed below you might note that the Nisqually Campground listed under *Olympia* is also a possibility for Tacoma.

WASHINGTON

Tacoma Campgrounds

☐ **DASH POINT STATE PARK** *(Open All Year)*
Reservations: www.parks.wa.gov/reservations/, (888) 226-7688
Information: (253) 661-4955, (360) 902-8844, www.parks.wa.gov
Location: 16 Miles (26 Km) N of Downtown Tacoma

GPS Location: 47.31722 N, 122.40667 W, 300 Ft

138 Sites – This campground along the shore of Puget Sound is not far north of Tacoma. However, in order to reach it you must find your way through the commercial and residential areas of Federal Way. The park has a very popular beach area good for beachcombing and even swimming since the tide bares a lot of sand which the sun warms. The campground itself is away from the water and off two loops. Only 27 of the sites have utilities, these will take RVs to 30 feet. A few no hookup sites will take RVs to 40 feet. One way to reach the park is to leave I-5 at Exit 143. Follow SW 320th westward for 4.5 miles (7.3 km). Turn right on 47th Ave. SW and drive north for .4 mile (.6 km). Now, at the T, turn left on SW Dash Point Road and you'll reach the campground entrance in .8 mile (1.3 km).

● **MAJESTIC MOBILE MANOR RV PARK**
　　(Open All Year)
Reservations: (800) 348-3144, www.majesticrvpark.com
Information: (253) 845-3144,
　　　　　　　　majesticrvpark@juno.com
Location: 5 Miles (8 Km) E of Downtown Tacoma

GPS Location: 47.20944 N, 122.33750 W, Near Sea Level

88 Sites – Majestic Mobile Manor is just what the name suggests. This is a mobile home park with a campground adjacent to it. The campground has a lot of long-term rigs closely packed on gravel. Sites are back-ins, they reach 75 feet. This is not a vacation park but if you are visiting Tacoma it's a place to base yourself. There is a swimming pool in summer. From I-5 just east of Tacoma take Exit 135 and head southeast on SR-167 toward Puyallup. The campground will be in your right in 3.7 miles (6.0 km).

● **GIG HARBOR RV RESORT** *(Open All Year)*
Reservations: (800) 526-8311
Information: (253) 858-8138, ghrv@comcast.net
Location: 11 Miles (18 Km) NW of
　　　　　　　Downtown Tacoma

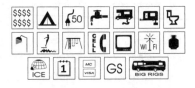

GPS Location: 47.34472 N, 122.59861 W, 100 Ft

105 Sites – Gig Harbor is the nicest of the campgrounds serving the Tacoma area. It is located on the far side of the Tacoma Narrows which is a problem if you are a commuter but not if you're a visiting tourist and can avoid rush hour traffic. Besides, central Gig Harbor is just down the road and has plenty of restaurants, shops, and harbor-side ambiance. The campground is located on a hillside which makes for an attractive park, but makes some sites a little difficult to get into with a big rig. This is a big-rig park, however, with large back-in and pull-thru sites to 75 feet. There's also a dedicated tent-camping area. Amenities include a summer-only swimming pool. To reach the campground from the Tacoma area take Exit 132 from I-5. Drive west and across the Narrows Bridge for 12 miles (19 km) and take the Burnham Drive NW exit. From the roundabout on the east side of the highway take the first exit (Burnham Dr. NW), which is signed for the campground, and follow Burnham Dr. for 1.2 miles (1.9 km) to the campground. It's on the left.

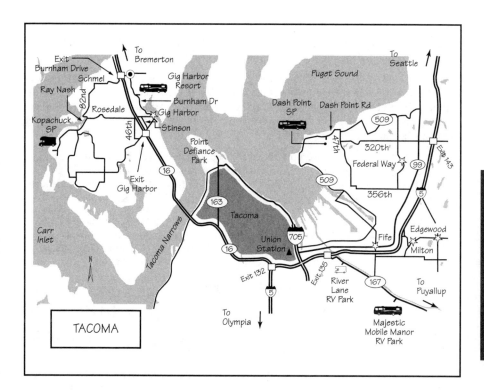

TACOMA

KOPACHUCK STATE PARK *(Open All Year)*
Information: (253) 661-4955, (360) 902-8844,
                www.parks.wa.gov
Location: 16 Miles (26 Km) W of Tacoma

GPS Location: 47.30833 N, 122.68167 W, 200 Ft

41 Sites – Kopachuck is a small state park located on the coast south of Gig Harbor. Many folks who live in the area call this their favorite local state park which is something considering there are so many similar waterside state parks on the Kitsap Peninsula. The attraction is the wide sandy beach, suitable for swimming, seafood gathering, and sunning. We've listed this one under Tacoma since it is technically not really on the Kitsap Peninsula and is relatively handy to Tacoma. Sites here are back-ins in a dark forest setting high above the beach. Narrow roads and narrow back-in sites limit RV size to about 35 feet. To reach the campground from the Tacoma area take Exit 132 from I-5. Drive west and across the Narrows Bridge for 9 miles (14.5 km) and take the Gig Harbor exit. Follow Stinson Ave. north for .8 mile (1.3 km) and turn left on Rosedale St. NW. Follow Rosedale east for 2.9 miles (4.7 km) and turn left on Ray Nash Dr. NW. Follow Nash, which becomes Kopachuck Dr. NW for 2.3 miles (3.7 km), the entrance is on the right.

TRI-CITIES

Despite the name the Tri-Cities area is composed of four cities: **Pasco, Kennewick,**

Richland, and **West Richland**. They are located at the confluence of the Columbia, Snake, and Yakima Rivers. The combined area population is about 170,000 which makes it the fourth largest population center in the state behind Seattle, Spokane, and Tacoma.

Since World War II the main economic engine of this region has been the **Hanford Nuclear Reservation** on the west side of the Columbia River about 20 miles to the north. Although Hanford no longer produces nuclear weapons it's still a major employer since clean-up operations continue. At times you'll see this in the area RV parks since workers from outside the area often live in them.

Farming and transportation are now the growth industries here. Although this is a very dry region the rivers make irrigation easy. The city is also a transportation hub. Highways meeting here include I-82, US-395 and US-12. I-84 passes not far to the south. There's also extensive commercial river traffic on the Columbia and Snake Rivers.

Amazingly, there's little in the way of a central business district here. The closest is central Richland, north of I-182 on the west bank of the Columbia. Nearby is Howard Amon Park, home to the **Columbia River Exhibition of History, Science, and Technology**. This museum has extensive displays covering Hanford and nuclear energy.

Tri-Cities Campgrounds

● **ARROWHEAD RV PARK** *(Open All Year)*
Res and Info: (509) 545-8206
Location: Pasco

GPS Location: N 46.25833, W 119.08278, 400 Ft

95 Sites – Arrowhead is a conveniently located older park with large sites. It's situated north of Pasco near the point where I-182, US-12, and US-395 intersect. Many sites here are rented long-term but there are usually sites available for travelers. There are 65 shaded RV sites, these are full-hookup back-ins and pull-thrus to 65 feet. There are also tent sites. From Exit 14B of I-182 drive north on US-395 for .8 mile (1.3 km) and exit at Kartchner St. Then drive east just .1 mile (.2 km) to Commercial St., turn right and you'll see the campground on the right in .4 mile (.6 km). There is also a Flying J at this exit.

○ **FRANKLIN COUNTY RV PARK** *(Open All Year)*
Res and Info: (509) 542-5982,
franklincountyrvpark@co.franklin.wa.us,
www.franklincountyrvpark.com
Location: Pasco

GPS Location: N 46.26778, W 119.17361, 500 Ft

59 Sites – This modern county RV park is on the grounds of the TRAC Event Center, which includes an indoor arena and exposition hall. Sites are paved back-ins and pull-thrus to 55 feet. Some are full-hookup sites, others just water and electric. Restrooms are in the arena building and in a building at the northwest corner of the park. From I-182 take Exit 9 and drive north on Road 68 for .5 mile (.8 km) to Burden Drive. Turn right and drive .2 mile (.3 km) to Convention Place. Now turn right and drive .2 mile (.3 km) to Home Run Road. Turn left and in .3 mile (.5 km) you'll see the RV parking on the left.

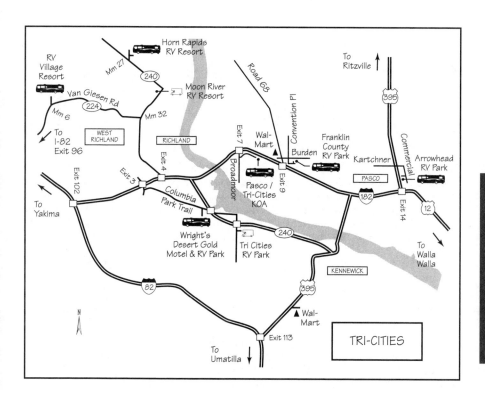

WASHINGTON

● **PASCO / TRI-CITIES KOA** *(Open All Year)*
Reservations: (800) 562-2495, www.koa.com
Information: 509 542-1357,
PascoKOA@pocketinet.com
Location: West Richland

GPS Location: N 46.27145, W 119.20632, 400 Ft

100 Sites – This is a large modern big-rig park that recently became a KOA. RV sites are back-ins and pull-thrus to 55 feet, all with full hookups. There's a heated swimming pool and a spa. Take Exit 7 from I-182 and head south on Broadmoor Blvd. Almost immediately turn left on St Thomas Drive and follow it for .8 mile (1.3 km) to the campground.

● **WRIGHT'S DESERT GOLD MOTEL AND RV PARK**
(Open All Year)
Res and Info: (509) 627-1000, desertgold2@msn.com,
wrightsdesertgold.com
Location: Richland

GPS Location: N 46.23944, W 119.25028, 300 Ft

89 Sites – This is an older motel and RV park with many permanent residents but it has a few sites available for travelers. There are pull-thrus to 60 feet and smaller back-in sites. Amenities include a pool and spa. Easiest access is from I-182 at Exit 3. Drive south on

Queensgate Drive for just a short distance and turn left onto Columbia Park Trail. Drive for 2.8 miles (4.5 km), the park is on the right.

● **HORN RAPIDS RV RESORT**
   Res and Info: (866) 557-9637,
                    (509) 375-9913,
                    info@hornrapidsrvresort.com,
                    www.hornrapidsrvresort.com
   Location: Richland

   GPS Location: 46.32731 N, 119.31475 W, 300 Ft

225 Sites – This huge RV park is the most modern and upscale in the Tri-Cities area. Sites are back-ins and pull-thrus to 70 feet. Roads and patios are paved, parking pads are gravel. Amenities include a swimming pool and spa. Like the other RV parks in the Tri-Cities area this one has many long-term residents. To reach the park take Exit 4 from US12 and travel north on the Bypass Highway for 4.1 miles (3.5 km). Turn left on SR-240 and follow it for 1.9 mile (3.1 km) to the park which is on the right.

● **RV VILLAGE RESORT** *(Open All Year)*
   Res and Info: (866) 637-9900
   Location: West Richland

   GPS Location: 46.29833 N, 119.38361 W, 400 Ft

100 Sites – This is a large big-rig park. Sites are back ins and pull-thrus to 55 feet, all with full hookups. There's a heated swimming pool and a spa. The campground is located to the west of the Tri-Cities. From I-82 take Exit 96 and follow SR-224 (Van Giesen Rd.) to the northeast for 5.9 miles (9.5 km) to the resort, it's on the left.

WALLA WALLA

Walla Walla (population 59,000) is in a fairly isolated location in southeast Washington state but well worth a visit. You may already be familiar with the town's name since it's known for its Walla Walla Sweet Onions, and also for the state's largest prison, the Walla Walla State Penitentiary.

For a time during the 1860s Walla Walla was Washington's largest city and was even expected to become the state's capital. This never did happen, but today's city has a handsome downtown area easily investigated on foot. The town also has two colleges: **Whitman College** near the center of town and **Walla Walla University** in the suburb of College Place.

Sweet onions aren't the only produce grown in the area. Visitors enjoy shopping for the onions as well as other local produce at the Walla Walla Farmer's Market, located at 4th and Main. The market is open from late spring until October from 9 AM to 1 PM on Saturdays and Sunday.

The surrounding region is also well-known for its wine with over 100 wineries. Like other wine areas Walla Walla has benefited with good restaurants and wine tasting possibilities.

During the westward expansion of the 1800s **Fort Walla Walla** was an important stop for wagon travelers. Fort Walla Walla Park is located southwest of the central district and is the home of the Fort Walla Walla Museum which has some of the original fort buildings

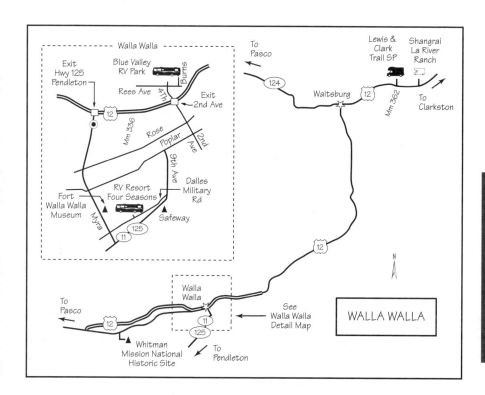

as well as other indoor and outdoor displays illustrating the area's history.

Six miles (10 km) west of Walla Walla along US-12 is **Whitman Mission National Historic Site**. This is the site of a mission established by Marcus and Narcissa Whitman in 1836. The Whitman Mission Massacre in 1847 caused the Cayuse War, the first of several Indian wars in the Oregon Territory.

Special events in Walla Walla include the **Balloon Stampede** in the middle of May and the **Walla Walla Sweet Onion Blues Fest** in the middle of July.

Walla Walla Campgrounds

● **BLUE VALLEY RV PARK** *(Open All Year)*
  Reservations: (866) 855-8282, www.bluevalleyrv.com
  Information: (509) 525-8282
  Location: Walla Walla

  GPS Location: 46.07667 N, 18.34250 W, 900 Ft

81 Sites – The Blue Valley is a nice big-rig resort next to an eighteen-hole public golf course. There are pull-thrus and back-in sites to 65 feet, all with full hookups but some paved and some gravel. Access is from US-12 north of town. Take the Second Ave. Exit near Mile 337. Drive north on 2nd and 4th for .2 mile (.3 km), turn right onto Rees and drive two blocks, turn left on Burns and the resort is ahead at the end of the block.

● **RV RESORT FOUR SEASONS** *(Open All Year)*
  Res and Info: (509) 529-6072, rvresort@gohighspeed.com
  Location: Walla Walla

GPS Location: 46.04667 N, 118.35639 W, 800 Ft

70 Sites – This campground on the southern edge of town has both well-kept long-term and traveler sites. It is a big rig resort with both back-in and pull-thru sites to 60 feet. Some parking is on pavement, other sites are grass covered. From US-12 take the City Center (2nd Ave) Exit near Mile 337. Drive south on 2nd for .6 miles (1 km) to Poplar St. Turn right on Poplar and drive west for .5 mile (.8 km) to 9th Street. Turn left on 9th and drive south .7 mile (1.1 km) to Dalles Military Road. Turn right on Dalles and in .6 mile (1 km) you'll see the campground on the right.

☐ **LEWIS AND CLARK TRAIL STATE PARK**
  (Open All Year)
  Information: (509) 337-6457, (360) 902-8844, www.parks.wa.gov
  Location: 23 Miles (37 Km) N of Walla Walla

GPS Location: 46.28806 N, 118.07194 W, 1,400 Ft

41 Sites – Lewis and Clark Trail State Park includes access to the Touchet River , decent for trout fishing. This is an older state campground that is best for smaller RVs and tents. It has sites on both sides of US-12. On the west are RV sites, back-ins to about 28 feet off a narrow circular drive. On the east side of the highway are tent sites on grass. Restrooms have flush toilets and coin-operated showers and there is a dump station. The campground is at Mile 362 of US-12, about 23 miles (37 km) north of Walla Walla.

WENATCHEE

Wenatchee (population 32,000) is located just below the point where the Wenatchee River joins the Columbia. The city is probably best known as the center of the apple-growing industry in Washington State.

Apples are featured at the **Washington Apple Commission Visitor's Center** at the north end of town, you'll see it on the right if you're driving to Wenatchee Confluence State Park. The **Wenatchee Valley Museum and Culture Center**, located downtown, has more about apples, but also about the history of the town.

A wonderful outdoor attraction in Wenatchee is the **Riverfront Park**. It features a paved 10-mile (16 km) loop trail that follows the river on both banks, with bridges at each end. It's great for bikes, walking, jogging, or even rollerblades.

Perched above the town to the south is the **Ohme Gardens**. The gardens, set in dry rocky terrain, are great. So is the view.

Wenatchee's big celebration is the **Washington State Apple Blossom Festival**. It features parades, dances, a carnival, a run, and an Apple Queen. The festival takes place at the end of April and beginning of May.

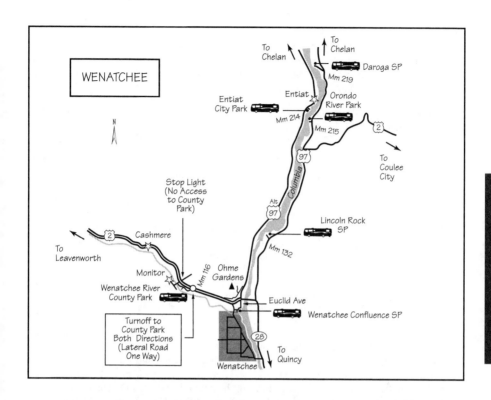

Wenatchee Campgrounds

☐ **WENATCHEE CONFLUENCE STATE PARK** *(Open All Year)*
Reservations: www.parks.wa.gov/reservations/, (888) 226-7688
Information: (509) 664-6373, (360) 371-2800, www.parks.wa.gov
Location: Wenatchee

GPS Location: 47.46028 N, 120.33028 W, 600 Ft

59 Sites – This park is conveniently located at the confluence of the Wenatchee and Columbia Rivers in the town of Wenatchee. A great trail system runs right by the park, it forms a loop with trails on both sides of the river and provides easy walking access to central Wenatchee, about 2 miles (3 km) away. Sites here are paved and up to 45 feet long. They are widely separated by beautiful lawns. From the intersection of US-97 and US-2 on the west side of the bridge over the Columbia north of Wenatchee turn south. In .4 mile (.6 km) turn left on Euclid Ave. following signs to the park. In another .4 miles (.6 km) turn left into the park entrance road, you'll reach the gate in another .2 miles (.3 km). Unlike the majority of Washington State campgrounds this park accepts reservations from April 1 to September 30.

○ **ENTIAT CITY PARK** *(Open April 15 to Sept 30 – Varies)*
Reservations: (800) 736-8428
Information: (509) 664-6373
Location: 14 Miles (23 Km) N of Wenatchee

GPS Location: 47.66778 N, 120.21889 W, 700 Ft

31 Sites – This medium-sized city park and campground has back-in sites to 45 feet. Tenters camp on grass nearby. The park is on the west bank of the Columbia River, a great location. There is also a boat launch here and extensive lawns. This campground is easy to spot from Alt US-97 and occupies most of the waterfront in the town of Entiat. This is about 14 miles (23 km) upstream from Wenatchee on the west bank.

○ **ORONDO RIVER PARK** *(Open April 15 to Sept 15 – Varies)*
Information: (509) 884-4700,
www.portofdouglas.org/recreation_
orondoriverpark.asp
Location: 15 Miles (24 Km) N of Wenatchee

GPS Location: 47.65675 N, 120.21451 W, 700 Ft

27 Sites – This is a Douglas County park with a boat ramp, swimming beach, and RV and tent camping. The 13 RV sites are back-ins on grass and gravel with some shade. Sites are short but it doesn't matter because you can back in as far as you need to with your wheels on the grass behind the sites. Tenters can pitch on grass next to the lake. The campground is located off US-97 some 14.9 miles (24.0 km) north of the Hwy 2 bridge at Wenatchee.

☐ **DAROGA STATE CAMPGROUND** *(Open March 5 to Oct 5)*
Information: (509) 664-6380,
Location: 18 Miles (29 Km) N of Wenatchee

GPS Location: 47.70887 N, 120.19730 W, 700 Ft

44 Sites – Daroga State Park is located on the east side of Lake Entiat. The RV sites and access road are paved back-ins and pull-thrus to 90 feet. They are on a hillside and have great views. There are also walk-in tent sites near the river. There's a day use area with a swimming beach and playground. The campground is located off US-97 some 18.1 miles (29.2 km) north of the Hwy 2 bridge at Wenatchee.

☐ **LINCOLN ROCK STATE PARK**
(Open March 7 to Oct 25 – Varies)
Reservations: www.parks.wa.gov/reservations/,
(888) 226-7688
Information: (509) 884-8702, (360) 371-2800,
www.parks.wa.gov
Location: 5 Miles (8 Km) NE of Wenatchee

GPS Location: 47.53500 N, 120.28333 W, 700 Ft

94 Sites – This very large state park is also upstream from Wenatchee and much closer than Daroga State Park. Lincoln Rock is on the east bank about 5 miles (8 Km) from Wenatchee. Sites here are widely spaced and separated by well-watered and manicured grass. They are big paved sites suitable for any rig, many are pull-thrus. A very park-like setting. In addition to the many campsites in the park there is a boat launch, tennis courts, and sports fields.

○ **WENATCHEE RIVER COUNTY PARK** *(Open All Year)*
Res and Info: (509) 667-7503, www.co.chelan.wa.us
Location: 4 Miles (6 Km) W of Wenatchee

GPS Location: 47.48500 N, 120.40944 W, 700 Ft

43 Sites – This very pleasant county park is located up the Wenatchee Valley from the town of Wenatchee. Noise is a bit of a problem in this park with the train tracks on one side and US-2 on the other, but it's not serious, you quickly

become accustomed to the occasional train. Sites are large paved back-ins to 45 feet and are arranged in pinwheels off circular drives. Drive west from Wenatchee on US-2 for 4 miles (6.4 km), the campground is on the south side of the highway at about Mile 115.5. You must turn off the highway to the east of the stoplight, there is no access to the park from the road with the stoplight.

WESTPORT

Although **Westport** (population 2,100) is just across the entrance of Grays Harbor from Ocean Shores the atmosphere is entirely different. Westport is very devoted to fishing, both charter and commercial. During the off season it seems almost derelict, but when the fish are running it is another story. The thing to do in Westport is take a charter fishing trip to catch salmon, halibut, tuna, or bottom fish. Also popular these days are boat trips out to the "whale hole" to watch the gray whales as they pause during their spring migration to Alaska during March, April, and May.

When you aren't out on the ocean there are other things to do in Westport. Along the waterfront next to the harbor there are a number of tourist shops and restaurants. Tourist sights include the **Westport Maritime Museum** and the privately owned **Westport Aquarium**. There is also a boat during the spring and summer that ferries walking passengers across to Ocean Shores.

Westport hosts its share of events, there's something almost every weekend during the summer months. Among them are the **Rusty Scupper Pirate Daze** the last weekend in

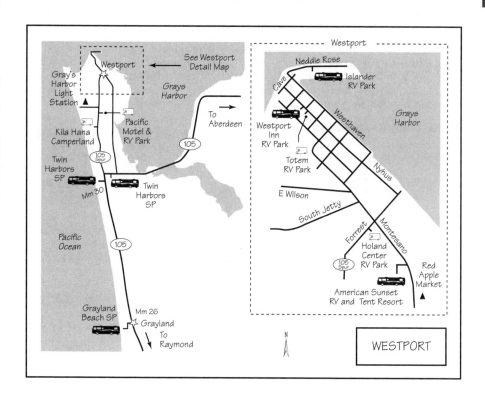

WASHINGTON

June, a **Kite Festival** in early mid July, the **Westport Art Festival** about the middle of August, and the **Westport Seafood Festival and Craft Day** on Labor Day. Check with the Chamber of Commerce for more events and exact dates.

Westport Campgrounds

● AMERICAN SUNSET RV AND TENT RESORT
    (Open All Year)
Reservations: (800) 569-2267
Information: (360) 268-0207,
                info@americansunsetrv.com,
                www.AmericanSunsetRV.com
Location: Westport

GPS Location: 46.89944 N, 124.10611 W, Near Sea Level

170 Sites – This is a nice large park located about .7 miles (1.1 km) from the dock area in Westport. The location means that the temperature here is warmer. The campground has less of a fisherman's camp atmosphere than those closer to the docks. In addition to the RV area (long back-ins to 50 feet and pull-thrus) there is a huge tent camping area and also a seasonal swimming pool. From the dock area in Westport proceed south on SR-105 for about a mile (1.6 km), the entrance will be on your right.

● **WESTPORT INN RV PARK** *(Open March 1 to Oct 31)*
Reservations: (800) 572-0177
Information: (360) 268-0111, coho@techline.com,
                www.westportwa.net/coho/rv/index.htm
Location: Westport

    GPS Location: 46.90969°N, 124.11605°W, Near Sea Level

76 Sites – This older park is conveniently located about a block from the Westport docks and marina. It's also a motel. Fishing charters can be arranged, they run two boats. It's easy to walk to the marina, shops and restaurants. Sites are all back-ins, RVs to 45 feet will fit although they'll project a bit into the driveway. The Westport Inn is on Nyhus between Coast Rd. and Harbor Ave.

● **ISLANDER RV PARK** *(Open All Year)*
Reservations: (800) 322-1740
Information: (360) 268-9166, info@westport-islander.com,
                www.westport-islander.com
Location: Westport

    GPS Location: 46.91194 N, 124.11528 W, Near Sea Level

57 sites – This campground sits next to the associated hotel. While the hotel is one of the nicer in town the RV park is a step down, although it is located overlooking the boat harbor. Sites are full-hookup pull-thrus to 40 feet although most are much shorter. The hotel and RV park are located at the northwest corner of the boat harbor, right where the road heads out along the northern breakwater.

☐ **TWIN HARBORS STATE PARK** *(Open All Year)*
Reservations: www.parks.wa.gov/reservations/,
                (888) 226-7688
Information: (360) 268-9717, (360) 371-2800,
                www.parks.wa.gov
Location: 1 Mile (1.6 Km) S of Westport

    GPS Location: 46.85778 N, 124.10639 W, Near Sea Level

297 Sites – This is a very large state campground just south of Westport. It is in two parts, one near the beach and the other across the highway. Only 49 sites have hookups and these are all closely grouped back-ins, some are 50 feet long. These sites have grills rather than fire pits and they are away from the ocean on the east side of the highway. The no hookup sites are much nicer and occupy both the beach side of the park and an area on the east side too. Some of these are 35 feet long, most are shorter, parking and tent-pitching is on grass. The dump station is free if you're staying in he park. The campground is located right at the junction where the stub road north to Westport meets SR-105. The entrance is on the road toward Aberdeen.

☐ **GRAYLAND BEACH STATE PARK** *(Open All Year)*
    Reservations: www.parks.wa.gov/reservations/, (888) 226-7688
    Information: (360) 267-4301, (360) 902-8844,
                 www.parks.wa.gov
    Location: 5 Miles (8 Km) S of Westport

    GPS Location: 46.79278 N, 124.09139 W, Near Sea Level

107 Sites – This state park is farther south than Twin Harbors but nicer with the sites arranged off 6 rings. They include almost 60 campsites with full hookups, some are 70 feet long. There is a nature trail through the dunes to the beach. From the intersection south of Westport where SR-105 from the south and SR-105 from Aberdeen meet, drive south 4.5 miles (7.3 km) to the entrance which is just south of the small town of Grayland. This park accepts reservations year-round.

WHIDBEY ISLAND

Whidbey Island stretches for 40 miles (65 km) from just north of Seattle to just south of Anacortes. It's a rural destination just a few miles from the Seattle metro area. However, the island isn't as crowded as you might expect, largely because access for Seattle residents requires a long drive or a ferry ride.

There are actually three ways to bring a vehicle onto the island. The only bridge is at the far north end across Deception Pass. The main ferry access is at the south end of the island from Mukilteo. This is only 25 miles (40 km) north of the Seattle business district and ferries are frequent, but they're expensive and during some tides access is difficult for big rigs. Finally, there's also a small ferry that operates from Port Townsend. This route doesn't bring nearly as many people onto the island as the other two.

With four state parks as well as commercial and local government campgrounds Whidbey has a lot to offer campers. An added bonus is that many of these campgrounds are near the beach.

Whidbey Island Campgrounds

☐ **DECEPTION PASS STATE PARK** *(Open All Year)*
    Reservations: www.parks.wa.gov/reservations/, (888) 226-7688
    Information: (360) 675-2417, (360) 902-8844, www.parks.wa.gov
    Location: 8 Miles (13 Km) N of Oak Harbor

    GPS Location: 48.39167 N, 122.64722 W, Near Sea Level

245 Sites – This large state park has a very impressive location offering views of Deception Pass, trails, fishing and swimming in a nearby lake, and excellent ocean beaches on Puget Sound. The camping areas are set in dense evergreens and

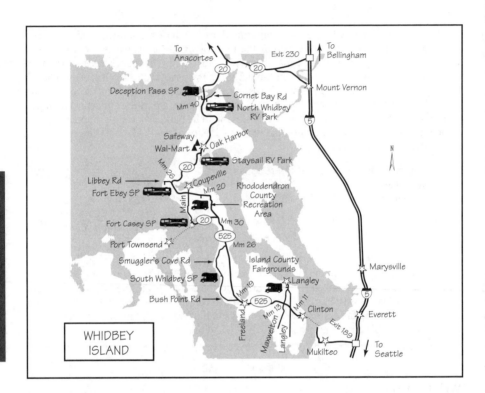

do not have views. Some of the hookup sites will take RVs to 35 feet although leveling may be difficult, the park is better for smaller rigs. Driving north on SR-20 on Whidbey Island watch for the Mile 40 marker. Turn left at the stoplight which is .8 miles (1.3 km) from the marker. From the Deception Pass bridge just drive south on SR-20 for a mile (1.6 km) to the stop light, the campground entrance will be on the right. This park accepts reservations year-round.

● **NORTH WHIDBEY RV PARK** *(Open All Year)*
Reservations: (888) 462-2674
Information: (360) 675-9597,
    managers@northwhidbeyrvpark.com,
    www.northwhidbeyrvpark.com
Location: 8 Miles (13 Km) N of Oak Harbor

GPS Location: 48.39056 N, 122.64556 W, 100 Ft

110 Sites – Located just a mile (1.6 km) from Deception Pass and right across from the entrance to Deception Pass State Park this campground is a nice commercial alternative to the state campground. Sites are paved pull-thrus to 50 feet and back-ins to 45 feet. Driving north on SR-20 on Whidbey Island watch for the Mile 40 marker. Turn right on Cornet Bay Road at the stop light which is .8 miles (1.3 km) from the marker, the campground will be in the right immediately after the turn. From the Deception Pass bridge just drive south on Highway 20 for a mile (1.6 km), turn left on Cornet Bay Road, the campground will be on the right.

○ **STAYSAIL RV PARK** *(Open All Year)*
   Information: (360) 679-5551, www.oakharbor.org
   Location: Oak Harbor

GPS Location: 48.28556 N, 122.65722 W, Near Sea Level

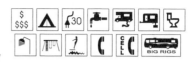

79 Sites – This is one of the most popular and least expensive campgrounds for big rigs on the Island. Sites are long back-ins, they have full hook-ups with 30 amp power. There are also 26 tent sites, these serve as no-hookup overflow sites for RVs if the other RV sites are full. This RV parking area is part of a large city park with large expenses of grass, restrooms with showers, a swimming lagoon, and walking trails. SR-20 makes an almost 90-degree bend in Oak Harbor. From the north continue straight at the turn, the road becomes South Beeksma Drive, and you'll reach the park in a block. From the south turn right at the bend.

☐ **FORT EBEY STATE PARK** *(Open All Year)*
   Reservations: www.parks.wa.gov/reservations/, (888) 226-7688
   Information: (360) 678-4636, (360) 902-8844, www.parks.wa.gov
   Location: 8 Miles (13 Km) SW of Oak Harbor

GPS Location: 48.22222 N, 122.76278 W, 100 Ft

54 Sites – Fort Ebey is one of 2 state parks on the Island that are former wartime gun batteries built to protect the approaches to Puget Sound. The campground here is in trees without views, sites are large enough for big RVs but maneuvering room is limited so very careful driving is required. Most sites are standard no-hookup sites, but there are 10 electricity-water sites. This park has extensive walking/ bike trails and a long beach. A small lake offers fishing for smallmouth bass. It's a popular hang gliding location too. To reach the campground leave SR-20 at about Mile 25 just north of Coupeville on Libbey Road and follow signs for 1.2 miles (1.9 km) to the park entrance.

○ **RHODODENDRON COUNTY RECREATION AREA**
   (Open April 1 to Oct 31)
   Information: (360) 679-7373
   Location: 12 Miles (19 Km) S of Oak Harbor

GPS Location: 48.20667 N, 122.65333 W, 200 Ft

10 Sites – This small county park is an inexpensive campground for tents and smaller RVs to about 25 feet. It's set in a dense grove of Douglas Fir and cedars. There is often a host. The campground is located just off SR-20 south of Coupeville. Turn west at the sign near Mile 20.

☐ **FORT CASEY STATE PARK** *(Open All Year)*
   Information: (360) 678-4519, (360) 902-8844,
        www.parks.wa.gov
   Location: 13 Miles (21 Km) S of Oak Harbor

GPS Location: 48.15722 N, 122.67389 W, Near Sea Level

35 Sites – Fort Casey is the second park located on the grounds of one of the former naval batteries set up to protect Puget Sound. Unlike Fort Ebey, the campsites here are set next to the water with great views, the ferry to Port Townsend docks right next to the campground. The sites have no hookups but some are back-ins to 40 feet. Easiest access is from the outskirts of Coupeville. Head south on South Main Street from SR-20 (near the pedestrian overpass), you'll reach the park entrance in 3.4 miles (5.5 km).

☐ **South Whidbey State Park** *(Open Feb 1 to Nov 30 – Varies))*
Reservations: www.parks.wa.gov/reservations/, (888) 226-7688
Information: (360) 331-4559, (360) 371-2800, www.parks.wa.gov
Location: 23 Miles (37 Km) S of Oak Harbor

GPS Location: 48.06000 N, 122.59417 W, 200 Ft

49 Sites – Sites in this campground are set in a grove of trees with no views. Most sites are suitable for RVs to 30 feet although a few of the utility sites will take 35 footers. To reach the campground head west from SR-525 on Bush Point Road at about Mile 19, just west of Freeland. The park entrance is on the left after 4 miles (6.4 km).

○ **Island County Fairgrounds** *(Open April 1 to Oct 1)*
Information: (360) 221-4677
Location: 35 Miles (56 Km) S of Oak Harbor

GPS Location: 48.03056 N, 122.40306 W, 200 Ft

60 Sites – The fairgrounds in Langley offer a good place to spend the night at the south end of the island, but not in August when they are reserved for the fair. Parking here is on grass with utility posts (electricity and water) scattered across the field. There is a self-service payment kiosk, the office here is open irregular hours. Restroom are available near the office, they have showers. There are no sewer drains at the sites but there is a dump station. From SR-525 near Mile 11 drive north on Langley Road, the fairgrounds entrance is on the left in 2.6 miles (4.2 km).

WINTHROP AND THE METHOW VALLEY

Since the opening of the North Cascades Highway the little town of **Winthrop** (area population 1,900) has become a four-season tourist Mecca. The town rebuilt itself as a western town by building false fronts on the buildings and covering the sidewalks with boardwalks. In the winter this is one of the top cross-country skiing areas in the state, and the surrounding hills are filled with summer hiking trails. There are a number of annual events celebrated in Winthrop including **Winthrop 49ers Days** during the second weekend of May, **Methow Valley Rodeos** on Memorial Day weekend and also Labor Day Weekend, **Winthrop Rhythm and Blues Festival** in mid-July, and the **Methow Valley Mountain Bike Festival** at the end of September. Check with the chamber of commerce for more information and to confirm dates.

Two miles (3 km) north of town is **Pearrygin Lake**. In the summer the lake offers a welcome respite from the relatively hot and dry countryside. There is a very popular state campground at the lake.

If you have a smaller vehicle you might want to drive the 19-mile (31 km) road up to **Harts Pass** and Slate Peak which at 7,448 feet is the highest point that can be driven to in Washington State. Consider yourself warned that much of this road is gravel and some sections have steep drop-offs and no guard rails. Trailers are not allowed on the latter portion of the drive beyond Ballard Campground. The road leaves SR-20 at Mazama which is about 14 miles (23 km) west of Winthrop.

Winthrop can get very crowded, particularly on weekends in the summer. The best way to handle it is to play along and enjoy it. There are many restaurants and small shops and the weather is usually great here on the dry side of the Cascades. There are a fine selection of nearby campgrounds to use as a base.

The surrounding countryside is mostly within the **Okanogan National Forest**. There is a ranger station on SR-20 just west of town where you can pick up information about interesting destinations and hikes in the national forest.

Winthrop and the Methow Valley Campgrounds

● **RIVERBEND RV PARK** *(Open All Year)*
Res and Info: (800) 686-4498,
(509) 997-3500,
reservations@riverbendrv.com,
www.riverbendrv.com
Location: 6 Miles (10 Km) S of Winthrop

GPS Location: 48.39111 N, 120.13528 W, 1,600 Ft

80 Sites – If you want to put some distance between yourself and the crowds in Winthrop but still want to be able to visit the town this is a good choice. The campground has back-ins and pull-thrus to 80 feet. It's located on the bank of the Methow River just north of Twisp, about 6 miles (10 km) down the valley from Winthrop.

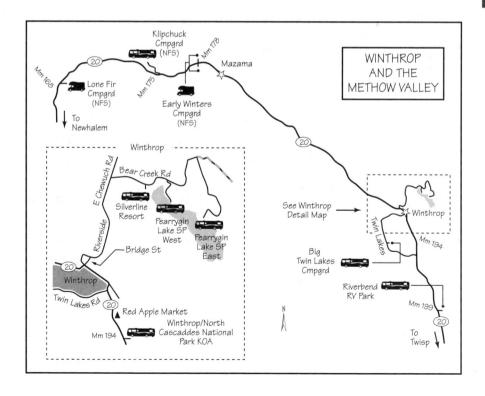

WASHINGTON

● **BIG TWIN LAKES CAMPGROUND**
(Open April 20 to Oct 31 – Varies)
Res and Info: (509) 996-2650, bigtwinlake@comcast.net,
www.methownet.com/bigtwin
Location: 4 Miles (6 Km) SW of Winthrop

GPS Location: 48.44750 N, 120.19861 W, 1,800 Ft

90 Sites – This is another campground located away from the madness of Winthrop. It occupies an open valley with a small lake. Parking is on grass with trees providing some shade, very pleasant. Sites are very long allowing rigs of any size to park here. This is a stocked lake so fishing is possible, only electric motors are allowed. There is swimming in the lake and you can rent paddle boats and rowboats. The campground is located off Twin Lakes Road. To reach it from Winthrop drive south 2.5 miles (4.0 km), or 5 miles (8 km) north from Twisp, and turn west on Big Twin Lake Road. In another 2 mile (3.2 km) you'll see the campground entrance on the right.

● **WINTHROP/NORTH CASCADES NATIONAL PARK KOA** *(Open April 15 to Nov 1)*
Reservations: (800) 562-2158, www.koa.com
Information: (509) 996-2258,
campkoa@mymethow.com,
www.methownet.com/koa
Location: 1 Mile (1.6 Km) S of Winthrop

GPS Location: 48.46250 N, 120.17028 W, 1,700 Ft

96 Sites – This is a well-run KOA, without a doubt the most popular commercial campground in the Winthrop area. Parking is on grass, there are back-ins and pull-thrus to 60 feet. The campground has a seasonal swimming pool. Because it is not actually in Winthrop the campground provides a shuttle bus. Watch for the entrance on the east side of the highway 1 mile (1.6 km) south of Winthrop and 7 miles (11.2 km) north of Twisp.

● **SILVERLINE RESORT**
(Open April 20 to Oct 20 – Varies)
Res and Info: (509) 996-2448,
silverline_resort@yahoo.com,
www.silverlineresort.com
Location: 2 Miles (3 Km) NE of Winthrop

GPS Location: 48.49361 N, 120.16417 W, 1,900 Ft

80 Sites – This is a very nice lakeside resort. They offer swimming in the lake, boat rentals, and mini golf. A great family vacation destination. There are back-ins and pull-thrus to 80 feet as well as many tent sites. From the point where SR-20 makes a 90-degree turn in central Winthrop drive north on Riverside Ave. which curves around and eventually turns into E. Chewuch Road. At 1.6 miles (2.6 km) from the 90-degree turn take the right onto Bear Creek Road. In .5 mile (.8 km) you'll see the entrance road on the right.

☐ **PEARRYGIN LAKE STATE PARK**
(Open March 31 to Oct 31 – Varies)
Reservations: www.parks.wa.gov/reservations/, (888) 226-7688
Information: (509) 996-2370, (360) 902-8844, www.parks.wa.gov
Location: 2 Miles (3 Km) NE of Winthrop

GPS Location: 48.49278 N, 120.15861 W, 1,900 Ft

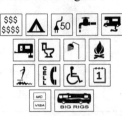

156 Sites – There are now two sections to this very popular

state campground. The original state campground (east campground) has 85 sites and the layout is normal for a state campground with mostly back-in sites off paved loops. Twenty-seven sites are pull-thrus to 60 feet. Everything is set on beautiful lawns. The second section (west campground) is a former commercial campground next door. It is accessed by a separate road, you'll reach it before you reach the original campground entrance. It has 71 sites including back-in side-by-side hookup sites and no-hookup sites along the lake. Sites here also reach 60 feet. From the point where SR-20 makes a 90-degree turn in central Winthrop drive north on Riverside Ave. which curves around and eventually turns into E. Chewuch Road. At 1.6 miles (2.6 km) from the 90-degree turn take the right onto Bear Creek Road. In .9 mile (1.5 km) from the turn you'll reach the entrance to the west campground, at 1.7 miles (2.7 km) the entrance to the east campground. Reservations are taken at this park from April 15 to October 31.

■ **EARLY WINTERS CAMPGROUND** *(Open April 15 to Sept 30 – Varies)*
Information: (509) 996-4003
Location: 15 Miles (24 Km) W of Winthrop

GPS Location: 48.59667 N, 120.44611 W, 2,200 Ft

12 Sites – This is a small and economical Okanogan National Forest campground with sites in two locations on either side of the highway. Sites reach about 30 feet in length. Both roads and parking pads are gravel. Water is from faucets. The campground is on both sides of SR-20 some 15 miles (27 km) west of Winthrop.

■ **KLIPCHUCK CAMPGROUND** *(Open May 15 to Sept 30 – Varies)*
Information: (509) 996-4003
Location: 18 Miles (29 Km) W of Winthrop

GPS Location: 48.59750 N, 120.51417 W, 2,100 Ft

46 Sites – Klipchuck is a larger Okanogan National Forest campground that is away from the highway yet easily accessible on a paved road. Paved loops run through the campground, the maximum site size is 34 feet. There's good hiking from this campground. The entrance road leaves SR-20 some 17 miles (27 km) west of Winthrop, then it's another 1.3 miles (2.1 km) to the campground.

■ **LONE FIR CAMPGROUND** *(June 1 to Sept 15 – Varies)*
Information: (509) 996-4003
Location: 24 Miles (39 Km) W of Winthrop

GPS Location: 48.58111 N, 120.62389 W, 3,600 Ft

27 Sites – Lone Fir is near the highway and quite a bit higher than the other two Okanogan National Forest campgrounds west of Winthrop. From here the next campground westward on the highway is Ross Lake. Some sites here will take 35 foot rigs if they are very carefully driven, the access road is paved but narrow with trees that could cause problems for larger RVs. The Lone Fir Loop Trail makes a nice walk. The campground is on the south side of SR-20 some 25 miles (40 km) west of Winthrop and 49 miles (79 km) east of Newhalem.

YAKIMA AND THE YAKIMA VALLEY

You'll probably be amazed by the many things to do and see in the Yakima area. The valley, stretching southeast from Yakima itself, includes the towns of Union Gap, Wapato, Toppenish, Zillah, Granger, Grandview, Sunnyside and Prosser. The Yakima Valley can

WASHINGTON

THE YAKIMA VALLEY IS WASHINGTON STATE'S WINE CENTER

be hot in the middle of the summer, spring and summer visits are great. Here are just a few of the offerings.

In **Yakima** (population 91,000) the **Yakima Valley Museum** is excellent, it has displays covering the Oregon Trail, Yakama Indians, Chief Justice William O. Douglas, and horse-drawn vehicles. Another good area museum is in Union Gap, this is the **Central Washington Agricultural Museum**. It does a good job on the agricultural aspect of the area's history. It's big with farm machinery, a tool museum, and 18 display buildings.

The irrigated Yakima Valley has long been an important fruit-growing center and in recent years has also become the wine center of Washington state. There are many **wineries with wine tasting rooms** and gift shops throughout the valley. The best way to visit is in your own vehicle, pick up a wine tour pamphlet and map at any visitor center or commercial campground. An added bonus is that throughout the valley you'll find stands offering fresh fruits and vegetables. Offerings vary, it just depends upon what is in season.

The huge 1.4 million-acre **Yakama Nation Reservation** stretches westward from the Yakima Valley all the way to Mt Adams. Near Toppenish you'll find a cluster of Yakama Nation-owned attractions including the **Yakama Nation Cultural Center** and restaurant, the **Yakama Nation Legends Casino**, and the **Yakama Nation Resort RV Park**.

The town of **Toppenish** (population 9,000) is the commercial center for the reservation. It is known for the outdoor murals painted on the buildings around town, some fifty of them in all. There's also the **American Hop Museum** with everything you ever wanted to know about hops.

The most popular annual event in the valley is probably the **Central Washington State**

Fair in the latter part of September and first of October, it offers a rodeo and the other things you would expect of a large state fair in an agricultural region.

Yakima and the Yakima Valley Campgrounds

● **CIRCLE H RV RANCH** *(Open All Year)*
   Res and Info: (509) 457-3683, circlehrvpark@msn.com,
          www.circlehrvpark.com
   Location: Yakima

   GPS Location: 46.59028 N, 120.47750 W, 1,100 Ft

64 Sites – This older but well-run RV park makes a good place to stay while visiting Yakima. It has a restaurant, a seasonal pool, mini-golf, and even free Wi-Fi. What more could you want? Paved back-in and pull-thru sites to 60 feet will take large rigs. To reach the campground take Exit 34 from I-82. Drive west on E. Nob Hill Blvd. and take the first right onto S. 18th Street. The campground is on the right in .3 mile (.5 km).

☐ **YAKIMA SPORTSMAN STATE PARK** *(Open All Year)*
   Reservations: www.parks.wa.gov/reservations/,
          (888) 226-7688
   Information: (509) 575-2774, (360) 902-8844,
          www.parks.wa.gov
   Location: 1 Mile (2 Km) E of Yakima

   GPS Location: 46.59222 N, 120.45500 W, 1,000 Ft

WASHINGTON

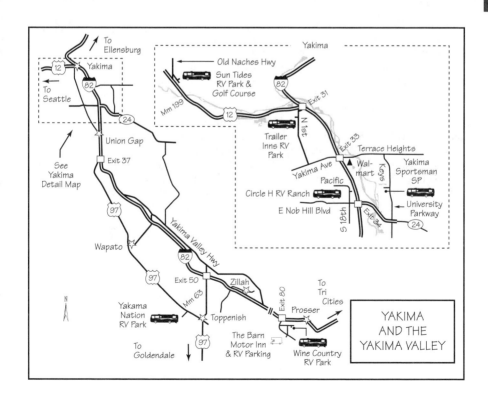

YAKIMA
AND THE
YAKIMA VALLEY

70 Sites – This is a heavily used campground due to its location near the city. The park offers the normal excellent state campground amenities in a convenient location. There are long sites to at least 50 feet, both back-ins off circles and pull-through side-by-side sites. There are hiking trails along the river and around the nearby pond. From I-84 in Yakima take Exit 33B southbound, Exit 33 northbound. Drive east on Terrace Heights Way for 1.3 miles (2.1 km), passing the Walmart. Then turn right on Keys Road and in 1.2 miles (1.9 km) you'll see the park entrance on the right.

● **YAKIMA TRAILER INNS RV PARK**
    (Open All Year)
    Reservations: (800) 659-4784, www.trailerinnsrv.com
    Information: (509) 452-9561, www.trailerinnsrv.com
    Location: Yakima

    GPS Location: 46.62222 N, 120.51194 W, 1,000 Ft

140 Sites – This commercial campground has an urban Yakima location with bus service and convenient access to the Yakima green belt bike trail nearby. There's an indoor pool with a spa and sauna room. Sites are back-ins and pull-thrus to 90 feet. Take Exit 31 from I-82 and drive .2 miles (.3 km) south on First Street, the entrance is on the right.

● **YAKAMA NATION RV PARK** *(Open All Year)*
    Reservations: (800) 874-3087, www.ynrv.com
    Information: (509) 865-2000, www.ynrv.com
    Location: 19 Miles (31 Km) S of Yakima

    GPS Location: 46.37806 N, 120.34472 W, 800 Ft

135 Sites – This large modern big-rig campground is conveniently located for visiting the wine tasting rooms in the Zillah area. A bonus is that both the Yakama Nation Cultural Center and Legends Casino are in the immediate area. The spacious campground has pull-thru and back-in sites to 65 feet, tent sites, and even rental teepees. Facilities include swimming pool and spa, a weight room, basketball and volleyball courts, and a very popular .8 mile walking and jogging track around the campground. Just next door is the Yakama Nation Cultural Center. It has a restaurant offering buffets and cultural favorites like salmon, buffalo, and fry bread. There is also a theater, a museum, a library, and a gift shop. The Legends Casino is about a half-mile from the campground. The campground is about 17 miles (27 km) south of Yakima. Driving south on I-82 from Yakima take the US-97 exit (Exit 37) and watch for the cultural center on the right in 14 miles (23 km) just north of Toppenish. It is well signed and located just west of the highway with excellent access.

● **WINE COUNTRY RV PARK** *(Open All Year)*
    Res and Info: (509) 786-5192, (800) 726-4969, winecountry@winecountryrvpark.com, www.winecountryrvpark.com
    Location: 1 Mile (2 Km) N of Prosser

    GPS Location: 46.21972 N, 119.78528 W, 700 Ft

135 Sites – Wine Country is a good big rig park just off I-82 near Prosser. As the name says, this is the heart of Washington's wine country. There's a pool and spa as well as large pull-thru sites to 60 feet, even a few tent sites. From I-82 about 45 miles (73 km) southeast of Yakima take Exit 80. Drive south to the first left, turn and drive eastward past

the rest area for .3 mile (.5 km), the campground entrance is on the right.

● **Sun Tides RV Park and Golf Course**
   (Open All Year)
   Res and Info: (800) 376-8025, (509) 966-7883,
                www.suntidesgolf.com
   Location: 5 Miles (8 Km) W of Yakima

   GPS Location: 46.63700 N, 120.59092 W, 1,100 Ft

60 Sites – This big-rig park is next to the 18 hole Sun Tides Golf Course. Sites are 65-foot full hookup pull-thrus. In addition to the golf course there's also an 18-hole championship putting course, a driving range, a pro shop, and a restaurant and lounge. From the intersection of I-82 and Hwy 12 north of Yakima (Exit 31) follow Hwy 12 west for 4.8 mile (7.7 km) to the stoplight at Old Naches Highway. Turn right and then right again on Pence Road to parallel the highway, the RV park entrance is on the left in just .2 miles (.3 km).

YAKIMA RIVER CANYON

The **Yakima River Canyon** is extremely scenic between Yakima and Ellensburg. It's worth your time to get off the freeway and take a look. SR-821 leaves the I-82 freeway about four miles (6 km) north of Yakima and follows the river for 27 miles (44 km) north to Ellensburg. The river is a favorite of fly fishermen and summer river rafters. A note of caution, keep your speed down, the authorities watch this road carefully.

The canyon is managed by the BLM and virtually all camping is at BLM sites. There are

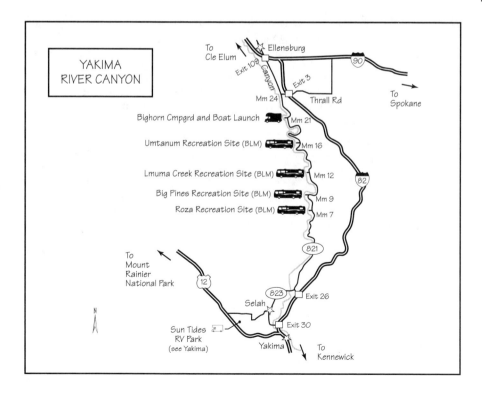

no hookups – but it's a beautiful place. The campgrounds below are listed from the Ellensburg end toward Yakima, from north to south, driving downstream. Note that things are in a state of flux here. Facilities are being improved and rates and opening dates are changing.

Yakima River Canyon Campgrounds

● **BIGHORN CAMPGROUND AND BOAT LAUNCH**
  (Open May 1 to Sept 15 – Varies)
  Location: 26 Miles (41 Km) N of Yakima

  GPS Location: 46.89418 N, 120.50003 W, 1,500 Ft

34 Sites – Bighorn Campground is the only private campground in the canyon. The spaces here are scattered unimproved spots in the trees along the river reached by poor dirt access roads. Some sites are fine for RVs to about 30 feet, in fact we've seen even larger rigs in here. The only facilities are portable toilets. This is a popular place for launching boats and rafts to float the river. The campground is located near Mile 22.

■ **UMTANUM RECREATION SITE** *(Open All Year)*
  Location: 21 Miles (34 Km) N of Yakima

  GPS Location: 46.85444 N, 120.47944 W, 1,400 Ft

7 Sites – This is a BLM site which has a large gravel parking lot as well as seven back-in sites as long as 60 feet. They have picnic tables and fire pits and handicapped-accessible vault toilets. There's also a footbridge across the river. The use (camping) fee is $15. The campground is located near Mile 16.

■ **LMUMA CREEK BLM RECREATION SITE** *(Closed In Winter)*
  Location: 17 Miles (27 Km) N of Yakima

  GPS Location: 46.81389 N, 120.45028 W, 1,300 Ft

7 Sites – This recreation site next to the river has a launch ramp and seven
campsites. It's a large gravel parking lot with the sites arranged around the perimeter, some right next to the river. Picnic tables and fire pits are provided and there are modern vault toilets. The campground is near Mile 12.

■ **BIG PINES BLM RECREATION SITE** *(Open All Year)*
  Location: 14 Miles (23 Km) N of Yakima

  GPS Location: 46.79333 N, 120.45583 W, 1,300 Ft

41 Sites – This site has been upgraded to a formal camping area. There are 41 sites, most are long paved back-ins but three are pull-thrus. Sites have tables, fire pits, and vault toilets are provided. This site is near Mile 9.

■ **ROZA RECREATION SITE** *(Closed In Winter)*
  Location: 12 Miles (19 Km) N of Yakima

  GPS Location: 46.76389 N, 120.45500 W, 1,200 Ft

5 Sites – This site is a large paved lot with a paved boat ramp and restrooms (vault toilets). It has the highest level of improvements of the BLM sites along the river but not necessarily the best campsites. The emphasis here is on the boat ramp. Camping is allowed in five sites arranged around the perimeter of the lot, sites have picnic tables and vault toilets. This site is near Mile 7.

Information Resources

See our Internet site at www.rollinghomes.com for Internet information links.

Bellingham

Bellingham Visitor Information Center, 904 Potter St, Bellingham, WA 98229; (360) 671-3990 or (800) 487-2032; tourism@bellingham.org

Chelan

Lady of the Lake, 1418 W Woodin Ave, Chelan, WA 98816; (509) 682-4584; info@lady-ofthelake.com

Lake Chelan Chamber of Commerce and Visitor Information Center, 102 East Johnson Ave (PO Box 216), Chelan, WA 98816; (509) 682-3503 or (800) 424-3526; info@lakechelan.com

Mill Bay Casino, 455 Wapato Lake Rd, Manson, WA 98831; (509) 687-6911 or (800) 648-2946

Wenatchee National Forest, Chelan Ranger District, 428 W Woodin Ave, Chelan, WA 98816; (509) 682-9004

Cle Elum and Roslyn

Cle Elum Chamber of Commerce, 401 W 1st St, Cle Elum, WA 98922; (509) 674-5958; cle_elum@cleelum.com

Coeur d'Alene, Idaho

Coeur d'Alene Post Falls Convention and Visitor Bureau, 105 N 1st St, Suite 100, Coeur d'Alene, ID 83814; (877) 782-9232

Ellensburg

Ellensburg Chamber of Commerce and Visitor Information, 609 North Main St, Ellensburg, WA 98926; (509) 925-3138 or (888) 925-2204; info@ellensburg-chamber.com

Forks and Western Sections of Olympic National Park

Forks Chamber of Commerce, Visitor's Center, 1411 S Forks Ave (PO Box 1249), Forks, WA 98331; (360) 374-2531 and (800) 443-6757; info@forkswa.com

Olympic National Forest Information Center, 551 S Forks Ave, Forks, WA 98331; (360) 374-7566

Grand Coulee

Coulee City Chamber of Commerce, 220 E Chelan St, Coulee City, WA 99115; (509) 632-5043 or (509) 681-2018

Grand Coulee Dam Area Chamber of Commerce, PO Box 760, Grand Coulee, WA 99133; (509) 633-3074 or (800) 268-5332; chamber@grandcouleedam.org

Grand Coulee Dam, Visitor Arrival Center, Grand Coulee Power Office, PO Box 620, Grand Coulee, WA 99133; (509) 633-9265

Soap Lake Chamber of Commerce, PO Box 433, Soap Lake, WA 98851; (509) 246-1821

Hood Canal

North Mason Visitors Info Center, 30 NE Romance Hill Road (PO Box 416), Belfair, WA 98528; (360) 275-4267

Ilwaco and Long Beach

Lewis and Clark Interpretive Center, 244 Robert Gray Dr SW, Ilwaco, WA; (360) 642-3029

Long Beach Peninsula Visitor Information, 3914 Pacific Hwy, Seaview, WA 98644; (360) 642-2400 or (800) 451-2542

Willapa National Wildlife Refuge, 3888 State Route 101, Ilwaco, WA 98624; (360) 484-3482; charlie_stenvall@fws.gov

Kitsap Peninsula and Bainbridge Island

Bainbridge Isle Chamber of Commerce, 590 Winslow Way E, Bainbridge Isle, Wa 98110; (206) 842-3700; info@bainbridgechamber.com

Kitsap Peninsula Visitor and Convention Bureau, 9481 Silverdale Way NW, Suite 281, Silverdale, WA 98383; (800) 337-0580; info@visitkitsap.com

Lake Easton and Lake Kachess

US Forest Service Visitor Information Center, 69805 Snoqualmie Pass Summit Road, Snoqualmie Pass, WA 98068; (425) 434-6111

Lake Pateros Region

Brewster Chamber of Commerce, 105 South Third St (PO Box 1087), Brewster, WA 98812; (509) 689-3464; info@brewsterchamber.org

Lake Wenatchee and Fish Lake Recreation Area

Lake Wenatchee Ranger Station, Wenatchee National Forest, Leavenworth, WA 98826; (509) 763-3103

Leavenworth

Leavenworth Chamber of Commerce, PO Box 327, Leavenworth, WA 98826; (509) 548-5807; info@leavenworth.org

Wenatchee National Forest, Leavenworth Ranger District, 600 Sherbourne, Leavenworth, WA; (509) 548-6977

Lewiston, Idaho and Clarkston, Washington

Clarkston Chamber of Commerce, 502 Bridge Street, Clarkston, WA 99403: (509) 758-7712

Hells Canyon National Recreation Area Headquarters, 2535 Riverside Dr, Clarkston, WA 99403; (509) 758-0616

Lewiston Chamber of Commerce, 111 Main Street, Lewiston #120, ID 83501; (208) 743-3531

Nez Perce National Historical Park – Spalding Site, 39063 US Hwy 95, Spalding, ID 83540; (208) 843-7001

Hells Canyon Tour Operators:

- Beamers Hells Canyon Tours, 1451 Bridge Street, Clarkston, WA 99403; (509) 758-4800
- River Quest Excursions, 4203 Snake River Ave Lewiston, ID 83501; (208) 746-8060 or (800) 589-1129; riverquest@cableone.net
- Snake Dancer Excursions, 1550 Port Drive, Suite B (PO Box 318) Clarkston, WA 99403; (509) 758-8927; sdexcursions@quest.net
- Snake River Adventures, 227 Snake River Ave., Lewiston, ID 83501; (208) 746-6276 or (800) 262-8874; sra1@lewistondsl.com

Maryhill

Goldendale Observatory State Park, 1602 Observatory Dr, Goldendale, WA 98620; (509) 773-3141

Maryhill Museum of Art, 35 Maryhill Museum Drive, Goldendale, WA 98620; (509) 773-3733; maryhill@maryhillmuseum.org

Moscow, Idaho and Pullman, WA and the Palouse

Moscow Chamber of Commerce, 411 South Main Street (PO Box 8936), Moscow, ID 83843; (208) 882-1800 or (800) 380-1801; staff@moscowchamber.com

Pullman Chamber of Commerce, 415 North Grand Ave, Pullman, WA 99163; (509) 334-3565 or (800) 365-6948

Moses Lake and the Potholes

Moses Lake Chamber of Commerce, 324 S Pioneer Way, Moses Lake, WA 98837; (509) 765-7888; information@moseslake.com

Mt Rainier National Park

Gifford Pinchot National Forest, Packwood Information Center, 13068 US 12, Packwood, WA 98361; (360) 497-1100

Mt Rainier National Park, 39000 Star Route 706 E, Ashford, WA 98304; (360) 569-6608

Mt St Helens National Volcanic Monument

Castle Rock Visitor Information Center, 147 Front Ave NW, Castle Rock, WA 98611; (360) 274-6603

Mt St Helens National Monument Visitor Center, 3029 Spirit Lake Hwy, Castle Rock, WA 98611; (360) 274-0962

Neah Bay

Lake Ozette Ranger Station, Olympic National Park, (360) 963-2725

Makah Museum and Cultural Center, PO Box 160, Neah Bay, WA 98357; (360) 645-2711

North Cascades National Park

North Cascade Chamber of Commerce, 59831 State Route 20, Marblemount, WA 98267; (360) 873-4150; chamber@marblemount.com

North Cascades NPS Complex, 810 State Route 20, Sedro Woolley, WA 98284; (360) 854-7200

North Cascades Visitor Center, State Route 20, Mile 120, Newhalem, WA; (206) 386-4495

North Cascades Wilderness Information Center, 7280 Ranger Station Rd, Marblemount, WA 98267; (360) 854-7245

Ocean Shores and the North Beaches Area

Ocean Shores Visitor Information Center, 120 W Chance a La Mer NW, Ocean Shores, WA 98569; (360) 289-9586

Washington Coast Chamber of Commerce, 2616 A State Route 109, Ocean City, WA 98569; (360) 289-4552; wacoast@techline.com

Okanogan Valley

Okanogan National Forest Headquarters, 215 Melody Lane, Wenatchee, WA 98801; (509) 664-9200

Omak Visitor Information Center, 401 Omak Ave, Omak, WA 98841; (509) 826-4218 or (800) 225-6625; omakvic@northcascades.net

Tonasket Information Center, 215 S Whitcomb Avenue, Tonasket, WA 98855; (509) 486-4543; contact@tvbrc.org

Olympia

Olympia-Lacey-Tumwater Visitor & Convention Bureau, 103 Sid Snyder Ave SW (PO Box 7338), Olympia, WA 98507; (360) 704-7544 or (877) 704-7500

Washington State Capitol Campus Visitor Information; (360) 902-8880

Port Angeles and the Northern Olympic National Park

Black Ball Ferry Line, 101 Railroad Avenue, Port Angeles, WA 98362; (360) 457-4491

Olympic National Park, 600 East Park Ave, Port Angeles, WA 98362-6798; (360) 565-3130

Olympic Peninsula Visitor Bureau, 338 W 1st St, #104, Port Angeles, WA 98362; (360) 452-8552 or (800) 942-4042

Port Angeles Chamber of Commerce, 121 E Railroad Ave, Port Angeles, WA 98362; (360) 452-2363; info@portangeles.org

Port Townsend

Port Townsend Chamber of Commerce Visitor Center, 440 12th St, Port Townsend, WA 98368; (360) 385-2722 or (888) 365-6978; info@jeffcountychamber.org

Seattle

Argosy Cruises, 1101 Alaskan Way, Pier 55, Ste 201, Seattle, WA 98101; (206) 622-8687 or (888) 623-1445; sales@argosycruises.com

Boeing Everett Tours; (360) 756-0086 or (800) 464-1476

King County Transit; (206) 553-3000

Museum of Flight, 9404 E Marginal Way S, Seattle, WA 98108; (206) 764-5720

Seattle Aquarium, 1483 Alaskan Way #59, Seattle, WA 98101; (206) 386-4300; contactus@seattleaquarium.org

Seattle Art Museum, 1300 First Ave, Seattle, WA 89101-2003; (206) 625-8900; webmaster@seattleartmuseum.org

Seattle Chamber of Commerce, 1301 5th Ave #2500, Seattle, WA 98101; (206) 389-7200

Seattle's Convention and Visitor Bureau, Visitors Information at Washington State Convention and Trade Center, 701 Pike St, Ste 800, Seattle, WA 98101; (206) 461-5800

Simply Seattle Visitor Info, 1600 1st Ave, Seattle, WA 98101; (206) 448-2207

Underground Tours, 608 1st Ave, Seattle, WA 98104; (206) 682-4646

Sequim

Dungeness National Wildlife Refuge, 33 S Barr Rd, Port Angeles, WA 98362; (360) 457-8451

Olympic Game Farm, 1423 Ward Rd, Sequim, WA 98382; (360) 683-4295

Seven Cedars Casino, 270756 Hwy 101, Sequim, WA 98382; (360) 683-7777

Sequim Chamber of Commerce, 1192 E Washington St (PO Box 907), Sequim, WA 98382; (360) 683-6197 or (800) 737-8462; info@sequimchamber.com

Skagit Valley

Anacortes Chamber of Commerce, 819 Commercial Ave #F, Anacortes, WA 98221; (360) 293-3832; info@anacortes.org

La Conner Chamber of Commerce, 606 Morris St, La Conner, WA 98257; (360) 466-4778

Mt Vernon Chamber of Commerce, 105 E Kincaid St #101, Mt Vernon, WA 98273; (360) 428-8547; info@mountvernonchamber.com

Snake River

Corps of Engineers, Clarkston Natural Resources Office, 100 Fair Street, Clarkston, WA 99403; (509) 751-0240; ClarkstonNaturalResources@usace.army.mil

Dam Info – To hear recorded information about when roads across the dams are open – (888) DAMINFO or (888) 326-4636

Ice Harbor Dam Visitor Center; 2339 Monument Dr, Burbank, WA 99232; (509) 547-2048; IceHarborParks&Recreation@usace.army.mil

Lower Granite Dam Visitor Center; (509)843-1493

Spokane

Spokane Visitor Information, 201 W Main Ave, Spokane, WA 99201; (509) 747-3230

Tacoma

Point Defiance Zoo and Aquarium, 5400 Pearl St, Tacoma, WA 98407; (253) 591-5337; pdzacomments@tacomaparks.com

Tacoma Art Museum, 1701 Pacific Ave, Tacoma, WA 98402; (253) 272-4258

Tacoma Regional Convention & Visitor Bureau, 1119 Pacific Ave, Ste 1400, Tacoma, WA 98402; (253) 627-2836; info@traveltacoma.com

Tri-Cities

Columbia River Exhibition of History, Science, and Technology, 95 Lee Blvd, Richland, WA 99352; (509) 943-9000 or (877) 789-9935

Tri-Cities Visitor and Convention Bureau, 7130 West Grandridge Blvd , Ste B (PO Box 2241), Kennewick, WA 99302; (509) 735-8486 or (800) 254-5824; info@VisitTRI-CITIES.com

Walla Walla

Fort Walla Walla Museum, 755 NE Myra Rd, Walla Walla, WA 99362; (509) 525-7703

Walla Walla Valley Chamber of Commerce, 29 E Sumach Street, Walla Walla, WA 98362; (509) 525-0850

Whitman Mission National Historic Site, 328 Whitman Mission Road, Walla Walla, WA 99362; (509) 529-2761

Wenatchee

Ohme Gardens County Park, 3327 Ohme Rd, Wenatchee, WA 98801; (509) 662-5785

Wenatchee Valley Convention & Visitors Bureau, 5 S Wenatchee Ave, Ste 100, Wenatchee, WA 98801; (800) 572-7753; info@wenatcheevalley.org

Westport

Grayland Beach Visitor Information, 2071 Cranberry Rd, Grayland, WA 98547; (360) 267-2003

Westport/Grayland Chamber of Commerce, 2985 S Montesano St (PO Box 306), Westport, WA 98595; (360) 268-9422 or (800) 345-6223

Westport Aquarium, 321 E Harbor St, Westport, WA 98595; (360) 268-0471

Westport Maritime Museum, 2201 Westhaven Dr (PO Box 1074), Westport, WA 98595; (360) 268-0078

Whidbey Island

Central Whidbey Chamber of Commerce, 905 NW Alexander, Coupeville, WA 98239; (360) 678-5434; director@centralwhidbeychamber.com

Deception Pass Visitors Center, 40751 State Route 20, Oak Harbor, WA 98277; (360) 675-9438

Oak Harbor Chamber of Commerce, 32630 State Route 20, Oak Harbor, WA 98277; (360) 675-3755

Winthrop and the Methow Valley

Winthrop Chamber of Commerce and Methow Valley Information Center, 202 Hwy 20 (PO Box 39), Winthrop, WA 98862; (509) 996-2125 or (888) 463-8469; info@winthrop-washington.com

Wenatchee National Forest Winthrop Visitor Information Center, 24 West Chewuch Rd, Winthrop, WA 98862; (509) 996-4003

Yakima and the Yakima Valley

American Hop Museum, 22 S B Street, Toppenish, WA 98948; (509) 865-4677; director@americanhopmusem.org

Central Washington Agricultural Museum, 4508 Main Street, Union Gap, WA 98903; (509) 457-8735 or (509) 248-0432; info@centralwaagmuseum.org

Cultural Heritage Center, Hwy 97 (PO Box 151), Toppenish, WA 98948; (509) 865-2800

Greater Yakima Chamber of Commerce, 10 N 9th St (PO Box 1490), Yakima, WA 98907; (509) 248-2021

Prosser Chamber of Commerce, 1230 Bennett Ave, Prosser, WA 99350; (509) 786-3177 or (800) 408-1517; info@prosserchamber.org

Yakima Valley Museum, 2105 Tieton Dr, Yakima, WA 98902; (509) 248-0747

Yakima Valley Visitors and Convention Bureau, 10 N 8th St, Yakima, WA 98901; (509) 575-3010 or (800) 221-0751

Yakima River Canyon

BLM Wenatchee Field Office, 915 N Walla Walla, Wenatchee, WA 98801; (509) 665-2100

WASHINGTON

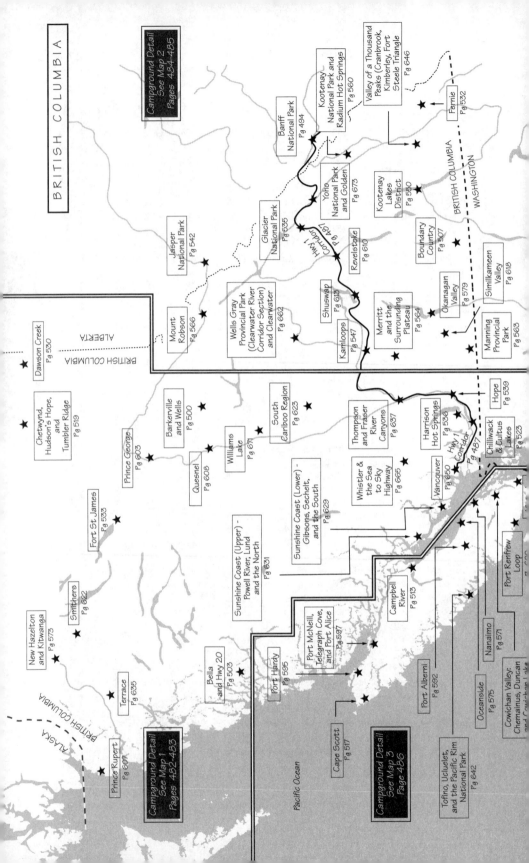

Chapter 6
British Columbia

It's easy to make the argument that British Columbia is the ultimate camping destination. The province offers both rugged and civilized seacoasts, islands, sophisticated cities, wilderness, and some of the most varied mountain terrain in the world.

Of course, unlike Washington and Oregon, British Columbia is in Canada, not the U.S. Fortunately, crossing the border is not very difficult. We've included a section about crossing the border, going both north and south, in the *Introduction* chapter of the book.

For most of us British Columbia is a spring, summer and fall destination. Vancouver Island, the Sunshine Coast, and Vancouver and the lower Fraser Valley have a marine climate. That means winter temperatures are generally above freezing but wet. The remainder of the province is much less temperate with higher elevations that mean cool winter temperatures and snow.

Although we have titled this chapter British Columbia it actually covers part of Alberta too. Some of the Rocky Mountain National Parks covered here; Jasper and Banff; are in that Province.

REGIONS AND THEIR CAMPGROUND RESOURCES

Vancouver Island

This large 250 kilometer (275 mile) long island offers Victoria, the sophisticated capital of the province, as well as remote beaches, northwest Indian culture (called First Nations in Canada), some of the best salmon fishing in the world, and pristine evergreen forests. Victoria is in the far south with a chain of mountains occupying the center ridge of the island. The east coast is relatively accessible with a good highway running all the way from Victoria up to Port Hardy in the far north. The rugged west coast of the island can only be reached in a few places using roads running west across the mountain spine.

Vancouver Island is easily accessible using frequent ferries from near Vancouver on the mainland. There are also ferry connections from Port Angeles and Anacortes in Washington and from Powell River at the upper end of the Sunshine Coast. There's even ferry service from Prince Rupert south to Port Hardy. All of these runs are described in our *Introduction* chapter.

From south to north the destinations covered in this chapter are: • *Victoria,* • *the Cowichan Valley* • *Port Renfrew Loop,* • *Nanaimo,* • *Oceanside,* • *Port Alberni,* • *Tofino, Ucluelet and the Pacific Rim National Park,* • *Campbell River,* • *Port McNeill, Telegraph Cove, and Port Alice,* • *Port Hardy, and* • *Cape Scott.*

Sunshine Coast

Stretching 100 kilometers (62 miles) north from the city of Vancouver along the mainland this region offers surprisingly good weather and warm water because it is in the rain shadow of Vancouver Island's mountains. The weather is very similar to that just to the west on the eastern side of Vancouver Island.

The Sunshine Coast is isolated. In the south a long inlet separates the region from Vancouver. It is necessary to use a ferry from Horseshoe Bay just north of Vancouver to Langdale. Then, after 81 km (50 miles) of two-lane paved road, you must take another ferry ride between Earl's Cove and Saltery Bay to reach the upper Sunshine Coast. From there you can backtrack or continue on by ferry from Powell River to Vancouver Island. There's no problem taking RVs on any of these ferries, see our *Introduction* chapter for more information.

Two sections of this chapter cover the Sunshine coast: • *Sunshine Coast – Lower* and • *Sunshine Coast – Upper.*

Vancouver and the Lower Fraser Valley

British Columbia's largest city is cosmopolitan and fun. Lots of people live downtown so there's always a lot going on. It's a pretty good-sized city with heavy traffic. Fortunately there are a good selection of campgrounds spaced around the perimeter, some with decent public transportation options.

The lower Fraser Valley is a fairly flat plain extending to the east from Vancouver. There are three destinations in this region described in this book: • *Chilliwack and Cultus Lakes,* • *Harrison Hot Springs, and* • *Hope.*

Interior

Much of the interior of British Columbia is mountainous. In the south the mountains run north and south and there are temperate valleys, often filled with lakes, between them. In the north there are mountainous areas as well as wide fairly flat plateaus. From north to south the interior destinations in this book are: • *Chetwynd, Hudson's Hope, and Tumbler Ridge,* • *Dawson Creek,* • *Prince Rupert,* • *Terrace,* • *New Hazelton and Kitwanga,* • *Smithers,* • *Fort St James,* • *Prince George,* • *Williams Lake,* • *Bella Coola and Hwy 20,* • *Barkerville and Wells,* • *Quesnel,* • *South Cariboo Region,* • *Mt Robson, ,* • *Wells Gray Provincial Park and Clearwater,* • *Kamloops,* • *Shuswap,* • *Revelstoke,* • *Glacier National Park,* • *Whistler and the Sea to Sky Highway,* • *Thompson and Fraser Canyons,* • *Merritt and the Surrounding Plateau,* • *Manning Provincial Park,* • *Similkameen Valley,* •

ELK IN A JASPER NATIONAL PARK CAMPGROUND

Okanagan Valley, • *Boundary Country,* • *Kootenay Lakes District,* • *Valley of a Thousand Peaks, and* • *Fernie.*

Canadian Rockies

Along the border between British Columbia and Alberta the Rocky Mountains have peaks to 12,000 feet. While not perhaps as high as some of those in Colorado these are some of the most rugged and impressive peaks in the entire chain. A large part of the border area is set aside as national parks. Destinations in this area in this book are: • *Jasper National Park,* • *Banff National Park,* • *Yoho National Park and Golden,* • *Kootenay National Park.*

GOVERNMENT LANDS AND THEIR CAMPGROUNDS

Provincial Park Campgrounds

British Columbia has an excellent system of provincial campgrounds. Prices are generally lower than commercial campgrounds in the areas where they are found. Only four provincial campgrounds listed in this book have electrical hookups, they are Porteau Cove and Alice Lake both in the • *Whistler and the Sea to Sky Highway* section and Juniper Beach and Steelhead , both in the *Canada Hwy 1* section.

There is a reservation system that includes most campgrounds. Our campground descriptions tell whether the individual campground being described takes reservations. Generally, some sites in a campground can be reserved and some cannot. Also, most camp-

BRITISH COLUMBIA

SCENIC PROVINCIAL PARK CAMPGROUND ON THE FRASER RIVER

grounds have a period at the beginning and end of the season when they are not busy and reservations are not available or required. Reservations are made through Discover Camping, you can use the internet (www.discovercamping.ca) or call (800) 689-9025, from outside Canada and the USA call (519) 826-6850. The reservation service is in effect from April 1 to September 15, telephone operators are only available from 7 am to 7 pm weekdays, 9 am to 5 pm on weekends and holidays. Reservations can be made up to three months in advance and must be made at least two days prior to your arrival. There is a reservation fee of $6.00 Canadian plus tax per site per night for the first three nights at a site, reservations exceeding three days pay a reservation fee for only the first three days as long as you do not change sites. An additional $5.00 charge is assessed for using the telephone rather than the internet to make reservations. There is a 14 day stay limit at most parks. Discounts of ½ off are available for B.C. residents over 65 years old after Labour Day and before June 15.

There is often a host at the larger provincial campgrounds. Provincial campgrounds no longer provide firewood for free although it is almost always available for purchase unless a fire ban is in effect. Sites in provincial campgrounds usually are separated by areas of undeveloped forest, sites vary in length, often with each one being different. Many provincial campgrounds will take larger rigs. See the individual campground write-ups for information about this. Generally, if there is a sani-station in a provincial campground there is an extra fee for its use, dumping is not included in the camping fee.

You can always use a credit card to pay for sites that you reserve by phone or on the internet. Some campgrounds will accept credit cards at the campground for payment, many will not. If we indicate that a provincial campground accepts credit cards that means that they are accepted at the campground itself, but usually only if the campground entrance station is in use when you enter. Be prepared to pay with cash whenever you visit a provincial campground.

National Park Campgrounds

The national park campgrounds vary a great deal. Some have full hookups, some have none. Almost all are great for tent campers and a few have been optimized for large RVs. See the individual campground write-ups for more information.

Not all campgrounds in the parks accept reservations, see the individual campground write-ups for more information. To make a reservation call (877) 737-3783 in Canada or (450) 505-8302 from outside North America. You can also make reservations on the Internet at www.pccamping.ca. Reservations can be made up to midnight of the day before you will arrive. There is an $10.80 Canadian fee per reservation.

Many larger national park campgrounds have entrance kiosks, but not all. If they do they will usually accept credit cards (Visa and Master Card).

One downside of the national parks is that there can be a number of fees. There is almost always an entrance fee to the national park. Of course there is also a camping fee. There's a fee for campfires and also a fee to use the sani-station. If you make a reservation there is a fee for that too.

Recreation Sites and Trails BC (RSTBC) Campsites

The BC Ministry of Forests formerly operated hundreds of small campgrounds throughout the province. Now responsibility for those campsites has been transferred to the BC Ministry of Tourism, Culture and the Arts and their Recreation Sites and Trails BC division. For the most part these are sites with minimal facilities, usually just picnic tables and outhouses. These sites fall into two categories: Managed With Fees and Managed Without Fees. There are no reservations for these sites and there is a 14-day stay limit. Some of the RSTBC sites listed in this book are the Managed Without Fees type. Many are infrequently serviced by volunteers. That means that it is important that you carry out your trash and leave the sites in at least as good condition as you found them. This type site is free. You'll find Forest Service Recreation Sites listed in the • *Cape Scott*, • *Chilliwack and Cultus Lakes*, • *Port Renfrew Loop*, • *Whistler and the Sea To Sky Highway,* and • *Similkameen Valley* sections of this Chapter.

CAMPGROUND LOCATION INDEX MAPS

On the following pages you'll find three Campground Location Index Maps for British Columbia. These maps show the approximate location of every campground as described in this chapter. The shaded areas show which section covers each campground shown. It's an easy matter to turn to the proper section where you'll find a detailed map, a description of the area, and detailed descriptions of all of the campgrounds. Note that there are four types of symbols used for the campgrounds:

- ■ Federal
- □ State
- ● Commercial
- ○ Local Government

BRITISH COLUMBIA

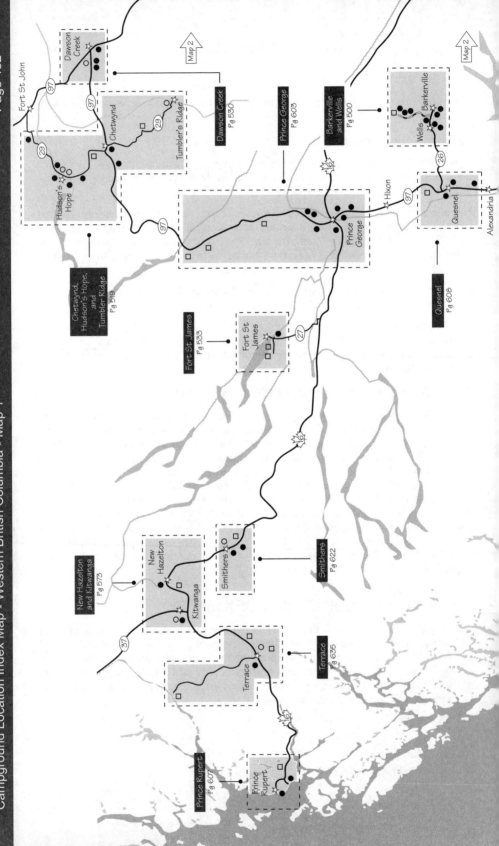

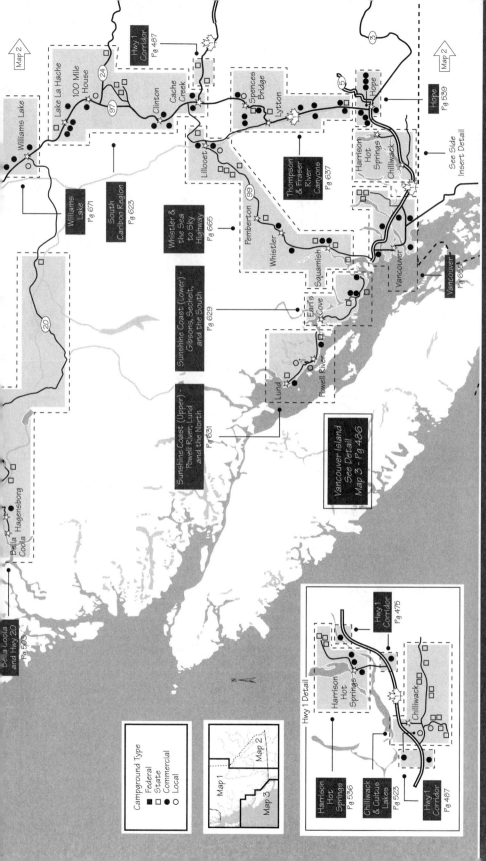

Campground Location Index Map * Western British Columbia * Map 1

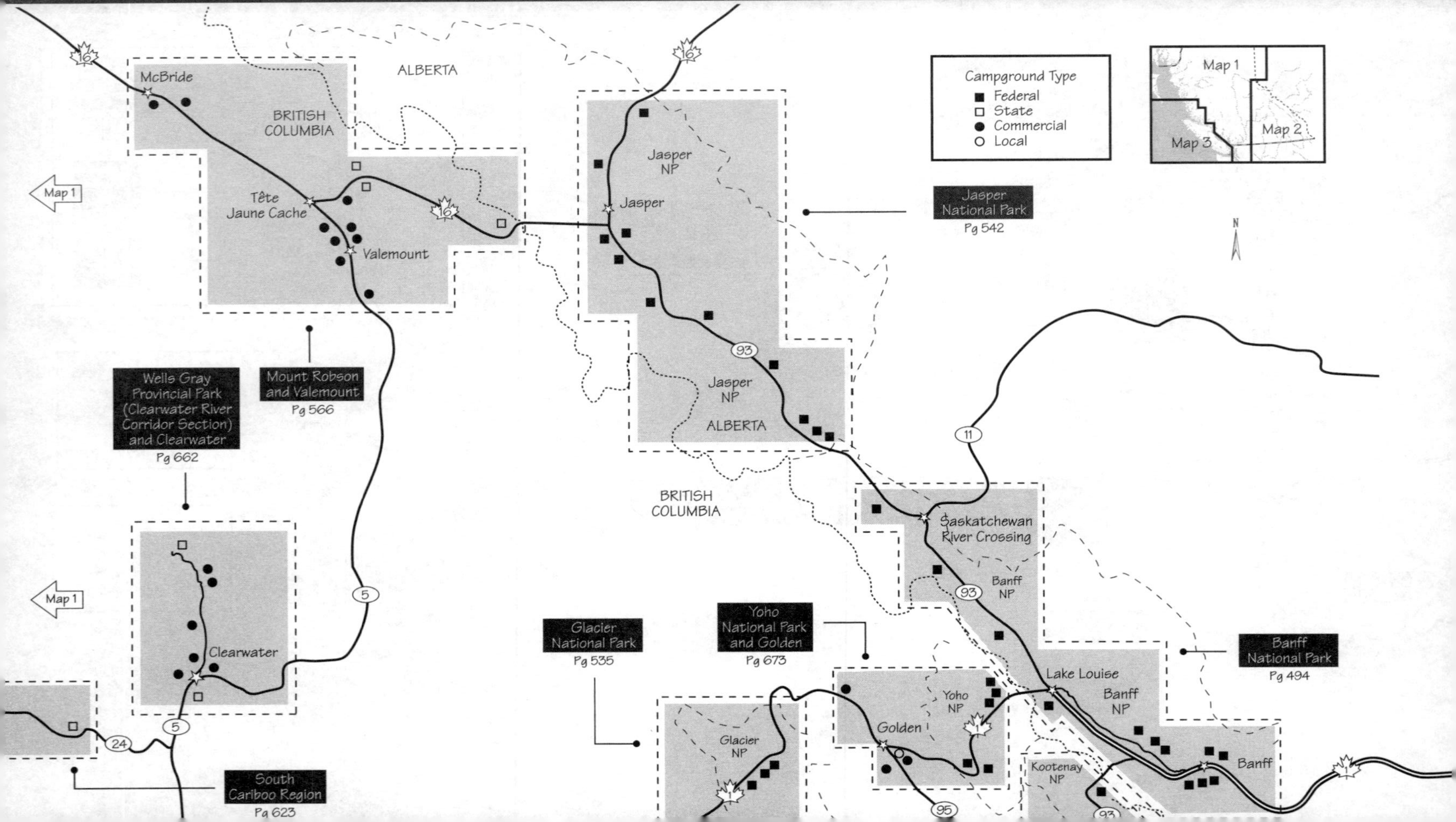

Campground Location Index Map * Eastern British Columbia * Map 2

Campground Type
■ Federal
□ State
● Commercial
○ Local

Jasper National Park
Pg 542

Banff National Park
Pg 494

Yoho National Park and Golden
Pg 673

Glacier National Park
Pg 535

Mount Robson and Valemount
Pg 566

Wells Gray Provincial Park (Clearwater River Corridor Section) and Clearwater
Pg 662

South Cariboo Region
Pg 625

Map 1
Map 2
Map 3

N

Jasper NP
Jasper
ALBERTA
BRITISH COLUMBIA

Saskatchewan River Crossing
Banff NP
Lake Louise
Banff
Kootenay NP
Yoho NP
Golden
Glacier NP

ALBERTA
BRITISH COLUMBIA
McBride
Tête Jaune Cache
Valemount
Clearwater

93
11
93
95
93
5
24
16

Map 1
Map 1

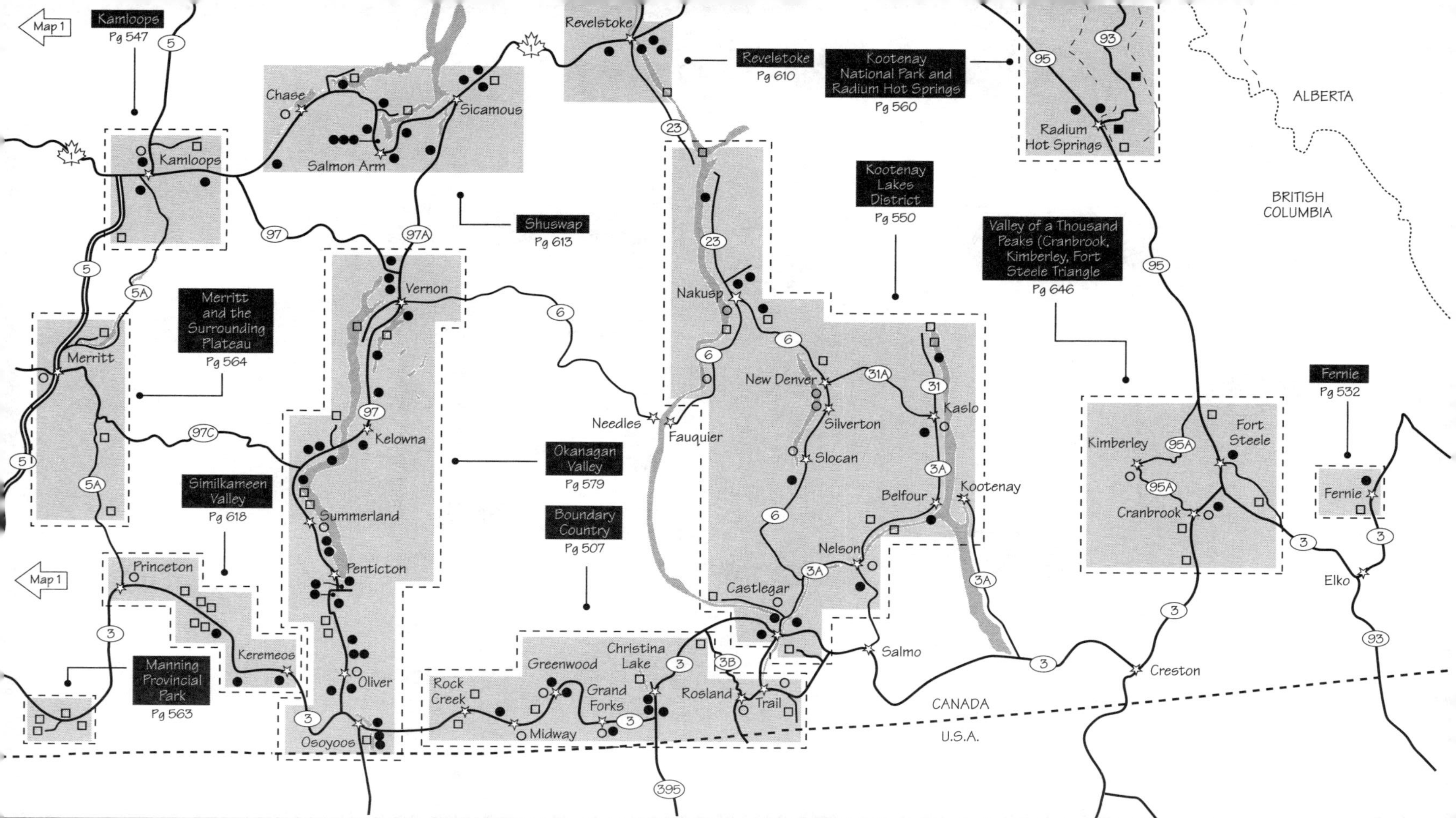

ALBERTA

BRITISH
COLUMBIA

Fernie
Pg 532

Fernie

Elko

Fort
Steele

Creston

Kimberley   Cranbrook

95A

95A

95A

Valley of a Thousand
Peaks (Cranbrook,
Kimberley, Fort
Steele Triangle)
Pg 646

Radium
Hot Springs

93

95

95

93

Kootenay National Park and
Radium Hot Springs
Pg 560

Kootenay
Lakes
District
Pg 550

Revelstoke
Pg 610

Kaslo

Kootenay

31

3A

Silverton

31A

Slocan

Belfour

New Denver

6

Nelson

Salmo

CANADA
U.S.A.

3A

Nakusp

23

6

Castlegar

Rossland

3B

Trail

Revelstoke

23

Fauquier

6

Needles

Christina
Lake

3

3.95

Grand
Forks

3

Greenwood

Sicamous

Okanagan
Valley
Pg 579

Boundary
Country
Pg 507

Midway

Shuswap
Pg 615

Salmon Arm

97A

Vernon

6

Rock
Creek

Chase

Kamloops
Pg 547

Kamloops

5

97

97

Kelowna

Summerland

Penticton

Oliver

Osoyoos

3

Merritt and the
Surrounding Plateau
Pg 564

Similkameen
Valley
Pg 618

Keremeos

97C

5A

Merritt

5A

Princeton

3

Manning
Provincial Park
Pg 563

5

5

Map 1

Map 1

Campground Location Index Map • Vancouver Island • Map 3

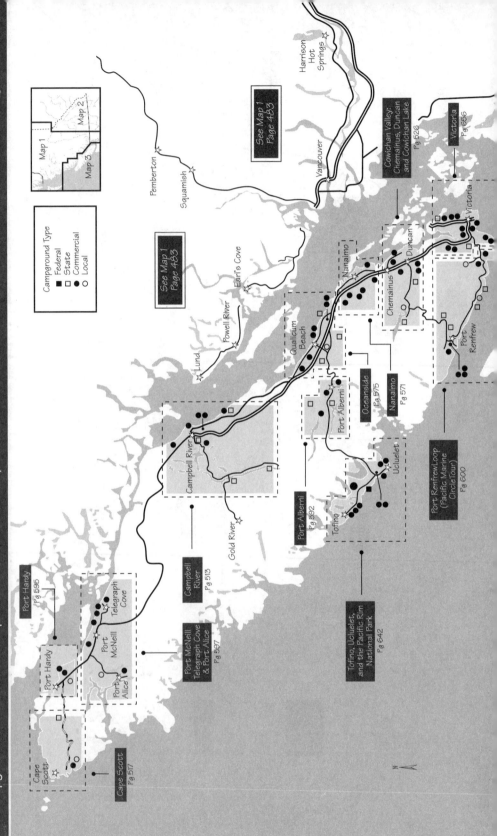

DESTINATIONS AND THEIR CAMPGROUNDS

TRANS-CANADA HIGHWAY (CANADIAN HWY 1)

Canadian Highway 1, the Trans-Canada Highway, is the main east-west highway across Canada. The mainland portion of the highway begins at zero in Horseshoe Bay just outside Vancouver. It runs eastward and is at 885 Km (550 miles) at the eastern border of Banff National Park in Alberta. That's as far as this guide goes. Large portions of the highway are two lanes wide and exits are not marked. For that reason the campgrounds listed below are only identified by exit number until they reach Hope and also in a short section near Kamloops, elsewhere they are listed by approximate distance from the zero mark at Horseshoe Bay.

This section of this guide follows Highway 1 as it ascends the Fraser River rather than following the Coquihalla Highway. The Coquihalla is a popular shortcut that runs from Hope to Kamloops and cuts 46 km (29 miles) off the east-west transcontinental route. For campgrounds along that section see the *Merritt and the Surrounding Plateau* section of this guide.

Note that many of the campgrounds along the Highway 1 corridor are described under other destination sections in this chapter. If so, we've given a page reference to make finding them easy.

Trans-Canada Highway (Canadian Hwy 1) Campgrounds

⮕ *Exit 14*

● CAPILANO RV PARK *(Listed under Vancouver, page 654)*

⮕ *Exit 37*

● BURNABY CARIBOO RV PARK *(Listed under Vancouver, page 654)*

⮕ *Exit 53*

● TYNEHEAD RV PARK *(Listed under Vancouver, page 655)*

⮕ *Exit 109*

● ROYALWOOD GOLF AND RV RESORT *(Open All Year)*
   Res and Info: (866) 895-7590, (604) 823-4111,
   www.royalwood-rv-park-resort.com
   Location: Hwy 1 Exit 109

   GPS Location: 49.12615 N, 122.08575 W, 100 Ft

82 Sites – This RV park is associated with the 18 hole golf course next door. Special rates are available for RV park guests. RV sites here are gravel off a gravel drive. Many are occupied by long-term guests. The available sites are mostly back-ins to 50 feet although there are just a few pull-thrus. Take Exit 109 from Hwy 1 and then travel southwest on the access road on the south side of the highway. It's .5 km (.3 miles) to the RV park entrance.

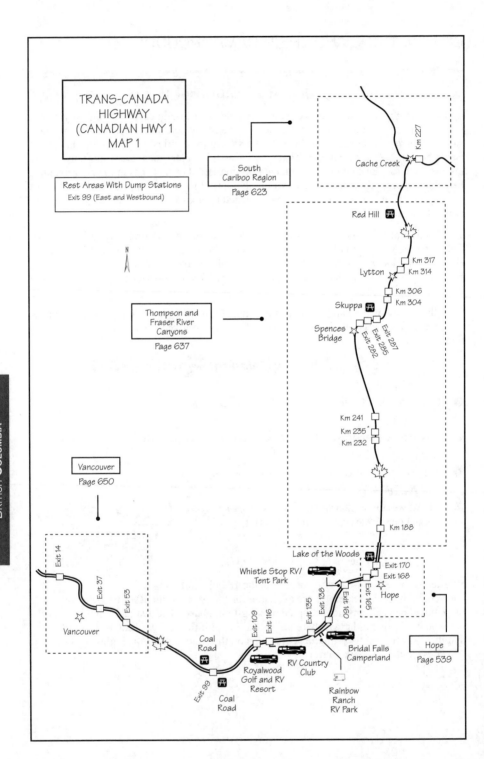

BRITISH COLUMBIA

TRANS-CANADA
HIGHWAY
(CANADIAN HWY 1
MAP 1

Rest Areas With Dump Stations
Exit 99 (East and Westbound)

South
Cariboo Region
Page 623

Cache Creek
Km 227

N

Red Hill

Km 317
Lytton   Km 314
Km 306
Skuppa   Km 304

Thompson and
Fraser River
Canyons
Page 637

Spences
Bridge   Exit 287
              Exit 285
              Exit 282

Km 241
Km 235
Km 232

Vancouver
Page 650

Km 188

Lake of the Woods

Whistle Stop RV/   Exit 170
Tent Park   Exit 168

Exit 14

Exit 37

Exit 53

Exit 138
Exit 135

Exit 165   Hope

Exit 160

Vancouver

Exit 109
Exit 116

Hope
Page 539

Coal
Road

Royalwood
Golf and RV
Resort

RV Country
Club

Bridal Falls
Camperland

Exit 99

Coal
Road

Rainbow
Ranch
RV Park

➔ *Exit 116*

● COTTONWOOD MEADOWS RV COUNTRY CLUB
   (Open All Year)
   Res and Info: (604) 824-7275,
                     camp@cottonwoodrvpark.com,
                     www.cottonwoodrvpark.com
   Location: Hwy 1 Exit 116

   GPS Location: 49.14364 N, 121.99944 W, 100 Ft

118 Sites – Cottonwood Meadows is a newer, nicely landscaped RV park located right next to the freeway and near a handy tourist information center. Sites here are pull-thrus and back-ins to 65 feet. Take Exit 116 from Hwy 1 and then follow the access road on the south side of the highway toward the east for .3 km (.4 mile) to the RV park entrance.

➔ *Exit 135*

● BRIDAL FALLS CAMPERLAND *(Open All Year)*
   Res and Info: (604) 794-7361, www.htr.ca
   Location: Hwy 1 Exit 135

   GPS Location: 49.18767 N, 121.74199 W, 200 Ft

300 Sites – This is a Holiday Trails membership campground that is also open to non-members. It's a very large place with good facilities. There's a water park next door for the kids and trails leading about a kilometer up the hill to Bridal Veil Trails Provincial Park. Sites here are paved or gravel back-ins or pull-thrus to 65 feet. Amenities include a swimming pool, spa, sauna, fitness center, restaurant, store, and liquor store. From Hwy 1 take Exit 135 and travel east on Bridal Falls Road, the access road on the south side of the highway. In 1.8 km (1.1 miles) you'll see the campground entrance on the right.

➔ *Exit 160*

● WHISTLE STOP RV/TENT PARK
   (Open March 30 to Nov 15)
   Res and Info: (604) 869-5132
   Location: Exit 160 of Hwy 1, 11 Km (7 Miles)
                     West of Hope

   GPS Location: 49.35125 N, 121.58528 W, 200 Ft

41 Sites – The Whistle Stop is a small campground with an convenient but unfortunate location between the highway and a busy railroad track. Parking here is in back-in sites to 55 feet on grass. There are full, partial, and no-hookup sites. Take Exit 160 from Hwy 1. Turn north and then follow the access road on the north side of the highway toward the west for .5 km (.3 mile) to the campground.

➔ *Exit 165*

● WILD ROSE RV PARK *(Listed under Hope, page 542)*

● HOPE VALLEY CAMPGROUND *(Listed under Hope, page 542)*

➔ *Exit 168*

● HOLIDAY MOTEL AND RV RESORT *(Listed under Hope, page 541)*

➔ *Exit 170*

● TELTE YET CAMPSITE *(Listed under Hope, page 540)*

BRITISH COLUMBIA

● **COQUIHALLA CAMPSITE** *(Listed under Hope, page 540)*

● **OTHELLO TUNNELS CAMPGROUND** *(Listed under Hope, page 541)*

  ➲ *Km 188 (Mile 117) from Horseshoe Bay*

☐ **EMORY CREEK PROVINCIAL PARK CAMPGROUND**
   (Listed under Thompson and Fraser River Canyons, page 641)

● **EMORY BAR RV PARK** *(Listed under Thompson and Fraser River Canyons, page 641)*

● **YALE CAMPGROUND** *(Listed under Thompson and Fraser River Canyons, page 641)*

  ➲ *Km 232 (Mile 144) from Horseshoe Bay*

● **ANDERSON CREEK CAMPGROUND**
   (Listed under Thompson and Fraser River Canyons, page 641)

  ➲ *Km 235 (Mile 146) from Horseshoe Bay*

● **UP TOWN RV PARK** *(Listed under Thompson and Fraser River Canyons, page 641)*

  ➲ *Km 241 (Mile 150) from Horseshoe Bay*

● **CANYON ALPINE RV PARK** *(Listed under Thompson and Fraser River Canyons, page 640)*

  ➲ *Km 282 (Mile 175) from Horseshoe Bay*

● **JADE SPRINGS CAMPGROUND**
   (Listed under Thompson and Fraser River Canyons, page 640)

  ➲ *Km 285 (Mile 177) from Horseshoe Bay*

● **KUMSHEEN RAFTING RESORT**
   (Listed under Thompson and Fraser River Canyons, page 640)

  ➲ *Km 287 (Mile 178) from Horseshoe Bay*

☐ **SKIHIST PROVINCIAL PARK** *(Listed under Thompson and Fraser River Canyons, page 640)*

  ➲ *Km 304 (Mile 189) from Horseshoe Bay*

● **SHAW SPRINGS CAMPGROUND**
   (Listed under Thompson and Fraser River Canyons, page 639)

  ➲ *Km 306 (Mile 190) from Horseshoe Bay*

☐ **GOLDPAN PROVINCIAL PARK**
   (Listed under Thompson and Fraser River Canyons, page 639)

  ➲ *Km 314 (Mile 195) from Horseshoe Bay*

○ **CAL WOOD RECREATION RESERVE**
   (Listed under Thompson and Fraser River Canyons, page 639)

  ➲ *Km 317 (Mile 197) from Horseshoe Bay*

● **ACACIA GROVE RV AND CABINS**
   (Listed under Thompson and Fraser River Canyons, page 639)

  ➲ *Km 365 (Mile 227) from Horseshoe Bay*

● **BROOKSIDE CAMPSITE** *(Listed under South Cariboo Region, page 625)*

  ➲ *Km 383 (Mile 238) from Horseshoe Bay*

☐ **JUNIPER BEACH PROVINCIAL PARK**
   (Open April 30 to Dec 31)
   Information: (250) 457-6794
   Location: 18 Km (11 Miles) E of Cache Creek

   GPS Location: 50.77996 N, 121.08077 W, 1,000 Ft

35 Sites – Juniper Beach is located along the Thompson River in a desert setting. Busy

BRITISH COLUMBIA

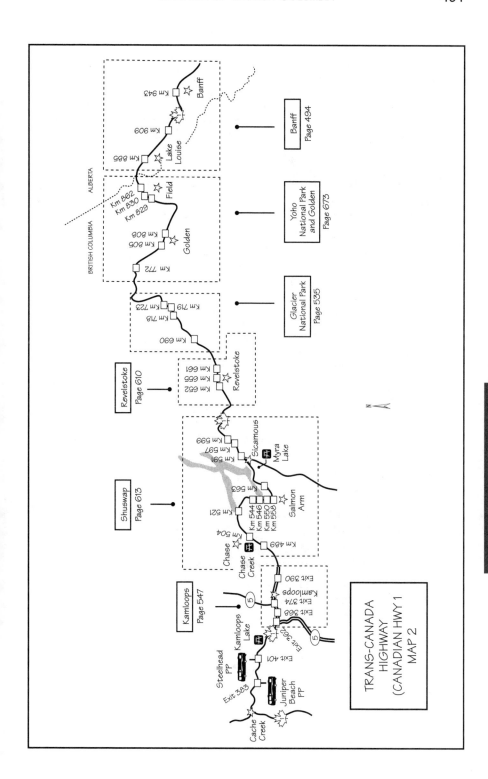

TRANS-CANADA
HIGHWAY
(CANADIAN HWY 1
MAP 2

railroad tracks run between the campground and the highway. There are 30 back-in sites to 40 feet with electric hookups as well as five sites for tents with pitching on grass. All sites have picnic tables and fire pits. There is a handicapped vault toilet and showers. At low water levels swimming is possible on a quiet swimming hole separated from the river. There is an overflow parking area for use if the campground is full, overflow campers pay a substantial fee. The park entrance road goes south to the river from a point that is 17.9 km (11.1 miles) east of Cache Creek and 52 km (32 miles) west of Kamloops.

➲ *Km 401 (Mile 249) from Horseshoe Bay*

☐ **STEELHEAD PROVINCIAL PARK**
   (Open May 1 to Oct 12)
   Information: (250) 377-8888
   Location: 35 Km (22 Miles) E of Cache Creek

GPS Location: 50.75612 N, 120.86461 W, 1,100 Ft

42 Sites – Steelhead is located at the foot of Kamloops Lake. It's a former commercial park so it isn't like most provincial parks. Like Juniper Beach, described above, it has electrical hookups, but only ten of them. The other 32 sites are no-hookup sites. Many are located with the hookup sites in a side-by-side configuration with others being informal pull-thru sites in a field. A small parking lot provides overflow camping for a fee. Some sites face the lake, some the river. There is a good beach on the lake and it is used for swimming and wind-surfing. The canoe float to Cache Creek from here is popular and fishing is good. The campground is on the north side of the highway some 35 km (22 miles) east of Cache Creek and the same distance west of Kamloops.

➲ *Exit 368*

● **KNUTSFORD RV PARK** *(Listed under Kamloops, page 548)*

➲ *Exit 374*

○ **KAMLOOPS EXHIBITION ASSOCIATION** *(Listed under Kamloops, page 548)*

● **SILVER SAGE RV PARK AND CAMPGROUND** *(Listed under Kamloops, page 549)*

➲ *Exit 390*

● **KAMLOOPS RV PARK** *(Listed under Kamloops, page 549)*

➲ *Km 489 (Mile 304) from Horseshoe Bay*

● **PONDEROSA PINES RV PARK** *(Listed under Shuswap, page 613)*

➲ *Km 504 (Mile 313) from Horseshoe Bay*

○ **CHASE LION'S RV PARK** *(Listed under Shuswap, page 613)*

➲ *Km 521 (Mile 324) from Horseshoe Bay*

● **SHUSWAP LAKE MOTEL AND RESORT CAMPGROUND** *(Listed under Shuswap, page 615)*

➲ *Km 544 (Mile 338) from Horseshoe Bay*

● **VIEWPOINT MOTEL AND RV PARK** *(Listed under Shuswap, page 615)*

➲ *Km 546 (Mile 339) from Horseshoe Bay*

● **PIERRE'S POINT FAMILY CAMPGROUND RESORT** *(Listed under Shuswap, page 616)*

➲ *Km 546 (Mile 339) from Horseshoe Bay*

● **SANDY POINT BEACH CAMPGROUND** *(Listed under Shuswap, page 616)*

➲ *Km 550 (Mile 342) from Horseshoe Bay*

● **SALMON RIVER MOTEL AND RV PARK** *(Listed under Shuswap, page 616)*

➲ *Km 558 (Mile 347) from Horseshoe Bay*

● **SALMON ARM CAMPING RESORT** *(Listed under Shuswap, page 616)*

➲ *Km 563 (Mile 350) from Horseshoe Bay*

● **HIDDEN VALLEY CAMPING AND RV PARK** *(Listed under Shuswap, page 617)*

➲ *Km 591 (Mile 367) from Horseshoe Bay*

● **HOMESTEAD RV AND CAMPING** *(Listed under Shuswap, page 617)*

➲ *Km 597 (Mile 371) from Horseshoe Bay*

● **SICAMOUS KOA KAMPGROUND** *(Listed under Shuswap, page 617)*

➲ *Km 599 (Mile 372) from Horseshoe Bay*

● **CEDARS CAMPGROUND** *(Listed under Shuswap, page 617)*

➲ *Km 599 (Mile 372) from Horseshoe Bay*

● **YARD CREEK CAMPGROUND** *(Listed under Shuswap, page 617)*

➲ *Km 652 (Mile 405) from Horseshoe Bay*

● **CANADA WEST CAMPGROUND** *(Listed under Revelstoke, page 611)*

➲ *Km 655 (Mile 407) from Horseshoe Bay*

● **LAMPLIGHTER CAMPGROUND** *(Listed under Revelstoke, page 612)*

➲ *Km 661 (Mile 411) from Horseshoe Bay*

● **REVELSTOKE KOA KAMPGROUND** *(Listed under Revelstoke, page 612)*

➲ *Km 690 (Mile 429) from Horseshoe Bay*

● **CANYON HOT SPRINGS** *(Listed under Glacier National Park, page 535)*

➲ *Km 718 (Mile 446) from Horseshoe Bay*

● **MT SIR DONALD CAMPSITE** *(Listed under Glacier National Park, page 536)*

➲ *Km 719 (Mile 447) from Horseshoe Bay*

● **LOOP BROOK CAMPSITE** *(Listed under Glacier National Park, page 536)*

➲ *Km 723 (Mile 449) from Horseshoe Bay*

● **ILLECILLEWAET CAMPSITE** *(Listed under Glacier National Park, page 536)*

➲ *Km 772 (Mile 480) from Horseshoe Bay*

● **CAMPERS HAVEN** *(Listed under Yoho National Park and Golden, page 674)*

➲ *Km 805 (Mile 500) from Horseshoe Bay*

○ **GOLDEN MUNICIPAL CAMPGROUND**
(Listed under Yoho National Park and Golden, page 674)

➲ *Km 808 (Mile 501) from Horseshoe Bay*

● **WHISPERING SPRUCE CAMPGROUND**
(Listed under Yoho National Park and Golden, page 676)

➲ *Km 829 (Mile 515) from Horseshoe Bay*

● **CHANCELLOR PEAK** *(Listed under Yoho National Park and Golden, page 677)*

➲ *Km 830 (Mile 516) from Horseshoe Bay*

● **HOODOO CREEK CAMPGROUND** *(Listed under Yoho National Park and Golden, page 677)*

➲ *Km 862 (Mile 536) from Horseshoe Bay*

■ **MONARCH CAMPGROUND – YOHO NATIONAL PARK**
(Listed under Yoho National Park and Golden, page 676)

BRITISH COLUMBIA

> ➭ *Km 862 (Mile 536) from Horseshoe Bay*

■ **KICKING HORSE CAMPGROUND** *(Listed under Yoho National Park and Golden, page 676)*

> ➭ *Km 885 (Mile 550) from Horseshoe Bay*

■ **LAKE LOUISE CAMPGROUNDS** *(Listed under Banff National Park, page 497)*

> ➭ *Km 909 (Mile 565) from Horseshoe Bay*

■ **CASTLE MOUNTAIN CAMPGROUND** *(Listed under Banff National Park, page 498)*

> ➭ *Km 943 (Mile 586) from Horseshoe Bay*

■ **TUNNEL MOUNTAIN VILLAGE 1** *(Listed under Banff National Park, page 498)*

> ➭ *Km 943 (Mile 586) from Horseshoe Bay*

■ **TUNNEL MOUNTAIN VILLAGE 2 AND TUNNEL MOUNTAIN TRAILER CAMPGROUND**
   (Listed under Banff National Park, page 499)

BANFF NATIONAL PARK

Banff was Canada's first National Park. The section of the park in the Bow Valley, roughly from Lake Louise to the townsite of Banff, is the most frequented part of the park and offers plenty to keep a visitor busy for a long time. It is also truly beautiful because it is ringed by some of the highest and most spectacularly rugged peaks in the world. A second and much smaller road, the **Bow Parkway**, offers a scenic and quiet alternative to the four-lane highway, and follows pretty much the same route except that it is on the east side of the Bow River instead of the west. You'll want to traverse the Bow Parkway at least once so you can stop occasionally and enjoy the valley. The distance between Banff and Lake Louise along the Bow Parkway and a short section of Hwy 1 near Banff is 56.6 km (35.1 miles).

Arriving on the Trans-Canada (Hwy 1) from the west you'll almost immediately see the exit for **Lake Louise**. This is the smaller of the two population centers of the park. Just off the highway to the west is what is known as the village of Lake Louise, it is really little more than a shopping center offering a tourist info centre, small stores, tourist services, and gasoline. Just past the village is a turn to the left for the giant Lake Louise Campground. If you go straight instead you will wind up the hillside for about 4 km (2.5 miles) to beautiful Lake Louise. There are big parking lots here but it is best not to try to take a very large rig or a trailer, the lots are big but still crowded. At the foot of the lake you'll see a huge hotel, the **Chateau Lake Louise**, it has been there in one form or another since 1890. You'll no doubt be part of a throng of visitors. You can walk through the hotel lobby and take some pictures from the lawn of the spectacular view featuring the emerald-colored lake and the glacier at the far end. Then you can explore part of the trail network along and above the lake, there are even a couple of teahouses where you can stop for refreshments.

At the lower end of the valley is the town of **Banff** with a population of about 7,500. This is the major population, business, and tourist center of the park. In addition to many park-type wonders in the area you'll find a wealth of shops and restaurants that rival any resort town. You'll also find a supermarket and other services required by RVers including some very big government-owned campgrounds. Banff is the largest town to be found inside any national park in either Canada or the U.S.

There are several interesting sights in the town area. It would be a good idea to make your first stop at the downtown **Park Information Centre** for local maps and information. The **Banff Springs Hotel** is one of the early Canadian Pacific Railways resort hotels and

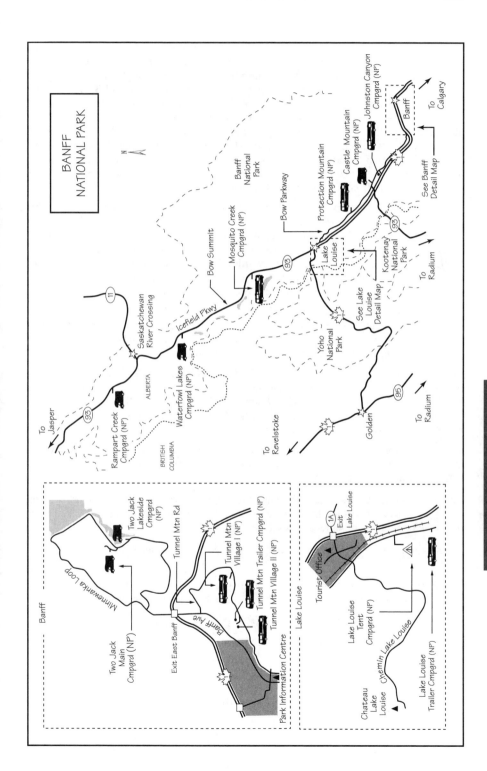

BANFF NATIONAL PARK

remains a fascinating place to visit. Just off the entrance road to the hotel is the road to the golf course, it leads past **Bow Falls** to a loop route through the golf course and can be a good place to see **elk**. They favor the course as a place to graze and relax. The original reason Banff was established was hot springs, you can visit the **Cave and Basin Centennial Center** built at the site of the original hot springs. You can't swim there any more but you will find lots to see. The **Sundance Canyon Trail** starts at the center and takes you along the Bow River to Sundance Canyon, about 7 kilometers (4.4 miles) round trip. If you do want to swim you can do so at **Upper Hot Springs**. Near Upper Hot Springs is the **Sulphur Mountain Gondola Lift** which takes you up to an observatory and restaurant high on Sulphur Mountain. There are two worthwhile museums in town of Banff, the **Whyte Museum of the Canadian Rockies** and the **Park Museum**.

There are several good drives in the Banff townsite area in addition to the one up to the Sulphur Mountain Gondola Lift. You can drive to an excellent viewpoint overlooking the town by following **Mt Norquay Drive**. It is on the far side of Highway 1 at the West Banff Exit and climbs about 300 meters in 5.8 kilometers (3.6 miles). From the East Banff Exit you can follow **Lake Minnewanka Road** to visit the ghost town of **Bankhead,** view **Lake Minnewanka** or take a commercial boat tour, then return on a loop drive past **Two Jack Lake** and **Johnson Lake.**

The **Icefields Parkway** enters Banff National Park from Jasper National Park to the north. See the *Jasper National Park* section of this chapter for information about the parkway north of the border between the two parks. The information below continues the description in that section and progresses from north to south.

The two parks meet at **Sunwapta Pass**. Thirty-two kilometers (29 miles) south of the pass the road crosses the North Saskatchewan River. To the west is the Howse Valley. The North Saskatchewan River and the Howse Valley were one of the early passes used by explorers and fur traders to cross the Rocky Mountains. Highway 11 heads east from here to Rocky Mountain House and Red Deer.

Thirty-five kilometers (22 miles) from the crossing the road crosses another pass. This is the Bow Summit and is even higher than Sunwapta Pass. At 2,067 meters (6,787 feet) this is the highest point on the parkway.

Bow Lake is one of the scenic highlights of the highway, you'll reach it in another 6 km (4 miles). Viewpoints along the highway let you look across the bright blue lake at the peaks beyond, don't forget to take some pictures.

The southern end of the parkway meets Hwy 1 some 35 kilometers (21 miles) south of Bow Lake.

The campground descriptions below are arranged from the north end of the park to the south near Banff townsite. Every one of these campgrounds is a national park campsite.

Banff National Park Campgrounds

■ **RAMPART CREEK CAMPGROUND – BANFF NATIONAL PARK**
    (Open June 25 to Sept 6 – Varies)
Information: (403) 762-1550
Location: 92 Km (57 Miles) N of Lake Louise

       GPS Location: 52.04194 N, 116.86750 W, 4,700 Ft

50 Sites – This is an older campground with rough and narrow interior roads. Some sites will take RVs to 35 feet, the others are smaller. This is the farthest-north Banff camp-

ground. It is 92 km (57 miles) north of Lake Louise and 37 km (23 miles) south of the Icefield Centre in Jasper National Park.

■ **WATERFOWL LAKES CAMPGROUND – BANFF NATIONAL PARK**
   (Open June 18 to Sept 6 – Varies)
Information: (403) 762-1550
Location: 60 Km (37 Miles) N of Lake Louise

GPS Location: 51.84250 N, 116.62083 W, 5,500 Ft

116 Sites – The campground is located on the south shore of Waterfowl Lake where the Mistaya River flows into the lake. Trails lead to Cirque and Chephren Lakes. This is another older campground with narrow access roads, some sites will take carefully-driven 35-foot RVs. The campground is 60 km (37 miles) north of Lake Louise and 69 km (43 miles) south of Icefield Centre.

■ **MOSQUITO CREEK CAMPGROUND – BANFF NATIONAL PARK**
   (Open All Year)
Information: (403) 762-1550
Location: 27 Km (17 Miles) N of Lake Louise

GPS Location: 51.63028 N, 116.33028 W, 6,000 Ft

32 Sites – Sites here are in trees on either side of a large open lot, and also in the lot. This open area can be cleared of snow, that's why this campground can stay open all year long. The sites themselves will take RVs to 30 feet while the open area will take any size. The campground is 27 Km (17 miles) north of Lake Louise and 102 km (63 miles) south of Icefield Centre.

■ **LAKE LOUISE CAMPGROUNDS – BANFF**
   NATIONAL PARK *(Open All Year)*

Reservations: www.pccamping.ca, (877) 737-3783
Information: (403) 762-1550
Location: Lake Louise

GPS Location: 51.41833 N, 116.17361 W, 5,000 Ft

395 Sites – The Lake Louise Campground is really two campgrounds sharing a common entrance station. One is an RV campground (called the trailer campground) with long pull-thru sites with electric and water hookups as well as a dump station. The other is for tenters (called the tent campground) and those in soft-sided RVs, the sites have vehicle parking at the site, not remote parking. There is also a nearby overflow campground with no hookups. The tent campground is completely surrounded by an electric fence to keep out bears. Tents and soft sided rigs (like tent trailers) are not allowed in the RV campground or overflow campground because they have no such fence. Due to bear activity tents and soft-sided trailers are not allowed to camp at Lake Louise during early spring (April/May) or late fall (Oct/Nov) so the tent campground is only open from June through September. Campfires are only permitted in the tent campground. Trails lead from the camping areas to the Lake Louise business area and to the lake. It's about .9 km (.5 mile) to the business area, 5 km (3 miles) to the lake.

■ **PROTECTION MOUNTAIN CAMPGROUND – BANFF**
   NATIONAL PARK *(Open June 25 to Sept 6 – Varies)*

Information: (403) 762-1550
Location: 16 Km (10 Miles) S of Lake Louise

GPS Location: 51.32722 N, 116.03750 W, 4,900 Ft

89 Sites – Protection Mountain Campground has two camping areas, one marked for RVs and one for tents. The RV area has some large sites suitable for RVs to 40 feet but caution is necessary since access roads are narrow and rough. Parking sites in the tent campground are very small. The campground is located off the Bow Parkway 16 km (10 miles) south of Lake Louise and 40 km (25 miles) north of the town of Banff.

■ CASTLE MOUNTAIN CAMPGROUND – BANFF NATIONAL PARK
   (Open June 4 to Sept 7 – Varies)
   Information: (403) 762-1550
   Location: 27 Km (17 Miles) S of Lake Louise

   GPS Location 51.26833 N, 115.91194 W, 4,700 Ft

43 Sites – This is a more commodious campground than Protection Mountain with wider driveways. Still it's most suitable for RVs only up to 35 feet, just a site or two will take a 40-footer. A restaurant and small store are nearby. The campground is located off the Bow Parkway 27 km (17 miles) south of Lake Louise and 37 km (23 miles) north of the town of Banff.

■ JOHNSTON CANYON CAMPGROUND – BANFF
   NATIONAL PARK *(Open June 4 to Sept 13 – Varies)*
   Information: (403) 762-1550
   Location: 23 Km (14 Miles) N of Banff

   GPS Location: 51.24222 N, 115.83750 W, 4,700 Ft

132 Sites – This campground is large enough to warrant a manned entrance station. Sites here are off three loops, a limited number of sites large enough for 40-foot RVs are available. You can walk up Johnston Canyon to take a look at two waterfalls. The campground is located off the Bow Parkway 34 km (21 miles) south of Lake Louise and 23 km (14 miles) north of Banff.

■ TUNNEL MOUNTAIN VILLAGE I – BANFF
   NATIONAL PARK *(Open May 4 to Oct 4 – Varies)*
   Reservations: www.pccamping.ca, (877) 737-3783
   Information: (403) 762-1550
   Location: 3 Km (2 Miles) E of Banff

   GPS Location: 51.19111 N, 115.52000 W, 4,700 Ft

618 Sites – Tunnel Mountain Village I is a huge place. It's the main Banff-area no-hook-up park and has good facilities. If you don't need hookups this is the place to stay, some sites will take RVs to 40 feet. The campground is located on the Tunnel Mountain Loop slightly farther from town than the Tunnel Mountain II and Tunnel Mountain Trailer campgrounds. Easiest access is from the eastern-most Banff off-ramp of Hwy 1. From the exit drive south on Banff Avenue for .8 km (.5 mile) and turn left on Tunnel Mountain Road. Follow the road as it winds up the hill, you'll see the campground entrance on your right in 3 km (2 miles). This access route lets you avoid downtown Banff which is congested. There is bus service into town from the campground. The distance to town is about 3 km (2 miles).

■ **TUNNEL MOUNTAIN VILLAGE II AND TUNNEL**
   MOUNTAIN TRAILER CAMPGROUND – BANFF
   NATIONAL PARK *(Open All Year)*

Reservations: www.pccamping,ca, (877) 737-3783
Information: (403) 762-1550
Location: 2 Km (1 Mile) E of Banff

GPS Location: 51.18833 N, 115.54000 W, 4,800 Ft

510 Sites – These two campgrounds share a common entrance with a manned entrance booth. After passing the booth you turn left for Tunnel Village II and right for Tunnel Mountain Trailer Campground. Both of these campgrounds are hookup campgrounds that have sites exceeding 60 feet but they are different. Tunnel Mountain II is the all-year campground here. There are wide paved access roads with sites set along the side, rigs parallel park. The campground is arranged this way to facilitate removal of snow in the winter. Sites have electrical hookups but no water or sewer, instead there is a sani-station. The Tunnel Mountain Trailer Campground, on the other hand, has full hookups. The 321 sites here are long pull-thrus arranged off gravel drives. This campground is only open from about May 6 - September 19 (Varies). Easiest access to these campgrounds is from the eastern-most Banff off ramp of Hwy 1. From the exit drive south on Banff Avenue for .8 km (.5 mile) and turn left on Tunnel Mountain Road. Follow the road as it winds up the hill, you'll see the campground entrance on your right in 5 km (3 miles). This access route lets you avoid downtown Banff which is congested. There is bus service into town from the campground. The distance to town is about 2 km (1 mile). Note that the Banff area also has an overflow area (in addition to the Two Jack campgrounds) with no hookups that is available when the other campgrounds are full.

■ **TWO JACK MAIN CAMPGROUND – BANFF NATIONAL PARK**
   (Open May 21 to Sept 7 – Varies)
Information: (403) 762-1550
Location: 10 Km (6 Miles) N of Banff

GPS Location: 51.22778 N, 115.50556 W, 4,800 Ft

380 Sites – This is a much less convenient place to stay than Tunnel Mountain, it tends to serve as the overflow camping area for Tunnel Mountain. The staff here recommends RVs no larger than 30 feet because sites are located off very tight loop roads. There are only two sites that will take RVs to 40 feet. To reach the campground drive north from the easternmost Banff entrance off ramp from Hwy 1. Turn right in .8 km (.5 miles) at the sign for Two Jack Campground and drive for 5.5 km (3.4 miles) to the entrance on your left. You'll pass the entrance to Two Jack Lakeside Campground before you reach the entrance to this campground. There is no bus service into Banff.

■ **TWO JACK LAKESIDE – BANFF NATIONAL PARK**
   (Open May 21 to Sept 13 – Varies)
Information: (403) 762-1550
Location: 8 Km (5 Miles) N of Banff

GPS Location: 51.21778 N, 115.50028 W, 4,600 Ft

74 Sites – Although they share a name this is a separate campground from Two Jack Main. It is usually considered to be more desirable because it has showers and will take slightly larger rigs. It's also quite a bit smaller and does not have a dump station, you have to go over to Two Jack Main and use theirs. Some sites are along the lake. To reach the

BRITISH COLUMBIA

campground drive north from the easternmost Banff entrance off ramp from Hwy 1. Turn right in .8 km (.5 miles) at the sign for Two Jack Campground and drive for 4.2 km (2.6 miles) to the entrance on your right. There is no bus service into Banff.

BARKERVILLE AND WELLS

From a junction 3 km (2 miles) north of Quesnel Hwy 26 leads east to Wells and Barkerville. It's a paved highway suitable for RVs. Wells is 76 km (47 miles) from the junction and Barkerville another 6 km (4 miles) beyond.

Wells (population 300) is an active town with a year-round population. It was formerly the company town for the Cariboo Gold Quartz Mine but today makes its living off the tourists attracted by nearby Barkerville, winter sports, gambling, and the Bowron Lake Provincial Park to the east. Wells offers stores, a gas station, galleries, and a museum. In winter the Troll Resort offers downhill skiing and both cross-country skiing and snowmobiling are popular. The first two campgrounds listed below are located in Wells.

Barkerville Historic Town started life as a gold rush town that was founded after Billy Barker made one of the most important strikes of the Cariboo gold rush here in 1862. The town was restored by the provincial government in 1958 and since that time Barkerville has been a popular tourist destination. The town itself is open year round, but most activities are available only during the summer season from mid-May to the beginning of September. During the season you'll be entertained by tours being led by costumed guides, gold-panning, shopping, and presentations at the Theatre Royal.

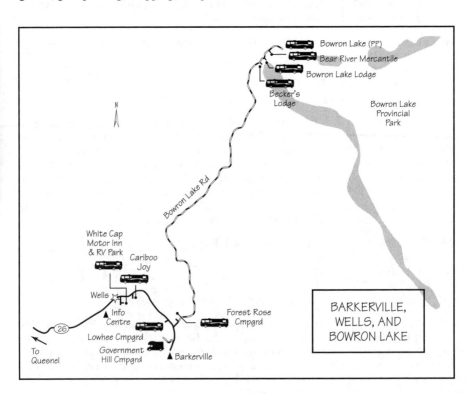

BARKERVILLE, WELLS, AND BOWRON LAKE

Just east of Wells via a 32 km (20 mile) gravel road is Bowron Provincial Park and Bowron Lake. We list 4 campground below that are located in this area. A popular attraction here is the canoe circuit. The circuit takes from six to 10 days, and covers 10 lakes, about 116 km (72 miles). There are 11 km (7 miles) of portages. Reservations are required to do the canoe circuit. Contact BC Provincial Parks for more information and to make reservations.

Barkerville and Wells Campgrounds

● **WHITE CAP MOTOR INN & RV PARK**
    (Open All Year)
    Res and Info: (250) 994-3489, (800) 377-2028,
               whitecap@goldcity.net,
               www.whitecapinn.com
    Location: Wells

    GPS Location: 53.10056 N, 121.56694 W, 4,000 Ft

22 Sites – The White Cap is a decent campground affiliated with the motel across the street. It's located in the town of Wells. Sites vary from tent and no-hookups to full-hookups that will take 40-footers. Restrooms are in the motel and also in a dedicated washroom, there are hot showers available for an extra charge. Computers with internet access are available in the lobby. As you enter Wells from the west continue straight ahead (don't turn left into the town), you'll soon see the White Cap sign pointing up the hill to the right.

● **CARIBOO JOY** *(Open June 1 to Sept 30 – Varies)*
    Res and Info: (250) 994-3463, www.cariboojoy.com
    Location: Wells

    GPS Location: 53.10222 N, 121.56389 W, 3,900 Ft

24 Sites – This small campground is located just outside Wells. It's another 4.5 km (2.8 miles) to Barkerville. Sites vary: a few are pull-thrus to 45 feet with full hookups but there are also partial hookup back-ins and tent sites. Watch for the campground on the right as you leave Wells heading east.

● **BARKERVILLE LOWHEE CAMPGROUND**
    (Open May 20 to Sept 30 – Varies)
    Reservations: (866) 994-3297,
               info@barkervillecampgrounds.ca
    Information: (604) 398-4414
    Location: Barkerville

    GPS Location: 53.08778 N, 121.51722 W, 4,000 Ft

87 Sites – Lowhee is the main former provincial park campground serving Barkerville. Sites here are back-ins to 45 feet. This campground has flush toilets, showers, and a dump station near the entrance. Follow Hwy 26 east from an intersection just north of Quesnel. In 73 km (45 miles) you'll enter Wells. Continue straight and in another 6 km (3.5 miles) you'll reach the campground entrance which will be on your right. The Barkerville historic town is another 2 km (1 mile) beyond the campground entrance.

● **BARKERVILLE GOVERNMENT HILL CAMPGROUND** *(Open June 15 to Sept 15)*
Information: (604) 398-4414
Location: Barkerville

GPS Location: *53.07556 N, 121.51222 W, 4,300 Ft*

23 Sites – Government Hill is the closest of three former provincial park campgrounds to historic Barkerville. The campground sits just above the parking lot and is for tenting and small rigs, some sites are suitable for RVs to 25 feet. Follow Hwy 26 east from an intersection just north of Quesnel. In 73 km (45 miles) you'll enter Wells. Continue straight and in another 4.9 km (3 miles) turn right at the sign onto a gravel road. The campground will appear in another 2.3 km (1.4 miles).

● **BARKERVILLE FOREST ROSE CAMPGROUND**
      (Open July 1 to Sept 2)
Reservations: (866) 994-3297, info@barkervillecampgrounds.ca
Information: (604) 398-4414
Location: Barkerville

GPS Location: *53.08639 N, 121.50694 W, 4,100 Ft*

56 Sites – The third of the former provincial park campgrounds serving Barkerville, it's the only one with pull-thru sites. Some will take 45-foot RVs. This campground is just a little farther from the historic town than Lowlee Campground, but still convenient if you have a tow car or don't mind a little hike. Follow Hwy 26 east from an intersection just north of Quesnel. In 73 km (45 miles) you'll enter Wells. Continue straight and in another 6.5 km (4 miles) turn left on the Bowron Lake Road. The campground is a short distance ahead on your left.

● **BECKER'S LODGE** *(Open May 1 to Sept 30)*
Res and Info: (250) 992-8864, www.beckerslodge.com
Location: Bowron Lake

GPS Location: *53.25318 N, 121.41541 W, 3,100 Ft*

30 Sites – Becker's has hookup sites for RVs as well as tent pads and support for those planning to canoe the Bowron Lakes. RV sites here are pull-thrus and back-ins with great views, electricity and water hookups are available but not sewer hookups or a sani-station. The nearest sani-station is near Wells. Other amenities and services include vehicle storage for canoeists, canoe rental, restaurant, and a small store. From Wells drive toward Barkerville for about 5 km (3 miles). Turn left at the sign for Bowron Lakes and follow the gravel road for 24.7 km (15.3 miles). There you will see the Becker's Lodge on the right. It is the first of the four camping areas at Bowron Lake.

● **BOWRON LAKE LODGE** *(Open June 15 to Sept 15)*
Information: www.bcadventure.com/bowron
Location: Bowron Lake

GPS Location: *53.25552 N, 121.41159 W, 3,000 Ft*

50 Sites – This is a simple campground with no hookups. Parking or tenting sites are along the lake and river in a large grassy field. Sites are separated by white rails. There are fire pits and picnic tables. Showers are included in the rate. To reach the campground follow the instructions above to Becker's Lodge. Continue for .5 km (.3 mile). The campground entrance is on the right.

● **BEAR RIVER MERCANTILE** *(Open May 1 to Sept 30)*
  Information: www.bowronlake.com
  Location: Bowron Lake

GPS Location: 53.25972 N, 121.40824 W, 3,000 Ft

15 Sites – The Bowron Lake Lodge has a small camping area near the lodge. There are picnic tables and fire pits. To reach the campground follow the instructions above to Becker's Lodge. Continue for 1 km (.6 mile). The campground entrance is on the right.

☐ **BOWRON LAKE PROVINCIAL PARK** *(Open May 15 to Sept 30)*
  Information: (778) 373-6107, www.bowronlakeinfo.com
  Location: Bowron Lake

GPS Location: 53.26031 N, 121.39233 W, 3,000 Ft

25 Sites – This campground is set in a grove of spruce near the lake and the Bowron Lakes ranger station. Sites are back-ins, some to 45 feet, with picnic tables and fire pits. To reach the campground follow the instructions above to Becker's Lodge. Continue for 2.1 km (1.3 mile). The campground is at the end of the road.

BELLA COOLA AND HWY 20

The trip out to Bella Coola shouldn't be lightly undertaken. From Williams Lake to Bella Coola is 448 km (278 miles). In addition to the distance RVers must consider the highway's rapid descent to the coast. It's no problem for small vehicles but a challenge for most RVs. Then, once you reach Bella Cool, a there's only one way out, you must retrace your steps.

The flip side of the coin is that this is a great trip. The drive out is very scenic with decent paved roads (other than The Hill) and little traffic. You'll see miles of both farmed and natural plateau country, cross Heckman Pass in Tweedsmuir Provincial Park South, and visit the Bella Coola Valley with its sea level wildlife viewing, fishing, and end-of-the-road ambiance.

"The Hill" or "The Precipice" is the descent from Heckman Pass at 4,879 ft to the Bella Coola Valley at 1,000 ft in a distance of 19 km (12 miles). This section of road is not paved. The most challenging section is the last 9 km (6 miles) which ends near Atnarko River Campground at the upper end of the valley. This section is one long grade of up to 18% with the cliff on one side and long drop-offs on the other. It's fairly narrow, has no guard rails, and there are two sharp switchbacks as well as other hairpin turns.

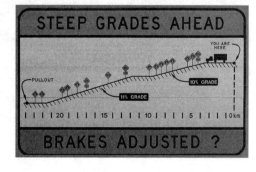

For small vehicles this grade is no real problem although drivers unaccustomed to mountain driving may find it unnerving. For large vehicles like RVs it's an obstacle to be overcome. Heading up and out presents few problems, just gear down and grind up the hill while watching ahead for downhillers who may be travelling too fast and out of control. Coming down, however, requires caution. It's important not to let your brakes get too hot. You can do this by gearing way down, using very slow speeds, and stopping when necessary to let the brakes cool. If you're overloaded or don't have good brakes don't consider descending the hill. If you are pulling a towed motorized vehicle, consider unhooking and driving the rigs separately.

The Bella Coola Valley stretches from the bottom of the hill westward to the ocean at the village of Bella Coola itself, a distance of 73 km (45 miles). Just a bit of the upper end is in Tweedsmuir Provincial Park, including two campgrounds. If you follow Hwy 20 down the valley, after 48 km (30 miles) you'll reach the farming town of Hagensborg. Another 23 km (14 miles) will bring you to the village of Bella Coola. Just beyond is North Bentinck Arm with docks, a bit of waterfront activity, and a waterfront park. All the way down the valley the highway is paralleled by famous fishing rivers, the Atnarko and the Bella Coola.

While the village of Bella Coola is at the end of the road, it's the town of Hagensborg that is your destination – that's where the RV parks are located. Both of the valley towns have grocery stores and supermarkets. If you're interested in the crafts produced by folks in the valley just ask around. Many artisans welcome visitors in their homes and even have small galleries. You'll also meet them at the farmer's market from June 1 to Sept 30 on Hwy 20 about 6 km east of Bella Coola.

Events in the valley include the **Bella Coola Rodeo** on the Canada Day (July 1) weekend, the **Discovery Coast Music Festival** in Mid July, and the **Bella Coola Valley Fall Fair** in early September.

A GRIZZLY BEAR AT A REST AREA NEAR BELLA COOLA

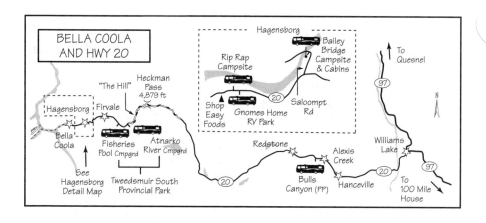

Fishing is one of the Bella Coola Valley's big draws. The Bella Coola and Atnarko Rivers and small creeks offer rainbows, cutthroat, and Dollies. Salmon runs include chinooks from mid-May to mid July, chums in late July, pinks in July and August, and cohos in September and October. **Bear viewing** can also be good since those fish attract large numbers of black and grizzly bears.

Bella Coola and Hwy 20 Campgrounds

☐ **BULL CANYON PROVINCIAL PARK** *(Open June 15 to Sept 15)*
Information: (250) 397-2523
Location: 121 Km (75 Miles) West of Williams Lake

GPS Location: 52.08847 N, 123.39399 W, 2,500 Ft

20 Sites – Bull Canyon is a pretty little campground on the bank of the Chilcotin River. It has a paved access road and gravel sites, four with timber-framed tent pads. There are 20 sites, two of them are pull-thrus to 55 feet. The remainder of the sites are back-ins, some to 60 feet. There is a water pump, tables, fire pits, and vault toilets. A pleasant trail follows the bank above the river, it makes a nice walk. The campground is on Hwy 20 74 miles (119 km) west of Williams Lake.

☐ **TWEEDSMUIR SOUTH PROVINCIAL PARK –**
   ATNARKO RIVER CAMPGROUND *(Open June 15 to Aug 15 – Varies)*
Information: (250) 397-2523
Location: 55 Km (34 Miles) East of Bella Coola

GPS Location: 52.40555 N, 125.91144 W, 1,000 Ft

30 Sites – Located right at the bottom of the famous grade into Bella Coola this is a simple campground along the Atnarko River. It has back-in sites for vehicles, some to 45 feet. There are no prepared tent pads but there are plenty of places to pitch a tent on forest duff or on the gravel vehicle pads. There is also a grassy area with picnic tables that can be used by five or six tents pitched close to each other. Bear-proof food lockers are provided. Water is from a hand pump. The campground is near the foot of "The Hill" on the south side of the highway, 72 km (45 miles) east of Bella Coola.

BRITISH COLUMBIA

☐ **TWEEDSMUIR SOUTH PROVINCIAL PARK –**
    FISHERIES POOL CAMPGROUND *(Open June 15 to Sept 30 – Varies)*

Information: (250) 397-2523
Location: 34 Miles (55 Km) East of Bella Coola

GPS Location: 52.37903 N, 126.08861 W, 600 Ft

11 Sites – This second Tweedsmuir South Provincial Park campground in the Bella Coola valley is also located on the Atnarko River, just above its confluence with the Bella Coola. Here there are nine back-ins and two tent sites. The vehicle sites are plenty long, to at least 40 feet, but narrow. They are adjacent back-in parking spaces in an open lot and are only one vehicle width wide. There is a kitchen shelter with a barrel stove, bear-proof storage lockers, and water is from a hand-operated pump. Camping in this campground is sometimes restricted to hard-walled camping units (no tents), due to large numbers of bears in the area. The campground is located on Highway 20, 16 km (10 miles) west of the Atnarko River Campground at the bottom of "The Hill" and 56 km (35 miles) east of Bella Coola.

● **BAILEY BRIDGE CAMPSITE AND CABINS**
    (Open May 15 to Oct 15 – Varies)

Res and Info: (250) 982-2342, www.baileybridge.ca
Location: 8 Km (5 Miles) East of Hagensbord

GPS Location: 52.40660 N, 126.49913 W, 200 Ft

27 Sites – This campground has a nice location on the banks of the Bella Coola River just outside Hagensborg. It's away from the main highway and has some large sites to 50 feet right along the river. Electricity is available at some sites. There are showers and vault toilets. Fishermen will appreciate the boat ramp and tackle shop. Cabins are also available. From the Atnarko River Campground drive west for 54 km (33.5 miles) and turn north on Saloompt Road. Saloompt leaves Hwy 20 at the eastern edge of Hagansborg. Drive for .8 km (.5 mile), the campground is on the left.

● **GNOMES HOME RV PARK**
    (Open April 15 to Oct 15 – Varies)

Res and Info: (250) 982-2504, gnome@belco.bc.ca,
                      www.gnomeshome.ca
Location: Hagensborg

GPS Location: 52.39108 N, 126.55347 W, 100 Ft

45 Sites – The Gnomes Home is the oldest of the Bella Coola area campground listed here. The sites are laid out to take advantage of the terrain and trees so they are not at all uniform. There are back-in and pull-thrus to 40 feet. Full hookup sites are available, as are partial and no hookup sites. Tenters will like the cooking shelter. The campground is located in Hagensborg. It's right on Highway 20, 58 km (36 miles) west of the Atnarko River Campground at the bottom of "The Hill" and 16 km (10 miles) east of Bella Coola.

● **RIP RAP CAMPSITE** *(Open May 1 to Oct 15 – Varies)*
    Res and Info: (250) 982-2752
    Location: Hagensborg

GPS Location: 52.39119 N, 126.55623 W, 100 Ft

26 Sites – This campground is virtually across the highway from the Gnomes Home described above, but just slightly closer to Bella Coola. It's a very well maintained and executed campground, you'll appreciate the details. The

name comes from the fact that the river bank here is lined with rip rap, huge chunks of rock placed to keep the river from eating away the bank. There are pull-thru and back-in sites to 40 feet with parking on grass for RVs and also some very nice tent and small rigs sites set in trees. A covered lounge area is great for tent campers on rainy days. It's possible to walk a river trial to bank-fishing locations and there's a nice platform perched on the rip rap for river watchers. See the Gnomes Home write-up above for directions to the campground.

BOUNDARY COUNTRY

Boundary Country is a scenic region just north of the border running east from the Okanagan Valley just north of the U.S. border. Hwy 3, the Crowsnest Highway, ties the region together and most of the campgrounds in this section are located near that highway. You'll find campgrounds in most towns and villages including Rock Creek, Midway, Greenwood, Grand Forks, Christina Lake, Trail, and Rossland. Other interesting nearby regions that are described in this chapter are • *Similkameen Valley*, • *Okanagan Valley*, • *Kootenay Lakes*, and • *Valley Of A Thousand Peaks*.

In the west this is a sparsely populated region with few people and small towns. The Crowsnest Highway follows the Kettle River until it reaches Midway, there the river flows south into the U.S. The river appears again at Grand Forks and joins the road again until just short of Christina Lake where it again departs south into the US. Continuing west you'll find three interesting destinations: Christina Lake, Trail, and Rossland.

Christina Lake is known as the warmest tree-lined lake in Canada. It looks deep and cold but in fact is fairly shallow, that's why it gets so warm. The village of Christina Lake grows from a winter population of about 1,000 to almost 6,000 in the summer. **Christina Lake Provincial Park** in town provides beach access but no camping. There are many summer family-oriented campgrounds in Christina Lake, we've picked four in the area that we think will appeal to travelers.

Trail (population 8,000) is home to the Teck Cominco smelter, it dominates the downtown area. The town is also home to many Italian immigrants and is well known for both its **Italian restaurants** and its **Fiesta Italiao** in September. The other major holiday in Trail is **Silver City Days** in May.

Up the mountain behind Trail is the former mining town of **Rossland** (population 3,500). The **Le Roy Mine** is no longer in operation but you can still visit, it is one of the top attractions in town. Actually, though, Rossland is known today as an outdoor sports town and home to the Red Mountain Ski Resort and miles and miles of mountain bike trails.

Boundary Country Campgrounds

☐ **JOHNSTONE CREEK PROVINCIAL PARK**
   (Open May 16 to Sept 18 – Varies)
Information: (250) 548-0076
Location: 7.1 Km (4.4 Miles) W of Rock Creek

GPS Location: 49.04528 N, 119.04972 W, 2,700 Ft

16 Sites – Johnston Creek is a small provincial campground. Sites are off an out and back road with a turn-around at the end. They're back-ins to 30 feet but most are smaller, about 25 feet long. A hand pump provides water and there are picnic tables and fire pits. There's a .5 km trail leading from the campground to Johnstone Creek Falls. This campground is located on the south side of Hwy 3 about 25.5 km (15.8 miles) west of Midway.

BRITISH COLUMBIA

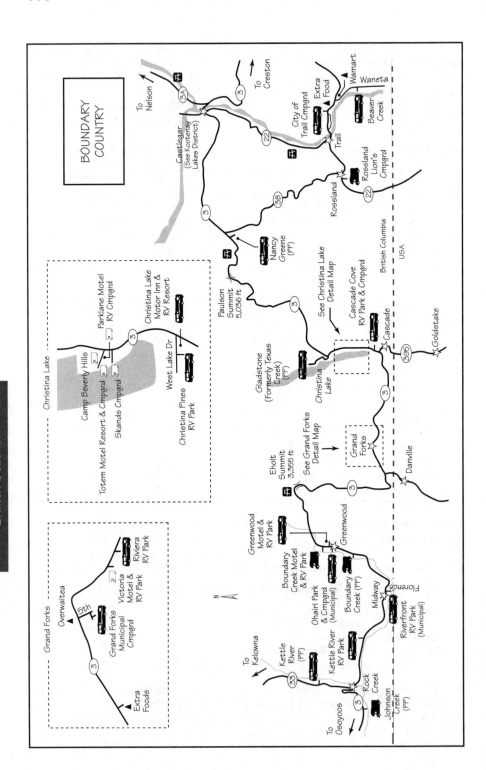

BOUNDARY COUNTRY

☐ **KETTLE RIVER RECREATION AREA**
   (Open April 25 to Sept 26 – Varies)
   Reservations: www.discovercamping.ca, (800) 689-9025
   Information: (250) 548-0076, info@campokanagan.com
   Location: 7 Km (4 Miles) NW of Rock Creek

   GPS Location: 49.11194 N, 118.98139 W, 2000 Ft

87 Sites – The campground at this park is set in dry country with huge pines. Sites here are long sites off two loops, there's nothing much to get in the way so even the largest RVs should have few problems in this campground. Sites have picnic tables and fire pits. The bed of the Kettle Valley Railroad runs though the park. Rails have been removed and the rail bed serves as a trail, this is part of the Trans Canada Trail and it cross the Kettle River on a bridge near the campground. Visitors swim and tube the Kettle River near the campground. The entrance is on Hwy 33 some 6.8 km (4.2 Miles) north of Rock Creek, the intersection of Hwy 3 and Hwy 33.

● **KETTLE RIVER RV PARK**
   (Open April 15 to Oct 15)
   Res and Info: (250) 446-2225 or (888) 441-2225,
            www.kettleriverrv.com
   Location: 8.5 Km (5.3 Miles) E of Rock Creek

   GPS Location: 49.04417 N, 118.88694 W, 1,900 Ft

46 Sites – This is a nice RV park located on the bank of the Kettle River in open country between Rock Creek and Midway. There are full-hookup pull-thrus to 100 feet. The campground is off Hwy 3 some 8.5 km (5.3 miles) east of Rock Creek and 10 km (6.2 miles) west of Midway.

○ **MIDWAY RIVERFRONT RV PARK**
   (Open April 15 to Oct 15 – Varies)
   Res and Info: (250) 449-2467, (250) 449-2222
   Location: Midway

   GPS Location: 49.00556 N, 118.77639 W, 1,900 Ft

19 Sites – This is a great little municipal campground next to the Kettle River in Midway. There are back-in sites to 35 feet and a small restroom. Tents can pitch on grass. Reservations are not only available, they're recommended. In Midway turn south on Florence St. which is just west of The Spot gas station and drive .8 km (.3 mile) to the campground, turn right just before the bridge. There's a dump station near the park, it's behind The Spot gas station, you pass it on the way to the campground.

☐ **BOUNDARY CREEK PROVINCIAL PARK**
   (Open May 16 to Sept 18 – Varies)
   Information: (250) 548-0076, info@campokanagan.com
   Location: 3 Km (2 Mile) W of Greenwood

   GPS Location: 49.05833 N, 118.69472 W, 2,300 Ft

18 Sites – This little campground borders Boundary Creek and is right next to the highway. Sites are fairly small: a couple would take 40 foot RVs but most won't, and maneuvering room is limited. It's best for RVs to 35 feet. The best sites are those near the creek. This is the historical site of the BC Copper Co. smelter and you'll find the stack and a slagheap near the campground. The campground is located on Hwy 3 just west of Greenwood.

BRITISH COLUMBIA

○ **OHAIRI PARK AND CAMPGROUND**
  (Open April 1 to Oct 30)
  Location: Greenwood

      GPS Location: 49.09139 N, 118.67806 W, 2,400 Ft

6 Sites – This municipal campground isn't very attractive. The RV sites are places to park on municipal land, it's a municipal park of sorts. The six sites have tables and fire rings and will allow parking any size RV. There's also a treed area suitable for tents. A park restroom building nearby has flush toilets, there's a dump station and a water faucet. Watch for the park on the west side of Hwy 3 in central Greenwood.

● **BOUNDARY CREEK MOTEL AND RV PARK** *(Open All Year)*
  Res and Info: (888) 518-4479, (250) 445-6641,
                www.boundarycreekmotel.com
  Location: Greenwood

      GPS Location: 49.09942 N, 118.67662 W, 2,400 Ft

6 Sites – This is a small motel with 5 back-in RV sites behind it.
They extend to 30 feet, the owner does have plans to make them longer. Restrooms with showers are available. The motel is in Greenwood on the west side of the highway.

● **GREENWOOD MOTEL AND RV PARK**
  (Open April 1 to Oct 31)
  Res and Info: (250) 445-6363,
                www.greenwoodcity.com/greenwood
                motel.html
  Location: Greenwood

      GPS Location: 49.09528 N, 118.67722 W, 2,400 Ft

11 Sites – This motel has an RV area. The back in sites are as long as 50 feet. They are full hookup sites The motel is on the east side of Hwy 3 in central Greenwood.

○ **GRAND FORKS MUNICIPAL CAMPGROUND**
  (Open May 15 to Oct 15 – Varies)
  Res and Info: (250) 442-5835, 250 443-4452
                www.city.grandforks.bc.ca/
                index.php/services/campground/
  Location: Grand Forks

      GPS Location: 49.03000 N, 118.44000 W, 1,600 Ft

48 Sites – Grand Forks has one of the best in-town municipal campgrounds you'll see. There are back-in sites to 45 feet as well as tent sites. RV sites have power and water hookups and there is a dump station, there are also some full-hookup sites. In winter, from Sept 15 to June 15 spaces are available on a weekly basis. Off Hwy 3 in central Grand Forks turn south on 5th street, the campground is in a park a short distance down the street. There's a swimming beach at the park and a supermarket just down the street.

● **RIVIERA RV PARK** *(Open All Year)*
  Reservations: (877) 700-2158, hosts@rivierarvpark.ca
  Information: (250) 442-1299,
  Location: Grand Forks

      GPS Location: 49.02472 N, 118.41889 W, 1,700 Ft

90 Sites – This is a neat park-like campground at the

BRITISH COLUMBIA

eastern edge of Grand Forks. Sites are back-ins and pull-thrus to 60 feet. All of the RV sites have full hookups, there are also five tent sites. The campground is situated next to the Kettle River and has its own little beach and swimming area. From Grand Forks proceed east on Hwy 3, just outside town you'll spot the campground on the right.

● **CASCADE COVE RV PARK AND CAMPGROUND**
  (Open April 1 to Oct 31)
  Res and Info: (250) 447-6662,
    cascadecovervpark@hotmail.com,
    www.christinalake.com/cascadecove
  Location: 1.6 Km (1 Mile) S of Christina Lake

GPS Location: 49.02250 N , 118.21778 W, 1,500 Ft

75 Sites – Cascade Cove doesn't sit right on the lake. Instead it is located on the outlet, a park-like location with its own beach on the river. The RV sites include full-hookup back-ins and pull-thrus to 60 feet, there are also a large number of tent sites. Heading east on Hwy 3 the campground entrance road is just .8 km (.5 mile) east of the intersection of Hwy 3 and Hwy 395 which comes north from the States.

● **CHRISTINA PINES RV PARK**
  (Open May 1 to Sept 15)
  Res and Info: (250) 447-9587
  Location: Christina Lake

  GPS Location: 49.03972 N, 118.21056 W, 1,500 Ft

100 Sites – The Christina Lake campground is a Holiday Trails membership campground. It accepts non-members but there are some restrictions on reservations. It isn't on the lake, but it does have a pool. Sites are fairly short here, most are 30-foot back-ins with a few slightly longer pull-thrus. All are full-hookup sites with parking on grass. There are also some tent sites. Amenities include the pool and mini-golf. In Christina Lake turn west off Hwy 3 onto West Lake Drive. Proceed about three blocks to Neimi Rd, turn left, and you'll see the park entrance on the left in about a block.

● **CHRISTINA LAKE MOTOR INN AND RV RESORT**
  (Open May 1 to Sept 30)
  Res and Info: (250) 447-9421, info@christinalakewmotorinn.com,
    www.christinalakemotorinn.com
  Location: Christina Lake

  GPS Location: 49.03972 N, 118.21056 W, 1,500 Ft

65 Sites – This facility in Christina Lake is not on the lake but is near the supermarket and other amenities of the village. RV sites are all paved back-ins of about 40 feet. They have electric and water hookups but no sewer, there is a dump station. There are also quite a few tent sites. Watch for the motor inn on the west side of Hwy 3 in Christina Lake.

☐ **GLADSTONE PROVINCIAL PARK** *(formerly Texas Creek)*
  (Open May 1 to Sept 21 – Varies)
  Reservations: www.discovercamping.ca, (800) 689-9025
  Information: (250) 548-0076
  Location: 8 Km (5 Miles) N of Christina Lake

  GPS Location: 49.12750 N, 118.24944 W, 1,500 Ft

63 Sites – This provincial park campground is located near the east side of Christina

Lake. Sites are all back-ins, many to 50 feet. Very few of the sites are right on the lake. There is a boat launch and 48 kilometers of hiking trails in the park including a lakeshore trail to the north. Swimming is possible from several small beaches below the campground. From the developed area of Christina Lake drive north about 3 km (2 miles), watch for the Gladstone or Texas Creek entrance road (East Lake Drive) on the left. Once on the access road it's another 4.3 km (2.7 mile) of paved surface to the campground.

☐ **NANCY GREENE PROVINCIAL PARK** *(Open June 1 to Sept 15 – Varies)*
    Information: (250) 837-5734, www.westkootenayparks.com
    Location: 29 Km (18 Miles) N of Rossland

        GPS Location: 49.26056 N, 117.94111 W, 4,100 Ft

14 Sites – This campground is next to Nancy Greene Lake, a beautiful sub-alpine body of water. The camping area here is really a paved parking lot, RVs back in along the edge. This parking arrangement means that large RVs will fit. The park has a nice 5 km trail around the lake as well as a swimming beach. Kayaking, canoeing, sailing and wind-surfing are popular in summer. There are also many other trails in the area, it's a popular cross-country skiing destination in the winter. The park is easy to find since it's right at the intersection of Hwy 3 and Hwy 3B. That's about 29 km (18 miles) north of Rossland and 24 km (15 miles) west of Castlegar.

○ **ROSSLAND LION'S CAMPGROUND**
    (Open May 1 to Canadian Thanksgiving – 2nd Monday in Oct)
    Information: (250) 362-5427, altdorfer@telus.net,
                    www.rossland.com/directory/lions_campground
    Location: Rossland

        GPS Location: 49.07750 N, 117.81833 W, 3,400 Ft

19 Sites – A nice little campground located just west of Rossland next to the local ballpark. It has tent and RV sites suitable for RVs to 35 feet. Restrooms here are modern with four rooms, each with sink, toilet, and shower. Because this campground is small and remote it's a good idea to call ahead to confirm availability. From Rossland drive west. The campground is on the south side of Hwy 22 just .5 km (.3 mile) west of the intersection of Highways 22 and 3B on the western edge of town.

○ **CITY OF TRAIL CAMPGROUND**
    (Open May 15 to Sept 15 – Varies)
    Res and Info: (250) 368-3144, tcoc@netidea.com
    Location: 5 Km (3 Miles) E of Trail

        GPS Location: 49.09134 N, 117.63917 W, 1,400 Ft

31 Sites – Trail's municipal campground has nicely land-
scaped tent and RV sites with water and electric hookups. Some hookup sites are pull-thrus, some but not all will take RVs to 40 feet. This is an easy campground to miss since there is no sign. It's 5.3 km (3.3 miles) east of the bridge over the Columbia in Trail on Hwy 3B on the north side of the road.

☐ **BEAVER CREEK PROVINCIAL PARK**
    (Open All Year As Weather Allows)
    Res and Info: (250) 367-9165
    Location: 8 Km (5 Miles) E of Trail

        GPS Location: 49.06694 N, 117.60472 W, 1,300 Ft

19 Sites – This small provincial campground overlooks the Columbia River. This is a campground managed by the local Kiwanis. RV sites are back-ins and some will take RVs to 45 feet although the narrow access roads require careful driving. A building with showers and flush toilets has been constructed near the entrance several hundred meters from the campsites. There are vault toilets in the campground. There is also a ball field and boat ramp. Services are available only during the peak season from May to September but the gates remain open for use without services. From the bridge over the Columbia in Trail head east on Hwy 3B for 6.3 km (3.9 miles) and turn south on Waneta Road (Hwy 22A). Coming from the east on Hwy 3B the turn is just past the Walmart. Follow Waneta Road for 3.1 km (1.9 miles), the campground entrance is on the right.

CAMPBELL RIVER

Campbell River (population 30,000) is probably best known as a fishing destination. The town is located on the east side of Vancouver Island at the south end of Discovery Passage, a place where there are extraordinary numbers of bait fish. The bait fish attract salmon year-round. The huge Tyee (large king) salmon are the most-desired prize, but you can also fish for sockeye (red), coho (silver), chum (dog) and pink salmon.

Because Campbell River is a fishing resort town you will find a wide variety of tourist facilities including RV parks, restaurants, and fishing charter operators.

One of the most interesting places to visit in Campbell River is the **Discovery Pier** (a saltwater fishing pier. It is located right next to the downtown boat harbor and juts out into Discovery Passage. Lots of fish are caught here, it's great fun to watch the action.

From Campbell River you can catch a small ferry across Discovery Passage to **Quadra Island**. You'll need to take a vehicle for transportation on the island, it is quite large. There's an excellent First Nations museum here called **Kwagiulth Museum** in Cape Mudge Village south of the ferry landing. There are also **petroglyphs** on display that have been moved here from nearby locations for protection from vandals.

Highway 28 leads westward from Campbell River through **Strathcona Provincial Park** to Gold River and the west coast of Vancouver Island. There are two large campgrounds in this largest of Vancouver Island's parks that are suitable for RVs. The park also has a number of hiking trails, particularly along the side road that leaves Highway 28 near the Buttle Lake Bridge and heads south along the east shore of Buttle Lake. Ninety-two kilometers (57 miles) from Campbell River the road reaches Gold River, a factory town for a pulp mill, and then continues another 14 kilometers (9 miles) to tidewater. From there you can ride the converted minesweeper MV Uchuck III which carries supplies to remote communities along the west coast of the island.

The campgrounds listed below run from south to north with the last ones west of Campbell River in Strathcona Provincial Park. The provincial park campgrounds are great for both tenters and RVers while the waterfront sites at the Ripple Rock RV Park are some of the most outstanding in North America, well worth the short drive on gravel to reach them.

BRITISH COLUMBIA

Campbell River Campgrounds

☐ **Miracle Beach Provincial Park** *(Open All Year)*
Reservations: www.discovercamping.ca, (800) 689-9025
Information: (250) 474-1336
Location: 16 Km (10 Mile) S of Campbell River

GPS Location: 49.849444 N, 125.095833 W, Near Sea Level

201 Sites – This is a large and very popular sea-side camp-
ground. It is one of the provincial parks with an entry gatehouse, a sign of how popular the park really is. The draw here is the beach, families love to spend their vacations camping in this park. Sites here are large enough to handle RVs to 45 feet. There are reduced services and fees from October 1 to April 30. The campground is located off Hwy 19A about 16 km (10 miles) south of Campbell River.

● **Salmon Point RV Resort and Marina**
     (Open All Year)
Res and Info: (250) 923-6605, (866) 246-6605,
       sales@salmonpoint.com,
       www.salmonpoint.com
Location: 10 Km (6 Miles) S of Campbell River

GPS Location: 49.88972 N, 125.12778 W, Near Sea Level

160 Sites – A large commercial RV resort on the
coast south of Campbell River. It offers large sites alongside a first-class marina. Some sites are beachside, some are inland from the marina under trees. Sites are back-ins, some to 60 feet, with parking on gravel or grass. Campfires are in a community fir pit. The resort has a fine swimming pool with an indoor hot tub, and an excellent restaurant. There is also a boat ramp. The campground is well-signed from Hwy 19A about 10 km (6 miles) south of Campbell River.

● **Campbell River Fishing Village and**
     RV Park *(Open All Year)*
Res and Info: (250) 287-3630,
       fishvil@oberon.ark.com,
       www.fishingvillage.bc.ca
Location: Campbell River

GPS Location: 50.00222 N, 125.23167 W, Near Sea Level

42 Sites – One of two small RV parks along Hwy 19A across the highway from the ocean just south of downtown Campbell River. The emphasis here is on fishing with guided trips available. This is an older campground but it's handy for access to central Campbell River. A bike trail runs along the beach across the street and you can easily walk in to town. A few of the sites here will take RVs to 40 feet, most sites are good for RVs to 25 or 30 feet. There is a community fire pit. From central Campbell River drive south, the campground is 2 km (1.2 miles) south of the Discovery Pier fishing dock.

● **Driftwood By The Sea RV Park and Cottages**
     (Open All Year)
Res and Info: (250) 203-0373, (888) 703-0373,
       driftwoodbythesea@telus.net,
       www.driftwoodbythesea.com
Location: Campbell River

GPS Location: 50.00413 N, 125.2326 W, Near Sea Level

British Columbia

28 Sites – This is the second RV park located just south of downtown Campbell River. Sites here are gravel back-ins to 70 feet separated by logs and have picnic tables but not fire pits. From central Campbell River drive south, the campground is 1.7 km (1.1 miles) south of the Discovery Pier.

● **THUNDERBIRD RV PARK** *(Open All Year)*

Res and Info: (250) 286-3344,
thunderbirdrvpark@shawbiz.ca,
www.thunderbirdrvpark.com
Location: Campbell River

GPS Location: 50.04278 N, 125.25000 W, Near Sea Level

90 Sites – This is a large park, conveniently situated,

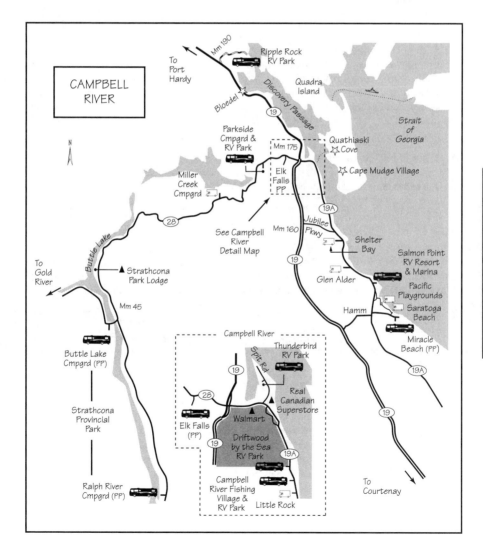

with good facilities. It's good for both big rigs and tent campers. It is located just outside Campbell River to the north on the Tyee Spit. It sits across the road from the ocean, a large ship loading pier is just to the south. There's a tidal estuary/river mouth behind the park and the sites overlooking it are the best in the campground with good views and a lawn behind the parking areas. Sites in the park are large pull-thrus and back-ins in a large gravel lot. Also available is a tent camping area at one end of the campground with grass for pitching. To reach the campground drive out the Spit Road from Hwy 19A in northeast Campbell River near the shopping centers. The campground is on the left about 1.1 km (.7 miles) from the cutoff from 19A.

☐ **ELK FALLS PROVINCIAL PARK** *(Open All Year)*
   Reservations: www.discovercamping.ca, (800) 689-9025
   Information: (250) 474-1336
   Location: 2 Km (1 Mile) W of Campbell River

   GPS Location: 50.03639 N, 125.29556 W, 100 Ft

122 Sites – This large provincial park campground is handy
because it is very near the city of Campbell River, just 1.5 km (.9 miles) to the west off Hwy 28 to Strathcona Provincial Park. Many sites are right along the Quinsam River which has runs of salmon. The 75-foot Elk Falls of the Campbell River is nearby. These are back-in sites, some to 55 feet. Toilets are vault-type except for flush toilets near the sani-station. There are good hiking trails from the campground. From October 1 to April 30 no services are available but the campground is open, fees are reduced.

● **PARKSIDE CAMPGROUND AND RV PARK**
   (Open April 1 to Oct 30)
   Res and Info: (250) 830-1428, parkside@xplornet.com,
                 www.parksidecampingrv.com
   Location: 6 Km (4 Miles) W of Campbell River

   GPS Location: 50.02893 N, 125.34520 W, 500 Ft

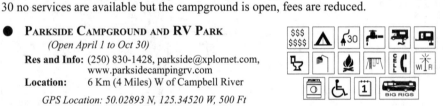

50 Sites – Here's a commercial RV park to the west side of Campbell River on the road out to Strathcona Provincial Park. The sites here are back-ins and pull-thrus to 55 feet. From its intersection with Hwy 19 on the west side of Campbell River go west on Hwy 28, the Gold River Highway. The campground is on the left in 5.9 km (3.7 miles).

● **RIPPLE ROCK RV PARK** *(Open April 1 to Oct 31)*
   Res and Info: (250) 287-7108,
                 ripplerockrv@brownsbayresort.com,
                 www.brownsbayresort.com
   Location: 23 Km (14 Miles) N of Campbell River
   GPS Location: 50.15944 N, 125.37250 W, Near Sea Level

65 Sites – This is a first class campground overlooking the sea north of Campbell River. It's nice enough that it wins lots of awards. Large pull-in and back-in sites have great views, patios, and full hookups. Amenities include a boat ramp, hot tub, very upscale game room, and of course, the view. Within a short walk is an associated marina with a restaurant and store known as Brown's Bay. The access road leaves Hwy 19 some 18 km (11 miles) north of Campbell River near Km 189. It's a 5.0 km (3.1 mile) gravel road.

☐ **BUTTLE LAKE CAMPGROUND – STRATHCONA**
 PROVINCIAL PARK *(Open April 15 to Oct 31)*

Reservations: www.discovercamping.ca, (800) 689-9025
Information: (250) 474-1336
Location: 48 Km (30 Miles) W of Campbell River

GPS Location: 49.83306 N, 125.62778 W, 700 Ft

85 Sites – A provincial park campground in a quiet location along the shore of Buttle Lake in Strathcona Provincial Park. Fishing is good in the lake and there are a number of hiking trails in the vicinity. The park has a sandy beach for sunning and swimming, canoeing and kayaking are popular on the lake, so is wind surfing when the weather is right. Large back-in sites will take rigs to 45 feet. The campground is located about 48 kilometers (30 miles) west of Campbell River along Hwy 28 to Gold River.

☐ **RALPH RIVER CAMPGROUND – STRATHCONA**
 PROVINCIAL PARK *(Open April 30 to Sept 30)*

Information: (250) 474-1336
Location: 73 Km (45 Miles) W of Campbell River

GPS Location: 49.63059 N, 125.52496 W, 700 Ft

85 Sites – The Ralph River Campground in Strathcona Provincial Park is more remote that the Buttle Lake Campground. It's also on the shore of Buttle Lake, but is located about 26 km (16 miles) off the main road to Gold River. The campground is set in a mixed evergreen forest. Interior roads and sites are gravel with back-ins to 50 feet. Larger rigs will find site access to require careful driving. The Shepherd Creek trailhead is just across the highway. From Campbell River drive west on Hwy 28 for 47.6 km (29.5 miles) to a Y. The road to Gold River goes west here, instead continue straight ahead for 26 km (16 miles) to the campground.

CAPE SCOTT

Cape Scott Provincial Park occupies the far remote northwest corner of Vancouver Island. The park is difficult to get to and doesn't get throngs of visitors. That makes it a great destination if you like to hike wild country and enjoy sometimes fighting the elements.

The park encompasses over 100 kilometers (62 miles) of coastline and 22,131 hectares (85 square miles) of rain-swept headlands and marshes. Expect inclement weather with rain and wind. The park is well-known for muddy hiking conditions so come prepared.

The short 2.5-kilometer (1.5-mile) trail to the beach at San Josef Bay is the most popular with visitors because it's easy and the trail well-maintained. Tent camping is allowed at San Josef Bay. Much longer hikes lead to remote Cape Scott (23.6 km), beaches at Experiment Bight (18.9 km), Nels Bight (16.8 km) and Nissen Bight (15 km), the abandoned Cape Scott settlement (12 km), and Eric Lake (3 km). Tent camping is allowed at Experiment Bight, Nels Bight, Nissen Bight, and Eric Lake.

The road to the park heads west from a junction near Port Hardy. From the highway to the park is a distance of 65 kilometers (40 miles), all except 2.4 km (1.5 miles) is gravel. Much of the distance you're on active logging roads requiring careful driving.

The road ends at a newly expanded parking lot. Trails begin here and lead to various

BRITISH COLUMBIA

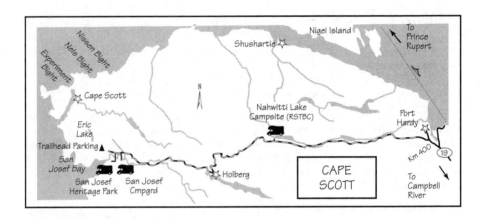

destinations including several places suitable for tent camping. Camping overnight in the parking lot is not allowed.

None of the campgrounds below offer hookups. Due to the sometimes narrow and rough gravel road these campgrounds are only suitable for smaller rigs, see the campground descriptions for specifics.

Cape Scott Campgrounds

● **SAN JOSEF HERITAGE PARK** *(Open All Year)*
   Res and Info: (250) 288-3682
   Location: 65 Km (40 Miles) W of Port Hardy

$\qquad$ *GPS Location: 50.68333 N, 128.25056 W, Near Sea Level*

12 Sites – This old homestead is the closest camping area to the provincial park parking area. The manager lives on-site so it makes a good place to leave your car if you are worried about break-ins at the lot while you're hiking in the park. It also makes a good place to camp for day hikes into the park. The area has been cleared and is a mowed lawn. Sites are set in the trees along the edge. There are picnic tables and fire pits, also an outhouse. Kayaks and canoes can be launched in the San Josef River at the campground. While the campground can take any size rig the access roads make about 30 feet the practical maximum size for RVs to this area. To reach the campground leave Hwy 19 some 1.9 km (1.2 miles) west of where the road goes north to the Port Hardy ferry terminal. The road is signed for Cape Scott Provincial Park and Holberg. For the first 2.4 km (1.5 miles) the road is paved, then it turns to gravel. At 43 km (27 miles) from the highway you'll reach Holberg. Continue on through town following Cape Scott signs. As you approach the park the road narrows to the point that bushes will brush the side of motorhomes. You'll come to a Y at 63 km (39 miles) from the highway, San Josef Campground is left (see below), take the right fork. There's another fork in just .5 km (.3 mile), the small provincial park parking lot is straight ahead .3 km (.2 miles). For San Josef Heritage Park turn left at the fork and you'll reach the campground in another .5 km (.3 mile).

○ **SAN JOSEF CAMPGROUND** *(Open All Year)*
   Information: (250) 956-4446, www.westernforest.com
   Location: 63 Km (39 Miles) W of Port Hardy

$\qquad$ *GPS Location: 50.68167 N, 128.23778 W, Near Sea Level*

13 Sites – This is a small wilderness campground provided by Western Forest Products, the local logging company. It is on the bank of the San Josef River, canoes and kayaks can be launched from this campground. There are back-in sites suitable for RVs to about 35 feet however the access roads make 30 feet the practical maximum size for this area. There are also outhouses, picnic tables, fire pits, and sometimes firewood, but no potable water. To find the campground just follow the instructions given for San Josef Heritage Park, the entrance road for this campground is just before the one for San Josef Heritage Park.

☐ **NAHWITTI LAKE CAMPSITE** *(Open All Year)*
Location: 23 Km (14 Miles) W of Port Hardy

GPS Location: 50.70417 N, 127.86250 W, 700 Ft

8 Sites – This is a small RSTBC campground located near (about 100 feet from the shoreline) Nahwitti Lake. The back-in sites here are suitable for RVs to about 25 feet. There are picnic tables, fire pits, and outhouses but no water except the lake. There is good trout fishing in the lake during June and July. The campground is on the north side of the highway to Holberg and Cape Scott some 23.4 km (14.5 miles) from the intersection near Port Hardy.

CHETWYND, HUDSON'S HOPE, AND TUMBLER RIDGE

Chetwynd (population 3,000) is located on the John Hart Highway (Hwy 97) between Prince George and Dawson Creek. It's much closer to Dawson Creek, only 102 km (63 miles) distant. Probably the most striking attraction of the town is the **chainsaw sculptures**, in fact, the town bills itself as the Chainsaw Sculpture Capital of the World. Many of them are on display outside the visitor center and are well worth a stop.

From Chetwynd Hwy 29 runs north to Hudson's Hope and then west to meet the Alaska highway north of Fort St. John. This is an interesting route since it passes by the two dams built to harness the Peace River. These two dams are a big part of the reason that every BC resident uses the word hydro instead of electricity in conversation. The largest of the dams is the **W.A.C. Bennett Dam**. It's off the main road about 11 km (7 miles) west of Hudson's Hope and behind it is British Columbia's largest lake, Williston Lake. There's a visitor centre at the dam with information about the dams, their construction, and the electricity they produce. The smaller dam, **Peace Canyon Dam**, is easier to reach since it's right off the road between Chetwynd and Hudson's Hope. It too has a visitor centre, this one focusing more on the history of the local area.

South of Chetwynd Hwy 29 leads some 92 km (57 mile) to **Tumbler Ridge.** This is a modern town built in 1981 to service the mining industry but it also serves as a center for outdoor activities in the surrounding area. Tumbler Ridge is known for the **dinosaur tracks** found in the vicinity and tours are available to go out and take a look.

The campgrounds below are located in Chetwynd, along the Hudson's Hope loop and also along the road toward Tumbler Ridge. There's a good selection of municipal, commercial and provincial campgrounds.

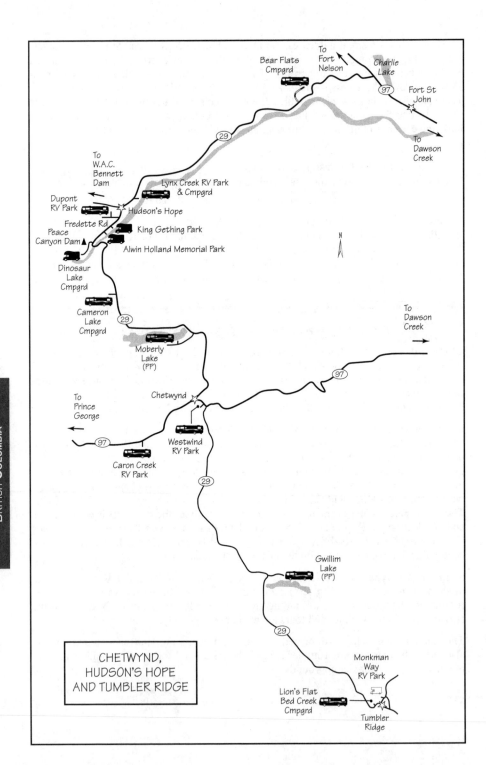

CHETWYND,
HUDSON'S HOPE
AND TUMBLER RIDGE

Chetwynd, Hudson's Hope, and Tumbler Ridge Campgrounds

● **CARON CREEK RV PARK** *(Open May 1 to Sept 30 - Varies)*
   Res and Info: (250) 788-2522
   Location: 13 Km (8 Miles) W of Chetwynd

   GPS Location: 55.62083 N, 121.81611 W, 1,900 Ft

40 Sites – As you approach Chetwynd from the west you'll find
Caron Creek RV Park right beside the highway. The sites here are full-hookup pull-thrus
to 70 feet. Watch for the park on the south side of Hwy 97 about 13 km (8 miles) west
of Chetwynd.

● **WESTWIND RV PARK** *(Open May 1 to Oct 31)*
   Res and Info: (250) 788-2190,
                    wwrvpark@hotmail.com
   Location: Chetwynd

   GPS Location: 55.68806 N, 121.60333 W, 2,000 Ft

60 Sites – This large park is an excellent place to
overnight in Chetwynd. There are ten tent sites as well as 50 full-hookup pull-thrus to
70 feet. There are good clean restrooms, a dump station, and a high pressure rig cleaning
station. The campground is on the south side of Hwy 97 about a mile outside the central
district of Chetwynd on the east side of town.

☐ **MOBERLY LAKE PROVINCIAL PARK** *(Open All Year)*
   Reservations: www.discovercamping.ca, (800) 689-9025
   Information: (250) 964-2243
   Location: 35 Km (22 Miles) N of Chetwynd

   GPS Location: 55.80889 N, 121.69417 W, 2,300 Ft

109 Sites – This provincial park is located on the south shore of Moberly Lake in a stand
of mature spruce and alders. It's open all year but services are limited Sept 1 through May
15. Sites are back-ins to 45 feet off paved access roads and there's plenty of maneuvering
room. There is a swimming beach and boat ramp, also a dump station. From Chetwynd
drive north toward Hudson's Hope on Hwy 29 for 19 km (12 miles). Turn left at the sign
for the park and drive 3.4 km (2.1 miles) west to the park entrance.

○ **CAMERON LAKE CAMPGROUND** *(Open May 1 to Sept 30 – Varies)*
   Information: (250) 783-9901, (250) 783-9154
   Location: 40 Km (25 Miles) N of Chetwynd

   GPS Location: N 55.88861, W 121.90361, 2,400 Ft

20 Sites – The campsites here are situated along Cameron Lake or back from the lake in
a treed area. Sites are large, some suitable for any RV, and are off a loop road. Amenities
include picnic tables, fire pits and vault toilets. Parking is on grass or gravel. An informal
day-use area has a small beach and swimming is popular, no power boats are allowed on
the lake. The camping area is off Hwy 29 some 24 km (15 miles) from Hudson's Hope
and 40 km (25 miles) from Chetwynd.

○ **DINOSAUR LAKE CAMPGROUND** *(May 1 to Sept 30 – Varies)*
   Information: (250) 783-9154
   Location: 8 Km (13 Mile) W of Hudson's Hope

   GPS Location: 55.98028 N, 122.00694 W, 1,600 Ft

50 Sites – This campground borders Dinosaur Lake, the reservoir behind the Peace Canyon Dam. Sites here are back-in parking lot style on gravel with room for RVs to 35 feet. At the end of each site is a picnic table and metal fire ring. A nearby day-use area has a swimming beach and boat ramp. The access road for this campground is off the entrance road for the Peace Canyon Dam visitor center. From Hudson's Hope drive 6 km (3.7 miles) west on Hwy 29 to the sign for the visitor center. Turn right and in 1 km (.6 mile) you'll spot the campground access road going right, the campground is 1.3 km (.8 mile) down this road.

○ **ALWIN HOLLAND MEMORIAL PARK** *(Open May 1 to Sept 30 – Varies)*
   Information: (250) 783-9901 or (250) 783-9154
   Location: 2.4 Km (1.5 Miles) W of Hudson's Hope

GPS Location: 56.00861 N, 121.95333 W, 1,400 Ft

12 Sites – This is a small municipal campground in heavy trees near the Peace River west of Hudson's Hope. Sites are small, the campground is best for tent campers, vans, and pickup campers. Amenities include picnic tables, fire pits, and outhouses. The campground entrance road is on the south side of Hwy 29 about 2.4 km (1.5 mile) west of Hudson's Hope.

○ **KING GETHING PARK** *(Open May 1 to Sept 30 – Varies)*
   Information: (250) 783-9901 or (250) 783-9154
   Location: Hudson's Hope

GPS Location: 56.02417 N, 121.92806 W, 1,600 Ft

15 Sites – Parking in this little municipal campground is on grass. Limited maneuvering room makes the park best for RVs to 35 feet. Each site has a picnic table and a metal fire ring. There are restrooms with flush toilets and coin-operated showers as well as a dump station and water fill station. Very convenient. The campground is on the south side of Hwy 29 just west of central Hudson's Hope.

● **DUPONT RV PARK** *(Open May 1 to Sept 30)*
   Res and Info: (250) 783-5460
   Location: Hudson's Hope

GPS Location: 56.02917 N, 121.91389 W, 1,600 Ft

8 Sites – This is a very neat little commercial RV park located right in Hudson's Hope. These are back-in full-hookup sites that can take RVs to 40 feet. In Hudson's Hope on Hwy 29 you'll see Fredette Road extending to the west. Follow Fredette road for about a block and a half to the park.

● **LYNX CREEK RV PARK AND CAMPGROUND**
       (Open May 1 to Sept 30 – Varies)
   Res and Info: (250) 783-5333, lynxrv@pris.ca,
                 www.lynxcreekrvpark.com
   Location: 6 Km (10 Miles) E of Hudson's Hope

GPS Location: 56.06833 N, 121.83444 W, 1,500 Ft

25 Sites – Lynx Creek is an excellent little full hookup campground located on the north shore of the Peace River. Most sites are long pull-thrus with water and electricity hookups. There is also lots of room for tent campers. Amenities include a dump site and mini golf. From Hudson's Hope drive east on Hwy 29 for 6 km (10 miles) the campground is on the right.

● **BEAR FLATS CAMPGROUND** *(Open May 1 to Sept 30 – Varies)*
Information: (250) 262-3205
Location: 53 Km (33 Miles) E of Hudson's Hope

GPS Location: 56.27000 N, 121.25028 W, 1,500 Ft

50 Sites – This camping area is a grassy clearing with scattered trees. Campsites are not defined. Electricity is by way of long cords from near the office. There are hot showers but restrooms are outhouses. There's a covered picnic area and a laundry. To reach the campground follow Hwy 29 west from its intersection with Hwy 97 near Charlie Lake for 21 km (13 miles) or 53 km (33 miles) east from Hudson's Hope.

☐ **GWILLIM LAKE PROVINCIAL PARK** *(Open May 20 to Sept 15 – Varies)*
Information: (250) 242-1146 or (250) 787-3407
Location: 45 Km (28 Mile) S of Chetwynd

GPS Location: 55.36000 N, 121.35778 W, 2,500 Ft

50 Sites – Gwillim Lake campground is on the north shore of Gwillim Lake, surrounded by mountains. The campground's sites are back-ins, some to 70 feet. The campground has a boat ramp and fishing in the lake is possible but not considered great. Water is from a hand pump. This is a beautiful location and the campground doesn't usually get a lot of use. From Chetwynd head south on Hwy 29, the road to Tumbler Ridge. The entrance road to the park is on the left after 45 km (28 miles).

○ **LION'S FLAT BED CREEK CAMPGROUND**
(Open May 1 to Sept 30 – Varies)
Information: (250) 242-3123
Location: Tumbler Ridge

GPS Location: N 55.12028 N, W 121.01750 W, 2,500 Ft

44 Sites – This district government campground is used by visitors, the Tumbler Ridge Monkman Campground on the far side of town is primarily used as a camp to house workers and we do not recommend it. Sites at Lion's Flat Bed Creek campground are back-ins, some with views of the creek. Sites are as long as 50 feet. There are restrooms, a dump station and the Flatbed Falls Interpretive Trail. The campground is located off Hwy 29 just south of Tumbler Ridge. Approaching from Chetwynd you'll see it just before reaching town.

CHILLIWACK AND CULTUS LAKES AREA

Two lakes south of Hwy 1 near Chilliwack offer great recreational opportunities to folks living in the Greater Vancouver area. They're an easy drive from the city.

Cultus Lake is by far the easiest to reach. It's located just 8 km (5 miles) south of Exit 119 of Hwy 1. This 4 km (2.5 mile) long lake is warm enough for water sports like swimming and skiing and hosts a provincial park with 4 campgrounds as well as a regional park campground. The area is highly developed as a tourist destination and has a waterpark.

Chilliwack Lake is just the opposite. This long narrow wilderness lake is undeveloped and has one campground, a provincial park, at the north end. The lake is 8 km (5 miles) long and is popular for fishing and nearby hiking trails.

Between the two lakes is the paved access road to Chilliwack Lake. Chilliwack Lake Road is 40 km (25 miles) long and is lined with RSTBC campgrounds, mostly along the Chilliwack River.

BRITISH COLUMBIA

Chilliwack and Cultus Lakes Area Campgrounds

☐ **CHILLIWACK LAKE PROVINCIAL PARK CAMPGROUND**
   (Open May 1 to Oct 10 – Varies)
   Information: (604) 986-9371
   Location: 45 Km (28 Miles) SE of Chilliwack

GPS Location: 49.09542 N, 121.45529 W, 2,100 Ft

146 Sites – The campsites in this campground are at the north end of 8 kilometer long Chilliwack Lake. The lake is popular for fishing, canoeing and kayaking, water-skiing, and even swimming although it's pretty cold. There are also a number of good trails, including the Trans Canada Trail, accessible in the park. Campsites here are gravel back-in sites off gravel roads, they allow plenty of maneuvering room and extend to 60 feet and longer. The campground has a good number of trees but is still fairly bright. The campground is on a plateau above the lake and does not have lake views. From Exit 119 of Hwy 1 near Chilliwack travel south on Vedder Road for 5.0 km (3.1 miles). Just before the bridge turn left onto Chilliwack Lake Road and follow it for another 40.2 km (24.9 miles) to the campground.

☐ **RIVERSIDE RECREATION SITE** *(Open All Year)*
   Res and Info: (604) 858-0020
   Location: 26 Km (16 Miles) SE of Chilliwack

GPS Location: 49.09526 N, 121.58271 W, 1,400 Ft

11 Sites – This is a small RSTBC campground located between a small stream which flows into the Chilliwack River and the Chilliwack Lake Road. Sites here are short, the campground is best for tent campers, vans, or pickup campers. They have picnic tables and fire pits and there are vault toilets. No potable water is provided. There is a camp host who manages the campground. Large evergreens shade the campground which is relatively dark. From Exit 119 of Hwy 1 near Chilliwack travel south on Vedder Road for 5.0 km (3.1 miles). Just before the bridge turn left onto Chilliwack Lake Road and follow it for another 20.6 km (12.8 miles) to the campground.

☐ **THURSTON MEADOWS RECREATION SITE** *(Open All Year)*
   Res and Info: (604) 858-0020
   Location: 22 Km (14 Miles) SE of Chilliwack

GPS Location: 49.07547 N, 121.74942 W, 600 Ft

50 Sites – This is a nice open RSTBC campground located on the bank of the Chilliwack River. It has back-in and parallel-style sites to 40 feet. They have picnic tables and fire pits and there are vault toilets. No potable water is provided. The campground has a host. From Exit 119 of Hwy 1 near Chilliwack travel south on Vedder Road for 5.0 km (3.1 miles). Just before the bridge turn left onto Chilliwack Lake Road and follow it for another 17.1 km (10.6 miles) to the campground.

☐ **ALLISON POOL RECREATION SITE** *(Open May 1 to Sept 5 – Varies)*
   Res and Info: (604) 858-0020
   Location: 19 Km (12 Miles) SE of Chilliwack

GPS Location: 49.07793 N, 121.79383 W, 500 Ft

8 Sites – This small RSTBC campground is located next to the Chilliwack River. It's popular with fishermen because it has good river access but is relatively quiet. Sites here

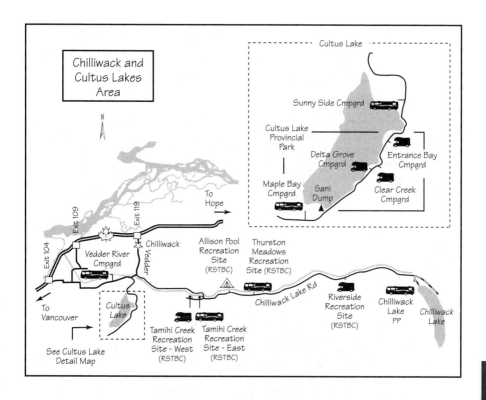

are not suitable for RVs. Some sites have picnic tables and fire pits and there is a vault toilet. No potable water is provided. The campground is gated and locked, call ahead to check availability for tent camping. From Exit 119 of Hwy 1 near Chilliwack travel south on Vedder Road for 5.0 km (3.1 miles). Just before the bridge turn left onto Chilliwack Lake Road and follow it for another 14 km (8.5 miles) to the campground.

☐ **TAMIHI CREEK RECREATION SITE** *(Open All Year)*
    Res and Info: (604) 824-2883
    Location: 14 Km (9 Miles) SE of Chilliwack

   GPS Location: 49.07099 N, 121.83840 W, 300 Ft

108 Sites – There are actually two RSTBC campgrounds here, Tamihi East and Tamihi West. Both are on the south shore of the Chilliwack River, Tamihi Creek runs between them. Tamihi East has 16 back-in or parallel-parking style sites off a large gravel lot next to the river so any size RV is OK. There is a large picnic shelter here. The much larger Tamihi West has smaller traditional sites in an open grass area and also in trees with sites to about 35 feet. Both camping areas have tables and fire pits, as well as vault toilets and hosts. No potable water is provided. From Exit 119 of Hwy 1 near Chilliwack travel south on Vedder Road for 5.0 km (3.1 miles). Just before the bridge turn left onto Chilliwack Lake Road and follow it for another 9.4 km (5.8 miles) to the campground.

○ **SUNNY SIDE CAMPGROUND – CULTUS**
    LAKE PARK *(Open April 1 to Sept 30)*

Res and Info: (604) 858-5253,
                sunnyside@cultuslake.bc.ca
Location: 8 Km (5 Miles) S of Chilliwack

GPS Location: 49.06708 N, 121.96358 W, 200 Ft

600 Sites – This huge campground has a variety of sites including many sites that are leased for the entire season. Traveler's will find many back-in full hookup sites to 40 feet with parking on dirt. There are also many no hookup tent sites. The campground features a long beach on Cultus Lake and is near a variety of other amenities in this resort community including water slides and golf. There's also a boat ramp. From Exit 119 of Hwy 1 near Chilliwack travel south on Vedder road for 6.1 km (3.8 miles). Turn left on Cultus Lake Road and follow it for 2.1 km (1.3 miles) to the campground entrance.

☐ **CULTUS LAKE PROVINCIAL PARK**
    (Open April 1 to Oct 12 – Varies)

Reservations: www.discovercamping.ca, (800) 689-9025
Information: (604) 986-9371
Location: 13 Km (8 Miles) S of Chilliwack

    GPS Location: 49.05515 N, 121.97103 W, 200 Ft

281 Sites – Cultus Lake is a very popular destination for folks on the lower mainland. It's a fairly large shallow lake so it gets plenty warm enough for watersports. It's also very accessible. There are four provincial park campgrounds along the eastern and southeastern shore of the lake. In order, from north to south, they area Entrance Bay (47 sites), Clear Creek (85 sites), Delta Grove (52 sites), and Mable Bay (73 sites). Sites are set in fairly heavy forest and are smaller than sites in many provincial park campgrounds, a few will take carefully driven RVs to 40 feet. Amenities include sandy swimming beaches, boat ramps, and a dump station. From Exit 119 of Hwy 1 near Chilliwack travel south on Vedder road for 6.1 km (3.8 miles). Turn left on Cultus Lake Road and follow it for 6.5 km (4 miles) to the campground check-in kiosk.

○ **VEDDER RIVER CAMPGROUND – CULTUS**
    LAKE PARK *(Open May 1 to Oct 31)*

Res and Info: (604) 823-6012
Location: 10 Km (6 Miles) S of Chilliwack

GPS Location: 49.09658 N, 122.00679 W, 100 Ft

195 Sites – While the Vedder River Campground is
managed as part of Cultus Lake Park is it is actually not near the lake. Instead, it is about 3 km (2 miles) northwest of the lake along the Vedder River. The Vedder is the same river as the Chilliwack River, but the name changes west of the bridge that crosses it 3 km (2 miles) east of the campground. The campground has tent sites with grass surfaces as well as back-in and pull-thru RV sites to 100 feet. From Exit 119 of Hwy 1 near Chilliwack travel south on Vedder Road for 8.9 km (5.5 miles). Turn right on Gleisbrecht Road and follow it north for .8 km (.5 mile) to the entrance kiosk.

COWICHAN VALLEY: CHEMAINUS, DUNCAN, AND COWICHAN LAKE

Chemainus (population 4,100) has become famous for the **murals** painted on the small town's buildings. It seems like everyone stops to take a look around, you might as well

too. You'll see the sign taking you east to Chemainus from the highway about 29 kilometers (18 miles) south of Nanaimo. There is quite a bit of parking, even for RVs. Footprints painted on the ground lead you from one mural to the next, and many shops have sprung up to sell you food and souvenirs.

Nearby Duncan (population 5,000) has totem poles, not murals. There are about 80 of them. Duncan also is home to the **Quw'utsun Cultural and Conference Center**. There you'll find a gift shop featuring Cowichan sweaters, a restaurant, and varied cultural attractions related to the Cowichan Fist Nation people. Duncan is also home to the **BC Forest Museum Discovery Centre**. The museum has 100 acres of logging displays and a narrow-gauge railway. It is located off Highway 1 just north of Duncan.

Duncan is situated right next to the **Cowichan River** which runs from Cowichan Lake to tidewater. This is an excellent fishing river, much of it open only to fly fishing. It has steelhead, brown trout and rainbow trout. There is a paved highway (Highway 18) to **Cowichan Lake** leading west from a point north of Duncan on Highway 1. Twenty-six kilometers (16 miles) up this road you will reach the small community of Lake Cowichan. From here web of paved and unpaved logging roads can take you to Bamfield, Port Renfrew, Carmanah Walbran Provincial Park and Nitinat Lake. Exercise caution when driving on them as some continue to be active logging roads. The paved route to Port Renfrew is described in the section in this chapter titled *Port Renfrew Loop.*

Cowichan Lake is one of the largest on Vancouver Island. The southern shore is unusual in that it has much warmer weather than the surrounding region, it has an average maxi-

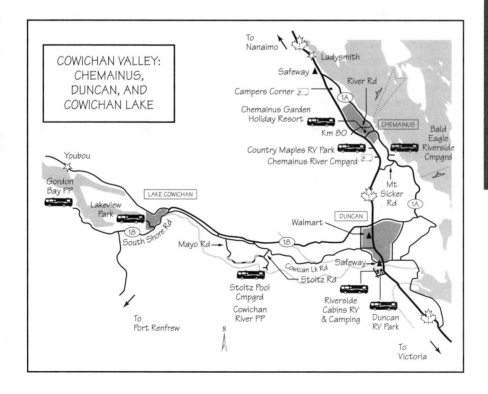

mum temperature of about 75 degrees Fahrenheit. Gordon Bay Provincial Park, the last campground described below, is a large campground perfectly positioned to take advantage of this fact.

Chemainus, Duncan, and Cowichan Lake Campgrounds

● **CHEMAINUS GARDEN HOLIDAY RESORT**
     (Open All Year)
     Res and Info: (250) 246-3569,
                   www.chemainusrvpark.ca
     Location: Chemainus

     GPS Location: 48.91750 N, 123.72722 W, 200 Ft

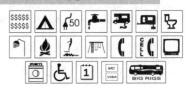

125 Sites – This is a very unusual campground. Campsites are set in extensive formal gardens complete with ponds full of Koi. New owners are proceeding with upgrade plans to turn the park into a community with both park models and RV sites to 80 feet. Additions also include a clubhouse and pool. Even better, this campground is within walking distance of Chemainus, you can walk to the center of town in about 10 minutes. From Chemainus drive south on Hwy 1A. Just outside town turn right on River Road. The campground entrance will be on your left in 1 km (.6 mile). From Hwy 1 you can take the River Road Exit for Chemainus, the campground will be on your right in 1.3 km (.8 miles).

● **BALD EAGLE RIVERSIDE CAMPGROUND**
     (Open All Year)
     Res and Info: (250) 246-9457, becamp@cow~net.com
     Location: 6 Km (4 Miles) S of Chemainus

     GPS Location: 48.88806 N, 123.68778 W, 100 Ft

60 Sites – Another campground convenient to Chemainus, this one is next to the Chemainus River and offers swimming in the river. Back-in sites at the center of the campground will take RVs to 45 feet. Easiest access is from Chemainus. Just drive south on the Chemainus Road, Hwy 1A, for 6 kilometers (4 miles). The campground is on the left.

● **COUNTRY MAPLES RV RESORT**
     (Open All Year)
     Res and Info: (250) 246-2078,
                   www.holidaytrailsresorts.com
     Location: Off Hwy 1, about 13 Km (8
                   Miles) North of Duncan

         GPS Location: 48.89611 N, 123.71587 W, 200 Ft

160 Sites – This is a membership park, but non-members are welcomed. It's a large nice park with sites in trees and in the open. Sites are back-ins and pull-thrus to 55 feet. Amenities include a swimming pool, swimming in the nearby river, a clubhouse, mini-golf, and an arcade. The entrance is on the west side of Hwy 1 near Km 76. This is 10 km (6 miles) north of the intersection with Hwy 19 to Lake Cowichan.

● **DUNCAN RV PARK** *(Open All Year)*
     Res and Info: (250) 748-8511
     Location: Duncan

     GPS Location: 48.77056 N, 123.70111 W, 200 Ft

85 sites – This older commercial campground is conveniently located within walking distance of downtown Duncan. For travelers there are pull-thru sites that will take RVs to 40 feet, also a lot of no-hookup tent sites near the river. Many sites here are filled with month-to-month residential rigs. Heading south from Duncan on Hwy 1 cross the bridge and take the first right onto Boys Road. Take another right in one block and the campground will be straight ahead.

● **RIVERSIDE CABINS RV AND CAMPING** *(Open All Year)*
   Information: (250) 746-4352
   Location: Duncan

   GPS Location: 48.76860 N, 123.70691 W, 200 Ft

80 Sites – This is another older commercial campground not far from the Duncan RV Park. Sites here are off gravel access roads with parking on gravel or grass. There are back-in sites to about 40 feet. Many of the sites here are filled with month to month residents. There is quite a bit of space for tent or no-hookup rig camping on grass. Water is from faucets. Heading south from Duncan on Hwy 1 cross the bridge and take the first right onto Boys Road. Continue .6 km (.4 mile) to the T at Allenby Road. Turn right and the campground is on the right.

☐ **STOLTZ POOL PROVINCIAL PARK CAMPGROUND – COWICHAN RIVER PROVINCIAL PARK** *(Open All Year)*

   Reservations: www.discovercamping.ca, (800) 689-9025
   Information: (250) 474-1336
   Location: 20 Km (12 Miles) W of Duncan

   GPS Location: 48.77306 N, 123.88861 W, 400 Ft

43 Sites – Cowichan River Provincial Park is located on the Cowichan River between Duncan and Cowichan Lake. From the campground there is access to hiking trails along the river, not to mention the river itself which is popular for fishing and for swimming and tubing in the summer. The campground is fairly new with back-in sites to 45 feet. There are also four walk-in tent sites. Water is from a hand pump. Access is from Hwy 18. Watch for the sign for the campground 15 kilometers (9.5 miles) from the Hwy 18 intersection with Hwy 1. Then drive another 5.0 km (3.1 miles) south to the campground entrance.

○ **LAKEVIEW PARK** *(Open All Year)*
   Res and Info: (250) 749-3350,
      www.town.lakecowichan.bc.ca/
      camping.shtml
   Location: 31 Km (19 Miles) W of Duncan

   GPS Location: 48.81893 N, 124.07604 W, 600 Ft

50 Sites – This nice municipal campground is on the south shore of Cowichan Lake not far from the town of Lake Cowichan at the east end of the lake. Sites here are gravel back-ins to 50 feet, some with power and water and the others with no hookups. There is a swimming beach and a boat launch. Follow Hwy 18 west from a point just north of Duncan. Drive 26 kilometers (16 miles) to the town of Lake Cowichan then another 1.4 kilometers (2.3 miles) on south shore road.

BRITISH COLUMBIA

□ **GORDON BAY PROVINCIAL PARK** *(Open All Year)*
Reservations: www.discovercamping.ca, (800) 689-9025
Information: (250) 474-1336
Location: 40 Km (25 Miles) W of Duncan

GPS Location: 48.83500 N, 124.19639 W, 600 Ft

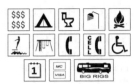

126 Sites – This large lakeside provincial campground is on
the warm south side of Cowichan Lake and features a swimming beach and boat launch.
The campground is open with full services from March 15 to October 31 and there is a
gatehouse. During the rest of the year self-contained RVs can overnight in the boat launch
area for a reduced fee. Sites are situated in a dense evergreen forest and are long gravel
back-ins, some exceeding 60 feet. To reach the park take Hwy 18 west from a point just
north of Duncan, drive 26 km (16 miles) to the town of Lake Cowichan, then another 14
km (9 miles) on South Shore Road.

DAWSON CREEK

Dawson Creek (population 13,000) is the kick-off point for a drive to Alaska up the
Alaska Highway. Don't confuse this town with Dawson City, the gold rush town located
on the Yukon River north of Whitehorse. Don't be deceived by the small population fig-
ure above, Dawson Creek really serves as an important services town in the agricultural
Peace River Block with a population of over 50,000 people.

The **Dawson Creek Visitor Information Centre** has brochures and pamphlets covering
sights and campgrounds north along the highway. It is located near the intersection of
Highway 49 and Highway 2 near the center of town. They can also give you information about road conditions farther north. It is in a complex called the **NAR (Northern
Alberta Railway) Park** which also houses the **Dawson Creek Station Museum** which
concentrates on the agricultural history of the area and the Alaska Highway. They have
an excellent film of the building of the Alcan, a good introduction. In the same complex
is the Dawson Creek Art Gallery. In the parking lot is the Mile Zero Cairn, claimed to be
the true Mile 0 of the Alaska Highway. There's also a second Mile 0 Marker in town, it's
a short two-block stroll away.

Another Dawson Creek attraction is the **Walter Wright Pioneer Village** at the Rotary
Park, there are historic buildings from before the highway was constructed. The park
is located near the intersection of the Hart (highway from Prince George) and Alaska
Highways.

Dawson Creek hosts the Fall Fair Exhibition and Pro Rodeo about the middle of August.

All of the campgrounds described below are located near the junction of Hwy 97 from
Prince George and the Alaska Highway at the northern edge of Dawson Creek. You'll
find them full of Alaska-bound travelers.

Dawson Creek Campgrounds

○ **MILE "0" RV CAMPSITE** *(Open May 1 to Sept 30)*
Information: (250) 782-2590, mile0campground@aol.com,
        www.citydirect.ca/mile0
Location: 2 Km (1 Mile) N of Dawson Creek

GPS Location: 55.77000 N, 120.26083 W, 2,200 Ft

100 Sites – This municipal campground is the nicest of

the Dawson Creek campgrounds with widely spaced sites separated by grass. There are back-ins and pull-thrus to 80 feet as well as tent sites. A picnic shelter makes things more comfortable for tenters, and there is an outdoor swimming pool (really a shallow cement pond called Rotary Lake) nearby as well as the Walter Wright Pioneer Village outdoor museum. From the intersection of Hwy 97 from Prince George and the Alaska Highway just north of Dawson Creek travel north for just a short distance, the campground is on the left.

● **NORTHERN LIGHTS RV PARK**
   (Open All Year)
   Res and Info: (250) 782-9433, (250) 219-0315 (Cell),
                  Nlrv2010@gmail.com, www.nlrv.com
   Location: 3 Km (2 Miles) W of Dawson Creek

   GPS Location: 55.76639 N, 120.29083 W, 2,200 Ft

80 Sites – The Northern Lights is located west of town. It overlooks Dawson Creek from a low hill. There are tent sites as well as back-ins and pull-thrus to 50 feet. From the intersection of Hwy 97 from Prince George and the Alaska Highway just north of Dawson Creek travel west on Hwy 97 for 2.4 km (1.5 mile) to the campground.

● **TUBBY'S RV PARK** *(Open All Year)*
   Res and Info: (250) 782-2584 , www.tubbysrvpark.com
   Location: Dawson Creek

   GPS Location: 55.76667 N, 120.26028 W, 2,200 Ft

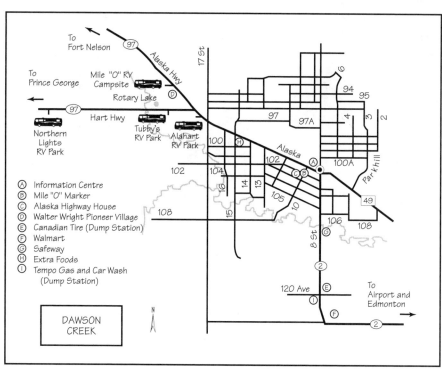

DAWSON CREEK

Ⓐ Information Centre
Ⓑ Mile "0" Marker
Ⓒ Alaska Highway House
Ⓓ Walter Wright Pioneer Village
Ⓔ Canadian Tire (Dump Station)
Ⓕ Walmart
Ⓖ Safeway
Ⓗ Extra Foods
Ⓘ Tempo Gas and Car Wash
   (Dump Station)

90 Sites – Tubby's RV Park has large pull-thrus to about 45 feet, some with full hookups. The campground has newly renovated restrooms and laundry. There is a large 3-bay RV wash out front. From the intersection of Hwy 97 from Prince George and the Alaska Highway just north of Dawson Creek travel west on Hwy 97 for .5 km (.3 mile) to the campground.

● **ALAHART RV PARK** *(Open All Year)*
   Res and Info: (250) 782-4702, alahart@pris.ca
   Location: Dawson Creek

   GPS Location: 55.76583 N, 120.25250 W, 2,200 Ft

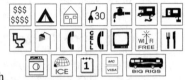

45 Sites – The Alahart is a motel and RV park with a restaurant out front along the highway. There are back-in and pull-thru sites to about 40 feet. The campground has many long-term residents. From the intersection of Hwy 97 from Prince George and the Alaska Highway just north of Dawson Creek travel south toward the city for just a short distance to the campground, it's on the right.

FERNIE

Fernie (population 5,000) is the center of commerce in the Elk River Valley. This valley extends to the north and Crowsnest Pass, the pass used by both Hwy 3 and the old Canadian Pacific Railroad to cross the Rockies. Part of Fernie's charm is its brick buildings, required by law after the town burned down in 1908. A favorite is the Fernie Courthouse. There is a free booklet available at the info centre that outlines a downtown walking tour

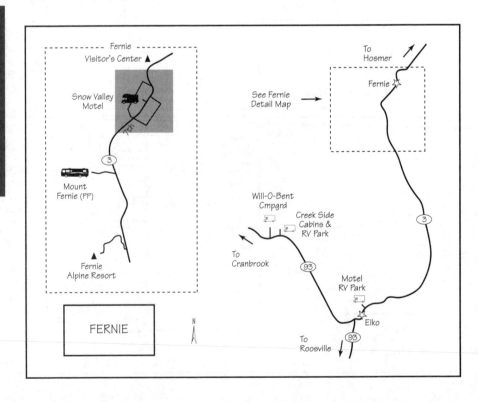

and points out the most interesting buildings. Fernie is a ski town, the **Fernie Alpine Resort** is a few miles south of town. In summer it's open for mountain bikes.

Fernie Campgrounds

● **SNOW VALLEY MOTEL** *(Open May 1 to Oct 31)*
 Res and Info: (250) 423-4421, (877) 696-7669,
   info@fernieaccomodations.com,
   www.snowvalleymotel.com
 Location: Fernie

GPS Location: 49.50972 N, 115.06306 W, 3,300 Ft

10 Sites – In winter this motel rents most sites on a seasonal basis (daily/weekly/monthly sites are sometimes available) but in the summer it caters to travelers and it's the closest campground to the center of town. Amenities include an indoors hot tub. Sites are small and reservations are taken for RVs to only 32 feet. Larger rigs are sometimes OK on a walk-in basis if the parking situation allows. Only two of the ten sites have sewer connections, the rest have electricity and water only. The hotel is located on the north side of the Crowsnest Hwy 3 (7th Ave.) as it passes through town between 10th and 11th Streets.

☐ **MOUNT FERNIE PROVINCIAL PARK**
   (Open June 1 to Sept 30 – Varies)
 Reservations: www.discovercamping.ca, (800) 689-9025
 Information: (250) 422-3003
 Location: 3 Km (2 Miles) S of Fernie

GPS Location: 49.48694 N, 115.09056 W, 3,400 Ft

43 Sites – This handy campground is located just south of town. The campground is situated on flat ground and sites are good size with several that will take RVs to 45 feet. The top loop may be useable outside the open dates depending upon weather, there is no fee for use outside the open dates. From Fernie drive south about 2.4 km (1.5 miles) and turn west on an .8 km (.5 mile) access road to the campground.

FORT ST JAMES

The **Fort St James National Historic Site** is located on the shore of Stuart Lake in the small town of Fort St James (population 2,000). This is the oldest established town in

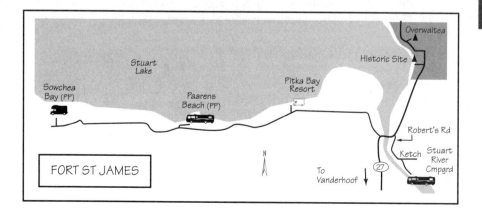

British Columbia. Highway 27, a 55 km (34 mile) paved road, leads up to Fort St James from Hwy 16 about 97 km (60 miles) west of Prince George.

The historic site is a former fur trading post. It was founded by Simon Fraser in 1806. These aren't the original buildings but some do date from the 1880s and they certainly do give a feeling of what life was like in a post like this. There are interpreters dressed in period costume on hand to tell you what it was like in the early days.

There are three campgrounds that are good bases for visits to the site. Two are lakeside provincial parks and the third is a commercial campground with hookups.

Fort St James Campgrounds

☐ **PAARENS BEACH PROVINCIAL PARK**
   (Open May 15 to Oct 30 – Varies)
   Reservations: www.discovercamping.ca, (800) 689-9025
   Information: (250) 964-3489
   Location: 8 Km (5 Miles) W of Ft St James

   GPS Location: 54.41889 N, 124.37861 W, 2,200 Ft

36 Sites – This park occupies a site on the south shore of Stuart Lake. These are back-in sites on a loop and an out and back stub road with sites near but not on the lake. Sites are fairly large and some will take RVs to 40 feet. They have picnic tables and fire pits. There's a beach and boat ramp. The road to the campground leaves Hwy 27 west of the bridge across the Stuart River just south of Fort St James. Follow the road west for 7.1 km (4.4 miles) to the campground.

☐ **SOWCHEA BAY PROVINCIAL PARK** *(Open May 15 to Sept 13 – Varies)*
   Reservations: www.discovercamping.ca, (800) 689-9025
   Information: (250) 964-3489
   Location: 11 Km, (7 Miles) W of Ft St James

   GPS Location: 54.41944 N, 124.44778 W, 2,200 Ft

30 Sites – Sowchea Bay is another provincial park located on the south shore of Stewart Lake. Unlike Paarens, many of this park's poorly defined sites are on the beach. They're arranged off two out and back stub roads. Limited site size and maneuvering room make this a campground for smaller RVs, up to about 30 feet. There's a hand water pump, vault toilets, picnic tables, fire pits, and a boat ramp. The road to the campground leaves Hwy 27 west of the bridge across the Stuart River just south of Fort St James. Follow the road west for 11.6 km (7.2 miles) to the campground. En route you'll pass Paarens Beach Provincial Park.

● **STUART RIVER CAMPGROUND**
   (Open May 15 to Oct 10 – Varies)
   Res and Info: (250) 996-8690
   Location: 3 Km (2 Miles) S of Ft St James

GPS Location: 54.40472 N, 124.25639 W, 2,200 Ft

35 Sites – This is a pleasant little privately owned campground situated on the Stuart River. It has docks and a launching ramp and serves as a small marina. Some sites here are along the river and others back from it. There are full, partial, and dry sites and with some maneuvering it is possible for 40 footers to use the campground. The access road to this campground leaves the highway north of the bridge across the Stuart River which

is south of Fort St James. It's called Robert's Road, follow it 1.8 km (1.1 mile) to the campground.

GLACIER NATIONAL PARK

Between Revelstoke and Golden the Trans-Canada Highway crosses 1,330 meter (4,365 foot) Rogers Pass. The pass is surrounded by Glacier National Park. Since the Trans-Canada is the main east-west highway in Canada there is no charge for driving through the park – as long as you don't stop. Fee collection stations are located at the park boundaries to the west and east of the park.

This region receives a great deal of precipitation, almost every day it either rains or snows. That means that a great deal of snow accumulates in the winter. Campgrounds here open late and backcountry travel permits are required because of the avalanche danger. When the weather is clear, though, this is a beautiful place.

Right at the top of the pass is the **Rogers Pass Centre** where you can stop to see films and exhibits about the park. You can also get information about the park's hiking trails. There's a motel next door with a coffee shop.

Two of the campgrounds listed below are national park campgrounds located inside the park. As in most Canadian national parks you have to pay a park entrance fee to stay in them, in addition to the campground fee. Here it's $7 Canadian per person or $18 per family.

Glacier National Park Campgrounds

● **CANYON HOT SPRINGS**
   (Open May 15 to Sept 25 – Varies)
   Res and Info: (250) 837-2420,
          www.canyonhotsprings.com
   Location: 35 Km (22 Miles) W of Rogers Pass
          Visitor Center

   GPS Location: 51.13833 N, 117.85722 W, 2,300 Ft

200 Sites – If you want to visit Glacier National Park but don't want to give up your hookups, this is the place. In addition to the hookups the campground has two hot spring swimming pools. There are good tent sites in trees and also back-in and pull-thru RV sites

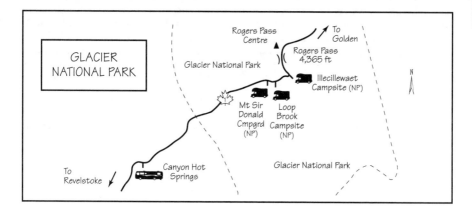

to 55 feet with electric and water hookups. The campground is on the south side of Hwy 1 midway between Revelstoke and the Rogers Pass Visitor Center in the park, it's 35 km (22 miles) from each.

■ **MT SIR DONALD CAMPSITE – GLACIER NATIONAL PARK**
   (Open July 1 to August 30 – Varies)
   Information: (250) 837-7500
   Location: 8 Km (5 Miles) W of Rogers Pass Visitor Center

   GPS Location: 51.26200 N, 117.55064 W, 3,500 Ft

15 Sites – This is a small national park campground located about 2 km west of Loop Brook Campsite. It has 15 back-in sites. Most are very small but a few are as long as 30 feet. There are picnic tables and vault toilets but no fire pits and no campfires allowed. The campground is on the south side of the highway some 8 km (5 miles) west of the Rogers Pass Visitor Center. There's a long paved pull-off just to the west of the campground entrance.

■ **LOOP BROOK CAMPSITE – GLACIER NATIONAL PARK**
   (Open July 1 to Sept 6 – Varies)
   Information: (250) 837-7500
   Location: 6 Km (4 Miles) W of Rogers Pass Visitor Center

   GPS Location: 51.25861 N, 117.53972 W, 3,700 Ft

20 Sites – This is a small national park campground with back-in sites suitable for RVs to about 25 feet. It's excellent for tent campers since it has a shelter cabin with a woodstove and restrooms with flush toilets and even a dish-washing sink with hot water. There's an interesting railroad history-related trail from the campground. Normally in the Spring the nearby Illecillewaet campsite opens a week or so earlier than this one. The campground is just a short distance off the highway on the south side some 6 km (4 miles) west of the Rogers Pass Visitor Center.

■ **ILLECILLEWAET CAMPSITE – GLACIER NATIONAL PARK**
   (Open June 24 to Oct 10 – Varies)
   Information: (250) 837-7500
   Location: 3 Km (2 Miles) W of Rogers Pass Visitor Center

   GPS Location: 51.27083 N, 117.50278 W, 4,024 Ft

60 Sites – This is the main Glacier National Park Campground. It wasn't designed for today's big rigs, maneuvering room and short sites limit use to RVs to about 30 feet. Some sites are along the river. The campground is located on the south side of the highway about 3 km (2 miles) west of the Rogers Pass Visitor Center.

HARRISON HOT SPRINGS

Harrison Hot Springs (Population 1,600) makes a great camping destination just 100 km (60 miles) east of Vancouver. The resort town sits at the south shore of Harrison Lake. This 40-mile long lake is very shallow out as far as Echo Island which you can see just offshore, but then the bottom drops to depths of up to 900 feet. Today it's a popular boating destination but in early days it was a steamboat route to the Cariboo gold fields.

Harrison's **beach** is one of its best features. It's wide and sandy. There's a swimming lagoon, lawns, even a boat launch. Actually, though, this is not a natural beach, a great deal of money has been spent to make it so nice. If you would like water a little warmer than that in the lake or the lagoon, you might try the **Public Pool** near the beach. A hot springs rises just west of town and water is piped to the pool. During the trip the water is cooled to a perfect soaking temperature of 38° C (100° F).

Like any resort town Harrison tries its best to keep you occupied. There are restaurants and shops, even a 9-hole golf course. There are also many trails near the town. Another way to attract visitors is annual festivals and events and Harrison has its share. Probably the best known is the **World Championship of Sand Sculpture** held on the beach during early September. Harrison is also a great place to see bald eagles, they congregate on the Harrison River south of town and can most easily be seen from the Morris Valley Road on the west side of the river north of its confluence with the Fraser at Harrison Mills. There's even a bald eagle festival at Harrison Mills at the end of November.

Harrison Hot Springs Campgrounds

● **GLENCOE MOTEL AND RV PARK** *(Open All Year)*
  Res and Info: (604) 796-2574
          www.glencoemotel.com
  Location: Harrison Hot Springs

  GPS Location: 49.30139 N, 121.78472 W, 100 Ft

27 Sites – This campground is located right in central Harrison Hot Springs, very near the pool and the beach. It is on the grounds of a small motel. There is tent camping on grass and a sink for tenters to do their dishes. RV sites

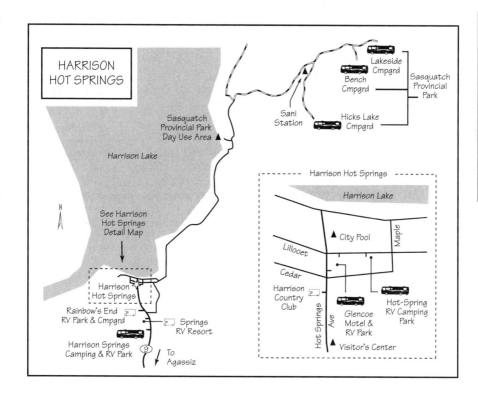

HARRISON HOT SPRINGS

Sasquatch Provincial Park Day Use Area ▲

Harrison Lake

N

See Harrison Hot Springs Detail Map

Harrison Hot Springs

Rainbow's End RV Park & Cmpgrd

Harrison Springs Camping & RV Park

Springs RV Resort

To Agassiz

Sani Station

Bench Cmpgrd

Lakeside Cmpgrd

Hicks Lake Cmpgrd

Sasquatch Provincial Park

Harrison Hot Springs

Harrison Lake

City Pool ▲

Lillooet

Cedar

Harrison Country Club

Maple

Glencoe Motel & RV Park

Hot Springs Ave

Hot-Spring RV Camping Park

Visitor's Center ▲

BRITISH COLUMBIA

are on grass or are paved, most will take RVs to about 35 feet although there are 3 long pull-thrus that will take 45-footers with careful maneuvering. Watch for the Glencoe on the east side of Hot Springs Avenue as you drive into the central area of Harrison Hot Springs. It's about two blocks from the lake.

● **HOT-SPRING RV CAMPING PARK** *(Open All Year)*
    Res and Info: (604) 796-3467, (866) 345-2225
    Location: Harrison Hot Springs

   GPS Location: 49.30222 N, 121.78361 W, 100 Ft

21 Sites – The Hot-Spring RV Camping Park is a small RV park right in central Harrison Hot Springs and across the street from the public swimming pool. Sites here are not huge but some will take 40-footers with slide-outs. The campground is located on the south side of Lillooet Ave. just east of Hot Springs Ave. Lillooet is the street that parallels the lake shore but one block back from the beach.

● **HARRISON SPRINGS CAMPING AND RV PARK**
    (Open April 1 to Oct 12)
    Res and Info: (604) 796-8900, www. harrisonsprings.com
    Location: 1 Mile (1.6 Km) S of Central Harrison Hot
                      Springs

   GPS Location: 49.28975 N, 121.78027 W, 100 Ft

65 Sites – This is a large campground just outside town. Sites are set in trees and narrow access roads require caution for big rigs. There are tent sites and many full-hookup back-ins to about 40 feet. Coming in to Harrison Hot Springs watch for the Harrison Hot Springs welcome sign on the right. The campground entrance is on the left in a short .2 mile (.3 km).

☐ **HICKS LAKE CAMPGROUND – SASQUATCH PROVINCIAL PARK**
    (Open March 14 to Oct 16 – Varies)
    Reservations: www.discovercamping.ca, (800) 689-9025
    Information: (604) 446-8325
    Location: 10 Km (6 Miles) NE of Harrison Hot Springs

   GPS Location: 49.34611 N, 121.71028 W, 800 Ft

71 Sites – This is one of those campgrounds located east of Harrison Hot Springs in Sasquatch Provincial Park. It's the nearest to town. Sites here are all back-ins off a large loop. A few sites reach 40 feet but most are shorter. A few are on the shore of Hicks Lake. There are no hookups but there is a dump station on the entrance road to the park which serves campers in all three campgrounds in the park. There is a boat ramp near the campground, Hicks lake has a 10 horsepower restriction. In Harrison Hot Springs drive east on Lillooet Ave. It soon turns north and follows the shore of Harrison Lake for 5 km (3.1 miles) to a Y. Turn right and in another 1.1 km (.7 miles) you'll come to another Y. Turn right and the road becomes gravel, you'll see a sani-station 2.9 km (1.8 miles) from the Y and in another .3 km (.2 mile) the campground entrance is on the right.

☐ **BENCH CAMPGROUND – SASQUATCH PROVINCIAL PARK**
    (Open May 16 to Oct 16 – Varies)
    Reservations: www.discovercamping.ca, (800) 689-9025
    Information: (604) 446-8325
    Location: 11 Km (7 Miles) NE of Harrison Hot Springs

   GPS Location: 49.36583 N, 121.69139 W, 800 Ft

64 Sites – This campground is near but not on Deer Lake, the Lakeside Campground is nearby. Sites here are all back-ins but tend to be larger than in Hicks Lake Campground with many 50-foot sites. Follow the directions for reaching Hicks Lake Campground above, then continue on another 1.3 km (.8 miles) to the entrance for the campground which will be on your right.

☐ **LAKESIDE CAMPGROUND – SASQUATCH PROVINCIAL PARK**
  (Open All Year)

Reservations: www.discovercamping.ca, (800) 689-9025
Information: (604) 446-8325
Location: 11 Km (7 Miles) E of Harrison Hot Springs

GPS Location: 49.36778 N, 121.68417 W, 700 Ft

42 Sites – Lakeside Campground is on the shore of Deer Lake. There is a boat launch, only electric motors are allowed on the lake. Sites here are back-ins and reach 45 feet but many have a good slope making RV parking difficult. The campground has full services only from March 21 to October 13, outside that time period camping is free but no services are available. To reach the campground follow the directions to Bench Campground above and then continue straight when you reach the Bench Campground entrance road.

HOPE

Hope (population 6,200) is probably best known as the setting for the filming of the cult movie classic ***First Blood***, the first of the Rambo movies. The peaceful little town couldn't be more unlike the one shown in the movie, but you can still see some evocative scenery that may remind you of the movie. If you visit the info centre they can tell you where to see locations that are shown in the movie, they can give you a pamphlet that details the locations of Rambo sites. Probably the best-known are various locations near the five **Othello Tunnels** in the Coquihalla Canyon Provincial Park to the east of town. There's a hiking trail through the tunnels.

Another attraction here are the two-dozen or so **chainsaw sculptures** scattered around town. They were created by local artist Pet Ryan and have turned Hope into the Chainsaw Carving Capital of British Columbia.

If you travel east of Hope you're beyond Hope. Get it? You'll probably hear this old joke several time when you visit but you might take it a little more seriously if you visit the **Hope Slide Viewpoint** located 16 km (10 miles) east of Hope on Hwy 3. You'll see that the entire face of the mountain to the north has slid into the valley. This happened fairly recently, on January 9, 1965. Four people were killed by the slide.

The highways near Hope can be a little confusing. The Trans-Canada Highway (Hwy 1) becomes Hwy 3 right at Hope and then east of town the main route goes north as Hwy 5 (the Coquihalla Highway) while Hwy 3 continues east. When traveling eastward to stay on Hwy 1 you actually have to exit the freeway at Exit 170 and drive north through Hope and up the Fraser River Valley. Through the Fraser River Valley Hwy 1 is a winding two-lane highway. Most modern eastbound through traffic follows the Coquihalla Highway (a toll road) and rejoins Hwy 1 in Kamloops.

BRITISH COLUMBIA

Hope Campgrounds

● **TELTE YET CAMPSITE** *(Open May 15 to Oct 15 – Varies)*
Res and Info: (604) 869-9994, chawath@uniserve.com
Location: Hope

     GPS Location: 49.38167 N, 121.44750 W, 100 Ft

30 Sites – This campground is located right in Hope on the
bank of the Fraser River. It's the most convenient place to stay
if you want to explore the town on foot. The campground is operated by the Chawathil
First Nation band, the campground name means "Up-River People" Campsite. Sites here
vary in size and configuration and most are large enough only for RVs to 35 feet but there
are two very long 60-foot pull-thrus. The restrooms are old but better than they look from
the outside. The entrance to the campground is off Water Avenue, the road that runs along
the river on the west side of the central area of the town. Easiest access is from Exit 170
where Hwy 1 exits the freeway when it becomes Hwy 3.

● **COQUIHALLA CAMPSITE**
     (Open All Year)
    Res and Info: (604) 869-7119, (888) 869-7118,
                hopecamp@telus.net
    Location: 1 Km (.5 Mile) E of Central Hope

     GPS Location: 49.38000 N, 121.42639 W, 300 Ft

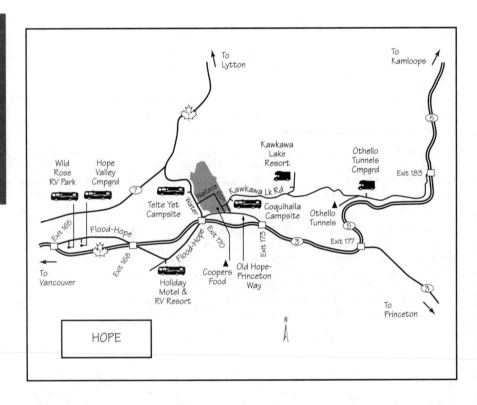

122 Sites – This campground is set in thick trees on the east side of Hope. Sites vary in configuration but some will take RVs to 45 feet. The largest part of the campground is non-hookup sites but there are some with electricity and water and ten long back-in sites with full hookups including TV. The campground is located along the Coquihalla River and some sites are next to a dike and walking trail along the river. To reach the campground take Exit 170 from Hwy 3. Follow old Hope-Princeton Way eastward along the north side of the highway for 1 km (.6 mile). Turn left on Seventh Avenue and in .2 km (.1 mile) turn right on Kawkawa Lake Road. You'll see the campground on the right in another .3 km (.2 mile).

● **KAWKAWA LAKE RESORT** *(Open April 1 to Sept 30)*
   Res and Info: (604) 869-9930, www.kawkawalake.net
   Location: 5 Km (3 Miles) E of Hope

   GPS Location: 49.38389 N, 121.39306 W, 300 Ft

63 Sites – Little Kawkawa Lake is located east of Hope. This campground is a fishing and family holiday resort with a boat ramp and swimming beach. Some of the sites will take RVs to 35 feet although most are smaller. To reach the campground follow the instructions given for the Coquihalla Campsite above. Continue east past the entrance to the Coquihalla Campsite, cross the river, and in another 2.3 km (1.4 miles) take the left at the Y and drive north along the east shore of the lake for another .5 km (.3 mile) to the campground.

● **OTHELLO TUNNELS CAMPGROUND**
   (Open All Year)
   Res and Info: (604) 869-9448, (877) 869-0543,
                    camp@othellotunnels.com,
                    www.othellotunnels.com
   Location: 6.5 Km (4 Miles) E of Hope

   GPS Location: 49.38083 N, 121.35361 W, 700 Ft

40 Sites – This park is just a 10 minute walk from the famous Othello-Quintette Tunnels walking trail. It's a great campground for tent campers and RVs to about 35 feet. The park has a rainy day shelter with a fireplace, a large barbecue for groups, a rainbow trout pond, a basketball hoop, and a game room. You can reach the campground by following the instructions given above for the Kawkawa Lake Resort and then taking the right fork of the Y at 2.3 km (1.4 miles) to continue another 3.4 km (2.1 miles) to the campground. Alternately, take Exit 183 from Hwy 5 (the Coquihalla Hwy) and travel south and west on the northwest side of the freeway for 3.2 km (2 miles) to the campground.

● **HOLIDAY MOTEL AND RV RESORT** *(Open All Year)*
   Res and Info: (604) 869-5352 info@holiday-motel.com,
                    www.holiday-motel.com
   Location: 1.9 Km (1.2 Miles) SW of Hope

   GPS Location: 49.35895 N, 121.46100 W, 300 Ft

18 Sites – This motel just outside Hope in Silver Creek has a small RV park in a gravel lot next to the motel. Some grass separates the sites. Most are back-ins, some will take RVs to 40 feet. From Hope drive southwest on the Flood Hope Road. Zero your odometer as you leave town and pass under the Crowsnest Hwy (Hwy 3) and in 1.2 mile (1.9 km) you'll spot the Motel/Campground sign on the left. The actual facility is a block back from the road.

● **HOPE VALLEY CAMPGROUND**
   (Open All Year)
   Res and Info: (604) 869-9857, (866) 869-6660
   Location: 5 Km (3 Miles) W of Hope

   GPS Location: 49.36639 N, 121.50694 W, 100 Ft

150 Sites – This former KOA is conveniently located west of Hope just off Hwy 1. Sites are set in
evergreens and range from tent sites to pull-thrus to about 55 feet. There is also a seasonal outdoor swimming pool. To reach the campground take Exit 165 from Hwy 1 and
travel eastward on the Flood-Hope road on the north side of the freeway for .7 mile to the
campground entrance.

● **WILD ROSE RV PARK** *(Open April 1 to Oct 31)*
   Reservations: (800) 463-7999, wildrose@uniserve.com
   Information: (604) 869-9842, (800) 463-7999,
   www.wildrosecamp.com
   Location: 6 Km (3.5 Miles) W of Hope

   GPS Location: 49.36583 N, 121.51361 W, 100 Ft

70 Sites – The Wild Rose is just down the highway from
the Hope Valley Campground. It's more open with fewer
trees and has tent sites as well as RV sites including pull-thrus to 60 feet. Parking is on
either gravel or grass. Take Exit 165 from Hwy 1 and travel eastward on the Flood-Hope
road for .5 km (.3) mile to the campground entrance.

JASPER NATIONAL PARK

Highway 16 crosses the Rockies through Yellowhead Pass. Jasper National Park encompasses most of this crossing of the Rockies. Right in the middle of the crossing you'll
find the town of **Jasper** (population 5,500) which serves as the service and administration
center of Jasper National Park just as Banff townsite does for Banff National Park. Many
of the attractions of the park are near the town, so are several very large campgrounds.

Jasper definitely reflects its roots as a division town on the Grand Trunk Pacific and Ca-
nadian Northern Railways. The town has a number of worthwhile sites to visit. The Park
Visitor Centre is near the center of town. There's also a museum, the **Jasper-Yellowhead
Museum**, with exhibits about the history of the park.

The Jasper area has its own mountain tram. The **Jasper Tramway** climbs the Whistlers
Mountain to a terminal at 2,285 meters (7,516 feet). From there you can climb a trail to
the summit at 2,464 meters (8,085 feet). Jasper also has its own old hotel, the **Jasper
Park Lodge**, located east of the townsite on Lac Beauvert and accessible off Maligne
Lake Road. The lodge also has an 18-hole golf course.

There are some interesting drives in the Jasper region. **Maligne Lake Road** leads eastward from the Jasper townsite area for 44 km (28 miles) to the very scenic **Maligne
Lake**. Along the way you can take a look at **Maligne Canyon** and **Medicine Lake**. At
Maligne Lake you can either rent your own canoe or take a commercial boat cruise on
this 22-kilometer-long mountain lake.

Another good drive is to follow Hwy 16 to the north as it follows the Athabasca River
on its descent to the eastern plains. Along the way the highway passes between two large

BRITISH COLUMBIA

lakes: Jasper and Talbot. Forty-four km (27 miles) from Jasper townsite is the junction with Miette Hot Spring Road. Turn right here, and in just 1.3 km (.8 miles) stop at the **Punchbowl Falls** pull-off and take the short walk to the overlook for the very scenic falls. If you continue along the road you will reach **Miette Hot Springs** some 17 km (10.5 miles) from the highway, Parks Canada operates a swimming pool complex here.

If you drive west you can follow Hwy 16 across **Yellowhead Pass** (1,131 meters, 3,711 feet), and into Mt Robson Provincial Park. **Mt Robson** is the highest mountain in the Canadian Rockies (3,954 meters, 12,972 feet). You can stop at the visitor center near the western border of the park some 62 km (39 miles) west of Yellowhead Pass. From the visitor center you have a spectacular view of the mountain. The reason it is so impressive is that the visitor center sits at an altitude of only about 850 meters (2,800 feet) and is only 11 kilometers from the mountain, you definitely get the full effect. Mt Robson Provincial Park is covered in the *Mt Robson and Valemount* section of this chapter.

Running north and south between Jasper National Park and Banff National Park is the 230 kilometer (143 mile) **Icefields Parkway**. It's one of the most scenic roads in North America and not to be missed. The north junction is right at Jasper townsite. Don't try to hurry along this highway. There is plenty of magnificent scenery and many places to stop, enjoy the view, and even take some hikes.

Like most Canadian national parks there is a day fee for the use of Banff and Jasper National Parks. It is possible to drive through Jasper on Hwy 16 without paying the fee, but not the Icefield Parkway. There are kiosks on both ends of the Parkway where the fee is collected.

As you travel south you'll soon come to the cutoff for **Highway 93A**. This loop road was formerly the main highway but has been bypassed by new construction. It's a little narrow and not in great condition so people driving large RVs probably won't like it. The old highway runs south along the western side of the valley parallel to today's road for about 25 kilometers and rejoins the Parkway near Athabasca Falls.

The old highway provides access to some interesting sights and locations. One is **Mt Edith Cavell Road**. This narrow road climbs 14.5 km (9 miles) to the foot of Mount Edith Cavell and the Angel Glacier. Trailers are not allowed on the road so if you have one you'll probably want to make this drive as a side trip from the Jasper area. Also worth a look is the **Athabasca Trail Exhibit** at the picnic area at the mouth of the Whirlpool River. The Athabasca Trail was another one of those cross-Rockies routes used by explorers and fur traders, it ascended the Athabasca River to this point from the east, then climbed the Whirlpool River through Athabasca Pass before descending to the Columbia River Valley.

Even if you don't take the Hwy 93A loop it's well worth the time to stop at **Athabasca Falls** at the southern end. The turn for Athabasca Falls from the Icefields Parkway is well marked, it is 31 km (19 miles) south of Jasper town site. The Athabasca River drops over a ledge and tumbles through a narrow canyon. Overlooks and a pedestrian bridge offer excellent views, a great place for pictures.

Sunwapta Pass (2,035 meters, 6,675 feet) marks the boundary between Jasper National Park and Banff National park. A few kilometers north of the pass is the huge **Columbia Icefield Centre**. This is an observatory with great views across the valley to the Athabasca Glacier and the Columbia Icefield. It also serves as the embarkation point for bus tours onto the glacier. Busses leave the Center and drive to edge of the glacier, there passengers change to special busses with huge tires called snocoaches to actually drive out onto the

BRITISH **COLUMBIA**

SPECIAL BUSSES CALLED SNOCOACHES TAKE YOU OUT ONTO THE COLUMBIA ICEFIELD

glacier. As an alternative you can drive to the foot of the glacier yourself and take a short hike for a close look. The Icefield Centre also houses a Parks Canada Visitor Centre.

For more about the Icefields Parkway south of the border of Jasper National Park see the section of this chapter titled *Banff National Park*, page 494.

Jasper National Park Campgrounds

■ **POCAHONTAS CAMPGROUND – JASPER NATIONAL PARK**
(Open May 5 to Canadian Thanksgiving – 2nd Monday in Oct)
Reservations: (877) 737-3783, www.pccamping.ca
Information: (780) 852-6176
Location: 40 Km (25 Miles) W of Jasper

GPS Location: 53.19722 N, 117.90917 W, 3,600 Ft

140 Sites – This large campground is located near the far east entrance to the park and away from the center of things. Many sites here are suitable for RVs up to 30 feet but a few will take 40-footers, the people at the entrance station know which ones they are. Two good hiking trails start here: Sulphur Skyline and Utopia Pass. The campground is located off Hwy 16 some 40 km (25 miles) east of Jasper and 8 km (5 miles) from the eastern entrance to the park.

■ **SNARING RIVER CAMPGROUND – JASPER NATIONAL PARK**
(Open May 20 to Sept 12 – Varies)
Information: (780) 852-6176
Location: 15 Km (9 Miles) E of Jasper

GPS Location: 53.01056 N, 118.08778 W, 3,300 Ft

66 Sites – This is another campground east of Jasper off Hwy 16. Sites are back-ins and some will take RVs to about 40 feet but access roads are narrow so the practical rig size limit here is about 35 feet. The entrance road is located 10 km (6 miles) east of Jasper and 39 km (24 miles) from the eastern entrance to the park. From the turnoff it's another 5 km (3 miles) on a paved road to the campground entrance.

■ **WHISTLER'S CAMPGROUND – JASPER NATIONAL PARK**
   (Open May 6 to Oct 12 – Varies)
   Reservations: (877) 737-3783, www.pccamping.ca
   Information: (780) 852-6176
   Location: 2 Km (1 Mile) S of Jasper

   GPS Location: 52.85083 N, 118.07639 W, 3,400 Ft

781 Sites – This is Jasper's largest campground. Sites are arranged off circular drives which are in turn located off a huge one-mile loop drive. Sites are well-separated, some will take 45-footers. Elk often graze in the park, particularly in the sites on the western border. The location is convenient with Jasper just a short drive away. From Jasper drive south on Hwy 93, the campground entrance is on the right in 2 km (1 mile).

■ **WAPATI CAMPGROUND – JASPER NATIONAL PARK**
   (Open All Year)
   Reservations: (877) 737-3783, www.pccamping.ca
   Information: (780) 852-6176
   Location: 3 Km (2 Miles) S of Jasper

   GPS Location: 52.85083 N, 118.07639 W, 3,500 Ft

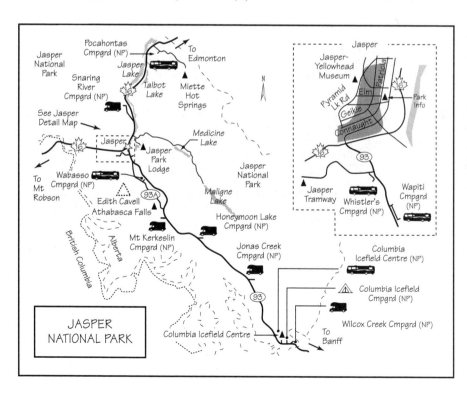

JASPER NATIONAL PARK

362 Sites – This is the second largest campground in the park and it too is near Jasper, just a short distance from the huge Whistler's Campground. Note the strange opening schedule, the campground serves as the winter campground for the park and also as a supplement to Whistler's Campground during busy times in the summer. Wapati puts its hookup rigs in a large paved lot that is also used as the winter campground. This lot will take RVs to 45 feet. From Jasper drive south on Hwy 93, the campground entrance is on the left in 3 km (2 miles).

■ **WABASSO CAMPGROUND – JASPER NATIONAL PARK**
    (Open June 23 to Sept 5 – Varies)
Reservations: (877) 737-3783, www.pccamping.ca
Information: (780) 852-6176
Location: 15 Km (9 Miles) S of Jasper

        GPS Location: 52.76333 N, 117.98806 W, 3,500 Ft

228 Sites – Wabasso is off a paved loop road called Hwy 93A that runs from 6 km (4 miles) south of Jasper on Hwy 93 to the cutoff on Hwy 93 near Athabascan Falls, 31 km (19 miles) south of Jasper. The campground has electrical hookups and no hookup sites to 30 feet as well as tent-only sites . The campground is 8.7 km (5.4) miles from the north end of the loop road, 15 km (9 miles) from the south end. The road is much better in the north, we recommend access from that direction.

■ **MT KERKESLIN CAMPGROUND – JASPER NATIONAL PARK**
    (Open June 23 to Sept 5 – Varies)
Information: (780) 852-6176
Location: 32 Km (20 Miles) S of Jasper

        GPS Location: 52.63444 N, 117.86639 W, 4,000 Ft

42 Sites – This is a smaller self-registration campground away from the Jasper area but convenient to Athabasca Falls. While some sites would take 40 foot RVs the access roads are narrow making the practical limit for this campground about 30 feet. It is 32 km (20 miles) south of Jasper and 65 km (40 miles) north of the Icefield Centre.

■ **HONEYMOON LAKE CAMPGROUND – JASPER NATIONAL PARK**
    (Open June 23 to Sept 5 – Varies)
Information: (780) 852-6176
Location: 52 Km (32 Miles) S of Jasper

        GPS Location: 52.55667 N, 117.68056 W, 4,600 Ft

35 Sites – This campground is next to Honeymoon Lake, several sites are along the lake-shore. Some sites will take RVs to 35 feet but most are smaller. It is 50 km (31 miles) south of Jasper and 47 km (29 miles) north of Icefield Centre.

■ **JONAS CREEK CAMPGROUND – JASPER NATIONAL PARK**
    (Open May 20 to Sept 5 – Varies)
Information: (780) 852-6176
Location: 76 Km (47 Miles) S of Jasper

        GPS Location: 52.41694 N, 117.39556 W, 5,200 Ft

25 Sites – Jonas Creek is another small campground just off the road. There are two long pull-thrus only suitable for RVs to about 35 feet due to limited maneuvering room. Other sites are good for RVs to about 30 feet. There are some nice walk-in tent sites on a small ridge a short distance above the campground but your car will be parked at the bottom of

the hill. There is also a cooking shelter at the bottom of the campground near the highway. Jonas Creek is located 76 km (47 miles) south of Jasper and 21 km (13 miles) north of Icefield Center.

■ **COLUMBIA ICEFIELD CENTRE – JASPER NATIONAL PARK**
   (April 1 to Oct 31)
   Information: (780) 852-6176
   Location: 97 Km (60 Miles) S of Jasper

   GPS Location: 52.22056 N, 117.22889 W, 6,500 Ft

At least 100 Sites – The Icefield Center has a large paved lot which can be used for camping. This is called an overflow camping area but it's kept open all of the time during the season and used for parking by RVs visiting the center. It's available even if the nearby campgrounds (a very limited number, particularly for big rigs) are open. It may seem like boondocking but it's not free and there are vault toilets next to the campground for evening use when the flush toilets at the center are not available. The Icefield Center is about 97 km (60 miles) south of Jasper and 129 km (80 miles) north of Lake Louise.

■ **COLUMBIA ICEFIELD CAMPGROUND – JASPER NATIONAL PARK**
   (Open May 20 to Oct 10 – Varies)
   Information: (780) 852-6176
   Location: 98 Km (61 Miles) S of Jasper

   GPS Location: 52.21972 N, 117.20417 W, 6,600 Ft

33 Sites – This is a campground for tents only. Amenities include cook shelters and a great view across the valley to the west. This campground is just 2 km (1 mile) south of the Icefield Centre.

■ **WILCOX CREEK CAMPGROUND – JASPER NATIONAL PARK**
   (Open May 19 to Oct 31 – Varies)
   Information: (780) 852-6176
   Location: 100 Km (62 Miles) S of Jasper

   GPS Location: 52.21778 N, 117.17972 W, 6,700 Ft

46 Sites – Wilcox Creek is set on the side of a mountain. There isn't enough room for back-in sites so everyone gets a pull-thru. Actually you park parallel next to your picnic table and fire pit and there are trees between sites. It's a nice arrangement and allows RVs to 35 feet to use what would otherwise be a cramped campground. Wilcox Creek is located 3 km (2 miles) south of Icefield Centre and 126 km (78 miles) north of Lake Louise.

KAMLOOPS

Kamloops (population 93,000) is so perfectly situated astride so many transportation corridors that it is inevitably an important crossroads and supply center. The town sits at the confluence of the North Thompson, the South Thompson, and the Thompson Rivers. It also is on both the Trans-Canada Highway (and at the northern junction of the Coquihalla) and the route of the Canadian Pacific Railway.

Because this is a large city it has a lot to offer. The central area hosts shopping and restaurants and the **Riverside Park** overlooks the place where the rivers meet. Probably the most interesting offering in Kamloops is the **Secwepemc Museum and Heritage Park**, owned and operated by the local First Nations people. This is an indoor and outdoor

BRITISH COLUMBIA

museum showing the history and culture of the original inhabitants of the area. Additionally, Kamloops has a museum, the **Kamloops Museum**, which relates the region's more recent history. In addition to the museums you can take a ride on the river in the restored **Wanda Sue**, a paddlewheel riverboat, or ride the rails behind a steam engine on the **Kamloops Heritage Railway**. Sixteen km (10 miles) east of Kamloops at Exit 390/391 you'll find the **BC Wildlife Park**, it features native BC wildlife including bears, wolves, mountain lions, and moose in natural-looking areas, it's great for kids.

Kamloops Campgrounds

● **KNUTSFORD RV PARK** *(Open March 1 to Oct 31)*
Res and Info: (250) 372-5380, (866) 777-1954,
              knutsfordcamp@hotmail.com
Location: 6 Km (4 Miles) S of Kamloops

GPS Location: 50.61694 N, 120.32167 W, 2,500 Ft

160 Sites – This is the most convenient commercial
campground to Kamloops. It's a neat modern campground that sits in a protected valley on the hillside south of the city. There are good tents sites as well as good back-in RV sites that will take RVs up to 45 feet. The big-box stores including Walmart are just 6 km (4 miles) down the hill. To reach the campground take Exit 368 from Hwy 1. Drive south up the hill for 5 km (3.4 miles), the campground entrance is on the right.

☐ **PAUL LAKE PROVINCIAL PARK** *(Open May 15 to Sept 15 – Varies)*
Information: (250) 377-8888
Location: 24 Km (15 Miles) NE of Kamloops

GPS Location: 50.75000 N, 120.10861 W, 2,700 Ft

90 Sites – Paul Lake Provincial Park is a popular swimming spot for
folks from Kamloops. The campground is on the hill about a quarter mile from the day use area so it's away from most of the activity. Some sites will take RVs to well over 45 feet. There are some good hiking trails at this park. From Highway 1 take Exit 374 and drive north on Hwy 5 toward Clearwater. In 5.2 km (3.2 miles) turn right on Paul Lake Road at a Husky gas station and drive another 18 km (11 miles) to the campground.

○ **KAMLOOPS EXHIBITION ASSOCIATION**
     (Open April 15 to Oct 15 – Varies)
Res and Info: (250) 314-9645 or (250) 572-6874
Location: Kamloops

GPS Location: 50.68923 N, 120.32775 W, 1,100 Ft

45 Sites – A close place to camp to the center of town is the Kamloops Exhibition Association, a fairgrounds and horse racing track. There's a golf course across the street. You'll probably want to check ahead by telephone to make sure the campsites will be available because major events sometimes preempt or fill the campground. These are long back-in sites suitable for any size rig, a few have full hookups. The facilities are best described as serviceable but rough, don't expect the standards of a normal RV park. From Highway 1 take Exit 374 and drive north on Hwy 5 toward Clearwater. In 3.2 km (2.0 miles) turn left on Mount Paul Way, in another .3 km (.2 mile) turn right on Chilcotin Road, then again turn left in .3 km (.2 mile). Once you make this turn the entrance is then on the left with the office in the nearest building. Check in here during normal business hours. If you're arriving when the office is closed continue to the campground, someone will come around to collect or you may have to pay when the office opens.

BRITISH COLUMBIA

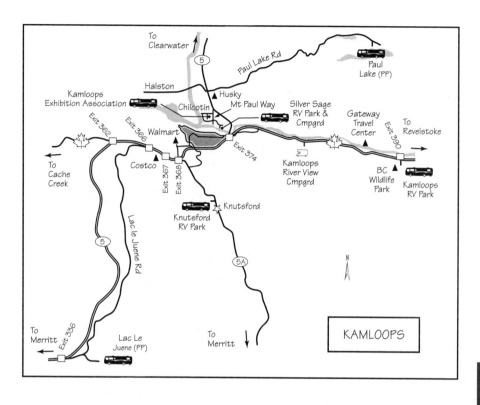

● **SILVER SAGE RV PARK AND CAMPGROUND**
   (Open April 1 to Oct 15)
   Res and Info: (877) 828-2077
   Location: Kamloops

GPS Location: 50.68095 N, 120.31892 W, 1,100 Ft

100 Sites – This is a traveler park located behind a residential RV park. The travel sites sit next to the river with a high dike between them and the residential section. All hookup sites are gravel surfaced back-ins to about 40 feet, they have electric and water hookups and there is a dump station in the park. About half the sites have no hookups with parking on grass, these are good for tent campers. There is a nearby restroom facility located just on the far side of the dike. From Highway 1 take Exit 374 and drive north on Hwy 5 toward Clearwater. In 3.2 km (2.0 miles) turn left on Mount Paul Way. Drive south on Mount Paul Way for 1.2 km (.7 mile), turn left on Athabasca Street W, and you'll reach the park in another .5 km (.3 mile).

● **KAMLOOPS RV PARK**
   (Open All Year – Reduced Facilities in
   Winter)

   Res and Info: (250) 573-3789,
                kamloopsrvpark@shaw.ca
                www.kamloopsrvpark.ca
   Location: 16 Km (10 Miles) E of Kamloops

GPS Location: 50.65444 N, 120.07639 W, 1,100 Ft

100 Sites – This is a big-rig campground located east of Kamloops along Hwy 1. There are tent sites as well as RV back-in and pull-thru sites for RVs to 60 feet. Take Exit 390 from Hwy 1 about 16 km (10 miles) east of Kamloops. The campground is on the south side of the highway.

☐ **LAC LE JEUNE PROVINCIAL PARK**
    (Open May 15 to Sept 15 – Varies)
    Reservations: www.discovercamping.ca, (800) 689-9025
    Information: (250) 377-8888
    Location: 35 Km (22 Miles) S of Kamloops

    GPS Location: 50.48639 N, 120.48917 W, 4,300 Ft

144 Sites – This is a large provincial park campground on Lac le Juene, on the plateau south of Kamloops. Sites here are long back-ins off wide paved access roads. This is a thinly treed area with lots of sunlight. Lac Le Jeune has good rainbow fishing and there is a fishing pier at the campground. There is also a swimming beach. There are extensive hiking trails in this area including an 8 km trail around the lake. From Kamloops follow Hwy 5, the Coquihalla Hwy south for 31 km (19 miles) to Exit 336, the Lac Le Jeune Rd. Follow this road east for 4 km (2.5 miles) to the park entrance.

KOOTENAY LAKES DISTRICT

The Kootenay Lakes district of Southeast British Columbia is dominated by three long lakes oriented in a north-south direction. Between these lakes are the rugged and very scenic Selkirk Mountains.

Farthest west is Arrow Lake, sometimes called Arrow Lakes since at one time there were two lakes. The Keenleyside Dam near Castlegar caused a rise in lake levels and combined the two. The present lake stretches all the way north to Revelstoke, a distance of 220 kilometers (136 miles). A road runs along the east side of the lake and **Nakusp** is the largest town along this road.

Castlegar, near the south end of Arrow Lake (population 7,000) is the crossroads of the Kootenay Lakes area. It sits at the confluence of the Kootenay and Columbia Rivers and the intersection of Highways 3 and 3A. Probably the most interesting thing about Castlegar is that is was the place selected by a group of Russian **Doukhobors** when they left Russia due to religious persecution and settled here in the early 1900s. Two sites are interesting to visit, **Zuckerberg Island Heritage Park** and its Russian Orthodox Chapel House and the **Doukhobor Village Museum**.

North of Castlegar is the **Slocan Valley** and **Slocan Lake**. It's the smallest of the three lakes and is located midway between the others. Hwy 6 runs along its east shore and there you'll find the small towns of **Slocan**, **Silverton**, and **New Denver**. This is a historical mining area, you'll find the mining town of **Sandon**, virtually a ghost town, in the mountains to the east and the **Silvery Slocan Museum** in New Denver. The mountains on both sides of this lake have great hiking trails including those in **Valhalla Provincial Park** just west of the lake which can be accessed on foot from Slocan.

Finally, on the east side of the region is **Kootenay Lake**. It's the largest natural lake in the province, some 156 km (97 miles) long and almost 6 km (4 miles) wide in places. The town of **Kaslo** is the northernmost city on the west side of the lake. It is known as the prettiest town in BC and has the **SS Moyle** on display. This is a steam sternwheeler that has been restored, it is thought to be the world's oldest passenger sternwheeler and is

A TRANQUIL EVENING PADDLE ON SLOCAN LAKE

in wonderful condition. Farther south are the very popular **Ainsworth Hot Springs** with a big outdoor pool. Even farther south is **Balfour**, a ferry port. From here you can catch a ferry to Crawford on the east shore of the lake, it's the world's longest free ferry ride, two hours round trip.

Nelson (population 9,500) occupies a beautiful site on the south shore of the west arm of Kootenay Lake. Originally a mining, and then an agricultural and timber town, Nelson has preserved its **historical buildings**. A pamphlet from the info centre will lead you around town and teach you a bit about Victorian architecture. When you've tired of that it's time to head down to **Lakeside Park** and relax on the beach or under the shade trees. Nelson has a city museum (the **Nelson Museum, Archives and Art Gallery**) and is home to the **Nelson Brewing Company** which gives tours. During the summer Nelson hosts **Artwalk**. Downtown businesses set themselves up as galleries and there are grand opening days toward the beginning of August and September.

The campgrounds descriptions below are arranged from south to north. First those near Arrow Lake, then Slocan Lake, and finally Kootenay Lake.

Kootenay Lakes District Campgrounds

● **CASTLEGAR RV PARK AND CAMPGROUND**
   (Open April 1 to Oct 31 – Varies)
   Res and Info: (250) 365-2337, (866) 687-7275,
                      info@castlegarRVPark.com,
                      www.castlegarRVpark.com
   Location: 3 Km (2 Miles) SW of Castlegar

   GPS Location: 49.27111 N, 117.67833 W, 1,400 Ft

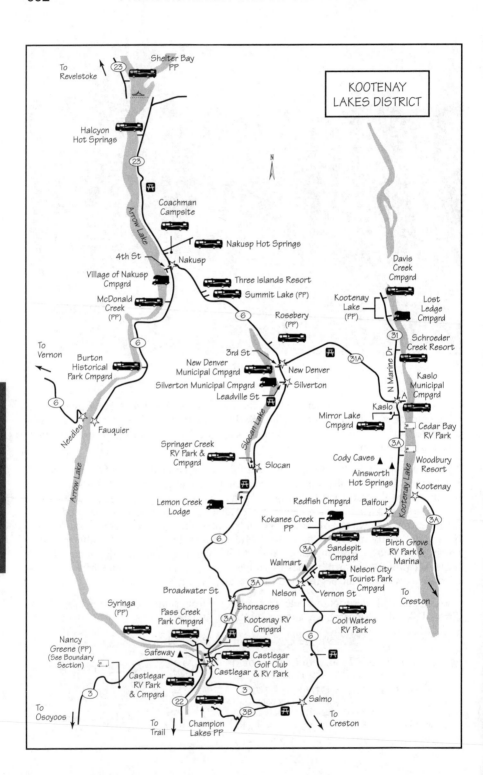

37 Sites – An good little campground located southwest of Castlegar with good camping for tents or RVs. RV sites are back-ins to 42 feet with parking on grass or gravel. The park is located on the south side of the Crowsnest Highway (Hwy 3) about 3.7 km (2.3 miles) to the southwest of Castlegar.

● **CASTLEGAR GOLF CLUB AND RV PARK**
    (Open April 15 to Oct 15 – Varies)
    Reservations: (800) 666-0324, www.golfcastlegar.com/home/tee-times/
    Information: (250) 365-5006, www.golfcastlegar.com
    Location: 6 Km (3 Miles NE of Castlegar

      GPS Location: 49.30620 N, 117.62044 W, 1,900 Ft

20 Sites – This is a new RV park associated with an 18-hole golf course outside Castlegar. Sites are back-ins to 50 feet with electric and water hookups. From Hwy 3A just north of Castlegar and south of the Kootenay River crossing turn east on Ootischenia Rd and follow it south for 1 km (.6 miles). Turn left on Columbia Road and follow it for .3 km (.2 mile). Turn left on Aaron Road and follow it for 1.3 km (.8 mile) to the golf club entrance.

● **KOOTENAY RV CAMPGROUND** *(Open All Year)*
    Res and Info: (877) 318-0008, (250) 365-5604,
              www.kootenayriverrv.ca
    Location: 3 Km (2 Miles) NE of Castlegar

      GPS Location: 49.31417 N, 117.63667 W, 1,300 Ft

43 Sites – This is an older residential RV park with a few sites for travelers. Sites can take RVs to 40 feet and have full hookups. There is a community fire pit but not individual campfires. From Hwy 3A just north of Castlegar and south of the Kootenay River crossing follow the entrance road west for a short distance to the campground.

○ **PASS CREEK PARK CAMPGROUND**
    (Open April 15 to Sept 30 – Varies)
    Res and Info: (250) 304-2062, passcreekpark@hotmail.com
    Location: 5 Km (3 Miles) N of Castlegar

      GPS Location: 49.33833 N, 117.66167 W, 1,400 Ft

32 Sites – This campground is in a small regional park. It's a government campground with an on-site manager. When sufficient water is available in the nearby creek a large pond is filled for swimming but some years this is not possible. When there's water this is a popular place, when there's not, it is not. Sites are back-ins suitable for any rig. Hookups may be added in the near future. You'll see this campground signed off Hwy 3A just north of Castlegar and north of the bridge over the Kootenay. Follow signs 3 km (2 miles) east, the entrance road is on the right.

□ **SYRINGA PROVINCIAL PARK** *(May 6 to Sept 30 – Varies)*
    Reservations: www.discovercamping.ca, (800) 689-9025
    Information: (250) 837-5734, www.westkootenayparks.com
    Location: 25 Km (16 Miles) W of Castlegar

      GPS Location: 49.35139 N, 117.89139 W, 1,400 Ft

61 Sites – This provincial park is on the southeast shore of Arrow Lake. Sites are all back-ins, many will allow longer RV combinations. There's a boat ramp and swimming beach at the park, also about 10 km of hiking trails. From Castlegar

drive north on Hwy 3A for about 3 km (2 miles). Take the cut-off marked for Robson to the left and follow the highway for 23 km (14 miles) to the park.

☐ **CHAMPION LAKES PROVINCIAL PARK** *(Open All Year)*

Reservations: www.discovercamping.ca, (800) , (604) 689-9025
Information: (250) 825-4212,
                championlakes@westkootenayparks.com
Location: 47 Km (29 Miles) SE of Castlegar

GPS Location: 49.18757 N, 117.61248 W, 3,500 Ft

95 Sites – This is a large but fairly remote provincial park. It's located southeast of Castlegar, BC and quite some distance off the highway. The campground is located between two of the three Champion Lakes. Swimming in the lakes is popular and there are some good hiking trails between them. Although the campground is open all year services are provided and a fee is charged only from June 1 to Sept 15. Snow is not cleared so sites may not be useable in winter. The RV sites are all back-ins and some are as long as 45 feet. There are also some sites designed solely for tent campers with tent pitching pads. Amenities include swimming beaches, hiking trails around the lakes, and canoe launch sites. From Castlegar drive southeast for 27 km (17 miles) on Hwy 3 until it meets Hwy 3B. Turn right and proceed another 8 km (5 miles), then turn right into Champion Lakes Road and you'll reach the campground in another 9.4 km (5.8 miles.

○ **BURTON HISTORICAL PARK CAMPGROUND**
   (Open May 1 to Sept 30 – Varies)

Res and Info: (250) 265-4982, Christine@burtonhistoricalpark.com,
                www.burtonhistoricalpark.com
Location: 34 Km (21 Mile) S of Nakusp

GPS Location: 49.99083 N, 117.88806 W, 1,500 Ft

28 Sites – This is a really pretty little campground set in a grassy park right along the shore of Arrow Lake. The sites are long back-ins off a gravel loop road that runs through the park. They have picnic tables and fire pits. There is a long beach area out front with a boat launch. It's on the lakeshore some 34 km (21 miles) south of Nakusp.

☐ **McDONALD CREEK PROVINCIAL PARK**
   (Open May 6 to Sept 30 – Varies)

Reservations: www.discovercamping.ca, (800) 689-9025
Information: (250) 265-3592
Location: 11 Km (7 Miles) S of Nakusp

GPS Location: 50.13278 N, 117.80583 W, 1600 Miles

46 Sites – The sites in this provincial park campground are all off an out and back access road with a turnaround at the end. Half of them are along Arrow Lake with direct access to the water. These are all long back-ins, big rigs are no problem. There's a swimming beach and boat ramp. The campground is located on the west side of Hwy 6 about 11 km (7 miles) south of Nakusp.

○ **VILLAGE OF NAKUSP CAMPGROUND**
   (Open May 1 to Oct 15 – Varies)

Res and Info: (250) 265-1061, camp@nakuspcampground.com,
                www.nakuspcampground.com
Location: Nakusp

GPS Location: 50.24361 N, 117.80694 W, 1,400 Ft

40 Sites – The Nakusp municipal campground has back-in sites off a paved access road. Some will take 35-foot RVs. Ten of these have electrical hookups. There's a dump station and restrooms with flush toilets and showers. The dump station is available to folks not staying at the campground, they must pay a $5 fee. This is a conveniently located campground within walking distance of central Nakusp. In central Nakusp, at the intersection of Hwy 23 from the north and Hwy 6 from the east, turn south on Hwy 6 toward Fauquier. In 1 km (.6 mile) turn right on 4th Street NW. Now turn left on 8th Ave. NW, you'll see the campground entrance on the right.

● **COACHMAN CAMPSITE** *(Open April 1 to Nov 15)*
   Res and Info: (250) 265-4212,
                  info@coachmancampsite.com
                  www.coachmancampsite.com
   Location: Nakusp

   GPS Location: 50.25611 N, 117.81667 W, 2,500 Ft

44 Sites – This is a summer vacation park with full, partial and no-hookup sites. RV sites are back-ins to 40 feet. The park has a swimming pool and offers mini golf. It's located at the northern end of Nakusp on the east side of Hwy 23.

● **NAKUSP HOT SPRINGS** *(Open May 15 to Oct 15 – Varies)*
   Res and Info: (866) 999-4528, (250) 265-4528,
                  www.nakusphotsprings.com
   Location: 11 Km (7 Miles) NE of Nakusp

   GPS Location: 50.29556 N, 117.68833 W, 2,500 Ft

30 Sites – The sites at this hot springs are located below the swimming pool area on a shelf above a roaring creek. These are back-ins to about 45 feet with electrical and water hookups. There's also a separate tent camping area and overflow camping for RVs. There are restrooms in the camping area with flush toilets and showers. There are two pools here, one warm and one hot. The camping fee doesn't cover use of the pool. The road up to the hot springs leaves Hwy 23 at the north end of Nakusp. It's 11 km (7 miles) on a paved road up to the hotsprings.

● **HALCYON HOT SPRINGS** *(Open All Year)*
   Res and Info: (250 265-3554, (888) 689-4699,
                  www.halcyon-hotsprings.com
   Location: 34 Km (21 Mile) N of Nakusp

   GPS Location: 50.51722 N, 117.89944 W, 1,500 Ft

40 Sites – Halcyon Hot Springs is an upscale resort overlooking Arrow Lake. The RV sites at this resort are located on a bench above the resort area. These are full-hookup sites with parking on gravel off gravel drives. Most RV sites are back-ins to 35 feet although three pull-thrus are 45 feet long. There is also a walk-in tent area with pitching on cedar chips. The four pools below aren't included in the price of the campground. From Nakusp drive north on Hwy 23 for 34 km (21 miles) to the campground.

☐ **SHELTER BAY PROVINCIAL PARK** *(Open May 6 to Sept 30 – Varies)*
   Information: (250) 837-5734
   Location: 48 Km (30 Miles) S of Revelstoke

   GPS Location: 50.63864 N, 117.92564 W, 1,400 Ft

17 Sites – This provincial park campground is simple with vault toilets, picnic tables, and

fire pits. Sites are back-ins to 40 feet. In addition to the formal sites there are six overflow sites. There is also a swimming beach and boat ramp. The campground is located on the northwest shore of Arrow lake near the west end of the ferry run from Shelter Bay to Galena Bay. It's on the Kootenay Lakes access route from Revelstoke via Hwy 23.

● **LEMON CREEK LODGE** *(Open May 1 to Oct 15 – Varies)*
Res and Info: (250) 355-2403, (877) 970-8090,
info@lemoncreeklodge.com
www.lemoncreeklodge.com
Location: 10 Km (6 Miles) S of Slocan

GPS Location: 49.69611 N, 117.49472 W, 1,800 Ft

36 Sites – This is a quiet rustic lodge about 2 km down a gravel road from the highway. There are 20 back-in sites to 40 feet off a gravel loop drive under pines. About half of the sites have electrical and water hookups, the rest are not serviced. There are showers and the lodge has a good restaurant. From Slocan drive south on Hwy 6 for 7.4 km (4.6 miles). Turn west on the gravel road, it's signed for the lodge, and follow it for 1.5 km (.9 miles), the lodge is on the left.

○ **SPRINGER CREEK RV PARK AND CAMPGROUND**
(Open May 1 to Sept 30 – Varies)
Res and Info: (250) 355-2266, (250) 355-2277,
www.slocancity.com
Location: Slocan

GPS Location: 49.76167 N, 117.46194 W, 1,800 Ft

24 Sites – This is Slocan's municipal campground. It's a modern campground with good facilities but doesn't have a particularly scenic location. Access roads and sites are gravel in a grove of cedar trees. Roads and sites are pleasantly irregular, sometimes it's hard to tell where you're supposed to camp. There are pull-thru and back-in sites, some to 50 feet. Five sites are full-hookup, fourteen are partial hookups with low amp power, and some sites are dry or tent sites. Firewood is free and there is a small charge to dump if you're staying at the campground, the charge is higher if you're a drop-in. The campground is located near the point where the access road to Slocan leaves Hwy 6, watch for it on the right after you turn toward town.

○ **SILVERTON MUNICIPAL CAMPGROUND**
(Open May 15 to Oct 15 – Varies)
Information: (250) 358-2472, administration@silverton.ca,
http://www.silverton.ca/rec/Camping.html
Location: Silverton

GPS Location: 49.95417 N, 117.36056 W, 1,700

30 Sites – This campground has sites in two locations. On the lakefront there is a group of small sites in a grove of trees, a few are lakefront sites. This area is best for tents and small camping vehicles. A block away back from the lake and along a creek is another group of back-in sites with parking on grass. These sites will take RVs to 35 feet. Both areas have restrooms with flush toilets and there are showers at the lakefront campground. There's a boat ramp at the lake. Access is easy. In Silverton turn toward the lake on Leadville St., it's signed for camping. Follow the road to the lake and the campground. To reach the second area turn left on the cross street at the lower campground, drive one block, turn left and drive one block to the area entrance.

○ **NEW DENVER MUNICIPAL CAMPGROUND**
(Open May 1 to Sept 30 – Varies)
Information: (250) 358-2316
Location: New Denver

GPS Location: 49.98750 N, 117.37583 W, 1,800 Ft

25 Sites – This is another municipal campground, this one with hookups. It's on the lake in New Denver and has back-in sites to 45 feet, some with electricity and water hookups, some dry. There are restrooms with flush toilets and showers, also a swimming beach, a marina, and a boat ramp. In New Denver turn toward the water on Third Street and follow it to the park.

☐ **ROSEBERY PROVINCIAL PARK** *(Open May 6 to Sept 16)*
Information: (250) 265-3952, (250) 837-5734, (866) 937-5734,
www.westkootenayparks.com
Location: 5 Km (3 Miles) N of New Denver

GPS Location: 50.03333 N, 117.40417 W, 1,800

36 Sites – Rosebery is a small provincial park. It has back-in and a few pull-thru sites to 45 feet off two out and back access roads with turnaround loops at the ends. Two sites have tent pads. It's pretty much an overnight stop, not a lot of amenities or interesting activities. From New Denver head north on Hwy 6, the campground entrance is signed on the right in about 5 km (3 miles).

☐ **SUMMIT LAKE PROVINCIAL PARK**
(Open May 1 to Sept 19 – Varies)
Information: (250) 489-8591, (250) 265-4710
Location: 15 Km (9 Miles) SE of Nakusp

GPS Location: 50.15444 N, 117.65417 W, 2,500 Ft

34 Sites – This campground is on the shore of Summit Lake. Sites are off a paved loop road, they're back-ins to 45 feet. Some of them are great lakeside sites. Other amenities include a swimming beach and boat launch. This lake is stocked with rainbows so fishing is popular. The campground is on the east side of Hwy 5 some 15.3 km (9.5 miles) SE of Nakusp and 31 km (19 miles) north of New Denver.

● **THREE ISLANDS RESORT** *(Open May 1 to Sept 30)*
Res and Info: (250) 265-3023, www.threeislandsresort.ca
Location: 13.7 Km (8.5 Miles) SE of Nakusp

GPS Location: 50.15833 N, 117.66278 W, 2,500 Ft

65 Sites – This RV Park occupies the northwest shore of 2-mile-long Summit Lake. There are back-in and pull-thru sites to 65 feet with parking on grass. About half of the sites are full-hookup, the remainder have electricity and water hookups. There's a swimming beach, boat ramp, dock, and boat rentals. This is a popular stocked fishing lake. The campground is on the northeast side of Hwy 5 about 13.7 Km (8.5 Miles) southeast of Nakusp.

● **COOL WATERS RV PARK** *(Open All Year)*
Information: (250) 354-1973, wdwebber@shaw.ca,
www.coolwatersrvpark.com
Location: 2 Km (1 Mile) S of Nelson

GPS Location: 49.46439 N, 117.28372 W, 2,300 Ft

BRITISH COLUMBIA

20 Sites – Cool Waters is a decent alternative campground for visiting Nelson, if you have some way to get in to town. Sites here are all back-ins to about 45 feet. They have electricity and water but there is are no sewer drains and no dump station. From Nelson drive south on Hwy 6 toward Salmo. The campground is on the right about 2 km (1 mile) out of town.

○   **NELSON CITY TOURIST PARK CAMPGROUND**
       (Open May 1 to Sept 30 – Varies)
     Information: (250) 352-7618, campnels@telus.net,
                          http://nelson.ca/EN/main/residents/
                          community-facilities/city-campground.html
     Location: Nelson

       GPS Location: 49.49750 N, 117.28611 W, 1,900 Ft

37 Sites – This small municipal campground occupies a sloping site in a residential neighborhood. It is possible for just a few RVs as large as 40 feet to get into the campground and park but maneuvering is difficult. The campground is best for tents and RVs to about 30 feet or smaller. The location is very convenient; the central area of town is less than a half-mile distant on city sidewalks. Easiest access is by turning east on Vernon or Baker Streets in central Nelson from Hwy 3A as it passes through town. In a few blocks the main route turns left to curve around the hillside. There are campground signs so you shouldn't miss the turn. You'll soon see the campground sign on the right, watch closely since if you drive past turning around is difficult.

☐   **KOKANEE CREEK PROVINCIAL PARK**
       (Open May 1 to Sept 30 – Varies)
     Reservations: www.discovercamping.ca, (800) 689-9025
     Information: (250) 825-4212, www.westkootenayparks.com
     Location: 18 Km (11 Miles) NE of Nelson

       GPS Location: 49.60528 N, 117.12139 W, 1,700 Ft

168 Sites – There are actually two campgrounds in this park. Coming from the direction of Nelson you'll first see Redfish Campground on the left. This is the smaller campground and sites are suitable only for tents and RVs to about 25 feet. It is open for a shorter season than the main campground. Just beyond, on the right, is Sandspit Campground. This is a large campground with an entry booth and sites suitable for RVs to 45 feet. It's on the lake side of the highway and there is a swimming beach as well as a boat ramp. During the off season it is possible for self-contained rigs to overnight in a parking lot. From Nelson head northeast on Hwy 3A for about 18 km (11 miles) to the campground.

●   **BIRCH GROVE RV PARK AND MARINA**
       (Open April 15 to Oct 31)
     Info and Res: (877) 247-8774, (250) 229-4275
     Location: 3 Km (2 Miles) W of Balfour

       GPS Location: 49.61889 N, 117.00111 W, 1,800 Ft

53 Sites – This is a lakeside summer resort campground. Most sites are back-ins to 35 feet. About 15 have full hookups, the remainder are dry sites. There's a dock, launch ramp, and marina here too. Reservations must be for at least a week. It's best to call ahead if you want to stay for even a short time to check on apace availability. The campground is located along the lake to the west of Balfour.

● **MIRROR LAKE CAMPGROUND**
  (Open April 15 to Oct 15)
  Res and Info: (250) 353-7102,
                www.mirrorlakecampground.com
  Location: 3 Km (2 Miles) S of Kaslo

  GPS Location: 49.87705 N, 116.90487 W, 1,800 Ft

125 Sites – This is a beautiful big camping area that slopes down to the west side of little Mirror Lake. Parking is on grass and sites vary, but many have water and electric hookups. RV sites are back-ins and pull-thrus to 45 feet. There's no sewer hookups but there is a sani-station and a truck is available for emptying tanks. There is a nice beach for swimming and rental boats are available. From Kaslo head south for 3 km (2 miles) to Arcolo Rd which is on the right. Turn here and the campground entrance is on the right in another .2 km (.1 mile).

○ **KASLO MUNICIPAL CAMPGROUND**
  (Open May 1 to Sept 30 – Varies)
  Res and Info: (250) 353-2662, kaslocampground@yahoo.ca,
                www.kaslo.ca
  Location: Kaslo

  GPS Location: 49.90948 N, 116.89890 W, 1,800 Ft

25 Sites – The sites in Kaslo's municipal campground are back-ins for RVs to 45 feet. There are water and electric hookups and a restroom with flush toilets and showers. Sites have picnic tables and firepits. To find the campground just follow A Street to its end near the water.

● **SCHROEDER CREEK RESORT**
  (Open April 1 to Oct 31)
  Res and Info: (250) 353-7383,
                inquiries@shroedercreekresort.com
                www.schroedercreekresort.com
  Location: 15 Km (9 Miles) N of Kaslo

  GPS Location: 50.03139 N, 116.90806 W, 1,800 Ft

80 Sites – Schroeder Creek is a camping resort and marina along the shore of Kootenay Lake. Many sites here have long term residents but many are available for travelers too. These are full-hookup sites, both back-ins and pull-thrus to 70 feet. There are also many no-hookup sites that are great for tenters with pitching on grass. The marina has a boat ramp and sheltered boat slips available. From Kaslo just follow the lakeside road, North Marine Drive, north for 15 km (9 miles) to the access road, it's on the right.

□ **LOST LEDGE CAMPGROUND - KOOTENAY LAKE**
  PROVINCIAL PARK *(Open All Year, Snow Not Cleared)*
  Information: (250) 825-4212
  Location: 23 Km (14 Miles) N of Kaslo

  GPS Location: 50.10083 N, 116.93833 W, 1,800 Ft

14 Sites – This campground is on the shore of Kootenay Lake. Sites are back-ins to 35 feet off a paved loop road. Some sites are on the lakeshore. There's a special handicap accessible site here, a gravel beach, and a boat ramp. From Kaslo drive north on the shore road, called Hwy 31 or North Marine Drive, for 27 km (17 miles), the campground is on the right.

☐ **DAVIS CREEK CAMPGROUND - KOOTENAY LAKE**
   PROVINCIAL PARK *(Open May 15 to Sept 15 – Varies)*

Information: (250) 825-4212
Location: 29 Km (18 Miles) N of Kaslo

GPS Location: 50.14111 N, 116.95056 W, 1,800 Ft

18 Sites – This campground is on the shore of Kootenay Lake. Sites are back-ins to 45 feet off a gravel loop, some on the lake shore. From Kaslo drive north on the shore road, called Hwy 31 or North Marine Drive, for 23 km (14 miles), the campground is on the right.

KOOTENAY NATIONAL PARK AND RADIUM HOT SPRINGS

The Kootenay National Park is essentially a corridor that follows the Banff-Windermere Highway from its crossing of Vermillion Pass down into the Columbia River Valley at Radium Hot Springs. Kootenay National Park is in British Columbia while Banff National Parkk is in Alberta, the border is the Continental Divide. The distance from the border down to the Radium Hot Springs is 95 km (58 miles). Of course Kootenay is one of a whole complex of connected national parks in the Canadian Rockies and this highway makes a good entry route if you happen to be coming from the right direction.

Most of the attractions in Kootenay lie along the highway. There are three summer campgrounds in the park. These are Marble Canyon, McLeod Meadows, and Redstreak

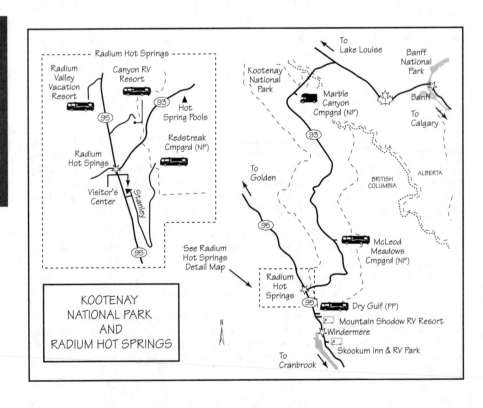

Campground. All are described below. Marble Canyon and McLeod Meadows are accessible from the Banff-Windermere Highway, Redstreak has an entrance from Radium Hot Springs. In winter these campgrounds are closed but there is another parking area known as Dolly Varden with vault toilets that serves as a campground. Dolly Varden is 34 km (21 miles) from Radium Hot Springs and is not described below since it is really not much more than a parking lot.

In addition to the campgrounds there are several good short trails along the highway. These include the Fireweed Trail at Vermillion Pass, Marble Canyon trail (88 km (55 miles) from Radium Hot Springs), the Paint Pots (88 km (55 miles) from Radium Hot Springs), and an interpretive trail at Olive Lake (13 km (8 miles) from Radium Hot Springs). There's also a visitor centre in the park (at Vermillion Crossing, 63 km (39 miles) from Radium).

The most popular attraction in the park, however, is actually very near the southern border. This is the **Radium Hot Springs** pools, a swimming area 3 kilometers from Radium. There are two pools here, a hot pool at 40° C (104° F). There is road access from the main park highway as well as a trail from Redstreak campground.

Radium Hot Springs (population 800) is located just outside the park. It's in the Columbia River Valley, also known as the Rocky Mountain Trench in this area. It is large enough to have restaurants and stores for supplies. One attraction here is a herd of bighorn sheep that often wander the streets of town. Below we list two campgrounds in town and another a few miles to the south. The park's Redstreak Campground is also only accessible from a road that starts in town.

There is a campfire fee in these national park campsites.

Kootenay National Park and Radium Hot Springs Campgrounds

■ **MARBLE CANYON CAMPGROUND – KOOTENAY NATIONAL PARK** *(Open June 24 to Sept 5 – Varies)*

Information: (250) 347-3367
Location: 87 Km (54 Miles) NE of Radium Hot Springs

GPS Location: 51.18500 N, 116.12000 W, 4,800 Ft

61 Sites – This campground is best for tents and smaller rigs. While restrooms do not have showers they do have hot water in the sinks. Sites are arranged off small loops that make maneuvering tough for larger rigs. There is one loop called the big site loop that has a few very long sites but it too is a small-circumference loop limiting access to RVs to about 35 feet long. The campground is the easternmost one in Kootenay National Park, it is 16 km (10 miles) from the intersection of Hwy 93 with Hwy 1 in Banff National Park and 87 km (54 miles) from Hwy 95 in Radium Hot Springs.

■ **McLEOD MEADOWS CAMPGROUND – KOOTENAY NATIONAL PARK** *(Open May 20 to Sept 5 – Varies)*

Information: (250) 347-3367
Location: 27 Km (17 Miles) NE of Radium Hot Springs

GPS Location: 50.76694 N, 115.94472 W, 3,600 Ft

98 Sites – The sites here are back-ins off 10 different loops. Sites and access are suitable for RVs to 45 feet. This campground, like others in this park, has hot water in the restroom sinks. The campground is 77 km (48 miles) from the intersection of Hwy 93

with Hwy 1 in Banff National Park and 27 km (17 miles) from Hwy 95 in Radium Hot Springs.

● **RADIUM VALLEY VACATION RESORT**
(Open April 1 to Nov 30)
Res and Info: (250) 347-9715,
www.radiumvalleyvacationresort.com
Location: Radium Hot Springs

GPS Location: 50.63085 N, 116.07717 W, 2,800 Ft

84 Sites – This is a beautiful modern condominium RV park with sites available for rental. The sites are pull-thrus and back-ins to about 80 feet. Some sites are full hookup and some are water and electric, there is a dump station. Amenities include a clubhouse, pool, spa, and playground. The Wi-Fi hotspot is in the clubhouse. From the intersection of Hwy 95 and Hwy 93 in the center of town drive north for 1.2 km (.7 miles), the entrance is on the left.

● **CANYON RV RESORT** *(Open April 15 to Oct 15)*
Res and Info: (250) 347-9564, www.canyonrv.com
Location: Radium Hot Springs

GPS Location: 50.62861 N, 116.06778 W, 2,800 Ft

130 Sites – This well run and popular commercial campground sits in a canyon just outside Radium Hot Springs. Sites are back-ins and pull-thrus to 55 feet. During the camping season this is a busy place, reservations are recommended, especially for big rigs. At the northern edge of Radium Hot Springs follow the sign east to the campground.

■ **REDSTREAK CAMPGROUND – KOOTENAY NATIONAL PARK** *(Open June 1 to Oct 10 – Varies)*
Reservations: (877) 737-3783, www.pccamping.ca
Information: (250) 347-3367
Location: 3 Km (2 Miles) SE of Radium Hot Springs

GPS Location: 50.62472 N, 116.06000 W, 3,300 Ft

242 Sites – This large national park campground is a good place to stay when visiting Radium Hot Springs, a trail leads to the pool from the campground. The hookup sites here are large and will take RVs to 45 feet. The campground is located inside the park but access is on a small road from the town of Radium Hot Springs. From the intersection of Hwy 93 from Banff and Hwy 95 in Radium Hot Springs go south .3 km (.2 miles). Turn left and then right and follow the campground access road for 2.4 km (1.5 miles) to the campground entrance.

☐ **DRY GULCH PROVINCIAL PARK CAMPGROUND**
(Open May 1 to Oct 11 – Varies)
Information: (250) 422-3003, ekparks@telus.net
Location: 3 Km (2 Miles) S of Radium Hot Springs

GPS Location: 50.58694 N, 116.03833 W, 3,100 Ft

26 Sites – Dry Gulch is a small provincial park set on a hillside. Most sites here are suitable for RVs to 30 feet although a couple would take rigs to 40 feet. The campground is located on the east side of Hwy 95 some 4.7 km (2.9 miles) south of the intersection of Highways 93 and 95 in Radium Hot Springs.

BRITISH COLUMBIA

MANNING PROVINCIAL PARK

This large provincial park is located on the Crowsnest Highway between Hope and Princeton. It's in the heart of the Cascade Mountains and water from the park goes both west to the Fraser River and east to the Similkameen and eventually the Columbia River. This is a big park with an area of 71,000 hectares. About 58 kilometers (36 miles) of Hwy 3 are inside the park.

The visitor facilities of the park are concentrated near the **Manning Provincial Park Resort**. Within a few miles you'll find a visitor centre, four drive-in campgrounds, a lakeside day-use area, and lots of short trails designed for folks not wanting to devote a whole day to a wilderness trek.

Actually, the hiking is where this park shines. One great feature is a road that climbs to the north from the intersection near the resort. It's paved to Cascade Lookout (8 km), then continues on as a gravel road to a parking lot near Blackwall Peak (additional 8 km). It's an easy way to get up to the sub-alpine elevations where the wildflowers go really wild during late July and August. Hiking trails lead from both parking areas on this road.

Manning has lakes too. Lightening Lake is accessed from a day-use area 2.7 km (1.7 mile) south from the intersection at the lodge, just a little closer than the Lightening Lake campground. There are actually three lakes – Lightening, Flash, and Strike. No motors are allowed but canoes and kayaks are fine.

In addition to the four drive-in campgrounds in this park there are many hike-in camping sites in the back country. Although the drive-in campgrounds are closed in the winter there is winter overnight vehicle camping. It's in the parking lot of the Lightening Lake day-use area and has no facilities other than a vault toilet. There's also a winter tent camping area called Lone Duck which is just beyond the Lightening Lake day-use area entrance. The park has one dump station, it's located a short distance off the highway about 1 km east of the intersection at the lodge. Watch for the sign.

The Manning Park Lodge, located on Hwy 3 at Km 60, serves as the center of services in the park. It offers a motel, pub, restaurant, and gift and grocery store.

Manning Provincial Park Campgrounds

☐ **COLDSPRING CAMPGROUND** *(Open June 3 to Oct 11 – Varies)*
Reservations: www.discovercamping.ca, (800) 689-9025
Information: (250) 840-8822
Location: Manning Provincial Park

GPS Location: 49.07419 N, 120.80646 W, 4,000 Ft

64 Sites – Coldspring Campground is next to the highway and is the only one of the park campgrounds located west of the lodge. Sites here are long back-ins to 50 feet. Restrooms are vault toilets and there is water available. The Canyon Nature Trailhead is at this campground. The entrance is near Km 58 of Hwy 3, this is 2.1 km (1.3 miles) west of the lodge.

☐ **HAMPTON CAMPGROUND** *(Open May 20 to Oct 11 – Varies)*
Reservations: www.discovercamping.ca, (800) 689-9025
Information: (250) 840-8822
Location: Manning Provincial Park

GPS Location: 49.06694 N, 120.72361 W, 3,700 Ft

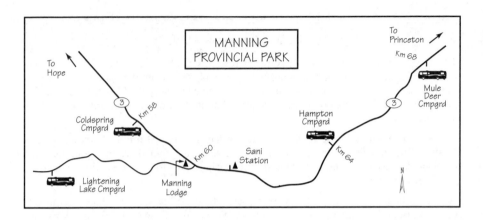

99 Sites – Hampton Campground is a modern provincial park campground with some sites large enough for RV combinations to 60 feet. This is one of the higher campgrounds in the park so it opens late. It's easily accessible from the highway. The entrance is on the north side of Hwy 3 near Km 64. That's 4.0 km (2.5 miles) east of the lodge.

☐ **LIGHTNING LAKE CAMPGROUND** *(Open June 6 to Oct 2 – Varies)*
   Reservations: www.discovercamping.ca, (800) 689-9025
   Information: (250) 840-8822
   Location: Manning Provincial Park

   GPS Location: 49.06194 N, 120.84417 W, 4,200 Ft

143 Sites – Lightening Lake is the largest of the campgrounds in the park. It is away from the main highway and adjacent to Lightning Lake. Some of the sites here will take RV combos to 60 feet and the restrooms have flush toilets and hot showers. This is also the campground where the host for all the campgrounds stays. The nearby day-use area offers a swimming beach and small boat rentals. From the lodge at Km 60 of Hwy 3 go south on the access road to Lightning Lake, it's 6.5 km (4 miles) to the campground

☐ **MULE DEER CAMPGROUND** *(Open May 20 to Oct 11 – Varies)*
   Reservations: www.discovercamping.ca, (800) 689-9025
   Information: (250) 840-8822
   Location: Manning Provincial Park

   GPS Location: 49.09083 N, 120.68056 W, 3,600 Ft

49 Sites – This is a very nice campground situated along the Similkameen River. It's right along the main highway so access is easy, it's also the lowest of the campgrounds in the park. That means that this is usually the first campground in the park to open each year. They're all back-in sites, many to 50 feet or more. The campground even has a water system and flush toilets. The campground entrance is at Km 68 of Hwy 3, this is about 8.9 km (5.5 miles) east of Manning Lodge.

MERRITT AND THE SURROUNDING PLATEAU

The town of Merritt (population 7,000) is the central town of the high plateau between the Okanagan Valley to the east and the Fraser River Canyon to the west. The modern Coquihalla Highway (Hwy 5) toll road connects the town to Hope in the south and Kamloops to the north and is now the main route for Hwy 1 transcontinental traffic. From Merritt another highway, the Okanagan Connector (Hwy 97C) runs eastward to Peachland in the Okanagan Valley.

Merritt hosts the **Merritt Mountain Music Festival** in July which attracts big-name country music stars for a week of concerts. It has attracted as many as 148,000 attendees. Even if you don't get there for the festival you'll see the bronzed hand prints of country stars displayed around town.

The first campground listed below is the Merritt municipal campground. The others are provincial park campgrounds some distance from the town. All of these are on lakes and are great mid-summer destinations due to the high and dry climate of this area.

Merritt and the Surrounding Plateau Campgrounds

○ **CLAYBANKS RV PARK** *(Open All Year)*
　Res and Info: (250) 378-6441, info@claybanksrv.com,
　　　　　　　　www.claybanksrv.com
　Location:　Merritt

　　GPS Location: 50.10472 N, 120.79306 W, 1,900 Ft

84 Sites – This municipal campground is located right in
Merritt. It has RV sites and tent sites and is used by travelers as well as longer term visitors to the area. Sites are back-ins and pull-thrus to 60 feet and are gravel pads separated

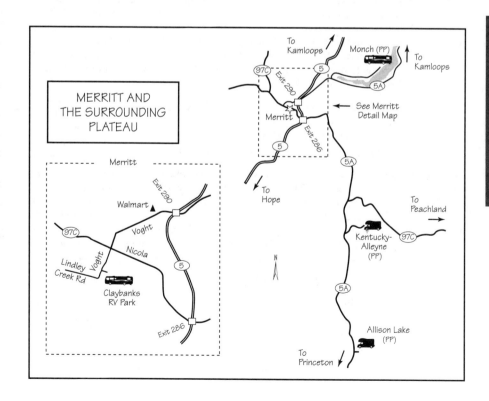

by grass. Most of the RV sites have full hookups and there's a dump station across the road from the entrance, Wi-Fi Internet access is available at the office. The easiest approach route is from Hwy 5 north of town. Take the Voght Street Exit (Km 290) and follow it southwest for 3.5 km (2.2 miles) through town to the park.

☐ **Monck Provincial Park** *(Open April 15 to Oct 31 – Varies)*
    Reservations: www.discovercamping.ca, (800) 689-9025
    Information: (250) 315-0253
    Location: 19 Km (12 Miles) NE of Merritt

      GPS Location: 50.17639 N, 120.53778 W, 2,200 Ft

120 Sites – This is a beautiful provincial park on the north shore of Nicola Lake. There are scattered Ponderosa pines on a sunny south-facing slope. Sites here are mostly back-ins, some are very long and suitable for any RV combination. There's also a swimming beach, boat ramp, trails, and a small store. From Merritt's Voght Street Exit at Km 290 of the Coquihalla Hwy drive northeast on Hwy 5A. In 8.4 km (5.2 miles) turn left onto a side road signed for Monch Provincial Park. Follow it 10.3 km (6.4 miles) to the park entrance, it's on the right.

☐ **Kentucky-Alleyne Provincial Park** *(Open May 14 to Sept 30 – Varies)*
    Information: (250) 378-5334
    Location: 35 Km (22 Miles) S of Merritt

      GPS Location: 49.90667 N, 120.56806 W, 3,300 Ft

58 Sites – Sites in this park are located in smaller camping areas along four lakes: Alleyne Lake, West and East Pond, and Kentucky Lake. Sites are back-ins and pull-thrus, some to 40 feet. Maneuvering room is tight so this campground is best for units to 35 feet. Swimming in the lakes is possible and there are some boat launches. These lakes are stocked with rainbows. In winter some vehicle campsites are accessible, vault toilets are available. Access to the park is off Hwy 5A some 31 km (19 miles) south of Merritt. Follow paved Bates Road for 3.5 km (2.2 miles) east to the park.

☐ **Allison Lake Provincial Park** *(Open April 15 to Sept 11 – Varies)*
    Information: (250) 840-8807
    Location: 58 Km (36 Miles) S of Merritt

      GPS Location: 49.68028 N, 120.60444 W, 3,000 Ft

24 Sites – This is a campground near Allison Lake, the lake is across the highway from the campground. Sites here are back-ins off a narrow access loop. Although some will take RVs to 40 feet the poor access and uneven sites make this campground best for RVs to 30 feet. There's a beach at the lake, a boat launch, and the lake is stocked with rainbows. During the off season the campground is not gated, there are no services and no fee during this period. The park straddles Hwy 5A some 58 km (36 miles) south of Merritt.

Mt Robson and Valemount

The view from the visitor center at Mt Robson Provincial Park is definitely one of the most impressive in the entire Rocky Mountain chain. From the visitor center at 850 meters (2,500 ft) you have an outstanding view of the entire southern face of the mountain which rises to 3,954 meters (12,972 feet.

If the weather isn't cooperating – or if you just want to wait until the next day for another

ENJOYING A REST STOP AT KINNEY LAKE

BRITISH COLUMBIA

view – there are two good provincial park campgrounds within a kilometer or so of the visitor center.

Or, perhaps you want to get an even closer look or maybe even see the north side of the mountain. For that you'll have to walk. The Berg Lake Trail is probably the best-known hike in British Columbia. From the trailhead near the visitor center it's 5 km (3 miles) to Kinney Lake for wonderful close-up views of the mountain. It's another 16 km (10 miles) to Berg Lake for a look at the north side. There are quite a few campgrounds along the way. Check at the visitor center for more information and to register if you decide to go.

If you don't want to stay in the park itself there are many other nearby choices. Both Valemount, 34 km (21 miles) to the south and McBride, 65 km (40 miles) to the west, have campgrounds. Both the park campgrounds and those in Valemount and McBride are described below.

Mt Robson and Valemount Campgrounds

☐ **Robson Meadows Campground**
   (Open May 15 to Sept 30 – Varies)
   Reservations: www.discovercamping.ca, (800) 689-9025
   Information: designbynature@telus.net
   Location: Mt Robson Provincial Park

   GPS Location: 53.03240 N, 119.24727 W, 2,700 Ft

125 Sites – Robson Meadows is by far the largest campground in Mt Robson Provincial Park. It's located on the south side of the highway opposite the visitor center. Sites here

are back-ins as long as 50 feet with plenty of maneuvering room. Amenities include a playground and there is a dump station.

☐ **ROBSON RIVER CAMPGROUND**
    (Open May 15 to Sept 6 – Varies)
    Information: designbynature@telus.net
    Location: Mt Robson Provincial Park

    GPS Location: 53.03240 N, 119.24727 W, 2,700 Ft

19 Sites – Robson River Campground is located about 1 km (36 mile) west of the visitor center. It has back-in sites to about 40 feet but the narrow access road makes 35 feet a more practical size. Many sites have tent pads. The little campground has flush toilets and showers. Trails run along the river.

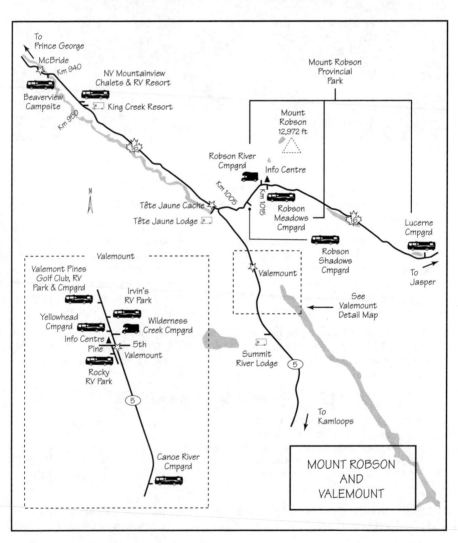

☐ **LUCERNE CAMPGROUND** *(Open May 15 to Sept 15)*
Information: designbynature@telus.net
Location: Mt Robson Provincial Park

GPS Location: 52.84930 N, 118.57250 W, 3,500 Ft

38 Sites – This campground is well away from the visitor center and two other vehicle accessible campgrounds in the park. It is located near the eastern edge of the park along Hwy 16, next to Yellowhead Lake. Vehicle accessible sites here are fine for any RV, there is one pull-thru and the rest are back-ins to about 50 feet. There are also two walk-in tent sites. There is a swimming beach. Water is from a hand pump.

● **VALEMOUNT PINES GOLF CLUB, RV PARK**
 AND CAMPGROUND *(Open April 1 to Oct 15)*
 Res and Info: (250) 566-4550, (250) 566-4627,
  pines@valemount.com
 Location: Valemount

GPS Location: 52.84814 N, 119.28985 W, 2,600 Ft

46 Sites – Valemount Pines is a nine hole course with camping at the front of the property near the highway. Sites are grass or gravel pull-thrus to 60 feet under scattered small pines. Sites are full, partial or no hookup and there is a dump station. A few sites are available in winter. At the northern edge of Valemount there's a bridge over Swift Creek. From the bridge drive north for 1.7 km (1.1 mile) to an entry road on the left.

● **IRVIN'S RV PARK** *(Open April 1 to Oct 30)*
 Res and Info: (250) 566-4781, www.irvinsrvpark.com
 Location: Valemount

GPS Location: 52.84275 N, 119.28343 W, 2,600 Ft

136 Sites – Irvin's is a large open big rig park in a large lot with no shade next to the highway. There are many tent sites as well as 80 full-hookup pull-thrus to 65 feet. At the northern edge of Valemount there's a bridge over Swift Creek. From the bridge drive north for 1 km (.6 mile) to an entry road on the right.

● **YELLOWHEAD CAMPGROUND AND RV PARK**
 (Open May 1 to Sept 30 – Varies)
 Res and Info: (250) 566-0078,
  camping@yellowheadcampground.com,
  www.yellowheadcampground.com
 Location: Valemount

GPS Location: 52.83682 N, 119.28291 W, 2,600 Ft

71 Sites – This campground is located along Swift Creek at the northern edge of Valemount. There are tent sites with water as well as back-in and pull-thru RV sites with electric and water hookups. There is a dump station. Wi-Fi is at a hotspot. At the northern edge of Valemount there is a bridge over Swift creek. From the bridge drive north for .4 km (.3 mile) to an entry road on the left

● **WILDERNESS CREEK CAMPGROUND** *(Open May 1 to Sept 30 – Varies)*
 Location: Valemount

GPS Location: 52.83555 N, 119.27675 W, 2,500 Ft

This is a no-hookup campground along Swift Creek with sites similar to what

you'd find in a forest service campground. It has back-in and pull-thru sites to 30 feet. There are picnic tables, fire pits, and portable toilets. At the northern edge of Valemount there's a bridge over Swift Creek. From the bridge drive north for .4 km (.3 mile) to an entry road on the right. Turn in there and follow the entry road at the right for .5 km (.3 mile) to the campground.

● **ROCKY RV PARK** *(Open April 15 to Sept 30 – Varies)*
   Res and Info: (250) 566-4141, rockyrvpark@gmail.com
   Location: Valemount

   GPS Location: 52.82974 N, 119.27927 W, 2,500 Ft

85 Sites – This former KOA has sites in a grove of pine trees. There are a large number of tent sites as well as pull-thru RV sites to 65 feet. This campground is in Valemount. It's on the west side of the highway about .3 km (.2 mile) south of the visitor center.

● **CANOE RIVER CAMPGROUND** *(Open April 1 to Oct 30)*
   Res and Info: (250) 566-4781, www.canoerivercampground.com
   Location: 8.5 Km (5 Miles) S of Valemount

   GPS Location: 52.774285 N, 119.256372 W, 2,600 Ft

121 Sites – Unlike the other Valemount campground Canoe River is located south of town. This is a big piece of property with sites concentrated well away from the office. Some no-hookup sites are at the back of the property along the Canoe River. There are back-in and pull-thru sites to 70 feet with water and electric hookups. Decent Wi-Fi covers some of the parking area and there is a dump station. From Valemount drive south on Hwy 5 for 8.5 km (5.3 miles), the campground is on the left.

● **NV MOUNTAINVIEW CHALETS**
   AND RV RESORT *(Open All Year)*

   Res and Info: (250) 569-0185,
                     n.v.mountainview@hotmail.com,
                     www.nv-mountainview.ca
   Location: 10 Km (6 Miles) E of McBride

   GPS Location: 53.22662 N, 119.99678 W, 2,500 Ft

46 Sites – This nice road-side campground has pull-thrus and back-ins to 80 feet. Amenities include a nice sauna and hot tub. The facility is located on the north side of Hwy 16 some 10 km (5 miles) east of McBride.

● **BEAVERVIEW RV PARK AND CAMPGROUND**
   (Open May 1 to Sept 30 – Varies)
   Res and Info: (250) 569-2513
   Location: 2 Km (1 Mile E of McBride)

   GPS Location: 53.30020 N, 120.12623 W, 2,300 Ft

56 Sites – This campground has pull-thru RV sites to 80 feet in an open field as well as back-in RV and tent sites in trees and along the Fraser River. It's located just east of McBride on the south side of the highway.

NANAIMO

Nanaimo (population 79,000) is the second largest city on Vancouver Island and British Columbia's third oldest incorporated town. The early reason for the town's existence was coal, big deposits close to tidewater were the economic driver. Today coal isn't mined here, there is little evidence that it ever was unless you know where to look. Nanaimo has three **ferry terminals**: north of the central area is Departure Bay with service to Horseshoe Bay on the mainland, south of town is Duke Point with service to Tsawwassen on the mainland, and there is also a small ferry to Gabriola Island. Actually, two even smaller ferries serve **Newcastle Island Provincial Park** and little **Protection Island** in the harbor.

The charm of Nanaimo is in its **waterfront**. There is a four-kilometer (2.5 mile) walking trail connecting a chain of parks. Look for **Swy-a-lana Lagoon Park** which is a man-made lagoon designed to attract marine life. Nearby is the pedestrian-only ferry out to **Newcastle Island**, a provincial marine park with a 7.5-kilometer (4.7-mile) trail that circles the island. At the southern end of the waterfront trail you are near the center of the city and several interesting sights. The **Bastion** is a blockhouse built by the Hudson's Bay Company in 1853, now it is the site of the Bastion Museum and a daily firing of cannons at noon during the summer. Nearby is the **Nanaimo Museum** with historical displays including a coal mine from the town's early days.

Nanaimo has a huge annual celebration known as the **Marine Festival** during the last

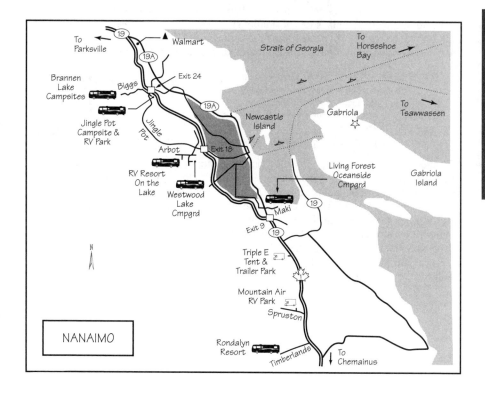

NANAIMO

half of July. The eagerly anticipated main event is the **World Championship Bathtub Race**.

Nanaimo Campgrounds

● **BRANNEN LAKE CAMPSITE** *(Open All Year)*
Res and Info: (866) 756-0404, (250) 756-0404,
                   brannenlake@shaw.ca,
                   www.brannenlake.com
Location: Nanaimo

GPS Location: 49.20321 N, 124.06437 W, 300 Ft

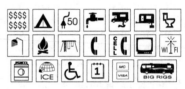

115 Sites – This campground about 2 km from Brannen Lake has a variety of campsites including long pull-thrus with full hookup and vehicle tent camping sites with no hook-ups. There is access to a swimming beach on the lake, a boat launch, and a heritage farm under the same ownership. From Exit 24 of Hwy 19 drive south and take the first right on Biggs Road. Follow Biggs for 2.4 km (1.5 miles) to the campground entrance which is on the right.

● **JINGLE POT CAMPSITE AND RV PARK**
      (Open All Year)
Res and Info: (250) 758-1614
Location: Nanaimo

GPS Location: 49.20361 N, 124.03306 W, 300 Ft

120 Sites – This is a beautifully landscaped park with lots of flowers. Sites are terraced on a hillside with plantings between sites. There are pull-thru spaces suitable for RVs to 45 feet for travelers as well as lots of smaller sites. The access to the campground is from Exit 24 of Hwy 19 as it bypasses Nanaimo to the west. Turn southwest and almost immediately you'll see the sign for the campground entrance on your left.

● **RV RESORT ON THE LAKE** *(Open All Year)*
Res and Info: (877) 826-9835, (250) 754-1975,
                   admin@resortonthelake.com,
                   www.resortonthelake.com
Location: Nanaimo

GPS Location: 49.16472 N, 124.00361 W, 600 Ft

150 Sites – This is a large popular RV park that slopes down toward Westwood Lake. There's no beach on the lake, instead a walking trail follows the lake shore from a nearby day-use park. Facilities include a large swimming pool and an upscale clubhouse, a hot tub, a community fire pit, tennis courts, and a putting green. It's great for big rigs with long back-ins to 60 feet and lots of maneuvering room. The access to the campground is from Exit 18 of Hwy 19 as it bypasses Nanaimo to the west. Head west and in just .5 km (.3 mile) take the left turn marked for the campground. Drive up the hill and at the Y in .6 km (.4 mile) take the right fork. You'll see the campground entrance on the left in another .4 km (.3 mile).

● **WESTWOOD LAKE CAMPGROUND** *(Open All Year)*
   Res and Info: (250) 753-3922, westwoodlake@shaw.ca,
                    www.westwoodlakecampgrounds.com
   Location: Nanaimo

   GPS Location: 49.16417 N, 123.99611 W, 600 Ft

66 Sites – This is a smaller campground also located near
Westwood Lake. The campground is just 100 yards or so
down the lake from the day-use park, it's easy to walk
over to the swimming beach. This campground has some excellent tent sites as well as
RV sites. A few RV sites are pull-thrus to 60 feet but most are back-ins to 35 feet. The
access to the campground is from Exit 18 of Hwy 19 as it bypasses Nanaimo to the west.
Head west and in just .5 km (.3 mile) take the left turn marked for the campground. Drive
up the hill and at the Y in .6 km (.4 mile) take the left fork. You'll see the campground
entrance on the left in another .3 km (.2 mile).

● **LIVING FOREST OCEANSIDE CAMPGROUND**
   (Open All Year)
   Res and Info: (250) 755-1755,
                    reservations@livingforest.com,
                    www.livingforest.com
   Location: Nanaimo

   GPS Location: 49.13028 N, 123.91278 W, 100 Ft

250 Sites – This is a large campground located about 5 ki-
lometers (3 miles) south of central Nanaimo overlooking the outlet of the Nanaimo River.
It's good if you want to be close to town. Sites are pull-thrus to 60 feet and back-ins to
35 feet. We prefer the sites overlooking the harbor. Swimming is on the river below the
campground. Wi-Fi is free at the office, available for a price at some sites. To reach the
campground from the north follow Hwy 19, the Nanaimo Parkway (bypass route) around
the west side of town. At the south end of town take Exit 9 and head back toward Nanaimo on Hwy 1. Drive two blocks and turn right on Maki. The campground is just ahead.

● **RONDALYN RESORT** *(Open All Year)*
   Res and Info: (800) 643-7552 or
                    (250) 245-3227,
                    rondalynresort@shaw.ca,
                    www.rondalynresort.com
   Location: Nanaimo

GPS Location: 49.04097 N, 123.90431 W, 100 Ft

120 Sites – This polished campground is some distance south of Nanaimo but the country location is very pleasant. There are back-in and pull-thru sites to 55 feet. Amenities
include a swimming pool, spa, par 3 golf course, restaurant, basketball court, and trout
pond and river fishing. Timberlands Road, the access road, goes west from Hwy 1 just
south of the Nanaimo Airport, about 10 km (6 miles) south of Nanaimo. Follow Timberlands for 2.3 km (1.4 mile) to the campground.

NEW HAZELTON AND KITWANGA

The Cassiar Highway leaves the Yellowhead Highway some 481 km (298 miles) west of
Prince George and 243 km (151 miles) east of Prince Rupert. It immediately crosses the

BRITISH COLUMBIA

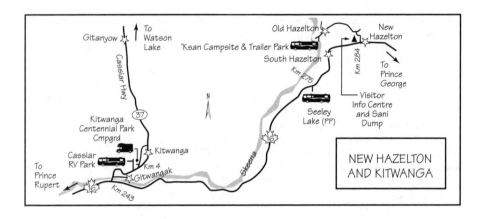

Skeena River Bridge and in just .3 km (.2 miles) a road goes east to **Gitwangak** which is home to a fine collection of totem poles. If you find these interesting there's another group at **Gitanyow** along a short road from the highway about 21 km (13 miles) to the north.

Three kms (2 miles) north of Gitwangak you'll come to **Kitwanga**. This is the home of the **Kitwanga Fort National Historic Site** (Battle Hill) and has a modern RV park and a very small village campground.

Forty-four km (27 miles) east of the Cassiar Junction is the Hazleton area. There are actually three towns called Hazleton. Both New and South Hazleton are along Hwy 16. Between them a road goes north to historic **Old Hazleton** which is the real attraction. Right at the junction there's a visitor info centre that is well worth a stop. Even the 5-mile road in to Old Hazleton is interesting since it crosses a **suspension bridge** across the Bulkley River. Old Hazleton itself is fun to visit mostly for the old buildings, many reconstructed and some still in use. Nearby is very popular **'Ksan Historical Village** which has seven very photogenic communal houses and a campground for RVs and tent campers. A good side trip is to continue north 13 km (8 miles) to **Kispiox** which has more totem poles.

New Hazelton and Kitwanga Campgrounds

● **'KSAN CAMPSITE AND TRAILER PARK**
    (Open May 1 to Oct 1)
Information: (250) 842-5940,
                gitanmaaxksan@bulkley.net,
                www.ksancampground.com
Location: Old Hazleton

GPS Location: 55.24972 N, 127.67778 W, 700 Ft

50 Sites – This campground sits next to the river near historic Old Hazleton and right next to the 'Ksan Historical Village and Museum. There are small back-in sites without hookups for tenters and small boondocking RVs as well as 60-foot pull-thru sites with full hookups arranged in a large grassy field. To reach the campground leave Hwy 16 near Km 284, there is a visitor center with a sani-station on the corner. Go north on the paved road. You'll cross an impressive suspension bridge at 1.6 km (1 mile), pass through a populated area, continue straight where the main road makes a 90-degree right at 6 km (3.7 miles) and at 7.4 km (4.6 miles) you'll see the campground entrance on your left.

☐ **SEELEY LAKE PROVINCIAL PARK** *(Open May 9 to Sept 30 – Varies)*
Information: (250) 638-8490
Location: Km 275 of Hwy 16

GPS Location: 55.19667 N, 127.68833 W, 1,000 Ft

20 Sites –Seeley Lake is adjacent although sites don't overlook the lake. Sites here are back-ins. A narrow access road makes this campground appropriate for RVs to about 35 feet although some sites would actually take 40-footers. This is a loop road that exits onto the highway a few hundred feet east of the main entrance. There are 20 sites, all have fire pits and picnic tables, some have tent pads. Restrooms are vault toilets. Water is from a hand pump. There is an overlook near the sites that allows great views of the lake and the mountains beyond, there's also a day use area near the campground entrance. Watch for the campground sign near Km 275 of Hwy 16 about 33 km (21 miles) east of the Yellowhead Highway - Cassiar Highway junction. It's on the south side of the highway.

● **CASSIAR RV PARK** *(Open May 1 to Oct 15)*
Res and Info: (250) 849-5799, inquiries@cassiarrv.ca,
                 www.cassiarrv.ca
Location: Kitwanga

GPS Location: 55.11444 N, 128.03361 W, 800 Ft

65 Sites – This campground is the most southerly along the Cassiar Highway and is a popular stop for Alaska travelers. There are tent sites as well as back-in and pull-thru sites to 80 feet. To reach the campground drive west from Km 4 of the Cassiar Highway on Barcalow Road. The campground is on the left in .6 km (.4 mile).

○ **KITWANGA CENTENNIAL PARK CAMPGROUND** *(Open As Weather Allows)*
Location: Kitwanga

GPS Location: 55.12889 N, 128.02389 W, 700 Ft

12 Sites – This is a simple village-run campground in Kitwanga. Sites are small back-ins to about 30 feet in a grove of trees. New vault toilets are provided as well as tables, fire pits, and firewood. Stays are limited to three days. Easiest access is from Km 4.2 of the Cassiar Highway. Follow Kitwanga Valley Road left for .6 km (.4 mile) to the Dollops service station. The campground is across the street.

OCEANSIDE

Oceanside is the tourist industry's name for one of the most popular family resort areas in Canada. The region is located on the east coast of Vancouver Island about 23 km (14 miles) northwest of Nanaimo. The two largest towns here are **Parksville** (population 10,000) and **Qualicum Beach** (population 7,000). Both are along the coast. The main north-south highway, Hwy 19, is inland here. A leisurely alternate route, Hwy 19A runs near the water. The beaches here are known for the shallow sandy stretches running far from shore that warm in the sun and make swimming in the ocean possible. In addition to the coast the area is overlooked by Mt Arrowsmith and there are a number of inland parks that make great destinations. There's lots to do in the area with beaches, boating, and golf the top attractions. You'll also find good day-trip destinations like the caves at Horne Lake Caves Provincial park, Butterfly World and Gardens, and Mt Arrowsmith hikes.

BRITISH COLUMBIA

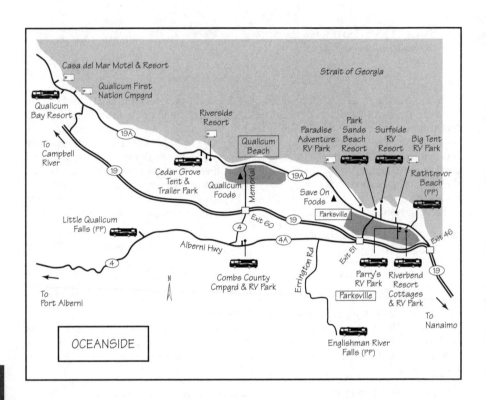

OCEANSIDE

Oceanside Campgrounds

☐ **LITTLE QUALICUM FALLS PROVINCIAL PARK**
   (Open April 30 to Sept 30)

Reservations: www.discovercamping.ca, (800) 689-9025
Information: (250) 474-1336
Location: 11 Km (7 miles) West of Qualicum Beach

GPS Location: 49.31000 N, 124.54694 W, 500 Ft

105 Sites – The attraction at this park is the Little Qualicum River which runs near the campground. There are hiking trails with overlooks of the canyon and falls, also places upstream suitable for swimming. There's better swimming nearby at Cameron Lake. The park is located off the Alberni Highway (Hwy 4) some 9.0 km (5.6 miles) west of the intersection of the highway with Hwy 19, the Inland Island Highway.

○ **COMBS COUNTY CAMPGROUND AND RV PARK**
   (Open May 15 to Sept 30)

Res and Info: (800) 925-3888, (250) 248-9371,
                  www.combscampground.com
Location: 13 Km (8 Miles) W of Parksville

GPS Location: 49.30426 N, 124.44482 W, 300 Ft

100 Sites – This campground isn't near the ocean, but it is near the tourist attractions of Coombs including Coombs

Country Market and Coombs Emporium. It also has great access to the attractions toward Port Alberni like Cathedral Grove and Little Qualicum Falls. There are tent sites as well as back-in and pull-thru RV sites to 50 feet, mostly in trees. There is a swimming pool, a hot tub, and a fishing pond. From Hwy 19 take Exit 60 onto Hwy 4 and travel south for 2.6 km (1.6 miles). Turn left on Hwy 4A and the campground entrance is on the left in only .8 km (35 mile).

☐ **ENGLISHMAN RIVER FALLS PROVINCIAL PARK**
   (Open April 30 to Sept 30 – Varies)
   Reservations: www.discovercamping.ca, (800) 689-9025
   Information: (250) 474-1336
   Location: 13 Km (8 Miles) SW of Parksville

   GPS Location: 49.24877 N, 124.35451 W, 600 Ft

103 Sites – Englishman River Falls is a nice provincial park inland from Parksville. There are two waterfalls nearby, trails, and in late summer when water volumes are down you can swim below one of the falls. Sites here are gravel surfaced off wide gravel drives. Many extend to 45 feet in length. From Parksville From Parksville follow the Alberni Highway (Hwy 4A) south. Zero your odometer when you pass under the Inland Island Highway (Hwy 19). In 3.1 km (1.9 miles) turn left on Errington Road. Follow Errington 8.4 km (5.2 miles) to the campground entrance.

● **QUALICUM BAY RESORT** *(Open All Year)*
   Res and Info: (250) 757-2003, (800) 663-6899,
                     info@resortbc.com,
                     www.resortbc.com
   Location: 13 Km (8 Miles) N of Qualicum Beach

   GPS Location: 49.40194 N, 124.62444 W, Near Sea Level

120 Sites – This is a campground set in trees with campsites around a pond. Swimming is in the pond. There's also an ice cream store out front. The park has tent sites as well as back-in and pull-thru RV sites to 50 feet. Zero your odometer at the point where Memorial Avenue in Qualicum Beach meets Highway 19A, the coastal highway. Memorial is the main north/south avenue through Qualicum Beach, it is an extension of the Port Alberni Highway. Drive west along the waterfront for 15.5 km (9.6 miles), the campground is on your left.

● **CEDAR GROVE RV PARK AND CAMPGROUND**
   (Open Easter to Canadian Thanksgiving – 2nd Monday in Oct)
   Res and Info: (250) 752-2442 ,
                     www.cedargrovervpark.ca
   Location: 5 Km (3 Miles) NW of Qualicum Beach

   GPS Location: 49.36194 N, 124.48389 W, Near Sea Level

111 Sites – This campground is located northwest of Qualicum Beach. Although it's next to the coastal highway the park is on the side of the road away from the beach. Swimming here is in the river behind the park. Sites are back-ins to 50 feet. Zero your odometer at the point where Memorial Avenue in Qualicum Beach meets Highway 19A, the coastal highway. Memorial is the main north/south avenue through Qualicum Beach, it is an extension of the Port Alberni Highway. Drive west along the waterfront for 6.9 km (4.3 miles), the campground is on your left.

● **PARK SANDS BEACH RESORT** *(Open All Year)*
   Res and Info: (250) 248-3171, (877) 873-1600,
                 www.parksands.com
   Location: Parksville

   GPS Location: 49.32222 N, 124.31250 W, Near Sea Level

94 Sites – The Park Sands is a tradition in Parksville,
long one of the most popular commercial campgrounds in the area. The campground is
adjacent to the beach and within walking distance of the malls and stores that line the
highway along here. There are two sections of the resort. Near the highway the sites are
older with parking on gravel and grass. Farther from the highway are larger sites with
paved parking areas, many suitable for RVs to 45 feet. The campground is open all year
but in winter takes self-contained rigs only as the restrooms are closed up.

● **SURFSIDE RV RESORT** *(Open All Year)*
   Res and Info: (250) 248-9713, relax@surfside.bc.ca,
                 www.surfside.bc.ca
   Location: Parksville

   GPS Location: 49.32300 N, 124.30647 W, Near Sea Level`

230 Sites – The Surfside is an upscale membership
campground with some privately owned sites put into a pool for rental. There are 230
sites in the park but about 50 are usually in the rental pool. They're big back-in and
pull-thru sites to 60 feet. The campground is located on the beach and has tennis courts,
a pool, and a clubhouse. The campground entrance road, Corfield Street, is about .6 km
(.4 miles) east of the Park Sands Beach Resort. Follow Corfield for .2 km (.1 mile) to the
resort entrance.

● **PARRY'S RV PARK** *(Open April 1 to Oct 31)*
   Res and Info: (250) 248-6242,
                 www.parrysrvpark.com
   Location: Parksville

   GPS Location: 49.31265 N, 124.28563 W, Near Sea Level

130 Sites – Parry's is a popular Parksville RV park.
It is not located on the ocean. Instead, it is located
just inland along the English River. There's a beach
on the river and a swimming hole. There are tent sites as well as back-in and pull-thru
RV sites to 55 feet. Amenities include a swimming pool. The location is very convenient
to the restaurants and other attractions in Parksville. From Hwy 19A just west of where
it crosses the Englishman River drive south on Martindale Road. The campground is on
the left after one block.

● **RIVERBEND RESORT COTTAGES AND RV**
   PARK *(Open All Year)*

   Res and Info: (800) 701-3033,
                 www.riverbendresort.bc.ca
   Location: Parksville

   GPS Location: 49.31402 N, 124.27897 W, 100 Ft

110 Sites – On the far side of the river from Parry's is the Riverbend Resort. There's no
swimming pool at the Riverbend but it too offers a beach and swimming holes in the

river. There are tent sites and full-hookup RV sites to 60 feet. The entrance to the campground is off Hwy 19A just east of where it crosses the Englishman River.

☐ **RATHTREVOR BEACH PROVINCIAL PARK**
   (Open All Year)
   Reservations: www.discovercamping.ca, (800) 689-9025
   Information: (250) 474-1336, (250) 248-9460
   Location: 2 Km (1 Mile) E of Parksville

   GPS Location: 49.32111 N, 124.26750 W, Near Sea Level

165 Sites – This is one of the most popular provincial parks in the system, the attraction is the wide beach. When the tide goes out the water recedes a long way, and when it come in over the hot sand it's nice and warm. Twenty-five sites are walk-in tent sites. Many RV sites are suitable for RVs larger than 45 feet, they are all back-ins. Reservations are required from the last week of June to Labour Day in September. The campground is open all year long but from October 16 to March 15 services are limited, there is a reduced fee during this period. The campground is located about 2 km (1 mile) east of Parksville on Highway 19A, the Island Highway.

OKANAGAN VALLEY

Canada's portion of the Okanagan River Valley stretches 200 km (125 miles) north from the U.S. border. The outstanding feature here is probably the weather, the average rainfall is only 9 inches per year because the North Cascades shelter the valley from storms coming from the Pacific.

When you add the valley's water to the weather the Okanagan becomes a perfect playground. Several lakes dominate the valley, the largest by far is Okanagan Lake, it's 170 km (105 miles) long. In summer they're plenty warm enough for swimming and have many very popular beaches. Boating of all kinds is extremely popular.

There are a number of small towns and three good-sized cities in the valley. Most are arranged off Highway 97 which runs up the center.

The most southern part of the region and stretching north to Penticton, is known for its fruit orchards and vineyards. Small towns line the road including **Osoyoos, Oliver,** and **Okanagan Falls.** There are also campgrounds along the lakes, not to mention fruit stands along the road and wineries to visit.

Farthest south of the three cities is **Penticton** (population 33,000). The town sits between two lakes: to the south is Skaha Lake and to the north is Okanagan Lake. There are excellent beaches on both lakes, several RV parks are located on the Skaha Lake shore. Penticton attracts a lot of visitors and has all the facilities they require. You can't miss the **S.S. Sicamous**, an old sternwheeler beached on the shore of Okanagan Lake, it is now a museum and there are hopes of restoring it to operating condition. The town has an excellent museum covering all aspects of the town's history. The **Okanagan Game Farm** is located about eight kilometers south of town on Highway 97, it has a good selection of animals from around the world. You'll also find no shortage of golf courses, water slides, and vineyards offering tours. Penticton hosts several celebrations including a Peach Festival during the second week of August and the Okanagan Wine Festival in October.

From Penticton Highway 97 follows the west side of Okanagan Lake to the north for 58 km (36 miles). There are a number of small towns on this side of the lake, as well as a

BRITISH COLUMBIA

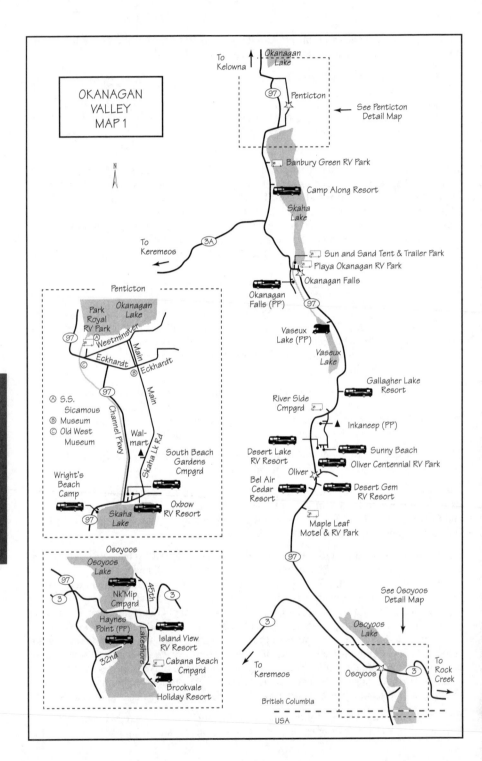

OKANAGAN
VALLEY
MAP 1

N

To
Kelowna

Okanagan
Lake

97 Penticton

See Penticton
Detail Map

Banbury Green RV Park

Camp Along Resort

Skaha
Lake

To
Keremeos

3A

Sun and Sand Tent & Trailer Park

Playa Okanagan RV Park

Okanagan Falls

Okanagan
Falls (PP)

97

Vaseux
Lake (PP)

Vaseux
Lake

Gallagher Lake
Resort

River Side
Cmpgrd

Inkaneep (PP)

Desert Lake
RV Resort

Sunny Beach

Oliver Centennial RV Park

Oliver

Desert Gem
RV Resort

Bel Air
Cedar
Resort

Maple Leaf
Motel & RV Park

97

See Osoyoos
Detail Map

Osoyoos
Lake

3

To
Keremeos

Osoyoos

3

To
Rock
Creek

British Columbia

USA

Penticton

Park
Royal
RV Park

Okanagan
Lake

97 Ⓐ Westminster

Eckhardt

Ⓒ

Ⓑ Eckhardt

Main

Main

Ⓐ S.S.
Sicamous

Ⓑ Museum

Ⓒ Old West
Museum

97

Channel Pkwy

Wal-
mart

Skaha Lk Rd

South Beach
Gardens
Cmpgrd

Wright's
Beach
Camp

97

Skaha
Lake

Oxbow
RV Resort

Osoyoos

Osoyoos
Lake

97

3

Nk'Mip
Cmpgrd

45th

3

Haynes
Point (PP)

Lakeshore

Island View
RV Resort

32nd

Cabana Beach
Cmpgrd

Brookvale
Holiday Resort

number of good campgrounds. Connecting the West Side to Kelowna is a long floating bridge similar to the ones used in Seattle.

Kelowna is the province's fourth largest city with a population of about 100,000 people. Like Penticton, Kelowna caters to visitors, there are many attractions devoted to them. Tours of vineyards and fruit-growing and packing operations are very popular, just check with the info centre to see what is available. The city is surprisingly pleasant with a number of excellent lake-side parks offering good beaches and a nice central downtown area. Kelowna hosts the Okanagan Wine Festival during the first week of October.

About 50 km (36 miles) north of Kelowna is the region's third large city, Vernon, with a population in the neighborhood of 35,000. Along the way watch for the signs for **Ellison Provincial Park** about 16 km (10 miles) south of Vernon, it is a fresh-water underwater park for snorkeling and scuba.

Vernon has fewer visitor attractions than the cities farther south. The **O'Keefe Ranch** is located 13 km (8 miles) to the north on Hwy 97 toward Kamloops. It is an early cattle ranch and is open to the public as a non-profit historic site, there is a mansion and several other buildings. Also a restaurant and camping area (see below).

Okanagan Valley Campgrounds

☐ **HAYNES POINT PROVINCIAL PARK** *(Open April 1 to Oct 11)*
   Reservations: www.discovercamping.ca, (800) 689-9025
   Information: (250) 548-0076, info@campokanagan.com
   Location: Osoyoos

   GPS Location: 49.01444 N, 119.45806 W, 900 Ft

41 Sites – The beauty of this park is that it is located on a long peninsula extending into Lake Osoyoos. Because of that, most sites are near the water since they are back-ins off a central road. Some sites here extend to 45 feet although many are much smaller. Swimming is possible in the lake and there's a boat ramp. There's also a short nature trail at the foot of the peninsula that offers pretty good birding in some seasons. There is also a boat ramp. This is a very popular park and has a seven day limit, reservations are definitely recommended. There's another attraction here too. RVers are allowed to camp in an overflow area that runs along the entrance road. You pay the same as you would in the campground but you're right next to the water. No tables, no fire pits, but you have your own beach. This overflow area serves as a safety valve for the entire Osoyoos region when campgrounds are full. The campground entrance road is off Hwy 97 some 2.9 km (1.8 miles) south of the intersection of Hwys 3 and 97 in Osoyoos. After turning east on the entrance road (32nd Ave) it's .5 km (.3 miles) to the park.

● **ISLAND VIEW RV RESORT** *(Open All Year)*
   Res and Info: (250) 495-7696, islandviewresort@telus.net
   Location: Osoyoos

   GPS Location: 49.02165 N, 119.43551 W, 1,000 Ft

110 Sites – This is a condominium park with sites available for rental. They are landscaped and paved full hookup, back-in sites to 50 feet. Each site has a small lawn and shrubs. The park is located across the road from the lake. Since sites are terraced many have good views. From Hwy 3 on the east side of the bridge over Lake Osoyoos drive south on Lakeshore Dr for 1.1 km (.7 mile) to the park.

● **BROOKVALE HOLIDAY RESORT**
    (Open May 1 to Sept 30)
Res and Info: (888) 495-7514, 250 495-7514,
                www.brookvalecampground.com
Location: Osoyoos

    GPS Location: 49.00444 N, 119.43611 W, 900 Ft

73 Sites – Sites here are back-ins (or pull-into's) across the road from the beach. This older park is best for RVs to 30 feet if it's full since parking and maneuvering room is limited. It could handle larger RVs off-season since many parking spots aren't bordered by anything that might get in your way. Almost all sites have electricity and water hook-ups, there are very few with sewer. There's no dump station but a sewer tank truck is sometimes available. From Hwy 3 on the east side of the bridge over Lake Osoyoos drive south on Lakeshore Dr. In 3.1 km (1.9 miles) you'll spot the Brookvale, it's on the left.

● **NK'MIP CAMPGROUND** *(Open All Year)*
Res and Info: (250) 495-7279,
                info@campingosoyoos.com,
                www.campingosoyoos.com
Location: 3 Km (2 Miles) NE of Osoyoos

    GPS Location: 49.03833 N, 119.44056 W, 900 Ft

320 Sites – This large campground is located on the east side of Osoyoos Lake. The large complex includes a 9-hole golf course, marina, Desert and Heritage Centre visitor center, and a winery. There's an indoor swimming pool a hot tub and a swimming beach. Sites here include tents sites as well as large back-ins to 60 feet. Some sites are along the waterfront. From the intersection in Osoyoos head east on Hwy 3. In 3.5 km (2.2 miles) turn north on 45th Street. You'll arrive at the campground entrance in about 1 km (.6 mile).

● **BEL AIR CEDAR RESORT** *(Open All Year)*
Reservations: (800) 801-0999
Information: (250) 498-2443, www.belaircedar.com
Location: Oliver

    GPS Location: 49.16889 N, 119.55861 W, 1,000 Ft

28 Sites – The Bel Air is a motel and RV park in southern Oliver. Sites here are back-ins and pull-thrus to 55 feet, most are full-hookup sites. Tent sites with grass for pitching are along the south fence. There's a swimming pool and spa. The campground is on the west side of Hwy 97 about 1 km (.5 mile) south of Oliver.

● **DESERT GEM RV RESORT** *(Open All Year)*
Res and Info: (888) 925-9966, (250) 498-5544,
                info@desertgemrv.com,
                www.desertgemrv.com
Location: Oliver

    GPS Location: 49.17250 N, 119.55417 W, 1,000 Ft

65 Sites – The Desert Gem is a modern big-rig park located right next to Hwy 97 as it passes through Oliver. All sites are full hookup. There are paved back-ins and pull-thrus to 60 feet. Watch for the campground at the southern edge of Oliver on the east side of the highway.

○ **Oliver Centennial RV Park**
(Open April 1 to Oct 15)
Reservations: (877) 965-4837
Information: (250) 498-6800, www.centennialrvpark.com
Location: Oliver

GPS Location: 49.18333 N, 119.54806 W, 1,000

60 Sites – This Oliver municipal campground is centrally located and very handy. It's right downtown and backs onto a bike trail along the Okanagan River with the city info centre next door. Sites here are mostly tents site and back-ins to about 45 feet, there are a few pull-thrus too. Parking is on grass with shade. Full and partial hookups are available and there's a dump station. The campground is located one block east of Hwy 97 in central Oliver.

● **Sunny Beach** *(Open All Year)*
Res and Info: (250) 498-4501
Location: Oliver

GPS Location: 49.20417 N, 119.54083 W, 900 Ft

25 Sites – This is one of two RV parks at the north end of little Tuc-El-Nuit Lake, situated just northeast of Oliver. Desert Lake RV Resort, described below, is the other. There are full-hookup back-ins and pull-thrus to 60 feet. Parking is on gravel off paved roads with trees for shade. There's a dock and swimming beach. Although access is possible directly from Oliver it is probably easier to drive to the park from the north. About 5.6 km (3.5 miles) north of Oliver on Hwy 97 turn right at the road marked for Inkaneep Provincial Park. Drive south for 2.9 km (1.8 miles) and you'll see the entrance road for both this park and Desert Lake RV Resort on the right. Sunny beach is the first of the two.

● **Desert Lake RV Resort** *(Open All Year)*
Res and Info: (250) 485-0158
Location: Oliver

GPS Location: 49.20389 N, 119.54139 W, 900 Ft

40 Sites – This is the second of two RV parks at the north end of Tuc-El-Nuit Lake. See Sunny Beach above for the other. This campground has many long term residents but also sites for vacationers. These are back-ins and pull-thrus to 60 feet with parking on gravel off paved access roads. There's a swimming beach. Although access is possible directly from Oliver it is probably easier to drive to the park from the north. About 5.6 km (3.5 miles) north of Oliver on Hwy 97 turn right at the road marked for Inkaneep Provincial Park. Drive south for 2.9 km (1.8 miles) and you'll see the entrance road for both this park and Desert Lake RV Resort on the right.

● **Gallagher Lake Resort**
(Open May 1 to Oct 16)
Reservations: (800) 562-9017,
                reservations@gallagherlakeresort.com
Information: (250) 498-3358
Location: 6 Km (4 Miles) N of Oliver

GPS Location: 49.24361 N, 119.52417 W, 1,000 Ft

British Columbia

155 Sites – This older campground has lots of tent sites, also partial and full-hookup RV sites. There are both back-in and pull-thru sites, some to 60 feet. The campground is on Gallagher Lake and offers swimming and fishing. There are also tennis courts. Wi-Fi is only available near the office. From Oliver drive north on Hwy 97 for 6 km (3.7 miles), the campground is on the right.

☐ **VASEUX LAKE PROVINCIAL PARK** *(Open All Year)*
   Information: (250) 548-0076
   Location: 6 Km (4 Miles) S of Okanagan Falls

   GPS Location: 49.29861 N, 119.53056 W, 1,000 Ft

12 Sites – The sites in this campground are back-ins off a short road which closely parallels Hwy 97 along the shore of Vaseux Lake. Most of the sites are on the lake. Due to a steep approach the sites here are best for RVs to about 30 feet that don't have a clearance problem. There's a swimming beach and this shallow lake is well-known as a bird watching destination, a small canoe or kayak would help to get you away from the highway and out on the lake. It's hard to miss this campground, driving south from Okanagan Falls it's on the right side about 6 km (4 miles) from town.

☐ **OKANAGAN FALLS PROVINCIAL PARK**
   (Open March 28 to Oct 12 – Varies)
   Information: (250) 548-0076
   Location: Okanagan Falls

   GPS Location: 49.34167 N, 119.58083 W, 1,100 Ft

25 Sites – This pretty little provincial park campground is just a short distance off the main road but it seems much more isolated. Sites here are off a paved loop road and some are as long as 40 feet although most are shorter. They're separated by lush lawn and shade trees. The campground adjoins the Okanagan River near the outlet of Skaha Lake. The falls it is named for are really more like rapids, but they are scenic. As Hwy 97 passes north through the little community of Okanagan Falls it jogs west and crosses the Okanagan River before turning sharply north. Just west of the river a road goes south along the west side of the river, follow it .3 km (.2 mile) to the campground entrance.

● **CAMP ALONG RESORT** *(Open April 1 to Oct 31)*
   Reservations: (800) 968-KAMP
   Information: (250) 497-6652 www.campalong.com
   Location: 6 Km (4 Mile) S of Penticton

   GPS Location: 49.40750 N, 119.60528 W, 1,400 Ft

80 Sites – This campground is set in an old apricot and pear orchard on a hilltop overlooking Skaha Lake. Views are spectacular from the sites at the eastern edge of the camp. It has tent sites and back-in RV sites to 45 feet. Unfortunately, site access is difficult for RVs over about 30 feet. Parking is on grass between the trees and most are full-hookup sites. The facilities are good and include a swimming pool. Wi-Fi is available at the office and a few sites nearby. Watch for the campground on the east side of the highway 3.1 km (1.9 miles) north of the intersection where Hwy 3A from Keremeos joins up with north-south Hwy 97. That's 8.4 km (5.2 miles) north of Okanagan Falls and 6.1 km (3.8 miles) south of Penticton.

● **WRIGHT'S BEACH CAMP**
  (Open March 15 to Oct 15)
  Res and Info: (250) 492-7120,
                www.wrightsbeachcamp.com
  Location: Penticton

  GPS Location: 49.45083 N, 119.60861 W, 1,100 Ft

230 Sites – Wright's is a beach-front campground on the northern shore of Skaha lake. The sites are back-in (or pull-in) sites with full hookups from very small to 50 feet in length. Many are right on the beach. There's the big beach with a swimming area as well as a pool. It's an easy place to find. From the intersection of the Channel Parkway and Skaha Lake Road drive west on Hwy 97 for .9 km (.5 mile), the campground is on the left.

● **SOUTH BEACH GARDENS CAMPGROUND**
  (Open May 1 to Sept 30)
  Res and Info: (250) 492-0628,
                www.southbeachgardens.com
  Location: Penticton

  GPS Location: 49.45333 N, 119.59472 W, 1,200 Ft

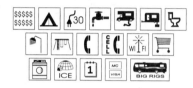

270 Sites – This is a large holiday campground located across the street from Skaha Beach. This one can be a little crazy when summer holidays are in full swing. There are tent sites as well as back-in and pull-thru RV sites to 48 feet. Amenities include mini golf. Traveling eastbound on Hwy 97 continue strait onto Skaha Lake Road at the point where Hwy 97 turns inland to run along the channel. In .2 km (.1 mile) turn left into the campground entrance.

● **OXBOW RV RESORT** *(Open March 15 to Oct 15)*
  Res and Info: (250) 770-8147, info@oxbowrvresort.com,
                www.oxbowrvresort.com
  Location: Penticton

  GPS Location: 49.45361 N, 119.59389 W, 1,200 Ft

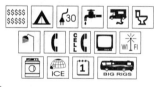

75 Sites – The Oxbow is a small but well-run family park
at the southern edge of Penticton. It's well-organized and spotless and our favorite place to stay in the area. Skaha Beach Park is just across the road. Sites are back-ins to 40 feet and a few long pull-thrus to 70 feet. Traveling eastbound on Hwy 97 continue strait onto Skaha Lake Road at the point where Hwy 97 turns inland to run along the channel. In .3 km (.2 mile) turn left into Skaha Place and then left again into the campground entrance.

● **SUMMERLAND CAMPGROUND RV PARK**
  AND TENTING *(Open June 22 to Sept 5)*
  Res and Info: (250) 494-0911, (800) 494-0911,
                info@summerlandcampground.com,
                www.summerlandcampground.com
  Location: Summerland

  GPS Location: 49.56833 N, 119.63028 W, 1,100 Ft

38 Sites – This vacation campground limits RV length to 28 feet. They have back-in sites partial and full hookup. There's also a swimming pool and the Sun-Oka Provincial Beach Park is just a short walk away. Wi-Fi is accessible near the office. Just south of Summerland on Hwy 97 turn east on Wharf Street, then in a block turn right on Towgood Place.

BRITISH COLUMBIA

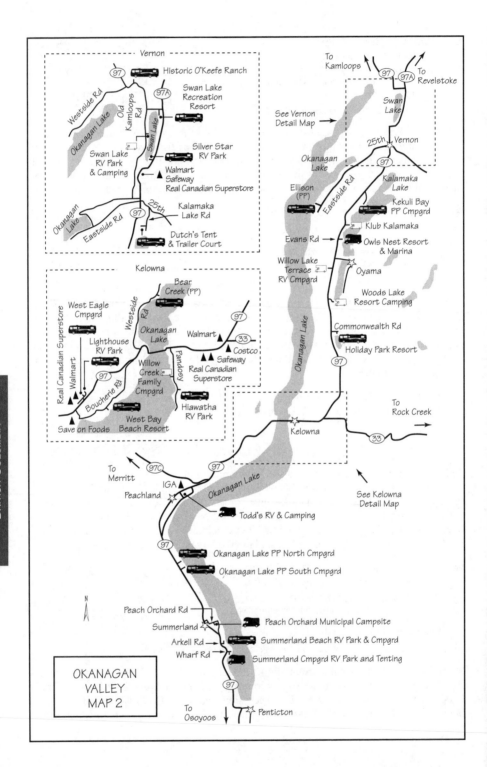

Vernon

97

Historic O'Keefe Ranch

97A

Swan Lake
Recreation
Resort

Westside Rd

Old Kamloops Rd

Swan Lake

Okanagan Lake

Silver Star
RV Park

Swan Lake
RV Park
& Camping

Walmart
Safeway
Real Canadian Superstore

25th

Eastside Rd

Okanagan Lake

97

Kalamaka
Lake Rd

Dutch's Tent
& Trailer Court

To
Kamloops

97   97A

To
Revelstoke

Swan
Lake

See Vernon
Detail Map

25th   Vernon

Okanagan
Lake

97

Eastside Rd

Ellison
(PP)

Kalamaka
Lake

Kekuli Bay
PP Cmpgrd

Klub Kalamaka

Evans Rd

Owls Nest Resort
& Marina

Willow Lake
Terrace
RV Cmpgrd

Oyama

Woods Lake
Resort Camping

Commonwealth Rd

Holiday Park Resort

Okanagan Lake

97

To
Rock Creek

Kelowna

Bear
Creek (PP)

Westside Rd

West Eagle
Cmpgrd

Real Canadian Superstore

Okanagan
Lake

Walmart

97

33

Costco

Lighthouse
RV Park

Pandosy

Safeway
Real Canadian
Superstore

Walmart

97

Willow
Creek
Family
Cmpgrd

Boucherie Rd

Hiawatha
RV Park

Save on Foods

West Bay
Beach Resort

Kelowna

33

To
Rock Creek

To
Merritt

97C

97

IGA

Peachland

Okanagan Lake

See Kelowna
Detail Map

Todd's RV & Camping

97

Okanagan Lake PP North Cmpgrd

Okanagan Lake PP South Cmpgrd

N

Peach Orchard Rd

Summerland

Arkell Rd

Wharf Rd

Peach Orchard Municipal Campsite

Summerland Beach RV Park & Cmpgrd

Summerland Cmpgrd RV Park and Tenting

97

OKANAGAN
VALLEY
MAP 2

To
Osoyoos

Penticton

The entrance is on the right. Wharf Street is 8.9 km (5.5 miles) north of Penticton and 49.4 km (30.6 miles) south of the west end of the Kelowna floating bridge.

● **SUMMERLAND BEACH RV PARK AND CAMPGROUND**
  (formerly Illahie Beach RV Park-Campground)
  (Open April 30 to Oct 1)

  Res and Info: (250) 494-0800,
  www.summerlandbeachrv.com
  Location: Summerland

  GPS Location: 49.58139 N, 119.64306 W, 1,100 Ft

140 Sites – This campground has beach frontage and the capability to take large RVs. About half of the sites here are long term residents but there are some 50 back-ins to 45 feet as well as tent sites. RVs are not parked along the beach but there are fire pits there. From Hwy 97 in Summerland the park is signed at Arkell Rd. Exit here and drive north for just a short distance to the park. This exit from Hwy 97 is 10.3 km (6.4 miles) north of Penticton and 47.9 km (29.7 miles) south of the west end of the Kelowna floating bridge.

○ **PEACH ORCHARD MUNICIPAL CAMPSITE**
  (Open May 15 to Sept 15)
  Res and Info: (250) 494-9649, www.peachorchard.ca
  Location: Summerland

  GPS Location: 49.60972 N, 119.65944 W, 1,300 Ft

125 Sits – This municipal campground has lots of tent sites and also many back-in RV sites to 35 feet. Many of the RV sites have electricity and water hookup and there is a dump station. Peach Orchard Beach and Rotary Beach are within easy walking distance just down the hill. Although there are not campfires at the sites there are community fire pits, also a tennis court and nearby boat ramp. To reach the park turn east at the traffic light in Summerland on Rosedale Ave. Almost immediately jog right on Biagioni Avenue until you reach Peach Orchard Road. Turn left here and you'll see the campground on the right in 1.1 km (.7 mile). The Rosedale traffic light is 14.7 km (9.1 miles) north of Penticton and 43.5 km (27.0 miles) south of the west end of the Kelowna floating bridge.

☐ **NORTH CAMPGROUND - OKANAGAN LAKE PROVINCIAL PARK**
  (Open May 15 to Sept 19 – Varies)
  Reservations: www.discovercamping.ca, (800) 689-9025
  Information: (250) 548-0076
  Location: 10 Km (6 Miles) S of Peachland

  GPS Location: 49.69083 N, 119.73333 W, 1,100 Ft

80 Sites – Although the entrance to this campground is high on the side of a steep hillside the sites are at shore level next to Okanagan Lake. They are located off two paved loops and are pretty closely spaced back-ins to 60 feet. Some sites are directly on the lake. There's a swimming beach, a boat launch, and a 1 km trail to the south campground. The access road to this campground is well marked on Hwy 97 between Summerland and Peachland. It's 25.5 km (15.8 miles) north of Penticton and 32.7 km (20.3 miles) south of the west end of the Kelowna floating bridge.

BRITISH COLUMBIA

☐ **SOUTH CAMPGROUND - OKANAGAN LAKE**
    PROVINCIAL PARK *(Open All Year)*

Reservations: www.discovercamping.ca,
            (800) 689-9025
Information: (250) 548-0076
Location: 11 Km (7 Miles) S of Peachland

GPS Location: 49.68167 N, 119.71806 W, 1,100 Ft

88 Sites – Sites at this provincial park campground are on the hillside along the road that loops down to the beach. They are back-ins to about 60 feet, maneuvering room is tighter here than at the north campground. There is a swimming beach and a trail to the north park. In the off season the gates are open and camping is allowed, but there are no services. The fee is low for off season camping. The access road to this campground is well marked on Hwy 97 between Summerland and Peachland. It's 24.4 km (15.1 miles) north of Penticton and 33.7 km (20.9 miles) south of the west end of the Kelowna floating bridge.

● **TODD'S RV AND CAMPING** *(Open April 15 to Oct 15)*
   Res and Info: (250) 767-6644, (866) 255-6864,
              www.toddsrv.com
   Location: Peachland

GPS Location: 49.78417 N, 119.70972 W, 1,100 Ft

85 Sites – Todd's is located right across the street from the beach. It has tent and back-in RV sites to 35 feet. There are both full and partial hookup sites and there is a community fire pit. The campground is located at the northeast end of Peachland. To reach it take Todd Road south from Hwy 97 to the beach. Then turn left and in a short distance you'll see the campground on the left. The Todd Road intersection is 38.4 km (23.8 miles) north of Penticton and 19.8 km (12.3 miles) south of the west end of the Kelowna floating bridge.

● **LIGHTHOUSE RV PARK** *(Open All Year)*
   Information: (250) 768-7644
   Location: Westbank

GPS Location: 49.84555 N, 119.60928 W, 1,400 Ft

40 Sites – A newer campground perched high on the hillside in Okanagan Landing above new stores and the highway with great views of Okanagan Lake. Because it is only 10 km (6 miles) south of the Kelowna Bridge this modern campground attracts many long-term campers who want a spot to stay close to the city, but it also makes a decent place for travelers who want the same thing. It's not primarily a family holiday site like most other campgrounds around the area. Sites are back-ins to 50 feet and pull-thrus to 70 feet with decent landscaping on terraces. In Westbank, 9.4 km (5.8 miles) south of the Kelowna bridge across Okanagan Lake, turn up the hill on Elk Road. In just a block turn right on Louis Drive and follow it for .6 km (.4 mile) up the hill past the entrance to West Eagle Campground to the Old Okanagan Highway. Turn left and you'll see the entrance on the right.

● **WEST EAGLE CAMPGROUND**
(Open May 1 to Sept 30)
Res and Info: (250) 768-7426, infoatrmdgroup.com
Location: Westbank

GPS Location: 49.84333 N, 119.60806 W, 1,300 Ft

80 Sites – This campground is situated in Westbank
on a hillside far above the highway, and stores. There is tent camping on grass as well
as pull-thru RV sites to 40 feet on dirt under trees. These include both full and partial
hookup sites. There is Wi-Fi access near the office. In Westbank, 9.4 km (5.8 miles) south
of the Kelowna bridge across Okanagan Lake, turn up the hill on Elk Road. In just a block
turn right on Louis Drive and follow it for .4 km (.2 mile) up the hill to the campground
entrance on the left.

● **WEST BAY BEACH RESORT**
(Open March 15 to Oct 15)
Res and Info: (250) 768-3004,
                www.westbaybeachresort.com
Location: Westbank

GPS Location: 49.83139 N, 119.57750 W, 1,100 Ft

70 Sites – West Bay Beach is a waterside vacation campground and quite close to Kelowna. It has a few pull-thru sites to 40 feet but most are back-ins, some to 37 feet. There's a
beach and boat ramp here, a tennis court, and also some llamas and alpacas that the kids
love. To reach the campground in Westbank turn east off Hwy 97 onto Boucherie Road
and follow it for 5.6 km (3.5 mile). Turn left onto Westbay Road and drive down to the
resort. Boucherie Road leaves Hwy 97 some 2.7 km (1.7 miles) from the west end of the
Kelowna floating bridge.

☐ **BEAR CREEK PROVINCIAL PARK**
(Open April 1 to Oct 10 – Varies)
Reservations: www.discovercamping.ca, (800) 689-9025
Information: (250) 548-0076, info@campokanagan.com
Location: 10 Km (6 Miles) NW of Kelowna

GPS Location: 49.92639 N, 119.51139 W, 1,100 Ft

122 Sites – This is a large lakeside provincial park divided by Bear Creek. Sites will take
RVs to 40 feet, all are back-ins. There is a swimming beach and a boat launch. Because
this is such a busy park reservations are essential. To reach the park turn north on Westside Road off Hwy 97 from an intersection just 1.6 km (1 mile) west of the west end of
the Okanagan Lake floating bridge. Follow Westside 8 km (5 miles) north to the park.

● **HIAWATHA RV PARK** *(Open March 1 to Sept 30)*
Res and Info: (888) 784-7275, (250) 861-4837,
                www.hiawatharvpark.com
Location: Kelowna

GPS Location: 49.84722 N, 119.48667 W, 1,100 Ft

75 Sites – The Hiawatha is one of the few camp-
grounds actually located in Kelowna. It's near the shore of Okanagan Lake but not on it.
There are sites for tenters as well as back-ins and pull-thrus to 40 feet. Amenities include
a pool and spa. From an intersection .6 km (.4 mile) east of the east end of the Okanagan Lake Floating Bridge turn south on Pandosy. Follow Pandosy south for 4.2 km (2.6

BRITISH COLUMBIA

miles), along the way it will become Lakeshore Rd. The campground entrance is on the left.

● **HOLIDAY PARK RESORT** *(Open All Year)*
Reservations: (800) 752-9678
Information: (250) 766-4255, www.sweetlife.com
Location: 10 Km (6 Miles) N of Kelowna

GPS Location: 50.00750 N, 119.39306 W, 1,400 Ft

570 Sites – This huge campground has mostly per-
manently located units but there are about 100 RV sites available for vacationers and travelers as well as condo sites that are in a rental pool. These are paved back-in big rig sites
to 75 feet. The campground is on the north end of Duck Lake and has lots of amenities
including indoor and outdoor swimming pools, tennis courts, hot tubs, sauna, and restaurant. It's an adult oriented place with lots of retired residents but children are welcome. To
reach the park head north from Kelowna on Hwy 97. After about 10 km (6 miles) you'll
see Duck Lake on the right and just beyond the north end find Commonwealth Road.
Turn right here and proceed .6 km (.4 mile) to the entrance.

● **OWLS NEST RESORT AND MARINA**
(Open May 1 to Oct 30 – Varies)
Res and Info: (250) 548-3830
Location: 18 Km (11 Miles) S of Vernon

GPS Location: 50.12222 N, 119.38250 W, 1,300 Ft

100 Sites – This campground is on the west shore of Ka-
lamalka Lake. The campground is on a steep hillside with access to sites requiring rigs to
negotiate paved but narrow and steep driveways inside the campground. Access is tight
and careful driving required. There are shaded tent sites as well as 30-foot back-ins with
full hookups. Amenities include a swimming beach, boat ramp, and marina. The access
road to the resort is Evans Road. From Kelowna travel north on Hwy 97 for 26 km (16
miles), the park entrance is on the east side of the highway. This is 18 km (11 miles) south
of Vernon.

□ **KEKULI BAY PROVINCIAL PARK CAMPGROUND**
(Open April 1 to Oct 31 – Varies)
Reservations: www.discovercamping.ca, (800) 689-9025
Information: (250) 545-8467
Location: 10 Km (6 Miles) S of Vernon

GPS Location: 50.18194 N, 119.34000 W, 1,400 Ft

70 Sites – This campground occupies a bench that overlooks the west shore of Kalamalka
Lake. There is a boat launch and swimming in the lake. Two yurts are available for rental.
Sites are open with no shade, most will take rigs to 45 feet and all are back-ins with gravel
surfaces. From Kelowna travel north on Hwy 97 for 42 km (26 miles), the park entrance
is on the east side of the highway. This is 10 km (6 miles) south of Vernon.

□ **ELLISON PROVINCIAL PARK** *(Open April 1 to Oct 31)*
Reservations: www.discovercamping.ca, (800) 689-9025
Information: (250) 545-9943
Location: 15 Km (9 Miles) S of Vernon

GPS Location: 50.17528 N, 119.44000 W, 1,300 Ft

71 Sites – This provincial park campground on the eastern shore of Okanagan Lake is in a beautiful setting. It's also the site of a fresh-water skin-diving park. Sites are well above the lake and a few are on a bluff with spectacular views. They are located off several paved loop drives. Sites are back-ins, some to about 40 feet. Caution is important with larger RVs there because maneuvering room is poor and there are big trees near the road. The park has a two swimming beaches and 6 kilometers of nature trails, also a boat ramp. From central Vernon follow 25th Ave. east. This soon becomes Okanagan Landing Road and then Eastside Road. After 16.3 km (10.1 miles) you'll reach the campground entrance.

● **DUTCH'S TENT AND TRAILER COURT** *(Open All Year)*
    Res and Info: (250) 545-1023
    Location: Vernon

    GPS Location: 50.23528 N, 119.26694 W, 1,300

75 Sites – Dutch's isn't on the water but it is a short walk from Kal Beach on the north shore of Kalamalka Lake. It's also just on the outskirts of Vernon. The park has tent sites as well as back-ins to 40 feet with hookups. There is also a dump station. To reach the park start in central Vernon where Hwy 97 (32nd St) crosses 25th Ave. Head east on 25th for just .2 km (.1 mile) to Hwy 6. Turn right onto Hwy 6 and follow it for .8 km (.5 mile) to Kalamalka Lake Rd. Turn right onto Kalamalka and follow it for 2.4 km (1.5 mile) the campground, the entrance is on the right.

● **SILVER STAR RV PARK** *(Open All Year)*
    Res and Info: (250) 542-2808,
        www.silverstarcampground.com
    Location: 3 Km (2 miles) N of Vernon

    GPS Location: 50.29750 N, 119.25583 W, 1,200 Ft

85 Sites – This campground is located just north of Vernon on the west side of Hwy 97 and on the east shore of Swan Lake. Sites are back-ins and pull-thrus to 75 feet, most with full hookups. Many back-ins sites are along the lake shoreline with tables on grass - nice sites. There's a heated outdoor pool. Watch for the park about 3 km (2 miles) north of town.

● **SWAN LAKE RECREATION RESORT** *(Open All Year)*
    Res and Info: (250) 558-1116, swanlakerec@telus.net,
        www.swanlakerecresort.com
    Location: 8 Km (5 Miles) N of Vernon

    GPS Location: 50.33639 N, 119.2461 W, 1,300

150 Sites – Most of the lots in this park are individually owned but are in a rental pool when the owners are not using the sites. These are beautiful RV sites, great for big RVs. Sites are back-ins to 50 feet and pull-thrus to 70 feet, all full hookup. Amenities include a swimming pool, spa and laundry. From Vernon head north on Hwy 97. About 8 km (5 miles) north of town Hwy 97 cuts off to the west toward Kamloops while Hwy 97A continues north to Armstrong. Take the turn onto Hwy 97 toward Kamloops and in just .3 km (.3 mile) turn left on Highland Road and proceed south a short distance to the park entrance.

BRITISH COLUMBIA

● **HISTORIC O'KEEFE RANCH**

Information: (250) 542-7868, info@okeeferanch.ca, www.okeeferanch.ca
Location: 13 Km (8 Miles) NW of Vernon

GPS Location: 50.36364 N, 119.28292 W, 1,100 Ft

10 Sites – This historic Okanagan Valley ranch offers tours, special events, and a restaurant. They also have a parking lot for overnighting RVers. This is just a gravel parking place with no facilities. Units must be self contained. Discounted entry passes are available for campers. From Vernon drive north on Hwy 97 for about 8 km (5 miles) to where Hwy 97 and Hwy 97A split. Turn left onto Hwy 97 and in 5 km (3.1 miles) you'll see the ranch on the right.

PORT ALBERNI

Port Alberni (population 18,000) is located at the eastern edge of the long narrow Port Alberni Inlet. That makes the town a west coast port although it's only 35 km (22 miles) from Qualicum Beach on the east coast of Vancouver Island. The main highway to the west coast's Pacific Rim region runs right through Port Alberni and there are good reasons to stop and spend some time.

Port Alberni is the home port for the **MV Frances Barkley**. This little ship steams down Alberni Inlet and makes deliveries to many little towns along the west coast. A day spent riding along is a popular trip. The ships depart from **Alberni Harbor Quay** which has additional attractions including shops, restaurants, and a maritime museum.

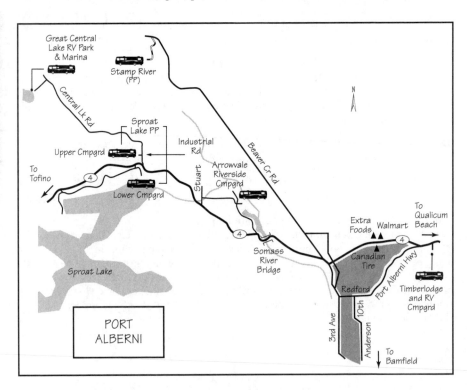

SPROAT LAKE IS HOME TO TWO HUGE MARTIN MARS FLYING BOATS

Another attraction in Port Alberni is **McLean Mill**. This is a designated national historical site and has an operating steam sawmill. You can get there by steam railroad from
central Port Alberni or drive directly to the mill location north of town.

About 5 kilometers (3 miles) beyond Port Alberni watch for the sign for Sproat Lake
Provincial Park. In addition to having a great campground, this lake is the home of two
huge **Martin Mars flying boats**. They were built during World War II and today are used
as water bombers for fighting forest fires. If they're not in use you'll see them anchored
just offshore from the park, really an unusual sight.

Port Alberni Campgrounds

☐ SPROAT LAKE PROVINCIAL PARK *(Open All Year)*
   Reservations: www.discovercamping.ca, (800) 689-9025
   Information: (250) 474-1336
   Location: 6 Km (4 Miles) W of Port Alberni

   GPS Location: 49.29139 N, 124.92667 W, 200 Ft

59 Sites – Sproat Lake is a very large lake located just west of Port
Alberni. Hwy 4 passes along its north shore. There are two camping areas in this provincial park. One is near the lake at the upper end of a day-use parking area. The second is
above on the far side of the highway. The lower campground is open all year but with no
services available and a reduced fee from October 16 to April 14. The upper campground
is open only from April 15 to October 15. The beach is popular for swimming, in summer
it also offers great views of two anchored WWII four-engine Martin Mars water bombers. We've seen black bears in this campground. Showers are available in the restroom
buildings near the beach. The sites in the upper campground are back-ins to 60 feet, those

in the lower campground are back-ins to about 40 feet. There are no handicap facilities in the upper campground and there is an 800 meter trail leading from the upper campground down to the showers and beach. To reach the park drive west from Port Alberni on Hwy 4 for 6 km (4 miles). You'll first see the sign for the upper sites on the right, then the lower ones and beach on the left.

● **ARROWVALE RIVERSIDE CAMPGROUND**
   (Open All Year)

   Res and Info: (250) 723-7948,
   www.arrowvalecottages.com
   Location: 2 Km (1 Mile) W of Port Alberni

   GPS Location: 49.28139 N, 124.86611 W, 100 Ft

40 Sites – This campground is in a country setting west of Port Alberni. This is a small farm with berry preserves and pies available for purchase. There are goats for the kids and swimming in the river below the campground. Parking is on grass, sites will take RVs to 45 feet. A few are pull-thrus. From Port Alberni head west on Hwy 4. Zero your odometer as you cross the Somass River bridge on the outskirts of town. In 3.4 km (2.1 miles) you'll see the campground sign pointing right. Turn here. In another .3 km (.2 mile) turn right following the campground sign. In another 1.6 km (1 mile) you'll come to a stop sign at a highway. The campground entrance is straight ahead across the highway.

● **TIMBERLODGE AND RV CAMPGROUND**
   (Open All Year)

   Res and Info: (250) 735-9415,
   www.timberlodgerv.ca
   Location: Port Alberni

   GPS Location: 49.26417 N, 124.75417 W, 400 Ft

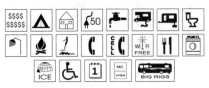

39 Sites – This motel with a campground behind it is right on the main highway entering Port Alberni from the east, it's hard to miss. There are 39 tent and back-in RV sites to 45 feet with full hookups. Additional amenities include an indoor pool (open only in summer, however), a sauna, and a restaurant.

☐ **STAMP RIVER PROVINCIAL PARK** *(Open All Year)*

   Reservations: www.discovercamping.ca, (800) 689-9025
   Information: (250) 474-1336
   Location: 13 Km (8 Miles) NW of Port Alberni

   GPS Location: 49.33775 N, 124.92320 W, 300 Ft

23 Sites – This small provincial park is a bit off the main highway but still popular. Trails lead to Stamp Falls and the fish ladder there, a great place to watch migrating salmon in the fall. The sites reach 40 feet in length. Tents pitch on the parking pads because there is a lot of underbrush that doesn't allow off-pad pitching and there are no tent pads. Water is from a hand pump. From October 16 to April 29 services are reduced and so are overnight fees. From Hwy 4 just west of the 90 degree right turn in western Port Alberni where Johnston Road becomes River Road take a right on Beaver Creek Road. Follow Beaver Creek Road 12.4 km (7.7 miles) to the park entrance, it's on the left.

● **Great Central Lake RV Park and Marina**
  (Open All Year)
Res and Info: (250) 723-2657, www.greatcentrallake.ca
Location: 12 Km (7 Miles) NW of Port Alberni

  GPS Location: 49.32238 N, 124.99375 W, 200 Ft

25 Sites – This is a small campground and marina at the south end of Great Central Lake. In addition to the fishing, this lake is known for Della Falls, the highest waterfall in North America, which is actually in Strathcona Provincial Park. Reaching the falls isn't easy, it requires a 35 km boat trip (a water taxi is available), then a 15 km (each way) hike. The campground has back-in and parallel-parking style RV sites to 35 feet both along and away from the water as well as tent sites with vehicle parking. To reach the park drive west from Port Alberni on Hwy 4 for 6 km (4 miles). Turn right on Industrial Road (the same road access the upper section of the Sproat Lake Provincial Park). Follow this road north for 6.1 km (3.8 miles) to the park.

PORT HARDY

Port Hardy (population 5,000) is the largest town at the north end of Vancouver Island. It's located at the end of the island's north-south Hwy 19. From Port Hardy the province operates ferries that travel even farther north, as far as Prince Rupert. As the commercial center of the northern island Port Hardy is the best place to pick up supplies. The town offers restaurants, gas stations, and shops with all the necessities.

Other nearby destinations described in this chapter that you will want to visit on the north

KAYAKING AT HOLBERG INLET NEAR PORT HARDY

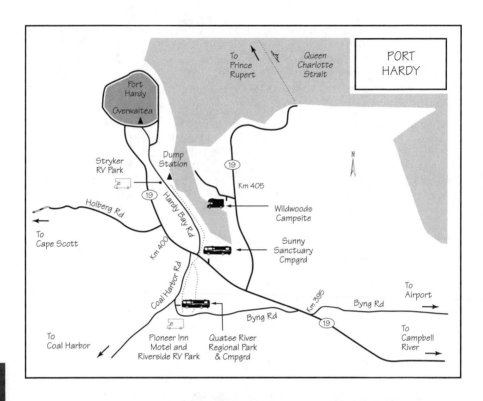

end of Vancouver Island are *Port McNeill, Telegraph Cove, and Port Alice* and *Cape Scott*.

Port Hardy Campgrounds

○ **QUATSE RIVER REGIONAL PARK & CAMPGROUND** *(Open All Year)*

Res and Info: (250) 949-2395, (866) 949-2395, quatse@island.net, www.quatsecampground.com

Location: 3 Km (2 Miles) S of Port Hardy

GPS Location: 50.69000 N, 127.48639 W, Near Sea Level

62 Sites – This campground is adjacent to the local fish hatchery and proceeds from the park help support the hatchery. Sites are wilderness-type with lots of trees and pretty good separation, many have hookups. The Quatse River runs next to the campground and many sites face it across the access loop road. Sites are back-ins and vary a great deal in size. A couple will take RVs to 40 feet but most are suitable for rigs to 30 or 25 feet. This is a good car-camping campground as some sites have grass and cars can park next to the tents. Restrooms are in the office building and are modern with flush toilets and showers. A walking trail runs through the campground and you can follow it along the river and then the waterfront to town, it's 5 km (3 miles) to the visitor center. To reach the campground take the Coal Harbor Road to the south from a point 1.3 km (.8 miles) west (in the direction of Port Hardy) of the ferry access road. In just 1.0 km (.6 mile) turn left on Byng Road, the campground will be on your left in another .2 km (.1 mile).

● **SUNNY SANCTUARY CAMPGROUND**
   (Open All Year)
Res and Info: (250) 949-8111, (866) 251-4556,
         camp@sunnysanctuary.com,
         www.sunnysanctuary.com
Location: 2 Km (1 Mile) SE of Port Hardy

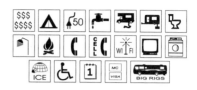

GPS Location: 50.69778 N, 127.47806 W, Near Sea Level

65 Sites – Sunny Sanctuary is a large campground with open unshaded sites, a decent campground good for rigs of any size. There's also good facilities for tent campers here with a grassy area to pitch tents and a room for cooking and washing dishes. This campground has the longest list of amenities in the Port Hardy area including pay Wi-Fi, TV hookups at some sites, large sites, a cooking area for tenters, and access to the community trail which leads in to town. From the intersection of Hwy 19 and the ferry access road continue .8 km (.5 miles) toward Port Hardy, the campground entrance is on the north side of the highway.

● **WILDWOODS CAMPSITE**
   (Open May 15 to Oct 15 – Varies)
Res and Info: (250) 949-675, pjranger@telus.net
Location: 5 Km (3 Miles) SE of Port Hardy

GPS Location: 50.70833 N, 127.47306 W, Near Sea Level

75 Sites – Wildwood is an older campground set in trees on uneven ground. There is limited maneuvering room and while a few sites will take RVs to 35 feet it's a challenging campground if you're over 30 feet long. The campground is off the ferry access road, 1.9 km (1.2 miles) from the junction with Hwy 19.

PORT MCNEILL, TELEGRAPH COVE, AND PORT ALICE

As you drive toward the north end of Vancouver Island from Campbell River there is a long stretch which is inland. Then, 185 km (115 miles) from Campbell River you reach the coast again. The main town here is Port McNeill, and for travelers Telegraph Cover is also a popular destination. Also, from just west of Port McNeill you can follow the road west to Port Alice, a gateway to the west coast's Quatsino Sound.

Port McNeill (population 2,700) is the second largest town on the north shore of Vancouver Island, only Port Hardy is larger. This is a logging and fishing town, it offers stores, restaurants and service stations. The town is also the ferry terminal for trips to Alert Bay and Sointula. For visitors the town offers the **North Island Discovery Center** which is a logging museum. Port McNeill is also a good place to take marine tours to see orcas, there are lots of them in the local waters of Johnstone Strait and Blackfish Sound.

Cluxewe Resort and Alder Bay Resort, the first two campgrounds listed below, are both oceanside campgrounds located respectively west and east of Port McNeill.

Telegraph Cove is much smaller than Port McNeill but seems to get almost as many visitors. This is really a privately owned destination dedicated to tourism. It's extremely photogenic, a dockside community clustered around a small rocky cove. Most people visit for the whale watching, fishing and kayaking. There are also restaurants, shops, a marina, and a campground. See the Telegraph Cove campground descriptions below for information on how to get to Telegraph Cove and the campground.

Finally, from a point 19 km (12 miles) west of Port McNeill, paved but winding Hwy 30

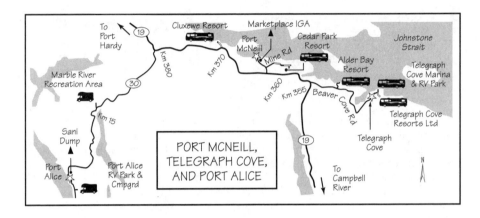

leads 31 km (19 miles) west to **Port Alice**. This is a neat little town on the shore of Neroutsos Inlet - which leads to Buchhotz Channel, Quasino Sound, and the Pacific Ocean. There's a waterside park, a seawalk, an information centre and a boat ramp so it's an easy place to access the west coast waters for kayaking or fishing.

Port McNeill, Telegraph Cove, and Port Alice Campgrounds

● **CLUXEWE RESORT** *(Open All Year)*
Res and Info: (250) 949-0378, (250) 949-7030,
                relax@cluxewe.com,
                www.cluxewe.com
Location: 10 Km (6 Miles) W of Port McNeill

GPS Location: 50.61250 N, 127.17250 W, Near Sea Level

130 Sites – A beachfront resort campground with back-in sites in several areas. Some are in the main all-weather RV parking area, mostly back from the water with no views with parking on gravel. Others are on a spit of land to the west between the ocean and the estuary of the Cluxewe River. Many of these sites front the beach or the estuary behind the spit. They are grassy sites perfect for tents and RVs to 35 feet. Finally, there are many back-in sites with parking on a nice grass lawn arranged around a play area, restrooms, and covered picnic pavilion. Many sites in this campground will take RVs to 45 feet. It's located west of Port McNeill, the .8 km (.5 mile) gravel access road goes north 8.9 km (5.5 miles) west of the Port McNeill cutoff.

● **ALDER BAY RESORT** *(Open All Year)*
Res and Info: (250) 956-4117, (888) 956-4117,
                abresort@island.net,
                www.Alderbayresort.com
Location: 15 Km (9 Miles) E of Port McNeill

GPS Location: 50.55944 N, 126.91167 W, Near Sea Level

125 Sites – This large sea-side resort offers great views across to Alert Bay. There's a marina and boat ramp here so it's a popular place for fishermen. It's a wide open campsite with no trees so you can take full advantage of the sun if it happens to be out when you visit. RV sites are back-ins and pull-thrus to 60 feet. The campground is on the Beaver Cove Road 4.2 km (2.6 miles) from its intersection with Hwy 19. You don't have to drive any gravel to get here.

● **TELEGRAPH COVE MARINA AND RV PARK**
   (Open May 1 to Sept 30)
   Res and Info: (250) 928-3163,
                    reservations@telegraphcome.ca,
                    www.telegraphcove.ca
   Location: 23 Km (14 Miles) E of Port McNeill

GPS Location: 50.54703 N, 126.82965 W, 100 Ft

48 Sites – This campground is close to the cove and its docks and restaurant, about .3 km (.2 mile). It is a modern big-rig park. All sites are back-ins, some to 50 feet. The sites occupy a hollow above the docks and some sites have views of them. Parking is on gravel and sites have picnic tables. Restrooms are located in the park but the boardwalks and other attractions are a short hike away. The Telegraph Cove road leaves Hwy 19 near Km 355 which is 6.9 km (4.3 miles) east of the cutoff to Port McNeill. This paved road will take you the 15.1 km (9.4 miles) to Telegraph Cove. When you arrive at Telegraph Cove the campgrounds are beyond, but you must stop to check in. Note that there are two campgrounds here, registration for this campground is not at the small store near the parking area. Instead, pass around the store to the right and you'll find the office on the second floor of the modern building ahead. Once you check in you turn left at the T and follow the paved road .3 km (.2 mile) to the campground entrance.

● **TELEGRAPH COVE RESORTS LTD**
   (Open May 1 to Sept 30)
   Res and Info: (250) 928-3131, (800) 200-4665,
                    www.telegraphcoveresort.com
   Location: 23 Km (14 Miles) E of Port McNeill

GPS Location: 50.54000 N, 126.82667 W, Near Sea Level

125 Sites – The campground here is well away from the cove, it's a .6 km (.4 mile) walk or drive up the hill on a gravel road. This older campground is set in dense trees in a small valley with no views. Some sites will take RVs to 45 feet, they are back-in sites. The Telegraph Cove road leaves Hwy 19 near Km 355 which is 6.9 km (4.3 miles) east of the cutoff to Port McNeill. This paved road will take you the 15.1 km (9.4 miles) to Telegraph Cove. When you arrive at Telegraph Cove the campgrounds are beyond, but you must stop to check in. Note that there are two campgrounds here, registration for this campground it at the small store near the parking area. Once you check in you turn right at the T and follow the gravel road .6 km (.4 mile) to the campground entrance.

○ **MARBLE RIVER RECREATION AREA** *(Open all Year)*
   Location: Hwy 30 to Port Alice

GPS Location: 50.52711 N, 127.43341 W, 200 Ft

32 Sites - This is a free campground provided by Western Forest Products, the local logging company. There are 32 back-in sites off two loops. These are long sites (to at least 50 feet) but limited maneuvering room means it's best for RVs to 35 feet. The Marble River runs by the campground and Alice Lake is just across the highway, there is a boat ramp at the lake. From Hwy 19 turn toward Port Alice on Hwy 30. You will reach the campground in 14.5 km (9.0 miles).

● **PORT ALICE RV PARK & CAMPGROUND**
   Res and Info: (250) 284-3422
   Location: Port Alice

GPS Location: 50.41986 N, 127.48102 W, Near Sea Level

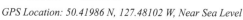

10 Sites – This small RV park is located adjacent to the Oceanview Restaurant in Port Alice. All sites are back-ins, some are full-hookup, the rest have electricity and water. Sites are closely spaced, about 35 feet long, and parking is on gravel and grass. Tenters can pitch on grass near the RVs. There is no dump station at the park but there's a free municipal dump station that you'll see just as you enter town. While the park overlooks the inlet the way the spaces are arranged means that only the end units can really see much of the water. When you reach Port Alice just continue until you spot the Oceanside Restaurant on the left. You'll see the RVs just beyond.

PORT RENFREW LOOP (PACIFIC MARINE CIRCLE TOUR)

The recent paving of formerly rough and dangerous logging roads between Cowichan Lake and Port Renfrew has opened some great new country for travelers along Vancouver Island's west coast. The tourism industry has dubbed the route the Pacific Marine Circle Tour. As a circle tour it's 255 km (158 miles) from Victoria, up the east coast to Duncan, inland to Cowichan Lake, across to Port Renfrew, and then back to Victoria along the Strait of Juan de Fuca.

From Cowichan Lake, not far inland from Duncan, you can drive the newly paved Harris Creek Main across the spine of the island to Port Renfrew. The distance is 55 km (34 miles). This is a good road and fine for RVs. It's well signed so navigation is not a problem. There are two RSTBC campgrounds along the way and they are described below.

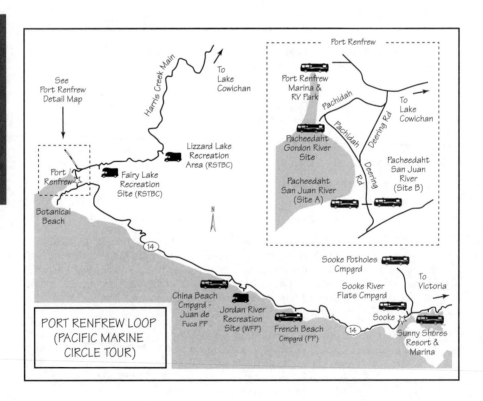

Port Renfrew (population 200) is northwest terminus Juan de Fuca Marine Trail and the southeast end of the Pacific Rim National Park's West Cost Trail. It's on the southern shore of the Gordon River and a Pacheedaht First Nation ferry shuttles folks across the river to hike the trail. Most visitors go out to **Botanical Beach** to see its tide pools and rocks. Port Renfrew is known for its halibut and salmon fishing, charters are available. Port Renfrew has three campgrounds, they are described below.

From Port Renfrew it's 74 km (112 miles) southeast along the coast on Hwy 14, the West Coast Road, to Victoria. Along the way you parallel the Juan de Fuca Marine Trail with many access points and campgrounds. Parts of this road actually aren't as good as the Cowichan Lake to Port Renfrew section, but careful driving will see you through. Six of the campgrounds along this section of highway are described below.

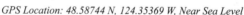

Port Renfrew Loop Campgrounds

☐ **LIZARD LAKE RECREATION AREA** *(Open May 20 to Oct 10)*
Location: 14 Km (9 Miles) E of Port Renfrew

GPS Location: 48.60778 N, 124.22719 W, 300 Ft

27 Sites – This RSTBC (Recreation Site and Trails BC) campground next to Lizard Lake is in three areas. The largest has 20 back-in vehicle sites to 30 feet. There are also two walk-in tent camping areas just a bit to the east. All have picnic tables and fire pits as well as vault toilets and are near the lake. No potable water is provided. Lizard Lake is stocked with rainbows and there is a fishing dock. Only boats without engines are allowed on the lake. This campground is 43 km (27 miles) from the town of Lake Cowichan and 14 km (9 miles) from Port Renfrew

☐ **FAIRY LAKE RECREATION SITE** *(Open May 20 to Oct 10)*
Location: 6 Km (4 Miles) E of Port Renfrew

GPS Location: 48.58744 N, 124.35369 W, Near Sea Level

36 Sites – This RSTBC campground is a large one. The sites are off a gravel loop road next to Fairy Lake. Sites are as long as 35 feet but restricted maneuvering room on the narrow rough access road makes 25 feet the maximum practical RV size here. A few sites are along the lake and there's a boat ramp. No potable water is provided. The lake has cutthroat and sea run Dolly Varden. The campground is 55 km (34 miles) from the town of Lake Cowichan and 6 km (4 miles) from Port Renfrew.

● **PORT RENFREW MARINA AND RV PARK**
   (Open May 1 to Oct 15 – Varies)
   Res and Info: (250) 483-1878, info@portrenfrewmarina.com,
            www.portrenfrewmarina.com
   Location: Port Renfrew

GPS Location: 48.58660 N, 124.40945 W, Near Sea Level

40 Sites – This marina and RV park near Port Renfrew is on a quiet estuary. It is the center of sports fishing in the area. Many fishing guides and other fishermen spend the summer here. There are back-in sites to about 40 feet. Low amp power is available to a few sites but is unlikely to be available to travelers. Water is trucked in and may be available. From Port Renfrew drive north on Deering Road for about 2.9 km (1.8 miles) until you have crossed the Deering Bridge #2. Turn left and you'll reach the marina in .5 km (.3 mile).

● **PACHEEDAHT GORDON RIVER SITE**
(Open May 15 to Sept 15 – Varies)
Location: Port Renfrew

GPS Location: 48.57737 N, 124.41244 W, Near Sea Level

54 Sites – This is a First Nation campsite on the beach on Port San Juan at the mouth of the San Juan River. Sites are irregularly sized and situated but many are along the water. Some are as long as 50 feet in length. Five have low-amp power hookups. There is small kiosk near the entrance that houses the office and offers a few snack items. Wi-Fi, flush toilets, and showers are also available there. From Port Renfrew drive north on Deering Road for 1.3 km (.8 mile). Take the left fork on Pachidah Road and drive another 1 km (.6 mile), you'll see the campground entrance on the left.

● **PACHEEDAHT SAN JUAN RIVER SITES** *(Open May 15 to Sept 15 – Varies)*
Location: Port Renfrew

GPS Location: 48.56226 N, 124.40037 W, Near Sea Level

37 Sites – This is another First Nation campsite, it's associated with the
one above. Sites here are located on the both sides of Deering Road just north of Port Renfrew. Some are on the beach of Port San Juan. They are irregular sites, some as long as 45 feet. The Pacheedaht Gordon River Site is nearby and offers showers and Wi-Fi to folks staying at the San Juan River Sites. From Port Renfrew drive north on Deering Road for .3 km (.2 mile), the camping area is on both sides of the road.

☐ **CHINA BEACH CAMPGROUND - JUAN DE**
    FUCA PROVINCIAL PARK *(Open May 14 to Sept 15 – Varies)*
Reservations: www.discovercamping.ca, (800) 689-9025,
Information: (250) 474-1336
Location: 32 Km (20 Miles) W of Sooke

GPS Location: 48.43464 N, 124.07725 W, 200 Ft

85 Sites – This large campground is located some distance inland from the beach, trails lead down to it. Sites are off a large gravel loop with several interior roads. They are gravel back-ins sites to 45 feet with picnic tables and fire pits. The campground is 32 km (20 miles) west of Sooke and 37 km (23 miles) east of Port Renfrew.

○ **JORDAN RIVER RECREATION SITE** *(Open All Year)*
Location: 29 Km (18 Miles) W of Sooke

GPS Location: 48.42125 N, 124.05184 W, Near Sea Level

30 Sites – Jordon River Recreation Site is a small beachside camping area run by Western Forest Products which conducts extensive logging operations on Vancouver Island. The site has back-in sites to 35 feet right next to the rocky beach as well as sites in trees nearby. There are vault toilets, picnic tables, and fire pits. The recreation site is 29 km (18 miles) west of Sooke and 40 km (25 miles) east of Port Renfrew.

☐ **FRENCH BEACH PROVINCIAL PARK CAMPGROUND** *(Open All Year)*
Reservations: www.discovercamping.ca, (800) 689-9025
Information: (250) 474-1336
Location: 19 Km (12 Miles) W of Sooke

GPS Location: 48.39358 N, 123.94232 W, Near Sea Level

69 Sites – The park has large gravel back-in sites to 50 feet off a wide

paved access road. There are views of the beach from some sites although this location is heavily wooded. Trails lead to the beach. During the winter the campground is open but services are reduced and fees are lower. The campground is located 19 km (12 miles) west of Sooke and 50 km (31 miles) east of Port Renfrew.

○ **SOOKE RIVER FLATS CAMPGROUND**
 (Open April 1 to Sept 30)
Res and Info: (250) 642-6076,
    camping@sookecommunty.com,
    www.sookecommunity.com/camping/
Location: Sooke

GPS Location: 48.38958 N, 123.70884 W, Near Sea Level

50 Sites – This is a community owned campground along the Sooke River just outside the town of Sooke, BC. There are tent sites in an area with trees as well as back-in RV sites to 40 feet. The RV sites have power and water, there is a sani-dump. Amenities include a kitchen shelter, playground, and boat launch. From Hwy 4 passing through Sooke, BC travel inland on Phillips Road. In .8 km (.5 miles), the campground entrance is on the right.

○ **SOOKE POTHOLES CAMPGROUND** *(Open May 20 to Sept 5 – Varies)*
Res and Info: (888) 738-0533, (250) 383-4627,
    http://blog.conservancy.bc.ca/ecotourism/potholes-campground/
Location: Sooke

GPS Location: 48.44316 N, 123.72109 W, 200 Ft

67 Sites – This campground is located in the Sooke River Valley just up the bank from the Potholes. This camping area is operated by The Land Conservancy and is located in the Sooke Potholes Regional Park. This location has long been known in the Victoria area as a fantastic recreation area featuring swimming in the "potholes" along the upper Sooke River. The Galloping Goose regional bike trail connects the potholes with central Victoria, a distance of 50 kilometers (31 miles). Sites here are small and are primarily tent sites with tables and fire pits although RVs to 26 feet are allowed. There is a picnic shelter with a large fireplace. From Sooke drive north on the Sooke River Road for 7.3 km (4.5 miles) to the entry booth. Pay here and then drive another 2.4 km (1.5 miles) to the campground.

● **SUNNY SHORES RESORT AND MARINA** *(Open All Year)*
Res and Info: (250) 642-5731, (855) 642-5731,
    info@sunnyshoresresort.com,
    www.sunnyshoresresort.com
Location: 3 Km (2 Miles) E of Sooke

GPS Location: 48.39034 N, 123.66450 W, Near Sea Level

75 Sites – Sunny shores has tent and RV camping as well as boat moorage and a boat ramp. RV sites are back-ins and pull-thrus to 55 feet. The resort is located off Hwy 14 about 3 km (2 miles) east of Sooke.

PRINCE GEORGE

Prince George (population 71,000) is by far the largest city of northern British Columbia. It's the commercial hub of the northern province and is large enough that it offers almost anything you could want in the way of supplies or services including a variety of big-box stores. For travelers Prince George is the last large city on the way north.

BRITISH COLUMBIA

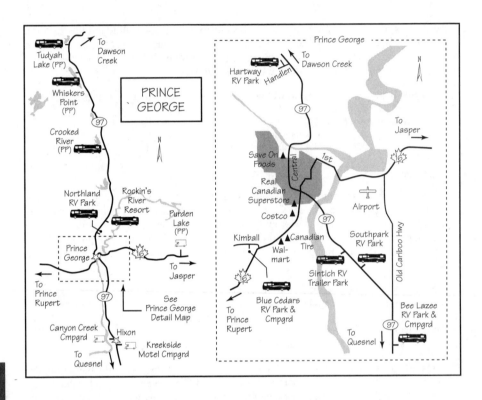

Visitor attractions in Prince George are limited but there are a few. For outdoor lovers there's **Forests of the World** on the University of British Columbia campus with several kilometers of nature trails featuring labels on local plants. Another walking area is **Cottonwood Island Nature Park**. The city has two good museums, the **Prince George Railway and Forest Industry Museum** and **Exploration Place**. Prince George is surrounded by pulp mills. One of them, **Canfor**, has good tours.

Prince George Campgrounds

● **BLUE CEDARS RV PARK AND CAMPGROUND**
    (Open All Year)

Reservations: (888) 964-7271, bluecedars@telus.net
Information: (250) 964-7272,
                www.bluecedarsrvpark.com
Location: 6 Km (4 Miles) SW of Prince George

GPS Location: 53.85917 N, 122.82139 W, 2,300 Ft

100 Sites – The Blue Cedars (formerly the Blue Spruce) is a great place to stop for the night if you're headed westward toward Prince Rupert or if you just want to have a convenient place to stay while visiting Prince George. Sites include spaces for tents as well as pull-thrus to 70 feet, but there are also partial and no hookup back-ins. The campground is located southwest of Prince George on the highway toward Prince Rupert. If you zero your odometer at the junction of Hwy 16 with Hwy 97 and head south on Hwy

16 you'll see the sign for the campground in 6.1 km (3.8 miles). Turn right and you'll reach the campground entrance in just a short distance.

● **Sintich RV Trailer Park** *(Open All Year)*
   Reservations: (877) 963-9862, info@sintichpark.bc.ca
   Information: (250) 963-9862 www.sintichpark.bc.ca
   Location: 6 Km (4 Miles) S of Prince George

   GPS Location: 53.85306 N, 122.71472 W, 2,100 Ft

130 Sites – This campground is a large one with many permanent residents. A large area, however, is set aside for short term use and travelers, including several tent sites in trees. Most sites here are back-ins or pull-thrus to 70 feet. The campground considers itself an adult park and says so on a sign out front. The Sintich is off Hwy 97 about 6 km (4 miles) south of Prince George.

● **Southpark RV Park** *(Open All Year)*
   Res and Info: (250) 963-7577, (877) 963-7275,
      mail@southparkrv.com,
      www.southparkrv.com
   Location: 8 Km (5 Miles) S of Prince George

   GPS Location: 53.84250 N, 122.69444 W, 2,200 Ft

53 Sites – Southpark is located at the southern approaches to Prince George. The campground can take tent campers and large rigs, there are pull-thrus to 100 feet. Also, this is a year-round campground. It's located right off Hwy 97 some 8 km (5 miles) south of town.

● **Bee Lazee RV Park and Campground**
   (Open May 1 to Sept 30)
   Res and Info: (250) 963-7263, (866) 963-7263,
      drone@pgonline.com,
      www.beelazee.ca
   Location: 15 Km (9 Miles) S of Prince George

   GPS Location: 53.78167 N, 122.65611 W, 2,200 Ft

65 Sites – The Bee Lazee is a good park for both tent campers and big rigs, as long as being near town isn't important. There is a seasonal swimming pool and good facilities including a coin RV wash. The campground is right next to the highway and has tent sites and pull-thrus to 60 feet. This park is located on the east side of Hwy 97 some 15 km (9 miles) south of Prince George.

● **Hartway RV Park** *(Open March 1 to Oct 30)*
   Res and Info: (250) 962-8848, (866) 962-8848
   Location: 10 Km (6 Miles) N of Prince George

   GPS Location: 54.00028 N, 122.80167 W, 2,300 Ft

40 Sites – Unlike most campgrounds near Prince George the Hartway is located north of town. Sites are mostly back-ins to 50 feet but there are just a few longer pull-thrus. This campground is just a little off the main road, you'll probably drive right by if you're not looking. Heading north from Prince George zero your odometer as you come off the bridge over the Nechako River. After 9.7 km (6 miles) turn left on Handlen Road. Go one block and turn right on Kelly Road, the campground is a block ahead.

● **NORTHLAND RV PARK**
  (Open May 15 to Oct 30 – Varies)
  Res and Info: (250) 962-5010, info@northlandrv.ca,
      www.northlandrv.ca
  Location: 15 Km (9 Miles) N of Prince George

  GPS Location: 54.03389 N, 122.76778 W, 2,400 Ft

42 Sites – The Northland has both tent and RV sites. Those for RVs are full-hookup back-ins to 25 feet and very long pull-thru sites, parking is on grass. Heading north from Prince George zero your odometer as you come off the bridge over the Nechako River. After 14.7 km (9.1 miles) you'll see the RV park on the right.

● **ROCKIN'S RIVER RESORT** *(Open May 15 to Oct 15)*
  Res and Info: (250) 971-2223, www.rockinsriverresort.com
  Location: 24 Km (15 Miles) N of Prince George

  GPS Location: 54.09806 N, 122.67056 W, 1,200 Ft

58 Sites – The Rockin's River Resort is situated along the Salmon River and just a short distance off Hwy 97. Sites here are pull-thrus to 65 feet with electricity and water and also riverside back-ins to 40 feet with no utilities. This too is a campground that many folks just don't see as they travel the highway, but it's worth a look. Heading north from Prince George zero your odometer as you come off the bridge over the Nechako River. After 24.5 km (15.2 miles) take a right on Salmon Valley Road. Turn right here and the campground is on the right.

☐ **CROOKED RIVER PROVINCIAL PARK**
  (Open May 15 to Sept 19 – Varies)
  Reservations: www.discovercamping.ca, (800) 689-9025
  Information: (250) 964-3489
  Location: 71 Km (44 Miles) N of Prince George

  GPS Location: 54.48194 N, 122.67444 W, 2,300 Ft

65 Sites – This popular provincial park campground north of Prince George surrounds little Bear Lake. Sites here are back-ins, some very long. Narrow access roads and uneven sites mean that drivers of large RVs will have to be very careful. Restrooms have flush toilets and showers, there is also a sani-station. The park has a day-use area with swimming beach as well as several hiking trails, including one around the lake. The campground is off Hwy 97 some 71 km (44 miles) N of Prince George.

☐ **WHISKERS POINT PROVINCIAL PARK**
  (Open June 1 to Sept 8 – Varies)
  Information: (250) 964-3489
  Location: 124 Km (77 Miles) N of Prince George

  GPS Location: 54.90722 N, 122.93472 W, 2,300 Ft

69 Sites – This campground is situated on a point on long McLeod Lake. Sites are back-ins, some very large and many right along the lake. The campground has a sani-station, swimming beach, and boat ramp. The camp is reached via an access road off Hwy 97 some 124 km (77 miles) north of Prince George.

BRITISH COLUMBIA

☐ TUDYAH LAKE PROVINCIAL PARK
(Open May 15 to Sept 30 – Varies)

Information: (250) 964-3489
Location: 144 Km (89 Miles) N of Prince George

GPS Location: 55.06056 N, 123.03028 W, 2,200 Ft

36 Sites – This campground is on the south shore of Tudyah Lake. The sites are in an open meadow environment so there's lots of light. There's a gravel boat launch and hand-operated water pump. The campground is located off Hwy 97 some 144 km (89 miles) north of Prince George.

PRINCE RUPERT

The northwest British Columbian city of Prince Rupert (population 15,000) is the real gateway to Southeast Alaska. Prince Rupert is at the end of a good paved road and is much closer to Alaska than Bellingham, the most southerly port for the state ferries. Even Alaskans living in Southeast use the city as a gateway, many think it well worth the effort to drive 1,450 or so kilometers (900 miles) through Canada to access the Lower 48. Incidentally, you can't get to Prince Rupert on the ferry from Bellingham, that boat doesn't stop here.

Prince Rupert is a very clean and well-organized little town with full services. It is the western terminus for one of Canada's few rail lines to the Pacific Ocean and dates from the early 1900s. Today the town continues to be an important port.

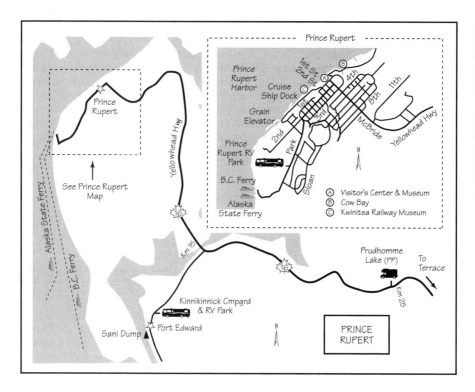

Probably the most interesting area of Prince Rupert for visitors is **Cow Bay**. This small waterfront area has historical buildings now housing restaurants, pubs, and gift shops. Also interesting is the **Museum of Northern British Columbia** at First and McBride overlooking the water. Other sights include the **Kwinitsa Railway Museum**, and the **North Pacific Historic Fishing Village** in nearby Port Edward with displays about the salmon canning industry that was the lifeblood of this region for many years.

Prince Rupert Campgrounds

○ **PRINCE RUPERT RV CAMPGROUND**
      (Park Avenue Campground) (Open All Year)

Res and Info: (250) 627-1000,
                www.princerupertrv.com
Location: Prince Rupert

   GPS Location: 54.29944 N, 130.34111 W, 100 Ft

120 Sites – This municipal campground is a popular place to stay for folks waiting to board the ferries just down the road. There are tent sites and back-in RV sites to 45 feet. Wi-Fi access is possible at the office. When you enter Prince Rupert just follow signs to the ferry docks. You'll find yourself on a wide highway called Park Avenue. The campground sign is on the right.

● **KINNIKINNICK CAMPGROUND AND RV PARK**
      (Open All Year)
Res and Info: (866) 628-9449, (250) 628-9449,
                rvpark@citytel.net, www.kinnikcamp.com
Location: Port Edward, 15 Km (9 Miles) S of Prince Rupert

   GPS Location: 54.22906 N, 130.29005 W, 100 Ft

27 Sites – While not actually in Prince Rupert the Kinnikinnick is nearby, and makes a good alternative to the Prince Rupert RV Park. It's located in Port Edward, along the route to the North Pacific Fishing Village Museum. The campground has back-in gravel sites that will take RVs to 45 feet. They are separated by vegetation and some have decent views. Full hookups are available and so are tent sites. The road to Port Edward leaves Hwy 16 about 11 km (6.8 miles) southeast of Prince Rupert and leads southwest. About 3.4 km (2.1 miles) from the junction you'll see the campground entrance on your left.

□ **PRUDHOMME LAKE PROVINCIAL PARK**
      (Open May 15 to Sept 15 – Varies)
Information: (250) 638-8490
Location: 20 Km (12 Miles) E of Prince Rupert

   GPS Location: 54.24083 N, 130.13472 W, 200 Ft

24 Sites – This provincial campground has sites for tents and RVs to about 30 feet. It's right off Hwy 16 about 20 Km (12 Miles) east of Prince Rupert.

QUESNEL

Quesnel (population 10,000) is a pleasant little town on the banks of the Fraser River. Since there are campgrounds near the center it's a fun place to spend the night. The **Quesnel Museum**, right next to the visitor center, is probably the best in the Cariboo. Quesnel was originally a Hudson's Bay trading post, the site is in the park along the river. The town has a nice **riverfront trail**. Pinnacle Provincial Park, just a few kilometers west of town has some great hoodoos. The big celebration in Quesnel is **Billy Barker Days**, held the third weekend in July.

Quesnel Campgrounds

● **AIRPORT INN MOTEL AND RV PARK**
   (Open All Year)
   Res and Info: (250) 992-5942, airportinn@shaw.ca
   Location: 2 Km (1 Mile) N of Quesnel

   GPS Location: 53.00861 N, 122.50639 W, 1,600 Ft

75 Sites – The Airport Inn is located just north of Quesnel and has long pull-thrus to 70 feet. Watch for it on the west side of Hwy 97 about 1.6 km (1 mile) north of town and .8 km (.5 mile) south of the junction for Hwy 26 going east to Wells and Barkerville.

☐ **TEN MILE LAKE PROVINCIAL PARK**
   (Open May 15 to Sept 30 – Varies)
   Reservations: www.discovercamping.ca, (800) 689-9025
   Information: (250) 397-2523
   Location: 10 Km (6 Miles) N of Quesnel

   GPS Location: 53.06778 N, 122.44306 W, 2,400 Ft

96 Sites – Ten Mile Lake Provincial Park has two campgrounds: Lakeside and Touring. Some sites are pull-thrus, sites reach 50 feet. The Lakeside campground offers reserva-

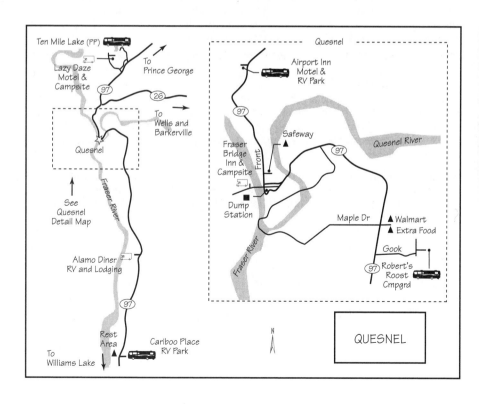

BRITISH COLUMBIA

tions, flush toilets, and coin-operated showers. The campground entrance is on the west side of Highway 97 some 10 km (6 miles) north of Quesnel.

● **ROBERT'S ROOST CAMPGROUND**
   (Open April 15 to Oct 15 – Varies)
   Res and Info: (888) 227-8877, (250) 747-2015,
             www.robertsroostcampsite.ca
   Location: 8 Km (5 Miles) S of Quesnel

   GPS Location: 52.95750 N, 122.42028 W, 1,900 Ft

70 Sites – This campground is located back in a residential area south of Quesnel. It's situated on little Dragon Lake. Sites are back-ins and pull-thrus to 50 feet, there are also tent sites. The campground has docks and a boat ramp. Heading south on Hwy 97 zero your odometer as you leave the bridge over the Fraser channel. In 5.5 km (3.4 miles) you'll reach Gook Road. Turn east there and drive another 1.9 km (1.2 miles) to the campground.

● **CARIBOO PLACE RV PARK**
   (Open May 1 to Oct 31)
   Res and Info: (250) 747-8555
   Location: 37 Km (26 Miles) S of Quesnel

   GPS Location: 52.70963 N, 122.45453 W, 1,700 Ft

70 Sites – This is a simple campground located along the highway south of Quesnel. It has tent sites as well as back-in and pull-thru sites to 55 feet with parking on grass. These are partial hookup sites without sewer, but there is a dump station. Heading south from Quesnel on Hwy 97 zero your odometer as you cross the Fraser River. The campground is on the left some 37 km (23 miles) south of this point.

REVELSTOKE

You'll probably be surprised at what this little town (population 6,500) on the Columbia River has to offer. The historic downtown area is well preserved and pleasant with restaurants, shops and even frequent evening entertainment in **Grizzly Plaza**. The town has the excellent **Revelstoke Railway Museum** as well as a local historical museum called the **Revelstoke Museum**.

As you might expect of a town in such a spectacular mountainous location, several of the best attractions are in the surrounding area. **Mount Revelstoke National Park** is right outside town. You can drive the Meadows in the Sky Parkway which climbs steeply for 26 kilometers and about 1,100 meters. Near the end of the road there's a parking lot and a shuttle bus will carry you another kilometer to the top for good views and nice walking paths. Because the road is steep with switchbacks trailers are not permitted. There is a small parking lot where you can leave your trailer near the entrance at the bottom.

There are two dams on the Columbia River above Revelstoke. The nearest to Revelstoke is called **Revelstoke Dam**. It is located 8 kilometers (5 miles) north of town on Highway 23 and has a good self-guided tour of the facility including a trip to the top of the dam for the view.

If you are heading west on Highway 1 in the direction of the Shuswap through Eagle Valley you might want to keep an eye open for a few roadside attractions that have been

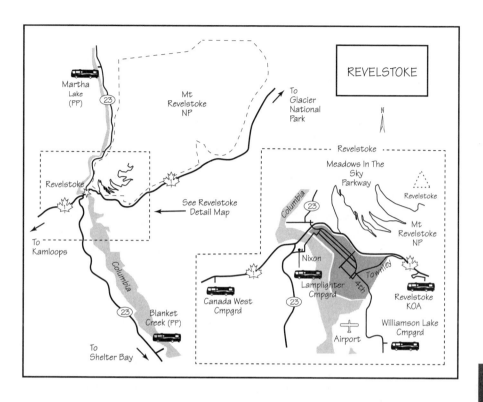

developed with travelers in mind. One of these is **Craigellachie** where the last spike of the transcontinental rail line was driven. This is really just a rest stop with plenty of parking and restrooms as well as a display. There are also a bevy of commercial attractions including **Crazy Creek Waterfall**, **Beardale Castle Miniatureland**, **Enchanted Forest**, and the **Three Valley Gap Chateau and Heritage Ghost Town**.

Revelstoke Campgrounds

● **CANADA WEST CAMPGROUND**
   (Open All Year)
   Res and Info: (250) 837-4420,
                    canadawest@revelstoke.com,
                    www.canadawest.revelstoke.com
   Location: 3 Km (2 Miles) W of Revelstoke

   GPS Location: 50.991389 N, 118.26278 W, 1,700 Ft

100 Sites – This is an older campground that has been spruced up. Sites have older electrical hookups mounted in boxes between the sites. Parking is on grass with back-in and pull-thru sites to 50 feet. Leveling can be difficult, particularly for larger RVs. Picnic tables and fire pits are provided. There is a swimming pool. The Wi-Fi here is only useable near the office. Access is easy, the campground is on the south side of Hwy 1 some 3 km (2 miles) west of Revelstoke.

☐ **BLANKET CREEK PROVINCIAL PARK**
   (Open May 6 to Sept 30 – Varies)
   Reservations: www.discovercamping.ca, (800) 689-9025
   Information: (250) 837-5734
   Location:　　24 Km (15 Miles) S of Revelstoke

GPS Location: 50.83306 N, 118.08306 W, 1,400 Ft

63 Sites – This provincial park campground is set in a former farm next to the Arrow Lake Reservoir on the Columbia River. There is a large circular lagoon for swimming which is rimmed with a sandy beach. Most sites are back-ins to 30 feet but a few will take 40 footers. To reach the campground drive south from Revelstoke on Hwy 23. Hwy 23 leaves Hwy 1 just west of the bridge over the Columbia just west of Revelstoke. It's 23.7 km (14.7 miles) to the campground entrance from the intersection.

☐ **LAMPLIGHTER CAMPGROUND**
   (Open May 1 to Sept 30 – Varies)
   Res and Info: (250) 837-3385, lampcamp@telus.net,
   　　　　　　　www.revelstokecc.bc.ca/lamplighter
   Location:　　Revelstoke

GPS Location: 51.00111 N, 118.21861 W, 1,400 Ft

50 Sites – This is one of those campgrounds that makes us want to spend a few extra days. It's neat and tidy, has a convenient location within a short hike or bus ride of the center of town, and is a pleasant place to stay. Parking here is on grass with good tent sites as well as back-in and pull-thru RV sites to 60 feet. Picnic tables and fire pits are provided. The free Wi-Fi reaches throughout the park. Easiest access is from Hwy 23 on the west side of the river. From the intersection of Hwy 1 and Hwy 23 drive south .3 km (.2 mile). Turn east on Nixon Road, in .3 km (.2 mile) you'll see the campground on the left.

● **REVELSTOKE KOA**
   (Open May 1 to Sept 30 – Varies)
   Reservations: (800) 562-8506, www.koa.com
   Information: (250) 837-2085, revkoa@yahoo.com,
   　　　　　　　www.revelstokekoa.com
   Location:　　5 Km (3 Miles) E of Revelstoke

GPS Location: 50.99139 N, 118.15389 W, 1,700 Ft

170 Sites – This is a nice KOA located outside town along the highway to the east. RV sites are smaller back-ins and pull-thrus to 50 feet. Swimming is in a pool. The Wi-Fi here only is useable near the office. To reach the campground drive 5 km (3 miles) east from the main Revelstoke central exit, the campground is on the south side of the highway.

● **WILLIAMSON'S LAKE CAMPGROUND**
   (Open April 15 to Oct 15 – Varies)
   Res and Info: (888) 676-2267, (250) 837-5512,
   　　　　　　　wlcamp@revelstoke.net,
   　　　　　　　www.williamsonlake
   　　　　　　　campground.com
   Location:　　5 Km (3 Miles) S of Revelstoke

GPS Location: 50.96828 N, 118.17164 W, 1,400 Ft

50 Sites – This campground, especially popular with locals, sits next to a small swimming lake south of town. There is a swimming beach, canoe and paddleboat rentals, and an 18 hole mini-golf course. Sites are smaller back-ins and pull-thrus to 75 feet. No-

hookup and tent sites are located along the lake. The Wi-Fi here is only useable near the office. From south Revelstoke drive south on 4th Street which soon becomes Airport Way. About 3.5 km (5.6 miles) south of town you'll see the sign for the campground on the left. There's a short access road in to the campground.

☐ **MARTHA CREEK PROVINCIAL PARK** *(Open May 6 to Sept 30)*
Information: (250) 837-5734,
information@westkootenayparks.com
Location: 18 Km (11 Miles) N of Revelstoke

GPS Location: 51.14941 N, 118.19958 W, 1,900 Ft

25 Sites – This is a small provincial park with a campground located on the shore of the Revelstoke reservoir north of Revelstoke. The sites are paved back-ins to 40 feet both overlooking and back from the lake. Many of these are sets of two individually rented sites right next to each other on the same pad. Additionally, there are two beautiful 60-foot parallel parking style sites that overlook the lake. Amenities include a sandy swimming beach, boat ramp, dock, and large grassy day-use area. From Hwy 1 on the north side of Revelstoke drive north on Hwy 23. You'll pass the Revelstoke Dam and after 17.7 km (10.7 miles) see the park entrance on the left.

SHUSWAP

Located north of the Okanagan, the Shuswap region is a popular summer family camping area. From early July to Labor Day the campgrounds are packed with vacationing families. The area is named after **Shuswap Lake** which is shaped a little like a big X. There are a few additional lakes too, most importantly Little Shuswap Lake, Adams Lake, and Mara Lake. The main towns are **Salmon Arm** (population 17,000), a good place for supplies, and **Sicamous** (population 3,000).

Water sports are the main attraction here, including **houseboating**. Sicamous is called the houseboat capital of Canada for good reason. It seems like hundreds of houseboats are cruising the lake during the summer season.

Shuswap Campgrounds

● **PONDEROSA PINES RV PARK** *(Open All Year)*
Res and Info: 250 577-3468
Location: 11 Km (7 Miles) SW of Chase

GPS Location: 50.71862 N, 119.77825 W, 1,100 Ft

26 Sites – This is a simple but nice RV park located right next to the highway to the west of Chase. There are tent sites as well as the grassy RV sites which are back-ins to 40 feet and pull-thrus to 70 feet. The RV park is located along Hwy 1 some 11 km (7 Miles) west of Chase, BC.

○ **CHASE LION'S RV PARK** *(Open May 1 to Sept 30 – Varies)*
Information: (250) 679-8470
Location: Chase

GPS Location: 50.82583 N, 119.69972 W, 1,100 Ft

20 Sites – This is a handy little campground if you aren't concerned about extra amenities. It has tent camping in a grassy field, back-in RV sites that will take RVs to 45 feet, full hookups, and restrooms with showers. It sits at the outlet of Little

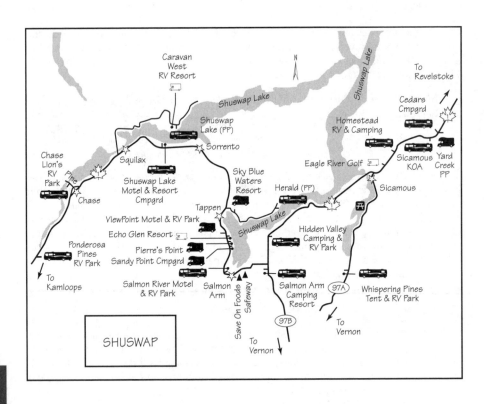

Shuswap Lake and has a boat ramp. We've found this place practically empty when everything in the area is full. From Shuswap Ave. in central Chase turn north on Pine Avenue, the campground is on the left in 1 km (.6 mile), just before the bridge.

SHUSWAP LAKE PROVINCIAL PARK
(Open May 1 to Oct 10 – Varies)
Reservations: www.discovercamping.ca,
          (800) 689-9025
Information: (250) 955-0861, (250) 955-0863
Location: 26 Km (16 Miles) NE of Chase

GPS Location: 50.91028 N, 119.43722 W, 1,100 Ft

272 Sites – This is a large and very popular campground in an ideal location on the north shore (more sun than the south shore) of the west arm of Shuswap Lake. It has an excellent beach. While the location is a little remote, the facilities here are supplemented by the Shuswap Lake Camp Store just outside the entrance which offers telephones, groceries and laundry. There are also restaurants and equipment rental outfits nearby. Copper Island, about 1 km offshore, is part of the park and has hiking trials. Some sites will accept RVs to 45 feet. In the off season it is possible for self-contained rigs to overnight in the day-use area parking lot for no fee. The road out to the campground leaves Hwy 1 some 8 km (5 miles) east of Chase. The campground entrance is at 18 km (11.2 miles).

● **SHUSWAP LAKE MOTEL AND RESORT**
   CAMPGROUND *(Open April 1 to Oct 15)*

Res and Info: (888) 587-0514, (250) 675-2420,
                  www.shuswaplakemotel.com
Location: Sorrento

   GPS Location: 50.87726 N, 119.47259 W, 1,200 Ft

12 Sites – This is a small and well cared for motel with a campground on the western outskirts of Sorrento. Sites are on grass or gravel, only four sites have hookups. These are pull-thru sites to 40 feet with electricity and water, there is no sewer for RVs available at the campground. Swimming is at a beach a short walk from the campground.

● **SKY BLUE WATERS RESORT** *(Open All Year)*
   Res and Info: (866) 835-4531, (250) 835-4531,
                     skybluewaters@hotmail.com,
                     www.skybluewatersresort.com
   Location: 16 Km (10 Miles) W of Salmon Arm

      GPS Location: 50.78034 N, 119.30989 W, 1,100 Ft

36 Sites – This is a rustic motel with a campground located next to it and overlooking Salmon Arm of Shuswap Lake. The resort has a boat ramp, dock, and swimming beach across the road from the hotel. Fortunately it's a relatively quiet road, although traffic heading for Herald Provincial Park does pass by here. Sites are back-ins or pull-ins to 35 feet and overlook the lake. To reach the resort leave Hwy 1 just north of Tappen. Follow Sunnybrae-Canoe Point Road for 1.8 km (1.1 miles) to the resort.

☐ **HERALD PROVINCIAL PARK** *(Open May 1 to Sept 30 – Varies)*
   Reservations: www.discovercamping.ca, (800) 689-9025
   Information: (250) 835-0103
   Location: 11 Km (7 Miles) E of Tappen

      GPS Location: 50.78722 N, 119.20528 W, 1,100 Ft

119 Sites – Like Shuswap Provincial Park, this campground is on the north shore of one of the arms of Shuswap Lake. This time it's Salmon Arm near Tappen. There's a good beach here too. This campground also can take RVs to 45 feet but it's a little less convenient than Shuswap since there is no store at the gate. A short hike will take you to impressive Margaret Falls. There's a boat ramp at the park. Self-contained rigs can camp in the day use area during the off season. To reach the campground leave Hwy 1 just north of Tappen. Follow the road along the north shore of the arm for 10.8 km (6.7 miles) to the entrance.

● **VIEWPOINT MOTEL AND RV PARK**
   (Open March 15 to Oct 15 – Varies)
   Res and Info: (250) 832-2833, www.viewpoint.ca
   Location: 10 Km (6 Miles) W of Salmon Arm

      GPS Location: 50.75043 N, 119.32551 W, 1,200 Ft

13 Sites – This is a beautifully maintained small motel and RV park overlooking the Salmon Arm of Shuswap Lake from a high point along Hwy 1. There are 13 back-in RV sites to 35 feet with parking on gravel. The ViewPoint is on the south side of the Trans Canada Highway, about 10 km (16 miles) west of Salmon Arm.

● **PIERRE'S POINT FAMILY CAMPGROUND RESORT**
  (Open May 15 to Sept 30 – Varies)
  Res and Info: (877) 832-9523, (250) 832-9523,
                    ppoint01@telus.net,
                    www.pierrespointcampground.com
  Location: 7 Km (4.5 Miles) NW of Salmon Arm

  GPS Location: 50.73806 N, 119.31722 W, 1,100 Ft

185 Sites – This is a good example of one of the family
vacation resorts scattered around the shores of Shuswap Lake. In fact, campers without
children are discouraged. Sites here tend to be small and the rigs really packed in. A few
sites are pull-thrus to 50 feet but most are back-ins to 30 feet or so. This campground is
full of smaller trailers and tents. Although there are many tenters there are few dedicated
tent sites, most have low-amp electricity and water. There's a huge beach with swimming
in the lake, a small store, a snack bar, and equipment rentals. You'll find Pierre's well-
signed between Tappen and Salmon Arm, about 7 km (4.5 miles) NW of Salmon Arm.

● **SANDY POINT BEACH CAMPGROUND**
  (Open May 15 to Oct 12)
  Res and Info: (250) 832-3793
  Location: 6 Km (4 Miles) NW of Salmon Arm

  GPS Location: 50.73034 N, 119.30995 W, 1,100 Ft

310 Sites – This is another large beachside family
campground on the south shore of Salmon Arm. Many sites are occupied by long term
guests. There are tent, partial, and full hookup sites. Most are back-ins to 30 feet. Amenities include a large beach area, boat ramp, and store. From Salmon Arm drive 6 km (4
miles) west. Turn south on Sandy Point Road and follow signs to the campground.

● **SALMON RIVER MOTEL AND RV PARK**
  (Open April 1 to Oct 30)
  Res and Info: (250) 832-6035
  Location: Salmon Arm

  GPS Location: 50.69356 W, 119.33068 W, 1,100 Ft

30 Sites – This is a motel with an RV park behind it on
the western approaches to Salmon Arm. Sites are back-ins to 40 feet and pull-thrus to 60
feet. The motel is on the north side of the highway at the western edge of Salmon Arm.

● **SALMON ARM CAMPING RESORT**
  (Open May 1 to Oct 1)
  Res and Info: (866) 979-1659, (250) 832-6489,
                    www.salmonarmcamping.com
  Location: 2 Km (1 Mile) E of Salmon Arm

  GPS Location: 50.70242 N, 119.22928 W, 1,600 Ft

66 Sites – This former KOA is located just east of Salmon
Arm. The sites here are back-ins to 40 feet and pull-thrus to 50 feet. The campground
has a heated pool and a hot tub. From central Salmon Arm drive east a short distance on
Hwy 1 to the intersection with Hwy 97B to Vernon. .Turn south onto Hwy 97B and the
campground entrance is on the right in .8 km (.5 mile).

● **HIDDEN VALLEY CAMPING AND RV PARK**
(Open All Year)
Res and Info: (866) 441-6159, (250) 832-6159 ,
www.hiddenvalleycampground.ca
Location: Hwy 1, 6 Km (4 Miles) NE of Salmon
Arm

GPS Location: 50.74775 N, 119.22472 W, 1,200 Ft

75 Sites – A well cared for RV park and campground east of Salmon Arm next to the highway. Sites are back-ins and pull-thrus, a few to 45 feet but most are smaller. From the intersection of Hwy 1 and Hwy 97B east of Salmon Arm drive north for 4.4 km (2.7 miles) and you'll see the campground entrance on the right.

● **HOMESTEAD RV AND CAMPING** *(Open All Year)*
Res and Info: (250) 836-2583,
homesteadcampground@yahoo.ca
Location: 5 Km (3 Miles) E of Sicamous

GPS Location: 50.86583 N, 118.92833 W, 1,100 Ft

109 Sites – This is an older family-run campground on the banks of the Eagle River along Hwy 1 east of Shuswap Lake. All parking is on grass, sites are back-ins and pull-thrus to 80 feet. Swimming is in a pool. Watch for the campground on the north side of the highway about 5 km (3 miles) east of Sicamous.

● **SICAMOUS KOA KAMPGROUND**
(Open May 1 to Oct 1)
Reservations: (800) 562-8506,
www.koa.com
Information: (250) 836-2507,
sicamouskoa@shaw.ca
Location: Hwy 1, 12 Km (8 Miles) E of
Sicamous

GPS Location: 50.88834 N, 118.84255 W, 1,100 Ft

68 Sites – This roadside KOA has back-ins to 50 feet and pull-thrus to 70 feet as well as tent sites. Amenities include a Wi-Fi hotspot and a heated pool. The campground is on the south side of the Trans Canada Highway about 12.3 km (7.6 miles) east of Sicamous.

☐ **YARD CREEK PROVINCIAL PARK** *(Open May 1 to Sept 30 – Varies)*
Location: 15 Km (9 Miles) E of Sicamous

GPS Location: 50.89778 N, 118.81250 W, 1,400 Ft

65 Sites – This is a small provincial park. While some sites would take RVs as long as 45 feet sites are not level and the roads are narrow making maneuvering for large rigs very difficult. The practical length limit at this park is about 30 feet. The campground is on the south side of the Hwy 1 about 15 km (9 miles) east of Sicamous.

● **CEDARS CAMPGROUND**
(Open May 15 to Sept 20 – Varies)
Res and Info: 877 836-3988, www.cedarsrvpark.com
Location: Hwy 1, 15 Km (9 Miles) E of Sicamous

GPS Location: 50.89695 N, 118.82381 W, 1,200 Ft

115 Sites – This large older campground is located right along the highway across from

BRITISH COLUMBIA

the entrance to Yard Creek Provincial Park. There are many tent sites as well as pull-thru RV sites to 70 feet. Amenities include a swimming pool and Wi-Fi hotspot. The campground is on the north side of Hwy 1 about 15 km (9 miles) east of Sicamous.

● **WHISPERING PINES TENT AND RV PARK**
   (Open May 20 to Sept 6)
   Res and Info: (250) 838-6775, whispines@hotmail.com
   Location: 18 Km (11 Miles) S of Sicamous

   GPS Location: 50.69599 N, 119.04197 W, 1,200 Ft

160 Sites – This campground is located well south of Sicamous along Hwy 97A. They have many tent sites as well as back-in and pull-thru RV sites to 50 feet. The park has a swimming pool. From the intersection of Hwy 1 and Hwy 97A east of Sicamous drive south on Hwy 97A for 18.4 km (11.4 miles) to the entrance, it's on the right.

SIMILKAMEEN VALLEY

The Similkameen Valley lies just to the west of the Lower Okanagan Valley. The Similkameen River begins in Manning Provincial Park and runs east through the valley to eventually join the Okanagan River. Highway 3, the Crowsnest Highway, runs the length of the valley.

For our purposes the west end of the valley is marked by the town of **Princeton**, population 3,000. The town is located at the confluence of the Tulameen and Similkameen Rivers. It has a western ranching and mining heritage and has decided to make itself into a western theme town. Visit the **Princeton Museum** which shows off the town's mining past and which also has a great fossil collection. There's a **Historic Walk** around the downtown area, check at the visitor center about this.

As you travel downstream from Princeton you'll pass through the little town of **Hedley**. This too was a mining town and has its own mining museum, the **Hedley Museum**.

Two provincial parks make good spots to stop for lunch or to stretch your legs. These are **Stemwinder** and **Bromley**. Both have campgrounds, described below. Bromley is a popular swimming hole on the Similkameen.

The town of **Keremeos**, population 1,500, marks the eastern end of the valley. Keremeos is best known for its fruit stands, this area is one of Canada's foremost fruit growing regions. There are also quite a few vineyards in the area. The town museum is the **Similkameen Museum**, located in an old jailhouse.

Just west of town a road leads across the **Red Bridge**, a covered railroad bridge now used as a highway bridge. It is a gravel road that leads some 48 km (30 miles) south to **Cathedral Provincial Park**. This is a wilderness park offering no vehicle camping, but is does have lots of hiking routes as well as hike-in tent camping locations.

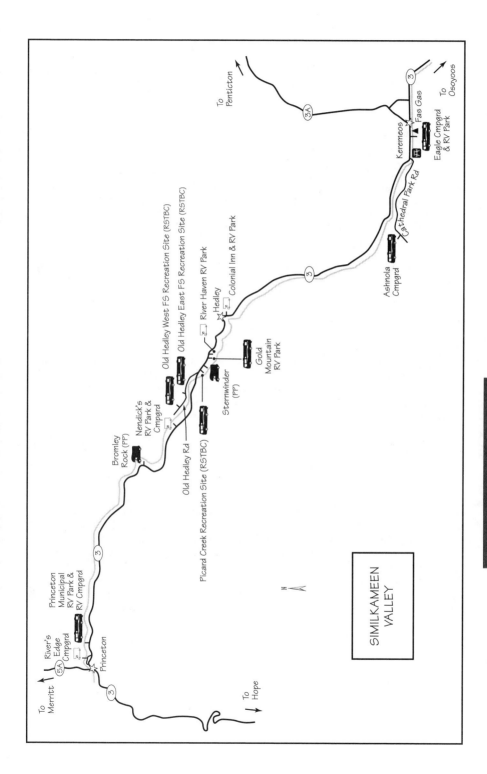

SIMILKAMEEN VALLEY

Similkameen Campgrounds

○ **PRINCETON MUNICIPAL RV PARK AND CAMPGROUND** *(Open May 1 to Sept 30)*

Res and Info: (855) 295-7355, (250) 295-7355,
info@princetonrvpark.ca,
www.princetonrvpark.ca
Location: Princeton

GPS Location: 49.46194 N, 120.47444 W, 2,100 Ft

73 Sites – This is the Princeton municipal campground. It is located on the south side of the Similkameen River just east of Princeton. All of the sites in this campground are back-ins along an access road running parallel with the river and highway. The sites on the river side are gravel surfaced, those on the road side are grass. Some sites are as long as 50 feet. These are electric and water sites, there are no sewers but there is a dump station. From central Princeton head east on Hwy 3, the campground is on the left.

☐ **BROMLEY ROCK PROVINCIAL PARK** *(Open April 15 to Oct 31)*
Information: (604) 476-9069
Location: 16.7 Km (10.4 Miles) W of Hedley

GPS Location: 49.41500 N, 120.26083 W, 1,800 Ft

17 Sites – The campground sites at this park are off a loop downstream from the day-use area. This is a spectacular setting with the Similkameen River running past huge rocks. The campsites are mostly back-ins but there are three pull-thus. The sites are small here and the campground is best for RVs no larger than 30 feet. During the off season the campground is accessible, there is no fee and no services available. Bromley Rock is on the north side of Highway 3 some 16.7 km (10.4 miles) west of Hedley. In the other direction it's 22.6 km (14 miles) east of Princeton.

☐ **OLD HEDLEY EAST AND WEST RECREATION SITES** *(April 15 to Oct 15)*
Location: 8.5 Km (5.3 Miles) W of Hedley

GPS Location: 49.38222 N, 120.17806 W, 1,800 Ft

25 Sites – These two RSTBC camping areas are located near each other just off Hwy 3. Both have parking on dirt under pines overlooking the Similkameen River. It's a quiet area and very easy to access in any size RV. There are a few picnic tables, some fire pits, and even vault toilets. There is no potable water provided. Watch for Old Hedley Road on the north side of Hwy 3 about 6.4 km (4 miles) west of Hedley. It's just east of a bridge over the Similkameen and, if you're coming from the west, is about 31 km (19 miles) east of Princeton. Follow Old Hedley Road west along the north bank of the river, you'll reach Old Hedley East in 2.1 km (1.3 mile) and Old Hedley West in 3.2 km (2 miles).

☐ **PICKARD CREEK RECREATION SITE** *(Open April 15 to Oct 15)*
Location: 6.0 Km (3.7 Miles W of Hedley

GPS Location: 49.37474 N, 120.14532 W, 1,700 Ft

16 Sites – This RSTBC site is set in sparse trees sloping gently down to the Similkameen River. Sites are generous and will take carefully driven large RVs. There is no potable water. The camping area is on the south side of Hwy 3 some 6.0 km (3.7 miles) west of Hedley.

BRITISH COLUMBIA

☐ **STERNWINDER PROVINCIAL PARK** *(April 15 to Oct 31)*
Information: (604) 476-9069
Location: 5.2 Km (3.2 Miles) W of Hedley

GPS Location: 49.37083 N, 120.13583 W, 1,700 Ft

27 Sites – This is a provincial park next to the highway and perched above the Similka-meen River. Sites are all back-ins, good for RVs to about 35 feet since maneuvering room is limited. The sites on the lower side of the loop are right on the river, those on the upper side are near the road. The campground is right on Hwy 3 some 5.2 km (3.2 miles) west of Hedley.

● **GOLD MOUNTAIN RV PARK**
   (Open May 1 to Oct 1)
Res and Info: (250) 292-8188, oldt-mtn@telus.net,
         www3.telus.net/GoldMountainRV/
Location: 4.4 Km (2.7 Miles) W of Hedley

GPS Location: 49.36667 N, 120.12806 W, 1,700 Ft

24 Sites – This is one of two similar campgrounds situated next to each other off Hwy 3 and sloping down to the Similkameen River. The place next door is called the River Haven RV Park. The campground has a few pull-thrus to 60 feet, the remaining sites are back-ins to 40 feet. Some are full-hookup sites but there are also quite a few sites with no sewer hookups. The campground is on the south side of Hwy 3 some 4.4 km (2.7 miles) west of Hedley.

● **ASHNOLA CAMPGROUND** *(Open April 1 to Sept 30)*
Information: (250) 499-5528, www.lsib.org
Location: 10 Km (6 Miles) W of Keremeos

GPS Location: 49.21111 N, 119.98333 W, 1,500 Ft

100 Sites – Ashnola is a First Nation campground located on the route to Cathedral Pro-vincial Park. This is a big campground and a convenient place to stay if you're planning to drive south to Cathedral Provincial Park on a day trip. There are also a number of RSTBC (Recreation Sites and Trails BC) campgrounds father down the road. The devel-oped sites at Ashnola Campground are back-ins, some to 40 feet. There's also a large area without developed sites but suitable for parking under scattered pines. Power is some-times available by stretching a cord. Restrooms have flush toilets and showers. From just west of Keremeos follow the Cathedral Park road for 8.2 km (5.1 miles) across the Red Bridge and to the campground.

● **EAGLE CAMPGROUND AND RV PARK**
   (Open All Year)
Res and Info: (250) 499-5439
Location: Keremeos

GPS Location: 49.20444 N, 119.86083 W, 1,300 Ft

26 Sites – This tidy campground is great if you're looking for a full-hookup park in the Keremeos area. There are full-hookup pull-thrus and back-ins to 60 feet with parking on grass and also shorter back-ins. There's also some dry camping. A bike and foot path runs by the campground and extends west to the Red Bridge. Watch for the campground entrance behind the Fas Gas station off Hwy 3 about a mile west of Keremeos.

BRITISH COLUMBIA

SMITHERS

Smithers (population 5,500) is situated on Hwy 16 some 371 km (230 miles) west of Prince George and 348 km (216 miles) east of Prince Rupert. The town is in the Bulkley Valley surrounded by mountains, a very scenic location.

To get out into those mountains you might drive up Kathlyn Glacier Road to a viewpoint overlooking **Twin Falls**. You can hike in to the **Kathlyn Glacier**. Another good nearby hiking destination is the **Babine Mountains Provincial Park** to the northeast of town. Along the way stop at the **Driftwood Canyon Provincial Park**, known for its fossil beds.

Smithers Campgrounds

○ **RIVERSIDE PARK** *(Open May 15 to Oct 15 – Varies)*
Information: (250) 847-1600
Location: Smithers

GPS Location: 54.78556 N, 127.14861 W, 1,500 Ft

50 Sites – This municipal campground is located below town on the bank of the Bulkley River. There are tent sites as well as back-in RV sites to 45 feet. Several hiking trails leave from the park. From central Smithers follow Main Street east to the park.

● **RIVERSIDE GOLF AND RV PARK**
    (Open May 1 to Oct 31)
Res and Info: (250) 847-3229
Location: 3 Km (2 Miles) E of Smithers

GPS Location: 54.76694 N, 127.12556 W, 1,600 Ft

56 Sites – This campground is located right alongside a golf course. There are tent and back-in sites as well as pull-thrus to 70 feet. Restrooms are in the basement of the reception building. The campground is located on the south side of Hwy 16 about 3 km (2 miles) east of Smithers.

● **FT TELKWA RV PARK** *(Open May 1 to Nov 1)*
Res and Info: (250) 846-5012, www.forttelkwa.com
Location: 13 Km (8 Miles) E of Smithers

GPS Location: 54.69135 N, 127.04489 W, 1,600 Ft

35 Sites – This RV park is located next to the Bulkley River. RV sites here are mostly full-hookup back-ins and pull-thrus to 60 feet. There are also tent sites. Amenities include a boat ramp and free pressure wash. From the bridge over the Bulkley on the east side of Smithers drive east on Hwy 16 for 12.7 km (7.9 miles), the campground is on the right.

☐ **TYHEE LAKE PROVINCIAL PARK**
    (Open May 13 to Sept 15 – Varies)
Reservations: www.discovercamping.ca, (800) 689-9025
Information: (250) 638-8490
Location: 14 Km (9 Miles) E of Smithers

GPS Location: 54.70861 N, 127.04056 W, 1,800 Ft

59 Sites – This beautiful campground is on the west shore of Tyhee Lake. Most sites are back from the edge of the lake in an aspen forest. All sites are back-ins, some to 45 ft. The

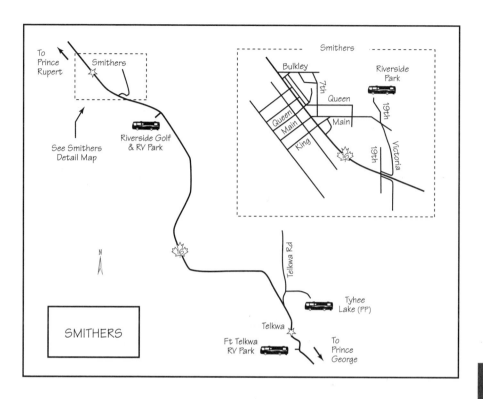

campground offers restrooms flush toilets and showers. There's also a day-use area with beach and boat launch. To reach the park head east from Smithers. Zero your odometer as you pass over the bridge that crosses the Bulkley River east of town. In 12.7 km (7.9 miles) turn left onto Telkwa Road. In .8 km (.5 mile) you'll see the entrance road to the park on the right.

SOUTH CARIBOO REGION

This region is a large area stretching all the way from Cache Creek in the south to Lac La Hache in the north, a distance of about 160 km (100 miles). It's a high plateau region with hot dry summers and cold winters.

Highway 97 runs the length of this region. You'll notice that small towns along the way have names like 70 Mile House and 100 Mile House. That's because this was the access route to the Cariboo gold fields (see *Barkerville and Wells* in this section) and the mileages in the name reflect their distance from Lillooet.

Cache Creek (population 1,100) sits at the junction of Hwy 1, the Trans-Canada Highway, and Hwy 97. Cache Creek has grocery stores, restaurants, fuel, a campground, and a dump station at the visitor centre. The **Hat Creek Ranch** is located about 11 kilometers north of Cache Creek and just west of Hwy 97 on Hwy 99. This historic ranch features a roadhouse and native village, also a restaurant and gift shop. Cache Creek celebrates **Grafitti Days** with a Car Mania automobile rally in June.

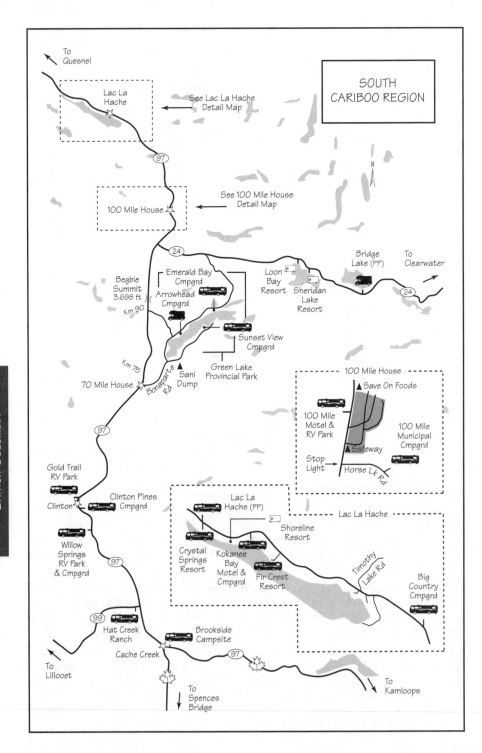

To Quesnel

Lac La Hache

See Lac La Hache Detail Map

SOUTH CARIBOO REGION

97

100 Mile House

See 100 Mile House Detail Map

N

24

Begbie Summit 3,698 ft
Km 90

Emerald Bay Cmpgrd

Arrowhead Cmpgrd

Loon Bay Resort

Sheridan Lake Resort

Bridge Lake (PP)

To Clearwater

24

Sunset View Cmpgrd

Green Lake Provincial Park

Km 75

70 Mile House

Bonaparte Rd

Sani Dump

100 Mile House

Save On Foods

100 Mile Motel & RV Park

Stop Light

Safeway

Horse Lk Rd

100 Mile Municipal Cmpgrd

97

Gold Trail RV Park

Clinton Pines Cmpgrd

Clinton

Willow Springs RV Park & Cmpgrd

97

Lac La Hache (PP)

Shoreline Resort

Crystal Springs Resort

Kokanee Bay Motel & Cmpgrd

Fir Crest Resort

Lac La Hache

Timothy Lake Rd

Big Country Cmpgrd

99

Hat Creek Ranch

Cache Creek

Brookside Campsite

97

To Lillooet

To Spences Bridge

To Kamloops

BRITISH COLUMBIA

Clinton (population 1,000) is not far north of Cache Creek, only 39 km (24 miles). Like Cache Creek Clinton offers stores, restaurants, and gas. Clinton has two campgrounds in town and another a few miles to the south. The town hosts a rodeo in May and the **Clinton Jamboree** in August.

100 Mile House (population 2,000) is the largest town along this section of highway. It has large supermarkets, services, restaurants, and fuel. We list two campgrounds in 100 Mile House.

The community of **Lac La Hache** (population 400) stretches about 18 km (11 miles) along the east shore of Lac La Hache. It's widely known as the longest town in the Cariboo but, truthfully, there are long distances between structures in this "town". Lac La Hache is good for boating and water sports. We list 5 campgrounds in the area and 3 of them are on the shore of the lake.

Near 100 Mile House Highway 24 branches off and heads east. This highway crosses an area of many lakes, a lot of them have lodges and campgrounds for fishermen. The nickname for this highway is the "Rainbow Road", it's known for the rainbow trout that inhabit many of the lakes. A lot of the lakes were stocked with trout in the 1940s and today the fish are thick. Bridge Lake Provincial Park, one of the campgrounds listed below, is along this highway and makes a good fishing base.

South Cariboo Region Campgrounds

● **BROOKSIDE CAMPSITE**
   (Open April 1 to Oct 31)

Res and Info: (250) 457-6633,
   brooksidecampsite@hotmail.com
   www.brooksidecampsite.com

Location: Cache Creek

GPS Location: 50.80972 N, 121.30667 W, 1,600 Ft

98 Sites – A very good campground located just outside Cache Creek on Hwy 97 toward Kamloops. There is tent camping on grass as well as back-ins to 35 feet and pull-thru sites to 70 feet. Amenities include a swimming pool and Cache Creek running through the park.

● **HAT CREEK RANCH** *(Open May 1 to Sept 30)*

Information: (250) 457-9722, (800) 782-0922,
   www.hatcreekranch.com

Location: 10 Km (6 Miles) W of Cache Creek

GPS Location: 50.88611 N, 121.40917 W, 1,600 Ft

30 Sites – Hat Creek Ranch is a historic site with a restaurant, gift shop, motel, and camping area. There are 8 back-in sites with electrical hookups as well as a large grass area for both tents and RVs with no hookups. Restrooms with showers are available. From Cache Creek drive north on Hwy 97 for 10 km (6 miles) to the intersection with Hwy 99. Turn east and in .6 km (.4 mile) the ranch is on the left.

● **WILLOW SPRINGS RV PARK AND CAMPGROUND**
   (Open May 15 to Sept 15 – Varies)

Res and Info: (250) 459-7046,
   www.willowspringscampground.com

Location: 6 Km (4 Miles) S of Clinton

GPS Location: 51.03222 N, 121.55028 W, 3,000 Ft

45 Sites – This is one of the prettier campsite you'll see along the highway with sites on grass sloping down to a small lake. Pull-thru sites will take RVs to 45 feet. Highway noise can be a problem here. It's located on the west side of Hwy 97 about 31 km (19 miles) north of Cache Creek and 6 km (4 miles) south of Clinton.

● **CLINTON PINES CAMPGROUND**
    (Open March 15 to Oct 15 – Varies)
    Res and Info: (250) 459-0030, clintonpines@xplorenet.com
    Location: Clinton

    GPS Location: 51.08361 N, 121.58972 W, 3,000 Ft

16 Sites – This is a small campground set in a landscaped former gravel pit. Sites include full and partial hookup sites including full-hookup pull-thrus to 60 feet. The campground is located on the southern border of Clinton on the east side of Hwy 97.

● **GOLD TRAIL RV PARK**
    (Open April 1 to Nov 15 – Varies)
    Information: (250) 459-2638
    Location: Clinton

    GPS Location: 51.09444 N, 121.58139 W, 3,000 Ft

50 Sites – This campground is located in central Clinton giving you walking access to the town's shops and restaurants. Sites are set on a grass lawn and will take RVs to 45 feet. It has its own restaurant.

☐ **SUNSET VIEW CAMPGROUND – GREEN LAKE**
    PROVINCIAL PARK *(Open May 13 to Sept 5)*
    Reservations: www.discovercamping.ca, (800) 689-9025
    Information: (250) 397-2523
    Location: 19 Km (12 Miles) E of 70 Mile House

    GPS Location: 51.34500 N, 121.30639 W, 3,500 Ft

54 Sites – This is one of three campgrounds in Green Lake Provincial Park. The campground will take RVs to 45 feet. This is a popular boating and water sports lake and the campground has a boat launch. Sunset View is on the south side of the lake and is easily accessed from a cutoff just south of 70 Mile House. In 8.5 km (5.3 miles) you'll reach a provincial park information shelter and dump station. Take the right fork there and in another 11.4 km (7.1 miles) you'll reach the campground entrance.

☐ **ARROWHEAD CAMPGROUND – GREEN LAKE**
    PROVINCIAL PARK *(May 13 to Sept 5)*
    Information: (250) 397-2523
    Location: 17 Km (10.5 Miles) E of 70 Mile House

    GPS Location: 51.39847 N, 121.25791 W, 3,500 Ft

16 Sites – Arrowhead is a nice little campground on the north shore of the lake with RV sites right along the beach. They are all back-ins, in pairs, most to 40 feet. The RVs in each of the pairs is separated from the other with cement barriers. Arrowhead Campground is on the north side of the lake and is easily accessed from a cutoff just south of 70 Mile House. In 8.5 km (5.3 miles) you'll reach a provincial park information shelter and dump station. Take the left fork there and in another 8.4 km (5.2 miles) you'll reach the campground entrance.

☐ **EMERALD BAY CAMPGROUND – GREEN LAKE
PROVINCIAL PARK** *(Open May 23 to Oct 2)*

Reservations: www.discovercamping.ca, (800) 689-9025
Information: (250) 397-2523
Location: 26 Km (16 Miles) E of 70 Mile House

GPS Location: 51.44319 N, 121.15962 W, 3,500 Ft

51 Sites – Emerald Bay is the largest north shore campground. It's in an aspen grove. Sites here are off two gravel loops, they are all back-ins, some to 45 feet. Some are near the lake shore. Water is from a pump, there is a swimming beach and a playground. Emerald Bay Campground is on the north side of the lake and is easily accessed from a cutoff just south of 70 Mile House. In 8.5 km (5.3 miles) you'll reach a provincial park information shelter and dump station. Take the left fork there and in another 17.4 km (10.8 miles) you'll reach the campground entrance.

○ **100 MILE MUNICIPAL CAMPGROUND** *(Open May 24 to Oct 1 – Varies)*

Information: (250) 395-2434
Location: 100 Mile House

GPS Location: 51.63667 N, 121.28972 W, 2,000 Ft

11 Sites – This small municipal campground has back-in sites in a pleasant location at the edge of town. It's easily accessible. A few of the formal sites will take RVs to 40 feet and there is an overflow area for larger rigs but some leveling is required in this area. A short trail leads to a small waterfall. In 100 Mile House turn east at the Husky gas station on Horse Lake Road, the campground is on the left in .5 km (.3 mile).

● **100 MILE MOTEL AND RV PARK**
(Open April 15 to Oct 1 – Varies)
Res and Info: (250) 395-2234
hunmotel@shaw.ca,
www.100milehouse.ca
Location: 100 Mile House

GPS Location: 51.64361 N, 121.29750 W, 2,000 Ft

48 Sites – This small motel in the town of 100 Mile House is handy for shopping or restaurants. It has pull-thru sites with electricity and water to 60 feet with parking on mixed gravel and grass. A large grassy tent camping area is in the rear and along the south side of the RV slots. Some sites have picnic tables, showers require payment, and there is a dump station. Watch for it on the west side of the highway .3 km (.2 mile) north of the Safeway supermarket.

● **BIG COUNTRY CAMPGROUND**
(Open May 1 to Sept 30)
Res and Info: (250) 396-4181,
www.100milehouse.ca/stay/resorts/
bigcountry.html
Location: 5 Km (3 Miles) S of Lac La Hache

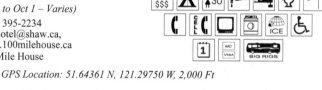

GPS Location: 51.79028 N, 121.40611 W, 2,800 Ft

41 Sites – This former KOA is the first Lac La Hache campground you'll reach if you're headed north. It's not on the lake. There are back-ins and pull-thrus sites to 60 feet. Amenities include a swimming pool. The campground is located 21 km (13 miles) north of 100 Mile House and 5 km (3 miles) south of the south end of Lac La Hache. It's on the east side of the road.

BRITISH COLUMBIA

● **FIR CREST RESORT**
(Open May 15 to Sept 15 – Varies)
Res and Info: (250) 706-9575, (250) 396-7337,
              resort.fircrest@gmail.com,
              www.fircrestresort.com
Location: Lac La Hache

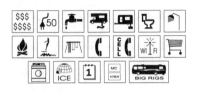

GPS Location: 51.83722 N, 121.56611 W, 2,700 Ft

90 Sites – This is one of the best big-rig campgrounds in the area. It has large pull-thru sites to 70 feet overlooking the lake and good facilities. Swimming is in the lake and there are canoe and bicycle rentals. As you enter Lac La Hache from the south watch for the road to the right to Timothy Lake Resort Area (Timothy Lake Road). Continue straight, in 6.8 km (4.2 miles) turn left at the sign for the resort at Fircrest Road and drive .5 km (.3 mile) to the campground. From the north the right turn onto Fircrest Road is 6.6 km (4.1 mile) from the Lac La Hache Provincial Park entrance.

● **KOKANEE BAY MOTEL AND CAMPGROUND**
(Open All Year)
Res and Info: (888) 399-7345, (250) 396-7345,
              info@kokaneebaycariboo.com,
              www.kokaneebaycariboo.com
Location: Lac La Hache

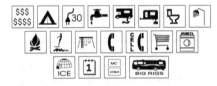

GPS Location: 51.84889 N, 121.58556 W, 2,700 Ft

50 Sites – Another shore-side Lac La Hache campground with waterfront sites and a pleasant atmosphere. Parking is on grass, there are large back-in sites to 45 feet and pull-thrus to 60 feet. There's swimming in the lake and there is a boat ramp. As you enter Lac La Hache watch for the road to the right to Timothy Lake Resort Area (Timothy Lake Road). Don't turn, in another 9.4 km (5.8 miles) you'll see the motel and campground on the left. From the north the resort is 4.2 km (2.6 miles) from the Lac La Hache Provincial Park entrance.

● **CRYSTAL SPRINGS RESORT**
(Open May 15 to Oct 15 – Varies)
Res and Info: (250) 396-4497,
              info@crystalspringsresort.ca,
              www.crystalspringsresort.net
Location: Lac La Hache

GPS Location: 51.85861 N, 121.64056 W, 2,700 Ft

60 Sites – A smaller but very pleasant lakeside resort. Campsites are down the hill from the office building which is on the access road to the waterfront portion of Lac La Hache Provincial Park. Some back-ins reach 45 feet in length. The park next door has a swimming beach and boat ramp. The resort is on the far side of the road from the Lac La Hache Provincial Park campground entrance.

☐ **LAC LA HACHE PROVINCIAL PARK**
(Open May 13 to Oct 2 – Varies)
Reservations: www.discovercamping.ca,
              (800) 689-9025
Information: (250) 397-2523
Location: Lac La Hache

GPS Location: 51.85972 N, 121.63972 W, 2,700 Ft

BRITISH COLUMBIA

83 Sites – This is a handy provincial park with facilities on two sides of the highway. Campsites are on the east side as is the dump station. There is also a swimming beach, picnic area, and boat ramp alongside the lake to the west. Camping sites are almost all back-ins with a few pull-thrus, some sites reach 50 feet in length. The park is located at the north end of the strip of facilities that line the east side of Lac La Hache.

☐ **BRIDGE LAKE PROVINCIAL PARK** *(Open June 15 to Sept 18 – Varies)*
Information: (250) 397-2523
Location: 60 Km (37 Miles) E of 100 Mile House

GPS Location: 51.48500 N, 120.69944 W, 3,700 Ft

16 Sites – This is a small and fairly remote provincial park. It's a handy place to stop if you are traveling the popular Hwy 24 between Hwy 97 and the Clearwater entrance to Wells Gray Provincial Park. The park has a boat ramp and is suitable for RVs to only 35 feet due to limited maneuvering room. It is located 52 km (32 miles) east of the 100 Mile House intersection with Hwy 97 some 8 km (5 miles) south of 100 Mile House.

SUNSHINE COAST (LOWER) – GIBSONS, SECHELT, AND THE SOUTH

Access to the Sunshine Coast is a 45-minute ferry ride from Horseshoe Bay across Howe Sound to Langdale. There are frequent ferries from Horseshoe Bay (approximately every two hours) so you don't have to worry much about your schedule there. If you plan to continue on to the upper Sunshine Coast you should check when you buy your ticket to

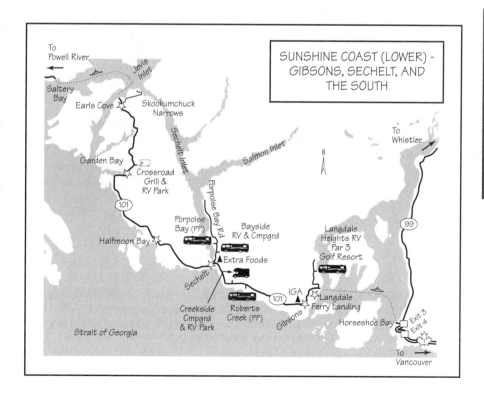

see when the Earls Cove to Saltery Bay ferry runs. Otherwise you might find yourself waiting for quite a long period at the dock in Earls Cove.

When you leave the boat in Langdale you are on the Sunshine Coast proper. Some folks call this area the Lower Coast. Highway 101 runs north near the coast for 79 kilometers (49 miles) through the communities of Gibsons, Roberts Creek, Sechelt, Halfmoon Bay, Madeira Park, and Pender Harbor to Earls Cove.

If you decide that you really love the lower Sunshine Coast you will find plenty of campgrounds along the way. There is a good provincial campground set in a cedar grove called Roberts Creek Provincial Park just 15 kilometers (9 miles) north of the Langdale ferry terminal and another larger one called Porpoise Bay Provincial Park about 23 kilometers (14 miles) north of the terminal. There are also a number of commercial campgrounds.

The **Skookumchuck Rapids** are famous world-wide. These are saltwater rapids, much like a river. In the narrows the salt water rushes both north and south, depending upon the tide. You'll want to be on hand when the tide changes at either high or low water so that you can see the flow change directions. You'll find that the best viewing times are easy to find in local papers, at the information centers, and even posted at the trailhead. To reach the narrows drive 6 kilometers (4 miles) east on Egmont Road from a point on Hwy 101 about 1 kilometer (.6 mile) south of the Earls Cove ferry landing. Park along the road in the parking lot and walk down an access road and then along a fine trail for a distance of 4 kilometers (2.5 miles) to the narrows.

Sunshine Coast (Lower) Campgrounds

● **Langdale Heights RV Par 3 Golf Resort**
(Open All Year)
Res and Info: (604) 886 2182, 800 234-7138,
kmbventures2009@hotmail.com,
www.langdaleheights.com
Location: 5 Km (3 Miles) N of Langdale Ferry Landing

GPS Location: 49.45917 N, 123.49694 W, 400 Ft

54 Sites – This campground and 9-hole par 3 golf course sit on a hillside overlooking Howe Sound. Back-in sites will take RVs to 45 feet. There is also a grassy tent camping area. Golf is included in the price of your campsite. From the ferry landing in Langdale head up the hill and in .8 km (.5 mile) take the first right onto the Port Mellon Highway. Take a left at the Y in 3.1 km (1.9 miles), the campground entrance is on the right 3.9 km (2.4 miles) from your turn onto the Port Mellon Highway.

☐ **Robert's Creek Provincial Park**
(Open June 15 to Sept 15 – Varies)
Information: (604) 885-3714, info@sunshinecoastparks.com,
www.sunshinecoastparks.com
Location: 18 Km (11 Miles) W of Langdale Ferry Landing

GPS Location: 49.44056 N, 123.67139 W, Near Sea Level

21 Sites – This small provincial park campground has sites that will take any size rig and there is beach access a 1.4 km (.9 mile) hike from the campground. In the off season tent campers may walk in and use the park, there is no fee. The park is located along Hwy 101 some 13 km (8 miles) west of Gibsons and 8 km (5 miles) southeast of Sechelt.

● **CREEKSIDE CAMPGROUND** *(Open All Year)*
Res and Info: (800) 565-9222,
                    (604) 885-5937,
                    creeksidecampground@dccnet.com,
                    www.baysidecampground.com
Location: 21 Km (13 Miles) W of Langdale Ferry
                    Landing

GPS Location: 49.44056 N, 123.70833 W, 100 Ft

38 Sites – This is a commercial campground with many long-term rigs but also with sites for travelers. It is located right along the highway in the small town of Wilson Creek, there is a small commercial mall next door. The campground has small back-in sites but a few will take RVs to 35 feet. Amenities include a swimming pool. The campground is located 16 km (10 miles) north of Gibsons and 5 km (3 miles) south of Sechelt, 2.9 km (1.8 miles) north of the Robert's Creek Provincial Park.

☐ **PORPOISE BAY PROVINCIAL PARK** *(Open All Year)*
Reservations: www.discovercamping.ca, (800) 689-9025
Information: (604) 885-3714, www.bcparks.ca,
                 www.sunshinecoastparks.com
Location: 31 Km (19 Miles) NW of Langdale Ferry Landing

GPS Location: 49.50667 N, 123.74806 W, Near Sea Level

94 Sites – This large provincial park campground is located east of Sechelt away from the main highway. It sits on Sechelt Inlet and has a swimming beach. Some of the sites reach 50 feet. There is also a tent camping area suitable for about 10 tents. This campground has flush toilets and hot showers for no charge. Campfires at individual campsites are not allowed although there are several community fire pits that can be used in the evening. The campground gate is open from April 15 to October 15, services are provided, and there is a fee. Off season the family campground gate is closed but you can camp for free at the group site with no services. To reach the campground drive north on Wharf Road in central Sechelt. After just .5 km (.3 miles) turn right on Porpoise Bay Road, the campground is on the left in 3.4 km (2.1 miles).

● **BAYSIDE RV AND CAMPGROUND** *(Open All Year)*
Res and Info: (877) 885-7444, (604) 885-7444,
                    baysidecampground@telus.net,
                    www.baysidecampground.com/
Location: 29 Km (18 Miles) NW of Langdale
                    Ferry Landing

GPS Location: 49.49139 N, 123.74722 W, 200 Ft

46 Sites – This new campground is built to provide lots of separation between sites, they aren't squeezed into a small area like in most commercial campgrounds. Sites are back-ins and pull-thrus to 75 feet. Despite the name this is not a waterside campground, but it's still a nice place. To reach the campground drive north on Wharf Road in central Sechelt. After just .5 km (.3 miles) turn right on Porpoise Bay Road, the campground is on the right in 1.5 km (.9 miles).

SUNSHINE COAST (UPPER) – POWELL RIVER, LUND AND THE NORTH

Powell River (population 22,000) was a forestry-dependant town for years , the pulp mill there was once the world's largest. In fact it remains something of a forestry town since

BRITISH COLUMBIA

it is still home to a working paper mill, with much reduced operations, now owned by Cataylist Paper. Today tourism is also an important force. Powell River occupies an area offering a full range of outdoor attractions including fishing, kayaking, scuba diving, canoeing, hiking, and golf. The town has all the amenities including good shopping for supplies, restaurants and public transit.

Powell River is actually made up of four communities. The farthest south is Westview. This is the first you will see when you arrive from the south, it has the ferry terminal and most of the services. North a few miles but south of the very short river that Powell River is named after is the original town site. It is actually called Townsite and is the site of the pulp mill as well as many residences. To the east of Townsite is a suburb built around Cranberry Lake, and north of the mouth of the Powell River is Wildwood.

While you will probably spend most of your time in Westview, you will find a visit to **Townsite** interesting. It has actually been designated a Heritage Area by the Canadian government. From the Mill Viewpoint you can see the chain of 10 cargo ship hulks that make up the breakwater for the paper mill harbor.

There are a wide selection of hiking trails available in the Powell River area. Probably the easiest and most accessible is a short trail north from Willingdon Beach Park along the bed of an old beachfront railroad. You'll find signs identifying different trees and also vintage logging equipment on display from the nearby museum. Another interesting trail is the wheelchair accessible trail circling nearby Inland Lake. For a more challenging

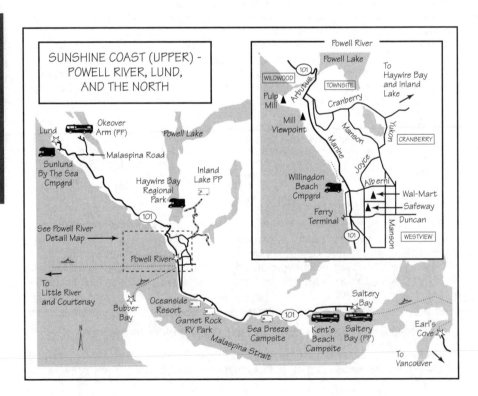

BRITISH COLUMBIA

trail consider the 165-kilometer (102-mile) Sunshine Coast trail from Sarah Point in the north to Saltery Bay.

You should drive the final 30 kilometers (19 miles) along Highway 101 to Lund. This is the northern end of Highway 101 which is said to stretch all the way south to Chile. **Lund** is a jumping-off point for boating the waters to the north. The historic Lund Hotel makes a good place to catch a meal and there's a friendly little RV park in town too.

Sunshine Coast (Upper) Campgrounds

☐ **SALTERY BAY PROVINCIAL PARK** *(Open All Year)*
   Reservations: www.discovercamping.ca, (800) 689-9025
   Information: (604) 885-3714
   Location: 1.1 Km (.7 Mile) N of Saltery Bay Ferry Landing

   GPS Location: 49.78250 N, 124.19278 W, Near Sea Level

42 Sites – This provincial park has two sections. From the south you'll first reach the campground, then there is a day-use area with a boat ramp a mile or so north of the campground. The campground is well known for its rocky little cove which is a popular scuba destination with an underwater statue. It's also a fun place to swim off the rocks and tiny beach. Camping sites are all back-ins, some as long as 65 feet. Tenters pitch on the parking pads. The campground has services and a fee from May 13 to September 15, off season it is open with no services and there is no fee. The campground is located less than a mile north of the Saltery Bay ferry dock, 26 km (16 miles) south of Powell River.

● **KENT'S BEACH CAMPSITE** *(Open All Year)*
   Res and Info: (604) 487-9386, kentsbeach@telus.net,
                    www.kentsbeach.com
   Location: 3 Km (2 Miles) N of Saltery Bay Ferry
                    Landing

   GPS Location: 49.78250 N, 124.21556 W, Near Sea Level

30 Sites – This commercial campground has a sea-side location with some sites right on the beach. Others are in an open area back from the water and even more up the hill on gravel in a clearing. Big rigs will have no problems using the upper camping area, the lower areas are also accessible to big rigs with careful driving. The campground is located 3.1 km (1.9 miles) north of the ferry landing, 24 km (15 miles) south of Powell River.

○ **WILLINGDON BEACH CAMPSITE** *(Open All Year)*
   Res and Info: (604) 485-2242,
                    reservations@willingdonbeach.ca,
                    www.willingdonbeach.ca
   Location: Powell River

   GPS Location:49.84750 N, 125.53056 W, Near Sea Level

76 Sites – This is the most popular campground in the area for travelers. It's located on the beach just north of the ferry terminal. You can walk to some of the Powell River shops and restaurants from here. Sites are fairly small and driveways narrow, most sites are suitable for RVs to about 30 feet although there are a few for RVs to 45 feet. For tent campers there are many grassy sites with picnic tables and fire pits as well as a covered area with a fireplace. There is a free dump station just south of the park in the parking area of Willingdon Beach Park. You'll find the park in Powell River along the waterfront north of the ferry docks at the north end of Willingdon Beach Park.

BRITISH COLUMBIA

WATERFRONT CAMPING AT THE WILLINGDON BEACH CAMPSITE

○ **HAYWIRE BAY REGIONAL PARK** *(Open All Year)*
Information: (604) 483-3231, (604) 483-1097
Location: 6 Km (4 Miles) NE of Powell River

GPS Location: 49.90556 N, 124.51722 W, 300 Ft

41 Sites – This regional campground is located northeast of Powell River on the east shore of Powell Lake. Due to the narrow gravel access roads and small sites it is suitable for RVs to about 30 feet. The route to the campground is signed from Powell River. From the intersection of Alberni Street and Joyce in Powell River head north on Joyce. In .1.5 km (.9 miles) at the T turn left on Manson Avenue and you'll soon enter the Cranberry Lake area. In 2.3 km (1.4 miles) at another T turn right onto Cranberry. In 1.6 km (1 mile) the road to the campground goes left. You'll reach a Y at .6 km (.4 miles), go left. The road now turns to gravel and in another 5.2 km (3.2 miles) the entrance to the campground is on the left.

● **SUNLUND BY THE SEA CAMPGROUND**
  (Open May 1 to Sept 30)
  Res and Info: (604) 483-9220, info@sunlund.ca, www.sunlund.ca
  Location: Lund

  GPS Location: 49.97889 N, 124.76194 W, Near Sea Level

33 Sites – Lund is a very small town clustered around a rocky cove. This great little campground is located within 100 yards of the bay but not within sight of it, there's a short trail to reach the boardwalk. As a jump-off point for boaters headed north into Desolation Sound the town is a virtual parking lot, not great for RVs. Fortunately this

campground allows access to the village without having to deal with that. The campground has full-hookup back-in sites to 35 feet and access is no problem if you drive carefully. Longer rigs can be accommodated with prior notice. As you approach Lund the road to Okeover Bay Provincial Park will let you know you're getting close (it's about 2.4 km (1.5 miles) to the south), watch for the campground signs. They'll take you left onto Larson Rd., then almost immediately to the right and then to the right again and down into the campground.

☐ **OKEOVER ARM PROVINCIAL PARK**
   (Open May 15 to Sept 15 – Varies)
   Location: 6 Km (4 Miles) E of Lund

GPS Location: 49.99194 N, 124.71528 W, Near Sea Level

18 Sites – This is a small provincial park located on Okeover Arm to the east of Lund. It's a popular put-in spot for kayakers. The campground is small but some sites reach 50 feet although access is difficult for large rigs. There are four tents sites with pitching pads near the entrance. The campground was in poor condition last time we visited. Malaspina Road leaves the highway about 2.4 km (1.5 miles) south of Lund. This paved road will take you directly to the park, a distance of 3.7 km (2.3 miles).

TERRACE

Terrace (population 19,000) is the largest city between Prince George and Prince Rupert. It's 580 km (360 miles) west of Prince George and 145 km (90 miles) east of Prince

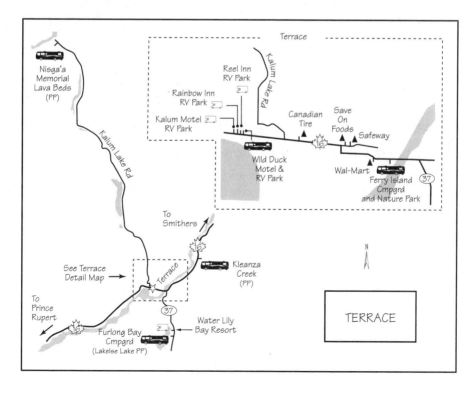

Rupert. The city offers a variety of services including repair facilities, supermarkets, restaurants, and campgrounds.

Probably the most interesting visitor attraction in this area is Canada's most recent lava flow. This is located in **Nisga'a Memorial Lava Bed Provincial Park** about 100 km (60 miles) north of Terrace. The flow dates from about two centuries ago. A paved road leads up to the park and there is a provincial park campground in the park, we describe it below.

We've listed a number of campgrounds for the Terrace area including commercial, city, and provincial park sites.

Terrace Campgrounds

☐ **KLEANZA CREEK PROVINCIAL PARK** *(Open May 10 to Sept 15 – Varies)*
Information: (250) 638-8490, nwescapesbc@telus.net
Location: 16 Km (10 Mile) NE of Terrace

GPS Location: 54.60139 N, 128.40222 W, 300 Ft

32 Sites – This is a smaller provincial park campground that sits next to Kleanza Creek in a historic mining area. It's a pretty site with evergreens and a creek which some sites overlook. Sites are very long and angled, they stretch to 60 feet. Water is from a hand pump. The circle at the end of the access road could be tough for very large coaches, disconnecting the tow car might be necessary. The campground is located off a short access road some 16 km (10 miles) northeast of Terrace.

☐ **FURLONG BAY CAMPGROUND**
    (Open May 13 to Sept 15 – Varies)
    Reservations: www.discovercamping.ca, (800) 689-9025
    Information: (250) 638-8490, nwescapesbc@telus.net
    Location: 19 Km (12 Miles) S of Terrace

GPS Location: 54.37861 N, 128.52528 W, 200 Ft

156 Sites – South of Terrace on Lakelse Lake is Lakelse Lake Provincial Park and its Furlong Bay Campground. The sites here are very long back-ins, some to 60 feet. Unfortunately, they are at right angles to the access road and have narrow entrances so it can take some work to get a big rig into them. This provincial park has flush toilets, showers, and a sani-station. There's also a swimming beach and boat launch. From Terrace head south on Hwy 37, it's 19 km (12 miles) to the campground entrance.

○ **FERRY ISLAND CAMPGROUND AND NATURE PARK**
    (Open March 15 to Sept 30 – Varies)
    Res and Info: (250) 635-3530, (250) 615-9657,
                ferryislandterrace@gmail.com
                www.terrace.ca/residents/leisure_services/ferry_
                island_campground1
    Location: Terrace

GPS Location: 54.51083 N, 128.57139 W, 200 Ft

103 Sites – Ferry Island is Terrace's municipal campground. It's located on an island in the Skeena River in a grove of cottonwoods. Many of the trees have faces carved in the bark. Sites are back-ins and pull-thrus to about 55 feet, most have electricity, picnic tables, and fire pits. Restrooms have flush toilets and showers. In Terrace you'll find the access road off Hwy 16 at the Skeena River crossing. There are actually two bridges and the access road is between them.

● **Wild Duck Motel and RV Park** *(Open All Year)*
    Res and Info: (866) 638-1511, (250) 638-1511,
                wildduck@telus.net,
                www.wildduckmotel-rv.com
    Location: Terrace

    GPS Location: 54.51833 N, 128.64417 W, 200 Ft

24 Sites – This is one of a series of small RV parks along the highway in this area. The Wild Duck has one very long pull-thru but most sites are back-ins to about 45 feet. Most sites are full hookups but a couple have no sewer. Restrooms with showers are provided. These parks are right on Hwy 16 at the west end of Terrace, about 3.1 km (1.9 mile) west of where Hwy 16 make two 90-degree turns to cross the railroad tracks.

☐ **Nisga'a Memorial Lava Beds Provincial Park**
    (Open May 9 to Sept 30 – Varies)
    Information: (250) 638-8490
    Location: 92 Km (57 Miles) N of Terrace

    GPS Location: 55.19500 N, 129.11361 W, 200 Ft

16 Sites – This provincial park campground is in an isolated situation near the lava beds. It's a nicely treed area and sites are back-ins to 65 feet off a paved loop road. Nearby is a small First Nation-run visitor center offering information about the area and also tours. From Terrace drive north on BC-113 (Kalum Lake Road) for 92 km (57 Miles) to the campground.

Thompson and Fraser River Canyons

On a map the Thompson and Fraser River Valleys appear to be the best route for a railroad or road from the coast at Vancouver to the interior of British Columbia. In fact, the rivers probably are the best route, but they certainly didn't prove to be easy routes. A trip through the canyons is interesting because it allows you to see the difficulties faced over the years by the people who needed to pass this way: first the Indians, then the fur traders, then the gold seekers, then the railroads, and finally the Trans-Canada Highway.

Leaving Cache Creek and heading south the highway crosses some high dry country and then descends to the level of the Thompson River. In many sections the road is built upon fill right in the river channel. At **Spences Bridge** the highway crosses over the river to the south shore.

The Thompson and the Fraser come together at **Lytton** (population 400), you might want to drive through town to the mouth of the Thompson to see the muddy Fraser and the much clearer Thompson come together. A bridge crosses the Thompson here and you may be tempted to follow the small paved road 69 km (43 miles) north along the east shore of the Fraser River to Lillooet which is located in the *Whistler and the Sea to Sky Highway* section of this chapter.

From Lytton south the highway is in the Fraser River Canyon. Notice that there are two sets of railroad tracks in much of the canyon. Eight kilometers (5 miles) south of Lytton there are two railroad bridges where both sets of tracks cross to opposite sides. This seemingly useless exercise was necessary since the first set of tracks had been built along the easiest route by the Canadian Pacific Railroad. When the Canadian Northern built their set of tracks later there was only room on the other side of the river.

BRITISH COLUMBIA

Fifty-four kilometers (33 miles) south of Lytton you will see the upper station of an aerial tram on the right side of the highway. You should at least stop and take a look. It is possible to walk down to the river here but the tram is much easier, it runs from April 1 to October 30. Below is **Hell's Gate**, a spot where the river flows so fast that the salmon have to use fishways to get through. Actually, before 1913 the fish could make it on their own, then railroad construction caused a slide that blocked the river to the fish much of the time. The fishways were constructed several years later to restore the run of salmon up the Fraser. The water level of the Fraser through here varies as much as 30 meters (100 feet) so at higher water levels you can't even see the top of the fishways. You may find it hard to believe but during the construction of the railroad a sternwheeler actually made it up the river through Hell's Gate.

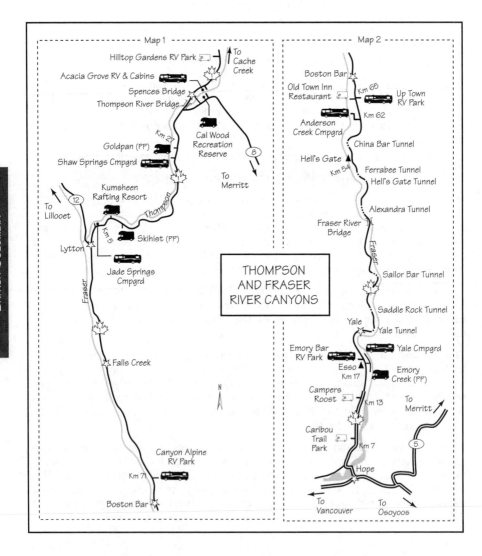

BRITISH COLUMBIA

Near Hell's Gate you will pass through 7 tunnels and cross a modern bridge across the river. This modern bridge replaced a much smaller suspension bridge, and that bridge remains, although it is only used by pedestrians. The walk from the highway down to the **Alexandra Bridge** is a nice short hike, the trail starts at Alexandra Bridge Provincial Park which is 10.3 kilometers (6.4 miles) south of the Hell's Gate tram station.

Thompson and Fraser River Canyons Campgrounds

● ACACIA GROVE RV AND CABINS *(Open All Year)*
Res and Info: (800) 833-7508, (250) 458-2227
www.acacia-rvpark-cabins.com
Location: Spences Bridge

GPS Location: 50.42497 N, 121.33441 W, 700 Ft

34 Sites – This is a nice motel and RV park next to the Thompson River in the small town of Spences Bridge. Sites are back-ins and pull-thrus to about 50 feet, some overlooking the river. The campground is just off the highway at the eastern edge of Spences Bridge. This is about 37 km (23 miles) east of Lytton.

○ CAL WOOD RECREATION RESERVE *(Open All Year)*
Location: Spences Bridge

FREE ⛺ 🔥

GPS Location: 50.42111 N, 121.33472 W, 700 Ft

20 Sites – This camping area is located on the south side of the Thompson River, across from Spences Bridge. Sites are ill-defined, but there are about 20 of them. With careful maneuvering RVs of any size find parking here although it's best for RVs to about 30 feet. Amenities include a few picnic tables, some rock fire rings, a vault toilet, and easy access to the beach. There is no potable water but there is a box for donations. To reach the camping area follow Hwy 8 from an intersection just west of Spences's Bridge and south of the highway bridge over the Thompson River. Follow Hwy 8 east for 1.8 km (1.1 mile) to the camping area.

☐ GOLDPAN PROVINCIAL PARK *(Open May 1 to Sept 30 – Varies)*
Information: (250) 455-2708
Location: 29 Km (18 Miles) E of Lytton

$ $$$ ⛺ 🔥

GPS Location: 50.34944 N, 121.38944 W, 700 Ft

14 Sites – This is a very popular little campground, probably because it is right on the river below the highway where everyone driving by sees it. The campground also attracts fishermen and river rafters. Once you get used to the commotion it's fun to watch the trains go by. Maneuvering room is tight for big RVs, the campground is suitable for RVs to about 30 feet. Sites are back-ins and water is from a hand pump. There's a place to park temporarily next to the entrance road, take a look at the sites that are available before you commit yourself. The campground is right off the highway 8 km (5 miles) west of the bridge at Spences Bridge on Highway 1 and 29 km (18 miles) east of Lytton.

● SHAW SPRINGS CAMPGROUND
     (Open April to Oct – Varies)
Information: (250) 458-2324
Location: 26 Km (16 Miles) E of Lytton

GPS Location: 50.33917 N, 121.39667 W, 700 Ft

30 Sites – This is an old restaurant with a neglected campground and a few motel rooms.

The sites here include pull-thrus that will take RVs to 40 feet. It's located 11 km (7 miles) west of the bridge at Spences Bridge and 26 km (16 miles) east of Lytton.

☐ **Skihist Provincial Park** *(Open April 30 to Sept 30 – Varies)*
Information: (250) 455-2708
Location: 8 Km (5 Miles) E of Lytton

GPS Location: 50.25333 N, 121.50917 W, 900 Ft

58 Sites – A nice provincial park campground set in pines above the highway in a spectacular section of the Thompson River Canyon. Some sites are suitable for RVs to 35 feet. This can be a very warm campground in the middle of the summer, this is a hot and arid region. There's an 8 km trail from the campground that offers great views of the canyon. The old Cariboo Wagon Road ran through this park and there are sometimes elk around. The access road up to the campground is 27 km (17 miles) from the bridge at Spences Bridge on Highway 1 and 8 km (5 miles) east of Lytton.

● **Kumsheen Rafting Resort** *(Open May 1 to Sept 6 – Varies)*
Res and Info: (800) 663-6667, www.kumsheen.com
Location: 5 Km (3 Miles) E of Lytton

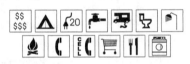

GPS Location: 50.25972 N, 121.53528 W, 700 Ft

50 Sites – This place is primarily a river rafting resort. It offers many different rafting tours as well as rock climbing. Facilities include a good restaurant, swimming pool, and hot tub. Most sites are for tents. RV sites are back-ins with a few suitable for RVs to 35 feet. A few low-amp electric hookups are available but most RV sites are without utilities. Call ahead to discuss options and make reservations. It's located 31 km (19.5 miles) west of the bridge at Spences Bridge and 5.6 km (3.5 miles) east of Lytton.

● **Jade Springs Campground**
　　(Open March 15 to Nov 15 – Varies)
Information: (250) 455-6662
Location: 3 Km (2 Miles) E of Lytton

GPS Location: 50.24944 N, 121.56278 W, 800 Ft

50 Sites – This treed site slopes from the highway down toward the Thompson River in the canyon below. There's a grocery store and café on the road above. Sites here are in evergreens off narrow gravel access roads, limited maneuvering room means the campground is best for tents and RVs to about 30 feet. Some sites have full hookups, there are also no-hookup sites. The campground is located about 3 km (2 miles) east of Lytton in the Thompson River Canyon, that's 111 km (68 miles) north of Hope.

● **Canyon Alpine RV Park**
　　(Open April 15 to Oct 15)
Res and Info: (604) 867-9734, (800) 644-PARK,
　　　　www.canyonalpinervpark.com
Location: 5 Km (3 Miles) N of Boston Bar

GPS Location: 49.91333 N, 121.44556 W, 600 Ft

31 Sites –This nice campground is set under big trees behind a motel. There are back-ins and pull-thrus to 60 feet. There's also a restaurant nearby. The campground is located about 5 km (3 miles) north of Boston Bar, that's 69 km (43 miles) north of Hope.

● **UP TOWN RV PARK** *(Open All Year)*
   Location: Boston Bar

   GPS Location: 49.86457 N, 121.44154 W, 500 Ft

7 Sites – This is a tiny campground right next to the high-
way and just south of Boston Bar. It has five 40-foot back in sites with full hook-ups and
a grassy area large enough for a couple of tents. Next door is a building with restrooms
and a laundry. Watch for it on the east side of the highway. It's so small you might miss it.

● **ANDERSON CREEK CAMPGROUND**
   (Open April 1 to Oct 31)
   Res and Info: (604) 867-9089
   Location: 61 Km (38 Miles) N of Hope

           GPS Location: 49.83972 N, 121.43250 W, 400 Ft

40 Sites – This campground has 15 RV sites and another 25 tent sites. Those for RVs are
off a gravel drive, parking is on grass. These are large back-in and pull-thru sites to 60
feet. The campground entrance is on the west side of the highway near a convenience
store, there's a good sign. A paved and then gravel road leads you under the railroad
tracks, a distance of .8 km (.5 mile) from the highway.

● **EMORY BAR RV PARK**
   (Hope River RV Park) (April 1 to Oct 31)
   Res and Info: (604) 863-0033, info@emorybarrvpark.com,
              www.emorybarrvpark.com
   Location: 16 Km (10 Miles) N of Hope

   GPS Location: 49.51960 N, 121.42101 W, 200 Ft

50 Sites – This newer big-rig RV park is set in open trees behind a gas station, store,
and restaurant. The operation is across the highway from the Yale Campground and the
Emory Creek Provincial Campground which are described below. Sites are back-ins and
pull-thrus to 60 feet off good gravel roads. The campground is located on the west side of
Hwy 1 in Yale, about 17 km (105 miles) north of Hope.

● **YALE CAMPGROUND** *(Open May 15 to Oct 15)*
   Information: (604) 863-2407, (604) 869-1133
   Location: 17 Km (10.5 Miles) N of Hope

   GPS Location: 49.52194 N, 121.41972 W, 300 Ft

50 Sites – This is an older park located on the east side of Hwy 1 across from a gas station and small store. The campground is managed from the store. The large sites in the
campground are pull-thrus to about 60 feet with parking on grass in a central cleared
area. Many other small sites without hookups are located off nearby loop roads. The
campground is located on the east side of Hwy 1 in Yale, about 17 km (10.5 miles) north
of Hope. It shares an entrance road with the Emory Creek Provincial Campground, described below.

☐ **EMORY CREEK PROVINCIAL CAMPGROUND** *(Open May 15 to Oct 15 – Varies)*
   Information: (604) 863-2443
   Location: 16 Km (10 Miles) N of Hope

   GPS Location: 49.51472 N, 121.41694 W, 200 Ft

34 Sites – Emory Creek Provincial Park is situated on a heavily treed shelf between the

BRITISH COLUMBIA

highway and the Fraser River. The trees serve to make the campground seem somewhat quiet and isolated even though it is near both railroads and the highway. The sites in this small campground are back-ins to 60 feet but limited maneuvering room limits the practical rig size here to about 35 feet. The campground entrance is on the east side of Hwy 1 about 16 km (10 miles) north of Hope.

TOFINO, UCLUELET, AND THE PACIFIC RIM NATIONAL PARK

As you drive east from Port Alberni toward the west coast of Vancouver Island you'll cross 250 meter (820 ft) Sutton Pass and then the road descends steeply and in another 10 kilometers (6 miles) you will reach a T intersection. Ucluelet is to the left (6 kilometers, 4 miles) and Tofino to the right (33 kilometers, 20 miles). Most of the Long Beach section of Pacific Rim National Park is also to the right. At this intersection there's a handy information centre. In the campground write-ups below this is called the Tofino-Ucluelet Junction.

If you turn north you will almost immediately enter **Pacific Rim National Park Reserve**. There are actually three scattered sections to this park: Long Beach, the West Coast Trail, and the Broken Islands Group. This section, Long Beach, stretches along the coast almost as far as Tofino. Several short roads lead to beach parking lots, overlooks, and trails. There is a daily use fee for using this park, the parking lots have self-service machines allowing you to buy a ticket allowing you to purchase a day pass. The machines accept coins, currency, and credit cards. Note that you do not have to pay a fee to drive through

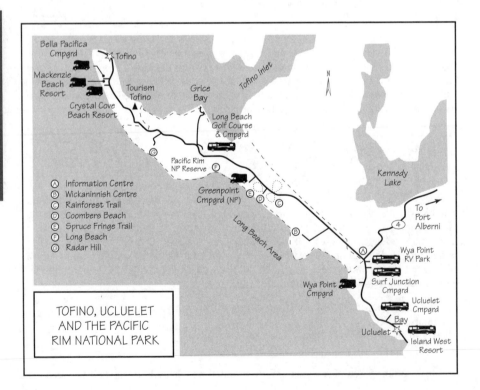

the park, just to park in it. If it is late you may want to drive on to Tofino and then return to explore the following day.

Almost immediately after entering the park you'll see the turn for **Wickaninnish Centre** which offers museum-type displays and a restaurant as well as wheelchair-accessible views and trails. The center overlooks **Wickaninnish Beach**. As you continue to drive north toward Tofino you'll pass turn-offs for the **Rainforest Trail, Coombers Beach** and **Spruce Fringe Trail, Green Point Campground, Long Beach**, and **Radar Hill**.

The section of road through the park is 23 kilometers (14 miles) long. When you leave the park you'll start seeing the outskirts of Tofino. The road passes turnoffs to several resorts, restaurants, and campgrounds and then arrives in little Tofino, the end of the road.

The town of **Tofino** (population 1,100) is quite small and very tourist oriented. You'll find studios, stores, and restaurants in a compact area. Down the hill are three docks: the crab dock, Fisherman's Wharf, and the government wharf. Much of the activity of the town is oriented around **Clayoquot Sound**. There are popular charter trips for fishing, whale watching and sightseeing. One popular destination is **Hot Springs Cove** which offers the only hot springs on Vancouver Island. A much shorter hop is to **Meares Island** where you can follow hiking trails through the rain forest. These are also excellent kayaking waters.

The big event of the year in Tofino is the **Pacific Rim Whale Festival** held during the last half of March and first weekend of April. It celebrates the spring gray whale migration.

Ucluelet (population 1,500) is to the south. It's much like Tofino but less expensive and more focused on fishing. Natural destinations in the area include the 8.5 kilometer **Wild Pacific Trail** and **Big Beach**. The **Ucluelet Aquarium** is great for both kids and adults.

Tofino, Ucluelet, and the Pacific Rim National Park Campgrounds

● **WYA POINT RV PARK** *(Open April 1 to Sept 30)*
   Res and Info: (250) 726-3401, www.wyapoint.com
   Location: Just S of the Port Alberni Road Junction

   GPS Location: 48.99142 N, 125.58746 W, 100 Ft

16 Sites – This campground is at a First Nation information center located just south of the Tofino-Ucluelet Junction. There is an affiliated campground for tents and very small rigs with a similar name described below. The RV sites here are back-ins to 45 feet with power and water hookups. Only self-contained rigs are accommodated since restrooms are only open during the operating hours of the visitor center.

● **SURF JUNCTION CAMPGROUND** *(Open April 1 to Oct 31)*
   Res and Info: (250) 726-7214, (877) 922-6722,
      www.surfjunction.com
   Location: .5 Km (.3 Miles) S of the Port Alberni Road Junction

   GPS Location: 48.98750 N, 125.58667 W, 200 Ft

49 Sites – This is one of the few campgrounds listed in this section that is not located next to the water. The campground caters to the surfing crowd, they drive to whichever beach has the best surf on any particular day. Surprisingly, it's also a good place to stay for other tenters and RVers because it has large well-separated back-in RV sites to 45 feet and a central location. There's also a great hot tub, surfing lessons, and surf equipment rentals. At the Tofino-Ucluelet Junction where the road from Port Alberni meets the coastal road turn left toward Ucluelet. The campground entrance is on the left in .6 km (.4 mile).

● **WYA POINT CAMPGROUND** *(Open April 1 to Sept 30)*
  Res and Info: (250) 726-3401, www.wyapoint.com
  Location: 2.4 Km (1.8 Mile) S of the Port Alberni Road Junction

  GPS Location: 48.97043 N, 125.60503 W, Near Sea Level

32 Sites – This First Nation campground is associated with the RV campground at the
visitor center described above. The sites here are small back-in vehicle accessible campsites to about 25 feet and walk-in campsites on the beach and in the forest above. Sites
have picnic tables and fire pits. The beach is a beautiful small one with access only from
the campground. From the Tofino-Ucluelet Junction drive south toward Ucluelet for 2.4
km (1.5 mile). Turn toward the ocean on the Willowbrea Road which is dirt and gravel
and fairly rough, only smaller vehicles with decent clearance should attempt it. It's 1.3
km (.8 mile) from the highway in to the campground.

● **UCLUELET CAMPGROUND** *(Open April 1 to Sept 30)*
  Res and Info: (250) 726-4355,
                    camp@uclueletcampground.com,
                    www.uclueletcampground.com
  Location: Ucluelet

  GPS Location: 48.94556 N, 125.55806 W, Near Sea Level

106 Sites – Located on the north shore of the inner boat harbor in Ucluelet, some sites
here have great views. The campground also has what may be the most scenically located
dump site in B.C. Some sites, particularly back away from the water, are suitable for RVs
to 45 feet. At the Tofino-Ucluelet Junction turn left toward Ucluelet. The campground
entrance is on the left in 6 km (3.7 miles).

● **ISLAND WEST RESORT** *(Open All Year)*
  Res and Info: (250) 726-7515, fish@islandwest.com,
                    www.islandwestresort.com
  Location: Ucluelet

  GPS Location: 48.94569 N, 125.54931 W, Near Sea Level

37 Sites – Like the Ucluelet Campground this campground is located next to the inner boat harbor in Uclue-
let. Campsites are scattered around the grounds of this marina and restaurant, the main
camping area is on a bluff above the marina. Some sites will take RVs to 45 feet. There is
a boat ramp, the marina, and a restaurant and pub on site. At the Tofino-Ucluelet Junction
turn left toward Ucluelet. In 6.5 km (4.0 miles) turn left on Bay Street and follow it down
the hill to the resort entrance.

■ **GREENPOINT CAMPGROUND – PACIFIC RIM**
  NATIONAL PARK *(Open April 2 to Oct 10 – Varies)*
  Reservations: www.pccamping.ca, (877) 737-3783,
  Information: (250) 726-3500
  Location: 11 Km (7 Miles) N of Port Alberni Road Junction

  GPS Location: 49.05468 N, 125.71923 W, Near Sea Level

112 Sites – The only national park campground in this park is usually booked solid, make
reservations if you want to stay here. The campground is located within easy strolling
distance of the beach. Most sites are vehicle sites as long as 70 feet but maneuvering
room is tight with narrow access roads and 90 degree turns into the sites. There are also
a few walk-in tent sites. Note that you do not need to pay the daily park fee to stay at

this campground or visit the beach below it, but you do need to pay the fee to visit other areas of the park. At the Tofino-Uclulet Junction turn right toward Tofino. In 10.6 km (6.6 miles) you'll see the campground entrance on the left.

● **LONG BEACH GOLF COURSE AND CAMPGROUND**
   (Open May 1 to Sept 30)
   Res and Info: (250) 725-3332, golf@island.net,
                     www.longbeachgolfcourse.com
   Location: 18.5 Km (11.5 Miles) N of the Port Alberni Road
                    Junction

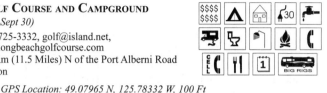

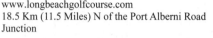
GPS Location: 49.07965 N, 125.78332 W, 100 Ft

83 Sites – This 18-hole golf course has an RV campground as well as a no-hookup wilderness type campground adjacent to the Tofino airport, inland from the national park. The RV sites are full-hookup back-ins site to 45 feet. There are 7 sites. The wilderness camping area is set in a heavy evergreen forest and has 76 campsites with back-ins to 35 feet. These sites have picnic tables and fire pits. From the Tofino-Ucluelet Junction drive north for 18.5 km (11.5 miles) to the access road to the golf course, it's on the right.

● **CRYSTAL COVE BEACH RESORT** *(Open All Year)*
   Res and Info: (877) 725-4213, (250) 725-4213,
                     info@crystalcove.ca,
                     www.crystalcovebeachresort.com
   Location: 29.1 Km (18.1 Miles) N of the Port
                    Alberni Road Junction

GPS Location: 49.12722 N, 125.90139 W, Near Sea Level

93 Sites – This resort is located about 2.4 km (1.5 miles) from Tofino next to MacKenzie Beach which is popular for sunning and even swimming. There are upscale rental cabins as well as the RV sites. The place is nicely landscaped. RV sites are back-ins to 35 feet. All sites have full hookups. At the Tofino-Ucluelet Junction turn right toward Tofino. In 29.1 km (18.1 miles) watch for the campground sign pointing west. This is about 3 km (2 miles) before you reach Tofino.

● **BELLA PACIFICA RESORT**
   (Open Feb 15 to Nov 1 – Varies)
   Res and Info: (250) 725-3400,
                     campground@bellapacifica.com,
                     www.bellapacifica.com
   Location: 27 Km (17 Miles) N of the Port Alberni Road
                    Junction

GPS Location: 49.13306 N, 125.90194 W, Near Sea Level

180 Sites – This resort, like the Crystal Cove Beach Resort described above, is on Mackenzie Beach. It's a good beach for lying in the sun. Ocean swimming is possible if you're tough or use a wet suit. There are well-spaced sites with no hookups as well as more crowded sites with hookups overlooking the beach. A few of these reach 35 feet but most sites are much smaller. This campground charges a $10 reservation fee in addition to the nightly fee shown above. At the Tofino-Ucluelet Junction turn right toward Tofino. In 29.5 km (18.3 miles) watch for the campground sign pointing west down Mackenzie Beach Road. This is about 3 km (2 miles) before you reach Tofino. Follow the road a short distance to the campground, it's on the right.

● **MACKENZIE BEACH RESORT** *(Open All Year)*
  Res and Info: (250) 725-3439, www.mackenziebeach.com
  Location: 29.5 Km (18.3 Miles) N of the Port Alberni Road
                  Junction

  GPS Location: 49.13216 N, 125.90212 W, Near Sea Level

61 Sites – This beach resort, in the same area as the two described
above, has RV sites behind the resort and tent sites along the beach in front. The RV
sites are back-ins to 30 feet with water and electric hookups. Amenities include a pool
and hot tub. At the Tofino-Ucluelet Junction turn right toward Tofino. In 29.5 km (18.3
miles) watch for the campground sign pointing west down Mackenzie Beach Road. This
is about 3 km (2 miles) before you reach Tofino. Follow the road a short distance to the
campground, it's on the left.

VALLEY OF A THOUSAND PEAKS (CRANBROOK, KIMBERLEY, FORT STEELE TRIANGLE)

The Kootenay Rockies cover the entire southeast corner of British Columbia. The region
runs east from the Okanagan Valley all the way to the true Rockies that form the border
between British Columbia and Alberta. Just west of the high Rockies is a wide valley,
sometimes called the Rocky Mountain Trench. It is said to run, in one form or another,
all the way from Mexico. Within this trench, near the Canadian border with the U.S., is a
region the publicists call the Valley of a Thousand Peaks. It's more commonly known as
the Cranbrook, Kimberley, Fort Steele Triangle.

Cranbrook (population 19,000) is the largest town in this part of British Columbia and
serves as the supply center for the region. Historically it's a railroad town, and the main
reason to visit is to see the **Canadian Museum of Rail Travel** . This museum has a large
collection of restored passenger rail cars and features seven from the famous Trans-Canada Limited dating from 1929. Cranbrook's summer festival is **Sam Steele Days** which
is held the third weekend in June.

Fort Steele, of course, is named for the same Sam Steele. The fort is a restoration of early
Fort Steele, which was a boom town during the East Kootenay gold rushes during the
1800s. The fort has over 60 restored buildings and townspeople dressed in costumes, a
living museum. The fort is generally considered a top visitor attraction and a visit takes
the better part of a day.

The final corner of the triangle is occupied by **Kimberley** (population 7,000). It's at
1,100 meters (3,600 feet) which makes it the highest town in British Columbia and second only to Banff in Canada. This is a former mining town, a company town for the
Sullivan Mine which operated for 92 years and produced lead, zinc, and silver. Today
the town has recreated itself with a Bavarian theme. The Bavarian center of the town is
the **Platzl**, a central square with the largest cuckoo clock in Canada. Bavarian restaurants
and shops complete the picture. The other big attraction in town is the old **Sullivan Mine**
with an information center, the Bavarian City Mining Railway, the mine portal and a
restored miners house. Kimberley is also a ski town with the **Kimberley Alpine Resort**
just outside town. Kimberley hosts its share of events including the **Kimberley Old Time
Accordion Championships** and **Julyfest** in July. Of course there's also an **Octoberfest**
in September.

The campgrounds in this section are arranged as if you were driving the Cranbrook, Kimberley, Fort Steele Triangle from the north in a counterclockwise direction. Wasa Lake

THE CUCKOO CLOCK IN THE PLATZL IN KIMBERLEY IS THE LARGEST IN CANADA

Provincial Park is located near the junction of Hwy 95 and Hwy 95A about 37 km (23 miles) north of Cranbrook. From there you can drive 29 km (18 miles) southwest on 95A to Kimberley where the Kimberley Riverside Campground is located. From Kimberley it's another 37 km (18 miles) down to Cranbrook. The next four campgrounds listed give you a good choice for a stay although Moyie Lake Provincial Park is some distance to the south. Finally, it's 13 km (8 miles) north to Fort Steele where two campgrounds provide a place to spend the night.

Cranbrook, Kimberley, Fort Steele Triangle Campgrounds

☐ **WASA LAKE PROVINCIAL PARK** *(Open May 1 to Sept 30)*
Reservations: www.discovercamping.ca, (800) 689-9025
Information: (250) 422-3003
Location: 35 Km (22 Miles) N of Cranbrook

GPS Location: 49.78111 N, 115.72833 W, 2,600 Ft

104 Sites – The campsites at Wasa Lake Provincial Park are near but not next to the lake. Virtually all sites here are back-ins (three are pull-thrus) to 50 feet. A highlight here is the paved walking or biking trail that runs all the way around the lake, a distance of 5 miles. There is also a swimming beach in the park on the lake. Wasa Lake is known as the warmest swimming lake in the Kootenays. One hundred km

(62 miles) south of Radium Hot Springs and 37 km (23 miles) north of Cranbrook Hwy 95 splits. Hwy 95A climbs to Kimberley in the west and Hwy 95 continues south to Fort Steele and Cranbrook. One and one-half miles south of this junction off Hwy 95 the road to Wasa Lake Provincial Park goes east to the campground. There is also access from another junction a short distance to the south.

○ **KIMBERLEY RIVERSIDE CAMPGROUND**
(Open April 15 to Oct 15)
Res and Info: (877) 999-2929, (250) 427-2929,
info@kimberleycampground.com,
www.kimberleycampground.com
Location: 6 Km (4 Miles) S of Kimberley

GPS Location: 49.63472 N, 115.99722 W, 3,200 Ft

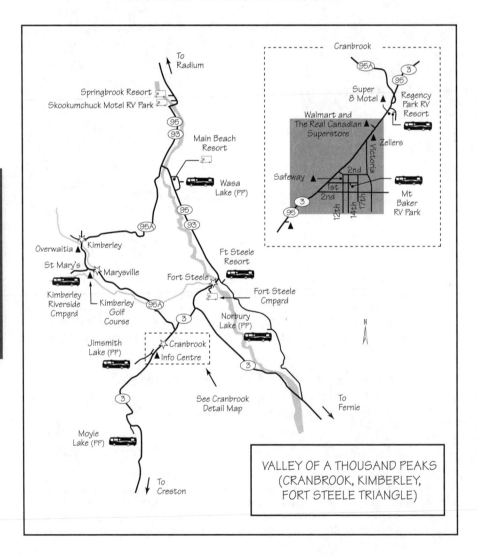

VALLEY OF A THOUSAND PEAKS
(CRANBROOK, KIMBERLEY,
FORT STEELE TRIANGLE)

145 Sites – You'll be amazed by this unusual municipal campground. It's new, a huge place with nice big sites. It's laid out more like an upscale housing development than a campground. The wide campground road leads past the office down to sites in three different areas. Sites are back-ins and pull-thrus to 85 feet. There's also a tent area. The office houses a store and also has a large "resort" (shallow) swimming pool out back. Wi-Fi is available in one location in the camping area. It's free but not available at all sites. Unfortunately the campground is about 5.6 km (3.5 miles) from Kimberley and there is no bus service so a vehicle is essential. The road to the campground, St. Mary's Road, leaves Hwy 95A some 2.9 km (1.8 miles) south of Kimberley on the northern edge of the town of Marysville. It climbs west for 2.7 km (1.7 miles), the campground is on the left.

○ **MT BAKER RV PARK** *(Open All Year)*
    Reservations: (877) 501-2288
    Information: (250) 489-0056,
                parkhost@mountbakerrvpark.com,
                www.mountbakerrvpark.com
    Location: Cranbrook

GPS Location: 49.50944 N, 115.76056 W, 3,000 Ft

76 Sites – Mt Baker is Cranbrook's municipal campground. It's located just a few blocks east of the central area of town so it's extremely convenient for travelers. A Safeway is only two blocks away. An older campground, there are many smaller sites but there are also pull-thrus to 60 feet. The camping area is on a sloping hillside so leveling can be difficult in some sites. There are also two separate grassy tent areas to accommodate many tents. Campfires are in a community fire pit. Easiest access is by following Second Street east 11 blocks from Hwy 95 as it passes through central Cranbrook. The park entrance is off First Street just east of 14th Ave.

● **REGENCY PARK RV RESORT**
    (Open All Year)
    Information: (250) 417-1119, regencyrvpark@shaw.ca
    Location: Cranbrook

    GPS Location: 49.53472 N, 115.73972 W, 3,000 Ft

48 Sites – This is a very simple big-rig campground. Sites are set in a large field with almost no trees. They're all long pull-thru and back-in sites to 80 feet or longer with full hookups. The campground sits right on the east side of Hwy 95 about 1 km (.6 mile) north of the Walmart at the north end of Cranbrook. Pull in to the campground entrance off 30th Ave.

□ **JIMSMITH LAKE PROVINCIAL PARK**
    (Open June 1 to Oct 11 – Varies)
    Information: (250) 422-3003
    Location: 3 Km (2 Miles) S of Cranbrook

    GPS Location: 49.48250 N, 115.84000 W, 3,600 Ft

34 Sites – This provincial park is located just outside Cranbrook to the south. It's a popular local swimming beach. There is also a boat ramp. The campground is behind the beach area on a hillside, sites are back-ins to 60 feet. At the southern edge of Cranbrook on Hwy 3/95 there is an info centre on the east side of the highway. Opposite it is the road to the campground. Follow signs for 4 km (2.5 miles) to the entrance gate.

☐ **MOYIE LAKE PROVINCIAL PARK**
(Open May 1 to Oct 30 – Varies)
Reservations: www.discovercamping.ca, (800) 689-9025
Information: (250) 422-3003
Location: 18 Km (11 Miles) S of Cranbrook

GPS Location: 49.37250 N, 115.84472 W, 3,000 Ft

111 Sites – This park is on the north shore of large Moyie Lake. There are swimming beaches and a boat launch at the park. Sites are back-ins to 60 feet. From October 1 to October 30 the campground gate is open, no services are provided, and there is no fee. The park is located 18 km (11 miles) south of Cranbrook on the west side of Hwy 3.

● **FORT STEELE RESORT** *(Open All Year)*
Res and Info: (250) 489-4268, resort@fortsteele.com,
www.fortsteele.com
Location: 15 Km (9 Miles) N of Cranbrook

GPS Location: 49.62139 N, 115.62444 W, 2,600 Ft

172 Sites – This is the closest campground to the Ft Steele park. It's a large campground sitting next to a gas station and store. Sites are back-ins and pull-thrus to 60 feet. Swimming is in a pool. The campground is located about a quarter-mile north of Fort Steel just off Hwy 95.

☐ **NORBURY LAKE PROVINCIAL PARK** *(Open All Year)*
Information: (250) 422-3003
Location: 29 Km (18 Miles) NE of Cranbrook

GPS Location: 49.53694 N, 115.48639 W, 2,700 Ft

46 Sites – Norbury Lake campground sits on the north shore of Norbury Lake. Peckham's Lake is nearby. A trail leads to that popular fishing lake. There are rainbows in Peckham's lake, power boats are prohibited on both lakes. The park is near Fort Steele and sites are back-ins to 60 feet, there's also good maneuvering room. This park has full services and a fee from May 15 to September 15. Off season there are no services and no fee but the campground gate is open. From the junction just north of Ft Steele follow signs 15.6 km (9.7 miles) southeast to the campground.

VANCOUVER

Vancouver is by far the largest population center for western Canada. With about 2.4 million people in the Greater Vancouver area it is about the same size as Portland or Seattle. The city is probably best known for its spectacular location. Mountains rise nearby both to the north and east. The ocean is not only to the west in the form of Howe Sound, but also, as Burrard Inlet and False Creek, to the north and south. To top it off there's the spectacular Lions Gate Suspension Bridge spanning the mouth of Burrard Inlet between Stanley Park and North Vancouver.

Highway access to Vancouver is decent but not great. Highway 1 from eastern Canada is a multi-lane freeway that enters the city from the east. Unfortunately, it does not connect with major highways from the U.S. so access from the south can be a little confusing. Most folks cross the border at the north end of the U.S. Hwy I-5 in Blaine, Washington. From there you can follow what appears to be the main road, Hwy 99, north into Vancouver. You will soon find yourself on boulevards and then cross into the downtown

BRITISH COLUMBIA

area, not the best place to be in a big RV. A better plan is to follow signs from the border that lead you up Hwy 15 (not a freeway but also not heavily trafficked) to connect with Hwy 1 to the east of Vancouver. From there you can use the freeway to get to Vancouver campgrounds to the north and east of downtown, travel north to Horseshoe Bay, or travel eastwards to the rest of the province.

Probably not too surprisingly, Vancouver got its start at about the same time as Portland and Seattle. The first European settlers to the area were fur trading companies that established forts along the Fraser River just to the east. Serious settlement of what is now Vancouver began in the 1850s. The large area now covered by Vancouver actually encompassed more than one small settlement. One of these was Granville, also called Gastown, today it is considered the place where Vancouver began.

In the beginning the city of Victoria, on Vancouver Island to the west, grew faster than Vancouver. Concern that Vancouver Island might be incorporated into the U.S. resulted in a concentrated British effort to develop the island, and gold discoveries up the Thompson and Fraser Rivers in the mountains east of Vancouver only gradually moved the center of population growth over to the mainland.

Other early events either precede or echo the histories of Portland and Seattle. Vancouver had its own serious fire in 1886, rebuilding resulted in many of the Gastown buildings you see today. The railroad reached Vancouver in the next year, and, just like Portland and Seattle, a direct and relatively easy to travel connection with the east really caused the city to take off.

As Canada's major west coast port Vancouver grew rapidly and continues to do so today. More freight passes through Vancouver than any other Canadian port, and by some measures Vancouver too is called the largest port on the west coast of North America.

The original **Gastown** settlement is at the base of a peninsula and didn't have a great deal of area for growth because it is hemmed in by water. As a result the city has spread off the peninsula to the north and south and today continues to grow to the east up the wide Fraser Valley.

The downtown peninsula is bounded on the north by Burrard Inlet and on the south by False Bay. Just south of Gastown is the city's **Chinatown**. To the west of these is the modern downtown area and farther to the west a primarily residential area known as the West End and also Stanley Park. Visitors from the U.S. will be impressed with Vancouver's cosmopolitan air, and also with the number of people who live near the center of town.

North of the peninsula, across Burrard Inlet, is North Vancouver, you reach it via the scenic Lions Gate Bridge. South of the Peninsula is a large residential area known as Central Vancouver which is also the location of the University of British Columbia.

More remote suburbs include Richmond, to the south, New Westminster, to the southeast, and Burnaby and Port Coquitlam to the east. You can go even farther and still consider yourself in the Vancouver metropolitan area. Delta and Surrey are to the south toward the U.S. border and to the east up the Fraser Valley are Langley and Abbotsford.

Vancouver has an excellent public transportation system. Pamphlets with details about service are available at the many info centres in Vancouver and on approaches to the city. The Coast Mountain Bus Company is the bus arm. It provides excellent bus service throughout the greater Vancouver area. Vancouver has a light rail transportation system

BRITISH COLUMBIA

too. This is known as SkyTrain. There is one line, it is underground downtown and above ground elsewhere. It runs southeastward from downtown and provides service to Burnaby, New Westminster, and Surrey. Trains run every 5 minutes or so. SeaBus passenger ferries connect downtown Vancouver with North Vancouver. The Vancouver terminal is near Canada Place, the North Vancouver terminal is Lonsdale Quay. From the quay there is bus service to many North Vancouver destinations. There are also tiny passenger ferries that chug around False Creek and are appropriately known as the False Creek Ferries. There are docks at many tourist destinations including Granville Island, Vanier Park, and Telus World of Science.

When you arrive in Vancouver on public transportation you will probably find yourself in the central business district. The new center of attraction for visitors is **Canada Place**. Now a combination cruise ship dock, convention center, hotel, shopping center, and theater, the very modern soaring tent-like building on a pier was originally build as a pavilion for the Expo86 fair. Canada Place is served by the SkyTrain light rail system.

Up the hill from Canada Place Granville Street has been closed to most traffic to become a European-style pedestrian mall. Along or near Granville you'll find lots of shopping. From its intersection with Granville you can follow Robson Street northwestward toward the West End and Stanley Park. Robson is lined with restaurants and boutiques.

Stanley Park is Vancouver's jewel. This huge park covers the entire tip of the peninsula occupied by Vancouver. It is a big place, there are miles and miles of trails as well as roads allowing you to tour the park in an automobile. A Seaside Promenade runs along the entire coastline of the park. Stanley Park is also home to the excellent **Vancouver Aquarium**. The Golden Gate-like Lions Gate suspension bridge makes a scenic jump from Stanley Park to North Vancouver.

If you head eastward from Canada Place you'll soon find yourself in historic **Gastown**. Cobblestone streets and well-maintained 19th-century buildings make the neighborhood stand out, and because it is a designated historic district the shops are open on Sundays.

Just southeast of Gastown is **Chinatown**. This is the second largest such area on the West Coast, only San Francisco's Chinatown is larger. In addition to the usual shops and restaurants you might want to visit the Dr. Sun Yat-sen Classical Chinese Garden which is located on Carrall Street between W. Pender and Keefer.

You can easily visit **North Vancouver** as a pedestrian by taking a ferry across Burrard Inlet. The SeaBus terminal is just east of Canada Place, ferries dock in North Vancouver at Lonsdale Quay. There's a farmers market at the quay as well as restaurants and shops. Busses to the sights in North Vancouver also depart from the quay.

Two popular attractions lie up the mountain. The first is the **Capilano Suspension Bridge**. This dizzying suspension foot bridge crosses the Capilano River at a height of 70 meters (230 feet). Higher on the same road is **Grouse Mountain** ski area. You can ride the gondola up to the ski slope for magnificent views of the city and hiking trails.

There are a number of attractions south of downtown also. One of the closest and most easily accessible is **Telus World of Science**. This is a science/technology museum housed in a 17-story ball originally built for Expo86. There is also an Omnimax theater. It is served by SkyTrain and also by the False Creek Ferries.

From Telus World of Science you can use the ferry to hop over to **Granville Island**, also accessible by car or bus. Not long ago this was little more than an area of old warehouses

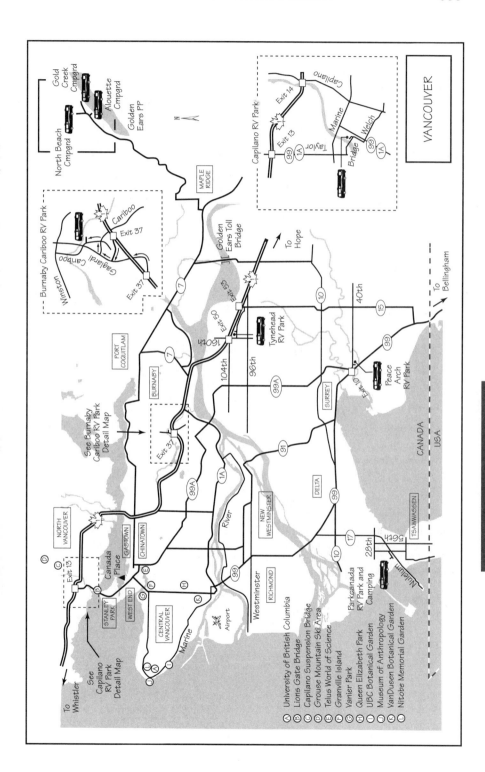

but it has been completely redone. Now there's a visitor information centre, a public market, the Emily Carr Institute of Art and Design, a marina, shops, restaurants, and theaters.

The area on the south side of False Bay is known as Central Vancouver. Attractions there are mostly grouped in Vanier Park and on the University of BC campus although there are also two excellent gardens. The first of these is **Queen Elizabeth Park**, a 130-acre park located on Little Mountain which offers views of the city. The **Bloedel Floral Conservatory** in the park is a dome-style greenhouse housing tropical plants and birds. The **VanDusen Botanical Garden** is nearby and offers 55 acres of beautiful gardens.

Vanier Park is located on the south shore of English Bay just west of Granville Island. In the park you'll find two museums. The **Vancouver Museum** is a regional history museum much more interesting then most of this genre, probably because Vancouver's history includes the coastal Indian cultures and also the European exploration of the Northwest. There's much more of the latter at the nearby **Vancouver Maritime Museum**. The park also has a planetarium and an astronomical observatory.

West of Vanier Park and occupying 1,900 acres on Point Grey is the University of British Columbia. The **Museum of Anthropology** here is excellent and covers, of course, the Pacific Northwest Indian cultures. The university campus has miles of hiking trails and beaches. Also on campus are the **Nitobe Memorial Garden**, a traditional Japanese garden and the **UBC Botanical Garden**.

Vancouver Campgrounds

● **BURNABY CARIBOO RV PARK** *(Open All Year)*
    Res and Info: (604) 420-1722, camping@bcrvpark.com,
                  www.bcrv.com, www.bcrvpark.com
    Location: Burnaby

    GPS Location: 49.24861 N, 122.91222 W, Near Sea Level

240 Sites – This is a convenient campground for folks approaching Vancouver from the east. It is located just off Hwy 1 and is near Burnaby Lake Regional Park which has good hiking trails. Sites are back-ins to 45 feet. There's an indoor swimming pool and Jacuzzi as well as a free internet station. The Lougheed Shopping Center is a short drive away. To find the campground take Exit 37 (Cariboo Rd.). You'll be on Gaglardi Way, drive north. Drive only a short distance and turn right at the Cariboo Rd sign. Again drive only a short distance and turn left on Cariboo Road. Now drive about .5 km (.3 miles) north and turn right on Cariboo Place, this is the entrance road to the campground. The route is signed so it is easier to drive than to read.

● **CAPILANO RV PARK** *(Open All Year)*
    Res and Info: (604) 987-4722,
                info@capilano rvpark.com,
                www.capilanorvpark.com
    Location: North Vancouver

    GPS Location: 49.32389 N, 123.13139 W,
    Near Sea Level

240 Sites – This campground is conveniently located in North Vancouver just north of the Lions Gate Bridge and near Hwy 1. It is also within easy walking distance of the Park Royal Shopping Centre. Sites are back-ins to 45 feet. Amenities include a pool and spa and internet lounge. There is good bus service into Vancouver from near the campground.

To most easily drive to the campground leave Hwy 1 at Exit 14. Drive south 1.8 km (1.1 miles). You will cross Marine Drive and continue south on Capilano Road, a paved two-lane road . Take a right on Welch Street, there is a sign for the RV park here. Follow Welch as it goes west and passes under the Lions Gate Bridge approach ramp, a distance of about .8 km (.5 mile). Turn right on Bridge Street and you'll see the park entrance on the right just as the road makes a 90° turn to the left.

● **PEACE ARCH RV PARK** *(Open All Year)*
    Res and Info: (604) 594-7009,
                www.peacearchrvpark.com
    Location: Surrey

    GPS Location: 49.07472 N, 122.81389 W, Near Sea Level

215 Sites – If you're willing to stay a little farther from Vancouver when you visit you'll find that the parks are less expensive than those right near town. There's beautiful landscaping around the office and in the garden near the swimming pool. This campground has larger sites than those in town including pull-thrus to 55 feet long. Free Wi-Fi is provided throughout the park. Bus service to town is available and the site is very convenient to the crossing into the U.S. The campground is located just off Hwy 99 about 10 km (6 miles) north of the U.S. border crossing at Blaine. Take Exit 10 for the King George Highway (Hwy 99A) northbound. Almost immediately turn right on 40th Street, the campground entrance is on the right in .3 km (.2 miles).

● **PARKCANADA RV PARK AND CAMPING**
    (Open All Year)
    Reservations: (877) 943-0685
    Information: (604) 943-5811, info@parkcanada.com,
                www.parkcanada.com
    Location: Delta

    GPS Location: 49.03250 N, 123.09222 W, Near Sea Level

124 Sites – This is an older park with many permanently parked rigs, but it's convenient to the Tsawwassen Ferry terminal for travel to Sidney near Victoria on Vancouver Island. Sites are back-ins and pull-thrus to 45 feet. Bus access to Vancouver is from a stop about a mile from the campground. The campground is located right next to Hwy 17 (the Tsawwassen access route) and adjacent to a recreational water park with big slides so it's tough to miss. If you follow Hwy 17 south from its intersection with Hwy 99 you'll see the campground sign indicating the right turn in about 8.4 km (5.2 miles). From the ferry terminal the turn is about 4.0 km (2.5 miles). Turn north on 52nd Street and then immediately left to parallel the highway, you'll reach the water park entrance in .8 km (.5 mile). Proceed into the parking lot, the campground office and gated entrance are on the far side straight ahead.

● **TYNEHEAD RV PARK** *(Open All Year)*
    Res and Info: (604) 589-1161, tynehead@telus.net,
                www.tynehead.com
    Location: Surrey

    GPS Location: 49.18833 N, 122.77167 W, 200 Ft

180 Sites – Tynehead is a park to the east of Vancouver. It's an older park. It's convenient to the Trans-Canada but public transportation is not conveniently accessed from the park. There are many long-term residents. Sites are back-ins and pull-thrus to 55 feet. In summer there's

a swimming pool. Access is probably easiest from Exit 53. Head south on Hwy 15 but turn right almost immediately on Tynehead Drive. Tynehead Drive will carry you around the north side of Tynehead Regional Park for 3.7 km (2.3 miles), the campground entrance will be on your right.

☐   **GOLDEN EARS PROVINCIAL PARK** *(Open All Year)*
    Reservations: www.discovercamping.ca, (800) 689-9025
    Information: (604) 466-8325
    Location: 19 Km (12 Miles) NE of Maple Ridge

    GPS Location: 49.32434 N, 122.46052 W, 500 Ft

409 Sites – This is a large provincial park, and it's fairly close to Vancouver. It's just a little far out for visitor to the city, but it's a great place to spend a few days if you aren't planning to commute. The park is named for the two peaks of Mt Blanshard. There are three large vehicle accessible campground along Allouette Lake: Allouette (206 sites), Gold Creek (148 sites), and North Beach (55 sites). One gate controls access to all three. The Gold Creek campground remains open all year long (if snow allows) but the two others open from about June 20 to September 5. Spaces are long back-ins allowing use by any size RV. Access is from the town of Maple Ridge, a suburb to the north-east of the city. From Maple Ridge the route to the campground leads east and north, it is well marked with official signs. In central Maple Ridge drive north a few blocks to east-west Dewdney Trunk Road and turn east. Follow Dewdney for a few blocks and turn north on 232nd St. Follow 232nd St north for 2.4 km (1.5 miles) and turn right on 132nd Ave. Now follow 132nd eastward and then north to the park and its campgrounds, a distance of 15.8 km (9.8 miles). The road changes names several times but the route is easy to follow.

VICTORIA

At the far south end of Vancouver Island the city of Victoria (population 360,000) has played many roles through the years. Originally the area was a popular First Peoples site, they harvested camas bulbs where Beacon Hill Park is today. In the 1840s the Hudson Bay Company selected a site on the excellent harbor for their western headquarters. Victoria soon became the capital city of the colonies of British Columbia and Vancouver Island. However, when Vancouver became the terminus for the transcontinental railroad Victoria remained the capital city, but slid into a long period of existence as a quiet tourist attraction and bastion of Britishness. Today the town is rapidly growing but still very pleasant. A great place to live or to visit.

The tourist business in Victoria probably can be dated to the construction of the huge Canadian Pacific Railway **Empress Hotel** in 1908. The hotel remains one of the most popular destinations for the millions of tourists that visit Victoria each year, quite a few on cruise boats from Seattle. Many come for the formal afternoon tea at the hotel. The downtown area, particularly near the hotel, is full of sights and activities for these tourists.

In the immediate vicinity you'll find the following sights, and more. At the **docks** in front of the hotel you can sign up for whale-watching tours or catch one of the tiny harbor ferries. The **Parliament Buildings** face the hotel across grass lawns, they're lighted at night and tours are available. The excellent **Royal British Columbia Museum** should not be missed, it has full-sized displays of natural history, cultural history, and the art and culture of the area's First People populations. Other attractions devoted to the daily tourists

VICTORIA'S HARBOR BUSTLES WITH ACTIVITY

BRITISH COLUMBIA

including Miniature World, Ann Hathaway's Cottage, the Royal London Wax Museum, Helmcken House, Craigdarroch Castle, the Maritime Museum, the Crystal Gardens, and the Undersea Gardens.

There are several reasons to get out and away from Victoria. Probably the most popular attraction outside the city are the **Butchart Gardens**. They fill a former limestone quarry next to Tod Inlet on the east side of the Saanich Peninsula. The gardens are well worth a visit and cover over fifty acres. Nearby are the **Butterfly Gardens** where you'll find thousands of butterflies in an enclosed garden.

Victoria Campgrounds

● **GOLDSTREAM PROVINCIAL PARK** *(Open All Year)*
   Reservations: www.discovercamping.ca, (800) 689-9025
   Information: (250) 474-1336
   Location: 11 Km (7 Miles) W of Victoria

   GPS Location: 48.46056 N, 123.55833 W, 300 Ft

173 Sites – This is a large provincial park campground conveniently located very near Victoria. The fine hiking trails are a bonus. The campground itself is set in very tall old trees, it's very impressive but also a little dark. Many sites are 45 feet long or more. Swimming is in the Goldstream River. Although the campground is open all year long, from November 1 to March 14 there are reduced fees because no water, firewood, or sani-station are available. The campground is located right off Hwy 1 as you descend from Malahat Summit into town.

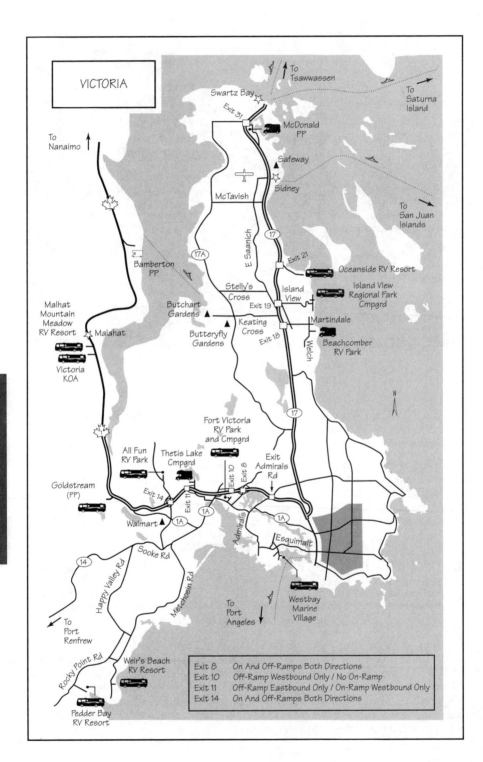

BRITISH COLUMBIA

VICTORIA

To Tsawwassen

Swartz Bay

Exit 31

To Saturna Island

McDonald PP

To Nanaimo

Safeway

Sidney

McTavish

To San Juan Islands

E Saanich

17

Bamberton PP

17A

Exit 21

Oceanside RV Resort

Stelly's Cross

Island View

Exit 19

Island View Regional Park Cmpgrd

Malhat Mountain Meadow RV Resort

Butchart Gardens

Martindale

Malahat

Butteryfly Gardens

Keating Cross

Exit 18

Welch

Beachcomber RV Park

Victoria KOA

N

17

Fort Victoria RV Park and Cmpgrd

All Fun RV Park

Thetis Lake Cmpgrd

Exit Admirals Rd

Exit 10

Exit 8

Goldstream (PP)

Exit 14

Exit 11

1A

1A

Admirals

1A

Walmart

Esquimalt

14

Sooke Rd

Happy Valley Rd

Metchosin Rd

To Port Angeles

Westbay Marine Village

To Port Renfrew

Rocky Point Rd

Weir's Beach RV Resort

Pedder Bay RV Resort

Exit 8	On And Off-Ramps Both Directions
Exit 10	Off-Ramp Westbound Only / No On-Ramp
Exit 11	Off-Ramp Eastbound Only / On-Ramp Westbound Only
Exit 14	On And Off-Ramps Both Directions

● **FORT VICTORIA RV PARK AND**
CAMPGROUND *(Open All Year)*

Res and Info: (250) 479-8112, info@fortvictoria.ca,
www.fortvictoria.ca
Location: Victoria

GPS Location: 48.46000 N, 123.44250 W, 100 Ft

300 Sites – This is a very large and well-run campground conveniently located near the freeway where Highway 1 enters Victoria from the upper island. There is good bus service in to town. Sites here are back-ins and pull-thrus to 55 feet, it's an excellent big-rig campground. The park is easily visible from Hwy 1 as you approach Victoria from the north. Take Exit 8 marked Helmcken Road and follow the signs on a roundabout route about 1.8 kilometers (1.1 miles) to the campground.

● **WESTBAY MARINE VILLAGE** *(Open All Year)*

Res and Info: (250) 385-1831, (866) 937-8229,
info@westbay.bc.ca,
www.westbay.bc.ca
Location: Victoria

GPS Location: 48.42556 N, 123.39528 W, Near Sea Level

61 Sites – This campground sits right on the shore of West Bay, there are views across Victoria's inner harbor of the city. It's a great place to watch the ships and floatplanes go by. You can also walk along waterfront bike paths right into town, a distance of about 4 kilometers (2.5 miles) or take the bus or the tiny harbor ferryboats. Sites are all back-ins, RVs to 45 feet will fit. This is a very popular campground, make reservations well in advance if you want to stay here. Follow signs from Highway 1 at the Admirals Road exit just west of Victoria. You'll drive south on Admirals Road for 4.5 kilometers (2.8 miles), turn left on Esquimalt Rd. and drive 1.4 kilometers (.9 miles), then turn right on Head and follow signs through the neighborhood to the campground.

● **PEDDER BAY RV RESORT** *(Open March 1 to Oct 31)*

Res and Info: (877) 478-1771, (250) 478-1771,
www.pedderbay.com
Location: 18 Km (11 Miles) W of Victoria

GPS Location: 48.34885 N, 123.57447 W, Near Sea Level

88 Sites – Pedder Bay is a new RV park perched above a marina to the southwest of Victoria. RV sites here are good for big rigs: they are back-ins and pull-thrus to 60 feet. They are separated by fences and hedges for privacy. There are also tent sites. Amenities include a coffee house; tackle shop; rental boats, kayaks, and bikes; and a boat ramp. Take Exit 8 from Hwy 1. Drive south for 1.2 km (.7 mile) to Hwy 1A, the Island Highway. Turn right and follow Hwy 1A for 8.4 km (5.2 miles) as it heads first west and then curves to the south, where it soon becomes Sooke Road. Turn left on Happy Valley road and drive for 7.1 km (4.4 miles). Turn right on Rocky Point Road and drive for 5.2 km (3.2 miles), the campground entrance road goes left there.

● **WEIR'S BEACH RV RESORT** *(Open All Year)*
   Res and Info: (250) 478-3323, (866) 478-6888,
                     www.weirsbeachrvresort.bc.ca
   Location: 16 Km (10 Miles) W of Victoria

   GPS Location: 48.35234 N, 123.54698 W, Near Sea Level

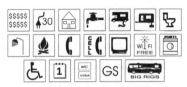

60 Sites – Weir's Beach is located west of Vancouver on the beach on the south side of the island. It's a modern campground with excellent facilities, not to mention a row of campsites facing a quiet beach. Sites are back-ins to 40 feet. One access route to the campground is to take Exit 8 from Hwy 1. Drive south for 1.2 km (.7 mile) to Hwy 1A, the Island Highway. Turn right and follow Hwy 1A for 5.8 km (3.6 miles) as it heads first west and then curves to the south, along the way becoming Sooke Road. Turn left on Metchosin Road and follow it for 11 km (7 miles), you'll see the park entrance on the left.

● **ALL FUN RV PARK** *(Open All Year)*
   Res and Info: 250 474-4546, www.allfun.bc.ca
   Location: Langford, North of Victoria

   GPS Location: 48.47127 N, 123.50053 W, 200 Ft

95 Sites – This campground is next to Western Speedway automobile racetrack in Langford on the northern edge of Victoria and is part of an entertainment complex that also includes batting cages, go karts, mini golf, an ice cream parlor, and a Sunday swap-an-shop. Sites are back-ins to 35 feet and pull-thrus to 45 feet. From Hwy 1 in Victoria take Exit 14 and drive north on Millstream Road. The RV park is on the right in 1.6 km (1 mile).

● **THETIS LAKE CAMPGROUND**
       (Open All Year)
   Res and Info: (250) 478-3845, thetislake@shaw.ca
   Location: Victoria

   GPS Location: 48.46194 N, 123.46833 W, 200 Ft

150 Sites – This is a commercial campground located right next to Thetis Lake Regional Park. You can easily walk out a back gate to reach the swimming beach. The campground has many semi-permanent residents but about 30 hookup sites for travelers. It slopes up a steep hill so access and sites limit vehicle size to about 30 feet for these sites. There are lots more tent sites on the hillside with vehicle access for only automobiles (no RVs due to very steep roads in this section). Access is easy from up-island. Take Exit 11 from Hwy 1, turn north, and the entrance to the regional park parking lot will be on your left. Turn in and drive past the parking lot entrance to the campground entrance. From the east there is no exit possible at Exit 11 so it's easiest to take Exit 8 for Hemcken Road, go 1.1 km (.7 mile) south, turn right on Hwy 1A. In 1.6 km (1 mile) turn right on Six Mile road and follow it for 1 km (.6 mile) under the freeway and into the campground on the far side.

● **BEACHCOMBER RV PARK** *(Open April 16 to Oct 15)*
   Res and Info: (250) 652-3800, info@beachcomberrv.com,
                     www.beachcomberrv.com
   Location: 13 Km (8 Miles) N of Victoria

   GPS Location: 48.55778 N, 123.36333 W, Near Sea Level

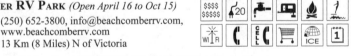

59 Sites – The campground has a great location right on the beach on the east side of

the Saanich Peninsula. It's for self-contained camping vehicles only because the only restroom facilities are port-a-potties. Most sites are on grass. They have electricity and water and there is a sani-dump. Some sites here are large but access is difficult for large rigs because of the narrow, steep access. Swimming is in the ocean. To find it follow Martindale Rd. east from Hwy 17 about 15.6 km (9.7 miles) south of the ferry docks in Schwartz Bay, 10.5 km (6.5 miles) north of the intersection of Hwy 1 and Hwy 17 near Victoria. Unfortunately there is no access to Martindale if you're southbound, you must exit 1.3 km (.8 miles) to the north on Island View Road, head east, and then turn right on Lochside Dr. to parallel the highway as you drive south to intercept Martindale. There's a long steep narrow access road down into the campground, but it is paved.

○ **ISLAND VIEW REGIONAL PARK CAMPGROUND**
   (Open May 15 to Sept 10 – Varies)
   Res and Info: (250) 478-3344, www.crd.bc.ca/parks/islandview
   Location: 16 Km (10 Miles) N of Victoria

   GPS Location: 48.57472 N, 123.36806 W, Near Sea Level

47 Sites – Another campground right on the beach on the east shore of the Saanich Peninsula. Facilities are simple but the setting is nice. There are long back-in RV sites near the beach and very nice tent and RV sites inland. Swimming is in the ocean. Note that there are no utility hookups at this campground. Water is available from a faucet, but not at sites. To reach the campground follow Island View Road from Hwy 17 about 14.4 km (8.9 miles) south of the ferry docks in Schwartz Bay, 11.8 km (7.3 miles) north of the intersection of Hwy 1 and Hwy 17 near Victoria. Drive 3 km (1.9 miles) east from Highway 17, then turn left when you reach the beach. The campground is at the north side of Island View Beach Regional Park parking lot.

● **OCEANSIDE RV RESORT** *(Open All Year)*
   Res and Info: (250) 544-0508,
      www.oceansideresortrv.com
   Location: Saanich

   *GPS Location: 48.58836 N, 123.37698 W,
      Near Sea Level*

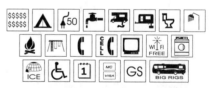

187 Sites – This is a beautiful modern big-rig park located not far south of the Swartz Bay ferry terminal. Sites are beautifully landscaped, and while the park is not right on the beach it is within strolling distance. There are back-in sites to 60 feet and pull-thrus to 70 feet. From the stoplight at Exit 21 on Hwy 17 turn east on Mt Newton X Road. Drive .5 km (.3 miles) and take the right fork onto Koa Road. Follow Koa for 1.1 km (.7 miles) to the campground.

☐ **MCDONALD CAMPGROUND, GULF ISLAND**
   NATIONAL PARK PRESERVE *(Open May 1 to Oct 10 – Varies)*
   Reservations: (877) 737-3783, www.pccamping.ca/parkscanada/
   Location: 2 Km (1 Mile) S of Swartz Bay

   GPS Location: 48.67310 N, 123.42540 W, 100 Ft

43 Sites – This is a no-hookup government campground located not far from the ferry terminal at Swartz Bay. Sites here are located in a dense forest on a knoll. They are back-in sites, some as long as 40 feet. However, roads are narrow and access difficult for large RVs so the practical maximum RV size here is 35 feet or shorter. Some sites have tent pads. Sites have fire pits and picnic tables and there are vault toilets. Water is from

faucets. Easiest access off Hwy 17 is from the Wain Road/McDonald Park Road Exit .1.9 km (1.2 miles) south of the Swartz Bay ferry landing. Drive east on McDonald Park Road for .5 km (.5/.62 miles), the park entrance is on the right.

WELLS GRAY PROVINCIAL PARK (CLEARWATER RIVER CORRIDOR SECTION) AND CLEARWATER

Clearwater (population 1,700) serves as the gateway to the Clearwater River Corridor section of Wells Gray Provincial Park. The small town stretches along the highway and offers a few restaurants, stores and campgrounds. There is also an info centre at the junction with Wells Gray Park Road, a good place to pick up information about facilities and conditions in the park.

Wells Gray Provincial Park is very large but much of it is pretty hard to reach. The southern portion of the park near Clearwater is the most accessible for RVers. This park is known for its waterfalls, you can see three of them by taking an easy three hour drive north from Clearwater. The road that leads from Clearwater into the park is not a major highway but also no particular challenge. It is paved all the way to Helmcken Falls, a distance of 47 kilometers (29 miles). From a junction just before you reach the falls an unpaved road continues on into the park to Clearwater Lake, another 28 kilometers (17 miles).

Spahats Falls is really in another park, Spahats Creek Provincial Park. It takes about 10 minutes to walk to the viewpoint where you see Spahats Creek fall about 60 meters out

DAWSON FALLS

of an impressive gorge and then flow into Clearwater Creek. The falls are 10 kilometers (6 miles) from the junction in Clearwater.

Thirty-five kilometers (22 miles) from the junction in Clearwater you enter Wells Gray Provincial Park. In just another few kilometers you'll see the parking area for the **Dawson Falls** viewpoint on the left. A short walk takes you to a viewpoint where you can see the Murtle River flow over a 20 meter drop.

The most famous of the falls in the park is undoubtedly **Helmcken Falls**. This is the fourth highest waterfall in British Columbia and an unusually memorable sight due to the volume of water and the massive amounts of spray rising into the air. The water falls into a fairly restricted bowl causing strong updrafts and heavy mists. The falls are 47 kilometers (29 miles) from the junction in Clearwater.

Wells Gray Provincial Park and Clearwater Campgrounds

● **CLEARWATER COUNTRY INN AND RV PARK**
   (Open April 1 to Nov 15)
   Res and Info: (250) 674-3121, (888) 242-3533,
                  park@clearwatercountryinnandrvpark.com,
                  www.clearwatercountryinnandrvpark.com
   Location: Clearwater

   GPS Location: 51.65167 N, 120.03194 W, 1,500 Ft

60 Sites – The easiest to find campground in Clearwater is probably this one. It is located behind a restaurant and motel on Hwy 5 just .2 km (.1 mile) east of the cutoff to Wells Gray Provincial Park. Sites here are back-ins and pull-thrus to 70 feet shadowed by tall evergreens. Amenities include a swimming pool.

● **DUTCH LAKE RESORT AND RV PARK**
   (Open May 1 to Nov 10 – Varies)
   Res and Info: (250) 674-3351, (888) 884-4424,
                  chris@dutchlake.com,
                  www.dutchlake.com
   Location: Clearwater

   GPS Location: 51.65167 N, 120.06278 W, 1,300 Ft

71 Sites – This campground is away from the business strip along the highway but easy to find and access. It's quiet and good for tenters and big rigs too with full-hookup pull-thru sites for RVs to 45 feet. It's on a lake with a restaurant overlooking the water. From the info centre at the junction of the Wells Gray Park Road and Hwy 5 drive west on the highway for 1 km (.6 miles). Turn right on the Old Thompson Highway and drive 1.1 km (.7 miles) northwest to Dutch Lake Road. Turn right here and you'll soon see the campground entrance on your right.

● **CLEARWATER VALLEY RESORT MOTEL**
   AND CAMPGROUND / KOA
   (Open May 1 to Oct 12 – Varies)

   Res and Info: (250) 674-3909, (888) 837-1161,
                  www.clearwatervalley.com
   Location: Clearwater
   GPS Location: 51.65314 N, 120.03980 W, 1.400 Ft

90 Sites – The KOA in Clearwater has nice large back-in and pull-thrus to 70 feet. Ameni-

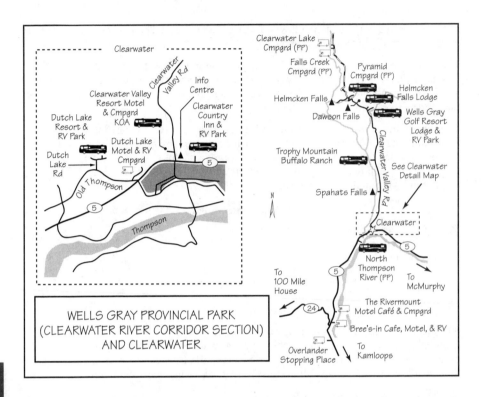

WELLS GRAY PROVINCIAL PARK
(CLEARWATER RIVER CORRIDOR SECTION)
AND CLEARWATER

ties include a swimming pool and mini golf. From Hwy 5 in Clearwater drive north on the Clearwater Valley Road for only .2 km (.1 mile), the entrance is on the left.

☐ **NORTH THOMPSON RIVER PROVINCIAL PARK**
   (Open May 1 to Sept 30 – Varies)
   Res and Info: (250) 674-2194
   Location: 5 Km (3 Miles) SW of Clearwater

   GPS Location: 51.62444 N, 120.08667 W, 1,400 Ft

61 Sites – This large provincial campground is near Clearwater just off the highway. The Clearwater and Thompson Rivers meet here, a few sites are on the Thompson River. Some sites will take RVs to 45 feet, all are back-ins. From the junction of the Wells Gray Park Road and Hwy 5 drive southwest on Hwy 5 five km (3 miles), the campground entrance is on the left.

● **WELLS GRAY GOLF RESORT LODGE AND**
     RV PARK *(Open April 15 to Oct 15 – Varies)*
   Res and Info: (250) 674-0009 or (877) 215-4653,
                     wellsgraygolf@bcresorts.com,
                     www.wellsgraygolf.bcresorts.com
   Location: 34 Km (21 Miles) N of Clearwater

   GPS Location: 51.93917 N, 120.048611 W, 2,100 Ft

60 Sites – A wonderful place to stay that is convenient to the park, has good facilities, offers creek-side parking, and is also a 9-hole golf course. The Helmcken Falls Lodge

with its restaurant is right next door and the campground offers great deals on camping/ golfing packages. Sites are back-ins and pull-thrus to 50 feet. From the intersection in Clearwater next to the info centre drive north on the park road for 34 km (21 miles), the entrance is on the right.

● **HELMCKEN FALLS LODGE** *(Open May 15 to Sept 15 – Varies)*
    Res and Info: (250) 674-3657, info@helmckenfalls.com,
                  www.helmckenfalls.com
    Location: 34 Km (21 Miles) N of Clearwater

    GPS Location: 51.93694 N, 120.05750 W, 2,100 Ft

24 Sites – This lodge and restaurant offers camping in a quiet field behind and below the lodge. It is a very good tent camping location with grass for pitching your tent and restroom facilities with showers. There are also back-in RV sites suitable for RVs to 45 feet but there are no sewer or dump facilities. It's right next door to the Wells Gray Golf Resort Lodge and RV Park so the location is good for day trips into the park to see the waterfalls. From the intersection in Clearwater next to the info centre drive north on the park road for 34 km (21 miles), the entrance is on the right.

● **TROPHY MOUNTAIN BUFFALO RANCH**
    (Open May 15 to Oct 15 – Varies)
    Res and Info: (250) 674-3095, info@buffaloranch.ca,
                  www.buffaloranch.ca
    Location: 20 Km (12 Miles) N of Clearwater

    GPS Location: 51.81548 N, 120.02629 W, 2,200 Ft

13 Sites – This ranch maintains a small campground. There are four tent sites and back-in and pull-thru RV sites to 40 feet. Sites have picnic tables and fire pits. There are two cabins available and there is an outdoor barbecue style restaurant specializing in Bison meat. From Hwy 5 in Clearwater drive north on the Clearwater Valley Road for 19.6 km (12.2 miles), the ranch entrance is on the left.

☐ **PYRAMID CAMPGROUND – WELLS GRAY PROVINCIAL PARK**
    (Open All Year)
    Information: (250) 674-2194, info@explorewellsgray.com,
                 www.explorewellsgray.com
    Location: 43 Km (27 Miles) N of Clearwater

    GPS Location: 51.97111 N, 120.11944 W, 2,700 Ft

50 Sites – This campground is inside Wells Gray Provincial Park about 4 kilometers from Helmcken Falls. Sites are large back-ins with some suitable for RVs to 45 feet. Tents must pitch on the gravel parking pads. There is a trail from the campground that leads 14 kilometers to Majerus and Horseshoe Falls on the Murtle River. The campground gates are open all year. From May 1 to September 30 there are fees, outside this period there are no services or fees. You can't miss this campground, the entrance is right at the junction of the paved road to Helmcken Falls and the gravel road to Clearwater Lake. It is 43 km (27 miles) north of Clearwater.

WHISTLER AND THE SEA TO SKY HIGHWAY

The Sea to Sky Highway is Hwy 99 as it climbs from Horseshoe Bay, just north of Vancouver, up into central British Columbia at Lillooet. Between Pemberton and Lillooet there are some steep hills. A few short sections reach a 15% grade, some longer sections are in the neighborhood of 10%. There are also switchbacks. Larger RVs do routinely travel this road but if you have reservations about the climbing or braking ability of your rig it is best to avoid the Pemberton to Lillooet section. The road is paved the entire distance.

Horseshoe Bay is just north of Vancouver, Hwy 1 leads directly to the ferry terminal there. Follow the signs for Whistler and Hwy 99 and you're on your way. The highway follows the shore of Howe Sound and in 44 km (27 miles) reaches Squamish.

Squamish (population 15,000) is the best supply center along the highway and a center for outdoor activity. Much of it revolves around the **Stawamus Chief** rock face and rock-climbing activities there, the mountain is just south of town. Squamish is also home to the

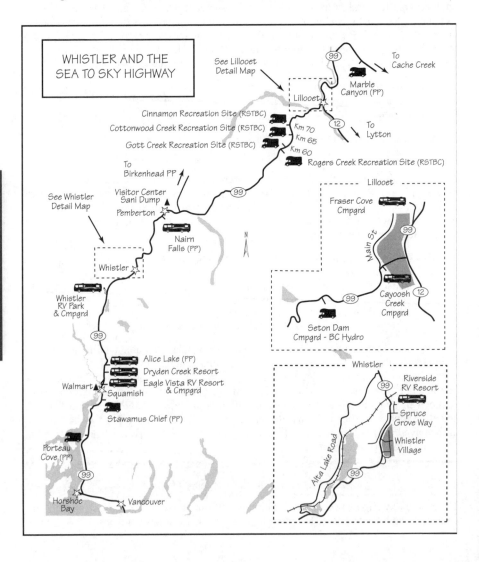

BC Museum of Mining and the **West Coast Railway Heritage Park**.

Whistler (population 10,000), the site of the Winter Olympics in 2010, is the next town along the way. Whistler is spread over quite a large area with condos and golf courses visible through the trees but the center of the action is Whistler Village. Large parking lots are located behind the village, in summer there should be plenty of room for you. Whistler village has pedestrian-only streets, it is modeled after the ski villages in the alps. Even if you don't ski you'll want to take a look.

Whistler has a commercial campground. If it's too crowded or not your style alternates are Nairn Falls Provincial Park which is 27 km (17 miles) toward Pemberton, or Whistler RV Park which is 19 km (12 miles) toward Squamish.

Just beyond Pemberton the highway climbs and the campgrounds get scarce. There are a number of RSTBC campgrounds along the road. They're small and most are suitable for only smaller rigs.

When you finally reach **Lillooet** you'll find that it is blessed with some decent campgrounds considering its remote location. Lillooet now has a population of 2,300 or so but for a very short time during the Cariboo Gold Rush in the early 1860s it was the second-largest town north of San Francisco. From here the Cariboo Wagon Road went north to the Cariboo Gold Fields. Lillooet sits at the bottom of the Fraser River Canyon and has a very hot (in summer) and dry climate. From here you can drive north to the Cariboo or south to Lytton and Highway 1 on paved roads.

Whistler and the Sea to Sky Highway Campgrounds

☐ **Porteau Cove Provincial Park** *(Open All Year)*

Reservations: www.discovercamping.ca, (800) 689-9025
Information: (604) 986-9371, seatoskyparks.com,
www.seatoskyparks.com
Location: 19 Km (12 Miles) S of Squamish

GPS Location: 49.55861 N, 123.23444 W, Near Sea Level

60 Sites – This campground occupies a narrow piece of land between the highway and the ocean. It's one of the few provincial campgrounds that has electrical hookups. RV sites are almost all back-ins, a few reach 50 feet in length, most are shorter. The campground gate is open all year. From March 1 to October 31 there are full services. From November 1 to February 28 there are reduced services and a reduced fee. Some of the sites are walk-in tent sites. Porteau Cove is popular with wind surfers and scuba divers, it has an artificial reef out front. There are also boat ramps and a dock. The campground is located off Hwy 99 some 24 km (15 miles) north of Horseshoe Bay and 19 km (12 miles) south of Squamish.

☐ **Stawamus Chief Provincial Campground**
(Open May 14 to Oct 17 – Varies)

Information: (604) 986-9371
Location: 3 Km (2 Miles) S of Squamish

GPS Location: 49.68167 N, 123.15306 W, 200 Ft

62 Sites – This is primarily a tent camping park used by people who are climbing the Stawamus Chief granite face that looms above the campground. Most sites are walk-ins, there is a cooking shelter. About 15 sites are accessible by vehicle; a few will take very small RVs to about 22 feet. Outside the open dates noted above the gates of the camp-

ing area are closed but tent campers can walk in and camp. The campground is located off Hwy 99 some 40 km (25 miles) north of Horseshoe Bay and 3 km (2 miles) south of Squamish. There is a rest stop along the highway here, a paved road runs about a quarter mile up the hill to the campground.

● **EAGLE VISTA RV RESORT AND CAMPGROUND**
   Res and Info: (604) 898-3343, (877) 898-3343
                 www.eaglevistarv.com
   Location: Squamish

   GPS Location: 49.72692 N, 123.13821 W, 100 Ft

63 Sites – Sites in this nice well-managed and maintained campground are back-ins and pull-thrus to 60 feet. Trees provide shade but this isn't a dark park. There's a rental yurt available and also a BBQ restaurant. From Hwy 99 as it passes through Squamish, turn east on Finch Drive at the stoplight near the Tim Horton's. After driving .5 km (.3 mile) turn left on Logger's Lane. Drive 1 km (.6 mile) and then turn right on Centennial Way. The campground is on the right in .2 km (.1 mile).

● **DRYDEN CREEK RESORTS** *(Open All Year)*
   Res and Info: (604) 898-9726,
                 info@drydencreek.com,
                 www.drydencreek.com
   Location: 6 Km (4 Miles) N of Squamish

   GPS Location: 49.76722 N, 123.13694 W, 200 Ft

51 Sites – This is a very pleasant campground set east and well back from the highway so road noise is minimal. It's set in big evergreens and has quite a few monthly rigs. There is an excellent area for pitching tents on grass as well as variously situated back-ins to 40 feet and a few large pull-thrus to 55 feet. Reservations are very important here, particularly for RVs, this is a popular place. The campground is located off Hwy 99 some 6 km (4 miles) north of Squamish and 50 km (31 miles) south of Whistler.

☐ **ALICE LAKE PROVINCIAL PARK**
        (Open March 15 to Oct 31 – Varies)
   Reservations: www.discovercamping.ca, (800) 689-9025
   Information: (604) 986-9371, www.seatoskyparks.com
   Location: 10 Km (6 Miles) N of Squamish

   GPS Location: 49.79194 N, 123.12611 W, 700 Ft

120 Sites – This large provincial park campground is another popular one due to its location near Vancouver and Whistler and the pleasant location. Sites are as long as 50 feet, 55 have electrical hookups. There are trails around the lake and to three other nearby lakes and two swimming beaches on Alice Lake. Campground gates are closed when snow falls, weather determines the opening and closing dates. Tent camping is allowed when the gates are closed. The campground is located off Hwy 99 some 10 km (6 miles) north of Squamish and 48 km (30 miles) southwest of Whistler.

● **WHISTLER RV PARK AND CAMPGROUND**
        (Open All Year)
   Res and Info: (888) 222-2154, info@whistlerrvpark.com,
                 www.whistlerrvpark.com
   Location: 16 Km (10 Miles) SW of Whistler

   GPS Location: 50.04458 N, 123.13088 W, 1,900 Ft

150 Sites – This large new RV park is situated on a flat terrace far above the highway with wonderful views. There are back-in and pull-thru sites to 60 feet as well as drive-in and walk-in tent sites in trees. This campground is the second closest to Whistler and is popular with winter-sports visitors. Winter rates are lower. The campground is located off Hwy 99 some 34 km (21 miles) north of Squamish and 16 km (10 miles) southwest of Whistler.

● **RIVERSIDE RV RESORT** *(Open All Year)*
   Res and Info: (877) 905-5533, (604) 905-5533,
                    info@whistlercamping.com,
                    www.whistlercamping.com
   Location: Whistler

   GPS Location: 50.13639 N, 122.95222 W, 2,100 Ft

155 Sites – Whistler has only one RV park and this is it. It's a nice upscale campground with sites in five areas. There are pull-thru full hookups to 60 feet in one area, a nice tent-only area near Fitzsimmons Creek, a back-in area with paved sites and electric and water hookups (to about 30 feet) on the hillside across the creek, a multi-use area (RV no-hookup camping or tents) nearby with gravel sites, and even a group camping area. It's very important to reserve well ahead if you wish to stay here, Whistler needs more campgrounds. Amenities include an 18-hole putting course, café, rentals of bikes and skis, a market, and a walking trail that runs past the park. Whistler Village is only a mile or so away, there's a shuttle or you can walk or bike on the nice paved trail that runs right through the park. There's also public bus service available. To reach the campground drive north from Whistler Village on Hwy 99. In 2 km (1.2 miles) turn right on Spruce Grove Way and then immediately left to follow the access road to the campground.

☐ **NAIRN FALLS PROVINCIAL PARK** *(Open May 13 to Oct 2 – Varies)*
   Reservations: www.discovercamping.ca, (800) 689-9025
   Information: (604) 986-9371, www.seatoskyparks.com
   Location: 27 Km (17 Miles) N of Whistler

   GPS Location: 50.29611 N, 122.81778 W, 800 Ft

92 Sites – Nairn Falls is a large provincial park that makes a good alternative in the Whistler area. Because it's some distance on the far side of Whistler from Vancouver it often has room for campers when other campgrounds within driving distance of Whistler are full. Many sites are large enough for RVs to 45 feet and longer. Water is from hand pumps. There are several good hiking trails including a popular 1.5 km (1 mile) trail to Nairn Falls. Although the gates to the campground are locked during the off season it is OK to walk in and tent camp, there is no fee for this. The campground is located off Hwy 99 some 27 km (17 miles) north of Whistler and 3 km (2 miles) south of Pemberton. You may find the nearby dump station in Pemberton to be handy, it's at the visitor center.

☐ **ROGERS CREEK RECREATION SITE**
   (Open When Weather Allows)
   Location: 32 Km (20 Miles) SW of Lillooet

   GPS Location: 50.53139 N, 122.15472 W, 3,000 Ft

7 Sites – An RSTBC (Recreation Sites and Trails BC) campground along Cayoosh Creek. Some spaces here have room for RVs to 25 feet. There are picnic tables, fire rings, and pit toilets. No potable water is provided. The campground is on the east side of Hwy 99 near Km 59. This is 65 km (40 miles) from Pemberton and 32 km (20 miles) from Lillooet.

☐ **GOTT CREEK RECREATION SITE** *(Open When Weather Allows)*
Location: 31 Km (19 Miles) SW of Lillooet

GPS Location: 50.53528 N, 122.13611 W, 2,700 Ft

3 Sites – This is another RSTBC campground along Cayoosh Creek. It is a little farther from the road, maybe 100 yards. The three sites will take RVs to 25 feet, two of them are creek-side. There are picnic tables, fire rings, and pit toilets. No potable water is provided. The campground is on the west side of Hwy 99 near Km 60. This is 66 km (41 miles) from Pemberton and 31 km (19 miles) from Lillooet.

☐ **COTTONWOOD RECREATION SITE**
   (Open When Weather Allows)
Location: 23 Km (14 Miles) SW of Lillooet

FREE ▲ ♨

GPS Location: 50.58306 N, 122.09167 W, 2,200 Ft

12 Sites – A third RSTBC campground along Cayoosh Creek. Cottonwood will take carefully driven 30-foot RVs and there's a circular drive although the turns are tight for 30-footers. There are picnic tables, fire rings, and pit toilets. No potable water is provided. The campground is on the west side of Hwy 99 near Km 68. This is 74 km (46 miles) from Pemberton and 23 km (14 miles) from Lillooet.

☐ **CINNAMON RECREATION SITE** *(Open When Weather Allows)*
Location: 19 Km (12 Miles) SW of Lillooet

FREE ▲ ♨

GPS Location: 50.61278 N, 122.10556 W, 2,100 Ft

11 Sites – This is the one of the largest of the RSTBC recreation sites along Cayoosh Creek. It can take RVs to 35 feet, the sites are located off a circular drive. There are picnic tables, fire rings, and pit toilets. No potable water is provided. The campground is on the west side of Hwy 99 near Km 72. This is 79 km (49 miles) from Pemberton and 19 km (12 miles) from Lillooet.

○ **SETON DAM CAMPGROUND – BC HYDRO** *(Open When Weather Allows)*
Location: 5 Km (3 Miles) W of Lillooet

GPS Location: 50.66778 N, 121.97639 W, 800 Ft

42 Sites – BC Hydro provides a very nice free campground just outside Lillooet near the Seton Lake Dam. Site are back-ins and will take RVs to 30 feet. There is a swimming beach nearby. From the intersection of Hwy 99 and Hwy 12 on the far side (east) of the Fraser River from Lillooet drive west across the river. Follow Hwy 99 for 5.5 km (3.4 miles), the campground entrance is on the left.

● **CAYOOSH CREEK CAMPGROUND**
   (Open April 1 to Oct 31 – Varies)
Res and Info: (250) 256-4180,
         cayooshcreek@lillooetbc.ca
Location: Lillooet

GPS Location: 50.68111 N, 121.92889 W, 500 Ft

41 Sites – This tidy little campground just outside Lillooet is the best place in the area for big rigs and not bad for tenters either. Tents are pitched in a grassy field. There are pull-thru sites that will take 45 foot RVs with no problem, they have electric and water hookups and there is a dump station. From the intersection of Hwy 99 and Hwy 12 on the

east side of the Fraser River from Lillooet drive west across the river. Follow Hwy 99 for .8 km (.5 mile), the campground entrance is on the left.

● **FRASER COVE CAMPGROUND**
   (Open All Year)
   Res and Info: (250) 256-0142, (800) 936-2040,
                    camping@frasercove.com,
                    www.frasercove.com
   Location: 2 Km (1 Mile) NE of Lillooet

GPS Location: 50.70861 N, 121.9111 W, 700 Ft

22 Sites – This campground has the most scenic location of all of the campgrounds in Lillooet. It winds down the bluff to the river on the bank opposite Lillooet. The old walking bridge across the river is just upstream and provides a handy way to walk in to town. Some sites will take RVs to 40 feet but maneuvering room is limited and there is a switchback, disconnect your tow car before entering. You might even walk in and take a quick look before committing yourself. Sites are full or partial hookup, tenting is available on the beach. This is usually a self-service campground with no attendant on site. From the intersection of Hwy 12 and Hwy 99 near Lillooet drive north on Hwy 12 toward Cache Creek and Clinton for 2.1 km (1.3 miles), the entrance is on the left.

☐ **MARBLE CANYON PROVINCIAL PARK** *(Open All Year)*
   Information: (250) 378-5334, blparks8@gmail.com
   Location: 48 Km (30 Miles) NE of Lillooet

GPS Location: 50.83361 N, 121.69306 W, 2,600 Ft

30 Sites – This small campground sits between two small lakes. It can only take tent campers and RVs to 25 feet. Water is from a hand pump. There's swimming in the lakes. The campground gate is open all year. From April 28 to October 1 there are services and a fee, outside that time services are limited and there is no fee. The campground is on Hwy 12 northeast of Lillooet. It's 48 km (30 miles) from Lillooet, 27 km (17 miles) from the intersection with Hwy 97 between Cache Creek and Clinton.

WILLIAMS LAKE

Williams Lake (population 12,000) is the Cariboo region's largest city. It's 233 km (145 miles) south of Prince George and 118 km (73 miles) south of Quesnel. It's a supply and service center for the region. The museum here is the large **Museum of the Cariboo Chilcotin** which has exhibits covering the gold mining history of the area.

In early July Williams Lake holds one of the largest rodeos in Canada, the **Williams Lake Stampede**. It's more than just the rodeo, there are lots of other cowboy celebration activities around town.

The town has a small selection of campgrounds, they including a good municipal site on the grounds of the Stampede.

BRITISH COLUMBIA

Williams Lake Campgrounds

○ **STAMPEDE CAMPGROUND** *(Open All Year)*
Res and Info: (250) 398-6718,
              campground@williamslakestampede.com,
              www.williamslakestampede.com
Location: Williams Lake

GPS Location: 52.12417 N, 122.12944 W, 1,800 Ft

80 Sites – This municipal campground is the most centrally located in Williams Lake, on the Williams Lake Stampede Rodeo Grounds. Sites are full, partial, and no-hookup, both back-in and pull-thru to 45 feet. Restrooms with hot showers are available and there is a free dump station that can be used by people not staying at the campground. Services are reduced in winter. The Stampede is at the end of June and first part of July, you'd undoubtedly find it hard to get in to the campground then. It's located off Hwy 20 just south (down the hill) of its intersection with Hwy 97 in Williams Lake.

● **CHIEF WILL-YUM RV SITE**
     (Open March 15 to Oct 15 – Varies)
Res and Info: (250) 303-4653
Location: Williams Lake

GPS Location: 52.11778 N, 122.00500 W, 2,000 Ft

44 Sites – This First Nation-owned campground is up the
hill behind a gas station and store on the eastern approaches to Williams Lake. There are

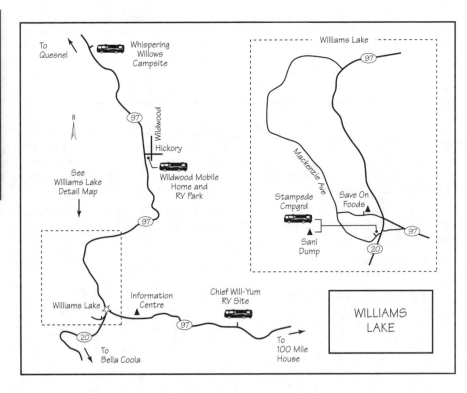

back-in and pull-thru sites, a few as long as 70 feet. There is also tent camping on grass. The campground is located on the north side of Hwy 97 some 5.6 miles (9 km) east of the intersection of Hwy 97 and Hwy 20 in Williams Lake.

● **WILDWOOD MOBILE HOME AND RV PARK**
 (Open All Year)
 Res and Info: (250) 989-4711. letscamp@wlbc.net
 Location: 13 Km (8 Miles) N of Williams Lake

 GPS Location: 52.21111 N, 122.08917 W, 2,800 Ft

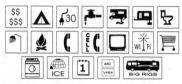

36 Sites – The Wildwood is a residential park located outside Williams Lake to the north. It has many permanently located units also some sites for travelers. These are gravel sites with full-hookups, both back-ins and pull-thrus to 50 feet. The campground is located on Hwy 97 some 13.7 km (8.5 miles) north of the intersection of Hwy 97 with Hwy 20 in Williams Lake.

● **WHISPERING WILLOWS CAMPSITE**
 (Open April 15 to Oct 1 – Varies)
 Information: (250) 989-2323
 Location: 21 Km (13 miles) N of Williams Lake

 GPS Location: 52.27278 N, 122.14306 W, 2,100 Ft

15 Sites – Sites in this rustic First Nation campground are located off a loop drive. Six back-in RV sites up front have electrical and water hookups. Parking here is on grass, check the surface to make sure it will support your rig. Other smaller sites are located off the loop and have no hookups. There is a sani-station. Restrooms have flush toilets and showers but condition varies, check before parking if you are not self-contained. The campground is located on Hwy 97 some 21.9 km (13.6 miles) north of the intersection of Hwy 97 with Hwy 20 in Williams Lake.

YOHO NATIONAL PARK AND GOLDEN

Yoho National Park is one of the many parks clustered in Canada's Rocky Mountains. It encompasses the region in which Hwy 1 and the Canadian Pacific Railroad make the steep climb up into the Rockies toward Kicking Horse Pass.

The park visitor center is just off Hwy 1 in the small town of Field. There are two campgrounds near each other and not far off the highway a few miles to the northeast.

One of the more popular attractions in the park is **Lake O'hara**. You can only access the lake and its trail system using a shuttle bus or by hiking the 12 km (7.5 miles) to the lake. Reservations are a necessity if you want to ride the bus, this is a popular destination and the number of visitors is limited. No reservation is necessary, however, if you walk. The lake is usually icebound until mid July.

Easier to reach is beautiful **Emerald Lake**, a 10 km (6 mile) drive north of the highway. There's a trail system here, the most popular is the 5 km (3 mile) trail around the lake.

Golden (population 4,000) is actually outside the park but is the main population and service center in the area. The town is on the banks of the Columbia River which is flowing north at this point. This is an attractive little town, known for its whitewater rafting and hang-gliding.

EMERALD LAKE IN YOHO IS ONE OF THE MOST SCENIC SPOTS IN CANADA

Remember that if you decide to stay in the campgrounds inside Yoho National Park you will have to pay the park fee in addition to the campground fee listed below.

Yoho National Park and Golden Campgrounds

● **CAMPERS HAVEN** *(Open May 1 to Nov 15)*
Res and Info: (800) 563-6122, (250) 340-8482,
noryon@hotmail.com
Location: 26 Km (16 Miles) W of Golden

GPS Location: 51.48944 N, 117.16194 W, 2,600 Ft

71 Sites – If you're looking for a quiet place to pull off the road with big sites and easy access Campers Haven fills the bill. Most of the RV sites are pull-thrus to 60 feet with full hookups. Parking is on grass. The entrance road intersects Hwy 1 some 26 km (16 miles) west of Golden, the campground is .5 km (.3 mile) from the highway so road noise is no problem.

○ **GOLDEN MUNICIPAL CAMPGROUND**
(Open All Year)
Res and Info: (250) 344-5412,
info@goldenmunicipalcampground.com,
www.goldenmunicipalcampground.com
Location: Golden

GPS Location: 51.29722 N, 116.95139 W, 2,600 Ft

105 Sites – An excellent place to stay if you want to explore the town of Golden. This is a

riverside campground but you're more likely to think of it as a railroad-side campground since the river is hidden from view by a dike but the railroad can still be easily heard as trains pass on the far side of the river. There are sites in a wooded area that are good for tents as well as sites suitable for RVs to 45 feet, both with and without hookups. The municipal swimming pool is nearby. To reach the campground from Hwy 1 head south on Golden's main street, 10th Ave. You'll cross the bridge over the river, then in two blocks turn left on 9th Ave and follow it .8 km (.5 mile) to the campground.

● **GOLDEN ECO ADVENTURE RANCH**
   (Open May 12 to Sept 30 – Varies)
   Res and Info: (250) 344-6825, gear@persona.ca,
                  www.goldenadventurepark.com
   Location: 6 Km (4 Miles) S of Golden

   GPS Location: 51.24278 N, 116.92278 W, 2,600 Ft

69 Sites – There are two separate campgrounds set in trees sharing a very upscale restroom and services building. One of the campgrounds is for tent campers (with vehicle parking at the sites) and the other has big RV sites. Most are pull-thrus with water and electric hookups, that will take RVs over 45 feet long. Sites are separated by vegetation so you're not competing with your neighbor for space to extend your awning. There's also a hang-gliding landing zone out in front of the campground, free entertainment! Drive south from Golden on Hwy 95 for 6 km (4 miles) from the bridge over the Columbia in town. Turn right on Nickelson road and after another .8 km (.5 mile) turn right on Canyon Creek Road. Drive another .5 km (.3 mile), turn right on McBeath Road and you'll soon

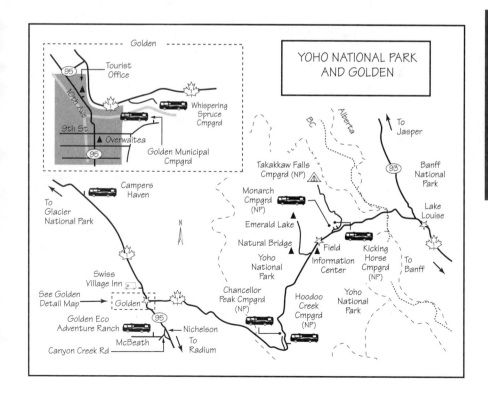

see the long entrance driveway on your right stretching across a field to the offices and then beyond to the campgrounds in the trees.

● **WHISPERING SPRUCE CAMPGROUND**
   (Open April 15 to Oct 15)
   Res and Info: (250) 344-6680,
         www.whisperingsprucecampground.com
   Location: 2 Km (1 Mile) E of Golden

   GPS Location: 51.30056 N, 116.94750 W, 2,900 Ft

140 Sites – This is an older campground that was obviously a KOA at one time. It's located just off the highway to the east of town in a subdivision with motels and other businesses. Watch for a herd of urban bighorn sheep in the neighborhood, they're usually around. There are a variety of site types including tent sites on grass and long pull-thrus suitable for RVs to 45 feet. Follow Hwy 1 east from the main Golden exit for 1.3 km (.8 miles), turn right and follow the access road for .5 km (.3 miles) to the campground.

■ **MONARCH CAMPGROUND – YOHO NATIONAL PARK**
   (Open May 1 to Oct 10 – Varies)
   Information: (250) 343-6783
   Location: 5 Km (3 Miles) E of Field

   GPS Location: 51.42083 N, 116.44194 W, 4,200 Ft

44 Sites – Monarch is a smaller campground that seems to act as an overflow area for the nearby Kicking Horse Campground. Actually, this is a very nice campground in its own right, better than Kicking Horse in some ways, including convenience. Also, sites are somewhat open with fewer trees than the other campgrounds. It's nice. Some sites here are walk-in tent sites and the rest are back-in sites suitable for RVs to about 30 feet although there are a couple sites that will take RVs to 40 or perhaps even 45 feet. There is a kitchen shelter. The campground is located along the Yoho Valley Road which goes north off Hwy 1 some 3.1 km (1.9 miles) east of the Field Visitor Center. After turning you'll see a sani-station on the left in .5 km (.3 miles) and the campground entrance on the left in .8 km (.5 miles).

■ **KICKING HORSE CAMPGROUND – YOHO NATIONAL PARK**
   (Open May 11 to Oct 4 – Varies)
   Information: (250) 343-6783
   Location: 3 Km (2 Miles) E of Field

   GPS Location: 51.42306 N, 116.43500 W, 4,200 Ft

92 Sites – A large campground with a variety of sites including both tent sites and long pull-thrus in an open field suitable for RVs longer than 45 feet. This is the most popular campground in the park. Arrive early! The campground is located along the Yoho Valley Road which goes north off Hwy 1 some 3.1 km (1.9 miles) east of the Field Visitor Center. After turning you'll see a sani-station on the left in .5 km (.3 miles), the Monarch Campground entrance on the left in .8 km (.5 miles), and the Kicking Horse Campground is to the left in 1.1 km (.7 miles).

■ **TAKAKKAW FALLS TENT CAMPGROUND – YOHO NATIONAL PARK** *(Open June 20 to Oct 1 – Varies Due to Snow)*
   Information: (250) 343-6783
   Location: 16 Km (10 Miles) E of Field

   GPS Location: 51.49897 N, 116.48563 W, 5,000 Ft

BRITISH COLUMBIA

35 Sites – Takakkaw is a walk-in tent campground located at the end of Yoho Valley Road. This is the same side road that runs by Monarch and Kickinghorse campgrounds. The campground is adjacent to and shares the parking for scenic Takakkaw falls. Vehicles do not park at campsites. You must walk the short distance although there is a cart to help schlep your gear. There's a kitchen shelter, food storage bins, and a kitchen shelter. Follow Yoho Valley Road for 13.9 km (8.6 miles) to the parking lot. This road is not suitable for trailers due to sharp switchbacks.

■ **HOODOO CREEK CAMPGROUND – YOHO NATIONAL**
      PARK *(Open June 24 to Sept 5 – Varies)*

Information: (250) 343-6783
Location: 24 Km (15 Miles) SW of Field

GPS Location: 51.22407 N, 116.570198 W, 3,600 Ft

30 Sites – Hoodoo is a day use area that allows overnight camping – for a fee. There are parking lot spaces, picnic tables, but no fire pits. There are also dry toilets. A sani-dump is nearby. The entrance to the day use area is on the east side of Hwy 1 some 23.2 km (14.4 miles) southwest of Field. Drive east on the paved access road for .6 km (.4 miles) to the campground.

■ **CHANCELLOR PEAK CAMPGROUND – YOHO NATIONAL**
      PARK *(Open June 3 to Sept 25 – Varies)*

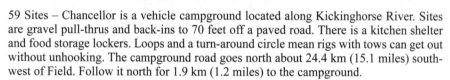

Information: (250) 343-6783
Location: 26 Km (16 Miles) SW of Field

GPS Location: 51.23618 N, 116.58547 W, 3,600 Ft

59 Sites – Chancellor is a vehicle campground located along Kickinghorse River. Sites are gravel pull-thrus and back-ins to 70 feet off a paved road. There is a kitchen shelter and food storage lockers. Loops and a turn-around circle mean rigs with tows can get out without unhooking. The campground road goes north about 24.4 km (15.1 miles) southwest of Field. Follow it north for 1.9 km (1.2 miles) to the campground.

Information Resources

See our Internet site at www.rollinghomes.com for Internet information links.

All British Columbia

BC Ferries, 1112 Fort Street, Victoria, BC, V8V 4V2; (888) 223-3779; customerservice@bcferries.com

Banff National Park

Banff National Park, Box 900, Banff, AB, T1L 1K2; (403) 762-1550

Banff Information Centre, 224 Banff Avenue, Banff, AB, T1L 1K2; Parks Canada (403) 762-1550, Banff/Lake Louise Tourism Bureau (403) 762-8421; banff.vrc@pc.gc.ca

Banff Park Museum, Banff Avenue Next To Bow Bridge (PO Box 900), Banff, AB, T1L 1K2; (403) 762-1558; banff.vrc@pc.gc.ca

Lake Louise Visitor Centre, By the Sampson Mall, Lake Louise; AB; (403) 522-3833; ll.info@pc.gc.ca

Whyte Museum of the Canadian Rockies, 111 Bear Street, Banff, AB, T1L 1A3; (403) 762-2291

Barkerville and Wells

Barkerville Historic Town, PO Box 19, Barkerville, BC, V0K 1B0; (250) 994-3332 or (888) 994-3332; barkerville@barkerville.ca

Wells Visitor Centre, 11900 Hwy 26, Wells, BC, V0K 2R0; (250) 994-2323 or (877) 451-9355; vic@wellsbc.com

Bella Coola and Hwy 20

Bella Coola Tourist/Visitor Info Booth; 628 Cliff St, Bella Coola, BC, V0T 1C0; (250) 799-5202 or (866) 799-5202; info@bellacoola.ca

Boundary Country

Grand Forks Visitor Centre, 524 Central Ave, Grand Forks, BC, V0H 1H0; (250) 442-5835; gftourism@shaw.ca

Greenwood Visitor Centre, 214 S Copper Ave, Greenwood, BC, V0H 1J0; (250) 445-6355; museum@shaw.com

Rossland Visitor Centre, 1100 Hwy 3B (Box 26), Rossland, BC, V0G 1Y0; (250) 362-7722; rosslandmuseum@netidea.com or museum@rossland.com

Trail Visitor Centre, 1199 Bay Ave Suite 200, Trail, BC, V1R 4A4; (250) 368-3144; tcoc2@netidea.com

Campbell River

Campbell River Visitor Centre, 1235 Shopper's Row, Campbell River, BC, V9W 2C7; (250) 830-0411 or (877) 286-5705; info@visitorcentre.ca

MV Uchuck III, PO Box 57, Gold River, BC, V0P 1G0; (250) 283-2515 or (877) 824-8253; info@mvuchuck.com

Chetwynd, Hudson's Hope, and Tumbler Ridge

Chetwynd Visitor Centre, 5217 North Access Rd, Chetwynd, BC, V0C 1J0; (250) 788-1943; tourist@gochetwynd.com

Hudson's Hope Visitor Centre, 9555 Beattie Dr, Hudson's Hope, BC, V0C 1V0; (250) 783-9154; hhinfo@pris.ca

Peace Canyon Dam Visitor Centre; (888) 333-6667

Tumbler Ridge Tourist/Visitor Info Booth, 270 Southgate Rd (Box 100), Tumbler Ridge, BC, V0C 2W0; (250) 242-3123; tourism@dtr.ca

W.A.C. Bennett Dam Visitor Centre, Williston Lake Reservoir, Canyon Dr, Hudson's Hope, BC; (888) 333-6667

BRITISH COLUMBIA

Chilliwack and Cultus Lake Area

Chilliwack Visitor Centre, 44150 Luckakuck Way, Chilliwack, BC, V2R 4A7; (604) 858-8121 or (800) 567-9535; info@tourismchilliwack.com

Cowichan Valley: Chemainus, Duncan, and Cowichan Lake

Chemainus Visitor Centre, 9796 Willow St, Chemainus, BC, V0R 1K0; (250) 246-3944; visitorcentre@chemainus.bc.ca

Duncan Visitor Centre, 361 Trans Canada Hwy, Suite Unit 8, Duncan, BC, V9L 3R5; (250) 746-4636 or (888) 303-3337; visitorinfo@duncancc.bc.ca

Ladysmith Tourist/Visitor Info Booth, 411B 1st Ave, Ladysmith, BC, V9G 1A4; (250) 245-2112; admin@ladysmithcofc.com

Lake Cowichan Tourist/Visitor Info Booth, 125 C South Shore Rd (Box 824) Lake Cowichan, BC, V0R 2G0; (250) 749-3244; info@lakecowichan.ca

Quw'utsun' Cultural and Conference Centre, 200 Cowichan Way, Duncan, BC, V9L 6P4; (250) 746-8119

Dawson Creek

Dawson Creek Visitor Centre, 900 Alaska Ave, Dawson Creek, BC, V1G 4T6; (250) 782-9595; info@tourismdawsoncreek.com

Fernie

Fernie Visitor Centre, 102 Hwy 3, Fernie, BC, V0B 1M5; (250) 423-6868; info@fernie-chamber.com

Fort St. James

Fort St. James National Historic Site (Box 1148), Fort St. James, BC, V0J 1P0; (250) 996-7191; stjames@pc.gc.ca

Fort St. James Visitor Centre, 115 Douglas Ave, Fort St. James, BC, V0J 1P0; (250) 996-7023 or (800) 608-7698; fsjchamb@fsjames.com

Glacier National Park

Mt Revelstoke and Glacier National Park, Box 350, Revelstoke, BC, V0E 2S0; (250) 837-7500; revglacier.reception@pc.gc.ca

Rogers Pass Discovery Centre; Hwy 1, 69 Km (43 Miles) East of Revelstoke; (250) 837-7500

Harrison Hot Springs

Harrison Hot Springs Tourist/Visitor Info Booth, 499 Hot Springs Rd (Box 255), Harrison Hot Springs, BC, V0M 1K0; (604) 796-5581; info@tourismharrison.com

Hope

Hope Visitor Centre, 919 Water Ave (Box 370), Hope, BC, V0X 1L0; (604) 869-2021 or (866) 467-3842; destinationhope@telus.net

Jasper National Park

Jasper National Park, Box 10, Jasper, AB, T0E 1E0; (780) 852-6176

Icefield Centre (Info Desk), 103 Km (64 Miles) South of Jasper on Icefield Parkway; (780) 852-6288

Jasper Information Centre, 500 Connaught Drive, Jasper, AB; Parks Canada (780) 852-6176, Jasper Tourism and Commerce (780) 852-6236

Jasper-Yellowhead Museum, 400 Pyramid Lake Rd, Jasper, AB; (780) 852-3013

Kamloops

Kamloops Visitor Centre, 1290 West Trans Canada Hwy, Kamloops, BC, V2C 6R3; (250) 372-8000 or (866) 372-8081; inquiry@tourismmkamloops.com

Kootenay Lakes District

Castlegar Visitor Centre, 1995 6th Ave, Castlegar, BC, V1N 4B7; (250) 365-6313; tourism@castlegar.com

Kaslo Visitor Centre, 324 Front St (Box 537), Kaslo, BC, V0G 1M0; (250) 353-2525; ssmoyie@klhs.bc.ca

Nakusp Visitor Centre, 92 6th Ave NW, Nakusp, BC, V0G 1R0; (250) 265-4234; nakusp@telus.net

Nelson Visitor Centre, 225 Hall St, Nelson, BC, V1L 5X4; (250) 352-3433; info@discovernelson.com

New Denver Visitor Centre, 202 6th Ave (Box 448), New Denver, BC, V0G 1S0; (250) 358-2719; vic@slocanlake.com

Slocan Tourist Visitor Info Booth, 1020 Giffin Rd (Box 50), Slocan, BC, V0G 2C0; (250) 355-2666; springr@telus.net

Kootenay National Park and Radium Hot Springs

Kootenay National Park, Box 220, Radium Hot Springs, BC, V0A 1M0; (250) 347-9505

Kootenay Park Lodge Visitor Centre, Hwy 93, 63 Km (39 Miles) East of Radium Hot Springs; (403) 762-9196; info@kootenayparklodge.com

Radium Hot Springs Pools, Hwy 93, 3 Km (2 Miles) East of Radium Hot Springs; (250) 347-9485; hot.springs@pc.gc.ca

Radium Hot Springs Visitor Centre, 7556 Main St E (Box 225), Radium Hot Springs, BC, V0A 1M0; Parks Canada: (250) 347-9485, Chamber of Commerce: (250) 347-9331; info@RadiumHotSprings.com

Manning Provincial Park

Manning Provincial Park, Gibson Pass Resort, Inc.; (250) 840-8822 or (800) 330-3321; camping@manningpark.com

Merritt And The Surrounding Plateau

Merritt Tourist/Visitor Info Booth, 2202 Voght St (Box 1105), Merritt, BC, V1K 1B8; (250) 378-0349

Merritt Mountain Music Festival; (250) 378-0965; info@merrittfest.com

Mt Robson and Valemount

British Columbia Visitor Centre @ Mt Robson, Hwy 16, Mt Robson Provincial Park, Mount Robson, BC, V0E 2Z0; (250) 566-4038; BCVCMtRobson@gov.bc.ca

Valemount Visitor Centre, 785 Cranberry Lake Rd, Valemount, BC, V0W 2Z0; (250) 566-9893; valemountvc@gmail.com

Nanaimo

Nanaimo Visitor Centre, 101 Gordon Street, Nanaimo, BC, V9R 5J8; (250) 756-0106 or (800) 663-7337; info@tourismnanaimo.com

New Hazelton and Kitwanga

Hazelton Visitor Centre, Junction of Hwys 16 and 62, 4070 – 9th Ave (Box 340), New Hazelton, BC, V0J 2J0; (250) 842-6071; info@newhazelton.ca

Oceanside

Parksville Visitor Centre, 1275 East Island Hwy (Box 99), Parksville, BC, V9P 2G3; (250) 248-3613; info@parksvillechamber.parksville.com

Qualicum Beach Centre, 2711 West Island Hwy, Qualicum Beach, BC, V9K 2C4; (250) 752-9532; info@qualicum.bc.ca

Okanagan Valley

Kelowna Visitor Centre, 544 Harvey Ave, Kelowna, BC, V1Y 6C9; (250) 861-1515; info@tourismkelowna.com

Oliver Visitor Centre, 36250 – 93rd St (CPR Station) (Box 460), Oliver, BC, V0H 1T0; (250) 498-6321 or (866) 498-6321; info@winecapitalofcanada.com

Osoyoos Visitor Centre, Junction of Hwys 3 and 97, 9912 Hwy 3, (Box 500), Osoyoos, BC, V0H 1V0; (250) 495-5070; visit@destinationosoyoos.com

Peachland Tourist/Visitor Info Booth, 5812 Beach Ave, Peachland, BC, V0H 1X7; (250) 767-2455; peachlandhamber@shawcable.com

Penticton Visitor Centre, 553 Railway St, Penticton, BC, V2A 8S3; (250) 493-4055 or (800) 663-5052; visitors@penticton.org

Summerland Visitor Centre, 15600 Hwy 97 (Box 130), Summerland, BC, V0H 1Z0; (250) 494-2686 or (877) 212-1015; summerlandchamber@shawbiz.ca

Vernon Visitor Centre, 701 Hwy 97S, Vernon, BC, V1B 3W4; (250) 542-1415 or (800) 665-0795; info@tourismvernon.com

Westbank Visitor Centre, 2376 Dobbin Rd, Westbank, BC, V4T 2H9; (250) 768-2712; wkvisitorcentre@gmail.com

Port Alberni

Alberni Valley Visitor Centre, 2533 Port Alberni Hwy, Port Alberni, BC, V9Y 8P2; (250) 724-6535; avcoc@alberni.net

Lady Rose Marine Services, 5425 Argyle Street (PO Box 188), Port Alberni, BC, V9Y 7M7; (250) 723-8313 or (800) 663-7192; ladyrosemarine@telus.net

Port Hardy

Port Hardy Visitor Centre, 7250 Market, (Box 249), Port Hardy, BC, V0N 2P0; (250) 949-7622; phcc@cablerocket.com

Port McNeill, Telegraph Cove, and Port Alice

Port McNeill Visitor Centre, 1594 Beach Drive (PO Box 129), Port McNeill, BC, V0N 2R0; (250) 956-3131 or (888) 956-3131; pmcc@island.net

Port Renfrew Loop (Pacific Marine Circle Tour)

Juan de Fuca Provincial Park, Hwy 14, Port Renfrew BC; (250) 474-1336

Prince George

Prince George Visitor Centre, 1300 – 1st Ave, Suite 101, Prince George, BC, V2L 2Y3; (250) 562-3700 or (800) 668-7646; info@tourismpg.com

Prince Rupert

Prince Rupert Visitor Centre, 100 First Avenue West (PO Box 669), Prince Rupert, BC, V8J 3S1; (250) 624-5637 or (800) 667-1994; prinfo@citytel.net

Quesnel

Quesnel Visitor Centre, 703 Carson Ave, Quesnel, BC, V2J 2B6; (250) 992-8716 or (800) 992-4922; qvisitor@quesnelbc.com

Revelstoke

Revelstoke Visitor Centre, 204 Campbell Ave (Box 490), Revelstoke, BC, V0E 2S0; (250) 837-5345 or (800) 487-1493; info@revelstokechamber.com

Similkameen Valley

Hedley Tourist and Visitor Information Booth, 712 Daly St, Hedley, BC, V0X 1K0; (250) 292-8787

Keremeos Visitor Centre, 427 7th Ave, Keremeos, BC, V0X 1N0; (250) 499-5225

Princeton & District Museum and Archives, 167 Vermillion Ave, Princeton, BC, V0X 1W0; (250) 295-7588

Princeton Visitor Centre, 105 Hwy 3 East, Princeton, BC, V0X 1W0; (250) 295-3103; chamber@nethop.net

South Similkameen Museum, 604 6th Ave, Keremeos, BC, V0X 1N0

Shuswap

Salmon Arm Visitor Centre, #101, 20 Hudson Ave NE (Box 999), Salmon Arm, BC, V1E 4P2; (250) 832-2230 or (877) 725-6667; info@visitsalmonarm.com

Sicamous Visitor Centre, 446 Main Street (Box 346), Sicamous, BC, V0E 2V0; (250) 836-3313; sicamouschamber@cablelan.net

Sorrento Visitor Centre, 2405B Centennial Dr, Sorrento, BC, V0E 2W0; (250) 675-3515; sorrentochamber@telus.net

Smithers

Smithers Visitor Centre, 1411 Court St, Smithers, BC, V0J 2N0; (250) 847-5072 or (800) 542-6673; info@tourismsmithers.com

South Cariboo Region

Cache Creek Tourist/Visitor Info Booth, 1270 Stage Rd, Cache Creek, BC, V0K 1H0; (250) 457-7661; cachecreekinfo@telus.net

South Cariboo Visitor Centre, 155 Airport Rd (Box 340), 100 Mile House, BC, V0K 2E0; (250) 395-5353 or (877) 511-5353; southcaribootourism@dist100milehouse.bc.ca

Sunshine Coast (Lower)

Gibsons Visitor Centre, 417 Marine Drive, Gibsons, BC, V0N 1V0; (604) 886-2374 or (866) 222-3806; ivic1@telus.net

Sechelt Visitor Centre, 5790 Teredo St, Sechelt, BC, V0N 3A0, (604) 885-1036; visitorinfo@dccnet.com

Sunshine Coast (Upper)

Powell River Visitor Centre, 4760 Joyce Ave, Powell River, BC, V8A 3B6; (604) 485-4701 or (877) 817-8669; info@discoverpowellriver.com

Terrace

Terrace Visitor Centre, 4511 Keith Ave, Terrace, BC, V8G 1K1; (250) 635-4944, (877) 635-4944

Thompson and Fraser Canyons

Hells' Gate Air Tram, 43111 Trans Canada Hwy, Boston Bar, BC, V0K 1C0; (604) 867-9277

Lytton Visitor Centre, 400 Fraser St, Lytton, BC, V0K 1Z0; (250) 455-2523; lyttoncofc@lyttonbc.net

Tofino, Ucluelet and the Pacific Rim National Park

Tofino Visitor Centre, 455 Campbell Street, Tofino, BC, V0R 2Z0; (250) 725-3414 or (888) 720-3414; info@tourismtofino.com

Ucluelet Aquarium, Main Street Waterfront Promenade, Ucluelet, BC; info@uclueletaquarium.org

Ucluelet Visitor Centre, 2791 Pacific Rim Hwy, Ucluelet, BC, V0R 3A0; (250) 726-4600; info@pacificrimvisitor.ca

Valley of a Thousand Peaks (Cranbrook, Kimberley, Fort Steele Triangle)

Cranbrook Visitor Centre, 2279 Cranbrook St N, Cranbrook, BC, V1C 4H60; (250) 426-5914 or (800) 222-6174; info@cranbrookchamber.com

Kimberley Visitor Centre, 270 Kimberley Ave, Kimberley, BC, V1A 0A3; (250) 427-3666 or (866) 913-3666; manager@kimberleychamber.com

Vancouver

Delta Visitor Centre, 6201 60th Ave, Delta, BC, V4K 4E2; (604) 946-4232; admin@deltachamber.com

Grouse Mountain Resorts Ltd., 6400 Nancy Greene Way, North Vancouver, BC, V7K 4R9; (604) 980-9311; info@grousemountain.com

Langley Visitor Centre, 2-7888 – 200th Street, Langley, BC, V2Y 3J4; (604) 888-1477; info@tourism-langley.ca

North Vancouver Visitor Centre, 124 West 1st St, Suite 102, North Vancouver, BC, V7M 3N3; (604) 987-4488; tourism@nvchamber.ca

Telus World of Science, 1455 Quebec Street, Vancouver, BC, V6A 3Z7; (604) 443-7443; info@scienceworld.ca

Vancouver Maritime Museum, 1605 Ogden Ave, Vancouver, BC, V6J 1A3; (604) 257-8300

Museum of Vancouver, 1100 Chestnut Street, Vancouver, BC, V6J 3J9; (604) 736-4431

Vancouver Visitor Centre, Plaza Level, 200 Burrard St, Vancouver, BC, V6C 3L6; (604) 683-2000, visitvancouver@tourismvancouver.com

Victoria

Sidney Visitor Center, 10382 Patricia Bay Hwy, Sidney, BC, V8L 3S8; (250) 656-0525; visitors@peninsulachamber.ca

Victoria Visitor Info Centre, 812 Wharf Street, Victoria, BC, V8W 1T3; (250) 953-2033 or (800) 663-3883; info@tourismvictoria.com

Wells Gray Provincial Park and Clearwater

Clearwater Visitor Centre, 416 Eden Rd, Suite 201, Clearwater, BC, V0E 1N0; (250) 674-2646; cwchamber@mercuryspeed.com

Whistler and the Sea to Sky Highway

Pemberton Visitor Centre, Hwy 99 and Pemberton Portage Rd, Pemberton, BC, V0N 2L0; (604) 894-6175; info@pembertonchamber.com

Squamish Visitor Centre, 38551 Loggers Lane, Suite 102, Squamish, BC, V8B 0H2; (604) 815-4994; info@squamishchamber.com

Whistler Visitor Centre, 4230 Gateway Dr, Whistler, BC, V0N 1B4; (604) 935-3357; visitorservices@tourismwhistler.com

Lillooet Visitor Centre, 790 Main St, Lillooet, BC, V0K 1V0; (250) 256-4308; lillmuseum@cablelan.net

Williams Lake

Williams Lake Visitor Center, 1660 South Broadway, Williams Lake, BC V2G 2W4; (250) 392-5025, (877) 967-5253

Williams Lake Stampede; (250) 392-6585, (800) 71-RODEO; info@williamslakestampede.com

Yoho National Park and Golden

British Columbia Visitor Centre @ Golden, 111 golden Donald Upper Rd, Golden, BC, V0A 1H1; (250) 344-7711; BCVCGolden@gov.bc.ca

Yoho National Park, Field, BC, V0A 1G0; (250) 343-6783

Text Index

686

Map Index

Campground Index

Bandon RV Park	Bandon	Commercial	109
Barkerville Forest Rose Campground	Barkerville and Wells	Commercial	502
Barkerville Government Hill Campground	Barkerville and Wells	Commercial	502
Barkerville Lowhee Campground	Barkerville and Wells	Commercial	501
Barton Park	West Cascades SB	Local Gov	264
Barview Jetty County Park	Tillamook	Local Gov	242
Bastendorff Beach Boondocking	Charleston	BLM	130
Bastendorff Beach County Campground	Charleston	Local Gov	130
Bay View State Park	Skagit Valley	WA St Pk	437
Bayside RV and Campground	Sunshine Coast - Lower	Commercial	631
Beach Loop RV Village	Bandon	Commercial	109
Beach Resort at Turtle Rock	Gold Beach	Commercial	149
Beach RV Park	Interstate 82 Corridor	Commercial	310
Beachcomber RV Park	Victoria	Commercial	660
Beachfront RV Park	Brookings	Local Gov	117
Beachside RV Park	Bellingham	Commercial	312
Beachside State Park Campground	Waldport and Florence	OR St Pk	249
Beacon Rock State Park	Columbia Gorge	OR St Pk	135
Bear Creek DNR Recreation Area	Port Angeles	WA DNR	413
Bear Creek Provincial Park	Okanagan Valley	BC Prov Pk	589
Bear Flats Campground	Chetwynd	Commercial	523
Bear Hollow County Park	John Day Country	Local Gov	165
Bear Mountain RV Park	Rogue-Umpqua SB	Commercial	230
Bear River Mercantile	Barkerville and Wells	Commercial	503
Bear Wallow Campground	La Grande	USFS	172
Beaver Bay Recreation Area	Lewis River Region	Local Gov	366
Beaver Campground	Lewis River Region	USFS	367
Beaver Creek Provincial Park	Boundary Country	BC Prov Pk	512
Beaverview RV Park and Campground	Mt Robson	Commercial	570
Becker's Lodge	Barkerville and Wells	Commercial	502
Bee Lazee RV Park and Campground	Prince George	Commercial	605
Beebe Bridge Park	Chelan	Commercial	317
Bel Air Cedar Resort	Okanagan Valley	Commercial	582
Belfair State Park	Hood Canal	WA St Pk	342
Belknap Hot Springs	West Cascades SB	Commercial	271
Bella Pacifica Resort	Tofino, Ucluelet	Commercial	645
Bellingham RV Park	Bellingham	Commercial	313
Bench Campground - Sasquatch PP	Harrison Hot Springs	BC Prov Pk	538
Bend/Sisters Garden RV Resort	Redmond and Sisters	Commercial	220
Beverly Beach State Park	Lincoln to Newport	OR St Pk	182
Beyond Hope Resort	Sandpoint	Commercial	425
Biak By The Sea Trailer Park	Tillamook	Commercial	242
Big Bar Campground	Hell's Canyon	USFS	155
Big Bend Campground	John Day Country	BLM	164
Big Bend Recreation Site	Prineville	BLM	217
Big Country Campground	South Cariboo Region	Commercial	627
Big Creek Campground	Hood Canal	USFS	344
Big Creek Campground	Mt Rainier NP	USFS	378
Big Lake and Big Lake West Campgrounds	West Cascades SB	USFS	268
Big Pines BLM Recreation Site	Yakima River	BLM	470
Big Pines RV Park	Willamette Pass Route	Commercial	282
Big Twin Lakes Campground	Winthrop	Commercial	464
Bighorn Campground and Boat Launch	Yakima River	Commercial	470
Birch Bay State Park	Bellingham	WA St Pk	313
Birch Grove RV Park and Marina	Kootenay Lake District	Commercial	558
Bird Track Spring Campground	La Grande	USFS	172
Black Beach Resort and RV Park	Republic	Commercial	419
Black Canyon Campgruond	Willamette Pass Route	USFS	278
Blackhorse Campground	Hell's Canyon SB	USFS	159
Blackwell Island RV Park	Coeur d'Alene	Commercial	322
Blanket Creek Provincial Park	Revelstoke	BC Prov Pk	612

Crystal Springs Resort	South Cariboo Region	Commercial	628
Cultus Lake Campground	Cascade Lakes	USFS	126
Cultus Lake Provincial Park	Chilliwack	BC Prov Pk	526
Curlew Lake State Park	Republic	WA St Pk	418
Cypress Grove RV Park	Interstate 5	Commercial	87
Daroga State Park	Wenatchee	WA St Pk	456
Dash Point State Park	Tacoma	WA St Pk	448
Davis Creek CG - Kootenay Lake Provincial Park	Kootenay Lake District	BC Prov Pk	560
Deception Pass State Park	Whidbey Island	WA St Pk	459
Deerwood RV Park	Eugene	Commercial	145
Delta Campground	West Cascades SB	USFS	274
Depot Park RV Park and Museum	John Day Country	Local Gov	163
Deschutes Campground - Cove Palisades SP	Warm Springs	OR St Pk	260
Deschutes River State Recreation Area	Interstate 84	OR St Pk	88
Desert Gem RV Resort	Okanagan Valley	Commercial	582
Desert Lake RV Resort	Okanagan Valley	Commercial	583
Detroit Lake State Park	West Cascades SB	OR St Pk	266
Devil's Lake RV Park	Lincoln to Newport	Commercial	179
Devil's Lake State Recreation Area	Lincoln to Newport	OR St Pk	180
Devil's Post Pile Recreation Site	Prineville	BLM	216
Dexter Shores RV Park	Willamette Pass Route	Commercial	277
Diamond Hill RV Park	Interstate 5	Commercial	80
Diamond Lake Campground	Rogue-Umpqua SB	USFS	233
Diamond Lake RV Park	Rogue-Umpqua SB	Commercial	233
Dinosaur Lake Campground	Chetwynd	Local Gov	521
Discovery Point Resort and RV Park	Reedsport	Commercial	225
Donley Service Creek River Access Park	John Day Country	BLM	165
Dosewallips State Park	Hood Canal	WA St Pk	346
Douglas County Fairgrounds	Roseburg	Local Gov	236
Dow Creek RV Resort	Hood Canal	Commercial	345
Driftwood By The Sea RV Park and Cottages	Campbell River	Commercial	514
Driftwood II Off Highway Vehicle Campground	Reedsport	USFS	222
Driftwood RV Park	Interstate 84	Commercial	91
Driftwood RV Park	Brookings	Commercial	117
Driftwood RV Park	Ilwaco and Long Beach	Commercial	349
Dry Gulch Provincial Park	Kootenay NP	BC Prov Pk	562
Dryden Creek Resorts	Whistler	Commercial	668
Duncan RV Park	Cowichan Valley	Commercial	528
Dunes Resort	Ocean Shores	Commercial	395
Dungeness Recreation Area	Sequim	Local Gov	435
Dupont RV Park	Chetwynd	Commercial	522
Dutch Lake Resort and RV Park	Wells Gray PP	Commercial	663
Dutch's Tent and Trailer Court	Okanagan Valley	Commercial	591
E & J RV Park and Days Inn	Ellensburg	Commercial	326
Eagle Campground and RV Park	Similkameen Valley	Commercial	621
Eagle Creek Campground	Columbia Gorge	USFS	137
Eagle Rock Campground	Rogue-Umpqua SB	USFS	234
Eagle Tree RV Park	Kitsap Peninsula	Commercial	352
Eagle Vista RV Resort and Campground	Whistler	Commercial	668
Eagles Hot Lake RV Park	La Grande	Commercial	170
Early Winters Campground	Winthrop	USFS	465
East Lake Campground	Newberry NVM	USFS	196
East Lake Resort	Newberry NVM	Commercial	195
Eco Park Resort	Mt St Helens NVM	Commercial	385
Eel Creek Campground	Reedsport	USFS	227

Eightmile Campground	Leavenworth	USFS	361
Elk Falls Provincial Park	Campbell River	BC Prov Pk	516
Elk Haven RV Park	Rogue-Umpqua SB	Commercial	235
Elk Lake Campground	Cascade Lakes	USFS	124
Elk River RV Park	Port Orford	Commercial	203
Ellensburg KOA Kampground	Ellensburg	Commercial	327
Ellison Provincial Park	Okanagan Valley	BC Prov Pk	590
Elwha Campground	Port Angeles	US Nat Pk	410
Elwha Dam RV Park	Port Angeles	Commercial	409
Emerald Bay Campground - Green Lake PP	South Cariboo Region	BC Prov Pk	627
Emerald Valley RV Park	Interstate 5	Commercial	79
Emigrant Lake (The Point) RV Park	Ashland	Local Gov	98
Emigrant Springs State Heritage Area	Interstate 84	OR St Pk	93
Emory Bar RV Park	Thompson	Commercial	641
Emory Creek Provincial Campground	Thompson	Commercial	641
Englishman River Falls Provincial Park	Oceanside	BC Prov Pk	577
Entiat City Park	Wenatchee	Local Gov	455
Eugene Kamping World	Eugene	Commercial	146
Eugene Premier Resorts RV	Eugene	Commercial	146
Evans Campground	Roosevelt Lake	US Nat Pk	422
Fairholm Campground	Port Angeles	US Nat Pk	412
Fairy Lake Recreation Site	Port Renfrew Loop	RSTBC	601
Fall Creek State Recreation Area	Willamette Pass Route	OR St Pk	278
Falls Creek Campground	Forks	USFS	333
Fallsview Campground	Hood Canal	USNF	346
Farewell Bend Campground	Rogue-Umpqua SB	USFS	232
Farewell Bend State Park	Interstate 84	Commercial	94
Farragut State Park	Sandpoint	ID St Pk	427
Fay Bainbridge State Park	Kitsap Peninsula	WA St Pk	353
Ferry Island Campground and Nature Park	Terrace	Local Gov	636
Fidalgo Bay Resort	Skagit Valley	Commercial	438
Fir Crest Resort	South Cariboo Region	Commercial	628
Fish House Inn	John Day Country	Commercial	164
Fish Lake BLM Campground	Malheur NWR	BLM	186
Fishhook Park	Snake River	Corps of Eng	443
Five Peaks RV Park	Wallowa Lake Region	Commercial	256
Fogarty Creek RV Park	Lincoln to Newport	Commercial	181
Forks 101 RV Park	Forks	Commercial	330
Fort Casey State Park	Whidbey Island	WA St Pk	461
Fort Ebey State Park	Whidbey Island	WA St Pk	461
Fort Flagler State Park	Port Townsend	WA St Pk	416
Fort Henrietta RV Park	Interstate 84	Local Gov	92
Fort Spokane Campground	Roosevelt Lake	US Nat Pk	423
Fort Steele Resort	Valley of 1,000 Pks	Commercial	650
Fort Stevens State Park	Astoria	OR St Pk	101
Fort Townsend State Park	Port Townsend	WA St Pk	414
Fort Victoria RV Park and Campground	Victoria	Commercial	659
Fort Worden State Park	Port Townsend	WA St Pk	415
Franklin County RV Park	Tri-Cities	Commercial	450
Fraser Cove Campground	Whistler	Commercial	671
French Beach Provincial Park Campground	Port Renfrew Loop	BC Prov Pk	602
French Pete Campground	West Cascades SB	USFS	274
Frissel Crossing Campground	West Cascades SB	USFS	275
Frog Lake Campground	Mount Hood	USFS	189
Ft Telkwa RV Park	Smithers	Commercial	622
Furlong Bay Campground - Lakelse Lake PP	Terrace	BC Prov Pk	636
Gallagher Lake Resort	Okanagan Valley	Commercial	583

Hee Hee Illahee RV Resort	Salem	Commercial	236
Hells Canyon Park	Hell's Canyon	Local Gov	155
Hells Canyon RV Resort and Marina	Lewiston and Clarkston	Commercial	364
Hells Gate Idaho State Park	Lewiston and Clarkston	ID St Pk	363
Helmcken Falls Lodge	Wells Gray PP	Commercial	665
Herald Provincial Park	Shuswap	BC Prov Pk	615
Herman Creek Campground	Columbia Gorge	USFS	136
Hewitt/Holcomb Park	Hell's Canyon	Local Gov	157
Hi Dee Ho RV Park	Sandpoint	Commercial	424
Hiawatha RV Park	Okanagan Valley	Commercial	589
Hicks Lake Campground - Sasquatch PP	Harrison Hot Springs	BC Prov Pk	538
Hidden Pines RV Park	Bend	Commercial	112
Hidden Valley Camping and RV Park	Shuswap	Commercial	617
Hilgard Junction State Park	La Grande	OR St Pk	172
Hillview RV Park	Lewiston and Clarkston	Commercial	364
Hi-Way Haven RV Park	Interstate 5	Commercial	82
Hobuck Campground	Neah Bay	Local Gov	385
Hobuck RV Park	Neah Bay	Local Gov	386
Hoh Olympic National Park Campground	Forks	US Nat Pk	332
Hoh Oxbow Washington State DNR CG	Forks	WA DNR	332
Hoh River Resort	Forks	Commercial	332
Holiday Motel and RV Resort	Hope	Commercial	541
Holiday Park Resort	Okanagan Valley	Commercial	590
Holiday RV Park	Ashland	Commercial	96
Home Valley Park	Columbia Gorge	Local Gov	136
Homestead RV and Camping	Shuswap	Commercial	617
Honey Bear Campground	Gold Beach	Commercial	147
Honeymoon Lake Campground	Jasper NP	Can Nat Pk	546
Hood Park Campground	Snake River	Corps of Eng	444
Hoodoo Creek Campground - Yoho NP	Yoho NP	Can Nat Pk	677
Hoodoo Patio RV Park	West Cascades SB	Commercial	273
Hoodoo's Camp Sherman Resort	Camp Sherman	Commercial	119
Hoodview Campground	Mount Hood	USFS	192
Hoover Campground	West Cascades SB	USFS	267
Hope Valley Campground	Hope	Commercial	542
Horn Rapids RV Resort	Tri-Cities	Commercial	452
Horseshoe Bend Campground	Rogue-Umpqua SB	USFS	234
Horsfall OHV Campground	Reedsport	USFS	228
Hot Spring RV Camping Park	Harrison Hot Springs	Commercial	538
Howard Miller Steelhead County Park	North Cascades NP	Local Gov	391
Hu Na Ha RV Park	Wallowa Lake Region	Local Gov	173
Humbug Campground	West Cascades SB	USFS	266
Humbug Mountain State Park	Port Orford	OR St Pk	204
Hunters Campground	Roosevelt Lake	US Nat Pk	422
Hunters RV and Gas	Lakeview	Commercial	176
Ice Cap Creek Campground	West Cascades SB	USFS	271
Icicle River RV Park	Leavenworth	Commercial	361
Idaho Power/BLM Boat Launch	Interstate 84	BLM	95
Ike Kinswa State Park	Cowlitz River Lakes Region	WA St Pk	324
Illahee State Park	Kitsap Peninsula	WA St Pk	352
Illecillewaet Campsite	Glacier NP	Can Nat Pk	536
Ilwaco / Long Beach KOA Kampground	Ilwaco and Long Beach	Commercial	349
Indian Creek Recreation Park	Gold Beach	Commercial	147
Indian Ford Campground	Redmond and Sisters	USFS	219
Indian Henry	West Cascades SB	USFS	265
Indian Mary Park Campground	Grants Pass	Local Gov	152
Indian Well Campground	Klamath Falls	US Nat Pk	170
Ireland's Ocean View RV Park	Gold Beach	Commercial	149
Iron Creek Campground	Mt Rainier NP	USFS	381
Irvin's RV Park	Mt Robson	Commercial	569

Island County Fairgrounds	Whidbey Island	Local Gov	462
Island View Regional Park Campground	Victoria	Local Gov	661
Island View RV Resort	Okanagan Valley	Commercial	581
Island View Trailer Park	Sandpoint	Commercial	424
Island West Resort	Tofino, Ucluelet	Commercial	644
Islander RV Park	Westport	Commercial	458
Islet Campground	Willamette Pass Route	USFS	279
Issaquah Village RV Park	Seattle	Commercial	432
Jackman Park BLM Campground	Malheur NWR	BLM	186
Jacks Landing RV Resort	Grants Pass	Commercial	151
Jade Springs Campground	Thompson	Commercial	640
Jantzen Beach RV Park	Portland	Commercial	210
Jefferson County Campground	Hood Canal	Local Gov	347
Jefferson County Fairgrounds	Warm Springs	Local Gov	259
Jefferson County Fairgrounds	Port Townsend	Local Gov	414
Jessie M Honeyman Memorial State Park	Reedsport	OR St Pk	222
Jetty Fishery Marina	Nehalem Bay	Commercial	193
Jimsmith Lake Provincial Park	Valley of 1,000 Pks	BC Prov Pk	649
Jingle Pot Campsite and RV Park	Nanaimo	Commercial	572
Joe Creek Waterfalls RV Camping	Interstate 5	Commercial	86
John Neal Memorial Park	Salem	Local Gov	240
Johnston Canyon Campground	Banff National Park	Can Nat Pk	498
Johnstone Creek Provincial Park	Boundary Country	BC Prov Pk	507
Jonas Creek Campground	Jasper NP	Can Nat Pk	546
Jones Bay and Osborne Bay Campgrounds	Grand Coulee	WA St Pk	340
Jordan River Recreation Site	Port Renfrew Loop	Local Gov	602
Jo's Motel & Campground	Crater Lake NP	Commercial	143
Joseph H Stewart State Recreation Area	Rogue-Umpqua SB	OR St Pk	231
Juniper Beach Provincial Park	Trans-Canada Hwy	BC Prov Pk	490
Junipers Reservoir RV Resort	Lakeview	Commercial	177
Kah Nee Ta High Desert Resort	Warm Springs	Commercial	257
Kalaloch Olympic National Park CG	Forks	US Nat Pk	333
Kamei Resort	Chelan	Commercial	316
Kamloops Exhibition Association	Kamloops	Local Gov	548
Kamloops Island Campground	Roosevelt Lake	US Nat Pk	420
Kamloops RV Park	Kamloops	Commercial	549
Kampers West Kampground	Astoria	Commercial	102
Kaslo Municipal Campground	Kootenay Lake District	Local Gov	559
Kawkawa Lake Resort	Hope	Commercial	541
Kekuli Bay Provincial Park Campground	Okanagan Valley	BC Prov Pk	590
Kelly's Brighton Marina	Nehalem Bay	Commercial	193
Kent's Beach Campsite	Sunshine Coast - Upper	Commercial	633
Kentucky-Alleyne Provincial Park	Merritt	BC Prov Pk	566
Kettle Falls Campground	Roosevelt Lake	US Nat Pk	420
Kettle River Campground	Roosevelt Lake	US Nat Pk	420
Kettle River Recreation Area	Boundary Country	BC Prov Pk	509
Kettle River RV Park	Boundary Country	Commercial	509
Kiahanie Campground	West Cascades SB	USFS	275
Kicking Horse Campground - Yoho NP	Yoho NP	Can Nat Pk	676
Kid Valley Campground	Mt St Helens NVM	Commercial	385
Kilchis River Campground	Tillamook	Local Gov	243
Kimberley Riverside Campground	Valley of 1,000 Pks	Commercial	648
King Gething Park	Chetwynd	Local Gov	522
Kinnikinnick Campground and RV Park	Prince Rupert	Commercial	608
Kitsap Memorial State Park	Kitsap Peninsula	WA St Pk	353
Kittitas County Fairgrounds	Ellensburg	Local Gov	327
Kitwanga Centennial Park Campground	New Hazelton	Local Gov	575
Klahowya National Forest Campground	Port Angeles	USFS	413

McDonald Creek Provincial Park	Kootenay Lake District	BC Prov Pk	554
McKenzie Bridge Campground	West Cascades SB	USFS	273
McLeod Meadows Campground	Kootenay NP	Can Nat Pk	561
Meadow Wood RV and Campground	Interstate 5	Commercial	85
Memaloos State Park	Columbia Gorge	OR St Pk	138
Merrill Lake Campground	Lewis River Region	WA St Pk	366
Merrill Mobil Manor and RV Park	Klamath Falls	Commercial	169
Metzler Park	West Cascades SB	Local Gov	262
Midway Riverfront RV Park	Boundary Country	Local Gov	509
Midway RV Park	Coos Bay	Commercial	140
Mid-Way RV Park	Interstate 5 Corridor	Commercial	302
Mike's Beach Resort on Hood Canal	Hood Canal	Commercial	346
Mile "0" RV Campsite	Dawson Creek	Local Gov	530
Mill Bay Casino	Chelan	Commercial	316
Millersylvania State Park	Olympia	WA St Pk	404
Millsite RV Park	Interstate 5	Local Gov	83
Milo McIver State Park	West Cascades SB	OR St Pk	264
Minam State Recreation Area	Wallowa Lake Region	OR St Pk	254
Mineral Springs Campground	Cle Elum and Roslyn	USFS	321
Minnie Peterson Washinton State DNR CG	Forks	Wa DNR	331
Miracle Beach Provincial Park	Campbell River	BC Prov Pk	514
Mirror Lake Campground	Kootenay Lake District	Commercial	559
Moberly Lake Provincial Park	Chetwynd	BC Prov Pk	521
Mona Campground	West Cascades SB	USFS	273
Monarch Campground - Yoho NP	Yoho NP	Can Nat Pk	676
Monck Provincial Park	Merritt	BC Prov Pk	566
Moon Mountain RV Resort	Grants Pass	Commercial	151
Mora Campground	Forks	US Nat Pk	330
Moses Lake Cascade Campground	Moses Lake	Local Gov	371
Moses Lake Sand Dunes	Moses Lake	Local Gov	374
Mosquito Creek Campground	Banff National Park	Can Nat Pk	497
Mossyrock Park	Cowlitz River Lakes Region	Local Gov	324
Mount Fernie Provincial Park	Fernie	BC Prov Pk	533
Mount Vernon RV Park	Skagit Valley	Commercial	437
Mountain Man RV Park	Oregon Caves NM	Commercial	197
Mountain View Holiday Trav-L-Park	Baker City	Commercial	105
Mountain View Motel and RV Park	Wallowa Lake Region	Commercial	255
Mountain View RV Park	Warm Springs	Commercial	260
Mounthaven Resort	Mt Rainier NP	Commercial	377
Moyie Lake Provincial Park	Valley of 1,000 Pks	BC Prov Pk	650
Mt Baker RV Park	Valley of 1,000 Pks	Commercial	649
Mt Hood Village Resort	Mount Hood	Commercial	187
Mt Kerkeslin Campground	Jasper NP	Can Nat Pk	546
Mt Sir Donald Campsite	Glacier NP	Can Nat Pk	536
Mt St Helens RV Park	Mt St Helens NVM	Commercial	383
Mt St Helens RV Resort	Mt St Helens NVM	Commercial	384
Mule Deer Campground	Manning Prov Pk	BC Prov Pk	564
Muleshoe Recreation Site	John Day Country	BLM	164
Nahwitti Lake Campsite	Cape Scott	RSTBC	519
Nairn Falls Provincial Park	Whistler	BC Prov Pk	669
Nakusp Hot Springs	Kootenay Lake District	Commercial	555
Nancy Greene Provincial Park	Boundary Country	BC Prov Pk	512
Nason Creek Campground	Lake Wenatchee	USFS	359
Natural Bridge Campground	Rogue-Umpqua SB	USFS	232
Neat Retreat RV Park	Interstate 84	Commercial	95
Nehalem Bay State Park	Nehalem Bay	OR St Pk	193
Nelson City Tourist Park Campground	Kootenay Lake District	Local Gov	558
Nesika Beach RV Park	Gold Beach	Commercial	147
Netarts RV Park	Tillamook	Commercial	244

New Denver Municipal Campground	Kootenay Lake District	Local Gov	557
Newberry RV Park	Bend	Commercial	113
Newhalem Creek Campground	North Cascades NP	US Nat Pk	393
Nisga'a Memorial Lava Beds Provincial Park	Terrace	BC Prov Pk	637
Nisqually Plaza RV Park	Olympia	Commercial	406
Nk'Mip Campground	Okanagan Valley	Commercial	582
Norbury Lake Provincial Park	Valley of 1,000 Pks	BC Prov Pk	650
North Campground - Okanagan Lake Provincial Park	Okanagan Valley	BC Prov Pk	587
North Thompson River Provincial Park	Wells Gray PP	Commercial	664
North Twin Lake Campground	Cascade Lakes	USFS	127
North Waldo Campground	Willamette Pass Route	USFS	279
North Whidbey RV Park	Whidbey Island	Commercial	460
Northern Lights Casino RV Park	Skagit Valley	Commercial	438
Northern Lights RV Park	Dawson Creek	Commercial	531
Northland RV Park	Prince George	Commercial	606
Nor'West RV Park	Bellingham	Commercial	313
Nottingham Campground	Mount Hood	USFS	190
NV Mountainview Chalets and RV Resort	Mt Robson	Commercial	570
Oak Fork Campground	Mount Hood	USFS	191
Oak RV Park	Interstate 5 Corridor	Commercial	302
Oak Slope Campground	Ashland	Local Gov	98
Oakridge RV Park	Willamette Pass Route	Commercial	278
Oasis RV Park	Interstate 84	Commercial	95
Ocean City State Park	Ocean Shores	WA St Pk	397
Ocean Mist Resort	Ocean Shores	Commercial	396
Oceanside RV Park	Charleston	Commercial	131
Oceanside RV Park	Gold Beach	Commercial	148
Oceanside RV Resort	Victoria	Commercial	661
Ochoco Divide Campground	John Day Country	USFS	166
Ochoco Lake Campground	Prineville	Local Gov	215
Odell Lake Lodge and Resort	Willamette Pass Route	Commercial	280
Odessa Creek Campground	Klamath Falls	USNF	169
Ohairi Park and Campground	Boundary Country	Local Gov	510
Ohanapecosh Campground	Mt Rainier NP	US Nat Pk	378
Okanagan Falls Provincial Park	Okanagan Valley	BC Prov Pk	584
Okanogan Bingo and Casino	Okanogan Valley	Commercial	401
Okanogan Fairgrounds RV Park	Okanogan Valley	Local Gov	401
O'Keefe Ranch	Okanagan Valley	Commercial	592
Ol Jo's Campground	Oregon Caves NM	Commercial	199
Olallie Campground	West Cascades SB	USFS	271
Old Camp Casino	Malheur NWR	Commercial	184
Old Hedley East and West Rec Sites	Similkameen Valley	RSTBC	620
Old Mill RV Park	Tillamook	Commercial	242
Oleover Arm Provincial Park	Sunshine Coast - Upper	Commercial	635
Oliver Centennial RV Park	Okanagan Valley	Local Gov	583
Ollokot Campground	Hell's Canyon SB	USFS	159
Olson's Resort	Neah Bay	Commercial	388
Olympia Campground	Olympia	Commercial	405
On The River Golf and RV Resort	Interstate 5	Commercial	83
Oregon 8 Motel and RV Park	Klamath Falls	Commercial	168
Oregon Campground	John Day Country	USFS	161
Oregon Dunes KOA Kampground	Reedsport	Commercial	228
Oregon Trails West RV Park	Baker City	Commercial	105
Orondo River Park	Wenatchee	Local Gov	456
Osoyoos Lake Veteran's Memorial Park	Okanagan Valley	Local Gov	399
O'Sullivan Sportsman's Resort	Moses Lake	Commercial	373
Othello Tunnels Campground	Hope	Commercial	541
Outback RV Park	Interstate 5 Corridor	Commercial	300

Outdoor Resorts Motorcoach Resort	Lincoln to Newport	Commercial	182
Owls Nest Resort and Marina	Okanagan Valley	Commercial	590
Oxbow RV Resort	Okanagan Valley	Commercial	585
Ozette Olympic National Park Campground	Neah Bay	US Nat Pk	388
Paarens Beach Provincial Park	Fort St James	BC Prov Pk	534
Pacheedaht Gordon River Sites	Port Renfrew Loop	Commercial	602
Pacheedaht San Juan River Sites	Port Renfrew Loop	Commercial	602
Pacific Beach State Park	Ocean Shores	WA St Pk	394
Pacific Campground and Overnight Trailer Park	Tillamook	Commercial	244
Pacific Pine RV Park	Waldport and Florence	Commercial	252
Packwood Overnights Events Tent	Mt Rainier NP	Commercial	379
Packwood RV Park	Mt Rainier NP	Commercial	379
Page Springs Campground	Malheur NWR	BLM	185
Palouse Falls State Park	Snake River	WA St Pk	443
Palouse Lions RV Park	Moscow	Local Gov	370
Panorama RV Park and Storage	Roosevelt Lake	Commercial	421
Paradise Campground	West Cascades SB	USFS	272
Paradise Cove RV Park	Mt St Helens NVM	Commercial	383
Paradise Creek Campground	Lewis River Region	USFS	367
Paradise Point State Park	Interstate 5 Corridor	WA St Pk	304
Park at the River	Wallowa Lake Region	Commercial	256
Park Lane Motel Suites and RV Park	Spokane	Commercial	444
Park Sands Beach Resort	Oceanside	Commercial	578
Parkcanada RV Park and Camping	Vancouver	Commercial	655
Parkside Campground and RV Park	Campbell River	Commercial	516
Parry's RV Park	Oceanside	Commercial	578
Pasco / Tri-Cities KOA	Tri-Cities	Commercial	451
Pass Creek Douglas County Park	Interstate 5	Local Gov	80
Pass Creek Park Campground	Kootenay Lake District	Local Gov	553
Pateros Memorial City Park	Lake Pateros	Local Gov	357
Paul Lake Provincial Park	Kamloops	BC Prov Pk	548
Paulina Lake Campground	Newberry NVM	USFS	197
Peabody Creek RV Park	Port Angeles	Commercial	408
Peace Arch RV Park	Vancouver	Commercial	655
Peach Beach Campground	Goldendale	Commercial	335
Peach Orchard Municipal Campsite	Okanagan Valley	Local Gov	587
Pear Tree Resort	Ashland	Commercial	97
Pearrygin Lake State Park	Winthrop	WA St Pk	464
Pedder Bay RV Resort	Victoria	Commercial	659
Pelton Park	Warm Springs	Local Gov	259
Pendleton/Mountain View KOA	Pendleton	Commercial	201
Pheasant Ridge RV Resort	Portland	Commercial	211
Phoenix RV Park	Salem	Commercial	239
Pickard Creek Recreation Site	Similkameen Valley	RSTBC	620
Pierre's Point Family Campground	Shuswap	Commercial	616
Pilot RV Park	Interstate 84	Commercial	92
Pine Point Campground	Mount Hood	USFS	192
Pine Rest Campground	Camp Sherman	USFS	120
Pine Springs Resort	Goldendale	Commercial	336
Pioneer Ford Campground	Camp Sherman	USFS	121
Pioneer RV Park	Interstate 84	Commercial	92
Pioneer Trails	Skagit Valley	Commercial	439
Pleasant Valley RV Park	Tillamook	Commercial	247
Plymouth Park	Interstate 82 Corridor	Corps of Eng	310
Pocahontas Campground	Jasper NP	Can Nat Pk	544
Point Campground	Cascade Lakes	USFS	125
Point Hudson Resort and Marina	Port Townsend	Commercial	416
Poison Butte Recreation Site	Prineville	BLM	217
Ponderosa Falls	Spokane	Commercial	447

Ponderosa Pines RV Park	Shuswap	Commercial	613
Porpoise Bay Provincial Park	Sunshine Coast - Lower	BC Prov Pk	631
Port Alice RV Park & Campground	Port McNeill	Commercial	599
Port Angeles / Sequim KOA	Port Angeles	Commercial	408
Port Ludlow RV Park	Port Townsend	Commercial	417
Port of Arlington Marina and RV Park	Interstate 84	Local Gov	91
Port of Cascade Locks Marine Park	Columbia Gorge	Local Gov	134
Port of Newport Marina and RV Park	Lincoln to Newport	Local Gov	183
Port of Siuslaw RV Park and Marina	Waldport and Florence	Local Gov	252
Port Orford RV Village	Port Orford	Commercial	204
Port Renfrew Marina and RV Park	Port Renfrew Loop	Commercial	601
Porteau Cove Provincial Park	Whistler	BC Prov Pk	667
Portland Fairview RV Park	Portland	Commercial	209
Portland-Woodburn RV Park	Interstate 5	Commercial	77
Portside RV Park	Brookings	Commercial	117
Potholes State Park	Moses Lake	WA St Pk	373
Potlatch State Park	Hood Canal	WA St Pk	342
Prairie Campground	Bend	USFS	112
Premier Resorts RV Park of Salem	Salem	Commercial	238
Premier RV Resort of Lincoln City	Lincoln to Newport	Commercial	181
Prince Rupert RV Campground	Prince Rupert	Commercial	608
Prince's Parking	Okanogan Valley	Commercial	399
Princess Creek Campground	Willamette Pass Route	USFS	280
Princeton Municipal RV Park	Similkameen Valley	Local Gov	620
Prineville Reservoir - Jasper Point Campground	Prineville	OR St Pk	214
Prineville Reservoir - Main Campground	Prineville	OR St Pk	214
Prineville Reservoir Resort	Prineville	Commercial	214
Pringle Falls Campground	Cascade Lakes	USFS	129
Promontory Park	West Cascades SB	Local Gov	264
Prospect RV Park	Rogue-Umpqua SB	Commercial	231
Protection Mountain Campground	Banff National Park	Can Nat Pk	497
Prudhomme Lake Provincial Park	Prince Rupert	BC Prov Pk	608
Pyramid Campground	Wells Gray PP	BC Prov Pk	665
Qualicum Bay Resort	Oceanside	Commercial	577
Quatse River Regional Park & Campground	Port Hardy	Local Gov	596
Quileute Oceanside Resort	Forks	Commercial	330
Quinault Beach Resort Casino	Ocean Shores	Commercial	396
Quinault Maritime Resort and RV Park	Ocean Shores	Commercial	397
Quinn River Campground	Cascade Lakes	USFS	126
Radium Valley Vacation Resort	Kootenay NP	Commercial	562
Rainbow Campground	West Cascades SB	USFS	265
Rainbow's End RV Park	Sequim	Commercial	435
Ralph River Campground	Campbell River	BC Prov Pk	517
Rampart Creek Campground	Banff National Park	Can Nat Pk	496
Rasar State Park	Skagit Valley	WA St Pk	437
Rathtrevor Beach Provincial Park	Oceanside	BC Prov Pk	579
Red Bridge State Park	La Grande	USFS	172
Redmond Expo Center RV Park	Redmond and Sisters	Commercial	218
Redmond/Central Oregon KOA	Warm Springs	Commercial	261
Redstreak Campground	Kootenay NP	Can Nat Pk	562
Regency Park RV Resort	Valley of 1,000 Pks	Commercial	649
Rest-A-While RV Park	Hood Canal	Commercial	345
Revelstoke KOA	Revelstoke	Commercial	612
Rhododendron County Recreation Area	Whidbey Island	Local Gov	461
Rice Hill RV Park	Interstate 5	Commercial	80
Richardson Park	Eugene	Local Gov	145
Riley Ranch County Campground	Reedsport	USFS	228

Rip Rap Campsite	Bella Coola and Hwy 20	Commercial	503
Ripple Rock RV Park	Campbell River	Commercial	516
Ripplebrook Campground	West Cascades SB	USFS	265
River Bridge Campground	Rogue-Umpqua SB	USFS	231
River Oaks RV Resort	Okanogan Valley	Commercial	399
River Rim RV Park	Redmond and Sisters	Commercial	218
River Walk RV Park	Coeur d'Alene	Commercial	322
Riverbend Resort Cottages and RV Park	Oceanside	Commercial	578
Riverbend RV Park	Winthrop	Commercial	463
Riverpark RV Resort	Grants Pass	Commercial	151
Rivers West RV Park	Interstate 5	Commercial	83
Riverside Cabins RV and Camping	Cowichan Valley	Commercial	529
Riverside Campground	Camp Sherman	USFS	119
Riverside Campground	West Cascades SB	USFS	268
Riverside Golf and RV Park	Smithers	Commercial	622
Riverside Park	Smithers	Local Gov	622
Riverside Recreation Site	Chilliwack	RSTBC	524
Riverside RV Resort	Brookings	Commercial	116
Riverside RV Resort	Whistler	Commercial	669
Riverside State Park	Spokane	WA St Pk	445
Riverview Trailer Park	Bend	Commercial	112
Riviera RV Park	Boundary Country	Commercial	510
Roamer's Rest RV Park	Portland	Commercial	211
Robbin's Nest Big Rig RV Park	Bandon	Commercial	109
Robert's Creek Provincial Park	Sunshine Coast - Lower	BC Prov Pk	630
Robert's Roost Campground	Quesnel	Commercial	610
Robinson Latah County Park	Moscow	Local Gov	369
Robson Meadows Campground	Mt Robson	BC Prov Pk	567
Robson River Campground	Mt Robson	BC Prov Pk	568
Rock Creek Campground	Cascade Lakes	USFS	126
Rock Creek Campground	Waldport and Florence	USFS	250
Rockin's River Resort	Prince George	Commercial	606
Rocky Point Resort	Klamath Falls	Commercial	169
Rocky RV Park	Mt Robson	Commercial	570
Rogers Creek Recreation Site	Whistler	RSTBC	669
Rogue Elk Park	Rogue-Umpqua SB	Local Gov	231
Rogue River RV Park	Rogue-Umpqua SB	Commercial	229
Rogue Valley Overnighters	Grants Pass	Commercial	150
Rolling Hills Mobile Terrace and RV Park	Portland	Commercial	209
Rondalyn Resort	Nanaimo	Commercial	573
Rosebery Provincial Park	Kootenay Lake District	BC Prov Pk	557
Rosland Campground	Bend	Local Gov	113
Rossland Lion's Campground	Boundary Country	Local Gov	512
Round Lake State Park	Sandpoint	ID St Pk	426
Royalwood Golf and RV Resort	Trans-Canada Hwy	Commercial	487
Roza Recreation Site	Yakima River	BLM	470
Rufous Corps of Engineers Dispersed Camping	Interstate 84	Corps of Eng	90
Rufous RV Park	Interstate 84	Commercial	90
RV Country Club	Trans-Canada Hwy	Commercial	487
RV Park of Portland	Portland	Commercial	210
RV Park Palouse Empire Fairgrounds	Moscow	Local Gov	370
RV Resort and Cannon Beach	Astoria	Commercial	104
RV Resort Four Seasons	Walla Walla	Commercial	454
RV Resort on the Lake	Nanaimo	Commercial	572
RV Village Resort	Tri-Cities	Commercial	452
Salem Campground and RVs	Salem	Commercial	239
Salmon Arm Camping Resort	Shuswap	Commercial	616
Salmon Harbor Marina	Reedsport	Local Gov	226
Salmon La Sac Campground	Cle Elum and Roslyn	USFS	320

Salmon Point RV Resort and Marina	Campbell River	Commercial	514
Salmon River Motel and RV Park	Shuswap	Commercial	616
Salt Creek Recreation Area	Port Angeles	Local Gov	410
Saltery Bay Provincial Park	Sunshine Coast - Upper	BC Prov Pk	633
Saltwater State Park	Seattle	WA St Pk	433
Sam Owen Campground	Sandpoint	USFS	426
San Josef Campground	Cape Scott	Commercial	518
San Josef Heritage Park	Cape Scott	Commercial	518
Sand and Sea RV Park	Lincoln to Newport	Commercial	181
Sand Beach ORV Campground	Tillamook	USFS	245
Sand Castle RV Park	Ilwaco and Long Beach	Commercial	349
Sandy Point Beach Campground	Shuswap	Commercial	616
Santiam Flats Campground	West Cascades SB	USFS	267
Scandia RV Park	Bend	Commercial	111
Scenic Beach State Park	Kitsap Peninsula	WA St Pk	353
Scenic Meadows RV Park	Wallowa Lake Region	Commercial	256
Schroeder Creek Resort	Kootenay Lake District	Commercial	559
Schroeder Park Campground	Grants Pass	Local Gov	152
Sea Bird RV Park	Brookings	Commercial	117
Sea Perch RV Resort	Waldport and Florence	Commercial	250
Sea Ranch RV Park	Astoria	Commercial	103
Seal Rocks Campground	Hood Canal	USNF	346
Seal Rocks RV Cove	Waldport and Florence	Commercial	249
Seaquest State Park	Mt St Helens NVM	WA St Pk	384
Seascape RV Park	Tillamook	Commercial	246
Sea-Tac KOA	Seattle	Commercial	433
Secret Camp RV Park	Gold Beach	Commercial	148
Seeley Lake Provincial Park	New Hazelton	BC Prov Pk	575
Sequim Bay State Park	Sequim	WA St Pk	434
Seton Dam Campground - BC Hudro	Whistler	Commercial	670
Seven Feathers RV Resort	Interstate 5	Commercial	84
Shadow Bay Campground	Willamette Pass Route	USFS	279
Shadow Mountain RV Park	Port Angeles	Commercial	411
Shady Acres RV Park	Oregon Caves NM	Commercial	198
Shady Firs RV Park	Mt Rainier NP	Commercial	380
Shady Pines Resort	Okanogan Valley	Commercial	402
Shady Tree RV Park and Campground	Interstate 90 Corridor	Commercial	306
Shamrock Village RV Park	Eugene	Commercial	145
Shaw Springs Campground	Thompson	Commercial	639
Sheep Bridge Campground	Cascade Lakes	USFS	127
Shelter Bay Provincial Park	Kootenay Lake District	BC Prov Pk	555
Shelter Cove Resort	Willamette Pass Route	Commercial	280
Shelton County Park	John Day Country	Local Gov	165
Sherwood Campground	Mount Hood	USFS	190
Shuswap Lake Motel and Resort Campground	Shuswap	Commercial	615
Shuswap Lake Provincial Park	Shuswap	BC Prov Pk	614
Sicamous KOA Kampground	Shuswap	Commercial	617
Silver Cove RV Resort	Mt St Helens NVM	Commercial	384
Silver Falls State Park	Salem	OR St Pk	239
Silver Fox RV Park	West Cascades SB	Commercial	264
Silver Lake Resort	Mt St Helens NVM	Commercial	384
Silver Ridge Ranch	Lake Easton	Commercial	355
Silver Sage RV Park and Campground	Kamloops	Commercial	549
Silver Springs Campground	Mt Rainier NP	USFS	380
Silver Star RV Park	Okanagan Valley	Commercial	591
Silverline Resort	Winthrop	Commercial	464
Silverton Municipal Campground	Kootenay Lake District	Local Gov	556
Silverwood RV Park	Coeur d'Alene	Commercial	323
Sintich RV Trailer Park	Prince George	Commercial	605
Skihist Provincial Park	Thompson	BC Prov Pk	640

Venice RV Park	Astoria	Commercial	103
Viento State Park	Columbia Gorge	OR St Pk	137
ViewPoint Motel and RV Park	Shuswap	Commercial	615
Village of Nakusp Campground	Kootenay Lake District	Local Gov	554
Village RV Park	Neah Bay	Commercial	386
Wabasso Campground	Jasper NP	Can Nat Pk	546
Waldport/Newport KOA	Waldport and Florence	Commercial	249
Wallowa Lake State Park	Wallowa Lake Region	OR St Pk	256
Wallowa Lion's RV Park	Wallowa Lake Region	Local Gov	254
Wallowa River RV Park	Wallowa Lake Region	Commercial	255
Wallowa Valley Stay N Wash RV Park	Wallowa Lake Region	Commercial	255
Wanapum State Park	Interstate 90 Corridor	WA St Pk	306
Wapati Campground	Jasper NP	Can Nat Pk	545
Wapato Lake Campground	Chelan	Commercial	316
Wasa Lake Provincial Park	Valley of 1,000 Pks	BC Prov Pk	647
Washington Park	Skagit Valley	Local Gov	439
Waterfowl Lakes Campground	Banff National Park	Can Nat Pk	497
Waterwheel Campground	Klamath Falls	Commercial	168
Wauconda RV Campground	Republic	Commercial	418
Wawawai County Park	Snake River	Local Gov	440
Waxmyrtle Campground	Reedsport	USFS	223
Webb County Park	Tillamook	Local Gov	245
Weir's Beach RV Resort	Victoria	Commercial	660
Wells Gray Golf Resort Lodge and RV Park	Wells Gray PP	Commercial	664
Wenatchee Confluence State Park	Wenatchee	WA St Pk	455
Wenatchee River County Park	Wenatchee	Local Gov	456
West Bay Beach Resort	Okanagan Valley	Commercial	589
West Eagle Campground	Okanagan Valley	Commercial	589
West South Twin Campground	Cascade Lakes	USFS	128
Westbay Marine Village	Victoria	Commercial	659
Westfall BLM Campsite	Hell's Canyon	BLM	156
Westport Inn RV Park	Westport	Commercial	458
Westwind RV Park	Chetwynd	Commercial	521
Westwood Lake Campground	Nanaimo	Commercial	573
Whalen Island County Park	Tillamook	Local Gov	245
Whaleshead Beach Resort	Brookings	Commercial	115
Wheeler County RV Park	John Day Country	Local Gov	165
Whiskers Point Provincial Park	Prince George	BC Prov Pk	606
Whispering Falls Campground	West Cascades SB	USFS	267
Whispering Pines RV Park	Cle Elum and Roslyn	Commercial	318
Whispering Pines Tent and RV Park	Shuswap	Commercial	618
Whispering Spruce Campground	Yoho NP	Commercial	676
Whispering Willows Campsite	Williams Lake	Commercial	673
Whistle Stop RV/Tent Park	Trans-Canada Hwy	Commercial	489
Whistler RV Park and Campground	Whistler	Commercial	668
Whistler's Bend County Park	Rogue-Umpqua SB	Local Gov	235
Whistler's Campground	Jasper NP	Can Nat Pk	545
White Cap Motor Inn and RV Park	Barkerville and Wells	Commercial	501
White River Campground	Mt Rainier NP	US Nat Pk	379
Whitehorse Park Campground	Grants Pass	Local Gov	152
Wilcox Creek Campground	Jasper NP	Can Nat Pk	547
Wild Duck Motel and RV Park	Terrace	Commercial	637
Wild Mare Horse Camp	Reedsport	USFS	229
Wild Rose RV Park	Spokane	Commercial	446
Wild Rose RV Park	Hope	Commercial	542
Wilderness Creek Campground	Mt Robson	Commercial	569
Wildhorse Casino RV Park	Pendleton	Commercial	202
Wildwood Mobile Home and RV Park	Williams Lake	Commercial	673
Wildwoods Campsite	Port Hardy	Commercial	597
Willaby Campground	Forks	USFS	333

ABOUT THE AUTHORS

For the last nineteen years Terri and Mike Church have traveled in Alaska, Mexico, Europe, Canada, and the western U.S. Most of this travel has been in RVs, a form of travel they love. It's affordable and comfortable; the perfect way to see interesting places.

Over the years they discovered that few guidebooks were available with the essential day-to-day information that camping travelers need when they are in unfamiliar surroundings. *Pacific Northwest Camping Destinations, Southwest Camping Destination, Traveler's Guide to Alaskan Camping, Traveler's Guide to Camping Mexico's Baja, Traveler's Guide to Mexican Camping, Traveler's Guide to European Camping, and RV and Car Camping Vacations in Europe* are designed to be the guidebooks that the authors tried to find when they first traveled to these places.

Terri and Mike live full-time in an RV: traveling, writing new books, and working to keep these guidebooks as up-to-date as possible. The books are written and prepared for printing using laptop computers while on the road.

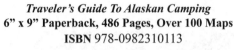
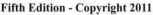

Traveler's Guide To Alaskan Camping
6" x 9" Paperback, 486 Pages, Over 100 Maps
ISBN 978-0982310113

Fifth Edition - Copyright 2011

A laska, the dream trip of a lifetime! Be prepared for something spectacular. Alaska is one fifth the size of the entire United States, it has 17 of the 20 highest peaks in the U.S., 33,904 miles of shoreline, and has more active glaciers and ice fields than the rest of the inhabited world. In addition to some of the most magnificent scenery the world has to offer, Alaska is chock full of an amazing variety of wildlife. Fishing, hiking, kayaking, rafting, hunting, and wildlife viewing are only a few of the many activities which will keep you outside during the long summer days.

Traveler's Guide To Alaskan Camping makes this dream trip to Alaska as easy as camping in the "Lower 48". It includes almost 500 campgrounds throughout Alaska and on the roads north in Canada with full campground descriptions, appropriate RV size for each campground, and maps showing exact locations. It also is filled with suggested things to do and see including fishing holes, hiking trails, canoe trips, wildlife viewing opportunities, and much more.

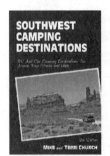

Southwest Camping Destinations
6" x 9" Paperback, 544 Pages, Over 100 Maps
ISBN 978-0974947198

Second Edition - Copyright 2008

B ryce Canyon, Carlsbad Caverns, the Grand Canyon, and Mesa Verde are among the 100 destinations covered in this travel guide for RVers and car campers. Native American sites and desert habitats are also of interest in this region, making it a great vacation destination for families with children. Maps are provided for each destination along with descriptions of tourist attractions and listings for more than 500 traveler campgrounds.

For those who want to escape to a warm climate in the winter there is a special "snowbird" chapter which gives details on top snowbird destinations in the southwest. Over 350 campgrounds are compared in destination like Palm Springs, Las Vegas, Lake Havasu and Parker, Needles and Laughlin, Yuma, Quartzsite, Phoenix, Mesa, Apache Junction, Casa Grande, and Tucson. This analysis is accompanied by maps showing the exact locations of campgrounds in these favorite destinations.

RV and Car Camping Vacations in Europe
6" x 9" Paperback, 320 Pages, Over 140 Maps
ISBN 978-0965296892

First Edition - Copyright 2004

P eople from North America love to visit Europe on their vacations. One great way to travel in Europe is by RV or car, spending the night in convenient and inexpensive campgrounds. It's a way to travel economically and get off the beaten tourist trail. It's also a great way to meet Europeans. Many of them travel the same way!

Most of us lead busy lives with little time to spend on planning an unusual vacation trip. With this book a camping vacation in Europe is easy. It tells how to arrange a rental RV or car from home, when to go and what to take with you. It explains the process of picking up the rental vehicle and turning it back in when you're ready to head for home. It describes a series of tours, each taking from a week to two weeks. The ten tours cover much of Western Europe and even the capitals of the Central European countries. The book has details about the routes and roads, the campgrounds to use, and what to do and see while you are there.

Traveler's Guide To Mexican Camping
6" x 9" Paperback, 576 Pages, Over 250 Maps
ISBN 978-0982310106

Fourth Edition - Copyright 2009

Mexico, one of the world's most interesting travel destinations, is just across the southern U.S. border. It offers warm sunny weather all winter long, beautiful beaches, colonial cities, and excellent food. Best of all, you can easily and economically visit Mexico in your own car or RV.

The fourth edition of *Traveler's Guide To Mexican Camping* is now even better! It has become the bible for Mexican campers. With this book you will cross the border and travel Mexico like a veteran. It is designed to make your trip as simple and trouble-free as possible. Maps show the exact location of campgrounds and the text gives written driving instructions as well as information regarding the size of RV suitable for each campground. In addition to camping and campground information the guide also includes information about cities, roads and driving, trip preparation, border crossing, vehicle care, shopping, and entertainment.

Traveler's Guide To Camping Mexico's Baja
6" x 9" Paperback, 256 Pages, Over 65 Maps
ISBN 978-0974947181

Fourth Edition - Copyright 2008

Sun, sand, and clear blue water are just three of the many reasons more and more RVers are choosing Mexico's Baja as a winter destination. The Baja is fun, easy, and the perfect RVing getaway. Only a few miles south of the border you'll find many great campsites, some on beaches where you'll camp just feet from the water.

Traveler's Guide To Camping Mexico's Baja starts by giving you the Baja-related information from our popular book *Traveler's Guide To Mexican Camping*. It then goes further. We've added more campgrounds, expanded the border crossing section, and given even more information about towns, roads, and recreational opportunities. Unlike the Mexico book, the Baja book is arranged geographically following Transpensinsular Highway 1 south. The book also covers nearby Puerto Peñasco. Like all our books, this one features easy-to-follow maps showing exactly how to find every campground listed.

Traveler's Guide To European Camping
6" x 9" Paperback, 640 Pages, Over 400 Maps
ISBN 978-0965296881

Third Edition - Copyright 2004

Over 350 campgrounds including the best choice in every important European city are described in detail and directions are given for finding them. In many cases information about convenient shopping, entertainment and sports opportunities is included.

This guide will tell you how to rent, lease, or buy a rig in Europe or ship your own from home. It contains the answers to questions about the myriad details of living, driving, and camping in Europe. In addition to camping and campground information *Traveler's Guide To European Camping* gives you invaluable details about the history and sights you will encounter. This information will help you plan your itinerary and enjoy yourself more when you are on the road. Use the information in this book to travel Europe like a native. Enjoy the food, sights, and people of Europe. Go for a week, a month, a year. Europe can fill your RV or camping vacation seasons for many years to come!

HOW TO BUY BOOKS
PUBLISHED BY ROLLING HOMES PRESS

Rolling Homes Press is a specialty publisher. Our books can be found in many large bookstores and almost all travel bookstores. Even if such a bookstore is not convenient to your location you can buy our books easily from Internet bookstores or even directly from us. Also, most bookstores will order our books for you, just supply them with the ISBN number shown on the previous pages or on the back cover of this book.

We maintain a website – **www.rollinghomes.com**. If you go to our website and click on the tab labeled *How To Buy* you will find instructions for buying our book from a variety of Web and storefront retailers as well as directly from us. The instructions on the website change periodically, they reflect the fact that we are sometime out of the country for long stretches of time. When we are not available we make arrangements to be sure that you can obtain our books quickly and easily in our absence.

Retailers and individuals can always obtain our books from our distributor:

Independent Publisher's Group
814 North Franklin Street
Chicago, Illinois 60610

(800) 888-4741 or (312) 337-0747

www.ipgbook.com